International Handbook of
PSYCHOLOGY

International Handbook of
PSYCHOLOGY

edited by

KURT PAWLIK

AND

MARK R. ROSENZWEIG

SAGE Publications
London • Thousand Oaks • New Delhi

© International Union of Psychological Science

First published 2000

SAGE Publications Ltd
6 Bonhill Street
London EC2A 4PU

SAGE Publications Inc
2455 Teller Road
Thousand Oaks, California 91320

SAGE Publications India Pvt Ltd
32, M-Block Market
Greater Kailash – I
New Delhi 110 048

British Library Cataloguing in Publication data

A catalogue record for this book is available from the British Library

ISBN 0 7619 5329 9

Library of Congress catalog record available

Typeset by Photoprint, Torquay, Devon
Printed in Great Britain by The Cromwell Press Ltd, Trowbridge, Wiltshire

Contents

Biographic Profiles

Editors

Kurt F. Pawlik is Professor of Psychology and Institute Director (1966–) and Dean, Faculty of Psychology and International Center for Graduate Studies, University of Hamburg, Germany. His main areas of teaching and research include the psychology of individual differences (and psychological assessment), neuropsychology, and environmental psychology. Since the late 1960s Pawlik served in numerous national and international scientific functions, as President of the German Society of Psychology, President of the Criminological Scientific Council at the Conseil de l'Europe, Strasbourg, Secretary-General and President of the International Union of Psychological Science, and, since 1998, as President of the International Social Science Council, Paris. He was awarded the Austrian Cross of Honors in Science and Arts.

Pawlik is author/co-author of over 180 publications (articles, chapters, and books), and editor/co-editor of scientific journals, including the following:

Hundleby, J. D., Pawlik, K., & Cattell, R. B. (1965). *Personality factors in objective test devices*. San Diego: Knapp.

Pawlik, K. (1966). *Dimensionen des Verhaltens*. [Dimensions of Behavior.] Bern, Switzerland: Huber.

Pawlik, K. (Ed.). (1982). *Diagnose der Diagnostik*. [Diagnosis of diagnostics.] (2nd ed.). Stuttgart, Germany: Klett. [Spanish ed.: *Diagnosis del diagnostico*. Barcelona: Herder, 1980.].

Pawlik, K. (Ed.). (1982). *Multivariate Persönlichkeitsforschung*. [Multivariate personality research]. Bern, Switzerland: Huber.

Pawlik, K., & Stapf, K. H. (Eds.). (1992). *Umwelt und Verhalten*. [Environment and behavior]. Bern, Switzerland: Huber.

Pawlik, K. (Ed.). (1998). Neuropsychology of consciousness. *International Journal of Psychology, 33*, 185–233.

Pawlik, K. (Ed.). (1983–). *Methoden der Psychologie* [Methods of psychology] (14 vols). Bern, Switzerland: Huber.

Psychologie [Teaching and research texts in psychology] (48 vols). Heidelberg, Germany: Springer. New Series: 6 vols. Göttingen, Germany: Hogrefe.

Pawlik, K. (Editor-in-Chief). (1996–). *European Psychologist*. Quarterly journal. Göttingen, Germany: Hogrefe.

Current address: Department of Psychology, University of Hamburg, Von-Melle-Park 11, 20146 Hamburg, Germany

Mark R. Rosenzweig is Professor of Graduate Studies in the Department of Psychology, University of California, Berkeley, where he has taught since 1951. His main activities are in research and teaching in biological psychology and in international psychology. He was given the American Psychological Association Distinguished Scientific Contribution Award in 1980 and its Award for Distinguished Contributions to International Psychology in 1997.

Rosenzweig was elected to the National Academy of Sciences, USA in 1979. He was awarded honorary doctorates by the University of Paris (1980) and l'Université Louis Pasteur, Strasbourg (1997). Rosenzweig served as a member of the Executive Committee of the International Union of Psychological Science (IUPsyS) from 1972 to 1996, and was IUPsyS vice-president, 1980–84, president, 1988–92, and past-president, 1992–96. He was co-editor of the *Annual Review of Psychology* from 1969 to 1994.

Rosenzweig is author, co-author, editor or co-editor of 300 publications (articles, chapters, and books), including the following:

Rosenzweig, M. R., Krech, D., Bennett, E. L., & Diamond, M. C. (1962). Effects of environmental complexity and training on brain chemistry and anatomy: A replication and extension. *Journal of Comparative and Physiological Psychology*, *55*, 429–437.

Rosenzweig, M. R. (Ed.). (1992). *International psychological science: Progress, problems, and prospects*. Washington, DC: American Psychological Association.

Rosenzweig, M. R. (Ed.). (1993). Psychology in developing countries and regions. [Publication of IUPsyS Presidential Symposium at the 15th International Congress of Psychology, Brussels.] *Psychology and Developing Societies, 5*(2).

Rosenzweig, M. R. (1996). Aspects of the search for neural mechanisms of memory. *Annual Review of Psychology, 47*, 1–32.

Rosenzweig, M. R. (1998). Historical perspectives on the development of the biology of learning and memory. In J. L. Martinez Jr. & R. P. Kesner (Eds.). *Neurobiology of learning and memory* (3rd ed., pp. 1–53). New York: Academic Press.

Rosenzweig, M. R., Leiman, A. L., & Breedlove, S. M. (1999). *Biological psychology: Introduction to behavioral, cognitive, and clinical neuroscience* (2nd ed.). Sunderland, MA: Sinauer Associates. (Translated into French, Italian, and Spanish.)

Rosenzweig, M. R. (1999). Continuity and change in development of psychology around the world. *American Psychologist, 54*(4), 252–259.

Rosenzweig, M. R., Holtzman, W. H., Sabourin, M., & Bélanger, D. (2000). *History of the International Union of Psychological Science*. Hove, UK: Psychology Press.

Current address: Department of Psychology-1650, University of California, 3210 Tolman Hall, Berkeley, CA 94720-1650, USA

International Editorial Advisory Board

John G. Adair is Professor Emeritus of psychology at the University of Manitoba, Winnipeg, Canada. He researches the social psychology of the science of psychology, especially methodology and research ethics, and most recently the process of indigenization and growth of psychological science in developing countries (see Special Issues of *International Journal of Psychology*, *30*(6), and *Applied Psychology: An International Review*, *48*(4)). He is recognized for his contributions to international psychology on the Executives of IUPsyS, IAAP, and SIP, on the organization of the 1996 International Congress program, and as coordinator of ARTS, an international program of training seminars for scholars from developing countries.

Current address: University of Manitoba, Department of Psychology, Winnipeg, MB, Canada, R3T 2N2

Rubén Ardila was born in Colombia and received his psychological training in his native country and in the USA. His Ph.D. degree in experimental psychology was granted by the University of Nebraska-Lincoln. He has done research in experimental analysis of behavior, history of psychology, professional issues, and the application of psychology to socio-economic development. Dr. Ardila has published 24 psychology books and more than 150 scientific papers in journals from several countries. He has been visiting professor in the United States, Germany, Spain, Argentina and Puerto Rico. He was President of the Interamerican Society of Psychology (SIP), and founder and first President of the Latin American Association for the Analysis and Modification of Behavior.

Current address: National University of Colombia, Bogotá, Colombia

Géry d'Ydewalle is currently Director of the Laboratory of Experimental Psychology at the University of Leuven (Belgium) and President of the International Union of Psychological Science. He obtained his Ph.D. from the University of Leuven, and has been visiting professor at Birkbeck College (London), the London School of Economics, and the University of Liège (Belgium). In 1992, he received the highest scientific award in Belgium, the Francqui Prize. He is member of the Belgian Royal Academy of Science. His current research interest is on visual information processing and memory.

d'Ydewalle, G. (1997). Visual perception at the edge of the century. In R. Fuller, P. N. Walsh, & P. McGinley (Eds.), *A century of psychology: Progress, paradigms and prospects for the new millenium* (pp. 241–251). London: Routledge.

d'Ydewalle, G., Desmet, G., & Van Rensbergen, J. (1998). Film perception: The processing of film cuts. In G. Underwood (Ed.), *Eye guidance in reading and scene perception* (pp. 357–367). Oxford: Elsevier.

Current address: Department of Psychology, University of Leuven, B-3000 Leuven, Belgium

Hiroshi Imada, Ph.D., Professor of Psychology and President of Kwansei Gakuin University, Nishinomiya, Japan. Born in 1934 in Nishinomiya, Japan. Graduated from the Department of Psychology, Kwansei Gakuin University in 1957, and from the Graduate School of University of Iowa, USA, in 1963 (Ph.D.). Post-doctoral study at the Institute of Psychiatry, University of London, 1968–69. Professor of Psychology of Kwansei Gakuin University since 1974. Executive Committee member of the International Union of Psychological Science since 1992. Publications: *Fear and anxiety* (1974, in Japanese); *Psychology of learning* (1996, in Japanese).

Current address: Department of Psychology, Kwansei Gakuin University, Uegahara, Nishinomiya, Hyogo 662, Japan

Cigdem Kagitcibasi is Professor of Psychology and Dean at Koc University in Istanbul, Turkey. She received her Ph.D. from the University of California, Berkeley. She is Vice-President of the International Union of Psychological Science, the Past President and Honorary Fellow of the International Association for Cross-Cultural Psychology, and a member of the Turkish Academy of Sciences. She received the American Psychological Association 1993 Award for Distinguished Contributions to the International Advancement of Psychology and the International Association of Applied Psychology 1998 Award for Distinguished Contribution to the International Advancement of Applied Psychology. She is the author of *Family and Human Development Across Cultures* (1996) and the co-editor of the *Handbook of Cross-Cultural Psychology*, vol. 3 (1997).

Current address: Psychology Department, Koc University, Cayir Cad. 5, 80860 Istinye, Istanbul, Turkey

Kevin McConkey is Professor of Psychology and President, Academic Board, University of New South Wales, Sydney, Australia. He holds BA (Hons) and Ph.D. from University of Queensland; is Fellow, Academy of the Social Sciences in Australia, Australian Psychological Society, American Psychological Association, and American Psychological Society; is Past President, Australian Psychological Society and Chair, National Committee for Psychology, Australian Academy of Science. He has interests in hypnosis, memory, and ethics; publications include: Kevin M. McConkey & Peter W. Sheehan (1995), *Hypnosis, memory, and behavior in criminal investigation*, and Steven J. Lynn & Kevin M. McConkey (Eds.) (1998), *Truth in memory*.

Current address: The University of New South Wales, School of Psychology, Sydney 2052, Australia

Lionel John Nicholas is an Associate Professor of Psychology at the University of the Western Cape, South Africa. He is editor of the South African Journal of Psychology, President of the Psychological Society of South Africa and executive member of the Professional Board for Psychology. His publications include:

Nicholas, L. J. (1994). Racism in higher education in South Africa: A challenge to counsellors. *British Journal of Guidance and Counselling*, 22(1), 119–125.

Nicholas, L. J., & Durrheim, K. (1996). Validity of the Rohrbaugh and Jessor Religiosity Scale. *Perceptual and Motor Skills*, *83*, 89–90.

Nicholas, L., Pretorius, T., & Naidoo, A. (1999). An historical perspective of career psychology in South Africa. In M. Watson & G. Stead (Eds.). *Career psychology: In the South African* (pp. 1–14). Pretoria, Van Schaik.

Current address: Centre for Student Counselling, University of Western Cape, PO Box X17, Belleville, 7535, Republic of South Africa

Juan José Sánchez-Sosa obtained his Licentiate in Psychology degree from México's National University (UNAM), and MA and Ph.D. from the University of Kansas, USA. He is full time faculty at UNAM since 1970. He has also taught at the University of California, Riverside and has served as member of doctoral dissertation defense committees by invitation to universities in Switzerland, the US and Spain. He is author/editor of six books and some 50 articles/chapters on health, educational and professional psychology. He was Editor of the *Mexican Journal of Behavior Analysis*, founding president of the Mexican Academy of Applied Psychophysiology and Biofeedback. He has also presided over the Mexican Psychological Society, the Mexican College of Psychologists, the Mexican Academy of Doctors in Social and Human Sciences, and served as Dean of UNAM's School of Psychology for two terms. He is currently Secretary General of the Union of Latin American Universities, and president of the International Society of Clinical Psychology (ISCP) for the year 2000.

Current address: Apartado Postal 22-211, 14091 Tlalpan, Mexico DF

Durganand Sinha (1922–98) was a distinguished cross-cultural scholar, an effective spokesman for psychology in the developing world, and a champion of the development of indigenous approaches to psychological research. He was educated at Patna University (India) and Cambridge (UK). Over a distinguished academic career he held appointments at Patna University, the Indian Institute of Technology (Kharaghpur), ANS Institute of Social Studies in Patna (as Director), and Allahabad University, where he was the first Head of its Psychology department. He was a Fellow and President of the International Association of Cross-Cultural Psychology, and had a distinguished research career with a number of books and articles focused on acculturation, deprivation, poverty, and psychology and national development.

Janet Taylor Spence retired in 1997 from the University of Texas at Austin as Ashbel Smith Professor Emeritus and Cowden Centennial Professor Emeritus. She is best known for her work on gender, a field in which she continues to contribute. Her recent publications include her 1993 article 'Gender-related traits and gender ideology: Evidence for a multifactorial theory', in *Journal of Personality and Social Psychology*, *64*, 624–635, and the 1995 chapter (with C. Buckner) 'Masculinity and femininity: Defining the undefinable', in P. Kalbfleisch, and M. Cody (Eds.). *Gender, power and communication in interpersonal relationships* (pp. 105–138). Hillsdale, NJ: Erlbaum Associates.

Current address: PO Box 465, Dennis, MA 02638, USA

Jan Strelau, Ph.D., is Senior Professor at the University of Warsaw, Poland, Head of the Department of Individual Differences, founder and chair of the Interdisciplinary Center for Behavior Genetic Research, University of Warsaw. He holds honorary doctor degrees of the University in Gdansk, Poland and University of Humanistic Sciences in Moscow, Russia. A member of the Polish Academy of Science and Academia Europaea, Strelau is Vice-President of the IUPsyS and Associate Editor of the journal *European Psychologist*. He has published over 20 books and about 200 papers in the domain of individual differences especially on temperament, among others: *Temperament, activity, personality* (Academic Press, 1983) and *Temperament: A psychological perspective* (Plenum Press, 1998).

Current address: Faculty of Psychology, University of Warsaw, Stawki 5/7, Waszawa, Poland

Lawrence Weiskrantz is Emeritus Professor of Psychology at the University of Oxford, where he was Professor from 1967 to 1993. He continues to carry out research on neuropsychological mechanisms of memory and perception, especially the brain mechanisms of blindsight and consciousness. His degrees are from Swarthmore College (B.A.), Oxford University (M.Sc.), and Harvard University (Ph.D.). He is a Fellow of the Royal Society of London, and a Member of the U.S. National Academy of Sciences.

Recent books include *Consciousness lost and found* (Oxford University Press, 1997) and *Blindsight* (Oxford University Press, 1986, updated 1998).

Current address: Department of Exp. Psycholgy, University of Oxford, South Parks Road, Oxford OX1 3UD, UK

Houcan Zhang is Professor of Psychology and Member of the Administrative Committee at Beijing Normal University, and Adjunct Professor at Jiangxi Normal University, People's Republic of China. She is Deputy Chairperson of the Educational Testing Research Association, the Ministry of Education PRC, and member of the Standing Committee of Chinese Psychological Society. She has been Vice-President of CPS and Council member of ITC. Currently Houcan Zhang is EC Member of IUPsyS.

She has authored several books and published about 80 articles in areas of experimental psychology, cognition, testing, statistics and educational measurement. Her books include *Statistics applied in psychology and education* (1987) and *Behavioristic psychology* (1996).

Current address: Department of Psychology, Beijing Normal University, Beijing 100875, China

Authors

Maria Amerigo was awarded her doctorate in Psychology in 1990 from the Complutense University of Madrid and is currently teaching and researching at the University of Castilla-La Mancha, where she is a Lecturer in Social Psychology. Her main area of research is situated within the field of Environmental Psychology, focusing particularly on the study of residential quality in public housing. She has participated in numerous international meetings and published a series of articles and monographs on this subject; The following serve as an example:

Amérigo, M. (1995). *Satisfacción residencial. Un análisis psicológico de la vivienda y su entorno*. Madrid: Alianza Universidad.

Amérigo, M., & Aragonés, J. I. (1997). A theoretical and methodological approach to the study of residential satisfaction. *Journal of Environmental Psychology, 17,* 47–57.

Current address: Faculty of Humanities, University of Toledo, Plaza de Padilla, 4, E-45071 Toledo, Spain

Juan Igazio Aragonés graduated as an industrial technical engineer from the Polytechnic University of Madrid (1971) and was awarded Doctor of Psychology by the Complutense University of Madrid (UCM) in 1983. He has held different professional positions in private industry and in the University and is currently Lecturer in Social Psychology at the UCM. He has co-edited various books, authored or co-authored articles and book chapters dealing with research areas in Environmental Psychology and in particular environmental cognition, residential settings, pro-environmental behavior and attitudes, disasters and risk perception.

Amérigo, M. & Aragonés, J. I. (1990) Residential satisfaction in council housing. *Journal of Environmental Psychology, 10,* 313–325.

Aragonés, J. I., & Amérigo, M. (Eds.). (1998). *Psicología ambiental*. Madrid: Pirámide.

Current address: Department of Psychology, Complutense University of Madrid, E-28223 Madrid, Spain

Rubén Ardila: see entry under International Editorial Advisory Board (p. xi)

Federico Bermúdez Rattoni is Head of the Department of Neuroscience of the Institute of Cellular Physiology at the National University of Mexico (UNAM). M.D. UNAM, 1979. He received his Ph.D. at the University of California, Los Angeles in 1984 and has been Professor of Neuroscience at UNAM since 1984. John Simon Guggenheim, fellow. He was a Visiting Professor to the Center for the Neurobiology of Learning and Memory, University of California, Irvine, 1990. He received the Syntex Award for Medical Research in 1993 and the National Investigator (SNI), Level III,

UNAM Prize for Research in 1998. The aim of his laboratory has been the study of the cortical biochemical mechanisms underlying formation and retrieval of aversive memories.

Bermúdez Rattoni, F., Introini-Collison, F. B., & McGaugh, J. L. (1991). Reversible lesion of the insular cortex by tetrodotoxin produce retrograde and anterograde amnesia for inhibitory avoidance and spatial learning. *Proc. Nat. Acad. Sci. (USA)*, *88*, 5379–5382.

Miranda, M. I., & Bermúdez Rattoni, F. (1999). Reversible inactivation of the NBM disrupts cortial ACh release and acquisition but not retrieval of aversive memories. *Proc. Nat. Acad. Sci. (USA)*, *96*, 6478–6482.

Current address: Departamento de Neurociencias, Instituto de Fisiologia Celular, Universidad Nacional Autónoma de México, 04510 Mexico, DF

Robert Burden is Professor of Applied Educational Psychology and Head of the School of Education at Exeter University, UK. Formerly a classroom teacher and school psychologist, he established the Master's degree professional training course in educational psychology at Exeter in 1991. Burden has held elected positions as Chair of the British Psychological Society's Division of Educational and Child Psychology and as President of the International Association of School Psychologists, from whom he received a lifetime achievements award for his contribution to International School Psychology. He is the author of more than eighty publications including *Psychology for language teachers* (1997) and *Thinking through the curriculum* (1998) (both with M. Williams).

Current address: School of Education, University of Exeter, Heavitree Road, Exeter EX1 2LU, UK

Michael Corballis was born in New Zealand, where he completed bachelors and masters degrees in mathematics and psychology. He completed his Ph.D. in psychology at McGill University in Montreal, Canada in 1965. He was on the faculty at McGill from 1968 to 1978, when he returned to New Zealand to take up a Chair of Psychology at the University of Auckland. His research interests are in laterality, visual cognition, the split brain, language, and evolution. He is author of a number of books, including *Human laterality* (1983), *The lopsided ape* (1991), and, with Stephen E. G. Lea, *The descent of mind* (1999).

Current address: Department of Psychology, University of Auckland, Private Bag 92019, Auckland, New Zealand

Juan D. Delius grew up in Argentina and studied biology at the Universities of Freiburg, Göttingen and Oxford. Later he taught animal psychology at the Universities of Durham and Bochum. He has been a Visiting Professor at the Universities of California, San Diego, of Mexico, Iztacala, of Buenos Aires, Argentina and of Barcelona, Bellaterra. He is now Professor of Experimental Psychology at the University of Konstanz, Germany. His research activities have ranged widely, from a field study on the behavior of skylarks to an inquiry on the processes of cultural evolution. At present he is interested in the biopsychological foundations of cognitive processes in animals and humans. Recent publications are:

Delius, J. D., & Siemann, M. (1997). Transitive responding in animals and humans: exaptation rather than adaptation? *Behavioural Processes*, *42*, 107–137.
Godoy, A. M., & Delius, J. D. (1999). Sensitisation to apomorphine in pigeons is due to conditioning, subject to generalisation but resistant to extinction. *Behavioural Pharmacology*, *10*, 367–378.

Current address: Allgemeine Psychologie, Universität Konstanz, Universitätsstr. 10, D-78434 Konstanz, Germany

Michel Denis is Senior Scientist at the National Center for Scientific Research (LIMSI, Université de Paris-Sud, Orsay, France). He is in charge of a unit of cognitive psychology in a computer science laboratory mainly dedicated to the design of human–machine interactive devices. His research on the cognitive and cerebral processes involved in the representation of space provides a basis for the development of computer-assisted navigational aids. He has published several books on mental imagery, language, and visuospatial cognition. Michel Denis is a member of the Executive Committee of the International Union for Psychological Science, in charge of interdisciplinary projects.

Current address: Groupe Cognition Humaine, LIMSI-CNRS, Université de Paris-Sud, BP 133, F-91403 Orsay Cedex, France

Sara L. Dolan, M.A., is an advanced graduate student in the Clinical Psychology program in the Department of Psychology at the University of Iowa. She works with Peter E. Nathan, studying influences on college student binge drinking, alcohol expectancies, and neuropsychological impairments in substance abusers.

Current address: 140 Spence Laboratories of Psychology, University of Iowa, Iowa City, IA 52242, USA

Pieter J. D. Drenth (Ph.D. in 1960) was trained as a psychologist at the Vrije Universiteit, Amsterdam and at New York University, New York. He has been Professor of Psychology at the Vrije Universiteit, Amsterdam since 1967. From 1982 to 1987 he served as Rector Magnificus (Vice Chancellor) of the Vrije Universiteit. From 1990 until 1996 he was President of the Royal Netherlands Academy of Arts and Sciences. At present he is Chairman of the Social Science Research Council in the Netherlands and Dean of the Faculty of Psychology and Education at the Vrije Universiteit, Amsterdam. He has written some 200 scientific articles and is (co-)author and (co-)editor of 27 books, the most well known of which may be: *Testtheorie* (Van Loghum

Slaterus, 1990) and *Handbook of work and organizational psychology* (Psychology Press, 1998).

Current address: Faculty of Psychology and Pedagogics, Department of Work and Organizational Psychology – Vrije Universiteit, De Boelelaan 1081c, NL-1081 HV Amsterdam, The Netherlands

Géry d'Ydewalle: see entry under International Editorial Advisory Board (p. xi)

Martha L. Escobar graduated with honors from the National Autonomous University of Mexico (UNAM). She received the Best Student Medals and Awards for her M.S. and Ph.D. studies in Neurosciences. Since then she has been working at the Cellular Physiology Institute of the UNAM. By 1991 she had carried out a research stay at the Bonney Center for the Neurobiology of Learning and Memory, University of California at Irvine. In 1994 she made a postdoctoral stay in the University of California at Berkeley. Currently, she is an Associated Professor at the Department of Neuroscience in the Cellular Physiology Institute, UNAM. Her main research interests include the study of neocortical long-term potentiation and its relationship with learning and memory processes, as well as the active-dependent synaptogenesis process.

Current address: Departamento de Neurociencias, Instituto de Fisiologia Celular, Universidad Nacional Autónoma de México, 04510 Mexico, DF

William K. Estes is Professor of Psychology, Emeritus at Harvard University and currently serves as Distinguished Scholar in Psychology and Cognitive Science at Indiana University. His career-long research effort has centered on experimental and theoretical analyses of human and animal learning and the development of mathematical models for learning, memory and decision making. Recent work is concerned with problems of fidelity and durability of human recognition memory. He is author of *Statistical models in behavioral research*, Hillsdale, NJ: Erlbaum Associates, 1991; and *Classification and cognition*, Oxford University Press, 1994.

Current address: Department of Psychology, Indiana University, Bloomington, IN 47405, USA

Rocio Fernandez-Ballesteros is Professor of Psychology at the Autonoma University of Madrid, teaching psychological assessment and evaluation at graduate, master and Ph.D. levels. She has authored more than 200 publications mainly devoted to psychological assessment and gerontology. A Past President of the European Association of Psychological Assessment and of the Division on Psychological Assessment and Evaluation of the International Association of Applied Psychology, she is Editor-In-Chief of the *European Journal of Psychological Assessment* and Editorial Board member of several national and international scientific journals in the field of psychology and gerontology. One of her specialities is program evaluation (UNESCO, European Commission, Spanish National Institute of Social Services).

Current address: Facultad de Psicologia, Universidad Autónoma de Madrid, E-28049 Madrid, Spain

Nico H. Frijda: born 1927 in Amsterdam, the Netherlands. Ph.D. 1956 University of Amsterdam. Full professor in experimental psychology, Amsterdam University, 1965–92. Professor extraordinarius in emotion studies, Amsterdam University, since 1992. Currently engaged in the study of elementary theoretical problems in emotion theory, as well as in some teaching. Publications include *The emotions*. Cambridge, England: Cambridge University Press, 1986; and The laws of emotion. *American Psychologist*, *43*, 349–358, 1988.

Current address: Department of Psychology, University of Amsterdam, Roeterstraat 15, NL-1018 WB Amsterdam, The Netherlands

Peter M. Gollwitzer received his Ph.D. at the University of Texas at Austin, USA (1981). From 1983 to 1993 he was at the Max-Planck-Institute for Psychological Research in Munich, where he headed the Intention and Action Research Group from 1988 to 1992. Since 1993 he has held the Chair of Social Psychology and Motivation at the University of Konstanz. His research interests cover a broad range of motivational and volitional issues. At present he holds a guest professorship at New York University and analyses how planning facilitates the initiation of goal-directed behavior and how it protects people's goal pursuits from unwanted distractions and intrusions. Recent publications are:

Gollwitzer, P. M. (1999). Implementation intentions and effective goal pursuit: Strong effects of simple plans. *American Psychologist*, *54*, 493–503.
Gollwitzer, P. M., & Bargh, J. A. (1996). (Eds.). *The psychology of action. Linking cognition and motivation to behavior*. New York: Guilford Press.

Current address: Universität Konstanz, Fachgruppe Psychologie, Postfach 55 60, D-78434 Konstanz, Germany

Benicio Gutiérrez-Doña is Associate Researcher of Psychology at the Universidad Estatal a Distancia, Costa Rica. He is also Clinical Psychologist in private practice. He received his B.A. in 1988, his Lic. in 1992 and his M.Sc. in 1996 from the Universidad de Costa Rica. From 1996 to 1998 he conducted studies for M.Sc. in Computer Sciences at Instituto Tecnológico, Costa Rica. Since 1999 he has worked on his dissertation at the Institute of Health Psychology of the Freie Universität of Berlin, Germany. His research focus lies on stress, coping, social support, personality, and life history.

Current address: Centro de Investigación Académica, Universidad Estatal a Distancia de Costa Rica, Costa Rica

Allan R. Harkness received his Ph.D. in Psychology from the University of Minnesota in 1989. His program within psychology was clinical, and he completed an internship at the Minneapolis Veterans Administration Medical Center. He is an Associate Professor and Director of Clinical Training in the Department of Psychology at The University of Tulsa in Tulsa, Oklahoma. He specializes in the assessment and clinical implications of individual differences in personality. Some recent publications include:

Harkness, A. R., & McNulty, J. L. (in press). Implications of personality individual differences science for clinical work on personality disorders. In P. T. Costa, Jr., & T. A. Widiger (Eds.). *Personality disorders and the five-factor model of personality* (2nd ed.). Washington, DC: American Psychological Association.

Harkness, A. R., & Lilienfeld, S. O. (1997). Individual differences science for treatment planning: Personality traits. *Psychological Assessment*, *9*, 349–360 (Invited article).

Current address: Department of Psychology, The University of Tulsa, 600 South College Avenue, Tulsa, OK 74104-3189, USA

Giyoo Hatano is a Professor of Educational Psychology at Keio University, Mita, Tokyo. He has been interested in studies on expertise, conceptual development and literacy acquisition. His publications include *Learning to read and write: A cross-linguistic perspective* from Cambridge University Press and chapters in *Handbook of education and human development*, *Handbook of cross-cultural psychology (2nd ed.)*, and *Handbook of child psychology (5th ed.)*. He is a foreign associate of National Academy of Education (US), and was given the Award for Outstanding Contribution to Educational Psychology 1998 by the International Association of Applied Psychology, Division of Educational, Instructional and School Psychology.

Current address: Human Relations, Keio University, Mita, Minatu-ku, Tokyo, 108-8345, Japan

Robert Hogan, Ph.D. University of California, Berkeley 1967; Professor of Psychology and Social Relations, The Johns Hopkins University 1967–82; McFarlin Professor of Psychology, University of Tulsa, 1982–present.

Hogan, R., Johnson, J. A., & Briggs, Sr. (Eds.). (1996). *Handbook of personality psychology*. San Diego, CA: Academic Press.

Current address: Department of Psychology, University of Tulsa, Tulsa, OK 74104, USA

Michael Hogg is Professor of Social Psychology, Director of the Centre for Research on Group Processes, and Director of Research for the Faculty of Social and Behavioral Sciences at the University of Queensland. He received his Ph.D. from Bristol University, and is a Fellow of the Academy of the Social Sciences in Australia. He has taught at Bristol University, Macquarie University, and Melbourne University, and was visiting Professor of Psychology at Princeton University. Michael Hogg is editor of the journal *Group Processes and Intergroup Relations*, and has published widely on group processes, intergroup relations, and social identity. A recent book, with Abrams, is *Social identity and social cognition* (Blackwell, 1999).

Current address: School of Psychology, University of Queensland, Brisbane, QLD 4072, Australia

Vera Hoorens is an Associate Professor of Social Psychology at the Katholieke Universiteit Leuven (Leuven University), Belgium. Her current activities include research on social cognition, particularly self-favoring biases in social comparison, and teaching various courses in the domain of general and social psychology. Some selected publications:

Hoorens, V. (1995). Self-favoring biases, self-presentation and the self-other asymmetry in social comparison. *Journal of Personality*, *63*, 793–817.

Hoorens, V., Remmers, N., & van de Riet, K. (1999). Time is an amazingly variable amount of money: Endowment and ownership effects in the subjective value of working time. *Journal of Economic Psychology*, *20*, 385–405.

Current address: Department of Psychology, University of Leuven, Teinsestraat 102, B-3000 Leuven, Belgium

Kayoko Inagaki is a Professor of Early Education and Developmental Science at the College of Education, Chiba University, Chiba. She has been studying the emergence and change of naive biology, and found that the initial form of autonomous biology is personifying and vitalistic. She also studies classroom discourse in mathematics, especially its cross-cultural differences. She is the co-editor of *The emergence of core domains of thought* from Jossey-Bass, and has published many articles in American and European journals and edited volumes.

Current address: 1-20-8 Togoshi, Shinagawa-ku, Tokyo, 142-0041, Japan

Qicheng Jing is Professor of Psychology at the Institute of Psychology, Chinese Academy of Sciences, China. He is also Honorary Research Scientist at the University of Michigan and Fellow of the Third World Academy of Sciences. He was a Fellow of the Center for Advanced Study in the Behavioral Sciences, USA, and Henry Luce Fellow of the University of Chicago. He is a Past President of the Chinese Psychological Society and Past Vice-President of the International Union of Psychological Science. His present research is on the cross-cultural study of cognition and aging. He has authored several books and published extensively in the areas of psychological systems, visual perception and child development. His books include *Colorimetry* (in Chinese, 1979) and *Concise encyclopedia of psychology* (Ed., in Chinese, 1991).

Current address: Institute of Psychology, Chinese Academy of Sciences, Beijing, 100012, China

Cigdem Kagitcibasi: see entry under International Editorial Advisory Board (p. xii).

Heidi Keller is Professor of Psychology at the University of Osnabrueck. She received her Ph.D. at Mainz University in 1975 and her habilitation at Darmstadt in 1984. Her major research interests concern the interplay of biology and culture for the definition of developmental trajectories. She has done extensive research in the area of early caregiver–child interaction and developed a culture-sensitive model of parenting. A longitudinal cross-cultural research program which is based on the model of parenting is currently investigated in different cultures. Recent publications:

Keller, H., Lohaus, A., Völker, S., Cappenberg, M., & Chasiotis, A. (1999). Temporal contingency as a independent component of parenting behavior. *Child Development, 70*(2), 474–485.

Keller, H. (1996). Evolutionary approaches. In J. W. Berry, Y. H. Poortinga, & J. Pandey (Eds.), *Handbook of cross-cultural psychology, Volume 1: Theory and method* (2 ed., pp. 215–255). Boston: Allyn & Bacon.

Current address: Department of Psychology, University of Osnabrück, Seminarstrasse 20, 49069 Osnabrück, Germany

Stephen E. G. Lea is Professor of Psychology at the University of Exeter, UK. He carries out research in animal cognition, behavioral ecology, human visual perception and economic behavior, and is one of the founders of economic psychology in Europe. He is best known for his research articles on pattern recognition in birds, and for bringing together ecological, economic and psychological approaches in the analysis of both human and animal behavior. His books include *Instinct, environment and behavior* (1984) and *The individual in the economy* (1987), as well as *The descent of mind* recently edited with Michael Corballis.

Current address: Department of Psychology, University of Exeter, Washington Singer Laboratories, Exeter EX4 4QG, UK

Willem J. M. Levelt is founding Director of the Max-Planck Institute for Psycholinguistics, Nijmegen, and Professor of Psycholinguistics at Nijmegen University. He has published widely in psychophysics, mathematical psychology, linguistics and psycholinguistics. Among his publications are *Speaking: From intention to articulation* (MIT Press, 1989) and, together with A. Roelofs and A. Meyer, 'A theory of lexical access in speech production' (*Behavioral and Brain Sciences*, 1999, 2, 1–38).

Current address: Max-Planck Institute, Wundtlaan 1, NL-6525 XD Nijmegen, The Netherlands

Keng Chen Liang received his B.S. and M.S. from the Department of Psychology, National Taiwan University and Ph.D. from the Department of Psychobiology, University of California, Irvine. He is now a Professor at the Department of Psychology, National Taiwan University, teaching Physiological Psychology and related courses. He also serves as the editor for the *Chinese Journal of Psychology*. His research focuses on the neural bases of learning and memory, particularly the roles of the amygdala and related structures in memory formation and retrieval for aversive and appetitive tasks. His recent publications include:

Liang, K. C. (1999). Pre- or posttraining injection of buspirone impaired retention in the inhibitory avoidance task: Involvement of amygdala 5-HT1A receptors. *European Journal of Neuroscience, 11*, 1491–1500.

Current address: Department of Psychology, National Taiwan University, 1 Roosevelt Road, Sec. 4, Taipei, Taiwan 10764, China

David Lubinski's interests circle around psychological measurement and assessing individual differences in human behavior. Using longitudinal methods, his empirical research is concentrated on the identification of different 'types' of intellectually precocious youth and the conditions for enhancing their educational and vocational development. With Camilla Benbow, he co-directs the Study of Mathematically Precocious Youth (SMPY), a longitudinal study of over 5000 intellectually talented participants, initially identified before age 13. His framework for studying talent development is best described in Lubinski and Benbow (2000), while a more overarching view of psychological orientation is found in Lubinski (1996, 2000).

Lubinski, D. (1996). Applied individual differences research and its quantitative methods. *Psychology, Public Policy, and Law, 2*, 187–203.
Lubinski, D. (2000). Assessing individual differences in human behavior: 'Sinking shafts at a few critical points.' *Annual Review of Psychology, 51*, 405–444.
Lubinski, D., & Benbow, C. P. (2000). States of excellence. *American Psychologist, 55*.
Lubinski, D., & Humphreys, L. G. (1997). Incorporating general intelligence into epidemiology and the social sciences. *Intelligence, 24*, 159–201.

Current address: Department of Psychology, Vanderbilt University, Nashville, TN 37203, USA

Ingrid Lunt is Assistant Dean of Research at the Institute of Education, University of London and Head of its Doctoral School. She was President of the European Federation of Professional Psychologists Associations (1993–99) and President of the British Psychological Society (1998–99). She is a member of the Executive Committee of the International Association of Applied Psychology. Her current research interests are professional psychology practice and education, higher professional education, inclusive education. She is leading a European Union funded research project to develop a European framework for Psychologists Training. Recent publications include:

Lunt, I. (1999). Unity through diversity: an achievable goal. *The Psychologist, 12*(10), 492–496.
Lunt, I. (1998). Psychology in Europe: challenges and opportunities. *The European Psychologist, 3*(2), 93–101.
Lunt, I., & Norwich, B. (1999) *Can effective schools be inclusive schools?*

Current address: Institute of Education, 25 Woburn Square, London WC1H 0AA, UK

Michelle L. Meade received her B.A. from Grinnell College and her M.S. from Washington University in St. Louis. Her masters research was concerned with effects of social contagion on memory, showing that if two people see the same scene and then one publicly recalls erroneous information about the scene, the other person will incorporate the wrong information into memory. In short, one person's false memories contaminate the other person's recollections. She is currently working towards her Ph.D.

Current address: Department of Psychology, Washington University, One Brookings Drive, St. Louis, MO 63130-4899, USA

Peter E. Nathan is University of Iowa Foundation Distinguished Professor of Psychology in the University of Iowa Department of Psychology. His current research interests include empirically supported psychological treatments. He also continues to study determinants of abusive drinking by American college students and to explore the reliability, validity, and utility of syndromal diagnosis. Before coming to Iowa, Nathan was Henry and Anna Starr Professor of Psychology and Director of the Center of Alcohol Studies, Rutgers University.

Current address: Department of Psychology, University of Iowa, E119 Seashore Hall, Iowa City, Iowa 52242, USA

Gabriele Oettingen did her dissertation at the Max-Planck-Institute for Behavioral Physiology in Seewiesen (Germany) and at the Medical Research Council in Cambridge (UK). From 1989 to 1998 she was a Senior Researcher at the Max-Planck-Institute for Human Development in Berlin (Germany). Since 1999 she has been a Visiting Professor at the Department of Psychology of New York University. Her research interests cover a broad range of motivational issues in educational, developmental, social, and cross-cultural psychology. She investigated the impact of educational style on peer interactions and status hierarchies, observed explanatory style and signs of depression in various political and socio-cultural contexts, and investigated cultural and educational factors that shape the development of efficacy and control beliefs. Her recent research focuses on the motivational role of various forms of thinking about the future in goal setting and goal disengagement. Recent publications are:

Oettingen, G. (1997). *Psychologie des Zukunftdenkens*. [The psychology of thinking about the future.] Goettingen: Hogrefe.
Oettingen, G. (2000). Expectancy effects on behavior depend on self-regulatory thought. *Social Cognition*.

Current address: Department of Psychology, New York University, 6, Washington Place, New York, NY 10003, USA

Kurt F. Pawlik: see entry under Editors (p. ix)

Ype H. Poortinga is Professor of Cross-Cultural Psychology at Tilburg University and, part time, at the University of Leuven. His most consistent research interest has been the conditions under which data obtained in different cultural populations can be meaningfully compared. His empirical work has dealt with a variety of topics, including information transmission, basic personality variables, and emotions in populations as far apart as Southern Africa, India and Indonesia.

Poortinga, Y. H. (1997). Towards convergence? In J. W. Berry, Y. H. Poortinga, & J. Pandey (Eds.). *Handbook of cross-cultural psychology* (2nd ed., Vol. 1, pp. 347– 387). Boston: Allyn & Bacon.

Poortinga, Y. H. (1998).Cultural diversity and psychological invariance: Methodological and theoretical dilemmas of (cross-)cultural psychology. In J. G. Adair, D. Bélanger, & K. L. Dion (Eds.). *Advances in psychological science*, (Vol. 1, pp. 229–246). Hove, UK: Psychology Press.

Current address: Department of Psychology, Tilburg University, PO Box 90153, NL-Le Tilburg, The Netherlands

José M. Prieto is Professor at Complutense University, Department of Individual Differences and Work Psychology. Secretary General of the International Association of Applied Psychology, Prieto is a Member of the Executive Committee of the Federation of Spanish Psychological Associations and, from 1981 to 1994, was a member of the Executive Board of the Spanish Psychological Association (COP). He served as President of the 23rd International Congress of Applied Psychology, Madrid 1994. His present field of research and development programs is Applied Cyberpsychology. In the past he focused on Personnel Assessment and Human Resources Training. He has published 130 papers in Spanish, English, French and Italian. He received the 1998 Award for services and contributions to the advancement of the profession of psychology internationally, conferred by the IAAP in San Francisco. Also a member of the editorial boards of 13 national and international journals on psychology. Invited professor in Paris, Montreal and Buenos Aires.

Current address: Department of Psychology, Complutense University of Madrid, Despacho 2218, Campus Somosaguas, E-28223 Madrid, Spain

Lea Pulkkinen, Ph.D., Professor of Psychology, University of Jyväskylä, Finland; leave of absence in 1996–2001 for the appointment as the Academy Professor (research professor) at the Academy of Finland. Director of the Centre of Excellence on Human Development and Its Risk Factors, University of Jyväskylä, Finland, 1996–2002. President of the Net University of Psychology (Psychonet) across six Finnish Universities. President of the International Society for the Study of Behavioural Development (ISSBD), 1991–96; Past President, 1996–2000. Member of the Academia Europaea 1989 to present. Visiting scholar at several universities in USA and UK in the 1990s. Research interest: longitudinal study of personality and social development from childhood to adulthood. Results published in international journals and books, e.g.:

Pulkkinen, L. (1998). Levels of longitudinal data differing in complexity and the study of continuity in personality characteristics. In R. B. Cairns, L. R. Bergman, & J. Kagan (Eds.), *Methods and models for studying the individual* (pp. 161–184). Beverley Hills, CA: Sage.

Current address: Department of Psychology, University of Jyväskylä, PO Box 35, FIN-40351 Jyväskylä, Finland

Henry L. Roediger, III is the James S. McDonnell Distinguished University Professor at Washington University in St. Louis. Since receiving his Ph.D. from Yale University in 1973, he has also taught at Purdue University, the University of Toronto, and Rice University. His research interests lie in human learning and memory, particularly retrieval processes. He has served as Editor of the *Journal of Experimental Psychology: Learning, Memory and Cognition* and of *Psychonomic Bulletin & Review*. A 1995 study by the Institute of Scientific Information reported that his research had the highest impact (in terms of average citations) in psychology during the period 1990–94.

Current address: Department of Psychology, Washington University, One Brookings Drive, St. Louis, MO 63130-4899, USA

Mark R. Rosenzweig: see entry under Editors (p. x).

Vladimir Mikhailovich Roussalov is Professor of Psychology at the Institute of Psychology, Russian Academy of Sciences, Moscow, Russia. He is Head of the Laboratory of the Psychology and Psychophysiology of Individuality. His current activities cover both research (methods of measurement) and teaching, his specialization being the field of personality and individual differences. Publications:

Roussalov, V. M., & Guseva, O. V. (1990). A shortened version of Cattell 16 PF (8PF). *Psichologichesky zhurnal*, No. 1, pp. 34–38.
Roussalov, V. M. (1987). A new version of adaptation of EPI. *Psichologichesky zhurnal*, No. 1, pp. 113–126.

Current address: Institute of Psychology, Russian Academy of Sciences, 13 Yaroslavskaya Str., 129366, Moscow, Russia

Michel Sabourin has been affiliated with the Department of Psychology of the University of Montreal since 1970. His past major research interests were in the area of altered states of consciousness and suggestibility, both in human and animals. Since 1985, Sabourin has pioneered in Quebec the development of legal psychology in research and professional practice; he has acted as consultant for jury trial preparation in over 25 criminal cases and has testified as expert witness in both Canada and the USA. Twice President of the Quebec College of Psychologists (1982–85, 1992–94), and President of the Canadian Psychological Association (1989–91). A past Editor of the *International Journal of Psychology* (1988–92), he is member of the Executive Committee and Treasurer of the International Union of Psychological

Science (IUPsyS). He has published over 40 articles and book chapters in different areas of psychology and has made over 75 presentations at major national and international congresses.

Mays, V. M., Rubin, J., Sabourin, M., & Walker, L. (1996). Moving towards a global psychology: Changing theories and practice to meet the needs of a changing world. *American Psychologist, 51*, 485–487.

Sabourin, M., Craik, F., & Robert, M. (Eds.). (1998). *Advances in psychological science: Volume 2: Biological and cognitive aspects.* Hove, East Sussex: Psychology Press.

Sabourin, M. (1999). The evolution of ethical standards in the practice of psychology: A reflection on the APA Code of Ethics. *Japanese Journal of Psychology, 70*, 51–64.

Current address: Department of Psychology, University of Montreal, PO Box 6128, Succ. Centre-Ville, Montreal (Quebec), Canada H3C 3J7

Ralf Schwarzer is Professor of Psychology at the Free University of Berlin, Germany. He is also Adjunct Professor at York University, Canada. He was Founding Editor of *Anxiety, Stress, and Coping: An International Journal.* Currently he is Past-President of the European Health Psychology Association, Fellow of the American Psychological Association, and President-Elect of the IAAP Health Psychology Division. His research focus lies on stress, coping, social support, self-efficacy, and health behavior change. Publications can be found at his website (www.psychologie.de/schwarzer).

Current address: Freie Universität Berlin, Institut für Arbeits-, Organisations- und Gesundheitpsychologie – WE 10, Habelschwerdter Allee 45, 14195 Berlin, Germany

Kenneth J. Sher, after completing his doctorate in clinical psychology from Indiana University (1976–80), served his clinical internship at Brown University (1980–81), and then took a faculty position at the University of Missouri (1981), where he currently holds the rank of Professor of Psychology. His primary interests are in the areas of alcoholism, etiology, and prospective research methodology. He has served as the Associate Editor of *Psychological Bulletin* and the *Journal of Abnormal Psychology.* He is a Fellow of the American Psychological Association and the American Psychological Society. He is the author of numerous scholarly publications and of the monograph, *Children of alcoholics: A critical appraisal of theory and research* (1991, University of Chicago Press).

Current address: Department of Psychology, University of Missouri, 200 S. 7th Street, Columbia, MO 65211, USA

Anne Helene Skinstad is currently Assistant Professor and Coordinator of the Substance Abuse Counseling Program at the University of Iowa. She is also principal investigator and director of the Prairielands ATTC, a technology dissemination project funded by the Substance Abuse and Mental Health Service Administration (SAMHSA), Center for Substance Abuse Treatment (CSAT). A clinical psychology graduate of the University of Bergen, Norway, her major research interests include substance abuse in women, female substance abusing offenders, adult survivors of sexual abuse, and substance abusers with personality disorders.

Current address: N-254 Lindquist Center, Division of Counseling, Rehabilitation, and Student Development, College of Education, University of Iowa, Iowa City, IA 52242-1529, USA

Henderikus J. Stam is Professor of Psychology at the University of Calgary and a member of the theory program in the Department of Psychology. He has written on the history of psychology in North America, particularly in the Progressive Era, the body in psychology, and is currently working on historical and theoretical problems in twentieth-century psychology. He is founding and current Editor of *Theory & Psychology*.

Current address: Department of Psychology, University of Calgary, 2500 University Drive, Calgary, Alberta, Canada T2N 1N4

Timothy Trull is Professor of Psychology at the University of Missouri. His research interests are in the areas of diagnosis and classification of mental disorders, personality disorders (particularly borderline personality disorder), psychometrics, the relationship between personality and psychopathology. Professor Trull is also an author of the textbook, *Clinical psychology: Concepts, methods, and profession.*

Trull, T. J., Useda, J. D., Conforti, K., & Doan, B. T. (1997). Borderline personality disorder features in nonclinical young adults: 2. Two-year outcome. *Journal of Abnormal Psychology, 106,* 307–314.

Trull, T. J., Widiger, T. A., Useda, J. D., Holcomb, J., Doan, B., Axelrod, S. R., Stern, B. L., & Gershuny, B. S. (1998). A structured interview for the assessment of the five-factor model of personality. *Psychological Assessment, 10,* 229–240.

Current address: Department of Psychology, 210 McAllester Hall, University of Missouri, Columbia, MO 65211-2500, USA

Carlo Umiltà is Professor of Neuropsychology in the Department of General Psychology of the University of Padua. He was President of the European Society for Cognitive Psychology (1993/4), Chairperson of the Executive Committee of the International Society for the Study of Attention and Performance (1994–8), and President of the Italian Neuropsychological Society (1985–8). His current research interests include the neuropsychology of spatial attention, selective attention, space representation, and executive functions.

Umiltà, C., & Moscovitch, M. (Eds.). (1994). *Attention and performance XV. Conscious and nonconscious information processing.* Cambridge, MA: MIT Press.

Umiltà, C. (1992). The control operations of consciousness. In A. J. Marcel & E. Bisiach (Eds.), *Consciousness in contemporary science* (pp. 334–356). Oxford: Clarendon.

Current address: Department of Psychology, University of Padova, Via Venezia, 8, I-35131 Padova, Italy

Pierre Vrignaud is research scientist at the INETOP (National Institute for Work and Vocational Guidance Studies). He holds a Ph.D. in Psychology from University Paris 5. His main topics of interest are differential psychology and psychometrics. He is author of several papers on these topics as well as questionnaires and software. He represents the 'Société Française de Psychologie' at the International Test Commission and provides expertise in assessment survey for the French Ministry of Education and international organizations.

Vrignaud, P. (1996). Les tests au XXIéme siècle. *Pratiques Psychologiques, 4,* 5–28.
Vrignaud, P., & Bonora, D. (1998). Literacy assessment and international comparisons. In Dan Wagner (Ed.). *Literacy assessment for out-of-school youth and adults.* Philadelphia: UNESCO/ILI.

Current address: Service de Recherche – INETOP/CNAM, 41, Rue Gay-Lussac, F-75005 Paris, France

Lenore E. A. Walker is a clinical and forensic psychologist and Director of the Domestic Violence Institute, a non-profit agency with offices around the world for training and education, research, and public policy initiatives in the area of domestic violence. In addition, Walker is a Professor and Coordinator of the Forensic Psychology Concentration in the doctoral program at Nova Southeastern University in Ft. Lauderdale, Florida. Author of 10 books and numerous book chapters and peer reviewed articles on domestic violence and violence against women and children, she has been a trainer for projects sponsored by the United Nations, NATO, WHO, and international governments. Her 1999 revision of her book *The battered woman syndrome* (Springer) integrates an update of the literature with her groundbreaking study on battered women.

Frequently asked to testify as an expert witness in courts in the U.S. and Canada, Walker pioneered the Battered Woman Self Defense for women who killed their abusers in self-defense. Her book, *Terrifying love: Why battered women kill and how society responds* (Harper/Collins, 1989) details some of these stories.

Current address: Center for Psychological Studies, Nova Southeastern University, 3301 College Avenue, Ft. Lauderdale, FL 33314, USA

Zhong Ming Wang is Professor of Industrial/Organizational Psychology and Executive Dean at School of Management, Zhejiang University in China. He is President of the Industrial/Organizational Psychology Division of the

Chinese Psychological Society. He is on the editorial boards of the *Chinese Journal of Applied Psychology*, *Applied Psychology*, *Journal of Cross-Cultural Psychology*, and the *Journal of Organizational Behavior and Human Decision Process*. His research areas include personnel selection/assessment, organizational decision-making and leadership. His publications include 'Psychology in China' in *Annual Review of Psychology* (1993) and 'Culture, economic reform and the role of I/O psychology in China' in *Handbook of industrial and organizational psychology* (1996).

Current address: Department of Psychology, Hangzhou University, Hangzhou 310028, China

Michael G. Wessells, Ph.D., is Professor of Psychology at Randolph-Macon College in Ashland, Virginia, USA. As Senior Psychosocial Consultant for Christian Children's Fund, he assists war-affected children and families in Angola, Kosovo, East Timor, and other countries. The author of many articles on the psychology of peace and nonviolent conflict resolution, he is Associate Editor of *Peace and Conflict: Journal of Peace Psychology*. He has served as President of the APA Division of Peace Psychology, as President of Psychologists for Social Responsibility, and as Chair of the Committee for the Psychological Study of Peace of the International Union of Psychological Science. His current research examines psychology of humanitarian assistance, post-conflict reconstruction, and the reintegration of former child soldiers.

Current address: Randolph-Macon College, Department of Psychology, Ashland, VA 23005, USA

Houcan Zhang: see entry under International Editorial Advisory Board (p. xiv).

Preface

This Handbook provides a convenient way to find authoritative, up-to-date information about psychological knowledge and research obtained around the world. It is part of the program of the International Union of Psychological Science (IUPsyS) to promote knowledge of psychology and to disseminate it widely. The Handbook is written at a level that makes it accessible to the educated public. It will also be used by students in many fields of psychology, as well as by specialists to find out about progress in fields of psychology other than their own.

Human behavior and human conscious experience are shaped and molded by numerous factors and driving forces, some of them universal in nature and others more specific to social or societal contexts, or individual conditions. Psychology, the science of human behavior and experience, has to address itself to this wide range of constitutive factors and the enormous variability in behavior and experience resulting therefrom. To the extent that human behavior and experience differ across cultures, it is not surprising that the approaches to psychology show variations across cultures and ethnic groupings. In this sense this Handbook constitutes a first attempt of its kind to present psychology from a broader international perspective and study human behavior and experience from more than one societal context.

Early plans for the Handbook go back to 1994–95 when the idea was developed between the IUPsyS Standing Committee on Communication and Publications and Ziyad Marar of Sage Publications, London, UK. Of course, for an international handbook of psychology one would, ideally, like to see each major field of psychology approached from several regional or cultural perspectives. It soon became obvious that such a demanding goal would not be feasible within the limits of time, cost, and pages inevitable for the Handbook. So the Editors devised a curtailed Handbook design that provided for an International Editorial Advisory Board (IEAB) to guide in the selection of leading specialist authors from different countries and regions of the world, each one expected to deal with the respective chapter topic in an international comparative manner. In order to expedite the international approach and, at the same time, facilitate balanced coverage across the full breadth of psychology as a science and a profession, the Editors developed a fine-grained chapter plan, with explicit lists of topics and contents to be covered in each chapter, also to provide for cross-reference and to avoid undue duplication.

Preparation of this chapter master plan was significantly assisted by the International Editorial Advisory Board and, at a later state, by the chapter authors themselves. The IEAB nominated possible authors for each of the planned chapters, attempting to name productive psychologists from all countries in which research is being done. The Editors then had the task of preparing a list of prospective authors, balanced by regions of the world and representing both sexes, and then recruiting authors. We were gratified that in many cases our first choices agreed to prepare chapters. Because the majority of psychological studies are conducted in Western Europe and North America, it is natural that most of the authors come from those regions, but we were also successful in recruiting authors from Asia, Latin America, and Oceania.

Several steps were involved in the preparation of the chapters, to make them as representative and useful as possible. Authors first submitted outlines of their chapters, then, after exchange with the Editors, submitted a first draft. The Editors discussed this draft with the author, who then submitted a revised draft. The revised draft was then sent for comments and suggestions to one or more members of the IEAB and to authors of related chapters. These comments and suggestions were then sent anonymously to the chapter author. In most cases, we were pleased that chapter authors were amenable to making changes to make their drafts more readable, to eliminate possible sources of misinterpretation, and to include further information they may have overlooked originally.

In a few cases, readers may notice differing points of view among chapters. This is to be expected in a developing field of study and research where complex problems are approached from different viewpoints. In some fields of psychology, there are also regional approaches to problems. Most of the chapters, however, could well have been written by an expert from a different country or region. In some cases, chapters are jointly written by authors from more than one country, or even from more than one continent.

We thank the authors for their skill and devotion in preparing expert and readable chapters, and in making knowledgeable critiques of other chapters. We thank the members of the IEAB for their wisdom in nominating authors and in critiquing draft chapters. Finally, we are happy to thank colleagues at Sage for their help in preparing this volume quickly and expertly. Our special thanks go to Ms. Angelika Quade in Kurt Pawlik's institute at the University of Hamburg for her devoted, untiring assistance in the preparation of this Handbook: from the first stages of chapter design, through manuscript solicitation and processing, until the final stages of proof-reading and indexing. This volume could not have taken its present shape without her continuous coordination and support.

Now we present this volume to the readers, hoping you will gain much pleasure and profit from it. Your comments are most welcome concerning scope and coverage of the Handbook and the content and presentation of particular chapters. These comments will help us in preparing the next edition of the Handbook.

Kurt Pawlik
Mark R. Rosenzweig

Part A
FOUNDATIONS AND METHODS OF PSYCHOLOGY

1

Psychological Science: Content, Methodology, History, and Profession

KURT PAWLIK AND MARK R. ROSENZWEIG

1.1 HUMAN BEHAVIOR AND EXPERIENCE

People have always had to study each other's behavior closely, but it was only in the nineteenth century that psychology emerged as an academic and scientific discipline, and only in the twentieth century that it also became a major field of professional activity. References to the human mind and how it may operate and translate into overt behavior can be traced back to specimens of written history, poetry, and philosophical speculations dating centuries B.C.E. In this sense, as the German psychologist Hermann Ebbinghaus pointed out, psychology has a long past, although it has only a short history. During the last one hundred years, psychological science has made tremendous strides, both in understanding behavior and mental processes and in applying this to practical problems, for example, in education and health, in industry and other work contexts, and in personal guidance and psychotherapy. This book illustrates the current scope of psychological science, its fields of basic and applied research, its methods and theories, and the wide range of its professional-psychological activities. It covers such diverse fields as learning over the life span, emotions and emotional disorders, memory processes and knowledge acquisition, and interpersonal behavior and group conflicts. It does so in an international perspective, bringing together editors and authors from around the world and drawing upon psychological research and professional expertise from different regions so as to give a balanced presentation with respect to cultures and ethnicity.

Relations of Psychological Science to Common-Sense Psychology

Modern scientific psychology differs importantly from what has variously been called folk psychology, lay psychology, common-sense, or implicit psychology. Common observations have led to a rich store of examples and beliefs about behavior, so that psychological discoveries may at times seem to be merely restatements of the obvious. But as Kelley (1992, p. 13) has pointed out, what is claimed to be 'obvious' is not obvious at all. Often the opposite of a finding would also be accepted as equally obvious. Also, folk psychology often includes contradictory principles. For example, many languages have a saying equivalent to 'You can't teach an old dog new tricks', and also another that holds 'You're never too old to learn.' The task of scientific psychology is to determine which of the apparently contradictory principles is correct, or under what circumstances one or the other is correct, and to formulate general principles relating age to ability to learn various kinds of material or skills. To the extent that a theorist challenges an audience's assumptions and practices, they will find the theory interesting, as Davis (1971, p. 311) pointed out. But even in the case of obvious beliefs, the role of scientific research is to add precision and reconcile apparent contradictions by identifying the conditions under which each of the different results will hold (Kelley, 1992, p. 15). Furthermore, comparative psychological research allows us to apply the methods of scientific inquiry to the study of folk psychology itself, yielding new insights into how people think people will behave, how they conceptualize human nature and behavior and its causes, including their own behavior.

As psychology began to develop as a scientific discipline and advance beyond folk concepts, it also led to unexpected discoveries and insights into human behavior, its evolution, its development, and its causes. A pertinent example is the discovery that a memory trace, once established, tends to persist in long-term memory. Failure to recall something from long-term memory is mainly (though not exclusively; see Estes, 1997) caused by faulty performance of memory search (retrieval) or recognition processes rather than genuine forgetting. It has been an important, far-reaching finding that past learning will not fade out by itself. Today this is widely recognized, for example in therapeutic practice, in the behavioral treatment of anxiety conditions. Here techniques have been developed to weaken learned fears, not by trying to erase the memory, but by enabling a patient to learn new, competing attitudes or behaviors. Another application of this same discovery led to modern techniques of neuropsychological rehabilitation of long-term memory performance in normal old-age.

In recent years, folk concepts about human behavior have become a focal point of research interests in connection with the notion of so-called indigenous psychology (see Section 1.2 below and Chapters 3, 18, and 30).

How Should Psychology Be Classified Among the Disciplines?

Originally philosophy was the trunk of general knowledge from which the sciences branched off. Thus, what we call physics used to be called 'natural philosophy'. In some countries there is still a tendency to assimilate psychology to philosophy, but in Europe and North America scientific psychology clearly diverged in its aims and methods from philosophy in the last century.

How is psychology classed among the sciences? An earlier (1991) and a more recent (1998) survey by the International Union of Psychological Science (IUPsyS) showed that psychology is classified differently in different countries and regions of the world. Some aspects of psychology suggest that it be classified with the biological sciences, whereas other aspects suggest that it belongs to the social sciences. The statutes of the IUPsyS state that it works to promote 'the development of psychological science, whether biological or social, normal or abnormal, pure or applied'. Responses to the 1991 IUPsyS questionnaire show that in different places, psychology is classified as a natural science, a biological or life science, a medical science, a behavioral science, a social science, an educational science, a humanity, or in a class of its own. In two-thirds of the national responses to the IUPsyS survey, psychology was classified differently at different universities within the same country, and even within the same university there may be psychology departments in different schools or faculties. Half the respondents from industrialized countries classified psychology as a biological or life science, and so did 33% of those from developing countries. On the other hand, half of the respondents from industrialized countries (but neither Canada nor the United States) also reported that at least some of their universities classified psychology as a humanity, but only 24% from developing countries did so.

In some universities, psychology was given a class of its own in 45% of the industrialized countries, but this is true in only two (11%) of the developing countries in our sample. In the United States, publications of the National Science Board and the National Science Foundation put psychology in its own class; its neighbors are, on the one side, the life sciences (including agricultural sciences and medical sciences) and, on the other side, the social sciences (including economics, sociology/anthropology, and political science).

Notwithstanding the variety of classifications of psychology in different countries and different universities, and in view of the research programs of modern psychology, it would be more accurate either to acknowledge that the domain of psychology overlaps those of biological, behavioral, and social sciences or, as many organizations already do, to give psychological science a class of its own (Rosenzweig, 1992, pp. 7–8).

One way to integrate biological and social lines of thinking and research within the discipline of psychology is to recognize and combine the structural (largely biological) and content (largely social) aspects of behavior. The basic principles of associative learning, for example, as described in Chapter 7, originate largely in innate properties of the central nervous system that mediate learning. These structural properties hold throughout a species and even across many species. Similarly the neurophysiology of speech resides in basic neurobiological structures whose characteristics are revealed in the way children of different ethnic backgrounds acquire their culture's language systems. At the same time, the nature and content of associations learned by any single person or the specificity of the sign system and grammar rules of any language are bound to culture and social milieus. Thus in the study of human learning or of language behavior, perspectives of structure and of content must become integrated, and the methodology of psychological science has to develop so as to provide for this approach from both a biological and a social perspective. As Pawlik (1994a) has argued, this combined sociobiological approach in the study of behavior makes for a unique role of psychology in the study of human nature (see also Section 1.3 below).

Growing Recognition of the Scientific Status of Psychology

The 1991 and 1998 IUPsyS surveys asked whether recognition of psychological research in the respondents' countries was increasing, remaining the same, or decreasing. Twenty-six of the 38 national responses stated that recognition is increasing, and only one response said 'decreasing.'

By now the national academies of science or similar organizations in most industrialized countries have psychologists among their members, and this is true for an increasing number of developing countries (Rosenzweig, 1992, Table 10, p. 62). The first psychologist was elected to the Third World Academy of Sciences in 1996. In 1982 the International Union of Psychological Science became a member of the International Council of Science (then called the International Council of Scientific Unions), the apex of international scientific organizations. Further evidence of recognition of the scientific status of psychology is presented and discussed by Rosenzweig (1992). A resource list of references on the state and development of psychology in different countries has been published by Imada (1996).

Dictionary Definitions of Psychology

Dictionary definitions of psychology in several countries of North America and Western Europe reflect general usage in defining psychology as a science, thus testifying to widespread acceptance of this status. Here are a few examples of such definitions:

The *Oxford English Dictionary* (2nd ed., 1989): '1.a. The science of the nature, functions, and phenomena of the human mind (formerly also of the soul) . . .

'c. In mod. usage, the signification of the word has broadened to include (a) The scientific study of the mind as an entity and its relationship to the physical body, based on observations of the behaviour and activity aroused by specific stimuli; and (b) The study of the behaviour of an individual or of a selected group of individuals when interacting with the environment or in a given social context. So experimental psychology, the experimental study of the responses of an individual to stimuli; social psychology, the study of the interaction between an individual and the social group to which he belongs' (vol. 12, p. 766).

The *Random House College Dictionary* (1984): '1. the science of the mind or of mental states and processes. 2. the science of human and animal behavior.'

The Larousse French dictionaries show a transition in definitions around 1960 from psychology as a branch of philosophy to psychology as a science. Emphasis on the scientific nature of modern psychology is also found, for example, in the *Grande dizionario della lingua italiana*

(1988) or in the German *Grosses Duden Lexikon* (Bibliographisches Institut, 1969) and *Brockhaus Enzyklopädie* (Bibliographisches Institut, 1996).

Chinese dictionaries define psychology as 'A science studying the objective laws of psychological activities' (*Xin Hua Dictionary*, 1980) and list fields such as developmental psychology, physiological psychology, and social psychology, as well as applied fields such as educational psychology, industrial psychology, medical psychology, sports psychology, art psychology, aviation psychology, and so on (*Ci Hai Dictionary*, 1989).

Why Does the Classification of Psychology Matter?

Plato wrote, 'What a country honors will flourish there.' Obtaining recognition of the scientific achievements of psychological research and its applications is both a reward for psychological investigators and practitioners and one of the conditions that fosters further achievements. Failure to obtain recognition for the scientific status of psychological research retards the further advance of such research and its applications. It also impairs recruitment of students to the field. Psychologists from various parts of the world testify to this, as the following examples show.

Writing from China and Hong Kong, Leung and Zhang (1995, p. 698) note '. . . that the classification of psychology has implications for its development. If psychology is classified as a science, funding is usually more adequate. The Institute of Psychology in China is under the Chinese Academy of Sciences, and the funding received is better than for other social sciences. In Hong Kong, psychology is classified as a laboratory-based subject, and funded better than economics and sociology. On the other hand, if psychology is grouped under humanities, equipment and technical support is often insufficient.'

Writing from Mexico, Diaz-Loving, Reyes-Lagunas and Diaz-Guerrero (1995) state that the fact that social sciences are considered there as part of humanities and not as sciences makes it difficult to obtain funding for research and hard to attract students and to obtain positions outside of academia for them.

In Australia, a report prepared for the National Committee of Psychology of the Australian Academy of Science (Australian Research Council Discipline Research Strategies, 1996) notes problems of funding for biological psychology due in part to 'The inadequacy of classifying psychology for funding purposes as a social science, and thus not recognising explicitly its essence as a behavioural science, or its crucial biological science aspect . . .' (p. 8).

1.2 FIELDS OF PSYCHOLOGY AS A SCIENCE

Some fields of psychology are defined in terms of the phenomena investigated, such as child psychology and learning theory, and this book contains many chapters devoted to such subject matter specialties. Other fields are defined in terms of the approaches or methods used, such as general psychology versus the study of individual differences, or basic research versus applied psychology. Let us consider a few such fields here, and they will be exemplified in several of the following chapters.

The study of general psychology is often contrasted with the study of individual differences. General psychology seeks to find principles and rules that apply to all people or members of a species, and we will see examples in such chapters as Chapter 5 on Perception and Chapter 7 on Memory. The study of individual differences emphasizes relatively persistent differences in the structure of behavior among persons or members of the same species; we will see examples in Chapter 16 on Personality and Individual Differences.

We saw above that psychology is sometimes classified as a biological science and sometimes as a social science. Similarly, within psychology the fields of biological psychology and social psychology are distinguished. Biological psychology, formerly called physiological psychology, is concerned with the relationships between biological processes, on the one hand, and behavior and mental processes, on the other. This approach will be examined in Chapter 4. Social psychology studies interactions within and among groups and the ways in which individuals influence or respond to each other. The social/societal bases of behavior are examined in Chapter 3.

Social psychology in turn is sometimes contrasted with cross-cultural psychology. Rather than assuming that social interactions and influences are invariant among all cultures, cross-cultural psychology examines to what extent they are the same and to what extent they differ. This approach is examined in Chapter 14. Beyond this, some psychological researchers emphasize that psychology itself is a social product, and there are active attempts to indigenize psychology, that is, to develop variants of psychology that are especially appropriate to specific societies and cultures or that will consider or incorporate implicit knowledge about human nature as it has developed in a society's system of traditions, beliefs, and values. Although indigenization has become a rather popular concept, several recent analyses have been critical of indigenization as a goal, as Adair and Kagitcibasi (1995) have discussed. Kagitcibasi (1992) favors an orientation or methodology oriented towards discovering indigenous reality, but she questions indigenization as a goal. The topic of indigenization of psychology is discussed in Chapter 18.

Basic psychology is sometimes contrasted with applied psychology, the former being concerned with discovering facts and laws of psychology and the latter with applying psychological principles, methods and knowledge to practical situations. Some writers consider theoretical psychology as yet another, distinct field of psychological science (see Section 1.5 below and Chapter 26). Although many psychologists devote their efforts principally to one or the other of these poles of activity, it is now widely accepted that basic research has often been inspired by practical observations and problems, and that attempts at application can provide important tests of the adequacy of psychological hypotheses and further theoretical developments. Therefore there is much communication and interaction between those who do basic research and those who apply psychological knowledge and principles. Many of the following chapters present not only basic research but also its applications in the various areas of psychology.

1.3 HUMAN BEHAVIOR AS A SHARED OBJECT OF STUDY

There are several other sciences that also have human behavior or aspects of it as their object of study. They can be clustered into three groups, depending on whether they follow a biological-medical, a social, or a predominately applied approach. In this section these 'correlated' sciences are briefly introduced, with an aim towards defining the specifics of psychology and its contributions as a science.

Correlated Biological-Medical Sciences

Though rooted conceptually in seventeenth to eighteenth-century philosophy, empirical psychology as an academic discipline grew out of physiology. Building on seminal contributions to the study of human perception by physiologists like Johannes Müller and Hermann Helmholtz, many first-generation university professors of psychology actually entered psychology after graduate study of medicine or physiology. Famous examples are Wilhelm Wundt (1843–1920), founder of the first University Laboratory of Psychology (1875) at the University of Leipzig, Germany, or William James (1842–1910) at Harvard University, USA, a founding father of empirical psychology in America. Close ties between physiology and psychology were typical not only in the founding years of academic psychology but continued ever since and now undergo an influential revival in modern neuroscience.

How can one differentiate between physiology and psychology? A common definition explains physiology as that 'branch of biology that deals with functions and activities of life or of living matter (as organs, tissues, or cells) and of the physical and chemical phenomena involved' (Merriam-Webster, 1983, p. 888). By contrast, psychology is commonly defined as the science of behavior and experience, its causes and consequences (effects). To the extent that one can gain knowledge about behavior and conscious experience by investigating correlated functions of living matter, like the central nervous system, physiology and psychology share a common object of study. At the same time they typically differ in study approach, with physiologists preferring to work 'upwards', from living organs' tissue towards behavior, whereas psychologists prefer working 'downwards', from complex behavioral data towards their biological roots. While both sciences must cooperate, especially in methodological terms, they maintain their independence, also as a safeguard against undue biological reductionism (in psychology) or undue mentalism (in physiology).

Similar relations hold between psychology and other biomedical specialties such as neurophysiology (physiology of the nervous system), endocrinology (physiology of endocrine glands), immunology (physiology of the immune system), genetics (science of hereditary bases of organismic variations), and human biology (also called anthropology by non-American authors and including the study of phylogenetic evolution of modern humans). Chapter 4 discusses these biological bases of human behavior and experience, while specifics of the biology of learning, perception, language behavior, emotion, and motivation are dealt with in the respective specialized chapters.

In research and in professional terms, psychology interfaces with the medical sciences both in clinical contexts and in the health sector at large, that is, in the assessment, prevention or therapy of psychological causes and effects of illnesses and diseases and in broader health-related issues, like health education. This holds especially for a field as interdisciplinary as mental health, where psychology and psychiatry (the clinical science of mental disorders) join force in investigating and treating mental disorders. Other examples of cross-disciplinary cooperation between psychology and medicine involve neurology (in the study and treatment of psychological disorders resulting from nervous system diseases and injuries), pediatrics (e.g., in children born prematurely), gerontology (in psychological care for the aged), and in all clinical disciplines (like gynecology) that involve intensive-care programs or deal with cancer and other severe forms of illness. Clinical and health psychology, psychopathology, neuropsychology, psychosomatics, and medical psychology are specialties developed in these contexts. They are covered in Chapters 21 and 22 (Clinical Psychology) and in Chapter 23 (Health Psychology).

A concept sometimes confused with psychology is psychoanalysis. The latter refers to a specific theoretical and therapeutic approach in studying and treating behavior disorders, mainly of the so-called neurotic type such as anxiety disorders or obsessive-compulsive disorders. Founded by the Viennese psychiatrist Sigmund Freud (1856–1939) around the end of the nineteenth century, psychoanalysis is based on the general notion that non-conscious processes play an important role in shaping a person's personality and, in case of unresolved conflicts, in the possible development of behavior disorders. Inaccessible in principle to direct observation, unconscious mechanisms are inferred from dream-content analysis, from a patient's verbal reports while under hypnosis, or in the course of (usually long-term) therapeutic interventions. Psychoanalysis developed into a school of thought of its own, with varying degrees of input to and from academic psychology in different countries. Today psychoanalytic therapy is but one of several methodologies of psychotherapy, some of them often more effective than psychoanalysis in terms of costs and outcome (see Chapter 22).

Correlated Social Sciences

The ancient Greek philosopher and founder of speculative-philosophical psychology, Aristotle (384–322 B.C.E.), is quoted for the programmatic statement 'ho ánthropos zōon politikón estin', or 'the human is a social being' (Aristotle, *Politeia*). True enough, the content of human behavior and its development cannot be described, let alone explained, without reference to the social system of which any one of us is a member and to which each of us contributes. The basics of this social context of human behavior are presented in Chapters 3 and 16, while specific social interactions in perception, learning, etc. come up in the respective topical chapters.

How does psychology's contribution to the study of human behavior differ from that of other social sciences, in particular sociology, political science, and economics? Sociology, the science of society, of social institutions and of social relationships, studies human behavior as part of these wider, collective structures and processes. By contrast, psychologists typically take off from the level of the individual. Often the two directions of study will prove complementary, for example in the study of social attitudes or in small-group research. By contrast, political science concentrates on the description and analysis of political (governmental and nongovernmental) institutions and processes and on structures of political action. Again there is overlap with psychology, as in the study of voting behavior or of interactions between government institutions and the individual. Finally, economics is the social science chiefly concerned with the study of the production, distribution and consumption of goods and services. Although this ties in closely with many facets of human behavior and with personal and collective values and preferences, cross-disciplinary cooperation between economics and psychology still leaves much to be desired.

Other social sciences correlated with psychology one way or another include ethnology (the description and analysis of behavior in its variations within and between cultures), human or social geography (the study of human behavior from a geographic-regional perspective), demography (the science of human population development), and public opinion research. Links and relationships between psychology and other social sciences are discussed in detail in Chapters 3, 27, and 31.

Other Cross-Disciplinary Links

Psychology fulfills an important role also as a resource science for education, particularly special education of the handicapped, in educational counseling and in vocational guidance (cf. Chapter 23). Beyond the health sector and education, other applied sciences closely linked with psychology include business administration, the legal sciences (especially criminology and penology – the descriptive and normative study of legal and administrative procedures in the treatment of offenders), marketing research, ergonomics (or human engineering) and – more recently – environmental sciences. In these fields psychological knowledge is sought and applied to develop more effective problem solving strategies; Chapters 24, 25 and 26 provide synoptic overviews.

Finally, psychology has traditional links with philosophy and epistemology (the descriptive and normative analysis of scientific knowledge acquisition) and is a contributing field of science to such multi-disciplinary sciences as neuroscience and cognitive science. Neuroscience covers the scientific study of the structure and functioning of the nervous system, including so-called behavioral neuroscience that specializes in the study of behavior and experience in a neurobiological context. Cognitive science refers to the scientific study of information processing, knowledge acquisition, and knowledge-guided action. Recently these two fields have become united into the new, still broader field of cognitive neuroscience (see Gazzaniga, 2000).

Other disciplines connecting with psychology are linguistics (the study of language, with the specialty of psycholinguistics), informatics (computer science), and artificial intelligence research. Chapter 31 looks in some detail into these cross-disciplinary linkages of psychological science.

Curiously enough, up to now there is hardly any scientific cross-breeding, let alone direct scientific cooperation between psychology and history, the branch of knowledge that studies, and attempts to explain, past records of human action and its contexts. The long-standing question, whether we are able to learn from history or unable to do so (see Hegel, 1840), becomes pertinent here. There have been recent claims to bring psychology, especially social psychology, into closer cooperation with history, and vice versa. This should prove instrumental in accounting for historical records and contexts within the laws of social behavior and, at the same time, identify these records and contexts as research input for constructing and testing theories in social psychology.

1.4 PSYCHOLOGICAL METHODOLOGY

The methods of psychological science are dealt with in detail in Chapter 2. They enable psychologists to gain knowledge about human behavior and conscious experience by systematic observation and experiment and to investigate, on the basis of such data, variations, dependencies, causes, correlates, and consequences of human behavior. In this way empirical generalizations become feasible and descriptive laws of behavior can be deduced and tested.

One important distinction in psychological methodology relates to the objectivity versus subjectivity of a method, that is, the degree to which its application and results prove independent of the persons applying the method, their explicit or implicit expectations, beliefs, or values. In the development of psychological methods over the past one hundred years, increasingly higher standards of objectivity and reliability have been achieved. Special methods like tests and questionnaires have been developed for the psychological assessment of individual differences in behavior (see Chapter 19). In addition, methods have been adapted from applied mathematics, numerical analysis, and statistics for the design of experiments, for behavioral measurement (scaling), descriptive data analysis (descriptive statistics), and for testing hypotheses (statistical inference). Depending on the kind of behavior under study, the data collected may be quantitative (numerical, like reaction-time measures) or categorical (qualitative, such as a client's narration in a clinical interview or a psychotherapy session). Different methods of analysis have been developed for quantitative and qualitative behavioral data. Since the 1960s, electronic computing facilities have come to play a growing role in psychological methodology, first only for (statistical) data analysis, then also in data acquisition and, more recently, in data condensation (for example, in multivariate personality research or in psychophysiology). Today, personal computers have become indispensable tools for psychologists, and special software has been developed for computer-assisted psychological data-acquisition, data-storage, and data-analysis, both in research and for practical-professional work as in psychological assessment and testing (see Chapters 2 and 19).

Varieties and Criteria of Psychological Methodology

Methods of psychological observation, experimentation and data analysis vary with the kind of behavior and the type of question studied. In experimental research, measures of behavior are investigated as a function of one or several experimental independent variable(s). For example, an investigator may study how the speed of learning a new psychomotor coordination task will depend on the pacing of learning trials or the kind of feedback offered to subjects. In the design of an experiment the choice of independent variables is determined by the hypotheses derived from the theory guiding the study.

By contrast, in survey research, psychological phenomena are investigated with respect to variations accessible through a subject sampling plan. For example, a sample of 120 sixth-graders may be assessed in tests of school motivation and in a questionnaire of self-reported parental support in order to study correlations between these two sets of variables. In this case 'natural' sources of variation (between families, social classes, etc.) are studied, which are beyond the investigator's control.

Cronbach (1957) has referred to these two types of methodology as experimental versus correlational psychology. They have one aspect in common: behavioral data are collected under standardized conditions. In contrast, in so-called field studies, data collection is devised so that it can take place in a person's natural environment, at home, at work, in leisure settings or in other situations, as required by a study design. In recent years, further development of portable computer-based methods for psychological and psychophysiological data acquisition have become immensely helpful in building up genuine field research in psychology (Pawlik, 1998).

Psychological methods must meet stringent methodological, especially psychometric, criteria to be considered adequate in scientific-professional terms. They are discussed at length in Chapters 2 and 19 and include, in addition to objectivity, standards of reliability (percentage of variance in the data attributable to 'true' sources of variation, as compared with accidental or 'error' variance) and validity (degree to which observed variations are due to the intended component of behavior and only to this component). Other quality standards of psychological methods refer, for example, to the sensitivity of a method and its culture-fairness (freedom from sub-population bias).

Ethics of Psychological Investigations

Next to standards of methodology, psychological research both with human and non-human participants (or 'subjects', as they were called in earlier literature) must also meet criteria of professional ethics. They are included in the codes of ethics devised by the psychological associations of many countries. Some may even be part of the legal codes in a country.

In research with human participants, the principle of informed consent is considered indispensable (with only few and special exceptions as in orderly penal procedure). Informed consent is a guiding principle in national professional codes of ethics for psychology (Leach & Harbin, 1997). It maintains that participants in a study or an assessment must be informed in advance as to the purpose and methods of that study or assessment and the use to be made of its results. On the basis of this information, opportunity

must be granted to voluntarily decline participation. Special rules of research ethics have been developed for research with handicapped persons and for clinical therapy research. In psychological assessment, testing, and counseling or therapy, psychologists are committed to assure strict confidentiality of results as related to concrete individuals. In Germany, for example, the penal code explicitly refers to psychologists, like doctors, attorneys or clergy, as being bound by the rule of personal confidentiality.

Many countries have passed laws concerning the use of animals in research, especially research involving pain or stress. Typically, regulations differentiate between species (for example, vertebrates versus non-vertebrates, with especially strict regulations for work with non-human primates) and include rules for animal care (housing, feeding, etc.).

Today in many countries funding agencies, universities and other institutions for psychological research have set up ethics committees to guide researchers and agencies in the preparation of research proposals and in granting decisions.

1.5 THEORETICAL PSYCHOLOGY

Theory development in psychology and a review of major theoretical systems in psychology are taken up in Chapter 29. A psychological theory is a system of statements, any one logically non-contradictory to all other statements in that same theory, which are developed (constructed) so as to account for a large number or range of phenomena in terms of fewer concepts (constructs), principles, or processes. In this way theories are parsimonious ('reductive' in the good sense of the word) and allow representation of many phenomena as a function of fewer theoretical terms. In a broad sense, these theoretical constructs, principles or processes are then said to explain the phenomena under consideration. Chapter 29 discusses alternative approaches to theory construction in psychology.

For example, a theory of anxiety disorders will attempt to explain the development of fear and of fear-responsive behavior on the basis of a few basic principles of learning and emotion (see, for example, Gray, 1982). In order for such a theory to be testable, it is indispensable that each term (concept, principle, or process) used in a statement be linked to relevant observables, that is, to operations of behavior observation. If a theory does not fulfill the requirement of operational definition, it will prove logically impossible to devise a test of its appropriateness in a way that can not immediately be declared improper by simply changing definitions of terms! Equally obvious, no matter how appropriate a theory may appear today for a given set of phenomena, new evidence tomorrow may change the picture or even disprove the theory. In psychology this has happened more than once. For example, the theory of general intelligence developed by Charles Spearman in the early twentieth century (Spearman, 1904), seemingly in good accord with then available evidence on intelligence test intercorrelations, was soon questioned by Cyril Burt and finally disproved empirically in 1934 by L. L. Thurstone (see Wolman, 1985, for a synoptic review).

It is this notion of relativity of scientific theories that led the Austrian-British philosopher Karl R. Popper (1974) to emphasize that the truthfulness of a theory can never be proven (in the full sense of the word); instead theories can only, and at best, be shown not to be in conflict with data at hand, that is, be non-falsifiable for the time being. Methods and criteria for theory testing constitute a classical topic of epistemology and have been dealt with extensively in modern analytical philosophy (see, for example, Lenk, 1975). Popper's falsifiability criterion has not remained undisputed, still most research in psychology has been guided by it, in addition to the criterion of replicability of a finding, that is, its independent confirmation by other researchers and in other laboratories.

In this Handbook pertinent theories of human behavior, of development and of mental functioning are reviewed in the respective chapters, most notably in Chapters 5–18.

1.6 History of Psychological Science

Standard histories of psychology have mainly been written from the viewpoints of Western Europe or North America, but the history of psychology has varied among different countries and regions of the world, as is reflected in some recent books (e.g., Gilgen & Gilgen, 1987; Sexton & Hogan, 1992) and symposia (e.g., Adair & Kagitcibasi, 1995; Pawlik & Rosenzweig, 1994). In every region of the world, systems of thought were concerned with human experience and behavior. Modern scientific psychology began in the German-speaking countries after the middle of the nineteenth century, and rapidly spread to North America, but it reached many developing areas of the world only after World War II.

In Europe and North America psychology developed from both philosophy and physiology, and from other disciplines as well. As Mueller (1979) noted, several lines of research that antedated psychology all led into the development of psychology in Europe and North America. These included the following lines:

- work on sensation and perception by physicists and biologists such as Newton, Young, Fechner, Helmholtz, and Wundt;
- work on localization of psychological functions in the nervous system by physiologists such as Bell and Magendie, Sechenov, Fritsch and Hitzig, and Hughlings Jackson;
- sociomedical work by investigators such as Pinel, Charcot, Freud, and early workers on mental testing such as Binet and Ebbinghaus;
- materialistic attempts to reduce life processes to chemistry and biology in the work of such scientists as Loeb and Jennings;
- Darwin's theory of evolution. This was congenial to and fostered the American interests in individual differences (the variation that makes natural selection possible). It also made the study of animal behavior appropriate as a pathway to the understanding of human beings, and it made the development of comparative psychology reasonable.

At the same time that psychology was evolving from a philosophical to a scientific enterprise in the latter half of the nineteenth century, this evolution was also favored by a transition in the organization of colleges and universities in many industrialized countries from strictly undergraduate institutions to organizations that included, and often specialized in, postgraduate education.

The growth of psychology was also fostered by the organization of courses, laboratories, scientific associations, journals, and congresses. In this regard, the development of psychology paralleled that of other sciences in the developed countries. Courses in psychology in the United States evolved from courses with such names as 'Intellectual Philosophy', 'Mental Philosophy', and 'Mental Science' that were taught in American colleges in the first half of the nineteenth century. Textbooks for such courses began to use the term 'psychology' in their titles by the 1830–40s, but courses entitled psychology became popular only in the 1870–80s. Large numbers of colleges were founded in the US by various churches, and later most of these became non-denominational. The formation of state universities was promoted by grants from the federal government. In the last third of the nineteenth century, the philanthropy of several wealthy individuals led to the founding of private universities with an emphasis on research and graduate studies. The widespread philanthropic support of American institutions of higher education is characteristic of the American scene and differentiates it from most other countries. Graduate programs in psychology soon emerged. In 1875 G. Stanley Hall received what was perhaps the world's first PhD degree in psychology from Harvard for work done with William James.

Laboratories were early seen to be necessary to pursue psychology in the Fechnerian–Wundtian tradition. The first laboratory of experimental psychology was established 1875 by Wilhelm Wundt at the University of Leipzig, to be followed in the German-speaking countries by the founding of institutes of psychology at the Universities of Bonn, Graz, and Kiel in the 1890s. Chapter 30 provides some comparative information on the development of psychology in different countries. By 1892, about 20 American colleges and universities had laboratories of psychology. As of 1900, laboratories of psychology had been founded at 41 US colleges and universities, more than in all the rest of the world.

Almost from the start of modern psychological research, investigators from different laboratories and institutions have met to discuss their research. This soon led to formation of local, then national, and international organizations to foster such meetings and encourage research. The world's oldest national psychological association is the American Psychological Association (APA), founded in 1892. This was part of the movement to establish disciplinary societies in the US, starting with the American Chemical Society in 1876. National psychological organizations were formed in France and in the United Kingdom in 1901, in Germany in 1904, in Argentina in 1908, and in Italy in 1910. For dates of formation of other national psychological organizations, see Table 30.1 in Chapter 30. In many developing countries, national psychological associations were formed only in the 1950s or even later.

By 1881 psychologists were discussing the need for an international meeting, and the first International Congress of Psychology took place in Paris in 1889. Subsequent International Congresses of Psychology have taken place every three to five years, with gaps caused by the two World Wars. Since 1951 these congresses have been organized by the IUPsyS, and since 1972 they have taken place every four years. The International Congresses of Psychology at Leipzig (1980), Acapulco (1984), Sydney (1988), Brussels (1992), and Montreal (1996) have each attracted about 4,000 participants. (For a history of the International Congresses of Psychology and the IUPsyS, see Rosenzweig, Holtzman, Sabourin and Belanger, 2000.) The 27th International Congress of Psychology takes place in Stockholm in 2000, and the 28th Congress is scheduled for Beijing in 2004.

Throughout its history, psychology has been shaped also by social events and movements. For example, the two World Wars had major effects on the development of psychology. In World War I, psychologists were active in testing and classifying recruits. This stimulated further applications of psychology in different fields also in the postwar years. During World War I, the annual number of psychological publications in German fell below those in English, and thereafter English maintained its predominance. In World War II, psychologists also aided in designing equipment, in preparing training materials and in giving psychotherapy to members of the armed forces. In the United States, the postwar years saw a tremendous expansion of psychology. Many returning soldiers went to colleges and universities on government scholarships, fostering the growth of academic psychology. Also, the government subsidized graduate programs, especially in clinical psychology, to aid in caring for veterans with psychological problems. Across the Atlantic Ocean, in Austria and Germany the terror regime of the Nazis and the war brought psychological research almost to an absolute halt (Pawlik, 1994b); it took more than a decade to succeed gradually in re-establishing a psychological university education after the war. On the other hand, World War II weakened the colonial powers, leading to independence of many Asian and African countries; this in turn strengthened the movement toward development of indigenous psychologies, relevant to different cultural contexts. All throughout its history, the development of psychology proved particularly sensitive to infringements of personal freedom and civil rights as has been shown, for example, by Jing (1994, and Chapter 30) for the so-called Cultural Revolution and its effects on the state of psychology in China.

1.7 PSYCHOLOGY AROUND THE WORLD: INTERNATIONAL DISTRIBUTION OF PSYCHOLOGISTS AND PSYCHOLOGICAL ORGANIZATIONS

International Distribution of Psychologists

The number of psychologists in the world has been increasing rapidly in the last decades. An estimate made for 1980 showed about 260,000 (Rosenzweig, 1982). By 1991 the total probably reached 500,000 according the 1991 IUPsyS survey (Rosenzweig, 1992), indicating approximately a doubling over a decade. By 2000, the total is undoubtedly close to one million.

In making these estimates, local definitions of 'psychologist' were used; that is, the numbers include those who are considered to be qualified to call themselves psychologists in each country. The amount of training for this differs greatly among countries. In the United States and Canada, most psychologists have a doctoral degree, and the others have master's degrees. In many other countries, four or five years of postsecondary education suffice, and in some countries as little as three years of postsecondary training are considered sufficient.

To put the worldwide number of psychologists into perspective, Rosenzweig (1992, pp. 19–21) compared it with the numbers of physicians and of neuroscientists, because the work of the latter groups parallels that of certain main groups of psychologists: those who provide health-services and those who are engaged in research and academic work. It appeared that in 1992 the total number of psychologists was about one twelfth the number of physicians in the world but about twenty times the number of neuroscientists.

Psychologists are distributed very unequally around the world. In the 1991 IUPsyS survey, the number of psychologists per million population was 550 in 11 industrialized countries outside of Eastern Europe, 83/million in four countries of Eastern Europe, 191/million in 14 developing countries outside of China, and 2.4/million in China. The numbers of psychologists engaged in research showed even greater inequality of distribution: 23/million in 15 industrialized countries and only 4.2/million in 15 developing countries.

The ratios of female to male psychologists in main regions of the world are summarized by Sexton and Hogan (1992, pp. 469–470) as follows. In European countries, 53% of all psychologists are women, in South American and Caribbean countries, 70% are women, but overall in Asian countries only 25% are women, although some Asian countries have high percentages of women. In the United States the percentage of doctorate degrees going to women had risen to 58% by 1990. Among these doctorates, the ratio of women to men was clearly larger in the areas of educational (2.38), developmental (2.36), school (1.89), social (1.74), counseling (1.52), and clinical psychology (1.42); these areas where women predominate in the US include all of the health-provider fields but are not limited to them. The ratio of women to men obtaining doctorates in the US in 1990 was

lowest in experimental (0.52) and industrial/organizational (0.75) psychology.

International Distribution of Psychological Organizations

Psychologists have formed many national, regional, and international psychological organizations, as well as organizations for specialized fields of psychology. Figure 1.1 shows some of these psychological organizations, as well as relations to some international bodies. In 1892 the first still-existing national psychological organization was formed – the American Psychological Association. As of mid-1999, 66 national organizations belong to the International Union of Psychological Science (IUPsyS), and more are joining every year. The IUPsyS traces its history back to the international committee that organized International Congresses of Psychology, after the first such Congress in Paris in 1889. There are also regional organizations, such as the Interamerican Society of Psychology (Sociedad Interamericana de Psicologia) or the Association de Psychologie Scientifique de Langue Française.

Among the international associations with individual memberships, the largest is the International Association for Applied Psychology (IAAP), founded in 1920. The IAAP and 10 other international organizations are affiliated with the IUPsyS.

The psychological organizations with individual members vary enormously in size, the largest being the American Psychological Association with about 87,000 full members as of 1999. These organizations perform many important functions, including holding regular scientific and professional meetings to help their members keep up-to-date on advances in their fields; publishing scientific and professional journals; helping to inform the public about psychological matters; striving for legislation to improve support for education, research, and professional representation; and cooperating with scientific and professional organizations of related disciplines.

1.8 Psychology as a Profession

If members of the public are asked what work psychologists do, some will reply that they conduct psychotherapy with individual clients and others will say that they teach in colleges and universities. These answers are correct as far as they go, but they do not begin to suggest, let alone encompass the wide variety of occupations psychologists perform or the variety of

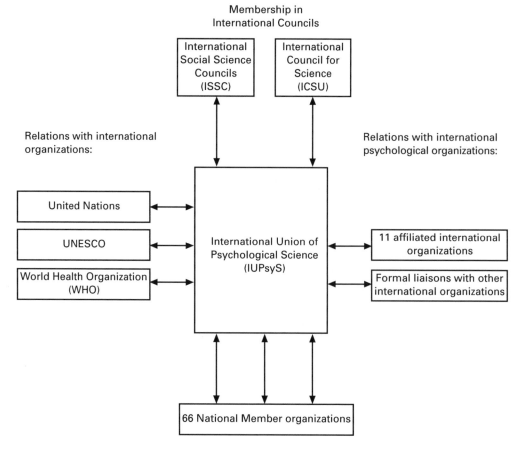

Figure 1.1   *Relations of the International Union of Psychological Science (IUPsyS) with other organizations*

their workplaces. Let us consider some of the variety of psychologists' occupations, drawing some of the following material from a publication of the American Psychological Association (APA) that takes up this topic at greater length than we can here (*Psychology/Careers for the twenty-first century: Scientific problem solvers*).

Many psychologists conduct research as their primary or secondary occupation. Some of this research takes place in laboratories where experimental conditions can be carefully controlled. Much of this laboratory research is conducted in universities, government agencies, and private organizations such as pharmaceutical firms. Some psychological research is carried out in the field, in offices and factories, public places, schools, and hospitals, where behavior is observed and recorded as it occurs naturally. Here psychologists study and contribute to the work environment, partly in what is called industrial/ organizational or personnel psychology. As the APA publication notes:

Psychologists study what makes people effective, satisfied, and motivated in their jobs; what distinguishes good workers or managers from poor ones; and what conditions of work promote high or low productivity, morale, and safety.

Some psychologists design programs for recruiting, selecting, placing, and training employees. They help make changes in the way the organization is set up.

Others help design the actual tasks, tools, and environments with which people must deal when doing their jobs. These specialists can also help design the products that organizations turn out and conduct research related to product design. For example, they play a big role in making computer hardware more user-friendly, which in turn contributes to both to operator performance in the workplace and product acceptability in the marketplace.

Psychologists with training in mental health and health care also deal with the health and adjustment of individuals in the work setting. They work with employee assistance plans that provide help with drug or alcohol addiction problems; they also foster healthy behavior. (American Psychological Association, 1996, p. 17)

Organizational/industrial psychologists work for private companies or in governmental agencies. Some have set up their own consulting firms. Still other psychologists work to promote physical and mental health. In some countries, many of these psychologists have a private practice, with clients and patients coming to the psychologist's office. In other countries, most health psychologists work in governmental agencies. According to the APA publication:

Increasingly, . . . psychologists in independent practice are contracting on either a part-time or full-time basis with organizations to provide a wide range of services. For example, a psychologist can join a health practice and work with a team of other health care providers, such as physicians, nutritionists, physiotherapists, and social workers to prevent or treat illness . . .

Psychologists also instruct students who are training to become health care professionals, such as physicians and nurses, about psychological factors involved in illness. And they advise health care providers already in practice about the psychological bases of much illness so that symptoms that are psychological in origin can be better diagnosed and treated. Psychologists involved in health care teams typically work in hospitals, medical schools, outpatient clinics, nursing home, pain clinics, rehabilitation facilities, and community health and mental health centers. (American Psychological Association, 1996, p. 19)

1.9 Organization of Study in Psychology

Academic and professional training in psychology vary, at times to a surprising degree, among universities and, still more so, among countries and regions; they also vary depending on institutional structures of higher education. In the present context only a brief summary presentation is feasible. We shall first look at the organization of study in industrialized countries.

One-Level versus Two-Level Study

Universities organized in the British College tradition – that is in Australia, North America and in the United Kingdom – still adhere to the two-level structure of separate undergraduate and graduate schools, whereas universities in most Continental European countries follow a one-level, continuous organization. Such structural differences in higher-education institutions also relate to differences in pre-university (secondary or high school-level) education in the respective countries and they have consequences, among others, for the organization of an academic curriculum. In the one-level structure, introductory (undergraduate) and advanced (graduate) curriculum components are organized within one and the same school, usually with significant and flexible interplay between the two.

A recent survey by Newstead and Makinen (1997) illustrates this point. They compared university training schedules in psychology from a survey conducted by the European Federation of Professional Psychologists' Associations and from additional reports obtained from 14 European countries. They found that 15 countries offer a one-level course in psychology and only five countries follow a two-level model of teaching. One implication of a one-level program is that almost all students completing the first years of study in psychology attempt to continue and complete the full course. This is different from the situation, for example, in the US where admission to graduate school is contingent upon a new selection procedure and by no means automatic after graduation from college with a major in psychology. As a result, significant numbers of students in the US complete an undergraduate program in psychology without continuing for graduate training in psychology. The design of an undergraduate program in psychology takes this into account. By contrast, the one-level program is oriented towards full-scale study in psychology from the first semester onwards.

Generalist versus Specialist Training Philosophy

The survey by Newstead and Makinen (1997) also highlights another source of variation in psychology course design: the difference between a generalist and a specialist training philosophy. Among European countries, the generalist model is followed in 12 countries. Notwithstanding some specialization among applied fields, typically in the last 2 years of a 5-year course, students are trained to acquire proficiency in all major fields of psychology and prepare for a wide sector, if not the full range of professional psychological activities. This is in marked contrast to the typical North American program which requires the student to choose one, often relatively narrow, field of specialization from the first or second graduate year onwards. While a generalist curriculum design emphasizes breadth of competence at the expense of possibly too early in-depth specialization, the specialist curriculum design builds on exemplary high competence in one or a few fields, at the necessary expense of overview and transfer of knowledge across fields. The relative merits and shortcomings of either model still await detailed analysis; quite likely, they will vary also with differences in the economic and educational state of development of a country.

Scientific-Academic versus Professional Training

By their tradition, universities strive for the highest scientific-academic standards of training. By the late 1960s in North America and about a decade later in Europe, this training philosophy was more and more challenged by growing demands for psychological practitioners prepared to enter professional work in schools and clinics, in private practice, in industry, etc. Different universities and countries reacted differently to this challenge. In North America, a new type of tertiary education institution came into existence: the Professional Schools of Psychology, no longer offering a research degree but a professional doctorate like the doctor of psychology (Psy.D.). At the same time, high-ranking university departments of psychology began to introduce comparable course programs, often also leading to a Psy.D. degree, many of them following the science-practitioner or Boulder model of the APA. As a rule, these programs contain an obligatory half- to one-year practical internship. In recent years similar specialized science-practitioner curricula have also been set up at some British universities.

In countries adhering to the one-level, generalist model of education in psychology, growing specialization and professionalization has recently given rise to a new kind of two-stage model of training, which assigns the professional-practical teaching to a post-graduate science-practitioner course in psychology. In Germany, for example, a federal law passed in 1998 requires psychology graduates after completion of the 5- to 6-year university course in psychology to enroll in a subsequent 3-year post-graduate training which will prepare them for a state examination ('approbation') pre-requisite for professional psychotherapeutic work. Such postgraduate programs combine advanced, specialized scientific and practical on-the-job training; they are organized by university departments in cooperation with practical-professional institutions like psychiatric or neurological hospitals, day-care centers, etc. Trainees are expected to hold a supervised part-time position in the respective field. The merits and likely shortcomings of such two-stage training models still await evaluation.

Psychology Training Outside North America and Europe

Today training in many countries outside North America and Europe resembles either the US-American or one of the European curricular plans, usually depending on historical ties in political-economic development. In Mexico, for example, students enroll in the psychology program immediately after completing high school with a baccalaureate degree, and training requires 5 to 6 years. Other Latin American countries follow a similar plan. In East African countries, the British model seems to prevail, whereas in West African countries it is the French type. Australia and New Zealand have programs similar to the US-American curriculum, as do Japan and China.

1.10 SOURCES OF INFORMATION ABOUT PSYCHOLOGY

Each chapter of this Handbook gives some general Resource References, as well as specific references to certain points in the chapter. The general references will help the interested reader to find more about the topic.

Like other sciences, psychology offers a broad spectrum of information sources, ranging from traditional forms such as books, monographs, and journals to the modern-technology information access via the Internet. In the early days of experimental psychology, psychological research was published in journals of philosophy or physiology. The first journals specifically devoted to psychology began to appear in the last quarter of the nineteenth century, among them such distinguished periodicals as the German-language journals *Archiv für Psychologie* (started in 1875) and *Zeitschrift für Psychologie* (started in 1885), the *American Journal of Psychology* (started in 1888), and *L'Année Psychologique* (started in 1895). With the exception of the *Archiv für Psychologie*, they all still continue in publication. In the early 1900s, psychological journals began to differentiate and multiply rapidly. According to a recent estimate (literature database PsycINFO, American Psychological Association) the world-wide total number of high-quality, peer-reviewed psychological or psychology-related journals is around 1,500; almost 17% of these are non-English language publications. Psychology journals differ in topical breadth, ranging from broad, general journals, addressing all fields of psychology, to more and more specialized journals (e.g., cognitive psychology, methods of psychological assessment or therapy). They also differ in regional coverage, from global journals (such as the *International Journal of Psychology* and the *International Journal of Applied Psychology*), through regional journals (such as the *American Psychologist*, the *European Psychologist*, and the *Scandinavian Journal of Psychology*), to primarily national journals (such as the Russian *Voprosi Psykhologi*, the *Rivista Mexicana de Psicologia*, or the *Indian Journal of Social Psychology*). And they vary in journal profile as to scientific research or professional-practical orientation.

Today English has become the major, global communication language, in psychology as in other fields. However, about 5% of journal publications in the PsycINFO database still appear in a language other than English. (This percentage is smaller than that of non-English journals partly because English-language journals tend to be published more frequently and to contain more articles per issue than do non-English language journals.) In the number of journal articles published per year, the major non-English languages of publication in psychology are German (with 1.54% of articles in the PsycINFO database), French (1.26%), Spanish (1.20%), Japanese (0.75%), Chinese (0.37%), and Russian (0.22%). In recent years there is growing trend towards usage of the English language even in publications from non-Anglophone countries. Maintaining sufficient accessibility of the so-called non-English-language or NEL literature has been of continuing concern to the International Union of Psychological Science. At the time of writing, there is a tendency for psychological NEL journals of basic research to gradually change towards an all-English format whereas professional journals serving psychological practitioners are more likely to stick to their national-language format.

Inevitably, NEL journal publications entail narrower limits in availability and accessibility of a contribution across countries and language areas. On the other hand, turning every psychological publication into English would involve the risk of alienating the language of psychology from the natural language of the people in a country. In addition, it would set higher thresholds for authors less fluent in English. The language issue becomes especially critical for introductory texts for schools and universities. The prevailing tendency in many NEL regions is to use the local language for introductory texts. As a result, the psychological textbook literature has seen a plethora of textbook translations since the 1950s. Foundations have even made special grants to support the translation of leading texts and resource books into languages (such as Chinese, Russian) which serve large regions of the world that otherwise have reduced access to psychological literature.

The rapid increase in number of annual publications in psychological science impelled psychologists, as early as the 1890s, to devise reference publications to guide readers through this ever-growing literature. Annual lists of psychological publications were first published in the *Zeitschrift fuer Psychologie und Physiologie der Sinnesorgane* beginning with volume one, 1890. In 1895 *L'Année Psychologique* published in its first volume a classified bibliography. This continued until 1905 when the service was expanded to provide abstracts of psychological publications. The American journal, *Psychological Review*, began in 1895 a separate publication, the *Psychological Index*, which listed psychological publications in 35 annual volumes until 1942, when it was merged into the *Psychological Abstracts*, started in 1927 by the American Psychological Association. *Psychological Abstracts* became the world-wide reference source for publications in psychology, appearing in its 74th volume in 2000. This journal publishes brief summaries of psychological book and journal publications, with full citations. Until 1988, *Psychological Abstracts* still aimed at world-wide coverage irrespective of the original language of a publication. With the continuing growth in number of annual publications in psychological science, the number of abstracts per *Psychological Abstracts* volume reached 33,000 by the mid-1980s. At that time, the APA set up the new abstract database, PsycINFO, which was accessible through on-line electronic networking (nowadays via internet service providers) and, soon thereafter, also off-line on CD-Rom (PsychLit). So starting 1988, the print version of *Psychological Abstracts* was limited to those abstracts from the PsycINFO database which came from Anglophone publications. It is expected (and already noticeable) that, with increasing accessibility of electronic database facilities, the printed version of *Psychological Abstracts* will steadily lose its importance. In addition to its wider coverage and prompt up-dating facility, PsycINFO also offers advanced means of automatic keyterm search analysis. Other electronic publication databases of relevance to psychology are MedLine, the medical literature abstract database published by the U.S. National Library of Medicine, and a number of specialized literature databases in the neurosciences, in environmental sciences, and in the social sciences at large (Social Science Citation Index).

Another type of secondary source publication in psychology developed in the 1950s: topical reviews, summary reports, and, more recently, statistically refined so-called meta-analytic studies. Volume 1 of the *Annual Review of Psychology* appeared in 1950. Published by the Annual Review Corporation, USA, the 51st volume appeared in 2000. Other Annual Review publications of interest to psychology are those in anthropology, genetics, immunology, medicine, neuroscience, physiology, public health, and sociology. (Of the 27 Annual Review publications, the psychological review ranks fourth in initial year of publication.) The *Annual Review of Psychology* covers the different specialties of psychology according to a several-year publication schedule, with more important fields reviewed every second or third year, others at longer intervals. Additional reviews and summary articles on methods of psychological assessment are covered in a special bibliographic and review source publication, the *Mental Measurement Yearbook*, now also available via electronic on-line internet services.

RESOURCE REFERENCES

Annual review of psychology. Palo Alto, CA: Annual Reviews, Inc. (Volume 51 in 2000).

Gleitman, H., Fridlund, A. J., & Reisberg, D. (2000). *Basic psychology* (5th Ed.). New York: W. W. Norton.

Gregory, R. L., & Zangwill, O. L. (Eds.). (1987). *The Oxford companion to the mind*. Oxford, UK: Oxford University Press.

Imada, H. (1996). Psychology throughout the world: A selected bibliography of materials on psychology published in English 1974–1995. *International Journal of Psychology*, *31*, 307–368.

Kazdin, A. E. (Ed.). (2000). *Encyclopedia of psychology*. (8 vols.). Washington, DC: American Psychological Association and New York: Oxford University Press.

Koch, S. (1959–1963). *Psychology: A study of a science* (vols. 1–5). New York: Oxford University Press.

Rosenzweig, M. R. (Ed.). (1992). *International psychological science: Progress, problems, and prospects*. Washington, DC: American Psychological Association.

Sexton, V. S., & Hogan, J. (Eds.). (1992). *International psychology: Views from around the world* (2nd ed.). Lincoln: University of Nebraska Press.

Zimbardo, P. G., & Gerrig, R. J. (1996). *Psychology and life*. New York: Harpercollins.

ADDITIONAL LITERATURE CITED

Adair, J. G. & Kagitcibasi, C. (Eds.). (1995). Development of psychology in developing countries: Factors facilitating and impeding its progress. *International Journal of Psychology*, *30*, 633–753.

American Psychological Association (1996). *Psychology/Careers for the twenty-first century: Scientific problem solvers*. Washington, DC: American Psychological Association.

Australian Research Council Discipline Research Strategies. (1996). *Psychological Science in Australia*. Canberra: Australian Government Publishing Service.

Bibliographisches Institut. (1969). *Das große Duden-Lexikon* (2 Ed.). Mannheim: Lexikonverlag.

Brockhaus – die Enzyklopädie in vierundzwanzig Bänden. 1996 (20 Auflage). Leipzig: Brockhaus.

Cronbach, L. J. (1957). The two disciplines of scientific psychology. *American Psychologist*, *12*, 671–684.

Davis, M. S. (1971). That's interesting! Towards a phenomenology of sociology and a sociology of phenomenology. *Science*, *1*, 309–344.

Diaz-Loving, R., Reyes-Lagunes, I., & Diaz-Guerrero, R. (1995). Some cultural facilitators and deterrents for the development of psychology: The role of graduate research training. *International Journal of Psychology*, *30*, 681–692.

Estes, W. K. (1997). Processes of memory loss, recovery and distortion. *Psychological Review*, *104*, 148–169.

Gazzaniga, M. S. (Ed.). (2000). *The new cognitive neurosciences*. Cambridge, MA: MIT Press.

Gilgen, A. R., & Gilgen, C. K. (Eds.). (1987). *International handbook of psychology*. Westport, CT, USA: Greenwood Press.

Gray, J. A. (1982). *The neuropsychology of anxiety*. Oxford: Clarendon Press.

Hegel, G. W. F. (1840). *Vorlesungen über die Philosophie der Geschichte*. [Lectures on the philosophy of history]. Berlin: Duncker und Humblot.

Jing, Q. (1994). Development of psychology in China. *International Journal of Psychology*, *29*, 667–675.

Kagitcibasi, C. (1992). Linking the indigenous and universalist orientations. In S. Iwaki, Y. Kashima, & K. Leung (Eds.), *Innovations in cross-cultural psychology* (pp. 29–37). Amsterdam: Swets & Zeitlinger.

Kelley, H. H. (1992). Common-sense psychology and scientific psychology. *Annual Review of Psychology*, *43*, 1–23.

Leach, M. M., & Harbin, J. J. (1997). Psychological ethic codes: A comparison of twenty-four countries. *International Journal of Psychology*, *32*, 181–192.

Lenk, H. (1975). *Pragmatische Philosophie* [Pragmatic philosophy]. Hamburg: Hoffmann und Campe.

Leung, K., & Zhang, J. (1995). Systemic considerations: Factors facilitating and impeding the development of psychology in developing countries. *International Journal of Psychology, 30*, 693–706.

Merriam-Webster. (1983). *Webster's Ninth New Collegiate Dictionary*. Springfield, MA: Merriam-Webster.

Mueller, C. G. (1979). Some origins of psychology as a science. *Annual Review of Psychology, 30*, 9–29.

Newstead, S. E., & Makinen, S. (1997). Psychology teaching in Europe. *European Psychologist, 2*, 3–10.

Pawlik, K. (1994a). Dimensions of complexity in psychology, with some extensions into neuroscience. *Science International, 58*, 21–23.

Pawlik, K. (1994b). Psychology in Europe: Origins and development of psychology in German-speaking countries. *International Journal of Psychology, 29*, 677–694.

Pawlik, K. (1998). The psychology of individual differences: The personality puzzle. In J. G. Adair, D. Bélanger, & K. L. Dion (Eds.), *Advances in psychological science. Vol. 1: Social, personal and cultural aspects* (pp. 1–30). Hove, UK: Psychology Press.

Pawlik, K., & Rosenzweig, M. R. (Eds.). (1994). Special issue. The origins and development of psychology: Some national and regional perspectives. *International Journal of Psychology, 29*, 665–756.

Popper, K. R. (1974). *Conjectures and refutations: the growth of scientific knowledge*. London: Routledge and Paul.

Rosenzweig, M. R. (1982). Trends in development and status of psychology: An international perspective. *International Journal of Psychology, 17*, 117–140.

Rosenzweig, M. R., Holtzman, W. H., Sabourin, M., & Bélanger, D. (2000). *History of the International Union of Psychological Science* (in press). Hove, UK: Psychology Press.

Spearman, C. (1904). 'General intelligence', objectively determined and measured. *American Journal of Psychology, 15*, 72–101.

Wolman, B. B. (Ed.). (1985). *Handbook of intelligence*. New York: Wiley.

Communications concerning this chapter should be addressed to: Professor Kurt Pawlik, Department of Psychology, University of Hamburg, Von-Melle-Park 11, 20146 Hamburg, Germany

2

Basic Methods of Psychological Science

WILLIAM K. ESTES

This review of research methods focuses on concepts and issues that cut across subject matter areas. The orientation is historical in part because understanding current issues depends on some knowledge of their origins. Historical trends are treated more systematically in Chapter 1 and methods specialized for particular research settings in other chapters of this volume.

2.1 THE NATURE OF PSYCHOLOGICAL DATA

When the new discipline of psychology branched off from philosophy and natural science in the late 1800s, it inherited a pressing need for new approaches to some longstanding problems, notably the relation between the physical and mental worlds. The ensuing century has seen a continuing reciprocal interaction between the development of specific researchable questions about the mental and behavioral activities of organisms and the crafting of methods that could yield answers. Progress in the early years was slow, in part because of the lack of any ready-made definition of what would constitute psychological data. As a temporary expedient, early psychologists borrowed methods for generating data from other disciplines – introspective reporting of mental activities from philosophy, observation of animal behavior from biology, recording of simple bodily processes from physiology and medicine.

Sharp, and in some instances long-continuing, controversies arose over the question of which type of data is natural and proper for psychology. A satisfactory answer had to come from experience as the alternatives were tested in actual research.

Data from Introspection

One group of early psychologists, the structuralists, tried to build a science of mind on data obtained from subjects ('observers') who introspected on such matters as the qualities of sensations. This movement was at the center of experimental psychology for decades, but went into a decline as it became apparent that the science so generated was encapsulated in the structuralists' highly technical literature and was not yielding findings with implications for life outside the laboratories.

A research method may continue in use, however, long after the philosophical or methodological movement in which it originated has passed into history. Introspection is a case in point. With the decline of structuralism, introspective methods lost favor as a source of psychological data. Then, gone but not forgotten, introspection re-emerged in the 1960s with the rise of cognitive science, in which verbal protocols were a major source of data and a basis for much theorizing on problem solving. But despite their new popularity, introspective methods continued to exhibit the same weakness that had aroused critics in the structuralist period – the lack of effective means of obtaining interpersonal agreement among scientists on the interpretation of introspective data.

As a consequence, the introspective method itself became a subject of research, and two developments led to substantial clarification of its scope and limitations. The first was a body of work, reviewed by Nisbett and Wilson (1977), converging on the conclusion that people have little or no direct access to either the bases or the properties of their own mental processes. The second was a series of studies of verbal protocols by Herbert A. Simon and others showing that when people are properly instructed and monitored, they can produce veridical reports of the contents, though not of the processes, of short-term memory. In this connection, Strack and Forster (1995, p. 352) conclude from a study of recollections of experiences that 'Self-reports appear to be useful indicators of underlying mechanisms only to the extent that it is sufficiently understood how such reports are generated.'

Data from Observations of Behavior

The gap left by the decline of structuralism was filled by the work of a rapidly growing legion of investigators who held that the observable behavior of organisms was the proper subject matter for psychology. This movement went through two distinct, though overlapping, stages. The first was the popularization of 'behaviorism' by John B. Watson, starting just before World War I and continuing to the peak of its influence in the 1940s. In this tradition, the sole subject of investigation was behavior in its own right, the purpose of research being to lay the groundwork for predictions of behavior and to develop techniques for its control or modification in practical situations. The most commonly used measures of behavior, frequencies or speeds of actions, were treated simply as indices of strength of response tendencies with no reference to underlying causes. Theory generated by

the research took the form of taxonomies of the classes of behaviors (responses) available to an organism and the types of stimulus conditions that controlled response strengths.

Beginning in the early 1950s, however, the dominance of behaviorism weakened, and the goals of research increasingly shifted from simply predicting what organisms do to accounting for how they acquire, process, and use information. Response frequencies and speeds continued to be the primary data, but now they served as indices of underlying processes.

The new orientation is well illustrated by a series of efforts to produce a method for tracing the time course of unobservable cognitive processes. In the 1860s, the Dutch physiologist Franciscus Donders had introduced a subtractive technique for estimating the duration of a mental process from reaction times. Donders reasoned that the difference between response time to a single stimulus known in advance and time to decide which of two stimuli occurs would provide an estimate of the duration of the process of discriminating the stimuli.

A century later, Donders' rationale was extended to the analysis of cognitive tasks used in research on information processing, among them visual search and speeded recognition (reviewed by Seymour, 1979). In a much-studied visual search task, a subject searches an array of stimuli, usually digits, letters, or words, and responds with a key press as soon as a predesignated target stimulus is identified. Response times plotted against the number of stimuli in the array typically yield an approximately linear function, anticipated on the supposition that search time is the sum of the times for processing individual stimuli in the search path.

In a speeded recognition task, an experimental trial has two parts: first, the subject views a target set of items, again usually random digits, letters or words; second, a test item is presented and the subject presses a 'yes' or a 'no' key to indicate whether the test item did or did not come from the target set. It has been of special interest that functions relating response time to set size are usually very similar in the two tasks, suggesting that the underlying processes of comparison and decision are basically the same in short-term memory search and visual search.[1] These and related results led to very wide use of response-time measurements to test hypotheses about the nature of mental representations in areas of psychology ranging from cognition to psychopathology during the 1970s.

As often happens with exciting new methods, enthusiasm for the potentialities of the extended subtractive method as a window to the mind had to come under stricter discipline as new findings began to show that the connection between response times and underlying processes was more complex than initially assumed. In particular, much evidence accrued for the prevalence of speed–accuracy tradeoffs in which subjects voluntarily sacrifice speed for accuracy when motivated to do so. Recognition of this complication does not rule out the use of response times to trace the course of cognitive processes, but it does mean that response time (or speed) and error data from a task must be considered jointly and, when feasible, analyzed within the framework of models of the speed–accuracy relationship. (See the volumes by Broadbent, Kantowitz, and Luce in Resource References.)

Data Generated by Neurophysiological and Neuroanatomical Techniques

The third major class of psychological data is discussed in Chapters 4 and 8 of this volume, and only a few salient trends will be mentioned here. From the founding of psychological science, one of its principal goals, well expressed by pioneers as diverse in their outlooks as William James and Wilhelm Wundt, was to achieve explanations of psychological phenomena in terms of brain function. Substantial research efforts directed toward this goal were mounted in the early decades of this century, but limitations on relevant knowledge and technology made for slow and uncertain progress.

The most important method developed during this period was ablation – surgically removing a structure from an animal's brain, then inferring the normal function of the ablated structure by observing what capability was diminished or eliminated. A risky aspect of this kind of inference, which only slowly gained wide appreciation, arises from the brain's enormous powers of reorganizing its function after damage. An animal's accomplishment of a task that normally depends on a particular brain structure, X, may, after ablation of X, be mediated by other structures not previously involved. Owing to this property of the brain, together with technical limitations on precision of the experimental procedures, some of the major results of ablation studies – for example, Karl S. Lashley's conception of mass action of the brain (essentially the antithesis of localization of function) – did not withstand the test of time.

Persistent failure of ablation research to reveal significant localization of psychological functions in the brain led to a schism between psychobiological research and the development of theories of learning and memory in the 1930s and 1940s. Some leading figures in the latter vein, notably Burrhus F. Skinner, even argued that the study of behavior should be conducted

entirely independently of biological psychology and should develop its own autonomous body of stimulus–response theory. Skinner's view continues to prevail among investigators in the tradition of operant conditioning and behavior modification, but for most others in the field it was undermined by a series of events.

The first of these was the appearance of Donald O. Hebb's *Organization of Behavior* (1949), which set forth a compelling case for a neurally based psychology of perception, learning, and memory. Prospects of realizing Hebb's goals would have been remote given only the methodology available to Lashley, but a new flourishing of biological psychology (now better known as behavioral neuroscience) was made possible by technological advances. Increasingly sophisticated ablation techniques were coupled with methods of observing and measuring activity levels in various parts of the nervous system of a living animal while tasks of interest are performed (for a thorough review of these developments, see the volume by Rosenzweig, Leiman, and Breedlove, and its translations, in Resource References). By the beginning of the 1990s, these methods were exerting significant impact on currently evolving theories of memory systems. It seems clear that there will be no reversal of this new trend.

Fruitful applications of techniques imported into psychology from neural science are not limited to the area of learning and memory. Psychopharmacological procedures, for example, are now enabling some progress in the search for biochemical bases of personality characteristics (Zuckerman, 1995). Motivation for this search is high, in part because of the hope for payoffs in the form of treatments for personality disorders.

2.2 GENERAL ASPECTS OF METHODOLOGY

Although specific research methods vary widely across the various psychological specialties, owing to differences in problems and constraints, some broad aspects of methodology are common to all. Among these, classification, measurement, and standardization call for special treatment. In each case, the discussion will be illustrated in terms of research domains for which the particular aspect has been of special importance.

Classification

Every science has found it necessary to develop schemes of classification in order to bring order to its heterogeneous objects of investigation and to guide application of research results. Thus, few concepts are as ubiquitously referred to in both the technical and the popular literature of science as the elements in chemistry, particles in physics, types of stars in astronomy, taxonomies of plant and animal forms in biology, and diagnostic categories in medicine.

However, all kinds of classification are not of comparable scientific importance. Kurt Lewin (1935) explicated for psychologists a persuasive argument that scientific progress in any field depends on a transition from an Aristotelian to a Galilean mode of classification. The Aristotelian mode originally referred to classification pursued in the attempt to capture the essences of natural objects but now simply characterizes the practice, common in the less mature sciences, of classifying as an end in itself. The Galilean mode, in contrast, denotes classification based on the dynamical properties of objects or on theoretical processes assumed to underlie them. Lewin seems to have intuitively discerned a fact that many investigators come to understand only by experience: it is easy to embellish existing classifications by adding new categories, but more difficult, and more rewarding, to demonstrate that entities differing greatly in their surface properties should be assigned to the same category.

In psychology, the presupposition of some of the most influential founders of major subdisciplines (for example, James, Kraepelin) was that Galilean categories initially defined by behavioral observations would prove to be associated with distinctive neurological processes that explained the lines of classification. Little empirical support for this vision was available during the lifetimes of James or Kraepelin, but they set a goal that has shaped the course of development of research methods over the ensuing century. As individual research specialties took form, efforts toward linking psychological to neurological classifications persisted, and even accelerated, though unevenly, because bursts of progress often had to wait on technological advances. Trends in the theoretical role of taxonomic efforts can be illustrated by means of capsule sketches of a few particular fields.

Memory

One of the currently most often cited passages in James's *Principles of Psychology* (1890), presents his distinction between primary and secondary memory – the predecessor of the long-enduring and now ubiquitous classification of memory phenomena in terms of short-term and long-term processes. Though almost lost from view for many decades, this classification re-emerged in the 1960s in conjunction with a burst of new methodologies for experimentally separating short- from long-term phenomena. The whole array of new methods and results of their application has been thoroughly reviewed by Crowder (1976).

The short-term/long-term distinction was formalized and partially quantified by Atkinson and Shiffrin (1968). Perhaps the most seminal aspect of their work was going beyond purely psychological research and drawing on evidence from studies of effects of brain damage on memory (for example, Barbizet, 1963; Milner, 1967). Atkinson and Shiffrin's model, refined in various ways by succeeding investigators, continues to this day to epitomize the short–long distinction for a great many psychologists and scientists in related fields from neurology to artificial intelligence.

In other domains of memory research, the development of theory has been even more closely tied to efforts toward classification. A categorization of long-term processes in terms of *episodic* versus *semantic* memory originated by Endel Tulving about 1970 has provided a widely accepted framework for research on all but very short-term memory down to the present. The episodic component is the subsystem that mediates the storage and retrieval of representations of individual learning episodes in their situational contexts; the semantic component mediates storage and retrieval of information, such as word meanings, that is not tied to particular episodes. In the work of John R. Anderson on general cognitive architectures, semantic memory has been categorized into declarative and procedural memory, the former being much the same as Tulving's semantic subdivision, the latter referring to retention and retrieval of motor or cognitive acts and skills.[2]

Tulving (1985) has reviewed the history of taxonomies of memory and interpreted them in terms of progress toward a categorization of memory processes that might reflect the lines of classification of underlying neural mechanisms and processes.

Learning

By the mid-1930s, the burgeoning literature on conditioning and animal learning flowing from the theories of Clark L. Hull, Ivan Pavlov, and Edward C. Tolman was straining the capability of psychologists to assimilate it. Thus the time was ripe for the effort toward classification that appeared in Hilgard and Marquis' *Conditioning and Learning* (1940). This volume presented an organization of the field that persists even in today's textbooks, and as perhaps its single most influential contribution, introduced the categorization of elementary learning processes in terms of classical versus instrumental conditioning. Despite strenuous efforts by Hull and others to make a theoretical case for a unified interpretation of conditioning and learning, methods of investigation are still largely organized in terms of Hilgard and Marquis's classification.

In the domain of human learning, one of the first significant classifications, *incidental* versus *intentional* learning, distinguishing learning that occurs in the absence or presence, respectively, of any known motive or instruction to learn, dates from the early 1900s. By mid-century a thorough review by McGeoch and Irion (1952) had established its wide applicability over the whole range of human learning from the memorization of word lists and simple trial-and-error learning to concept formation and categorization.

A very active current strain of research is concerned with identifying processes of *explicit*, or conscious, and *implicit*, or unconscious, memory that may underlie intentional and incidental learning, respectively (Jacoby, 1991). However, issues about the necessity of these distinctions seem incapable of settlement by verbal arguments supported only by purely experimental attacks at the psychological level. Thus, attention is shifting to experimentation augmented by mathematical modeling or by correlating behavioral data with those obtained via techniques of brain imaging (Gabrieli, 1998).

Personality and Psychopathology

Taxonomies have been a dominant theme in psychopathology from its earliest days. A prime exemplar of Aristotelian classification appears in the many editions (1952 to 1994) of the American Psychiatric Association's *Diagnostic and Statistical Manual of Mental Disorders* (DSM). The DSM established, and evidently cast in stone, the collection of diagnostic categories of psychoses and neuroses (mania, depression, schizophrenia, hysteria, . . .) that was taken over by the budding new specialty of clinical psychology in its post World War II period of expansion and has provided the framework for much of its research on problems of diagnosis of mental and behavioral disorders (Nathan & Langenbucher, 1999).

Efforts to progress toward the Galilean mode within psychiatry drew on psychoanalytic theory for interpretations of the diagnostic categories. Clinically oriented psychologists, in particular a group associated with Hull's laboratory in the 1940s, made a vigorous effort to bring some of the psychoanalytic interpretations into the laboratory for experimental tests, but ultimately even leading proponents of this approach had to conclude that it did not prove productive (Sears, 1944).

More promising alternatives had been foreshadowed by Kraepelin in the late 1800s. In the hope of uncovering neurological processes that might underlie diagnostic categories, Kraepelin mounted a program of psychological studies of sensory–motor phenomena that paved the way for the experimental psychopathology that began to flourish in the 1950s. Even today, progress toward relating psychopathological symptom categories to experimental results is meager, but, nonetheless, Kraepelin's prescience is being borne out by new developments in psychopharmacology and genetics. For example, tangible progress is currently being made in relating the fluctuations in behavioral symptoms seen in manic and depressive disorders to activity levels of neurotransmitters in the brain and in identifying genetic factors underlying schizophrenia. Thus, it may yet become possible to realize the long-term goal of defining diagnostic categories of mental disorders in such a way that assignment of an individual to the proper category dictates the appropriate form of treatment.

In the broader area of psychology of personality, efforts toward theory have been even more closely tied to classification (though other approaches to research and theory in personality psychology have their adherents, as discussed in Chapter 16 of this volume). The evolution and present status of taxonomic approaches, with special attention to the preeminent taxonomic unit, *personality trait*, has most recently been given a thorough review by Funder (1991). The trait concept had already risen to prominence by the end of the second decade of the twentieth century when a classic article by Floyd and Gordon Allport explicated the classification and measurement of traits in terms that quickly became standard and have undergone little in the way of basic change over subsequent decades. A quite different taxonomic approach was taken by Henry A. Murray, who developed the thesis that classification of people's behavioral dispositions in terms of motives is more fundamental than classification in terms of traits. Regardless of views on that issue, both forms of classification continue to be central to personality theory.

Developmental Psychology

Owing to the overweening influence of Jean Piaget, classification has been the principal mode of theorizing in the domain of cognitive development over most of its history down to the present decade. In Piaget's theorizing, the central concept was a classification of cognitive structures. His system had empirical, mathematical, and psychological aspects. Knowledge structures were distilled from the cognitive tasks used in Piaget's research on children; these were related in his theorizing to mathematical structures involving groups and lattices and also to his classification of developmental stages (Piaget, 1970). The way in which much of the research of psychological scientists on cognitive development over many decades was instigated and molded by this body of theory has been thoroughly reviewed in a special section of the journal *Psychological Science* (July, 1996; Charles J. Brainerd, guest editor).

Recent trends in developmental research and theory are marked by a shift in the focus of taxonomic efforts from tasks and stages to cognitive, motor, and perceptual modules that develop concurrently in the child from birth as a function of maturational and experiential processes. Notable advances are currently being reported in the interpretation of these apparently dissociable modules in terms of dynamic systems theory (Bertenthal, 1996).

Psychological Measurement

Measurement Theory

In the textbooks of psychology and all but a very few specialized journals, measurement is synonymous with scores on psychological tests, most often developed and used with no concern about formal properties of underlying scales or dimensions. By analogy to older sciences, however, measurement should be expected to enter pervasively into every facet of psychological theory. How it should enter is a difficult question. In historical fact, theory has progressed without explicit attention to formal aspects of measurement in most areas of psychological science – learning and memory, thinking and reasoning, mental development, personality and social interaction. Measurement theory has played a role in psychophysics but has been central only to research on decision and choice. The reasons for this state of affairs were debated in a series of articles running through several issues of the journal *Psychological Science* in 1992 (beginning with reviews of a mammoth multi-volume treatise on foundations of measurement just completed by an eminent group of authors, David Krantz, Duncan Luce, Patrick Suppes, and Amos Tversky, assembled from psychology, mathematics, and philosophy), but the debate led to no clear resolution.

Lack of time for measurement to permeate psychology is certainly not a factor. In 1860, Gustav Fechner published his classic work on measurement of the magnitude of sensation, but research stemming from this seminal event proceeded for nearly a century before theoretical issues concerning measurement were finally brought to the attention of the greater community of psychologists by Stevens (1951). The centrality of measurement to psychophysics (and therefore to psychology in Stevens's view), is pointed up by the fact that in his listing of the seven main problems of psychophysics, five had to do with measurement. However, going beyond psychophysics, Stevens presented his now famous classification of types of measurement scales:

- Nominal: requiring merely the assignment of numbers to objects, like the numerals on athletes' jerseys;
- Ordinal: reflecting a systematic ordering of objects, like the numbering of checks in a checkbook;
- Interval: having equal units but an arbitrary zero point, like the Celsius scale of temperature;
- Ratio: having equal units and an absolute zero, like distance.

This taxonomy has been greatly refined and elaborated by succeeding investigators, but its broader importance lies in bringing home to psychological scientists the existence of the different kinds of measurement scales that may find application in different kinds of research problems. The necessity of taking account of the distinctions in particular cases has been a debatable issue, however. One much-publicized question concerns the types of measurement scales that need to be assumed for proper application of various statistical methods. The question is theoretically interesting, but the evolution of statistical methods for psychological researchers and means of validating their application has gone forward vigorously without waiting on an answer.

It seems puzzling that the most elaborate and formally impressive theoretical structure that presently exists in psychological science, the array of measurement models with its associated taxonomy, could have evolved over the last half century with an empirical focus almost exclusively limited to a particular type of decision making that derives from economics and game theory and has remained outside the scope of most cognitive modeling.

The link between measurement and decision making was forged by the epoch-making work of John von Neumann and Oscar Morgenstern in the 1940s. Their general treatment of games and economic behavior set simultaneously the framework within which theories of decision making have developed down to the present and the accompanying focus on a type of decision problem in which people make choices between alternatives that take the form of gambles, insurance packages, or the like. Thus, the domain of application of measurement theory has continued to be largely limited to the class of decision problems defined by combinations of utilities and probabilities.

The Measurement of Intelligence

Perennially one of the central problems of psychology, the assessment of intelligence has had a history dominated by practical concerns and almost wholly uncontaminated by interaction with formal measurement theory. In the early 1900s, a pioneering experimental psychologist, Alfred Binet, was called from his laboratory to help with the problem of classifying poorly performing children in Paris schools by level of mental ability – in particular, distinguishing those who could profit by continued schooling from those who could not. Like his famed predecessor Francis Galton, Binet had been exploring simple laboratory tasks that might plausibly be related to mental ability, and he evidently had learned enough to turn away from that intellectually appealing but practically unpromising approach. Thus, the intelligence test that Binet and his collaborator, Theodore Simon, produced to meet the needs of the schools was heavily weighted with items constructed by modifying and elaborating the laboratory tasks to make them more similar to activities that occur in school (Binet & Simon, 1908). Through successive revisions, the Binet–Simon test set the framework within which the field would develop and the standard against which all new candidates would be evaluated.

Not surprisingly, given the history of intelligence testing, efforts toward theoretical interpretations of test performance have focused, not on studying the role of putative causal variables in an individual's background and learning history, but on analyzing intercorrelations of test scores in order to identify hypothetical mental factors that may underlay performance. The first, and in some respects the most important of these efforts was initiated a few years after the construction of the Binet–Simon test by Charles Spearman. His insight was that a matrix of inter-item correlations could be accounted for on the assumption of one underlying factor of general ability (termed g) plus a large number of special abilities whose effects were specific to single tasks or types of tasks. The existence of a general ability factor has seemed natural to many people, psychologists and others; consequently, though its popularity has waxed and waned many times over the years, the g factor is still under active investigation.

Among the alternatives to Spearman's model that have appeared, the most influential has been Louis Thurstone's multiple factor theory, originated in the 1930s. The basic assumption of Thurstone's approach is that the mental structure underlying test performance constitutes a relatively small set of factors, all of about equal status. Starting, like Spearman, with a matrix of inter-item correlations, Thurstone extracted from a given matrix a set of factors that satisfied not only technical requirements but also criteria of psychological meaningfulness. Test data could then be scored for individuals' *loadings* on each factor and the subset of items found that correlated most highly with each factor. The item subsets so obtained constitute tests for abilities, for example, arithmetical or spatial reasoning, that are less general than g but more general than Spearman's special abilities. In a currently popular line of taxonomically oriented research, the intermediate-level abilities are grouped into classes that are thought to correspond to broad types of intelligence, for example, crystalline versus fluid.

It seems less than ideal that conceptions of intelligence should continue to be grounded mainly in analyses of test data, isolated from research and theory on higher mental processes. The isolation is so nearly complete that no reference to intelligence is to be found in most textbooks of cognitive psychology, information processing, or cognitive science. The actual course of development was perhaps inevitable given the early definitions of intelligence in terms of 'what the tests measure' and the disappointing results of studies seeking correlations between performance on simple laboratory tasks and 'intelligence quotients'. However, the time now seems ripe to couple new approaches to intelligence in the information-processing tradition with developments in artificial intelligence, which from its beginnings has focused on the processes responsible for intelligent behavior rather than on the assessment of intelligence.

The near future of this field may also be marked by increased interest in the biological bases of intelligence. Extensive twin studies, interpreted in terms of increasingly powerful statistical models, have begun to yield quantitative estimates of the contribution of heredity. And concurrent research in microbiology seems to offer the prospect of uncovering the specific genetic and biochemical bases of some individual differences in intelligence. This line of research is exciting, not only for the potential theoretical advances, but for the possibility of remedying intellectual deficits by pharmacological methods. However, realizing this possibility may depend on the parallel development of more powerful theories of how cognitive processes generate intelligent performance.

Standardization

The benefits and costs of standardization versus innovation in research designs and procedures are frequently in conflict and an optimal balance is not easily achieved. Innovation is an essential condition for progress, but when overdone it can hinder efficiency. In principle, for the purpose of gaining the most possible information from each individual experiment, it is ideal to craft the method to fit the demands of the particular research problem addressed. But in practice, a satisfactory compromise must be found between this ideal approach and the need for some degree of standardization.

Some of the benefits of standardization are obvious. Using similar methods for related experiments, whether done by the same or by different investigators, makes for economy of description in research reports and facilitates the task of collating the results. The common observation that experimental reports in psychological journals are typically much longer than those in biology or physics is due in part to the much greater standardization of methods in the older sciences. However, it is not feasible to redress the imbalance by imposing severe restrictions on length of method descriptions by psychologists because idiosyncratic differences among related experiments with respect to instruction of subjects, preliminary training in experimental procedures, and the like can have large effects on results. It is surely no accident that the average length of Method sections of articles has steadily increased over the years as psychological scientists have gained appreciation of the importance of apparently minor differences in procedures between studies.

Unfortunately, carrying standardization too far can inhibit creativity. Frequently an innovative method designed by an investigator to attack a previously refractory problem is immediately taken up with such enthusiasm by others that the journals are swamped with a wave of closely related applications of the new method that quickly runs into diminishing returns. Some highly visible examples in experimental psychology are George Sperling's partial report procedure for estimating the information gained by observers from brief stimulus displays, Saul Sternberg's method of measuring speed of short-term memory search, and the free-recall procedure popularized by the first studies of clustering in semantic memory. Each of these lines of research has been highly fruitful, but it may be questioned whether the scientific advances have been commensurate with the volume of often highly redundant experiments churned into the literature. Excessive enthusiasm for currently popular research paradigms seems to reflect a tendency toward economy of effort that is manifest also in other contexts, for example, the dependence on group testing of experimental subjects in much research on decision making and the heavy reliance on questionnaires as surrogates for actual observations of behavior in personality and social psychology.

How the present uneasy compromise among the competing needs for innovation, standardization, and economy of journal space might be improved is a difficult question. Significant innovations in methods are richly rewarded by prizes, awards, and promotions. However, significance depends on a rare combination of talent and luck, and many innovations obstruct progress toward desirable standardization. Efforts toward standardization are needed, but they typically receive little notice and therefore meager payoff. Possibly scientific societies could help by providing forums for informed discussion of the issue at meetings or in working groups. Also, societies might try to develop means for storing and keeping accessible full descriptions of methods, perhaps via the internet, thus relieving journals of the need to publish more than brief summaries of methods.

2.3 RESEARCH DESIGN

Many forms of empirical investigation resemble psychological research in some respects but differ in others. A detective investigating a crime or a scholar trying to ascertain the authorship of a literary work may be as thorough in determining facts and critically evaluating evidence as a research psychologist but differs with respect to objectives. The former seeks only to produce or update a historical record by settling the question of what happened in particular cases. The latter seeks to arrive at conclusions that hold for broad classes of events and situations and thus can provide the basis for predictions of what may be expected to happen on future occasions.

This review is confined to research methods that are intended to advance psychological knowledge and theory. Two essential facets of methods that can advance knowledge are controlled comparison and replication. In psychology, most knowledge comes from experiments, which always incorporate these properties. However, for some subdomains, notably animal behavior, psychopathology, and social psychology, experiments are often impractical and ways must be found to conduct observations of behavior under conditions that allow achievement of the objectives of controlled comparison and replication to some degree. The research methods reviewed in this chapter are mostly experimental in character, but deviations from the strict demands of formal experimental design receive attention as appropriate.

Experimental Methods

Research Settings and 'Ecological Validity'

A central issue for most areas of psychological research concerns the setting in which empirical investigations are conducted. It was assumed by the great pioneers who forged the general methodology of experimental psychology during the half-century from Ebbinghaus (1885) to Woodworth (1938) that advances in theory and in methods for application of research results would derive mainly from studies pursued in the laboratory under strictly controlled and usually artificial conditions. That assumption has governed the main stream of psychological research down to the 1990s. However, the entire period has been marked by outbursts of dissent by investigators impatient with the discipline of the laboratory.

At the start of human experimental psychology, Hermann Ebbinghaus (1885/1964) felt that the demands of getting the study of memory under way on a firm footing required the use of very simple procedures with artificial materials (the now familiar 'nonsense syllables'). His results proved so influential that, except for Edward Lee Thorndike's efforts to apply rudimentary human learning theory to education, the tradition of restricting research on human learning and memory to artificial laboratory situations remote from application held sway for three-quarters of a century. This tradition was epitomized in the extensive studies of verbal paired-associate and serial list learning by Leo Postman, Benton Underwood, and their followers in the 1950s, simultaneously admired by many psychologists for their scientific quality and criticized by others for their limited scope and presumed lack of relevance to practical affairs. During the later decades of the 1900s, exchanges of polemics if anything increased in frequency and visibility, centering on the issue of 'ecological validity' – that is, the question of whether laboratory settings for research can be representative of those that occur in everyday life. For the most part, the mainstream of research proceeds undisturbed by polemics, but with laboratory experimentation occasionally augmented by studies designed to obtain information about behavior (or products of behavior) outside of laboratory settings. These forays into non-laboratory environments have been especially fruitful when designed to gain evidence pertaining to specific theoretical issues or predictions (e.g., Anderson & Schooler, 1991; Bahrick, 1984).

Single-Variable, Experimental-Control Designs

Undoubtedly the longest entrenched and most durable research method in the experimental areas of psychology is the single-variable experiment. In the simplest form of the experiment, performance observed in the presence and in the absence of an experimental variable is compared under conditions intended to ensure that any difference in performance actually reflects an effect of the variable. That the qualification is critically important can be illustrated by a historical example. In one of the few experiments attributed to the philosopher-psychologist William James, done about 1890, he set out to test the widely held doctrine of *formal discipline*, according to which memory capacity is increased by practice on any task that exercises memory. The specific approach of James and several students was to investigate whether practice in memorizing poetry strengthens a general skill, that is, whether effects of the practice transfer to materials other than those used in the practice. They memorized selections from a particular poem by Victor Hugo, measuring the time required, then tried to train their memories by practicing with selections from other poets every day for a month. Finally, as a test of transfer, they memorized new selections from Hugo's poem. Some slight improvement was reported, but no amount of improvement would have been definitive because one does not know whether it might have occurred over the same interval in the absence of the practice.

James and his students should be credited with a pioneering effort on an important and difficult problem, but their approach was defective in important respects. A major advance on their method would have required the addition of a second group of participants who memorized the same passage initially, then, without the practice on works of other poets, were tested after a month on the new selections from Hugo.

Although the fact was not yet familiar to psychologists in James's time, adding the feature of random assignment of subjects to groups is similarly important. The possibility must be faced that group differences in final performance might arise simply as a result of individual differences among subjects in the ease with which they could memorize the particular poems used in the final session. Random assignment does not preclude this possibility, though it does ensure that such subject effects will tend to average out over a series of experiments. But even these improvements in design are not enough to ensure a valid result. It might be, for example, that the particular passages of poetry used in the initial and final sessions differed in difficulty of memorization. Random assignment of passages to sessions would improve matters; or the experiment might be replicated with two new groups who would have the same procedures except for an interchange of the passages used in the initial and final sessions. Finally, one could not expect to arrive at a conclusion about transfer of practice effects unless, at a minimum, similar experiments were conducted with study materials other than poetry, a point well appreciated by later investigators.

The moral to be drawn from this example is that the single-variable experimental-control design, though superficially simple, can serve to advance knowledge only if applied with close attention to the requirements of a fully controlled comparison, which often is achievable only with a series of experiments. Ronald A. Fisher, from whose work in the 1920s flowed many of the principles of experimental design that guide research today, set the goal of planning self-contained experiments whose results could stand alone. But however appropriate that goal may have been for research on fertilization of crops, Fisher's original area of concern, the test of time has shown it not to be well suited to psychological science. The way in which advances in knowledge deepen investigators' understanding of the factors that may contaminate experimental-control comparisons and limit the generalizability of conclusions from single experiments has come to be well appreciated by editors of psychological journals, many of whom now favor articles reporting multiple experiments whose results converge on the problem at issue.

There are drawbacks, however, to relying on single-variable experiments, even in sequences or clusters, as the principal means for exploring a rich research domain. Addressing a research question by means of many single-variable experiments has disadvantages with respect to cost and efficiency, for often many of the experiments share a common control procedure. Further, the behavior being studied may depend on combinations of variables in ways that cannot be revealed by single-variable experiments. And, perhaps most important, it may be difficult to bring the results of multiple experiments together to yield an answer to the question that motivated them, as can conveniently be illustrated by reference again to the transfer-of-practice problem.

Continuation of experimental attacks on the doctrine of formal discipline brought in some of the most famous names in the history of psychology. Among the immediate successors of

James was Thorndike, who collaborated with Robert S. Woodworth in a series of transfer studies employing diverse materials and procedures. The common design had three stages: first, the subjects were tested for accuracy on a task (for example, estimating areas or crossing out all instances of a designated letter on a printed page), then they were given practice on the task with a particular set of stimuli, and, finally, they were tested with different stimuli from the same category. By and large, the substance of their results has been credited with severely undermining the conception of formal discipline, but the results of individual studies were in many instances inconsistent, precluding any general conclusions.

Factorial Design

Although Thorndike and Woodworth could scarcely have done better in the early 1900s, present-day investigators could improve on their approach by using Fisher's principle of factorial design (Fisher, 1937). In a factorial design, two or more experimental variables that could be studied separately instead become the factors in a single experiment, subject to the requirement that each level of any factor is combined equally often with each level of every other factor. A likely source of some of the inconsistencies in Thorndike and Woodworth's transfer studies is that particular task manipulations may have different effects on transfer depending on values of other experimental variables, such as amount of practice. One could evaluate such interrelations and at the same time increase the power of the study to reveal transfer with an experiment in which effects of task differences were measured following several different amounts of practice. If, for example, three of Thorndike and Woodworth's tasks were used together with three levels of practice, the design could be compactly represented by the matrix

	P1	P2	P3
T1	10	10	10
T2	10	10	10
T3	10	10	10

where T1, T2, and T3 denote the tasks and P1, P2, and P3 the levels of practice (one of which could be set at zero as a control measure); and we assume that 10 experimental subjects are assigned to each cell.[3] The scores might be performance on the final test expressed as a percentage of performance on the initial test, the preference of many early investigators, including Thorndike and Woodworth, or, perhaps better, just differences between final and initial performance.

Compared with the alternative of conducting several single-variable experiments each representing just two of the cells in the matrix, the factorial design is almost unbelievably powerful, yielding additional information about interactions with virtually no loss of efficiency for evaluating the effects of the individual factors.

It is unfortunate that in the psychological literature discussions of the principles and values of factorial design nearly always appear in textbooks of psychological statistics, creating the impression that the design is merely a special case of analysis of variance (ANOVA). The point needs emphasis that the principles of factorial design are fundamental and most of the values are realized whether or not the data from a study are analyzed by means of an overall ANOVA.

In the broad domain of experimental psychology, single-variable, experimental-control and multi-variable, factorial designs continue in active use with the choice of method for specific problems being a matter of judgment. The single-variable design is useful for preliminary exploration of a problem and for experiments intended to test hypotheses or theoretical predictions under conditions that can be specified in advance. Although the factorial design is highly efficient when appropriate, realization of the efficiency requires that the way be paved by exploratory work that yields information about the number of factors that should be included and the appropriate levels of each factor.

Regression Designs

As a science matures, emphasis tends to shift from determining the presence or absence of effects of experimental variables to disclosing systematic relationships between these variables and a performance measure. For this purpose, the single-variable design has been extended to become what is now known as a regression design. In the Thorndike and Woodworth experiment on estimating areas of figures, for example, the investigators might have assigned different groups of subjects to different amounts of practice, yielding as the main result a curve of average final test performance as a function of practice time. There would have been no obvious motivation for the extension in the early 1900s, but there would be today, for there are now available theoretical models from which one can derive the predicted form of the practice curve.

In a further extension, termed multiple regression, the relation between final test performance and a number of different independent variables (for example, practice time, size and area of test figures, and amount of reward for accuracy) could be studied simultaneously. From analysis of the multiple regression results, one could determine which, if any of the independent variables influence performance, and for these the form of the relationship.

Quasi-Experimental and Correlational Designs

In many areas of psychology, including personality, social psychology, and psychopathology, the designs discussed above are often inapplicable, either because it is not possible to assign subjects randomly to conditions or because variables that are of interest as possible causal factors are not amenable to experimental manipulation. In such cases, investigators sometimes resort to heuristic methods, termed quasi-experiments, in which subjects are asked to imagine what their responses would be under a missing control condition. However, there has been little progress toward achieving inter-investigator agreement on the interpretation of these heuristics.

A more common tactic in the personality and social areas is to dispense with efforts at strict control of putative causal variables in favor of correlational approaches. Multiple correlation methods are somewhat analogous to multivariable experimental designs but with fewer constraints. For example, in a study aimed at the determinants of a personality characteristic, subjects may be rated, by themselves or by other observers, for their degree of manifestation of the characteristic. Then the ratings can be correlated with personality or ability test scores or with reported frequency of participation in relevant activities. From the correlational data, the relative degree of dependence of ratings on each of the other variables can be estimated (Keren & Lewis, 1993b)

In some research areas, it is common to see studies that appear on the surface to allow controlled comparisons of the effect of an independent on a dependent variable but that are actually correlational in character. This situation frequently arises in studies of signal detection and recognition memory. In the familiar detectability model for such situations, it is assumed that detection of a signal or recognition of a stimulus depends in part on an individual's criterion for making positive judgments. In a common type of experiment, subjects are given instructions or incentives intended to modify the subjects' criteria and it is determined whether estimates of criteria derived from the data are systematically related to level of performance on tests of detection or recognition. Significant relationships are often interpreted as signifying effects of criteria on performance. However, the relationships are correlational, and all that is known is that performance was affected by some

properties of the actual independent variables –
the differential instructions or incentives.

Longitudinal and Cohort Designs

The study of mental development and aging is
one of the few categories of psychological
research that is not amenable to fully controlled
experimentation. The research objective is always to trace the course of development or
decline of some aspect of behavior, most commonly an ability, over time and uncover the
causal factors responsible for the changes. Two
basic types of research design are available. In a
longitudinal design, the same individual subject
or group is given some type of test on a
sequence of occasions that are typically spaced
by intervals of one or more years. For some
kinds of tests, performance on later tests may be
influenced by subjects' experiences on earlier
ones, raising difficult problems of interpretation.
And for all kinds of tests, this design has practical drawbacks: most important is the fact that
whatever the intended duration of a study, some
subjects may be lost part way through the
sequence of tests so that such standard measures
as group means become almost uninterpretable;
this hazard is especially serious when a study
requires comparisons on successive tests for
groups that are treated differently in some
respect (for example, groups of school children
who learn in different environments).

The drawbacks of longitudinal studies are
mitigated or eliminated by use of *cohort* designs
in which the tests associated with different ages
are given to different groups of subjects. For
example, in a study of growth of vocabulary,
word counts might be obtained at a particular
time for three different groups of children having mean ages of 2, 3, and 4 years. But now a
new problem arises: the groups may differ not
only in mean age but also in other factors such
as family background or amount of preschool
experience that could affect vocabulary.

In developmental research on young children,
most of problems can be handled reasonably
satisfactorily because studies can usually be
limited to durations over which the same children can be observed on successive tests in
order to obtain genuine longitudinal comparisons.
In the currently very active domain of research
on aging, however, comparisons of young,
middle-aged, and elderly adults typically extend
over periods of many years, so that longitudinal
comparisons are rarely feasible and cohort
designs must be relied on. Unfortunately, all of
the same hazards of cohort designs arise in
research on effects of aging as in developmental
studies, but even more acutely because subjects

recruited for different adult age groups often
come from very different populations.

Various measures can be taken to mitigate the
hazards of cohort designs. One is to make use
of 'lagging'. In a lagged cohort design, sets of
cohorts are studied beginning at different times.
For example, cohorts of subjects with mean ages
of 30, 50, and 70 years might be studied in the
spring of 1980 and another set of similar cohorts
in the spring of 1990. Any significant difference
or interaction between test performance for the
two sets of cohorts would indicate the presence
of factors relevant to performance that would
be confounded with age within either cohort.
Another useful measure is to conduct a longitudinal study with the same experimental conditions and type of subjects over a limited time
span, say 1980 to 1990 in the example, and
compare the longitudinal trends with the trends
within sets of cohorts.

Implementing these measures is a strenuous,
time-consuming, and expensive task, but for
some purposes, the effort may be worthwhile.
When an investigator is concerned only with
practical questions of how to deal with people of
differing ages in some situation, a simple cohort
design may suffice, possible confoundings of
age with other variables simply being ignored.
But when concern is with understanding the
processes, psychological or neurophysiological,
implicated in age-related changes in cognitive
abilities, it must generally be essential to use all
available tactics that can aid the pursuit of
generalizable conclusions. An example of the
kind of research program that may be needed
is described in Schaie (1989) for a study of
age-related changes in perceptual speed during
adulthood that employed a combination of
longitudinal and lagged cohort designs.

Observational Methods

Owing to the strong influence of physical scientists on the establishment of the earliest psychological laboratories, experimentation has been
the preferred research method for psychological
science throughout its history. However, field
observation plays an important role in specialties that face special difficulties in implementing
fully controlled experiments.

Animal Behavior and Learning

The context for the first studies of animal behavior and learning by psychologists was a substantial body of information generated by biologists such as Jacques Loeb and H. S. Jennings
in the early 1900s with a combination of experimental and observational methods. Theory
derived from their work almost dropped from

view during a wave of enthusiasm for learning theories based mainly on data from experiments on conditioning and maze learning. However, naturalistic observation received new impetus in the 1940s under the leadership of the founders of ethology, Konrad Lorenz and Nikolaas Tinbergen (reviewed by G. Gottlieb in Hearst, 1979, cited in Resource References). Ethology is devoted to the observational study of animal behavior in natural habitats, and, in particular, the demonstration of genetically programmed behavioral routines associated with foraging, mating, territoriality, and the like, that seem to make unnecessary, even in the higher organisms, much of the learning that is the focus of laboratory approaches.

The gap between the ethological and the laboratory traditions has narrowed over the years as a consequence of several developments. One of these was a new line of work by some influential ethologists, notably Robert Hinde, in which it was demonstrated that some of the processes of learning theory could be studied effectively in behaviors that occur in animals' natural habitats. Another was the engagement of some experimentally trained biologists and psychologists in research on species-specific behaviors that are found only in natural settings, for example, communication among bees, foraging by ants, navigation by birds. This development has been thoroughly reviewed by Gallistel (1993), who has used the output of such studies in his formulation of mathematical models for animals' cognitive representations of time and space and for mechanisms of response timing and navigation.

Human Behavior in Social Settings

Because by tradition, if not by definition, the subject matter of social psychology is behavior that occurs in social settings, its investigators cannot rely as heavily on experimental methods as do those in most other fields of psychological science. Much of its data must come from observations of people in situations where their behavior depends mainly on the activities of others. But if the data are to generate scientific knowledge and theory, the observations must be as disciplined as those made in an experimental laboratory.

Most generally, studies of social behavior must be planned so that controlled comparisons of the same kind that characterize experimental studies can be achieved to some degree. For some purposes, actual experiments can be contrived, as when the people in a research situation other than the subject are confederates of the investigator, trained to react toward the subject in specific ways called for by the design of the study. But more often, behavior must be observed as it occurs spontaneously in natural settings. To illustrate some of the problems of control that arise, suppose that an investigator wishes to study the reactions of bystanders to victims of accidents in relation to age of the bystander. Because real accidents are too infrequent and unpredictable to provide material for research purposes, accidents will have to be simulated. Contriving the simulation requires a number of decisions. A locale must be chosen, and because the frequency of different types of bystanders must be expected to vary with location, several locations differing with respect to presumably relevant characteristics would be desirable. Similarly, properties of the victim, such as age, ethnic category, and mode of dress, may be important, so several victims differing systematically on these properties would be needed.

The significance of some decisions is less obvious. For example, research on diurnal cycles of physiological and psychological processes has shown that differences in speed and efficiency of information processing between young and elderly adults vary widely as a function of time of day; thus this factor also must be manipulated so as to eliminate confoundings with other factors. Still another consideration, generally much more important in observational than in experimental research, is experimenter bias. In the hypothetical study, the experimenter would be responsible for categorizing the behavior of bystanders, for example, as being responsive or unresponsive to the plight of the victim, and these judgments might be affected by characteristics of the experimenter. It may not be possible to eliminate effects of bias completely, but they can be reduced by various measures, including appropriate training of the experimenter (discussed in an extensive review of systematic observational methods by Weick, 1968).

Conducting observational research that can yield scientific knowledge is not easy, as is highlighted by this example. However, the stakes are high for social psychologists because empirical generalizations and models deriving from their research often can only be adequately tested by observation of social interactions in natural settings.

2.4 METHODS OF ANALYSIS OF DATA

The Treatment of Quantitative Data

Central Tendencies and Error Estimates

Because behavioral data are typically very noisy compared with those of biology or physics, the first step in analyzing a set of data is nearly always to sort observations into classes and compute measures of central tendency, usually means (averages) or medians, for the classes.[4] These descriptive statistics capture possible effects of independent variables, and plots of means against values of independent variables bring out functional relationships.

To prepare the way for any conclusions about effects or trends, it is essential to estimate experimental error, which in psychological experiments may come from individual differences among subjects, uncontrolled variation in effects of extraneous variables that may influence performance, sampling of stimuli or other materials, or error in operation of measuring instruments. The estimate of error may be obtained directly or indirectly in various ways, but the most common procedure is the direct computation of a *probable error*, a statistic taken over from physics and engineering by the earliest experimental psychologists.[5]

There is wide agreement in the present-day literature on research methodology that presentations of means in tables or figures should routinely be accompanied by measures of variability, for example standard deviations of the distributions of scores from which means are computed or standard errors of the means. Present-day journal editors often advise that this routine be followed, but it sometimes seems that the editors are working against a tide of apathy. The wisdom of such advice was well appreciated by some of the earliest experimental psychologists, perhaps owing to their familiarity with physical science. However, a survey of a sampling of psychological research journals from the 1880s to the 1990s has shown that progress toward uniformity in reporting measures of variability has been agonizingly slow and that uniformity is still far from fully achieved (Estes, 1997).

Significance Testing

The reason for this less than optimal state of affairs may lie in the strong preference shown by the majority of psychological researchers for going directly from descriptive measures to tests of statistical significance.[6] The familiar *t* test and its more general relative *analysis of variance* have become so wildly popular that a recent survey of a sample of British and American journals in several areas of psychological research showed the use of these statistics to be close to 100%.

The widespread dependence on significance tests has almost, but not quite, drowned out the voices of persistent critics of their use. The objections take several forms. A perennially popular one is the claim that the tests are ill

conceived, because effects of experimental variables can never be exactly zero; therefore, a hypothesis of exactly zero difference between means can never be accepted and it makes no sense to test the hypothesis statistically. The reply by equally persistent users of significance tests is that the claim of illogicality is merely a matter of semantics. In practice, obtaining a *t* value too small to meet a criterion of significance in a given situation leads a researcher, not to claim that a true difference is zero, but only to conclude that, without further evidence, it would be imprudent to take any action that depends on the difference being different from zero.

Pursuing the apparently endless debates between critics and defenders of significance testing may not be a very constructive enterprise, for reliance on the procedure is justified mainly by the results of long-term use, just as is reliance on any research method or instrument. There is indubitably a hazard that significance testing may tend to crowd out other, more informative, statistical procedures; however, the hazard is widely recognized and excellent treatments of methods for going beyond testing are now available (as witness Keren and Lewis, 1993a; Tukey, 1977; or the new journal *Psychological Methods*).

An aspect of significance testing that unfortunately receives less attention than efficiency at guarding against false claims of experimental effects is *power*, the probability of failing to reject the hypothesis of no effect when it is false. Ways of estimating power are described in standard texts, but in practice estimates are rarely reported. In traditional experimental areas such as psychophysics, learning and memory, or human factors research, it seems adequate for investigators' judgments about sizes of data sets needed for satisfactory reliability to be guided by prevailing practices and feedback from critics. But in some areas of research in social psychology and personality, surveys have shown that power is generally so low as to preclude definitive findings from many individual studies.

Meta-analysis, a method for mitigating this weakness, has recently become popular in these and related areas. In a meta-analysis, one assembles a collection of studies all bearing on a particular question or issue and computes an overall estimate of the probability that a null hypothesis can be rejected at a specified significance level. Thus a single conclusion is derived from a set of studies that may vary widely among themselves in the extent to which they support the conclusion. This technique is evidently seen as a boon to many researchers whose main concern is to arrive efficiently at recommendations for action. However, it clearly is at odds with a longstanding tradition of experimental psychology that, when confronted with studies that disagree in their implications for an important issue, one should continue experimenting with variation of conditions till the disparities are resolved.

Scaling Theory

A basic assumption of much cognitive theory is that people's perceptions or memories of objects can be represented as points in a psychological space. In this context, scaling refers to methods that take data such as judgments of similarities among objects in a collection as input and use formal algorithms to determine scales of psychological distance among the representations. These distances, together with assumptions about the metric structure of the space, are entered into models that predict performance on judgmental tasks such as categorization in the same or related situations.[7] The development of scaling theory has mainly followed a different path than that of general measurement theory, and scaling theory has entered into a wider range of cognitive models and a greater diversity of practical applications.

A very common problem in applications of psychological science is that of quantifying people's judgments of complex phenomena. The problem is especially acute in the use of expert judgments, for example, judgments of risk associated with economic policies, judgments of quality of artistic performance, judgments of social values of investments. A solution is to have the judges produce numerical ratings of risk, quality, or value, then to use well-developed procedures to analyze the ratings in terms of concepts and measures derived from statistical or psychological theory. Illustrations of the power of this technique in action are reported by Hammond, Harvey, and Hastie (1992) for applications in which value judgments from the public and from scientific consultants were the basis for policy recommendations that resolved community conflicts over police procedures and water reclamation plans.

The Treatment of Qualitative Data

Some psychological data are intrinsically qualitative, for example, movies of classroom activities, observations of patients' behavior by hospital personnel, records of occurrences of single events. The last category is the most amenable to analyses akin to those done for quantitative data by analyses of variance and related methods. In preparation for systematic analysis, event frequencies are often entered in contingency tables, which are similar in form to

Table 2.1 *Answers to the question 'Did you vote in the last election?'*

Response	Educational Level		
	Grade School	High School	College
Yes	20	27	18
No	12	5	14

data matrices prepared for factorial analyses of variance. For example, suppose that in a study of voter behavior in relation to educational level, frequencies of participants' answers to the question 'Did you vote in the last election?' were as shown in Table 2.1. A method termed log-linear analysis (assuming a multinomial probability distribution of cell entries) would yield estimates of main effects and interactions of the row and column variables similar to those that would arise from an analysis of variance.

The technique of cluster analysis, requiring even weaker assumptions, has found frequent applications to problems of organization in memory. In some well-known early instances, a subject's protocol in free recall of a word list was scored for the distances (numbers of intervening items) separating occurrences of particular recalled words; then these distances served as input to a computer program that yielded as output a diagram revealing any tendency for semantic clustering. The underlying idea was that an individual's memorial representation of a studied list is not a chronologically ordered sequence of studied items, but rather a tree-like structure in which representations of words having similar meanings appear in the same branch or adjacent ones whereas words dissimilar in meaning appear in relatively widely separated branches. On the assumption that the individual generates a response protocol on a recall test by going through the structure in a systematic fashion, words with similar meanings would, then, be expected to occur close together in the protocol even if they were widely separated in the studied list. Frequent confirmation of this expectation by cluster analyses was a major factor behind the high interest in organization of semantic memory in the 1960s (Crowder, 1976).

2.5 THEORETICAL MODELS

In common usage, as distinguished from formal logic, the term *model* denotes any theoretical formulation that includes assumptions about the structures and processes responsible for performance in a given domain and that allows exact derivations of implications of the assumptions. Analysis of variance (strictly speaking the linear model of which it is a special case) meets the definition, but its structure is the same in all applications and parameter estimates from a particular data set are not expected to carry over to any other situation. For scientific modeling, in contrast, striving for generality is the sine qua non. The structure of a scientific model is chosen to enable rigorous specification of what is assumed in a particular scientific theory or hypothesis, and the minimal criterion of success is that the model provide an economical description of significant aspects of behavior in some class of situations. The following discussion focuses on the methods used to generate the theoretical assumptions of models of behavioral and cognitive phenomena, to derive testable predictions, and to draw inferences about processes that underlie observed performance. Because extant models vary widely with respect to abstractness and scope, it is convenient to organize the discussion by means of a rough classification into *laws*, *descriptive-analytic models*, and *process models*. These model types can only be briefly characterized in this section, but more extensive treatments are included in Resource References.

Laws

Though the term model did not come into common use among psychologists until the 1950s, efforts to formulate mathematical models actually date from the earliest days of scientific psychology. In the tradition of the physical sciences, the goal of research in sensory psychophysiology in the eighteenth and nineteenth centuries was strongly oriented toward the formulation of scientific laws. Formally, a law is simply a model, but it has the connotation of being firmly established, and, in practice, it has the special limitation of referring only to a single functional relationship. Among the earliest instances in psychological science is Bloch's law, which states that the effect of a visual stimulus briefer than about 100 ms is proportional to the product of intensity and duration. A more famous example is Weber's law, dating from the early nineteenth century, which states that a just discriminable change in a stimulus is a constant fraction of its intensity. Though later research showed that this relation only holds accurately within restricted ranges of intensities, the appellation *law* is merited by virtue of its holding closely enough for practical purposes in a great variety of situations, ranging from measuring people's visual and auditory capabilities to designing concert halls. Further, Weber's law

enters in some fashion into many later laws and models. For example, it was basic to Fechner's formulation of a logarithmic relation between psychological and physical stimulus magnitudes. In the Weber–Fechner tradition, the formulation of laws has continued even as the scope of psychophysics has broadened to include diverse judgmental processes.[8] A notable recent addition to the collection of laws deriving from psychophysics is the 'universal law of stimulus generalization' proposed by Shepard (1987).

In the domain of animal learning and behavior, the *matching law*, distilled from a large body of operant conditioning research by Richard J. Herrnstein, expresses a proportionality between rate of responding and rate of reinforcement (usually reward). Originally formulated with reference to operant conditioning and simple trial-and-error learning, applicability of the matching law has been demonstrated for a wide variety of human behaviors in economic and political contexts (Herrnstein, 1990).

Descriptive-Analytic Models

Laws may be viewed as a special case of a broad class of descriptive-analytic models (abbreviated *descriptive* in the remainder of this section) whose purpose is to generate abstract representations of trends or patterns in data that are simpler in form and more general than the original descriptions recorded during experiments. An especially simple example of this type of model is the *constant ratio rule*, originally formulated by Frank R. Clarke in the late 1950s for speech communication but subsequently found to hold widely for data obtained in studies of letter and word recognition and preferential choice. The data typically take the form of matrices in which rows correspond to stimuli and columns to responses and a cell entry is the frequency (or probability) with which the row stimulus evoked the column response. The constant ratio rule expresses the property that the ratio of the probabilities of any two responses to a given stimulus is independent of the number of responses available.

A common method for constructing descriptive models is to define derived measures, that is, parameters, which may reflect relationships not apparent in the raw data. In the case of stimulus–response data matrices, a perennial question is whether the probability $p_{i,j}$ of a subject's making response j to stimulus i depends only on the subject's ability to discriminate stimulus i from others or also on a bias for making response j regardless of the stimulus. The prevailing method of dealing with this question is Luce's similarity-choice (or biased-choice) model (Luce, 1977), in which the probability $p_{i,j}$ is assumed to be expressible as the product of a parameter $s_{i,j}$ (similarity of stimulus i to stimulus j) and a parameter b_j (bias for response j). For all but very small data matrices, the number of similarity parameters is uncomfortably large; however, constraints suggested by theoretical assumptions or considerations of practicality are imposed to reduce the number, and the most commonly used version of the model has only one parameter, s, representing the similarity between any two non-identical stimuli.

Application and testing of the model involves a step termed *estimation*. In current practice, a computer program is given a set of guessed values of the parameters, computes theoretical predictions of the data values and a measure of error (the average disparity between predicted and observed values), then repeats the procedure for a new set of parameter values and continues till a set of values is found that minimizes the error. Often, only a portion of the data of an experiment is used in the estimation procedure, and a critical test of the model is the goodness with which, using the parameter estimates so obtained, it can predict the remainder of the data.

In some instances, descriptive models arise from experience with *normative* (sometimes termed *prescriptive*) models, which prescribe how people (or machines) should perform in order to optimize some kind of payoff. The process can be illustrated in terms of the signal detection model of perception and recognition. About 1950, an already well-established mathematical theory of statistical decision was used by electrical engineers as the basis for a theory of an ideal detector, that is, a machine that would yield the best possible performance at detecting faint signals in communication networks. Soon after the success of this effort had been demonstrated, a psychologist, John A. Swets, and an engineer, Wilson P. Tanner, Jr., proposed that human performance in perceiving near-threshold stimuli might be described by the signal detection model. Reinterpreting the ideal detector as a descriptive model, Swets and Tanner showed how the two parameters of the model could be estimated from performance data, thus transforming the raw data into derived measures of accuracy and bias. One parameter, known as d', reflects the observer's ability to discriminate a stimulus from background noise; the other, commonly denoted C, reflects response bias (specifically, the observer's criterion for reporting presence of the stimulus). Once the utility of the model had been demonstrated for the interpretation of psychophysical and simple perceptual experiments, it was extended to recognition memory with d' interpreted as a measure of an individual's ability to distinguish presence versus absence of the trace of a perceived stimulus in memory and C as the individual's bias toward reporting recognition of a stimulus. This model now appears ubiquitously in studies of recognition memory, either as a constituent of broader models of recognition or simply as a device for computing measures of accuracy and bias from performance on recognition tests.[9]

The tactic of reinterpreting a normative model as a descriptive model is frequently employed in the domain of cognitive science and human decision making, the normative model being an information-processing machine in the former case and the idealized 'rational man' of statistical decision theory and classical economics in the latter. The success in these applications has not approached that achieved by signal detection theory, but the normative models have often provided useful frameworks for the development of descriptive models and useful baselines for informative comparisons of people's achievement on cognitive tasks with what is theoretically possible.[10]

Process Models

A process model includes representations of the cognitive processes and structures assumed to underlie performance in some class of phenomena, for example, those of short-term memory, visual imagery, or two-person interactions. Often a process model is portrayed only in the familiar flow diagram with boxes representing components of the model and arrows signifying lines of influence or interactions. At this immature stage, a model can serve at most as an aid to organizing and communicating a programmatic theory. When the construction is completed by adding computational assumptions, the result is a mathematical or computer model that simulates aspects of performance and generates testable predictions of behavior.

Perhaps the most important function of process models is to enable tests of the individual theoretical assumptions embodied in a model. The procedure for testing is to formulate a pair of 'nested' process models for a given set of phenomena and compute predictions of performance from each for an appropriate experiment. One member of this pair, the full model, includes all of the structures and processes hypothesized to be essential components; the other member, the baseline model, is the same except for the deletion of the one component whose status is at issue. Goodness of the predictions of these two versions of the model are compared, for example, by means of a likelihood ratio test, and if the fit of the full model to the data proves significantly better than that of the baseline model, the test is taken to support the theoretical assumption included only in the full model.

Applications of this procedure appear in current research programs for a wide range of problems, including, for example, tests of assumptions about roles of forgetting in paired-associate learning, inhibition in simple cognitive tasks, curvilinear utility functions in decision making.[11] The basic reasoning is the same in all cases, though the technicalities of implementation vary. A more formal presentation of this method of hypothesis testing, together with full illustrative applications, is given in Wickens (1982) in Resource References. Special aspects of methodology that arise in process models of language processing are discussed by McKoon and Ratcliff (1998). Activity in this arena has recently reached a new height of intensity, with the combined efforts of mathematicians, computer scientists, and mathematical psychologists producing a succession of solutions to problems of model comparison that had long appeared to be intractable. Several notable advances in methods for comparing models that differ in complexity and numbers of free parameters were presented in a special symposium at the 1999 meeting of the Society for Mathematical Psychology (Santa Cruz, CA, 1 August, 1999) and abstracts will be published in a forthcoming issue of the *Journal of Mathematical Psychology*.

Increasingly, models of perception and cognition have structures adopted from neural network theory. Empirical evaluation of these 'connectionist' (or 'parallel, distributed processing') models follows the same principles that apply to classical mathematical models. However, their use for purposes of testing hypotheses about underlying cognitive processes runs into extremely difficult problems of inference because in connectionist models the processes do not have distinct representations. Issues of representation and formal methodology that arise in this new strain of theoretical research are discussed in many chapters of Posner (1989), cited in Resource References, and, at a more technical level, by Suppes, Pavel, and Falmagne (1994).

2.6 Postscript

Over the past century, the basic research methods of psychological science have evolved in reciprocal interaction with the generation of an agenda of research problems, the accrual of results, and the emergence of formal theory. At the level of specific experimental techniques, technological advances have fueled an exponential increase in capabilities for gaining information about relations between brain and behavior. In the domain of data analysis, inputs from mathematics, statistics, and late in the century, computer science have similarly enhanced the power of methods and models for bringing research results to bear on theoretical problems. At the level of general methodological issues, debates concerning, for example, the relation between mind and body, the nature of psychological data, and the choice between naturalistic and artificially simplified experimental settings have not moved toward any clear settlements, but they have served to motivate efforts to sharpen some of the classical concepts of psychology and to broaden the once excessively restricted domain of behavioral research.

Acknowledgement

Preparation of this chapter was supported by Grants SBR 93-17256 and SBR 96-10048 from the National Science Foundation.

Notes

1. Methods of testing hypotheses about these processes are given in Townsend and Ashby (1983) and in numerous subsequent publications by Townsend.

2. Research on cognitive architectures, with special attention to Anderson's system, is thoroughly reviewed in the chapter by Newell, Rosenbloom, and Laird in *Foundations of Cognitive Science* (see Posner, 1989, Resource References).

3. The cell size of 10 in the example is arbitrary of course. The principle for choosing cell size in a real experiment is, first, to estimate on the basis of any relevant knowledge how many subjects would be needed to yield stable group means for a particular factor (task or amount of practice in the example), then to distribute that number of subjects as equally as possible over the cells in the row or column of the design matrix corresponding to that factor.

4. Henceforth, for brevity, reference will be only to means.

5. Probable error of a mean is defined as the range of scores around the true mean of the parent distribution (assumed to be normal) that would include approximately 50% of sample means if many samples were drawn. The *standard error* is similarly defined except that it includes approximately 68% of sample means.

6. Informally, *significance*, in this context, denotes confidence that an observed result, for example, a

difference between means for experimental and control groups, is unlikely to have arisen solely from fluctuations of subject sampling or random errors of measurement.

7. See Resource References for a review of scaling methods in cognitive modeling by Nosofsky (1992).

8. The present scope of the Weber–Fechner legacy is well portrayed by Geissler, Link, and Townsend (1992) in Resource References.

9. Basic concepts of signal detection theory and applications relevant to this discussion are given by Macmillan and Creelman (1991), cited in Resource References.

10. The role of normative models in human cognition is reviewed in Shiffrin and Steyvers (1997); the role in decision making is reviewed in Coombs, Dawes, and Tversky (1970) in Resource References.

11. All of these variations are treated by Dowling, Roberts, and Theuns (1998), cited in Resource References. That volume also includes discussions of uses of graph theory in modelling of knowledge spaces and processes of social interaction.

Resource References

Atkinson, R. C., Herrnstein, R. J., Lindzey, G., & Luce, R. D. (Eds.). (1988). *Stevens' handbook of experimental psychology* (2nd ed.). New York: Wiley.

Broadbent, D. E. (1971). *Decision and stress*. London: Academic Press.

Coombs, C. H., Dawes, R. M., & Tversky, A. (1970). *Mathematical psychology*. Englewood Cliffs, NJ: Prentice-Hall.

Dowling, C. E., Roberts, F. S., & Theuns, P. (1998). *Recent progress in mathematical psychology*. Mahwah, NJ: Erlbaum.

Geissler, H.-G., Link, S. W., & Townsend, J. T. (1992). *Cognition, information processing, and psychophysics: Basic issues*. Hillsdale, NJ: Erlbaum.

Hearst, E. (Ed.). (1979). *The first century of experimental psychology*. Hillsdale, NJ: Erlbaum.

Howell, W. C. (1994). Human factors and the challenges of the future. *Psychological Science, 5*, 1–7.

Kantowitz, B. H. (Ed.). (1974). *Human information processing: Tutorials in performance and cognition*. Hillsdale, NJ: Erlbaum.

Keren, G., & Lewis, C. (1993a). *A Handbook for Data Analysis in the Behavioral Sciences: Vol. 1 Methodological issues*. Hillsdale, NJ: Erlbaum.

Lindzey, G., & Aronson, E. (1968). *The handbook of social psychology: Vol. 1: Theory and method* (3rd ed.). New York: Random House.

Luce, R. D. (1986). *Response times: Their role in inferring elementary mental organization*. New York: Oxford University Press.

Macmillan, N. A., & Creelman, C. D. (1991). *Detection theory: A user's guide*. Cambridge: Cambridge University Press.

Nosofsky, R. M. (1992). Similarity scaling and cognitive process models. *Annual Review of Psychology, 43*, 25–53.

Pervin, L. A. (1990). *Handbook of personality: Theory and research*. New York: Guilford Press.

Posner, M. I. (Ed.). (1989). *Foundations of cognitive science*. Cambridge, MA: MIT Press.

Rosenzweig, M. R., Leiman, A. L., & Breedlove, S. M. (1998a). *Psychobiologie*. Brussels & Paris: De Boeck Universite. (French translation by Nicole Bonaventure and Bruno Will of the first edition, 1996.)

Rosenzweig, M. R., Leiman, A. L., & Breedlove, S. M. (1998b). *Psicologia biologica*. Milan, Italy: Casa Editrice Ambrosiana. (Italian translation by Patrizia S. Bisiacchi and Arnaldo Cassini of the first edition, 1996.)

Rosenzweig, M. R., Leiman, A. L., & Breedlove, S. M. (1999). *Biological psychology: An introduction to behavioral, cognitive, and clinical neuroscience* (2nd ed.). Sunderland, MA: Sinauer.

Wickens, T. D. (1982). *Models for behavior: Stochastic processes in psychology*. San Francisco: Freeman.

Additional Literature Cited

Anderson, J. R., & Schooler, L. J. (1991). Reflections of the environment in memory. *Psychological Science, 6*, 396–408.

Atkinson, R. C., & Shiffrin, R. M. (1968). Human memory: A proposed system and its control processes. In K. W. Spence, & J. T. Spence (Eds.), *The psychology of learning and motivation: Advances in research and theory* (pp. 89–105). New York: Academic Press.

Bahrick, H. P. (1984). Semantic memory content in permastore: Fifty years of memory for Spanish learned in school. *Journal of Experimental Psychology: General, 113*, 1–29.

Barbizet, J. (1963). Defect of memorizing of hippocampal-mammillary origin: A review. *Journal of Neurology, Neurosurgery, and Psychiatry, 26*, 127–135.

Bertenthal, B. I. (1996). Origins and early development of perception, action, and representation. *Annual Review of Psychology, 47*, 431–459.

Binet, A., & Simon, T. (1908). Le Developpment de l'intelligence chez les enfants [Development of intelligence in children]. *L'Année Psychologique, 14*, 1–94.

Crowder, R. G. (1976). *Principles of learning and memory*. Hillsdale, NJ: Erlbaum.

Ebbinghaus, H. (1885). *Memory* (Reprint 1964. Originally published in 1885). New York: Dover.

Estes, W. K. (1997). On the communication of information by displays of standard errors and confidence intervals. *Psychonomic Bulletin & Review*, *4*, 330–341.

Fisher, R. A. (1937). *The design of experiments* (2nd ed.). London: Oliver and Boyd.

Funder, D. C. (1991). Global traits: A neo-Allportian approach to personality. *Psychological Science*, *2*, 31–39.

Gabrieli, J. D. E. (1998). Cognitive neuroscience of human memory. *Annual Review of Psychology*, *49*, 87–115.

Gallistel, C. R. (1993). *The organization of learning*. Cambridge, MA: MIT Press.

Hammond, K. R., Harvey, L. O., Jr., & Hastie, R. (1992). Making better use of scientific knowledge: Separating truth from justice. *Psychological Science*, *3*, 80–87.

Hebb, D. O. (1949). *Organization of behavior: A neurophysiological theory*. New York: Wiley.

Herrnstein, R. J. (1990). Behavior, reinforcement, and utility. *Psychological Science*, *1*, 217–224.

Hilgard, E. R., & Marquis, D. G. (1940). *Conditioning and learning*. New York: D. Appleton-Century.

Jacoby, L. L. (1991). A process-dissociation framework: Separating automatic from intentional uses of memory. *Journal of Memory and Language*, *30*, 513–541.

James, W. (1890/1950). *The principles of psychology. Vol. II*. New York: Dover.

Keren, G., & Lewis, C. (1993b). *A handbook for data analysis in the behavioral sciences: Vol. 2 Statistical issues*. Hillsdale, NJ: Erlbaum.

Lewin, K. (1935). *A dynamic theory of personality: Selected papers*. New York: McGraw-Hill.

Luce, R. D. (1977). The choice axiom after twenty years. *Journal of Mathematical Psychology*, *15*, 215–233.

McGeoch, J. A., & Irion, A. L. (1952). *The psychology of human learning* (2nd ed.). New York: Longmans, Green.

McKoon, G., & Ratcliff, R. (1998). Memory-based language processing: Psycholinguistic research in the 1990s. *Annual Review of Psychology*, *49*, 25–42.

Milner, B. (1967). Amnesia following operation on the temporal lobes. In O. L. Zangwill & C. W. M. Whitty (Eds.), *Amnesia* (pp. 109–133). London: Butterworth.

Nathan, P. E., & Langenbucher, J. W. (1999). Psychopathology: Description and classification. *Annual Review of Psychology*, *50*, 79–107.

Nisbett, R. E., & Wilson, T. D. (1977). Telling more than we can know: Verbal reports on mental processes. *Psychological Review*, *84*, 231–259.

Piaget, J. (1970). Piaget's theory. In P.H. Mussen (Ed.), *Carmichael's manual of child psychology* (3rd ed.). New York: Wiley.

Schaie, K. W. (1989). Perceptual speed in adulthood: Cross-sectional and longitudinal studies. *Psychology and Aging*, *4*, 443–453.

Sears, R. R. (1944). Experimental analysis of psychoanalytic phenomena. In J. McV. Hunt (Ed.), *Personality and the behavior disorders Vol. 1* (pp. 306–322). New York: Ronald Press.

Seymour, P. H. K. (1979). *Human visual cognition*. New York: St. Martin's Press.

Shepard, R. N. (1987). Toward a universal law of generalization for psychological science. *Science*, *237*, 1317–1323.

Shiffrin, R. M., & Steyvers, M. (1997). A model for recognition memory: REM – retrieving effectively from memory. *Psychonomic Bulletin & Review*, *4*, 145–166.

Stevens, S. S. (1951). Mathematics, measurement and psychophysics. In S. S. Stevens (Ed.), *Handbook of experimental psychology* (pp. 1–49). New York: Wiley.

Strack, F., & Forster, J. (1995). Reporting recollective experiences: Direct access to memory systems? *Psychological Science*, *6*, 352–358.

Suppes, P., Pavel, M., & Falmagne, J.-C. (1994). Representations and models in psychology. *Annual Review of Psychology*, *45*, 517–544.

Townsend, J. T., & Ashby, F. G. (1983). *Stochastic modeling of elementary psychological processes*. Cambridge: Cambridge University Press.

Tukey, J. W. (1977). *Exploratory data analysis*. Reading, MA: Addison-Wesley.

Tulving, E. (1985). On the classification problem in learning and memory. In L.-G. Nilsson, & T. Archer (Eds.), *Perspectives on learning and memory* (pp. 67–94). Hillsdale, NJ: Erlbaum.

Weick, K. E. (1968). Systematic observational methods. In G. Lindzey, & E. Aronson (Eds.), *The handbook of social psychology* (2nd ed.). *Vol. 2: Research methods* (pp. 357–451). Reading, MA: Addison-Wesley.

Woodworth, R. S. (1938) *Experimental psychology*. New York: Holt.

Zuckerman, M. (1995). Good and bad humors: Biochemical bases of personality and its disorders. *Psychological Science*, *6*, 325–332.

Communications concerning this chapter should be addressed to: Professor William K. Estes, Department of Psychology, Indiana University, Bloomington, IN 47405, USA

3

Behavior in the Social Context

VERA HOORENS AND YPE H. POORTINGA

3.1 INTRODUCTION

Humans are a social species. This social nature provides the basic rationale for the present chapter's focus on the interaction between individual human organisms and their social context. First, we explore the reasons *why* humans are social beings and briefly consider the broad implications of this characterization. Next, we go somewhat more deeply into the question what it *means* to be social. In other words, how does an individual function whose primary mode of existence is that of a group member rather than of a solitary individual? After that, we consider some important 'natural' social groups and we briefly discuss their role in shaping human behavior. Against this background, we describe designs and strategies used by researchers to study the interaction between humans and their social context. A separate section is devoted to the relationship between biological underpinnings of behavior and the cultural context. While in the past these were treated as competing or contrasting influences in explanations of

behavior, their interactive nature has become more central in recent times. In the penultimate section of this chapter, we address some constraints and paradoxes in the explanation of social behavior. The final section offers a brief overview of the different psychological fields and of related disciplines that focus on the social context of human behavior.

3.2 THE ORIGINS AND DIMENSIONS OF BEING SOCIAL

Origins of Being Social

For both ontogenetic and phylogenetic reasons, humans can be characterized as social beings. *Ontogenetically*, newborn humans are characterized by a remarkable immaturity that renders them dependent for a long time on others for survival and growth (Björklund, 1997). It is clear that infants are critically dependent on their primary caregivers for the fulfillment of even the most basic needs. Most of us spend the extended period from infancy until sexual and social maturity and reaching socio-economic independence mainly within the nuclear or extended family. The emotional bonds of this early period form a blueprint for later relationships and continue to provide the context for our psychological functioning through adulthood. Throughout life, most of our behaviors are influenced by present, past, or anticipated interactions with others. As we argue later on, this holds in part even for those 'covert' behaviors that seem intrinsically private and individual, such as feeling, wishing and thinking.

There can be no doubt that the origins of being social are to be found in the *phylogenetic* and *cultural* history of humanity. From our hunting and gathering ancestors onwards the primary mode of existence has always been in small groups. Only with the advance of technology, first in the form of agriculture and animal husbandry, and very recently in the form of industrial production, more complex societies have arisen. We share our primary mode of existence with non-human primates such as chimpanzees and bonobos, with whom we show a striking genetic resemblance. Needless to say it may be tempting to assume that our social behavior patterns shared with these species must be genetically determined. However, caution is warranted against interpreting similarities in behavior across genetically related species as evidence of biological determination. For instance, until a few years ago the extrapolation to the human species of male dominance, so clearly observable in the behavior of chimpanzees and other ape species, seemed obvious and straightforward. Since then the description of the more gentle social interactions of the bonobo has shown the danger of such a generalization (De Waal, 1996).

Still, one may ask what the likely consequences are of this ontogenetic and phylogenetic background for human behavior. First, like other species humans show such a strong *tendency to seek the company of others* and to form and maintain at least a minimal number of stable relationships, that numerous researchers since Freud have conceptualized a fundamental 'need to belong' (e.g., Bowlby, 1969; Fiske, 1992). Such a need may well derive from the phylogenetic survival value of living in small groups (Baumeister & Leary, 1995). Even in urban societies, most humans still spend the better part of their life within the context of relatively stable (even though not invariable and not unchangeable) small groups.

Second, and related to the former point, it seems that humans are *pervasively dependent on each other* for the fulfillment of a variety of needs and motives. A solitary individual cannot fulfill many important life tasks. In addition, the degree to which one individual reaches his or her goals often has direct consequences for the degree to which others attain or miss theirs. Even the seemingly total and unidirectional dependence of the infant on its caregivers has aspects of mutuality. Indeed, caregivers are usually rewarded for their care as the infant meets their emotional needs or desires and fulfills their own aspirations. Mutual dependence or, as psychologists tend to call it, social interdependence, is a ubiquitous characteristic of people's behavioral environment.

Third and at the most general level, human behavior is *behavior in and between small groups* rather than the behavior of the isolated individual. This implies that solitary situations are not the most natural context for human behavior, but that they are rather the exception. Such a group-as-baseline view renders many 'enigmatic' findings on human behavior more readily understandable. For instance, people seem to form groups, to identify with new groups and to behave as established members of them with an amazing ease and speed. Research using the so-called 'minimal group paradigm' has shown that categorizing individuals into groups on the basis of an ad hoc procedure, for example, assigning them randomly to a 'forest' party and a 'sea' party, is sufficient to start treating others as either 'out-group' or 'in-group' members (Tajfel, 1982).

Dimensions of Being Social

What does it mean to be social? There are various ways to formulate an answer to this question, leading to different taxonomies of social behavior. Many answers that may be extracted from the literature include a classification of cognitive, affective, and motivational tasks that need to be fulfilled for a person to function as an individual and a group member. Here we refer to three task categories: understanding, engagement, and coping.

The most fundamental task is *social understanding*. The basis for social understanding is distinguishing between oneself and others. For example, in the theory of Piaget (1972) the external world and the subject are undifferentiated for the newborn. Contacts between the body and objects become the source of the distinction between external and internal. Soon the recognition of persons, and even of specific persons follows (to the delight of young parents!). Later distinctions between one's own group and other groups, between different other groups, and between fellow-humans and members of other species come about. Such distinctions delineate entities – oneself, individuals, groups, species – that need to be understood somehow in order to create a certain degree of predictability and controllability of one's environment and oneself. Social understanding further includes perceiving, categorizing and interpreting behaviors, searching for causes and consequences, and processing verbal information. These processes of categorization, attribution, and evaluation result in a more or less elaborated personal and social identity (some authors prefer to think in terms of multiple identities), more or less elaborate mental representations of one's own and other groups (Moscovici, 1984), and more or less stable attitudes towards a variety of groups and individuals (Eagly & Chaiken, 1993).

Based on the understanding of the social world (including oneself), humans *engage* in different modes of sociality or in different ways of relating to others. Fiske (1992) mentions four basic modes of sociality that alone or in combination with each other structure human social interaction and cognition. These are communal sharing (social behavior based on a sense of unity and solidarity), authority ranking (social behavior based on a hierarchical ranking of group members), equality matching (social behavior based on a strictly balanced exchange assuming equality of group members), and market pricing (social behavior based on cost–benefit calculations and profit maximization). Besides these fundamental modes of engagement, more specific choices are to be made. For instance, given an equality matching or a market-pricing interaction, one of various social exchange principles may be selected with each of them defining equality or fairness along different dimensions of comparison. Preferences for certain principles may depend on individual characteristics such as one's sex, but also on situational and cultural characteristics (e.g., Major, Bylsma, & Cozzarelli, 1989).

Finally, humans cannot foresee all possible consequences of their social engagements, nor do they have complete personal control over them. They have to *cope* with these consequences. According to Lazarus and his associates (e.g., Lazarus & Folkman, 1984), different types of appraisal determine whether social interactions, roles, positions, and other events and situations are *experienced* as stressful. Primary appraisal consists of evaluating whether an event is positive, negative, or neutral with respect to one's well being. The subsequent stage of secondary appraisal occurs after one has decided that an event is, or may become damaging to one's well-being – in other words, after the event has been categorized as threatening, harmful, or challenging. In this case, one assesses whether one's resources and abilities

are sufficient to overcome this harm, threat, or challenge. The combined outcomes of both primary and secondary appraisal determine the degree to which stress is experienced as a result of being confronted with a given event or situation. Efforts to cope with the stress of unwanted and/or unforeseen consequences of social interactions are of two kinds: changing the interaction itself (problem-focused coping), or changing one's emotional and cognitive responses to its consequences (emotion-focused coping). In turn, coping tasks may be complicated or facilitated by supportive interactions with others. One important finding is that social support or social interactions which are meant to be helpful, may be beneficial in some circumstances but harmful in others. This is not too surprising if one realizes that 'helpful' interactions are often unsolicited and inappropriate given a person's immediate needs, and that they thus may become social stressors in themselves.

3.3 INDIVIDUALS AND THEIR (NATURAL) GROUPS

One may argue that after infancy, there appears to be an even more basic choice, preceding the one between modes of sociality. This is the decision whether or not to be with others in the first place. In some circumstances, humans may choose between different degrees of companionship. However, this freedom of engagement is culturally bound and often limited to strictly defined groups of others, as a rule more so for women than for men. For example, in most cultural populations the category of 'family' allows little freedom of choice for an individual to seek or to avoid its members' presence, whereas the categories of 'friends' and 'acquaintances' do. In the present section we focus on natural groups, i.e. entities of social organization that are characteristic of the way of life in most, if not in all societies.

Social Interactions in Childhood

As already mentioned, social interactions of young children predominantly take place within one setting, namely, the family. For a long time, psychologists believed that the infant's attachment to its primary caregiver was no more than a learned or secondary reaction to the fulfillment of an infant's primary need for food by the caregiver. Impetus for change came from the famous experiments by Harlow and his associates (e.g., Harlow, 1958). They provided rhesus monkeys reared in isolation with different types of 'surrogate mothers'. These monkeys showed a strong preference for a soft and warm surrogate mother covered with comfortable cloth over a hard and cold surrogate mother made of naked wire. Contrary to what a naïve use of learning principles (with emphasis on reinforcement) had led to believe, the monkeys even did so when they were dependent on the latter 'mother' for the provision of food.

It is a pervasive assumption that the interaction qualities of the family and particularly those of the primary caregiver shape a child's later interactions, relationships, and even personality characteristics (see, for instance, Hartup & Van Lieshout, 1995). Currently much attention is being paid to Bowlby's (1988) attachment theory, in which security (versus insecurity) in the relationship with the mother is the key concept. Depending on whether they feel secure or insecure in this interaction, infants are believed to develop a secure attachment style characterized by closeness and trust or an insecure attachment style, such as avoidance of rejection or ambivalence between seeking closeness and avoiding rejection. Quite often, the early acquired attachment style is believed to characterize the individual for life (e.g., Parkes, Stevenson-Hinde, & Marris, 1991).

In the early interactions with parents and siblings, and later on in the interactions with other family members, peers, teachers, etc., the child develops an identity that is personal but that at the same time may be qualified as a social identity. Experience with family roles is the first confrontation with social roles or with prescriptive expectations concerning the behavior of individuals who occupy a certain position. In a broader sense, the child learns about roles and role expectations concerning him or her and others and about the positions that exist in any social setting. By the time the child goes to primary school it has already acquired an extensive repertoire of actions that allow it to participate in a variety of activities within a range of settings and with numerous persons (Barker & Wright, 1951).

The significance of others for human ontogenetic development is not a matter of discussion; the irreparable damage to development in those rare cases of children reared in isolation preempts any debate. However, there are strong differences of opinion as to how the relationship between the developing individual and the social context is best conceptualized. In maturation theories primacy is given to the biological growth and development of the human organism. Learning theorists take a predominantly empiristic stance; the individual acquires the behaviors that are reinforced by the social environment. The relationship between person and environment is conceptualized in yet another way in traditions that are associated with Vygotsky (1978). In this view, higher mental (i.e., typically human) psychological functions are *culturally* mediated; they have to be present in the society before the individual can acquire them. Initially, broad functions – such as the ability for abstract thinking – were thought to have originated in this way. Later on, cultural mediation has been postulated to operate on a more specific level – such as cognitive algorithms. This has led to research traditions on everyday cognition and situated learning in various cultural settings (Cole, 1996).

There are substantial differences in socialization patterns between cultural populations. Some of these concern specific developmental tasks like responding to the expectations of parents about the age of onset of walking. So-called parental ethnotheories are thus part of the environment with which children interact. In addition, broader patterns have been suggested, such as a relationship between the degree of food accumulation and socialization towards autonomy in traditional societies. When there is high food accumulation, as among agriculturists, socialization is directed towards dependence, especially for girls; when food accumulation is low, as among hunter-gatherers, socialization is more directed towards independence and more equal for boys and girls (cf. Segall, Dasen, Berry, & Poortinga, 1999).

Extensions of the Social Context

Growing up in a complex society implies becoming part of a number of groups. After the family, kindergarten and primary school are the groups that typically constitute the first expansion of one's social world. Later on, individuals engage in a variety of other formal and informal groups – such as high school classes, neighborhood friendship groups, sports clubs, and, later on, work teams and romantic relationships – thus further expanding and complicating the social world, especially in complex, urban-industrialized societies.

Interactions with others depend on the social perceptions of actors. Is the other a member of one's own group, and if so, what is this person's position or status? Depending on their status, individuals have differential rights and privileges. Those with a similar status display more evidence of solidarity (mutual liking, higher frequency of contacts). Interaction patterns are further controlled by intricate cultural rules, concerning, for instance, forms of address (Brown & Levinson, 1987) and exchange of compliments (Barnlund & Araki, 1985).

If an interaction partner is not a member of one's in-group, it is likely that the actor's opinions and attitudes are more negative than if the other is an in-group member. In-group favoritism and out-group discrimination have been studied extensively with both small and large groups. At the level of nations, ethnocentrism and stereotyping are the most central foci of interest. Although the 'us' versus 'them' distinction does not *always* come with a negative bias towards the out-group, the tendency in this direction has been demonstrated to be widespread (see Brewer and Campbell, 1976, for a study on thirty ethnic groups in East Africa). Research has shown, for example, that intergroup attraction is positively related to cultural similarity and opportunities for contact. However, individuals who share their membership of certain groups, but who in addition differentially belong to other groups, tend to treat each other as in-group members rather than as out-group members (Vanbeselaere, 1987). Quite clearly, findings like these have political implications for the formation of national identities in multiethnic societies as well as for the opportunities they offer for Machiavellian manipulation.

3.4 How Social Behavior is Studied

Research on social interaction has always been shattered over different fields in psychology and over a variety of related sciences. Focusing on psychological research, one major division is between developmental stages. Developmental psychologists typically study changes over time in parent–child interactions within the nuclear and extended family and in peer interactions in later childhood as well as in further stages of life. Social psychologists, in contrast, are mainly concerned with the social behavior of adults. Another division has to do with geographic parameters. Until the end of the twentieth century, most American and European psychologists – in other words, those psychologists who dominate the field – have tended to focus their observations on individuals of their own American and European cultural background to postulate universal insights in human behavior. Despite the growth of cross-cultural psychology, 'other societies' still tend to be considered the domain of cultural anthropology.

An impressive arsenal of data-gathering methods and techniques is at the disposal of researchers. Observation of actual interactions is the most general mode of data collection. For infants and young children, naturalistic observation is the method of choice, both for studying interaction patterns holistically and for the assessment of specific variables, such as direction of gaze. However, one also finds a range of other methods, like recordings of psychophysiological responses to the environment and reports by others, especially reports by parents of their children's behavior.

Most researchers are strongly concerned with distinguishing the phenomena of interest from ambient events. The widespread preference for research in standard settings (such as the laboratory) and for the use of standardized methods (such as questionnaires and tests) derives from this concern. For example, mother–child attachment may be studied using the so-called 'strange situation' in which the mother is requested to leave her child with a stranger for a given period of time. This procedure allows for a standardized assessment of the child's responses to separation and reunion (Ainsworth, Blehar, Waters, & Wall, 1978). Several authors have raised the question whether such a procedure is culturally appropriate. In other words, are identical results to be expected in societies where young children spend their time in day care centers as in societies where children stay with their mother on an almost continuous basis?

With older children and adults another method can be used, namely, self-reports. These are often gathered using standardized questionnaires. As they are often quick and easy to apply they are frequently used. However, there is ample evidence that responses to questionnaires tend to be distorted by response styles. The most pervasive response style is the tendency to answer in a socially desirable manner. Other examples of response styles that may distort questionnaire findings are the tendency to say 'yes' rather than 'no' and the tendency to avoid or to seek extreme values on response scales.

The experiment continues to be the most preferred method for the study of social interactions. It presupposes a systematic manipulation by the researcher of hypothesized situational determinants of behavior. This happens through the creation of various experimental conditions and the random allocation of subjects to these conditions.

One general assumption underlying experimental research is the belief that important elements of people's social context can be manipulated separately from each other. This implies that experimenters can sovereignly define the research setting and manipulate those elements of it that they deem relevant for the participants' behavior. Obviously, such assumptions are not always realistic and this may make experimental research vulnerable. Moreover, many aspects of social behavior do not lend themselves readily to strict experimentation, either because this would lead to an ethically unacceptable treatment of persons, or because the behavior of interest cannot be isolated from the social context. The frequent use of quasi-experimental designs is a consequence of these limitations. Quasi-experiments use existing groups of subjects and they incorporate a variety of procedural and statistical refinements to account for the nonrandom allocation of subjects to conditions and for the often limited control on treatments (Cook & Campbell, 1979). However, the extent to which proper controls can be realized and alternative explanations may be eliminated is limited. This becomes particularly evident if one considers behavior in its cultural context. Here subjects are inherently linked to the cultural population they belong to, and it is difficult if not impossible to disentangle in a study the behavior of interest from the broader context. A somewhat similar problem concerns the disentanglement of age and cohort effects on developmental processes. Rather complex cross-sequential research designs are needed to unravel various components that contribute to the variance in a given data set (Adam, 1978).

However, contemporary challenges to the experimental method do not derive primarily from questions about the limited accuracy of data due to weaknesses of design. They derive from the rejection of the assumptions on which the experimental paradigm is based. There are objections to the rigid prescriptions of standardized experimental procedures and measurement instruments, as well as to the presumed status of psychological traits and processes as if these have a quality of objective reality (Gergen, 1973). The traditional idea that psychological concepts refer to an objective reality is questioned. Rather such concepts are considered to be culture bound and mere expressions of a particular time; they are historical. This postmodernist critique comes in many forms and variations. It emphasizes either the (historical) contextuality of scientific concepts, as in Kessen's (1979) dictum about the American child as a cultural invention, or the uniqueness of individual life trajectories, or the need for indigenous psychologies to complement, if not to replace, Euroamerican concepts that can only be irrelevant elsewhere. Well known is Gergen's (1982) social constructionism, which states that behavior as well as our thinking about behavior is entirely contextual.

Those who argue against constructionism and postmodernism tend to emphasize the importance of objectivity and the replicability of procedures. They stress the importance of striving for valid data and interpretations. Statements that cannot be validated with methods that are independent of the person of the researcher have been frowned upon for a long time in scientific psychology. We expect that in the future, the demonstration of validity will continue to be the main standard for the evaluation of a study's merits.

3.5 THE SOCIETAL MATRIX

The social context of human behavior cannot be fully described by merely identifying natural groups such as nuclear and extended families, and by analyzing the interaction patterns that occur within them. These groups are part of a broader society and the manner in which this society is organized affects how they function. At the same time, if societal factors affect human behavior through their impact on natural groups, the proximal processes of family interaction can also attenuate societal influence (Bronfenbrenner & Ceci, 1994).

One category of building stones of society consists of societal *norms*, i.e., more or less cogent and widely shared behavioral expectations that are crystallized in explicit laws. Two emphases are possible. The first stresses the conventional character of many norms. From this point of view, norms are social agreements about how to behave in certain situations or even about which opinions are proper. The other view is that norms are based on *values*, i.e., affective–cognitive representations of what is morally good or bad. Values may be so much part of our lives that we take them for granted until a violation temporarily enhances their salience and elicits efforts to make them explicit.

At a more mundane level, social interactions are governed by a variety of rules that generally refer to desirable courses of action. Many rules have come about for practical reasons. For instance, rules in sports are installed for the pragmatic purposes of knowing how to begin, where to play, when to stop, and who the winner is. Needless to say, within a context of conflict or competition for scarce resources, personal or group interests may masquerade as values and be the true reason behind efforts to establish rules that foster them. For instance, while striving for alternative rules of distribution, subgroups that feel deprived may obscure their material interests by stressing values such as fairness.

Societies further shape behavior through their *institutions*. These may be defined as habitualized actions that are socially defined as the 'right way to do things'. The social agreement that is at the basis of an institution also includes a definition of the different actors that are assumed to perform these actions (e.g., Charon, 1987). Institutions are established to meet demands faced by society. Cultural anthropologists have linked early economic development from hunting and gathering towards agriculture and animal husbandry to the pressures of increasing population density. Once in place, these new forms of economic subsistence allowed for still higher population densities and for the emergence of more complex societies and diversified institutions.

The implications of this development for social interactions can perhaps best be illustrated with some recent developments. The technological changes of the last centuries, including the recent information technology revolution, have important implications for the magnitude, the number, and the complexity of different groups humans belong to. In contrast to our ancestors, present-day individuals almost inevitably get in touch with others who belong to different religious, cultural, and socio-economic groups. They are thus exposed to different worldviews, preferences, and life-styles. In addition, interactions with fellow group members may now happen on very different levels of interpersonal proximity, ranging from regular face-to-face contact via phone calls to electronic mail. They may even be largely unidirectional as in the case of television broadcasting and the use of websites. However, probably the most striking consequence of the multiple group structures of modern societies is that they allow for role reversals to occur. Individuals may hold different roles in different groups and therefore, even hierarchical relationships may reverse depending on the specific role at hand. This is in sharp contrast with traditional society where the fixed social structure and its psychological consequence of more authoritative and paternal relationships make role reversal rather unthinkable.

The impact of techno-economic developments on behavior can hardly be emphasized too strongly. The GNP of a nation is a strong predictor of a wide range of social variables, including the value dimension of individualism–collectivism, gender role ideology, and reported feelings of satisfaction and happiness (Georgas, Van de Vijver, & Berry, 1999). Of course, GNP is a simple outcome variable related to complex economic processes, and it is highly confounded with the average number of years of school education in a country. However, we should not underestimate the degree to which the financial wealth of a nation allows its members a degree of control over their lives that individuals living in poorer countries cannot even dream of.

Of course, other institutionalized domains should not be ignored. Notably, religious institutions which have been mainly a subject of anthropological analysis, may have a profound impact on the behavior of even non-believing members of a society. As far as they are a cultural fact, religious dogmas, symbols and beliefs provide powerful standards for regulating social behavior (Vergote, 1993).

3.6 RELATIONSHIPS BETWEEN BIOLOGY AND CONTEXT

One remarkable feature of the history of psychology is the intensive battle between social and biological perspectives. Since the dualism between body and soul, each with a separate existence (*materia*), was given up, no one has denied either that human behavior has biological underpinnings or that it is influenced by environmental events. Biological and environmental factors co-determine behavior in different and often complicated ways. There is evidence suggesting that environmental conditions affect biological processes. These, in turn, influence social behavior. If one considers that social behavior, in its turn, can change the social environment, the interdependence of social and biological factors is clear. However, when it comes to any more precise specification of these processes, essential, often time-bound, differences in perspectives remain between research traditions.

During a few decades before 1990, much theorizing on social behavior emphasized the impact of the social environment. Overt behavior – including social behavior – was seen as the outcome of learning processes. The remarkable cross-cultural variation in human behaviour continues to provide credit for learning as an explanatory principle, especially if learning is not limited to classical conditioning and contingency learning but taken to include imitation and rule learning.

Challenges to traditional behaviorism and cognitive psychology have originated from various fields of biology (cf. Chapter 4). Analysis of the nervous system, especially the brain, has greatly expanded with advances in cognitive neuroscience, biochemistry, and (psycho)-physiology. At the same time, developments in sociobiology and (human) ethology have led to the emergence of evolutionary psychology.

Perhaps the most significant insight from ethology is that the distinction between learning and instinct is less absolute than previously believed. On the one hand, the Watsonian assumption that each response may be equally easily coupled with each stimulus has turned out to be incorrect. On the other hand, seemingly fixed action patterns, like song in birds, do show variations under unusual environmental stimulation. In human ethology observational studies have revealed essential similarities in parent–infant interaction patterns across a wide range of societies, such as the universal presence of kissing as a sign of affection. Moreover, it has been pointed out that identical principles may underlie behavior expressions that differ in appearance. Eibl-Eibesfeldt (1979, 1989) has argued that such similarities are also evident in culturally specific customs like the diverse greeting procedures that are found around the world. His conclusion was that 'there exists a universal grammar of social behavior' (1979, p. 22).

The criterion of universality has been used frequently to argue for the biological determination of behavior. Aggressive behavior may serve as an example. Taking criminal violence as a standard, all over the world and across a wide range of ages men display more aggression than women do, with a maximum in late adolescence and early adulthood. This pattern coincides with age-related increases and decreases in the level of testosterone, a hormone of which men have more than women do. At the same time, cross-cultural differences in aggression rates exist that cannot be correlated with testosterone levels. It is now generally accepted that early deterministic explanations of aggressive acts as being biologically driven – proposed, for example, by Lorenz – are outdated (Herbert, 1988; Segall, Ember, & Ember, 1997). A more complex picture of human aggression is emerging, including biological and social determinants as well as interactions between them (cf. Chapter 4).

An approach to social behavior driven by evolutionary theory came with sociobiology. Its main breakthrough was the explanation of altruistic behavior among social insects as being compatible with evolution models. By serving the interests of family members and of their reproductive success, an organism may also enhance the reproduction of the genes that are shared between them, thus rendering altruism and self-interest compatible. Sociobiologists had little hesitation in extending this argument to the social behavior of humans. Many findings have been quoted in support, such as the higher rate of homicide by fathers of their stepchildren as compared with homicide of own-children, the pervasive presence of ingroup–outgroup distinctions, and ethnocentrism and nationalism. Whereas sociobiology and early forms of evolutionary psychology were mainly concerned with demonstrating the biological determination of social behavior, more recent theorizing is shifting towards interactionist positions. From this point of view, conditions in the social environment trigger genetically available modes of action (cf. Chapter 14).

The main topic of interest in biological explanations of social behavior is the demonstration and explanation of sex differences. These differences are seen as phylogenetically evolved dispositions resulting from differences between the optimal reproduction strategies of women and men. Studying with samples from thirty countries, Buss and colleagues (Buss et al., 1990) found considerable similarities in the traits young men and women like to see in their mates. Both across genders and across countries mutual attraction, intelligence, and a dependable character were highly valued. However, there were some sex differences that consistently emerged across countries (the term 'gender differences' that is popular in the social sciences seems inappropriate here). Men valued physical appearance somewhat more, while women gave somewhat more importance to the earning capacity of their prospective partners. These findings are said to match traditional reproductive roles, where a woman is interested in a good provider for herself and her children while a man is looking for a woman capable to bear his children, with so-called secondary sex characteristics like breast development being a sign of fertility. At the same time, it should be noted that cross-cultural differences (with men and women agreeing within societies) were much larger than the observed sex differences. Hence, it is not surprising that the evolutionary interpretation of 'gender' differences in mate preferences is still being disputed (e.g., Eagly & Wood, 1999).

3.7 LIMITATIONS, CONSTRAINTS, AND PARADOXES

In this section we attempt to consider social behavior from a metaperspective. We examine some aspects of the relationship between the study of social behavior and the context in which it takes place. We also raise some issues that are critical for the development of the field itself.

Constraints on Interpretation

Probably the most serious limitation in the study of social behavior lies in the fact that we are simultaneously the observer and the observed. Its obbligato character does not diminish the relevance of the notion that with respect to our social and cultural context we are like fish that only note the importance of water when they are outside of it. What we often do not seem to realize is the multifacetedness of contextual influences. We already mentioned the changing notions of childhood over historical times. We also referred to the emergence of indigenous

psychologies as a reaction against the ethnocentric character of the topics studied in Euro-
american psychology and against its ethnocentric methods and theories (Sinha, 1997).
Going beyond psychology, we should be struck
by the disciplinary dominance of our interpretations. For example, the rapid Japanese industrial
development and, later on, the emergence of the
Asian tigers has been attributed to decision
making, leadership styles, (collectivist) in-group
relationships, and (Confucian) values, while in
the economic literature a convergence of political and economic factors has been put forward.
The unexpected economic upheavals that took
place in these countries in the late 1990s have
shown the limitations of economic science, but
we should realize that they are also quite incompatible with such psychological explanations as
mentioned.

Much of the above has to do with the often
post hoc interpretation of data and with the fact
that scientists tend to look for convergent rather
than for discriminant evidence when testing
their theories. We have already alluded to difficulties in demonstrating evolutionary adaptations. These difficulties have been made explicit
by Gould (1991). He argues that a given characteristic of the human species may not have come
about for the function it presently fulfills. It may
also have arisen either 'accidentally' or through
natural selection for a function that it does not
anymore fulfill. Long after its emergence, such a
characteristic may have proved useful and come
to be used (i.e., 'coopted') for its current role.
Needless to say, similar problems of multi-
interpretability occur when adaptations are invoked at more proximal levels, like customs or
cultural conventions.

The (Un-)Predictability of Social Behavior

Research on social behavior has generated a
wealth of useful empirical knowledge. Apart
from the general issues that have been mentioned at various places in this chapter, research
on social behavior has produced a variety of
more specific insights that are surprising and
sometimes even disturbing. Many of these
results can now be found in any introductory
text in the field (e.g., Feldman, 1998; Hewstone,
Stroebe, & Stephenson, 1996). For example, in
two-party mixed-motive interdependence situations (the so-called 'prisoner's dilemma game'),
surprisingly often individuals choose to defect
on each other and thus to harm their joint well
being. While interpreting our own behavior and
other people's behavior, we tend to attribute
other people's successes and our own failures to

situational factors, whereas we more readily
attribute other people's failures and our own successes to the actor's personal characteristics.

Zimbardo constructed a simulated prison and
found that the behavior of mentally healthy
students who were randomly assigned to the
roles of 'prisoners' and 'guards' changed dramatically as a function of their 'new' group
membership – a change that he captured under
the label of 'deindividuation'. Even more well
known are the shocking obedience experiments
in which Milgram showed that when com-
manded to do so, almost everyone of us is
capable of hurting and even killing an innocent
other – at least, as long as the relative proximity
of the 'victim' and the 'commander' fulfills
certain requirements. It should be noted that
these phenomena were mainly discovered and
validated within research traditions relying on
the experimental method and on standardized
assessment scales. Therefore, we venture to disagree with viewpoints that reject the experimental paradigm.

Nevertheless, we would argue that the importance of many findings is overrated because
researchers are too pretentious about the explanatory power of their data. A statistically significant
difference appears to be the final goal of many
experiments, with the level of significance being
treated as if it reflects the size or importance of
the explained component of variance (Cohen,
1994). In addition, there is a tendency to overestimate the quality of representation in measurement. Generalizations to broad domains are
often made on the basis of a small set of stimuli
or items. The validity of such interpretations
is then extremely vulnerable. This is particularly worrisome in culture-comparative research,
where equivalence of domains and methods of
measurement often is presumed rather than
demonstrated (Van de Vijver & Leung, 1997).

Some scholars interpret this situation as an
indication of the relative recency of the field.
Consequently, they envisage a world to be won
by further and methodologically even more
sophisticated research. It is important to realize,
however, that there are inherent limits to the
predictability of social behavior and of developmental pathways. In this respect, we tend to
agree with postmodern and constructionist
research traditions. In our view, however, the
solution should not be sought in the introduction
of ideographic methods in which the principles
of objective measurement and validation are
given up. We would rather propose that alternative conceptualizations be developed in which
the predictable and the unpredictable, or the
explainable and the unexplainable, are more
clearly demarcated.

Such a demarcation is possible with non-linear dynamics, like 'chaos' or 'catastrophe' models. Sometimes we tend to identify these with *un*predictability, i.e. allowing any possible outcome. However, chaos and catastrophes in physical systems are characterized by unpredictability within well-described boundaries. Whether these boundaries are deterministic or probabilistic does not matter for the present argument. Taking the famous example of weather forecasts, chaos theory does make clear the uncertainty in predictions beyond a few days. At the same time, it equally allows for long-term regularities, like low temperatures in winter or high rainfall during the monsoon season.

We fully realize the danger of interpreting any unexpected change in behavior as chaos. However, this can be avoided if precise theoretical models guide research. Not surprisingly, this way of thinking is rapidly gaining attention. For instance, it is a fascinating idea that stage transitions in ontogenetic development and the emergence of higher stages can be described in terms of non-linear dynamics (e.g., Van Geert, 1994). More generally, humans may show a variety of possible courses of action. At the same time constraints limit the set of alternatives that are open to them. While it may be impossible to predict which course of action from that set a given individual will choose at any given time, it is possible and fruitful to delineate the constraints governing his or her behavior (Poortinga, 1997).

The Primacy of Group Membership: Some Further Considerations

Besides its contribution to psychological knowledge on the functioning of groups and individuals, the aforementioned minimal group paradigm has far-reaching implications for the methodology of studying behavior in a social context. In this respect, a remarkable contradiction is found with researchers who wonder about the amazing strength of the minimal group paradigm and yet neglect its potential relevance in everyday research practice. Imagine the situation in which research participants arrive at a laboratory in order to perform an 'individual' task. It may be sufficient that four or five participants arrive simultaneously and that they are collectively addressed as 'participants' or 'guests' by individuals who introduce themselves as 'experimenters' to temporarily activate a certain social identity in the participants. From this point of view, we may indeed wonder to which degree certain findings on so-called individual behavior are in fact findings on social behavior. Thus, many studies comparing human behaviors in 'individual' versus 'social' situations can be said to actually compare behaviors in *different types of* essentially social situations.

The minimal group paradigm can also be used to illustrate another methodological paradox. Above we have argued that the effectiveness of the paradigm is demystified if we assume that humans behave primarily as group members rather than as solitary individuals. This justifies the assumption that behavior in groups and social situations should be treated as the true baseline of human functioning, rather than the behaviors in isolation that have typically fulfilled this role. In other words, in contrast to common research practice it is perhaps not the effect of group membership or the presence of others that is to be explained, but the effect of their absence (Hoorens & Poortinga, in preparation). A number of enigmatic findings fall into place if the central question is reformulated as to how and to which degree behavior changes when it is displayed in isolation rather than in the presence of or in coaction with others.

At the same time, behavioral patterns that seem obvious while mainly viewing humans as solitary individuals may become *less* straightforward. For instance, in interactions characterized by social interdependence and by a partial conflict of interests between the participants – such as in the prisoner's dilemma game – people often make behavioral choices that maximize their own immediate outcomes while jeopardizing the group result that also includes their personal share. Consequently, the group result deteriorates to such a degree that each individual's total outcome becomes markedly less than optimal – hence the notions of 'social traps' and 'social fences'. Even in situations of stable interdependent relationships and in which there is no conflict of interest at all, lose–lose agreements are reached rather than win–win agreements (Thompson & Hrebec, 1996). Thus, we would seem ill equipped for optimally functioning in our natural habitat. Part of the solution appears to be that in many cases the sum of the individual inputs that are necessary for a group to survive successfully, is lower than the sum of the input needed from an individual for his or her solitary survival. If this is true, there is no point for an individual group member to invest the maximum of his or her energy and capacities in the realization of group goals, as he or she may necessarily do when acting alone.

Social Research and Social Reality

Many classics of social research have emerged from researchers' dismay or wonder over societal problems. One example is the research tradition on social dilemmas that took off after Hardin's (1968) description of the 'tragedy of the commons'. Using the overgrazing of the meadows of a traditional village as a case in point, Hardin showed how individual gain (a larger number of cattle for one farmer) and communal loss (overgrazing of the commons) can go hand in hand. The relevance of this view for research on environmental exploitation is obvious.

Another instance is the research program by Darley and Latané (for an overview see Latané & Nida, 1981) on the 'bystander effect'. This is the phenomenon that people are more likely to help a fellow human being in need when they are alone with the victim than when they are in the company of others. The starting point of Darley and Latané's research program was the fate of a young woman who was stabbed to death while tens of witnesses did nothing to help rescue her. These and other instances give ground to the impression that fundamental questions on human behavior may take specific incidents as their starting point and that they tend to be formulated on the basis of a mixture of scientific interest and societal concern.

A focus on practically relevant questions is highly recommendable and starting social and behavioral research from apparent societal problems seems only laudable. However, it creates a nagging uncertainty to realize how much our knowledge is grounded in the vicissitudes of what happens to strike researchers' attention. In the case at hand, much research on helping behavior has focused on single acts of helping behavior in sudden and rather severe emergencies and between strangers. In reality by far most helping behavior is towards members of one's in-group.

The intimate relationship between research and reality that characterizes social behavioral phenomena also works the other way around. The results of social and behavioral research may affect reality itself (Gergen, 1973). Through mass media and classroom coverage certain findings may spread so widely beyond the scientific community that they become common knowledge. People may even deliberately try to alter their own behavior, depending on the moral value that they attach to insights derived from research. Paradoxically, to the degree that it is appealing and successful, analysis of human behavior may render itself obsolete. In the 1950s, for instance, Asch reported his famous studies on conformism. He showed that even highly educated people often follow a majority that is clearly and undoubtedly wrong. Since then, a decrease in conformist behavior has been noted in a number of studies (Bond & Smith, 1996). Several explanations for this change have been advanced. However, it is not unreasonable

to argue that widely reported and often shocking demonstrations of human conformity and obedience have contributed to a heightened awareness of the dangers of behaving in accordance with the acts and commands of others and to a strengthened desire to resist this tendency.

3.8 Pertinent Fields and Disciplines

As we have seen in this chapter, human behavior in its social context is the focus of study in various subdisciplines of psychology. First among these is social psychology, encompassing the scientific study of all forms of social behavior. A range of textbooks and handbooks is available (e.g., Feldman, 1998; Hewstone, Stroebe, & Stephenson, 1996). One subfield of social psychology is social cognition. It studies how we understand our social environment. This subfield borrows heavily from basic knowledge on human perception, learning, memory, and thought processes. Another subfield is social interaction. It studies, among other topics, exchange modalities, such as equity, equality, and need. These subfields have relevance for, and are often inspired by, applied domains of psychology such as organizational and community psychology.

In cross-cultural psychology the emphasis is on one particular kind of context in respect of which there are pervasive differences, namely culture. Cross-cultural research does not only deal with the sociocultural environment, but also with ecocultural factors. By incorporating information from diverse cultural contexts it extends the range of behavioral variation, thus allowing for a much broader perspective than can be obtained within the boundaries of a single society (Berry et al., 1997). The third subdiscipline that should be mentioned is developmental psychology. One of its foci is on the interactions of the individual with significant others during various phases of the life course. These others vary systematically; from the mother in early infancy via peers in adolescence, to one's own spouse and children in adulthood and to grandchildren in old age (e.g., Shaffer, 1994).

When considering the position of social psychology and related subdisciplines among other sciences, the most important distinction is between natural and social sciences. Psychology belongs to both these broad domains. Many perspectives on individual functioning presume the application of methods and theories from biological sciences like neurology, physiology, and biochemistry. The new emergence of biological approaches to the study of social behavior grounded in ethology and evolutionary theory has been referred to before. As a social science, psychology is unique in that it is directed at the individual level. Other social sciences are oriented towards the supra-individual level of social institutions.

Among these other social sciences, in our view cultural anthropology is the most pertinent to the study of individual behavior in a social context. It also has the widest scope as it deals with virtually all aspects of human life and activities, be it from the perspective of humans as culture-bearers (Levinson & Ember, 1996). In ethnographies, cultural anthropologists have described the way of life of people of a large number of societies. Anthropologists always have been concerned with psychology (notably in the tradition of culture-and-personality or psychological anthropology; Bock, 1988). This is even more so with the recent shift from an emphasis on (technological) artifacts and societal structure (i.e., culture as external context) towards psychological concerns. The meanings of customs and institutions as the members of a cultural population experience them have become a focus of attention (i.e., culture as internalized).

Cultural anthropology is fascinating for psychologists because of its reliance on the observation of behavior in natural settings, because of its theories, and especially because of its data. Ethnographies open our eyes for the full range of variation in human social interaction patterns. An extensive data record, the Human Relations Area Files, makes this record accessible (Murdock, 1983). One neat example is the finding across 250 societies that infants tend to be carried in cradles when the average temperature during some part of the year drops below 10°C, while arm and sling carrying is predominant in warmer societies (Whiting, 1981). Apparently, urine leaking on one's clothes is too disagreeable in cold weather.

Within Western societies, the discipline closest to social psychology is sociology. It may be defined as the study of social institutions, including the family, work organizations and the state. These institutions determine the contexts in which social behavior takes place and by which it is constrained. Sometimes sociological and social psychological studies show close overlap. This is the case, for instance, for studies on topics such as attitudes, values, positions, and roles.

By now a variety of social sciences have emerged that deal with a particular kind of institutions or of modes of social interaction at a societal level. Thus, political science is concerned with the state and how it is organized to carry out its administration and its regulating functions, as well as with relationships between nations. Economics, and more specifically macroeconomics, is concerned with the exchange of resources at the societal level. The relationship with social psychology is quite evident in the case of microeconomics or consumer psychology – the study of individual economic behavior. Journals like the *Journal of Consumer Research* publish research by economists and psychologists alike, and many studies on consumer behavior use social-psychological concepts and are based on social-psychological theories. Although economics and psychology are characterized by very different assumptions, points of view, and criteria for the selection of relevant research questions, here they may find themselves studying identical phenomena. It is possible that such overlapping interests give rise to the emergence of multidisciplinary fields that often have an applied focus.

While considering the rather vague boundaries between various disciplines that are concerned with human behavior, one might expect a tendency towards integration. However, we should not forget that practising social and behavioral sciences is a form of human behavior, just as much as choosing between friends to play tennis with or as persuading our students that their hard work will eventually lead to fascinating insights. As such, the influence of processes that make us prefer familiar situations and objects above unknown ones and that give rise to in-group versus out-group biases also apply here. Thus, even if content-related boundaries lose much of their meaning scientists are apt to defend the right of 'their' science to survive as an independent and unique approach of human behavior within the social context.

Resource References

Berry, J. W., Poortinga, Y. H., Pandey, J., Dasen, P. R., Saraswathi, T. S., Segall, M. H., & Kagitcibasi, C. (Eds.). (1997). *Handbook of cross-cultural psychology* (2nd ed., Vols. 1–3). Boston: Allyn & Bacon.

Bock, P. K. (1988). *Rethinking cultural anthropology: Continuity and change in the study of human action.* New York: Freeman.

Cole, M. & Cole S. R. (1996). The development of children (3rd ed.). New York: Freeman.

Feldman, R. S. (1998). *Social psychology* (2nd ed.). Upper Saddle River: Prentice-Hall.

Flick, U. (Ed.). (1998). *The psychology of the social.* New York: Cambridge University Press.

Hewstone, M., Stroebe, W., & Stephenson, G. M. (Eds.). (1996). *Introduction to social psychology: A European perspective* (2nd ed.). Oxford: Blackwell.

Himmelweit, H., & Gaskell, G. (Eds.). (1990). *Societal psychology*. Newbury Park: Sage.

Kaplan, P. S. (1998). *The human odyssey: Life-span development* (3rd ed.). Pacific Grove: Brooks/Cole.

Keller, H. (Ed.). (1998). Lehrbuch Entwicklungspsychologie [Textbook of developmental psychology]. Bern: Huber.

Segall, M. H., Dasen, P. R., Berry, J. W., & Poortinga, Y. H. (1999). *Human behavior in global perspective: An introduction to cross-cultural psychology* (2nd ed.). Boston: Allyn & Bacon.

Shaffer, D. R. (1994). *Social and personality development* (3rd ed.). Pacific Grove: Brooks/Cole.

ADDITIONAL LITERATURE CITED

Adam, J. (1978). Sequential strategies and the separation of age, cohort, and time-of-measurement contributions to developmental data. *Psychological Bulletin, 85*, 1309–1316.

Ainsworth, M. D. S., Blehar, M., Waters, E., & Wall, S. (1978). *Patterns of attachment*. Hillsdale, NJ: Erlbaum.

Barker, R. G., & Wright, H. S. (1951). *One boy's day: A specimen record of behavior*. New York: Harper.

Barnlund, D. C., & Araki, S. (1985). Intercultural encounters: The management of compliments by Japanese and Americans. *Journal of Cross-Cultural Psychology, 16*, 9–26.

Baumeister, R. F., & Leary, M. R. (1995). The need to belong: Desire for interpersonal attachments as a fundamental human motivation. *Psychological Bulletin, 117*, 497–529.

Björklund, D. F. (1997). The rule of immaturity in human development. *Psychological Bulletin, 122*, 153–169.

Bond, R., & Smith, P. B. (1996). Culture and conformity: A meta-analysis of studies using Asch's (1952b, 1956) line judgment task. *Psychological Bulletin, 119*, 111–137.

Bowlby, J. (1969). *Attachment and loss* (Vol. 1). New York: Basic Books.

Bowlby, J. (1988). *A secure base: Parent-child attachment and healthy human development*. New York: Basic Books.

Brewer, M., & Campbell, D. T. (1976). *Ethnocentrism and intergroup attitudes: East African evidence*. New York: Sage.

Bronfenbrenner, U., & Ceci, S. J. (1994). Nature-nurture reconceptualized in developmental perspective: A bioecologial model. *Psychological Review, 101*, 568–586.

Brown, P., & Levinson, S. C. (1987). *Politeness: Some universals in language usage*. Cambridge: Cambridge University Press.

Buss, D. M. et al. (1990). International preferences in selecting mates: A study of 37 cultures. *Journal of Cross-Cultural Psychology, 21*, 5–47.

Charon, J. M. (1987). *The meaning of sociology* (2nd ed.). Englewood Cliffs: Prentice-Hall.

Cohen, J. (1994). The earth is round ($p < .05$). *American Psychologist, 49*, 997–1003.

Cole, M. (1996). *Cultural psychology: A once and future discipline*. Cambridge: Belknap.

Cook, T. D., & Campbell, D. T. (1979). *Design and analysis issues for field settings*. Chicago: Rand McNally.

De Waal, F. (1996). *Good natured: The origins of right and wrong in humans and other animals*. Cambridge: Harvard University Press.

Eagly, A. H., & Chaiken, S. (1993). *The psychology of attitudes*. Fort Worth: Harcourt Brace Jovanovich.

Eagly, A. H., & Wood, W. (1999). The origins of sex differences in human behavior: Evolved dispositions versus social roles. *American Psychologist, 54*, 408–423.

Eibl-Eibesfeldt, I. (1979). Human ethology: Concepts and implications for the sciences of man. *Behavioral and Brain Sciences, 2*, 1–57.

Eibl-Eibesfeldt, I. (1989). *Human ethology*. Hawthorne: Aldine de Gruyter.

Fiske, A. P. (1992). The four elementary forms of sociality: Framework for a unified theory of social relations. *Psychological Review, 99*, 689–723.

Georgas, J., Van de Vijver, F. J. R., & Berry, J. W. (1999). *Ecosocial indicators and psychological variables in cross-cultural research*, under review.

Gergen, K. (1973). Social psychology as history. *Journal of Personality and Social Psychology, 26*, 309–320.

Gergen, K. (1982). *Towards transformation in social knowledge*. New York: Springer.

Gould, J. (1991). Exaptation: A crucial tool for an evolutionary psychology. *Journal of Social Issues, 47*, 43–65.

Hardin, G. R. (1968). The tragedy of the commons. *Science, 162*, 1243–1248.

Harlow, H. F. (1958). The nature of love. *American Psychologist, 13*, 673–685.

Hartup, W. W., & Van Lieshout, C. F. M. (1995). Personality development in social context. *Annual Review of Psychology, 46*, 655–687.

Herbert, J. (1988). The physiology of aggression. In J. Groebel, & R. A. Hinde, (Eds.), *Aggression and war* (pp. 58–71). Cambridge: Cambridge University Press.

Hoorens, V., & Poortinga, Y. H. (in preparation). *On the social psychology of solitariness*.

Kessen, W. (1979). The American child and other cultural inventions. *American Psychologist, 34*, 815–820.

Latané, B., & Nida, S. (1981). Ten years of research on group size and helping. *Psychological Bulletin, 89*, 308–324.

Lazarus, R. S., & Folkman, S. (1984). *Stress, appraisal, and coping*. New York: Springer.

Levinson, D., & Ember, M. (Eds.). (1996). *Encyclopedia of cultural anthropology* (Vols. 1–4). New York: Henry Holt.

Major, B., Bylsma, W. H., & Cozzarelli, C. (1989). Gender differences in distributive justice preferences: The impact of domain. *Sex Roles, 21*, 487–497.

Moscovici, S. (1984). The phenomenon of social representations. In R. M. Farr, & S. Moscovici (Eds.), *Social representations* (pp. 3–69). Cambridge: Cambridge University Press.

Murdock, G. P. (1983). *Outline of world cultures* (6th ed.). New Haven: HRAF Press.

Parkes, C. M., Stevenson-Hinde, J., & Marris, P. (Eds.). (1991). *Attachment across the life cycle*. London: Tavistock/Routledge.

Piaget, J. (1972). *The principles of genetic epistemology*. London: Routledge.

Poortinga, Y. H. (1997). Brown, Heisenberg, and Lorenz. Predecessors of twenty-first-century psychology? In R. Fuller, P. N. Walsh, & P. McGinley (Eds.), *A century of psychology. Progress, paradigms and prospects for the new millennium* (pp. 1–15). London: Routledge.

Segall, M. H., Ember, C. R., & Ember, M. (1997). Aggression, crime, and warfare. In J. W. Berry, M. H. Segall, & C. Kagitcibasi (Eds.), *Handbook of cross-cultural psychology* (2nd ed., pp. 213–254).

Sinha, D. (1997). Indigenizing psychology. In J. W. Berry, Y. H. Poortinga, & J. Pandey (Eds.), *Handbook of cross-cultural psychology* (2nd ed., Vol. 1, pp. 129–169). Boston: Allyn & Bacon.

Tajfel, H. (1982). *Social identity and intergroup relations*. Cambridge: Cambridge University Press.

Thompson, L. & Hrebec, D. (1996). Lose-lose agreements in interdependent decision making. *Psychological Bulletin, 120*, 396–409.

Vanbeselaere, N. (1987). The effects of dichotomous and crossed social categorizations upon intergroup discrimination. *European Journal of Social Psychology, 17*, 143–156.

Van de Vijver, F. J. R., & Leung, K. (1997). *Methods and data analysis for cross-cultural research*. Thousand Oaks: Sage Publications.

Van Geert, P. (1994). *Dynamic systems of development: Change between complexity and chaos*. London: Harvester Wheatsheaf.

Vergote, A. (1993). What the psychology of religion is and what it is not. *International Journal for the Psychology of Religion, 3*, 73–86.

Vygotsky, L. S. (1978). *Mind in society: The development of higher social processes*. Cambridge, MA: Harvard University Press.

Whiting, J. W. (1981). Environmental constraints on infant care practices. In R. H. Munroe, R. L. Munroe, & B. B. Whiting (Eds.), *Handbook of cross-cultural human development* (pp. 155–180). New York: Garland.

Communications concerning this chapter should be addressed to: Professor Vera Hoorens, Department of Psychology, University of Leuven, Tiensestraat 102, B-3000 Leuven, Belgium

4

Psychology in Biological Perspective

MARK R. ROSENZWEIG AND KENG CHEN LIANG

4.1 THE SCOPE AND AIMS OF BIOLOGICAL PSYCHOLOGY

Psychology is both a biological and a social science, as Chapter 1 points out. The present chapter emphasizes the biological aspects of psychology, just as Chapter 3 emphasizes the social aspects. Both aspects must be taken into account for a comprehensive view of psychology, and at some points in this chapter we note interactions between biological and social variables in determining behavior and experience. The relevance of the biological approach for many fields of psychology is demonstrated by the fact that biological bases of behavior are mentioned in most of the following chapters.

The field that studies biological aspects of psychology and biological contributions to psychology has been given several names. Originally it was called 'physiological psychology' when 'physiology' was used to designate what we now call biomedical sciences. As specialized fields broke off from physiology – including biochemistry, immunology, and neurochemistry

– and as new fields were introduced – including genetics and endocrinology – the designation 'physiology' became too narrow, so the more inclusive term 'biological psychology' became more appropriate. Other terms sometimes used for this field include 'physiology and behavior' and 'behavioral neuroscience'.

The development of neuroscience as an integrated but multidisciplinary field in the last quarter of the twentieth century benefited biological psychology (behavioral neuroscience). Through the progress of neuroscience, biological psychology strengthened its ties and interactions with neighboring sciences and advanced its program of research and applications.

Biological psychology is concerned with both similarities and differences among individuals. The anthropologist Clyde Kluckhohn observed that each person is in some ways like all other people, in some ways like some other people, and in some ways like no other person. We can extend this observation to the much broader range of animal life. In some ways each person is like all other animals (e.g., we all need to ingest complex organic nutrients), in some ways like all other vertebrates (e.g., having a spinal column), in some ways like all other mammals (e.g., nursing as a baby), and in some ways like all other primates (e.g., having a hand with an opposable thumb and a relatively large, complex brain). These similarities and differences make it instructive to compare species and individuals in regard to behavior and biology, as we will note in some examples. This is also a theme of Chapter 19.

The Scope of Biological Psychology

The scope of biological psychology is indicated by the following list of some of the main fields it encompasses. For each major field, we state a question to indicate its relevance. Some of these topics will be discussed later in this chapter or taken up in other chapters.

1. Biological foundations of behavior.
   What is the biological 'machinery' on which behavior depends?

   Functional neuroanatomy: The nervous system and behavior.
   What are the main structures of the nervous system and how is each involved specifically in behavior?

   Neurophysiology: Generation, conduction, transmission, and integration of neural signals.
   How is information coded, transmitted and processed in the nervous system?

   Psychopharmacology: Neurotransmitters, drugs and behavior.
   How do neurons transmit signals chemically, and how can this be affected by drugs?

   Psychoneuroendocrinology: Hormones and behavior.
   How do hormones affect reproductive parental and social behavior?

   Psychoneuroimmunology: The immune system and behavior.
   How does the immune system interact with the endocrine and nervous systems in determining behavior?

2. Evolution and development of the nervous system.
   How does an evolutionary approach help in understanding behavior?

   Evolution of brain and behavior.
   How are brain differences among species related to differences in their behavioral capacities?

Life-span development of the brain and behavior.
How are brain development and change over the life span related to behavior?

3. Sensory processes and perception.

   General principles of sensory processing.
   What principles of functioning and biological mechanisms hold for all sensory modalities?

   Processing in the different sensory modalities: Touch and pain, hearing, vestibular perception, taste and smell, vision.
   What are some of the structural adaptations that enable different sensory receptors to respond to different kinds of stimuli?

4. Movements and actions.
   How are mental or cognitive processes translated into behavior? See Section 4.5.

5. Motivation and regulation of behavior.

   Sex: Evolutionary, hormonal, and neural bases.
   How do sex hormones help to organize the early development of the nervous system?

   Homeostasis: Active regulation of internal states.
   What mechanisms help to keep bodily conditions relatively constant but also responsive to calls for activity?

   Biological rhythms, sleep, and dreaming.
   How are various bodily functions, such as hormone levels, neural activity, and muscle tonus, regulated during wakefulness and various states of sleep, including dreaming?

   Affection and affiliation.
   How are affection and social attachment affected by levels of certain hormones?

6. Emotions and mental disorders.

   Emotions, aggression, and stress.
   What regions of the brain are particularly involved in emotions?

   Psychopathology: Biological bases of behavior disorders.
   How are certain mental disorders related to abnormalities of brain chemistry and anatomy?

7. Cognition.

> Biological perspectives on learning and memory.
> *How are changes in learning and memory over the life span related to changes in the nervous system?*
>
> Neural mechanisms of learning and memory.
> *What regions of the brain are involved in conditioning? (See the last part of Section 4.4.)*
>
> Language and cognition.
> *What brain regions are particularly involved in language? What treatments can aid recovery of language following a stroke?*

Biological Psychology has been a Major Part of Modern Psychology from the Start

Biological psychology has been a major part of psychology from the start of modern psychology in Europe and North America in the nineteenth century. For a brief history of biological psychology, see Rosenzweig (2000). Biological psychology remains a major field of research and instruction in the main English-speaking countries, and in some other countries. There are several current textbooks in the field; some are listed in the Resource References of this chapter. Reviews of advances in biological psychology appear in such publications as the *Annual Review of Psychology*, *Annual Review of Neuroscience*, *Trends in Neuroscience*, *Trends in Cognitive Science*, *Behavioural and Brain Sciences*, and *Current Opinions in Neurobiology*.

4.2 RELATIONS BETWEEN BIOLOGICAL AND SOCIAL PSYCHOLOGY

The influences of both genetics and experience on behavior and mental functions (nature and nurture) are discussed in Chapter 3 and we will add a bit to that discussion here. The authors of Chapter 3 note the long-standing historical contest between proponents of social and biological perspectives. Stating that no one now denies either that human behavior has biological underpinnings or that it is influenced by environmental events, they claim that this is about as far as agreement goes. Here we take a further step, indicating how the biological approach is helping to understand the means and mechanisms by which some of the social/experiential factors influence behavior.

For studying and understanding many kinds of behavior, biological and social perspectives offer complementary avenues. In other cases, biological and social factors continuously interact and affect each other. We will give examples of both kinds.

As Chapter 3 emphasizes, concrete social behaviors are largely learned. A major field of biological psychology is investigating the biological mechanisms of learning and memory storage – how these processes occur, where in the nervous system they occur, how and why different kinds of learning vary over the life span. Some of these questions about learning and memory are taken up later in Section 4.4, and they are treated more fully in Chapter 8. Biological research complements social and cognitive research on learning and memory.

Emotional aspects of behavior are important in social psychology. Biological research and theorizing about emotion go back to the nineteenth century and continue actively today, as Chapter 12 reports. Biological research on emotion complements social and cognitive research on emotion.

In some cases social behavior is determined, in part, by biological factors. For example, social attachment and affection are determined in part by levels of the neuropeptide hormones oxytocin and vasopressin, which are secreted by neurons of parts of the hypothalamus. These neuropeptides are also involved in many aspects of reproductive and parental behavior; this is true in humans and other mammalian species (Carter, 1998). Recent research indicates that not only the concentration of vasopressin but also the distribution of vasopressin receptors among brain regions helps to determine social behaviors (Young, Nilsen, Waymire, MacGregor, & Insel, 1999). A rodent species, the prairie vole, known for its fidelity and sociability, was found to have a gene that determines where and when the vasopressin receptor is turned on; this gene is not present in two promiscuous and less social vole species. The investigators then inserted the prairie vole gene into house mice, which are not highly social and are promiscuous. When the genetically altered mice were given vasopressin, the males significantly increased their contact with females, a response not seen in normal male house mice. Impressed that a single gene can alter social behavior, the investigators now plan to study variation of the distribution of the vasopressin receptor among humans, especially because most psychiatric disorders are characterized by abnormal social attachments.

In other cases, biological and social factors continuously interact and affect each other in an

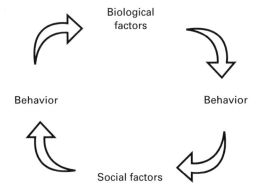

Figure 4.1 *Relations between biological factors, behavior, and social factors. There are continual reciprocal interactions among these factors*

ongoing series of events as behavior unfolds. This is indicated in Figure 4.1.

For example, the level of testosterone in a person's circulation affects his dominance behavior and aggression in social groups. The dominance may be exhibited in a great variety of social settings, ranging from playing chess to physical aggression. In several studies in humans and primates, the level of testosterone correlates positively with the degree of dominance and with the amount of aggression exhibited. Winning a contest, whether a game of chess or a boxing match, raises the level of testosterone; losing a contest lowers the level of testosterone. The altered level of testosterone in turn is one of the factors that determine the display of dominance and aggression in the social group, and this has further repercussions. Thus, at any moment the level of testosterone is determined, in part, by recent dominance-submissive social experience, and the level of testosterone determines, in part, the degree of dominance and aggression. Of course, social/cultural factors also help to determine the frequency of aggression; as Chapter 3 points out, cross-cultural differences in rates of aggression exist that cannot be correlated with hormonal levels, and ways of expressing aggression and dominance are determined in part by sociocultural factors.

The neurotransmitter serotonin is another of several biological factors correlated with the magnitude of aggression, but in this case the correlation is negative; that is, the greater the aggression, the lower the concentration of serotonin. Serotonin seems to help suppress aggression. Serotonin concentration also varies with social experience; levels of serotonin decline as the individual's position in a social group rises. For further discussion and references to the involvement of testosterone and

serotonin in dominance and aggression, see Rosenzweig, Leiman, and Breedlove (1999, pp. 423–424).

4.3 BODILY SYSTEMS BASIC TO BEHAVIOR

Understanding the operation of the body is essential for research on biological foundations of psychology. While different organs were speculated to be the site of the mind or soul in ancient times, it is now well established that the nervous system is critical in coordinating behavior and mental functions by receiving information from various parts of the body, processing incoming and stored information, and sending orders to muscles and glands. The nervous system does not accomplish its task alone; it works together with the endocrine system and the immune system.

The Nervous System

The nervous system is composed of neurons, about a trillion of them in the case of the human body, and extensively varied in morphology and function. A typical neuron (Figure 4.2) contains a cell body, or soma, that subserves the maintenance and integration functions, and also branches, including many dendrites, which are involved in receiving signals, and an axon, which is involved in transmitting signals. Communication in the nervous system is highly convergent and divergent. A neuron receives multiple inputs at its dendrites or soma, and sends output through its axon to multiple target sites. The axon terminals form connections with dendrites or soma of the recipient neurons by specialized structures called synapses. The small gap (20 nanometers) between the presynaptic terminals and postsynaptic sites requires signal transmission to be mediated by different chemicals called neurotransmitters. Direct electrical transmission across certain synapses also exists at some sites in the nervous system of invertebrates and even vertebrates.

While attention has been focused on neurons in discussing the biological bases of mental function, the nervous system contains as many, or probably even more, glial cells, which are essential for the vitality and functioning of neurons. They regulate the chemical environment of neurons, remove debris and repair damage after injury. Certain types of glial cells (Schwann cells or oligodendrocytes) wrap their processes around some axons to form a myelin sheath, which not only provides protection but also increases the signal conduction velocity of the myelinated axon. Degeneration of the

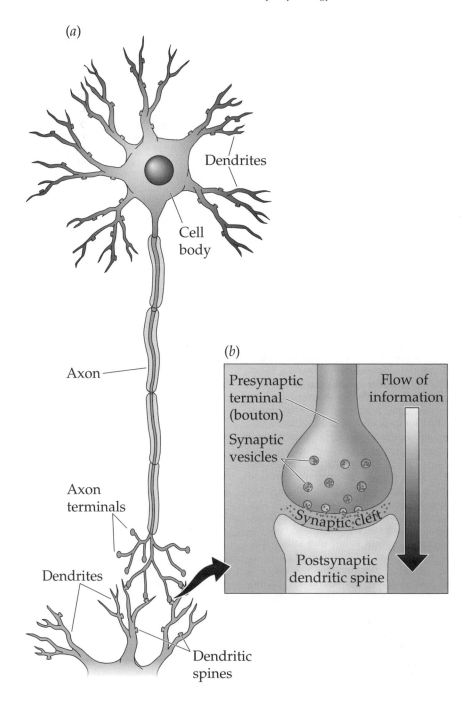

Figure 4.2   *A typical neuron. The neuron (a) receives signals at its dendrites and cell body (soma); the information is integrated by the cell body, and an output signal may be conducted down the axon to its terminals and thence to synapses on other neurons. The presynaptic terminal (b) contains synaptic vesicles which are filled with molecules of neurotransmitters. When the neurotransmitter molecules (represented as dots in the diagram) are released into the synaptic cleft, they bind to receptor molecules and can stimulate or inhibit the postsynaptic neuron. (Adapted with permission from Rosenzweig, Leiman, & Breedlove, 1999.)*

myelin sheath due to autoimmune diseases may lead to conduction failure and as a consequence result in disorders of motor behavior such as multiple sclerosis.

Although organisms are capable of reacting to stimuli of various types (visual, auditory, tactile, etc.), the nervous system transduces (codes) all the sorts of stimulus energies as a single form of signal: alteration in electrical potentials across the neuronal membrane. The neuron actively maintains a resting potential of about 70 mV, the interior of the neuron being electrically negative in relation to the exterior. The transduction of stimuli into neural signals depends on exchange of electrically charged ions through various channels (or gates) in the neuronal membrane controlling the permeability of ions. Lowering the membrane potential of an axon to its threshold sets off an action potential. This signal is all-or-none, self-propagating and non-decremental, which results from sequential activation and deactivation of voltage-dependent sodium and potassium channels. Some properties of neuronal coding are related to behavior of ion channels. For example, because the action potential is all-or-none, its amplitude cannot code the stimulus intensity. However, some nerves code the intensity of stimuli by their firing rate (the frequency of action potentials). After an action potential there is a brief absolutely refractory period and then a relatively refractory period, during which the membrane is hyperpolarized (more negative inside than in the resting state) because the rectifier potassium channels remain open. A stronger stimulus is needed to bring the hyperpolarized membrane potential to the firing threshold. The higher the stimulus intensity, the sooner the hyperpolarization will be overcome. Thus a strong stimulus generates more frequent firing of action potentials than does a weak stimulus.

Neural impulses reaching axon terminals open calcium channels leading to a series of biochemical events and eventually causing the presynaptic terminal to release neurotransmitter molecules, which cross the synaptic cleft and bind to specific protein molecules called receptors located on the postsynaptic membrane. The binding alters the permeability of ion channels directly in so-called ionotropic receptors or indirectly through a second messenger system in so-called metabotropic receptors. Both result in excitatory or inhibitory effects on the postsynaptic neuron. It is critical to note that mental activity is related to inhibition as well as to excitation of neurons. For example, visual experience is induced by light impinging on the retina causing hyperpolarization and thus inhibition of the rod receptors; the rods are normally depolarized due to opening of some positive ion channels in darkness. Likewise, generation and modulation of some behaviors are due to inhibition of neurons that exert tonic inhibition on the motor pathway. The entire output of the cerebellum is inhibitory. It is also critical to note that activation of a single input rarely fires the postsynaptic neuron. Instead, firing of the postsynaptic neuron is decided by spatial summation of excitatory and inhibitory inputs from various sources and temporal summation of inputs impinging within a time limit. The convergence of multiple synaptic activity in determining firing of a neuron is the basis of the fact that processing of stimuli, as well as responses to them, is often modulated by various factors such as arousal, attention, emotion, or motivation.

The human nervous system contains a central and a peripheral division. The central nervous system (CNS) contains the brain and spinal cord, and the peripheral division contains cranial and spinal nerves innervating peripheral targets including sensory receptors, muscles, or visceral organs. Those nerves carrying information from and to the viscera and involved in control of their activity form the autonomic nervous system (ANS) which is further divided into the sympathetic and parasympathetic branches. The activity of the ANS has been implicated in motivational and emotional functions, as discussed in Chapters 11 and 12, respectively. The spinal cord processes information from sensory receptors, delivers motor orders to the muscles, and serves as a relay between the brain and the periphery. The brain contains a central core known as the brain stem including the medulla, pons, midbrain, thalamus, and hypothalamus. Around the brain stem are the basal ganglia and limbic system. All these structures are largely covered by the cerebral cortex, which is most developed in the human being; it can be further divided into the frontal, temporal, parietal, and occipital lobes in each hemisphere. While the two sides of the central nervous system are grossly symmetrical, functional and structural asymmetries are demonstrated in the cerebral cortex and other brain loci. Cells in the cerebral cortex group into layers while those in other structures group into aggregations called nuclei. Different subdivisions are involved in different functions, as is discussed in related chapters.

Sensory, motor, and mental functions are represented at many levels of the nervous system. Different types of information processing may be undertaken by neural circuits of distinct levels. One type of operation is to combine information from both sides of the body to derive a third dimension of perception that is not naturally reflected in the surface of the receptor organ. An example is localizing auditory or

visual stimuli in the environment. Sound localization depends on the difference in intensity,
time of arrival, or phase of sound waves as they
impinge the two eardrums. Stereopsis (visual
depth perception) depends on the fact that the
image of a stimulus farther or nearer than the
fixation point falls on non-corresponding positions of the two retinas (retinal disparity). The
auditory localization mechanisms have been
studied especially in owls and bats, animals that
depend of auditory localization to prey in the
dark. Some auditory neurons in the brain stem
receive convergent inputs from the two cochleae.
These neurons are able to detect sounds from
specific locations which create a particular temporal delay in action potentials from the two
ears (Carr & Konishi, 1990). In the visual system, the convergence of bilateral information
does not take place until the primary visual
cortex. However, in higher order visual cortical
areas, there are regions in which neurons
specialize in detecting visual depth (Poggio &
Poggio, 1984).

In general, the nervous system appears to
observe a division of labor. Various properties
involved in a behavioral function rely on different groups of neurons within each level. This
principle is best attested by the multiple visual
representation areas in the cerebral cortex. Information concerning the form, color, motion, and
position properties engages different cells in the
primary visual cortex (area V1); this information
is then dispatched to specific higher-order
regions of the visual cortex. Information concerning form and color flows through a ventral
stream of neural pathways to the inferotemporal
cortex (the 'what' pathway), whereas that concerning motion and position flows dorsally to
the parietal lobe (the 'where' pathway) (Mishkin
& Ungerleider, 1982). It also appears that the
amount of neural tissue devoted to representing
a function is related to the fineness of discrimination or control in this function. This 'more is
better' principle is well demonstrated by the
large magnification factor in the foveal as compared with the peripheral regions of the primary
visual cortex.

While the gross distribution of various functions in different parts of the CNS is largely
determined by evolutionary and genetic factors,
it is now well established that the fine structure
of these representations is by no means static
and varies from individual to individual. The
anatomy of neural tissue subserving a function
is subjected to fine-tuning by experience. For
example, the cortical representational area for a
specific finger can be enlarged by repeated use
in a discriminative task or shrunk by depriving it
of sensory input (Buonomano & Merzenich,
1998). This experience-dependent plasticity of

the nervous system may serve as part of the
biological basis of personality or idiosyncratic
individual differences.

The Endocrine System

The endocrine system contains several endocrine glands, which are involved in regulation of
a constellation of physiological and behavioral
functions such as glucose utilization, conservation of fluid and ions, and facilitating sexual
maturation and behavior. The endocrine system secretes hormones into the blood stream,
through which they are carried to all parts of the
body. Thus, in contrast to the swiftness of signal
transmission and the specificity of target activation in the nervous system, signals in the endocrine system travel at a much slower velocity
and activate a much wider array of targets.

To affect the target tissue, hormones must
bind to specialized receptor molecules. Many
hormones bind to receptors on the membrane of
target cells, just as neurotransmitters do, and
they activate a second messenger biochemical
cascade to alter metabolic functions of the cell.
But steroid hormones (including those released
from the adrenal cortex and sex glands) enter the
cells by penetrating through the membrane and
binding to receptors in the cytoplasm. The
hormone–receptor complex is transferred into
the nucleus. In the nucleus, the complex is able
to regulate expression of specific genes, which
in turn direct protein synthesis in the cytoplasm
and hence change cellular functions. Thus, while
nerve impulses induce a relative short-latency
and brief-duration response, hormones often
induce a long-latency and long-lasting response.
Therefore, hormones can prime the peripheral
tissue and create a suitable internal milieu appropriate for later brisk action of neural signals.

Activity of the endocrine system is under
hierarchical control, which provides one example of interactions between the endocrine and
the neural systems. Neurons in certain nuclei of
the hypothalamus secrete various releasing hormones into the median eminence, whence they
are sent by the portal vein system to stimulate
the anterior lobe of the pituitary gland to secrete
different tropic hormones. These in turn regulate
the activity of the adrenal glands, the gonads
and the thyroid gland. Steroid hormones secreted
by the peripheral endocrine glands or the pituitary
enter the CNS and bind to receptors in the
hypothalamus or elsewhere in the brain to exert
an inhibitory feedback control on the secretion
of various releasing or tropic hormones.

It is important to note that the action of
hormones is not limited to regulating endocrine

activity; they also participate in a constellation of physiological and behavioral functions. Receptors for hormones are found in widespread brain areas and are activated by hormones secreted from peripheral or central endocrine cells or neurons in numerous brain regions that also contain peptide or hypothalamic hormones. In many cases these peptide hormones, and other neuropeptides as well, coexist with traditional neurotransmitters in the nerve terminals and are co-released with them for transmission or modulation purposes. Hormones exert various kinds of effect on the nervous system. For example, sex hormones have been shown to have an organizational effect and an activational effect on sex functions. The former refers to the fact that early in development, the presence or absence of the male sex hormones switches the growth of the brain structures into a male or female mode and fosters the development of peripheral sex organs and secondary sexual characteristics. The activational effect refers to the fact that as the organism reaches sexual maturation, the release of sex hormones primes sexual behavior.

It should be mentioned that some hormones have other actions in addition to endocrine function. For example, infusion of corticotropin-releasing hormone (CRH) into the cerebral ventricles causes a wide spectrum of physiological and behavioral effects, including increased peripheral sympathetic outflow, inhibition of gastric motility and secretion, inhibition of feeding and sexual behavior, increased grooming, defensive withdrawal, and startle behavior. Such effects are present after hypophysectomy or adrenalectomy and hence independent of the pituitary–adrenal axis. These responses resemble those that occur under the state of fear or anxiety, leading to the suggestion that CRH may act as a central anxiogenic (anxiety-inducing) mediator (Dunn & Berridge, 1990). As mentioned in Chapter 8, several stress-released hormones such as adrenaline, glucocorticoid, adrenocorticotropin (ACTH), vasopressin, and cholecystokinin influence memory in various aversive or appetitive learning tasks. Post-training administration of these hormones can enhance later retention. The effect appears not to depend on endocrine target tissue because some fragments or analogs of these hormones devoid of endocrine activity are also effective. It has been proposed that the stress-released hormones may act as endogenous memory modulators to facilitate storage of stressful experience (McGaugh, 1989). A stress-released hormone capable of coping with the stress during confrontation but also engraving the lesson

in memory storage would increase survival and be highly adaptive from an evolutionary perspective. However, not all effects of stress-released hormones are beneficial. High levels of glucocorticoid in the peripheral tissue caused by prolonged stress may induce a constellation of harmful effects, which Hans Selye called the exhaustion phase of the general adaptation syndrome (Selye, 1956). In addition, high levels of glucocorticoid may activate certain neural receptors in the hippocampus and increase the vulnerability of hippocampal neurons to possible insults in daily life and thus accelerate aging (Sapolsky, 1992).

The Immune System

More and more evidence indicates intimate interactions between mental activity and the immune system. This system defends an organism from harmful foreign biological substances introduced into the body. So-called natural killer cells, members of the immune system, roam around the body to destroy infected cells or cancer cells. In addition, cells infected by viruses may secrete a peptide named interferon to suppress further reproduction of the virus. These are nonspecific actions of the immune system. Immune responses may also attack specific targets. Cells located in the thymus gland, bone marrow, spleen, and lymph nodes induce chemically mediated and cell-mediated immune reactions in detection of invading microorganisms. The B-lymphocytes, which originate in the bone marrow, release immunoglobulins into the body fluid; these act as antibodies that bind specifically to the unique protein (antigen) on the membrane of invaders and result in destruction of the invading cells. On the other hand, the T-lymphocytes, which originate in the thymus, have antibody attached on their membrane; they directly attack the invading microorganisms and destroy them or enhance their destruction by other cells. Cells in the immune system communicate with cytokines such as interleukins; these chemicals are synthesized and released by white blood cells to detect soluble toxic products from invading microorganisms and cause other white cells to proliferate. These cytokines may also provide information to other body systems as explained in the next paragraph.

Stress or psychological reactions to it have profound effects on immunoactivity. Emotional disturbance due to depression or highly stressful life events, such as school examinations or marital disruption, compromises the ability of the immune system and increases susceptibility to infectious diseases, autoimmune disorders, cardiac disease, and cancer. Animal studies have shown that enhancement or suppression of immune activity can be elicited by conditioned stimuli through a classical conditioning procedure (Ader & Cohen, 1993). These and other data suggest that there are three-way interactions among the neural, endocrine, and immune systems. The central nervous system influences the immune response through the autonomic nervous system and hypothalamic–pituitary axis. Sympathetic noradrenergic fibers innervate the thymus and spleen and affect functions of the immune cells. Receptors for neuropeptides are present on the membrane of these cells. Opiate blockers antagonize the suppression of the natural killer cells induced by intermittent shock stress, suggesting involvement of the endogenous opioid system. CRH and glucocorticoid have a profound immunosuppression effect. As noted in Chapter 12 on emotion, amygdaloid neurons are activated by emotional stimuli. Thus, through projections from the central amygdaloid nuclei to the paraventricular nucleus, stress could enhance release of CRH, which eventually releases glucocorticoid to suppress immune activity. Such effects may provide a biological mechanism by which social factors affect physiological conditions, such as vulnerability to contagious diseases or carcinogenic agents.

Conversely, cytokines released by immune cells or the CNS may act on the brain to affect neural activity (Rothwell & Hopkins, 1995). They bind to hypothalamic neurons, through which they influence secretion of various hormones, including increased release of ACTH, prolactin, and growth hormones but decreased release of luteinizing hormones. Behaviorally, the most conspicuous effect of cytokines given centrally or peripherally is to induce fever, and this appears to be mediated by release of CRH. In addition, cytokines may increase the amount of slow-wave sleep. These effects are part of the normal reaction to infection. It has therefore been proposed that the immune system may serve as a sensory channel informing the CNS of our internal chemical environment.

4.4 METHODOLOGY IN BIOLOGICAL PSYCHOLOGY

Major aspects of methodology in research in biological psychology will first be presented and discussed. Then we will illustrate these considerations by reviewing briefly the search for the neural mechanisms of classical (Pavlovian) conditioning.

Biological Psychology Studies Both Humans and Nonhuman Animals

Biological psychology manipulates and observes psychological variables just as do all other fields of psychology, and thus employs in general the methodology of psychology depicted in Chapter 2. However, to delineate the somatic contribution to behavior and mental functions, biological psychology needs to draw evidence from studies combining methods of psychology with those of other disciplines such as neuroscience, pharmacology, immunology, and endocrinology. These methods allow the investigator to probe into relevant bodily systems. Further, in contrast to many other fields of psychology that focus their research mainly on human beings, biological psychology investigates both human and nonhuman species. Study of animal subjects is justified for two reasons. First of all, from an evolutionary perspective, the bodily systems subserving mental activity, like any other biological features, are under the pressure of natural selection and have evolved over a long period of time as a consequence of adaptation to the environment. Behavioral functions have also evolved, as suggested by Charles Darwin (1872) in his book, *The Expression of the Emotions in Man and Animals*. Therefore, as stated in Section 4.1, common components may underlie mental functions of both humans and other species in terms of their structural bases or operational mechanisms. Investigating the brain function of animals can therefore contribute significantly to our understanding of that of humans. This expectation is substantiated by numerous findings suggesting shared biological bases of human and nonhuman behavior illustrated in various chapters of this book. A few examples from the rich literature in this area include parallel processing of different visual properties (e.g., hue, shape, and movement) in separate brain regions, hormonal influences in sexual development, and engagement of the amygdala by emotional arousal.

The second reason for employing animal studies is purely methodological. For one thing, studies of development or life-span changes in behavior and neural mechanisms are more practical to conduct in animals whose life spans are much shorter than our own. For another, invasive manipulation or assessment of brain functions cannot be performed in human subjects except under special circumstances. In rare cases, human bodily systems may be perturbed by natural causes or probed experimentally for therapeutic purposes (such as stimulation during surgical rectification of epilepsy); the ensuing behavioral symptoms may suggest relationships between structure and function. In the history of biological psychology, neurological findings have often served as good starting points in the history of biological psychology. However, follow-up animal studies are necessary to formally test and establish such inferences because damage produced by nature is seldom as well defined as experimental ablation or manipulation in animals. Various types of somatic or behavioral intervention can be applied to animals in a humane manner and also precisely in terms of time and location to unravel the relationships between body and behavior. Nonetheless, recently developed techniques such as functional brain imaging and magnetic brain stimulation allow us to measure or alter directly human brain activity and close the gaps in our knowledge between brain functions in humans and other species.

Even though mental functions across species may indeed vary with evolutionary status, the correspondence of particular sets of behavior from one species to another is hard to establish. When the neural mechanism of mental functions is inferred from animal studies, animal behavior is often used in the sense of a model for the mental function concerned. For example, imprinting behavior may serve as a model for filial attachment, and various types of aggression induced by different kinds of stimuli can model aspects of anger. The model system bears similarities to what is being modeled, but the two need not be identical. Such similarities could be based on different grounds. Some of them are based on apparent similarity in behavior, such as self drug-administration by animals as a model of addictive behavior. Some of them bear an essential theoretical component of the modeled function, as mastering certain tasks indicates declarative learning. Of course, inferred similarities must always be cross-checked by independent methods and by attempts to invalidate them.

Biological Psychology Uses a Variety of Approaches

To delineate the relationships between the bodily systems and mental functions, biological psychologists may adopt different approaches including somatic intervention, behavioral intervention, and correlation (Figure 4.3).

In somatic intervention, the investigator manipulates specific parts of a bodily system and assesses the consequence on mental/behavioral functions. The general strategy of manipulating a bodily system is to activate or suppress its function. Activation of a neural structure can be accomplished by applying weak electric currents

of appropriate intensity or by local infusion of drugs stimulating receptors inducing excitatory postsynaptic potentials (EPSP) or blocking receptors inducing inhibitory postsynaptic potentials (IPSP). Local infusion of drugs blocking EPSP or inducing IPSP will have opposite effects. Pharmacological manipulation of the biochemical cascade linked to receptors also serves a similar end and allows further dissection of the intracellular events critical for behavior. Permanent suppression of a neural function can be achieved by destruction of the tissue with various types of lesion. However, administration of local anesthetics or drugs that block sodium channels can cause temporary and reversible lesions of the affected tissue.

Interactions between the somatic system and mental function are by no means unidirectional; behavioral experience may alter structural or functional properties of the neural, hormonal, and immune systems. Such effects are typically revealed by behavioral intervention in which behavioral or mental functions are manipulated and consequences in bodily systems are detected. Changes in the brain may be anatomical, physiological, or neurochemical. Anatomical changes include increase in axonal branches, dendritic arborization, or synaptic formation after exposure to an enriched environment or after certain types of learning experience. Physiological changes may be expressed as increase of evoked responses to input stimuli or alteration in membrane electrotonic properties tested either in vivo or in vitro. Neurochemical changes may include increases or decreases of cellular energy utilization, receptor binding, enzyme activity, release or reuptake in neurochemicals or hormones, protein synthesis, or gene expression.

Studies in biological psychology may also adopt the correlational approach in which behavioral and somatic variables are measured simultaneously in each of a group of subjects, so that the extent to which the two measures covary can be measured. For example, the neurophysiological activity of a specific structure may correlate with behavioral performance during acquisition in a new learning task. In another case, the level of androgen or glucocorticoid may correlate with the social hierarchical status of monkeys in a colony. Structural or functional abnormalities may correlate with the severity of mental dysfunction in schizophrenic patients.

The interventional approaches help to find cause-and-effect relationships between the independent and the dependent variables. In contrast, the correlational approach cannot determine any causal relationship between the two measures. However, this by no means reduces its importance in biological psychology research, because

(a) Manipulating the body may affect behavior

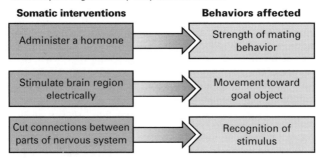

(b) Experience affects the body

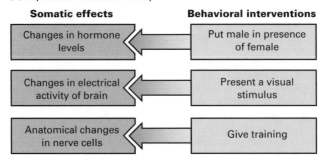

(c) Bodily and behavioral measures covary

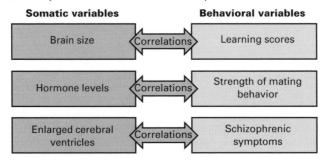

(d) Biological psychology seeks to understand all
     these relationships

Figure 4.3   *Different approaches to investigation: somatic intervention, behavioral*
intervention, and the correlational approach. (Reproduced with permission from
Rosenzweig, Leiman, & Breedlove, 1999, Figure 1.3.)

the presence of a correlation between two measures suggests future intervention studies, and lack of correlation may help to limit the domain for further investigation. Even when a causal relationship between two variables has been established, correlational studies still provide additional information. Based on the evidence that disrupting the function of a somatic structure alters a specific type of behavior, one can conclude that the somatic structure exerts critical influence on that behavior, but there is no guarantee that the structure is normally engaged when the behavior is performed in nature. However, if some somatic measures in that structure co-vary with the behavioral performance under natural conditions, it is more likely that the structure is inherently engaged in carrying out the behavior. Therefore, discovery of somatic mechanisms underlying mental functions relies on convergent evidence from studies using different approaches in biological psychology research.

Some Issues Involved in Different Approaches and Methods

How to reach a specific interpretation for the effect of a treatment is one of the major concerns in biological psychology research. Consider, for example, the use of lesions to evaluate the role of a structure in a function. It appears to be straightforward to ablate the structure and observe the effect. However, removing a block of tissue or making electrolytic or radio frequency lesions destroys not only the soma but also fibers of passage from other regions. Better specificity may be achieved by employing excitotoxins that damage only cell bodies but spare the fibers of passage. Neurotoxins invading particular types of neural elements may cause selective depletion of specific transmitters. For example, 6-hydroxydopamine (6-OHDA) is often used to deplete central dopamine for examination of its role in motivational or motor behavior. Likewise, side effects of a pharmacological agent often, if not always, prevent a clear interpretation of specific influences on behavior. Specificity of pharmacological studies may be achieved by administration of several drugs sharing the same intended action but with different side effects, or by counteracting the agonist effect with specific antagonists.

To employ treatments with specific influences on the nervous system does not necessarily guarantee a clear-cut interpretation of the finding. Two further sources of complication should be noted. One comes from the fact that the bodily system is dynamic. As noted in Section 4.3, structures in the nervous system are intimately interconnected with a multitude of convergent and divergent fibers and are highly reactive. Perturbation at one point causes not only local changes but also changes in adjacent or even remote areas. For example, lesions or chemical depletion may cause a constellation of compensatory reactions in the remaining system and the resultant behavioral deficit could be attributed either to loss of the ablated components or reactive changes in the surviving components. In the case of depletion, replacement of the depleted substance may differentiate the two possibilities, which are really hard to resolve in lesion studies. Stimulation of neural tissue by electrical or pharmacological means may affect not only activity of the stimulated area but also that of connected regions. Thus, caution must be used in assigning any effect, and hence the function inferred from the presence of such an effect, directly to the manipulated structure.

The second complication comes from the fact that behavior is subject to multiple influences, and quite different underlying causes may result in the same or similar changes in explicit behavior. To take studies of learning and memory as an example, treatments given prior to learning tasks may affect acquisition performance by changing sensory-motor or motivational processes instead of learning ability. Thus, influences on performance should be ruled out before a conclusion on learning per se can be reached. The post-training treatment regimen may avoid such confounding, and effects thus produced could be due to influence on storage processing of the learned information. Sometimes, behavior may involve different phases of processing, each of which may extend over a period of time. Treatments that cause permanent and irreversible effects on the nervous system may not be able to dissect the neural structures engaged at different stages of the process. For example, permanent lesions made post-training in a structure cannot distinguish whether it affects memory formation or memory retrieval. Yet reversible and temporary lesions administered at different phases may well serve such a purpose.

Another major concern in methodology is how to choose, from a whole array of available techniques, the appropriate ones that can detect or affect the relevant somatic events, which vary tremendously in both the spatial and temporal dimensions. As noted in Section 4.3, the basic structural and functional unit of the nervous system is the neuron. Yet mental activity may be related to episodes occurring at subordinate levels, such as the synapse, intra-cellular organelles, and specific molecules, or at superordinate levels such as neural networks, maps, systems, or even the entire CNS. The dimensions of these

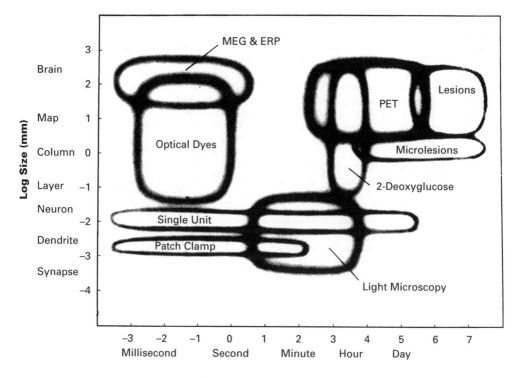

Figure 4.4 *Brain measures appropriate to different spatial and temporal dimensions of neural processes. (Abbreviations: ERP, event-related potential; MEG, magneto-encephalography; PET, positron emission tomography.) (Reproduced from Churchland & Sejnowski,* Science, *1988, Figure 3, with permission of the authors and* Science.)

structures vary from 10^{-7} to 10^2 mm. Different kinds of signal arise in these structures and may last for different periods of time varying from milliseconds, in the case of action potentials, to a whole life span, in the cases of increases or decreases of neural elements or the consequence of gene mutation. Methods presently available have constraints in both the spatial and temporal dimensions within which they can best function. For example, recording single unit activity accurately follows the signals from an individual neuron with a temporal resolution of milliseconds, but this technique is inadequate to detect the slower activity changes over a larger population of neurons. On the contrary, event-related potentials or the electroencephalogram (EEG) reflect massive field potential changes from an extensive region, but are unable to locate or distinguish the relative contribution of neural elements within that region. Figure 4.4 shows the spatial and temporal dimensions of neural processes appropriate for several methods.

It should be noted that the strength of a technique may not be an inherent property but should be judged in relation to the dimensions of

the phenomenon to be studied. Improvement of techniques in a reductionistic direction (say, from EEG to unit activity to patch-clamp recording of a single channel) has contributed much to the advancement of our knowledge of neural basis of behavior. However, Bullock (1993) has rightly reminded the field that some aspects of brain function may be imbedded in the integrative aspects of neural activity, which should be brought out by methods with appropriate spatial and temporal scales.

Biological Psychology Draws Conclusions from Convergent Evidence

Based on the above discussion on methodology, it is clear that biological psychology has to rely on evidence from various lines of studies to establish relationships between the somatic system and mental function. The reasons can be recapitulated as follows.

(a) The neural substrate underlying a mental function may involve mechanisms from the molecular to the system levels and engage somatic events with different durations. No method could cover the whole spectrum of neural events. Moreover, an apparently unitary behavioral or mental function may include sub-processes or sub-stages, each of which may have different neural substrates. Thus, studies using different methods yield findings on different facets of the relation, and only integration of all findings can generate the global picture.

(b) To achieve specificity of the treatment and reach valid interpretation of the observed effect, convergent evidence from studies using different methods is required.

(c) Studies adopting interventional approaches and the correlational approach may be complementary to substantiate the assertion that a particular somatic process is normally engaged in a mental function under natural conditions.

(d) Biological psychologists are interested in the extent of generalization of neural mechanisms underlying specific behavioral functions from one species to another, including humans.

The Neural Bases of Classical Conditioning

The search for neural bases of classical conditioning may be used to illustrate the dependence on convergent evidence in biological psychology. Ivan P. Pavlov established the behavioral principles of conditioning in a series of publications that began near the end of the nineteenth century (e.g., Pavlov, 1906). He later attempted to account for conditioning in terms of hypothetical irradiation of electrical activity across the surface of the cerebral cortex, but the irradiation was inferred from the behavior and was not based on direct observations and did not provide a satisfactory explanation. Later workers brought newer techniques to the search for the mechanisms and neural circuits involved in conditioning.

Psychologist/neuroscientist Richard F. Thompson and his colleagues, as well as other groups, have studied extensively the neural circuitry involved in eyelid conditioning in rabbits (for review, see Thompson & Kim, 1996). The task involves pairing of a tone (the conditioned stimulus, CS) with an air-puff (the unconditioned stimulus, US) administered to the eye; the air-puff causes the unconditioned response (UR) – blinking of the eye or closure of the eyelid. An early correlational study showed good correlation between activity of neurons in the hippocampus and the performance of the conditioned response (CR): the activity increased during acquisition only if the CS and US were paired and predicted the appearance and maturation of the CR. A behavioral intervention study showed that training experience enhanced synaptic efficacy in the hippocampus: after eyeblink conditioning, stimulation applied to the perforant path (an input to the hippocampus) of trained animals evoked larger monosynaptic population spikes in dentate granule cells. Enhanced responses in pyramidal neurons persisted even in the hippocampal slices taken from trained animals and assessed in vitro, suggesting that the changes had become intrinsic to the hippocampus. Similar neuronal activity model was also detected in the cerebellum. Unit activity changes in the deep cerebellar nuclei – especially the interpositus nucleus – also preceded and predicted the performance of the CR.

The roles of these two structures were distinguished by somatic intervention studies. Lesions of the cerebellum or the interpositus nucleus abolished acquisition in simple delayed classical conditioning but had no effect on performance of the UR, which ruled out involvement of performance factors and suggested a causal role of this structure in the task. In contrast, hippocampal lesions had little effect on acquisition or expression of CR in the simple delayed classical eyelid conditioning, suggesting that activity in the hippocampus did not bear any necessary role in CR performance. Yet hippocampal lesions did abolish learning in more complex paradigms such as trace conditioning and conditional or reversal discrimination learning, suggesting that the hippocampus subserves a different role than the cerebellum. The trace conditioned response has been compared to human declarative memory because awareness of the CS–US temporal contingency is a prerequisite for successful acquisition in trace conditioning (Clark & Squire, 1998).

The circuit and mechanism involved in the conditioned reflex engaging either structure was further delineated by use of a constellation of methods. For example, in the cerebellar circuitry, temporary and reversible lesions were used to distinguish between structures mediating plasticity and those mediating the output from the plastic site, which could not be properly dissociated by permanent lesion studies. Inhibitory chemical agents or local cooling were applied to either the anterior interpositus nucleus, which presumably is a major site of plasticity, or to its efferent sites such as the superior cerebellar peduncle and the red nucleus. The general findings were that suppression of the interpositus nucleus during training blocked performance in acquisition and the animals showed no trace of retention after the blockade was lifted and no saving if subjected to retraining. On the other hand, suppressing sites efferent to the interpositus nucleus during training blocked performance in acquisition, but the animals showed excellent performance in testing once the suppression was lifted, suggesting that the suppressed site was not essential for plasticity to occur.

Long-term depression (LTD) occurring in the cerebellar Purkinje cells has been proposed as a mechanism for plasticity underlying simple classical conditioning. LTD involves activation of glutamate metabotropic receptors. A recent study utilizing the newly developed gene-knock-out technique produced mice who did not express a specific type of metabotropic glutamate receptors (*mGluR1*). The results showed that these mutant mice were deficient both in LTD and eyeblink conditioning (Aiba et al., 1994), suggesting a correlation between a neural mechanism and behavior.

The involvement of the cerebellum and hippocampus in classical conditioning has also been investigated in human beings. Studies using positron emission tomography (PET) found that eyeblink conditioning in humans increased glucose metabolism or local cerebral blood flow of the cerebellar and hippocampal areas, among other regions, consistent with the findings from rabbits (Timmann et al., 1996). Furthermore, patients with unilateral cerebellar pathology were not able to acquire a conditioned eyeblink response (Bracha, Zhao, Wunderlich, Morrissy, & Bloedel, 1997). In contrast, amnesic patients with damage in the hippocampal area could acquire an eyeblink conditioned response in a delayed conditioning paradigm but failed to do so in a trace conditioning paradigm (Clark & Squire, 1998), again replicating the findings in nonhuman species. Thus, all the results from human and nonhuman studies employing various techniques converge in indicating that the cerebellum plays a critical role in mediating classical conditioning of certain somatic reflexes.

4.5 MOTOR BEHAVIOR: REFLEXES, MOVEMENTS AND ACTIONS

The behavior of people and other animals displays a great variety, ranging from relatively simple reflexes to coordinated movements and extending to complex acts or action patterns. Usually we are interested in acts or action patterns – complex, sequential behaviors, frequently oriented towards a goal – but even reflexes can tell us much about the principles of behavior and its bodily mechanisms.

An additional reason for taking up motor behavior here is that most of the chapters in this book omit this topic, simply assuming that mental or cognitive processes will be translated into behavior or into inhibition of behavior. Some psychologists and investigators in related disciplines, however, have made progress in studying how activity of muscles and glands is evoked and coordinated.

Reflexes

In the seventeenth century, the philosopher René Descartes noted that some responses appear to occur automatically to certain stimuli. He supposed that the neural energy of the stimulus is conducted to the spinal cord and there reflected (whence the term 'reflex') back out to the muscles, eliciting the response. At that time, the difference between sensory nerves and motor nerves had not yet been recognized. This was achieved early in the nineteenth century by Charles Bell and François Magendie, and it gave rise to the concept of the reflex arc. Late in the nineteenth and early in the twentieth century, investigators such as Charles Sherrington studied the laws of reflex action. Sherrington and Ivan Pavlov believed that behavior could be understood as a chain of successive reflexes, but this view was later shown to be over-simple. Rather, much behavior, ranging from locomotion to speech, appears to be organized by plans or programs that are established before acts occur, rather than each movement being triggered by the previous one. For example, walking is governed in part by a program integrated at the level of the spinal cord, as shown in studies with animals in which the spinal cord has been separated surgically from the brain (Brown, 1911). Not only can such animals walk on a treadmill, but they can continue to do so after transection of the dorsal roots deprives them of sensory input. Thus, walking appears to rely on an intrinsic motor program rather than being a sensory-instigated reflex.

In the case of speech, older explanations in terms of sensory-response units, each triggering the next, have given way to explanations in terms of plans in which each speech unit is placed in a larger pattern. Sometimes units are misplaced, although the pattern is preserved: 'Our queer old dean', said English clergyman William Spooner, when he meant, 'Our dear old queen'. (Spooner was so prone to mix up the order of sounds in his sentences that this type of error is called a spoonerism.) Such mistakes reveal a plan: the speaker is anticipating a later sound and executing it too soon. A chain of reflexes would not be subject to such errors.

Even in terms of reflexes, behavior is more complicated than originally supposed. For one thing, reflexes can be modified and acquired through training, and the concept of conditioned reflexes has been important, beginning early in the twentieth century, as described earlier in this chapter and more fully in Chapter 6. For another, there is *selective potentiation* of reflexes and of the underlying neural circuits.

Selective Potentiation

Selective potentiation refers to the fact that, at any given time, the activity of certain neural circuits is enhanced, whereas activity of other circuits is inhibited. For an example of operation of this principle, consider how an animal is able to walk over rough, uneven terrain. Walking involves two phases of movement in each leg: (1) the swing phase when the limb is off the ground and swinging forward; this is initiated by the flexion reflex, and (2) the stance phase, providing support and propulsion, involving the extension reflex. Normally, these two phases are evoked in succession by a generator circuit in the spinal cord, but what happens when an obstacle is encountered? For example, what happens if during movement a tap is delivered to the front of the paw? This is the part of the foot that is most likely to encounter something that might trip the animal or push its foot out from under it.

Experiments on this have been done with cats in which the spinal cord was separated surgically from the brain. Forssberg, Grillner, and Rossignol (1975) found that the same stimulus to the front of the foot could evoke either flexion or extension, depending on the phase of the leg movement when the tap was delivered. In the swing phase, the tap elicits flexion in all the joints of the leg; this lifts the leg and may allow it to clear an obstacle that might otherwise trip the cat. If the same tap is delivered as the cat is starting the stance phase, the stimulation elicits or strengthens the extension reflex, so a moving object that might have swept the cat's foot out from under it is less likely to do so. Thus, a given stimulus does not by itself determine a reflex response; the response is determined also by the state of the animal at the time of stimulation. The principle of selective potentiation can also be applied to some questions of motivation discussed in Chapter 11.

As well as selective potentiation, there is *selective inhibition*. A familiar example is the inhibition of the limb and neck muscles during sleep. Sometimes this inhibition does not exactly coincide with sleep. Many people have had the unpleasant experience of feeling paralyzed just before going to sleep or just after waking; a survey of the general population in Germany

and Italy showed that about 6% have had this experience (Ohayon, Zully, Guilleminault, & Smirne, 1999). There is also the pathological condition known as cataplexy in which a person, although remaining conscious, suddenly loses muscle tone and falls to the ground in moments of emotion, especially laughter. While investigating cataplexy, researchers in the Netherlands found that muscle tension in the legs of normal subjects declined markedly during laughter (Overeem, Lammers, & van Dijk, 1999). This may explain why expressions like 'weak with laughter' occur in many languages.

Chronic selective inhibition of the facial musculature is well known in Parkinson's disease, and recently it has been reported for patients with schizophrenia (Kring, 1999). Compared with nonpatients, schizophrenia patients exhibit few outward signs of emotion, although recordings from facial muscles reveal very small, subtle facial activity characteristic of different emotions. In response to emotional stimuli, schizophrenia patients report experiencing as much emotion as nonpatients. Thus the social interactions of the patients are impaired by their lack of normal facial responses. Here is another case where biological condition affects social relations.

Varieties of Motor Behavior

Table 4.1 presents a classification in which motor behavior is arranged in a hierarchy, with simple reflexes at the top, proceeding next to more complex movements, and then to more complex acts, ranging from locomotion to acquired skills. Even the reflexes can be modified by conditioning, as we have seen, to response to new or altered stimuli. The examples toward the bottom of the table rely less and less on innate reflex arcs.

Levels of Control of Motor Behavior

The control of motor behavior is implemented at several different levels of the nervous system, depicted in simplified fashion in Figure 4.5. Motor neurons in the ventral horn of the spinal cord or the brain stem send out axons to innervate muscles of the body and face regions. These fibers generally release acetylcholine which acts on nicotinic receptors. A motor neuron along with its innervated muscle fibers constitutes a motor unit. For example, muscles for eye movements have an innervation ratio (axons to muscle fibers) of roughly one to three, while those in the leg have a ratio of one to several hundreds. The fewer the number of muscle fibers a motor neuron innervates, the finer is the

Table 4.1   *A classification of movements and acts*

Movements	Examples
Simple reflex	Stretch, knee jerk, sneezing, startle, eye blink, pupillary contraction
Posture and postural changes	Standing, rearing, lying, balancing, sitting, urination posture
Sensory orientation	Head turning, touching, eye fixation, sniffing, ear movement, tasting
Acts	
Locomotion	Walking, creeping, running, crawling, swimming, stalking, flying, hopping
Species-typical action patterns	
Ingestion	Tasting, chewing, biting, sipping, drinking
Courtship display	Sniffing, chasing, retreating
Escape and defense	Hissing, spitting, submission posture, cowering
Grooming	Washing, preening, licking
Gestures	Grimacing, tail erection, squinting, tooth baring, smiling
Acquired skills	Speech, tool use, dressing, painting, sculpting, driving a car, sports, dancing

Source: Rosenzweig et al., 1999.

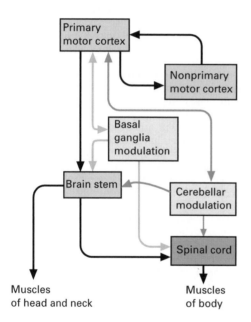

Figure 4.5   *Brain structures involved in motor control. (Adapted with permission from Rosenzweig, Leiman, & Breedlove, 1999.)*

motor control. Motor neurons that innervate the same muscle aggregate into nuclei or columns and may extend over several spinal segments. Spinal motor neurons receive inputs from skin, joints, tendons, and muscles. Such somatosensory information is capable of activating spinal reflexes for maintaining posture (the stretch reflex), protection from injury (the flexion reflex), and so forth. While these reflexes are mediated through intra- or inter-segmental circuitry linked by excitatory or inhibitory synapses within the spinal cord, they are nonetheless subjected to modulation by experience and other psychological factors. This is accomplished by supraspinal inputs conveying signals to control locomotion, orientation, posture and balance, species-specific behavior, and skilled motor acts. However, the spinal cord should not be viewed as merely a relay device that translates the central or peripheral inputs into motor acts. Evidence indicates that in vertebrates, spinal circuits subserve the function of a central pattern generator that engenders rhythmic motor activity for locomotion (Grillner et al., 1995). Spinal motor neurons thus coordinate their intrinsic patterns of activity with extrinsic information from various sources and serve as the final common pathway of the motor system.

Direct central inputs to spinal motor neurons arise from the cerebral cortex and some brainstem nuclei. These descending fiber tracts exert excitatory and inhibitory influences on the motor neurons. The cortical area subserving motor functions is mainly located in the frontal lobe. The primary motor cortex shows *somatotopic organization*; that is, motor control of adjacent body parts is mapped into adjacent regions of the primary motor cortex, and the amount of cortical tissue devoted to a specific body part reflects its fineness of motor control; thus the motor representation of parts involved in tool manipulation (hands and fingers) and speech (lips and tongue) are disproportionately huge. The corticospinal tract (also called the pyramidal tract due to its wedge shape in the medulla) arises from pyramidal neurons in the motor cortex. This tract contains large-diameter and fast-conducting axons and is involved in control of fine movements in arms, hands, and fingers. Damaging this tract in monkeys impairs manual dexterity but without significant effects on locomotion and reaching (Lawrence & Kuypers,

1968a). Fibers from the brain stem nuclei projecting to spinal motor neurons belong to the extra-pyramidal system, and damage in this system in monkeys leads to deficits in locomotion and posture (Lawrence & Kuypers, 1968b).

Behavioral neuroscientists began to understand how the motor cortex commands movements by monitoring cortical neuron discharges in monkeys performing specific motor acts. Activity of single neurons did not bear a clear-cut relationship with some types of movements. In a series of studies, Georgopoulos (1997) trained monkeys to make arm movements in reaching to eight possible target directions elicited by signals in those directions; he recorded neuronal firing in the primary motor cortex simultaneously with the movement. Plotting the discharge rates of specific neurons against various directions of movements revealed a direction-tuning curve in the response of many motor neurons. That is, a neuron altered its firing rate according to the direction of the reach. Each neuron fired most frequently at one of the directions, and slowed down as the deviation from this best direction increased. However, the movement was not determined solely by the neuron coding the movement direction as its best direction. Instead, a population of neurons was activated shortly prior to and during the movement, and the vector sum of population activities correlated best with the direction of movement. In a follow-up study to distinguish whether such activity is motor-related or sensory-related, Georgopoulos and collaborators trained the monkey to perform a delayed reaching task. A signal 90 degrees away from the intended movement appeared and soon turned off. The monkey had to wait for a period after the signal disappeared and then reach in the intended direction. Recording from a population of cortical neurons showed the summation vector gradually shifting from the signal direction to the reaching direction during the waiting period, similar to a mental rotation of movement.

The nature of neural coding for mental features has been an issue fundamental to research in biological psychology. The so-called 'single neuron doctrine' suggests that activity of single neurons is capable of forming unitary mental representations, whereas other theories insist that representation of mental activity relies on ensembles of neurons. While both views have strength and weakness in guiding research and interpreting findings, the results of Georgopoulos give one of the best examples that traits of behavior (direction of movement in this case) are represented by collective activities in a population of neurons.

Some brain structures do not project directly to the spinal cord but nonetheless exert a profound influence on motor functions; one set is the basal ganglia. The basal ganglia contain several distinct but interconnected parts. This structure receives inputs from most of the cerebral cortex and the thalamus as well as dopaminergic projections from the brainstem. Output of the basal ganglia, flowing through its complicated internal circuitries, is funneled to the frontal cortex and brainstem. The basal ganglia circuitry appears to modulate limb and eye movement. It may be involved in representation of serial order of learned and innate motor sequences. In tasks involving sequential movements, basal ganglia neurons fired 100 ms or more in advance of the activity of muscles (Kermadi & Joseph, 1995). Neuronal discharges in the supplementary motor area, a major target of the basal ganglia, have been shown to be selective to sequences of movements with a specific order (Tanji & Shima, 1994). Parkinson's disease involves degeneration of dopaminergic fibers projecting to the basal ganglia, disrupting functional balance in the basal ganglia circuitry and resulting in movement difficulties. Patients with obsessive–compulsive disorder are preoccupied with recurrent stereotypic sequence of behavior or thoughts. Recent evidence shows that they have functional abnormality in, among others, the basal ganglia (Saba, Dastur, Keshaven, & Katerji, 1998).

We mentioned the cerebellum in the last part of Section 4.4 in regard to its role in conditioning, but the importance of the cerebellum in regard to motor control was recognized even earlier, because injuries to the cerebellum cause impairments in motor coordination. Various parts of the cerebellum receive cerebral cortical and other central inputs through pontine nuclei as well as peripheral inputs from the spinal cord and vestibular nuclei. Inputs to the cerebellum are carried by the mossy fibers and climbing fibers. These inputs exert convergent excitatory effects on Purkinje neurons, which are the major output neurons of the cerebellar cortex. Axons of the Purkinje cells form inhibitory synapses onto the deep cerebellar nuclei, which in turn project to the motor cortex and other frontal regions and to motor neurons in the brain stem and spinal cord. The access of the cerebellum to an intricate set of information and to both pyramidal and extrapyramidal motor systems as well as its orderly intrinsic organization have invited speculation on the function it subserves and the mechanism to accomplish the function. In the Marr and Albus model (Albus, 1971), the cerebellar Purkinje cell with its two inputs functions as a learning-machine capable of detecting and reducing error from a preset criterion. The vestibulo-ocular reflex (VOR) refers to swift movement of the eyeball in a direction opposite to head turning in order to maintain a stable visual image. The involvement of the cerebellum in experiential modification of VOR supports this idea (Ito, 1998). This learning ability may play an important role in a function generally attributed to the cerebellum: coordination of motor programming or timing for rapid or automatic multi-joint complicated movement. Growing evidence has indicated that the cerebellum is involved not only in motor learning but also in other higher cognitive functions such as language and verbal working memory (Desmond & Fiez, 1998).

To students in biological psychology, the most challenging question concerning the study of the motor system is how the brain transfers emotion, motivation, visual signals, verbal instructions, as well as self-generated thoughts including plans, intention, and will into motor behavior. Recent evidence begins to address this issue, yet the picture is far from clear. In rats and cats, the midbrain periaqueductal gray (PAG) appears to mediate some reactions elicited by emotional stimuli (Bandler & Shipley, 1994). Part of its input derives from the limbic cortex, hypothalamus, and amygdala, all of which are implicated in emotional functions (see Chapter 12). Stimulating different parts of the PAG arouses various kinds of species-specific defensive behavior. Evidence has shown that fibers projecting from the central amygdaloid nucleus to the central gray mediate the freezing response during fear conditioning (LeDoux, 1995).

Another critical structure in this regard is the basal ganglia. A dorsal part of the basal ganglia (dorsal striatum) appears to be critical for associating an operant response to a specific stimulus reinforced by rewards (McDonald & White, 1993). Much attention has recently been paid to the nucleus accumbens lying at the ventral side of the basal ganglia. This structure receives multimodality sensory information from the limbic system. It is innervated by brainstem dopaminergic fibers, the activity of which has been implicated in expectancy of reward (Schultz, 1998). The nucleus accumbens gains access to motor function by way of the frontal cortex and the extrapyramidal system. Manipulating functions of the nucleus accumbens has been shown to alter performance in instrumental learning tasks including those using addictive drugs as reward (Kalivas & Nakamura, 1999), suggesting the importance of this structure in interfacing motivational and motor circuits (Morgenson, Jones, & Yim, 1980).

How thoughts lead to acts remains largely a mystery. The finding that readiness potentials recorded from humans performing voluntary acts preceded subjective awareness of intending to move by 350 to 400 ms (Libet, 1985) remains most intriguing to anyone contemplating the relationship between intention and movement. Most, if not all, of motor behavior acts on or reacts to stimuli in the environment. Thus, the motor system must work intimately with the sensory systems. The primary motor cortex receives direct projections from the somatosensory cortex. Motor neurons responsible for moving a specific part of the body receive information from sensory neurons responsive to stimulation in that part of the body. These fibers may provide rapid feedback during manipulation and account for the findings that a tactile signal is 75 ms faster in eliciting a hand movement than a visual signal (Evarts, 1974). The visual system nonetheless provides critical information in guiding motor acts. In reaching, saccadic eye movements and head turning precede the hand movement. If the eyes and head are prevented from moving, the reaching movement misses the target. The premotor cortex is a cortical region that lies just rostral to the primary motor cortex; it participates in preparing externally guided sequential movements. The dorsal part of this region receives information from the parietal cortex (Wise, Boussaoud, Johnson, & Caminiti, 1997), which receives the dorsal stream of visual information flow involved in detecting spatial cues. It is interesting to note that neurons in some sectors of the parietal cortex and frontal cortex show receptive fields of both visual and somatosensory stimuli. In some neurons of these regions, the receptive field to visual cues was shown to be modified by hand movements (Graziano & Gross, 1995). Reaching cannot rely totally on the retinotopic coordinate to locate the target. As the head or body turns to different directions, images of objects located at different positions in the space may fall on the same spot of the retina. Yet visual responses of some neurons in the parietal lobe could be modified by the position of gaze (Andersen, Bracewell, Barash, Gnadt, & Fogassi, 1990): neuronal discharge to a stimulus at the same retinotopic position was differentially amplified as a monkey fixated its eyes at different locations in space. Such amplification varying as a function of the gaze position allows transformation of a retinotopic coordinate into a head-centered or body-centered reference and facilitates reaching movement. Thus the parietal region may be an important region in coordinating sensorimotor function in an extrapersonal space.

Motor behavior should not be viewed only as the output of mental activity. It also sometimes contributes to enrich mental functions. Active manipulation of an object with the hands and fingers generally aids our perception of the shape and surface texture of the object. Furthermore, organisms from human infants to many other species show a natural tendency to imitate motor behavior of others. Recently some neurons in the rostral part of the ventral premotor cortex in monkeys were found to discharge not only when the monkey grasped or manipulated objects, but also when the monkey observed the same acts performed by another individual. It is proposed that these so-called 'mirror neurons' enable an organism to detect and understand the mental states of conspecifics. Such a function might be related to forming a 'theory of mind', which is essential for development of high order cognitive social interactions (Gallese & Goldman, 1998). A similar mirror system for recognition of gesture has also been detected in humans by positron emission tomography focusing on a region including Broca's area. The presence of such an observation/execution matching function in a brain area critical for language has invited speculation on its role in the evolution of the human communication system (Rizzolatti & Arbib, 1998).

4.6 SOME MAIN PRINCIPLES OF BIOLOGICAL PSYCHOLOGY

Material in this and other chapters of the book illustrate some main principles of biological psychology. We conclude and summarize this chapter by listing these principles here.

Communication among different parts and systems of the body occurs by means of three kinds of messages – neural, hormonal (endocrine), and immune system messages – and combinations of these kinds of messages also occur.

Most neural, hormonal, and immunological communication involves specialized receptor molecules that respond to only particular messenger molecules. Some receptor molecules are located in cell membranes and others are located inside the cells.

There are both excitatory and inhibitory messages in the neural, hormonal, and immune systems.

The neural, hormonal, and immune systems show cyclical changes in activity ranging in length from less than a day, about a day (circadian), to about a year (circannual) or more.

The neural, hormonal, and immune systems are all subject to modification by experience and learning.

The brain changes throughout life, as a function of both endogenous (intrinsic) and exogenous (extrinsic) factors and influences.

The nervous system is composed of separate cells that are distinct structurally, metabolically, and functionally.

The same stimulus input is represented at several levels and locations in neural sensory systems, and different kinds of analyses are made at the different levels and locations.

Behavioral interventions cause both behavioral and somatic effects, and somatic interventions cause both somatic and behavioral effects.

Social stimuli affect some neural and hormonal systems, and some neural and hormonal activities affect social behavior.

There is a basic cascade of neurochemical events that, continued to different lengths, can lead to a whole series of different effects, from neural conduction and behavioral activity to formation of long-term memory. Followed for a few steps, it ensures neural conduction and synaptic transmission; followed further it yields prolonged alteration in neural function that underlies phenomena such as habituation; continuation to a later stage yields memory storage and long-term potentiation; further continuation can lead to structural changes. Thus the neurochemical cascade deals with processes that span the time range from milliseconds to years.

Normally the entire brain is active all of the time; specific behavioral and cognitive activities increase or decrease the levels and patterns of activity of particular regions of the brain.

Different neural events differ widely in their spatial and temporal extents, so studying them requires techniques with different spatial and temporal resolutions. The discovery of new techniques and combinations of techniques is making it possible to study with increasing adequacy and accuracy the bodily processes that underlie behavior.

Specific mental functions usually involve coordination of neural activities among multiple brain sites and are regulated by multiple neurochemical systems in the brain.

Biological psychology and neuroscience study not only the processes and characteristics that hold for groups of persons or animals but also those that make individuals unique.

Stable percepts and personality traits are based on brain processes that are dynamic in terms of synaptic connections and biochemical processes.

An evolutionary perspective is essential to biological psychology. It offers two different but complementary emphases: (1) continuity of behavior and biological processes among species because of common ancestry, and (2) species-specific differences in behavior and biology that have evolved in adaptation to different environments.

An evolutionary approach often suggests hypotheses that may account for behaviors and their mechanisms, but these, like other hypotheses, must be tested thoroughly against other hypotheses before they are accepted or rejected.

Research in biological psychology can be applied to problems of human health and well-being, and attempts to make such applications also benefit research by providing tests of the adequacy of current findings and conclusions.

RESOURCE REFERENCES

Feldman, R. S., Meyer, J. S., & Quenzer, L. F. (1997). *Principles of neuropsychopharmacology.* Sunderland, MA: Sinauer.

Gazzaniga, M. S. (Ed.). (2000). *The new cognitive neurosciences* (2nd ed.). Cambridge, MA: MIT Press.

Mountcastle, V. B. (1998). *Perceptual neuroscience: The cerebral cortex.* Cambridge, MA: Harvard University Press.

Panksepp, J. (1998). *Affective neuroscience: The foundations of human and animal emotions.* New York: Oxford University Press.

Rosenzweig, M. R., Leiman, A. L., & Breedlove, S. M. (1998a). *Psychobiologie.* Louvain-la-Neuve, Belgium: DeBoeck Université. (French translation of first U.S. edition, 1996.)

Rosenzweig, M. R., Leiman, A. L., & Breedlove, S. M. (1998b). *Psicologia biologica.* Milan, Italy: Casa Editrice Ambrosiana. (Italian translation of first U.S. edition, 1996.)

Rosenzweig, M. R., Leiman, A. L., & Breedlove, S. M. (1999). *Biological psychology: Introduction to behavioral, cognitive, and clinical neuroscience* (2nd ed.). Sunderland, MA: Sinauer.

Rosenzweig, M. R., Leiman, A. L., & Breedlove, S. M. (In press, 2000). *Psicologia biologica.* Barcelona: Ariel. (Spanish translation of second U.S. edition, 1999.)

Zigmond, M. J., Bloom, F. E., Landis, S. C., Roberts, J. L. & Squire, L. R. (1999). *Fundamental neuroscience.* San Diego: Academic Press.

ADDITIONAL LITERATURE CITED

Ader, R., & Cohen, N. (1993). Psychoneuroimmunology: Conditioning and stress. *Annual Review of Psychology, 44,* 53–85.

Aiba, A., Kano, M., Chen, C., Stanton, M. E., Fox, G. D., Herrup, K., Zwingman, T. A., & Tonegawa, S. (1994). Deficient cerebellar long-term depression and impaired motor learning in mGluR1 mutant mice. *Cell, 79,* 377–388.

Albus, J. S. (1971). A theory of cerebellar function. *Mathematical Bioscience, 10,* 25–61.

Andersen, R. A., Bracewell, R. M., Barash, S., Gnadt, J. W., & Fogassi, L. (1990). Eye position effects on visual, memory and saccade-related activity in areas LIP and 7A of Macaque. *Journal of Neuroscience, 10,* 1176–1196.

Bandler, R., & Shipley, M. T. (1994). Columnar organization in the midbrain periaqueductal gray: modules for emotional expression. *Trends in Neuroscience, 17,* 379–389.

Bracha, V., Zhao, L., Wunderlich, D. A., Morrissy, S. J., & Bloedel, J. R. (1997). Patients with cerebellar lesions cannot acquire but are able to retain conditioned eyeblink reflexes. *Brain, 120,* 1401–1413.

Brown, T. G. (1911). The intrinsic factors in the act of progression in the mammal. *Proceedings of Royal Society* (London), *84,* 308–319.

Bullock, T. H. (1993). Integrative systems research on the brain: Resurgence and new opportunities. *Annual Review of Neuroscience, 16,* 1–15.

Buonomano, D. V., & Merzenich, M. M. (1998). Cortical plasticity: from synapses to maps. *Annual Review of Neuroscience, 21,* 149–186.

Carr, C. E., & Konishi, M. (1990) A circuit for detection of interaural time differences in the brain stem of the barn owl. *Journal of Neuroscience, 10,* 3327–3246.

Carter, C. S. (1998). Neuroendocrine perspectives on social attachment and love. *Psychoneuroendorinology, 23,* 779–818.

Clark, R. E., & Squire, L. R. (1998). Classical conditioning and brain systems: The role of awareness. *Science, 280,* 77–81,

Darwin, C. (1872). *The expression of the emotions in man and animals.* London: Murray.

Desmond, J. E., & Fiez, J. A. (1998). Neuroimaging studies of the cerebellum: Language, learning and memory. *Trends in Cognitive Sciences, 2,* 355–361.

Dunn, A. J., & Berridge, C. W. (1990). Physiological and behavioral responses to corticotropin-releasing factor administration: Is CRF a mediator of anxiety or stress responses? *Brain Research Review, 15,* 71–100.

Evarts, E. V. (1974). Sensorimotor cortex activity associated with movements triggered by visual as compared to somesthetic inputs. In F. O. Schmitt & E. G. Worden (Eds.), *The neurosciences: Third study program* (pp. 327–337). Cambridge, MA: MIT Press.

Forssberg, H., Grillner, S., & Rossignol, S. (1975). Phase dependent reflex reversal during walking in chronic spinal cats. *Brain Research, 85,* 103–107.

Gallese, V., & Goldman, A. (1998). Mirror neurons and the simulation theory of mind-reading. *Trends in Cognitive Science, 2,* 493–501.

Georgopoulos, A. P. (1997) Voluntary movement: computational principles and neural mechanisms. In M. D. Rugg (Ed.), *Cognitive neuroscience* (pp. 131–168). Cambridge, MA: MIT Press.

Graziano, M. S. A., & Gross, C. G. (1995). The representation of extrapersonal space: A possible role for bimodal visual-tactile neurons. In M. S. Gazzaniga (Ed.), *The cognitive neurosciences* (pp. 1021–1042). Cambridge, MA: MIT Press.

Grillner, S., Deliagina, T., Ekeberg, O., el Manira, A., Hill, R. H., Lansner, A., Orlovsky, G. N., & Wallen, P. (1995) Neural networks that coordinate locomotion and body orientation in lamprey. *Trends in Neurosciences, 18*, 270–279.

Ito, M. (1998). Cerebellar learning in the vestibulo-ocular reflex. *Trends in Cognitive Science, 2*, 313–321.

Kalivas, P. W., & Nakamura, M. (1999). Neural systems for behavioral activation and reward. *Current Opinion in Neurobiology, 9*, 223–227.

Kermadi, I., & Joseph, J. P. (1995). Activity in the caudate nucleus of monkey during spatial sequencing. *Journal of Neurophysiology, 74*, 911–933.

Kring, A. M. (1999). Emotion in schizophrenia: Old mystery, new understanding. *Current Directions in Psychological Science, 8*, 160–163.

Lawrence, D. G., & Kuypers, G. J. M. (1968a). The functional organization of the motor system in the monkey. I. The effects of bilateral pyramidal lesions. *Brain, 91*, 1–14.

Lawrence, D. G., & Kuypers, G. J. M. (1968b). The functional organization of the motor system in the monkey. II. The effects of lesions of descending brain-stem pathways. *Brain, 91*, 15–36.

LeDoux, J. E. (1995). Emotion: Clues from the brain. *Annual Review of Psychology, 46*, 209–235.

Libet, B. (1985). Unconscious cerebral initiative and the role of conscious will in voluntary action. *Behavioural and Brain Sciences, 8*, 529–566.

McDonald, R. J., & White, N. M. (1993). A triple dissociation of memory systems: Hippocampus, amygdala and dorsal striatum. *Behavioral Neuroscience, 107*, 3–22.

McGaugh, J. L. (1989). Involvement of hormonal and neuromodulatory system in the regulation of memory storage. *Annual Review of Neuroscience, 12*, 255–287.

Mishkin, M., & Ungerleider, L. (1982). Contribution of striate inputs to the visuospatial functions of parieto-preoccipital cortex in monkeys. *Behavioural Brain Research, 6*, 57–77.

Morgenson, G., Jones, D. L., & Yim, C. Y. (1980). From motivation to action: Functional interface between the limbic system and the motor system. *Progress in Neurobiology, 14*, 69–97.

Ohayon, M. M., Zully, J., Guilleminault, C., & Smirne, S. (1999). Prevalence and pathological associations of sleep paralysis in the general population. *Neurology, 52*, 1194–2000.

Overeem, S., Lammers, G. J., & van Dijk, J. G. (1999). Weak with laughter. *Lancet, 354*, 838.

Pavlov, I. P. (1906). The scientific investigation of the psychical faculties or processes in the higher animals. *Science, 24*, 613–619.

Poggio, G. F., & Poggio, T. (1984). The analysis of stereopsis. *Annual Review of Neuroscience, 7*, 379–412.

Rizzolatti, G., & Arbib, M. A. (1998). Language within our grasp. *Trends in Neurosciences, 21*, 188–194.

Rosenzweig, M. R. (2000). Biological psychology. In A. E. Kazdin (Ed.), *Encyclopedia of psychology, Vol. 1* (pp. 420–425). Washington, DC: American Psychological Association and New York: Oxford.

Rothwell, N. J., & Hopkins, S. J. (1995). Cytokines and the nervous system II: Actions and mechanisms of action. *Trends in Neurosciences, 18*, 130–136.

Saba, P. R., Dastur, K., Keshavan, M. S., & Katerji, M. A. (1998). Obsessive-compulsive disorder, Tourette's syndrome, and basal ganglia pathology on MRI. *Journal of Neuropsychiatry & Clinical Neurosciences, 10*, 116–117.

Sapolsky, R. M. (1992). *Stress, the aging brain and the mechanisms of neuron death*. Cambridge, MA: MIT Press.

Schultz, W. (1998) Predictive reward signal of dopamine neurons. *American Journal of Physiology, 80*, 1–27.

Selye, H. (1956). *The stress of life*. New York: McGraw-Hill.

Tanji, J., & Shima, K. (1994). Role for supplementary motor area cells in planning several movements ahead. *Nature, 371*, 413–416.

Timmann, D., Kolb, F. P., Baier, C., Rijntjes, M., Muller, S. P., Diener, H. C., & Weiller, C. (1996). Cerebellar activation during classical conditioning of the human flexion reflex: a PET study. *Neuroreport, 7*, 2056–2060.

Thompson, R. F., & Kim, J. J. (1996). Memory systems in the brain and localization of a memory. *Proceedings of the National Academy of Sciences of the United States of America, 93*, 13438–13444.

Wise, S. P., Boussaoud, D., Johnson, P. B., & Caminiti, R. (1997). Premotor and parietal cortex: Corticocortical connectivity and combinatorial computations. *Annual Review of Neuroscience, 20*, 25–42.

Young, L. J., Nilsen, R., Waymire, K. G., MacGregor, G. R., & Insel, T. R. (1999). Increased affiliative response to vasopressin in mice expressing the V1a receptor from a monogamous vole. *Nature, 400*, 766–768.

Communications concerning this chapter should be addressed to: Professor Mark R. Rosenzweig, Department of Psychology-1650, University of California, 3210 Tolman Hall, Berkeley, CA 94720-1650, USA

Part B
INFORMATION PROCESSING AND HUMAN BEHAVIOR

5

Sensation/Perception, Information Processing, Attention

GÉRY d'YDEWALLE

5.1 HISTORY

Although perception has always been an important area of research in psychology, its research prominence and focus have changed as a function of the history of psychology. The founders of psychology were heavily involved in perception research, partly due to the heated debate concerning the necessity of distinguishing sensory and perceptual experiences. While some scholars (particularly Helmholtz, 1867) claimed that our perceptual experience is built or constructed from our sensations, others claimed that the distinction between sensation and perception is an artificial one and that we can only reach our sensory feelings through a process of abstraction. The debate emerged in all fields of perception but it was particularly evident when trying to explain visual depth perception. While Hering (1879) advocated a direct fusion of the images from the two eyes into a single image which he called the Cyclopean eye, Helmholtz defended the position that the two images are separately processed, and much later in the

processing, there is a merging through higher-order 'unconscious inferences'. The earliest developments of perception research were more in agreement with the distinction between sensory and perceptual experiences as it fitted better in the Zeitgeist. This Zeitgeist is now typically called the structuralist approach, because it involved breaking down experience into constituent sensations using a method of analysis known as introspection. Structuralism, which reached its peak between 1870 and 1910 with the work of Wundt in Germany and Titchener in America, was an attempt to explore the mind in a manner analogous to the chemical analysis of substances; the laws of the mind would be revealed by a careful study of its elements and their relationships, and the elements of the analysis were sensations.

The advent of behaviorism between World Wars I and II basically put perception research to rest in North America, with a few notable exceptions in the field of psychophysics (see Boring, 1942). Indeed, the method of introspection proved to be unprofitable and even invalid, according to the scientific premises in which the founder of behaviorism, John Watson, wanted to develop a truly scientific psychology: trained observers frequently disagreed in their introspection; introspective data could not easily be quantified; and most importantly, many mental processes are simply not available to self-observation. Psychophysics was a tolerable branch of scientific psychology, as in most psychophysical studies participants typically have only to provide a 'yes' or 'no' answer to a question about a presented stimulus. Behaviorism concentrated upon simple stimulus–response relationships, and tended to treat stimuli as essentially simple events confronting organisms. Accordingly, they bypassed the issue of perception; only external stimuli reaching the organism and leading to a response were important.

Gestalt psychology, which developed in Europe at about the same time as behaviorism in North America, provided a wealth of new perceptual phenomena but the explanatory basis (in particular, the innateness and physiological basis of visual illusions) was then not well accepted. The classic work of the Gestalt school on perceptual organization was restricted to demonstrations of a number of phenomena, such as the figure–ground segregation and the role of different grouping principles or so-called Gestalt laws, without much concern for the underlying perceptual mechanisms (only referring quickly to a possible physiological basis) or for the functional role of these phenomena in the wider context of other kinds of processing taking place in the visual system. As a theory of perception, it can be said that Gestalt psychology failed badly, although it can also be asserted that the Gestalt approach was, within limits, brilliantly successful as it continues to exert a significant influence on the more recent psychology of perception. As to the sensation–perception discussion, Gestalt psychology strongly defended the position that perceptual experience is first, and only through an abstracting process of our consciousness could we reach our sensations. Therefore, the perceptual experience is more than, and different from the sum of all our sensations.

The early stages of cognitive psychology in the 1950s, as for example the 'New-Look' psychology, gave perception research an additional, new issue: the importance of top-down versus bottom-up processes. Top-down processes are processes that are driven by the organism's prior knowledge and expectations, rather than by the sensory input; bottom-up processes are driven solely by the sensory input. The new issue was to some extent related to the sensation–perception distinction: when one acknowledges the impact of higher-order cognitive processes,

one implicitly accepts the distinction. Not surprisingly, the cognitive psychologists gave more importance to top-down processes. The 'New-Look' psychologists typically had an interest in Freudian or other psychodynamic theories, despite their strong adherence to the experimental methodology. For example, Postman, Bruner, and McGinnies (1948) reported that it took longer to recognize 'taboo' words than control words when they are presented with a tachistoscope. More dramatically, Lazarus and McCleary (1951) reported that after certain words had been paired with electric shock, they took longer to recognize, and that even before the recognition thresholds were reached the words induced physiological responses in observers. Bruner and Goodman (1947) carried out an investigation into children's ability to judge the size of coins and found that the perception of size was influenced by the value of a coin, the effect being greater with children from poorer homes.

However, as with Gestalt psychology, early cognitive psychologists largely restricted their research activities to demonstrations of top-down influences, without serious attempts to provide detailed scrutinies of the nature of the underlying processes. Methodologically, most experiments were very weak. For example, the delayed responses to taboo words could be a response effect (i.e., the observer wishing to be absolutely sure before uttering a taboo word); poor children are expected to be less familiar with higher-value coins, etc. Nevertheless, the findings could only reinforce the idea that perception is a constructive process, steered by higher-order cognitive influences.

Top-down approaches were then strongly qualified by James J. Gibson's influence, leading to theories of direct perception; that is, perception without top-down processes, without any inferential steps, intervening variables, or associations. During World War II Gibson worked on the applied problems of pilot selection and testing. Flying clearly demanded accurate perception of space. Gibson became convinced that perception from aircraft made important use of information from the ground and the sky, and that this information was in the form of patterns of movement, the flowing textures which arise as a result of motion picture relative to the ground. Gibson's preliminary analysis of the situation is shown in Figure 5.1. If we examine light arriving at the eyes in real situations we find that it is structured: highly complex and rich in information. A single momentary retinal image may be impoverished but this is not true of the arrays of nested solid visual angles through which the head and the eyes sweep

Figure 5.1　*Flowing textures as a function of movement (Gibson, 1950)*

during normal perceiving. As we come to understand more about these arrays and the potential information contained in the structure, the less frequently shall we need to invoke further indirect, cognitive processes in explanations of seeing. Gibson (1950) believed in 'invariances' of perception, whereby the environment provides an active organism with a continuous and stable flow of rich information. His direct theory, involving strong interactions between the environment and the organism, is therefore often called an 'ecological' approach.

To some extent, perception psychology reached a point where no substantial theoretical progress could be expected. Several theories were advanced which tried to provide convincing evidence for their viewpoint (top-down versus bottom-up approaches; direct versus indirect theories, etc.) but there were no real breakthroughs. More substantial progress was made in the research fields of memory and attention in the early 1960s, thus outside perception, and this progress was made possible by the advent of the information-processing approach and the emergence of a new umbrella science, cognitive science. While the information-processing research focused heavily on unraveling underlying mental processes, the cognitive science approach, with its links to artificial intelligence, brought forward yet a further research issue, the nature of mental representations. It is partly with the background of these two developments (research on information processing and mental representations) that Marr's (1982) posthumous book on 'vision' was so particularly welcome among psychologists working in the field of perception research. It is worthwhile noting that the subtitle of his book explicitly refers to the two issues of processing and representation: 'A computational investigation into the human representation and processing of visual information'. Many consider the book as the most

important development in perceptual theory for many years.

To introduce Marr's book here in a nutshell is next to impossible. Marr had specialized knowledge of mathematics (his first training), physiology, computer science, and experimental psychology. His theory was developed and articulated as a function of whatever the four disciplines could offer to understand seeing. The starting point for seeing is the image on the retina; the end point is our awareness of the world. We seem to have a picture of the world available to us whenever our eyes are open. But the truth is that light stops at the retina. There can be no actual picture in our heads, only a firing of a large number of neurons. It follows that this neural activity represents the world symbolically, and we must therefore understand the nature of the symbolic processes. Marr argues that symbolic representations of various aspects of the world, initially obtained through the retinal image, are combined into the descriptions which we call seeing. Marr's theory is that perception proceeds as an information-processing device and that this system is organized into successive stages. We first start with the retinal image which could be conceived as a spatial distribution of light intensities across the retina. The detection of abrupt changes in neighboring intensity values produces a 'raw primal sketch' containing lines, edges, etc. Thereafter, those elements are interconnected using inter alia the Gestalt principles of grouping (see further in the section on two-dimensional perception), and leading to the full primal sketch (basically, the outlines of the objects in the picture). The next stage, leading to a 2½-D sketch, makes explicit the orientation and rough depth of the visible surfaces; it is as if a 'picture' of the world is beginning to emerge, but note however that at this level what is emerging is organized with reference only to the viewer (viewer- or subject-centered representation); it is not yet linked to a stable, external environment. In the next stage, the 3-D representation, shapes and orientation become explicitly organized in an object-centered framework, that is to say, in a manner that is independent of particular positions and orientation on the retina. Finally, this representation is matched with stored objects in a our memory; the matching implies at last cognitive and memory processes.

To reach a particular stage, a variety of computational processes is assumed, and those processes have been the focus of much recent empirical research. Many details of Marr's analyses are now either changed, rejected, or confirmed. What is more important for the psychology of perception is the influence of its programmatic nature: Marr's book launched a concerted effort and a renewed interest in the field, not only among psychologists but also (or rather primarily) among neuroscientists and computer vision people.

In recent years there has been increased interest in building neuron-like models of visual and auditory perception in which representations of the world are expressed in terms of activities in neuron-like units. Such 'connectionist' models have some apparent advantages. They appear, at least in principle, more biologically plausible. They provide a relatively easy way to think about a number of parallel computations. Perceptual learning is easy to conceive through weight adjustments (the reinforcement of excitatory or inhibitory 'connections' between neuron-like units and the weakening of others). Finally, most models have the property of 'distributed' processing: a representation is framed in terms of activities over a large set of simple units, and different patterns of activities in the same units refer to different representations. Such PDP (Parallel Distributed Processing) models are particularly powerful when applied to pattern and object classification. For a good introduction to connectionism, see Quinlan (1991).

5.2 From Sensations to Full-Fledged Perception in the Real World

Sensations

Psychophysics and the Concept of Threshold

There are sounds we cannot hear, contours we cannot see and odors we cannot smell. Psychophysics is about thresholds, their measurement and the debate about what they are. Psychophysics thus does more than providing techniques for exploration of the senses; it has given rise to theories of thresholds, and it has unfolded the issue about finding ways to measure and compare sensation, leading to measurement theories.

Two types of thresholds are typically distinguished in sensory research. Absolute thresholds are measures of the least amounts of physical energy needed in order to detect the stimulus, while difference thresholds (also sometimes called relative or discrimination thresholds) represent the minimum changes in the physical world in order to be perceived as difference. There are several techniques available to define the threshold empirically. In the methods of limits, the stimulus is systematically increased or decreased till the observer changes the response. The essence of the method of constant stimuli is that a set of comparison stimuli are

selected to present against one standard stimulus; the difference between the standard and comparison stimuli is randomized on each presentation and the observer must say which of the two stimuli is larger (or smaller, louder, etc.). The adjustment method involves fixing the value of the standard stimulus while setting the comparison stimulus to a value which is obviously different. The observer is then instructed to alter the setting of the comparison stimulus until the two stimuli appear equal. Tracking procedures vary stimulus values continuously while the observer attempts to maintain them just around threshold. Staircase procedures are based on the method of limits but include rules for the selection of stimuli which are based on the observer's immediately preceding response.

In 1954 Tanner and Swets published an influential paper in which they proposed to apply the theory of signal detection in defining thresholds. Let us illustrate the theory in defining the absolute threshold. On each trial, the observer has to decide that the stimulus (or signal, in the theory of signal detection terminology) is present, or that it is absent; and the signal may be present or absent. The following matrix represents the situation, inserting the usual terminology of the theory of signal detection:

	Yes response	No response
Signal	Hit	Miss
No signal	False alarm	Correct rejection

When there is no signal, there is then random noise (N): it represents the activity in the organism in the absence of stimulation. When the stimulus is available, we get a second distribution which is called the signal plus noise distribution (S + N). If the incoming stimulus is strong, then there will be a correspondingly greater separation between the N and S + N distributions. The observer needs to set a criterion when the difference between the two distributions is large enough to decide that there was a signal. The criterion, usually designated β (beta), is also known as the 'likelihood ratio'. The criterion is a personal decision, and as such may be affected by attentional set and instructions. The distance between the two distributions can be used as an index of the sensitivity of the observer, and is known as d' (d prime): d' is defined as the difference between the means of the two distributions divided by their variances.

Table 5.1

Physical stimulus	100.00	102.00	104.04	106.12	108.24	110.40
JND at	102.00	104.04	106.12	108.24	110.40	112.61
Difference	2.00	2.04	2.08	2.12	2.16	2.21
JND step	1	2	3	4	5	6

It is clear that the theory of signal detection has been successful as applied in psychophysics. The techniques of the theory of signal detection will have a lasting place in sensory psychology, and even beyond psychophysics. The main reason for its success is that its techniques offer a genuine way out of the problem of disentangling response (β) and sensitivity (d') effects in detection and other situations.

In his research on the difference thresholds of weight sensations, Weber (1846) discovered an important finding which was later elevated to the status of a law, Weber's law. If you start with a weight of 10 grams, you need to add 200 milligrams in order to feel a difference (the Just Noticeable Difference, JND); if you start with 100 grams, you need to add not 200 milligrams but 2 grams. The JND is thus not a fixed value but a ratio of the standard:

$$\Delta I/I = k$$

where ΔI is the JND change in the intensity of the new stimulus, I is the standard stimulus and k is the constant for a particular sensory modality (but differs from one sense to another one). This means that the smaller k is, the more sensitive we are for a particular sense; it allows sensitivity comparisons between senses.

Fechner's (1860) insight was that the size of the JND might parallel the strength of sensations. For example, starting with 100 g, the first JND will be 2 g. Next, substitute 102 g as a new standard and measure another JND. This will occur at 104.04 g (102 g + 2.04 g). Proceeding in this manner for a number of successive determinations of sequential JNDs, Table 5.1 gives the results obtained.

This means that to produce incremental, arithmetic steps in sensation, the physical stimulus must grow geometrically. As geometric progressions are equivalently described as logarithmic, the essence of Fechner's law can be described very simply: sensation is a logarithmic function of stimulus intensity, or:

sensation = k log (stimulus intensity)

Stevens (1957) challenged the Fechnerian indirect ways to measure sensations by proposing a number of what he believed to be more direct ways of measuring sensations. The two best-known techniques are magnitude estimation and cross-modal matching. In a magnitude estimation task, the observer is presented with two extremes of the stimulus range and asked to assign a number to each of them; thereafter, the entire range of stimuli is presented in random order and the observer assigns a number to each to match the resulting sensation. In a cross-modal matching task, the observer communicates the subjective intensity of a stimulus via another modality; for example, the perceived brightness of a light may be matched by adjusting the loudness of a tone or the force exerted on a lever. If observers' ratings in a magnitude task are plotted in logarithmic form on one axis of a graph, and stimulus intensities are represented in logarithmic form along the other axis, a linear function will emerge. The log-log relationship can be expressed in an equivalent form:

$$S = aX^b$$

where S is the subjective response, X is the stimulus intensity, a is the weighting function (allowing different units of measurement), and b is the exponent giving the rate of growth of sensation. This equation is known as the power function, and is the way in which most direct scaling data are presented (see Chapter 2).

In the recent history of psychophysics, there have been numerous attempts to reconcile the laws of Fechner and Stevens. For example, Norwich and Wong (1997) developed a more complete form of Fechner's law, as applied to the sensation of pure tones and which embraces the usual logarithmic and power functions.

Senses

The following paragraphs summarize briefly the state of our knowledge about the psychophysics of our senses. For more detail on stimulus and receptor matters, the structure of the eye, the inner ear, and other sense organs, and on the brain regions involved in perception, readers are referred to Rosenzweig, Leiman, and Breedlove (1999).

As to the sensation of light, we need to distinguish two physical properties and their corresponding psychological effects in the observer. Light energy is a band of electromagnetic radiation. Variation in its intensity is a major determinant of perceived brightness. It can also vary in wavelength, the distance between the peaks of two successive waves, which is a major determinant of perceived color (hue). It is the main task of psychophysics to relate the physical properties to their perceptual effect (i.e., intensity | brightness, and wavelength | color).

As to the psychophysics of light intensities, a major research track has been directed to the issue of light adaptation. The role played by the retina in light adaptation has always been a concern of both physiologists and psychologists, and is typically discussed under the general heading of 'lower-level processing'. While earlier it was believed that when retinal function is understood, then the psychophysical data will be understood, or, more precisely, that the data will be predicted with very few assumptions about what the brain does further. However, psychophysical data have been shown to be totally inconsistent with a retinal explanation, due to a failure to separate a model of retinal physiology from a model relating the physiology to behavioral phenomena. Moreover, the variety of retinal cells should give pause to anyone attempting to model the retina; for the primate, the anatomist has distinguished at least two horizontal cell, 10 bipolar-cell, and 20 to 40 amacrine cell types (see Dacey, 1996), and it must be added that intracellular recording from the cells of the primate retina is still in its infancy (Hood, 1998).

One well-known type of context effect in light perception goes by the name of simultaneous contrast. A patch of gray will look darker if surrounded by a light border and lighter if surrounded by a dark border. This effect results in part from the interaction of cells in the retina which tend to suppress one another's activity through a process called lateral inhibition. One cell, responding vigorously to a bright light, reduces the activity of adjacent cells. However, not all brightness illusions can be explained by such low-level mechanisms. For example, Adelson (1993) demonstrated that the brightness percept is also strongly influenced by the perceptual organization of the stimuli. Simple modifications of the stimuli that should have little effect on low-level mechanisms greatly alter the strength of the illusion.

Beyond light intensity variations, color sensations can be ordered by reference to two further dimensions: hue (defined mainly by the wavelength) and saturation (defined by the spectral purity of the color). The first question about the mechanisms that underlie color vision concerns the way in which the different wavelengths are transduced into a retinal discharge. There is good agreement that this is done by the joint action of three different cone types in the retina, each of which has a somewhat different sensitivity curve: one is particularly sensitive in the short-wave region of the spectrum, the second to wavelengths in the middle range, and the third

to the longer wavelengths (Bowmaker & Dartnall, 1980; MacNichol, 1986). A second question concerns the way the receptor output is coded to produce color sensation. A leading approach is the opponent-process theory of Hurvich and Jameson (1957). They assume that there are three neural systems, each of which corresponds to a pair of antagonistic sensory experiences: red–green, blue–yellow, and black–white. The first two determine perceived hue; the third determines perceived brightness. In a multi-stage color model, de Valois and de Valois (1993) have shown that successive cortical processes are necessary to account for the full range of color phenomena.

As in visual sensation, the psychophysics of audition (psychoacoustics) separate three dimensions of the physical stimulus and its corresponding auditory response: the intensity of the stimulus (and its corresponding loudness), its frequency (pitch perception), and the mixing of the frequencies (the timbre). The auditory system is organized tonotopically, such that the frequency of a stimulating sound is mapped onto a location along the basilar membrane within the cochlea, providing a place code; for example, low-frequency tones lead to a maximal displacement of hair cells in the apical part of the basilar membrane and high-frequency tones lead to a maximal displacement of hair cells in the bottom part of the basilar membrane. (It should be noted that there are two types of hair cells; although people have about 3,500 inner hair cells and about 12,000 outer hair cells, the inner hair cells account for most of the fibers in the auditory nerve and seem to play the major role in hearing.) In addition, cells exhibit frequency selectivity throughout the auditory pathway to the cortex. This tonotopic organization provides a basis for spectral analysis of sound.

While the older studies concentrated on the nature of the relationship between variations of the physical stimulus and the auditory response, the important role of time and time-varying properties in the stimulus has become increasingly clear. Temporal relations have been clear enough in the application to speech perception, but now it is becoming evident that such temporal relations are a necessary component of auditory perception in general. Also new is the outcome of several profile analyses showing that the recognition and discrimination of sounds is greatly enhanced when not only the spectral peaks (formants) are taken into account; listeners can monitor the output of more than one critical band of frequencies simultaneously and thereby can achieve better performance than they would by listening only to the critical frequency band containing the signal. The most persistent and resistant research problem concerns the ability of listeners to process simultaneously but separately several acoustic signals. The signal combination provides a very complex pressure waveform that through an oscillograph is a meaningless jumble. How does the listener separate the voice signal from the truck outside, and so on? Several competing solutions (cognitive, Gibsonian, computational, etc.) have been presented and the debate continues; for a good review, see Hirsh and Watson (1996).

The phenomenological description and quantification of smells is notoriously problematic. Despite the occasional development of a vocabulary for a specific application (e.g., wine tasting), there remains an essential resistance of olfaction to verbalization (Classen, 1993). This practical difficulty is mirrored on the level of theory by the inability of psychophysics, after a century of research, to specify the perceptual dimensions of olfaction (Cain, 1978). Stimulus intensity and pleasantness-versus-unpleasantness have been proposed as dimensions (Berglund, Berglund, Engen, & Ekman, 1973; Jones, Roberts, & Holman, 1978), but no satisfactory scheme for organizing odor quality exists. Understanding how the olfactory system encodes and decodes information is difficult, given the lack of a clear physical energy to characterize smell (as wavelength for color vision, or frequency for auditory pitch); moreover, similar chemical substances can sometimes have different odors and some substances with different chemical formulas can smell alike. Olfaction is critical to the survival of lower animals, while in humans it has been considered less important than the other senses. Nevertheless, a relationship between olfaction and sex seems likely also in humans. Olfactory acuity in women seems better at ovulation than during menstruation and there is evidence that olfactory cues (i.e., human pheromones) among women can synchronize the menstrual cycle and that odors serve as attractants to the opposite sex.

Taste is a sense which is relatively poorly developed in humans, at least compared with vision and audition. Behavioral investigators believe that there are four basic qualities of taste: sour, sweet, salty, and bitter. In the mouth there are specialized receptor organs, called taste buds, which are sensitive to chemicals dissolved in water. The average person possesses about 10,000 such taste buds. Much work is now done to test the specificity hypothesis which states that different fibers carry the message of the taste buds to the brain. Electrical recording studies have indeed shown that fibers are differentially sensitive to the chemicals which are the bases of the four basic qualities of taste.

There are of course many other senses: haptic sense, kinesthesis and vestibular senses, and skin senses (including pressure, warmth, cold, and pain). Research on pain perception is perhaps most developed, through the existence of a well-articulated theory: the gate-control theory of Melzack (Melzack & Wall, 1965). According to the theory, sensations of pain result from activation of certain nerve fibers in the skin which lead to specific centers of the brain for pain perception. When the fibers are activated, say by an injury, the neutral 'gate' to the brain is opened for pain sensations. There is another set of neural fibers that, when activated, reduce the effects of the pain fibers and close the gate to the pain sensations.

Intermodal Aspects of Sensation

Synesthesia (basically, a sensation in one sensory modality leading to a sensation in another modality) has not been studied extensively. This is regrettable because it potentially could lead to a better picture of how senses relate to each other. There are several possibilities how synesthesia may emerge. Some researchers use the term 'crosstalk' to refer to the perceptual consequences potentially direct links between the several sensory channels, while a feedback solution emphasizes the role of top-down, higher cognitive influences arising in a high level of the brain's neural activity. Crosstalk and feedback mechanisms may in fact each underlie different types of synesthesia. For a good discussion, see Grossenbacher (1997).

Sensory systems have evolved to work together, and normally, different sensory cues are synchronized both in space and time. However, discordant cues from different modalities can have powerful effects on perception, as illustrated by the so-called McGurk effect, wherein a speaker lip expresses the syllable 'ga' in time with the sound 'ba' (McGurk & McDonald, 1976). The perception is of neither 'ga' nor 'ba' but a synthesis of the two, 'da'. Similarly, in ventriloquism the sight of movement compels one to believe it is also the source of the sound.

Perceptual Organization

Two-Dimensional Perception

The visual system deals with scenes and complex objects which are composed of simple components (visual features). A single visual feature activates neurons in many different cortical areas. Much of what is known about the visual features comes from biological studies that use single-cell recordings in the visual cortex. Those studies were pioneered by Hubel and Wiesel (1968) who identified three types of cells. Simple cells respond when the eye is exposed to a line stimulus at a particular orientation and position within the visual field. A complex cell also responds to a bar, line, or edge in a particular orientation but it does not require that the stimulus be at a particular place. Hypercomplex cells require not only that the stimulus be in a particular orientation but also that it be of a particular length.

When several objects are present simultaneously in the visual field, mechanisms are required to group or bind together visual features that belong to each object and to separate or segment them from features of other objects. The two issues are called the grouping (binding) and segmentation problems, and they are of course related to the old Gestalt laws of grouping and figure–ground perception. Modern research re-activated the two issues, by looking at their physiological basis, by providing a computational basis for the groupings, and by scrutinizing the role of attention. We discuss the three approaches separately here, although it must be added that they are often studied together.

A major challenge in neurophysiology is to understand how the neural activity in the numerous active zones leads to a unified percept of the visual scene. The anatomical basis is a dense network of connections that link the visual areas. Within this network, feedforward connections transmit signals from lower-order visual cortical areas such as V1 or V2 to higher-order areas. In addition, there is a dense web of feedback connections which, despite their anatomical prominence, remain functionally mysterious. We are now sure that feedback connections from higher-order areas (e.g., monkey area V5/MT) serve to amplify and focus activity of neurons in lower-order areas, and that they are important in the differentiation of figure from ground, particularly in the case of stimuli of low visibility. Grossberg (1997) proposed a detailed neural model (called FACADE) to generate context-sensitive perceptual groupings from visual inputs. The model suggests a functional role for cortical layers, columns, maps, and networks, and proposes homologous circuits for VI and V2 with larger-scale processing in V2. Modeled circuits simulate parametric psychophysical data about boundary grouping and illusory contour formation, which form the basis of FACADE neural theory of visual perception.

Following the framework of the computational approach of Marr (1982), bottom-up models of visual processing assume that figure–ground organization precedes object recognition. In fact, this was also defended by Gestalt psychology. The assumption seems logically necessary: how can object recognition occur before a region is labeled as figure? However, some behavioral studies find that familiar regions are more likely to be labeled figure than less familiar regions, a problematic finding for bottom-up models. Therefore, several interactive accounts (e.g., Vecera & O'Reilly, 1998) have been proposed in which figure–ground processes also receive top-down input from object representations in a hierarchical system. Interactive models offer an alternative conception of visual processing to bottom-up models.

Do grouping and segmenting require attention? According to Gestalt psychology, grouping precedes attention. Considering the recent discovery of the complexity of the neural circuits that are involved in grouping and taking into account the new highly interactive functional models of grouping, one needs to assume that there are several stages of processing in grouping: attention may be unimportant at earlier stages, but critical at later stages. Vecera and Behrmann (1997) tested an apperceptive agnosic (for apperceptive agnosia, see Neuropsychology of Perception in Section 5.3) patient, J. W., in tasks involving both spatial attention and preattentive grouping. J. W. had intact spatial attention: he was faster to detect targets appearing at cued locations than to targets appearing at uncued locations. However, his preattentive processes were severely disrupted. Gestalt grouping and symmetry perception, both thought to involve preattentive processes, were impaired in J. W. Also, he could not use Gestalt grouping cues to guide spatial attention. The results suggest that spatial attention is not completely dependent on preattentive grouping processes and vice versa. Preattentive grouping processes and spatial attention may mutually constrain one another in guiding the attentional selection of visual stimuli, but the two processes are isolated from one another. In Moore and Egeth (1997), participants reported which of two horizontal lines was longer. Dots in the background, if grouped, formed displays similar to the Müller–Lyer illusion or Ponzo illusion (see Figures 5.2 and 5.3). Despite inaccurate reports of what the patterns were, participants' responses on the line-length discrimination task were clearly affected by the two illusions. The results suggest that Gestalt grouping does occur without attention. In conclusion, most theories of visual perception assume that before attention is allocated within a scene, visual information is parsed according to the Gestalt principles of organization.

Several studies examined the nature of the psychological processes that underlie the Gestalt principles of grouping by proximity (Figure 5.4), grouping by regularity (Figure 5.5), and

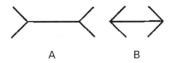

Figure 5.2   *Müller–Lyer illusion*

Figure 5.3   *Ponzo illusion*

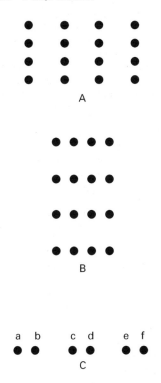

Figure 5.4   *Grouping by proximity*

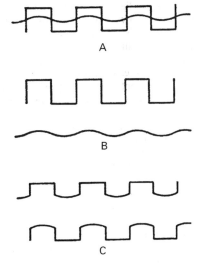

Figure 5.5   *Grouping by regularity*

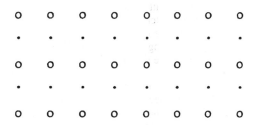

Figure 5.6   *Grouping by similarity*

grouping by similarity (Figure 5.6). One problem facing any computational model incorporating a number of the grouping principles is that of resolving the conflict arising when several principles suggest mutually exclusive organizations. The goal is to find the strongest visual grouping principle (e.g., van Lier & Wagemans,

1997) but it is fair to conclude the findings are rather contradictory; the observed superiority of one principle likely depends on the nature of the stimulus materials, the attentional requirements, etc.

Bregman (1990) showed that auditory organization is performed by a wide range of grouping principles which are very similar to the visual ones. Godsmark and Brown (1998) present a computational framework within which conflicts between the auditory grouping principles are resolved by a context-sensitive mechanism. The mechanism exhibits several properties consistent with human auditory organization. Additionally, as grouping principles operate in complete independence, the framework allows any number of further grouping principles to be incorporated.

Three-Dimensional Perception

As the retinal image is a two-dimensional picture, we achieve visual depth perception through basically two types of cues: binocular disparity cues and monocular depth cues. Any image differs a bit on the two retinas (provided the stimulus is not too far away), and the difference is called binocular disparity. The smaller the disparity, the further is the focused object located in a three-dimensional space. However, even with only one eye, people see reasonably good depth because the distance can be inferred from monocular cues. Here are a few monocular cues: size (smaller appearing objects are farther away), texture gradients (the more fine grained, the larger the distance), linear perspective, inter-position (an object blocking out the view of another must be closer), and motion parallax (images of nearby objects sweeping across the field of vision faster than far away objects). One of the most interesting features of three-dimensional vision is that it relies on many sources of information. Data from different cues must be merged coherently and flexibly. The middle temporal visual area (MT) of the cortex seems to be important in stereoscopic vision. Electrical stimulation of clusters of disparity-selective MT neurons biases perceptual judg-ments of depth, and the bias is predictable from the disparity preference of neurons at the stimu-lation site (De Angelis, Cumming, & Newsome, 1998).

The major determinant of sound location is the signal difference in the two ears. The signal may differ in intensity in the two ears: when the sound occurs to the right side, the sound wave reaching the right ear will be slightly more intense than that reaching the left. A second difference involves time interval: a sound on the left will strike the left ear fractions of a second before it reaches the right ear. Sound location is also heavily influenced by the expectations of the observer: the sound is located where it is expected to be originated. We need to rely on the expectations, because the ear difference does not help us to locate the sound in the vertical dimension and because the same ear difference often misleads us due to echo effects (sounds reaching us indirectly through echoing in a closed space). More details about auditory depth perception and auditory localization can be found in Middlebrooks and Green (1991).

Perception of Motion

Neuronal processes underlying perceived motion While motion detection at the early stage of cortical visual processing has been seen in area V1 of the primates, a number of studies have demonstrated a close link between the discriminative capacity of motion-sensitive neurons at subsequent stages – particularly area MT – and perceptual sensitivity to direction of motion. However, basic knowledge of the neural substrates of motion perception has largely come from research with nonhuman primates, and it was assumed that the general mechanisms are to hold for the human visual system as well. Neuropsychological studies, in conjunction with recent advances in functional brain imaging tools, have yielded initial support to this assumption.

Absolute and relative object motion percep-tion If the eyes are stationary, a stationary object will elicit a stationary image and a mov-ing object will elicit a moving image, thus providing a basis for visual perception of object motion. In fact, the eyes are seldom stationary, even when one is staring at a stationary object. Image movement results from the eyes moving past a stationary object as well as from a moving object. Accordingly, to achieve visual percep-tion of object motion, the origin of any image movement must be determined. One way to achieve this is for the visual system to register both image movement and eye movements, and to compare them (Wertheim, 1981). Of course, the registration of eye movements must not only concern movement of the eyes within the head, but also indirect movement due to head and body motion. This is usually called the absolute motion hypothesis.

Unfortunately, the registration of both image movement and eye movement is insufficient to explain the great sensitivity for object motion perception. Thus, other sources of information are needed to explain perception of object motion. One such source is suggested by the relative motion hypothesis. For example, a mov-ing object appears to move fast if objects surrounding it move slowly, and slowly if sur-rounding objects move fast. The most striking of such phenomena is induced movement (Duncker, 1929). The moon viewed against clouds on a windy night provides an example. The moon, otherwise phenomenally stationary, is seen to drift in the opposite direction to the clouds' movement. Sensitivity of movement-sensitive neurons tends to decrease with eccentricity, which might help explain why motion is more readily attributed to relatively central areas of attention (the moon); in addition, neurons with larger receptive fields are sensitive to higher velocities, which might explain why motion is more readily attributed to relatively small areas (the moon being typically smaller than the clouds). Many experiments show that induced movement entails neither image movement nor eye movement (Reinhardt-Rutland, 1988).

Apparent movement When two lights are spaced a slight distance apart in the dark and then lit alternately at certain intervals, rather than perceiving two lights being lit alternately, the observer sees only one light that appears to move back and forth, and this is called apparent motion. The distance between the two lights is a critical factor along with the temporal separation and brightness of the stimuli (Korte, 1915). If the temporal separation is increased then, according to one of Korte's laws, the physical separation must be increased accordingly if apparent motion is to be optimally maintained. The question then arises whether apparent movement depends upon successive stimulation of separate retinal (and therefore cortical) points or of points located separately in perceived space. At least two studies (Attneave & Block, 1997; Rock & Ebenholtz, 1997) suggest that retinal separation is not critical. For example, Rock and Ebenholtz (1997) created conditions where phenomenal separateness was experienced even when only one region of the retina is stimulated; under such conditions movement is experienced. Conversely, when separate retinal points are stimulated in such a manner that the source will not be experienced in two localities but, rather, in only one, movement is not experienced. This implies that neural interaction between two loci of excitation (on any level) cannot be a general explanation of apparent movement. Apparent or stroboscopic motion depends upon conditions in which each stimulus in the alternating cycle is perceived as located in a different place in space, even when that perception entails stimulation of the same region of the retina.

Event perception and biological motion Observers are remarkably good in detecting structures in an assembly of moving stimuli. Perceiving such a structure is called event perception, following the pioneering work of Johansson (1973, 1975). Event perception is particularly compelling in the perception of biological motion. Biological motion refers to conditions where the available stimulus material is confined to small lights attached to the major points of a moving actor. Despite the drastic impoverishment of the stimulus information (a set of lighted points; see Figure 5.7B), observers organize the swarm of moving dots immediately in a vivid percept of a human figure (see Figure 5.7A). Two components need to be distinguished in a biological motion display. First, the assembly of moving stimuli specifies a particular object, namely a human figure; and it is necessary that the point-lights be in motion

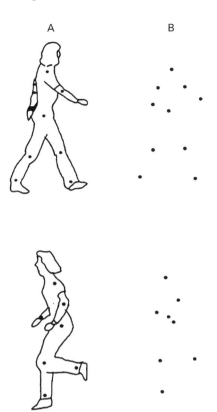

Figure 5.7 *Biological motion*

before a three-dimensional human figure can be recognized. Second, the figure is not only in motion; the figure appears to perform a particular action (walking, dancing, etc.) which is easily identifiable. While observing the moving dots, the perceiver makes successive eye fixations; the question then arises how the images of the successive fixations are integrated into the biological motion. Verfaillie, De Troy, and Van Rensbergen (1994) introduced small changes in the display during the saccadic eye movement between two fixations, in order to unravel the processes involved in the transsaccadic integration; during the saccade, changes can be inserted and will not be noticed by the observer as the visual image is suppressed during a saccade. Verfaillie et al. (1994) observed that small left–right position changes of the walker between two fixations are not easily noticed while a change in depth orientation is quickly discovered. This converges with neurophysiological evidence. Single-cell recordings of cells in the inferotemporal cortex of monkeys (Perrett, Harries et al., 1989; Perrett, Oram et al., 1991) have shown cells' high tolerance for changes in the position of the object, with a striking specificity for particular in-depth orientations exhibited by a majority of the neurons.

Perceiving a Stable and Meaningful World

Object Constancies

The information on the retina is continuously changing, despite a stable physical world. The retinal size of an object depends on its distance as well as its size; as an object moves away from the observer, its retinal image shrinks. The shape of the retinal image of an object also depends on the angle from which it is viewed. Depending on the location of the source of light, the brightness of an object also changes. Our body, head and eyes are continuously moving, and still we see the objects at the same position. This stability of size, shape, brightness, color, and position of objects is known as perceptual constancy. In research on perceptual constancies, it is crucial to make the distinction between proximal and distal information. Proximal stimuli are the physical energy patterns that strike the retinal receptors; distal stimuli are the objects at a distance that give rise to the proximal stimuli. That perception of objects is tied to the distal rather than the proximal stimulus suggests that observers typically assign a familiar shape, size, etc. to the object based on experience. While direct, Gibsonian psychology holds that sensory information is overabundant for the observers' needs in perceiving a stable world, indirect perception emphasizes an active process for stabilizing a perceived world.

Shape perception is often called a mid-level vision phenomenon because it does not require recognition. Two-dimensional visual stimuli have the same shape if there exists a transformation of spatial scale (e.g., magnification) or a rotation in the picture plane that renders them identical; similarly, three-dimensional objects have the same shape if their volumes can be equated by size changes or a combination of rotations about three spatial axes. Relatively little is known about the physiological mechanisms in shape perception but researchers have located neurons in the inferotemporal cortex that respond better to some shapes than to others, even when the shapes are not identified with specific previously learned objects.

Objects in their Interaction with Other Objects and Embedding Scenes

Most models of visual object perception (e.g., Biederman, 1987; Marr, 1982) view the apprehension of a particular object in an image as exclusively based on a data-driven and pre-conceptual recovery of the object's features from the retinal image. Research on object perception in full-scene context, however, suggests that this view may need to be modified if one wishes to model more than the perception of unanticipated, isolated objects. Several studies recording eye-movement patterns across line-drawings of natural scenes or real pictures have consistently shown shorter first fixations on objects likely to appear in a given scene than objects unlikely to be encountered in that scene (for a review, see De Graef, 1998; Figure 5.8). The dominant view is that during the first glance at a scene a scene-specific schema is automatically activated; since the schema presumably contains knowledge about the typical make-up and contents of the scene being viewed, its activation will generate expectations about what objects are likely to be present in that scene and what the typical features of these objects are. Consequently, the perception of context-consistent objects will merely require detection of the features suggested by a global scene-schema. However, alternative explanations exist. As Henderson, Pollatsek, and Rayner (1987) point out, objects within a scene are semantically related; the shorter identification may be due to a priming from one fixated object to the next fixated object. This alternative account does not need a processing of the scene; one merely needs to assume that data-driven access to an object representation primes related object representations. The observed scene-context effects may also be the product of post-perceptual and task-dependent guessing strategies. Much of the current research is directed to discover whether scenes indeed do affect directly perceptual processing of objects (De Graef, Christiaens, & d'Ydewalle, 1990; De Graef, De Troy, & d'Ydewalle, 1992).

Figure 5.8 *Improbable dumptruck in theater scene*

5.3 Topical Issues

Attention

When William James (1890) first delineated the varieties of attention more than a century ago, one major categorical boundary was the distinction between passive and active attention. The modern terms are usually bottom-up versus top-down, stimulus-driven versus goal-directed, or preattentive versus attentive processing; processing may depend on the properties of the image exclusively, while at other times it may be under strict control according to the observer's goal. Two major categories of image properties eliciting preattentive processing need to be distinguished: stimuli that differ substantially in one or more simple visual attributes (e.g., color, orientation, motion, etc.; often called feature singletons, or more simply singletons or features) from their background, and abrupt visual onsets.

We have already discussed the role of attention in perceptual grouping and segmentation; we suggested that the early stages of grouping do not require attention (see Sensations in Section 5.2). Here we address the grouping issue in the identification of an object. Treisman and Gelade (1980) proposed a model that may account for the role of attention (and inattention) in object perception. In particular, they claimed that feature information (e.g., color and orientation) of objects is processed preattentively and in parallel by lower-level perceptual mechanisms before being integrated or conjoined at a particular location to form a perceptual object. Integration is said to occur in one of three ways: (1) by focusing attention at a particular location in space and thereby invoking automatic integration of all features indexed to that location into a perceptual object; (2) in the absence of focused attention but influenced by general knowledge of properties of particular objects; and (3) in the absence of focused attention and general knowledge about the objects, thereby producing incorrect or illusory conjunctions. Thus, when the visual system processes novel stimuli, such that feature integration cannot be guided by prior experience with them, focused attention is necessary to ensure accurate conjunctions of features.

In the past, attention was viewed as similar to a spotlight directed to regions of space, 'illuminating' the objects there. However, there have been two changes. First, the metaphor has been replaced by a zoom-lens model, suggesting that there is a gradient of attentional coverage and that its zooming may vary as a function of stimulus properties as well as the observer's goal. Second, there has been considerable research showing that the basis for attentional selection is not only space-based but may also be object-based. Experiments designed to provide evidence for object-based accounts must demonstrate that a given finding is due to the allocation of attention to a locationally invariant object representation and not to spatial location. Evidence for object-based theories of attention falls into two broad categories. Locations or features in an image can be probed that differ according to their relationship to object structure but that do not differ in spatial location or separation. Attention may also be directed to moving objects, which by definition involves continuously changing spatial locations. Within each of these two categories, many specific techniques have been devised and are reviewed in Egeth and Yantis (1997). Logan (1996) presents a theory (CODE or COntour DEtector theory) that integrates space-based and object-based approaches to visual attention; CODE clusters nearby items into perceptual groups that are both perceptual objects and regions of space, thereby integrating object-based and space-based approaches to attention.

The deployment of attention from one stimulus to another takes time; a substantial body of research has explored the temporal characteristics of attentional deployment. For example, observers in Müller and Rabbitt (1989) fixated the center of a display while four boxes were present in the periphery; they had to detect a signal in one of the boxes; the remaining boxes did not contain the signal. Before the presentation of the signal, the observers received a cue that was either the brief brightening of one of the four boxes (peripheral cue) or the presentation of an arrow at the center of the display that pointed at one of the boxes (central cue). Performance was examined as a function of the stimulus-onset asynchrony (SOA) between the cue and the signal. Central cues elicit a shift of attention which is slow but more sustained, while peripheral cues produce a quick rise but are short-lived. Similar findings have been obtained in numerous studies.

If attention, like a spotlight, moves continuously through space, then more time to shift is predicted when a greater distance needs to be moved. However, it is now well established that attention can be shifted from one location to another one without necessarily a concomitant movement of the eyes. Is the shift then in an analog, continuous fashion, or accomplished abruptly (without any actual movement)? Converging evidence is now available to suggest that the relocation of attention is mainly distance independent, an argument against the analog nature of the movement.

Although we are far from a complete understanding of the brain structures which are involved in attention, we have enough information to know that very specific brain areas carry out computations that, when taken together, provide amplification of the attended events. Following Posner, Rothbart, and Thomas-Thrapp (1997), there are two major periods related to the achievement of attention. The first period is between 3 and 6 months of age. During this period, the infant achieves a high level of ability to shift attention to a visual stimulus and develops the capacity to anticipate its occurrence; much of this development depends on the maturation of a brain network that includes parietal, thalamic, and midbrain mechanisms related to shifting attention to targets. A second important period begins later in the second year of life (involving more the frontal parts of the brain), and provides the child with the ability to exercise voluntary control in a more flexible fashion; the development of this system allows more complex forms of anticipation and the effective control of language and internal thought.

Perceptual Learning

Perceptual learning consists of extracting previously unused information or identifying what external properties are available to be picked up by observers. No doubt, the ecological, direct approach of perception, with its emphasis on the direct perception of information from the world, has been the driving research force in this field. It needs to be acknowledged that the field of perceptual learning is not a homogeneous one, and is not necessarily the exclusive research domain of the direct approaches in perception. It is one of the few fields in perception where a rich literature with lower animals is also available. Psychophysicists have distinguished between peripheral, specific adaptations and more general, strategic ones, and between quick and slow perceptual learning processes. Cognitive psychologists, on the other hand, have distinguished between learning mechanisms driven by feedback (supervised learning) and those without feedback (unsupervised learning), instead operating on the structure inherent in the environmentally supplied information. Goldstone (1998) reviews the field in mainly human perceptual learning and classifies the research endeavors as a function of four basic mechanisms: attentional weighting, imprinting, differentiation, and unitization. The four mechanisms are remarkably similar to the three basic processes which Macintosh and Bennett (1998)

derive from perceptual learning in animal conditioning experiments: differential latent inhibition of common and unique elements; the establishment of unified representations of complex stimuli by associations between their elements; and the establishment of inhibitory associations between the unique elements of stimuli that occur apart.

By attentional weighting, perception becomes adapted to the environment by increasing the attention to perceptual features that are important, and by decreasing attention to irrelevant features. This mechanism is particularly important in categorical perception; observers are better able to distinguish between physically different stimuli when the stimuli come from different categories than when they come from the same category. An example is the discrimination of speech sounds where boundaries differ among languages. In birdsong, with training, birds develop brain neurons with highly specific receptive fields. With imprinting, internalized detectors develop for repeatedly presented stimuli, and these detectors increase the speed and accuracy with which the stimuli are processed. Although evidence for neural implementations for such detectors is available, most studies rather support a more functional description; that is, a device that explains the selective processing of repeatedly presented patterns. By differentiation, stimuli that were once psychologically fused together become separated, while unitization involves the construction of single functional units that can be triggered when a complex configuration arises.

Early Development of Perception

According to most traditional developmental theories (e.g., Piaget, 1936), newborns are endowed with only a very limited and simple repertoire of sensorimotor behaviors that are gradually, and slowly in stages, integrated. Perceptual capacities of very young babies were therefore assumed to be very limited. The early behavior of the neonate is essentially random and insensitive to contextual information. According to James (1890), the world of an infant must be a 'blooming, buzzing confusion'.

Most current research shows that this view is totally obsolete. To clarify the reconceptualization of the developmental aspects of perception, a clear separation needs to be made between perceptual control and guidance of actions on the one hand, and the perception and recognition of objects and events, on the other hand. For example, most infants do not reach for an object hidden by an occluder until they are about 9 months old; nevertheless, infants as young as 3 months old show evidence that they represent the continuity and solidity of the hidden objects when the test measures the visual fixation by the infant. While the first task requires perceptual control of action, the second task taps more directly the perceptual capacity of the child.

The habituation paradigm is foundational to the study of perception by infants. Infants are presented with a specific stimulus for a number of trials until their attention declines. Infants' attentiveness declines over trials because as they develop a stored representation of the stimulus it becomes less interesting; conversely, the novel stimulus should reinstate responsiveness. The findings converge to show that infants begin to store frequently repeated perceptual information from birth on.

One of the first tasks for the infant is to ascertain which features in the optic array comprise objects distinct from other objects. As early as 3 months, infants perceive two objects as distinct if they are separated in depth or move independently; however, they do not yet perceive boundaries between objects that are stationary and adjacent, even if the objects differ in color, texture, and form. Further perceptual learning is here required, and it may take one full year before the segmentation is achieved at the level of what adults are able to do.

A consistent but still largely unexplained finding is that neonates look longer at human faces (particularly their mothers' faces) than other configurations, even when the other configurations contain all the features of a human face (eyes, mouth, nose, etc.) in a scrambled order. Some theories claim that very young infants are biased toward the perception of low spatial frequencies (large-scale pattern information as in faces) but this does not explain the finding, because other symmetrical patterns are not as successful as faces in attracting the visual attention of the infants.

Gibson and Walk (1960) created an apparatus that contains an apparent cliff but the deep side is covered with clear glass strong enough to support babies who might venture beyond the edge. Generally, human babies over 6 months of age and many animals (even rats which were reared in darkness without visual experience) avoid going over the cliff; other animals proceed over the cliff without hesitation. Campos, Langer, and Krowitz (1970) tested 6- to 18-week-old infants (who are not yet able to crawl) by placing them on the edge and measuring their heart rates. When babies were placed facing the deep side, their heart rates changed considerably. Thus even very young infants responded to the depth cues, suggesting that at least some part of depth perception, as with other land animals, may be innate.

Cross-Cultural Research

The central aim of cross-cultural studies of perception is to investigate perceptual processes by comparing groups which differ in their cultural and ethnic characteristics or live in different environments. Numerous perceptual phenomena have been scrutinized using a cross-cultural methodology. Typically, older studies suggested one or another explanation, and current research mainly confirms the older explanations with some qualifications in some cases (Russell, Deregowski, & Kinnear, 1997). We restrict the presentation here to two issues: pictorial perception and geometric illusions.

The oldest issue is the pictorial perception. Hudson (1960) discovered that some of his observers in Africa interpreted thematic apperception test pictures as if they had lacked the ability to perceive pictorial depth; that is, the ability to 'see' that a picture represents an array of three-dimensional objects distributed in space. Within his group of observers in South Africa, western European children were found to have difficulties with perception of pictorial depth on their entry to school but showed a significant improvement by the end of their primary education. No analogous improvement was found in his black schoolchildren, and both they and some black graduate teachers performed badly. The report of Hudson's studies evoked a number of replications and extensions. Hudson considered two factors to be important in correct pictorial perception: educational achievement and intellectual endowment. More recent studies typically confirmed the importance of the first factor. Intelligence has not been an important predictor but Witkin's concept of field-dependency emerged as a significant variable in several studies. According to Witkin et al. (1954), individuals differ greatly in the degree to which they respond to distortions of the environment. Field-dependent observers base their judgment largely on the visual surroundings; field-independent observers rely more on themselves and hence are not so quickly led astray by distortions of the visual field.

Rivers (1905) was probably the first to conduct a systematic cross-cultural study of geometric illusions, as for example the Müller–Lyer illusion (see Figure 5.2). Following his pioneering work, the field lay fallow for half a century until Segall, Campbell, and Herskovits (1966) renewed interest in these problems. If we restrict here the discussion to one of the geometric illusions, the Müller–Lyer illusion, non-Western groups are less prone to the illusion than the Western controls. Segall et al. (1966) postulated that there are ecological and cultural factors which influence susceptibility to geometric illusions. For figures constructed of lines meeting in nonrectangular junctions, there will be a learned tendency among persons dwelling in carpentered environments to rectangularize those junctions, to perceive the figures in perspective, and to interpret them as two-dimensional representations of three-dimensional objects. On the whole, much of the current work has confirmed the carpentered-world hypothesis.

Neuropsychology of Perception

It must be acknowledged that neuropsychology has been blooming in recent years, as a part of a greater convergence of psychology and the neurosciences. Theories of perception profited from this development as several processes were validated through the discovery of particular clinical cases where the behavioral disturbance could only be explained by the inability of the patients to carry out a particular process. At the same time, progress in basic research on perception provided the clinical neuropsychologist with powerful frameworks and more concrete tools in trying to understand the nature of a perceptual disturbance, leading possibly to better remedial training. We restrict our presentation here to three major classes of perceptual disturbances, visual agnosia, hemineglect, and prosopagnosia, as the three are prime examples of fruitful interactions between neuropsychology and perception research.

The term visual agnosia is usually taken to imply that the perceptual disorder is not a consequence of general intellectual-cognitive deterioration, language impairment, or lower-level (that is, at the level of the eye, and more particularly the retina) visual dysfunction; the patient still 'sees' everything, but fails to go beyond the sensory information to achieve object perception. There are many forms of visual agnosia. As early as 1890, Lissauer distinguished between what he termed 'apperceptive' and 'associative' visual agnosias. In more modern terminology, following Marr (1982), apperceptive visual agnosia corresponds to processing problems before achieving a 3-D image; patients with associative visual agnosia fail to give the percept (the 3-D image) meaning by linking it to previous experience (the matching stage with memory representations, following Marr).

Lissauer's apperceptive or associative distinction is still often used as a starting point in identifying the various types of visual agnosia, but the issues raised by modern studies of visual agnosia demand a richer type of theory. It is precisely here that the approach of Marr (or its derivations) appears to be so fruitful. For example, there are patients who are able to see color, to distinguish small differences in brightness and wavelength on psychophysical testing but are unable to fulfill a task requiring shape information including copying, matching, and identification; they have a severe impairment in constructing a viewer-centered representation. The transition from a viewer-centered representation to an object-centered one is often impaired in visual agnosia patients with posterior lesions of the (mainly but not exclusively) right cerebral hemisphere; they experience disproportionate difficulty in identifying objects that are drawn overlapping each other, or in identifying objects from pictures degraded by the removal of edge information. The problems of constructing an object-centered representation are particularly salient among patients with posterior parietal lobe lesions of the right cerebral hemisphere; those patients typically have no problems in identifying objects taken from conventional views, but with unusual (but not necessarily unfamiliar) views, they are at a loss (Warrington & Taylor, 1973, 1978). A remarkable feature of associative visual agnosia is that, for some patients, it can be very category-specific. For example, Warrington and Shallice (1984) describes a patient who faced no particular problems in identifying inanimate objects but failed largely to identify living things.

One of the most intriguing of all perceptual disorders is unilateral neglect. Neglect is typically encountered in patients with right cerebral injuries, for whom it affects the left side of space. Patients with left-sided neglect following right hemisphere injury seem to ignore stimuli that fall to their left. Central mechanisms must be involved, as clearly demonstrated by Bisiach and his colleagues (Bisiach, Capitani, Luzzatti, & Perani, 1981; Bisiach & Luzzatti, 1978) who asked their (Italian) patients to imagine that they were in the central square (Piazza del Duomo) of Milan, facing the cathedral, and to describe what they would be able to see. The descriptions of the left-neglect patients were mostly found to involve the buildings on the right side (from the patient's imagined viewpoint) of the square; buildings on the left were not described. If then asked to imagine themselves standing on the steps of the cathedral, looking away from it, they described the buildings they had neglected to describe before because those now fell to their right in the imagined view.

Neglect need not be confined to visual perception and can affect the left side of tactile and auditory space as well. A number of theories have been proposed to try to account for unilateral neglect. According to Heilman (1979), the disorder is primarily attentional in nature, and numerous further studies suggest that neglect may rather involve an impairment of automatic than deliberate aspects of attentional orienting. In Bisiach's view, neglect is due to damage to an internal spatial framework that then interferes with the patient's ability to form a mental representation of one of the two sides of real or imagined space. The debate between proponents of attentional and representational theories is lively, and appears likely to continue for some years.

Faces have always occupied a special place in neuropsychology. Part of the reason for this is that they are considered to be 'special' stimuli (Farah, Wilson, Drain, & Tanaka, 1998). Striking is Yin's (1969) demonstration of the inversion effect, the tendency for recognition of faces to be differentially impaired (relative to that of other 'mono-oriented' stimuli such as houses) by turning the stimulus upside-down. Some brain-injured individuals are unable to recognize familiar faces yet recognize familiar bodies or voices (prosopagnosia). Certain neurons of some primates selectively fire to face stimuli only. Babies only 30 minutes old are adept at orienting towards faces. Much of the recent neuropsychological work on face recognition has exploited neuroimaging techniques in order to determine whether different regions of the human brain respond to faces selectively (Gorno Tempini et al., 1998; Kanwisher, Tong, & Nakayama, 1998). With the currently available evidence, one can conclude that parts of the inferior temporal cortex are critically involved in face recognition.

There are again many types of face processing disorders. In order to capture the specific problem of any prosopagnosia patient, Bruce and Young (1986) developed a model in which several processing units are assumed (see Figure 5.9). The model has been immensely popular in neuropsychology; it includes the analysis of facial expressions, analysis of the mouth and tongue movements involved in speaking (facial speech analysis), and types of directed (intentional) visual processing. Bruce and Young (1986) postulate a set of face recognition units

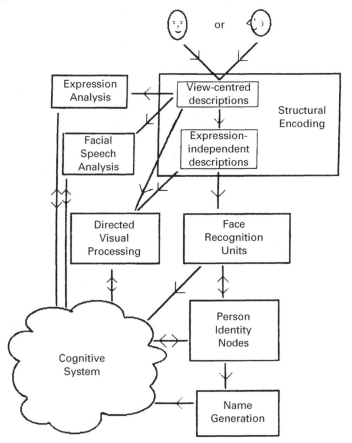

Figure 5.9 *Face processing (Bruce & Young, 1986). Reproduced with permission from the* British Journal of Psychology, © *The British Psychological Society*

that form a link between structural encoding of the face's appearance and person's identity nodes that provide access to stored information concerning known people. From Figure 5.9, the inspiration from Marr's computational approach is obvious.

5.4 WHERE IS PERCEPTION RESEARCH TO GO IN THE NEXT DECADE?

From several parts in this chapter, it is apparent that the computational approach of Marr, or more generally the information-processing paradigm, has the potential to enrich considerably research on perception. The discussions demonstrate how such a framework can integrate top-down and bottom-up processes, despite Marr's original emphasis on bottom-up mechanisms, leaving the cognitive processes for further investigation. The more recent advent of connectionism does not really change the picture. Connectionism gives only minor attention to perception, and as a whole discards top-down cognitive influences. There are of course notable exceptions modeling top-down and bottom-up interactions. Despite some initial (and convincing) successes in modeling psychological processes, we feel that connectionism is already almost out of the field of visual perception.

In what direction is perception research likely to go in the near future? We believe that more attention will be given to unraveling the power of the human perceptual system by analyzing more complex perceptual events, moving from psychophysical studies on simple stimulus patterns to fully-fledged capturing of important perceptual events. Based on the earlier work within the information-processing paradigm, scrutinizing the basic processes will push the field well beyond the more illustrative studies of Gestalt psychology, cognitive psychology or a Gibsonian direct approach.

RESOURCE REFERENCES

Baird, J. C. (1997). *Sensation and judgement: Complementarity theory of psychophysics.* Mahwah, NJ: Lawrence Erlbaum Associates.

Bregman, A. S. (1990). *Auditory scene analysis: The perceptual organization of sound.* Cambridge, MA: MIT Press.

Coren, S., Ward, L. M., & Enns, J. T. (1999). *Sensation and perception.* Fort Worth, TX: Harcourt.

Egeth, H. E., & Yantis, S. (1997). Visual attention: Control, representation, and time course. *Annual Review of Psychology, 48,* 269–297.

Gilkey, R. A., & Anderson, T. R. (1997). *Binaural and spatial hearing in real and virtual environments.* Hillsdale, NJ: Lawrence Erlbaum Associates.

Goldstone, R. L. (1998). Perceptual learning. *Annual Review of Psychology, 49,* 585–612.

Hirsh, I. J., & Watson, C. S. (1996). Auditory psychophysics and perception. *Annual Review of Psychology, 47,* 461–484.

Hood, D. C. (1998). Lower-level visual processing and models of light adaptation. *Annual Review of Psychology, 49,* 503–535.

Laming, D. (1997). *The measurement of sensation.* Oxford, UK: Oxford University Press.

Moore, B. C. J. (1997). *An introduction to the psychology of hearing.* London: Academic Press.

Pashler, H. E. (1998). *The psychology of attention.* Cambridge, MA: MIT Press.

Rock, I. (Ed.). (1997). *Indirect perception.* Cambridge, MA: MIT Press.

Rosenzweig, M. R., Leiman, A. L., & Breedlove, S. M. (1999). *Biological psychology: An introduction to behavioral, cognitive and clinical neuroscience* (2nd ed.). Sunderland, MA: Sinauer Associates, Inc.

Leading Journals

Journal of Experimental Psychology: Human Perception and Performance
Perception and Psychophysics
Perception

ADDITIONAL LITERATURE CITED

Adelson, E. H. (1993). Perceptual organization and the judgment of brightness. *Science, 262,* 2042–2044.

Attneave, F., & Block, G. (1997). Apparent movement in tridimensional space. In I. Rock (Ed.), *Indirect perception* (pp. 277–290). Cambridge, MA: MIT Press/Bradford.

Berglund, B., Berglund, U., Engen, T., & Ekman, G. (1973). Multidimensional analysis of twenty-one odors. *Scandinavian Journal of Psychology, 14,* 131–137.

Biederman, I. (1987). Recognition-by-components: A theory of human image understanding. *Psychological Review, 94,* 115–147.

Bisiach, E., Capitani, E., Luzzatti, C., & Perani, D. (1981). Brain and conscious representation of reality. *Neuropsychologia, 19,* 543–552.

Bisiach, E., & Luzzatti, C. (1978). Unilateral neglect of representational space. *Cortex, 14,* 129–133.

Boring, E. G. (1942). *Sensation and perception in the history of experimental psychology.* New York: Century.

Bowmaker, J. K., & Dartnall, H. J. A. (1980). Visual pigments and rods and cones in a human retina. *Journal of Physiology, 298,* 501–511.

Bruce, V., & Young, A. (1986). Understanding face recognition. *British Journal of Psychology, 77,* 305–327.

Bruner, J. S., & Goodman, C. C. (1947). Value and need as organizing factors in perception. *Journal of Abnormal and Social Psychology, 42,* 33–44.

Cain, W. S. (1978). History of research on smell. In E. C. Carterette & M. P. Friedman (Eds.), *Handbook of perception* (Vol. 6A, pp. 197–229). New York: Academic Press.

Campos, J. J., Langer, A., & Krowitz, A. (1970). Cardiac responses on the visual cliff in preloco-motor human infants. *Science, 170,* 196–197.

Classen, C. (1993). *Worlds of sense.* New York: Routledge.

Dacey, D. M. (1996). Circuitry for color coding in the primate retina. *Proceedings of the National Academy of Sciences, USA, 93,* 582–588.

De Angelis, G. C., Cumming, B. G., & Newsome, W. T. (1998). Cortical area MT and the perception of stereoscopic depth. *Nature, 394,* 677–680.

De Graef, P. (1998). Prefixational object perception in scenes: Objects popping out of schemas. In G. Underwood (Ed.), *Eye guidance in reading and scene perception* (pp. 313–336). Oxford, UK: Elsevier.

De Graef, P., Christiaens, D., & d'Ydewalle, G. (1990). Perceptual effects of scene context on object identification. *Psychological Research, 52,* 317–329.

De Graef, P., De Troy, A., & d'Ydewalle, G. (1992). Local and global contextual constraints on the identification of objects in scenes. *Canadian Journal of Psychology, 46,* 490–509.

de Valois, R. L., & de Valois, K. K. (1993). A multistage color model. *Vision Research, 33,* 1053–1065.

Duncker, K. (1929). Über induzierte Bewegung. *Psychologische Forschung, 12,* 180–259.

Farah, M. J., Wilson, K. D., Drain, M., & Tanaka, J. N. (1998). What is 'special' about face perception? *Psychological Review, 105,* 482–498.

Fechner, G. T. (1860). *Elemente der Psychophysik.* Leipzig: Breitkopf und Hartel.

Gibson, E. J., & Walk, R. D. (1960). The 'visual cliff'. *Scientific American, 202,* 64–71.

Gibson, J. J. (1950). *The perception of the visual world.* Boston: Houghton Mifflin.

Godsmark, D., & Brown, G. J. (1998). Context-sensitive selection of competing auditory organizations: A blackboard model. In D. F. Rosenthal & H. G. Okuno (Eds.), *Computational auditory scene analysis.* (pp. 139–155). Mahwah, NJ: Lawrence Erlbaum Associates.

Gorno Tempini, M. L., Price, C. J., Josephs, O., Vandenberghe, R., Cappa, S. F., Kapur, N., & Frackowiak, R. S. J. (1998). The neural systems sustaining face and proper-name processing. *Brain, 121,* 2103–2118.

Grossberg, S. (1997). Cortical dynamics of three-dimensional figure-ground perception of two-dimensional pictures. *Psychological Review, 104,* 618–658.

Grossenbacher, P. G. (1997). Perception and sensory information in synaesthetic experience. In S. Baron-Cohen & J. E. Harrison (Eds.), *Synaesthesia: Classic and contemporary readings* (pp. 148–172). Oxford, UK: Blackwell.

Heilman, K. M. (1979). Neglect and related disorders. In K. M. Heilman & E. Valenstein (Eds.), *Clinical neuropsychology* (pp. 268–307). New York: Oxford University Press.

Helmholtz, H. (1867). *Handbuch der Physiologischen Optik.* Hamburg: Voss.

Henderson, J. M., Pollatsek, A., & Rayner, K. (1987). Effects of foveal priming and extrafoveal preview on object identification. *Journal of Experimental Psychology: Human Perception and Performance, 13,* 449–463.

Hering, E. (1879). *Handbuch der Physiologie der Sinnesorgane.* Leipzig: Vogel.

Hubel, D. H., & Wiesel, T. N. (1968). Receptive fields and functional architecture of the monkey striate cortex. *Journal of Physiology, 195,* 215–243.

Hudson, W. (1960). Pictorial depth perception in subcultural groups in Africa. *Journal of Social Psychology, 52,* 183–208.

Hurvich, L. M., & Jameson, D. (1957). An opponent-process theory of color vision. *Psychological Review, 64,* 384–404.

James, W. (1890). *The principles of psychology.* New York: Holt.

Johansson, G. (1973). Visual perception of biological motion and a model for its analysis. *Perception & Psychophysics, 14,* 201–211.

Johansson, G. (1975). Visual motion perception. *Scientific American, 232,* 76–88.

Jones, F. N., Roberts, K., & Holman, E. W. (1978). Similarity judgments and recognition memory for common spices. *Perception & Psychophysics, 24,* 2–6.

Kanwisher, N., Tong, F., & Nakayama, K. (1998). The effect of face inversion on the human fusiform face area. *Cognition, 68,* B1–B11.

Korte, A. (1915). Kinematoskopische Untersuchungen. *Zeitschrift für Psychologie, 72,* 193–296.

Lazarus, R. S., & McCleary, R. A. (1951). Autonomic discrimination without awareness: A study of subception. *Psychological Review, 58,* 113–122.

Lissauer, H. (1890). Ein Fall von Seelenblindheit nebst einem Beiträge zur Theorie derselben. *Archiv für Psychiatrie und Nervenkrankheiten, 21,* 222–270.

Logan, G. D. (1996). The CODE theory of visual attention: An integration of space-based and object-based attention. *Psychological Review, 103,* 603–649.

Mackintosh, N. J., & Bennett, C. H. (1998). Perceptual learning in animals and humans. In M. Sabourin, F. Craik, & M. Robert (Eds.), *Advances in psychological science, Vol. 2: Biological and cognitive aspects* (pp. 317–333). Hove, UK: Psychology Press.

MacNichol, E. F., Jr. (1986). A unifying presentation of photo-pigment spectra. *Vision Research, 29,* 543–546.

Marr, D. (1982). *Vision: A computational investigation into the human representation and processing of visual information.* San Francisco: Freeman.

McGurk, H., & MacDonald, J. (1976). Hearing lips and seeing voices. *Nature, 264,* 746–748.

Melzack, R. D., & Wall, P. D. (1965). Pain mechanisms: A new theory. *Science, 150,* 971–979.

Middlebrooks, J. C., & Green, D. M. (1991). Sound localization by human listeners. *Annual Review of Psychology, 42,* 135–159.

Moore, C. M., & Egeth, H. (1997). Perception without attention: Evidence of grouping under conditions of inattention. *Journal of Experimental Psychology: Human Perception and Performance, 23,* 339–352.

Müller, J. H., & Rabbitt, P. M. A. (1989). Reflexive and voluntary orienting of visual attention: Time course of activation and resistance to interruption. *Journal of Experimental Psychology: Human Perception and Performance, 15,* 315–330.

Norwich, K. H., & Wong, W. (1997). Unification of psychophysical phenomena: The complete form of Fechner's law. *Perception & Psychophysics, 59,* 929–940.

Perrett, D. I., Harries, M. H., Bevan, R., Thomas, S., Benson, P. J., Mistlin, A. J., Chitty, A. J., Hietanen, J., & Ortega, J. E. (1989). Frameworks of analysis for the neural representation of animate objects and actions. *Journal of Experimental Biology, 146,* 87–113.

Perrett, D. I., Oram, M. W., Harries, M. H., Bevan, R., Hietanen, J. K., Benson, P. J., & Thomas, S. (1991). Viewer-centered and object-centered encoding of heads analysed at the single cell level in the temporal cortex of the rhesus macaque. *Experimental Brain Research, 16,* 153–170.

Piaget, J. (1936). *La naissance de l'intelligence chez l'enfant.* Neuchâtel, Switzerland: Delachaux & Niestlé.

Posner, M. I., Rothbart, M. K., & Thomas-Thrapp, L. (1997). Functions of orienting in early infancy. In P. J. Lang, R. F. Simons, F. Robert, & M. T. Balaban (Eds), *Attention and orienting: Sensory and motivational processes* (pp. 327–345). Mahwah, NJ: Lawrence Erlbaum Associates.

Postman, L., Bruner, J. S., & McGinnies, E. (1948). Personal values as selective factors in perception. *Journal of Abnormal and Social Psychology, 43,* 142–154.

Quinlan, P. (1991). *Connectionism and psychology: A psychological perspective on new connectionist research.* New York: Harvester Wheatsheaf.

Reinhardt-Rutland, A. H. (1988). Induced movement in the visual modality: An overview. *Psychological Bulletin, 103,* 57–71.

Rivers, W. H. R. (1905). Observations on the senses of the Todas. *British Journal of Psychology, 1,* 321–396.

Rock, I., & Ebenholtz, S. (1997). Apparent motion based on phenomenal location. In I. Rock (Ed.), *Indirect perception* (pp. 249–264). Cambridge, MA: MIT Press/Bradford.

Russell, P. A., Deregowski, J. B., & Kinnear, P. R. (1997). Perception and aesthetics. In J. W. Berry, P. R. Dasen, & T. S. Saraswathi (Eds.), *Handbook of cross-cultural psychology, Vol. 2: Basic processes and human development* (pp. 107–142). Boston, MA: Allyn and Bacon.

Segall, M. H., Campbell, D. T., & Herskovits, M. J. (1966). *Influence of culture on visual perception.* Indianapolis, IN: Bobbs-Merrill.

Stevens, S. S. (1957). On the psychophysical law. *Psychological Review, 64,* 153–181.

Tanner, W. P., & Swets, J. A. (1954). A decision-making theory of visual detection. *Psychological Review, 61,* 401–409.

Treisman, A. M., & Gelade, G. (1980). A feature-integration theory of attention. *Cognitive Psychology, 12,* 97–136.

Van Lier, R., & Wagemans, J. (1997). Perceptual grouping measured by color assimilation: Regularity versus proximity. *Acta Psychologica, 97,* 37–70.

Vecera, S. P., & Behrmann, M. (1997). Spatial attention does not require preattentive grouping. *Neuropsychology, 11,* 30–43.

Vecera, S. P., & O'Reilly, R. C. (1998). Figure-ground organization and object recognition processes: An interactive account. *Journal of Experimental Psychology: Human Perception and Performance, 24,* 441–462.

Verfaillie, K., De Troy, A., & Van Rensbergen, J. (1994). Transsaccadic integration of biological motion. *Journal of Experimental Psychology: Learning, Memory, and Cognition, 20,* 649–670.

Warrington, E. K., & Shallice, T. (1984). Category-specific semantic impairments. *Brain, 107,* 829–854.

Warrington, E. K., & Taylor, A. M. (1973). The contribution of the right parietal lobe to object recognition. *Cortex, 9,* 152–164.

Warrington, E. K., & Taylor, A. M. (1978). Two categorical stages of object recognition. *Perception, 7,* 695–705.

Weber, E. (1846). Der Tastsin und das Gemeingefühl. In E. Weber (Ed.), *Handwörterbuch der Physiologie, 3,* 481–588.

Wertheim, A. H. (1981). On the relativity of perceived motion. *Acta Psychologica, 48*, 97–110.

Witkin, H. A., Lewis, H. B., Hertzman, M., Machover, K., Meissner, P. B., & Wapner, S. (1954). *Personality through perception.* New York: Harper.

Yin, R. K. (1969). Looking at upside-down faces. *Journal of Experimental Psychology, 81*, 141–145.

Communications concerning this chapter should be addressed to: Professor Géry d'Ydewalle, Department of Psychology, University of Leuven, B-3000 Leuven, Belgium

6

Conditioning and Experimental Analysis of Behavior

RUBÉN ARDILA

This chapter describes the current state of the study of conditioning, the experimental analysis of behavior, its conceptual and methodological foundations, the main psychological processes that are included (habituation, sensitization, classical conditioning, operant conditioning, stimulus control of behavior, complex learning, verbal behavior, etc.), and the applications to social problems.

Because memory processes are presented in Chapter 7, and the neurobiology of learning is the topic of Chapter 8, they are not referred to in this chapter, except when it is necessary to do so in order to better understand the processes of conditioning and the experimental analysis of behavior.

The processes investigated have been studied with both human and nonhuman participants. At the present time research is in progress with a large number of species, but probably more emphasis is given to work with human partici-

pants than to work with nonhuman subjects. However, in this chapter both human and nonhuman research will be included.

6.1 SCOPE OF THE FIELD

The study of learning and conditioning is a field of research that began with Thorndike (1898, 1911) and Pavlov (1927).

At the present time conditioning and experimental analysis of behavior has greatly influenced other areas of psychology, and has applications in biology, evolution, and anthropology. It is a very active area of laboratory research, with nonhuman and human participants. It is also a large field of application concerned with the traditional areas of psychology (clinical, industrial/organizational, educational, social, sport, and forensic psychology), and the nontraditional areas (community behavior analysis, racism, violence, sexism, drug abuse, sexual coercion, social isolation, ecological psychology, and many others).

Perspective and Assumptions

The conceptual foundations of behavior analysis have been the subject of study for a number of psychologists and philosophers for the last 20 years. B. F. Skinner had always been very interested in philosophical issues. He stated (1974) that behaviorism was the philosophy of the science of behavior. This philosophy has been developed by several thinkers (see for instance Day, 1980; Morris, 1988, 1998; Rachlin, 1994; Smith, 1986; and Zuriff, 1985, among other authors).

Behavior analysis can be described as a natural science of behavior comprising three subdisciplines: the experimental analysis of behavior for *basic research* elucidating fundamental behavioral processes; *applied* behavior analysis for the application of these processes, derivative technologies, and research methods for clinical and community problems; and the *conceptual analysis of behavior*, for historical, philosophical, theoretical, and methodological investigations.

As Morris (1998) says, the experimental analysis of behavior (EAB) involves *conceptual analysis* as a matter of course – ontological assumptions. The EAB seeks: (a) to describe functional relations between classes of responses and classes of stimuli, and (b) to demonstrate the reliability and generality thereof, and thus their lawfulness. The dependent variable is the probability of an organism's response as a function of independent variables, which occur in real time.

On the other hand, *applied* behavior analysis employs basic behavioral processes, research methods and derivative procedures, in order to prevent and alleviate problems of social importance. Applied behavior analysis is accountable on seven dimensions: its procedures are applied to problems of relatively immediate social importance; its behavioral measures are valid and reliable; its procedures are described in sufficient technological detail for replication; its research methods are analytic; its effectiveness is socially significant; its generality is demonstrated across time, settings, and behaviors; and it is relevant to an overall conceptual system of behavior (Baer, Wolf, & Risley, 1987). Applied behavior analysis has derived from the EAB with 'their procedural emphases of reinforcement, punishment, and discriminative-stimulus contingencies as behavior-analytic environmental variables, their reliance on single-subject designs as the formats of analysis and proof, and their consistent use of the Skinner box as their arena' (p. 313). However, in the last decades, applied behavior analysis has been characterized by seven key words: applied, behavioral, analytic, technological, conceptual, effective, and capable of appropriately generalized outcomes.

The importance of a conceptual analysis has been pointed out since the beginning of the EAB. Skinner (1947) stated that 'what is needed is a theory of behavior' (p. 27). The task of conceptual analysis consists in '*accounting for* behavior, or *explaining* behavior, in a very broad sense *understanding* behavior' (p. 26). The conceptual analysis includes metatheory and philosophy, history and historiography, methodology, and system and theory. Metatheory and philosophy analyze behavior-analytic assumptions. System and theory refer to the nature of behavioral explanations and the behavior interpretation of cultural, social, and individual activities. Methodology is interested in examining concepts, terms, the unit of analysis, research goals, etc. History and historiography refer to the development of behavior analysis as a discipline.

The epistemology of behavior analysis has been influenced by naturalism, materialism, associationism, empiricism, behavioral biology, and pragmatism. Psychological pragmatism operationalized successful working into prediction and control as the goals for a science of behavior. From the point of view of empiricism, it was stated that what was necessary was to develop objective definitions for psychology's subjective terms, and exclude whatever was not logically or empirically definable from its subject matter.

The influence of behavioral biology in behavior analysis comes from Darwin (see Boakes, 1984). Contemporary behavior analysis adheres to upward continuity across species in biology and behavior, with the possibility of behavioral processes unique to human beings; to research practices derived from Claude Bernard's work in experimental medicine; and to behavioral adaptation in terms of its consequences in a way similar to natural selection (Skinner, 1981).

Naturalism as a frame of reference for behavior analysis assumes that behavior is lawful and orderly, and suitable for scientific investigation.

It is important to indicate that behavior analysis does not embrace logical positivism and conventional operationalism (see Smith, 1986). The hypothetical-deductive model of theory building, theory testing, and explanation, is not accepted by the experimental analysis of behavior. Skinner's positivism is a descriptive positivism, not a logical one. His operationalism is concerned with the workability of terms and concepts, not just with agreement about what they proscriptively meant (Skinner, 1963). His theory building is inductive and empirical, not deductive and hypothetical.

A Brief History

The psychology of learning, conditioning and the experimental analysis of behavior as fields of research is traced to Edward L. Thorndike and Ivan P. Pavlov at the end of the nineteenth century. However in a broader sense this history goes back to the naturalism of Aristotle and in general of Hellenic Greek philosophy. The role of Descartes, empiricism, British association-ism, the ideas of Locke, and Hume, have been documented in the history of behavior analysis (Kazdin, 1978; see also Kantor, 1959).

The interest in the physiological processes responsible for reflex behavior inspired the work of Ivan M. Sechenov (1829–1905) and of Ivan P. Pavlov (1849–1936). Sechenov found that the vigor of an elicited response does not invariably depend on the intensity of its triggering stim-ulus, and a very faint stimulus could produce a large response. Sechenov tried to apply his find-ings to voluntary behavior, and suggested that complex forms of behavior (including both actions and thoughts) that occur in the absence of an obvious eliciting stimulus are in fact reflexive responses; the eliciting stimuli are so faint as to be unnoticeable. Voluntary behaviors and thoughts are elicited by faint inconspicuous stimuli, according to Sechenov.

The behavior of an organism changes throughout its lifetime, and can be altered by experience. Sechenov did not center his work on this problem, but considered that reflex respon-ses depend on a pre-wired neural circuit con-necting the sense organs to the relevant muscles. Ivan Pavlov, on the other hand, showed that not all reflexes are innate and that new reflexes to stimuli can be established through mechanisms of association.

Pavlov's work came to be known as *classical conditioning*. It will be described in detail later on, due to its central importance in the contem-porary research on conditioning. Pavlov was interested in the influence of the central nervous system on the functioning of the organism, and devoted his early work to the efferent nerves of the heart and to digestive physiology. In 1904 Pavlov was awarded the Nobel Prize for Physi-ology for his research work, basically on diges-tive physiology.

The work on conditioning started with an interest in the way dogs learned to anticipate feeding episodes. Classical conditioning enables animals to take advantage of the orderly sequence of events in the environment and learn which stimuli tend to go with which events. Wolfsohn and Snarsky, in Pavlov's laboratory, performed the first systematic studies of clas-sical conditioning; they centered their interest in the salivary glands. Snarsky, in one of the earl-iest experiments, gave dogs sour water, artifi-cially colored black. After eliciting salivation with black sour water, he found that the dogs would also salivate to plain black water, or to the sight of a bottle containing a black liquid (see Boakes, 1984).

The work of Pavlov was known in the West after the translation of his publications, some of them into German, French, or English. In 1927 his collected works were published in English and the study of conditioning developed rapidly in the English-speaking world. John B. Watson (1878–1958) was greatly influenced by Pavlov and classical conditioning; his psychological system, *behaviorism*, has some of its roots in Pavlov.

Besides classical conditioning, another impor-tant landmark in the study of learning and behavior was *operant conditioning*. This work was basically developed by B. F. Skinner (1904–1990) in a series of papers and books beginning in 1930 and going up to 1990. This formulation of behavior arose out of observa-tions of animal performance in a type of experi-ment that Skinner invented, the bar-pressing activity of an organism (initially a rat, later on a pigeon and many other species).

Both instrumental learning (Thorndike, 1898, 1911) and Pavlovian conditioning (Pavlov, 1927) had been studied before Skinner. Researchers only appreciated the differences between these two 'types' of learning due to the work of Miller and Konorski (1928). They pas-sively flexed a dog's leg in the presence of a stimulus and paired this compound event with the presentation of food. After a number of such pairings the dog started to lift its leg spon-taneously when the stimulus was presented. This was considered a conditioned response, at vari-ance with Pavlov's principle of stimulus sub-stitution. According to this principle, exposure to stimulus–outcome pairings endows the stim-ulus with the capacity to act as a substitute or surrogate for the outcome and thereby to elicit the same response. Miller and Konorski noted that the ability of the stimulus to control leg flexion could not be explained in terms of it becoming a substitute for food. For this reason they argued for a second form of conditioning which they termed Type II. Skinner later argued for a Type II conditioning (Pavlov's was Type I), pointing out that Pavlov's principle could not explain why hungry rats learn to press a freely available lever for food.

The experimental analysis of behavior as a system was proposed by Skinner, based on operant conditioning. This is a development more along the lines of Thorndike's learning by selecting and connecting under the law of effect. Skinner recognized two kinds of learning (Type S and Type R), and he placed more emphasis upon the kind of learning which is under the control of its consequences.

The experimental analysis of behavior, operant conditioning and its numerous applications, will be presented later on in this chapter. The study of learning, on the other hand, has been influenced by the so-called 'cognitive revolution' in psychology (see the series *The Psychology of Learning and Motivation*, from 1967 up to now, especially the recent volumes edited by Bower). The area has diversified and become broader. The contributions of Thorndike, Pavlov, the early comparative psychologists, Watson, Skinner, etc., have been complemented by the work of cognitive psychologists.

Definitions of Basic Concepts

Learning is a central psychological process and several definitions of the concept have been proposed. They can be summarized in the definition presented in Squire's (1992) *Encyclopedia of Learning and Memory*: 'Learning refers to changes in behavior as a result of experience' (p. 349).

A more detailed definition states that 'Learning is an enduring change in the mechanisms of behavior involving specific stimuli and/or responses that results from prior experience with similar stimuli and responses' (Domjan, 1998, p. 13).

We will make use of our definition: 'Learning is a relatively permanent change of behavior that occurs as a result of practice' (Ardila, 1991, p. 18). In this definition learning is characterized by change, by relative permanence, and by practice. The role of reinforcement in learning is considered very relevant but not as a necessary condition. All relatively permanent behavioral changes that are the result of practice (reinforced or not) are considered learning.

Other important definitions in this area are:

Type S Learning. The conditioning of responding behavior; the letter 'S' is assigned because reinforcement is correlated with stimuli.

Type R Learning. The conditioning of operant behavior; the letter 'R' is used because the response is correlated with reinforcement.

Extinction. Reduction of the instrumental response that occurs because the response is no longer followed by the reinforcer.

Chaining. Consists of a sequence of discriminated operants such that responses during one stimulus are followed by other stimuli that reinforce those responses and set the occasion for subsequent ones.

Fading. A procedure for transferring control of responding from one stimulus or set of stimuli to another by gradually removing one while the other is gradually introduced.

Prompting. A prompt is a supplemental stimulus that raises the probability of a correct response. There are physical prompts and verbal prompts. They are frequently used in behavior modification programs, especially with children.

Shadowing. A procedure used when studying attention. Subjects are asked to shadow the attended message, emitting vocal responses that sound similar to those of the shadowed message (see Donahoe & Palmer, 1994).

Equivalent classes. A stimulus class usually produced through conditional discrimination in matching-to-sample, that includes all possible emergent relations among its members, is called an equivalent class. Stimuli that are members of an equivalent class are likely also to be functionally equivalent.

What is the Experimental Analysis of Behavior?

From the above presentation of the development of conditioning and learning, we can now turn our attention to the experimental analysis of behavior as a system. The experimental analysis of behavior (EAB) is a natural-science approach to the understanding of behavior regulation. It is concerned with controlling and changing the factors that affect the behavior of organisms. The experimental analysis of behavior implies a general scientific approach that includes assumptions about how to study behavior, methods and procedures to carry out the analysis, a systematic body of knowledge, and practical implications for society and culture (see Poling, Methot, & LeSage, 1995).

Behavior analysis is the scientific investigation of the interaction of organisms with the social and physical environment (see Ardila, 1993). It is the philosophical position of this approach that behavior is a function of its consequences. What happens following a response changes the future probability of that response.

If we observe that the behavior increases we say that the consequence was positively reinforcing; if the rate decreases, we say that the consequence was aversive. Ferster and Skinner (1957) described this in the following way: 'When an organism acts upon the environment in which it lives, it changes that environment in ways which often affect the organism itself. Some of these changes are what the layman calls rewards, or what are generally referred to technically as reinforcers: when they follow behavior in this way they increase the likelihood that the organism will behave in the same way again' (p. 1).

6.2 HABITUATION AND SENSITIZATION

Organisms adapt to the environment in many ways. Psychology has been influenced by the concepts of Darwinian evolution since the last decades of the nineteenth century, and the idea of *adaptation* has been central in the discipline since the early beginnings of psychology as a science. Adaptation is the process whereby the biological and behavioral characteristics of individuals come to be ones which favor survival and reproduction in their particular environment.

The benefit conferred by an adaptive feature can be assessed in terms of its contribution to Darwinian fitness. It is not easy to identify truly adaptive features, and to relate them to the solution of particular survival problems. In general, adaptation refers to successful adjustment to some external factors, and is a core concept in psychological explanations.

Habituation is one of the simplest forms of adaptation. It will be taken up in relation to the concept of sensitization and to the concept of reflex.

The Concept of Reflex

A *reflex* is an automatic reaction to external stimulation. A reflex involves an eliciting stimulus and a corresponding response that are linked. Presentation of the stimulus is followed by the occurrence of the response, and this response rarely occurs in the absence of the stimulus.

In a simple reflex the central nervous system receives a message from a sense organ and converts this directly into instructions for muscular contraction or glandular secretion. For example, an increase in illumination on the retina results in a reflex contraction of the iris so

that the pupil of the eye becomes smaller, cutting down the amount of light falling on the retina.

Reflexes constitute much of the behavioral repertoire of newborn infants, both nonhuman and human. Evolution has selected those repertories for their survival value to the individual and to the species. Inborn reflexes are common to the members of a given species. Learned reflexes – for instance conditioned reflexes – are specific for an individual organism. Conditioned reflexes have been one of the central topics in the psychology of learning, and the concept of conditioning has been investigated both in psychology and biology for several decades.

Adaptiveness of Habituation and Sensitization

Habituation is the decrease in responsiveness resulting from repeated stimulation. It is generally regarded as a form of learning, although it involves loss of responsiveness rather than acquisition of new responses. Habituation shows many typical features of learning including extinction and generalization. The adaptation of an organism to its environment is helped by habituation processes. Habituation reflects how an individual sorts out what to ignore and what to respond to. It is the end product of processes that help to organize and focus behavior in the ocean of ongoing stimulation.

Sensitization, on the other hand, is the increase of responsiveness. Like habituation, it is a fundamental feature of how organisms adjust to their environment. Habituation and sensitization occur in nearly all species and response systems.

Theoretical Explanations of Sensitization and Habituation

Habituation has been distinguished from sensory adaptation and from fatigue. A temporary hearing loss due to repeated exposures to a loud noise is sensory adaptation (and not habituation). The reflex response can fail to occur if the muscles involved become incapacitated by fatigue. In habituation the organism ceases to respond to a stimulus, even though it remains capable of sensing the stimulus and of making the muscle movements required for the response; the response fails to occur because changes in the nervous system block the relay of sensory neural impulses to the motor neurons (see Peeke & Petrinovich, 1984, for a detailed description of habituation, sensitization, and behavior).

Habituation is response-specific: an organism may stop responding to a stimulus in one aspect of its behavior while continuing to respond to the stimulus in other ways. Habituation is also stimulus-specific: a habituated response will quickly recover when a new stimulus is introduced.

The current theoretical explanation of habituation and sensitization is called the dual-process theory of habituation and sensitization. It assumes that there are different types of underlying neural processes responsible for increases (sensitization) and decreases (habituation) in responsiveness to stimulation. The habituation and the sensitization processes are not mutually exclusive. Both may be activated at the same time, and the behavioral outcome of the processes depends on which process is stronger. Habituation and sensitization are said to compete for control of behavior.

This theory has many applications, particularly in the area of perceptual learning. A number of investigations have been carried out in order to relate habituation and sensitization to other learning processes, especially *classical conditioning*. We will refer to this important research area next.

6.3 CLASSICAL CONDITIONING: FOUNDATIONS AND MECHANISMS

Respondent Behavior

Respondent conditioning, classical conditioning, or Pavlovian conditioning are equivalent terms. They refer to the transfer of control from one stimulus to another. Classical conditioning is considered as a 'type' of learning different from operant conditioning (also named instrumental conditioning or Skinnerian conditioning). Classical conditioning and operant conditioning are the main two areas of the psychology of learning, although social learning (Bandura, 1986) is also considered a very important 'type' of learning particularly for human beings. Research on classical conditioning began with Pavlov, and has developed in many countries of the world, not only in Russia.

When the probability of a response is determined by events that precede it, the behavior is classified as *respondent*. When the probability depends on the events that follow it, the response is classified as *operant*. Respondent behavior is to a large extent automatic and involuntary, although even voluntary behavior may have a conditioned-response function. In the particular case of human beings, classical conditioning accounts for an important segment of behavior, including emotional behavior.

Conditioned and Unconditioned Stimuli and Responses

All organisms are born with a set of reflexes, that are particular to the species. Human beings are born with an array of responses that are elicited by specific stimuli. The term *unconditioned stimulus* (US) refers to the eliciting event that is invariant, biologically based and not learned. *Unconditioned response* (UR) is the behavior evoked by the unconditioned stimulus (US). When an unconditioned stimulus elicits an unconditioned response, the relationship is called a reflex.

A *conditioned stimulus* (CS) is an arbitrary stimulus, such as a tone in the classical Pavlovian situation, that when it is associated with an unconditioned stimulus (US) – food in the Pavlovian situation – elicits a response. If the tone (CS) now elicits a response, the response to the tone is called a *conditioned response* (CR).

Originally the CS (tone) did not elicit the salivary response (UR). After several pairings the stimulus is presented alone and it now elicits a response: tone evokes salivation. The response has been learned. The association has been established between tone and salivation. See Figures 6.1 and 6.2 for the classical experimental situation, and for a diagram of the procedure.

Proximity does not guarantee conditioning, but it is necessary that the CS be a reliable predictor of the US (see a review of associative learning in Wasserman & Miller, 1997).

Many of the important concepts of conditioning and learning came from Pavlov's work. Not only the terms unconditioned stimulus, unconditioned response, conditioned stimulus, and conditioned response, but also respondent acquisition, the laws of the reflex (intensity magnitude, law of latency, law of the threshold), temporal summation, the law of reflex fatigue, respondent extinction, spontaneous recovery,

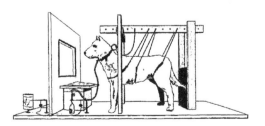

Figure 6.1 *Pavlovian salivary conditioning experimental preparation. A cannula attached to the dog's salivary duct conducts drops of saliva to a data-recording device*

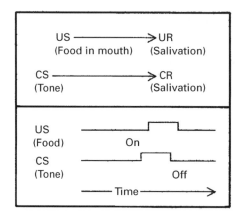

Figure 6.2   *Respondent conditioning. An arbitrary stimulus such as a tone (CS) is presented just before food is placed in the dog's mouth (US). After several pairings of tone and food, the tone is presented alone. If the tone alone now elicits salivation, it is called a conditioned stimulus (CS), and salivation to the tone is a conditioned response (CR)*

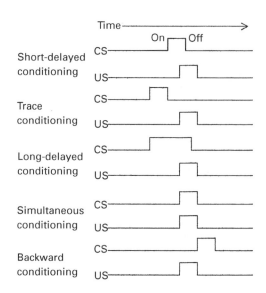

Figure 6.3   *Classical conditioning procedures*

generalization, discrimination, etc. The influence of the Pavlov school on the study of learning, conditioning, and behavior in general, has been decisive.

Classical Conditioning Procedures

In an experimental procedure it is possible to make several arrangements between CS and US. This has given origin to a number of procedures, as presented in Figure 6.3.

(a) *Simultaneous conditioning* consists of exposing subjects to a CS in conjunction with a US at the same time. The critical feature of simultaneous conditioning is that the CS and the US are presented concurrently.

(b) *Short-delayed conditioning* involves delaying the start of the US slightly after the start of the CS on each trial. This is the most frequently used procedure for classical conditioning. The critical feature of the short-delayed conditioning is that the CS starts each trial, and the US is presented after a brief delay, usually less than one minute. The CS may continue during the US or end as soon as the US starts.

(c) *Trace conditioning* is similar to short-delayed conditioning but the US is not presented until some time after the CS has ended. This leaves a gap between the CS

and the US, which is called the trace interval.

(d) *Long-delayed conditioning* is similar to short-delayed conditioning but the US is delayed much longer, usually between 5 and 10 min. There is no trace interval. The CS remains until the US occurs.

(e) *Backward conditioning*. In this procedure the US occurs shortly before, not after, the CS. The technique is called backward conditioning because the CS and US are presented in a 'backward' order compared with the other procedures.

Second-Order Respondent

Pavlov conducted experiments in what was called second-order conditioning: this procedure extends the transfer of control to events that have not been directly associated with the unconditioned stimulus. In first-order conditioning a neutral stimulus is paired with an unconditioned stimulus (US); after several pairings, the control of the response to the US is transferred to the neutral stimulus. In second-order conditioning, on the order hand, control is transferred to events that have not been directly associated with the US. These events gain control over the response because of their pairing with a conditioned stimulus (CS).

In one of these cases, Pavlov paired the tick of a metronome with food. The sound of the metronome came to evoke salivation. Because

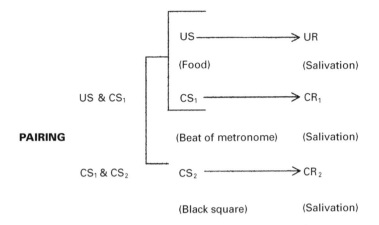

Figure 6.4 *First- and second-order conditioning. The second-order conditioned stimulus (CS₂) comes to elicit the conditioned response (CR) even though it has never been directly paired with the US*

the beat of the metronome was directly associated with the US, it is called a *first-order conditioned* stimulus (CS₁). Once the ticking sound reliably elicited salivation, Pavlov paired it with the sight of a black square. Following several pairings of the metronome beat with the black square, the sight of the black square (CS₂) evoked salivation. The black square is termed a *second-order conditioned* stimulus because it acquires control of the CR by its pairing with a first-order CS. It is important to indicate that the second-order CS (the black square) evoked the conditioned response (salivation) even though it was never directly paired with food. See Figure 6.4 for a comparison of first-order and second-order conditioning.

Pavlov considered that second-order conditioning had weak effects, but later research has indicated that it can have strong effects on behavior. Second-order conditioning is important because it extends stimulus control to events that have not been directly paired with the unconditioned stimulus. Phobic reactions can be examples of this type of conditioning. In behavior therapy this concept has been used to explain the acquisition and maintenance of a number of maladaptive behaviors.

Classical Conditioning Today

Pavlov's findings have been extended in many laboratories around the world. The contemporary work is based on the extensions of research of many investigators, among them Rescorla (see 1967, 1980, 1988; Rescorla & Wagner, 1972).

Although classical conditioning is typically investigated in laboratory situations, with human and nonhuman participants, a number of situations outside the laboratory can be explained by the classical conditioning findings. Classical conditioning is most likely to develop when one event reliably precedes another in a short-delayed CS–US pairing, and this occurs in many aspects of life. Stimuli in the daily environment occur in an orderly temporal sequence, because of the physical constraints of causation. Social institutions and customs ensure that things happen in a predictable order. Whenever certain stimuli reliably precede others, classical conditioning may take place.

Domjan (1998) mentions as examples of the prevalence of classical conditioning: conditioning of sexual behavior, infant and maternal responses during nursing, acquired food preferences and aversions in humans, etc. Turkkan (1989) describes a larger number of such situations. The conditioning of emotions and many procedures used in health psychology (among them systematic desensitization and flooding) are based on classical conditioning.

We will turn now to the other extensive area of research in the field of learning and conditioning, that is operant conditioning.

6.4 OPERANT CONDITIONING

An Area of Research and Applications

Operant conditioning is a general theoretical orientation that applies the techniques and concepts of instrumental learning to the full range of human and animal behavior. It is a system derived from the work of B. F. Skinner (1938, 1953, 1971, 1990). Its origins can be traced to Thorndike (1898, 1911), Watson (1913, 1930), and Pavlov (1927).

Operant conditioning seeks to identify the environmental determinants of behavior by means of an experimental analysis. All behavior is assumed to have its ultimate origins in the environment. The past and present environments of the individual affect behavior through the principle of reinforcement. The ancestral environment of the individual affects behavior through genetic mechanisms whose effects are summarized by the principle of natural selection. Both natural selection and reinforcement hold in common the belief that future behavior may be understood by examining the consequences of past behavior. In the case of natural selection, behaviors and structures are selected if they enhance reproductive fitness. In the case of reinforcement, behaviors are strengthened if they have been followed by critical events termed reinforcers. Lever pressing, if followed by food, would likely be strengthened in rats; talking, if followed by attention, would likely be strengthened in humans.

In operant conditioning it is assumed that the behavior of all organisms, human and non-human, is ultimately shaped by the environment. The aim of operant conditioning is to analyze the interaction between the organism and its environment into a three-term sequence or contingency. The product of the experimental analysis is to identify the environmental events (discriminative stimuli) that determine the occurrence of the behavior (operant) and of the environmental events (reinforcers) necessary for the acquisition and maintenance of the behavior. The term 'operant' is used in order to emphasize that this behavior operates on the subsequent environment to produce certain consequences.

Contingencies

Operant conditioning is interested in describing and explaining the relationship between behavior and the environmental events: antecedents and consequences. This relationship is called a contingency. It includes three components: (A) Antecedent events, (B) Behavior, and (C) Consequent events. This ABC or contingency lies in the center of behavior analysis and has been studied from the experimental and practical point of view.

Antecedent events (A) refer to stimuli before the behavior, such as sound, lights, gestures, instructions, etc. Behaviors (B) are the acts themselves (some response that the organism performs). Consequences (C) refer to events that

follow behavior. The description of behavior depends on understanding the types of antecedent events and consequences that influence behavior and how they operate.

The investigation of the antecedents of behavior includes the *contexts* in which behavior and *consequences* occur. The study of *consequences* is usually given priority in operant conditioning, more than the antecedents of behavior. This is due to the fact that many antecedent events acquire their influence because of their association with certain consequences. Understanding antecedent events is facilitated by outlining different consequences. In order to alter a particular behavior (in a behavior modification program), a consequence must be dependent or *contingent upon* the occurrence of that behavior: behavior change takes place when certain consequences are contingent upon performance. We say that a consequence is contingent when it is delivered only after the target behavior has been performed (and is otherwise not available). The noncontingent delivery of consequences does not result on systematic changes in a preselected target behavior.

The Principle of Reinforcement

Reinforcement refers to the increase in the frequency of a response when that response is immediately followed by certain consequences. As stated before, the consequence that follows behavior must be contingent upon behavior. A *reinforcer* is a contingent event that increases the frequency of behavior. Reinforcers have been classified as positive and negative: a *positive reinforcer* is an event that, presented after a response has been performed, increases the frequency of the behavior that follows. On the other hand, *negative reinforcers* are events that, removed after a response has been performed, increase the behavior preceding their removal.

Positive reinforcement is the process of increasing the frequency of a response that is followed by a favorable event (positive reinforcer). A positive reinforcer is defined by its effect on behavior. If an event follows a behavior and the frequency of that behavior increases, the event is a positive reinforcer. An increase in the frequency or probability of the preceding behavior is the defining characteristics of a positive reinforcer.

Positive reinforcers can be *primary* or *unconditioned* (food, water, etc.), or *secondary* or *conditioned*. Primary reinforcers serve as such without special training. Secondary or conditioned reinforcers, on the contrary, are not automatically reinforcing but acquire their reinforcing properties by being paired with events that are already reinforcing (primary reinforcers, or other secondary reinforcers already acquired). Stimuli or events that were once neutral may acquire reinforcing properties. In daily life there are many instances of conditioned reinforcers: money, praise, grades, etc., that acquired reinforcing value through learning. If a neutral stimulus is repeatedly presented prior to or along with a reinforcing stimulus, the neutral stimulus becomes a reinforcer.

When a conditioned reinforcer is paired with many other reinforcers it becomes a *generalized conditioned reinforcer*. Examples are attention, approval, affection, and money. Generalized conditioned reinforcers are very effective in altering behavior because they have been paired with a variety of events that are themselves reinforcing (attention may by followed by physical contact, smiles, affection, etc.).

What is a positive reinforcer for one person may not be such for another one. Also an event can be a positive reinforcer for a person under one situation and not under other circumstances (praise, touching). There is no guarantee that a particular event will be reinforcing. This has important implications in applied behavior analysis programs.

Negative Reinforcement

The removal of an aversive agent contingent upon a response is called negative reinforcement. It refers to the increase in the frequency of a response by removing an aversive event immediately after the response has been performed. An event is a negative reinforcer only if its removal after a response increases performance of that response. A negative reinforcer, like a positive reinforcer, is defined solely by its effect on behavior.

Reinforcement (positive or negative) always refers to an increase in behavior. Negative reinforcement requires an ongoing aversive event that can be removed or terminated after a specific response has been performed. For instance very loud music is an aversive stimulus, and to terminate it can be reinforcing. The behavior that terminates the loud music (screaming, swearing, making a threat) is negatively reinforced because it was followed by elimination of the aversive event. In the future the behavior of screaming, swearing, and threatening will increase.

Because the use of negative reinforcement requires the presentation to the individual of some aversive event – that can be removed or reduced immediately after he or she responds – negative reinforcement is seldom used in applied behavior analysis programs. The undesirability of using aversive stimuli has been demonstrated, and positive procedures are always preferred.

There are two types of negative reinforcers, primary and secondary. *Primary negative reinforcers* include shock, loud noise, intense stimuli, and are not learned. *Secondary negative reinforcers*, on the other hand, are conditioned or learned: aversive events become aversive by being paired with events that are already aversive.

Negative reinforcement is different from punishment, and in general from avoidance. This research topic, avoidance learning, has been investigated in the operant conditioning laboratory, and the differences among avoidance, escape, and punishment have been spelled out.

Punishment, Avoidance and Escape

Punishment is defined as the presentation of an aversive event or the removal of a positive event following a response, which decreases the frequency of that response (Kazdin, 1994, p. 38). Azrin and Holz (1966) had defined that 'punishment is the reduction of the future probability of a specific response as a result of the immediate delivery of a stimulus for that response. The stimulus is designed as a punishing stimulus; the entire process is designated as punishment' (p. 381).

It is important to indicate that punishment is defined only by the effect on behavior. Punishment is operative only if the frequency of a response is reduced. It has been found that in many cases the reduction of the punished behavior is not permanent.

In one type of punishment, an aversive event is presented after a response (being reprimanded or slapped after engaging in some behavior is an example of this kind of punishment). The second type of punishment implies the removal of a positive event after a response (losing privileges is one example). In general terms, punishment always refers to procedures that decrease a response. In contrast, negative reinforcement increases the response.

Avoidance is the performance of a behavior that postpones or averts the presentation of an aversive event. *Escape*, on the other hand, is the performance of a behavior that terminates an aversive event. In the escape situation the organism receives the aversive event, and leaves the situation (escapes). In the avoidance situation the response is emitted before the aversive event takes place. For instance the person runs away when he or she is getting wet in the rain (he or she escapes the rain). In the other case the person runs before getting wet (avoids the rain).

This area of research is an example of the interaction between classical and operant conditioning. The conditioned aversive event elicits an escape response (classical conditioning) that is negatively reinforced (operant conditioning). For a description of operant-Pavlovian interactions, including many other research areas, see Davis and Hurwitz (1977).

The Premack Principle

A new way of considering the effects of reinforcement came about with the work of Premack (1965). He indicated that allowing an individual to engage in certain responses can be used as a reinforcer. When an individual is given the opportunity to select among various responses, behaviors performed with a relatively high frequency can reinforce behaviors performed with a relatively low frequency. In other words, a higher-probability behavior can reinforce a lower-probability behavior.

In more formal terms, the Premack principle says: of any pair of responses or activities in which an individual engages, the more frequent one will reinforce the less frequent one (Premack, 1965, p. 132). To determine what behaviors are high or low in frequency requires observing the activities a person performs when given the opportunity to engage in behavior without restraints (what the person does in his/her free time, on the weekends, at the end of work or at the end of school, etc.).

A behavior observed to occur more frequently can be used to follow and reinforce a lower-frequency behavior. For many children, playing with friends is performed at a higher frequency than studying. If the higher-frequency behavior (playing) is made contingent upon the lower-frequency behavior (studying), the lower-probability behavior will increase.

Timberlake and Allison (1974) have attempted to explain the effectiveness of making one response contingent upon another. They state that the individual is deprived of opportunities to perform the desired (high-probability) behavior, when the behavior is made contingent upon completing some other response (low-probability behavior). This response-deprivation hypothesis states that performance of the target response increases in order to overcome the decreased rate (deprivation), of the preferred response.

The Premack principle has given origin to a new way of studying reinforcement. A large number of applications have been found. One of the main foundations of the new area of *behavioral economics* (see Green & Kagel, 1987, 1990) is the Premack principle. Probably this line of research will continue to be very important in the near future as a new way of conceptualizing reinforcement.

When a behavior is emitted, it is not always followed by reinforcement. As a matter of fact, not all classes of responses have consistent consequences. The reinforcement of some responses but not others is called partial reinforcement, and intermittent reinforcement. Schedules can arrange reinforcement on the basis of response number, time, or the rate of responding. Number, time, and rate can be combined in diverse ways to produce complex schedules.

The study of schedules gave origin to a systematic investigation of behavioral relations, and laid the foundations of a behavioral technology. The book by Ferster and Skinner (1957) *Schedules of Reinforcement* that originated the whole area of research and application, was evaluated by Cheney 40 years later in the following terms: '*Schedules* was one the first extensive presentations of single-subject behavior research to appear in the literature since Ebbinghaus's work 44 years earlier. The demonstration of such control and predictability had never been seen in behavior science before. In this regard *Schedules* was a major contribution to the formation of an independent science of behavior relations' (Cheney, 1997, p. ix).

6.5 COMPLEX LEARNING, STIMULUS CONTROL, AND VERBAL BEHAVIOR

Complex Learning

The complexities of behavior can be understood according to discriminations and differentiations arranged into appropriate chains of patterns. One of the goals of the experimental analysis of behavior has been the understanding of complex behavior using the basic tools of analysis, and a large amount of work has been done in that direction for several decades. Problem-solving, imitation, concept learning, insight, cognition, and many other basic psychological processes have been investigated using the conceptual frame of reference of the experimental analysis of behavior. Only a few examples of this work will be presented here.

People often do what others do, and our culture looks for and reinforces similarity, both in saying and in doing. There is spontaneous imitation in humans, and also learned imitation. Bandura (1986) has done research in social learning and imitation and argued that a cognitive theory of observational learning is required.

Complex behavior cannot be learned by observation until the component skills have been mastered. It is impossible to fly a plane by mere observation; when the separate skills have been acquired, observing others can provide information on how to sequence complex performances, especially with corrective feedback. It has also been found that the anticipated consequences of imitation determine whether an imitation response will occur. Individuals who expect positive outcome are likely to perform actions they have witnessed, and those who expect negative consequences are less likely to imitate such actions. From an operant perspective, imitation is most likely to occur in situations in which it has been reinforced previously, and is unlikely in situations in which it has been extinguished or punished.

Bandura has considered that 'the more interesting effect of modeling is what I call "abstract modeling". From observing examples, people derive general rules and principles of behavior which permit them to go beyond what they see and hear' (Bandura in an interview with Evans, 1980, p. 160).

This leads us to the study of *equivalence classes*. They are the cumulative products of selection after a learner has been exposed to a series of differential training procedures called contextual discriminations. In a *contextual discrimination*, a stimulus guides one response in one stimulus context and the same stimulus guides a different response in a second stimulus context. In other words, the environment–behavior relation selected by a reinforcer depends on the context in which the guiding stimulus appears. Equivalence classes play a crucial role in the development of complex environment–behavior relations.

Differential Responding

Stimulus control refers to a change in behavior that occurs when either a discriminative stimulus (S^D) or an extinction stimulus (S^Δ) is presented. When the discriminative stimulus is presented, the probability of response increases; when the extinction stimulus is presented, the probability of response decreases.

When an organism makes a response in one situation but not in another, we say that it *discriminates* between the situations. The simplest way to train a differential response or discrimination is to reinforce an operant in one

situation and withhold reinforcement in the other. A pigeon is reinforced for pecking the key in a Skinner box when a red light is present and not when a green light is present. It learns to discriminate between the two stimuli and to respond when the key is illuminated with the red light.

In everyday life human behavior is changed by signs, symbols, spoken words, or gestures. When social or nonsocial events precede operant behavior and affect its occurrence, they are called controlling stimuli.

The current work on stimulus and response *generalization*, learning factors in stimulus control, *equivalence*, and *context* cues, etc., has led to the discovery of a number of behavioral laws that have been applied in many settings (see Catania, 1992).

Verbal Behavior

Some of the most complex behaviors that humans engage in are concerned with language. The experimental analysis of behavior has given origin to a highly original way of studying language, thinking, and problem solving which is centered on what is called *verbal behavior* (see Hayes, 1989; Hayes, Hayes, Sato, & Ono, 1994; Skinner, 1957). It is clear that humans are social animals, and that an important aspect of human social behavior involves the regulation of the actions of others by speaking, writing, signing, and gesturing. The study of verbal behavior is concerned with the performance of a speaker and the environmental conditions that establish and maintain such performance. Verbal behavior refers to the vocal, written, and gestural performances of a speaker, writer, or communicator. This behavior operates on the listener, reader, or observer, who arranges for reinforcement of the verbal performance.

Verbal behavior affects the environment *indirectly*, while nonverbal behavior affects the environment directly. In a nonverbal situation, the person performs a behavior (lifting a glass, for instance) that produces an effect (change in perceptual stimulation because of the change in position of the glass). On the contrary, verbal behavior only works through its effect on other people ('Bring me the glass, please'). It is important to make clear that verbal behavior includes gestures, body movements, and other ways of indirectly operating on the environment through its effects on others, and not only talking. Manual signing is an example of this.

Rule-governed behavior, a very active area of research and applications, is a term used to describe the behavior of the listener. Verbal behavior is used to specify the performance of the speaker. The two concepts are closely related, of course. Rule-governed behavior includes the effects of instructions, advice, maxims, and laws on the listener's behavior. Rules are seen as complex discriminative stimuli, and the principles that govern stimulus control also regulate the behavior of the listener.

The practice of the *verbal community* refer to the customary ways that people reinforce the behavior of a speaker. The contingencies that regulate verbal behavior arise from the practices of people in the community. This concept, verbal community, implies that verbal behavior is established and maintained by the reinforcing practices of the community or culture.

The study of verbal behavior has been very controversial and given origin to many polemics. Some linguists consider that the principles of operant conditioning cannot be applied to the study of language. In spite of those criticisms, the area of verbal behavior has advanced considerably and is integrated with the study of symbolic behavior, problem solving, and cognition. Verbal behavior has progressed beyond Skinner (see Hayes, 1989). Verbal behavior is concerned with tacts, mands, intraverbal responses, echoic responses, textual responses, the three-term contingencies in natural speech, equivalence relations, and similar problems. For some international contributions to the area of verbal behavior see Gottschalk and Lolas (1987); Gottschalk, Winget, Gleser, and Lolas (1984).

6.6 Applied Behavior Analysis

Learning and its Applications

Since its beginning as a laboratory science, behavior analysis has been concerned with practical applications. Even in the early period of emphasis on basic research with rats and pigeons, the possibility of applying behavioral analysis to relevant social issues was a central concern of a number of investigators, including Skinner (1953).

The principles of conditioning and the experimental analysis of behavior have been applied in many areas of social relevance. Applications in the fields of environmental protection, clinical psychology, health, job effectiveness, sport training, violence prevention, poverty, sexism, racism, contingency management in institutions, and peace and conflict resolution, and so forth, are examples of the work in this discipline of applied behavior analysis.

As an example of applications we can mention *behavior therapy*. At the early stages of development, it was called conditioning therapy. It is based on the work of Pavlov, Bechterev, and Watson and learning theory. In the last decades the approach called cognitive–behavior therapy has been one of the main trends in clinical psychology at the international level. In behavior therapy neurotic behavior is seen as learned behavior. The application of learning theory to clinical problems promised to carry the discipline beyond diagnosis, and to close the gap between the laboratory and the clinic. One of the basic foundations of behavior therapy is the belief that behavioral disorders are essentially learned responses, and that modern learning theory has much to teach clinicians concerning the acquisition and extinction of such responses.

Another example of applications is *behavior analysis in education*. It refers to the application of conditioning and learning principles to educational problems, including all the educational system: from pre-school days to post-university education. Applied behavior analysis studies learning processes in 'special' populations (mentally-retarded people, gifted students, individuals with learning disabilities, blind persons, highly creative men and women, etc.), and the normal population (high school students, university students, and so forth).

In applied behavior analysis, the dominant view is social learning theory, which recognizes the importance of both environmental and cognitive influences and their interaction. This applies to the clinical area (cognitive-behavior therapy), the educational area (applied behavior analysis in education, the cognitive-behavioral approach), and to other fields. As Kazdin (1994) pointed out: 'The overall questions of applied behavior analysis concern the extent to which principles developed in laboratory research can be useful in developing effective treatment, education, and rehabilitation programs and the extent to which human behavior can be altered in significant ways to improve functioning in everyday life' (p. 26).

Because the focus of the discipline is on the environmental events that directly alter behavior, the principles, research designs, observational techniques, methods of analysis, and so forth, transfer readily to an applied science. Applied behavior analysis is a field of study that is focused on the applications of the principles, methods, and procedures of the science of behavior.

Concentration on *research* is one of the characteristics of applied behavior analysis. Another one is the emphasis on changing *behavior*, more than changing cognitions or feelings (although a behavior change produces changes in cognition and feelings). Emphasis is on *human* behavior, and in *socially relevant* problems. Rule-governed behavior, instructions, and contingency management are given great importance.

As indicated previously, in the last few decades applied behavior analysis has been characterized by seven key words: applied, behavioral, analytic, technological, conceptual, effective, and capable of appropriately generalized outcomes. Examples of this applied work can be found in journals such a *Behavior Therapy, Journal of Applied Behavior Analysis, Behaviour Research and Therapy, Journal of Behavior Therapy and Experimental Psychiatry, Behavior Modification, Behavioral Interventions, Cognitive and Behavioral Practice, Revista Mexicana de Análisis de la Conducta/Mexican Journal of Behavior Analysis, Análisis y Modificación de Conducta, Scandinavian Journal of Behavior Therapy, Science et Comportement, Verhaltenstherapie, Japanese Journal of Behavior Therapy*, and many others, in several countries of the world.

Applications to Society and Cultural Design

In the early stages of applied behavior analysis, work was centered on more 'traditional' aspects of applied psychology: clinical problems, industrial/organizational issues, educational factors, etc. In more recent times the applications have covered a new spectrum of areas: youth violence, racism, productivity, sexism, child maltreatment, conflict resolution, drug abuse, community psychology, and many others (Mattaini & Thyer, 1996; Plaud & Eifert, 1998).

The larger context of this approach to social issues is *cultural design* and the work on *cultural practices*. Sociocultural phenomena constitute the most crucial level of selection, besides genetic selection and operant selection (Skinner, 1981). Cultural practices are a special case of operants: behavior transmitted among individuals and across generations. They are maintained by established and relatively stable networks of reinforcement, usually social in nature. A group that shares a culture is a cultural entity, and culture is defined by Skinner as the contingencies of social reinforcement maintained by a group. Nations, families, communities, and organizations are groups, according

to this definition. Cultural practices require a system of interlocking social reinforcement that is necessary to stabilize the social practice.

Cultural design refers to the explicit planning, establishing and stabilization of cultural practices, cultural entities, and cultures (see Biglan, 1995; Glenn, 1991; Guerin, 1994; Lamal, 1991; also Harris, 1979).

6.7 CONCLUSIONS

Conditioning and learning have come a long way since the early days of Pavlov, Thorndike, Watson, and Skinner, up to the present time with the emphasis on rule-governed behavior, verbal behavior, applications to social issues, cultural design, and even designs of societies like Walden Two (Skinner, 1948) and Walden Three (Ardila, 1990).

The emphasis on large-scale applications, and the hopes for a better world based on science, and particularly in psychology as the science of behavior, was made clear by Skinner (1971):

> Almost all our major problems involve human behavior, and they cannot be solved by physical and biological technology alone. What is needed is a technology of behavior, but we have been slow to develop the science from which such a technology might be drawn ... The role of natural selection in evolution was formulated only a little more than a hundred years ago, and the selective role of the environment in shaping and maintaining the behavior of the individual is only beginning to be recognized and studied ... A scientific analysis ... raises questions concerning 'values'. Who will use a technology and to what ends? Until these issues are resolved, a technology of behavior will continue to be rejected, and with it possibly the only way to solve our problems. (pp. 22–23)

Behavior analysis is interested in cultural evolution because changes in culture alter the social conditioning of individual behavior. The analysis of cultural evolution suggests how the social environment is arranged and rearranged to support specific forms of human behavior. And as we have just seen from the above quotation by Skinner, behavior analysts suggest that the solution to many social problems require a technology of cultural design.

At the beginning of a new century and a new millennium – according to the Western civilization calendar – the interest in the planning of the future, and in new scenarios, has become a crucial topic. The contribution of behavior analysis to these issues can be very relevant.

From the basic experimental work with animals done in the early twentieth century by Pavlov and Thorndike to the contemporary interest in the future and in large-scale social planning, there is no doubt that conditioning and the experimental analysis of behavior have come a long way.

RESOURCE REFERENCES

Ardila, R., López López, W., Pérez-Acosta, A. M., Quiñones, R., & Reyes, F. D. (Eds.). (1998). *Manual de análisis experimental del comportamiento* [Handbook of experimental analysis of behavior]. Madrid, Spain: Editorial Biblioteca Nueva.

Blackman, D. E., & Lejeune, H. (Eds.). (1990). *Behaviour analysis in theory and practice*. Hove, UK: Erlbaum.

Catania, A. C. (1998). *Learning* (4th ed.). Englewood Cliffs, NJ: Prentice-Hall.

Donahoe, J. W., & Palmer, D. C. (1994). *Learning and complex behavior*. Boston: Allyn & Bacon.

Lattal, K. A., & Perone, M. (Eds.). (1998). *Handbook of research methods in human operant behavior*. New York: Plenum Press.

Lee, V. L. (1988). *Beyond behaviorism*. Hillsdale, NJ: Erlbaum.

Pavlov, I. P. (1927). *Conditioned reflexes*. London: Oxford University Press.

Pierce, W. D., & Epling, W. F. (1995). *Behavior analysis and learning*. Englewood Cliffs, NJ: Prentice-Hall.

Poling, A., Methot, L. L., & LeSage, M. G. (1995). *Fundamentals of behavior analytic research*. New York: Plenum Press.

Sidman, M. (1988). *Tactics of scientific research. Evaluating experimental data in psychology*. Boston: Authors Cooperative.

Journals

Behavioral and Physiological Science (previously *Conditional Reflex*, and *Pavlovian Journal of Biological Science*).
Integrative Behavioral and Physiological Science
Journal of the Experimental Analysis of Behavior
Journal of Applied Behavior Analysis
Learning and Motivation
The Behavior Analyst

Database

PsycSCAN: Behavior Analysis and Therapy (founded in 1995. Published by the American Psychological Association, Division 25).

ADDITIONAL LITERATURE CITED

Ardila, R. (1990). *Walden three*. New York: Carlton Press.

Ardila, R. (1991). *Psicología del aprendizaje* [Psychology of learning] (22nd ed.). México: Siglo XXI Editores.

Ardila, R. (1993). *Síntesis experimental del comportamiento* [Experimental synthesis of behavior]. Bogotá: Editorial Planeta.

Azrin, N. H., & Holz, W. C. (1966). Punishment. In W. K. Honig (Ed.), *Operant conditioning: Areas of research and application* (pp. 380–447). New York: Appleton-Century-Crofts.

Baer, D. M., Wolf, M. M., & Risley, T. R. (1987). Some still-current dimensions of applied behavior analysis. *Journal of Applied Behavior Analysis, 20*, 313–327.

Bandura, A. (1986). *Social foundations of thought and action: A social cognitive theory*. Englewood Cliffs, NJ: Prentice-Hall.

Biglan, A. (1995). *Changing cultural practices*. Reno, NV: Context Press.

Boakes, R. (1984). *From Darwin to behaviorism*. New York: Cambridge University Press.

Bower, G. H. (Ed.). (1967). *The psychology of learning and motivation* (Vols. 1–35). New York: Academic Press. (Currently edited by D. Medin.)

Catania, A. C. (1992). *Learning* (3rd ed.). Englewood Cliffs, NJ: Prentice-Hall.

Cheney, C. D. (1997). Foreword I. In C. B. Ferster & B. F. Skinner, *Schedules of reinforcement*. Reprinted: Acton, MA: Copley Publishing Group.

Davis, H., & Hurwitz, H. M. B. (Eds.). (1977). *Operant-Pavlovian interactions*. Hillsdale, NJ: Erlbaum.

Day, W. F. (1980). The historical antecedents of contemporary behaviorism. In R. W. Rieber & K. Salzinger (Eds.), *Psychology: Theoretical-historical perspectives* (pp. 203–262). New York: Academic Press.

Domjan, M. (1998). *The principles of learning and behavior* (4th ed.). Pacific Grove, CA: Brooks/Cole.

Evans, R. L. (1980). *The making of social psychology. Discussions with creative contributors*. New York: Gardner Press.

Ferster, C. B., & Skinner, B. F. (1957). *Schedules of reinforcement*. New York: Appleton-Century-Crofts.

Glenn, S. (1991). Contingencies and metacontingencies: Relations among behavioral, cultural, and biological evolution. In P. A. Lamal (Ed.), *Behavioral analysis of societies and cultural practices* (pp. 39–73). New York: Hemisphere.

Gottschalk, L. A., & Lolas, F. (1987). *Estudios sobre análisis del comportamiento verbal* [Studies of the analysis of verbal behavior]. Santiago, Chile: Editorial Universitaria.

Gottschalk, L. A., Winget, C. N., Gleser, G. C., & Lolas, F. (1984). *Análisis de la conducta verbal* [Analysis of verbal behavior]. Santiago, Chile: Editorial Universitaria.

Green, L., & Kagel, J. H. (Eds.). (1987, 1990). *Advances in behavioral economics*, Vol. 1 and 2. Norwood, NJ: Ablex.

Guerin, B. (1994). *Analyzing social behavior. Behavior analysis and the social sciences*. Reno, NV: Context Press.

Harris, M. (1979). *Cultural materialism: The struggle for a science of culture*. New York: Random House.

Hayes, S. C. (Ed.). (1989). *Rule-governed behavior*. New York: Plenum Press.

Hayes, S. C., Hayes, L. J., Sato, M., & Ono, K. (Eds.). (1994). *Behavior analysis of language and cognition*. Reno, NV: Context Press.

Kantor, J. R. (1959). *Interbehavioral psychology*. Chicago: Principia Press.

Kazdin, A. E. (1978). *History of behavior modification. Experimental foundations of contemporary research*. Baltimore, MD: University Park Press.

Kazdin, A. E. (1994). *Behavior modification in applied settings* (5th ed.). Pacific Grove, CA: Brooks/Cole.

Lamal, P. A. (Ed.). (1991). *Behavioral analysis of societies and cultural practices*. New York: Hemisphere.

Mattaini, M. A., & Thyer, B. A. (Eds.). (1996). *Finding solutions to social problems. Behavioral strategies for change*. Washington, DC: American Psychological Association.

Miller, S., & Konorski, J. (1928). Sur une forme particulière des reflexes conditionnels. *Comptes Rendus des Seances de la Societé de Biologie et de ses Filiales, 99*, 1155–1157.

Morris, E. K. (1988). Contextualism: The world view of behavior analysis. *Journal of Experimental Child Psychology, 46*, 289–323.

Morris, E. K. (1998). Tendencias actuales en el análisis experimental del comportamiento [Current trends in the experimental analysis of behavior]. In Ardila, R., Lopez Lopez, W., Pérez-Acost, A. M., Quiñones, R., & Reyes, F. D. (Eds.), *Manual de análisis experimental del comportamiento* [Handbook of experimental analysis of behavior]. Madrid, Spain: Editorial Biblioteca Nueva.

Peeke, V. S., & Petrinovich, L. (Eds.). (1984). *Habituation, sensitization, and behavior*. New York: Academic Press.

Plaud, J. J., & Eifert, G. H. (Eds.). (1998). *From behavior theory to behavior therapy*. Boston: Allyn and Bacon.

Premack, D. (1965). Reinforcement theory. In D. Levine (Ed.), *Nebraska Symposium on Motivation*

(pp. 123–180). Lincoln, NE: University of Nebraska Press.

Rachlin, H. (1994). *Behavior and mind: The roots of modern psychology*. New York: Oxford University Press.

Rescorla, R. A. (1967). Pavlovian conditioning and its proper control procedures. *Psychological Review, 74*, 71–80.

Rescorla, R. A. (1980). *Pavlovian second-order conditioning*. Hillsdale, NJ: Erlbaum.

Rescorla, R. A. (1988). Pavlovian conditioning: It's not what you think it is. *American Psychologist, 43*, 151–160.

Rescorla, R. A., & Wagner, A. R. (1972). A theory of Pavlovian conditioning: Variations in the effectiveness of reinforcement and nonreinforcement. In A. H. Black & W. F. Prokasy (Eds.), *Classical conditioning II: Current research and theory* (pp. 64–69). New York: Appleton-Century-Crofts.

Skinner, B. F. (1938). *The behavior of organisms*. New York: Appleton-Century-Crofts.

Skinner, B. F. (1947). Experimental psychology. In W. Dennis (Ed.), *Current trends in psychology* (pp. 16–49). Pittsburgh, PA: University of Pittsburgh Press.

Skinner, B. F. (1948). *Walden two*. New York: Macmillan.

Skinner, B. F. (1953). *Science and human behavior*. New York: Macmillan.

Skinner, B. F. (1957). *Verbal behavior*. New York: Appleton-Century-Crofts.

Skinner, B. F. (1963). Behaviorism at fifty. *Science, 140*, 951–958.

Skinner, B. F. (1971). *Beyond freedom and dignity*. New York: Knopf.

Skinner, B. F. (1974). *About behaviorism*. New York: Knopf.

Skinner, B. F. (1981). Selection by consequences. *Science, 213*, 501–504.

Skinner, B. F. (1990). Can psychology be a science of mind? *American Psychologist, 45*, 1206-1210.

Smith, L. D. (1986). *Behaviorism and logical positivism: A reassessment of the alliance*. Stanford, CA: Stanford University Press.

Squire, L. R. (Ed.). (1992). *Encyclopedia of learning and memory*. New York: Macmillan.

Thorndike, E. L. (1898). Animal intelligence: An experimental study of the association processes in animals. *Psychological Review Monograph, 2* (No 8).

Thorndike, E. L. (1911). *Animal intelligence: Experimental studies*. New York: Macmillan.

Timberlake, W., & Allison, J. (1974). Response deprivation: An empirical approach to instrumental performance. *Psychological Review, 81*, 146–164.

Turkkan, J. S. (1989). Classical conditioning: The new hegemony. *The Behavioral and Brain Sciences, 12*, 121–179.

Wasserman, E. A., & R. R. Miller (1997). What's
elementary about associative learning? *Annual
Review of Psychology, 48,* 573–607.

Watson, J. B. (1913). Psychology as the behaviorist
views it. *Psychological Review, 20,* 158–177.

Watson, J. B. (1930). *Behaviorism.* New York:
Norton.

Zuriff, G. E. (1985). *Behaviorism: A conceptual
reconstruction.* New York: Columbia University
Press.

Communications concerning this chapter should be addressed to: Professor Rubén Ardila, National University of
Columbia, Bogotá, Columbia

7

Memory Processes

HENRY L. ROEDIGER, III AND MICHELLE L. MEADE

Contemplation of the marvels of human memory is one of the oldest topics in the Western tradition. Lucid descriptions of the puzzles provided by memory were included in the dialogues of Plato and the discourses of Aristotle. Philosophers provided 2,000 years of interesting theorizing and speculation before the methods of science were directed at the issue of how memory works. The starting point for scientific exploration of memory was the great experimental work begun by Hermann Ebbinghaus (1850–1909) in 1879, culminating in publication of *Über das Gedächtnis* in 1885 (with an English translation published in 1913 with the title, *Memory: A contribution to experimental psychology*). In this chapter we briefly summarize the modern understanding of human memory from the perspective of experimental psychologists. However, many different traditions exist among scholars and researchers studying memory, from humanistic traditions in fields such as history and literature to other scientific approaches from neurobiology, cognitive neuroscience, and animal learning and behavior. We make occasional reference to these other fields, but concentrate here on research from experimental psychology.

We begin the chapter with two historical landmarks of the field. Next we turn to some basic methods that are commonly used and some fundamental findings that have resulted from these methods. Following this section comes a brief consideration of theories of memory phenomena. We next include an experiment in some detail that provides a sample of research and how it is conducted. Finally, we consider some ways the psychology of memory has had an impact on applied issues outside the laboratory.

7.1 TWO APPROACHES TO THE STUDY OF MEMORY

Ebbinghaus's scientific achievement was remarkable. He was the first person to empirically study memory, so he could not rely on the knowledge gained in past experiments to guide his own research. In light of such conditions, one may have expected the first advances in the study of memory to have been small ones, perhaps a few poorly crafted, ill-controlled experiments leading to results that could not be replicated by later researchers. However, nothing could be further from the truth in this case. Ebbinghaus developed impeccable scientific methods and collected data that have proved reliable; all his main experimental results have been replicated.

Ebbinghaus developed his own materials, invented an ingenious method of measuring retention, and examined many variables that have potent effects on memory. The materials were three-letter nonsense syllables (e.g., ZAK, FER), which were intended to minimize the influence of past language skills on learning new information. He placed these syllables in long lists and tried to memorize them by reading aloud each item in time to a metronome so as to guarantee control over study time. After reading the list, he would try to recite it. If he did not succeed, he would read it and again attempt to recite it from memory. The measure of learning was then the number of these study/test trials (or the amount of time) that it would take to reach the criterion of one perfect recitation. This measure is called a trials-to-criterion measure of learning.

But how to measure retention at some later point, say a week later? Ebbinghaus could have tried to recall the list, but he memorized so many there was no way to keep them straight. Further, he realized that even if he could not recall the list, this failure might not indicate that all traces of it had vanished from memory. Ebbinghaus solved the problem by developing his ingenious relearning and savings method. When he wanted to test his retention at some later point, he would again present the list to himself and try to recite it, repeating the process until he could again correctly recall the entire list. The smaller number of trials needed to relearn the list than had been required to learn it on the first occasion provided a measure of savings. He expressed this difference as a function of the number of possible trials that could be saved multiplied by 100 to create a percentage savings score. So, for example, if it took 15 trials to learn the list on the first occasion, but only five trials to perform the same feat a week later, the savings score would be $15 - 5 \div 15 \times 100$ for 66% savings, in this case. Of course, if the list took 15 trials to relearn, then the savings score would be zero (it took as many trials to relearn the list as it took to learn in the first place) and no measurable retention of the list would be obtained. The savings measure permits detection of retention when other measures such as recall or even recognition might

fail. (However, even if savings is zero, that does not necessarily mean that no effect of the prior experience remains; it just means that this measure failed to detect it.)

Ebbinghaus (1885/1913) conducted several year's worth of research with his new methods and reported the results in his book. He showed some findings that are obvious – longer lists take more trials to learn than shorter lists – but many others which were less obvious. For example, presentations of lists that were spaced apart in time led to better long-term retention (greater savings) than did massed presentation of the lists, or when the same list was repeatedly read in succession. Besides his elegant results (all obtained with himself as the only subject!), Ebbinghaus also provided an excellent analysis of statistics, developed an early mathematical model (of forgetting), provided a good account of the problem of experimenter bias, and created what may have been the first example of competitive hypothesis testing in experimental psychology. Ebbinghaus started the scientific study of memory off on a sure footing and many others followed his lead. He began what was later called the verbal learning tradition in the study of memory.

Another important tradition in the study of memory derives from a book by a British psychologist, Frederic Bartlett (1886–1969) in 1932. In *Remembering: A study in experimental and social psychology*, Bartlett performed rather casual experiments using prose materials and pictures. He argued that these were more like materials people encountered in their daily lives than were nonsense syllables and he made a point of testing people in more natural settings rather than under strict laboratory conditions. Bartlett showed how people would often recall material inaccurately, but that the errors were often plausible ones. For example, in recalling a native American folktale called 'The war of the ghosts' that contained supernatural details unfamiliar to his British college students, Bartlett noted that the students would often drop out these peculiar elements or, if the elements were recalled, subjects would give the elements a new meaning to make them fit better with the way they organized the story, a process he called rationalization. Bartlett developed the concept of schemata to explain the assimilation and later reconstruction of events. People interpret events of the world through their current knowledge structures, or schemata, and these organizational schemes also guide recall.

Bartlett emphasized the constructive nature of remembering: remembering was not the consultation of lifeless memory traces stored in the brain, but rather an active construction using bits of past experience woven together with current expectations and knowledge. This emphasis on construction and studying more lifelike situations was different from the verbal learning approach and much later inspired researchers to look outside the laboratory to study the phenomena of human memory (Neisser, 1978).

Ebbinghaus and Bartlett were both pioneers, each developing unique styles of research and differing perspectives on remembering. Both have left a long legacy of research. Much of the best research in the field arises from a combination of these approaches, by researchers who attempt to take the interesting memory phenomena that can be observed in the world and to bring them into more tightly controlled laboratory situations for careful study.

7.2 Experiments on Memory: Logic, Methods, and Findings

Studies of human memory typically have at least two distinct phases: a study phase and a test phase. In the study phase people are exposed to some events or material and in the test phase they are queried in some way about their memory for the earlier experience. Occasionally, in naturalistic studies of remembering, people might be asked to recall events from earlier in their lives, such as the earliest memory that they can retrieve from their childhoods (Waldfogel, 1948) or their classmates during their senior year in high school (Williams & Hollan, 1981). In the former example, the accuracy of the response cannot be checked (did the retrieved event actually occur early in their lives, or is it an experience described by a parent later?). In the second example, the recollections could be checked with yearbooks when available. However, in general, experimental psychologists like to gain control over the study phase of the experiment by presenting materials in the laboratory, like both Ebbinghaus and Bartlett did. When the experimenter has control over the conditions of study, then more secure inferences can be made about what is later retained (Schacter, 1995b).

The Encoding–Storage–Retrieval Framework

Psychologists have found it useful to conceive of the learning/memory process as composed of three stages: encoding (or acquisition) of information, storage (or retention), and retrieval (or accessing the memory). Encoding is the first stage that occurs during study and refers to accurate intake or perception of the event. Storage, or retention, is the second stage and refers

to maintenance of the information over time; presumably, encoding an event produces some change in the nervous system and this change (often referred to as a memory trace) persists over time. Retrieval is the process of accessing the information later when it is needed. Whenever an event is successfully remembered, all three stages must be intact: the event was encoded, stored, and retrieved. When a person fails to remember an event, one or more of the stages failed. Pinpointing which stage failed is often difficult.

These three stages are logically necessary, but in practice it is difficult to separate them cleanly (Watkins, 1990). For example, when does encoding of an event end and storage or retention begin? How can we know exactly what information is stored after an experience? If an event cannot be remembered, how can we determine at which stage the fault lies? These questions cannot be answered conclusively. In addition, as we will see later in the chapter, the three stages are intertwined. The cues most effective for retrieval depend critically on how information was encoded and stored.

Although encoding and storage are difficult to separate, statements about storage and retrieval can sometimes be made based on experimental evidence. Consider an experiment by Tulving and Pearlstone (1966). They gave high school students lists of words to remember that belonged to common categories. So, students heard 'Furniture – dresser, lamp; Birds – eagle, parakeet; Trees – elm, hickory,' and so on, for 24 categories with two words in each category, so 48 words in all. The students were told to remember the words for a later test. After the list was presented, students were given a free recall test in which they were asked to recall words in any order; in this condition they recalled, on average, 18.8 words. So, information about this many items was successfully encoded, stored, and retrieved. We can then ask about the fate of the other 29. Were they never perceived or encoded in the first place? This seems unlikely, because the words were presented rather slowly, at the rate of one word per 2 s, but the possibility cannot be totally ruled out. Were the words encoded, but then somehow 'lost' from storage before the test? Or were the words (or some of them) successfully encoded and stored, but the subjects failed to retrieve them?

Tulving and Pearlstone (1966) employed a second condition to help answer the last question. They presented another group of subjects with the same lists under the same conditions, but tested them with a cued recall test rather than a free recall test. In the cued recall test subjects were given the category names (Furniture – ? Birds – ? Trees – ?) and asked to recall list items in response to these cues. Now subjects recalled 35.8 items, or nearly twice as many as the free recall group was able to produce. The category names served as powerful retrieval cues, enabling subjects to recall much more information than they could without cues (free recall). But, you might think, perhaps the cues were not really effective but subjects simply guessed items in the category when given the category names. Tulving and Pearlstone were aware of this potential criticism and took several steps to rule it out. For example, the category members were not the first ones that occur on free association tests, but somewhat less common (and therefore harder to guess) members. So, for example, the birds were not *robin* and *sparrow*, but *eagle* and *parakeet*.

Based on these data, Tulving and Pearlstone (1966) made a critical distinction between information that is available in memory and that which is accessible. Any particular memory test (free recall, cued recall, recognition, and others, as discussed below) permits an assessment of the information that is accessible from memory, or the information retrievable under a particular set of test conditions. The information that is accessible, however, may not sufficiently represent the quantity of information that is available (or stored) in memory. No test provides an accurate assessment of exactly what has been stored in memory. We can say from the data presented above that in these experimental conditions more information was available for subjects tested with free recall than they were able to access. They free recalled only about 19 of the words but could have recalled around 36 under cued recall conditions. (In fact, the free recall subjects took a cued recall test after the free recall test and improved to about the level of the subjects given the cued recall test.) So, more information was available (stored) than was accessible (retrievable) under free recall conditions. Cued recall provided an estimate of 36 words recalled. But what about the remaining 12? Were they not encoded? Did they fade from storage? Or were they potentially retrievable with more powerful cues? We cannot say, short of finding the more powerful cues that might elicit their recall.

Distinguishing among encoding, storage, and retrieval is quite useful, even if there are gray areas in the use of these terms. Likewise, it is useful to distinguish between information that is available (stored) in memory and that which is accessible (retrievable) on any particular test, even though we can only measure the latter concept and not the former. At least the distinction prevents researchers from making the mistake, all too common in the history of memory research, of assuming that performance on a particular memory test provides an accurate measure of what a subject has encoded and stored. We will use these distinctions and terms throughout the remainder of the chapter.

Four Dimensions of Memory Experiments

Jenkins (1979) provided a useful way of thinking about experiments on human memory. He noted that researchers conducting experiments on the topic must make choices along four dimensions, whether or not that particular dimension is of interest in the experiment. These four dimensions are (1) the type of subject or person being tested, (2) the material used for the experiment, (3) the orienting tasks (or the features of the setting in which the people are tested), and (4) the type of test used to assess retention. If these four factors are placed in a plane and considered together, as in Figure 7.1, the appearance is one of a tetrahedron (although it is difficult to get this vision across on a two-dimensional page). The basic point is that all experiments on human memory involve choices in this four-dimensional space.

Consider the Tulving and Pearlstone (1966) experiment just described. The subjects were high school students, the materials were categorized word lists, and the subjects were all given

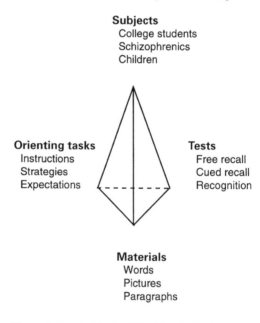

Subjects
College students
Schizophrenics
Children

Orienting tasks
Instructions
Strategies
Expectations

Tests
Free recall
Cued recall
Recognition

Materials
Words
Pictures
Paragraphs

Figure 7.1   *Jenkins' (1979) Tetrahedral Model of Memory Experiments. The variable of interest in a psychology experiment must be considered within the context of other variables which are held constant.*

intentional learning instructions during the study or encoding phase, meaning that they were told to pay attention to the words because they would later be tested on their memory for the words. So, these three factors were all held constant. The fourth factor, the type of test used, was the independent variable of interest. Some subjects received a free recall test whereas others were given a cued recall test. Subjects tested with cued recall produced more words on the test than those tested with free recall.

Jenkins' (1979) tetrahedral model of memory experiments illustrates that any experiment is created with some limited variables, or factors, of interest, and yet the study is conducted in the context of other variables, or factors, that are held constant. This position is referred to as *contextualism*: every experimental result is embedded in the context of other factors that were held constant. Appreciation of this point leads naturally to questions that should always be borne in mind. Would the finding from a particular experiment hold if other dimensions were manipulated? In the present case, if different types of subjects, or different materials, or other instructions prior to encoding were given, would cued recall still exceed free recall? There can be no a priori answers to such questions without the requisite program of research, yet researchers often implicitly assume that what they have found under their particular limited set of experimental conditions will generalize broadly to other conditions. Sometimes later research shows this to be true, but often later research will show that some exciting finding occurs only under a narrow set of conditions. The finding may still be of interest for theoretical or practical reasons, but its generality may not be great.

Jenkins' (1979) model provides a useful way of surveying some main findings about memory. We will consider each of the four factors in turn and discuss some of the variables that have been manipulated. We will describe some of the variables that have been shown to have powerful effects on most standard tests of memory involving recall and recognition. However, our generalizations will come with a ceteris paribus clause (all other things being equal). That is, the generalization holds under most conditions, but it is often possible to manipulate factors in the other three dimensions that would at least affect the magnitude of the experimental effects. In some cases the effect could be eliminated or even reversed under other conditions. Because our net is so wide in this brief sketch, we cannot review the literature exhaustively. We consider materials, orienting tasks and the experimental setting, the type of subject, and finally the type of tests.

Materials

Psychologists have studied memory for virtually every imaginable type of material. In the realm of verbal materials, lists of nonsense syllables and lists of words are common. In general, the more similar nonsense syllables are to real words, the better they are remembered. In addition, words that are frequently used are generally easier to recall than are words less frequently used. Phrases, sentences, paragraphs, and stories have been studied and, in general, the more meaningful and familiar the material is, the better it is remembered. Not surprisingly, when the words of a sentence are scrambled, they are remembered more poorly than when the sentence is presented intact. This points to an important feature of encoding: the 'same' material (the same words, in this case) can be well or poorly remembered depending on how it is presented. If it is presented in a coherent sentence it can be grasped and assimilated with past knowledge more easily. In the jargon of cognitive psychology, the sentence is more easily recoded (Miller, 1956). The same holds true even for lists of words. If they are organized in a meaningful fashion, they are more easily remembered than if presented randomly.

Retention for many types of nonverbal material has also been studied. Pictures, usually in the form of simple line drawings of common objects (a ladder, a helicopter) can be presented, with recall measured by having subjects produce names of the pictures. Pictures are better recalled and recognized than are the same items presented as words, even when the mode of response is verbal (which would seem to give the advantage to words, which are produced in the same form as the one in which they were presented). Faces are another popular material and some have argued that humans have special mechanisms for remembering faces, due to their importance to survival. In fact, some researchers have argued that the human brain has a special module or processor for faces and their retention, given their importance to human existence (see Bruce, 1988). Videotapes and complex pictures are sometimes used as stimuli for memory experiments, too. The idea behind using these types of stimuli is to study nonverbal memory; however, line drawings can be named, faces can be described (a bald man, with glasses, a high forehead) and so can complex pictures and videotapes. When psychologists want to study material where all reasonable types of verbalization are excluded, they turn to snowflakes (Neath & Knoedler, 1994) or kaleidoscope pictures (Wright, Santiago, Sands, Kendrick, & Cook, 1985) and use recognition procedures by testing with, for example, some snowflakes that are the same as those that were studied and some that are different, with the task being for subjects to recognize the previously presented snowflakes.

Psychologists often present materials visually, but some types of material such as words or digits can be presented auditorily and often interesting differences occur between these modalities. In addition, various types of non-verbal sounds can be presented for later recall or recognition: music, tones, or various sounds (popcorn popping, birds chirping, etc.). In the olfactory modality, people can sniff various smells and be asked to recall or to recognize them later. In fact, olfactory memory is interesting because different patterns sometimes emerge than with other classes of stimuli. Rounding out the modalities, people can also be tested for various objects touched against their bodies or for various tastes, although these modalities are rarely used in memory experiments.

Orienting Tasks and Settings

This category of variables refers to many aspects of the experimental context, including instructions subjects are given, the particular version of a task they are provided, the strategies they might use, whether the independent variable is manipulated between subjects (so each subject receives only one condition) or within subjects (so each subject participates in each condition). The potential number of such settings variables is quite large.

In memory research, one basic instructional variable that must be decided for each experiment is whether to use intentional learning instructions (they are told they will be tested so they should learn the material) or incidental learning instructions (they are not forewarned about the later memory test when given the material). Suppose subjects are to be exposed to a list of 50 words and they are asked to rate the pleasantness of each word on a scale of 1 to 7, just to insure they pay attention to the words. Later, they will be asked to recall the words. If one group of subjects is warned, prior to the task of rating the words, that they need to remember the words for a later test, this would constitute an intentional learning condition. If the subjects were not forewarned, the condition would be one of incidental learning. That is, the learning of the list of words would be incidental to what subjects perceived their main task to be, viz., rating the pleasantness of the words. In general, intentional learning instructions produce greater retention than do incidental learning instructions, but this effect depends on the nature of the orienting task (rating pleasantness, in this example) given to the subjects. Actually, with

pleasantness ratings, there would be little or no difference between incidental and intentional learning instructions. The reason is that when subjects rate words for pleasantness the task encourages thinking about the meaning of words, just as intentional learning instructions do. Because processing words for their meaning is a critical ingredient in remembering them, pleasantness rating encourages the type of processing that provides good retention and so, even with incidental learning instructions, recall and recognition of the words would be good (Craik & Lockhart, 1972). With tasks that do not encourage encoding of meaning, such as noting whether the word is printed in upper case or lower case letters, giving intentional learning instructions would typically reveal superior retention to incidental learning conditions.

Another factor of interest is the type of orienting task itself. Craik and Tulving (1975) had subjects exposed to words under incidental learning instructions. They were presented with a question and were asked to answer 'yes' or 'no' to the question in relation to the word that was presented immediately after the question. To take one example, consider the word BEAR given with the following three questions: Is it in upper case letters? Does it rhyme with CHAIR? Is it an animal? Subjects answered questions by pressing a key to indicate yes or no, as fast as possible. Other questions were similar to these (Is it in lower case letters? Does it rhyme with SOCK? Is it a type of bird?) but the answer was no. Later subjects were given a recognition test and required to select words they had recently studied from others that had not been presented. The results are shown in Figure 7.2 for items for which the answer to the question was yes. The outcome is dramatic: although all items were exposed for the same length of time, the split second encoding operation performed by the

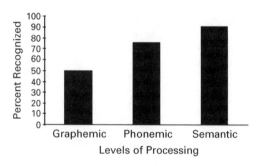

Figure 7.2 Data from Craik and Tulving (1975). Those items encoded on a deep level were better remembered than those items that were encoded on a shallow level. Chance performance was 33%.

subjects in answering the questions greatly affected the later memorability for the words. Asking questions that required analysis of meaning (Is it an animal?) produced much higher recognition than did analysis of the word's phonemic properties (Does it rhyme with CHAIR?), which in turn led to greater recognition than questions that called attention only to graphemic, visual properties of the word (Is it in upper case letters?). These results point again to the power of encoding processes: the outside world provides information to the senses, but whether it will be later remembered depends on the type of processing accorded the information.

Under intentional learning conditions, subjects can be given different strategies for use in learning material. Bower (1972) gave students lists of 20 pairs of words to remember, such as *thumbtack-pickle*. One group was told to silently rehearse (to repeat over to themselves) each pair until the next pair appeared on the screen. A second group was told to form interactive images between the referents of the two words. That is, they should imagine a thumbtack being pushed into a pickle. Later, both groups were given a test in which they were given the lefthand member of each pair (thumbtack – ?) and asked to recall the righthand member. Bower found that people who simply repeated the two words recalled about 45% of the words whereas the group that formed images recalled close to 75%. So, the instruction to use mental imagery increased recall by 30% over the strategy that most people use for memorizing, rehearsing information to themselves! In general, recoding verbal information in terms of mental images is a powerful aid to memorizing and therefore this strategy is a prominent ingredient in many memory improvement books and programs. Rehearsing information often has small or negligible effects on recall, even when rehearsal occurs over prolonged periods.

Some memory improvement books suggest that forming bizarre images helps more than using ordinary images. In the above example, the thumbtack and pickle should be made large and perhaps grotesque to engender the greatest mnemonic effect. However, the experimental evidence on this issue is mixed: some studies find that bizarre images help, whereas other studies do not. Why? One factor at work seems to be another contextual variable mentioned above, whether subjects are tested by having common and bizarre images in the same list or in different lists. When subjects form bizarre images to some items and common images to others, all within the same long list, they remember bizarre images better. However, when all items in the list are encoded either with bizarre or with common imagery, then often no difference exists in recall of the two types (McDaniel & Masson, 1985).

This outcome leads to a further point about encoding: when events are distinctive or salient, such as one bizarre image among many common ones, people often remember that event better. When events in our lives are powerful or emotional (either good or bad), we typically remember them very well. In fact, such events have been given the name flashbulb memories (Brown & Kulik, 1977) because they seem recorded as in a photographic flash. It is wrong to think of these powerful memories as literal photographs, because some research has shown that even when we think memories have this crystal clear quality, we can sometimes be quite wrong. However, distinctive, emotional events are usually remembered quite well.

Subjects

Psychologists have tested memory abilities of virtually all types of people. There are studies of college students, of children, of infants, of the mentally retarded, of depressed people, of schizophrenics, of older adults, of bilingual and trilingual individuals, of people with superior memories, of brain-damaged patients, of people receiving electroconvulsive therapy, and on and on. That said, we must admit that the greatest bulk of the research has been conducted with university students. Because most of the researchers in human memory are professors, students represent an abundant resource. We might make an analogy to the science of genetics by saying that college students are the *Drosophila* of human memory research. Just as geneticists use these fruit flies to work out the laws of genetics (fruit flies have relatively simple genetics, are easy to breed, and have short life spans), so researchers in human memory use college students. Like *Drosophila* to genetics researchers, college students have advantages for memory researchers as a population to study. They are usually intelligent, they are motivated, and millions of years of evolution have adapted them to their current niche in society: they participate in the educational system where they are given material to memorize for some 15–20 years, reaching expert level by the time they are in the university. Therefore, students represent an excellent model system for the study of human memory.

The problem of generality then arises: if the laws of memory are worked out with student populations, will they generalize to other groups? Of course, we might expect most other populations to perform worse over all than students, who are young, intelligent, and expert memorizers. In general, that is the case: young children and older adults, for example, both show generally poorer recall and recognition than do college students. So do depressed people, schizophrenics, brain-damaged individuals, and so on. However, the critical question is whether the generalizations about the effects of variables change with these other factors. Considering some of the findings in the preceding sections, does the effect of forming mental images, or the advantage of meaningful processing, or the effect of sentential organization change dramatically when different populations are tested? The answer to all these questions is no. In fact, at the risk of too broad a generalization, we can say that the effect of most variables is similar across numerous subject populations. There are a few exceptions to this claim, one of which will be considered in the next section, but as a general rule, different populations of people respond to powerful memory variables in much the same way. If a variable (such as imagery) has a positive effect in one group (college students), it probably will also have a positive effect in another group (children).

One fascinating topic is whether there is a small group of people who have memory abilities spectacularly better than those in the normal population. Do some people have photographic memories? Although some people do have extraordinarily good memories, the word *photographic* is probably too strong. One remarkable mnemonist was a Russian named Shereshevski, who was studied by Luria (1968). He could perform remarkable feats of memory and had great powers of mental imagery, as Luria documents in his fascinating book, *The mind of a mnemonist*. However, few others can duplicate his talents. Nonetheless, other mnemonists often have great powers, even if different from those of Shereshevski. An Indian named Rajan Mahadevan has a spectacular memory for numbers and has memorized pi (3.141592 . . .) to over 31,000 decimal places! Since pi is nonrepeating, a test of Rajan's memory is to give him five or ten digits and ask if this series of digits can be found in the first 31,000 digits of pi. He can decide yes or no within a matter of seconds with remarkable accuracy (Vogl & Thompson, 1995). Other mnemonists have specialized knowledge of the Bible or the Talmud, or have memorized telephone directories or dictionaries. Whether these remarkable people simply have radically different memory systems from the rest of us or instead use the same basic mechanisms as ordinary people but with greater efficiency is not known.

Tests that Assess Memory

Over the past century, many standard laboratory paradigms have been used to assess memory. We can broadly classify these tests as explicit memory tests or implicit memory tests. Explicit tests are, as the name implies, tests that provide direct or explicit queries about past experience. If subjects are asked to recall the list of pictures they recently saw in an experiment, their high school classmates, or the people they saw yesterday, these are explicit tests of memory. Implicit memory tests also measure the effects of past experience, but they do so indirectly through measuring transfer of past experience in current behavior without any instruction to retrieve from the past. For example, suppose you read the word *perspicacious* in a book yesterday. Today you are describing an intelligent acquaintance to one of your friends and you call her *perspicacious* in the course of the conversation. If you have never used that word before, you probably did it today because you read it yesterday. Therefore, we can say that reading it yesterday primed your use of the word today. Implicit memory tests are those that measure this kind of priming, although measured more formally than in this example. We first consider explicit measures of memory and then turn to implicit measures.

Explicit measures capture our conscious recollection of the past. Most of the experimental work on memory in the last century has used explicit measures. If people are given a list of 20 words and asked to recall them in any order, the task is free recall; if they were asked to recall them in the strict order in which they had been presented, the task would be serial recall. Both these are explicit measures of retention. Paired associate learning was exemplified above; people are given pairs to study (*thumbtack-pickle*) and later given one member of the pair and asked to recall the other. In describing an experiment in an earlier section, we discussed another cued recall test in which subjects were given category names (such as Birds) as an aid to recalling words presented with them in a list (eagle, parakeet). Cues can also be used that were not included in the material to be studied. For example, if the word *elephant* had been presented in a list of words, *tusk* might be given as an extra-list retrieval cue for that item.

Recognition procedures have also been described in this chapter. In general, people are given material to study (say, 100 pictures) and then are tested by giving them the studied pictures and a large number of other pictures with the instruction to identify the ones they saw earlier. If they see the studied and nonstudied pictures one at a time and are instructed to say *yes* or *old* and *no* or *new*, the test is called a free choice (or yes/no) recognition test. The subject makes a choice (yes/no or old/new) about each item. A forced choice recognition test involves giving subjects a studied item paired with one or more nonstudied items and asking them to pick the single studied item in the group. Free choice recognition tests are rather like true/false tests used in educational assessment, whereas forced choice tests are like multiple choice tests.

Throughout much of the history of research on human memory, people selected a convenient test and studied problems of memory via its use. Researchers could spend whole careers studying, say, processes involved in free recall or in recognition. The implicit assumption is that 'memory is memory' and that all tests reveal the same process, with some tests (say, recognition) more sensitive than others (say, free recall). Test paradigms were considered as what other scientists called preparations: once one has developed a sensitive task or preparation, it is used repeatedly. Although this research strategy can produce dividends in deep understanding of a limited range of problems, in the long run it seems misguided. The reason is that tests are not equivalent and do not measure the same 'thing' (such as strength of a memory trace). Often, the same variable can be shown to have different effects on various measures of memory. Consider the effects of frequency of words in the language. As noted above, high-frequency words are better recalled than low-frequency words when other characteristics (part of speech, length, etc.) are held constant. We might be tempted to explain this by saying that high-frequency words create stronger memory traces than do low-frequency words. However, when recognition measures are used, it turns out that low-frequency words are better recognized than are high-frequency words! For other variables there might be an effect on recall, but no effect on recognition. Therefore, recall and recognition cannot be considered as measuring 'the same memory' with differing sensitivity.

A useful perspective for thinking about the relation between the encoding and testing of memories is *transfer appropriate processing* (Bransford, Franks, Morris, & Stein, 1979). In general, performance will be better on tests to the extent that the processes engaged by the test match those used in encoding the materials. Let us consider an example. In an experiment by Stein (1978), subjects studied words such as 'knIfe' and answered one of two questions about it. In one case, the question asked about visual features ('Does the word have a capital I in it?') whereas the other type of question forced subjects to think about the meaning of the word, such as in 'Does _____ have a steel blade?' This

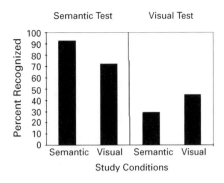

Figure 7.3 *Data from Stein (1978). Items are best remembered when the study conditions match the test conditions, exemplifying the principle of transfer appropriate processing.*

experiment is similar to one we discussed earlier in which we reported that, on a standard recognition test, questions encouraging the processing of meaning led to better recognition memory. However, Stein's experiment used two different kinds of recognition tests. One was the standard forced choice test in which subjects picked out a studied word from among nonstudied words (e.g., trUck, knIfe, relAy, and sCene). As can be seen in Figure 7.3 on the left, the prior work was replicated on this test, with semantic encoding conditions producing better recognition than the condition that required people to examine letters. However, consider the other kind of recognition test in which people were tested on their ability to recognize the visual appearance of the words they had just seen. Now the test consisted of a forced choice test like this – kNife, knIfe, kniFe, knifE – with subjects required to pick the form of the word they had studied. As shown on the right side of Figure 7.3, performance on this recognition test was the opposite to that on the standard test, with better recognition following prior attention being drawn to the appearance of the word during the encoding phase. Despite the fact that subjects encoded the same words in the same ways, the tests brought out different aspects of the encoded experience. A test that measured recognition of visual appearance was aided more by prior attention to the visual appearance of the words than by attention to their meaning; a test that measured recognition of meaningful aspects of prior experience benefited more from prior attention to the meaning of the words than by attention to their appearance. This pattern of results exemplifies the principle of transfer appropriate processing.

As noted above, implicit memory tests measure retention indirectly. The study phase of the typical form of these tests is much like it is for explicit memory tests. Usually subjects are exposed to either words or pictures under either intentional or incidental learning conditions. However, the test is quite different from those of explicit tests, because subjects are not told to remember events from their past. Instead, they are given another task to perform that is ostensibly unrelated to prior events in the experiment. For example, if subjects have been exposed to a list of words such as *elephant, accordion,* and *thimble,* then sometime later in the experimental session they might be told that their next task is to complete fragmented words with the first word that comes to mind. One version of the task, called word stem completion, provides subjects with the first three letters of words and asks them to say the first word that comes to mind. Some of the stems would correspond to previously studied words (ele____, acc____, thi____) and many other stems would not. In a different version of the task, called word fragment completion, subjects are provided with fragmented forms of words such as e_e_h_n_ and asked to guess what the words are, again with some fragments referring to previously studied words and others not. In both these tasks, the results of hundreds of experiments demonstrate that subjects are more likely to complete the word stems or word fragments with words that have been recently studied. For example, if *elephant* has not been studied, the probability of completing the word fragment with this word might be .30, whereas if the word had been studied, the completion rate might be .60. This 30% benefit is attributed to priming; prior study of the word primed word completion.

Psychologists became interested in these implicit memory tests because the outcome of experiments using implicit memory measures is often quite different from those using explicit measures. Implicit measures of memory reveal the influence of prior experience on behavior and so reflect a type of memory, but it is a very different type from that revealed by explicit memory tests such as recall and recognition. For example, some patients who have suffered brain damage lose most of their ability to remember new information, a condition called anterograde amnesia. Their forgetfulness is extreme; if they receive a list of words to remember and then are asked to recall or to recognize the words after a short retention interval, they may not even remember having heard a list, much less the particular words that were in the list! Performance on all explicit memory tests is quite poor for such patients.

The natural interpretation of this amnesia is that the centers in the brain responsible for encoding and storing new information have been

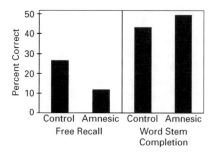

Figure 7.4 *Data from Graf, Squire, and Mandler (1984). Although amnesic patients perform worse than controls on an explicit, free recall test, there is no difference between the performance of the two groups on the implicit, word stem completion test.*

damaged. However, in the 1960s British psychologists Elizabeth Warrington and Lawrence Weiskrantz (1968) discovered that such patients showed perfectly normal patterns of priming on implicit memory tests, a finding replicated many times now. The results of one such replication by Graf, Squire, and Mandler (1984) are shown in Figure 7.4. Subjects in the experiment were either amnesic patients or control subjects matched on age and level of education. All subjects were shown lists of words and then given either a free recall test or a word stem completion test. As seen on the left side of Figure 7.4, patients were much worse than controls on the free recall test, which is no surprise. However, in the word stem completion results shown on the right, patients showed as much priming as did control subjects. The benefit from prior study of the words was normal for these patients, which may indicate that encoding and storage of information was intact. The amnesic patients' difficulty seems to be in retrieving the information when asked to remember it; the processes of conscious recollection have been disrupted. This pattern of results reveals a dissociation between measures of memory: performance on one set of tasks (explicit memory tasks) is greatly affected by brain damage, whereas performance on the other type of task (priming on implicit memory tests) is affected very little, if at all. This outcome represents an exception to the generalization made in the previous section that most individual difference variables affect the overall level of performance in memory experiments, but do not interact with these variables.

Many experimental variables also affect explicit and implicit measures of memory differently. For example, manipulation of intentional versus incidental learning instructions during study has little effect on implicit tests such as word stem and word fragment completion and neither does study time for individual items, massed presentation of items, and other factors such as the type of orienting task (rating words for appearance or for their meaning). The study of priming on implicit memory tests has burgeoned over the past 20 years and there is now a substantial literature on the topic, with general references provided in the Resource References. We should note here that there are many different types of implicit memory tests besides word stem and word fragment completion, so the claims we made above hold for these tests but not necessarily for all implicit tests.

We close this section by returning to the theme at the beginning: we cannot talk about 'memory' as if it is one entity. There are many ways of measuring memory and they reveal different processes and systems at work. It is misguided to think of memory as being all of one type, or of variables having a general effect across all types of settings, tasks, and people. Interactions or dissociations among measures of memory are the rule and not the exception.

7.3 Theories of Memory

There are dozens of theories of memory, which represents something of an embarrassment of riches. The presence of so many theories in the field reflects little agreement on which theory (or even which approach) is correct. Therefore, our aim in this section is to describe several categories of theories of memory rather than just one or two theories. First, however, we consider a theory that is widely accepted and is built into our way of talking about memory, but which is known to be untrue.

Strength Theory

One simple and appealing idea, built into many theories, goes like this: experiences in the world are coded into the nervous system in terms of memory traces, which vary in strength; some traces are strong (leading to good retention) whereas others are weak. For example, in a simple memory experiment in which subjects are presented with 30 words for later recall or recognition, some words might be said to leave stronger traces than others. These would be the words that tend, across subjects, to be well recalled and well recognized. Other words would lay down weaker traces. A representation of this idea is shown in Figure 7.5. A word must have considerable trace strength to be recalled because recall requires more strength than does recognition. The abscissa in the figure represents hypothetical traces of words labeled A, B, C, D,

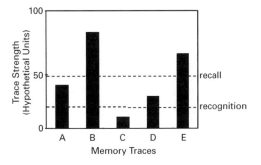

Figure 7.5 *A visual representation of a strength theory of memory: hypothetical memory traces and the threshold they must reach in order to be recognized, recalled, or both.*

and E whereas the ordinate represents strength of these traces. The figure accounts for why some words are recalled and others are not; similarly, the effect of experimental variables that generally increase retention, such as study time, can also be described as increasing trace strength. Words studied longer have stronger traces than those studied for less time.

The theory as portrayed in the figure can also account for the finding that often words can be recognized if they cannot be recalled. The threshold (represented by the horizontal line) for the amount of strength needed to succeed on a recognition test is lower than that for a recall test. More trace strength is required for recall than for recognition.

The simple strength theory of memory, as described in the previous paragraphs and as portrayed in Figure 7.5, can explain many basic facts about memory: why some items are recalled and others are not, why experimental variables affect retention, and why recognition is often more sensitive than recall, in the sense that items can be recognized when they cannot be recalled. The theory is simple and accords with our common sense way of describing memories as strong or weak. So, what is wrong with it? Basically, although it accounts for some facts, the theory fails to explain most of the interactions or dissociations described in the preceding sections. If the sole determinant of retention is memory strength, how does one account for differing patterns of performance as a function of the type of test given? According to the simple strength theory, tests differ only in their threshold for performance. In an earlier section, we noted that high-frequency words are better recalled (have higher strength) than low-frequency words. On the other hand, low-frequency words are better recognized than high-frequency words. Strength theory cannot explain such effects very easily, without making assumptions that undercut the theory. How can one and the same trace be stronger on a recall test but weaker on a recognition test? Similar types of problems crop up in comparing priming on implicit memory tests with recall and recognition on explicit tests, because such comparisons often reveal very different patterns of performance on the two types of test. There is no simple way to account for these differences in terms of a strength account and we can therefore reject it (for these and other reasons). However, the idea of memory strength is remarkably resilient and survives in many modern theories despite the fact that it has never worked. We consider below some promising alternatives, ones that try more realistically to deal with the variety and complexity of the data about memory.

Interference Theory

Interference theory was developed to explain forgetting. Strength theory's simple (and vacuous) account of forgetting is that, over time, the strength of traces simply wanes and therefore forgetting occurs. McGeoch (1932) mounted an attack on this simple decay or disuse theory of forgetting and argued that interference theory provides a more potent explanation.

There are two main types of interference, both quite important in certain situations. Proactive interference refers to the inhibiting effects that prior events have on recall or recognition of events learned later. Retroactive interference refers to the inhibiting effects on memory for some target event of other events occurring after the target event. So, for example, suppose you park your car in a large lot every day and your task each evening is to find it. The fact that you will sometimes go to where you parked it yesterday reveals proactive interference, or the interfering effect of prior events. If you were asked to determine where you parked your car seven days ago, retroactive interference would also come into play: the places you had parked the car in the intervening six days would also interfere with your recollection.

Proactive and retroactive interference are descriptive terms, referring to general classes of events that affect retention. The mechanisms believed to be responsible for interference are response competition (for both proactive and retroactive interference). That is, when asking 'where did I park my car a week ago?' the prior events and more recent events all compete as answers and the problem is selecting the correct answer from among these competitors. Another

factor, unlearning/recovery, also has been invoked to explain retroactive interference. The general idea is that learning a new experience (parking your car today) may cause forgetting ('unlearning') of previous experiences, such as where you parked it yesterday, which causes forgetting but also helps to update memory. However, unlearning does not seem permanent, because these inhibited responses can be shown to increase over time (Wheeler, 1995) and therefore to exert interference. Anderson and Neely (1996) provide a recent overview of inhibitory factors in remembering.

Memory Systems Theories

The guiding assumption of this class of theories is that several different cognitive systems underlie human memory. It is wrong to think of 'memory' as a single entity; rather, there are multiple memory systems and the reason that performance can differ so dramatically across various measures of memory is that different systems are responsible for these effects. Among the most generally agreed upon memory systems are the following: short-term memory (sometimes called primary memory or working memory), episodic memory, semantic memory, procedural memory, and perceptual memory. Let us discuss each in turn, albeit briefly.

Short-term or working memory, as the name implies, is responsible for the ability to hold, maintain, and use information over short periods of time. For example, the span of immediate memory for most people is around seven items, plus or minus two (Miller, 1956). That is, for stimuli such as words, digits, or letters, most people can remember between five and nine items in the correct order, with the average being seven (which is why local phone numbers are seven digits long). This short-term (or working) memory capacity seems to be different from other types of memory in the sense that working memory has been shown to remain intact when other types of memory are impaired. For example, amnesic patients (who have an obvious memory impairment) are often able to remember telephone numbers for a short time and other types of information demanding use of working memory. There may be more than one type of working memory, specialized verbal and nonverbal systems. Baddeley's (1986) influential theory of working memory postulates these distinct capacities and offers a systematic view of the available evidence.

Episodic memory (sometimes called long-term memory for events) refers to a person's ability to recollect the events of one's life. The hallmarks are that the events are personal ones and that they occurred at a particular time and a particular place in the past. Therefore, to recollect these events, an individual must be directed to (and able to) retrieve from a particular time and place. When subjects are asked to remember the words from a list presented five minutes ago, or to recall their first week of college, or to remember their first trip on an airplane, these are all queries of the episodic memory system. It is this system that is damaged in amnesic patients. They can remember events over the short term, but they cannot retrieve from long-term episodic memory.

Semantic memory refers to general knowledge of the meaning of facts, people and events. If you are asked for the definition of a platypus, or who Winston Churchill was, or the capital of Japan, these would all be queries of the semantic memory system. When new episodes occur in our lives, we interpret them through our past knowledge (through semantic memory) to represent them as meaningful episodes, but semantic memory and episodic memory seem otherwise separate. To return to amnesic patients, often their brain damage does not affect semantic memory – they still know the meaning of words, history they learned in school, and they might still be able to play chess well if they could do so before their injury. The problem they seem to have is in remembering personal events. Semantic memory is ahistorical and impersonal; recalling the time and place of the occasion when you first heard about Winston Churchill would not be necessary to knowing who he was and what he did.

Episodic and semantic memory are together sometimes called declarative memory. These systems permit people to make declarations about their past. We say 'I remember that . . .' when referring to episodic memories, or 'I know that . . .' when referring to semantic memories. Non-declarative memory systems are all the other systems.

Procedural memory is considered the system responsible for motor actions. Riding a bicycle, serving a tennis ball or, for that matter, walking and running are complex motor skills that must be learned. The systems that support these processes are different from others we have considered above.

Finally, there are also perceptual representation systems that maintain a memory for the perceptual objects of the world as they impinge on the individual. These representations are believed to be stored in brain areas in which the experiences were first processed in the visual, auditory, or other perceptual systems. For example, priming in implicit memory tests such as word fragment completion and word stem completion is mediated by such perceptual representation systems.

These five systems do not exhaust the possibilities, which may extend to as many as 15–20 in some counts. However, the ones listed above are generally agreed upon. We next consider an alternative approach.

Processing theories

In processing or procedural approaches, the basic assumption is that the brain/mind is composed of many different types of processes or procedures that can function in many ways. What we call 'memory' is a very general property of cognition in that experience changes the way a person interacts with the environment. The processing approaches try to account for the many different kinds of mnemonic skill by invoking the idea that any task has many component processes involved in it. Each task has a somewhat different set and arrangement of components from any other task.

The components of a task are difficult to define precisely, except at a broad level. For example, some memory tasks seem to respond strongly to manipulations of meaning or to conceptual information. These tasks (like recognition memory, for example) are not much affected by changes in perceptual/surface characteristics such as modality of presentation (auditory or visual) of information, but they are greatly affected by differences in orienting tasks (judging the case of words versus a meaningful judgment such as rating pleasantness). Therefore, recognition seems to represent a conceptual or meaningful task. On the other hand, implicit memory tests such as word stem and word fragment completion are affected in an opposite way by these variables. Manipulations of meaning have little effect, whereas manipulations of perceptual characteristics of the stimuli, such as modality of presentation, have a large effect on these tests. Therefore, these implicit memory tests are called perceptual tests, whereas explicit tasks such as recognition and free recall are referred to as conceptual tests (Blaxton, 1989). Perceptual processes are preeminent in the former tests, conceptual processes in the latter tests.

A general point made by processing theorists is that there are no dedicated memory systems in the human brain. Rather, there are a variety of all-purpose systems, with one purpose being to retain after-effects of experience. The perceptual memory systems, from this perspective, are perceptual systems used to analyze incoming information from the outside world and that also happen to change as a function of past experience. Procedural memory can be viewed in the same way. The nervous system changes as we practice a skill and these changes can be seen as procedural memory. However, all systems use procedures. Even in episodic memory experiments, how the query is presented to retrieve past experience determines the procedures used and the answer provided.

The emphasis on processing approaches to memory is the interactive nature of cognition. Although it is useful for some purposes to dissect the cognitive world into different capacities (perceiving, attending, remembering, thinking), all these processes interact. We cannot think about a problem without perceiving its features and having them call up ideas from the past. Similarly, we cannot perceive a complex scene without considerable past experience or knowledge that is stored in the brain. Perceiving requires memory just as memory requires perceiving. The processing approaches to cognition, sketched here, try to confront the interactive complexity of cognition (see Resource References for references on these points of view).

Mathematical Models

Theorists who endorse the memory systems and processing points of view attempt to cover wide territory, to account for differences from many tasks, many subject populations, and many variables. Theorists who use mathematical models typically endorse a different strategy as fruitful. This approach often considers rather limited situations, such as recognition memory, but develops highly specified models for the task of interest. The assumption is that proceeding this way – providing specific models that should be testable – will provide a useful way of conceptualizing memory. Thus, for example, exquisite and detailed models have been developed for the Sternberg (or item-recognition) paradigm in which a series of digits is given (6 1 8 5 3 9) and then after the list presentation, one digit is given as a test item. If the digit matches (8), the subject pushes a yes key as quickly as possible; if it does not match (4), the no key is pressed. Much interesting work has come from studying this item recognition task (Sternberg, 1975) and elegant models have been proposed (and falsified).

More ambitious models have attempted to account for a range of phenomena. One such model is the Search of Associative Memory (SAM) model by Raaijmakers and Shiffrin (1981). They proposed that memory could be conceived as a large associative network and

further specified a number of assumptions about how associations are formed during study episodes and retrieved during recall and recognition tests. The model has been used to make quantitative predictions in many different kinds of recall and recognition experiments. Although we cannot review the achievements here, the theory has impressively predicted a large range of results and shows the power of mathematical modeling in furthering our understanding of memory.

In this section of the chapter, we have provided several general approaches to theory development within modern cognitive psychology. As we have noted, many theories of memory exist and theorists approach the topic from different perspectives and select various patterns of results to explain. There is no single comprehensive theory of memory that has met with general acceptance.

7.4 A Sample Experiment: Roediger and McDermott (1995)

Psychologists interested in memory have usually measured accuracy of recollections in recall and recognition. The primary error they have examined is the error of omission, or forgetting – the inability to recollect something once known. However, another class of errors that people make is that of commission rather than omission – people can remember events differently from the way they happened or, in the most profound case of error, they can remember events that never happened at all. Thus far this chapter has dwelt on processes affecting accuracy in performance. Therefore, for the sample experiment we will focus on an experiment in which subjects make frequent errors.

Roediger and McDermott (1995, Experiment 2) tested 30 undergraduate students in a straightforward paradigm using 24 lists of words. The lists were produced from word association norms and the words were strongly associated. For example, one list was *smooth, bumpy, road, tough, sandpaper, jagged, ready, coarse, uneven, riders, rugged, sand, boards, ground,* and *gravel*. These words are the ones produced in a word association test to the word *rough*, but notice that rough is not included in the list. We refer to *rough* as the critical nonpresented item. In the experiment the 24 lists were arbitrarily divided into three sets of eight and each subject studied 16 lists. The lists were presented auditorily at the rate of one word every 1.5 s, after which the subjects received a signal that indicated they should either recall the list for 2 min or perform mental arithmetic for 2 min. After

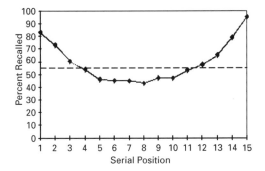

Figure 7.6 *Data from Roediger and McDermott (1995), Experiment 2. The probability of recalling the critical, nonpresented lure was slightly higher than the probability of recalling one of the words presented in serial positions in the middle of the list.*

eight lists subjects recalled the words in any order as soon as the list had been presented (free recall), whereas after the other eight lists they performed arithmetic problems. The reason for doing this was to examine the effects of recall on a later recognition test. Before describing the recognition test, we describe the results obtained in recall.

Presented in Figure 7.6 are the primary results from the recall test. The function shown is called a serial position curve, because it plots probability of recall on the ordinate and the ordinal position of the presented item on the abscissa. So, the first point is the average probability of recall of the first item in the lists, and so on. Note that recall of the first few items and the last few items is better than that for the middle items. This characteristic almost always occurs in immediate retention of a series; good recall of the first few items is called a *primacy effect* and superior recall of late items is a *recency effect*. However, for present purposes the dashed line represents the data point of most

interest. This line represents false recall, or recall of the critical nonpresented word (*rough* in our sample list above) that was not presented in the list. Obviously, average recall of this item was very high, at 55%. In fact, false recall of the critical nonpresented words was actually higher than for words that were presented in the middle of the list! Later experiments have generally shown that free recall of the critical nonpresented word is about the same as, or a little higher than, recall of the words presented in the middle of the list.

After hearing 16 lists and recalling eight of them, the subjects then received a recognition test in which they were instructed to decide whether each word was old (studied in the lists) or new (not studied). In addition, for each word they said was old, they were asked to judge whether they could remember when the word originally occurred in the list or if they just knew that the word had occurred but could not actually remember the moment of its occurrence. This remember/know judgment captures a person's experience during recollection and is often used to measure remembering of experiences as distinct from the feeling of familiarity that can occur without true remembering (Tulving, 1985). The recognition test consisted of 96 words, 48 of which had been studied (targets) and 48 of which had not been studied (lures or distracters). Among the lures were the 16 words that were the critical lures, words such as *rough* that were associated to list words but not actually presented.

The recognition results are presented in Table 7.1. The top two rows represent correct recognition (calling a studied word 'old', or the hit rate) whereas the bottom three rows represent false recognition (that is, calling a word that was objectively nonstudied 'old'; this is called a false alarm). Looking at the first column, which shows overall recognition, the most striking result can be seen by comparing the data in the top two rows, representing correct recognition

Table 7.1 *Data from Roediger & McDermott (1995) Experiment 2. Proportion of items recognized as a function of studied words (targets), unstudied words (critical lures and unrelated lures), and remember and know judgments*

	Recognition	Remember	Know
Targets			
Study + recall	.79	.57	.22
Study + arithmetic	.65	.41	.24
Critical lures			
Study + recall	.81	.58	.23
Study + arithmetic	.72	.38	.34
Unrelated lures	.14	.03	.11

of targets, with that in the next two rows showing false recognition of critical lures. (The first
and third rows represent the case in which
recognition occurred after recall; the second and
fourth rows indicate recognition that did not
follow recall.) Remarkably, the false alarm rate
for the critical lures equaled or even slightly
exceeded the hit rate for the target items. In
addition, prior recall of the studied list increased
both the hit rate and the false alarm rate for
overall recognition. Both the hit rate for targets
and the false alarm rate for critical lures greatly
exceeded the false alarm rate for lures from lists
that were not studied, whose data are shown in
the bottom row.

The second and third columns in Table 7.1
shows the breakdown of the overall recognition
rate into remember and know responses. Look
first at the data for unrelated lures in the bottom
row and see that the false alarms are usually
deemed to be items known to be on the list, but
that their actual occurrence cannot be remembered. This pattern makes sense, of course,
because the lure items were not actually on the
list. However, the top four rows show a very
different pattern. For the target items, subjects
say that they can remember the moment of
occurrence for most items that were called 'old'.
That makes sense, because the items actually
had been presented. However, exactly the same
pattern occurred for the critical lures: despite the
fact that they had not been studied, subjects not
only falsely recognized them as having been
presented, but also said they could remember the
actual occurrence of the words on the list! In
addition, when subjects had previously recalled
the list, the illusion of remembering was even
stronger.

The Roediger and McDermott (1995) experiment shows a simple laboratory technique that
produces dramatic levels of false recall and false
recognition. Unlike other work showing distortions of memory, this experiment was carried
out under conditions that should encourage
accurate responding. Subjects were tested for
recall immediately after list presentation with an
instruction warning them not to guess and the
technique used (free recall) is often thought to
be relatively error free because subjects set a
high criterion for responding (and indeed few
errors occurred, except for recall of the critical
nonpresented word). In addition, the recognition
test occurred relatively soon after the recall test.
The instruction for subjects to make remember/
know judgments is believed to make subjects
more aware of the basis of their responses and to
make them more carefully monitor their responses for accuracy. In addition, use of word lists
(rather than prose or slide sequences) is often
thought to encourage accuracy. Nonetheless,

despite all these conditions that normally
encourage accuracy, high rates of false recall
and false recognition occurred.

The most likely interpretation of the
Roediger–McDermott (1995) results is that subjects thought of the critical word during presentation of the list and then later confused their
private thoughts with the overt presentation of
list words. The general point is that people are
always drawing inferences, going beyond the
literal information in their environments. What
we remember of experiences may be some blend
of what actually happened and what we were
thinking while the events were happening.

7.5 APPLICATIONS OF RESEARCH

Research on human memory has been applied in
many settings. Because the coverage in this
chapter has been selective, not all the basic
research that could be applied has been covered
here. We will provide vignettes of applications
to issues of practical importance. Because the
issues of memory pervade thought in many
different contexts, the implications of basic
research for these applied topics can be wide-
ranging.

The demands on memory in modern life are
greatly increasing. Complicated telephone systems, computer systems, fax systems, cameras,
videorecorders, automobiles and the like give
rise to increasing cognitive demands, often on
memory. Simply the number of passwords and
telephone numbers that must be retained
exceeds the capacity of many people. Psychologists' expertise is often brought to bear on these
practical problems. In particular, telephone companies and computer companies hire many psychologists to work on making equipment use-
able by taking the human factor into account.
These human factors psychologists, as they are
called, try to engineer complex systems so that
they can be used with relatively few errors by
their human operators. For example, as discussed above, early research sponsored by telephone companies in England and the United
States showed that the largest number of digits
that could be remembered without error on an
immediate test was seven, so telephone numbers
were made seven digits long. Similarly, these
psychologists showed that numbers are better
remembered if they are grouped or chunked, so
the typical way telephone numbers in the United
States are presented is in groups of three, then
four, as in 792-3948. In France, telephone numbers consist of eight digits and are presented as
four sets of two-digit numbers: 79-23-94-81.
Human factors psychologists must consider

other processes besides memory, but complex mechanisms created by engineers must be configured with attention to the limited capacity of working memory of the humans who use them. Psychologists often help devise the person/machine interface.

Research on human memory is also applied by educational psychologists. After all, one central issue in education (perhaps the central issue) is transmission of knowledge from the instructor and textbook to the student, so that the student can learn and remember the information. Therefore psychologists have spent much time studying how to organize and present information in textbooks, how to lecture, and similar topics. One problem is transmitting information obtained from basic research on human memory to educators who might be able to use it. Still, many findings from psychology have found their way into educational practice.

Psychologists have also designed programs of cognitive rehabilitation. For example, many medical conditions, such as Alzheimer's disease, impair cognitive functioning in general and memory functioning in particular. Cognitive psychologists have devised programs that will ameliorate (but certainly not cure) severe difficulties that people have in remembering.

Relatedly, psychologists have also studied memory improvement techniques and have developed courses and written books on memory improvement that offer general advice. Many mnemonic techniques have been known since ancient times, but modern cognitive psychologists have studied specific aspects of advice provided in these systems to see which features of the techniques really work. For example, if imagery is used in a mnemonic device, is it necessary for the images to be bizarre ones for them to be effective? As discussed above, the answer is not clear-cut, but selective use of bizarre imagery on especially difficult items should improve performance.

Cognitive psychologists who study memory are also often called upon as expert witnesses in legal situations that turn on the vicissitudes of human memory. Three types of case will be mentioned here. First, many cases turn on eyewitness identification. If a witness to a crime identifies a suspect as the culprit, this fact represents powerful evidence in the courtroom. But how accurate are eyewitnesses? Much research has been conducted on this topic, with the finding that witnesses can sometimes be wrong, but quite confident that they are right. Conditions that foster mistaken eyewitness identification have been discovered and psychologists testify about this research in court cases.

A second type of court case concerns children's testimony. Can children serve as reliable witnesses? How accurate are their recollections? Under what conditions are they likely to be accurate? When might they be misled into making false accusations? These issues are central in cases in which children are the primary witness or the only witness. Therefore, developmental psychologists who study memory development serve as experts in these cases.

A third type of court case, much in the news in the United States, Canada, and the United Kingdom in recent years, concerns cases of recovered memory after long delays. In a typical case a woman in her 30s or 40s undergoes psychotherapy for depression or some other problem. The therapist may inquire about her experiences during childhood in the normal course of therapy. In the process of talking about her childhood, or in response from questions and demands from the therapists, the patient may recover memories of unpleasant events from that period. In the most dramatic cases, she may remember being physically or sexually abused by her father, by an uncle, or by a teacher. In some cases, these recovered memories during therapy are the first inkling that the patient had of such abuse. One interpretation is that the events experienced were so horrible that they were repressed, or banished to an unconscious state, and then recovered during the course of therapy. Another interpretation is that the events never happened at all and the 'memories' were manufactured during the course of therapy, perhaps via suggestions from the therapist and other mechanisms (Lindsay & Read, 1994).

The issues in such recovered memory cases are very complex and present challenges to the legal system when they are taken to court. Psychologists testify as expert witnesses. Although different shades of opinion exist on the general veracity of these recovered memory claims, many researchers believe that recovered memories of abuse should only be accepted as critical testimony when there is converging evidence of abuse from some other source (hospital records, other witnesses, etc.). The vagaries of memory are well known, especially after long delays, and much evidence points to the suggestibility of memory as a potent source for these memories.

7.6 Conclusion

This chapter has provided an overview of the experimental psychology of human memory. As noted at the outset, research in several other traditions also contributes important insights to our understanding of human memory. These include studies from neuropsychology (study of brain-damaged patients), from neurobiology (studying neural underpinnings of memory, usually with animal models), from neuroimaging (studying neural processes in intact humans whose brains are scanned by modern neuroimaging techniques while they are learning or retrieving information), from developmental psychology (studying memories of children and older adults), and from other directions, too. The study of human memory has become increasingly interdisciplinary. Keep in mind, then, that the perspective offered in this chapter is only one of many that are useful. However, the insights and research of experimental psychologists have defined the study of human memory in important ways.

RESOURCE REFERENCES

Bjork, E. L., & Bjork, R. A. (Eds.). (1996). *Memory.* San Diego, CA: Academic Press. This is an excellent collection of chapters on virtually all the topics included in this chapter and many more.

Ceci, S. J., & Bruck, M. (1995). *Jeopardy in the courtroom: A scientific analysis of children's testimony.* Washington, DC: American Psychological Association. A thoroughgoing analysis of the issues related to children's memory and their ability to testify in court cases.

Engelkamp, J., & Zimmer, H. D. (1994). *Human memory: A multimodal approach.* Seattle: Hogrefe and Huber. An excellent book with an emphasis on motor aspects of remembering. (Originally published in German as *Das menschlike Gedächtnis*, Gottingen: Hogrefe and Huber.)

Foster, J., & Jelicic, M. (1999). *Memory: Systems, processes, of function?* Oxford, UK: Oxford University Press. This book contains chapters by proponents of both processing and systems approaches to the study of human memory.

Graf, P., & Masson, M. E. J. (Eds.). (1993). *Implicit memory: New directions in cognition, development and neuropsychology.* Hillsdale, NJ: Erlbaum. A collection of essays about implicit memory that covers the central aspects of this area of research.

Neath, I. (1998). *Human memory: An introduction to research, data, and theory.* Pacific Grove, CA: Brooks/Cole. A fine undergraduate textbook on the subject.

Payne, D. G., & Conrad, F. G. (Eds.). (1997). *Intersections in basic and applied memory research.* Mahwah, NJ: Erlbaum. This book contains chapters in which authors explore a variety of practical issues in which memory research makes a useful contribution.

Schacter, D. L. (1995a) *Memory distortion: How minds, brains, and societies reconstruct the past.*

Cambridge, MA: Harvard University Press. An interesting collection of chapters on errors of memory.

Schacter, D. L. (1996). *Searching for memory: The brain, the mind and the past.* New York: Basic Books. A highly readable tour through the phenomena of human memory. Although the book is intended for a general audience, its author is a leading researcher. This book is a good starting place for someone just coming to the field.

Tulving, E. & Craik, F. I. M. (Eds.). (2000). *The Oxford handbook of memory.* Oxford, UK: Oxford University Press. This recent handbook contains chapters by leading experts on the primary topics in the study of memory.

ADDITIONAL LITERATURE CITED

Anderson, M. C., & Neely, J. H. (1996). Interference and inhibition in memory retrieval. In E. L. Bjork & R. A. Bjork (Eds.), *Memory* (pp. 237–313). San Diego: Academic Press.

Baddeley, A. D. (1986). *Working memory.* Oxford: Clarendon.

Bartlett, F. C. (1932). *Remembering: A study in experimental and social psychology.* New York: Cambridge University Press.

Blaxton, T. A. (1989). Investigating dissociations among memory measures: Support for a transfer appropriate processing framework. *Journal of Experimental Psychology: Learning, Memory, and Cognition, 15,* 657–668.

Bower, G. H. (1972). Mental imagery and associative learning. In L. Gregg (Ed.), *Cognition in learning and memory.* New York: Wiley.

Bransford, J. D., Franks, J. J., Morris, C. D., & Stein, B. S. (1979). Some general constraints on learning and memory research. In L. S. Cermak, & F. I. M. Craik (Eds.), *Levels of processing in human memory* (pp.331–354). Hillsdale, NJ: Erlbaum.

Brown, R., & Kulik, J. (1977). Flashbulb memories. *Cognition, 5,* 73–99.

Bruce, V. (1988). *Recognising faces.* London: Erlbaum.

Craik, F. I. M., & Lockhart, R. S. (1972). Levels of processing: A framework for memory research. *Journal of Verbal Learning and Verbal Behavior, 11,* 671–684.

Craik, F. I. M., & Tulving, E. (1975). Depth of processing and the retention of words in episodic memory. *Journal of Experimental Psychology: General, 104,* 268–294.

Ebbinghaus, H. (1885). *Über das Gedächtnis* [Memory: A Contribution to Experimental Psychology]. New York: Dover Publications.

Graf, P., Squire, L. R., & Mandler, G. (1984). The information that amnesic patients do not forget.

Journal of Experimental Psychology: Learning, Memory, and Cognition, 10, 164–178.

Jenkins, J. (1979). Four points to remember: A tetrahedral model of memory experiments. In L. S. Cermak & F. I. M. Craik (Eds.), *Levels of Processing in Human Memory* (pp. 429–446). Hillsdale, NJ: Erlbaum.

Lindsay, D. S. & Read, J. D. (1994). Psychotherapy and memories of childhood sexual abuse: A cognitive perspective. *Applied Cognitive Psychology, 8,* 281–338.

Luria, A. R. (1968). *The mind of a mnemonist: A little book about a vast memory.* New York: Basic Books.

McDaniel, M. A., & Masson, M. E. (1985). Altering memory representations through retrieval. *Journal of Experimental Psychology: Learning, Memory, and Cognition, 11,* 371–385.

McGeoch, J. A. (1932). Forgetting and the law of disuse. *Psychological Review, 39,* 352–370.

Miller, G. A. (1956). The magical number seven, plus or minus two: Some limits on our capacity for processing information. *Psychological Review, 63,* 81–96.

Neath, I., & Knoedler, A. J. (1994). Distinctiveness and serial position effects in recognition and sentence processing. *Journal of Memory and Language, 33,* 776–795.

Neisser, U. (1978). Memory: What are the important questions. In M. M. Gruneberg, P. E. Morris, & R. N. Sykes (Eds.), *Practical aspects of memory* (pp. 3–24). San Diego, CA: Academic Press.

Raaijmakers, J. G., & Shiffrin, R. M. (1981). Search of associative memory. *Psychological Review, 88,* 93–143.

Roediger, H. L., & McDermott, K. B. (1995). Creating false memories: Remembering words not presented in lists. *Journal of Experimental Psychology: Learning, Memory, and Cognition, 21,* 803–814.

Schacter, D. L. (1995). Memory distortion: History and current status. In D. L. Schacter, J. T. Coyle, G. D. Fischbach, M. M. Mesulam, & L. E. Sullivan

(Eds.), *Memory distortion* (pp. 1–43). Cambridge, MA: Harvard University Press.

Stein, B. S. (1978). Depth of processing reexamined: The effects of precision of encoding and test appropriateness. *Journal of Verbal Learning and Verbal Behavior, 17,* 165–174.

Sternberg, S. (1975). Memory scanning: New findings and current controversies. *Quarterly Journal of Experimental Psychology, 27,* 1–32.

Tulving, E. (1985). Memory and consciousness. *Canadian Psychology, 26,* 1–12.

Tulving, E., & Pearlstone, Z. (1966). Availability versus accessibility of information in memory for words. *Journal of Verbal Learning and Verbal Behavior, 5,* 381–391.

Vogl, R. J., & Thompson, C. P. (1995). The specificity and durability of Rajan's memory. In A. F. Healy & L. E. Bourne, Jr. (Eds.), *Learning and memory of knowledge and skills: Durability and specificity.* California: Sage Publications.

Waldfogel, S. (1948). The frequency and affective character of childhood memories. *Psychological Monographs, 62* (whole No. 291).

Warrington, E. K., & Weiskrantz, L. (1968). A new method of testing long-term retention with special reference to amnesiac patients. *Nature, 217,* 972–974.

Watkins, M. J. (1990). Mediationism and the obfuscation of memory. *American Psychologist, 45,* 328–335.

Wheeler, M. A. (1995). Improvement in recall over time without repeated testing: Spontaneous recovery revisited. *Journal of Experimental Psychology: Learning, Memory and Cognition, 21,* 173–184.

Williams, M. D., & Hollan, J. D. (1981). The process of retrieval from very long-term memory. *Cognitive Science, 5,* 87–119.

Wright, A. A., Santiago, H. C., Sands, S. F., Kendrick, D. F., & Cook, R. G. (1985). Memory processing of serial lists by pigeons, monkeys, and people. *Science, 229,* 287–289.

Communications concerning this chapter should be addressed to: Professor Henry L. Roediger, Department of Psychology, Washington University, One Brookings Drive, St. Louis, MO 63130-4899, USA

8

Neurobiology of Learning

FEDERICO BERMÚDEZ RATTONI
AND MARTHA ESCOBAR

This chapter reviews recent literature on the neural mechanisms involved in the acquisition (learning) and retrieval (memory) of information. We will examine some proposed models that explain how and which parts of the central nervous system are related to the processes of acquiring, storing, and retrieving information. Accumulating evidence shows that limbic structures like the hippocampus and amygdala, as well as the cerebral neocortex, basal ganglia, and cerebellum are involved in the processes related to the formation and storage of memories. As we will see, the neurons of these areas can change the strength of their electrical responses as a function of prior inputs. We will review studies that show how the so-called short-term and intermediate-term memories appear to depend on the activation at a cellular level of different molecules (neurotransmitters, second messengers, and early genes), and that protein synthesis is necessary for the formation of long-term memory. In Section 8.3, we will focus on recent studies on memory formation, emphasizing several brain circuits that handle different sensory modalities, giving examples of those proposed circuits. Finally in Section 8.4, we will review mnemonic effects and some

proposed animal models of neural degenerative diseases – Parkinson's, Huntington's, and Alzheimer's diseases – and their implications for memory formation and retrieval.

8.1 INTRODUCTION

To understand the brain mechanisms that underlie the processes of learning and memory we should first define those processes. Most neurobiologists and psychologists agree that *learning* is the process by which we acquire new knowledge, and *memory* is the process by which we can store and retrieve that knowledge. Additionally, we should add a third element that is known as memory *consolidation*; that is, the process beginning just after the acquisition of information and by which the information can be stored for a long period of time.

During our life span we learn facts that we can use for short or very long periods of time. For instance, if we would like pizza for dinner, we learn the phone number of the pizza restaurant nearby. Minutes later when we are enjoying the pizza we do not remember the phone number any more. This is an example of transitory memories that last for a short period of time which are called *short-term memory* or *working memory*. However, there are more persistent memories that last for months or years, as when we remember our friends at school or our grandmother's cakes. Those are called *long-term memories*. The classification of memories according to their duration was initiated in 1885 by Hermann Ebbinghaus in his work entitled *Uber das Gedachtnis* (About memory). This German researcher initiated the first systematic analysis of human memory.

Since ancient Greece, philosophers have wondered how we acquire knowledge. At the end of the nineteenth century, Ivan Petrovich Pavlov, a Russian psychologist, initiated one of the most influential approaches to the study of learning: classical conditioning. Pavlov postulated after several experiments that certain rules applied to the induction of conditioning. For instance, the *conditioned stimulus* (CS) should be presented before the *unconditioned stimulus* (US), otherwise the conditioning was weak or there was no conditioning at all. Furthermore, the two stimuli should be presented separated by an optimal period of time. That is, if the interval between stimuli is too long, e.g., the CS is presented one hour before the US, there is no conditioning or it is weaker. Later it was found that the optimal interval between stimuli presentation to obtain the best conditioning varies with the tasks; for instance, for the eye blink reflex in mammals it is 200 ms; for the gill withdrawal reflex in *Aplysia*, 0.5 s; for operant bar pressing it is about 2 s. However, there are cases of conditioning in which extensive delays do not prevent effective conditioning. This is the case for conditioned taste aversions in which food followed hours later by vomiting and cramps produce reliable food aversions. Moreover, this kind of conditioning violates the putative equivalence of stimuli, which is the assumption that any CS can be associated with any US, by clearly showing that the taste of food is more prone to be associated with gastric consequences than its color, texture, or shape in the food aversion or food preference context. Almost fifty years of research initiated by psychologist John Garcia and co-workers have convincingly demonstrated that conditioned taste aversion is a highly specialized, dedicated form of learning that associates signals generated during consumption of food with the delayed visceral consequences of its ingestion. In this regard, Robert Ader and Nicholas Cohen demonstrated in the 1970s–80s, by using the paradigm of conditioned taste aversions, that it is possible to produce increments or decrements of immune system responses (Bures, Bermúdez-Rattoni, & Yamamoto 1998).

There are other forms of learning that are not related to association of stimuli, such as *habituation* and *sensitization*. Habituation is one of the simplest forms of learning, in which the organism comes to ignore the recurrent presentation of a weak or non-noxious stimulus. That is, the naturally occurring behavioral response gradually diminishes its strength or its probability of occurring. An example of habituation is when we wear a hat or cap. At the beginning we are aware of our cap, but, as time goes by, we forget that we are wearing it. However, several days after not having worn it, if we put it on the awareness response comes back. This latter process is called dishabituation. Sensitization is another simple form of learning, in which an organism increases its response to a previously presented noxious or threatening stimulus. This is the case when we experience an earthquake, and later we become afraid (sensitized) at any environmental vibration or noise. This form of learning can be reversed by *habituation*. In our example of an earthquake, after several harmless environmental vibrations or noises, we would not experience fear any more.

8.2 SYNAPTIC PLASTICITY

All neurobiologists would agree that information is acquired, stored, and retrieved by the brain. The Spanish anatomist Santiago Ramón y Cajal proposed in the 1890s that the nervous system is composed mainly of nerve cells separated by small spaces, later called synaptic clefts, that provide communication paths among nerve cells. We now know that all brains consist of individual cellular units or neurons. Unfortunately, up to the present time we do not understand completely how the brain encodes memory as a biological entity. However, the brain's cellular architecture provides some clues on how it performs this function. All brains consist of multiple cellular units or neurons. Most neurons have the same parts: a dendritic tree, cell-body, axon, and synaptic buttons (see Figure 4.2). The majority of neurons communicate with each other across a synaptic space by means of molecules called neurotransmitters and neuromodulators. In mammalian brains, billions of neurons interconnect in vast networks of even more numerous synapses. The brain accomplishes all of its remarkable activity through networks of neurons. It is unlikely that a single neuron encodes a specific memory; rather, ensembles of neurons participate in maintaining a representation that serves as a memory. Such ensembles require dynamic interactions among neurons and an ability to modify these interactions, this implies a need for use-dependent changes in synaptic function.

Several researchers proposed the term *synaptic plasticity* to describe the changes that might facilitate the communication among nerve cells. This term refers to the possibility of inducing long-lasting changes that may or may not be reversible. Hebb (1949) increased our understanding of how networks of neurons might store information with the provocative theory that memories are represented by reverberating assemblies of neurons. Hebb acknowledged that a represented memory cannot reverberate forever and that some alteration in the network must occur to provide both a permanent trace in the assembly to make it likely to reconstruct it as a memory. Hebb formalized this idea in what it is known as Hebb's postulate: 'When an axon of cell A is near enough to excite a cell B and repeatedly or persistently takes part in firing it, some growth process or metabolic change takes place in one or both cells, such that A's efficiency, as one of the cells firing B, is increased' (Hebb, 1949, p. 62).

Many of the current advances in our knowledge of synaptic changes occurring during learning were made using the nervous system of a simple invertebrate animal *Aplysia*, the Latin name for a kind of sea slug (Kandel & Hawkins, 1992b). Other examples of invertebrate species used as learning models are the conditioning of food preference in the garden slug, *Limax maximus*, and conditioning of phototaxis using another marine mollusc *Hermissenda crassicoris*. One of the advantages of using this kind of preparation is the relative simplicity of the nervous system of invertebrates. For instance the central nervous system of *Aplysia* consists of a few ganglia, containing altogether about 20,000 neurons. One of them, the abdominal ganglion, controls the movement of two large exposed organs, the gill and the siphon. The gill is used to obtain oxygen from the water, and the siphon is a small organ above the gill that is used to eject seawater and waste. Eric Kandel and his associates initiated their investigations using very simple reflexes presented by *Aplysia* in its natural environment. When the siphon or the mantle shelf that covers it is gently touched, the defensive reflex (unconditioned reflex) retracts both the gill and the siphon to protect them. After several years of investigation these authors were able to identify the neuronal system that subserves the reflexes, and the cellular and molecular changes that occur in the nerve cells during the habituation, and sensitization, as well as the simple conditioning of the withdraw reflex. As we will see, similar molecular and cellular changes have been found in a model developed from a region of the mammalian brain, the hippocampus.

A Model for Learning in the Hippocampus

Some of the recent advances in our knowledge in the synaptic changes related to experience have been found in vertebrates in one region of the limbic system, the hippocampus. As we noted, the division of memory into short-term and long-term derived almost entirely from the work of cognitive psychology. A similar idea has emerged from studies of neurological patients with memory impairments. The scope and severity of human amnesia can best be appreciated in the noted patient H.M. (Scoville & Milner, 1957), whose difficulty has been described as a complete anterograde amnesia – an inability to learn new information after the onset of the amnesia – that causes him to forget the episodes of daily life as rapidly as they occur. H.M. became amnesic in 1953 as the result of a bilateral surgical excision of the medial temporal region performed in an effort to relieve severe epilepsy. The removal was intended to include the amygdala, the parahippocampal gyrus, and the anterior two-thirds of the hippocampus (Figure 8.1). As a result of the surgery, H.M. became profoundly amnesic. Although the epileptic condition was markedly improved, he could accomplish little, if any, new learning; and he appeared to have lost his memory for events that occurred during several years preceding surgery. He retained older memories, and he had a good vocabulary, normal language skills, and an IQ in the normal to bright-normal range. Yet his impairment in new learning was so severe that he required constant supervisory care. He could not learn the names or faces of the persons whom he saw regularly. Having aged since his surgery, he does not now recognize a photograph of himself. This kind of study, as well as experimental work carried out in rodents and primates, reveals the participation of the hippocampus in learning and memory processes.

In 1973, an important discovery made by Tim Bliss and Terje Lomo about hippocampal physiology opened an important door for better understanding the neurobiology of learning and memory. They found that brief, high-frequency electrical stimulation of an excitatory pathway to the hippocampus produced a long-lasting enhancement in the strength of the stimulated synapses (Bliss and Lomo, 1973). This effect is now known as long-term potentiation (LTP). Long-lasting changes in synaptic strength, such

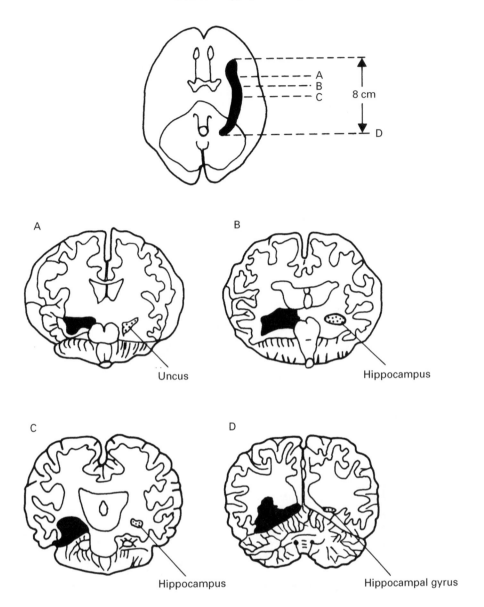

Figure 8.1 *Cross-sections show the estimated extent of removal of portions of the medial temporal pole, hippocampus, and parts of the hippocampus gyrus (dark color) in the patient H.M. Surgery was a bilateral, single-stage procedure, but one side is shown intact here for illustrative purposes. (Adapted from Kandel et al., 1995.)*

as LTP, are thought to underlie learning and memory. LTP is a form of activity-dependent synaptic plasticity that has been investigated mainly in the hippocampus, and a similar phenomenon has also been observed in the rat and cat neocortex where the modifications that subserve certain forms of learning and memory are likely to reside.

To understand LTP, let us describe briefly the gross anatomy of the hippocampus. The hippocampus consists of two thin sheets of neurons folded onto each other. One sheet is called the dentate gyrus and the other sheet is called Ammon's horn. Ammon's horn (cornu ammonis, CA) has four divisions, of which we will refer to only two: CA1 and CA3. The entorhinal cortex sends information to the hippocampus through a bundle of axons called the perforant path. Perforant path axons synapse on neurons of the dentate gyrus. Dentate gyrus neurons give rise to axons (mossy fibers) that synapse on cells in CA3. The CA3 cells give rise to axons that branch. One branch leaves the hippocampus via the fornix. The other branch, called the Schaffer

collateral, forms synapses on the neurons of CA1. These connections are summarized in Figure 8.2 A. Owing to its very simple architecture and organization, the hippocampus is an ideal place to study synaptic transmission in the mammalian brain. Although LTP was first demonstrated at the perforant path synapses on the neurons of the dentate gyrus, today most of the

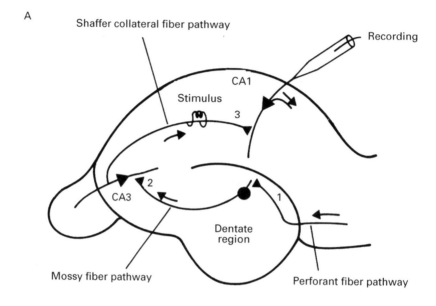

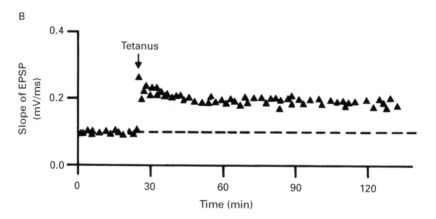

Figure 8.2   *A. There are three major afferent pathways in the hippocampus. The perforant pathway (1) from the entorhinal cortex forms excitatory connections with the granule cells of the dentate gyrus. The granule cells give rise to axons that form the mossy fiber pathway (2). This pathway connects with the pyramidal cells in area CA3 of the hippocampus. The CA3 cells project to the pyramidal cells in CA1 by means of the Schaffer collaterals (3). B. The effect of long-term potentiation in a cell in the CA1 region of the hippocampus is shown in this plot of the slope of the excitatory postsynaptic potentials in the cell. The slope is a measure of synaptic efficacy. Excitatory postsynaptic potentials (EPSPs) were recorded from outside the cell. (Adapted from Nicoll, Kauer, & Malenka, 1988.)*

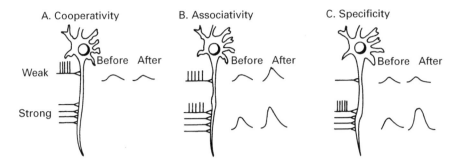

Figure 8.3 *Long-term potentiation in area CA1 of the hippocampus shows cooperativity, associativity, and specificity. A. Tetanic stimulation of the weak input alone does not cause long-term potentiation in the pathway (compare the potential before and after tetanus). B. Tetanic stimulation of the strong and weak pathways together causes long-term potentiation in both of them. C. Tetanic stimulation of the strong input alone causes long-term potentiation in the strong pathway but not in the weak. (Modified from Nicoll, Kauer, & Malenka, 1988.)*

experiments on the mechanism of LTP are performed on the Schaffer collateral synapses on the CA1 pyramidal neurons in brain slice preparations.

In a typical experiment, the effectiveness of the Schaffer collateral synapse is monitored by giving a bundle of presynaptic axons a brief electrical stimulus and then measuring the size of the resulting excitatory postsynaptic potentials (EPSPs) in a postsynaptic CA1 neuron (Figure 8.2 B). Usually such a test stimulation is given every minute or so for 15–30 min to ensure that the baseline response is stable. Then, to induce LTP, the same axons are given a tetanus, which is a brief burst of high-frequency stimulation (typically 50–100 stimuli at a rate of 100/s). Usually this tetanus induces postsynaptic changes, and subsequent test stimulation evokes an EPSP that is much greater than it was during the initial baseline period. In other words, the tetanus has caused a modification of the stimulated synapses so that they are more effective. Other synaptic inputs onto the same neuron that did not receive tetanic stimulation do not show LTP. Therefore, hippocampal LTP is input specific.

One remarkable feature of this plasticity is that it can be induced by a brief tetanus, lasting less than a second, consisting of stimulation at frequencies well within the range of normal axon firing. A second remarkable feature of LTP is its longevity. LTP induced in CA1 of awake animals can last hours or even days. Thus, this form of synaptic plasticity has attracted interest as a candidate mechanism in the formation of memory.

To produce LTP, it is necessary to use a strong stimulus that activates several afferent

fibers together. This cooperative activity has associative features similar to those encountered in classical conditioning. Like memory, LTP can be generated rapidly and is prolonged and strengthened with repetition and, importantly, it exhibits associative properties. This indicates that activity in an input that is strong enough to elicit LTP can help generate LTP in synapses on the same cell activated by a 'weak input' (incapable of eliciting LTP by itself), if the activity in the two inputs occurs within a finite temporal window. The associative property of LTP has often been considered a cellular analogue of associative learning. These features of LTP are illustrated in Figure 8.3.

Mechanisms of LTP

Excitatory synaptic transmission in the hippocampus is mediated by glutamate receptors. Na^+ ions passing through the α-amino-3-hydroxy-5-methyl-4-isoxazole propionate (AMPA) subclass of glutamate receptor are responsible for the EPSP at the Schaffer collateral-CA1 pyramidal cell synapse. CA1 neurons also have postsynaptic N-methyl-D-aspartate (NMDA) receptors. These glutamate receptors have the unusual property that they conduct Ca^{2+} ions, but only when glutamate binds and the postsynaptic membrane is depolarized. Thus, Ca^{2+} entry through the NMDA receptor specifically signals when pre- and postsynaptic elements are active at the same time. Considerable evidence now links this rise in postsynaptic $[Ca^{2+}]_i$ to the induction of LTP. The rise in $[Ca^{2+}]_i$ is believed to activate two protein kinases: protein kinase C and calcium-calmodulin-dependent protein

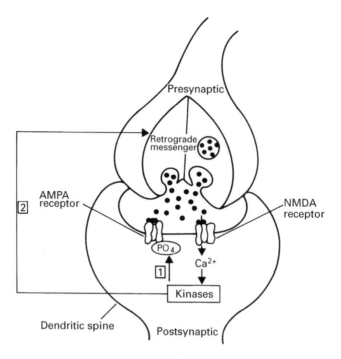

Figure 8.4 *Mechanisms of LTP. Ca^{+2} entering through the NMDA receptor activates protein kinases. This can cause LTP (1) by changing the effectiveness of postsynaptic AMPA receptors or (2) by generating a retrograde messenger that leads to a lasting increase in neurotransmitter release. (Modified from Bear, Connors, & Paradiso, 1996.)*

kinase II (see Figure 8.4). Pharmacological inhibition of either kinase blocks the induction of long-term potentiation.

Following the rise in postsynaptic $[Ca^{2+}]_i$ and the activation of the kinases, the molecular trail that leads to a potentiated synapse may actually branch. One path appears to lead toward an increased effectiveness of the postsynaptic AMPA receptors, perhaps by way of phosphorylation. The other branch may lead toward an increased presynaptic release of neurotransmitter. If this second possibility occurs, then there must be a signal that travels from the postsynaptic neuron to the presynaptic axon terminal. Such a signal is called a retrograde messenger, see Figure 8.4. A number of potential retrograde messengers (nitric oxide, carbon monoxide, platelet activating factor, and arachidonic acid) have been studied. However to date there is still no agreement on the identity of the elusive retrograde messenger involved in LTP. Whereas enzymatic modification of pre-existing synaptic proteins may be sufficient to change synaptic efficacy for modest periods of time, it seems necessary to invoke additional mechanisms to account for the maintenance of LTP for days or weeks. Recent work indicates that

these latter components of LTP may, in fact, involve altered gene expression.

Functional Significance

Although LTP is the leading candidate for a synaptic mechanism responsible for the encoding of memory, it remains unclear whether it is actually used during real learning to store information. This is a difficult question to address experimentally, and a conclusive answer cannot be given at this time, but several lines of evidence are consistent with an important role for LTP in certain forms of learning and memory. In rodents, in which the hippocampus is particularly important for spatial memories, infusion of an NMDA receptor antagonist blocks LTP induction and spatial learning at the same concentrations, while having no effect on a visual discrimination task that does not require hippocampal function. The targeted gene knockout of various protein kinases that impaired LTP also impaired spatial learning, although the degree of deficit in learning did not necessarily correlate directly with the degree of impairment in LTP. Third, as a rat explores a novel environment and presumably learns about it, the synaptic efficacy increases in the hippocampus, but that increase is not due to the motor activity itself. Most evidence firmly supports a role for LTP in learning and memory. However, an unequivocal experimental demonstration of a contribution of LTP to memory is hampered by our lack of knowledge of the biological basis of memory and of the ways in which memories are represented in ensembles of neurons, the existence of a variety of cellular forms of LTP, and the likely resistance of distributed memory stores to degradation by treatments that incompletely disrupt LTP.

The cerebral neocortex as a whole, or certain circumscribed cortical regions, is considered to be the principal site for the storage of memory. Studies of LTP in the cerebral neocortex developed subsequently, but have progressed less rapidly than those in the hippocampus. Experimental data describing the phenomenology and the mechanisms underlying LTP have accumulated in the neocortex, particularly in the visual, somatosensory, motor, and prefrontal cortices. In the developing visual cortex, LTP has been induced by afferent tetanic stimulation at relatively low frequencies, for long duration. Thus, particular attention has been given to the parameters of cortical LTP, and the differences between these and those effective in inducing hippocampal LTP. In the motor cortex, associative LTP following the combined activation of separate sites as well as homosynaptic LTP following activation of single pathways has been reported, and these types of synaptic plasticity have been suggested as being a basis for a certain type of motor learning. Finally, in the insular cortex, a region of the temporal cortex implicated in the acquisition and storage of different aversive motivated learning tasks, it has been suggested that in vivo tetanus-induced LTP of this area is a possible mechanism for the memory-related functions performed by this area of the cortex.

Protein Synthesis

Persistent kinases are likely to contribute to the maintenance of a synaptic modification, but apparently only for a limited time (minutes to hours). After that, a requirement for long-term memory is the synthesis of new proteins. These proteins are probably used to assemble new synapses. The possible role of new protein synthesis in memory has been investigated extensively since the 1960s after the introduction of drugs that selectively inhibit the assembly of proteins from messenger RNA. Protein synthesis inhibitors can be injected into the brains of experimental animals as they are trained to perform a task, and deficits in learning and memory can be assessed. These studies reveal that if brain protein synthesis is inhibited at the time of training, the animals learn normally but fail to remember when tested days later. A deficit in long-term memory is also often observed if the protein synthesis inhibitors are injected shortly after training. However, the memories become increasingly resistant to inhibition of protein synthesis as the interval between the training and the injection of inhibitor is increased. In invertebrates, repeated application of sensitizing stimuli causes a form of long-term memory that can last many days. The application of protein synthesis inhibitors at the time of training has no effect on sensitization measured hours later but completely blocks development of the long-term memory. Likewise, inhibition of protein synthesis at the time of a tetanus has no effect on the induction of LTP in the hippocampus. However, instead of lasting days to weeks, the synaptic potentiation gradually disappears over a few hours.

In the case of synapses that are strengthened after learning, it appears that proteins are used to construct new synapses (see below). In the mammalian nervous system, one approach has been to compare a brain structure in animals that have or have not had the opportunity to learn several tasks. Thus, putting a laboratory rat in a complex environment filled with toys, as well as other rats, has been shown to increase the number of synapses per neuron in the occipital cortex by about 25% as compared with the animals that remained in their home cages. Another approach has been to investigate structural changes after long-term potentiation in the hippocampus. It appears that LTP is also accompanied by an increased number of excitatory synapses. It is important to recognize that there are limits to structural plasticity in the adult brain. Large changes in brain circuitry are generally confined to critical periods of early life. But it is now very clear that the end of a critical period does not necessarily signify an end to changes in the structure of axon terminals or the effectiveness of their synapses.

Structural Changes

The idea that experience can alter the structure and function of cells in the adult central nervous system, improving learning and memory, has been proposed for a long time. Thus, brain morphological changes as a neurobiological substrate of memory were postulated by Santiago Ramón y Cajal, Jerzy Konorski, and Donald O. Hebb. In the twentieth century, several attempts to explore the possible relation between learning and neuronal plasticity have been made. An early and well-known example is the work of Rosenzweig, Bennett, and Diamond (1972; see Rosenzweig, 1996), which was the first to establish experimentally that differential rearing of rats (isolation, social housing, and enriched environments) was associated with striking changes in cortical thickness and dendritic branching. Since then, experimental manipulations of experience have shown that increasing the complexity of the housing environment, maze training, avoidance conditioning, and sensitization, results in neuronal growth in a variety of species (Bailey & Kandel, 1993).

Evidence for changes in synapse number with LTP in the CA1 region first came from studies by Lynch and his co-workers in 1980 who reported that electrical stimulation that produced LTP either in vivo or in vitro also led to a rapid increase in the number of synapses on dendritic shafts (Lee, Schotter, Oliver, & Lynch, 1980). This observation was confirmed and extended in the slice preparation by Chang and Greenough (1982) who also found a rapid increase in the number of shaft synapses per unit area and, in addition, an increase in the number of sessile spine synapses in slices exposed to LTP compared with equivalent low-frequency stimulated control groups. This stimulus-induced synaptogenesis in the hippocampus seems tightly correlated with LTP.

Several experiments have also demonstrated structural changes within sensorimotor regions of the brain after motor training. The most direct test of the involvement of synapse formation or retention in memory is to examine adult animals following training. In rats given extensive training on multiple maze patterns, visual cortex pyramidal neuron dendritic fields were larger than in handled controls. Unilateral visual exposure to maze training produced by contact eye-occlusion in split-brain rats produced unilateral dendritic field increases, ruling out general hormonal, metabolic, motor, or other non-learning aspects of the training procedure as a source of this effect (Chang & Greenough, 1982). In another unilateral paradigm, rats trained to reach into a small enclosure for food had larger dendritic fields in layer V pyramidal cells in the forelimb sensorimotor region of the cortex, a region essential to the performance of this task. Greenough and co-workers compared the effect on synaptic connectivity in the cerebellar cortex of neuronal activity associated with motor learning and with stereotypic activity arising from repetitive exercise. They placed adult rats in one of four experimental conditions: acrobatic conditioning, in which they were required to traverse an increasingly difficult series of elevated obstacles for food reward over a 30-day period; forced exercise on a treadmill; voluntary exercise on a running wheel to which the animals had free access; and inactivity, in which rats were kept in standard laboratory cages. The number of synapses per cerebellar Purkinje cell was elevated by acrobatic motor learning and was unaffected by exercise. These results suggest that only those aspects of activity that are related to the acquisition of a particular learning task lead to changes in synaptic organization.

The structural changes should require the synthesis and/or redistribution of various neuronal proteins, and several studies have demonstrated increased protein synthesis after behavioral training (see Rosenzweig, 1996). Furthermore, various inhibitors of protein and RNA synthesis can have amnesic effects if given near the time of training and can prevent training-induced changes in neuronal morphology (Bailey & Kandel, 1993). In this regard, studies in long-term potentiation, inhibitory avoidance task and conditioned taste aversion (Izquierdo, 1994) indicate that the progress of learning and memory processes implicates an early involvement of glutamatergic NMDA, AMPA, and metabotropic receptors regulated by cholinergic and γ-aminobutyric acid (GABAergic) transmission. This is followed by a phase sensitive to Ca^{2+}/calmodulin dependent protein kinases and still later by a phase sensitive to protein synthesis inhibitors. In another series of studies, Lamprecht and Dudai (1996) using conditioned taste aversion task, showed the relevance of immediate-early gene C-fos for the encoding of long-term memory, supporting the molecular hypothesis asserting that the encoding of long-term memory traces involves modulation of neuronal gene expression. The specific mechanisms by which experience could influence neuronal structure remain to be determined.

8.3 LOCALIZATION OF MEMORY FUNCTION

Studies of patients with brain lesions have provided the foundations of our knowledge about the biological organization of human memory. As we have seen in patient H.M., lesions in humans have produced dramatic memory dysfunction that provide clues about what brain regions are necessary for which memory processes. However, it should be pointed out that brain lesions alter not only the damaged structure, but also affect multiple connected brain systems. Therefore, special care is required when drawing conclusions based on the effects of brain lesions upon specific memory functions. Complex cognitive functions have been assigned to specific areas of the brain. We must be aware that localization of cognitive function does not imply that a specific function is mediated exclusively by one region of the brain. In fact, most functions require the integrated action of neurons on circuits from different regions, thus for Schacter and Tulving (1994) memory systems and brain circuits are not isomorphic. That is, one can have one brain circuit mediating multiple memory systems, or conversely many brain circuits might combine to mediate a particular memory system. Thanks to the recently developed techniques such as functional magnetic resonance imaging (fMRI) and positron emission tomography (PET), it is now possible to visualize activity presumably related to memory processes in the healthy brain. With the lesion studies and the studies using the non-invasive new techniques we have now a much clearer picture of what structures are involved in different processes of memory and how they participate. As mentioned, the fact that medial temporal or diencephalic lesions spares long-term memories has encouraged the view that the cortex is the ultimate repository of consolidated long-term memory.

We will now focus on the functions of some of the major association cortical areas, the prefrontal, and the medial temporal association areas. After many years of research on the role of different cortical areas, many researchers agree that each association area appears to be specialized in function, although all association areas participate in more than one cognitive function.

Temporal Lobe

One of the most intriguing and controversial studies implicating the neocortex of the temporal lobe in the storage of declarative memory traces was performed on living humans in the work of Wilder Penfield, mainly during the 1950s. In this work, as part of surgical treatment for severe epilepsy, patients had their brain electrically stimulated at numerous locations prior to ablation of the seizure-prone region. Electrical stimulation of the temporal lobe occasionally produced more complex sensations than those obtained with stimulation in other brain areas. In a number of cases, Penfield's patients described sensations like hallucinating sounds or recollecting past experiences. This is consistent with reports that epileptic seizures of the temporal lobes can evoke complex sensations, behaviors, and memories. However, there is no way to prove with certainty whether the complex sensations evoked by temporal lobe stimulation are recalled memories.

There is a group of interconnected structures in the medial temporal lobe that appear to be of great importance for the consolidation of declarative memory. As we mentioned, our understanding of the neural basis for declarative memory began with studies on the patient H.M., who after removal of most of the hippocampal formation and its associated medial temporal lobe structures, suffered a profound impairment in new learning (Scoville & Milner, 1957). Because the macaque monkey brain is similar in many ways to the human brain, macaques are frequently studied to further understand human amnesia. The monkeys are often trained to perform a task called delayed non-matching to sample (DNMS). In this type of experiment a monkey faces a table that has several wells in its surface. It first sees the table with one object on it covering a well. The object might be a square block (the sample stimulus). The monkey is trained to displace the object so that it can obtain a food reward in the well under the object. After getting the food, a screen is put down to prevent the monkey from seeing the table for some period of time (the delay interval). Then, the animal gets access to the table again, but now there are two objects on it, one is the same as before, and another is new. The monkey's task is to displace the new object (the non-matching object) in order to get another food reward. In the early 1980s, experiments performed by Mortimer Mishkin and his colleagues at the National Institute of Mental Health and Larry Squire and his co-workers at the University of California, San Diego, demonstrated that severe deficits on the DNMS task resulted from bilateral medial temporal lesions in macaque monkeys. Their performance in this task was close to normal if the delay between the sample stimulus and the two stimuli was short (a few seconds). This result is very important because it indicates that the monkey's perception was still intact after the ablation, and it was able to remember DNMS procedure. However, when the delay was increased from a few seconds to a few minutes, the lesioned monkey made increasingly more errors choosing the non-matching stimulus. The monkeys with medial temporal lesions appeared to provide a good model of human medial-temporal-lobe amnesia. As with H.M., the amnesia involved declarative rather than procedural memory, it seemed more anterograde than retrograde – a loss of information gained before the onset of the amnesia – and new long-term memory was more impaired than short-term memory. This animal model provides us with a window for understanding the neural basis of human memory.

In experiments using rodents similar results have been reported. In particular, lesions of the hippocampus affect spatial and temporal memories. To explore the spatial effects of hippocampal lesions the Morris Water Maze has been employed. It consists of a large water tank in which an animal has to find and remember the location of an underwater transparent acrylic platform submerged in a black circular pool. After several trials in which the animal is randomly released from different points of the tank, it learns to reach the platform. Hippocampal lesioned animals have great difficulty to find and remember the platform, despite the fact that they show good swimming abilities and are sensitive to cold water. In this regard, it has been reported that in humans the hippocampus and insular cortex show increased activity when subjects are remembering mental routes of mental navigation during a PET session.

The amygdala is another medial temporal structure, related to anxiety and emotional memory. James McGaugh and his associates at the University of California, Irvine, showed in a number of studies that functional inactivation of the amygdala, just after the learning trial, induced amnesia for affectively influenced memory. Later on, this group of researchers found that retention could be enhanced by post-training administration of stress-related hormone drugs, such as vasopressin, adrenocorticotropic hormone (ACTH), and corticosterone, suggesting that memory storage could be modulated by the action of endogenous neurotransmitters and hormones released by emotionally arousing stimulation (see Cahill & McGaugh, 1998). Recently it has been found in a PET study that amygdala activation correlates with individual differences in recall for emotional, but not for neutral, film clips.

Diencephalic System

One of the brain regions most associated with memory and amnesia is the diencephalon. This is not surprising, considering that the diencephalon is heavily connected with the temporal lobes. The three regions of the diencephalon implicated in the processing of recognition memory are the anterior and dorsomedial nuclei in the thalamus and the mammillary bodies in the hypothalamus. Large midline thalamic lesions in monkeys produce relatively severe deficits on the delayed non-match to sample task. These lesions damage the anterior and dorsomedial nuclei of the thalamus, producing retrograde degeneration in the mammillary bodies. There have been reports for many years

suggesting a relationship between human amnesia and damage to the diencephalon. A particular dramatic example is the case of an individual known as N.A., who in 1959 at the age of 21, was a radar technician in the US Air Force. One day he was assembling a model in his barracks, while behind him a roommate played with a miniature fencing foil. N.A. turned at the wrong moment and was stabbed through the nose. Many years later when a CT scan was performed, the only obvious damage was a lesion in his left dorsomedial thalamus. After his recovery, N.A.'s cognitive ability was normal but his memory was impaired. He had relatively severe anterograde amnesia and retrograde amnesia for a period of about 2 years after the accident. Although N.A.'s amnesia was less severe than H.M.'s, the quality was strikingly similar. Further support for a role of diencephalon in memory comes from Korsakoff's syndrome. Korsakoff's syndrome, commonly results from chronic alcoholism and is characterized by confusion, confabulations, severe memory impairment, and apathy. The majority of cases of Korsakoff's syndrome present lesions in the dorsomedial thalamus and the mammillary bodies.

Prefrontal Cortex

One of the most obvious anatomical differences between primates (especially humans) and other mammals are that primates have a large frontal lobe. The rostral end of the frontal lobe, the prefrontal cortex, is particularly highly developed. One reason for thinking that the prefrontal cortex may be involved in learning and memory is that it is interconnected with the medial temporal lobe and diencephalic structures. Some of the first evidence suggesting that the frontal lobe is important for learning and memory came from experiments performed in the 1930s employing a delayed response task in monkeys as well as other tasks including a delay period. Experiments conducted more recently suggest that the prefrontal cortex is involved with working memory for problem solving and the planning of behavior. One piece of evidence comes from the behavior of humans with lesions in the prefrontal cortex. These people usually perform better than those with medial temporal lesions on simple memory tasks such as recalling information after a delay period. However, in other complex tasks, humans with prefrontal damage show marked deficits. In this regard, in a recent study using fMRI, it has been reported that increments in the left prefrontal activation (anterior portion of the inferior prefrontal gyrus) occur when subjects make semantic versus non-semantic decisions about words. Even though the left frontal activation is more related to semantic processing associated with language, increased activity of this area has also been reported after non-verbal stimuli, such as looking at faces (Haxby et al., 1996). Finally it should be mentioned that increased activity in the frontal lobe has also been found during the performance of self-ordering pointing, a task in which the subjects are required to point to a different design on each card presented (on a sequence of playing cards) until all eight designs have been selected. In this condition, the subjects had to maintain an on-going record of the stimuli that they had already selected. Thus, it seems that the frontal lobe is related to strategic memory that subserves declarative memory in problem-solving and reasoning (Gabrieli, 1998).

In animal studies, Joaquín Fuster at the University of California in Los Angeles, and Kisou Kubota and Hiroaki Niki at the Primate Center at Kyoto, Japan, found that there are subgroups of cells that respond at different phases during a learning task. Monkeys that were implanted with microelectrodes into the prefrontal cortex were subjected to a DNMS task. During training, the researchers found that one group of neurons significantly increased its firing rate when the stimulus was presented to a monkey, another group of cells increased firing during the delay period between stimulus and response, and finally another group of cells increased its activity during the time that the animal was given the response (Fuster, 1995). Similar results have been found by Patricia Goldman-Rakic at Yale University, using eye movements as a response in a modified delayed non-match to sample task. This consists in a delayed saccade task, in which a monkey fixates on a spot on a computer screen and a target is briefly flashed at a peripheral location. After the target disappears, there is a variable-length delay. At the end of the delay period, the fixation spot goes off, and the animal must make a saccadic movement to the remembered location of the target. The authors found that some groups of the neurons keep firing between the stimulus presentation and when the animal gives the response. The authors called this group of neurons 'memory fields' because their activity corresponds to a mental state (working memory) interposed between the stimulus presentation and the emission of the responses (Goldman-Rakic, 1992b).

Finally, another example of a cortical area containing neurons that appear to retain working memory information is the lateral intraparietal cortex (area LIP). The responses of many neurons in area LIP show patterns that suggest a working memory function. Neurons in the LIP area keep firing throughout the delay period in which there is no stimulus, until saccadic movements finally occur (Goldman-Rakic, 1992b).

8.4 MODELS FOR DEGENERATIVE DISEASES

Some human diseases can produce memory impairment. Analysis of these abnormalities has provided some critical insights into the mechanisms underlying learning and memory processes. As people live longer by taking advantage of improved treatments for the infectious and cardiovascular diseases that were once unavoidably fatal, the incidence of degenerative disorders of the brain has increased. A degenerative disorder is one in which the disease process is progressive. Three of the most frequent and devastating degenerative disorders, each named for the physician who first described it, are Parkinson's disease, Huntington's disease, and Alzheimer's disease, and each disease involves the destruction of specific sets of neurons in rather distinctive ways.

Parkinson's disease

The most common disorder affecting the basal ganglia is named after the English physician who first described it in 1857. Patients with Parkinson's disease have difficulty initiating movements. Their movements are slower, and they lack the ability to generate spontaneous movements. Because of the increased tone, their muscles become rigid and they show a characteristic resting tremor, most prominently in their hands and fingers. If the disease is not treated these signs gradually worsen, eventually rendering patients completely unable to move voluntarily. Parkinson's patients also present cognitive impairments, mainly in spatial, temporal, and reference memory. For instance, they show a defective performance determining the sequential order of different stimuli. With respect to procedural memory, Parkinson's patients show severe deficits in learning motor skills. In the 1950s there was a major breakthrough in our understanding of this disease when investigators discovered that the neurotransmitter dopamine is severely depleted in the brains of patients with Parkinson's disease. This depletion results from the degeneration of dopaminergic neurons in the substantia nigra that project to the striatum, where they are critical for controlling the processing of information by the basal ganglia.

Huntington's Disease

The basal ganglia are also implicated in another serious neurological disease, described in 1872 by the American physician George Huntington, on the basis of cases that he, his father, and his grandfather had observed in their practices. This disease generally begins in the patients' late 30s and early 40s. It is characterized by four features: heritability, chorea (incessant, rapid, jerky movements), dementia, and death 15 or 20 years after onset. This disease, now called Huntington's disease, affects men and women with equal frequency, about five cases per 100,000 people. Huntington observed that the disease occurred in clusters within families and followed certain patterns of inheritance.

Huntington's patients present severe impairments in anterograde memory (especially retrieval of words, phrases, images, sounds, and maze tasks) as well as retrograde memory (especially retrieval of facts and faces). These findings suggest that the main cognitive problem in Huntington patients is the access to the information during retrieval, instead of an impairment in the information storage.

Huntington's disease involves the loss of cholinergic and GABAergic neurons in the corpus striatum. The death of these nerve cells is thought to cause chorea. The impaired cognitive functions and eventual dementia may be due either to a concomitant loss of cortical neurons or to the disruption of normal activity in the cognitive portions of the basal ganglia. It is now possible, using imaging techniques, to demonstrate selective loss of neurons in the caudate nucleus of a living patient with Huntington's disease.

Alzheimer's Disease

The German physician Alois Alzheimer (1907) was the first to describe a case of progressive forgetfulness leading to loss of all mental faculties within a few years in a previously healthy woman in her late 40s. Studying the patient's brain at postmortem, Alzheimer observed major wasting of the cerebral cortex. Using stains that deposited silver salts in the nerve cells and examining thin slices of the stained brain under the microscope, Alzheimer saw that the brain was filled with large collections of fibrils tangled in collections within the nerve cell bodies of the cortex. The progressive loss of mental abilities seen in this patient, and later in other relatively young patients whose brains at autopsy revealed the dramatic nature of the degenerative process, became known as Alzheimer's dementia. Alzheimer's disease (AD) has some of the general features of both Parkinson's and Huntington's diseases. As in Parkinson's disease, specific changes occur in brain chemistry. Several neurotransmitters are lost, especially within the cerebral cortex. As with Huntington's disease, some signs have indicated that inheritance is high in certain families, but Alzheimer's families have, until recently, been too rare to study in detail. After many cases were studied, age of onset became less important as a distinguishing characteristic, and the progressive loss of mental abilities became more important. Because the disease does not generally appear until a person's late 60s, and because the early symptoms of forgetfulness may be very subtle, a solid diagnosis prior to advanced signs and symptom is very difficult.

Several groups have reported that there are several deficits in cholinergic markers in the cerebral cortex of AD patients. Additionally, treatment of aged, non-demented humans with muscarinic antagonists (blockers of acetylcholine function) induced memory impairment resembling that present in AD. These findings are consistent with animal studies that show increased cognitive sensitivity to scopolamine (an acetylcholine competitive blocker) with age. The reduction in cholinergic cortical afferentation in AD was subsequently correlated with the partial degree of cognitive impairment. The dramatic reduction in presynaptic cortical cholinergic markers is reflected by a loss of neurons in the cholinergic basal forebrain including the nucleus basalis magnocellularis (NBM), also called nucleus of Meynert, the major source of cortical cholinergic innervation. Although the mechanisms leading to the degeneration of cholinergic neurons in the nucleus basalis Meynert are unknown, it has been speculated that neuronal death may result from the accumulation of neurofibrillary tangles in these neurons. The body of evidence accumulated by biochemical, pharmacological, and behavioral studies in the intervening years has supported the view that central cholinergic systems play a significant role in cognition impairment. Moreover recent studies underline the participation of other neurotransmitter systems such as excitatory amino acids as part of the etiology of AD.

As mentioned, AD results, at least in part, from a deficit in acetylcholine neurotransmission due to a degeneration of the large cholinergic neurons located in the NBM (Whitehouse et al., 1982). During the last decades of the twentieth century many animal models for degenerative disorders were developed. In animals, it has been demonstrated that lesions of the NBM produced severe impairments in cognitive function. In addition, cortical cholinergic activity has been correlated with recovery of associative functions in a wide variety of cognitive models. Thus, it has been demonstrated that grafts of fetal brain containing acetylcholine produce functional recovery from injury in brains of adult animals. Neurons of the NBM seem to be the major population of cells in the central nervous system expressing receptors to nerve growth factor (NGF), a peptide discovered by Nobel Prize laureate Rita Levi-Montalcini in the middle of the twentieth century. Rita Levi-Montalcini showed that this peptide produced growth of cell neurites in a dish preparation. Later it was demonstrated that when NGF was injected into the rat cortex, it was retrogradely transported to cell bodies of the NBM, and hippocampal transected neurons are able to respond to exogenously added NGF. Furthermore, a number of studies have demonstrated that NGF treatments induce recovery of degeneration of lesioned cholinergic neurons and ameliorate spatial memory impairments in aged rats and in animals with NBM lesions. Today a variety of strategies using NGF, and similar developed peptides, to inhibit or retard neurodegeneration in the brain, and to promote the survival and biochemical recovery of damaged neurons are under investigation.

8.5 Concluding Remarks

In this chapter, we have seen that the neural mechanisms for the formation of memories can reside in synaptic modifications. Moreover, it has been possible to identify some of the molecular mechanisms that lead to this synaptic plasticity. Thus, sequential events are represented first as changes in the electrical activity of the brain, then as second messenger molecules, and next as modifications of existing synaptic proteins. These temporary changes are converted to permanent ones by altering the structure of the synapse. In many forms of memory, this involves new protein synthesis and the assembly of new microcircuits. Our brain is constantly undergoing rewiring, to a certain degree, to adapt to life experiences.

Learning and memory are not confined to a single place in the brain. In the formation of memories it appears that highly processed sensory information coming from the cortical association areas is fed into the medial temporal cortex and processing goes on there and in the associated structures of the diencephalon, before memories are finally stored in a more permanent form in the neocortex.

At the end of the chapter we reviewed how analysis of some human diseases such as Parkinson's, Huntington's, and Alzheimer's, which produce memory impairment, has provided some critical insights into the mechanisms underlying learning and memory processes, since each disease involves the destruction of specific sets of neurons, and therefore different neurotransmitter systems.

Resource References

Gabrieli, J. D. E. (1998). Cognitive neuroscience of human memory. *Annual Review of Psychology, 49,* 87–115.

Goldman-Rakic, P. S. (1992a). La memoria funcional y la mente. *Scientific American, 194,* 68–75. (Spanish edition.)

Goldman-Rakic, P. S. (1992b). Working memory and the mind. *Scientific American, 267,* 110–117.

Kandel, E. R., & Hawkins, R. D. (1992a). Bases biológicas del aprendizaje y de la individualidad. *Scientific American, 267,* 49–57. (Spanish edition.)

Kandel, E. R., & Hawkins, R. D. (1992b). The biological basis of learning and individuality. *Scientific American, 194,* 78–86.

Malenka, R. C. (1995). LTP and LTD: Dynamic and interactive processes of synaptic plasticity. *The Neuroscientist, 1,* 35–42.

Milner, P. M. (1993). The mind and Donald O. Hebb. *Scientific American, 268,* 104–109.

Rosenzweig, M. R., Leiman, A. L., & Breedlove, S. M. (1999). *Biological psychology: An introduction to behavioral, cognitive, and clinical neuroscience* (2nd ed.). Sunderland, MA: Sinauer Associates.

Rosenzweig, M. R., Leiman, A. L., & Breedlove, S. M. (in press, 2000). *Psicología Biológica.* Barcelona: Editorial Ariel. (Spanish translation of the second U.S. edition, 1999.)

Additional Literature Cited

Alzheimer, A. (1907). Über eine eigenartige Erkrankung der Hirnrinde. *Allgemeine Zeitschrift für Psychiatrie und Psychisch-Gerichtliche Medizin, 64,* 146–148.

Bailey, C. H., & Kandel, E. R. (1993). Structural changes accompanying memory storage. *Annual Review of Neuroscience, 55,* 397–426.

Bear, M. F., Connors, B. W., & Paradiso, M. A (1996). *Neuroscience: Exploring the brain.* Baltimore, MA: Williams and Wilkins.

Bliss, T. V. P., & Lomo, T. (1973). Long-lasting potentiation of synaptic transmission in the dentate area of the anaesthetized rabbit following stimulation of the perdurant path. *Journal of Physiology (London)*, *232*, 331–356.

Bures, J., Bermúdez Rattoni, F., & Yamamoto, T. (1998). *Conditioned taste aversion: Memory of a special kind.* Vol. 31 Oxford Psychology Series. Oxford, UK: Oxford Science Publications.

Cahill, L., & McGaugh, J. L. (1988). Mechanisms of emotional arousal and lasting declarative memory. *Trends in Neurosciences*, *21*(7), 294–299.

Chang, F. L. F., & Greenough, W. T. (1982). Lateralized effects of monocular training and dendritic branching in adult split brain rats. *Brain Research*, *232*, 283–292.

Fuster, M. (1995). Frontal cortex and the cognitive support of behavior. In J. L. McGaugh & F. Bermúdez Rattoni. *Plasticity in the central nervous system, learning and memory* (pp. 149–160). Hillsdale, NJ: Erlbaum.

Haxby J. V., Ungerleider, L. G., Horwitz, B., Maisog, J. M., Rapoport, S. I., & Grady, C. L. (1996). Face encoding and recognition in the human brain. *Proceedings of the National Academy of Sciences of USA*, *93*, 922–927.

Hebb, D. O. (1949). *The organization of behavior: a neuropsychological theory.* New York: Wiley.

Izquierdo, I. (1994). Pharmacological evidence for a role of long-term potentiation in memory. *FASEB Journal*, *8*, 1139–1145.

Kandel, E. R., Schwartz, J. H., & Jessel, T. M. (1995). *Essentials of neural science and behavior.* Englewood Cliffs, NJ: Prentice-Hall.

Lamprecht, R., & Dudai, Y. (1996). Transient expression of c-fos in rat amygdala during training is required for encoding conditioned taste aversion memory. *Learning and Memory*, *31*, 31–41.

Lee, K. S., Schotter, F., Oliver, M., & Lynch, G. (1980). Brief bursts of high-frequency stimulation produce two types of structural change in rat hippocampus. *Journal of Neurophysiology*, *44*, 247–258.

Nicoll, R. A., Kauer, K. A., & Malenka, R. C. (1988). The current excitement in long-term potentiation. *Neuron*, *1*, 97–103.

Rosenzweig, M. R. (1996). Aspects of the search for neural mechanisms of memory. *Annual Review of Psychology*, *47*, 1–32.

Schacter, D. L., & Tulving, E. (1994). *Memory systems* (pp. 1–38). Cambridge, MA: MIT Press.

Scoville, W. B, & Milner, B. (1957). Loss of recent memory after bilateral hippocampal lesions. *Journal of Neurology and Neurosurgery Psychiatry*, *20*, 11–12.

Whitehouse, P. J., Price, D. L., Struble, R., Clarke, A. W., Coyle, J. T., & DeLong, M. R. (1982). Alzheimer's disease and senile dementia: Loss of neurons in the basal forebrain. *Science*, *217*, 1237–1239.

Communications concerning this chapter should be addressed to: Professor Frederico Bermúdez Rattoni, Departamento de Neurociencias, Instituto de Fisiologia Celular, Universidad Nacional Autónoma de México, 04510 Mexico, DF

9

Psychology of Language

WILLEM J.M. LEVELT

The psychology of language is the study of how we produce and understand language, how we read and write, and how we acquire these skills. These will also be the main topics of this chapter. Their discussion will be preceded by some remarks on language evolution and by two short sections on language as a generative system and on the history of the discipline. Language is the species-specific communication system of *homo sapiens*. As a product of evolution, it provided selective advantage to our ancestral hunter-gatherer clans that roamed the African savannahs. Much has been speculated about what exactly provided the evolutionary cutting edge of language. Dunbar (1996) stressed its role in social bonding. Primates regulate their bonding largely through grooming, and the time spent on grooming – up to 20% of the waking day – is directly related to group size. Early *homo sapiens* should have groomed some 40% of the day in order to maintain social cohesion in clans of typically one to two hundred members. Language is obviously an attractive alternative. Conversation can be conducted among several participants, who can be outside each other's tactile reach. More importantly, conversation has always been an

indispensable means of exchanging information about one's intentions, beliefs, fears, hopes, joys, that is about mental states. Such a device must have attained substantial significance for the one primate that has a 'theory of mind'. Sole among the great apes, our species has developed the ability to attribute mental states (such as intentions and beliefs) to our conspecifics in order to explain and predict their behavior (Tomasello & Call, 1997), and we understand our own behavior in similar terms. This ability allows us to monitor the state of the social network in which we participate and to act accordingly. Language is a marvelous device for exchanging information about mental states. How often do we use expressions such as 'Peter wants to leave', 'Sue hopes to come'? But mental states tend to be recursive and that is easily grasped by saying such things as 'Mary thinks that Peter wants to leave', or 'I don't believe that Mary thinks Peter wants to leave'.

The evolution of human culture is unexplainable without assigning a central role to language. The ability to converse makes it possible to share information of almost any kind. We use language to exchange useful experiences, to transmit traditional skills to our children, to plan joint actions of various kinds, etc.

Though the selective advantages of having a language are obvious, we will never be able to explain the present structure of natural language from the history of selective pressures that shaped it. That history has been irrevocably lost. Quite different from what Wundt (1900) supposed to be the case, all existing languages are highly complex systems; there are no peoples with simple languages. The long co-evolution of culture and genetic endowment has universally done its work. What kind of complex system is a natural language?

9.1 WHAT IS LANGUAGE?

The major function of language is to share information about whatever is relevant or dear to us. This 'aboutness' is one of the core features of language. Language is referential: 'the dog' (usually) refers to a particular dog; 'a dog' refers to one that has not yet been introduced in the conversation. 'I' refers to the present speaker. By saying 'yesterday' you pick out the day before today. Most words have meanings that can be used to refer to persons, objects, states of mind, or to even quite abstract states of affairs, such as 'democracy'. Language is, in addition, predicative. It is used to say something about these referents: 'the dog is limping', 'I am thirsty', 'yesterday was my birthday'. Predication is language's core business. When you say 'Tom drove his new car from Paris to Rome', you are predicating something about an agent (Tom), namely that he is driving some theme (his new car) from some source localization (Paris) to some goal localization (Rome). Agent, theme, source, and goal are the 'arguments' or 'thematic roles' of this proposition. There are other thematic roles that can be expressed in language, such as 'experiencer' ('John' in 'John loves flowers') and recipient ('John' in 'Mary gave John some flowers'). The predicate plus the thematic roles assigned form the sentence's 'argument structure'.

Closely connected to predication is modification. When you say 'his new car' you are modifying or further specifying 'car' by 'his' and 'new'. You can easily turn predication into modification to make reference more specific: 'the dog that is limping' or 'the limping dog'.

The versatility of language is largely due to its generativity. We can talk about just everything and to do so, we produce ever new utterances. That would not be possible with a fixed set of expressions, such as 'how are you today' and 'beg your pardon'. Rather, language allows us to combine and recombine a fixed set of elements to produce ever new composite expressions. For instance, every language has a small, fixed set of consonants and vowels ('phonemes'). They can be combined in particular ways for building new words: 'tran' is a possible word in English, but 'rtan' is not. Every language has a set of morphemes (some 20,000 for the English of a normal native speaker). Most of them are simple, meaningful words, such as 'dog', 'follow', 'green', 'you'. But others are meaningful elements that cannot stand alone as a word: 'un-' (as in 'undo'), '-s' (as in 'dogs'), '-ed' (as in 'walked'), etc. A large part of a language's generativity resides in combining and recombining morphemes, to create more and more complex words; there is no end to what we can do: 'vaccin' $\Rightarrow$ 'vaccinate' $\Rightarrow$ 'prevaccinate' $\Rightarrow$ 'prevaccination' $\Rightarrow$ 'anti-prevaccination' $\Rightarrow$ etc. This is called morphological or lexical productivity. There is, finally, syntactic generativity. In speaking, we combine words to create ever new phrases and sentences. There is no obvious limit here either. For every sentence we can create a more complicated one that contains it: 'Peter wants to leave' $\Rightarrow$ 'Mary thinks Peter wants to leave', 'I don't believe that Mary thinks Peter wants to leave' $\Rightarrow$ etc. Some languages, such as Turkish, do most of their work with lexical generativity. Others, such as English or Chinese, capitalize on syntactic generativity.

All languages have a generative system for dealing with the semantics of predication and modification, all have generative phonology and morphology for coining new words, and all have generative syntax for creating ever new sentences. Linguists have also noticed surprisingly universal properties for each of these generative systems. There is no semantic system without agents, patients, or recipients. There is no phonological system without phonemes and syllables. There is no syntactic system without verbs. However, as the archive of analyzed languages expands, linguists discover that many of their hypothesized universals turn out to be strong tendencies at best. Languages have evolved to solve similar problems in quite different, often idiosyncratic ways. Most European languages, for instance, have terms for 'left' and 'right'. Their semantics of space makes a major divide between what is left and what is right of the speaker; this is called 'deictic perspective' (Levelt, 1996). But other languages partition space in quite different ways. Speakers of the Guugu Yimithirr in Australia, for instance, use an 'absolute perspective', roughly equivalent to our north–south. They would happily say the equivalent of 'I have a fly on my north cheek' and change it to 'south cheek' when reorienting by 180 degrees. Syntactically, all European languages have phase structure; they chunk words together into meaningful, contiguous phrases, such as 'the big elephant', and phrases can become part of larger phrases, such as 'on the big elephant'. But many Australian languages have no obvious phrase structure. Words that belong together semantically or syntactically are spread out all over the sentence, with other words intervening. Also Latin belonged to this class of free word-order languages. Finally, it is not even the case that all of the world's 5–10 thousand languages are spoken languages. There also exist natural sign languages. Most of them developed in deaf communities. These languages are as complex and versatile as spoken languages.

9.2 HISTORY

Language and its use has always been a topic of great fascination. Its systematic study goes at least back to the sixth century B.C.E., when the great Indian linguist, Panini, devised the first systematic theory of the sound structure of language. This sophisticated system of phonology was orally transmitted to our present day. Explicitly studying the psychology of language is, however, a much more recent enterprise. The term 'psychology of language' ('Psychologie der Sprache') was coined mid-nineteenth century by the German linguists Steinthal and Lazarus. Evolution theory was in the air. Linguists already had a good understanding of how the Indo-European languages had evolved over the last two to three millennia. But they were entirely in the dark (as we still are) about the original natural causes that gave rise to language. Their guess was that language would naturally arise in the human mind. The origin of language would ultimately be explainable from psychological principles. 'Fortunate advances in linguistics presuppose a developed psychology',[1] Steinthal wrote in 1855, but alas, such a psychology did not exist. The 'psychology of language' was invented *pour besoin de la cause*. It was Wilhelm Wundt who took up the challenge. He went all out to lay the psychological foundations for a theory of language origins. Although that theory has long been abandoned, the spin-off of his two-volume *Die Sprache* (1900) has been substantial. With the greatest psychologist of his time dedicated to the psychology of language, it had become a respectable discipline, which easily adopted the work of many others, such as the work by Galton, Ebbinghaus, Marbe, and Watt on verbal memory

and word associations, Binet's efforts to measure vocabulary size, Meringer and Mayer's (1896) classical study of spontaneous speech errors, Broca and Wernicke discovering the left brain's involvement in the production and comprehension of speech, Huey's experimental studies of reading, Clara and William Stern's (1907) first thoroughly data-based study of children's language acquisition and so on. The psychology of language had become established.

The European tradition, continued by Bühler, Claparède, Vigotsky, Piaget, and many others has always been a mentalistic one. Language, after all, is a mental device. In North America the psychology of language increasingly eschewed mentalistic theories or explanations. Dominant behaviorism considered language behavior to be a system of conditioned reflexes, an opinion forcefully defended in the ultimate monument of that tradition: Skinner's *Verbal Behavior* (1957). North America needed the so-called 'cognitive revolution', vigorously stirred by Noam Chomsky, George Miller, Jerome Bruner, and others, to return to a mentalistic psychology. The mood of change had its terminological effects. The new generation of cognitive psychologists coined 'psycholinguistics' for what had previously been called 'psychology of language'.

The American cognitive revolution exerted a major influence on late-twentieth century psychology of language. Language came to be considered as a biological endowment of the human mind, the generative system unfolding quickly during the first years of life, stimulated by linguistic interaction with caretakers and peers. The mature, generative system came to be studied as part and parcel of a complex information processing system, which performs the high-speed feats of speaking and language comprehension. Entirely new approaches were developed to study the implementation of the component linguistic processes in the human brain.

9.3 PRODUCING AND UNDERSTANDING SPEECH

The systematic experimental analysis of speech production and comprehension has produced growing insight in what is called the 'functional architecture' of language, the network of psychological processing components involved in the generation and comprehension of language. Figure 9.1 is a schematic diagram of this processing network. I will call it a 'blueprint' to stress that it is as much a way to summarize the plethora of research findings, as a guide to

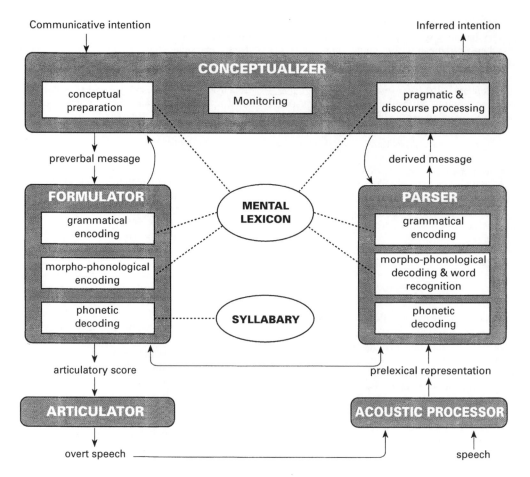

Figure 9.1   *Blueprint of the language user. Processing components involved in the production and comprehension of speech*

research: each component, its way of operating, its distinguishableness from or interaction with other components, its cerebral implementation, is or should be the topic of our research efforts.

In conversation, speaking and listening are closely bound. A participant is both speaker and listener and the verbal interaction is often a joint enterprise among participants to accomplish some goal of mutual interest. What a speaker is going to say is at any moment dependent on the state of the interaction, the attentional states of the interlocutors and their common ground (H. H. Clark, 1996).

Speaking

The left side of the diagram shows the component processes involved in the process of speaking. Its input is called the 'communicative intention'. Almost every verbal move in conversation

is made to affect an interlocutor in some way. The intended effect is the speaker's communicative intention. The first step for a speaker is to consider how the intended effect can be brought about. Imagine the speaker wants his interlocutor to lend him her bike. How to accomplish this? The military approach is to make a command: 'Lend me your bike!'. But this approach may deter a listener as being too direct; it can be more effective to ask whether the other party is able or willing to lend her bike: 'Can/will you lend me your bike?' A very careful approach would be to ask 'Would you know how I can get there – it is really too far to walk?' Such dances of politeness in conversation are universal in human cultures, as Brown and Levinson (1987) have pointed out. A speaker will estimate which move is most appropriate in the present circumstances. The move you opt for is the 'message' you are going to express. Messages come in three main varieties or 'moods'. You can declare something, for instance assert that the dog is limping; you can be imperative, for instance by commanding your interlocutor to lend you a bike, or your message can be an interrogative one, for instance when you ask what time it is.[2]

Whatever the content of a declarative, imperative, or interrogative message you opt to express, it must have an argument structure. In addition, the predicate and the arguments in the message must ultimately be expressible in words. Therefore, a message consists of 'lexical concepts', concepts such as DOG, LIMP, LEND for which there are words in the speaker's language.[3] The arguments in your message refer to entities such as the agent, the recipient, the location of your predication. How to cast them in terms of lexical concepts? The referring function of language is at work here. You will try to make an effective reference for your interlocutor. If you can truthfully refer to the same person as 'the plumber', 'my friend', or 'the giant', then which concept will you choose to activate for your interlocutor? If the interlocutor happens to know the tall man, but not that he is a plumber or your friend, you had better conceptualize the referent as 'giant'. This procedure of selecting an effectively referring concept is called 'perspective taking' (Levelt, 1996). Even two-year-old children show surprising flexibility in perspective taking (E.V. Clark, 1997).

A speaker's intention may be more complex than to express a single message. When you are asked to describe your apartment, you must decide what to say first, what next, etc. That is called the speaker's 'linearization problem' (Levelt, 1989). Most speakers will make an imaginary tour, beginning at the front door and going from room to room in some connected fashion. Linearization is always a problem when complex information is to be expressed. Try, for instance, to explain the game of chess to somebody. Linearization is also at stake when we tell a story, when we talk about personal events we were involved in (and this is most speakers' dearest occupation). Linearization, developing the plot, is one important aspect of our narrative skill, but there are many more, such as foregrounding and backgrounding of information, introducing referents in the story, etc.

Perspective taking and linearization are both ways to guide the interlocutor's attention. Still another way is to focus or defocus arguments for the listener. When you say 'I have a dog', you are introducing a new entity for your interlocutor, namely your dog. You focus it by using the full noun 'dog' and by giving it pitch accent. Your next sentence can be 'it limps'. You now defocus the same argument by using a pronoun

('it') to refer to it. That signals to the listener that it is the same argument you just introduced. But now you focus the limping for your listener, the newly introduced predicate.

Any message must ultimately get formulated. This involves a trio of operations: grammatical, phonological, and phonetic encoding. Grammatical encoding begins by retrieving words from the 'mental lexicon'. That is the repository of words we have built up in the course of our lives. Normal, educated persons will have some 50–100 thousand words available (Miller, 1991). Retrieving words proceeds in two steps. We first access what can be called 'the syntactic word' or the 'lemma', defined as the information about the word's syntactic properties, such as that it is a noun, or that it is a transitive verb. Quickly thereafter (van Turennout, Hagoort, & Brown, 1998) we access the word's 'phonological code', which is used in phonological encoding (see below).

Assume the speaker begins to formulate the message PEOPLE UNDERSTAND. It consists of a predicate (UNDERSTAND) plus an argument in the role of experiencer (PEOPLE). These are two lexical concepts, and they activate the corresponding lemmas in the speaker's mental lexicon. There is always some competition with other meaning-related lemmas (such as *comprehend* when *understand* is the target).[4] The amount of competition determines the speed at which the lemma can be retrieved from the mental lexicon (Roelofs, 1992). Here the retrieved lemmas are a verb (*understand*) and a noun (*people*). The next step in grammatical encoding is to couple the retrieved lemmas syntactically. The lemma *understand* has a syntactic slot for a subject and that subject should express the experiencer argument. The noun *people* is of the correct syntactic category to fill that slot and it also fits the experiencer role. The syntactic coupling (or 'unification') succeeds and the result is a small syntactic tree *people understand*, with the lemmas in this particular order. Such output of grammatical encoding is called a 'surface structure'. We can, of course, encode far more complex syntactic structures and we normally do this incrementally: we begin with the initial parts of the sentence and then 'grow' it to the end. That makes it possible for a speaker to begin uttering a sentence even before it is fully constructed syntactically. The most detailed theory of how speakers accomplish this feat is Kempen's (submitted).

As grammatical encoding is proceeding, phonological encoding dogs it as closely as possible. Shortly after the lemmas *people* and *understand* are selected, their phonological codes become available as well. A word's phonological code is, by and large, its string of phonemes. For the word 'people' this is the string /p/, /i/, /p/, /e/, /l/.[5] For 'understand' it is the string /u/, /n/, /d/, /e/, /r/, /s/, /t/, /æ/, /n/, /d/. All phonemes of a word become simultaneously available (see Levelt, Roelofs, & Meyer, 1999 for details of the experimental evidence on these and other aspects of phonological encoding). These phonological codes plus the syntactic tree are used by the speaker to construct the syllables and the prosody of the utterance.

How are syllables constructed? The evidence is that they are incrementally built up, starting at the beginning of the word. For 'understand', for instance, the speaker first concatenates /u/ and /n/, which completes a legal English syllable /un/. Then /d/, /e/, and /r/ are concatenated into a next syllable /der/, and then follows the composition of the last syllable /stænd/. Notice what happens if the speaker is rather producing the utterance 'people understand it'. The syllabification would now becomes /un/-/der/-/stæn/-/dit/; there is no syllable /stænd/ here. A word's syllabification is variable and context dependent. That is because syllabification straddles lexical boundaries; the syllable /dit/ belongs to both the words 'understand' and 'it'. This variability of syllabification makes it unlikely that syllables are stored in the speaker's lexicon. They are, rather, generated 'on the fly' as phonological encoding proceeds.

Generating the prosody of an utterance involves the metrical grouping of words into phrases and the assignment of intonation. The listener can use these cues to decode the syntax of the utterance and to detect what is focused or defocused by the speaker. In English, Dutch, German, and many other languages (but not in Turkish) speakers generate an intonation contour with pitch accent on the head word of the last phrase in the sentence. For the simple sentence 'people understand' this word is 'understand', which gets pitch accent on its stressed syllable /stænd/. This is followed by a so-called 'boundary tone'. If the mood of the speaker's message is declarative, pitch will normally drop on the last syllable. In the example this happens to be the same syllable as the pitch accented one (/stænd/). But it will be the syllable /dit/ in the utterance 'people understand it'. The boundary tone is very informative about the mood of an utterance. If the mood is interrogative, as in 'people understand it?', the boundary tone tends to go up.

The final step in the speaker's formulating process is phonetic encoding. The whole purpose of phonological encoding is to build a pronounceable structure. But how do the articulators know how to execute the pronunciation?

Let us return to the syllables. Syllables such as /un/ and /der/ and /stæn/ and /dit/ have been produced so often by a normal speaker that they are overlearned articulatory motor patterns. It is most likely (though not yet proven) that they are stored in the forebrain as whole syllabic gestures, and retrieved as soon as they turn up in grammatical encoding. These gestural patterns are further adapted to the current metrical and intonational plan. In addition, we adapt the loudness and intonational excursion of our speech to the environmental conditions, such as prevailing noise and distance from the interlocutor. The outcome of phonetic encoding and hence of the speaker's formulation process (see Figure 9.1) is an 'articulatory score', which can be executed by the articulatory system.

Speech articulation is the most complex motor behavior we can produce. Some hundred different muscles are involved in the generation of some 10–15 consonants and vowels per second. This high speed is only possible because these speech sounds are coarticulated (A. Liberman, 1996). When you say 'cool' you are already rounding your lips for the vowel /u/ when you pronounce the initial consonant /k/; you will not lipround the /k/ in /kill/. As a consequence, consonants and vowels do not appear as distinct entities in the speech signal (like letters in printed words). The listener has the formidable task of reconstructing them from the continuously flowing signal. I will not review the articulation process here, but see Levelt (1989) and Kent, Adams, and Turner (1996).

Monitoring and Self-Repair

The speech we hear most is the speech we produce ourselves. We can not only attend to our own overt speech, but also to our 'inner speech' which keeps babbling during our waking hours and which we misattribute as the speech of others when we dream or when we are in an acute schizophrenic state. It is not exactly known what inner speech is. Jackendoff (1987) and Wheeldon and Levelt (1995) provide theoretical and empirical arguments respectively for the supposition that it is a phonological code, roughly like the output of grammatical encoding. Whatever it is, we can attend to it and parse it just as we parse what is said to us by others. That gives us the ability to monitor our own speech production and correct impending trouble even before articulation has begun. This was probably done by the speaker who said

and further to the *ye-* uh to the green dot.

Here the word 'yellow' got interrupted within its first syllable. What does the speaker do when communicatively disruptive trouble shows up in internal or overt speech? Levelt (1983) provided evidence that speech gets halted immediately upon detection of such trouble. But detection can be relatively slow, for instance when the speaker is just initiating a new clause and has little attention available for self-monitoring. In that case, halting may follow several words after the trouble spot, as in:

And from *green* left to pink – er from blue left to pink.

When we speak we monitor for two classes of trouble. The first one is appropriateness, as in:

I am trying to *lease*, or rather sublease my apartment.

Here the speaker noticed that what she said is potentially ambiguous or underspecified for her interlocutor and she repaired it by becoming a bit more specific. The second class of trouble is all-out error. That happened in the yellow/green and green/blue errors above. We may also detect and correct syntactic error, as in

What things are this kid – is this kid going to say correctly?

or any other type of formal error.

When we interrupt our speech, we often signal to the listener that there is trouble and the kind of trouble. If it is appropriateness that is at issue, we drop in an editing term such as 'or rather' or 'I mean'. If it is all-out error, we may say 'no', 'sorry', or just 'uhm'. The factual repair is produced quite systematically. Almost always the speaker takes up and completes the interrupted syntax (Levelt, 1983).

Speech Comprehension

When we listen to someone else, our main business is to find out what the speaker intends to convey (Hörmann, 1976). Just as speech production, this involves a multilevel processing system. A first step is an initial acoustic analysis of the incoming signal. One thing most listeners are good at is 'streaming', following a speaker's voice amidst all sorts of interfering noise from the environment. We can even attend to a single voice when several people are talking at the same time – the so-called cocktail party effect. We probably especially attend to those aspects of the speech signal that give contrastive information on vowels (telling 'put' from 'pot' from 'pat' from 'pet') and on consonants (telling 'sea' from 'fee' from 'bee' from 'me'). Maybe we already detect whole syllables, at least stressed syllables. It is not well known what exactly is extracted from the noisy speech signal during

this initial stage, but it does have a name: the 'prelexical representation'.

The real parsing of speech requires phonetic decoding in the first place. As mentioned, the units of speech such as phonemes, syllables, words, prosodic phrases, are not freestanding units in the speech stream. One of the paramount problems in automatic speech recognition is the segmentation of the speech signal, in particular segmenting it into words. Human listeners do this mostly easily and automatically. How do they do it? Let us first consider the English listener. In numerous experiments, Cutler and her colleagues have shown that a main word segmentation strategy is to postulate a word boundary just before a heavy syllable (see Cutler & Clifton, 1999 for a review). A heavy syllable in English is one with a full, non-reduced vowel, a syllable that usually receives primary or secondary word stress. Using this strategy, a listener will correctly spot the beginning of words like 'boy', 'beacon', 'article', etc. The listener will mis-parse for words in the speech stream such as 'alert' or 'connect'. How often will the listener, using this method, segment correctly when listening to normal fluent talk? In about 90% of the cases, Cutler and Carter (1987) computed. The segmentation strategy works well for stress-timed languages, such as English, Dutch, or German, but it is not a universal one. In a stress-timed language there is a rhythmic alternation of strong and weak syllables and listeners capitalize on that rhythmic property of their native language for the purpose of segmentation. The main discovery of the cross-linguistic research project of Cutler and her colleagues is that listeners can always exploit the rhythmic properties of their language to derive word boundary information. But these rhythmic properties vary substantially across languages. There is good experimental evidence now that Japanese listeners are particularly sensitive to the characteristic moraic rhythm of their language (a word like *Honda* consists of three timing units or morae, *Ho-n-da*), whereas French, Spanish, and Catalan listeners have been shown to utilize the dominant syllable rhythm of their languages.

Can listeners exploit the speech signal to extract information on phrasal constituency? Some typical experiments in the psychology of language show that they can, to some extent at least. For instance, Levelt, Zwanenberg, and Ouweneel (1970) had four female native speakers of French read texts that contained an ambiguous sentence. Here is an example with its two versions (with their unambiguous English translations):

A. *Il veut vendre cet objet / volé à son ami*
(He wants to sell that object / stolen from his friend)
B. *Il veut vendre cet objet volé / à son ami*
(He wants to sell that stolen object / to his friend)

The text preceding the target sentence made it completely unambiguous and rarely did a speaker notice any ambiguity. The two versions (A and B) were spliced out of their texts: the 'context' versions. After having read the texts, the speakers were informed about the potential ambiguity of the target sentences. Now they were asked to read them as unambiguously as they could in either version (A and B). This provided the 'isolated' versions (A and B) of the sentences. The context and the isolated versions of the sentences were presented to groups of native French listeners. They were explicitly informed about the ambiguity of the sentences they were going to hear, and invited to judge which interpretation had been intended by the speaker. They were correct in 75% of the isolated cases (significantly different from the 50% chance level) and there was no significant bias towards the one or the other interpretation. This means that speakers can explicitly provide disambiguating prosodic information if asked to do so. For the versions spoken in context the correct score dropped to 60%. This still differed significantly from chance, but also from the 75% above. Clearly, speakers do not bother much to provide disambiguating prosodic information if the semantic context does the work already. An acoustic analysis of the context versions of the example sentence above showed that the cues they provide are of two kinds. In the A version, but not in the B version, there is a slight pause between *objet* and *volé*, indicating a phrasal break. In addition, that break is further marked by a marked pitch movement: in the A version *objet* ends at a high tone, *volé* begins at a low tone, whereas there is intonational continuity in the B version.

Cutler, Dahan and van Donselaar (1997) concluded their comprehensive review of research in listeners' exploitation of prosodic cues to syntax by saying that listeners can pick up cues that mark a break. A prosodic break is quite likely to mark a syntactic break, as is the case in the above examples. However, speakers often do not mark syntactic boundaries prosodically, as was the case in most of the text-embedded sentences above. Hence, listeners must have additional ways of parsing a sentence syntactically.

The initial segmentation of word-like and phrasal units is the listener's stepping stone to further morpho-phonological decoding of the speech signal. Central here is the process of word recognition. The core result of word recognition research since Morton's (1969) seminal publication is that an incoming speech signal causes multiple word activation in the listener's mind. Words compatible with a given stretch of speech are simultaneously activated by it. Such a set of co-activated word candidates is technically called a 'cohort' (Marslen-Wilson & Welsh, 1978). Models of word recognition give varying accounts of how a cohort gets resolved. How does the listener reduce it to a single, most likely solution, the recognized word? Here is an example of cohort reduction as originally proposed by Marslen-Wilson and Welsh: The listener receives as input the spoken word signal *trespass*. The first stretch of speech, *tr* activates words in the listener's mental lexicon that begin with 'tr-', such as 'trap', 'tremble', 'treasure', 'treat' and, of course, 'trespass'. All of them are compatible with this word-initial speech segment. This is called the 'word-initial cohort'. When as much as *tre* has come in, incompatible words, such as 'trap' and 'treat' are deactivated, whereas compatible words such as 'tremble' and 'treasure' are further activated. When the input signal has come as far as *tres*, only a few candidate words remain, among them 'treasure' and 'trespass'. Uniqueness is reached when the listener has taken in as much as *tresp*; 'trespass' is the only word in English that has 'tresp' as word-initial part. Reaching this so-called 'uniqueness point', the listeners can recognize the word and experiments show that they often do. Notice that the word can be recognized before it has fully sounded. That is often the case (dependent on where the uniqueness point is located) and that can help the listener to 'predict' the upcoming word boundary.

But the situation is more complicated than this. Most words have other words embedded in them. In *trombone* there is the word 'bone', and indeed 'bone' gets activated when you listen to 'trombone'. When you hear *start* you will coactivate 'star', 'tar', 'are', 'tart' (see Frauenfelder & Floccia, 1998 for a comprehensive review of research in word recognition). To make things even worse, there are often embedded words across word boundaries. Given the uncertainties of initial word segmentation, these can also play a role. For instance, the speech signal *first acre* will not only activate 'first' and 'acre', but also 'stay', 'steak', and 'take' (Cutler & Clifton, 1999). Modern theories of word recognition (see Frauenfelder and Floccia's review) explain how the ensuing within-cohort competition is efficiently resolved with optimal speed. Indeed, word recognition is very fast and often results before the word's end has sounded.

Many words that we encounter while listening to running speech are morphologically complex (though languages differ substantially in this respect, see Section 9.1 above). They can be inflected forms, such as the past tense: 'walk-ed' and pluralization: 'tree-s'. They can also be derivationally complex words, such as nominalizations: 'walk-er' and verbalizations: 'vaccin-ate'. There is increasing evidence that listeners attend to words as wholes, but also to their constituent morphemes. Listeners follow a 'double' or 'parallel route' in parsing morphologically complex words (Baayen, Dijkstra, & Schreuder, 1997). For instance, when a Dutch listener hears a plural form (such as 'tree-s' in English), the speed of recognition is determined by the frequency of occurrence in language use of that plural word.[6] But if the same listener hears a singular form (such as 'tree' in English), the speed of recognition is determined by the sum of singular and plural word frequencies. In other words, it is determined by the frequency of the stem (the frequency of 'tree', whether occurring with or without plural inflection). For an excellent review of morphological decoding, see Schriefers (1998). It may be useful for a listener to parse morphology, in particular inflection. In many languages grammatical decoding would be all but impossible without the listener's attending to inflectional markers. In German, for instance, listeners would be at a loss to distinguish between 'Der Peter rief den Hans an' (Peter called up Hans) and 'Den Peter rief der Hans an' (It was Peter that Hans called up) if they did not notice the nominative versus accusative case marking on the determiners, 'der' versus 'den' (the prosody of the two sentences can be the same).

As soon as words and their inflections are recognized, their syntax and semantics become available for the grammatical decoding of the utterance. This is, by and large, decoding the argument structure. Like word recognition, grammatical decoding is an incremental operation. It begins as soon as the first word is recognized and develops with every further recognized word or morpheme. Also, grammatical decoding is 'omnivorous': it ingests everything, uses any kind of information it encounters. The relevant information can be syntactic, but in many cases the listener uses semantic or pragmatic cues just as fast as syntactic ones. This immediate and massive use of whatever useful cues we can pick up is necessary, because almost every utterance we listen to is multiply ambiguous. The utterance 'my pupil' is ambiguous, because 'pupil' can mean 'part of the eye' or 'student'. A listener will not notice the ambiguity when hearing 'my eye's pupil' in which the 'part of the eye' interpretation is strongly invited. Only very precise reaction time measurements show that the alternative 'student'

meaning is temporarily activated, but then quickly suppressed. As listeners, we are rarely aware of the fact that almost any word we encounter has multiple meanings. In order to derive the argument structure of an utterance, information of the kind 'Who did what to whom', we are much dependent on recognizing the verb or verbs in an utterance. Encountering the word 'see', we know immediately that it must induce the argument structure 'someone sees something' and we will try to assign other words or phrases in the sentence to these 'someone' and 'something' roles. But this is not without problems either, because we will often meet local syntactic ambiguities as we proceed. The 'something' argument of 'see', for instance, can be an entity such as a person or an object ('I see the signpost'), but it can also be an event ('I see the weather change'). This can easily lead to parsing trouble, as in reading the following newspaper headline (from Altmann, 1997):

Crowds rushing to see Pope trample six to death

Certainly, the newspaper did not intend to convey that the Pope trampled six to death, but it is a possible reading of this sentence. That this ambiguity goes unnoticed is due to a combination of parsing strategies we have as readers or listeners. One is that we prefer the simplest possible syntactic structure compatible with the data. When reaching 'see', we prefer to assign the 'something' role to a simple noun phrase (like 'Pope') rather than to a more complex complement clause (like 'Pope trample six to death'). Also, we tend to take early decisions. We can close the argument assignment of 'see' as soon as we get to 'Pope' and we simply take the risk that we must revise it later on. These and other syntactic parsing strategies have been the topic of intensive research, see Frazier and Clifton (1996).

Clearly, other considerations will help us as well to cope with local ambiguities. We use all sorts of circumstantial evidence to zoom in on one solution rather than another. Our knowledge of the world tells us that wherever a Pope goes, crowds assemble to see him. There is increasing evidence that different knowledge sources, such as syntax, semantics and knowledge of the world, affect our parsing in parallel and almost immediately (Kempen, 1998; Tanenhaus & Trueswell, 1995).

Grammatical decoding, in particular the assignment of argument structure, strongly interacts with what is called 'pragmatic and discourse processing' in the diagram of Figure 9.1. In order to derive what the speaker intended to convey, the listener must find out what referents the speaker is referring to by means of the various arguments. 'The Pope' – which Pope?, 'six' – six what?, etc. Here the listener draws heavily on general knowledge, on knowledge of the conversational situation and on what was said before in the current discourse. An example of the latter is this. When somebody tells me 'My car has broken down. The battery is flat', the speaker is making a definite reference by means of the phrase 'the battery'. Which battery is intended? There was no previous talk about a battery. Still, I will immediately infer that it must be the battery of the broken-down car, mentioned in the previous sentence. I can make this inference because I know that cars have batteries. I also tacitly assume that my inter-locutor is 'cooperative' – there would be little gain in conversation if we tried to trick our listeners into drawing the wrong inference[7] (H. H. Clark, 1992). In quick interactions, refer-ring can be quite indirect, but still solvable. Nunberg (1979) presents the example of one waiter in a restaurant telling the other: 'The hamburger wants the bill'. Here 'the hamburger' apparently refers to the customer who had a hamburger, not the hamburger itself. The ambi-guity is easily resolved given shared knowledge of the situation. Still, the ease with which we resolve such ambiguous reference is a miracle. Inferring the referents of arguments in discourse is a major stumbling block for artificial language comprehension technology. That also holds for inferring the referents of pronouns. In their review of discourse comprehension, Noordman and Vonk (1998) discuss various cues that lis-teners use in guessing the referents of pronouns. When you hear 'Harry won the money from Albert, because he . . .', your first hunch will be that 'he' refers back to Harry, the topic of the sentence. But when you hear 'Harry trusted Albert, because he . . .', you will guess that 'he' refers back to Albert. How come? The inference is initiated by 'because'; the speaker is going to explain why Harry trusted Albert. The typical explanation here is some quality of the person trusted. This is only one of many subtle determi-nants of pronoun interpretation.

It will often be the case that a listener, in spite of tremendous skills of interpretation, does not succeed in deriving the speaker's intention. That is not dramatic – we are, in fact, accustomed to it and we possess a whole arsenal of interactive strategies to solve ambiguities of reference in conversation. Here is one example from H. H. Clark (1996, p. 172), the major study of these skills. Brenda and Alva are discussing paintings along the wall:

> Brenda: *that green is not bad, is it, that land-scape?*
> Alva: *What the bright one?*
> Brenda: *Yes.*

> Alva: **It's*[8]*
> Brenda: **Well it's* not very bright, no I meant the *second one along*.*
> Alva: **Oh, that one over* there.*

Here the correct reference of the original 'that green' is progressively cleared up in extensive interaction between the interlocutors. In produc-ing and understanding speech we negotiate meaning.

9.4 ACQUIRING LANGUAGE

It has always surprised psycholinguists that the complex skills of language use develop so early in the life of a child. By the age of 12 to 14 months infants master basic phonetic operations, such as distinguishing the consonants and the vowels of their native language and producing the language's most frequent syllables. At the age of 18–20 months most toddlers have a vocabulary of about 50 words, but then comes the 'word spurt': soon new words are added at a rate of some 8–10 per day, one per waking hour. With the expansion of the vocabulary, the child begins to make the relevant phonological dis-tinctions and with each new word it learns how the word can figure in a particular type of argument structure. Grammatical encoding and decoding begin to shape up by the end of the second year of life. Surely, the five-year-old is not yet an accomplished native speaker, but the basic system is up and running. Evolution clearly designed us to be skilled linguistic com-municators early in life, but it is unknown how this is programmed in our genome.[9] Moreover, that consideration does not provide us with enough restrictions to explain this early pattern of development. Only detailed observational and experimental analysis can help us unravel the forces that drive early language development.

The various components depicted in Figure 9.1 have their own developmental pattern. The maturation of a component is in some cases quite autonomous, in other cases quite inter-active. Surprisingly autonomous is the early maturation of phonetic encoding and decoding. A newborn baby is already able to distinguish native from non-native prosody. The womb is a low-pass filter and the fetus is able to pick up the low-frequency rhythm of the mother's ton-gue. Two-month-old infants can distinguish [ba] from [pa], [bæ] from [dæ] from [gæ], [wa] from [ja], [ma] from [na], [da] from [di] from [du], etc. In other words, they can pick up phonetic distinctions, such as voicing, place of articula-tion, nasality, that may turn out to be relevant for the acquisition of their native language. But when they approach the end of the first year of life, infants become increasingly insensitive to phonetic distinctions that are not relevant to their native language. Whereas six-to-eight months old Japanese babies readily distinguish between [ra] and [la], they loose this sensitivity by the age of ten to twelve months. Infants become 'phonologically deaf' to most non-native sound distinctions (see Jusczyk, 1997, for a review of speech perception during the first year of life).

A similar development is apparent in production. A normal infant begins to babble at the age of about seven months. Babbles are repetitive and alternating syllabic patterns, such as [ba-ba], [gi-gi] or [di-ti]. These first utterances are entirely meaningless. Rather, infants begin building up a syllabary by attending to the auditory effects of their own spontaneous articulations. Only when the basic system is functioning (around the age of 12 months), do they begin to prefer producing native syllables over non-native ones. And only then, one or a few of these babbles begin to denote a person, animal, or action. In other words, meaning is not the driving force behind the child's initial phonetic development; these skills develop autonomously during the first year of life in a sufficiently rich speech environment.

Building up a mental lexicon is a highly interactive enterprise. By the end of the first year, the infant already comprehends a few words. This probably drives the first attempts at production; syllabic patterns that approximate the auditory effects of known words are selected to make the appropriate reference. The simple coupling of syllabic patterns to referents soon gives way to a tripartite development. The first aspect is phonological development. As more and more protowords are added to the lexicon, more and more syllabic patterns must be kept apart to make the relevant meaning distinctions. Somewhere between 1;6 and 2;6 children solve this problem by 'phonologizing' their proto-lexicon. Initially, their protowords are whole articulatory gestures, but slowly they start attending to word beginnings, to word ends and to vowels as independently variable segments (C. C. Levelt, 1994). This provides them with a powerful 'bookkeeping' system for distinguishing words in any of these positions: [pin] from [tin], [tin] from [tan], [pin] from [pit], etc. Also, during the same period, they develop basic skills in coupling two or more words prosodically. The first multiword utterances superficially sound like single words uttered in succession. And indeed, the constituent words often have long pauses between them. But more precise measurements show that non-final words in such utterances are shorter than final ones and that intonation drops from non-final to final words; early multiword utterances are generated as wholes (Branigan, 1979).

A second aspect is the initial development of word meaning. During the first year of life, children have acquired basic knowledge about persons, animals, objects, actions, events and the first words are attempts to denote some of them. They tend to pick out whole objects (dog, chair) and whole actions (go, put), not parts of them. Although children assume that different words have different meanings, they quite early know that you can use different words to refer to the same entity, as one child (age 1;7) did when indicating his bowl of cereal first by 'food', then by 'cereal' (E. V. Clark, 1997). Perspective taking is an early skill.

The third and most dramatic aspect is the acquisition of word argument structure. A child's first two-word utterances can perform various functions, such as to express location ('there book'), possession ('baby shoe'), event structure ('hit ball'), etc. There is beginning argument structure for the expression of declarative ('big boat'), interrogative ('where ball?') and imperative ('more milk') moods. The need to express more complex argument structure is the first trigger for the emergence of syntax. A child acquiring an inflecting language, such as English, French, or German, begins to mark argument structure by inflection towards the end of the second year. Words for actions begin to become inflected for tense (progressive, past, present) as in 'Christy forgot milk' (Bowerman, 1990; child's age 1;11). This marks them syntactically as verbs. For each newly acquired verb, the child learns how to map its semantic arguments onto syntactic roles. In the example, the verb 'forget' puts the agent argument ('Christy') in syntactic subject position and the theme argument ('milk') in first object position.

The way in which verbs map their semantic arguments onto syntactic roles varies considerably. Take the verb 'give'. One month later, the same child produced 'I give mommy a bottle'. Here, the agent ('I') is again in subject position, but the theme argument ('a bottle') does not end up in first, but in second object position. It is the recipient argument ('mommy') that becomes the first object in the sentence. In spite of these differences between verbs, children initially make surprisingly few errors in their syntactic rendering of semantic arguments when they acquire new verbs. But errors do appear much later on, when the child has already mastered a substantial number of verbs. By then the child has sufficient experience with verbs to discover more general patterns in the syntactic realization of argument structure. A child will then occasionally overgeneralize such patterns.

Take so-called 'mental verbs', such as in 'something pleases / excites / bores / surprises / scares somebody'. All these verbs put the stimulus argument ('something') into subject position and the experiencer argument ('somebody') in object position. But there are other mental verbs, such as 'like' or 'hate' that do it the other way round: 'Somebody likes/hates something'. When a child at a later age acquires a less frequent verb of the latter type, such as 'enjoy', she may erroneously put it in the wrong class and make the error 'I saw a picture that enjoyed me' (child aged 6;6 – example from Bowerman's (1990) analysis of these developmental patterns). By the age of twelve, children still occasionally err on Latinate verbs, such as 'donate', patterning them after non-Latinate near-synonyms (such as 'give') to produce errors like 'he donated the church some money'.

As these examples show, important aspects of acquiring the syntax of the native language are lexically driven (E. V. Clark, 1995). The child first learns each verb's typical syntactic frame and only later generalizes these frames to particular general kinds, for instance how to make a complement construction ('I'll help you to find the butter' – see Bloom, Tackeff, & Lahey, 1984). But there is much more to be acquired in syntax, such as the construction of questions, the use of pronouns, the appropriate use of negation, etc. Linguists try to discover patterns of syntactic acquisition that hold cross-linguistically, in an effort to uncover universals of our linguistic endowment (see Weissenborn, Goodluck, & Roeper, 1992).

To become a native language user, the child must acquire more than phonology, meaning, and syntax alone. In order to act through language, the child must become versed in a variety of conversational skills: the ways of turn taking and turn giving, the ways in which to phrase intentions politely and indirectly, the appropriate addressing forms, etc. Each of these begins to develop quite early in life, but full competence is not reached before puberty. This is especially apparent for the skill of narration. The child must learn to guide the listeners attention by making use of various linguistic devices. For instance, in an English-language narration one can use tense marking to foreground an event against a background for the listener. The child (3;9) who describes a scene with a boy and a frog in it as 'The frog got out, when he's sleeping' focuses the listener's attention on the frog's action by using past tense and marks the boy's sleeping as background by using progressive tense. The child narrator will also try to keep the listener's attention focused on some agonist, once introduced, by using pronominal

reference (as the three-year-old above did by using 'he' when referring to the boy that had been introduced earlier). And the narrator will package the information in chunks or 'paragraphs' that the listener can oversee. Young children do not know how to do that. They often introduce each bit of information independently with 'And then . . .'. As these skills develop, narration becomes more and more cohesive. See Berman and Slobin (1994) for an extensive study of how narrative skills are acquired by children in different language communities. It shows that our narrative skills are not in full swing before we reach adolescence.

In literate cultures, finally, the child will have to acquire the culture's writing system. It usually takes years of training for a child to become a skilled reader and writer.

9.5 READING AND WRITING

Evolution did not design us to become users of written language. The widespread use of writing systems is so recent in human history that our genome has not been affected by any selective advantage that a writing system might provide. The cultural evolution of writing systems involves a discovery and an invention. The discovery is that continuous speech is based on underlying discrete units, in particular words, syllables, phonemes. This discovery was made, long ago, in oral cultures. Panini, for instance, developed a detailed, orally transmitted theory of the phonemic structure of language. The invention was to map any of these unit types onto visual symbols. This greatest of all cultural inventions has been an exceedingly difficult process. It succeeded twice, or at most three times in the course of our cultural history, first to the Sumerians a good five millennia ago, then to the Chinese some four millennia ago (though they may have had access to already existing writing systems) and finally to the Olmec and Maya in Central America around 200 B.C.E. It is even much more recent – in fact not much more than a century ago – that mostly Western cultures began to impose literacy as a general educational requirement.

The challenge to the psychologist of language is to explain the apparent fact that most of us are indeed able to acquire a writing system and to become fluent readers. Clearly, the skill is parasitic on two pre-existing skills, language and visual pattern recognition. For a major part reading is language comprehension as discussed in Section 9.3 above, only the input is visual instead of auditory. Following (visual versus auditory) word recognition, the two processes largely coincide. The remaining differences concern the absence of prosodic cues to phrasal parsing in reading (though partly compensated for by the presence of commas and dots), and the more dominant use of low-frequency words and low-frequency syntactic patterns in written texts. A major difference, also, is that reading is not an interactive process, where meaning is 'negotiated' between interlocutors; the reader is alone in deciphering the author's intention.

As hunter/gatherers we evolved refined pattern recognition. We became fast saccadic scanners, quickly detecting and recognizing small visual patterns that are of potential relevance to us, such as shapes of leaves, fruits, silhouettes, footprints. That ability is marshaled when we scan a text. A skilled reader scans some five to six words per second, fixating about 80% of the content words in a text. This is about twice the rate of normal spoken language understanding. The fixation of about 200 ms usually suffices to recognize the word.

The process of visual word recognition has become a major topic in reading research. When the script is alphabetic, the graphemic units to be recognized are letters or letter combinations that represent phonemes. These overlearned units are activated in the visual system by the characteristic contour patterns in the visual input. The ordered pattern of graphemic units activated by a fixated word has direct, parallel access to the orthographic word representation in the mental lexicon; this often suffices to recognize the word, in particular when the word is high-frequent. In addition, the graphemic units also activate 'their' phonemes and the reader can 'assemble' the word from the string of phonemes. This is, in fact, the only way for a reader to handle a new word or non-word, such as 'flork'; it is also what a child does in the first stage of learning to read. This phonemic assembling route remains active in the fluent reader; it gives access to the phonological word representation in the mental lexicon. It is often the faster route for the recognition of less frequent words, words we have less visual experience with. Quite probably the direct visual and indirect phonemic processes are mutually reinforcing in skilled reading (see Perfetti, 1999 for a review of reading comprehension).

The one most critical step in acquiring a script is to become aware of the linguistic units that are to be encoded by the visual symbols, or in other words to repeat the original cultural discovery. This is relatively easy if the unit is a word. Children develop word awareness without much effort. But none of the existing writing systems, including Chinese script, is a pure word-to-symbol matching system; there is always phonology involved. It is harder for children to become aware of syllables as spoken language units. That is what a Korean child must acquire in order to learn Korean syllabic script. But most difficult for children is to become aware of phonemes. There is no spontaneous awareness of phonemes in illiterate cultures, it is absent in illiterates living in literate cultures and many children never acquire reliable phonemic awareness, in spite of extensive training. It is not surprising that phonemic units do not stand out in spoken language. The articulatory gestures that realize successive phonemes substantially overlap in time, different from words and syllables. As a consequence, the acoustic word pattern does not contain discrete temporal units that correspond to phonemes. One can be a normal, fluent, and even skilled language user without having more than a rudimentary ability to become aware of the phonemic structure of a word. Persistent lack of phonemic awareness is a major cause of dyslexia (I. Y. Liberman & Shankweiler, 1991). It is, however, a short-sighted misnomer to call dyslexia a language disorder;[10] it is not.

9.6 CONCLUDING REMARKS – LANGUAGE AND THE BRAIN

It has always been a challenge for the psychology of language to dissect the implementation of language skills in the brain. Traditionally it was responded to by combining the study of language disorders with post-mortem brain anatomical research. The advent of modern brain imaging technology, such as positron emission tomography (PET), functional magnetic resonance imaging (fMRI), magnetic encephalography (MEG), and the registration of event-related electrical brain potentials (ERP) has dramatically changed the possibilities to meet the challenge, because language processes can now be detected and localized in the intact living brain. For reviews of these important developments see Brown and Hagoort (1999), Stemmer and Whitacker (1998), the chapter by Friederici in Friederici (1998), and the section on language in Gazzaniga (2000).

ERP and MEG, with their millisecond time resolution, provide on-line measures of the brain's dealings with linguistic tasks. For instance, when a subject reads or listens to a sentence, every new content word releases a negative brain potential, peaking around 400 ms after word onset. The better a word fits the semantic context, the smaller the N400 response. This N400 is probably generated in the anterior temporal lobes. Other ERP components are particularly sensitive to syntax rather than to semantics and they are generated in other cortical regions. Such findings support the view that syntactic and semantic operations, as much as they interact in sentence understanding, are subserved by separate, specialized systems in the brain (Friederici, 1998).

The precise localization of specialized regions, however, requires the measurement of metabolic activity in the brain by means of PET or fMRI. Such measurements have already undermined the classical notion that the vicinity of Broca's area in the left inferior frontal lobe has an exclusive role in speech production. Rather, this region is as much involved with speech comprehension, in particular with rapid phonetic and syntactic processing.

The psychology of language is now firmly functioning in the larger context of the cognitive neurosciences.

ACKNOWLEDGEMENTS

I am grateful to Eve Clark and to Anne Cutler for their help in the preparation of this chapter.

NOTES

1. 'Glückliche Fortschritte in der Sprachwissenschaft setzen eine entwickelte Psychologie voraus.'

2. Speakers express other kinds of messages as well. We often use expressives such as 'heavens' (or worse) and what H. H. Clark (1996) has called 'collaterals', such as 'uhm'.

3. I will denote lexical concepts by capitals.

4. I will denote lemmas by italics.

5. Phonemes are represented by symbols from the International Phonetic Alphabet (IPA) between slashes '/'. I will only slash the beginning and end of the string or delete slashes entirely when there can be no ambiguity.

6. Word frequency counts are intensively used in psycholinguistic research, because word frequency is one of the strongest determinants of word recognition latency and of word production latency. The best frequency count for English, German, and Dutch is the one published on CDROM by CELEX and distributed by the Linguistic Data Consortium.

7. We do do this occasionally, but that can only be successful just because an interlocutor doesn't expect it to happen.

8. Stretches in between '*' marks indicate speech overlap between the speakers.

9. The only information available is the involvement of chromosome 7 in three different developmental disorders that have a strong linguistic dimension: autism, developmental dysphasia, and William's syndrome.

10. If a society suddenly requires all of its children to acquire bike riding (as is factually the case in Holland), some otherwise perfectly normal children will turn out to find this very hard. By the same reasoning they apparently have a disorder of locomotion, a pathology in urgent need of medical intervention.

RESOURCE REFERENCES

Brown, C., & Hagoort, P. (Eds.). (1999). *Neurocognition of language*. Oxford: Oxford University Press.

Clark, E. V. (1993). *The lexicon in acquisition*. Cambridge: Cambridge University Press.

Clark, H. H. (1997). *Using language*. Cambridge: Cambridge University Press.

Friederici, A. (Ed.). (1998). *Language comprehension. A biological perspective*. Berlin: Springer.

Jusczyk, P. W. (1997). *The discovery of spoken language*. Cambridge, MA: MIT Press.

Kintsch, W. (1998). *Comprehension: A paradigm for cognition*. Cambridge: Cambridge University Press.

Levelt, W. J. M. (1989). *Speaking: From intention to articulation*. Cambridge, MA: MIT Press.

Pinker, S. (1994). *The language instinct*. London: Allan Lane.

Slobin, D. I. (Ed.). (1985). *The crosslinguistic study of language acquisition*. 2 Vols. Hillsdale, NJ: Lawrence Erlbaum Associates.

Stemmer, B., & Whitacker, H. A. (Eds.). (1998). *Handbook of neurolinguistics*. San Diego, CA: Academic Press.

ADDITIONAL LITERATURE CITED

Altmann, G. T. M. (1997). *The ascent of Babel*. Oxford: Oxford University Press.

Baayen, R. H., Dijkstra, T., & Schreuder, R. (1997). Singulars and plurals in Dutch: Evidence for a parallel dual route model. *Journal of Memory and Language*, 37, 94–117.

Berman, R. A., & Slobin, D. I. (1994). *Relating events in narrative: A crosslinguistic developmental study*. Hillsdale, NJ: Lawrence Erlbaum Associates.

Bloom, L., Tackeff, J., & Lahey, M. (1984). Learning *to* in complement constructions. *Journal of Child Language*, 11, 391–406.

Bowerman, M. (1990). Mapping thematic roles onto semantic functions: are children helped by innate linking rules? *Linguistics*, 28, 1253–1289.

Branigan, G. (1979). Some reasons why successive single word utterances are not. *Journal of Child Language*, 6, 411–421.

Brown, P., & Levinson, S. (1987). *Politeness: Some universals in language usage*. Cambridge: Cambridge University Press.

Clark, E. V. (1995). Language acquisition: The lexicon and syntax. In J. L. Miller & P. D. Eimas (Eds.), *Speech, language, and communication* (pp. 303–337). San Diego, CA: Academic Press.

Clark, E. V. (1997). Conceptual perspective and lexical choice in language acquisition. *Cognition, 64*, 1–37.

Clark, H. H. (1992). *Arenas of language use*. Chicago: University of Chicago Press.

Clark, H. H. (1996). *Using language*. Cambridge: Cambridge University Press.

Cutler, A., & Carter, D. M. (1987). The predominance of strong initial syllables in the English vocabulary. *Computer Speech and Language, 2*, 133–142.

Cutler, A., & Clifton, C. (1999). Comprehending spoken language: Blueprint of the listener. In C. Brown & P. Hagoort (Eds.), *Neurocognition of language*. Oxford: Oxford University Press.

Cutler, A., Dahan, D., & van Donselaar, W. (1997). Prosody in the comprehension of spoken language: A literature review. *Language and Speech, 40*, 141–201.

Dunbar, R. (1996). *Grooming, gossip, and the evolution of language*. London: Faber and Faber.

Frauenfelder, U., & Floccia, C. (1998). The recognition of spoken word. In A. Friederici (Ed.), *Language comprehension. A biological perspective* (pp. 1–40). Berlin: Springer.

Frazier, L., & Clifton, C. (1996). *Construal*. Cambridge, MA: MIT Press.

Gazzaniga, M. (Ed.). (2000). *The cognitive neurosciences* (2nd ed.). Cambridge, MA: MIT Press.

Hörmann, H. (1976). *Meinen und Verstehen*. Frankfurt: Suhrkamp.

Jackendoff, R. (1987). *Consciousness and the computational mind*. Cambridge, MA: MIT Press.

Kempen, G. A. M. (1998). *Sentence parsing*. In A. Friederici (Ed.), *Language comprehension. A biological perspective* (pp. 213–228). Berlin: Springer.

Kempen, G. (submitted). Human grammatical coding. Manuscript. Leiden University.

Kent, R. D., Adams, S. G., & Turner, G. S. (1996). Models of speech production. In N. J. Las (Ed.), *Principles of experimental phonetics* (pp. 3–45). St. Louis: Mosby.

Levelt, C. C. (1994). *The acquisition of place*. Leiden: Holland Institute of Generative Linguistics Publications.

Levelt, W. J. M. (1983). Monitoring and self-repair in speech. *Cognition, 14*, 41–104.

Levelt, W. J. M. (1996). Perspective taking and ellipsis in spatial descriptions. In P. Bloom, M. A. Peterson, L. Nadel, & M. F. Garrett (Eds.), *Language and space* (pp. 77–108). Cambridge, MA: MIT Press.

Levelt, W. J. M., Roelofs, A., & Meyer, A. S. (1999). A theory of lexical access in speech production. *Behavioral and Brain Sciences, 22*, 1–38.

Levelt, W. J. M., Zwanenburg, W., & Ouweneel, G. R. E. (1970). Ambiguous surface structure and phonetic form in French. *Foundations of Language, 6*, 260–273.

Liberman, A. (1996). *Speech: A special code*. Cambridge, MA: MIT Press.

Liberman, I. Y., & Shankweiler, D. (1991). Phonology and beginning reading: A tutorial. In L. Rieben & C. A. Perfetti (Eds.), *Learning to read: Basic research and its implications* (pp. 3–17). Hillsdale, NJ: Lawrence Erlbaum Associates.

Marslen-Wilson, W., & Welsh, A. (1978). Processing interactions and lexical access during word recognition in continuous speech. *Cognitive Psychology, 10*, 29–36.

Meringer, R., & Mayer, K. (1896). *Versprechen und Verlesen*. Stuttgart: Goschensche Verlag. (Reissued, with introductory essay by A. Cutler and D. A. Fay (1978). Amsterdam: John Benjamins.)

Miller, G. A. (1991). *The science of words*. New York: Freeman.

Morton, J. (1969). The interaction of information in word recognition. *Psychological Review, 76*, 165–178.

Noordman, L., & Vonk, W. (1998). Discourse comprehension. In A. Friederici (Ed.), *Language comprehension. A biological perspective* (pp. 229–262). Berlin: Springer.

Nunberg, G. D. (1979). The non-uniqueness of semantic solutions: Polysemy. *Linguistics and Philosophy, 3*, 143–184.

Perfetti, C. A. (1999). Comprehending written language: A blueprint of the reader. In C. Brown & P. Hagoort (Eds.), *Neurocognition of language*. Oxford: Oxford University Press.

Roelofs, A. (1992). A spreading-activation theory of lemma retrieval in speaking. *Cognition, 42*, 107–142.

Schriefers, H. (1998). Morphology and word recognition. In A. Friederici (Ed.), *Language comprehension. A biological perspective* (pp. 101–132). Berlin: Springer.

Skinner, B. F. (1957). *Verbal behavior*. New York: Appleton-Century-Crofts.

Steinthal, H. (1855). *Grammatik, Logik und Psychologie*. Berlin.

Stern, C., & Stern, W. (1907). *Die Kindersprache*. Leipzig: Barth.

Tanenhaus, M. R., & Trueswell, J. L. (1995). Sentence comprehension. In J. L. Miller & P. D. Eimas (Eds.), *Speech, language and communication*. San Diego, CA: Academic Press.

Tomasello, M., & Call, J. (1997). *Primate cognition*. Oxford: Oxford University Press.

Van Turennout, M., Hagoort, P., & Brown, C. (1998). Brain activity during speaking: From syntax to phonology in 40 milliseconds. *Science, 280,* 572–574.

Weissenborn, J., Goodluck, H., & Roeper, T. (1992). *Theoretical issues in language acquisition.* Hillsdale, NJ: Lawrence Erlbaum Associates.

Wheeldon, L., & Levelt, W. J. M. (1995). Monitoring the time course of phonological encoding. *Journal of Memory and Language, 34,* 311–334.

Wundt, W. (1900). *Die Sprache.* 2 Vols. Leipzig: Kröner.

Communications concerning this chapter should be addressed to: Professor William J. M. Levelt, Max-Planck Institute, Wundtlaan 1, NL-6525 XD Nijmegen, The Netherlands

10

Knowledge Acquisition and Use in Higher-Order Cognition

GIYOO HATANO AND KAYOKO INAGAKI

This chapter reviews what psychologists know about knowledge acquisition and knowledge use in higher-order cognition or thinking as goal-directed activities involving transformations of mental representations. It focuses on problem solving and comprehension. These are, we believe, two major manifestations of higher-order cognition, because they have clear adaptational values that are complementary: whereas comprehension is a coherence-seeking process through which people can grasp what the world is like, problem solving is search in a space of alternatives which enables people to change the world as they want. We incorporate findings from research on cognitive development (including expertise), because cognitive development is almost equivalent to the knowledge acquisition through problem solving and comprehension, and shows what a long-term consequence of these higher-order cognitive activities is like. We also refer very briefly to experimental cognitive psychology of the constituent processes of higher-order cognition, concepts and deduction as examples.

This chapter emphasizes the active, constructive, and creative nature of the mind, that is, that humans have a tendency to interpret what they observe and to find problems to solve, not to absorb information presented to them or to try to solve externally imposed problems. At the same time, it emphasizes roles of cognitive, biological, and sociocultural constraints (enabling and restricting factors and conditions) that are imposed on the working of the mind.

10.1 HISTORY AND BASIC CONCEPTS

Brief History of the Study of Higher-Order Cognition

Studies of higher-order cognition, thinking, knowledge, or reasoning date back at least to Aristotle. Even within the framework of experimental investigation, such studies have a long history of more than 120 years, as a number of psychologists in the nineteenth century engaged in empirical, though rather introspective, studies of thought. However, higher-order cognition was not a popular topic in psychology until recently. This was because, among others, behaviorism, the dominant paradigm in psychology from the 1920s to the early 1950s, barred the studies that relied on such mentalistic notions as representation, hypothesis, and interpretation. These studies were almost completely suppressed in North America, where behaviorism was very powerful. Studies of higher-order cognition survived slightly better on the European continent, where behaviorism was less salient, and were led by scholars who were interested in human development and education as well as in intelligence and creativity – the German Gestalt school represented by M. Wertheimer and K. Duncker (known for studies on productive thinking and insight), L. S. Vygotsky (higher mental functioning), and J. Piaget (logical operations as internalized actions).

Higher-order cognition resurfaced as a legitimate topic in psychology after the cognitive revolution in the 1950s, which is now often called its first wave. However, studies of higher-order cognition were not in the mainstream until the mid-1970s (with notable exceptions, such as Bruner, Goodnow, and Austin's 1956 study on hypothesis testing, Newell and Simon's 1972 study on information-processing models of problem solving, and a few others). Most of the successful cognitive studies in the early years were concerned with vision and language, and to a lesser extent, with memory, probably because these functions could be researched by manipulating stimuli and observing the corresponding response changes. Post-Piagetian cognitive developmental research was established toward the end of the 1970s.

Thus, studies on higher-order cognition have become an indispensable and integral part of psychology just in the last quarter of the twentieth century. Although still far fewer than studies of memory or language, the number of publications on thinking in the wide sense has increased in such general cognitive psychological journals as *Cognitive Psychology* and *Cognition*, and even a new journal specifically devoted to thinking, *Thinking and Reasoning*, began publication in 1995. Such topics as discourse understanding, concepts and categories, analogy and other forms of informal reasoning, and conceptual development seem to draw the particular attention of cognitive psychologists. Moreover, cognitive studies on thought processes constitute almost a majority in such related areas as instructional and social psychology. Last but not least, studies on higher-order cognition are

encouraged and supported by partner sciences in cognitive science.

Active, Constructive, and Creative Mind

As the history of psychology indicates, research on higher-order cognition is not compatible with behaviorism in many aspects. This is obvious in terms of methodology. Research on higher-order cognition has to use, almost inevitably, mentalistic notions and terms, even though the studies themselves are performed using rigorous scientific experimental methods.

Equally important is that behaviorists and higher-order cognition investigators tend to be radically different in characterizing human beings. Whereas behaviorists generally assume that organisms including humans are passive and idle, proponents of higher-order cognition assume them to be active. According to behaviorists (especially C. L. Hull and his followers), organisms become active only when they are exposed to painful stimulation, physiological deficits like hunger and thirst, and other stimuli conditioned on the preceding two (Hunt, 1965). In contrast, most investigators of higher-order cognition believe that humans, and animals with advanced traits (traits that have appeared relatively recently in evolution) to some extent, are active, curious, and inclined to interact with physical and social environments if and only if they are given such opportunities.

Also, unlike behaviorists who assume that learning occurs only by external reinforcement, investigators of higher-order cognition regard human minds as constructive in the sense that they spontaneously coordinate pieces of information to build more and more coherent systems of knowledge. The latter investigators assume rewards or punishments work through being mediated by the interpretation of the learning organism. They may even assume that learning or the construction of knowledge is based on internal feedback, such as consistency within pieces of presented information or with prior knowledge (Hunt, 1965).

Moreover, most investigators of higher-order cognition assume that humans are creative in the sense that they generate new ideas that transcend what they have experienced and what they already know. Although whether the new ideas are significant or novel for other people depends on context, the investigators believe that creativity itself is ubiquitous (Ward, Smith, & Vaid, 1997). This view is in opposition to the views that creative thinking is distinct from other types of thinking or that there is only a small number of creative people. Such views are apparently supported by some psychologists as well as by many lay people.

Key Constituent Notions: Forms of Knowledge

Before discussing what has been learned about knowledge acquisition and use in higher-order cognition, we first present some of the basic notions in the field and their definitions. We will start with the term 'mental representation'. This term means pieces of information in the mind that represent features of the external environment. Biologically, it is often claimed, mental representation has evolved for the sake of the survival of individual organisms and species. Because the survival for animals with advanced traits presupposes being able to eat without being eaten, they have to mentally represent the current state of the world and use it when they decide how to behave. More or less stable mental representations, which are based on accumulated experiences, articulated into objects or phenomena in the world and actions on them, are called 'knowledge' or 'beliefs' (often used interchangeably by psychologists, though philosophers reserve the former term only when it is believed to be veridical).

Human minds abstract empirical rules from the regularities of experiences (Holland, Holyoak, Nisbett, & Thagard, 1986). Each empirical rule can be described as a condition–action pair (called a production rule), like 'If X, then do Y'. Such empirical rules can readily represent the knowledge we have that indicates how to deal with objects and phenomena, like 'If it is too warm and the windows are shut, open them'. The rules can represent our factual knowledge by extending the action part to include the sending of an internal message, e.g., 'If you have a one-dollar bill, then you can change it for four quarters'. Thus, it does not seem totally impossible to approximate all human knowledge in terms of a set of a large number of these rules. Such a set is often called a 'production system'.

However, other elaborate forms of knowledge are also involved in higher-order cognition. We will mention just some of them here. First, a set of empirical rules are integrated into representations of what specific objects and phenomena are like; these are called concepts or schemas. They appropriately summarize our general and static knowledge about entities; for instance, our concept of dogs represents what we expect for any dog unless specified otherwise (e.g., has four legs, wags its tail when pleased). Concepts or schemas serve as building blocks in higher-

order cognition, because (a) they neatly mobilize related clusters of rules, (b) they are interrelated and constitute a conceptual structure, and (c) they can easily be combined directly (e.g., 'dog house' meaning 'kennel') or by predicates (e.g., dogs are animals). Some schemas are used to describe a sequence of events (e.g., dining at a restaurant) instead of entities, and these are called scripts.

Second, people may construct, also based primarily on empirical rules, mental models. Unlike concepts or schemas, mental models are dynamic, embodied, and often temporary representations of a particular object or situation. They change in response to mentally exerted actions and thus can be used for mental simulation. How vividly mental models indicate a concrete object or situation varies from context to context and from individual to individual.

Third, people are supposed to have theories in selected domains. The term, 'theories' means coherent bodies of knowledge that involve causal explanatory understanding. How similar ordinary people's naive or intuitive theories are to theories scientists have is still an open question, but the former certainly have something more than a collection of facts and/or procedures to obtain desired results. Explanatory mechanisms distinguish theories from other forms of knowledge, such as the restaurant script.

Fourth, procedural knowledge includes strategies, that is, chains of actions to perform a given task or classes of such action chains sharing performance goals and resource allocations. Because our ability to retain or manipulate several pieces of information at a time is limited, we often rely on strategies that can reduce the processing load, even though they may not be the most efficient way to perform the task.

Finally, humans possess knowledge about knowledge, which is called 'metacognitive knowledge'. Metacognitive knowledge plays an important role in higher-order cognition, especially when it is regulated consciously and intentionally.

Concepts and Categorization

Concepts are the most frequently studied and probably the best understood elaborate forms of knowledge, because they are the building blocks of higher-order cognition, as mentioned above, and are small enough for experimentally controlled investigations. Studies of concepts exemplify how complicated the relationships are between individual pieces of experience and the form of knowledge accumulating them. We will review these studies focusing on concepts' most salient function, categorization.

How can people classify new instances into the proper categories? In other words, in what form are concepts represented in the human mind? There are three major models (Medin, 1989): the classic model, the probabilistic model, and the theory-based model. (There is another prominent model of categorization, the connectionist network model, but we will not discuss it in this chapter.) The classic model, which is sometimes called the rule model, assumes that a concept is defined by common, criterial characteristics. Those entities and events that possess these characteristics, and only those, are classified into that concept. Early experiments on concept attainment (e.g., Bruner, Goodnow, & Austin, 1956) were all based on this model. They investigated how humans could identify the defining attributes based on the exemplars of a given concept.

The probabilistic model was proposed as an alternative to the classic model, because the classic model failed to explain some important phenomena (Medin, 1989). For example, there are everyday concepts (e.g., furniture) for which it is difficult to create a set of defining characteristics; there are marginal instances that we cannot classify with confidence (e.g., whether a television set belongs to the category of furniture); and some instances are more representative than others (e.g., a sofa is a better exemplar of furniture than a hat-rack). A 'prototype' version of this model (e.g., Rosch, 1975) assumes that a concept is indicated by a summary representation of many instances belonging to that concept. Common characteristics included in the summary representation are not defining, but serve as probabilistic cues for the category membership. Proponents of this version assert that a concept is best represented by a prototype that has modal characteristics of all instances, and that other instances are graded in terms of their similarities to the prototype.

Another version of this model assumes that a concept in the mind is represented by a set of instances that have been presented and stored (e.g., Nosofsky, 1988), although it shares the assumption that there are no defining characteristics. The summation of a measure of similarity between the new instance and each of the stored instances of a given category determines whether it belongs to this category. In either version, categorization is based on a similarity metric; what differs between the versions is whether the summary representation of properties shared by a majority of members is in the form of a prototype. The process of concept acquisition is, according to this model, to accumulate exemplars (and to build a prototype representing them).

The third, the theory-based model, is against the models that are based on similarity. It points out that similarity alone cannot explain why we have a particular concept (Murphy & Medin, 1985); for instance, why do we possess a category combining animals and plants in spite of the many perceptual differences, but not a concept of humans and dolls? It asserts that the properties that are shared by a majority of exemplars are not independent but correlated, or more accurately, causally connected (e.g., birds have wings, and are light in body weight, in order to fly).

However, as Medin (1989) hints, concepts are both formed based on similarities of instances and embedded in larger networks. Sometimes their integrated representation is salient, and other times they are taken as a collection of constituent instances. These features seem to be shared by all abstract forms of knowledge.

Reasoning: Deduction and Induction

By using forms of knowledge, human beings solve a variety of problems, that is, change the initial state into the goal state under an imposed set of constraints. Similarly, they understand or interpret what the target is like, again relying on an assumed set of constraints. Such processes inevitably involve reasoning. Reasoning (or inference, which is used as the synonym) can be defined as a goal-directed and constrained step-by-step transformation of mental representation or knowledge. It is not limited to logically valid or plausible transformations, but, unlike daydreaming, it has to be controlled by the reasoner's reasoning rules as well as by domain-specific knowledge. It is obvious that reasoning is critically important in higher-order cognition, because knowledge can seldom be applied to new situations as it is. In other words, knowledge is useful only when appropriately expanded by reasoning. However, reasoning is almost never a salient component in problem solving or comprehension. Most investigators in this field assume that basic deductive and inductive reasoning abilities are shared by participants in their studies. We will briefly examine whether ordinary people can solve reasoning tasks and if they can, how they do so.

Deduction

There have been many laboratory studies on deductive reasoning. Initially, the investigators were interested in examining whether children as well as ordinary adults can reason in accordance with ways prescribed by logicians. However, as research progressed, the interest has shifted to clarifying reasoning strategies and the knowledge used in reasoning. Now we know, with certainty, that people often employ content-specific reasoning procedures, based on the substantive interpretation, even when they are presented with logical reasoning problems that can (and should) be solved purely syntactically.

Wason's (1966) selection task is one that has been extensively studied. This task gives participating students a conditional rule in the form of 'if *p* then *q*'. They are also given four cards, each of which shows *p*, not-*p*, *q*, or not-*q* on one side or the other. They are required to decide which of the cards must be turned over to determine whether the rule is true or false. The logically correct choice is to select the *p* card (which may have not-*q* on its back) and the not-*q* card (which may have *p* on its back) only. Participants seldom make this correct choice when the conditional rule has arbitrary content (e.g., If a card has a vowel on one side, then it has an even number on the other). Rather, they tend to make various errors, of which the most common is to select the cards corresponding to *p* and *q*.

However, soon after the original publication by Wason it was shown that for certain formally equivalent rules indicating realistic content, the *p* and not-*q* cards are selected much more often (Johnson-Laird, Legrenzi, & Legrenzi, 1972). For example, for rules such as 'If a person is to drink alcohol, then he must be at least 20 years old', the *p* (drinking alcohol) and not-*q* (not yet 20 years old) cases are chosen frequently. This finding could be interpreted as showing that people can handle realistic conditional rules only. However, Cheng and Holyoak (1985) proposed an alternative interpretation: rules that can be interpreted as expressing relations of permission or obligation tend to induce the correct choice. In other words, conditional regulations are understood in terms of permission or obligation schema which are pragmatic reasoning schema based on obligatory relations. To support their proposal, Cheng and Holyoak demonstrated that facilitation could be obtained for an abstract permission rule, 'If one is to take action A, then one must satisfy precondition *P*'.

Moreover, more recent findings indicate that a rule may be interpreted differently depending on one's perspective, or put differently, one's selection is focused on the cases that are related most directly to one's own goals (Holyoak & Cheng, 1995). For example, 'If an employee works on the weekend, then that person gets a day off during the week', may be interpreted either as 'If an employee works on the weekend, then the employer must grant a day off during the week' (from an employee's perspective indicating the obligation of an employer), or 'If an employee works on the weekend, then that person may

take a day off during the week' (from an employer's perspective indicating the obligation of an employee, because it is equivalent to 'If an employee takes a day off during the week, then that person must have worked on the weekend').

To summarize, people do not solve logical reasoning problems as abstract, logical ones. Although some in the field have proposed formal rules allegedly explaining everyday reasoning performance (e.g., Rips, 1994), none of the proposals were firmly supported empirically. People may often use, as claimed by Cheng and Holyoak, pragmatic rules which are in specificity in between formal rules and domain-specific rules. If so, it would be interesting to research how such inference rules are acquired and how they are triggered.

Another prominent paradigm in deductive reasoning research is the mental models theory proposed by Johnson-Laird (1983). This theory assumes that human reasoning consists of constructing a series of mental models, each representing a true possible situation of a given premise. Once these mental models are constructed, one can ascertain whether a conclusion holds in them – the conclusion is possible if it holds in at least one of the models; necessary if it holds in all the models; and impossible if it never holds. In other words, the theory treats deduction as an extension of discourse comprehension (see Section 10.4). Johnson-Laird and Byrne (1995) claim that it can explain the findings not only by Cheng and Holyoak but also by others. Although all its details have not yet been specified, it is a highly promising alternative in the study of human reasoning.

Induction

In contrast to the large number of studies on deduction, induction has not been a popular topic in experimental cognitive psychology (Holland et al., 1986). This is probably because there is no obviously correct answer for induction, and whether one's answer is appropriate depends on the reasoner's goal, prior knowledge, and context.

However, this makes induction tasks highly useful for assessing reasoners' knowledge in research on knowledge acquisition. For example, how far reasoners inductively project a property observed in an entity depends on their understanding of the concept the entity belongs to and the conceptual structure including the concept (e.g., if a goldfish has a heart, it is likely that all fish have a heart).

The observed individual differences in inductive reasoning tasks are usually explained in terms of different prior knowledge, though logically it is possible to attribute them to different levels and modes of reasoning. A great majority of psychologists assume, though implicitly, that humans are not as different in basic reasoning ability as in domain-specific knowledge.

10.2 KNOWLEDGE ACQUISITION

People become increasingly competent with the accumulation of experiences over the course of years. Almost all people acquire competence in some domains rapidly and easily, whereas in other domains the acquisition of increased competence takes a long time and requires laborious effort. The former domains, which are called privileged or core domains, concern naive theories or coherent bodies of knowledge, the acquisition of which has been vital for the survival of our species. Good examples include those that deal with objects in space and their movement (naive physics), the human mind (naive psychology), and the human body as well as other animals and plants (naive biology). The latter domains, called non-privileged or peripheral domains, represent organized bodies of knowledge (and sets of skills for using the knowledge) that an individual acquires through his or her profession or hobby. Thus people often vary widely in the extent of mastery in these domains. Chess, cooking, and making diagnosis by reading X-ray films exemplify these domains.

Researchers studying conceptual development have dealt primarily with the former domains and those studying expertise have been concerned with the latter. However, these two lines of study share a focus on the construction and elaboration of domain-specific knowledge under constraints, and their findings are complementary. In what follows we define the term 'domain' in a wide sense to deal with both the issue of conceptual development and of expertise; it refers to a range of problem-solving and understanding circumscribed by a common set of constraints or a system of knowledge as produced by these constraints. Here the term 'constraints' refers to conditions or factors that facilitate the process of problem solving, comprehension, or aquisition of knowledge by restricting its possible range.

Characterizing Knowledge Acquisition

How is the human knowledge system acquired? We can derive from studies on the long-term acquisition of knowledge by humans four interrelated characterizations.

Knowledge is Acquired by Construction

The first characterization indicates that knowledge is acquired by construction; it is not acquired by transmission alone (Resnick, 1987). That knowledge is constructed is a corollary of the 'Zeitgeist' among contemporary cognitive researchers, that is, that human beings are active agents of information processing and action. Humans interact with the environment, find regularities, and construct condition–action rules and more elaborate forms of knowledge. Humans acquire knowledge richer than the knowledge they are presented with, or even invent knowledge which has never been presented, often as a byproduct of their problem solving and/or comprehension activity. Knowledge can be transmitted to some extent, but transmitted knowledge becomes usable in a variety of situations only after it is reconstructed, that is, interpreted and connected to the prior knowledge of the learner.

Knowledge Acquisition Involves Restructuring

The second characterization of knowledge acquisition is that it involves restructuring; that is, not only does the amount of knowledge increase but also one's body of knowledge is reorganized as more and more pieces of knowledge are acquired (Rumelhart & Norman, 1978). Conceptual change or a fundamental change of a concept is the best known example of the restructuring of knowledge (Carey, 1985). Knowledge systems before and after the conceptual change may sometimes be locally incommensurable; that is, some pieces of knowledge in one system cannot properly be translated into the other, as exemplified by the shift from the children's undifferentiated heat/temperature concept to the adults' two separate concepts of heat and temperature.

However, restructuring includes milder and more subtle forms and other levels than concepts. Concepts can be substantially modified, but the old and new concepts are not incommensurable (e.g., the concept of animals is expanded to include birds, fish, and insects); relationships between concepts can also change; the same phenomenon may be explained differently as causal devices change; and so forth. Condition–action rules may also be differentiated or amalgamated. In any case, the occurrence of restructuring can be attributed to the creative mind of humans, because it necessarily involves the deconstruction of knowledge that has had some adaptive value.

Process of Knowledge Acquisition is Constrained

The third characterization denotes that the process of knowledge acquisition is constrained (Gelman, 1990; Keil, 1981). As a consequence the acquisition of some forms of knowledge are easy, but others are difficult. The construction and successive revision of knowledge in a domain takes place under the same set of constraints so that the acquired knowledge in the domain is often similar, if not identical, between different individuals. Many cognitive theorists agree that the process of construction is constrained both by innate tendencies and by acquired prior knowledge (i.e., by cognitive constraints).

In actual studies, however, investigators differ widely in the importance they assign to each of the constraints; investigators who focus on conceptual development consider innate constraints to be critical, whereas those studying expertise emphasize prior knowledge as constraints in the target domain. Therefore, more detailed discussion on constraints will be given below separately for conceptual development and expertise.

Knowledge is Acquired Domain by Domain

The fourth characterization indicates that most knowledge is acquired domain by domain. Recent cognitive studies have demonstrated that individual competence varies considerably from domain to domain. In research on conceptual development, Piaget's stage theory, which posited that an individual's competence depended on his or her logico-mathematical structures applicable across domains, has been challenged or even rejected by many current researchers (Siegler, 1978). Many of these researchers believe that, because each domain is under a different set of constraints, the course and process of development vary from domain to domain; in other words, knowledge is acquired, in part, in a unique fashion in each domain.

Investigators of expertise (e.g., Chi, Glaser, & Rees, 1982) have also asserted that the most critical determinant of problem-solving competence is not the general ability, but the relevant domain-specific knowledge. A scientific inquiry or an everyday attempt to understand the world usually takes place within a particular domain. Knowledge produced through such an activity is also incorporated into the relevant domain only. Thus, knowledge is usually acquired separately for each domain, although a small number of pieces of knowledge are shared by a number of domains (e.g., knowledge about literacy or measurement), and analogical transfer or generalization of knowledge based on the recognized isomorphism across domains may sometimes occur (Holyoak & Thagard, 1995).

Conceptual Development

Here we will concentrate on the emergence of and later development in three core domains. Results obtained in recent studies generally show that the privileged domains are differentiated early, due to innate constraints, but the knowledge system in the domains is restructured, probably a few times, before it becomes an adult version.

Emergence of Core Domains of Thought

A growing number of researchers of conceptual development have argued that even young children possess more or less coherent bodies of knowledge about important aspects of the world. They assume that such bodies of knowledge often constitute naive 'theories' containing ontological distinctions, coherent organizations among pieces of knowledge, and causal devices or explanations as essential components (Wellman, 1990). A majority of researchers now agree that by about six years of age children have acquired autonomous core domains of thought: naive physics, naive psychology (or a theory of mind), and naive biology (Wellman & Gelman, 1998). Considering that human beings are a distinctly social species, use objects as tools as well as inhabit the physical world, and possess physiological bodies that must be fed and kept healthy, it is plausible that children are endowed with capabilities to construct naive theories about psychological, physical, and biological phenomena early in life. We present below a few supporting findings from recent studies.

Current studies concerning the early acquisition of physical knowledge have revealed that infants expect an inanimate object to move in accord with the physical principles – action on contact, no action at a distance, continuity (objects exist continuously and move on connected paths) and so on – and are surprised if its motion apparently violates them (Spelke, 1991). In addition, Spelke, Phillips, and Woodward (1995) reported that by the end of the first year infants differentiate between an inanimate object motion and human action; for human actions they consider person's direction of gaze or expression of emotion to be important, while they reason the object motion in accord with the physical principles. This suggests that infants' reasoning already depends upon domain-specific systems of knowledge as far as physics and psychology are concerned.

Simons and Keil (1995) reported that before acquiring detailed factual knowledge, children possess 'abstract' knowledge, for instance, assume different insides for animals and artifacts. When asked to choose one from three photographs of an animal inside, a machine inside and an aggregate substance (e.g., a pile of rocks, or blocks), preschool children consistently picked different insides for animals and artifacts. In addition, when they erred, they tended to assign natural kind inside (e.g., rocks) to the animals and artifact inside (e.g., blocks) to the artifacts.

Wellman, Hickling and Schult (1997) indicated, through both experimental studies and natural language analyses, that young preschool children appropriately apply causal reasoning to psychological, physical, and biological phenomena. Children of 3 and 4 years of age were presented with scenarios consisting of three different types of desired actions and asked if the protagonist could do the desired action, and then required to justify their judgments. The three types of desired actions were: (a) voluntary actions, which the protagonist can do if he wants to perform them (e.g., jump on the floor); (b) physically impossible actions (e.g., floating in the air without any support); and (c) biologically impossible actions (e.g., staying the same size forever). These authors found that not only the 4-year-olds but also the 3-year-olds generated appropriate causal explanations differentially for the possibility of these three types of actions, although offering biological explanations for biological phenomena was somewhat difficult for the 3-year-olds. Moreover, analyses of younger children's speech in everyday life supported the findings from the experimental studies.

Conceptual Change and Elaboration

That children have naive theories about the important aspects of the world does not mean that their theories are the same as intuitive theories that lay adults have. What changes occur in naive theories or their constituent concepts is a popular topic in conceptual development research.

With regard to naive psychology or theory of mind, Wellman (1990) claims that the first conceptual change (or theory change) is from a desire psychology to a belief–desire psychology at around age 3; the desire psychology that 2-year-old children are supposed to possess is based only on an understanding of simple desire as the determinant of human behavior, whereas the belief–desire psychology involves understanding that people possess belief as well as

desire. From age 3 to 6 a second conceptual change occurs within this belief–desire psychology; it is a change from a copy-container theory of mind, i.e., a static mind, to an interpretive-homuncular theory, i.e., an active and constructive mind. After 6 years of age the change involves an increase in the proficiency in children's belief–desire reasoning. Children elaborate and consolidate an interactive view of representation and an active-homuncular theory of mind.

Hatano and Inagaki (1996) characterize the initial form of young children's biology as personifying and vitalistic in nature, and describe what needs to be incorporated and/or modified for this biology to become the lay adult's intuitive biology. Weaknesses in young children's biology are (a) limited factual knowledge; (b) a lack of inference based on complex, hierarchically organized biological categories; (c) a lack of mechanistic causality; and (d) a lack of conceptual devices in biology. During the early elementary school years, children gradually overcome weaknesses (a) to (c) through conceptual change. This change is almost universal, at least among children growing up in highly technological societies. However, the authors claim, the acquisition of conceptual devices of truly biological nature (e.g., 'evolution', 'photosynthesis') requires systematic teaching, and only a limited portion of older children and adults may learn them even with good biological instruction.

To generalize, later conceptual development in privileged domains does not proceed as easily as earlier development. More specifically, whereas earlier conceptual changes are universal and spontaneous, later changes in naive theories which occur by incorporating scientific concepts and correcting 'misconceptions' are difficult to induce. Clement (1982), for example, reported that even after taking a mechanics course, more than 70% of the college students who majored in engineering continued to give erroneous answers for everyday mechanics problems (e.g., what direction of force acts on a coin that is tossed straight up into the air?); they still maintained the misconception, 'motion implies a force'.

Constraints in Conceptual Development

Innate constraints, which can best be described as preferences and biases, are presumed to play a significant role, especially in the initial acquisition of naive theories, whereas prior knowledge as constraints operate to a greater extent later in conceptual development. Innate constraints should serve to direct attention, and restrict the range of hypothesis space to be searched. A unique set of constraints in each privileged domain draws attention to relevant aspects of the target objects or phenomena so that even young children can distinguish those which should be interpreted within the domain from those which should not. In the case of naive biology, for example, there seems to be a set of constraints that direct attention to those aspects of living things that distinguish them from non-living things, such as possessing the capacity for self-initiated movement (Gelman, 1990).

Another set of innate constraints serves to eliminate in advance a large number of logically possible interpretations or hypotheses. Again, an example from naive biology might clarify this point. As demonstrated by Garcia (1981), even rats tend to attribute their bodily disturbance to eating a novel food. It seems likely that humans are endowed with similar constraints – trying to find a cause among a variety of foods for diarrhea, or seeking a physical cause for a cut. In other words, it is assumed that, because those tendencies and biases in the search enable humans to explore possible interpretations highly selectively, they can reach, in most cases, a reasonable interpretation promptly, and thus can accumulate pieces of knowledge constituting a core domain of thought.

How innate constraints are represented in the brain is yet to be known, but recent studies on autism suggest that naive psychology may have a dedicated cognitive mechanism, which autistic individuals lack. In fact, autistic individuals reveal a clear dissociation between psychological and physical understanding. For example, Baron-Cohen (1995) reported that they show disproportionately lower performance on the theory of mind task, such as a false belief task, while their performance concerning physical causation is often excellent. The false belief task was designed to examine whether children can understand that a person's behavior is caused by his or her false belief, and normal children 4 years of age and older succeed in this task without difficulty (e.g., Wimmer & Perner, 1983). Moreover, it has been pointed out that, even if some autistic individuals acquire theory of mind, they do so with great difficulty (see Section 10.5).

The notion of innate constraints does not exclude roles of experience, however. Peterson and Siegal (1997) found that deaf children raised by hearing parents, and thus without fluent signing conversational interaction, had selective deficits in naive-psychological reasoning, whereas deaf children raised in families with a fluent signer did not show such deficits. This suggests that conversational experience with a significant other contributes to the development of naive psychological understanding.

To generalize, even in privileged domains, knowledge is acquired through problem solving and comprehension within each domain, but that process is greatly enhanced by innate constraints.

Expertise

As mentioned earlier, there are a large number of domains in which people can gain expertise. These domains vary with respect to several important dimensions: some are knowledge-rich, and others are knowledge-poor; some require speed, while others do not; novel problems are continuously given in some, whereas the same set of problems is repeatedly presented in others; and some involve interpersonal competition or collaboration, while others are solitary. What is required to be qualified as an expert tends to vary accordingly. Therefore, the only characterization that is applied to all domains of expertise, in addition to the general features of knowledge acquisition mentioned at the beginning of this section, is as follows. Experts have acquired their domain-specific competence through experience in the domain over thousands of hours, which often takes the form of training called 'deliberate practice' (Ericsson, Krampe, & Tesch-Römer, 1993). In contrast to the early and easy acquisition of knowledge in the privileged domains, the process of gaining expertise in non-privileged domains is time-consuming and requires much effort, mainly because the latter is not helped by innate constraints, and this makes knowledge acquisition much harder, especially at the initial phase (see below).

Let us describe a few characteristics of experts, more specifically, their patterns of competence and kinds of underlying knowledge, observed in a number of domains. A cautionary note is needed here. In knowledge-rich domains experts are characterized primarily by their exceptional abilities for solving problems and understanding the relevant entities in the domain, but we will not discuss these aspects here, because they will be reviewed in Sections 10.3 and 10.4. All of the studies reported below used memory or simple performance tasks.

Knowledge Organized into Perceptual Chunks

Experts not only possess a great amount of domain knowledge but also have the knowledge organized into useful chunks (higher-order units involving a number of individual pieces) that can be triggered readily by perceptual cues. This finding was obtained first in the domain of chess. Chase and Simon (1973) demonstrated that chess experts recalled chessboard position patterns taken from actual games, which were presented for 5 s in each trial, more accurately and in a smaller number of trials than novices, although the difference disappeared for random board patterns. Moreover, the experts reported a cluster containing more pieces in the pattern than the novices. In other words, the experts' chunks were larger than the novices'. This perceptual superiority that was found among expert chess players has been replicated in other domains, such as in the game of Go, in reading circuit diagrams, in memorizing melodies, and in interpreting X-ray plates.

Knowledge as chunks cannot be applied across domain boundaries. Good evidence for this was provided by Oura and Hatano (1988). Musically experienced college students and elementary school children, both of whom had had about 5 years of piano training in classic music, and inexperienced college students, were presented a melody (an unfamiliar commercial song having clear tonality) auditorily and were asked to reproduce it. The results indicated that the musically experienced students were superior to the inexperienced ones, regardless of age, in the speed of acquisition as well as the eventual level of mastery of the melody. Two types of control experiments revealed that the superiority of the experienced students was not because they had a better memory in general. When asked to remember a short poem, the college students, regardless of their music experience, learned it faster than the children. Moreover, if the presented melody was a non-tonal (modal) Japanese folk song, the superiority of the musically experienced students disappeared; all three groups showed a comparably poor performance.

Knowledge Needed to Connect Components Meaningfully

Mckeithen, Reitman, Rueter, and Hirtle (1981), using computer programmers differing in skill levels (experts, intermediates, and beginners), examined the details of knowledge organization that these programmers possessed. The participants were presented with a computer program in either a normal or scrambled form for five 2-min study trials, and immediately after each trial, they were asked to write as much of the program as they could recall on a blank sheet. The results indicated that for the normal version of the program, the experts recalled the largest amount correctly, the intermediates could recall less, and the beginners recalled the least, but these differences disappeared for the scrambled version. The skill-related differences in correct recall for the normal version increased in later

trials, which was different from similar studies in other domains, such as chess or Go, in which the experts' superiority was revealed only at the initial trials. This was because, the authors interpret, the programmers needed several trials to understand the functions and structures of the program. This finding implies that programmers' knowledge does not consist of perceptual chunks. Instead, it is to organize programming components meaningfully, which is similar to what enables us to comprehend discourse (see Section 10.4).

In another experiment the participants were presented with a series of words taken from a program and written on cards (one word per card), and asked to learn at their own pace so that they could recall them later. The recall orders for each subject were analyzed and the details of individual programmers' clusters of key programming concepts were inferred. The beginners, whose programming knowledge was poor, seemed to use very general mnemonic techniques for memorizing and recalling the words; their patterns of recall showed a variety of common-language associations to the programming concepts, such as clusters of words with common first letters and lengths, or words alphabetized by first letters. In contrast, the experts recalled key programming language words in meaningful clusters; their organizations contained words grouped according to their function in the program. The intermediate programmers showed mixtures of programming and common-language associations.

Speed, Accuracy and Automaticity

It is not surprising that experts can solve problems and perform tasks in the target domain more quickly and accurately than novices, but the expert–novice difference is sometimes impressive. For example, abacus learners acquire, as they gain expertise, fast, accurate, and automated skills for operating the instrument (Hatano, 1997 for a review). Because people can learn to operate an abacus in a few hours, subsequent training is geared almost entirely to accelerating the speed of the operation. As a result of extensive training, abacus operation tends to be gradually interiorized to such a degree that most abacus masters can solve calculation problems by mental simulation. Because such mental operation is no longer constrained by the speed of muscle movement, it is much quicker than operating a real abacus.

Experts' mental calculation, unlike real abacus operation, is not entirely free from errors, but the accuracy is still at a respectable level. It is reported that a 4th-grade (10-year-old) girl, who became a junior national champion, could solve 30 printed multiplication problems, 3 digits by 3 digits (e.g., 148×395) or 4 by 2 (3519×42), in 58 s. This was surprising, but her net calculation time was even shorter – she needed this amount of time for writing the answers down. Thus, she could solve the same number of problems requiring the inverse operation (e.g., $277836 \div 78$) in 31 s, because the number of digits in the answers was nearly a half. She made just one error on these 60 problems.

Abacus experts' calculation is highly automatic. Experienced abacus operators can converse during calculation, even without the instrument. Needless to say, the conversation cannot be very serious – usually just a short and simple factual or preferential question–answer exchange, but this is still impressive, because most ordinary people cannot speak even a word while performing a mental calculation. Therefore, abacus experts are characterized in terms of three types of knowledge: (a) a cluster of specific condition–action rules for adding and subtracting numbers that enable them to run the four operations very fast, (b) a mental model of an abacus for mental abacus operation, and (c) metacognitive knowledge that monitors the execution of operations with a minimal processing load. Evidence suggests that in general, experts in operating devices or instruments seem to develop similar types of knowledge.

Constraints in Expertise

Unlike in conceptual development, innate constraints do not work in gaining expertise. Instead, prior knowledge as cognitive constraints plays an important role. The acquisition of knowledge proceeds slowly at the early stages of expertise. After a certain amount of domain-specific knowledge accumulates, the acquisition of new pieces of knowledge is accelerated, because prior domain-specific knowledge starts to work as constraints. Domain-specific knowledge serves to direct one's attention to relevant aspects. Moreover, it serves to eliminate in advance a large number of logically possible interpretations. Therefore, such domain-specific knowledge not only helps problem-solving and understanding, but also enhances the acquisition of new pieces of knowledge in the domain.

10.3 Problem Solving

This section is concerned with the solution of problems that we do not know how to solve. Our lives are full of problems in the wide sense, that is, we continuously strive to produce changes in the environment or in ourselves, but many of these challenges are not taken as problems in the real sense, because we already know how to solve them; executing a solution routine usually requires some effort, but no search. For example, washing one's face or cleaning one's teeth may be regarded as problem solving only when the water supply is suspended or toothpaste is unavailable.

To study problem solving experimentally, we need a problem that the participant, most often a college student, does not know how to solve. Moreover, for the experimenter's convenience, it is desirable that the problem can be solved in most cases in a short period of time. Thus, earlier studies on problem solving often used puzzles.

Process of Problem Solving

Problem Representation

Problems must be represented before their solution processes start. According to Newell and Simon (1972), the representation of a problem includes four components: (a) the initial state to start with, (b) the goal state to be reached, (c) a set of operators or actions that can be taken to change the current state, and (d) path constraints that restrict the range of successful paths to the solution. With these four components, puzzles such as the Tower of Hanoi (a favorite task among cognitive psychologists) can be neatly defined (assuming that there are tests to determine whether the goal has been achieved without violating the constraints). Let us take the three-disk version of the Tower of Hanoi as an example: there are three pegs, A, B, and C on a board; the initial state has all three disks of decreasing size on peg A, and the goal state is to have all three on peg C. This puzzle's only operation is to move disks, with two constraints: (a) only one disk can be moved at a time, and (b) a smaller disk must always rest on a larger disk when two or more disks are placed on the same peg. The search involves finding a path from the initial to the goal state in a problem space that includes 27 possible states. Because the components of this problem representation are clearly defined, the Tower of Hanoi and similar puzzles are often called well-defined problems.

Other problems are ill-defined. For instance, writing an essay is a typical ill-defined problem, because in this case it is not clear what the goal state is, what operators are available, etc. Still other problems fall in between. For example, many of the textbook problems in such subjects as mathematics and physics are well-defined for experts, but not so for students, because students may not have access to all possible operators, or know what constraints are imposed. As we will see below, these problems in knowledge-rich domains may be represented differently according to the solvers' domain knowledge.

Search Strategies

Problem solving can be defined as the search in a problem space (consisting of all states that can potentially be reached by applying available operators). The problem space may be too large for an exhaustive or 'brute-force' search, because its size increases exponentially with the number of steps needed to reach the goal state. Chess has a problem space of about 10^{20} states; other games (e.g., Go) have an even larger problem space. Thus, human problem solvers often rely on a heuristic search, trying to find a reasonably good solution with a reasonable amount of time and effort.

Heuristic search often presupposes domain-specific knowledge relevant to the target problem (e.g., knowledge that suggests a promising part of the problem space). However, as proposed by Newell and Simon (1972), there are several general heuristic search methods, among which means–ends analysis is the best known. This involves searching for an operator that effectively reduces the difference between the goal state and the current state. When no such operators can be applied, it tries to create the needed condition for the application of one of them. Means–ends analysis is usually much more efficient than relying on either a forward or backward search alone.

Decomposition and Planning

Complex problems that we often encounter in our daily lives can be divided into relatively independent subproblems. We can find a solution for the entire problem much more efficiently if we can aptly decompose the problem. For example, the problem of reducing one's weight can effectively be solved by eating food containing fewer calories and burning more calories through physical exercise. As this example suggests, another way to accelerate problem solving is by planning before executing the steps of a solution. It would be almost inconceivable to build a house without drawing its blueprint or write a novel without outlining its plot beforehand.

How Knowledge Operates in Problem Solving

Puzzles as typical examples of well-defined problems can be solved without prior knowledge (except for understanding the instructions), although experiences of solving the same or similar puzzles may make finding the solution more efficient. Interestingly, puzzles often require the solver to perform a move that seems to increase the distance from the goal state.

Most other problems in our lives, many of which are ill-defined, presuppose prior domain-specific knowledge to solve them successfully. Because the acquisition of such prior knowledge takes a long time, studies examining whether such knowledge makes a difference in problem solving have to compare experts and novices. Thus research on problem solving (as well as on comprehension) is often concerned with the expert–novice difference and expertise.

It is not easy to choose appropriate problems both for novices and experts; good problems for novices may not be problems for experts, because experts often possess 'problem schemas' by which they can recognize classes of problems and apply ready-made routines. However, some compromise may be possible. When the same problems are presented, experts are less likely than novices to make errors or take unnecessary steps, but a more interesting finding is that experts and novices use different heuristics in solving problems.

Simon and Simon (1978) compared in detail the processes of solving simple kinematics problems by an experienced and a less-experienced participant. These participants were asked, for example, to find the average speed of a bullet within a gun barrel half a meter long, assuming that it accelerates uniformly and leaves the muzzle at a speed of 400 m/s, how long the bullet remains in the gun after it is fired, etc. Both participants evoked an equation, inserted the known quantities into the equation, and found an unknown quantity by solving the equation. This cycle might be applied repetitively or recursively. The authors found that the novice searched for an equation that contained the quantity sought. If the equation could not be applied, then he turned his attention to one of the unknowns in that equation and proceeded to look for an equation that contained the new target. In other words, the novice relied on means–ends analysis or backward chaining. In contrast, the expert searched for an equation that would immediately yield a new quantity, and continued to test equations until the quantity sought was generated. In short, the expert used forward-chaining heuristics. The authors interpreted these results to mean that the expert's apparently more primitive approach was based on his physical intuition, that is, his ability to construct a mental representation of the situation in which the components described in the problems were causally connected. If the forward generation of new quantities is totally unguided, it must lead the problem solver to unnecessary steps or blind alleys. Therefore, experts must be, though unconsciously, guided by the quantity sought.

Moreover, even when the same problem is given, experts and novices may represent it differently. Chi, Feltovich, and Glaser (1981) indicate that experts, unlike novices, categorize physics problems by the laws of physics. These categories elicit relevant knowledge structures to represent the problems, and these structures indicate potentially useful solution methods.

Oura and Hatano (1998) indicate that novices and junior experts represent the task of playing a given piece of music quite differently. For novices, the problem is to shift from a slow and error-prone performance to a smooth and accurate one. Thus, they adopt repetitive exercise as an action that will probably lead them to the goal state. In contrast, for junior experts, the problem is to transform their structural and hierarchical understanding of a piece into an actual performance that conveys this understanding to an audience. For this purpose, they search among a variety of dynamic, temporary, and phrasing parameters. In fact, these authors found that a junior expert player, in her exercise, kept trying to coordinate two perspectives in her mind, that is, the perspective of herself as the player and the perspective of listeners. When she was allowed as much practice as she wanted, she repeated the piece 45 times before finishing, during which the tempo of the performance was slightly varied from one rendition to another.

How Knowledge Is Acquired in Problem Solving

As indicated in Section 10.2, gaining expertise often takes years. This implies that solvers cannot acquire much domain knowledge by solving a single problem. However, it has been shown that repeatedly solving well-defined problems like puzzles enables solvers to find the solution path promptly and to acquire strategies that can be applied to similar problems. Such learning or knowledge acquisition probably takes the form of combining old condition–action rules to produce a more efficient new rule, replacing a general rule that requires computation by a set of specific rules, and/or adding a new rule that makes the solution process better guided (Anderson, 1983; Anzai, 1987). For example, if there are two condition–action rules for transforming state A into state B, and state B into state C, a new, combined rule transforms state A directly into state C (called composition). Solvers

may find bad moves that lead them to a blind alley or to a previous state, and also recognize good moves that lead closer to the goal state, avoiding the bad moves. New condition–action rules avoiding bad moves and choosing good moves are thus added. All these condition–action rules enable solvers to find the correct solution promptly for the type of problems they have solved in the past using less efficient procedures, but these rules cannot be applied to other types of problems, because they are situation-specific. In other words, through solving the same kinds of problems repeatedly, solvers become routine experts, that is, experts who are distinguished in terms of their speed, accuracy, and automaticity.

Solvers acquire richer knowledge through their attempts to solve problems in knowledge-rich domains. For example, solvers are likely to acquire knowledge that enables them to represent problems aptly and to apply an appropriate solution routine (e.g., a law in physics). Solvers may learn about goal states, operators, and path constraints by solving an ill-defined problems (e.g., writing a novel). And through the solution of a series of novel problems, solvers may learn about the target entities that are dealt with in problem solving (e.g., raising animals may lead to a more accurate and elaborate concept or schema of what the raised animals are like). As a result, they may become able to build mental models of the target when needed, in other words, to gain adaptive expertise. Unlike routine experts, adaptive experts are expected to be able to solve novel problems in the domain, because they have grasped the meaning of solution routines in terms of changes in the target entities (Hatano & Inagaki, 1986).

Analogy and Transfer

As mentioned above, domain-specific knowledge is critical in solving problems; solvers represent a problem and search for a solution using this knowledge. Does this mean that almost no transfer occurs across domains, in other words, that the knowledge gained in one domain is not used in solving problems in other domains? This question has been examined under the name of analogical transfer, because transfer across domains requires the recognition of relational or structural similarity between the original and the target problems, which is the essence of analogy (Gentner & Markman, 1997). If the problem spaces of the target and the source are mapped, one can choose a path for the target that is structurally similar to the successful path in the source.

Gick and Holyoak (1980) examined whether college students could solve a problem through cross-domain transfer. The transfer problem to be solved was what is known as the 'tumor problem'. This problem concerns a doctor who has to figure out how to use radiation to destroy a tumor deep inside the body without injuring the patient's healthy tissues in the process. Because if rays are used that are intense enough to destroy the tumor, they will, apparently necessarily, injure the healthy tissues, this problem is known to be difficult for many people. A solution that can be used in this and similar cases is to give low-intensity rays from different directions at the same time so that they can converge on the tumor.

When Gick and Holyoak presented this tumor problem without any preceding problem, only about 10% of college students successfully solved it. However, of those who had previously read another story (called a 'fortress story') and were instructed to make use of it, 75% could find a satisfactory solution. The fortress story is apparently not similar to the tumor problem at all. In it, a general is trying to capture a fortress and needs to get his army to the fortress at full strength. Since the entire army cannot pass safely along any single road, the general sends his soldiers in small groups through several roads simultaneously, so that they can arrive at the fortress at the same time. What is common between the two situations is that it is necessary to divide the whole into smaller components so that each component can go through, and to recombine the components so that the whole can be reconstructed at the critical place.

Interestingly, when another group of college students read the fortress story but were not told to make use of it, only 20% could find a satisfactory solution for the tumor problem. Gick and Holyoak interpreted this result as consistent with their model of analogy; that is, before two domains are mapped, an appropriate source domain must be selected, and this process is the hardest one in analogy. Although creative human minds often try to apply to a novel problem seemingly relevant knowledge from another domain, finding the really applicable knowledge in other domains remote from the target appears to be very difficult.

However, in everyday life we do not choose a domain that best fits the problem in question. Rather, we examine only a very limited number of familiar domains as potentially useful source analogs. Because of this, even children can sometimes make use of analogies. In other words, we may have underestimated people's ability to transfer by focusing on laboratory

studies in which a stringent criterion of successful transfer is adopted.

10.4 COMPREHENSION

Comprehension or understanding (terms we use interchangeably) are defined differently by different authors, but here we adopt the following, comprehensive definition: comprehension is a process through which a coherent and plausible interpretation is adopted for the pieces of information gathered from both outside (through perception) and inside (through memory) about a target object or phenomenon. The above definition is based on Piaget (1978), who defined the term as the solution of the problem of 'the "how" and "why" of the connections observed and applied in action', but includes implicit forms of understanding. In other words, we assume that a coherent and plausible interpretation produces differentiated and appropriate predictions about the target but may not always lead to a verbal explanation for them. Our definition is also based on Kintsch's (1998) conceptualization, but unlike him, we assume that a process of coherence-seeking or multiple constraint-satisfaction can involve mechanisms other than spreading activation, that is automatic and effortless.

Understanding enables us to build enriched, stable, coherent, and usable representations of the world, which often serve as the basis for solving problems, that is, for changing the world as one desires. In this sense, understanding is an investment in an unknown future, and the human tendency to seek understanding can be considered adaptive. Thus the coherence-seeking process may take the form of a comprehension activity that is necessarily a time-consuming and effort-intensive process (Hatano, 1998). Comprehension activity often offers multiple interpretations at one time, and compares their plausibility carefully by deriving and testing predictions from each of the interpretations being considered. It is not a process in which one holds onto the first idea that comes to mind or one waits for a single interpretation to emerge through spreading activation. Comprehenders may feel uncertainty or puzzlement. Scientific inquiry is prototypical of this activity (e.g., Dunbar, 1995).

Categorization as Understanding

Recognizing something that is ambiguous as an instance of a concept or schema constitutes understanding, because it is adopting a coherent and plausible interpretation of a set of observed features of the target based on relevant concepts or schemas. Once we understand the target object or phenomenon, we can make sense of the observations and can remember them much more easily (e.g., Bransford & Johnson, 1972). Moreover, we can decide reasonably how to treat the target.

The diagnosis of disease by reading X-ray films is a good example of such tasks of categorization or identification. The same disease does not always produce the same appearance on the film, and there can be several diseases that have similar appearances. Therefore, reading X-ray films involves many inferences and requires a constraint-satisfaction process to reach a diagnosis. This is undoubtedly a process heavily dependent on prior knowledge, in which experts and novices would be expected to differ.

Lesgold et al. (1988) compared the ability to make accurate diagnosis by reading X-ray films of expert radiologists with novice ones. The participants were asked to report a diagnosis after being shown chest X-ray films for 2 s, and their protocols were analyzed. It was found that compared with the novices, the experts reported more varied findings (i.e., attributed specific properties to the film or the patient), their reasoning chains were longer, and a greater number of their findings were connected to at least another finding. The authors interpreted these results as follows: 'The data support a view of the expert as doing more inferential thinking and ending up with a more coherent model of the patient shown in the film' (p. 317).

However, experts and novices do not make the same observations and then interpret them differently based on their different amounts of knowledge in natural settings. In a further study the participants were required to examine the film as long as desired, while thinking aloud, and to dictate their formal diagnostic reports. Qualitative analysis of the protocols revealed that the experts exhibited more flexibility and tuned better their schemas in the perception of features in the film to the specific case with which they were working. They could discount most of the obvious film features that the novices were likely to be misled to judge as evidence of disease symptoms, by using a mixture of technical knowledge about how the films were made and a better-developed perception of the features.

Diagnosing films apparently requires simple outputs, i.e., whether there are pathological changes, and what kind of disease the changes are due to. However, the process of understanding is more dynamic and interactive than the top-down process of applying the relevant schema stored in memory or the bottom-up

process of summarizing and abstracting collected pieces of information. Perception, inference, and memory retrieval are inextricably connected. We assume that this is true for other processes of understanding.

Discourse Comprehension

Comprehension of discourse (including both narrative and expository text) is one of the most popular topics in the study of higher-order cognition. Here, the input information is in the form of a spoken or written sentence, and the comprehender's job is to form a coherent whole from individual sentences. Versions of schema theory (e.g., Schank & Abelson, 1977) were predominant in earlier studies. Schemas, each describing a sequence of actions or a set of constituent elements (e.g., a restaurant schema composed of the actions of being seated, ordering, being served, and paying) were supposed to be triggered by key words called headers (e.g., dinner) and then to control the comprehension process in a top-down fashion. However, as pointed out by Kintsch (1998), such top-down views have limitations; discourse comprehension is basically bottom-up, and it is much more flexible and context-sensitive than predicted from the schema theory.

Most contemporary investigators assume that to understand a story (i.e., a narrative text) is to build a micro-world in which these events described in it are likely to occur. Kintsch (1998) calls this micro-world the 'situation model'. In addition to the textbase that consists of those elements and relations that are explicitly described in the text itself, the situation model involves pieces of information that make the textbase coherent, complete, and interpretable in relation to prior knowledge. These pieces of information are inferred from both the text and prior knowledge. Multiple situation models may be constructed from one and the same text (e.g., differing in the coverage or the mode of representation).

When people understand a story, they will make inferences that are not given in the text. They sometimes infer that an event occurred, even though it is not explicitly written (e.g., from the sentence, 'He took a train for Tokyo', the reader infers that the subject bought a train ticket); other times, the reader infers how an event occurred, although the text does not give any concrete details. (From the sentence, 'He bought a ticket with coins', one infers, 'He used a vending machine.') Still other times, readers connect two adjacent propositions. (From the two sentences, 'Taro wanted to buy a CD player at a discounted price. He went to a shop in

Akihabara', one infers, 'Taro went to Akihabara to buy a CD player there.') How many inferences are spontaneously generated may depend on the readers, texts, and modes of reading. Graesser, Singer, and Trabasso (1994) claim that the inferences that are needed to explain why given events occur and to establish coherence of the text tend to be induced spontaneously as the text is being processed. Kintsch (1998) proposes that a coherent situation model is built based on these presented and inferred propositions through constraint-satisfaction, more specifically, spreading activation within the network of interrelated propositions.

Local situation models for a short sequence of events are further integrated into a global model in seeking overall coherence or a good story. This step may involve intentional processing. Let us take Spiro's classic experiment (1977) as an example. Participating students in his experiment read the following story: Bob and Maggie were an engaged couple. Maggie wanted to have babies, whereas Bob did not. They had a serious dispute about having a baby. When the students read it, they would predict, based on their prior knowledge, that the couple's marriage would fail. However, the experimenter told the participants that the story was true and Bob and Maggie were married and living happily. This information was inconsistent with the read story, and thus the students often tried to recover coherence by generating additional information that could reduce the incongruity they sensed; for example, the couple reached an agreement after a long discussion, the couple agreed to have just one baby, and so on. In fact, when the participants were asked to recall what had been explicitly indicated in the story, they tended to insert such additional pieces of information, especially long after the presentation of the story. Such an apparent inconsistency is seldom included in a well-organized actual text, but studies using experimentally designed defective texts (e.g., in Collins, Brown, & Larkin, 1980) have revealed that text comprehension may require a number of effortful attempts to instantiate, coordinate, and even insert pieces of information.

Almost all people are very experienced in discourse comprehension because it is a major medium of human communication. However, knowledge about the topic of the discourse still makes a difference, especially in the generation of inferences. As a result, more knowledgeable people can build a richer situation model than less knowledgeable ones. They learn more, especially when the text is less coherent and thus requires comprehension activity on the part of comprehenders. Schneider, Korkel, and Weinert (1989) demonstrated that students who knew a lot about the soccer game not only remembered details of a given story about soccer better, but also made more inferences and recognized contradictions in the text more often than their contemporaries who knew little about soccer.

Comprehension of Procedures and Targets

Just knowing the procedures to achieve goals differs from knowing how and why they work. By possessing knowledge to build mental models of the procedure–target combination (what the target is like and how it is changed by various procedures), we can grasp how and why these procedures work, modify the procedures flexibly, and even invent new procedures. Building such models may be through a process of comprehension.

Kieras and Bovair (1984) showed that having a 'device model' (a mechanical version of the procedure–target model) that describes the internal mechanism of a piece of equipment enhances not only the participants' learning how to operate the equipment but also their inventing more efficient procedures than the ones they have been taught. Their first experiment compared two groups, i.e., a model group and a rote group. The participants in the model group were presented with the device model in a fantasy context before being given procedural instruction, whereas those of the rote group learned the identical operating procedures of the equipment by rote. It was observed that the model group learned the procedures faster, retained them more accurately, and executed them more efficiently than the rote group. More interestingly, the model group could simplify inefficient procedures much more often than the rote group, indicating the benefit of their deeper understanding. The second experiment showed that the model group could infer the procedures much more easily than the rote group, again showing the significance of learning with understanding. The final experiment showed that what was critical was the knowledge about the internal structures of the components of the equipment, not the context of fantasy.

In the experiments by Kieras and Bovair (1984) described above, an externalized form of the standard device model was presented and explained. Active human minds often ask the questions 'how' and 'why', even when they know that a given procedure works, and may construct the procedure–target model through comprehension activity. For example, the recipe for bonito sashimi sometimes induces comprehension activity, because it is not just the slicing of raw fish, but involves steps of roasting the skin-covered surface quickly at a high temperature and putting the roasted side into icewater (Hatano, 1998). People may wonder why such a recipe is required, and if they comprehend it, they can modify it flexibly when they have to meet a different set of constraints, e.g., when there is no ice or no source of searing heat. To understand a given procedure is, as in this example, to find a plausible interpretation for how and why it works, in other words, what kind of effect each step of the procedure has on the target entity of the procedure.

We sometimes engage in an even more ambitious attempt to reconstruct a procedure from its product in our daily lives, which is similar to the scientific inquiry that tries to model a process from its observed outcomes. For example, we may want to reproduce an unfamiliar but tasty dish (Hatano, 1998). In an experiment, college students who were given a slice of perch mousse and asked to find how it had been made by tasting it (more specifically, to indicate its recipe) seemed to engage in comprehension activity. They often proposed ideas that they eventually discarded themselves. For example, they offered a number of possible ingredients, but rejected some of them both from their taste and knowledge about cooking. They expressed their feelings of uncertainty or puzzlement, as well as insight.

Although there have been few studies, prior knowledge seems critical for the understanding of procedures. First, prior knowledge enables comprehenders to think of hypotheses. Second, it serves as constraints in the pursuit of coherence and plausibility.

Understanding by Analogy

Plausible interpretations can be found in a variety of ways. When people encounter a novel object or phenomenon, they may try to understand it by likening it to a highly familiar object or phenomenon. For example, at the time of Iraq's invasion into Kuwait, many Americans (partly through the campaign by the government) likened Saddam Hussein to Hitler, and thus justified their bombing of Iraq. Interestingly, some objected to the military action by analogizing the Persian Gulf war to the Vietnam war. This illustrates how people try to understand a novel phenomenon by referring to their past experience that they think is most similar, and how their reactions to the phenomenon are mediated by their analogy (Holyoak & Thagard, 1995).

Using analogy, humans map their knowledge about the source to the present case (target), so that they can make a coherent interpretation of the set of observations for the target. Mapping involves search and thus goes beyond the retrieval of prior knowledge, often resulting in the production of new pieces of knowledge. In this sense, analogies are the key to creativity; they are often very useful in everyday cognition (Hatano, 1998) as well as in scientific reasoning (Dunbar, 1995) to generate hypotheses.

It should be noted, however, that this enterprise of understanding by analogy is entirely dependent on the analogist's possessing highly familiar source that is subjectively similar. In children, because such familiar sources are limited, we often observe their heavy reliance on a few particular sources. Anthropomorphism or personification can be regarded as one such attempt. Although young children are able to classify entities into ontological categories, they apply their knowledge about humans to other animate objects or even to inanimate objects, when they have to infer or interpret an object's unknown attributes or reactions (Carey, 1985; Hatano & Inagaki, 1996).

The analogies young children make may involve structurally inaccurate mapping (e.g., mapping the relationship between humans and food to that between plants and water), and induce biased reasoning (e.g., neglecting the roles of nutrients in the soil and photosynthesis). Young children may carry analogy beyond its proper limits and produce false inferences, as revealed in typical examples of animistic reasoning. However, they can generate 'educated guesses' by analogies, relying on their only familiar source analog of a person (Holyoak & Thagard, 1995), and animistic errors and/or overattribution of human characteristics to non-human animate objects should be regarded as negative byproducts unluckily produced by this process of reasoning. Even a highly productive scientist like Kepler was misled by analogies at the beginning of his career (Gentner et al., 1997).

Comprehension Monitoring

To comprehend well, it is necessary to assess one's extent of understanding, and to take appropriate action based on that assessment. However, whether one understands is not obvious (whereas whether one has solved a problem can be recognized more clearly). To put it differently, every task of comprehension is inevitably ill-defined. Therefore, how well people can monitor their own understanding and how this monitoring ability develops are interesting questions in the study of comprehension.

Research on comprehension monitoring has shown that younger children tend to miss the insufficiency or inconsistency of a given message more often than older children or adults, but another line of research on metacomprehension has revealed that even college students tend to have this 'illusion of comprehension' (Glenberg & Epstein, 1985). College students often believe that they understand a given text, though in fact they do not, at least as assessed by a multiple choice test.

As suggested by Schneider et al. (1989), it is likely that the more and less knowledgeable people differ in their ability to accurately estimate the degree of coherence among pieces of information and the adequacy of their comprehension. Humans seem to have a general tendency to make sense of their observations and actions, in other words, to derive coherent and plausible interpretations. However, judging whether the achieved understanding is adequate is a totally different issue. The criterion of adequacy may vary from context to context. Therefore, only those who have performed many similar ill-defined tasks of understanding in the target domain can assess it accurately.

10.5 The Brain and Higher-Order Cognition

Unlike with vision and motion, there have been very few successful studies connecting a specific aspect of higher-order cognition to specific areas of brain activity until quite recently. This was because the major experimental findings of brain science came from studies of monkeys and other nonhuman mammals, whose higher-order cognition, if any, is very limited. These experimental findings were supplemented by clinical reports on human patients who suffered from local brain damage. However, such damage is seldom restricted to a particular area of the brain. Moreover, as time passes, the damage may be compensated for by newly formed connections that are not available in the normal brain.

New, non-invasive imaging technologies, such as PET and fMRI, have started to change this situation, because we can now observe patterns of activation in the normal brain as a person performs specified experimental cognitive tasks. Although it is highly unlikely for us to find any dedicated cognitive mechanisms in the brain for problem solving or comprehension – because higher-order cognition is a compound process consisting of a number of constituent subprocesses – we may be able to identify those areas that are critically important for specific types of problem solving or comprehension. These technologies provide a powerful means to investigate higher-order cognition, if they are skillfully

combined with the manipulation of stimuli and the assessment of behavioral responses that psychological studies have developed.

However, it should be noted that the current imaging technologies still have limitations for investigating higher-order cognition. First, whereas their spatial resolution is high (they can locate the areas of activation with an error of millimeters), their temporal resolution is not high enough to specify the time course of rapid mental processes. This is especially true for PET; presently we can measure patterns of activation by PET only after a participant has been performing the same type of task for a few minutes. Researchers of higher-order cognition need more advanced technologies with high temporal resolution than are currently available, such as event-related fMRI. Second, because so many areas in the brain are usually activated by a complex cognitive task, it is necessary to set up a control condition, and the unique pattern of activation for a specific task is estimated by subtracting the pattern for the control task from the observed pattern for the target task. However, we do not have a good rationale for choosing the appropriate control condition, in other words, to equate other parameters than the critical one between the target and control tasks, either for problem solving or comprehension. For example, since almost every task of higher-order cognition requires a high information-processing load, its control task must also be cognitively demanding, but we do not yet know how best to choose such a control task.

Executive Control Function of the Frontal Lobe

One form of thinking can be regarded as interiorized action. More specifically, instead of exerting a series of motor actions on physical objects or moving one's own body parts in sequence, it is mentally operating on and changing mental representations of the targets. In other words, this form of thinking is controlled manipulation of mental models (i.e., mental representations that can be modified in response to mental actions). Many investigators assume that such thinking has the control devices and targets of control, and that the frontal lobe operates as the control system, which regulates the condition–action rules, concepts or schemas, and mental models stored in the parietal and temporal lobes (e.g., Holyoak, 1990).

The frontal lobe plays an important role in a variety of cognitive functions including thinking. Cabeza and Nyberg (1997) conclude, based on their review of PET studies of higher-order cognitive processes (although very few of them dealt with thinking), that the frontal lobe was involved 'in almost all cognitive processes' (except for bottom-up perceptual processes). This is probably due to its assumed role in the executive control of cognition. Stuss and Benson (1986), based on an extensive review of frontal lesion studies, propose several functions of the frontal lobe, such as planning and ordering sequential behavior, establishing, maintaining, and changing a mental set, and monitoring one's behavior. As Benson (1994) declares, reported clinical cases clearly indicate that damage to the prefrontal association cortex impairs the executive control of higher mental activities, although it seldom affects intelligence measured by conventional tests. It seems reasonable to assume that the frontal lobe is the control system for thinking defined as the goal-directed manipulations of mental representations.

It is far less certain where rules, concepts and other forms of elaborate knowledge are stored or how they are represented in the brain. However, imaging studies have begun to offer some interesting observations.

Category-Specific Imapairment and Differential Activation

According to clinical reports on human patients who have had a focal brain lesion, there are cases in which performances on highly similar tasks are differentially damaged. Some of these reports are highly relevant here, especially when combined with imaging studies revealing differential activation. Although the experimental tasks used were as simple as identification or naming tasks, the results suggest that knowledge about different types of entities – e.g., living things (represented by animals) and nonliving things (represented by human-made physical tools) – are stored in different locations in the brain. Such results reinforce views that entities belonging to different ontological categories (humans, nonhuman animals, plants and nonliving things), which are considered to be distinguished based upon schemes of mind (Atran, 1998), have specialized neural mechanisms acquired through evolution (Caramazza & Shelton, 1998).

Damasio, Grabowski, Tranel, Hichwa, and Damasio (1996) made one such pioneering attempt to combine clinical observation and imaging to examine whether knowledge about different classes of entities can be segregated. They prepared three naming tasks for different categories of entities, that is, for proper names of famous persons, basic category names of animals, and names of tools. They first administered these tasks to a large number of adults

who had single and stable lesions in various parts of the brain. They found that all but one of the 30 participants who showed poor naming performances had damage in the left hemisphere. More interestingly, they found that poor naming performances for the three categories were associated with damage in different areas of the brain: poor identification of person names was associated with damage in the left temporal pole (TP), animal names with that in the left inferotemporal (IT) (mostly anterior), and tool names with that in the posterolateral IT. None of the participants who showed normal naming performances had damage in these areas.

They then gave the same three naming tasks to normal right-handed participants while their regional cerebral blood flow (rCBF) was measured by PET. The control task was to say 'up' or 'down' when presented with unfamiliar faces oriented correctly or upside down. As expected, a statistically significant increase in rCBF was observed in the left TP/IT for each of the naming tasks. Moreover, person naming activated the left TP but not the left IT, whereas animal and tool naming activated the left IT and a restricted portion of the left TP. Tool naming activated the area more posterior and more lateral than an area for animal naming. To summarize, Damasio et al. (1996) obtained nicely converging evidence for the involvement of multiple regions of the left cerebral hemisphere, located outside the classic language area for word naming, and also for differential activation in anatomically separable regions of the brain in processing words for distinct kinds of items, i.e., humans, animals, and tools.

However, not all studies using PET identified the same sectors for seemingly the same categories (Caramazza & Shelton, 1998). Although we are sure that damage in different areas of the brain tends to produce correspondingly differentiated patterns of disorder, we are not confident that these areas are mainly responsible for cognitive tasks that tap into different ontological categories.

Functional Localization and Plasticity in the Human Brain

An important finding for knowledge acquisition obtained by recent imaging studies is that each part of the human brain is genetically assigned some particular functions that can be performed very well, but each can do other things if needed. This bounded plasticity is probably the key for us to understand how fast and easy learning in privileged domains can take place on the one hand and slow and laborious learning in non-privileged domains on the other.

We can see an exciting example of bounded plasticity in research on theory of mind, in which we can have three sets of data: (a) brain activation patterns among healthy people while solving theory of mind tasks, (b) cognitive and neural investigations of autistic individuals who are supposed to have genetically determined deficits in their theory of mind, and (c) the investigations of brain-damaged patients who have selective impairments in their theory of mind. We will first discuss a functional neuroimaging study by Fletcher et al. (1995) as an example of (a). They found by using PET that when compared with a 'physical' sequence of events, the comprehension of mentally-caused sequences of events (i.e., so-called 'theory of mind' stories, understanding of which requires a sophisticated attribution of mental states) activated a specific area of the left medial frontal cortex (Broadmann's area 8).

With regard to (b), as described in Section 10.2, autistic individuals show inferior performance in 'theory of mind' tasks, though their performance in tasks concerning physical causation is intact. Moreover, Happé et al. (1996), using patients with Asperger syndrome (to simplify, a mild form of autism), provided data suggesting that autistic individuals are impaired in the development of normal brain systems supporting naive psychological reasoning and understanding. More specifically, whereas among the normal individuals, Broadmann's Area 8 was highly active during reading theory of mind stories and answering a question, this area was not active among the individuals with Asperger syndrome. Instead, the stories activated an adjacent area (Broadmann Area 9/10 in left medial frontal cortex). This area was activated in the normal people, but to a much less extent than the above area responsible for attributing mental states to others.

These results are consistent with the idea that there is a special area in the brain for attributing mental states, that this area does not function well among people with Asperger syndrome, and that a neighboring area may develop capacities to compensate for the mentalizing function to some extent. Probably due to this substitution, some children with autism can develop an understanding of theory of mind, although it occurs much later than in the normal people. Moreover, they still reveal some limitations, for example, that fail to distinguish shouting in a noisy environment from shouting because of anger.

More recently, as for (c), Happé, Brownell, and Winner (1999) examined 'theory of mind' in adults who had had a stroke in the right hemisphere, a group of people known to reveal

pragmatic and social difficulties. The participants showed inferior performance in understanding materials requiring the attribution of mental states to non-mental materials, which were of the same difficulty among healthy elderly individuals and left hemispheric patients. The authors claim that their results support the notion of a dedicated cognitive system for theory of mind, and suggest that a healthy right hemisphere is needed for properly attributing mental states. However, it should be pointed out at this stage that, even if there is a dedicated system for theory of mind, defining its location in the brain will require many further studies, because exact locations of activation and/or damage differ even among carefully performed studies.

10.6 Socializing Higher-Order Cognition Research

Until the late 1980s, after the first wave of the cognitive revolution, most cognitive researchers concentrated on the study of symbol manipulation within the individual head, ignoring the sociocultural context that surrounds the individual (Gardner, 1985). As a result, it was often overlooked that our competence in daily life is heavily dependent on our continuous interaction with other people and tools.

Through the second wave of the cognitive revolution, however, many cognitive researchers were prepared to accept that the cognitive process, among others, higher-order cognition, can be greatly influenced by sociocultural situations. Within the cognitive science community, those views that emphasize the role of the environment, the context, the social and cultural setting in cognition have gained favor (Norman, 1993). The views are referred to by several different names, but here we use 'sociocultural' to represent all those views that assume that cognition occurs not just in the head but as a continuous interplay between an acting person's mind and the external environment. In this final section we discuss contributions from these sociocultural views to knowledge acquisition and use.

Acquisition of Knowledge through Participation in Practice

Sociocultural views indicate that knowledge is acquired usually through participating in culturally organized practices that involve a variety of sociocultural constraints and that are interesting and/or significant to the participants (Goodnow, Miller, & Kessel, 1995). Although the constraints in practices are to support participants' performance, rather than knowledge acquisition, repeated participation enhances the skills and knowledge needed to perform well in these practices.

Sociocultural constraints in practices include (a) artifacts which are shared by a majority of people of the community or its subgroup, and (b) the behavior of other people, interactions with them, and social contexts created by them. Because the artifacts, such as physical facilities and tools, social institutions and organizations, documented pieces of knowledge, and common sense and beliefs, direct people's attention and eliminate a great number of possible interpretations in advance, people can usually identify quite easily what they should do in practices, and also acquire knowledge and skills they need rather promptly. Likewise, most of what we do and acquire in practices is affected by other people. Our attention is often directed to what other people look at and we tend to take into account ideas proposed by others.

This analysis applies to everyday activities as well as to culturally valued practices related to production, ritual, etc. When the mastery of effective knowledge and skills requires extensive experience, the practice often takes the form of apprenticeship. In apprenticeship, the novice is initially assigned to relatively simple and peripheral parts of the practice, and comes to fulfill gradually more difficult and central parts as he or she gains better local knowledge and skills, and the understanding of the total practice. For example, Lave (1988) reported that apprentice tailors in Liberia are given such jobs as fixing buttons, which are simple and easy to repair but constitute authentic and essential parts of tailoring. Socioculturalists claim that participation in practices (including apprenticeships) tends to successfully support the knowledge acquisition of a great majority of ordinary people.

Knowledge is Situated

Human knowledge acquisition is situated in the contexts in which experience occurs and cannot help but be influenced by various features of these contexts. Because the most important contexts for knowledge acquisition and use are the practices people participate in repeatedly, it is heavily influenced by the characteristics of these practices (Greeno & MMAP, 1998). For example, when a practice is oriented toward solving a fixed class of problems skillfully, participants tend to become experts distinguished in terms of speed, accuracy, and automaticity. In contrast, when successful participation in practice requires flexibility and adaptiveness, they may learn to adapt their knowledge and skills to new situational demands.

Acquired knowledge is also situated in the sense that it reflects the history of its acquisition and use. Although textbooks of a given domain summarize a body of knowledge as a set of propositions, the knowledge that individuals 'possess' in their head includes representations of a more personal, concrete nature. For example, knowledge in the form of a formula or law is often accompanied by some preferred examples (e.g., those that were used when the formula was first introduced and those that the learner was able to solve for the first time by applying the formula). It may also be accompanied by the social context of its acquisition (e.g., how the teacher explained it and how other students reacted). These personal representations often serve as clues for retrieving the formula when it is appropriate. Proponents of the sociocultural views emphasize that much of our acquired knowledge is sociocultural in origin, and as such involves the internalization of sociocultural constraints so that they can work within the mind (as mental models of tools and other people).

Distributed Cognition

Individuals engaging in any collective activity often constitute a distributed system of cognition. None of them possess all the pieces of knowledge needed for successfully conducting the activity. In some cases, each of the members knows well what he or she has to do, but knows only partially what is being done by other members and/or by the system as a whole. In other cases, individuals behave based on their own motivation without an agreed division of labor. Even without a 'director' who monitors individual actions so that they can be coordinated, the system seems to function smoothly and productively. This smooth collective activity of a group whose members' knowledge is limited is attributed again to sociocultural constraints working in the activity. More specifically, these individuals select an alternative from their behavioral and conceptual repertoires that is in accordance with other individuals' behaviors (social constraints), and with shared artifacts (cultural constraints). Thanks to these constraints, the coordination of individual actions can be achieved without conscious planning or monitoring.

A good example of a distributed system of cognition is a team navigating a ship (Hutchins, 1995). Ship navigation is based on local problem solving. Although there is a captain, he does not control everything or know all that goes on.

In principle, each member of the team has to perform his job only when a particular condition occurs. However, mutual aid is given fairly often, and is appreciated, because, if there were no mutual aid, one member's failure to do his job could destroy the entire operation. To make this possible, there must be some overlap among the pieces of knowledge each member has. Since members move from one job to another as they gain expertise, more expert members usually know about less expert members' jobs. Moreover, members may know other members' jobs if they interact often.

Division of labor in distributed cognition does not have to be agreed upon in advance. In group problem solving and collective comprehension activity, different views are offered, based on participants' cognitive and social positions. When a team consists of members of varied backgrounds, it is likely that different problem representations or interpretations are offered, and different forms of reasoning are induced. Agents of higher-order cognition are more often people constituting a team, at least temporarily, than isolated individuals.

RESOURCE REFERENCES

Carey, S. (1985). *Conceptual change in childhood.* Cambridge, MA: MIT Press.

Chi, M. T. H., Glaser, R., & Farr, M. J. (Eds.). (1988). *The nature of expertise.* Hillsdale, NJ: Erlbaum.

Goodnow, J., Miller, P., & Kessel, F. (1995). *Cultural practices as contexts for human development.* San Francisco: Jossey-Bass.

Holyoak, K. J., & Thagard, P. (1995). *Mental leaps: Analogy in creative thought.* Cambridge, MA: MIT Press.

Keil, F. (1998). Cognitive science and the origins of thought and knowledge. In W. Damon (Ed.), *Handbook of child psychology* (5th edition), Vol. 1 (R. M. Lerner, Ed.), *Theoretical models of human development* (pp. 341–413). New York: Wiley.

Kintsch, W. (1998). *Comprehension.* New York: Cambridge University Press.

Newell, A., & Simon, H. A. (1972). *Human problem solving.* Englewood Cliffs, NJ: Prentice-Hall.

Siegler, R. S. (Ed.) (1978). *Children's thinking: What develops?* Hillsdale, NJ: Erlbaum.

Smith, E. E., & Osherson, D. N. (1995). *An invitation to cognitive science* (2nd edition). Vol. 3: *Thinking.* Cambridge, MA: MIT Press.

Ward, T. B., Smith, S. M., & Vaid, J. (Eds.). (1997). *Creative thought: An investigation of conceptual structures and processes.* Washington, DC: American Psychological Association.

ADDITIONAL LITERATURE CITED

Anderson, J. R. (1983). *The architecture of cognition.* Cambridge, MA: Harvard University Press.

Anzai, Y. (1987). Doing, understanding, and learning in problem solving. In D. Klahr, P. Langley, & R. Neches (Eds.), *Production system models of learning and development* (pp. 55–97). Cambridge, MA: MIT Press.

Atran, S. (1998). Folkbiology and the anthropology of science: Cognitive universals and cultural particulars. *Behavioral and Brain Sciences, 21,* 547–609.

Baron-Cohen, S. (1995). *Mindblindness: An essay on autism and theory of mind.* Cambridge, MA: Bradford Books.

Benson, D. F. (1994). *The neurology of thinking.* New York: Oxford University Press.

Bransford, J. D., & Johnson, M. K. (1972). Contextual prerequisites for understanding: Some investigations of comprehension and recall. *Journal of Verbal Learning and Verbal Behavior, 11,* 717–726.

Bruner, J. S., Goodnow, J. J., & Austin, G. A. (1956). *A study of thinking.* New York: Wiley.

Cabeza, R., & Nyberg, L. (1997). Imaging cognition: An empirical review of PET studies with normal subjects. *Journal of Cognitive Neuroscience, 9,* 1–26.

Caramazza, A., & Shelton, J. R. (1998). Domain-specific knowledge systems in the brain: The animate-inanimate distinction. *Journal of Cognitive Neuroscience, 10,* 1–34.

Chase, W. G., & Simon, H. A. (1973). Perception in chess. *Cognitive Psychology, 4,* 55–81.

Cheng, P. W., & Holyoak, K. J. (1985). Pragmatic reasoning schemas. *Cognitive Psychology, 17,* 391–416.

Chi, M. T. H., Feltovich, P. J., & Glaser, R. (1981). Categorization and representation of physics problems by experts and novices. *Cognitive Science, 5,* 121–125.

Chi, M. T. H., Glaser, R., & Rees, E. (1982). Expertise in problem solving. In R. J. Sternberg (Ed.), *Advances in the psychology of human intelligence, vol. 1* (pp. 7–76). Hillsdale, NJ: Erlbaum.

Clement, J. (1982). Students' preconceptions in introductory mechanics. *American Journal of Physics, 50,* 66–71.

Collins, A., Brown, J. S., & Larkin, K. M. (1980). Inference in text understanding. In R. J. Spiro, B. C. Bruce, & W. F. Brewer (Eds.), *Theoretical issues in reading comprehension: Perspectives from cognitive psychology, linguistics, artificial intelligence and education* (pp. 387–407). Hillsdale, NJ: Erlbaum.

Damasio, H., Grabowski, T. J., Tranel, D., Hichwa, R. D., & Damasio, A. R. (1996). A neural basis for lexical retrieval. *Nature, 380,* 499–505.

Dunbar, K. (1995) How scientists really reason: Scientific reasoning in real-world laboratories. In R. J.

Sternberg & J. E. Davidson (Eds.), *The nature of insight* (pp. 365–395). Cambridge, MA: MIT Press.

Ericsson, K. A., Krampe, R. T., & Tesch-Römer, C. (1993). The role of deliberate practice in the acquisition of expert performance. *Psychological Review, 100*, 363–406.

Fletcher, P. C., Happé, F., Frith, U., Baker, S. C., Kolan, R. J., Frackowiak, R. S. J., & Frith, C. D. (1995). Other minds in the brain: a functional imaging study of 'theory of mind' in story comprehension. *Cognition, 57*, 109–128.

Garcia, J. (1981). Tilting at the paper mills of academe. *American Psychologist, 36*, 149–158.

Gardner, H. (1985). *The mind's new science.* Basic Books.

Gelman, R. (1990). First principles organize attention to and learning about relevant data: Number and the animate–inanimate distinction as examples. *Cognitive Science, 14*, 79–106.

Gentner, D., Brem, S., Ferguson, R., Wolff, P., Markman, A. B., & Forbus, K. (1997). Analogy and creativity in the works of Johannes Kepler. In T. B. Ward, S. M. Smith, & J. Vaid (Eds.), *Creative thought: An investigation of conceptual structures and processes* (pp. 403–459). Washington, DC: American Psychological Association.

Gentner, D., & Markman, A. B. (1997). Structure-mapping in analogy and similarity. *American Psychologist, 52*, 45–56.

Gick, M. L., & Holyoak, K. J. (1980). Analogical problem solving. *Cognitive Psychology, 12*, 306–355.

Glenberg, A. M. & Epstein, W. (1985). Calibration of comprehension. *Journal of Experimental Psychology: Learning, Memory, and Cognition, 11*, 702–718.

Graesser, A. C., Singer, M., & Trabasso, T. (1994). Constructing inferences during narrative text comprehension. *Psychological Review, 101*, 371–395.

Greeno, J., & Middle-school Mathematics through Applications Project Group. (1998). The situativity of knowing, learning, and research. *American Psychologist, 53*, 5–26.

Happé, F., Brownell, H., & Winner, E. (1999). Acquired 'theory of mind' impairments following stroke. *Cognition, 70*, 211–240.

Happé, F., Ehlers, S., Fletcher, P., Frith, U., Johansson, M., Gillberg, C., Dolan, R., Frackowiak, R., & Frith, C. (1996). 'Theory of mind' in the brain: evidence from a PET scan study of Asperger syndrome. *NeuroReport, 8*, 197–201.

Hatano, G. (1997). Learning arithmetic with an abacus. In T. Nunes & P. Bryant (Eds.), *Learning and teaching mathematics: An international perspective* (pp. 209–231). Hove, UK: Psychology Press.

Hatano, G. (1998). Comprehension activity in individuals and groups. In M. Sabourin, F. Craik, & M. Robert (Eds.), *Advances in psychological sciences, vol. 2: Biological and cognitive aspects* (pp. 399–418). Hove, UK: Psychology Press.

Hatano, G., & Inagaki, K. (1986). Two courses of expertise. In H. Stevenson, H. Azuma, & K. Hakuta (Eds.), *Child development and education in Japan* (pp. 262–272). New York: Freeman.

Hatano, G., & Inagaki, K. (1996). Cognitive and cultural factors in the acquisition of intuitive biology. In D. R. Olson & N. Torrance (Eds.), *Handbook of education and human development: New models of learning, teaching and schooling* (pp. 683–708). Cambridge: Blackwell.

Holland, J. H., Holyoak, K. J., Nisbett, R. E., & Thagard, P. R. (1986). *Induction.* Cambridge, MA: MIT Press.

Holyoak, K. J. (1990). Problem solving. In D. N. Osherson, & E. E. Smith (Eds.), *Thinking: An invitation to cognitive science, vol. 3* (pp. 117–146). Cambridge, MA: MIT Press.

Holyoak, K. J., & Cheng, P. W. (1995). Pragmatic reasoning with a point of view. *Thinking & Reasoning, 1*, 289–313.

Hunt, J. M. (1965). Intrinsic motivation and its role in psychological development. In D. Levine (Ed.), *Nebraska symposium on motivation, vol. 13* (pp. 189–282). Lincoln, NE: University of Nebraska Press.

Hutchins, E. (1995). *Cognition in the wild.* Cambridge, MA: MIT Press.

Johnson-Laird, P. N. (1983). *Mental models.* Cambridge, UK: Cambridge University Press.

Johnson-Laird, P. N., & Byrne, R. M. J. (1995). A model point of view. *Thinking & Reasoning, 1*, 339–350.

Johnson-Laird, P. N., Legrenzi, P., & Legrenzi, S. M. (1972). Reasoning and a sense of reality. *British Journal of Psychology, 63*, 395–400.

Keil, F. (1981). Constraints on knowledge and cognitive development. *Psychological Review, 88*, 197–227.

Kieras, D. E., & Bovair, S. (1984). The role of a mental model in learning to operate a device. *Cognitive Science, 8*, 255–273.

Lave, J. (1988). *Cognition in practice.* Cambridge, UK: Cambridge University Press.

Lesgold, A., Glaser, R., Rubinson, H., Klopfer, D., Feltovich, P., & Wang, Y. (1988). Expertise in a complex skill: Diagnosing X-ray pictures. In M. T. H. Chi, R. Glaser, & M. J. Farr (Eds.), *The nature of expertise* (pp. 311–342). Hillsdale, NJ: Erlbaum.

Mckeithen, K. B., Reitman, J. S., Rueter, H. H., & Hirtle, S. C. (1981). Knowledge organization and skill differences in computer programmers. *Cognitive Psychology, 13*, 307–325.

Medin, D. L. (1989). Concepts and conceptual structure. *American Psychologist, 44*, 1469–1481.

Murphy, G. L., & Medin, D. L. (1985). The role of theories in conceptual coherence. *Psychological Review, 92*, 289–316.

Norman, D. A. (1993). Cognition in the head and in the world: An introduction to the special issue on situated action. *Cognitive Science, 17*, 1–6.

Nosofsky, R. M. (1988). Exemplar-based accounts of relations between classification, recognition, and typicality. *Journal of Experimental Psychology: Learning, Memory, and Cognition, 14*, 700–708.

Oura, Y., & Hatano, G. (1988). Memory for melodies among subjects differing in age and experience in music. *Psychology of Music, 16*, 91–109.

Oura, Y., & Hatano, G. (1998). *Specific and generalized others in mind*. Paper presented at the 15th meeting of International Society for the Study of Behavioral Development, Bern.

Peterson, C. C., & Siegal, M. (1997). Domain specificity and everyday biological, physical, and psychological thinking in normal, autistic, and deaf children. In H. M. Wellman and K. Inagaki (Eds.), *The emergence of core domains of thought: Children's reasoning about physical, psychological, and biological phenomena* (pp. 55–70). San Francisco: Jossey-Bass.

Piaget, J. (1978). *Success and understanding*. London: Routledge & Kagan Paul.

Resnick, L. B. (1987). Constructing knowledge in school. In L. S. Liben (Ed.), *Development and learning: Conflict or congruence?* (pp. 19–50). Hillsdale, NJ: Erlbaum.

Rips, L. J. (1994). *The psychology of proof*. Cambridge, MA: MIT Press.

Rosch, E. (1975). Cognitive representations of semantic categories. *Journal of Experimental Psychology: General, 104*, 192–233.

Rumelhart, D. E., & Norman, D. A. (1978). Accretion, tuning and restructuring: Three modes of learning. In J. W. Cotton & R. Klatzky (Eds.), *Semantic factors in cognition* (pp. 37–54). Hillsdale, NJ: Erlbaum.

Schank, R. C., & Abelson, R. P. (1977). *Script, plans, goals and understanding: An inquiry to human knowledge structures*. Hillsdale, NJ: Erlbaum.

Schneider, W., Korkel, J., & Weinert, F. E. (1989). Domain-specific knowledge and memory performance: A comparison of high- and low-aptitude children. *Journal of Educational Psychology, 81*, 306–312.

Simon, D. P., & Simon, H. (1978). Individual differences in solving physics problems. In R. S. Siegler (Ed.), *Children's thinking: What develops?* (pp. 325–348). Hillsdale, NJ: Erlbaum.

Simons, D. J., & Keil, F. C. (1995). An abstract to concrete shift in the development of biological thought: The 'insides' story. *Cognition, 56*, 129–163.

Spelke, E. S. (1991). Physical knowledge in infancy: Reflections on Piaget's theory. In S. Carey & R. Gelman (Eds.), *The epigenesis of mind: Essays on biology and cognition* (pp. 133–169). Hillsdale, NJ: Erlbaum.

Spelke, E. S., Phillips, A., & Woodword, A. L. (1995). Infants' knowledge of object motion and human action. In D. Sperber, D. Premack, & A. J. Premack (Eds.), *Causal cognition* (pp. 44–78). Oxford: Clarendon Press.

Spiro, R. J. (1977). Remembering information from text: The 'state of schema' approach. In R. C. Anderson, R. J. Spiro, & W. E. Montague (Eds.), *Schooling and the acquisition of knowledge* (pp. 137–165). Hillsdale, NJ: Erlbaum.

Stuss, D. T., & Benson, D. F. (1986) *The frontal lobes*. New York: Raven press.

Ward, T. B., Smith, S. M., & Vaid, J. (1997). Conceptual structures and processes in creative thought. In T. B. Ward, S. M. Smith, & J. Vaid (Eds.), *Creative thought: An investigation of conceptual structures and processes* (pp. 1–27). Washington, DC: American Psychological Association.

Wason, P. C. (1966). Reasoning. In B. M. Foss (Ed.), *New horizons in psychology*, Vol. 1. Harmondsworth, UK: Penguin.

Wellman, H. M. (1990). *The child's theory of mind*. Cambridge, MA: MIT Press.

Wellman, H. M., & Gelman, S. A. (1998). Knowledge acquisition in foundational domains. In W. Damon (Ed.), *Handbook of child psychology* (5th edition.), Vol. 2 (D. Kuhn & R. Siegler, Eds.), *Cognition, perception and language* (pp. 523–573). New York: Wiley.

Wellman, H. M., Hickling, A. K., & Schult, C. A. (1997). Young children's psychological, physical and biological explanations. In H. M. Wellman and K. Inagaki (Eds.), *The emergence of core domains of thought: Children's reasoning about physical, psychological, and biological phenomena* (pp. 7–25). San Francisco: Jossey-Bass.

Wimmer, H., & Perner, J. (1983). Beliefs about beliefs: Representation and constraining function of wrong beliefs in young children's understanding of deception. *Cognition, 13*, 103–128.

Communications concerning this chapter should be addressed to: Professor Giyoo Hatano, Human Relations, Keio University, Mita, Minatu-ku, Tokyo, 108-8345, Japan

11

Motivation

PETER M. GOLLWITZER, JUAN D. DELIUS, AND GABRIELE OETTINGEN

Motivation is the study of the processes that cause animals and humans to exhibit varying sets of behavior at different times. Some examples of such behavior sets are eating, fighting, socializing, achieving, and studying. Traditionally, one distinguishes between biopsychological and sociopsychological approaches to the processes that cause these behaviors (Reeve, 1997). The processes addressed by the first tradition are principally physiological and those by the second tradition mainly cognitive. The biopsychological perspective has been particularly successful in the analysis of so-called biological motives common to animals and humans, such as hunger, aggression, or sex. The sociopsychological perspective has been effective in the analysis of so-called cognitive motives largely restricted to humans, such as power or achievement needs. To the extent that modern psychology has come to accept that all psychological processes are due ultimately to physiological activity, the division is now somewhat arbitrary. Nevertheless, explanations of biological motives, even when concerning humans, are mainly offered in terms of largely factual physiological mechanisms (neuronal activation, hormone secretions, etc.), whereas cognitive motives are mainly explained in terms of psychological constructs (intending, planning, executing, etc.). These constructs, modern neuroimaging techniques notwithstanding, can not yet be easily

related with physiological events. This validates the dual approach offered in this chapter. Still, in some cases we have offered an integration of biopsychological and sociopsychological approaches, and other examples of such integration are given in Chapter 4. We look forward to further integration of these two approaches in the years to come.

11.1   THE BIOPSYCHOLOGICAL PERSPECTIVE

All organisms, including humans, are the product of biological evolution, a peculiar game that certain organic molecules with not perfectly self-replicating properties started up about four billion years ago. This observation is basic to the biopsychological perspective on motivation. Organisms are biological machines which are dedicated to the survival and reproduction of their genes, the present day descendants of these molecules (Dawkins, 1989). All behavior is the final product of a phylogenetic (evolutionary), ontogenetic (developmental), and physiogenetic (physiological) cascade of causes and effects. The biopsychological study of motivation is principally concerned with the last stages of this chain of events but at times it must also attend to their evolution and development. Genetics and learning for example play a role in determining why some people over-eat and others under-eat, why some are aggressive and others timid, and so on. The modern biopsychological perspective, which originated with Claude Bernard and Charles Darwin during the nineteenth century, assumes that most behaviors of humans and other advanced animals are the consequences of a varied and interacting number of causal factors and processes, which can not be easily subsumed under one global theory or even a limited number of different theories. This is best conveyed by describing some of the mechanisms underlying the most salient biological motivation systems.

Thirst

The life functions of all organisms are based on physico-chemical reactions that take place in an aqueous medium and work best when there is a certain salt/water mixture. The circulation of some animals furthermore depends on a certain volume of blood. More than 90% of the human body consists of water, about a third of it in a chemically bound form. Water losses are continuously incurred through respiration, perspiration, urination, and defecation. Drinking water or very watery solutions is by far the main mechanism by which water deficits are compensated. Water saving through excretion of more concentrated urine, avoidance of dry foods, suppression of sweating (to the possible detriment of thermoregulation!), and other mechanisms can help temporarily but will not prevent death if water is not drunk within a couple of days (De Caro, 1986). Water swallowed wets the mouth. This stimulates chemo- and mechanoreceptors in the mouth by diluting the concentrated (salty tasting) and lesser (parched sensation) saliva secreted during water deprivation and relieves the drinking drive for some time. The sensory receptors send neural signals that reach an area of the hypothalamus responsible for integrating the neural messages about the lack or presence of water in the mouth and elsewhere. Its activity correlates well with the subjective feeling of thirst. However, filling the mouth with water and spitting it out again does not inhibit thirst for long. Only when water filling the stomach is sensed by mechanoreceptors and chemoreceptors is the neural center more lastingly inhibited. However, if the passage of the water to the intestine is blocked (in animals) thirst recurs after a while. A longer lasting quenching of thirst occurs only when the water is allowed to pass into the intestinal tract and from there into the blood. Here it replenishes the loss in blood volume which goes along with water deficits and increases the venous blood pressure sensed by baroreceptors near the heart. Loss of blood pressure is known to be an important elicitor of thirst because of the verbal report and drinking behavior by humans after massive bleeding. An increase in venous pressure decreases the hypothalamic thirst drive, but still not definitively.

A more lasting inhibition of thirst occurs when water-diluted blood reaches the anterior hypothalamus and water finds its way by diffusion into osmoreceptive neurons, swells them and causes them to fire neural signals that massively inhibit the neighboring hypothalamic thirst center. They are called osmoreceptors because they respond to the salt/water concentration differences between their outside and inside giving rise to osmotic pressure. In fact the same optimal salt/water concentration is vital for all body cells. The osmoreceptors act as samplers of that variable. We know that these cells are crucially important for the regulation of thirst because water-satiated animals will begin to drink copiously again if a minute quantity of concentrated saline solution is experimentally injected into the anterior hypothalamus. They overdrink drastically and as soon as the injection effect wanes they begin to urinate profusely. Generally, an excess of water intake can be compensated by an increased diuretic activity of the kidneys. This activity is regulated by many of the same factors that control drinking, but of course in an opposing manner. When their supply with blood decreases, the kidneys secrete a substance into the blood that activates the hormone angiotensin. Among other things this active form of angiotensin is capable of inducing drinking through special brainstem chemoreceptors that activate the hypothalamic thirst center. The hypothalamic osmoreceptors on the other hand do not only induce thirst but also lead to the secretion of the hormone vasopressin by the pituitary gland (hypophysis). Vasopressin reaches the kidneys via the blood circulation and acts to reduce their water excretion. The hypothalamic thirst drive activates the essential and largely innate swallowing of water, but of course only if water is directly available. Most often the quenching of thirst requires learned responses such as walking to a well and drawing water from it. Some drinking may also be motivated less by the osmotic needs of the body than by the fact that a solution contains substances such as caffeine or alcohol for which there is no real bodily need but which are capable of directly stimulating neural mechanisms responsible for a sensation of well-being or pleasure (see below).

Hunger

The life functions of all animals require the intake of carbohydrates, fats, proteins, vitamins, salts, and trace elements to replenish the loss of solid matter which occurs through excretion and respiration after metabolic turnover (Leeg, 1994). Deprivation of food induces the motivating state of hunger, which is stronger the longer the deprivation lasts. When we eat a meal, chemoreceptors and mechanoreceptors in the mouth, pharynx, and stomach signal to an area of the hypothalamus which functions as a satiation center. This area in turn temporarily inhibits a neighboring hypothalamic area functioning as a hunger center. It appears that inhibition is based on the synaptic transmitter serotonin and that hunger activation involves the synaptic transmitter noradrenaline. Fenfluoramine, a pharmacological blocker of noradrenaline, is used to control excessive eating by very obese individuals. When the food mass enters the intestine, chemoreceptors induce the secretion of the hormone cholecystokinin, which enters the blood stream and among other things, stimulates the satiety area of the hypothalamus. When food reaches the upper intestine, digestion has progressively broken down carbohydrates into glucose, fats into fatty acids and glycerin, proteins into amino acids, and trace elements have been freed from organic molecules. Vitamins are not modified and salts are dissolved. All of these substances enter the bloodstream and are transported to all the cells of the body where they are further metabolized in the service of the life-supporting functions.

We have already mentioned the need for salts in connection with the maintenance of a precise water/salt balance in the body cells. The regulation of salt appetite is mediated by the same osmoreceptors which are also important for thirst regulation; but more immediately it is simply the pleasant taste that salt confers to food which normally ensures that we take up enough salt. A fall in salt concentration signaled by the hypothalamic osmoreceptors might even cause a relative upgrading of the hedonic value of the taste of salt. Any excess in salt intake that might occur through this rough and ready mechanism causes the kidney to excrete more salt than it normally does, at the cost of extra water loss. This increased salt excretion is elicited by aldosterone, a hormone secreted by the adrenal glands. Exaggerated ingestion of salt provokes increased thirst. The drinking that normally follows restores the osmotic state of the body's cells but also indirectly enables the disposal of salt through increased urine production.

Glucose (blood-sugar) is the main metabolic fuel for the cells and is thus required in appreciable quantities, not least so by the nervous system. Nevertheless, its concentration in the blood should not exceed a certain measure because too much glucose has a poisonous effect, as in diabetes. To prevent this, glucoreceptors in the hypothalamus activate the satiety center inhibiting any further eating. Also, under the influence of the hormone insulin, the lack of which causes diabetes, the liver regulates blood glucose levels by converting it into the starch glycogen, which it stores. This glycogen is converted back into glucose, under the influence of the hormone glucagon, when the glucose level falls again. Both insulin and glucagon are secreted by the pancreas gland under hypothalamic neural control.

Fatty acids can also supply metabolic energy except in neurons that are fully glucose-dependent. The latter, however, can benefit from the fact that the liver can convert glycerin into glucose. Glycerin and fatty acids, recombined to fat, can however also be stored in special adipose cells located under the skin and elsewhere in the body. While storing fat, these cells secrete leptin, a hormone which has a satiating effect when it reaches the brain (Kalat, 1997). Some people may in fact be obese because their brain is genetically under-sensitive to leptin or because their leptin is chemically aberrant (Rosenzweig, Leiman, & Breedlove, 1999). However, there certainly are other causes of obesity, such as individual differences in the basal metabolic turnover controlled by the hormone thyroxin. The mechanism that causes fat cells to release fatty acids and glycerin, which serve as energy sources during extended physical exercise or long-term fasting, is not yet clear. Although we have left out many of details, it should be obvious that the intake of carbohydrates and fats is normally regulated homeostatically, ensuring the maintenance of a fairly constant body weight. Increased levels of metabolites of these substances are sensed and these signals cause a satiation of hunger. However, these post-resorptive satiation signals arise too late to be relevant for the loss of appetite that normally limits the size of a meal. The latter arises from the much faster feedback originating from the food passage through mouth and stomach.

There do not seem to be any sensors comparable to the glucose or leptin receptors which could ensure the separate regulation of ingestion of proteins, vitamins, and trace minerals. Less definite regulatory mechanisms seem to ensure that we eat enough of them. One such mechanism is our preference for varied rather than monotonous food. The pleasurable connotation of eating is much reduced if we persistently eat the same tasting food. This habituation causes us to seek some variety in foods. There are some hypotheses about how this may be implemented neurally. Chances are that the varied diet that comes about in this manner ensures a balanced intake. There are also learning processes that help to ensure a balanced diet. Vitamin deficits are known to induce a feeling of sickness. Ingestion of food which contains the missing vitamin quite rapidly brings relief. Animals, and probably also humans, can associate this relief with the taste and odor of the food which they ate shortly before, and will then seek it out later. Conversely, animals and humans also learn to associate sickness with the taste and odor of food which they ate earlier. This aversion to the taste or odor of the particular food is virtually beyond conscious control. This device, of course, ensures the avoidance of poisonous foods.

It is possible that as in the case of salt appetite, deficits and excesses of particular substances or elements may affect states of the brain in ways that subjectively feel like cravings for or aversions to foods containing these substances. These states may be equivalent to the special hungers that we at times are able to identify in ourselves: a definite appetite for sweets, for meat, for vegetables, or some other kind of food. Childhood experience also influence taste preferences and might result in diet customs such as the eating of hot Indian curries or of American 'junk-food'. Cultural fashions can also lead to a conscious regulation of food intake with the aim of maintaining sportive fitness or social attractiveness. Anorexia, a life-threatening under-eating which arises often in adolescent girls, is exacerbated by a learned beauty-of-slimness fad. Culture often connects the simple act of eating and drinking with complex ceremonies (formal dinners, tribal feasts) that serve social needs more than the need for nutrition. Or again, the hunger motive may underlie complex cognitive operations such as organized hunting or commercial agriculture. But even at this sociocognitive level genetics can affect eating habits. Certain human populations are genetically unable to digest lactose (milk-sugar) as adults and therefore some of these groups bleed rather than milk their cattle.

Sleep and Wakefulness

The necessity of keeping oneself fed and hydrated obviously requires physical and mental activity. The satisfaction of most other motives usually also involves activity. Even when all needs seem satisfied there is still an intrinsic motive for intermittent activity. It serves to keep the neuro-musculo-skeletal movement apparatus in a fit condition. There is also an intrinsic exploration or curiosity drive that makes us survey the environment, inspect novel items, and generally acquire knowledge that may be useful later (Schneider & Schmalt, 1994). All this requires a state of wakefulness associated with a heightened responsiveness to external stimuli and a general readiness for behavioral action. But activity is also connected with increased chemical turnover and physical stress due to the drain on metabolic resources and wear on body structures. These must be replenished and repaired in periods of rest. In humans as well as in animals, the cycles of activity and rest are organized on the basis of a daily rhythm (Pinel, 1997). Diurnally active animals, humans included, tend to sleep at night and be awake during the day. In nocturnally active animals this pattern is reversed. Even when humans or animals are experimentally kept in a constantly lit, even-temperatured, sound-insulated, clockless, artificial environment they persist with an activity/rest cycle that is close to 24 hours in duration, the so-called circadian rhythm. It is driven by a neuro-humoral oscillator (biological clock) with the nucleus suprachiasmaticus and the pineal gland (epiphysis) as interacting elements. The basic rhythm, however, is modulated by homeostatic processes. Temporary deprivation of sleep or activity is partly compensated by a relative lengthening of subsequent sleep or activity phases.

Wakefulness is largely determined by the activity of a dense network of neurons along the axis of the brainstem. It receives collateral signals from all sensory stimuli and is capable of activating most cortical circuits. This is reflected by high frequency, small amplitude oscillations seen in electroencephalograms (EEG). As a person becomes drowsy and falls asleep, EEG recordings are dominated by low frequency, large amplitude oscillations. This slow wave sleep is periodically interrupted by episodes of EEG activity very similar to that seen during waking, although the person remains asleep. Rapid eye movements (REM sleep) can be observed through the sleeping person's closed eyelids. If a person wakes up during this phase she/he mostly reports having been dreaming. Deprivation of REM sleep for a night increases the number and length of REM sleep phases during the next night. This indicates that the organism needs REM sleep. The function of this dream sleep is not totally clear but animal studies have suggested that its prevention interferes with the consolidation of memories. It may serve to reorganize cognitive information that accumulates during wakefulness. Both types of sleep and their alternation are controlled by nuclei of the midbrain and thalamus, where the synaptic transmitter serotonin may be involved together with the epiphysial hormone melatonin in inducing the basic sleeping state. The addition of the transmitter acetylcholine induces REM episodes whereas wakefulness state may be maintained by the synaptic transmitter noradrenaline. Noradrenaline and serotonin have already been implicated in the regulation of hunger and satiety, and acetylcholine is among other things the transmitter that acts at the neuro-muscular endplates. Thus the same transmitters are acting in the regulation of different behaviors in different parts of the nervous system. Certain affective disorders are associated with sleep-irregularities and precisely timed doses of melatonin can bring relief. In any case, disturbance of the various mechanisms of sleep results in symptoms such as insomnia, sleepwalking, or narcolepsy.

Aggression and Fear

Survival and reproduction are dependent upon individual organisms securing environmental resources. When resources are freely available, as for example water in a humid country, there is no need to fight for them. However, food acquisition by predatory species entails hunting, and the prey may resist. Both predators and prey may engage in aggressive attack and defensive fleeing during such encounters. This agonistic behavior is often similar to that seen in intraspecific interactions, as individuals of the same species often have to compete for resources such as food or shelter. Intra-specific antagonism may also occur during competition for social resources, such as mating partners or allies. Such agonism often develops over prospective resources such as winter-barren land in expectancy of its summer fertility, or over social status in expectancy of prime access to all kinds of resources. Moreover, agonistic behavior may be supported by social groupings such as families, tribes, or nations. These conflicts take on the character of wars as the size of the groups involved increases and as weapons potentiate the group's power to injure and kill. Xenophobia, sectarianism, obedience, and fanaticism are some cognitive/cultural factors that can exacerbate aggression.

Fighting is connected with risk of injury and thus aggression is often balanced by fear. This frequently results in threat behavior. The individual development of agonistic motivation is driven by genetically determined behavioral dispositions which are modulated by experience. It is easy to breed genetically increased aggressiveness; fighting fish, cocks, and dogs being examples. Children probably become more aggressive if they discover that aggression is more often followed by reward than by punishment. Agonistic behavior is mainly controlled by non-homeostatic mechanisms, triggered by situational factors such as pain, offence, jealousy, or frustration (Renfrew, 1997). Nevertheless, deprivation from channeled, socially accepted aggressive outlets such as competitive sports or verbal disputes might lead to increased aggressive drive in at least some individuals. Frustrated children are more likely to behave aggressively to a bystander if they have previously experienced an aggressive scene than if they have not. Sensory information about situations provoking anger or fear is apparently transmitted by a special thalamo-amygdalar pathway. Stimulation through electrodes implanted into a neural circuit that extends from the amygdala through to the nucleus striae terminalis, the medial hypothalamus, and the medial midbrain elicits agonistic behavior in animals. In humans, responses such as slapping a medical attendant, accompanied by an angry facial expression, were observed when stimulation of the amygdala was necessary as a pre-surgical exploration. Male animals and humans generally are more prone to show aggression than females. In animals this is mediated by the hormone testosterone (Rosenzweig, Leiman, & Breedlove, 1999). Castrated male animals display less aggression than normal males and in both humans and animals testosterone injections heighten readiness for aggression. In female animals the pregnancy hormone progesterone appears to increase readiness for defensive aggression when offspring are threatened.

Sex and Parenthood

The central property of genes is replication. Sexual reproduction, a common complication of gene replication, is advantageous but also costly. Advantageous, because it enables the mixing of parental genes and thus guarantees offspring diversity. This increases the chance that some offspring will succeed in a permanently changing environment. Costly, because in many species it requires the synchronized coupling of ovum and sperm within the body of the female who then also bears the costs of pregnancy and in mammals, lactation. Sex is energetically cheap for males but they must compete for females. Females must be choosy about males, who are co-responsible for the genetic quality of their offspring. Females assess the quality of males and their willingness to continue investing in the common progeny after mating. The dominance of monogamy in human cultures is likely derived from the poor prospects single mothers have of raising healthy progeny under rough conditions. In many species, a maintained pair bond is essential for successful parenting. Males' reproductive efforts could be wasted if they do not contribute to the welfare of their offspring. Love probably strengthens this pair-bonding. Among humans, cultural customs produce much variation in courtship and partnership habits. The role that off-reproductive mating plays in pair maintenance is probably why sex is connected with intense pleasure. The dissociation of sexual activity from reproduction by contraceptive technology has reduced sex to a largely hedonic motive.

The existence of women and men is determined by the sex chromosomes. An XX fertilized ovum is predetermined to develop into a female, an XY fertilized ovum to develop into a male. However, this only determines whether the embryos develop female or male reproductive organs. Occasionally occurring XO (only one X chromosome) individuals develop neither testes nor ovaries. The differences in female and male behavior, or rather in the details of brain structures that control these differences, come about through a more complicated mechanism. A few weeks before birth the testes of male (human) embryos secrete testosterone which biases brain development in a male direction. Female embryos have no such burst of testosterone, nor indeed of estrogen, as the ovaries exhibit no perinatal activity. This allows the relevant brain structures to go on developing undisturbed (Kalat, 1997). Quite early in life these brain differences have the consequence that girls tend to learn to speak earlier than boys and boys are more prone to show rough-and-tumble (fighting) play than are girls. At puberty (testes secreting again testosterone, ovaries secreting for the first time estrogen), the brain differences determine that most girls begin to develop an interest in boys and most boys are attracted to girls. Why some do not and become homosexual rather than heterosexual is not yet altogether clear. For a proportion of male homosexuals it seems likely that brain differentiation is partly blocked by a mutant gene located on their X chromosome.

Readiness for the sex act, or libido, is in part influenced by the presence of circulating testosterone in males and, to a lesser extent, circulating estrogen and progesterone in females. Erotic stimuli and stimulation bring about mating readiness in both sexes. In males, more than females, this arousal is helped by the novelty of erogenous stimuli. This so-called Coolidge effect is an easily demonstrable phenomenon in male animals. They appear to tire if the same female is repeatedly presented but show renewed sexual efforts if a new receptive female is presented. Sexual arousal results in penile and clitoral erections and lubricatory gland secretions. This entails the expansion of vein irrigated cavernous tissue and glandular contractions under the control of nervous signals from the brain. Mechanostimulation of penile and vaginal tissue results in ejaculation of sperm in the male and contractions of the vaginal walls in the female. Both events are associated with a sensation of pleasure (orgasm), due to neural signals transmitted to the brainstem reward areas. The contractions associated with female orgasm may be coupled with a particularly effective transport of sperm to the uterus. The release of mature ova by the ovary occurs at four-weekly intervals and menstruation is connected with the post-ovulatory sloughing off of tissue lining the uterus. This tissue develops within the cycle in preparation for the possible implantation of a fertilized ovum and is rejected if such implantation does not take place. A complicated interaction between hypophysial and ovarial hormone secretions regulates the ovulatory/menstrual cycle. In contrast to many animals, the cycle has little influence on the day-to-day sexual receptivity of the human female. Even the widespread intercourse bar connected with menstrual bleeding is probably culturally sanctioned and not physiologically determined (Abramson & Pinkerton, 1995).

When implantation occurs and gestation begins, female libido is at first not inhibited despite a much changed hormonal situation. This suggests that sexual receptivity in the human female, additionally to fertilization also supports pair-bonding. As birth approaches, the hypophysial hormone prolactin readies mammary gland tissue for milk production. Emotional attachment to the baby seems to be facilitated by mechanical stimulation of the uterus wall during child birth. When the baby nurses, an innate response activated by low blood glucose, this stimulates through a quite direct neural pathway the secretion of oxytocin, another hypophysial hormone that causes the release of milk.

Parental care is the most basic form of genetically driven altruism (Rosenblatt, 1996). Although genes are essentially selfish in their operations, the evolutionary game allows that carriers of identical genes (e.g., offspring, kin) can benefit from genetically instructed altruistic behavior. The gene sets of children are of course combinations of half-sets of maternal and paternal gene copies. They can rely on being the preferred recipients of altruistic parental attention. Parents are prepared to bestow advantages on their children at cost to themselves but mothers more so than fathers. Mothers can nearly always be certain of their maternity whereas fathers may have been cuckolded and could be caring for a child that is not their own.

Social Motivation

Many animal species are highly social. Much of this is based on familial clans, involving a kind of extended parenting. This genetically driven kind of altruism provides graded benefits for all blood-relations. Relatives have a proportion of genes in common, high if the relationship is close, low if the relationship is distant. Aunts and uncles are typically prepared to act parentally to nephews and nieces. However, social dispositions can also develop among non-related persons. If I do something good for someone, it is not unreasonable to expect I might have a favor returned later. This altruism is founded on a reciprocal strategy promoted by friendships and/or cultural groups that make reciprocity their rule or tradition (Zahn-Waxler, Cummings, & Iannoty, 1991). Division of labor, where some people are hunters, others are farmers, others are cooks, and so on, is more efficient than each individual in a group trying to do everything. A division of labor however, increases dependence on the mutual exchange of services and goods.

Animals living in social groups are often capable of extensive social learning. Trans-generational traditions or protocultures (song protocultures in birds, food-washing cultures in monkeys, for example) and even proper cultures can develop as a result provided that the repertoire of traditions is sufficiently rich. The elements of culture are transmitted to individuals and come to reside as long-term memory traces in their brains and contribute to determining their behavior. Long-term memory traces are constellations of synaptic connections between neurons modified by learning, social in this particular case. These elements of culture, sometimes called memes (Dawkins, 1989), are packages of information that multiply through social learning and have some superficial similarities to genes. Genes are also packages of information but they reproduce by biochemical means. Memes are engaged in cultural evolution, which has similarities to biological evolution (Delius, 1991). Through memetically (rather than genetically) driven dispositions, they can bring about a meme-based altruism (for example, among members of trans-racial religions such as Muslims and Catholics) and promote meme-based aggression (for example strife between religious groups such as Catholics and Lutherans). This altruism and agonism is of a predominantly cognitive nature. Indeed, it is argued that the selection pressure for the evolution of primate intelligence arose mainly from the necessity to efficiently cope with the complexities of the social environment. Shifting alliances, coalitions, squabbles, and struggles with or against group members are usually necessary to obtain the best possible life quality for oneself and one's family.

Learned Motives

Biological motives are conventionally (and not totally incorrectly) considered as essentially innate and their development as genetically driven. However, as we have already seen, among many animals motivated behavior is rarely based on only genetically determined mechanisms. Learning processes usually refine or even create part of the mechanisms that control behavior. The capacity to learn is a genetically instructed mechanism evolved to take advantage of the possibility of improving the behavioral apparatus of an individual on the basis of experience. Genetically instructed because the synaptic connectivity modifications that underlie learning and memory formation are biochemical processes that require gene activity. Biologically motivated behavior is often prone to modifications by learning because the satisfaction of motives is usually associated with the activation of a positive hedonic state that is widely broadcast from the midbrain to throughout the forebrain by a ramified reward circuit using dopamine as a transmitter. Endorphines, natural morphine-like neuromodulators, also intervene. We know about this circuit because animals and humans with electrodes implanted in the relevant brain areas will learn to repetitively perform some arbitrary response such as lever pressing to get brief weak electric pulses delivered to these areas. Conversely, the thwarting of motivational goals is associated with the broadcast of a hedonically negative signal through a punishment system. Both these reinforcement signals are strong agents in bringing about synaptic modifications.

Apart from primary rewards and punishments such as the satisfaction of thirst, the achievement of sexual orgasm, or conversely the pain of being bitten, initially neutral stimuli can acquire secondary reward or punishment properties. For example, animals exposed to a particular sound before receiving painful electric foot-shocks learn to flee from that stimulus to avoid being shocked, and persist in doing so for a long time, although the shock may have been disconnected in the meanwhile. They show all the signs of fear when they hear the sound even though it is innocuous by itself. They have acquired a conditioned or learned emotional fear response that is sufficient to motivate an escape response. Some human phobias (of knives or of heights, for example) are thought to be acquired through such associative learning (Mook, 1996). Conversely, monkeys who have been taught that plastic chips thrown into vending machines will yield desirable tit-bits such as peanuts or grapes, once well trained, will work for hours on end, pressing a lever for the occasional reward of chips. This learned motive also causes them to hoard chips in particular places and to steal chips from each other, things that humans tend to do with money. These learned motives may represent incipient cognitive motives, and help to remind us that in the last analysis cognitive motives are biological, in the sense that they are based on information processing in the brain. Whether for example the monkeys are consciously aware of the stand-for quality of their chips or not is debatable. On the other hand, conscious reasoning is no longer considered a necessary attribute of cognitive operations in humans. We are often only very dimly or not at all aware of many of the cognitive processes that determine our behavior.

Summary

The biopsychological approach to motivation assumes that organisms including humans are primarily biological machines synthesized under the control of inherited genes and operating for the purpose of these genes' survival and reproduction. Behavior must be understood as fulfilling aspects of that overall function and as the product of the physiological machinery of individual organisms that, although grown under genetic control, is subject to adaptive modifications through learning. Through learning, the machinery is open to the influence of memes, cultural determinants of behavior that may act to support the organism's survival and reproduction or that may indeed promote only their own persistence and multiplication. The mechanisms of the motivation processes underlying different sets of behavior are varied and intricate, as befits the varied and complicated functions they fulfil.

11.2 THE SOCIOPSYCHOLOGICAL PERSPECTIVE

Three sets of phenomena have traditionally been of concern in the field of human motivation for personality and social psychologists: (a) the selection of a certain course of action, (b) the energizing of the implied behaviors, and (c) the regulation of these behaviors. In other words, motivation refers to what type of goals people choose, and how they go about implementing them: when and how goal-directed behavior gets started, is energized, sustained, and stopped. Taking this broad and comprehensive perspective, any field in social psychology (e.g., helping others, aggression, inter-group relations) may potentially be analyzed from a motivational viewpoint, and this extends not only to how people behave in social situations, but also to their social thoughts and feelings.

The lay concept of motivation points solely to energizing. People are referred to as *un*motivated when they fail to exert effort and do not live up to their potential. This narrow definition of motivation, however, reflects an important insight. Issues of what people *can* do, that is, their cognitive capabilities and limitations, are just the starting point of a motivational analysis which commonly attempts to discover the determinants and processes that underlie a person's willingness to use his or her potential.

The history of motivational theory can be summarized in terms of how the basic nature of human functioning and development is conceived. Early theories portrayed the human as a machine-like, reactive organism compelled to act by internal and/or external forces beyond our control (e.g., instincts, needs, drives, incentives, and so forth). According to Weiner (1992), prototypical theories are the psychoanalytic theories of Freud, Hull's learning theory, or Lewin's field-theoretical approach. These theories imply that if one could just push the right buttons, motivation would result. There is no room for conscious reflection and attempts at self-regulation. Instead, motivational forces transmit their energy outside of awareness, establishing a state of balance or equilibrium (referred to as arousal reduction, self-preservation, or need satisfaction).

More modern theories construe the human as God-like (Weiner, 1992). Accordingly, people are seen as all-just and all-knowing final judges of their actions. Expectancy-value theories (e.g., Atkinson, 1957) and attribution theories (e.g., Weiner, 1992) are based on this metaphor. Expectancy-value theories assume that people choose goals rationally based on comprehensive knowledge about the expected value and the probability of goal attainment. Attribution theories propose that the motivational determinants of a person's behavior are the causal explanations of prior action outcomes. The human is seen as an amateur scientist who systematically explores the causes of his or her past behaviors. The types of causes discovered are expected to affect the person's readiness to engage in these or related behaviors by influencing affects and expectations. However, even though people may be quite knowledgeable, they are imperfect decision-makers and evaluators (i.e., they only possess a bounded rationality).

Present-day theories of motivation go one step further. Human beings are construed as flexible strategists. The focus is on the different tasks a person has to perform when transforming wishes into actions (Gollwitzer, 1990; Heckhausen, 1991). Accordingly, humans are conceived of as highly flexible organisms who readily adjust to task demands. When choosing goals, people apparently try to live up to the ideal of being all-knowing and all-just by processing all of the available information and weighing it impartially. However, when the implementation of an already chosen goal is at issue, people are determined to achieve the desired ends. As a consequence, we become partial, favoring the implementation of the chosen goal. The desirability and feasibility of the chosen goal are seen in the most positive light, and the focus of attention is on the chosen goal. Although this determination to achieve the chosen goal invokes a machine metaphor, recent research contradicts this image of the goal-driven human. Goal achievement is rather a highly strategic undertaking that demands the flexible use of self-regulation skills.

In the following sections, selected issues are presented which characterize present-day social-psychological research on motivation. We will address research on (a) motives and needs, (b) expectations, attributions, and control beliefs, and (c) goal setting and goal striving.

Motives and Needs

Research on motives highlights the relation between motivation and affect (McClelland, 1985). Any motivated behavior is pulled by the anticipated affect associated with so-called natural incentives. Such incentives are attached to situations and actions that are important for the survival of the human species (e.g., affiliation, influence, intellectual mastery). Accordingly, it is proposed that there are a limited number of natural incentives, each of which shows an inborn relation to a specific cluster of emotions. The individual's preferences for certain types of incentives are defined as the individual's motive dispositions.

Socialization is said to teach which situations are associated with what kind of natural incentives and their respective affective experiences. In addition, people are assumed to acquire the skills which allow them to successfully approach desired incentives. McClelland distinguishes three basic groups of motives: the achievement motive, the power motive, and the affiliative motives (i.e., sex, affiliation, and intimacy). As

food is the reward or incentive for hunger, so is improving one's performance on a given task the incentive for the achievement motive. The incentive of the power motive is having impact, control, or influence over another person, a group, or the world at large. How this impact or influence is established depends on the individual's socialization. There are the crude ways of attacking others physically, but also the more sophisticated routes of persuading or teaching others. Finally, the incentives for the affiliative motives extend to sexual pleasures (sexual motive), being together with people (need for affiliation), and experiencing harmony, concern, and commitment (intimacy motive). All of these motives may entail a fear or avoidance component. Trying to meet a standard of excellence may not be motivated solely by hope for success, but also by fear of failure, and spending one's spare time affiliating with others may not be determined solely by the anticipated positive feelings of togetherness, but also by a high fear of rejection.

In principle, all humans are seen as possessing the various motives described. There are vast differences, however, in motive strength. This can be assessed by exploring both the array of situations a person interprets in terms of a given motive (e.g., a person high in need for power interprets all kinds of situations as power-related) and the intensity of the anticipated affect associated with having acquired respective incentives. Commonly this is done with the Thematic Apperception Test (TAT) which contains pictures of scenes loosely related to the motive measured. In the Achievement TAT, for instance, one picture shows an employee knocking at his boss's door. Participants who take the test are instructed to give free reign to fantasy, talking about what happens in the picture, how the depicted scenario came about, what the depicted persons think, and what will happen next.

This procedure (often referred to as the operant assessment procedure) is based on the idea that the presented pictures will trigger motive-related thoughts which will then be expressed in free fantasy. Respondent assessment procedures (i.e., the standard self-report questionnaires) are less appropriate, because they also reflect the values people hold with respect to a certain motive. Most people know that achievement, for instance, is highly valued in our society, and many have learned to value it highly themselves. But when it comes to actually behaving in an achievement-oriented manner in a given situation, a person who highly values achievement may nevertheless spontaneously pick up the affiliative cues present in this situation, and opt towards enjoying togetherness rather than achieving – because her achievement need is lower than her need for affiliation. A person's spontaneous fantasy production as stimulated by TAT pictures should reflect such preferences, and therefore should provide a more valid assessment of a person's motive dispositions than do self-report questionnaires.

More recent research has attempted to link the activation of different motives to different hormonal responses. An activated power motive leads to an increase in noradrenaline and adrenaline, whereas an activated achievement motive is associated with an increase of the hormone arginine-vasopressin (McClelland, 1995). The affiliation motive has been linked to the neurotransmitter dopamine. It is assumed that each motive is linked to specific hormonal responses that in turn facilitate motive-specific behaviors. People's motives have also been observed to affect the functioning of the immune system. For example, power-motivated people become ill more frequently and more severely when their attempts to acquire social influence are repeatedly frustrated or when they become targets of influence attempts by others.

Being high on a certain motive implies a recurrent concern for acquiring the respective incentives. People high on the affiliation motive perform affiliative acts frequently and energetically, readily perceive affiliative cues in the environment, and quickly detect affiliative networks. Also, predictions of the professional success of managers are strikingly accurate, particularly if one considers the motive dispositions in achievement (high), power (high), and affiliation (low) in concert. However, attempts to predict behaviors from motives commonly fail when engagement in these behaviors is based on conscious reflection. When it comes to choosing, between courses of action, tasks of differing difficulty, or persisting on a given task or leaving the field, people deliberate on the feasibility and desirability of the alternative courses of action. As it turns out, people do not determine the feasibility and desirability of an action solely on the basis of their motive dispositions, but also by thinking about their skills, the intricacies of the situation, and the expected value of the respective course of action.

Expectations, Attributions, and Control Beliefs

One of the first attempts to integrate these aspects of motivation was made by Atkinson (1957) in his risk-taking model. He proposed that the subjective probability of success and the task's incentive value conjointly affect task choice, both variables being influenced by the perceived difficulty of the task. Whereas easy tasks lead to a high subjective probability of success (direct function), they also possess low incentive value (inverse function) because the anticipated affect associated with success (pride) is lowest for easy tasks. The reverse is assumed for difficult tasks. Atkinson suggested that multiplying probability of success and incentive value will give a good estimate of whether a person will choose to work on a task, especially when the obtained score is weighted by the approach and avoidance components of his or her achievement motive (hope for success and fear of failure, respectively). The prediction is that primarily success-motivated individuals will choose tasks of medium difficulty, whereas failure-motivated people prefer easy or very difficult tasks. Research supports the model for predictions on task choice, but the model fails to account for the quantity and quality of task performance once people have started to work on the chosen tasks.

Elaborations of the model (Heckhausen, 1991) added further expectation-related concepts and differentiate various aspects of the incentive value of task performance. The incentive value of task performance is not simply determined by anticipated pride and shame. Positive self-evaluations, praise from significant others (e.g., teachers, parents), the instrumentality of task performance to super-ordinate long-term goals, and extrinsic side-effects (e.g., when an achievement task has affiliative benefits) must also be considered. In addition, Heckhausen points out that even if there are many potential positive incentives, one will only be motivated to strive for them if one expects that (1) the behaviors one is capable of performing will lead to successful task performance, and (2) successful task performance will lead to the incentives (i.e., possesses high instrumentality).

There is a further type of incentive that needs to be taken into consideration. Certain behaviors may possess an incentive value in and of themselves. This is most apparent when people fiercely engage in activities (e.g., hang-gliding) that serve no ostensible purpose. The associated flow-experience and complete absorption makes people seek such activities for no other reason but performing the activity. This is difficult to interpret in terms of expectancy-value theorizing which claims that people engage in action to achieve certain ends that are a consequence of having acted successfully.

Atkinson's model has also been elaborated by attribution theorists (Weiner, 1992) who attempted to understand changes in expectations and incentive value in terms of the attributions made for past performances. Success and failure may be interpreted as caused by internal (e.g., ability, effort) or external factors (e.g., task difficulty, luck). Ability and task difficulty are more stable causal factors than effort and luck. Weiner shows that the stability of success or failure attributions affects people's expectations of successful task performance (stable attributions lead to high or low expectations, respectively), whereas the internality of performance outcome attributions relates to affect (internal attributions produce more pride or shame, respectively).

Weiner also discovered that the approach component of the achievement motive (hope for success) is associated with attributing failure to luck or lack of effort and success to ability, whereas the avoidance component is linked to attributing failure to lack of ability and success to luck. Research on aggression also points to the importance of attributions for people's readiness to retaliate. Our anger and readiness to retaliate in response to the aggression of others are less related to the damage that was done to us, but rather to our interpretation of the aggressive act as intentional. Similarly, attributions also affect whether we help people in need. Interpreting the plight of victims as caused by their own irresponsible behaviors leads to less helping as compared with causal interpretations of their plight in terms of uncontrollable, external factors.

People develop personal styles of explaining positive and negative events (Seligman, 1990). An optimistic attributional style is the tendency to make more stable and global attributions for positive than for negative events, leading to expectations that positive events will be more persistent and pervasive than negative events. If, in addition, positive events are attributed to internal causes more than are negative events, strengthened self-esteem results. An optimistic attributional style predicts success at school, work, and sports, as well as physical and mental health (e.g., lack of depression).

Recognition of the motivational importance of expectations and attributions was the starting point of the cognitive revolution in the psychology of motivation. The revolution has progressed and has introduced further cognitive concepts such as control beliefs and goals. The most prominent theoretical explication of control beliefs is Bandura's (1997) self-efficacy theory. Self-efficacious individuals hold the firm belief that they possess the potential to execute the kinds of behaviors that a given task demands. People acquire this belief by reflecting on their own relevant past behaviors, observing the behaviors of similar others, being evaluated by significant others (e.g., teachers), and observing their own physiological reactions when challenged by a given task. High self-efficacy beliefs

are associated with choosing aspiring goals, exerting strong efforts to attain these goals, and persisting in the face of obstacles and hindrances.

Goal Setting

Determinants of Goal Setting

Research on the determinants of goal setting distinguishes between assigned goals and self-set goals. Whether people adopt goals assigned by others depends on variables that facilitate persuasion (e.g., the legitimacy and trustworthiness of the person who assigns the goal and whether the recipient manages to integrate the assigned goal with the goals he or she already holds). The adoption of self-set goals depends on the perceived desirability and feasibility of anticipated goal attainment, judged in comparison to potential alternative goals. Moreover, people differ in their preference for setting goals with certain structural features or contents. For example, people who generally think about their actions in concrete versus abstract terms also prefer to set themselves concrete versus abstract goals, respectively. People who construe their self as an ideal (which they intrinsically desire to attain) set goals with a positive outcome focus (i.e., goals focusing on establishing and keeping positive outcomes), whereas people who construe their self as an ought which they feel compelled to reach set goals with a negative outcome focus (i.e., goals that focus on avoiding and getting rid of negative outcomes).

For goal setting in the achievement domain it matters what kind of implicit theories people hold on the nature of ability. If people believe that ability is fixed and cannot easily be changed, they choose performance goals (i.e., goals geared at trying to find out through past performance how capable one is). If, however, people believe that ability can be improved by learning, they choose learning goals (i.e., goals geared at trying to learn more about on how one can successfully carry out the task at hand).

People's needs, wishes, and higher order goals also influence the type of goals that are set. Once specific higher order goals are formed (e.g., to become a physician), the latter determine the contents of lower order goals (i.e., goals describing what has to be done to achieve the higher order goal). Moreover, a person's concept of what he or she could possibly become (i.e., the possible self) provides the individual with thematic conceptions of what future selves he may strive for. Finally, the contents of goals tend to reflect people's needs. For example, strong autonomy, competence, and social integration needs lead to fewer materialistic goals and promote self-realization goals.

Processes of Goal Setting

Goal setting is based on reflective and reflexive processes. With respect to reflective processes, various ways of goal setting can be differentiated (Oettingen, 1997). First, the heightened sense of efficacy that is based on having successfully attained a prior goal stimulates the setting of ever more challenging goals. Second, people show a greater readiness to set themselves goals when they have exhaustively deliberated the desirability and feasibility of their wishes (i.e., potential goals). Third, when people are lured into planning the implementation of a potential goal, they tend to commit themselves to it.

Finally, recent research demonstrates that feasibility of goal attainment is not always reflected in people's goal setting, in the sense that only goals with high probability of success are chosen (Oettingen, 2000). When people positively fantasize about a desired future outcome, they set themselves goals independent of perceived feasibility. In other words, people who indulge in positive fantasies about desired future outcomes commit themselves to goals irrationally; they are too committed when probabilities of success are low, and not committed enough when probabilities of success are high. Such irrational goal commitments are also observed with people who are caught up in ruminations about aspects of the present reality that stand in the way of reaching one's fantasies. When people are mentally contrasting their positive fantasies with the impeding negative reality, however, their goal setting strictly reflects perceived feasibility. Strong goal commitments emerge when the perceived feasibility is high, and no goal commitment at all is found when the perceived feasibility is low.

Accordingly, when the perceived feasibility of goal attainment is high, the mental contrasting of positive fantasies about the future with negative aspects of the impeding reality is an effective route to creating strong goal commitments. For instance, when an overweight person who is confident of her ability to lose weight contrasts his or her positive fantasies about successful weight loss with his or her thoughts about the present negative reality (e.g., bad eating habits, the hardships of exercising), a strong goal commitment can be expected. Strong goal commitments will not occur, however, when people (even highly confident people) fail to contrast their positive fantasies about the desired future with the negative reality and instead mentally indulge in their desired future or are caught up in ruminations on negative aspects of the present reality (thus losing sight of their desired future).

For applied psychologists who attempt to strongly commit people to beneficial behavioral goals (e.g., health goals, academic goals, interpersonal goals), these findings imply that along with promoting people's confidence in their own capabilities, making them mentally contrast their positive fantasies about the future with negative aspects of the impeding reality is critical. Merely encouraging people to 'think positive' about their future does not lead to strong goal commitments, even if expectations of success are high. Moreover, the contrasting procedure helps people to refrain from setting themselves goals in domains where expectations of success are low, as contrasting leads to recognizing the probability of success. People who are caught up in persevering fantasies about a desired future or in persevering ruminations about a negative reality ignore the feasibility of potential goals and thus are at risk to commit themselves to goals that cannot be attained.

Goals may also become reflexively activated outside of awareness (Bargh & Chartrand, 1999). Strong mental links develop between the cognitive representations of situations and the goals that people chronically pursue within them. As a consequence of this repeated and consistent pairing in the past, such goals become automatically activated when the person enters the relevant situation. The automatically activated goal then guides behavior, without the individual choosing or intending the respective goal-directed line of action. There has been a reflective choice of the goal in the past, but this conscious choice is now bypassed. If, for example, a person has repeatedly and consistently chosen social gatherings (e.g., parties) to discuss work problems, the contextual cues associated with parties will sooner or later trigger behaviors serving this goal outside of awareness.

Goal Striving

Goal Content Effects

Successful goal striving is determined by how goals are framed and what contents they specify. The following structural features of goals are important. Challenging goals that are spelled out in specific terms lead to a higher attainment rate than modest specific goals or challenging but vague ('do your best!') goals. Proximal goals that relate to what the individual does in the near present or will do in the future are superior to distal goals that point far into the future. Apparently, proximal goals allow for more performance feedback and make it easier to monitor progress towards the goal. Goals with a positive outcome focus produce a promotion orientation geared at achievement, which facilitates goal pursuit, whereas goals with a negative outcome focus produce a prevention orientation geared at acquiring security, which hampers goal pursuit. Learning goals lead to better performances than performance goals, as the former allow for a more effective coping with failure than the latter by making people view set-backs as cues to focus on new behavioral strategies. Accordingly, behavior becomes oriented towards mastering the causes of the set-backs, which ultimately furthers goal attainment. Performance goals are less detrimental, however, when they are framed as approach goals (e.g., I want to get good grades) as compared with avoidance goals (e.g., I do not want to get bad grades).

Moreover, the thematic content of goals matters. Goals covering issues of autonomy, competence, and social integration are said to further intrinsic goal pursuit and thus lead to better performance in the sense of greater creativity, higher cognitive flexibility, greater depth of information processing, and more effective coping with failure. The side effects of such goal pursuit are positive well-being and higher life satisfaction. People who set themselves goals such as making money, becoming famous, and acquiring high status, experience a reduced level of well-being as compared with goal contents such as cultivating one's relationships to friends or becoming active in community services. This is particularly true for individuals who feel a strong self-efficacy, implying that people who successfully implement materialistic goals are particularly at risk for low well-being. Holding a high proportion of achievement and power goals is also linked to reduced well-being, whereas a high proportion of intimacy goals enhances it. The effects of goals on subjective well-being are also influenced by how well people's goal contents match the motives of achievement, affiliation, power, and intimacy. People with strong achievement and power motives and goals of the same theme as well as people with strong affiliation and intimacy motives and goals of the same theme report higher emotional well-being than people whose motives and goals are mismatched.

Planning

Experience tells us that it is often a long way from goal setting to goal attainment. Having set a goal is just a first step, commonly followed by a host of implemental problems that need to be successfully solved. These problems are manifold and pertain to initiating goal-directed actions and bringing them to a successful ending. To solve these problems effectively a person may plan how she wants to attain the chosen goal.

Research on implemental mind-sets (Gollwitzer, 1990) has shown that planning the implementation of a set goal creates a cognitive orientation that facilitates getting started with goal-directed actions. People with an implemental mind-set become closed minded in the sense that they are no longer distracted by irrelevant information. They are, however, very effective in processing information related to the implementation of set goals. Moreover, desirability-related information is processed partially, favoring pros over cons, and analysis of feasibility-related information favors illusory optimism. This optimism extends to the illusion of control over behavioral outcomes, a person's self-concept of possessing important skills and aptitudes, and to their perceived vulnerability to both controllable and uncontrollable risks. These features of the implemental mind-set favor goal attainment as they allow the individual to effectively cope with problems of goal striving such as being distracted by irrelevancies, doubting the attractiveness of the pursued goal, or being pessimistic about its feasibility.

Set goals commit people to attaining the specified future (outcome or behavior), but they do not commit people to when, where, and how they want to attain it. Such additional commitments can be added, however, by planning one's goal pursuit via forming so-called implementation intentions that take the form of 'if I encounter situation x, I intend to perform the goal-directed behavior y' (Gollwitzer, 1999). Difficult to reach goals (e.g., healthy eating) benefit greatly from being furnished with implementation intentions. As implementation intentions spell out links between situational cues and goal-directed behavior, by forming such intentions people pass on the control of goal-directed behavior to environmental cues. This facilitates the initiation of goal-directed actions. First, the mental representations of the specified situational cues become highly activated, making these cues more accessible. Situational cues specified in implementation intentions are thus more easily detected, remembered, and more readily attended to than comparable non-intended situations. Second, action initiation becomes automated. Goal-directed behaviors specified in implementation intentions are initiated immediately and effortlessly in the presence of the critical situations. Even patients with frontal lobe injuries (who are known to be plagued by deficient conscious and effortful control of behavior) benefit from implementation intentions. But it is not only the problem of action initiation that is ameliorated by implementation intentions. Resistance to temptation, fighting bad habits, and escaping the unwanted influences of competing goals activated outside of the person's awareness can also be facilitated.

Next to forming implementation intentions there are other effective forms of planning. The task of planning can be approached in a more reflective way as is entailed in mental simulations that explore possible routes to achieving one's goal (so-called process simulations; Taylor, Pham, Rivkin, & Armor, 1998). If such process simulations are applied repeatedly, they further goal attainment, such as achieving good grades in academic exams. Apparently, repeated mental simulations of how to achieve the goal also result in firm plans.

Action Control Strategies

Goal attainment is often hampered by competing goals. The issue of competing goal pursuits has been paid particular attention in theorizing on action control (Kuhl & Beckmann, 1994). Successful goal attainment implies that a current guiding goal has to be shielded from competing goals (e.g., the goal of making a phone call from the competing goal of tidying up one's messy desk). A number of different, but compatible control strategies are differentiated, such as attentional control, emotional control, motivational control, and environmental control. Through environmental control, for example, the individual prevents the derailing of an ongoing goal pursuit by removing competing temptations or enticements from the situation in which goal pursuit is to occur.

Whether and how effectively these strategies are used depends on the current control mode of the individual. An action-oriented person concentrates on the planning and initiation of goal-directed action, responds flexibly to contextual demands, and uses control strategies effectively. Things are quite different with a state-oriented person as he or she cannot disengage from incomplete goals and is thus caught up in uncontrollable perseveration of thoughts related to aversive experiences or in dysfunctional thoughts about future successes. Action- and state-orientation may be induced by situational variables (e.g., a surprising event, persistent failure), but are also founded in a personal disposition.

Recent research on state orientation as a personality attribute has discovered a further volitional handicap called self-infiltration. State-oriented individuals readily misperceive assigned goals as self-generated, and the degree of such false self-ascriptions is closely associated with reduced enactment of self-chosen as compared with assigned goals. These findings have stimulated a new theoretical perspective on action orientation versus state orientation, based on the assumption that the volitional control of action is a result of the cooperation of various subsystems (i.e., intention memory, extension memory, intuitive behavior control, and object recognition). Action orientation versus state orientation are parameters that modulate the cooperation between these systems thus leading to different kinds of action control with different outcomes.

Successfully resolving goal conflicts is not only an issue of shielding an ongoing goal pursuit from competing goal pursuits (Cantor & Fleeson, 1994). There is also the possibility of creative integrations, where new goals are formed which serve both of the conflicting goals (e.g., affiliation and achievement goals can be reconciled by taking on very important or responsible communal roles). Moreover, in an attempt to meet higher order goals (e.g., graduating from high school) people can strategically link behavioral goals that on the surface appear in conflict (e.g., when being with people and studying are reconciled by studying in groups). Finally, people may always resort to disengaging from one of the conflicting goals (e.g., by using the mental contrasting procedure described above).

Mobilization of Effort

A different line of research is concerned with how people avoid failures through increased effort (Wright, 1996). A person's readiness to exert effort turns out to be directly determined by the perceived difficulty of the task at hand. As the perceived difficulty increases so does the person's effort expenditure, unless the task is recognized as unsolvable. But there is a second limit to the linear increase of effort expenditure in response to heightened task difficulty: a person's potential motivation.

Potential motivation is determined by need-related variables (i.e., strength of the related need or higher order goal, the incentive value of the task, and the instrumentality of task completion for need satisfaction or attainment of the higher order goal). If the level of potential motivation is low, people do not find it worthwhile to extend more effort when an easy task becomes more difficult. This is because the upper limit of effort expenditure (suggested by the potential motivation) is low and thus reached quickly. If potential motivation is high, however, an increase in difficulty is matched by investing more effort, and this responsiveness holds up to high levels of difficulty. This is because the upper limit of effort expenditure (suggested by the potential motivation) is high and thus reached only after much effort.

Discrepancy Reduction

When failure occurs people do not give up on their goal pursuits but experience a discrepancy that needs to be closed. In Bandura's (1997) theory, goals have no motivational consequences per se. They only specify the conditions that allow for a positive or negative self-evaluation. If the set goal is attained through one's actions, a positive self-evaluation prevails; whereas staying below one's goals leads to a negative self-evaluation. The individual thus is seen as pushed by the negative self-evaluation associated with the discrepancy, and pulled by the anticipated positive self-evaluation that is intrinsically linked to closing the gap between the status quo and the goal (i.e., the performance standard). This implies that goals stimulate effortful action toward goal attainment only when people recognize a discrepancy between the status quo and the set goal. Bandura therefore proposes giving frequent feedback as a powerful means of stimulating goal pursuit. However, people are expected to engage in efforts to reduce the experienced discrepancy only when they feel self-efficacious.

Carver and Scheier (1998) propose a different discrepancy reduction theory of goal pursuit. Based on cybernetic control theory, the central conceptual unit of their analysis is the negative feedback loop. Carver and Scheier highlight the hierarchical organization of goal pursuit and thus assume a cascading loop structure. Goal-directed behavior is usually regulated at the middle level ('Do-goals') with action at higher levels ('Be-goals') suspended until the individual becomes self-aware. When discrepancies on the 'Be-level' or the 'Do-level' are discovered, lower level goals or behaviors geared at discrepancy reduction are triggered.

People are assumed to consult their outcome expectations when discrepancy reduction is hampered; in case of high expectations people keep trying, whereas low expectations lead to giving up. A positive affective response as a consequence of goal attainment is not assumed, nor is the detection of a discrepancy assumed to be associated with negative affect. Rather, the speed of progress in discrepancy reduction is seen as the source of positive or negative feelings in a person's goal pursuit. The intensity of these feelings is again regulated in a negative feedback loop. If the speed meets a set reference criterion, positive feelings result, whereas negative feelings are experienced with any speed that stays below this criterion.

Research on self-defining goals demonstrates, however, that people do not necessarily have to move downwards (i.e., to lower level goals) when trying to close goal discrepancies. When it comes to 'Be-goals' that specify a desired identity (such as being a good parent, an excellent scientist, or a very religious person) there are many different, alternative ways to indicate to oneself and others that one possesses the aspired identity. If one has failed to attain an indicator or has discovered that an indicator is out of reach (e.g., important discoveries for a scientist), one can compensate by striving for alternative indicators (e.g., supervising students). People who have set themselves self-defining goals and still feel committed to attain them readily respond to experiences of falling short with such compensatory efforts.

Summary

Social-psychological perspectives on motivation first focused on identifying the determinants of motivation. This search has moved from motives, needs, and incentives to more cognitive determinants, such as expectations, attributions, control beliefs, and goals. With the recent focus on goals, the issue of self-regulation of behavior has become prevalent. The human is conceived as a flexible strategist. This concept leads to a focus on the analysis of reflective and reflexive psychological processes that guide the successful attainment of desired outcomes.

ACKNOWLEDGEMENTS

J. D. D. thanks Dr. M. Siemann (Konstanz) for much help during the preparation of the manuscript.

RESOURCE REFERENCES

Bandura, A. (1997). *Self-efficacy: The exercise of control*. New York: Freeman.

Carver, C. S., & Scheier, M. F. (1998). *On the self-regulation of behavior*. Cambridge, UK: Cambridge University Press.

Gollwitzer, P. M., & Bargh, J. A. (Eds.). (1996). *The psychology of action: Linking cognition and motivation to action*. New York: Guilford Press.

Heckhausen, H. (1989). *Motivation und Handeln*. Berlin: Springer-Verlag.

Heckhausen, H. (1991). *Motivation and action*. Berlin: Springer-Verlag.

Kalat, J. W. (1997). *Biological psychology* (6th ed.). Pacific Grove: Brooks Cole.

McClelland, D. (1985). *Human motivation*. Glenview, IL: Scott, Foresman & Co.

Mook, D. G. (1996). *Motivation: The organization of action* (2nd ed.). New York: Norton.

Pinel, J. P. J. (1997). *Biopsychology* (3rd ed.). Boston: Allyn and Bacon.

Reeve, J. (1997). *Understanding motivation and emotion* (2nd ed.). Fort Worth: Harcourt Brace.

Rosenzweig, M. R., Leiman, A. L., & Breedlove, S. M. (1999). *Biological psychology: An introduction to behavioral, cognitive, and clinical neuroscience* (2nd ed.). Sunderland, MA: Sinauer Associates.

Schneider, K., & Schmalt, H. D. (1994). *Motivation* (2. Auflage). Stuttgart: Kohlhammer.

Weiner, B. (1992). *Human motivation*. Newbury Park: Sage Publications.

ADDITIONAL LITERATURE CITED

Abramson, P. R., & Pinkerton, S. D. (Eds.). (1995). *Sexual nature, sexual culture*. Chicago: Chicago University Press.

Atkinson, J. W. (1957). Motivational determinants of risk-taking behavior. *Psychological Review, 64,* 359–372.

Bargh, J. A., & Chartrand, T. L. (1999). The unbearable automaticity of being. *American Psychologist, 54,* 462–479.

Cantor, N., & Fleeson, W. (1994). Social intelligence and intelligent goal pursuit: A cognitive slice of motivation. In W. Spaulding (Ed.), *Nebraska Symposium on Motivation* (Vol. 41, pp. 125–180). Lincoln: University of Nebraska Press.

Dawkins, R. (1989). *The selfish gene* (2nd ed.). London: Oxford University Press.

De Caro, G. (Ed.). (1986). *The physiology of thirst and sodium appetite*. New York: Plenum.

Delius, J. D. (1991). The nature of culture. In M. Dawkins, T. Halliday, & R. Dawkins (Eds.), *The Tinbergen legacy*. London: Chapman & Hall.

Gollwitzer, P. M. (1990). Action phases and mindsets. In E. T. Higgins & R. M. Sorrentino (Eds.), *Handbook of motivation and cognition: Foundations of social behavior* (Vol. 2). New York: Guilford Press.

Gollwitzer, P. M. (1999). Implementation intentions: Strong effects of simple plans. *American Psychologist, 54,* 493–503.

Kuhl, J., & Beckmann, J. (Eds.). (1994). *Volition and personality: Action versus state orientation*. Göttingen, Germany: Hogrefe.

Leeg, C. R. (1994). *Appetite: Neural and behavioral bases*. London: Oxford University Press.

McClelland, D. (1995). Achievement motivation in relation to achievement-related recall, performance, and urine flow, a marker associated with release of vasopressin. *Motivation and Emotion, 19,* 59–76.

Oettingen, G. (1997). *Die Psychologie des Zukunftdenkens* [The psychology of thinking about the future]. Göttingen, Germany: Hogrefe.

Oettingen, G. (2000). Expectancy effects on behavior depend on self-regulatory thought. *Social Cognition, 18,* 101–129.

Renfrew, J. W. (1997). *Aggression and its causes*. New York: Oxford University Press.

Rosenblatt, J. S. (1996). *Parental care: Evolution, mechanisms and adaptive significance*. San Diego: Academic.

Seligman, M. E. P. (1990). *Learned optimism*. New York: Knopf.

Taylor, S. E., Pham, L. B., Rivkin, I. D., & Armor, D. A. (1998). Harnessing the imagination: Mental simulation, self-regulation, and coping. *American Psychologist, 53,* 429–439.

Wright, R. (1996). Brehm's theory of motivation as a model of effort and cardiovascular response. In P. M. Gollwitzer & J. A. Bargh (Eds.), *The psychology of action. Linking cognition and motivation to behavior*. New York: Guilford.

Zahn-Waxler, C. Cummings, F. M., & Iannoty, R. (1991). *Altruism and aggression*. Cambridge: Cambridge University Press.

Communications concerning this chapter should be addressed to: Professor Peter M. Gollwitzer, Universität Konstanz, Fachgruppe Psychologie, Postfach 55 60, D-78434 Konstanz, Germany

12

Emotions

NICO H. FRIJDA

12.1 WHAT IS AN EMOTION?

Emotion is one of the three main areas of psychology, in its traditional division into cognition, conation, and emotion. Emotions are often considered to form the main source of action. Yet, for a very long time emotion was not a central topic in psychology. Only since about 1960 has it re-entered the interest of psychologists. This long neglect had several causes. One was the behaviorist distaste of subjective experience. Another was the lack of a consensual definition.

Defining Emotions

That there is no generally accepted definition of emotions is in part because emotions involve so many different component phenomena. More precisely, the concept 'emotion' is used to denote a large variety of phenomena, both in daily interaction and in scientific discourse.

These include feelings, evaluations of and cognitions about objects and events, the establishment or disruption of relations with them, physiological arousal, facial expressions, and shifts in the control of behavior and thought that sometimes cause the individual to act contrary to reason. Emotions are multicomponential phenomena. Each of the component phenomena can form the core of a definition of emotions, and actually have done so. It thus is not uncontroversial to define emotions by one of them, the more so because the various components do not always all occur together. It is a basic fact about emotions that the intercorrelations between components are far from unity (Lang, 1984).

Emotions have been defined as feelings (e.g., Wundt, 1902), with the other components being viewed as caused by the them. In the early decades of the twentieth century emotions were often defined as modes of autonomic physiological reaction (or as the sensations coming from those reactions). During the 1960s, cognitions took a prominent place, and emotions were defined as a sort of judgments, or as cognitive attributions of felt autonomic arousal (Schachter & Singer, 1962).

The diversity of phenomena, and the fact that they do not always appear together has led to defining emotions instead as processes or dispositions underlying the phenomena. Emotions can be seen as a mental state 'behind' the phenomena. That mental state has sometimes been equated with the feeling, sometimes as an internal 'nonpropositional signal' (Oatley, 1992), and more often functionally, as the activated disposition to deal with certain contingencies (e.g., Ekman, 1982; Tomkins, 1962).

The dispositional notions represent an important shift in approaching emotions: a shift towards understanding them in terms of underlying mechanisms, rather than of patterns of phenomena. This is important in particular because the distinctions among the phenomena may not correspond to those among underlying processes. For instance, everything that can be grouped together as emotions may not derive from similar processes (LeDoux, 1996). Also, phenomena may not so much cause one another, but underlying processes may. These processes need not be thought of primarily in neurological terms. They can be conceived of in psychological, functional terms, that is, in terms of what they achieve or are meant to achieve.

These definitional issues are relevant for this major question: do creatures without conscious, reportable feelings have emotions? If emotions are defined by feelings, the answer of course is no. If they are defined by underlying processes, the answer is yes. The emotions of human adults, infants, and animals may differ in some respects, but still be basically similar. Indeed, the eliciting conditions of many behaviors and physiological reactions, their behaviors and physiological reactions themselves, and relevant brain structures and brain chemistries, are very similar (Panksepp, 1998). It is a plausible and useful assumption that animals and infants have emotions, and that one can learn very much from studying them for understanding the emotions of human adults. This is the standpoint taken in this chapter, and of most current theorists. Emotions are viewed as dispositional structures, to be defined functionally, and analyzed not only from conscious awareness or with respect to conscious awareness. The role and function of conscious feelings in emotions is an issue in its own right.

Emotions, Moods, and Well-Being

Definitions of emotion also diverge because some include all states that have one important phenomenon in common, for instance feelings of pleasure or displeasure, or the affective evaluation of objects, while others are more restrictive. It is indeed common to restrict the term emotion to that subclass in which the phenomena are elicited by a stimulus or event, and are of relatively short duration. Moods are usually split off by their longer duration or the absence of a clear object. Sentiments (e.g. 'I hate that person') are dispositions; the term sentiment is used for more or less permanent emotional attitudes, while emotion is usually reserved for acute reactions to an eliciting event. Other major concepts (e.g., well-being or happiness) are best seen as integrations of previous emotions (Kahneman, 1999).

12.2 DIFFERENT EMOTIONS

Emotion Taxonomy

What emotions are there, and how do they differ? All languages, of course, distinguish different emotions, but the differences differ in size. The emotion words in the given languages thus suggest a structure of more basic processes. When subjects are asked to rate the similarity between emotion words, the resulting similarity indices indeed show a hierarchical organization. Emotion words tend to divide into positive and negative ones (with often a group of neutral ones such as surprise). These large groups each consist of smaller clusters. The words in each of those clusters all appear to be variants of one 'kind' of emotion. Rage, irritation, anger, and hate, that themselves are part of the lowest level in the hierarchy, all can be seen as variants of anger.

The kinds of emotion are often considered to represent discrete emotion categories (Izard, 1977). They are often referred to as *basic emotions*. A typical set of such categories is the one found by Shaver, Wu, and Schwartz (1992): *anger, disgust, sadness, fear, joy, surprise, love, pity*. The sets of basic emotions found by such methods show considerable similarity between studies, and between languages (Shaver et al., 1992). Differences between studies and languages do, however, exist, and some words (e.g., *hope*, and *jealousy*) shift greatly from one cluster to another, and do not really belong in any one of them.

The findings on hierarchical structure of word similarities, and the notion of basic emotions, have led to the hypothesis that each emotion is a variant of one such basic emotion, or at most of the blend of two or three (e.g., Plutchik, 1980). The data do not support this idea: subjects cannot unambiguously assign all emotion words to one supposed basic emotion (Reisenzein,

1995). The supposition of an exhaustive hierarchy is unnecessary, even with a basic emotions concept. Some emotion words may refer to a particular component (e.g., *excitement* may refer to any emotion with pronounced autonomic arousal), and other to an eliciting circumstance (e.g., *jealousy*).

Differences Between Emotions

Language may not be the best way to approach the problems of discovering meaningful psychological distinctions. Not all emotion words point to distinct psychological phenomena; they may originate in cultural theory, social rules, or moral perspectives. The theoretical approach called social constructivism in fact finds emotion distinctions along these latter lines (see contributions in Harré & Parrott, 1996).

Moreover, analysis of words and their relationships forces one into a categorical view of emotions that may not be appropriate to the phenomena and processes. Emotion words do not all have sharply distinct meanings. Each refers to a 'fuzzy class', characterized by a prototype around which individual instances cloud in irregular fashion (Fehr & Russell, 1984). Emotions themselves may not really fit into distinct, discrete classes. They can be viewed as mental states that vary along the continuous dimensions of pleasantness and activation (Wundt, 1902; Russell & Barrett, 1999). Categorial labels then might just refer to some ill-defined region in that two-dimensional space, perhaps further specified by prototype scripts (Russell & Barrett, 1999).

Different emotions may also, however, correspond to different variants of a particular component. One has often proposed that different emotions correspond to different feelings; the basic emotions might correspond to irreducibly different feelings, sometimes referred to as *qualia* (e.g., Oatley, 1992). This point of view is problematic, because the only criterion for different feelings consists in the application of different words.

Emotions may be distinguished by any other component; the major emotion categories may be defined in terms of patterns of autonomic response, for instance. More theoretically grounded is to distinguish them by supposed dispositions that, when activated, generate particular patterns of components. This is the most common view of basic emotions: as basic mechanisms or dispositions (Buck, 1999; Ekman, 1982; Izard, 1977; Plutchik, 1980; Tomkins, 1962). Authors do not fully agree as to which should be distinguished. Ekman (1982) distinguished joy, sadness, fear, anger, disgust, and surprise; he later added contempt; others include shame, guilt, and affection.

How to identify such dispositions? Ekman (1982) has taken universal facial expressions as the cue to biological dispositions; the cue has been considered a weak one (Russell, 1994). One may also take a functional perspective. One may assume a small set of dispositions to deal with different major adaptational challenges (e.g., Buck, 1999; Ekman, 1982; Plutchik, 1980; Tomkins, 1962). Fear can be viewed as the disposition to deal with environmental threat, anger to deal with social obstacles or power rivalry, surprise with unexpected events, joy with success, affection with potential mates. This approach appears particularly appropriate if the dispositions are understood as evolutionary products for dealing with these contingencies (Cosmides & Tooby, 2000; Plutchik, 1980), and as being based upon dedicated neural structures, for which there indeed exists some evidence (e.g., LeDoux, 1996; Panksepp, 1998; see below).

Investigators do not agree about which emotion categories are basic ones (Ortony & Turner, 1990), and whether the very notion of basic dispositions is meaningful (see relevant section in Ekman & Davidson, 1994). Emotions may be just bundles of response components mutually influencing each other (they are *synchronized*; Scherer, 2000), and jointly called up by a given event as appraised by the subject. Emotion categories may reflect frequently recurring contingencies (Scherer, 2000), or just social and linguistic habits (Mandler, 1984). Which of the approaches, the basic emotions approach, or the multicomponential bundle approach, best explains the phenomena is still unclear. Findings on brain mechanisms will probably decide.

12.3 Emotional Phenomena

The major emotional components will be briefly discussed.

Motivational Change

Certain behaviors and feelings involve 'urges' (Tomkins, 1962): strivings that appear to interrupt ongoing goals and voluntary behavior, and cause a shift in goal priorities. They thus manifest a change in control of behavior.

Motivational aspects, and the mode of control of behavior, have in fact been considered as defining emotions in early philosophical psychology. What we now call emotions were formerly called *passions*, from the Greek ψαθημα, implying passivity, and opposed to the concept of *action*. The same feature coined its Latin equivalent, *affectus*. Motivational change is one of the phenomena that defines emotions, bringing up the important ethical issue of responsibility for one's emotions. Arnold (1960) defined emotional experience as experienced action tendency; Frijda (1986) defined emotions as states of action readiness, the latter defined as states of readiness to achieve a particular kind of subject–environment relationship.

Varieties of motivational state, as derived from behavior or from reports of experience, differentiate between emotions. Arnold (1960) defined different emotions as different action tendencies, and Frijda (1986) as different forms of action readiness (such as readiness to achieve proximity, hostile encounter, dominance, or general increase or loss of readiness to relate). Indeed, there are distinct relations between how one labels one's emotion and felt state of action readiness (e.g., Frijda, 1986; Roseman, Wiest, & Swartz, 1994).

Feeling

Feeling, subjective experience, has often been considered the central emotion component. Since the eighteenth or nineteenth century (but not before), emotions have been defined as feelings. But the nature of feelings is not immediately clear

It has been proposed that different emotions correspond to different qualia. As mentioned earlier, it has been proposed that all emotional feelings are variants of a few emotional qualia (e.g., Izard, 1977; Oatley, 1992). The hypothesis has not appeared tenable (Reisenzein, 1995).

A major core element of emotional feelings are the feelings of pleasure and pain. According to introspective studies by Wundt (1902), they are the only affective *qualia*, that is, experiences that cannot be reduced to body sensations and cognitions; the properly emotional in the feelings corresponds to the experiences of pleasure and pain, rather than body sensations such as those of autonomic arousal, as was proposed in theory of Schachter and Singer (1962).

Body sensations played an important role in the theory of emotional feelings of William James (1884), known as the James–Lange theory. Different feelings, presumably, correspond to different patterns of feedback from autonomic response. Such feedback returned in the theory of Schachter and Singer (1962). The distinctiveness of different feelings was thought to come from the feedback of autonomic arousal, complemented by cognitive attributions of their cause. The theory was not supported by the

evidence. Other proposed distinctive body sensations are those coming from facial expression (facial feedback theory; Izard, 1977; Tomkins, 1962). Although none of these body sensations appear indispensable to characterize an experience as an emotional feeling they do contribute to the quality of emotional feelings, and may play a role in their impact (Damasio, 1994). Reported body feelings corresponds to different emotions, as labeled by the subjects.

Further differentiation of feelings derives from associated cognitions. Different emotional experiences, say, of fear or joy, do not only differ in pleasantness, activation, and body feelings. They obtain their specificity largely from several other aspects. One of the major ones is *appraisal awareness*, that is, awareness of what the emotion is about. This 'aboutness' of feelings, also called their *intentional character*, is a general aspect of emotional feelings (Frijda, 1986; Oatley, 1992). It constitutes the cognitive component of emotional feelings, and may well be what distinguishes emotional feelings from moods. Appraisal awareness refers to the individual's awareness of what the emotional event may do or offer to him or her, or what he or she could or could not do to cope with it (Lazarus, 1991). Different emotions correspond to different forms of appraisal awareness, as has been abundantly shown in self-report studies (see the contributions and references in Schorr, Scherer, & Johnstone, 2000).

As just mentioned, emotional feelings also include awareness of motivational state, or state of action readiness. The various self-reported feeling aspects correspond to actual appraised emotion-eliciting aspects of events, actual states of action readiness (as inferred from behavior), and actual autonomic reactions only to a limited extent. Much in self-reports may well derive from preconceptions and post-hoc constructions (Parkinson, 1995; Rimé, Phillipot, & Cisamolo, 1990).

An important additional aspect of emotional feelings is the *significance* of the emotion to the individual (Frijda, 1986): his or her acceptance or rejection of the emotion, and its felt implications for self-esteem and the likely reactions of others. Emotion significance differs between emotions, between individuals, and between cultures (Mesquita, Frijda, & Scherer, 1997). It is what determines emotion control.

Affect

In this chapter, I use the term for the feelings of pleasure and pain, and for the processes underlying them. Those processes may be manifest in the perception of liked and disliked objects, rather than feelings (Zajonc, 1994). They may also operate nonconsciously, without the feelings, particularly at low process intensities (Zajonc, 1994). Subliminal exposure of pleasant or unpleasant stimuli (smiling face, spider) appear to influence later affect ratings of neutral stimuli (e.g., Murphy & Zajonc, 1993), or to facilitate conditioning (Öhman, 2000).

Pleasure and pain are opposite poles of one continuum of feeling (Russell & Barrett, 1999). The underlying mechanisms, however, are probably separate and to some extent independent (Ito & Cacioppo, 1999). The two processes can be simultaneously active, resulting in ambivalence and in the often only moderate negative correlations between separate positive and negative affect ratings. The two mechanisms also have different properties. For instance, positive affect tends to increase sociability and creativity (Isen, 1999), whereas negative affect does not do the opposite; negative affect shows *negativity bias*, a steeper increase of intensity with stimulus magnitude than positive affect (Ito & Cacioppo, 1999). Positive and negative mood have different effects on thinking strategies (Fiedler & Bless, 2000). Measurements of pleasure and pain (e.g., by rating scales) usually reflect some form of integration of feelings over time that do not relate in a simple manner to pleasure at specific moments (Kahneman, 1999).

Autonomic Reactions

Emotions have sometimes been defined as patterns of autonomic physiological responses (changes in heart rate, blood pressure, skin temperature, electrodermal or psychogalvanic skin responses). According to the James–Lange theory, different emotions should correspond to different patterns of autonomic response. Empirical research, by and large, has not supported that theory. All 'excited' emotions are, it has been argued, accompanied by an overall autonomic arousal pattern that serves energy mobilization; this has been called the *emergency response*, in the classic analysis by Cannon (1927). Different response patterns do in fact occur (for instance during active and passive coping), but do not correspond to different emotions like anger and fear (Cacioppo, Bernston, Larsen, Poehlman, & Ito, 2000). Ekman, Levenson, and Friesen (1983) reported findings suggesting that certain patterns do differentiate between basic emotions, but these findings may have been spurious (Cacioppo et al., 2000), or reflect differences in muscular effort.

Emotional Behavior

A major subject for research has been expressive behavior, defined as behavior suggesting an emotion in a person, that is by and large unlearned and universal in the species concerned. The designation 'expressive behavior' or 'expression' is misleading. It suggests that the behavior serves to express feelings, which is a theoretical interpretation that may not be correct (Frijda & Tcherkassof, 1997).

The most studied is facial expression (see Russell & Fernandez-Dols, 1997). Important descriptive analysis and evolutionary interpretations were given by Darwin (1872). Precise scoring methods have been developed (MAX by Izard, 1971; FACS by Ekman and Friesen, in Feldman & Rimé, 1991). High degrees of inter-observer agreement are obtained when selected posed facial expression photographs are rated in terms of a small set of emotion categories (such as Ekman's, 1982, categories). The agreements (and correspondence with the categories the expressions were meant to convey) range between 98% (for joy) and 56% (for contempt) in Western cultures; in illiterate cultures, they were appreciably lower, but still far above chance (Ekman, 1994; also, Izard, 1971). The amounts of agreement are probably influenced by the research methods used (Russell, 1994), but still sufficient to demonstrate similarity in identifying emotions from the face that is largely culture-independent (Ekman, 1994). The evidence has been interpreted as showing that facial expressions are parts of the neural dispositions for basic emotions (Ekman, 1982, 1994). This view has been contested by Fridlund (1994). Facial expressions do not strictly correspond to particular emotions. According to Fridlund, facial expressions have nothing much to do with emotions; they are also shown in the absence of emotion, and are sensitive to context, such as the presence of an audience. Their function is to influence other individuals, and not to express emotions. This function of expressions is, however, not incompatible with their usually resulting from emotions. Expressive behaviors may well be understood as 'coping behaviors' (Lazarus, 1991) for dealing with the emotional events, which includes influencing others by threats or calls for help (Frijda & Tcherkassof, 1997).

There are many other forms of expression: posture, voice intonation and cries, whole-body movements (Feldman & Rimé, 1991). Sophisticated coding systems for postures and body movements have been developed, but so far little research has been devoted to their specific relationships with emotions. Laughter and crying of course are whole-body reactions of a complex and ill-understood nature (Ruch, 1993).

Vocal expression of emotion has been studied by using standard or fake sentences, with varying intonations. They can be recognized about as well as facial expression photographs, and that in different linguistic groups (Johnstone & Scherer, 2000).

Emotions also induce more general behaviors, such as angry aggression, fearful flight, desirous approach. Some of these behaviors are innate, species-specific behaviors (modes of threat and attack, of fear responses such as freezing, running, and hiding), others are learned. Expressive behaviors rather generally are part of more encompassing behavioral patterns, and some expressive patterns also are whole-body responses (crying and laughter are notable examples).

Both innate and learned behaviors can largely be understood as coping behaviors; the surprised facial expression can be seen as an orienting response, and laughter as a play response signaling playful interaction (Darwin, 1872; Frijda & Tcherkassof, 1997; Ruch, 1993). The behaviors that co-occur or follow each other in given situations tend to have similar functions, such as self-defense, hostility, play (nonserious interaction), affinity, as Van Hooff (1982) found in analysis of chimpanzee behavior. Such functional equivalence is the cue for interpreting emotions as motivational states, *action tendencies* (Arnold, 1960) or *states of action readiness* (Frijda, 1986).

Cognitive Changes

Emotions can strongly influence cognitive processes. First, there is the arousal of attention, and the effects of the distribution of attention, as these are notable, for instance, in memory of emotional incidents (Christianson, 1992). Attention allocation also helps in producing the inverted U-curve, that is, improvement of performance with moderate emotions and disturbing it with strong ones. Positive mood states tend to improve recall of positive memories, and negative moods of negative memories (Clore & Gasper, in press). Positive emotions and moods tend to improve cognitive flexibility and originality (Isen, 1999); for instance, after giving subjects an unexpected gift, they score better on tests of cognitive flexibility. Social judgments are influenced by mood states, positive moods making them more favorable, and negative ones, more negative (Forgas & Vargas, in press). Emotions may make judgments more tenaciously held, more resistant to change by incompatible

information (see contributions in Frijda, Manstead, & Bem, in press).

Emotion Regulation

Practically all emotional reactions are being controlled to some degree, as evident from the relatively few instances in which this is not so (blind panic or anger, alcohol disinhibition, disinhibiting group influences). Emotion regulation appears to be so ubiquitous that it can be counted among the emotion mechanisms.

Emotion regulation is not only caused by social norms, as regulation in animals shows. According to Gray (1987), behavioral inhibition is elicited by aversive response consequences, or their anticipation. These aversive consequences may come from social censure, but also from undesired disruption of group harmony or from the harm that one might inflict upon others by unrestrained response. The latter controlling influences are not unique to humans but are also observed in primates (De Waal, 1996). Further sources of emotion control are the negative effects of emotions upon motor and cognitive performance. These various sources of regulation determine various other emotional manifestations, such as consideration for other people (or animals), and the whole level of social emotions that make smooth social interaction possible. Studies of patients with orbitofrontal damage illustrate how much the gamut of emotional reactions is impoverished when regulatory emotional reactions are interfered with (Damasio, 1994).

Emotion regulation proceeds along a number of different roads, such as appraisal change, response suppression, seeking distraction. The different procedures are being extensively discussed and studied in the literature (e.g., Gross, 1999).

12.4 EMOTION ELICITATION

General Framework

Emotion elicitation can be described in a general way as due to the appearance or termination of events that are intrinsically pleasant or unpleasant, or to the appearance or termination of events that signal or announce such pleasant or unpleasant events. This generalization comes from behaviorist psychology (Mowrer, 1960), where it was phrased in terms of the actual or signaled increase and decrease of positively and negatively reinforcing stimuli. The two times four contingencies (those for actual events, and those for signaled ones) can account for the elicitation of different emotions. The anticipation of an unpleasant event, for instance, would cover the antecedents of fear (fear being defined by escape or avoidance tendency, or fearful feeling), and the termination of a pleasant event, as well as the advent of an unpleasant one, that of any negative emotion. Further refinements were introduced by Gray (1987), by adding omission of an expected event and, more importantly, the availability or non-availability of coping behavior. Anticipation of the termination of a pleasant event would lead to fear if escape or avoidance appears possible, anger if hostile behavior belongs to the subject's repertoire, and sadness or despair if there is nothing he or she can do about it. Additional contingencies, and thus the antecedent conditions for further emotions, are based upon the likelihood of future events, and distinctions among who or what caused them (Scherer, 2000). In addition, so-called non-hedonic or cognitive emotions (surprise, interest, curiosity) are evoked by unexpected events (Meyer, Schützwohl, & Reisenzein, 1993).

Motivational Relevance

The same events can be described at a somewhat more integrative level. According to a large number of theorists, emotions are evoked by events that are relevant to the individual's concerns, motives, major goals, or well-being (Frijda, 1986; Lazarus, 1991; Mandler, 1984; Oatley, 1992; Stein & Trabasso, 1992). Events that appear favorable for reaching the goal or the concern's satisfaction generate pleasant emotions, and those that appear to obstruct its achievement generate negative emotions. An event of which the relevance is unclear may evoke surprise or curiosity. Different contingencies of goal achievement or non-achievement (loss of a goal or definitive impossibility of achieving it) cause sadness, someone obstructing progress causes anger, and so forth. The approach finds its support mostly in self-report studies on goals achievement contingencies and emotions (e.g., Oatley, 1992; Stein & Trabasso, 1992). In fact, the various contingencies mentioned in the previous subsection closely match the goal-relevant ones.

Many emotions result from motivational relevance in a more specific sense: from, innately or on the basis of learning, recognizing persons and objects as fit for satisfying certain motives. Falling in love, lust, curiosity, and enjoyments can be understood in this way (Kubovy, 1999; Rozin, 1999).

Appraisal

It is evident that emotions are only rarely elicited by intrinsically affective stimuli alone. Most emotions result from the meaning of events, that is, by their links to future stimulus events or to conditions for which the events are relevant. Psychological processes thus intervene between the actual eliciting events and the emotional reaction.

The processes are collectively referred to as *appraisal processes*. They form the core of appraisal theory, or cognitive emotion theory (Arnold, 1960; Frijda, 1986; Lazarus, 1991; Oatley, 1992; Scherer, 1999; Smith & Ellsworth, 1985; see also the contributions in Schorr, Scherer, & Johnstone, 2000). Appraisal theory makes a number of different points. First, there are processes that turn a perceived event into one with hedonic value. These processes may be disturbed, for instance by damage to the brain region named the amygdala (see below), and under the influence of drugs (many antidepressants render the individual more indifferent). Second, different emotions correspond to different contingencies as appraised, and they correspond to appraised contingencies rather than to different objective stimulus contingencies. Without adequate appraisal, a personal loss may not evoke sadness. Third, many aspects of these contingencies are subject-dependent anyway, such as the role of the available coping repertoire.

A large amount of research has sought to verify which appraisals correspond to which emotions. Most of that research consists of asking subjects to recall an incident of a number of emotions as identified by name ('please recall an incident when you were angry'), and to fill out a questionnaire asking to rate the role of each of a number of appraisal components (e.g., was the event favorable or harmful to your goals? how controllable did the event appear? was someone responsible for that event?). On the whole strong correspondence was found between particular emotions and particular appraisal patterns. It is, however, unclear to what extent this provides evidence that these appraisals are the emotions' causal antecedents. Self-report results may report emotional experiences rather than their antecedents, or be due to post-hoc constructions (Parkinson, 1995, and contributions in Schorr, Scherer, & Johnstone, 2000). Experimental research to find support for this aspect of the theory also exists, showing, for instance, that fear depends both upon outcome uncertainty and anticipated danger, but it is still modest.

There are more important points. Different individuals may appraise the same events differently, and thus differ in their emotions. The differences may be due to different expectations, different cognitive schemas that steer inferences from actual events, and different things that individuals desire or strive for. Individuals may also differ in the extent to which the features of different contingencies are actually picked up, or are expected to be present when in fact they are not. Appraisal theory thus tries to account for individual differences in emotions, and changes in emotion from moment to moment.

By including cognitive variables among emotion antecedents, appraisal theory substitutes the notion of *situation* for that of *stimulus*, in describing emotion antecedents. Stimuli rarely occur in isolation, and their effects usually depend upon a wide context that includes the individual's history as well as situational context (e.g., effects of social support, ways out under stress, awareness of coping repertoire called self-confidence).

Recognition that situations rather than stimuli elicit emotions explains that given events may have multiple emotional meanings, that are relevant to different concerns and allow different appraisals. Events may simultaneously or successively evoke various and even opposite emotions. Event–emotion links are therefore best described as sets of *mechanisms*, the outcomes of which may conflict (e.g., 'oppression causes anger' and 'oppression causes submission'), the appraisal details allowing one or the other are often hard to specify in advance (Elster, 1999).

Intrinsically Affective Stimuli and Conditions

Both accounts of emotion elicitation include the basic assumption that particular stimuli or conditions are intrinsically pleasant or unpleasant. The term is used for innately liked or disliked stimuli and conditions (like sweet taste and physical pain), as well as for stimuli that are liked or disliked due to early habit formation (like most food preferences; see Rozin, Haidt, & McCauley, 2000). Further emotion elicitors derive from these intrinsically affective stimuli and conditions by association, other forms of learning, or inference. Some stimuli do not properly innately elicit affect or emotion, but may innately facilitate the formation of liking or dislike, or facilitate the formation of conditioned avoidance or approach reactions. This is the *preparedness hypothesis* (see Öhman, 2000); the hypothesis is illustrated by the easily acquired fear of snakes, spiders, heights, and the like.

Intrinsically affective stimuli are those that behaviorist theory considers *primary reinforcers*. They include more than tastes and pain and other bodily discomfort. When near-universality among humans (and, in relevant cases, communality with primates and other higher animal species) is taken as evidence, they include sexual visual stimuli (young female forms) for human

males, and friendly, distressed, and angry facial and vocal expressions (Fridlund, 1994). Other intrinsic affective stimuli are actually constellations. For instance, novel stimuli tend to be liked and evoke interest (Ito & Cacioppo, 1999), but 'novelty' of course is not an elementary stimulus attribute. The things people strive for, and that form the satisfaction conditions of concerns, all are complex, and related in obscure ways to elementary stimuli. These conditions include the presence of particular individuals that offer occasion for clinging (bases for 'love'; Bowlby, 1969), familiar stimuli (Zajonc, 1968), being accepted or liked by familiar conspecifics (the basis of social bonding; Baumeister & Leary, 1995). They also include the states that define suprapersonal values (e.g., justice, personal freedom, interpersonal consideration), that may form motives and give rise to vehement emotions when threatened or achieved. Likewise, the elementary causes or implications of such an important concern as that for self-esteem are far from clear. There also are certain types of action that intrinsically produce positive affect, but cannot be properly characterized as 'events'. Examples are unimpeded functioning, play in the young of the species, and performing beyond habitual levels of functioning (Kubovy, 1999; Rozin, 1999).

General Conditions for Emotion Arousal

Emotions in the sense of reactions involving more than just feelings, but including behavioral inclinations or physiological change, require more involved conditions than just the presence of the stimuli or conditions just mentioned. Emotions tend not to result from mere presence of something pleasant or unpleasant, but from change over what was already present or what was expected. Emotion arousal, and emotional intensity, depend upon current level of adaptation, that itself depends upon previous and expected events (Parducci, 1995). Comparison processes play a very important role. Sometimes, it is the comparison with what could have been that counts; this is so, for instance, in the sharp emotions of regret; when you just missed the bus it feels worse than when it had left ten minutes ago (Landman, 1993). In other cases, it is the comparison with what others have that counts, as in envy.

Furthermore, whether an emotion is aroused by a given contingency (say, threat, or loss, or goal achievement) depends upon the availability or non-availability of possibilities for coping. Emotion is absent (or at least, most emotion components are) when the subject possesses a routine way to cope with the contingency.

Danger does not evoke fear if the subject knows how to deal with it, as does a well-trained mountain climber. Felt emotion, autonomic arousal, and behavioral disturbance occur only when no routine way is available, or when there was uncertainty about coping prior to succeeding. Joy and pride result from success to the degree that success was uncertain before (Weiner, 1985). In learning avoidance behavior in response to signals that electric shock will come, such signs are present in early phases of learning but disappear, once the animal has learned to escape smoothly and in time (Strongman, 1987). Some uncertainty about how to cope successfully and on time appears one of the conditions for emotions.

Appraisal of a given stimulus event may vary vastly, due to assessed meanings, the individual's history and cognitive schemata, and the specific context. This implies that a given event may tend to elicit conflicting emotions. A sexual stimulus may activate lust, and its context (or the very response of lust) may activate interpersonal consideration, or fear of consequences.

12.5 COGNITION AND EMOTION

Appraisal processes involve cognitive processes. Thus, cognitions influence emotion arousal, and modifying cognitions may modify emotions. Lazarus (1991) reports earlier experimental studies illustrating this: different task instructions, when viewing emotional material, changed emotional response. This notion has been taken up in cognitive behavioral therapy (e.g., Beck, 1976).

Their role in emotion elicitation has given rise to vivid controversies and debate, in part because emotion and cognition have been traditionally opposed, and in part because the very notion of cognition is unclear and ambiguous. It is sometimes taken to refer to conscious thought and deliberation, and sometimes to the processing of information, whether conscious or unconscious (Leventhal & Scherer, 1987).

Different levels of cognitive processes can be distinguished. Teasdale and Barnard (1993) distinguished propositional and implicational (or schematic) levels, the first referring to mere factual information representation, as in a verbal statement, and the second to information representation including mental images and links to feelings and actions. Propositional information does not influence emotions; only implicational information does. The distinction seeks to account for the fact that not all relevant knowledge

has emotional consequences; the abstract knowledge that spiders do no harm, and verbal warnings that smoking causes cancer, often have none. Power and Dalgleish (1997) further, in their SPAARS model added associative and analogical representations. Associations (as between a conditioned stimulus and the unconditioned electric shock) and analogical representations (raw affective stimuli and their images), however, are not what most investigators would call 'cognitive'. That is to say that, although most interesting emotions have cognitive antecedents, some elementary emotions do not. This is so in particular because the effects of conditioning (notably traumatic conditioning, such as severe electric shock after a light flash) may become fully independent from recall of the original unconditioned affective stimulus; they cannot be corrected by information about harmlessness of the conditioned stimulus (LeDoux, 1996).

Even in arousing emotions that heavily depend upon cognitive antecedents, noncognitive elements play a key role. Potential emotion antecedents evoke emotions only when and because they have links to intrinsically affective stimuli or conditions – by associations, images or earlier feelings (Frijda, 1988); it probably is what makes them 'implicational'.

12.6 FUNCTIONS OF EMOTIONS

Evolutionary considerations suggest that emotions have a function, or had so in the evolutionary past. Different emotions apply to different adaptational contingencies: fear to physical or other threats, anger to social conflicts of interest or power conflicts, disgust to coping with the dangers of inappropriate food intake or contamination (Plutchik, 1980; Rozin, Haidt, & McCauley, 2000; Tomkins, 1962). That type of functional analysis is current in ethology and in evolutionary perspectives on emotions (e.g., Cosmides & Tooby, 2000).

In general, emotions can be said to have the function of detecting hedonic or concern-relevant events, and to modify or maintain the individual's relationship with the environment. Detection is ensured by the various appraisal mechanisms, as well as by their end result, affect. Affect is the 'common currency' in terms of which the impact of different events can be compared, and response resources can be distributed (Ito & Cacioppo, 1999).

Furthermore, emotions are functional because they allow flexible adaptation to the various adaptational contingencies. Emotions involve behavioral flexibility, rather than fixed action patterns, which is a major difference with reflex behavior. The motivational states of readiness command different behaviors, as circumstances require and the behavior repertoire allows. Flexibility is the mark of emotions because emotions may profit from innate repertoires, learning, and cognition (Ekman, 1982; Frijda, 1986; LeDoux, 1996; Panksepp, 1998; Rolls, 1999; Scherer, 1999; Tomkins, 1962).

In addition to dealing with adaptational dilemmas, an important domain of emotion function is the regulation and even the constitution of interpersonal relationships and social harmony (Harré & Parrott, 1996). Many emotions serve to control interaction within groups. Shame enforces behavior in agreement with social habits, and guilt feelings motivate re-establishment of social equilibrium after having inflicted harm on someone else (Baumeister, Stillwell, & Heatherton, 1994); these interpretations are based both upon the conditions under which shame and guilt occur, and upon their consequences. Shame displays, for instance, tend to appease ill-will after transgressions, as was shown when experimental stooges upset supermarket displays and did, or did not, manifest embarrassment (Keltner & Buswell, 1997).

Emotions like sympathy, liking, and affection also establish and maintain social bonds. They enhance social cohesion in groups and support social adaptation. For instance, prior to feeding time chimpanzees often indulge in mutual grooming and kissing; when this happens, fights for the food are less frequent than otherwise (De Waal, 1996). Social emotions (loyalty, empathy, liking for social harmony) may sometimes dominate self-directed emotions, particularly in so-called interdependent or collectivist cultures (Markus & Kitayama, 1991). Moreover, emotions appear to function in social cohesion by the almost universal tendency to share one's emotions with others, who then may share that with third parties (Rimé, Finkenauer, Luminet, Zech, & Philippot, 1997).

The various behaviors, including facial expressions, can be understood as being instrumental to the various adaptational goals. The surprise expression can be viewed as an orientation response, fear expressions as self-protective responses, and crying as an alarm call. This functional perspective can be applied in subtle fashion. For instance, submission can be viewed as a non-aggressive solution to conflicts of power and interest. The solution can be achieved by signaling one's submission by, for instance, glance avoidance and making oneself look small. Several emotions can be interpreted as forms of submission, and as involving submission displays. Embarrassment, shame, guilt, respect, and humility, can all be viewed from that angle (Harré & Parrott, 1996).

The examples suggest that emotions were not merely functional in the distant evolutionary past. Theory has to account for the fact that emotions often are more of a nuisance than a help, such as the sufferings of grief and the behavioral interferences caused by nervousness. One of the efforts at explanation is the inverted-U-curve hypothesis: emotions improve performance and adaptation at moderate levels of intensity, but may be detrimental at high levels.

12.7 Brain Mechanisms

History

A hundred years ago, it was shown that emotions specifically depend upon lower brain centers. Removal of a dog's cortex did not eliminate anger responses (it in fact enhanced them), but transection of the brain at the level of the thalamus did. Later, it appeared that the responses involved the hypothalamus rather than the thalamus. Somewhat later, Klüver and Bucy (1937) discovered severe interference with emotional sensitivity after damage to the temporal lobes. The various discoveries led MacLean (1990) to his *triune brain* hypothesis: the 'reptilian brain' (brainstem core and related structures) ensured basic biological functions, such as feeding and sex; the paleomammalian brain or limbic system contained the provisions for emotions and social feeling; the neomammalian brain or newer cerebral cortex was related to emotions only for guidance and control. The tripartite partition of the brain is not generally accepted, but formed a heuristic in research and functional description.

I will give a brief overview of some of the findings in the analysis of brain mechanisms in emotions; it will include only a fraction of what has been discovered over the last decades. I will discuss the findings from a functional point of view, organizing them by major functions that brain research has helped to outline. Important sources are Buck (1999), LeDoux (1996), MacLean (1990), and Panksepp (1998).

Affect Mechanisms

Throughout the brain, there are sites sensitive to opioid substances, including the endogenous opioids such as endorphins and enkephalins. Opioids are closely linked to pleasure and to behaviors linked to stimulus acceptance (attention, facial reactions in the case of sensory stimuli). Opioid production is enhanced by rough-and-tumble playing, grooming in primates, sexual satisfactions. Opioid antagonists tend to decrease several of these activities.

Different kinds of liking (e.g., food tastes and smells, sexual pleasures) probably are linked to different sites. Taste and smell liking, for instance, appear to involve mechanisms in the orbitofrontal cortex (Rolls, 1999). A number of different neuropeptides are also involved.

Serotonin and periventricular (PVG) pathways probably are relevant in pain and other unpleasantness.

Activation Mechanisms

Attentional arousal and readiness to process relevant information is an essential aspect of emotions. Hence it is useful to mention the role of cortical arousal (Lindsley, 1951), determined or influenced by what was then called the *ascending reticular activating system* (ARAS), and that was a neural correlate of attentional arousal. Cortical arousal, EEG desynchronization, corresponds with attentional arousal or wakefulness.

More central to emotion are the phenomena of tonic activation or action readiness. Such readiness is evident, for instance, in intracranial self-stimulation (ICSS): animals may work hard, and for extended periods, to deliver themselves electrical stimulation at particular brain sites. The ICSS phenomena led to the hypothesis that these sites represented pleasure and pain 'centers'. There were, however, a number of puzzling findings, incompatible with that hypotheses; for instance, in humans, only in some places does stimulation evoke feelings of pleasure or pain. This led to the hypothesis of a *Seeking System* (Panksepp, 1998) or *Behavioral Activation System* (BAS; Gray, 1987), or to a 'reward system' (Rolls, 1999) that links stimuli for which it is sensitized to interest in and efforts towards obtaining those stimuli – a *wanting* rather than a *liking* system (Berridge, 1999). Although closely linked, pleasure and the activation of the seeking or wanting system appear to be distinct, and can be separately activated (Berridge, 1999).

The ICSS brain sites, too, are found throughout the brain, most concentrated in the medial forebrain bundle that traverses the hypothalamus towards the nucleus accumbens, septum, frontal cortex and the amygdala, and in those latter structures. The system is activated by dopamine (the mesolimbic and mesocortical dopamine systems). Dopamine generally plays an important role in interest and activation, as illustrated in the film *Awakenings*, and in the effects of cocaine and amphetamine.

Appraisal Mechanisms

As mentioned, temporal lobe damage severely impairs emotional discrimination. Animals lose their usual fears of humans and novel objects; they do not avoid objects that they had learned to avoid. They may respond sexually to animals from other species, and to inanimate objects. They try to eat inedible or unusual objects. The deficits appear to be caused specifically by damage to the amygdala (Weiskrantz, 1956).

LeDoux (1996) extensively showed that fear conditioning cannot be established after amygdala ablation (at least, it becomes considerably more difficult to do so), nor is established conditioning maintained. Other findings suggest that the amygdala may more generally be essential for emotional appraisal (Rolls, 1999). It appears to be a key point in linking perceived events to their affective value, both in a positive and in a negative sense, at least with respect to learned or conditioned stimuli. The amygdala thus may be essential for establishing the links between events and their affective implications. They may or may not be involved in affect arousal by unconditioned stimuli.

Discrimination Mechanisms

Appraisal of a total situation may lead to activation of a different emotional response from that which would be activated by the major or core aspects of that situation. Evidently, the brain is capable of on the spot modification of its learned or unlearned emotional reactions. That this is so appears from the effects of damage to the orbitofrontal cortex. Such effects are vividly described and discussed by Damasio (1994). Patients with such damage behave like psychopaths, and lack consideration as well as emotional foresight. On the basis of such and other findings, Rolls (1999) interprets the main role of the orbitofrontal area in emotion to be the rapid change of emotional reactions from what given stimulus events usually or primarily evoke. For the moment, the experimental evidence (on response to reward reversals) is mainly restricted to gustatory rewards, however.

Specific Emotional Mechanisms

There are a number of neural dispositions for particular modes of dealing with the environment or for dealing with particular contingencies. They play a key role in the arousal of particular emotions, as defined behaviorally and by feeling. These dispositions are sensitive to neurochemical influences, some of which tend to be different for different systems. The following is borrowed mostly from Panksepp (1998). The identification of these neural dispositions supports the hypothesis that emotions have a biological basis, as well as the notion of basic emotions.

For instance, some brain circuits are of central importance in anger. Anger, one may infer, involves the activation of that circuit. Electrical stimulation of sites on that circuit, in cats, induces attack towards an animate object in its field of vision, combined with signs of excitement (hissing, piloerection). The attack and excitement die down within seconds after stimulation stops. Humans that are stimulated in equivalent locations, or that suffer from irritation in those areas, report violent rage attacks. The circuit includes sites in the medial amygdala, the ventrolateral hypothalamus, and down to places in the midbrain (the periacquaductal gray). Activity of the circuit is supported by the neuropeptide called substance P. In normal animals, the circuit receives its information from elsewhere, for instance from regions in the orbitofrontal cortex where different sorts of information are integrated (for instance, the information on expectations and their nonfulfillment, which constitute frustration).

A major circuit has likewise been established that is essential for fear (or at least, for major forms of fear). Upon electrical stimulation, the animal may freeze, or make efforts to escape; it also may vocalize in ways as it does when faced with danger. The circuit includes the central and lateral amygdala, the anterior-medial hypothalamus, and midbrain periacquaductal gray, so again including evolutionary very old brain regions. In humans, stimulation is accompanied by a sense of foreboding. The circuit is sensitized by various neurochemical agents, among which the peptide corticotropin release factor (CRF) is pre-eminent.

Panksepp (1998) likewise describes circuits that are responsible for maternal care and, presumably, for the various urges and emotions that motivate and attend it; in humans, we call them affection, love, and tenderness. Damage to this *care* system (in the preoptic area, the hypothalamus, and midbrain) essentially eliminates maternal behavior in female rats, and injections of the peptides oxytocin and prolactin in some locations induce it. Interestingly, oxytocin is also involved in delivery and milk secretion. Neurochemically, the physical and emotional aspects of maternal caring belong together. Also interestingly, oxytocin plays a stimulating role in both male and female sexual activity, as well as in response of infants to their mothers, in responses to stroking, and in the attenuation of various forms of aggression.

As already mentioned, social bonds and various social pleasures are accompanied by increases in brain opioids. Opioids have a corresponding important role in the brain system linked to sadness or separation distress; Panksepp (1998) labels it the PANIC system. From the ancient midbrain periacqaductal grey (PAG) upwards to the medial thalamus, the septal area and the preoptic areas (just in front of the hypothalamus), up to the anterior cingulate cortex are circuits responsible for crying, or its animal counterpart, the distress call. Lesions in all the relevant circuits diminish or abolish distress calls, stimulation in those circuits induce them, whereas opioid antagonists enhance them and opioids (including morphine) again attenuate. The midbrain PAG circuits for separation distress intermingle with those that mediate physical pain, which make it plausible that, at least at that level, the two feelings resemble each other, and perhaps sensitivity to the cues of separation from caretakers or other attachment figures.

12.8 CULTURE AND EMOTIONS

The preceding sections contain ample evidence that emotions are based in biological, wired-in mechanisms of affective sensitivity, appraisal, and action readiness change. At the same time they wear the stamp of culture. There is wide cultural diversity.

Emotion taxonomies differ from culture to culture, or at least from one language to another. Numbers of emotion words vary between seven (for the Chewong in Malaysia), and two thousand (for English; Russell & Barrett, 1999). Many words are untranslatable between languages, and when they are, meanings may differ substantially (Russell, 1994; Wierzbicka, 1994). Although the structures of the emotion word sets in different language tend to yield similar basic concepts, there also are important differences (Shaver, Wu, & Schwartz, 1992). Basic emotions distinguished in cultural lore may be very different. In Hindu philosophy, for instance, the basic emotions are joy, sorrow, anger, sexual passion, energy or heroism, disgust, and amazement (Shweder & Haidt, 2000).

Differences exist in the relative importance of the various dimensions of cognitive appraisal and action readiness. For instance, magical influence is an important appraisal aspect in African cultures, and negligible in Western ones (Mesquita et al., 1997, for a review). The focality of given emotions (e.g., shame) varies as a function of differences in the prominence of concerns for social propriety and self-esteem (Mesquita et al., 1997).

Although basic mechanisms and emotional sensitivities may well be universal, the actual phenomenology of emotion may differ, and their roles in society may make the 'same' emotions (say, the emotion of aggressive self-assertion, in English called anger) in practice to be quite different ones (Harré & Parrott, 1996). There is no contradiction between the two conclusions of universality of basic mechanisms and cultural variability of specific emotions. As we saw, almost all aspects of emotion are influenced by cognition or other forms of acquired information. We discussed this in connection with emotion elicitors, with the sources of emotion referred to as motives or concerns, and in the forms taken by response repertoires. Culture as such is built-in in emotion in people's sensitivity for what others do or might do, and in the processing of symbolic information.

On the other hand, when methods of research allow such comparison, the variance of emotions and their manifestations due to culture appears much smaller than the variance due to types of emotions (see discussion of the work of Scherer in Mesquita et al., 1997).

12.9 CONCLUDING REMARKS

Emotion psychology has shown considerable progress over the last several decades. The progress is in various domains. One domain is that of theory. There has been a significant shift from emphasis upon phenomena to underlying mechanisms. The old oppositions between emotion and reason, and nature and nurture, have for all practical purposes been resolved as theoretical issues. Progress can also be seen in the field of empirical research. Cognitive influences have come to be a focus of interest, as also has research into cognitive and noncognitive determinants, and their respective roles. Finally, the advances in techniques, findings, and conclusions in the neuropsychology of emotion has been tremendous. Emotion has found a place in the brain, as it has in psychology as a whole.

RESOURCE REFERENCES

Frijda, N. H. (1986). *The emotions*. Cambridge: Cambridge University Press. (Italian: *Emozione*. Bologna: Il Mulino.)

Kahneman, D., Diener, E., & Schwarz, N. (Eds.). (1999). *Well-being. The foundations of hedonic psychology*. New York: Russell Sage.

LeDoux, J. (1996). *The emotional brain*. New York: Simon & Schuster.

Lewis, M., & Haviland, J. M. (Eds.). (2000). *Handbook of emotions* (2nd ed.). New York: Guilford Press.

Meyer, W.-U., Schützwohl, A., & Reisenzein, R. (1993, 1997). *Einführung in die Emotionspsychologie, Band I; Band II. Evolutionspsychologische Theorien*. Bern: Huber.

Oatley, K., & Jenkins, J. M. (1996). *Understanding emotions*. Oxford: Blackwell.

Panksepp, J. (1998). *Affective neuroscience*. Oxford: Oxford University Press.

Rimé, B., & Scherer, K. R. (Eds.). (1989). *Textes de base en psychologie: Les émotions*. Paris/Genève: Delachaux et Niestlé.

Schorr, A., Scherer, K. R., & Johnstone, T. (Eds.). (2000). *Appraisal processes in emotion: Theory, methods, research*. Oxford: Oxford University Press.

Strongman, K. T. (1987). *The psychology of emotion* (3rd ed.). Chichester: Wiley.

ADDITIONAL LITERATURE CITED

Arnold, M. B. (1960). *Emotion and Personality* (Vols. I and II). New York: Columbia University Press.

Baumeister, R. F., & Leary, R. M. (1995). The need to belong: Desire for interpersonal attachment as a fundamental human motivation. *Psychological Bulletin, 117*, 497–529.

Baumeister, R., Stillwell, A. M., & Heatherton, T. F. (1994). Guilt: an interpersonal approach. *Psychological Bulletin, 115*, 243–267.

Beck, A. T. (1976). *Cognitive therapy and the emotional disorders*. New York: International Universities Press.

Berridge, K. C. (1999). Pleasure, pain, desire, and dread: Hidden core processes of emotion. In D. Kahneman, E. Diener, & N. Schwarz (Eds.), *Well-being: The foundations of hedonic psychology* (pp. 525–557). New York: Russell Sage.

Bowlby, J. (1969). *Attachement*. London: Hogarth Press.

Buck, R. (1999). The biological affects: A typology. *Psychological Review, 106*, 301–336.

Cacioppo, J. T., Bernston, G. G., Larsen, J. T., Poehlman, K. M., & Ito, T. A. (2000). The psychophysiology of emotion. In M. Lewis & J. Haviland (Eds.), *Handbook of emotions* (2nd ed.). New York: Guilford.

Cannon, W. B. (1927). The James–Lange theory of emotion: A critical examination and an alternative theory. *American Journal of Psychology, 39*, 106–124.

Cannon, W. B. (1929). *Bodily changes in pain, hunger, fear and rage* (2nd ed.). New York: Appleton.

Christianson, S.-A. (1992) *The handbook of emotion and memory. Research and theory.* Hillsdale: Erlbaum.

Clore, G., & Gasper, K. (in press). Feeling is believing. In N. H. Frijda, A.S. Manstead, & S. Bem (Eds.), *Emotions and beliefs: The influence of thinking upon feeling.* Cambridge: Cambridge University Press.

Cosmides, L., & Tooby, J. (2000). Evolutionary psychology and the emotions. In M. Lewis & J. M. Haviland (Eds.), *Handbook of emotions* (2nd ed.). New York: Guilford.

Damasio, A. (1994). *Descartes error. Emotion, reason, and the human brain.* New York: Avon Books.

Darwin, C. (1872). *The expression of emotions in man and animals.* London: John Murray (3rd ed., P. Ekman (Ed.). 1998, Chicago: University of Chicago Press).

De Waal, F. B. M. (1996). *Good natured: The origins of right and wrong in humans and other animals.* Cambridge, MA: Harvard University Press.

Ekman, P. (Ed.). (1982). *Emotion in the human face* (2nd ed.). New York: Cambridge University Press.

Ekman, P. (1994). Strong evidence for universals in facial expression: A reply to Russell's mistaken critique. *Psychological Bulletin, 115,* 268–287.

Ekman, P., & Davidson, R. (Eds.). (1994). *The nature of emotion: Fundamental questions.* New York: Oxford University Press.

Ekman, P., Levenson, R. W., & Friesen, W. V. (1983). Autonomic nervous system activity distinguishing among emotions. *Science, 221,* 1208–1210.

Elster, J. (1999). *Alchemies of the mind.* Cambridge: Cambridge University Press

Fehr, B., & Russell, J. A. (1984). Concept of emotion viewed from a prototype perspective. *Journal of Experimental Psychology: General Section, 113,* 464–486.

Feldman, R. S., & Rimé, B. (Eds.). (1991). *Fundamentals of nonverbal behavior* (pp. 163–199). Cambridge: Cambridge University Press.

Fiedler, K., and Bless, H. (2000). The formation of beliefs at the interface of affective and cognitive processes. In N. H. Frijda, A. S. Manstead, & S. Bem (Eds.). *Emotions and beliefs: The influence of feeling upon thinking.* Cambridge: Cambridge University Press.

Forgas, J. P., & Vargas, P. T. (in press). The effects of mood on social judgement and reasoning. In M. Lewis & J. Haviland (Eds.), *Handbook of emotions* (2nd ed.). New York: Guilford.

Fridlund, A. J. (1994). *Human facial expression: An evolutionary view.* New York: Academic Press.

Frijda, N. H. (1988). The laws of emotion. *American Psychologist, 43,* 349–358.

Frijda, N. H., & Tcherkassof, A. (1997). Facial expression and modes of action readiness. In J. A. Russell & J. M. Fernandez-Dols (Eds.). (1997) *The psychology of facial expression* (pp. 78–102). Cambridge: Cambridge University Press.

Frijda, N. H., Manstead, A. S., & Bem, S. (Eds.). (in press). *Emotions and beliefs: The influence of feeling upon thinking.* Cambridge: Cambridge University Press.

Gray, J. A. (1987). *The psychology of fear and stress* (2nd ed.). Cambridge: Cambridge University Press.

Gross, J. J. (1999). Emotion and emotion regulation. In L. A. Pervin & O. P. John (Eds.), *Handbook of personality: Theory and research* (2nd ed.). New York: Guilford.

Harré, R., & Parrott, W. G. (Eds.). (1996). *The emotions: Social, cultural and biological dimensions.* Thousand Oaks, CA, Sage.

Isen, A. M. (1999). Positive affect. In T. Dalgleish & M. Power (Eds.), *The handbook of cognition and emotion* (pp. 521–539). New York: Wiley.

Ito, T. A., & Cacioppo, J. T. (1999). The psychophysiology of utility appraisals. In D. Kahneman, E. Diener, & N. Schwarz (Eds.), *Well-being: The foundations of hedonic psychology* (pp. 470–488). New York: Russell Sage.

Izard, C. E. (1971). *The face of emotion.* New York: Appleton-Century-Crofts.

Izard, C. E. (1977). *Human emotions.* New York: Plenum Press.

James, W. (1884). What is an emotion? *Mind, 9,* 188–205.

Johnstone, T., & Scherer, K. R. (2000). Vocal communication of emotion. In M. Lewis & J. M. Haviland (Eds.), *Handbook of emotions* (2nd ed.). New York: Guilford.

Kahneman, D. (1999). Objective happiness. In D. Kahneman, E. Diener, & N. Schwarz (Eds.), *Well-being: The foundations of hedonic psychology.* (pp. 3–25). New York: Russell Sage.

Keltner, D., & Buswell, B. N. (1997). Embarrassment: Its distinct form and appeasement functions. *Psychological Bulletin, 122,* 250–270.

Klüver, H., & Bucy, P. C. (1937). 'Psychic blindness' and other symptoms following temporal lobectomy in rhesus monkeys. *American Journal of Physiology, 119,* 252–353.

Kubovy, M. (1999). On the pleasures of the mind. In D. Kahneman, E. Diener, & N. Schwarz (Eds.), *Well-being: The foundations of hedonic psychology* (pp. 134–154). New York: Russell Sage.

Landman, J. (1993). *Regret: The persistence of the possible.* New York: Oxford University Press.

Lang, P. J. (1984). Cognition in emotion: Concept and action. In C. E. Izard, J. Kagan, & R. B. Zajonc (Eds.), *Emotions, cognition and behavior* (pp. 192–226). New York: Cambridge University Press.

Lazarus, R. S. (1991). *Emotion and adaptation.* New York: Oxford University Press.

Leventhal, L., & Scherer, K. (1987). The relationship of emotion to cognition: A functional approach to a semantic controversy. *Cognition and Emotion, 1,* 3–28.

Lindsley, D. B. (1951). Emotion. In S. S. Stevens (Ed.), *Handbook of experimental psychology* (pp. 473–516). New York: Wiley.

MacLean, P. (1990). *The triune brain in evolution: Role in paleaocerebral functions*. New York: Plenum Press.

Mandler, G. (1984). *Mind and body: The psychology of emotion and stress*. New York: Norton.

Markus, H. R., & Kitayama, S. (1991). Culture and the self: Implications for cognition, emotion, and motivation. *Psychological Review, 98*, 224–253.

Mesquita, B., Frijda, N. H., & Scherer, K. R. (1997). Culture and emotion. In: P. R. Dasen & T. S. Saraswathi (Eds.), *Handbook of cross-cultural psychology* (Vol. 2, pp. 255–298). Boston: Allyn & Bacon.

Morris, W. N. (1999). The mood system. In D. Kahneman, E. Diener, & N. Schwarz (Eds.), *Well-being: The foundations of hedonic psychology* (pp. 169–189). New York: Russell Sage.

Mowrer, O. H. (1960). *Learning theory and behavior*. New York: Wiley.

Murphy, S. T., & Zajonc, R. B. (1993). Affect, cognition, and awareness: Affective priming with optimal and suboptimal stimulus exposures. *Journal of Personality and Social Psychology, 64*, 723–739.

Oatley, K. (1992). *Best laid schemes: The psychology of emotions*. Cambridge, UK: Cambridge University Press.

Öhman, A. (2000). Fear and anxiety: Evolutionary, cognitive, and clinical perspectives. In M. Lewis & J. M. Haviland (Eds.), *Handbook of emotions* (2nd ed.). New York: Guilford.

Ortony, A., & Turner, T. (1990). What's basic about basic emotions? *Psychological Review, 97*, 315–331.

Parducci, A. (1995). *Happiness, pleasure, and judgment*. Mahwah, NJ: Erlbaum.

Parkinson, B. (1995). *Ideas and realities of emotion*. London: Routledge.

Plutchik, R. (1980). *Emotion: A psychoevolutionary synthesis*. New York: Harper & Row.

Power, M., & Dalgleish, T. (1997). *Cognition and emotion: From order to disorder*. Mawah, NJ: Erlbaum.

Reisenzein, R. (1995). On Oatley and Johnson-Laird's theory of emotion and hierarchical structures in the affective lexicon. *Cognition and Emotion, 9*, 383–416.

Rimé, B., Finkenauer, C., Luminet, O., Zech, E., & Philippot, P. (1997). Social sharing of emotions: New evidence and new questions. In W. Stroebe & M. Hewstone (Eds.), *European review of social psychology* (Vol. 7). Chichester: Wiley.

Rimé, B., Phillipot, P., & Cisamolo, D. (1990). Social schemata of peripheral changes in emotion. *Journal of Personality and Social Psychology, 59*, 38–49

Rolls, E. T. (1999). *The brain and emotion*. Oxford: Oxford University Press.

Roseman, I. J., Wiest, C., & Swartz, T. S. (1994). Phenomenology, behaviors, and goals differentiate discrete emotions. *Journal of Personality and Social Psychology, 67*, 206–221

Rozin, P. (1999). Preadaptation and the puzzles and properties of pleasure. In D. Kahneman, E. Diener, & N. Schwarz (Eds.), *Well-being: The foundations of hedonic psychology* (pp. 109–133). New York: Russell Sage.

Rozin, P., Haidt, J., & McCauley, C.R. (2000). Disgust. In M. Lewis & J. M. Haviland (Eds.), *Handbook of emotions* (2nd ed.). New York: Guilford.

Ruch, W. (2000). Exhilaration and humor. In M. Lewis & J. M. Haviland (Eds.), *Handbook of emotions.* (pp. 605–616). New York: Guilford.

Russell, J. A. (1994). Is there universal recognition of emotion from facial expression? A review of the cross-cultural studies. *Psychological Bulletin, 115*, 102–141.

Russell, J. A., & Barrett, L. F. (1999). Core affect, prototypical emotional episodes, and other things called 'emotion': Dissecting the elephant. *Journal of Personality and Social Psychology, 76*, 805–819.

Russell, J. A., & Fernandez-Dols, J. M. (1997). *The psychology of facial expression.* (pp. 78–102). Cambridge: Cambridge University Press.

Schachter, S., & Singer, J. (1962). Cognitive, social and physiological determinants of emotional state. *Psychological Review, 63*, 379–399.

Scherer, K. R. (1999). Appraisal theory. In T. Dalgleish & M. Power (Eds.), *Handbook of cognition and emotion*. Chichester: Wiley.

Scherer, K. R. (2000). Emotions as episodes of subsystem sychronization driven by nonlinear appraisal processes. In M. Lewis, & I. Granic (Eds.), *Emotion, development, and self-organization*. New York: Cambridge University Press.

Shaver, P., Wu, S., & Schwartz, J. C. (1992). Cross-cultural similarities and differences in emotion and its representation: A prototype approach. In M. Clark (Ed.), *Review of personality and social psychology* (Vol. 6, pp. 175–212). Beverley Hills: Sage.

Shweder, R. A., & Haidt, J. (2000). The cultural psychology of the emotions: Ancient and new. In M. Lewis & J. M. Haviland (Eds.), *Handbook of emotions* (2nd ed.). New York: Guilford.

Stein, N., & Trabasso, T. (1992). The organization of emotional experience: Creating links between emotion, thinking, and intentional action. *Cognition and Emotion, 6*, 225–244.

Teasdale, J. D., & Barnard, P. (1993). *Affect, cognition, and change*. Mawah, NJ: Erlbaum.

Tomkins, S. S. (1962). *Affect. Imagery and consciousness. Vol. 1: The positive affects*. New York: Springer.

Van Hooff, J. A. R. A. M. (1982). Categories and sequences of behavior: Methods of description and analysis. In K. R. Scherer & P. Ekman (Eds.), *Handbook of methods in nonverbal behavior research* (pp. 362–439). Cambridge: Cambridge University Press.

Weiner, B. (1985). An attributional theory of achievement motivation and emotion. *Psychological Review, 92,* 548–573.

Weiskrantz, L. (1956). Behavioral changes associated with ablation of the amygdaloid complex in monkeys. *Journal of Comparative and Physiological Psychology, 49,* 381–391.

Wierzbicka, A. (1994). Everyday conceptions of emotion: A semantic perspective. In J. A, Russell, J.-M. Fernandez-Dols, A. S. R. Manstead, & J.

Wellenkamp (Eds.), *Everyday conceptions of emotion* (pp. 17–48). Dordrecht: Kluwer.

Wundt, W. (1902). *Grundzüge der physiologischen Psychologie* (Vol. 3) [Foundations of physiological psychology] (5th ed.). Leipzig: Engelmann.

Zajonc, R. B. (1968). The attitudinal effects of mere exposure. *Journal of Personality and Social Psychology, Monographs, 9* (2, part 2).

Zajonc, R. B. (1994). Can emotions be unconscious? In P. Ekman & R. J. Davidson (Eds.), *The nature of emotion: Fundamental questions* (pp. 293–297). New York: Oxford University Press.

Communications concerning this chapter should be addressed to: Professor Nico H. Frijda, Department of Psychology, University of Amsterdam, Roeterstraat 15, NL-1018 WB Amsterdam, The Netherlands

13

Consciousness and Conscious Experience

CARLO UMILTÀ

13.1 HISTORY

Scientific psychology began in the nineteenth century as the study of those mental processes that are accompanied by conscious experience. When William James defined psychology as the science of mental life, he actually meant *conscious* mental life. For about half a century there had been investigations concerning psychophysical laws, sensory processes, memory, intelligence, and hypnosis. Almost every investigator in these areas believed that consciousness was the key to studying mental events.

In the early part of the twentieth century, however, prominent scholars, like Ivan Pavlov and John Watson maintained that it was scientifically improper to deal with consciousness, because we can only observe physical behavior and brain events. As a consequence, human personal experience became almost a taboo subject in science. Behaviorism banned consciousness, and other mentalistic concepts, as a legitimate topic of investigation from mainstream experimental psychology. However, the study of consciousness survived in other areas of psychology. The contrast between conscious and nonconscious processes was at the core of psychoanalytic theories (Erdelyi, 1985), and of the study of dreaming (Foulkes, 1990) and hypnosis (Kihlstrom, 1985). Also, in social psychology research was to some extent concerned with consciousness (Uleman & Bargh, 1989). However, these studies did not directly address the issue of the relative contributions of conscious and nonconscious processes in cognition, which is of current concern in experimental psychology.

The turning point came when it became increasingly clear that a substantial amount of cognitive processing occurs independent of consciousness (for brief historical reviews, see Reber, 1992; Velmans, 1991). Earlier scholars, like Hermann Helmholtz (unconscious inferences) and Francis Galton in the nineteenth century, and the Wuerzburg school at the beginning of the twentieth century, had already realized that much cognitive processing takes place outside of consciousness. However, it was the discovery, in the late twentieth century, of a number of strikingly neuropsychological syndromes that made a really compelling case for the existence of nonconscious cognitive processes, and thus pointed to the need of consciousness as an explanatory construct.

By following the pioneering work of Clark Hull and Edward Thorndike in the first part of the twentieth century, the earliest studies with normal subjects touched on the issue of learning without consciousness or incidental learning (Reber, 1965). These studies, however, were plagued by problems of methodology and questions over the degree to which incidental learning was truly incidental and how much awareness there was on tasks that purportedly showed learning without consciousness. In the 1970s, papers on consciousness were published by respected investigators (Mandler, 1975; Posner, 1978; Shallice, 1972). They were instrumental in making consciousness a legitimate topic of investigation. Although severe problems of definition, theory, and methodology continued to plague the experimental study of consciousness, the attitude had changed; these difficulties were now seen as problems to be confronted and solved rather than as fatal flaws that question the legitimacy of research on consciousness.

13.2 Conscious versus Nonconscious Processing

Many studies with healthy persons investigated the processing of unattended information to collect evidence about nonconscious processing. In them, the term 'attended' is taken to mean 'conscious', whereas the term 'unattended' is taken to mean 'unconscious'. The first relevant studies were those that went under the rubric of *subliminal perception*, in which the stimuli were presented using techniques designed to ensure that the material was not consciously processed.

Nonconscious Processing in Normal Subjects

Three main experimental paradigms were used: dichotic listening, parafoveal presentation, and visual masking. They involve looking for indirect evidence of nonconscious processing, that is for the influence of the outcome of nonconscious processing on the outcome of conscious processing.

Dichotic Listening

In dichotic listening tasks, subjects are simultaneously presented with different messages to each ear, and are asked to attend to only one, ignoring the other. The task requires them to repeat back the message delivered to the attended ear. When questioned afterwards about the message delivered to the unattended ear, they are unable to report its meaning, or even the language in which it was spoken. However, they are able to report some of its physical characteristics, like whether it was speech or a tone.

In one of the earliest studies, Lewis (1970) found that the speed at which words delivered to the attended ear were repeated was influenced by semantically related words delivered to the unattended ear. Semantically unrelated words had no effect. In another study (Corteen & Wood, 1972), subjects were conditioned to expect a mild electric shock when they heard certain words. Subsequently, they participated in a dichotic listening experiment, in which, while they shadowed the attended message, the words previously associated with electric shocks were sometimes presented to the unattended ear. Although they claimed to have been unaware of the words in the unattended ear, the shock-associated words continued to produce changes in galvanic skin response. This occurred also with different words that were semantically related to the conditioned ones.

Such studies are cited as evidence that the processing of the unattended, nonconscious message includes the analysis of meaning. Their several replications (Velmans, 1991) indicate that the results are reliable. It is possible, however, that words in the unattended ear briefly attract attention and subjects become momentarily aware of the unattended words (Holender, 1986). If one cannot be certain that the message to the unattended ear has never become aware, the dichotic listening paradigm cannot provide a sound basis for the notion of nonconscious processing in the unattended ear.

Parafoveal Presentation

The rationale is very similar to that of dichotic listening. Subjects are asked to focus attention on stimuli shown at fixation and to ignore stimuli presented outside the fovea. In a study (Underwood, 1976), a foveal ambiguous word, that is a word with several meanings, acted as the target, whereas a task-irrelevant word (the flanker) was presented in the parafoveal area. The subject could not report the flanker, which, however, biased the meaning of the target word. For example, the target word *palm* was interpreted as being related to plants or to body parts, depending on the meaning of the flanker (i.e., *tree* or *hand*).

The biasing influence of the meaning of unattended, parafoveal flankers on the reported meaning of foveal, attended targets is open to the same criticisms that can be leveled at dichotic listening studies (Holender, 1986). Because one cannot be absolutely certain that the subject never became aware of the flanker, it is not safe to rely on the subject voluntarily not paying attention to the to-be-ignored stimuli.

Visual Masking

Under strict pattern-masking conditions, a stimulus cannot be reported because of data limitation, rather than because of a voluntary strategy on the subject's part. If the masking procedure is really effective, the masked stimulus cannot be reported, no matter how hard the subject tries to report it. Therefore, the best available evidence of nonconscious processing originates from studies that used masking.

In a lexical decision task, subjects are asked to decide as soon as possible whether a letter string is a word or not. In 'priming' studies the target letter string is preceded by a prime, that is by a task-irrelevant word. Normally, both the prime and the target are presented suprathreshold and are both consciously processed. A prime such as *bread* facilitates the lexical decision for a semantically associated word, like *butter*, in comparison to a nonassociated word, like *nurse*. In 'masked priming' studies, the prime is masked and is not consciously perceived. It may, however, continue to facilitate the response to the following target. That is evidence of nonconscious processing of the masked prime. Marcel (1980) used two types of mask for the prime. When masked by a pattern, the prime was effective and produced facilitation, whereas with a random noise mask, the prime was not effective and did not produce facilitation. Marcel proposed that the pattern mask prevents access to consciousness by disrupting perceptual integration, but does not prevent nonconscious access to semantic knowledge. In contrast, the noise mask degrades the stimulus early in processing, and thus prevents access to semantic knowledge.

Methodological Problems

The effects of unattended stimuli were extremely sensitive to subtle differences in the experimental procedures. That produced heated discussions over the reliability of the results and their interpretation. The controversies were mostly concerned with the criteria that were used to determine consciousness in the subject, and the correct type of technique for determining thresholds (Styles, 1997).

The logic underlying the paradigms of dichotic listening, parafoveal presentation, and visual masking is that nonconscious information processing can be demonstrated by a dissociation between two indexes. One indicates unavailability of information to consciousness. The other indicates availability of information even though it is not available to consciousness.

Many investigators measured the first index solely in terms of subjective reports. But one should be very cautious in concluding that information was not available to consciousness merely because the subject denies having been aware of the stimulus. It is sounder to determine the absence of consciousness on the basis of tasks that measure discriminative capability. In particular, one should use present/absent tasks, which require subjects to distinguish between the presence or absence of a stimulus, or forced-choice tasks, which require discriminating among a set of known stimuli. Marcel's (1980) experiments, and subsequent experiments in which his methodology was adopted, are especially convincing because they demonstrate the effects of the masked word, even when subjects cannot detect it, as evidenced by the fact that they cannot discriminate between its presence or absence.

Cheesman and Merikle (1985) proposed the distinction between a 'subjective' threshold and an 'objective' threshold. When the stimulus is below the subjective threshold, subjects claim they cannot see it, but may still be able to make a better than chance judgment about its presence/absence. The objective threshold is the point in perceptual processing below which subjects are at chance level at deciding whether the stimulus is present or absent. Holender (1986) maintained that it is the objective threshold that must be used to assess nonconscious processing. In contrast, Cheesman and Merikle maintained that the subjective threshold may be used, on condition that one can provide evidence that stimuli presented below that threshold produce *qualitatively* different effects from stimuli that are presented above it (see Section 13.3 below).

Nonconscious Processing in Brain-Damaged Patients

Neuropsychological studies have provided evidence showing that information that cannot be overtly recognized is processed outside consciousness. There are a number of examples in the literature of the way in which processing and consciousness can break down following brain damage (Farah, 1994; Köhler & Moscovitch, 1997; Styles, 1997). These are termed dissociations between preserved implicit (nonconscious) and impaired explicit (conscious) knowledge. Explicit knowledge is defined as knowledge of a particular aspect of stimulation that can be expressed as conscious experience. Implicit knowledge refers to knowledge of a particular aspect of stimulation that is revealed in task performance, but is not accompanied by a corresponding conscious experience.

Although the essence of many neuropsychological studies dealing with nonconscious processing is the indirectness of the testing procedure, an important distinction should be made between types of task and types of process (Young & De Haan, 1992). The use of the terms 'explicit' and 'implicit' is better reserved to refer to the nature, conscious or nonconscious, of the *processing*. In contrast, to characterize *tasks*, the terms 'direct' or 'indirect' should be used. A direct task directly inquires about a given ability, and performance is dependent on that ability. On an indirect task, assessment of the ability in question is incidental and the task ostensibly measures something else. In most patient studies, implicit processing was inferred on the basis of performance in indirect tasks.

Cortical Blindness

Damage to the primary visual cortex causes blindness in parts of the visual field (scotomas). Complete lack of visual conscious experience is revealed by standard tests. However, it is now well established that some cortically blind patients possess preserved implicit knowledge about visual stimuli that fall in the scotoma. This preserved implicit knowledge is usually referred to as 'blindsight' (Weiskrantz, 1986).

Blindsight was initially tested by direct tasks that required the patients to perform forced-choice responses to stimuli shown in the scotoma. For example, a brief visual stimulus was presented in one of several locations within the scotoma. The patients were asked to guess where the target was presented by moving their gaze, or by manually pointing to the stimulated location, or by making a verbal response such as 'top' or 'bottom'. Despite subjective impression of engaging in random guessing, and the absence of any reportable awareness of the stimulus, their localization judgements were surprisingly accurate. The forced-choice guessing procedure was also used to demonstrate that some patients are able to detect stationary or moving stimuli, to discriminate the direction of movement, and even to discriminate between different stimulus orientations.

Several criticisms were leveled at the forced-choice guessing procedure, the more damaging of which was that patients' performance might reflect residual awareness of visual stimuli, which may be qualitatively different from normal conscious vision (Köhler & Moscovitch, 1997). The critical point is again that lack of consciousness is established solely on the basis of subjective reports, that is the patients' claim that they do not see the stimuli. Because of that, a number of indirect tasks were introduced to examine the effects produced by information

delivered to the scotoma on processing that occurs in the intact field.

When normal subjects are asked to respond to the second of two flashes that are presented in rapid succession, reaction time is slower than when a single flash is presented. In a cortically blind patient, Corbetta, Marzi, Tassinari, and Aglioti (1990) found that reaction time to the target flash presented in the intact part of the visual field was slower when a preceding flash was presented in the scotoma than when only the target flash was presented. The inhibitory effect occurred even though the patient was never aware of being presented with two flashes, and always perceived a single flash in the intact field. Similar indirect tasks showed a number of effects attributable to stimulation of the scotoma: interfield summation, inhibition of saccade execution, threshold resetting, tilt of the subjective vertical, color after-images, and perceptual completion.

Prosopagnosia

Bilateral lesions of the occipitotemporal region may cause an impairment in visual processing of faces that is termed prosopagnosia. Prosopagnosic patients are able to discriminate a face from a non-face but cannot identify specific individuals. However, a substantial body of evidence has been accumulating that indicates that prosopagnosic patients possess implicit knowledge about face familiarity and face identity.

De Haan, Young, and Newcombe (1987) asked a prosopagnosic patient to categorize a printed *name* as belonging to an actor or a politician. Simultaneously with each name, a task-irrelevant, to-be-ignored photograph of an actor's or politician's face was presented. Normal subjects are slower at categorizing the names when the face comes from a different category than when it comes from the same category. Although the patient was severely impaired at categorizing the faces overtly, he showed interference from different-category faces.

Neglect

Neglect is a disorder that generally follows posterior parietal damage and results in patients' failure to report or even orient to stimuli occurring on the contralesional side of space. Often the deficit manifests itself in the visual, auditory, and tactile modalities. There are two main hypotheses attempting to explain neglect. According to the representational hypothesis (Bisiach & Vallar, 1988) neglect is caused by a deficit in the ability to form a whole representation of space. Patients do not react to stimuli originating from the affected region because that region is impoverished or absent in their internal representation of space. The attentional hypothesis (Kinsbourne, 1987) maintains that each hemisphere is responsible for shifting attention in the contralateral direction in either region of space. Damage to one hemisphere (generally, the right hemisphere) causes an imbalance in favor of shifts contralateral to the intact side, thus rendering orienting towards the affected side (generally, the left side) difficult or impossible.

Standard tests show that patients are completely unaware of stimuli in the affected hemispace. However, indirect tasks reveal that they may process to a remarkably high degree information presented in that hemispace. Làdavas, Paladini, and Cubelli (1993) reported a patient who could not read aloud words presented in the left field, nor judge their lexical status or semantic content. He could not even detect the presence of a string of letters. However, response to a word in the intact right field was faster when the word was preceded by a brief presentation of an associated word in the impaired field. The patient indirectly showed semantic priming caused by words presented in the affected field, even though he was unable consciously to process any of their attributes.

Amnesia

Amnesic patients, with either focal brain lesions in the medial temporal lobe or degenerative brain disorders, demonstrate retention of information about events for which they disclaim any memory (Moscovitch, Goshen-Gottstein, & Vriezen, 1994). They are catastrophically poor in direct tasks, which require explicit recollection, such as recognition and recall. In contrast, they can show near-normal performance in indirect tasks, which do not make direct reference to the past, but rather assess memory by showing changes in behavior with experience or practice, in the absence of a subjective experience of remembering.

An often-used indirect task is stem or fragment completion, which shows the increased likelihood that a word stem will be completed with a previously studied word (Schacter, Chiu, & Ochsner, 1993). In this task, the first letters of a word are presented (e.g., *mot*, for *motel*) and the patient is asked to complete the stem with the first word that comes to mind. Priming effects are obtained when probability of completion of studied words is above the baseline guessing rate and exceeds that of nonstudied words. Fragment completion is similar, except that a word fragment is presented (e.g., - *t* - *i* - *g*, for *string*) instead of the stem. Amnesic patients consistently show normal or near-normal priming, even though their memory for the studied words is severely impaired when it is tested

directly. A similar pattern of results is obtained when pictures, rather than words, are used. Identification of degraded line drawings of familiar objects improves in amnesic patients, if they previously have seen the intact drawing, even though their explicit memory for the drawing is nearly null.

A controversial issue concerning dissociations between explicit and implicit memory is the assumption that direct and indirect tasks are 'process pure' (Rugg, 1995). A task may ostensibly be indirect, yet performance on it may be contaminated by explicit knowledge. Similarly, implicit knowledge may influence performance on what is ostensibly a direct task. An alternative approach has been developed by Jacoby, Toth, and Yonelinas (1993). It is termed 'process dissociation procedure' and requires a condition in which conscious and nonconscious processes have the same effects on performance, and a second condition in which the two processes operate in opposition to each other. Results from these two conditions can be combined so as to quantify the relative contributions of explicit and implicit memory to the ability to retrieve studied items. However, the procedure rests on the assumptions that conscious and nonconscious processes are independent and that their influence in the two conditions is invariant.

Models of the Dissociation

Three explanations have been proposed to account for the dissociation between explicit and implicit knowledge (Köhler & Moscovitch, 1997). One is that specialized neural mechanisms are disconnected from, and because of that do not convey the output of their processing to, the higher-level neural system(s) that subserve(s) consciousness. The explicit/implicit dissociation would reflect a disconnection between intact specialized mechanisms and intact consciousness system(s). Another explanation is that consciousness system(s) receive(s) degraded output from damaged mechanisms. Degraded information nonconsciously manifests its effects on indirect tasks, but is insufficient for being consciously processed in direct tasks. Identical mechanisms would subserve both explicit and implicit knowledge, the only difference being that, when lesioned, these mechanisms produce low quality output, which cannot give rise to consciousness. Because explicit and implicit knowledge would be subserved by the same mechanisms, they should be qualitatively similar. The third explanation is that the lesion destroys mechanisms that are necessary for demonstrating explicit knowledge through direct tasks, whereas performance in indirect tasks depends on different mechanisms, which do not have access to consciousness. Input would always be processed in parallel by mechanisms that send their output to consciousness and by mechanisms that do not. The lesion destroys the former, leaving the latter (nearly) intact. Because they are thought to be subserved by different mechanisms, explicit and implicit knowledge might be qualitatively different.

These accounts make alternative predictions and likely apply to different forms of the explicit/implicit dissociation. The explanation based on disconnected but otherwise intact mechanisms predicts that patients' performance in indirect tasks should very closely resemble that of normal subjects in the same tasks. The explanation based on degraded output from damaged mechanisms predicts that patients should perform worse (a quantitative difference) than normal subjects in indirect tasks. The explanation based on independent mechanisms for performance in direct and indirect tasks predicts the presence of qualitative differences between patients and normal subjects.

13.3 QUALITATIVE DIFFERENCES

There is evidence that processes that are accompanied by conscious experience are qualitatively different from those that occur without any concomitant conscious experience. These qualitative differences were among the criteria that Cheesmann and Merikle (1985) adopted to substantiate the distinction between conscious and nonconscious processes.

In a study by Marcel (1980), subjects were shown three letter strings, one after another, and were asked to make lexical decisions to the first and third string. On some trials, the first string was a context word, which was followed by an ambiguous word (the prime), then by a target word. Examples are *save - bank - money* and *save - bank - river.* The lexical decision time to the third word indexed which meaning of the ambiguous word had been accessed. In one condition, the prime was presented unmasked, at an exposure duration of 500 ms, so that all words were consciously available. Results showed selective priming of the target: only the meaning of the prime related to the meaning of the context word was activated. The prime *bank* facilitated response to *money* but not to *river.* When the prime was presented for 10 ms and was pattern masked, so that subjects claimed to be unable to detect it, unselective priming occurred, and all meanings of the ambiguous word were accessed. The prime *bank* facilitated both *money* and *river.*

Negative priming refers to the slowing of responses to recently ignored stimuli. For example, with visually superimposed outline forms, subjects can be instructed to attend to the red figure and to ignore the superimposed green one, or vice versa. Negative priming manifests itself as a slowing of the response, relative to a control condition, when the previously ignored item is presented as a target on the next trial. Two explanations have been offered for negative priming, and both invoke some form of inhibition. One is that activation of the distracter representation is reduced and this inhibition is still effective when the next trial is presented. The other is that the distracter representation is denied access to the response system and its isolation from the control of action must be overcome when, on the next trial, the distracter requires a response.

In the flankers task (Eriksen & Eriksen, 1974), subjects are presented with a string of letters (e.g., SSFSS) and asked to give a discriminative response to the central letter (the target) and ignore the other letters (the distracters). The relation between the target and the distracters on the first, prime trial and the target on the subsequent, probe trial can be manipulated. When the second target is again F, the response to it is speeded up, indicating the usual positive priming effect. When the second target is instead S, the response is slowed down, indicating negative priming. Fuentes and Humphreys (1996) used a modified version of the flankers task to test the impaired and the intact visual fields of a patient with extinction, that is with a form of neglect that manifests itself when both visual fields are simultaneously stimulated. Results indicated a qualitative difference between processing of distracters in the two visual fields. In the intact field negative priming was found, whereas in the impaired field there was positive priming when the previously ignored distracter was re-presented as the target on the probe trial.

13.4 FUNCTION(S) OF CONSCIOUSNESS

A crucial issue concerns what the function(s) of consciousness might be. If part of human cognitive processing is conscious, it is reasonable to assume, from a Darwinian stand point, that consciousness should have some function (Reber, 1992). However, this assumption is not universally accepted. Velmans (1991) has argued that consciousness plays no role in cognitive processing, not even in those higher order processes that render it possible to choose among alternative courses of action, to plan and time their execution, and to make decisions (executive processes). Of course, Velmans does not deny that we are conscious of those processes. However, he distinguishes between processes and the results of processes. Although one can have conscious access to some of the results of processes, one never has conscious access to the operations they perform. Therefore, conscious access cannot have a causal role in cognitive processing. What instead plays a role is focal attention. But consciousness and focal attention are confounded; processes that are at the focus of attention are accompanied by focal attention, and when focal-attentive processing is absent, consciousness also is absent.

No doubt attention is closely associated with consciousness: both are capacity limited and slow acting, both involve working memory, both operate in series and use processing resources, both intervene in planning and decision making. However, there are reasons for keeping them separated (Umiltà, 1992). Attention is not always necessary for the product of a process to access consciousness. It is a privileged route to consciousness, but not the only one available. There are cases in which consciousness is accessed bypassing attention. In a dichotic listening task, some 'special' unattended words (e.g., the listener's name) gain immediate access to consciousness. In the case of well-learned routines, it is possible to be conscious of performing an action without paying attention to it.

The available evidence suggests that consciousness plays a causal role in mediating inhibition; inhibitory processes may not take place unless the stimuli are consciously processed. In the Marcel (1980) study, one of the meanings of a consciously perceived word was inhibited when the other meaning was selectively activated by the context word. In contrast, when the prime word did not access consciousness, both meaning were activated. The Fuentes and Humphreys (1996) study showed that the representations of distracters that did not access consciousness were not inhibited. It must be stressed that the inhibitory processes themselves are not necessarily conscious. It is the fact that the representations that need to be inhibited are conscious that allows inhibition to take place.

Also, a study by Libet (1985) provided evidence in support of the notion that consciousness is instrumental in allowing inhibition of ongoing cognitive processes. He developed a procedure that enabled subjects to establish the instant they experienced a wish to perform a spontaneous act involving no preplanning (a simple flexion of the wrist or fingers). The time of the conscious intention to act was obtained from the subject's report of the spatial position of a revolving dot on a clockface when he/she

became conscious of wanting to move. Simultaneously, Libet recorded from the scalp the electrophysiological readiness potentials that occur about 550 ms before execution of voluntary acts. The wish to act was consciously experienced about 200 ms *before* execution of the voluntary act, that is it *followed* the readiness potentials by about 350 ms. The conclusion was that activation of the neural mechanisms that eventually lead to an action begins nonconsciously. Also, it was found that the decision to act could still be consciously inhibited during 150–200 ms after experiencing the conscious intention. Libet proposed that the role of consciousness would be that of either permitting or preventing the motor implementation of the intention to act. In the absence of conscious experience, execution of the movement could not be prevented.

13.5 THEORIES OF CONSCIOUSNESS

Several theories posit that it is the activity of a unitary mechanism, which may have a unitary brain representation, that gives rise to consciousness (Umiltà, 1992). Other theories posit instead that consciousness arises as a result of interactions among various brain mechanisms (Dennett & Kinsbourne, 1992). Also, there are theories that posit that consciousness arises from the binding of disparate neural elements into an integrated pattern by an oscillating 35–75 Hz signal (Crick & Koch, 1990; Singer, 1993). Of the three most influential theories of consciousness, to be described next, Shallice's is of the interactionist type, Schacter's is of the unitary type, whereas Baar's is ambiguous.

Baar's (1988) theory relies on three components: expert processors, a global workspace, and contexts. Expert processors are specialized nonconscious processors, reminiscent of Fodor's (1983) modules. They are extremely efficient in narrow domains, work autonomously, display their output in the global workspace, receive messages from the global workspace, and form coalitions. The global workspace is a device devoted to system-wide dissemination of information, which broadcasts global messages to all expert processors. In the global workspace new links between expert processors are formed, producing new coalitions. Contexts are pre-established coalitions of expert processors that can influence global messages without themselves entering the global workspace. They are devices that constrain conscious contents in the workspace without being conscious themselves. Only the contents of global workspace are conscious. Outputs from the expert processors that win the competition to reach the global work-space are broadcast throughout the system. If one thinks that representations become conscious by entering the global workspace, the theory is of the unitary type. If one thinks that representations become conscious by being disseminated throughout the whole system, the theory is of the interactionist type.

Shallice's (1992) theory has several components, the most important among which are specialized processors, schemata, a contention scheduling system, and a supervisory attentional system (SAS). The specialized processors are akin to Baar expert processors. The schemata are well-learned, highly specific programs for routine actions and thoughts. Many schemata can be concurrently activated through the specialized processors and memory traces, and the competition among them is resolved by another specialist system, contention scheduling. Contention scheduling automatically selects among activated schemata by means of excitation and lateral inhibition. Routine actions and cognitive processes depend on the selection operations that are carried out by contention scheduling. When nonroutine actions and cognitive processes are needed, top-down biasing of schemata is provided by SAS. It operates by the application of additional excitation and inhibition to schemata, which changes the probability of selection by contention scheduling.

One might think of one of these components as the conscious part of the model, thus transforming Shallice's theory into one of the unitary type. That is what Baddeley (1992) did by equating his central executive with SAS. However, Shallice maintained that the contents of consciousness do not correspond to the contents of SAS, but rather they correspond to the flow of information between the control components when there is concurrent and coherent operation of them on information from schemata.

Schacter's (1990) theory shares most of its components with Baar's and Shallice's theories. These are special-purpose modules, an executive system, a declarative/episodic memory system, and a procedural/habit system. The key feature of the theory is the existence of a phenomenal consciousness component. It acts as the link between the special-purpose modules and the executive system, which controls and guides the activities of the special-purpose modules. The executive system would not operate if its contents had not been mediated by consciousness. The theory posits that representations become conscious because of what happens inside the phenomenal consciousness component. Because what matters for consciousness is the fact of being inside a specific component, rather than

informational exchange among components, Schacter's theory is clearly of the unitary type.

13.6 A PRIVILEGED BRAIN LOCUS FOR CONSCIOUSNESS?

The theories outlined above propose different solutions to the problem of how consciousness is represented in the brain. The main difference concerns whether consciousness is linked to activity in one, privileged part of the brain, or instead it originates from interactions among several brain structures. Dennett and Kinsbourne (1992) in particular have criticized the idea that consciousness depends on the activity of a single brain mechanism, which they called the Cartesian theater model, after the pineal gland in Descartes' brain. A modern version of this model can be found in Gray (1995), who has proposed that the unitary brain mechanism of consciousness is the subicular area, which belongs to the septohippocampal system.

The explicit/implicit dissociations described earlier are domain specific because they occur in one single domain. That seems to militate against the possibility that there exists a unitary neural structure subserving consciousness. If there were a general-purpose consciousness system, then a focal lesion to it should produce patients showing the explicit/implicit dissociations across a number of different domains, possibly all domains. No such patient has been described so far. That supports the notion that consciousness arises from many independent consciousness systems that may be separately lesioned (Umiltà & Zorzi, 1995). Note that the three explanations of the explicit/implicit dissociations (see above) apply to either a unitary consciousness system or multiple consciousness systems.

Those states in which there is a general severe alteration in consciousness seem instead to contradict the notion of multiple consciousness systems. In this context, one should consider a basic distinction between the capacity for consciousness and the contents of consciousness (Zeman, 1997). The former depends on the normal activity of the upper brainstem and related areas of the thalamus (the reticular activating system), whereas the latter are supplied by cortical areas. The domain-specific dissociations between explicit and implicit knowledge occur when some of the contents of consciousness are lacking because of focal cortical lesions. Coma, a state of unconsciousness in which the eyes are closed and the sleep–wake cycle is absent, occurs when the reticular activating system is lesioned and the capacity for consciousness is lost. Of particular interest is the vegetative state (Giacino, 1997; Zeman, 1997), which, in a sense, is the converse of coma because the reticular activating system is still functional whereas all cortical functions are lost or gravely impaired. The vegetative state shows that there can be wakefulness without consciousness. Patients have the eyes open and are awake, but demonstrate no evidence of being conscious. Importantly, the contents of consciousness are lacking across all domains, even though reports hint at the possibility of preserved implicit knowledge (Barbur, Watson, Frankowiack, & Zeki, 1993; Menon et al., 1998). However, that is not necessarily evidence against the presence of multiple consciousness systems. The vegetative state results from acute insults or chronic diseases that affect the entire cortex. Therefore, it might well be that consciousness is lacking in every domain, not because a unitary consciousness system is lesioned but rather because all consciousness systems are damaged.

Other altered states of consciousness (minimally conscious state, akinetic mutism, and locked-in syndrome; Giacino, 1997) are less interesting from this point of view because in them the contents of consciousness are, to a certain extent, preserved, whereas in the vegetative state, the contents of consciousness are completely absent. It is possible that, as happens in the vegetative state, in the case of less severe alterations of consciousness, all consciousness systems are damaged, although to a lesser degree.

Resource References

Baars, B. J. (1988). *A cognitive theory of consciousness.* Cambridge: Cambridge University Press.

Crick, F., & Koch, C. (1990). Towards a neurobiological theory of consciousness. *Seminars in Neurosciences, 2,* 263–275.

Foulkes, D. (1990). Dreaming and consciousness. *European Journal of Cognitive Psychology, 2,* 39–55.

Giacino, J. (1997). Disorders of consciousness: Differential diagnosis and neuropathologic features. *Seminars in Neurology, 17,* 105–111.

Kihlstrom, J. F. (1985). Hypnosis. *Annual Review of Psychology, 36,* 385–418.

Köhler, S., & Moscovitch, M. (1997). Unconscious visual processing in neuropsychological syndromes: A survey of the literature and evaluation of models of consciousness. In M. D. Rugg (Ed.), *Cognitive neuroscience.* Hove: Psychology Press.

Marcel, A. J., & Bisiach, E. (Eds.). (1992). *Consciousness in contemporary science.* Oxford: Oxford University Press.

Milner, A. D., & Rugg, M. D. (Eds.). (1992). *The neuropsychology of consciousness.* London: Academic Press.

Reber, A. S. (1992). The cognitive unconscious: An evolutionary perspective. *Consciousness and Cognition, 1,* 93–133.

Styles, E. A. (1997). *The psychology of attention.* Hove: Psychology Press.

Umiltà, C., & Moscovitch, M. (Eds.). (1994). *Attention and performance XV: Conscious and nonconscious information processing.* Cambridge, MA: MIT Press.

Velmans, M. (1991). Is human information processing conscious? *Behavioral and Brain Sciences, 14,* 651–726.

Additional Literature Cited

Baddeley, A. D. (1992). Working memory. *Science, 255,* 556–559.

Barbur, J. L., Watson, J. D. G., Frackowiack, R. S. I., & Zeki, S. (1993). Conscious visual perception without V1. *Brain, 116,* 293–302.

Bisiach, E., & Vallar, G. (1988). Hemineglect in humans. In F. Boller and J. Grafman (Eds.), *Handbook of neuropsychology* (Vol. 1). Amsterdam: Elsevier.

Cheeseman, J., & Merikle, P. M. (1985). Word recognition and consciousness. In D. Besner, T. G. Waller, & G. E. MacKinnon (Eds.), *Reading research: Advances in theory and practice* (Vol. 5). New York: Academic Press.

Corbetta, M., Marzi, C. A., Tassinari, G., & Aglioti, S. (1990). Effectiveness of different task paradigms in revealing blindsight. *Brain, 113,* 603–616.

Corteen, R. S., & Wood, B. (1972). Autonomous responses to shock associated words in an unattended channel. *Journal of Experimental Psychology, 94,* 308–313.

De Haan, E. H. F., Young, A., & Newcombe, F. (1987). Face recognition without awareness. *Cognitive Neuropsychology, 4,* 385–415.

Dennett, D. C., & Kinsbourne, M. (1992). Time and observer: The where and when of consciousness. *Behavioral and Brain Sciences, 15,* 183–247.

Erdelyi, M. H. (1985). *Psychoanalysis: Freud's cognitive psychology.* New York: Freeman.

Eriksen, B. A., & Eriksen, C. W. (1974). Effects of noise letters upon the identification of a target in a non-search task. *Perception and Psychophysics, 16,* 143–149.

Farah, M. J. (1994). Visual perception and visual awareness: A tutorial review. In C. Umiltà & M. Moscovitch, *Attention and performance XV: Conscious and nonconscious information processing.* Cambridge, MA: MIT Press.

Fodor, J. A. (1983). *Modularity of mind.* Cambridge, MA: MIT Press.

Fuentes, L. J., & Humphreys, G. W. (1996). On the processing of extinguished stimuli in visual neglect: An approach using negative priming. *Cognitive Neuropsychology, 13,* 111–136.

Gray, J. A. (1995). The contents of consciousness: A neuropsychological conjecture. *Behavioral and Brain Sciences, 18,* 659–722.

Holender, D. (1986). Semantic activation without conscious identification in dichotic listening, parafoveal vision and visual masking. *Behavioral and Brain Sciences, 9,* 1–66.

Jacoby, L. L., Toth, J. P., & Yonelinas, A. P. (1993). Separating conscious and unconscious influences on memory: Measuring recollection. *Journal of Experimental Psychology: General, 122,* 139–154.

Kinsbourne, M. (1987). Mechanisms of unilateral neglect. In M. Jeannerod (Ed.), *Neurophysiological and neuropsychological aspects of spatial neglect.* Amsterdam: North-Holland.

Làdavas, E., Paladini, R., & Cubelli, R. (1993). Implicit associative priming in a patient with left visual neglect. *Neuropsychologia, 31,* 1307–1320.

Lewis, J. L. (1970). Semantic processing of unattended messages using dichotic listening. *Journal of Experimental Psychology, 85,* 225–228.

Libet, B. (1985). Unconscious cerebral initiative and the role of conscious will in voluntary action. *Behavioral and Brain Sciences, 8,* 529–566.

Mandler, G. (1975). *Mind and emotion.* New York: Wiley.

Marcel, A. J. (1980). Conscious and preconscious recognition of polysemous words: Locating the selective effects of prior verbal context. In R. S. Nickerson (Ed.), *Attention and performance VIII.* Hillsdale, NJ: Erlbaum.

Menon, D. K., Owen, A. M., Williams, E. J., Minhas, P. S., Allen, C. M. C., Boniface, S. J., & Pickard, J. D. (1998). Cortical processing in persistent vegetative state. *Lancet, 352,* 200.

Moscovitch, M., Goshen-Gottstein, Y., & Vriezen, E. (1994). Memory without conscious recollection: A tutorial review from a neuropsychological perspective. In C. Umiltà & M. Moscovitch, *Attention and performance XV: Conscious and nonconscious information processing.* Cambridge, MA: MIT Press.

Posner, M. I. (1978). *Chronometric explorations of mind.* Hillsdale, NJ: Erlbaum.

Reber, A. S. (1965). *Implicit learning of artificial grammars.* Unpublished Masters Thesis, Brown University.

Rugg, M. D. (1995). Memory and consciousness: A selective review of issues and data. *Neuropsychologia, 33,* 1131–1141.

Schacter, D. L. (1990). Toward a cognitive neuropsychology of awareness: Implicit knowledge and anosognosia. *Journal of Clinical and Experimental Neuropsychology, 12,* 155–178.

Schacter, D. L., Chiu, C.-Y. P., & Ochsner, K. N. (1993). Implicit memory: A selective review. *Annual Review of Neuroscience, 16,* 159–182.

Shallice, T. (1972). Dual functions of consciousness. *Psychological Review, 79,* 383–393.

Shallice, T. (1992). Information processing models of consciousness. In A. J. Marcel & E. Bisiach (Eds.), *Consciousness in contemporary science.* Oxford: Oxford University Press.

Singer, W. (1993). Synchronization of cortical activity and its putative role in information processing and learning. *Annual Review of Physiology, 55,* 349–374.

Uleman, J. S., & Bargh, J. A. (Eds.). (1989). *Unintended thought.* New York: Guilford.

Umiltà, C. (1992). The control operations of consciousness. In A. J. Marcel & E. Bisiach (Eds.), *Consciousness in contemporary science.* Oxford: Oxford University Press.

Umiltà, C., & Zorzi, M. (1995). Consciousness does not seem to be linked to a single mechanism. *Behavioral and Brain Sciences, 18,* 701–702.

Underwood, G. (1976). Semantic interference from unattended printed words. *British Journal of Psychology, 67,* 327–338.

Velmans, M. (1991). Is human information processing conscious? *Behavioral and Brain Sciences, 14,* 651–726.

Weiskrantz, L. (1986). *Blindsight: A case study and implications.* Oxford: Oxford University Press.

Young, A. W., & De Haan, E. H. F. (1992). Face recognition and awareness after brain injury. In A. D. Milner & M. D. Rugg (Eds.), *The neuropsychology of consciousness.* London: Academic Press.

Zeman, A. (1997). Persistent vegetative state. *Lancet, 350,* 795–799.

Communications concerning this chapter should be addressed to: Professor Carlo Umiltà, Department of Psychology, University of Padova, Via Venezia, 8, I-35131 Padova, Italy

Part C
SOCIAL PROCESSES AND BEHAVIORAL DEVELOPMENT

14

Developmental Psychology I: Prenatal to Adolescence

HEIDI KELLER

14.1 CONCEPTIONS OF DEVELOPMENT

Development constitutes the essence of human life. Folk conceptions and philosophical treatises over the centuries as well as the scientific study of development during the last decades have largely focused on child development, although Charlotte Bühler during the 1920s/1930s in Vienna already represented the view that development comprises the whole life span.

The scientific interest in children and childhood was on the one hand linked to the influence of education in developmental sciences at the turn of the nineteenth century (as an example, the journal *Pedagogical Seminary* was founded in 1891). On the other hand, childhood was perceived as a state of immaturity which promised to shed light on the origins of psychological processes. Wilhelm Wundt in Leipzig promoted this expectation as well as Karl Bühler in Vienna.

The interest in child psychology found its first expressions in extensive descriptive data collections based on diaries that psychologists, such as the couples Scupin and Stern published about their own children. Controlled observation, mainly administered during longitudinal assessments (the same individuals are observed on several occasions over time), has remained the favorite methodological tool of developmental psychology, despite a short period of experimental child psychology during the 1950s and 1960s. And even the scientific value of diaries has been rediscovered recently. Thus, the scientific study of child development qualifies as expression of the Zeitgeist emphasizing specific topics and tools.

The expertise of psychologists from different cultures has nourished a growing awareness about the cultural conceptions of the child as being part of an indigenous view of human psychology (cf. Doi, 1978; Enriquez, 1993; Nsamenang, 1992; Sinha, 1996). The cultural accounts of developmental processes form a special challenge to developmental theories, since the definition of the life span differs across cultures, thus questioning a consensual understanding of development from birth to death. Mainly rooted in religion, circular views incorporating ancestral states are contrasted with Western linear thinking (Erny, 1968). In Western Cameroon, the prenatal period until the naming ceremony about 7 days after birth when the umbilical cord falls off, forms one developmental stage in which the child is considered as not yet being human, since it still belongs to the spirits; also in Hindu or Buddhist views, life does not end with death, not only due to spiritual continuation, but also due to reincarnation. The different patterning of the life course in different cultures, therefore, underscores the fact that there is not one normative developmental pathway with possible deviations but different, however equally appropriate and adaptive, developmental trajectories.

A Brief Glance at the History of Developmental Theories

Theories of human development and particularly child development, as documented in the psychological literature, mainly refer to Euro-American tableaus of describing, explaining, and predicting planful changes during ontogenesis. Textbook chapters on the history of developmental psychology often refer to the individual achievements of forefathers like G. Stanley Hall (1844–1924), James Mark Baldwin (1861–1934), William Stern (1871–1938), or Arnold Gesell (1880–1961), to name just a few. It is interesting that women, often teaming with their husbands like Clara Stern and Charlotte Bühler, remain largely unnoticed when historical milestones are celebrated.

The main concern of the early developmentalists remains today the most compelling question of developmental psychology: the interplay between biology and culture. This discussion is rooted in the dichotomous view on development as expressed in the *tabula rasa* metaphor on the one hand, that had been developed by English empiricist philosophers such as John Locke attributing development completely to the effect of sensory input, and on the other hand in the nativist view, based on René Descartes' or Wilhelm Leibnitz' philosophical accounts stating that specific ideas are inborn

and Jean Jacques Rousseau's treatise on natural growth and maturation.

Hall introduced, among other ideas, the extension of Haeckel's recapitulation theory beyond embryonic development with the claim that ontogenetic development from birth to adolescence recapitulates the phylogenetic development of the species. As early as 1895, James Mark Baldwin promoted the modern view that the developmental question is not about whether nature or nurture shape ontogenesis, but how they interact. With his segmentation of the life course into phases and stages and the formulation of the principles of assimilation and accommodation, he was most influential in the theorizing of Jean Piaget. William Stern conceptualized the interplay between heredity and environment along the principles of convergence. Individual dispositions converge with environmental factors. According to Stern, the milieu can only exert effects if there are dispositions that are receptive to the particular effects (Stern, 1923), a thought that was later reformulated by Norbert Bischof (1996) as 'inborn environment'. Arnold Gesell was especially concerned with growth which he also conceived of as the result of the interplay between inheritance and environment, with a special emphasis on continuity ('continuous self-conditioning'; Gesell, 1928, p. 57). Beyond his theoretical contributions, special merits are certainly due to his methodological approach of developing observational tools and techniques. Mainly interested in physical maturation, he documented a wealth of careful observations in a special observation room and introduced the frame-by-frame analysis of filmed material, his 'cinemanalysis'. Even today observation studios in psychological laboratories all over the world are called 'Gesell domes'.

The giants in developmental theorizing introducing modern times are without any doubt Jean Piaget (1896–1980) and Lev Semenovich Vygotsky (1896–1934) whose influences are still present, Piaget's mainly in the cognitive developmental domain and Vygotsky's mainly with respect to cultural psychology. Piaget is predominantly associated with his invariant sequence of ontogenetic stages of cognitive development (sensorimotor stage, 0–24 months; preoperational stage, 2–4 years; concrete operations, 7–12 years; stage of formal operations, 12–16 years) and the mechanisms constituting developmental progress: assimilation as the adaptation of the environment to the mental concepts of the infant/child and accommodation as the adaptation of the child's mental concepts to the environment, both aiming at equilibrium. But he himself was rather interested in formulating a theory of genetic epistemology. Thousands of empirical studies have been inspired by his theoretical accounts since the 1960s. Evidence about infants' early capabilities and competencies, domain-specific learning mechanisms (versus general-purpose models) as well as the cultural shaping of cognitive mechanisms challenge his conceptions. Nevertheless his tremendous oeuvre will remain an especially valuable contribution to developmental theorizing also for the future. Vygotsky whose life span covered only 38 years, introduced a different Zeitgeist when he founded his theoretical approach on Marxist ideology. According to him, the child constructs the mind through social experiences. Especially his conception of the 'zone of proximal development' (the distance between the actual and the potential level of development which can be reached with the help of expert partners) has stimulated developmental research tremendously. He formulated, partly together with Aleksander Romanovich Luria, the history of human development as moving to successive transitional points where development becomes directed into new channels by achieving new levels of functioning. In particular the cultural psychology school relies much on Vygotsky's formulations with a present new shift of attention after the recent political changes in Eastern European societies.

This treatment of theoretical viewpoints is cursory and selective, highlighting significant contributions for the understanding of the main conceptual issues relating to children's development. For further conceptions of development, especially relating to a life span view, the reader is referred to the introductory section of Chapter 15.

Evolutionary Psychology: A Modern View about Development

The prevalent eclectic theoretical orientations that form the background of contemporary empirical research to a large extent combine fragments from different origins with respect to different developmental domains. We promote the theoretical approach of evolutionary or Darwinian psychology in this chapter, representing a biologically based, however explicitly contextually-culturally shaped account of human behavior and development. The evolutionary perspective has the capacity to analyze developmental processes from an encompassing, yet detailed theoretical framework, even with the claim for a unitary theory. Yet, the reception of evolutionary theorizing has not been unequivocally positive. On the contrary, it seems to challenge metaperspectives on the human nature,

thus provoking skeptical and even hostile reactions. Nevertheless, its acceptance is increasing, especially due to its capacity to provide answers for the central developmental concerns:

- the interplay between culture and biology,
- the question of continuity and plasticity, and
- the sequence of developmental tasks.

Evolutionary theorizing starts on the assumption that humans as well as other species aim at replicating their genes. The life history represents a holistic strategy for the optimal achievement of this ultimate goal. Although the individual acts as a 'carrier of genes' (Hamilton, 1964), social behavior and psychological functioning have evolved as important tools which enable the individual to pursue these 'interests', implicitly as well as explicitly, effectively. Psychological development is contingent upon environmental conditions, defining adaptation as a context dependent specialization. In order to be able to react flexibly to environmental demands, individuals are considered to be equipped with open genetic programs (Mayr, 1974; for gene–environment interaction see Chapter 15), mainly consisting of devices for the easy learning of specific environmental information at particular times during ontogeny. This view supports the evidence of critical periods in a non-deterministic way. Central tendencies canalize the content and timing of learning. The human capacity for life-long learning, often named plasticity, thus does not imply randomness or infinite possibilities as sometimes claimed by lifespan psychologists.

In evolutionary terms individual life histories can be described as – mostly implicit and nonconscious – trade-offs between different components of fitness,[1] mainly survival and growth (requiring somatic effort) and reproduction (requiring reproductive effort), consisting of mating effort and parental investment. Accordingly, the duration of phases or stages during the life cycle differs with different contexts. This framework therefore allows to capture cross-cultural differences in the patterning of life cycles in terms of contextual adaptations as well as interindividual differences. It is assumed that culture, and hence also norms and value systems, evolved during phylogeny in order to facilitate the functioning of social groups which had to increase the number of members beyond genetic relatives for better exploitation of resources and more effective defense against predators. Also cultural patterns, thus, are considered as following the reproductive logic of fitness optimizing. This argument does not claim, however, that every single behavior or any cultural achievement has an adaptational function.

Evolutionary developmentalists have proposed socialization models which identify developmental trajectories contingent upon the childhood context. The availability and abundance of resources is associated with a special way of caring for the offspring (parenting effort) which then leads to particular qualities of the infant–parent relationship which have somatic consequences in terms of timing of puberty. Reproductive styles can consequently be more quantitatively oriented (low resources, low parental investment, insecure child–parent attachment, early onset of puberty, early age at first childbirth, many offspring, close spacing of children, low parental investment towards own offspring), or more qualitatively oriented (abundant resources, high parental investment, secure infant–parent attachment, later onset of puberty, later age at first childbirth, fewer offspring, high parental investment in one's own offspring), thus supporting intergenerational continuity.

Since individuals have to solve their developmental tasks by partitioning the different fitness components across the life span, life trajectories are supposed to form coherent responses to environmental demands, thus expressing structural continuity. Evolutionary thinking can be viewed as extending the classical culture and personality school, especially the approach by Beatrice and John Whiting. These scholars assigned a crucial role to the context or ecology for shaping the economy and social structure of a society which then influences child-rearing practices and childhood experiences. These form a special blueprint for later personality development (Figure 14.1).

During the 1950s, the Whitings set up a comparative research design in six different cultural contexts (Orchard Town in New England, Juxtlahuaca in Mexico, Tarong in the Philippines, Taira in Japan, Khalapur in India, and Nyansongo in Kenya), that was aimed at demonstrating empirically this interplay of ecology, culture, and psychology. This study program will be taken into consideration at different places in the course of this chapter.

Evolutionary theorizing is different from psychological developmental theories in several important ways. Adult functioning is not conceived of as the developmental goal, but the whole life span, especially the pattern of developmental phases is an evolutionary end product. Predictions from evolutionary theorizing are not restricted to specific developmental domains, but cover the whole array of psychological functioning and allow one to address interindividual, differential and cross-cultural differentiation at the same time. Evolutionary assumptions can be tested also in modern industrialized societies, although even some evolutionary theorists (cf. Tooby & Cosmides, 1992) express their concerns about the applicability to modern men. Finally, evolutionary assumptions allow one to test prospectively proximate functioning, thus being open for support as well as rejection of specific hypotheses. In any case, evolutionary theorizing adds a new dimension to the understanding of development by asking: Why and how could this behavior and development possibly contribute to the fitness of this particular person?

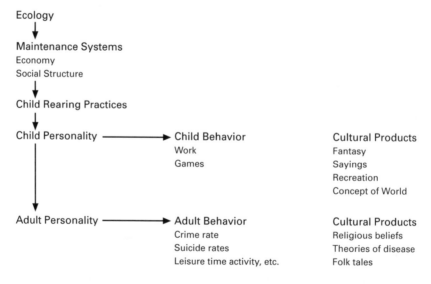

Figure 14.1   *A system's view on behavioral development (adapted from B. B. Whiting, 1963, p. 5)*

14.2 BEGINNINGS

The Prenatal Period

Although the beginning of life is functionally defined when the mother's and father's germ cells join, the understanding of the onset of life is nevertheless largely culturally determined. As we have already argued, the cultural view might postpone the beginning of (social) life even after actual birth. In Western societies on the other hand, there has been a heated discussion about the prenatal actual beginning of life before birth in the context of abortion laws. From a biological perspective, any human being begins life as a zygote with a diameter of 0.14 mm and with a weight of a fifteen-millionth of a gram. Remarkable quantitative and qualitative changes occur during the 9 months of pregnancy, preparing the fetus for extra-uterine life. Pregnancy can be divided into three different periods. The *germinal period* covers the time from conception to implantation about 8–10 days later. The *embryonic period* lasts for about 6 weeks from the attachment of the blastocyst to the uterus until the end of the eighth week when the major organs are shaped. At the end of this period, the organism begins to react to direct stimulation that the mother will not notice until the end of the fourth month due to the tinyness of the embryo. The developmental sequence of the embryo is followed by the cephalocaudal (from head to feet) and the proximodistal pattern (from the inner part to the periphery). The *fetal period* covers the time from 9 weeks after conception until birth. The fetal period prepares the organism for extra-uterine life in terms of receptability of stimulation and refining patterns of motor activity, although the newborn is extremely altricial, that is, physiologically premature caused by the limitation of the birth canal with respect to brain size. The fetal period is characterized by a high level of motor activity occurring spontaneously as well as in response to stimulation. At about 17 weeks, the activity rate declines due to brain development which allows for more inhibitory control, resuming by the end of the sixth month. Fetal activity seems to be crucial for normal limb development. During the last 4–5 months of pregnancy, infants respond with heart rate changes to light penetrating the mother's womb and to sounds. And it seems to be evident that they recognize after birth what they have been exposed to regularly during the last two or three months of pregnancy. Experiments with mothers reading text passages regularly several times a day for 3 months or playing the same music again and again have supported the assumption of fetal learning. The uterine environment and, thus, the mother's physiology and psychology affect the fetus in various ways by chemical messages through the wall of her abdomen, the placenta, and the umbilical cord. Physical cues are transmitted by the mother's activity rate and patterns of movement.

Supportive as well as detrimental influences can be specified. Supportive factors which facilitate the transition to parenthood are constituted by a good health condition and an acceptant and relaxed psychology of the expectant mother. In particular paternal and family support reduce maternal stress and increase the readiness for allocating investment to the expected child. On the other hand, father's absence has detrimental effects on infant and child mortality as demonstrated by the South American Ache people (Hill & Hurtado, 1991).

The regular experience of a substantial degree of the stress secretions adrenaline and cortisone has sizable effects on the fetus' motor activity in terms of irritability and hyperactivity with an increasing probability for miscarriage or premature delivery and developmental disturbances after birth, such as disorders of eating, sleeping, and elimination. In large parts of the world, extreme malnutrition is the major threat of maternal and infants' lives. Several studies have demonstrated that in times of famine spontaneous abortions, stillbirths, and death at birth increase remarkably. Also less serious conditions like malnourishment, usually associated with low economic security and unstable living arrangements, have consequences with respect to birth defects, premature birth, or small-for-date babies. On the other hand, intervention programs have demonstrated that with food supplement in impoverished areas, health status conditions and also intellectual development can be substantially improved. Since measles immunization reaches about 80% of the Western as well as the non-Western world, this disease has more or less disappeared as a major teratogenetic factor. However, a new threat for children's lives has appeared since the 1980s with the AIDS virus. Although more than 6,000 pregnancies in the USA are affected by AIDS, it is a much bigger problem in some African or Asian societies. About 50% of the babies of HIV positive mothers become affected by the virus passing through the placental barrier or by exposure to mother's blood during delivery. The problems increase further when the mothers, or, in two-parent families, even both parents die early, leaving their children orphaned. The Zambian government runs programs addressing especially the situation of these children.

Drugs such as medication, coffee, alcohol, nicotine, cocaine, and heroine are again more

Western-biased dangers to children's and of course mothers' health. Smoking is one of the few known factors associated (though not causally linked) to the Sudden Infant Death Syndrome (SIDS) – the unexpected death of otherwise healthy babies, especially during the first 6 months of life. Serious alcohol consumption during pregnancy is significantly associated with the fetal alcohol syndrome (FAS), including an abnormal small head with an underdeveloped brain, eye abnormalities, congenital heart disease, and facial malformations. Mental retardation can occur even if the full FAS is not seen.

Generally the teratogenic effects are most disastrous if damage occurs during the first weeks of pregnancy. If individual organs have already developed, their susceptibility to detrimental effects is highest during their initial growth period. The effects are interindividually variable. Not all infants exposed to a specific substance at a specific time develop the same consequences. General genetic, health, and contextual factors of mothers and babies individualize the effects.

Birth and the Newborns' Condition

The fact of birth is a memorable event with special rites and ceremonies all over the world. In industrialized cultures, hospital birth is the rule with medical technology determining the experiences to a large extent. Delivery is often a painful experience so that many modern mothers decide to take anesthetics, especially peridural anesthesia which affect 'only' the lower part of the body. In cases where labor is difficult and especially painful or the baby is not in the head-first position, the baby is delivered by Cesarean section. During the last decades, the practice of Cesarean section has come under serious criticism, since it obviously increased disproportionally in frequency in some hospitals on Fridays. On the other hand, medical intervention saves the lives of thousands of infants and mothers.

At the beginning of the normal birth process, infants produce adrenaline which facilitates the absorption of the liquid from the lungs and, thus, breathing and increases the blood flow. The pressure through the birth canal provides the infant with tactile and vestibular experiences which are supposed to influence the regulation of behavioral states like sleep, wakefulness, or fussiness. Any medication affects the attentional system of the infant and thereby bonding and attachment processes. During the process of delivery, infants may experience oxygen deficits which can be very harmful for brain development. The American anesthesiologist Virginia Apgar developed in 1953 a quick screening technique of the neurological condition of the infant which continues to be used worldwide. The Apgar Test consists of a rating (0, 1, 2) of five vital signals (heart rate, respiratory effort, muscle tone, reflex responsivity, and color). The test is administered 1, 5, and 10 minutes after birth. The optimal score is 10. A score of 4 or below necessitates immediate medical intervention.

Studies conducted in the 1970s documented that early relationship formation, especially on the part of the mother (bonding), might be facilitated by extended contact between mother and newborn. Although these results could not be replicated satisfactorily, they had beneficial societal consequences in changing the usual hospital routines. Rooming-in (the infant stays in the mother's room for the day or even over night) was introduced and appreciated especially by first-time mothers. Also fathers' attendance at delivery was supported. The presence of fathers, however, is not popular or even taboo in many non-Western cultures where the delivering woman is surrounded by other women of her kin or village supporting and guiding her. There are also cultures where the expectant mother gives birth without the assistance of anybody else. An expectant Eipo mother in Papua New Guinea who feels that she is close to delivery separates from her community. She gives birth in a kneeling position which is popular across different cultures and evaluated by gynecologists as the physiologically most appropriate way to deliver. She might even decide about the life of the newborn during the first minutes, since resources for subsistence in the small valleys are restricted.

One of the major risks which threatens a more or less normal pregnancy concerns preterm birth at a gestational age (from conception to birth) less than 37 weeks and low birth weight less than 2,500 grams, possibly based on fetal growth retardation. Ten percent of all births in the USA are preterm with the special risks of immature lungs, digestive and immune systems. Besides teratogenic factors, especially living in poverty contexts and reproductive patterns associated with these risk factors, like very young age at first birth, poor health of the mother, and close spacing of children, define the reality of large, mainly rural populations of non-Western societies. In India, the prevalence of low birth weight babies according to the above definition ranged between 26–57% in urban slums and 35–41% in rural communities, according to national statistics of 1987–1988 compiled by UNICEF. A 1993–1994 survey of the Deepak Charitable Trust in a rural area of the state of Gujarat reports 38% of low birth weight babies.

Low birth weight increases the risk of neurological deficiencies, impairment of growth potential and decrease in intellectual capacities. Prematurity can be compensated during the course of the following development, especially when the family context is affluent and supportive.

The Equipment of the Newborn

The normal full-term baby enters the world well prepared for the first developmental tasks to master. Crucial for survival and development is a special caregiving environment. Therefore infants ought to be able to attract and maintain the attention of their caregivers. The special combination of facial features like a large head in relation to the body, a round face, relatively large eyes, and a prominent forehead constitute the 'Kindchenschema' (babyness) that Konrad Lorenz (1969) had identified to attract attention and elicit caregiving responses also in other species than humans. Commercial industry is taking advantage of this stimulus pattern in distinct ways and also comic heroes are designed accordingly. However, not all infants are equally attractive and also human parents make a difference. Mothers of less attractive newborn girls were more attuned to other people than mothers of attractive girls (Langlois, Ritter, Casey, & Sawin, 1995). This differential treatment albeit often denied from a moral perspective, is in line with evolutionary considerations about preferred allocation of investment to the offspring who promises greatest reproductive value. Attractiveness, especially in terms of body and facial symmetry, constitutes certainly a powerful evolutionary tool. Interestingly one of the aims of Indian baby massage is to enhance symmetry. Also the sad, but still numerous cases of neglect, abuse, and infanticide mainly follow an implicit evolutionary logic: they are more frequent in step-families (which include about 80–90% of step-fathers), in low economic circumstances, young parents (mothers less than 20 years) and directed more to disabled or malformed infants during the first six months of their lives (Daly & Wilson, 1988).

The resemblance that a baby has with the mother and especially the father is a further significant denominator of the newborn. Due to paternal insecurity, mothers of newborns like to assure the resemblance of the baby with the paternal line in order to secure the future paternal investment. Resemblance checks decrease with increasing age of the baby. Also the sex of the baby and the ordinal position are biological marker variables with a tremendous impact on developmental trajectories.

Any normal full-term infant is equipped with a set of functioning senses and the capacity and motivation to attend to the environment and to learn. Research activities since the 1950s have accumulated convincing evidence about infants' preparedness for active participation in development and have terminated a view of infancy as being the era of the 'buzzing blooming confusion' that William James had assumed, or as being the reflex creature without cortex that William Stern had in mind. The slogan of the 'competent infant' appeared, who can see and hear at birth and before, who is receptive to touch, responds to movement, can differentiate between different tastes and smells, and has functioning thermoreceptors. The pieces of information from different sensory systems can be interrelated. Newborns usually try to locate a noise with orienting movements of the eyes and the head. Newborns are able to direct their attention selectively to environmental cues, especially movement, contour, and contrast. They prefer novel, but not too discrepant information over familiar, and complex, but not too complex information over simple. With their short memory span of about 1 second, they detect contingencies between external events as well as person-based contingencies. They develop expectations about the occurrence of events. Another special capacity of newborns consists in the ability to segment spoken language into linguistic units (phonemes); the ability to process any spoken language becomes restricted to the mother tongue after a few weeks. Nevertheless, other research has shown that children can acquire a second language with native facility if they start the second language by age 7. Recent research has furthermore indicated that newborns have a rudimentary knowledge of biological and physical concepts.

Newborns' Behavioral States

Newborns' behavior is patterned into psychophysiological states. Extensive long-term observations of newborns by ethologically oriented scholars like Peter Wolff in the 1960s have painted a differentiated picture of different levels of arousal and activity associated with distinct modes of brain activity. Newborn babies all over the world spend most of their time, about 16 from 24 hours, asleep, yet in two different sleeping states. Quiet sleep is characterized by low muscle tone and motor activity and regular breathing. REM sleep is characterized by Rapid Eye Movements with a higher muscle tone and more motor activity, like startles, facial grimaces, and irregular breathing. Newborns begin their sleep cycle with REM sleep, lasting for about 20 minutes, then to fall into quiet sleep for about the same time span. After two to three months, this pattern reverses in industrial countries, indicating a major shift to diurnal regulation and, thus, adult sleeping patterns. Babies in other parts of the world, however, continue to wake up several times during the night and nurse. This is related to sleeping arrangements which follow different cultural scripts. Infants in the Western world are trained very early to sleep alone in their own cot or bed and even room, thus expressing an early emphasis on the development of independence. Members of cultures with permanent contact between infant and caregiver stressing relatedness more than independence, favor co-sleeping arrangements. As John Whiting reviewed in the 1960s, mothers slept with their infants in 2/3 of the societies that he had assessed. But also the co-sleeping practices can vary tremendously. In urban slum areas in India, the whole family sleeps on the floor in the only room of the house. If there is a bed available, the father will sleep on it, possibly also his brother, if he lives with the family. In West Cameroonian Nso farmers, the mother sleeps in her bed, the children behind her, the youngest one closest to her. The mother faces the door in order to protect her children from bad spirits which might wish to harm the baby or take it back. The father sleeps alone in his own house or room.

Also waking time is differentiated into two states according to arousal and activity level. Alert inactivity is a state of concentrated attentiveness to the environment with only low motor activity. Babies in the state of alert inactivity are most interested in social interactions. Active wakefulness describes increased motor activity which might lead to irritability and distraction. Two transitory states between waking and sleeping can be observed. One can be described as drowsiness with low motor activity and eyes glazed; the other can be categorized as fussiness with high motor irritability, often leading to crying. It is interesting that in the Western literature crying is described as a behavioral state. This is due to the extended duration of crying in Western babies as compared with infants who are carried a good portion of the day. !Kung San babies have the same crying frequencies as American babies, similar cry curves over the day with an evening peak and a similar cry curve over the first months with a peak at about 2 months of age. However, their cry durations are significantly shorter than that of American babies.

There are tremendous interindividual differences within all of these areas. Infants differ with respect to their activity levels, having different needs concerning the amount of sleep which often diverge from their parents' needs and expectations, they differ in their amounts of crying, their attention spans vary, the learning rates are different, the transitions between the states are more or less smooth. These interindividual differences are mainly captured by two integrative concepts in the literature: temperament and emotional regulation.

The Study of Temperament and Emotional Regulation

The vast interest in the study of temperament in infants and small children that arouse, astonishingly without any reference to the older European temperament research in personality, can be traced back mainly to the New York longitudinal study conducted by Alexander Thomas and Stella Chess in the late 1950s. With questionnaire data that the two pediatricians collected from parents of a broad socioeconomic and ethnic variety, they tried to identify the stylistic components of behavior, with respect to nine behavioral traits which were then combined into three types:

- easy babies who made up about 40% of the sample with regular rhythms, neutral to positive mood, and adaptable to new situations;
- difficult babies who were mainly irregular in their rhythms and had difficulties to adapt to new situations with a negative mood made up 20%;
- slow to warm-up babies covering another 15% of the sample needed more time to adapt to new situations than easy babies with a tendency to withdraw, but in a mild style with neutral mood.

The field expanded with different scholars defining a wide variety of temperamental dimensions, like sociability, emotionality, reactivity, self-regulation. These temperament researchers basically assume that temperamental differences are correlated with physiological parameters and that temperament is genetically based and stable from the beginning. Twin studies comparing monozygotic twins sharing 100% of alleles with dizygotic twins or siblings (sharing 50% of alleles), have been conducted in order to estimate similarities and differences in behavior with respect to the genetic influence. A second method assesses the correlation between genetically related and adopted siblings with respect to the exhibition of particular behaviors. Empirical evidence clearly demonstrates that genetic influence cannot be demonstrated shortly after birth. This might possibly be due to the birth experience or the strong effect of biorhythms on the behavior. From 4 months on, temperamental differences seem to be stable and from 6 months on, the genetic influence on temperamental dimensions is relatively visible (40–60%). However, similar estimations are reported also for intelligence and other personality traits like aggressiveness, implying that temperament is not more genetically based than other personality traits. Thus, the question remains open what differentiates temperament from inter-individual differences in behavior in general or personality in particular.

Shared environmental influences like the impact of parental education or socioeconomic circumstances do not influence temperamental traits. Non-shared environmental influences like pre- and perinatal conditions, differential parental treatment associated with sex or sibling position on the other hand, exert substantial influences on temperamental traits, also validating again evolutionary assumptions about the effects of differential parental investment. There are interesting ethnic differences: cross-cultural researchers have reported differences in activity level between Caucasian and non-Caucasian babies; Chinese-American and Mayan babies seem to be more placid and less active as compared with Euro-American babies. Patricia Greenfield and Carla Childs (1991) have integrated slow movement patterns of Zinancantec Indian babies which might be genetically rooted into a cultural contextual perspective when they report that slow movements are cultural highly valued in this community and shape the developmental context from intrauterine experiences until mate preferences.

Recently – maybe due to the conceptual and methodological problems associated with the study of temperament – emotional reactivity and regulation is regarded as a specific area of research. Based on discrete emotion theory, it is assumed that infants are equipped with basic emotions at birth, like joy, fear, anger, disgust, and distress. These emotions communicate the mood and viability of the infant and regulate approach and avoidance behaviors towards familiar and unfamiliar persons and objects. In particular the dynamic aspects of emotion, like arousability and intensity are related to the physiological underpinnings. Also vagal tone and the release of cortisol have been associated with the internal regulation of novelty and stress. There is, however, no one-to-one equivalence of physiological and behavioral manifestations of emotions, thus stressing the view that emotional experience is regulated in different functional systems. This differentiation allows the baby to learn the expression of emotions according to cultural scripts as well as the possibly adaptive strategy of deception concerning emotions in specific social contexts.

14.3 Relationship Formation as the First Integrative Developmental Task

The Cultural Formation of a Primary Social Matrix

Psychological development synthesizes a biologically based, yet culturally shaped conception of the self. Crucial for this integrative achievement is the acquisition of a social identity, based on social relationships. Accordingly, the development of primary relationships, the construction of a social matrix, is an early universal developmental task across cultures. However, the social contexts and the cultural scripts differ.

The seminal contributions of John Bowlby and Mary Ainsworth since the late 1960s have alerted researchers to the importance of developing attachment towards the primary caregivers, especially the mother, as a phylogenetically evolved behavioral system. The formation of a specific attachment quality at the end of the first year is assumed to be based on preceding interactional experiences, mainly maternal sensitivity as the prompt, consistent, and adequate response to infants' cues, especially distress, and organizes the consequent social and cognitive behavioral development. Three attachment qualities were identified in Mary Ainsworth's original Baltimore sample of 105 children: secure attachment (B-attachment) comprises about 70% of the sample and is mainly defined as proximity seeking after distress; insecure avoidant attachment (A-attachment) with 20% of the sample consists mainly in contact avoiding after distress; insecure ambivalent attachment (C-attachment) with 10% of the sample consists of proximity seeking as well as avoiding behaviors after distress. A fourth type was later added by Mary Main as a disorganized (D) pattern of attachment consisting mainly of unpredictable and inappropriate, but intensive behaviors like stereotypical movements or freezing of movements. The attachment quality is supposed to be translated during the next two years into an internal working model which comprises representations of the self, the caregiving persons and the relationships. Mary Ainsworth developed a laboratory assessment procedure, the Strange Situation Test, in order to assess the quality of attachment. During a field study in Ganda, she had observed that Ganda babies became distressed and upset when their mothers left the room in the family's home. Since American East-Coast babies were not especially irritated when their mothers left the room, she set up a standard procedure of separations, stranger contact, and reunion episodes in a laboratory in order to increase the stress on the baby so that the attachment system becomes activated. The procedure itself, which had been originally invented as a cultural adaptation, i.e. increasing stress in US-American babies, soon became a standardized tool, also used for cross-cultural comparisons, thus ignoring the idea that attachment as well as its expression might vary across cultures.

Cross-cultural studies of infants' social experiences as well as microanalytical observations of early interactional exchanges allow one to describe the early interactional patterns more precisely than the rating-based evaluations of attachment researchers. Humans display a universal repertoire of infant-oriented behavior supporting and maintaining preverbal dialogues. They create the frame for eye contact with continuous looking, they imitate smiles and vocalizations and they talk to infants with a special language register – baby talk or motherese – which has been observed in very different languages like Mandarin Chinese or German, consisting of a high pitch, simple structure, and prosodic contours. During the first weeks of infants' lives, these behavioral competencies are practiced until they culminate in the third month of life with extended periods of mutual eye contact framing an intensive interactional exchange of mimical and vocal/verbal behaviors. During this time, interindividual differences also become most pronounced. After the three months' period infants' interest in eye contact declines, although parents continue monitoring their infants' view until the end of the first year. Interindividual differences in infants' amount of eye contact, especially during the three months focal time period, and the developmental course over the first year have been demonstrated to be dependent upon mainly two characteristics of caregivers' behavior which seem to be independent of each other: contingency and warmth. Contingency represents the promptness of the parental response towards the infant's interactional signals. A substantial amount of parental reactions occurs within a second, thus, stressing the intuitive nature of parenting. This time window is within infants' memory capacity and allows the perception of causality with a sense of self as a causal agent as a consequence. Warmth conveys positive emotionality and attunement to the baby and is mainly embedded in emotional sharing and close bodily proximity. Parental warmth lays ground for the acquisition of conceptions of belongingness and interrelatedness (Keller, Lohaus, Völker, Cappenberg, & Chasiotis, 1999). The differential patterns of interactional exchange around the third month of life allows the assessment of interactional quality much earlier than attachment theory has proposed with the end of the first year.

The interactional patterns that have been described so far are mainly based in facial exchange and characteristic for Western-biased care arrangements. There are, however, other parental care systems prevalent during the early months that can be identified across different cultures which are equally part of the phylogenetic inheritance. The first and most basic parenting system is constituted by primary care. Although being part of any caregiving surrounding, it might constitute the sole system of parenting, especially in poverty contexts where infant mortality is high and therefore individual bonds of the mother to her children are usually not very intensive. Leigh Minturn and William Lambert have described a pattern of nursing in response to crying as the only maternal attention towards infants in the context of the Six Culture Study initiated by Beatrice and John Whiting for Indian Rajput villagers. Marten de Vries, having observed Masai babies, makes the interesting statement that infants that were fussy and of difficult temperament could more easily survive a year of extreme famine than infants that had been classified as of easy temperament. The fussier babies could alert their mothers' attention more than the easier babies and received more nursing.

A second parenting system which affords a higher parental investment consists of the body contact system ('back and hip cultures' according to John Whiting who sees their prevalence in the warm regions of the world). Body contact implies close proximity and thus warmth as a major socialization medium. Continuous infant carrying is reported from many different parts of the world, such as Africa, Papua New Guinea, Indonesia, South America, with foraging people or wandering pastoral groups demonstrating the highest amounts of infant carrying. Parenting effort in terms of the body contact system allows the mother to care for her baby and continue at the same time with her subsistence activities and daily chores. Child care becomes a co-occurring activity with the child never being alone, but at the same time never being the center of attention.

The third system of parenting is constituted by body stimulation as an exclusive dyadic activity. Body stimulation provides the infants with extensive motor experiences which foster the early development of a body self. This parenting system can be identified, for example, in African societies where babies are held and rocked in an upright position. The Indian custom of baby massage constitutes another example of body stimulation.

The fourth caregiving system consists of face-to-face interactions which are prevalent in the Western industrialized world and in the middle and upper middle classes of non-Western societies. The display of face-to-face interaction, including verbal/vocal exchange, as a socialization context is obviously related to the caregiver's experience of formal schooling (Greenfield & Cocking, 1994), especially language-based social interactions and instructions. Caregiving contexts with extended face-to-face exchange usually do not have extended body contact contexts. US-American babies are carried only half as often as Gusii babies. In fact, carrying and body contact mainly constitute reactions towards distress in Western contexts. Face-to-face exchange requires an exclusive focus of attention from the caregiver towards the infant and therefore represents a costly investment strategy.

The most prominent mode of caregiving all over the world, however, consists of varying composites of these different systems which accentuate different caregiving behaviors differently and, thus, provide infants with diverging experiences in the process of developing a sense of self (Keller, in press).

Although the mother is the primary caretaker in virtually all cultures, there are nevertheless substantial differences with respect to the definition of family and accordingly the composition of the social environment for the infant. In the Western world, the mother spends more than 90% of the waking time with the infant and is usually the only one to address all the infant's needs. In an extended or joint household as in Africa or India, mothers usually attend to distress, whereas social play and physical exercises might be mainly performed by grandmothers or siblings forming multiple caretaking arrangements. Child care can also be understood as the obligation of a whole village when family literally means the place where the fire burns, as in rural parts of the Ivory Coast. In particular the role of fathers has received a lot of attention in the 1970s and 1980s in the literature. Although the factual involvement with infants might be usually small, covering not much more than presence during about an hour of infants' waking time in Western studies, with a few known exceptions of high paternal involvement like the Aka Pygmies in Central Africa, the indirect effects of father's presence and support are significant as the detrimental effects of father's absence, especially for small children, e.g. in the South American Ache, have revealed. The early relational experiences form the starting points for different developmental trajectories or pathways across the lifespan.

By about 3 months of age, infants have achieved a neurological and behavioral organization that enables them to venture for new developmental tasks. Robert Emde and colleagues have labeled this developmental transition as the first bio-behavioral shift. In fact, in very different cultures a developmental transition is celebrated during this age span. In India, rituals are performed that expose the infant to the sun. In Cameroonian Fulani pastorals, infants are introduced into the social community. Western infants are expected to sleep through the night. To what extent infants from different cultures undergo the same maturational and neurological processes at this time is an open question. The acquisition of the diurnal rhythm in Western babies seems not to be a maturational achievement in the first place, but the result of applying implicit or explicit developmental and educational theories of parents (cultural scripts). We have already reported that sleep–wake states develop differently in different cultural contexts. Similarly the motor precocity of African babies might result from prior experiences with the body stimulation system, when Kipsigis babies from rural Kenya are taught to walk from the eighth week on (Bril, 1989). At the other extreme, South American Ache children start walking at 23 months on average. It can be assumed that the differential nature of the early experiences has consequences for the consequent patterns of development. There is, however, not much empirical evidence from longitudinal studies in non-Western cultures. In the following section, we will therefore concentrate on developmental consequences related primarily to face-to-face contexts.

Developmental Consequences of Early Relationship Formation

Attachment theory presented one of the first prospective approaches for developmental predictions on the assumption that the quality of attachment organizes future developmental outcomes. Securely attached children have been demonstrated to be socially more competent in interactions with their peers in preschool classes, develop more reciprocal and mutually rewarding friendships, perform better on cognitive tasks, and show less developmental problems in the following years. Also interaction researchers could document that the mode and quality of interactional patterns at about three months of age have co-occurring as well as consequent developmental consequences. The infant's amount and quality of eye contact as well as maternal interactional contingency can be related to the amount of infant crying at the same developmental time span. Consequences in different developmental domains have been identified during the following years in terms of later relationship quality, quality of exploration during the preschool years, timing of language acquisition, and development of disorders and problems during the preschool years. Interaction diagnostics and therapy programs have resulted from those studies. These developmental pathways are part of evolutionary socialization models when reproductive styles are related to early childhood experiences which seem to be especially mediated by the acquisition of early relational concepts.

Thus the quality of the early interactional experiences may have psychological, social, and somatic consequences. Not only shaping the structure of behavioral development, but also timing of the acquisition of developmental milestones seem to be influenced in a non-random way. The early onset of psychological achievements such as object permanence, exploration, and language, is supported by a secure early relationship quality that allows the child to direct its available energy actively to its own developmental progress. The early onset of somatic markers such as puberty, on the other hand, seems to be related to insecure and unstable patterns of early relationship formation.

14.4 THE COMPETENT CHILD: TODDLERS AND PRESCHOOLERS

Cultural Conceptions of Competence and Learning

In many different cultures, a next developmental transition is assumed at the age of about 2 years. US-American parents regard 'the terrible twos' as a new challenge for family development. On the South Pacific Island of Fiji, children at about 2 years gain *Vakayalo*, meaning that they are now responsible for their actions because they are able to tell right from wrong. Also Hudson Bay children have gained *iluma* or reason at 2 years (cf. Cole & Cole, 1996). Weaning at about 2 years initiates a new developmental stage in the Northwest Cameroonian Nso children who start to organize games with their peers to rehearse social roles like *Awowonie*. This mother and father game comprises household chores as well as selling, singing and dancing, funeral ceremonies, child rearing, and hunting.

Besides the struggle for independence, especially in Western societies, the emerging mental capabilities and competencies and the accompanying social responsibilities form this developmental transition. However, cultures differ with respect to their definition of competence and the modes to acquire it. Cross-cultural studies asking whether the Piagetian stages of intelligence development are universal, have identified a different conception of competence comprising social cooperation, duty and responsibility, respect and harmony in many agrarian African and Asian societies as an alternative to the Western ideal of analytical reasoning.

The differential evaluation of components constituting competence seems to be dependent on the affordances of the eco-cultural context. Based on a study comprising 21 samples from different cultures, John Berry (1976) demonstrated that there is a relationship between ecological conditions and the cognitive style of field dependence/independence. Foraging people were more independent in their perception when perceiving more details within a comprehensive visual field. This capacity allows good spatial orientation. Agrarian people for whom this ability is not crucial for survival, on the other hand, scored lower in those tasks.

The preferred and culturally esteemed modes of learning also differ across cultures. The development of Western analytical intelligence is based on formal instruction and schooling. Cultural tools like reading, writing, and calculating are acquired, independent of the daily life context. Children are expected to be curious and to ask questions in order to acquire knowledge which forms their individual action potential. Cultures stressing social competence as part of intelligence rely on observational learning within the daily life context for which the child is responsible when deciding when and how long to observe and practice. The child is rather an apprentice in this participatory learning environment where asking questions often seems to be inappropriate. The acquired competence contributes to the 'shared knowledge' of the family or primary social group. The context dependency of learning has also been documented for Brazilian street children who can calculate their trading transactions very effectively without showing any transfer to school math.

Emerging Mental Capabilities

The achievement of toddlerhood and the preschool years with the most significant developmental consequences consists in the dawning of representational thinking. The concrete and solid world of the infant becomes complemented by and transformed into a mental world that allows insightful and rational actions. Three cognitive milestones open this new territory: emerging language starting at about one year; the understanding of the concept of time at about 2½ years; and finally the developing theory of mind at about 3½ to 4 years (cf. Bischof-Köhler, 1998). These achievements allow the child to integrate the early conception of the self as being composed from self-recognition, agency, relatedness, and body awareness in different degrees with expectations about social relationships such as empathy and reciprocity. This integration results in the establishment of a system of norms and values.

A long and interesting debate is documented in the behavioral sciences as to whether these capacities are uniquely human or whether they also characterize the behavior of other species, especially nonhuman primates. Wolfgang Köhler (1921) was the first to document that chimpanzees do not only follow trial and error during problem solving, but come to 'insightful' solutions by mental probing when they visually scan the problem situation (how to reach a banana) to come up spontaneously with a correct solution after a short while (to use boxes as platforms). However, Birch (1945) experimentally documented with six chimpanzees, aged 4–5 years, that the 'insight' was largely dependent on prior experiences. Nevertheless, today there seems to be no doubt that at least rudimentary forms of cognitive representations and language are existent in nonhuman primates. Chimpanzees can produce utterances and learn a symbol language (Premack & Premack, 1983). They can interpret relational functions (like 'smaller than'), they can learn to perform simple mathematical calculations and follow verbal instructions (cf. Dunbar, 1996). The vocal production of different primate societies have been identified as communicative in nature. They inform each other about approaching individuals and their social ranks (Cheney & Seyfarth, 1994). Also simple forms of anticipation have been observed when chimpanzees collect stones before they set out for an area where nuts are growing which they crack (Boesch & Boesch, 1990). They can recognize themselves in a mirror and have a rudimentary focus of social cognition when they demonstrate that they understand the intention of others. Again Wolfgang Köhler had observed that the chimpanzee Sultan demonstrated to a younger female how to reach a banana after having observed that she did not understand what Köhler wanted her to learn. With the understanding of the intentions and desires of others, deception and cheating co-evolved. Volker Sommer reports many examples of 'tactical deception' among primates in his book 'Lob der Lüge' (praise the lie) (1992).

However, nonhuman primates do not produce language spontaneously. Neither do they have the strong desire to learn the names of things or to name objects. Also language trained chimpanzees do not display a distinct motivation to teach language to their offspring and they do not keep the stones with which they crack the nuts for the next occasion.

Representational Development

Humans have developed new dimensions to the prerequisites by the flexible use of capacities and the extension of mental action beyond the actual situation. Only humans organize their past experiences and their future plans on an ongoing time axis. They can think about own and others' mental states and manipulate these mentally. Most important, however, seems to be the uniquely human desire to accumulate knowledge. Humans are curious, they prefer novelty over familiarity, they explore their surroundings, and they ask questions. Daniel Berlyne (1960) even proposed to conceive of epistemic curiosity as an independent motive. Although childhood is especially characterized as an exploratory stage, curiosity and the motive to become knowledgeable and understanding remain lifelong motors of human development.

Language Development

Two hypotheses have been developed for explaining and locating the occurrence of language during human history. The dominant view relates the emergence of language to the developing tool use about 50,000 years ago. The production and the use of tools are regarded as being linked to verbal instructions. Robin Dunbar (1996), however, argues that language developed as long as about 500,000 years ago, mainly to stabilize larger social groups ('acoustical grooming'). The social character of early language acquisition seems to support this theoretical account.

Human infants are equipped with the cognitive and sensory capacities to learn language from birth on. They prefer human language over other sounds and decode meaningful language units (phonemes) from the verbal input. They are motivated to produce sounds which are culturally unspecific, until about the 9th month and start afterwards with cultural 'jargoning' (Cole & Cole, 1996). Language acquisition is embedded in the early social exchange with the primary caregivers. Despite the universal occurrence of characteristics of infant-directed speech (motherese, baby talk) with high frequency, high pitch, pronounced contours, simple structure, and many repetitions, early language acquisition also follows distinct cultural scripts. Caregivers express cultural norms and values and, thus, the cultural communication code with the early language input. Senegalese Wolof mothers address more statements and questions to their infants than French mothers who modulate and adapt their utterances more to the babies' signals (Rabain-Jamain & Sabeau-Jouannet, 1997). Although language development starts at birth, the occurrence of the first (proto-)words, mainly 'mom' or 'dad', around the 10th to the 14th months demarcates a developmental milestone.

Language development proceeds then as a continuous process with three different knowledge systems interacting: prosodic competence is based on the recognition and production of rhythmical language units; linguistic competence allows development of meaning of words and phrases; and pragmatic competence directs the adequate communicative usage of phrases in different contexts (cf. Grimm & Wilde, 1998).

Children in most diverse cultural contexts obviously go through a one-word stage which is usually followed by a brief two-word period. By about 18 months, infants have acquired the 50-words limit from which they expand their vocabulary with an enormous developmental speed. By 16 years, about 60,000 words constitute adult language. The 50-words threshold demarcates the qualitative reorganization of the early lexicon. Children have acquired the abstract cognition that things have names. They are now ready to form immediately an idea about the meaning of an unknown word in an otherwise familiar and structured context ('fast mapping'). Newly acquired words may be overgeneralized when the children address all adult males as 'dad' or name all animals as dogs. On the other hand, they overdiscriminate word meanings when they restrict a word to a specific specimen, like duck only for plastic ducks, not for real animals (cf. Grimm & Wilde, 1998). The reorganization of language development following the 50-word register includes grammar learning, a decrease in the production of nouns and an increase in verbs and adverbs, most pronounced between 27 and 31 months. Syntax becomes now important as a bootstrapper, especially for abstract meanings. This developmental stage also covers phrase building which further allows decoding the meaning of non-obvious and non-concrete words.

About 13 to 20% of US-American and German children are 'late talkers', since they have not yet acquired 50 words by the age of 2 years. Half of these late talkers have caught up with normal language performance by the age of 3 to 4 years. However, 6 to 10% of these populations have developed pathology which also extends to cognitive and socio-emotional development.

Language development obviously is not based on the genetically fixed Language Acquisition Device (LAD) that Noam Chomsky had proposed in 1975. Besides, language development can only

partly be explained by reward and imitation. Language acquisition depends largely on the participation of children in social interactions with experienced tutors. Michael Tomasello and his colleagues (1993) demonstrated that children learned the meaning of words when objects were named which were part of children's ongoing activities and when mothers named words which were part of children's activities. This intuitive didactic (cf. also 'zone of proximal development') is a component of the parenting repertoire and is displayed by parents from different cultures across developmental domains, from Western style language acquisition to learning to run errands in Nigerian Yoruba toddlers. Although some cultural accounts on parameters of early language input exist, not much is known about language acquisition processes from non-Western cultures, including the fact that many non-Western children are raised in more than one mother tongue (Mohanty & Pradesh, 1993).

The Theory of Mind

The notion of a theory of mind was introduced by David Premack and G. Woodruff with their programmatic article 'Does the chimpanzee have a theory of mind?' (1978) and describes the capacity to think about own and other mental states in terms of desires and beliefs. It is assumed that basic conceptions of domains like physics, biology, and psychology are inborn and organized parallel to scientific theories. The slogan of the child as an intuitive scientist allows one to describe cognitive development as restructuring different domains according to the respective level of knowledge. The cognitive world of the child is understood as complex, but unitary. This view contradicts Piaget's view which described children's difficulty to reason about other peoples' mental states with egocentrism as an immature stage of development.

Researchers differ in their opinions about the exact onset of a theory of mind. 'Boosters' (cf. Chandler, Fritz, & Hala, 1989) acknowledge social referencing (refer visually to the mother in ambiguous situations) as early as the first year as an index of a theory of mind which is followed by symbol play during the second year and the recognition of others' mental states and emotions in three-year-olds. 'Scoffers' restrict the theory of mind to the competence to recognize false beliefs. In particular the following experimental situation to assess false beliefs by Heinz Wimmer and Josef Perner (1983) has received tremendous attention.

In a doll play situation, the doll 'Maxi' puts candies into one drawer and then leaves the room. The candies are then relocated by the adult experimenter into a different drawer. Maxi returns and the participating child is asked where Maxi will look for the sweets.

Most three-year-old children answer that Maxi will look into the drawer where the candies actually are, without acknowledging that Maxi has no information about the relocation. Only 3½- to 4-year-old children can recognize the false belief. There is scarce evidence from other cultural backgrounds about the timing of the development of reasoning about other peoples' thinking. Jeremy Avis and Paye Harris (1991) presented a similar hiding story to Baka children from Southeast Cameroon. These children too could give the right answers somewhere between 3 and 5 years.

Only at that age do children understand the relationship between accessibility of information, the resulting knowledge and possibility of actions in others and themselves. As a consequence, children apply the view about right and wrong opinions for themselves as well as for others. At the same age, children begin to disentangle causality and intentionality. Until then, they attribute an intention to any event, even in the inanimate world. This new achievement opens the door for deceiving others intentionally, which occurs first at about 4½ years. They are now able to describe the perspective of another person correctly, start referential communication, such as referring to the informational level of another person and start to differentiate appearance from reality. John Flavell and colleagues have demonstrated this differentiation with examples like a sponge that appeared to be a rock and a stone that appeared to be an egg. Chinese, Japanese, British, and US-American three-year-olds were likely to answer incorrectly, four-year-olds seemed to be in a transition state and five-year-olds finally seemed to be able to differentiate fact from fancy consistently. Older siblings seem to accelerate the development of a theory of mind, thus underlining the impact of non-parental socialization influences.

Social Cognition

The main social cognitive progress that toddlers achieve is the development of empathy. Empathy describes the sharing and understanding of the emotional state or intention of another person as distinct from oneself. Thus empathy is different from emotion contagion which might already occur in infants when they start crying upon hearing other babies cry. Doris Bischof-Köhler (1989) has studied empathy with the following quasi-experimental design. Children from 15 to 24 months played with an adult playmate in a laboratory room. Suddenly a teddy bear lost its arm or a spoon broke. The adult displayed open distress. The children reacted with four different patterns of behavior. The 'empathic helper' understood the situation, tried to help and to console the playmate. 'Helpless-confused' children felt obviously uncomfortable, sometimes seemingly concerned, but without knowing what to do. 'Emotionally infected' children started crying themselves, because they obviously could not attribute the distress to the adult, but rather felt it themselves. 'Unconcerned children' finally continued playing without paying attention to what had happened to their playmate. It is interesting that the achievement of empathy was directly related to the ability to recognize oneself in a mirror. The classical procedure to assess mirror recognition consists in confronting the infant who has been marked with something unusual in the face, like a red nose or a black dot on the cheek with the mirror image. All self-directed behaviors, including self-naming, are interpreted as indicating self recognition. All children classified as 'empathic' had recognized themselves in the mirror. The 'confused' and the 'emotionally infected' children were obviously in a transition state of self recognition with avoiding the mirror image; the 'concerned' children finally did not recognize themselves in the mirror. Having developed the representation of a distinct image of the self allows also the distinct perception of the emotional reality of another person. Based on maturational mechanisms, empathy can only occur during the second year of life, whereas mirror recognition might occur several months earlier. Later stages of empathy development during early childhood (~ 3–6 years) are related to language and symbol use. Empathy can then be expressed in more subtle ways even for people who are not present. Between 6 and 9 years finally, children start to understand the reality of other persons beyond the actual situation with acknowledging the effects of illness or poverty, thus beginning to become aware of societal concerns.

The development of empathy can be regarded as an important precursor for the prosocial motive of sympathy which enables the child to help and support others; however, also other factors like mood and perceived competence modulate the actual behavior in a concrete situation. Prosocial behaviors, like sharing, helping, and cooperating with others, are part of the evolutionary heritage. Due to evolutionary theorizing, altruism first developed in the context of kin selection, since supporting genetic relatives seemed to improve the own inclusive fitness (nepotistic altruism). However, with the necessity of enlarging the size of social groups for better resource acquisition and protection against predators, reciprocal altruism developed, since it became beneficial to help others, if returns could be expected. The representation of time even enabled our ancestors to postpone the expected returns into the future. The expectations of reciprocity become a major link between individuals and foster group cohesion. A balanced reciprocity account of giving and taking seems to be part of social relationships in most diverse cultural environments, even in ritualized ways like the Potlatch of native North American Indians or the Kula that Bronislaw Malinowski so vividly described in the 'Argonauts of the Western Pacific' (1979).

Doris Bischof-Köhler points to negative social consequences which also become accessible with the development of empathy, like envy, gloating, ill will, and aggression. Some authors also understand guilt as a consequence of empathic identification in terms of feeling responsible for the other's situation. These tendencies are also rooted in humans' evolutionary heritage.

The Development of Gender Identity

After having established a basic sense of self, children are ready for the next developmental task, i.e. to acquire their gender identity at about 2 years. Gender identity denotes the self-representation of the sex or gender, whereas the gender role is assigned to the social display of the identity. One of the earliest theoretical proposals for the explanation of the developmental processes of gender identity is rooted in Sigmund Freud's stage model of development. Starting from the assumption that all biological drives have the goal of survival and procreation of the species, the fundamental sex drive (libido) is conceived of as the motor of development. Sexual gratification proceeds during development through stages that denote the parts of the body that satisfy the drive. The first stage is the oral stage, where the mouth is the primary source of pleasure. In the second year of life the anal stage focuses on sphincter control. During the fourth year, the phallic stage, the genitals become the center of pleasure seeking. During this stage, the developmental pathways of boys and girls begin to diverge. Boys develop sexual feelings for their mothers and often express the wish to marry her. Girls mainly experience penis envy. Between 6 and 7 years, the turmoil calms down in a latency stage which lasts until puberty. During the latency stage, the sexual desires are suppressed, instead adult skills and values are acquired. During puberty, sexuality reappears in the genital phase and is now directed towards mating partners.

Especially for boys, identification with the father is achieved by solving the conflicts related to the Oedipus complex (the analogous Electra complex for female development is not similarly elaborated). Feelings of anxiety and guilt as directed at the father while desiring the mother, are transformed into identification with the father, at the same time laying the foundation for moral development (the super ego).

Freud was attacked from many different perspectives for his speculative theorizing. Although his stage model may need reformulation, he should nevertheless receive credit as one of the few early scholars who claimed that childhood development is central for adult personality formation.

Social learning theorists have proposed that observation and imitation are the roots of development in general and sex role adoption in particular, thus excluding the emotional character of Freudian identification. Observation and imitation are complemented by parental reward and prohibition/punishment strategies that are especially salient for sex-typical activities (like rough and tumble play).

During recent decades, by far the most attention has been given to the cognitive approach proposed by Lawrence Kohlberg (1966) which is based on Jean Piaget's cognitive developmental theory. According to this view, the child constructs the gender concept actively like any other cognitive schema. Identity formation is pursued through several consecutive stages. Children start by becoming aware of categorical differences between the sexes. Mostly based on parameters of outer appearance, like body shape or hair style, they are able by 2 to 3 years of age to differentiate men from women. This view is in line with evolutionary theorizing which postulates epigenetic rules that facilitate the acquisition of gender-related information early in life (cf. Daly & Wilson, 1988). The next stage consists in recognizing similarities with the one or other sex. At about 3 years, children are able to label themselves as boys or girls and have thus acquired the basic or core gender identity. The next stage concerns gender stability when children begin to understand that sex roles do not change over time, which is followed by gender constancy, the independence of the gender schema of situation or context. Even wearing a dress, a boy remains a boy. Gender schema theorists have modified the original Kohlbergian approach with supplementary assumptions, that children's gender schema knowledge nourishes the interest in gender-linked activities and behavior.

With the establishment of the core gender identity (stage 1), children's preferences in fact become biased against sex. Boys do not want to play with girls and do girlish things and vice versa. The gender topic controls children's activities to a large extent and they develop marked preferences for their own sex.

The Emergence of Moral Standards

Children are now ready to become aware of the evaluation of behavior, of what is considered to be good or bad, right or wrong in their family. The earliest awareness of moral standards are children's assessments of the evaluative response of their caregivers. This view implies that in the beginning moral standards are imposed from outside, especially from the experience with powerful others, ascribing cultural standards a prominent place for defining the content of moral obligations. Jean Piaget proposed to conceive of this 'morality of constraints' as heteronomous morality. He told children pairs of stories in which a child causes a mishap – in one case pursuing a selfish interest and in the other case an effort to be helpful. He then asked the children evaluative questions about the stories. Until middle childhood, children's evaluations are guided by the amount of the mishap without taking the intention into consideration. With increasing interactions with peer groups, the heteronomous standards are replaced by autonomous morality which is based on an understanding of norms and rules as arbitrary agreements. Through the process of internalization, the external knowledge becomes part of the inner psychological functioning and part of the conception of the self. Based on the achievements of the theory of mind, an inner voice observes and guides the evaluation of self and others. This inner voice constitutes the conscience and acts as the keeper of moral standards. Shame and guilt are moral emotions that develop during the second until the sixth year (Erikson, 1976). The internal standards are visible in behavior which becomes regulated through self control. Related to self control is the ability for compliance with caregivers' demands. The ability to inhibit immediate impulses is based on the newly acquired capacity of time representation, allowing to plan ahead.

The developmental status of the child that is about to enter middle childhood reflects the emotional experiences as well as the cognitive achievements in his or her behavioral organization that are expected from the cultural scripts constituting the symbolic environment in which their developmental pathways are embedded.

14.5 CHILDHOOD: SOCIAL PRIMING AND COGNITIVE APPRENTICESHIP

Childhood demarcates the developmental period that begins around the 6th year of age and lasts until the beginning of puberty. Although the worlds of childhood differ remarkably across cultures, the beginning forms again a pancultural transition. In Germany, mandatory school attendance starts at 6 years of age. The Ifaluk of Micronesia believe that 6-year-old children begin to perform valued adult behaviors, like the ability to work, to adhere to social norms and demonstrate compassion for others (Lutz, 1987). The Ngoni of Malawi associate the loss of milk teeth around 6 years of age with more independence and responsibilities (Read, 1968). At about 6 years, Kenyan Kipsigis children are considered as mature enough to perform small purchases (Harkness & Super, 1983). The Cameroonian Nso children start understanding why the social norms are supposed to be the way they are, why there are taboos, and why they should be respected. They run errands, and tether goats and chickens.

This transition marks maturational, social, and cognitive changes which extend the children's range of action to the larger cultural context by the assignment of responsibilities.

Cultural Conceptions of Childhood

The enormous differences of childhood in different cultures were summarized by Urie Bronfenbrenner (1977) as the two worlds of childhood when he described the lives of US-American and those of former Soviet Union children. His report clearly demonstrated that different political ideologies have a tremendous impact on socialization contexts and activities that are adhered to children within these contexts. Cross-cultural evidence, however in line with sociobiological thinking, indicates that the differing worlds of childhood (as well as adulthood) are mainly shaped by the availability of economic resources and the respective level of industrialization.

The Western child extends his home range and starts exploring the physical surroundings on its own or with friends and peers. In particular the detailed description of Roger Barker and Herbert Wright (1951) of 'One Boy's Day' in 'Midwest', USA, has evidenced that adults' supervision over children's time has tremendously decreased. The streets and empty urban lots became the attractive places to be, especially for boys. Martha Muchow has reported similar observations from pre-war Hamburg in Germany where a distant department store became a favorite location with boys, who were more adventurous and enterprising than girls. Except for exploration and play, children's days are largely structured by school attendance and extra-curricular classes like sports, ballet, and drama. In contrast to their agrarian, foraging, or pastoral non-Western counterparts, Western children's activities are either part of their education or recreation. Although many parents promote group activities, so that their youngsters rehearse social behavior, the socialization goals are focused on individual performance and achievement.

Enlarging the ecology with peers is also part of the Nso farmers' childhood socialization in West Africa. Peers learn from each other, playing adult roles in coffee plantations, uninhabited houses, or corners of the central compound. Each child brings his or her own basket with food which they eat together at midday. Out of their own curiosity, they leave the compound searching for firewood, hunting rabbits, fetching water, harvesting bush nuts. Also sex-segregated activities are common when boys play and form 'secret societies' to which girls do not have access. Sibling care is part of the daily program of children at that age with girls being more involved than boys.

The West African pastoral Fulani child's activities during this age span also mainly consist of informal learning from the activities of others and from stories. These children gradually start running minor errands and become primed into the significance of cattle in the society. Especially boys might be given the task of keeping the calves from straying into huts or eating grain. Cattle education preoccupies boys' time at this period as they learn the types of grass which most appeal to the cattle and general dietary needs of herds. Girls start accompanying their mothers to sell butter, milk, or cosmetics fabricated from leaves and bark of trees. They learn to prepare the special Fulani shelter and other household utensils. On attaining 7 or 8 years of age, the male child is initiated by circumcision, and he immediately abandons the feminine world.

Still another world of childhood is characterized by children's participation in the labor force, outside the social protection of the family or the village. Especially children from urban slums have to contribute to the family income, mostly by trading on their own in the streets of the big cities. There is, however, also a substantial number of children living in the streets and supporting themselves. In 1985 UNICEF estimated that there were 100 million street children in the world. Most of them continue to maintain contact with their families. Violence against children living in streets is a major threat in many parts of the world.

Reorganization of Mental Skills

Starting at about 5 years, changes in brain structure and function have important consequences for mental development. The change in the electroencephalogram (EEG) is especially dramatic. Until about 5 years, awake children display more theta activity, which is characteristic of adult sleep, than alpha waves, which characterize adult attentional processes. After a phase of equal amounts of theta and alpha activity between 5 and 7 years, alpha activity becomes predominant, thus establishing the adult pattern. Myelinization, the process in which neurons become covered with the fat substance myelin, increases and allows higher speed of transmission of nerve impulses, the numbers of synapses (connections between neurons) increases and the EEG activity becomes more synchronized. At about 8 years, these activities reach a plateau and remain stable thereafter. These maturational changes allow children more complex functioning of their mental activities. The formation of explicit action plans, the emerging self-reflection, the extension of the memory span accompany these maturational changes which, however, cannot be causally linked (Case, 1992). Jean Piaget (1983) directed special attention to concrete operations as the emerging new form of thought. These mental actions or operations allow to combine, separate, and transform information following logical laws, however still restricted to concreteness in terms of tangible objects or thoughts about objects. According to his general cognitive developmental theory, Piaget assumed that concrete operations transform all psychological domains. He assumed that general principles are acquired, like conservation and reversibility. Conservation denotes that a property (like sex and gender) or a substance (like amount of liquid) remain the same, although appearance or shape might vary. Reversibility or negation describe the understanding of the possibility or impossibility of reversing states and actions. Piaget proposed specific and most creative experimental procedures for assessing diverse mental capabilities.

The most popular conservation task starts with the presentation of two identical glasses filled with the same amounts of liquid. The experimenter asks the child whether the amounts are the same in the two glasses. If the child agrees, the experimenter pours the content of one glass into a smaller and thinner glass and asks the child whether the higher rise of liquid in the new glass still represents the same amount of liquid or more or less. Children about 3 to 4 years old insist that there is more liquid, since they can only focus on a single dimension or attribute. Only around age 8, can children consider the height and circumference of the glasses and make correct judgments.

Piaget's conclusions are nevertheless challenged by discoveries like the domain and context specificity of cognitive functioning as well as the procedural character of mental activity. Cross-cultural studies have shown that the performance of cognitive capacities mainly relies on the familiarity of problem and material.

The Social World of Childhood

The most dramatic change in the lifestyle in middle childhood is the significant increase in time that children spend with peers as compared with their parents. Nevertheless the peer group is differently defined in different cultures. In the Western world, the peer group is composed of self-selected age mates who share interests and attitudes. However, accessibility like the neighborhood or parental selection of contexts like school classes, holiday preferences, friends' network and the like, play a major role. In the Arabian world, the peer group is constituted mainly by family members, the most intimate one being constituted of siblings, followed by cousins and finally neighbors as a more distant peer group.

Yet siblings play a special role in children's development not only in traditional societies. Being raised with siblings creates a distinct socialization climate, especially with respect to the ordinal position or birth rank that a child inherits. Frank Sulloway (1997) recently documented with a wealth of biographical information that the ordinal position within a family may constitute rather predictable developmental challenges in terms of becoming more conservative or more creative, as one example. Psychological interest in sibling research became especially evident in studies which tried to assess the developmental transition from a one-child family to two-children families with the necessity to reorganize the family system. For the parents this transition constitutes the second major task of family development after the transition to parenthood with the first child. There is evidence that the second child experiences less unshared attention from the parents, especially the mother's, since the added demands on the mother's attention reduce her interaction time. It can further be assumed that especially inexperienced Western mothers have developed more trust and security in their competence of child care, so that their interactional style becomes less anxious and tense and thus more emotionally warm. But siblings also influence each other

directly as studies, especially of cognitive development, have demonstrated. Children with siblings seem to be advanced with respect to social perspective-taking skills as compared with single children, and younger siblings appreciate the advice provided by their older siblings when they consult more with their sibling than with a friend in mastering tasks.

But relationships between siblings can be conflictual and stressful at the same time. With the parental investment theory, John Trivers proposed a sociobiological account of differences in parents' allocation of investment in boys and girls depending on the available resources. Parents should tend to invest more in their girls in poor contexts, since their reproductive success is less variable than that of boys who in turn should be 'preferred' under affluent circumstances. There are historical as well as contemporary data confirming this view. On the other hand, the preference for sons over daughters, e.g. in India, extends also to poverty contexts. More research is needed, especially tackling the interaction between sex and birth position, to better understand these processes.

The peer group is often contrasted with family constituting 'external influences' on children's development. These comparisons, however, seemingly compare apples with pears. Children do not become friendly or hostile because their peers are friendly or hostile. As we have argued earlier, there is developmental continuity translating early interactional experiences into a working model of the self which facilitates the acquisition of specific personality traits in interaction with genetic predispositions. The first follow-up studies of attachment research in the 1970s documented that securely attached children have smooth and rewarding relationships with their peers. On the psychological basis laid by the early relationship formation, social roles within the peer groups are negotiated, social ranks are established, and the experience of reward and frustration shapes the continuous process of personality development. Thus, the subtle and organizational influence of early family environment and the following socialization contexts need longitudinal research where previous and concurrent influences can be compared; self reports (questionnaires) administered during children's middle childhood obviously cannot capture the developmental dynamics adequately.

Numerous studies have investigated children's play groups and analyzed their interactional format as well as the group structure and its dynamics. The ways in which children are helpful and constructive to each other, observe rules, cheat each other, behave aggressively, are insecure, plus their physical attractiveness, make children popular, neglected or rejected. Children who are rejected often differ from popular children in many respects. Except for attractiveness, they may have difficulties in assessing social situations correctly and accordingly behave inadequately. Assessment difficulties may be related to distraction or distortion of the perception due to difficult family backgrounds. Children from poor families may be insecure; battered children or those from neglectful and abusing families may want to hide their problems. Children from immigrant families are often confronted with value systems at school and in peer groups that are different from those promoted at home, which may result in conflict in all contexts.

Piaget (1932/1965) concluded from his observations and interviews that boys and girls play different games and play the same games differently. Although his view has found support as well as contradiction, there is nevertheless a clear sex segregation to be stated during this developmental period. Children engage primarily in same-sex groups and may even avoid the other sex. Boys' activities seem to be more competitive, aggressive, stressing physical strength, whereas girls are more interested in domestic activities and relationships. Girls congregate mostly in pairs or three friends, whereas boys gather in larger groups with less intimate personal relationships. Similarity seems to be the basis for friendships. The sex differentiation of behavioral development prepares children for different sex roles. Competition and cooperation form the two dominating and discriminating value systems. Although cultural and societal values, especially in the industrialized societies, may change, children's behavioral preferences during middle childhood obviously do not alter dramatically.

Moral Reasoning and Moral Behavior

Moral judgments are reflected in meaning structures that undergo qualitative changes during development. Based on Piaget's conceptions of developmental progress from heteronomous to autonomous orientations, Lawrence Kohlberg proposed a widely accepted modified stage theory (see Kohlberg, 1966, 1976). He conducted a 30-year longitudinal study with 72 male participants who were 10 to 16 years when first assessed. The main modifications based on six assessments consisted in the definition of six stages which form three levels: the preconventional level comprises stage 1, heteronomous morality, and stage 2, instrumental morality. Heteronomous morality is governed by avoidance of punishment from an egocentric point of

view without recognizing the interests of others. Instrumental morality implies that rules are followed only if there is a personal and immediate interest. The conventional level (level II) comprises stage 3, good-child morality, and stage 4, law-and-order morality. The good-child morality which first appears at about 10 to 11 years of age, integrates social relations as a necessary part of the moral perspective. Children no longer depend on external qualifications for their judgments of right or wrong, but take reciprocal relations, shared feelings, and agreements into consideration. Stage 4 (law-and-order morality) concerns the institutionalization of social relationships. The group takes priority over the individual.

The post-conventional level (level III) comprises stage 5, social-contract reasoning, and stage 6, universal ethical principles. Social-contract reasoning expresses an obligation to the law, focusing again more on an individual, but socially responsible level. Universal ethical principles finally do not represent an empirical stage, but a deontological position. Later authors, including Elliot Turiel and colleagues, have argued that the types of rules described for the stages, especially personal concerns, conventions, and morality, do not represent an ontogenetic line of development, but are already differentiated early during development, yet have developmental contents. Personal concerns are defined as rule systems, created by the individual. Conventions concern the social expectations of a group that are consensually followed by the individuals. Moral rules finally concern social regulations that are rooted in encompassing principles of justice and welfare.

There is an extensive and ongoing debate about the universality or relativity of moral standards. Kohlberg's theory has undergone extensive cross-cultural testing. Lutz Eckensberger and Roderick Zimba conclude that, from a comprehensive review of cross-cultural data, stages 2 to 4 seem to exist transculturally, but that also cultural specifications are apparent. A variety of perspectives on morality has been offered across cultures, like the Indian moral of duty, the Confucian principle of *giri-vinjo* (obligation), or the Javanese principles of *hormab*, respect for older people, and *rukunas*, describing harmony in social relations. These conceptions might be related to Carol Gilligan's conception of morality of care and responsibility that she contrasted as female morality with Kohlberg's male view. However, many questions concerning indigenous conceptions of morality remain open.

There is another open question concerning the relationship of children's reasoning about moral issues and their concrete actions. Research clearly indicates that there is no one-to-one concord-ance between the level of moral reasoning and the respective actions. Sociobiology explains this discrepancy on the assumption that people in the first place pursue their own interests, that is, genetic interests. Regulating ideas are never-theless important, since cooperation generally promises also better individual success ('the true egoist cooperates').

The Changing Sense of Self

With the shift in social behavior and cognition, the sense of self also alters remarkably, and children are capable of reporting about them-selves, their feelings and attitudes. The signifi-cant dimensions that reorganize the internal representation of the self concern physical appearance, social comparisons with peers, activities that are mastered, and psychological characteristics. Children, but also adults with different cultural backgrounds, differ with respect to the way they describe themselves. Individuals from Western cultures describe themselves in terms of their psychological attributes, stressing especially their uniqueness and their activities, whereas members of traditional cultures describe themselves predominantly in terms of their social relationships, like being a daughter, a friend.

At about 6 years of age, children discover that internal experiences and outer appearance might diverge; at about 8 years psychological differ-entiation becomes complemented with the dis-covery that one individual person can have differ-ent, even contradictory feelings or intentions.

At around the same time, the appreciation of others concerning one's own person becomes vital for the evaluation and estimation of the self. Thus, self-esteem which was intricately intertwined with the perceptual sense of self finds expression in the reflexive self that is now emerging.

14.6 ADOLESCENCE: FAMILY FOUNDATION OR EDUCATIONAL MORATORIUM

Adolescence as the transformation phase between childhood and adulthood is not only shaped by cultural influences, but constitutes itself a culture-specific phenomenon. In traditional societies, children have now acquired the behavior, the skills, and the knowledge to participate in adult life, found a family, and contribute to the fam-ilies' subsistence. There is a continuous transition from childhood to adulthood (cf. Saraswathi, 1999). In Western societies as well as middle and upper classes of traditional societies, adoles-cence represents a culturally defined educational moratorium, disrupting the continuity between childhood and adulthood. In most cultures, tran-sitional rituals are celebrated ('rites de passage'), introducing the new social status. The cultural diversity of adolescence phases was first docu-mented by Margaret Mead in 1928 (Mead, 1928/1961), an achievement that certainly is not negated by the criticism concerning her methods of data collection.

Puberty and Maturational Changes

Puberty is the main somatic marker of ado-lescence. The development of the reproductive system with its endocrinological changes, but also the changes in body shape and growth mark distinct developmental changes. Puberty in males is initiated by interaction among the hypothala-mus, the pituitary gland, and the testes, finally discharging gonadotropins into the blood. These hormones stimulate the testes to produce testos-terone which initiates changes in the body development. The most visible male somatic markers are the growth spurt and the spermarche. The growth spurt refers to a sudden increase in height where boys might acquire about 22 cm in a relatively short period of time. The testes begin to produce sperm cells which are released spontaneously for the first time, usually during sleep. The first ejaculations occur as nocturnal emissions (wet dream). Boys develop muscles and strength.

Puberty in females is also related to the inter-action of hypothalamic activity with the pituitary glands releasing gonadotropic hormones which stimulate the ovaries to produce estrogen and progesterone triggering the physical develop-ment necessary for reproduction. Menarche is the visible somatic marker of puberty in girls. Girls also have a growth spurt, however less pronounced than boys. Girls develop breasts and their hips acquire their specific shape due to fat deposit. Evolutionary theorists argue that the hip–waist ratio is a universal descriptor of attractiveness, independent of stature.

There are vast interindividual differences in the timing of puberty. The average age at which puberty begins in today's industrialized societies is between 12 and 13 years for girls and 13 to 14 years for boys. The onset of puberty has become markedly earlier over recent decades, mainly related to better nutritional provision. However, the historical changes are not as marked for boys as they are for girls. Data from poverty contexts indicate that menarche is reached on the average at 15 to 17 or even 18 years. Interindividual variability associated with early and late matura- tion has been related to social development, per- sonality formation, and development of deviant behavior. The results are contradictory: some studies indicate that early-maturing boys are psychologically and socially more mature, other studies portray early-maturing boys as more anxious, less exploratory, and less curious than late-maturing boys. The latter view is also sup- ported by data indicating that early-maturing boys are more likely to smoke, use drugs, drink alcohol, and may even get into conflict with the law. The picture for early-maturing girls even seems to be more negative. They have problems with their stature, being taller and heavier than late-maturing girls and, maybe even more im- portant, than boys. They seem to be less emo- tionally stable and self-controlled and seem to be at risk for drug and alcohol abuse or deviant behavior, such as shoplifting and running away.

Sociobiology offers an interesting perspective on early and late maturation when addressing not only the consequences, but also highlight- ing the precursors. As we have outlined earlier, evolutionary models describe developmental pathways from early social and economic child- hood experiences, mediated by quality of attach- ment and emotional balance to the onset of puberty. Among others, studies from New Zeal- and, the United States, and Germany indicate that, especially for girls, the early childhood context – particularly divorce of the parents, all the more if this occurred during the first five years of the child's life – accelerates onset of puberty.

Changing Social Relationships

The peer groups of middle childhood acquire a new quality during adolescence. Especially in Western industrialized societies, cliques with about six youngsters who are in regular touch with each other, constitute the primary peer group. Crowds, as a larger collection of people forming 'reputation-based collectives', define a looser social organization. Nevertheless, crowds set standards and define trends and prestige, so the crowd puts pressure on peers to conform. Peer pressure is especially influential during the early years of adolescence.

Adolescents in traditional societies have at- tained adult status. The male Nso adolescents from Cameroon are now admitted to the manly activities of the community and the secret so- cieties which women do not have access to. Nso girls, as many other adolescent girls in traditional societies, marry and start having children.

Parent–Child Relationship

Adolescence has been characterized, especially in European philosophy and poetry, as a period of increased instability, turmoil, with inevit- able emotional conflict with parents. In Western societies, adolescence is a developmental time span where children develop distance from their parents and parental attempts to control the children contradict the liberation tendencies of children, who rather seek advice and guidance from their peers. The visibility of specific youth cultures which openly express divergence from the prevailing adult values often masks the fact that most youth continue to have warm and friendly relationships with their parents. As empirical studies have revealed, adolescents and their parents are generally in agreement on important issues like religion, family planning, and moral issues. Contradictions often refer to more marginal areas like hairstyle, mode of dressing, and time for coming home at night. In the public discussion of developmental influ- ences, peer influence is often overestimated. However, finding the own way is largely depend- ent on the cultural scripts for individuation. Con- forming to parental and family values, respect- ing the assigned role, and behaving accordingly are no matters of negotiation in many traditional societies. 'Mammy woteri' and 'Baa woteri' are Nso Cameroonian adolescent girls and boys who are at the end of the apprenticeship stage, and can do almost everything that the mother does (household chores, child care), and all that is considered as the duty of the father in a house- hold – disciplining the young ones, clearing the farms, and tapping palm wine. Generally the family's role remains important, also during this life stage and across cultures.

Cognitive Development

Adolescent thinking mirrors the transition to adult cognitive functioning. Piaget labeled his last stage of intelligence development as formal operational thinking. It mainly differs from concrete operations by the ongoing mental capability to consider all aspects of a problem or a situation at the same time.

Formal operational thinking allows one to develop hypotheses about possible outcomes of problems or situations and evaluate them com- paratively. With this new achievement, thinking about thinking becomes possible and complex metacognitive systems of reasoning are devel- oped. Related to this ability is second-order thinking, which allows one to follow different lines of thinking with their respective logical implications at the same time. Domain-specific increase of knowledge can be regarded as a second motor of changes in reasoning and thinking. Information-processing theories explain the flexible and integrative thinking of adolescents as a result of using more efficient strategies of information management.

The universality of formal operational thinking has been addressed as controversially as the other stages of intelligence development. On the one hand, it is argued that formal operations are necessary in order to meet the demands of adult roles and the responsibilities of adult life in any culture. However, even in middle class US-American samples, only 30–40% solve the problems proposed by Jean Piaget and Bärbel Inhelder as characterizing formal operational thinking. This specific problem solving capacity can be improved by instruction and tutoring. The interindividual differences in achieving and mastering this mode of thinking clearly perpetuate into adulthood. Sex differences, with males outperforming females in the Piagetian task, revealed the importance of the context for activating specific modes of thinking. Obviously, more boys will be interested in science contexts which mainly constitute the experimental tasks. As well as the importance of the context expressing differential interests, different strategies and modes of thinking may also exist and vary according to sex. Mathematicians have identified two successful strategies to solve mathematical tasks, with boys preferring a more analytic procedural/functional problem solving style and girls a more holistic intuitive, predicative, but equally successful strategy. The evidence that training and tutoring increase the ability for formal operational thinking includes the cross-cultural variability for attendance of formal schooling. However, Piaget himself acknowledged that difficult contextual conditions and a different exposure to training might enhance or delay the attainment of developmental stages. The analysis of these different contextual demands challenges cultural psychologists to identify and analyze indigenous ways of thought development.

Acquiring a Metaperspective on the Self

In the psychological literature, adolescence is often considered as the time span where identity formation sets the major developmental task. In particular the conception of Erik Erikson (1968) accentuated adolescence as the time to resolve the developmental crisis on the basis of the results of earlier developmental tasks. Successful graduation would be the favorite developmental goal, but impairment of the life cycle might also result. The basic developmental challenges of the preceding life stages consisted in establishing trust and autonomy, taking initiative and developing industry. These characteristics have to be synthesized together with the physical changes, cognitive skills, social experiences, and expectations for the future into one's adult sense of self. These views on the self can differ with respect to successful integration, as James Marcia (1980) concluded from interviews with male college students. He developed four identity patterns which can be described as 'identity diffusion' (the adolescent tried out several identities without finding his/her own way; the prevalence of identity diffusion decreases from the pre-highschool years to the college upper class years); 'identity achievement' (the adolescent has made choices concerning self-evaluation, social commitments, and occupational goals and has set up plans for the future; this pattern increases over time); 'foreclosure' (describing committed adolescents, but without having gone through any form of identity crisis; being relatively stable with about 35% over the age-groups studied), and 'moratorium' (describing an identity pattern of adolescents who experience an identity crisis and take their time out in order to develop their own perspective; this pattern also remains relatively stable over the age groups, covering about 12–28%).

Generally, the different cultural socialization scripts and practices find their expression in different conceptions of the selves that can be described as independent or individualistic and interdependent or collectivistic. Hazel Markus and Shinobu Kitayama (1998) described the independent construal of the self as expressing the notion of a distinct and separate person with an emphasis on unique personal attributes organized as distinctive wholes, abstracted from social responsibilities and duties. This actional self conception is conceived of as independent, assertive, competitive, self-assured, self-sufficient, and direct. The interdependent construal of the self describes the person as fundamentally connected with other human beings, who subordinates individual interests to the collectivity by being attentive, respectful, dependent, emphatic, self-controlled, dutiful, self-sacrificing, conforming, and cooperative. These different culturally defined identity conceptions are acquired during developmental pathways which can be described as continuous processes of synthesizing socializatory experiences beginning at birth or even earlier with means of constructing and co-constructing one's own reality.

ACKNOWLEDGEMENTS

The information presented in this chapter is largely based on Keller (1997, 1998b) and Cole and Cole (1996). I thank Yovsi Relindis for the insights into the Cameroonian Nso and Fulani cultures.

NOTE

1. Evolutionary theory conceives of inclusive fitness as being the resultant of one's own reproductive success plus the reproductive success of genetically related individuals.

RESOURCE REFERENCES

Berry, J. W., Poortinga, Y. H., Pandey, J., Dasen, P. R., Saraswathi, T. S., Segall, M. H., & Kagitcibasi, C. (1996). *Handbook of cross-cultural psychology* (2nd ed., 3 vols.). Needham Heights, MA: Allyn and Bacon.

Cole, M., & Cole, S. R. (1996). *The development of children* (3rd ed.). New York: Freeman.

Hill, K., & Hurtado, A. M. (1996). *Ache life history: The ecology and demography of a foraging people.* New York: Aldine de Gruyter.

Kagitcibasi, C. (1996). *Family and human development across cultures: A view from the other side.* Mahwah, NJ: Lawrence Erlbaum.

Kao, H. S. R., & Sinha, D. (Eds.). (1997). *Asian perspectives on psychology.* New Delhi: Sage.

Keller, H. (Ed.). (1997). *Handbuch der Kleinkindforschung* [Handbook of infancy research] (2nd ed.). Bern: Huber.

Keller, H. (1998a). Diferentes cominhos de socialização até a adolescência. *Revista Brasileira de Crescimento e Desenvolvimento Humano* [Brazilian Journal of Human Growth and Development], *8* (1–2), 1–14.

Keller, H. (Ed.). (1998b). *Lehrbuch Entwicklungspsychologie* [Textbook of developmental psychology]. Bern: Huber.

Keller, H. (in press). Human parent–child relationships from an evolutionary perspective. *American Behavioral Scientist* Special Issue with the topic 'Evolutionary psychology: Potential and limits of a Darwinian framework for the behavioral sciences'.

Keng, C. H. (Ed.). (1991). *Child development. Preschool children.* Malaysia: Pelanduk Publishing.

Munroe, R. L., & Munroe, R. H. (1975). *Cross-cultural human development.* Prospect Heights, IL: Waveland Press.

Nsamenang, A. B. (1992). *Human development in cultural context. A Third World perspective.* Newbury Park: Sage.

Papalia, D. E., & Wendkos Olds, S. (1992). *Psicologia del Desarrollo. De la infancia a la adolescencia* [Developmental psychology. From infancy to adolescence]. New York: McGraw-Hill.

Saraswathi, T. S. (Ed.). (1999). *Culture, socialization, and human development.* New Delhi: Sage.

Whiting, B. B. (Ed.). (1963). *Six cultures: Studies of child rearing.* New York: Wiley.

Leading Journals

Child Development
International Journal of Behavioral Development
Developmental Psychology

ADDITIONAL LITERATURE CITED

Avis, J., & Harris, P. L. (1991). Belief–desire reasoning among Baka children: Evidence for a universal conception of mind. *Child Development, 62,* 460–467.

Barker, R. G., & Wright, H. F. (1951). *One boy's day: A specimen record of behavior.* New York: Harper Brothers.

Berlyne, D. E. (1960). *Conflict, arousal, and curiosity.* New York: McGraw-Hill.

Berry, J. W. (1976). *Human ecology and cognitive style: Comparative studies in cultural and psychological adaptation.* New York: Sage/Halsted.

Birch, H. G. (1945). The relation of previous experience to insightful problem-solving. *Journal of Comparative Psychology, 38,* 367–383.

Bischof, N. (1996). *Das Kraftfeld der Mythen. Signale aus der Zeit, in der wir die Welt erschaffen haben* [The force field of myths. Signals from an area in which we created the world]. München: Piper.

Bischof-Köhler, D. (1989). *Spiegelbild und Empathie. Die Anfänge der sozialen Kognition* [Mirror recognition and empathy. The beginnings of social cognition]. Bern: Huber.

Bischof-Köhler, D. (1998). Zusammenhänge zwischen kognitiver, motivationaler und emotionaler Entwicklung in der frühen Kindheit und im Vorschulalter [Relationships between cognitive, motivational and emotional development in infancy and childhood]. In H. Keller (Ed.), *Lehrbuch Entwicklungspsychologie* [Textbook of developmental psychology] (pp. 317–316). Bern: Huber.

Boesch, C., & Boesch, H. (1990). Tool use and tool making in wild Chimpanzees. *Folia Primatologica, 54,* 86–99.

Bril, B. (1989). Die kulturvergleichende Perspektive: Entwicklung und Kultur [The cross-cultural perspective: Development and culture]. In H. Keller (Ed.), *Handbuch der Kleinkindforschung* [Handbook of infancy research] (1st ed.) (pp. 71–88). Heidelberg: Springer.

Bronfenbrenner, U. (1977). Toward an ecology of human development. *American Psychologist, 32,* 513–531.

Case, R. (1992). The role of the frontal lobes in the regulation of cognitive development. *Brain and Cognition, 20*(1), 51–73.

Chandler, M. J., Fritz, A. S., & Hala, S. M. (1989). Small-scale deceit: Deception as a marker of 2-, 3-, and 4-year-olds' early theories of mind. *Child Development, 60,* 1263–1277.

Cheney, D. L., & Seyfarth, R. M. (1994). *Wie Affen die Welt sehen.* München: Hanser; (1990). *How monkeys see the world: Inside the mind of another species.* Chicago: University of Chicago Press.

Chomsky, N. (1975). *Reflections on language.* New York: Pantheon Books.

Daly, M., & Wilson, M. (1988). *Homicide.* New York: Aldine.

Doi, L. T. (1978). Amae: A key concept for understanding Japanese personality structure. In R. J. Corsini (Ed.), *Reading in current personality theories* (pp. 213–219). Ithaca, NY: Peacock Publishers.

Dunbar, R. (1996). *Grooming, gossip and the evolution of language.* London: Faber & Faber.

Enriquez, V. G. (1993). Developing a Filipino psychology. In U. Kim & J. W. Berry (Eds.), *Indigenous psychologies: Research and experience in cultural context* (pp. 152–169). Newbury Park, CA: Sage.

Erikson, E. H. (1968). *Identity: Youth and crisis.* New York: W. W. Norton.

Erikson, E. H. (1976). *Identität und Lebenszyklen* [Identity and life cycles]. Frankfurt: Suhrkamp.

Erny, P. (1968). *L'enfant dans la pensée traditionnelle de l'Afrique noire.* Paris: Le livre africain.

Gesell, A. (1928). *Infancy and human growth.* New York: McMillan.

Greenfield, P. M. & Childs, C. P. (1991). Developmental continuity in biocultural context. In R. Cohen & A. W. Siegel (Eds.), *Context and development* (pp. 135–159). Hillsdale, NJ: Erlbaum.

Greenfield, P. M., & Cocking, R. R. (Eds.). (1994). *Cross-cultural roots of minority child development.* Hillsdale, NJ: Erlbaum.

Grimm, H., & Wilde, S. (1998). Im Zentrum steht das Wort [In the center is the word]. In H. Keller (Ed.), *Lehrbuch Entwicklungspsychologie* [Textbook of developmental psychology] (pp. 445–473). Heidelberg: Springer.

Hamilton, W. D. (1964). The genetical evolution of social behaviour. *Journal of Theoretical Biology, 7,* 1–52.

Harkness, S., & Super, C. M. (1983). The cultural construction of child development: A framework for the socialization of emotion. *Ethos, 11,* 221–231.

Hill, K., & Hurtado, A. (1991). The evolution of premature reproductive senescence and menopause in human females: An evaluation of the 'grandmother hypothesis'. *Human Nature, 2*(4), 313–350.

Keller, H., Lohaus, A., Völker, S., Cappenberg, M., & Chasiotis, A. (1999). Temporal contingency as a independent component of parenting behavior. *Child Development, 70*(2), 474–485.

Kohlberg, L. (1966). A cognitive-developmental analysis of children's sex role concepts and attitudes. In E. E. Maccoby (Ed.), *The development of sex differences.* Stanford, CA: Stanford University Press.

Kohlberg, L. (1976). Moral stages and moralization: The cognitive-developmental approach. In J. Lickona (Ed.), *Moral development behavior: Theory, research and social issues.* New York: Holt, Rinehart and Winston.

Köhler, W. (1921). *Intelligenzprüfungen an Menschenaffen.* Berlin: Springer; (1973). *The mentality of apes,* 2nd ed. Boston: Routledge & Kegan Paul.

Langlois, J. H., Ritter, J. M., Casey, R. J., & Sawin, D. B. (1995). Infant attractiveness predicts maternal behaviors and attitudes. *Developmental Psychology, 31,* 464–472.

Lorenz, K. (1969). Innate bases of learning. In K. H. Pribram (Ed.), *On the biology of learning* (pp. 13–93). New York: Harcourt.

Lutz, C. (1987). Goals, events, and understanding Ifaluk emotion theory. In D. Holland & N. Quinn (Eds.), *Cultural models in language and thought.* Cambridge: Cambridge University Press.

Malinowski, B. (1979). *Argonauten des westlichen Pazifik.* Frankfurt: Syndikat; (1964). *Argonauts of the Western Pacific.* London: Routledge & Kegan Paul.

Marcia, J. E. (1980). Identity in adolescence. In J. Adelson (Ed.), *Handbook of adolescent psychology.* New York: Wiley.

Markus, H., & Kitayama, S. (1998). The cultural psychology of personality. *Journal of Cross-Cultural Psychology, 29*(1), 63–87.

Mayr, E. (1974). Behavior programs and evolutionary strategies. *American Sciences, 62,* 650–659.

Mead, M. (1928/1961). *Coming of age in Samoa.* New York: Dell.

Mohanty, A. K., & Pradesh, P. (1993). Theoretical despairs and methodological predicaments of developmental psychology in India. Some reflections. In T. S. Saraswathi & B. Kaur (Eds.), *Human development and family studies in India* (pp. 104–121). New Dehli: Sage.

Piaget, J. (1932/1965). *The moral judgment of the child.* New York: Free Press.

Piaget, J. (1983). Piaget's theory. In P. H. Mussen (Ed.), *Handbook of child psychology: Vol. 1: History, theory and methods.* New York: Wiley.

Premack, D., & Premack, A. (1983). *The mind of an ape.* New York: Norton.

Premack, D., & Woodruff, G. (1978). Does the chimpanzee have a theory of mind? *The Behavioral and Brain Sciences, 1,* 515–526.

Rabain-Jamain, J., & Sabeau-Jouannet, E. (1997). Maternal speech to 4-month-old infants in two cultures: Wolof and French. *International Journal of Behavioral Development, 20*(3), 425–451.

Read, M. (1968). *Children of their fathers: Growing up among the Ngoni of Malawi.* New York: Holt, Rinehart & Winston.

Sinha, D. (1996). Indigenizing psychology. In J. W. Berry, Y. H. Poortinga, & J. Pandey (Eds.), *Handbook of cross-cultural psychology, Vol. 1: Theory and method* (pp. 129–169). Boston: Allyn & Bacon.

Sommer, V. (1992). *Lob der Lüge. Täuschung und Selbstbetrug bei Tier und Mensch* [Praise the lie. Deception and self-deception in man and animal]. München: C. H. Beck.

Stern, W. (1914/1923). *Psychologie der frühen Kindheit* [Psychology of early childhood]. Leipzig: Quelle & Meyer.

Sulloway, F. (1997). *Der Rebell der Familie. Geschwisterrivalität, kreatives Denken und Geschichte.* Berlin: Siedler; (1997). *Born to rebel: Birth order, family dynamics, and creative lives.* New York: Vintage Books.

Tomasello, M., Kruger, A. C., & Ratner, H. H. (1993). Cultural learning. *Behavioral and Brain Sciences, 16,* 495–552.

Tooby, J., & Cosmides, L. (1992). The psychological foundations of culture. In J. H. Barkow, L. Cosmides, & J. Tooby (Eds.), *The adapted mind. Evolutionary psychology and the generation of culture* (pp. 19–136). New York: Oxford University Press.

Wimmer, H., & Perner, J. (1983). Beliefs about beliefs: Representation and constraining function of wrong beliefs in young children's understanding of deception. *Cognition, 13,* 103–128.

Communications concerning this chapter should be addressed to: Professor Heidi Keller, Department of Psychology, University of Osnabrück, Seminarstrasse 20, 49069 Osnabrück, Germany

15

Developmental Psychology II: Adulthood and Aging

LEA PULKKINEN

15.1 THE DYNAMICS OF ADULT DEVELOPMENT

In this chapter, developmental dynamics is described from three viewpoints: lifespan psychology, life-course sociology, and behavior genetics. The choice of the viewpoints for the description of the dynamics of adult development in this chapter was affected by several facts: all three viewpoints are needed for understanding human development; they represent the most modern conception of adult development; and they are more applicable to normal development and empirically more testable than clinically based psychodynamic theories. Theory and research on adult development is rather sparse compared with child development, and only recently has a wider interest in it arisen. An attempt has been made to incorporate material from a variety of cultures, but at present relatively little work on adult development is available on non-Western cultures.

Lifespan Developmental Psychology

In the history of developmental psychology, the time continuum of the life span can be found in philosophers' writings over centuries (Reinert, 1979), but it was empirically discovered by Charlotte Bühler's works (1933) in Germany. Her conception of developmental psychology covering the entire life span became rapidly known in the United States, and in other continents soon after World War II through psychological textbooks. The principles of lifespan psychology have, however, been more systematically formulated during the past 30 years.

Lifespan theory and research is concerned with interindividual regularities and differences, and intra-individual plasticity in development (Baltes, Lindenberger, & Staudinger, 1998). It assumes that various adaptive processes are involved in individuals' lives from conception into old age, and identifies three major influence systems on lifespan development: (1) age-graded influences (e.g., education and marriage) which shape individual development in a relatively normative way; (2) history-graded

influences (e.g., a war) which make development different across historical periods; and (3)
non-normative influences (e.g., an accident)
which may have powerful effects on an individual's development. Lifespan developmental psychology incorporates both person-centered (holistic) and function-centered approaches. The
function-centered approach means focusing on a
category of behavior, such as cognition, personality, and emotion, and describing the lifespan
changes in the processes associated with them.
In this chapter, adult development is first described on the basis of function-centered
research. The chapter ends with a more holistic
approach which considers a person as a system
and connects age periods of development into a
pattern of lifetime individual development.

In lifespan psychology, development is
defined 'as selective age-related change in adaptive capacity' (Baltes, Staudinger, & Lindenberger, 1999, p. 479). It includes not only growth-
oriented notions of development, but is also
open to other kinds of changes and to different
means of attaining the same developmental outcome. The lifespan model of *selective optimization with compensation* (SOC) introduced by
Margret and Paul Baltes and their colleagues in
the 1990s incorporates processes involved in
successful development and successful aging. It
means that any process of human development
involves selection of goals, optimization of
means, and compensation of losses. Lifespan
psychology pays attention to the developing
person's contribution to the creation of his or
her own development (Brandtstädter, 1998).
Individuals steer their physical, cognitive, socio-
emotional and personality development by setting goals, making choices, and constructing
strategies for coping with various developmental
challenges (Nurmi, 1997). On the basis of the
Berkeley Longitudinal Study, Clausen (1993)
concluded that individuals demonstrate a 'planful competence' that powerfully influences the
course of their lives. The planful competence
involves self-confidence, intellectual commitment, and dependable effectiveness, and it affects choices and the quality of decisions people
make.

The view which emphasizes freedom of individual decision and action may have a Western
bias associated with an individualistic cultural
base as argued by Kagitcibasi (1988). According
to her, dependency and conformity expectations
for the preservation of the family and the society
are higher in subsistence-level societies. The
history of the conception that individuals are
able to select the paths they follow dates back to
the 1920s, but only recently this kind of constructionist view of individuals in shaping their
own development has become popular among

Western social scientists. It may overlook the
constraining life circumstances for a great number of people in the world who do not have the
options to choose from.

Life Course Theory

From Socialization to Life Course

A research paradigm which emphasizes the
effects of environmental factors on development
is known as socialization. After World War II,
increasing attention was focused on the heightened influence of family as a socializing agent in
childhood development. Diverse social and
demographic changes were presumed to affect
family socialization, and socialization as a
research paradigm was strong in the 1960s.
However, due to an inability to address concerns
such as continuity, change, and human agency,
the socialization perspective was not regarded as
adequate for the description of many aspects of
adult development over the life span of an
individual. A shift in framework from socialization to life course took place in the 1970s.

The Principles of Life Course

Life course sociology sheds light on the contextual factors of development. The life course
of individuals can be described in terms of
social trajectories, such as education, work, and
family. They interact with developmental trajectories; for instance, cognitive functioning is
related to education and career. Human development takes place in a cultural context in a
complex way (Valsiner & Lawrence, 1997).
Different social structures create specific roles
for individuals to fulfill. Brandtstädter (1998)
argues that development is essentially a cultural
product, but cultures are largely the end products of personal and collective activity. The
effects of cultural context on development were
powerfully addressed by Urie Bronfenbrenner
in the early 1970s (Bronfenbrenner & Morris,
1998). Issues on culture-bound tests and theories, differences in person–culture interaction,
and social circumstances that affect the construction of an individual's life course have been
critically discussed within cross-cultural psychology (e.g., Nsamenang, 1992; Valsiner &
Lawrence, 1997).

The first principle of the life course is that
social trajectories are affected by *historical time
and culture* (Elder, 1998). The second principle
of the life course is known as *human agency*
which means that individuals construct their
own life course within the opportunities and
constraints of historical time, culture, and social
circumstances. It assumes that individuals have

options to choose from; the assumption which has been questioned by cross-cultural psychologists. The life course theory also includes two other primary principles: *timing of lives* and *linked lives*. The former means that the developmental impact of life events (e.g., childbirth) on transitions is affected by the time when they occur in a person's life. Some events may be considered timely or ill-timed in relation to age norms. The principle of linked lives suggests that lives (e.g., the lives of family members) are lived interdependently.

Modern societies change rapidly, and therefore, the year of one's birth may expose the individual to different historical worlds in terms of, say, educational opportunities and economic situations. They cause *cohort effects* which mean that social change differentiates the life conditions of successive cohorts. For instance, the drastic income loss during the Great Depression in the USA in the 1930s affected younger children, particularly boys, more strongly than older children because younger children were more dependent on their parents and could not participate as much in working for the family's well-being.

Conceptual Distinctions

Life span specifies the temporal order of two or more life stages. The periods of life span include prenatal stage (conception to birth), infancy and toddlerhood (birth to age 3), early childhood (3 to 6 years), middle childhood (6 to 12 years), adolescence (12 to about 20 years), young adulthood (20 to 40 years), middle age (40 to 65 years), and late adulthood or old age (65 years and over). Instead, the concept of *life course* refers to the interdependence of age-graded trajectories, such as work and family. These concepts differ from the concept of *life history* which commonly refers to an individual's life events in chronological order. *Life organization*, on the other hand, means the coherence of the life history which the individual has constructed. Furthermore, *life structure* refers to an individual's subjective account of his or her life pattern at a given age, *life stage* to a socially defined position such as adolescence or advanced age, and *life cycle* to a reproductive process in a human populations such as the family cycle.

Genetic Factors in Development

Contextual factors affect development in interaction with genetic factors. Information about the role of genetic factors in development has been gained, especially in studies involving twins and adopted children (Plomin & Petrill, 1997). Genetic influence can be described in terms of *heritability*, a statistic that describes the proportion of observed differences between individuals that can be attributed to genetics. Recent studies have shown notable genetic influences on individual differences in personality and cognitive development, and their continuity over time. About half of the interindividual variance in personality measures is explained by genetic factors. Genetics also plays an important role in many close relationships; for instance, people choose partners who are similar to themselves (called assortative mating). For cognitive development, research has shown (Pike & Plomin, 1997) that: (1) genetic factors primarily contribute to the stability of intelligence during development; (2) specific cognitive abilities such as verbal and spatial ability are largely attributable to the same genes; (3) behavioral traits are influenced by many genes; and (4) performance in scholastic achievement and intelligence tests is affected by the same genetic factors. Effort is needed for scholastic achievement, but effort alone does not explain individual differences in achievement independent of ability.

Developmental genetic studies have revealed that heritability increases with age. Regarding the intelligence quotient (IQ), for example, heritability is about 40% in childhood, 60% in early adulthood, and 80% in later life. These findings may sound surprising because it seems that environmental factors should become more important as life experiences accumulate. The increasing genetic component is understandable on the basis of person–environment transaction. Within the constraints of social circumstances, individuals select environments which in favorable conditions facilitate matching their genetic dispositions and accentuating their genetic propensities; it is called proactive person–environment transaction. Another type of person–environment transaction is called reactive which means that individuals experience and interpret the same environment in different ways and react to it differently. A third type of person–environment transaction is called evocative and it refers to the fact that people react to an individual's characteristics, such as temperament or personality traits, intelligence, motivation, and physical functioning capacity.

Although genetic factors help to explain individual differences in personality and cognitive functioning, a large part of the variance is not genetic in origin. Such nongenetic environmental influences include prenatal and postnatal nutrition, illness, and parenting. The investigation of nongenetic effects is difficult because of their complexity. For instance, a *shared* family *environment* explains a large part of the variance of intelligence scores in childhood but has a negligible effect in adulthood. As previously stated, an explanation for this phenomenon is that individuals select different aspects from their environments to interact with. This is called a *nonshared environment* because the environmental effects are not shared by individuals living in the same environment equally. The effect of nonshared environment on individuals in relation to the effect of shared environment increases with age.

15.2 COGNITIVE DEVELOPMENT

Developmental Trends in Sensory and Psychomotor Functioning

The senses are sharpest and physical functioning, in general, is at its peak in young adulthood, from the early twenties to early thirties. A decline becomes evident in middle age (Papalia, Olds, & Feldman, 1998). Gradual hearing loss begins, however, already in adolescence. Hearing loss proceeds more quickly in men than in women. One-third of people between 65 and 74 have suffered enough hearing loss to cause them difficulties in hearing what people say, and this proportion increases with age.

As for vision, the decline is related to the fact that the lens of the eye becomes progressively less flexible. Age-related visual problems occur in near vision, dynamic vision, sensitivity to light, visual search, and speed of processing visual information. In old age, difficulties may appear in perceiving depth or color and in sensitivity to visual contrast. The other senses – taste, smell, and sensitivity to pain and temperature – also generally begin to decline after age 45, but do so more slowly in women than in men. In old age, sensitivity to taste declines, which may worsen appetite or cause overcompensation by the adoption of a highly seasoned or oversalted diet.

Strength and coordination of the lower body decline gradually, whereas upper body strength is retained longer. Endurance remains more undiminished than strength. Overall, people generally lose about one-fifth of their adult strength by age 70, and about half of it by their eighties. The decline is related to the loss of muscle mass which is increasingly replaced by fat. Muscle strength can, however, be retained by weight lifting and other exercise. Reaction time slows by one-fifth between age 20 and 60.

The consequences of declines in reaction time, vision, coordination, and motor skills on performances such as skilled industrial work, typing, or driving are, however, compensated for by knowledge and judgment based on experience, and by personality characteristics

such as conscientiousness and prudence. Therefore, in many occupations middle-aged people are better workers than younger adults. This notion contrasts with the increasing age discrimination being met on labor markets in many countries which may engender anxiety about the future among those facing middle age.

Developmental Trends in Cognitive Abilities

Early studies on intelligence and cognitive development that began with children showed a linear growth of cognitive capacity with age until late adolescence but a gradual decline in adulthood. Negative conclusions of cognitive development in adulthood were revised when new methodological approaches and theoretical conceptualizations emerged. It was found that a *cross-sectional design*, used in earlier studies, provided information about the differences between different age groups rather than about changes in the individual. Such cross-sectional comparisons may produce cohort effects because younger and older adults have typically lived in different environments in terms of, for instance, the quality and length of education.

Another approach to the study of cognitive development has been a *longitudinal design*, in which the same people are studied more than once. Longitudinal studies with repeated tests over time have shown an increase in intelligence at least until middle age. In any longitudinal study, attrition, that is, the loss of some of the participants, affects the generalizability of the results. It is possible that poorer scorers drop out more often than higher scorers, and that experience with testing situations favors people.

The drawbacks of both cross-sectional and longitudinal research have prompted researchers to make use of a *sequential design*. It combines the cross-sectional and longitudinal designs: several cross-sectional samples of different ages are assessed over a certain period of time. Schaie and his colleagues applied this approach in the Seattle Longitudinal Study of Adult Intelligence (Schaie, 1994) that began in 1956. Their random sample included 500 participants: 25 men and 25 women at five-year age intervals from age 20 to 70. The original participants were tested every seven years, and new participants were added. The total sample tested by 1994 included 5,000 participants.

Variability in Developmental Patterns

The test battery included in the Seattle Longitudinal Study consisted of five timed tests: verbal meaning, number, word fluency, spatial orientation, and inductive reasoning. A standard measure in the study of adult intelligence is the *Wechsler Adult Intelligence Scale (WAIS)*. It comprises of 11 subtests for verbal (information, comprehension, arithmetic, and similarities) and nonverbal (mastering a maze, identifying the missing part of a picture) performance. On the basis of the scores obtained in subtests, a verbal IQ, a non-verbal IQ, and a total IQ can be calculated. In the Seattle Longitudinal Study, developmental trends were investigated for intellectual abilities separately.

No uniform pattern of age-related changes in intellectual abilities was found (Schaie, 1994). Most individuals maintained their cognitive abilities until age 60, and many individuals improved their performance in some tests. Even then a reduction did not emerge in all or even most areas. Cognitive abilities generally increased until about age 40, remained stable until about age 60, and then incurred minor losses by age 70. There was, however, enormous variability among individuals and abilities in developmental patterns. Some individuals showed declines in young adulthood, and some did better at age 70 than the average young adult. Some abilities tended to decline early; others tended to remain stable or even increase until age 70. People with higher scores were healthier, wealthier, better-educated, and had more stable marriages, intelligent spouses, and stimulating lives. These factors are related. The findings show that cognitive development is intertwined with psychosocial development.

Fluid and Crystallized Intelligence

To understand why different abilities show different developmental patterns, Horn and Cattell proposed a distinction between fluid and crystallized intelligence in the 1960s. Fluid intelligence involves perception and reasoning, in the other words, the ability to solve problems that require speed in perceptions and information processing but little previous knowledge, while crystallized intelligence is manifested in vocabulary and general information and involves the ability to remember and use information. Crystallized intelligence is more dependent on education and cultural background than fluid intelligence.

Fluid intelligence peaks during young adulthood, but crystallized abilities do not show steeper decrement until the late 70s (Birren & Schaie, 1990). It has been suggested that fluid intelligence is determined by neurological status, whereas crystallized intelligence is largely affected by cultural experience. A meta-analysis of 91 studies (Verhaeghen & Salthouse, 1997), which included a comparison between subsamples

under and over 50 years of age, showed that there is already a negative correlation between age and performance in fluid intelligence among 18- to 50-year-olds. This means that age-related decline does not *only* emerge after the age of 50. The decline accelerates over the adult lifespan, most notably in speed, reasoning, and episodic memory.

Closely related to the Cattell–Horn theory of fluid and crystallized intelligence is a *two-component model* which identifies two categories of intellectual functioning: the mechanics and pragmatics of cognition (Baltes et al., 1999). The mechanics of cognition are genetically predisposed, whereas the pragmatics of cognition are associated with acquired knowledge. For instance, perceptual speed and reasoning are abilities that involve mechanics and parallel fluid intelligence. They show monotonic decline during adulthood. Verbal knowledge and fluency are more pragmatic abilities and parallel crystallized intelligence. They start to decline only in very old age. The Berlin Aging Study conducted with participants aged 75 to 105 years showed that the degree of distinctiveness between different aspects of mechanics and pragmatics of intelligence decreased significantly in old age (Lindenberger & Baltes, 1997). This means that abilities become more interrelated, and the age trajectories between the abilities become smaller as age increases. All abilities tend to decrease in very old age due to general brain-related deterioration.

Qualitative Changes in Cognitive Capacities

Relativistic Thinking and Wisdom

A qualitative difference in the cognitive competence of younger and older people has been suggested by Labouviev-Vief (1985). Piaget's theory assumes a development toward abstract, hypothetical reasoning which is free from subjectivity and cultural contamination. The ability to think abstractly and use scientific reasoning develops in adolescence. Consequently, 'mature' reasoning should involve a denial of subjectivity. However, older adults who typically do not perform as well as younger ones in formal reasoning tend to be subjective, to personalize the tasks set, to consider the affective dimensions involved, to consider alternative interpretations, and to suggest multiple answers.

In relativistic thinking or postformal thought, they also tend to utilize life experiences. Labouviev-Vief (1985) argues that subjective, intuitive reasoning exists parallel to objective, rational reasoning. They balance and enrich each other, suggesting that wisdom is a synthesis of reason and emotion. Wisdom has also been defined as expert knowledge of the fundamental pragmatics of life, i.e., as part of the pragmatics of intelligence (Baltes et al., 1999). It may grow in later adulthood, especially if individuals have had certain kinds of experience and professional background. Wisdom is a cognitive and motivational metastrategy which protects against the fragmentation of knowledge and enhances the optimization of one's virtues. It consists of the knowledge and skills involved in the interpretation and meaning of life.

Age and Creativity

Creativity has been operationalized by tests of *divergent thinking* which show a capacity to come up with a number of novel and yet acceptable solutions to problems. In contrast, *convergent thinking*, the capacity to arrive at a single correct answer to a problem, characterizes an intelligent person (Gardner, 1998). Creative individuals are above average in intelligence, but extremely high intelligence does not predict high creativity.

Divergent thinking as well as the number of publications, paintings, and compositions peak, on average, around age 40. Creativity varies, however, depending on the field. Poets, mathematicians, and theoretical physicists are most productive around age 30, whereas novelists, philosophers, social scientists, and historians increase their productivity through their fifties. A masterpiece may appear at any age. It is characteristic of creative individuals to start early and be very productive, even into old age.

Highly creative individuals differ from their peers more in personality characteristics such as willingness to take risks, motivation, and persistence than in cognitive abilities, although they generally exhibit at least two distinct cognitive strengths and stick to a selected domain (Gardner, 1998). Their family background is often comfortable and exhibits a high work ethic. Personal losses and stress in childhood are also common. Creative adults differ in many respects from prodigies who have mastered a domain at an early age, yet in both cases, a factor that differentiates the highest achievers from others is the large amount of time invested in work and practice.

Age and Learning

The concept of intelligence has historically been associated with the ability to learn, but common measures of intelligence do not normally test learning ability. In his *triarchic theory of intelligence*, Sternberg (1997) suggests a broad conception of the learning and thinking abilities underlying human intelligence. 'Intelligence comprises the mental abilities necessary for adaptation to, as well as shaping and selection

of, any environmental context.' (p. 1030). Intelligent people can respond flexibly to challenging situations. Sternberg divides intelligence into three components: the analytical, the creative, and the practical, which collectively affect learning.

Research results suggesting a decrease in fluid intelligence with age raise questions as to whether intelligence is related to learning, whether it is possible to compensate for losses by practicing skills, and whether learning is possible in old age. The tasks of learning are traditionally associated with childhood and youth, but formal training for many individuals now extends long into young adulthood. With shifting career patterns, many adults continue to learn until retirement and beyond. In some Western countries, about half of all adults participate in continuing education. With age-adjusted instruction, older people can learn new information and skills, such as how to use computers, although often more slowly than younger ones. In this context, older people show a plasticity and modifiability in cognitive performance, and they can benefit from training.

15.3 Personality Development

Behavioral Attributes and Dispositions

Temperament

Definitions of temperament usually refer to the biological bases of behavior, although the term temperament has also been used to refer to style of behavior or primary reaction patterns without reference to the underlying biological processes. Rothbart and Bates (1998) define temperament as 'constitutionally based individual differences in emotional, motor, and attentional reactivity and self-regulation' (p. 109). Genetic inheritance, maturation, and experience influence temperament. Reactivity, which is modulated by self-regulatory processes, can be measured in terms of the onset, duration, and intensity of affective reactions such as fear and anger. Rothbart and Bates emphasize that temperament processes are open systems. This means that experiences influence the development of temperament. It may also mean that what are normally understood as personality traits are largely aspects of temperament differentiated in the course of life experience.

There are several theories concerning the structure of interindividual differences in temperament. The broad behavioral tendencies, quite generally accepted among researchers, are: (1) extraversion, approach, or positive affect; (2) inhibition, anxiety, or harm-avoidance;

(3) irritability or anger; and (4) affiliativeness or social reward dependence (Rothbart & Bates, 1998). These tendency categories are reminiscent of the four-fold temperaments: sanguine, melancholic, choleric, and phlegmatic, respectively, identified by ancient Greco-Roman physicians. Longitudinal studies show that there is significant continuity between childhood temperamental characteristics and adult outcomes, for instance, between a child's irritability and subsequent undercontrolled behavior such as criminality. An individual's temperament may become an organizing force in his or her development.

Trait Models

Trait models are taxonomies of personality traits developed to facilitate the communication of interindividual differences in behavioral characteristics. They are structures of personality description, not structures of personality. The number of traits that researchers have used in the description of personality has varied substantially. Over the past decades, a reasonable consensus has been reached on five factors: Extraversion (e.g., active, assertive, enthusiastic, outgoing), Agreeableness (generous, kind, sympathetic, trusting), Conscientiousness (organized, planful, reliable, responsible), Neuroticism (anxious, self-pitying, tense, worrying), and Openness to Experience (artistic, curious, imaginative, of wide interests). Each covers a broad domain of individual differences (Caspi, 1998) and includes a number of more specific personality dimensions. The five factors have emerged at different ages, in different cultures, and with different methods. They have been interpreted as representing important dimensions of people's social survival needs, providing information about individuals' adaptational potential, and depicting the dimensions used in the judging of other people. Criticism of this consensus has also been presented (Block, 1995): the descriptive system is atheoretical, the interpretation and naming of factors is subjective, and the extracted dimensions are dependent on the variables included in the analyses. Jack Block suggests that the construct 'Five Factor Approach to personality description' be used instead of the 'Five Factor Model of personality'.

The number of factors that adequately describes personality is still debated. Shortly before his death, Eysenck (1997) argued that Agreeableness and Conscientiousness are primary rather than higher-order factors. A meta-analysis of 14 studies on children, adolescents, and adults confirmed this argument (Digman, 1997). Two higher-order factors emerged. One, called alpha, was principally formed by the dimensions Agreeableness, Conscientiousness, and Emotional Stability on one pole and by Hostility, Heedlessness, and Neuroticism on the other. The second higher-order factor, called beta, covered the dimensions Extraversion and Openness to Experience. These constructs form links between the Five Factor Model and Eysenck's original temperament theory of Extraversion and Neuroticism.

Digman (1997) gave different interpretations to these factors: Factor alpha describes socialization, whereas Factor beta represents personal growth. In parallel to this notion, the largest environmental influences and the lowest heritabilities were found in the Factor alpha dimensions, whereas the smallest environmental influences and the highest heritabilities were found in the Factor beta dimensions (Vernon, Jang, Harries, & McCarthy, 1997). The Factor beta dimensions correlate with intellectual abilities as revealed by a meta-analysis of several studies (Ackerman & Heggestad, 1997).

A two-dimensional framework with four-fold prototypical behaviors has guided the longitudinal studies of personality development by Block (1993) in the United States and Pulkkinen (1996b) in Finland. The four prototypes are reminiscent of the temperament categories, and their dimensions are similar to the factors alpha and beta. The prototypes include undercontrolled behavior, such as aggression; overcontrolled behavior, such as compliance; ego-resilient behavior, such as constructiveness; and ego-brittleness, such as anxiety. These prototypes show continuity over time and they are associated with typical adult outcomes, for instance, aggressive or undercontrolled behavior in childhood predicts criminality in adulthood.

The Person-Oriented Approach

The person-oriented approach is an alternative or complementary approach to the variable-oriented study of personality (Block, 1971). It aims at a more holistic view of personality which 'emphasizes the close dependency of individual functioning and individual development on the social, cultural, and physical characteristics of the environment' (Magnusson & Stattin, 1998, p. 686). The person-oriented approach means that individuals are not described and compared in terms of isolated variables (as in the variable-oriented study) but in a configuration of several variables. There are many methodological tools for the study of the patterning of structures such as the Q-sort technique, pattern analysis, cluster analysis, latent profile analysis, configural frequency analysis, latent transition analysis, log-linear modeling, and the multivariate P-technique (Magnusson & Stattin, 1998).

One of the person-oriented approaches to personality is to identify individual differences in terms of personality types. The concept of type does not refer here to discrete categories because individuals differ in their degree of 'fit' in the category prototype (York & John, 1992). In the Finnish Longitudinal Study of Personality and Social Development in which the development of about 80% of a random sample of females and males has been studied from childhood to early middle age, personality styles (or types) in adulthood were studied considering personality traits, life orientation, and behavioral activities (Pulkkinen, 1996b). Personality types obtained replicated the types that Block (1971) identified with the participants of the Berkeley Longitudinal Study. The use of the hierarchical clustering technique made it possible in the Finnish study to group the types into more general categories, i.e., to three replicable personality types that have emerged in several studies (Caspi, 1998). One-fourth of women and men were characterized by the personality type called Conflicted. It included negative emotionality and interpersonal conflicts. Two personality types described adjustment. The division between adjusted and conflicted personality types was rooted in the quality of emotional and behavioral regulation in childhood, and individuals tended to remain in the same category from early adulthood to mid-adulthood.

Stability and Change in Personality Characteristics

Although it is difficult to prove that there are no absolute changes in personality characteristics during adult years, longitudinal studies suggest that Neuroticism tends to decline and Conscientiousness/Dependability, Self-confidence, Outgoingness, and Cognitive Commitment tend to increase (Caspi, 1998). Individual changes may, however, differ from this general pattern. For instance, Jones and Meredith (1996) found that, in spite of the general increase in Cognitive Commitment from age 18 to 30 (expressed by the means of the group), Cognitive Commitment decreased significantly in 31% of the participants during this period. Thus group statistics may be rather meaningless for the prediction of continuity in an individual's personality characteristics. In general, there is very little evidence for age-related losses in self and personality functions until the late seventies, but more discontinuity in the functional status of personality can be seen in individuals above age 85 (Baltes et al., 1998).

Longitudinal studies show notable stability of interindividual differences in personality traits over time. Especially in adulthood, such stability exists in all five factors of personality (Costa & McCrae, 1994). In general, stability is higher at mature ages than in childhood, which suggests that a psychological organization of personality forms with age (Caspi, 1998). In addition to stability of phenotypically similar characteristics over time, indicated by, for instance, a significant correlation of aggression scores measured at different ages, continuity has also been found between phenotypically different attributes such as aggression and criminality measured at different points of time. The latter is called *heterotypic continuity*. A correlation can be interpreted as an indicator of heterotypic continuity if the obtained coherence can be inferred from a genotypic attribute underlying both behaviors. Continuity is, however, often interpreted as heterotypic without a sound theoretical basis. Temperament or the four-fold prototypical behaviors introduced by Block and Pulkkinen are examples of constructs that have been used in the interpretation of heterotypic continuity.

Self-System

Multiple Selves

Personality characteristics are observable by other people. An individual's own conception of his or her personality and its continuity is integrated by self. A view of self, including both positive and negative attributes, is formed through social comparisons. Comparison with peers for self-evaluation, or rather, for personal competence assessment, becomes salient in middle childhood (Harter, 1998). This process is supported by socializing agents such as parents, teachers, and peers. During early adolescence when abstract thinking develops, an adolescent becomes capable of constructing an abstraction of the self, for instance, as intelligent. Seeing himself or herself as intelligent is based on the combination of such attributes as successful at school and innovative. Such abstractions are typically isolated self-attributes without a coherent organization.

Linking one abstraction to another becomes possible in middle adolescence, but attempts to resolve the contradictions inherent in the opposite poles of the continuum, being both cheerful and depressed, for example, reveals the lack of maturity. 'An awareness of the opposites within one's self-portrait causes considerable intrapsychic conflict, confusion, and distress' (Harter, 1998, p. 573). In late adolescence, higher-order abstractions that represent the coordination of single abstractions make it possible to develop a more integrated theory of self. Opposing attributes do not produce a conflict; they can be accepted under terms such as flexibility, inconsistency, or moodiness. These higher-order abstractions help relieve the troublesome contradictions within the self.

In addition to actual attributes included in the *real self*, adolescents have conceptions of what they would like to be, i.e., of an *ideal self*. Its development is related to an early representation of what others want them to be. Some discrepancy is motivating, but a high discrepancy may be indicative of maladjustment such as depression. A third type of self-image, the *ought self*, refers to the attributes that one believes he or she should possess. A high discrepancy between the real self and the ought self may produce negative emotions. The identification of self-images has also been made in the time dimension. The real self represents immediate and *actual* self, whereas the *possible selves* represent both the hoped for and dreaded selves. They can be approached or avoided; they have a motivational function.

According to the old self-theory of William James, individuals who have a positive self-concept in areas where they desire high achievement, have high *self-esteem*. A high discrepancy between the real and ideal selves may result in low self-esteem. Empirical research on different age groups has confirmed that competence in areas that individuals consider important correlate more highly with overall self-esteem than competence in domains deemed unimportant. Self-esteem may even increase in old age (65 years or over) due to *self-efficacy* which is higher in older than younger age (Dietz, 1996). Self-efficacy means an evaluation based on a sense of competence.

Studies on the stability of self-representation show that there is a decline in positive self-judgment in preadolescence, after which self-evaluation gradually becomes more positive. The increase in personal autonomy during adolescence provides opportunities to select activities in which one is competent. *Self-concept* is relatively stable in adulthood, although short-term changes in self-concept may occur. This stability is related to the selection of information and experiences; people avoid information that threatens their view of self. They construct a sense of continuity over time for the *I-self* (I as an agent) and for the *Me-selves* (characteristics recognized by others). A great majority of people over the age of 85 think that they are essentially the same people they have always been, although most people perceive that some of their characteristics have changed (Troll & Skaff, 1997).

Unfavorable self-evaluations may be associated with depression or other negative outcomes, and preoccupation with self may interfere with work and interpersonal relations. Overestimation in self-judgment, on the other hand, may produce an egoistic self-image which also has a negative influence on interpersonal relationships. Developmental processes of self-image with regard to underlying mechanisms and transition rules have not yet a coherent empirical foundation (Harter, 1998).

Growth Models

The growth of self is inherent in Western humanistic and psychodynamic theories. Oriental philosophies may have different views of human growth. Humanistic theories stress the potential for positive development. People can take charge of their lives and direct it toward creativity and self-realization. Maslow (1954) identified a hierarchy of needs from the level of basic physiological needs to safety needs, belongingness and love needs, esteem needs, and finally self-actualization needs. *Self-actualization* involves self-fulfillment and the realization of one's potential. Its attainment is rare; self-actualized people have special characteristics such as creativity and a strong sense of values. The theory states that needs on the more basic level have to be largely satisfied before people can satisfy needs on a higher level. This principle has been seriously questioned. In non-Western cultures, the hierarchy of needs may be different. For instance, social belongingness needs may be at the top of the hierarchy, not self-actualization.

An influential lifespan theory about personality development by Erik H. Erikson (1950) exemplifies the growth of self through age stages. His theoretical framework was psychoanalytical, and therefore he analyzed self development in terms of ego. Ego is an aspect of personality that operates on the reality principle and seeks acceptable means of gratification. The theory covers eight stages across the life span. Erikson argues that a psychosocial crisis in early adolescence concerns *group identity* versus *alienation*, and in late adolescence *individual identity* versus *role diffusion*. Marcia (1980) has proposed a model for the resolution of the identity crisis. He distinguished four identity statuses on the basis of exploration of and commitment to a certain mode of action or way of thinking. An individual's identity status may be different in different domains, such as religion, politics, and vocational career. Although identity diffusion (no exploration, no commitment) declines with age, many people remain diffused in some domains into adulthood. In general, exploration seems to be a process typical of young people, whereas commitment is typical of adults.

15.4 Socio-Emotional Development

Both conceptually and theoretically, the study of socio-emotional development is close to that of personality development. Therefore, they are often regarded together. In this section, social development is discussed in terms of socio-emotional relationships, emotions, and dimensions of interpersonal behavior.

Social Relationships

Adult Attachment

Attachment refers to an affectionate and reciprocal relationship between two people. The advantages of the child's secure attachment to his or her parents continue into adolescence and adulthood. Bowlby claimed in the 1970s that the attachment relationship a child forms with the primary caregiver results in a prototypical internal working model of close relationships which affects the formation of close relationships even in adulthood. Four prototypes of adult attachment were distinguished by Bartholomew and Horowitz (1991): secure (positive self image – positive image of others), dismissing (positive self – negative others), preoccupied (negative self – positive others), and fearful attachment (negative self – negative others). There is some evidence suggesting that adults with different attachment styles differ in their interpersonal relationships, overall adjustment, and personality characteristics, and that these differences extend into later adulthood and old age (Diehl, Elnick, Bourbeau, & Labouviev-Vief, 1998). For instance, secure individuals are less neurotic, more extraverted, and more agreeable than the rest.

Securely attached adults generally have securely attached children; they respond to their infants most sensitively, which is a basis of secure attachment. Serious aggression and other behavior problems in children are related to insecure attachment in mothers and in their children. These observations have led van IJzendoorn (1997) to present a developmental socioemotional model of antisocial behavior, in which attachment is related to the type and level of moral reasoning and which could, in part, explain the risk of violence in the insecurely attached.

Friendships

'A friendship consists mainly of being attracted to someone who is attracted in return, with parity governing the social exchanges between the individuals involved' (Hartup & Stevens, 1997, p. 355). The developmental significance of friendship in children and adolescents has been studied with many methods, but less is known about it beyond adolescence. A differentiation between *deep structure* and *surface structure* of friendship helps shed light on the role of friendship across the life course.

As summarized by Hartup and Stevens (1997), mostly Western research shows that the deep structure of friendship, which refers to the social meaning of relationships, is developmentally stable. Trustworthiness and understanding are attributes given to a friend both at school age and in older age. The deep structure of friendship can be described as symmetrical reciprocity. In contrast, the surface structure of friendship, which refers to the actual exchanges between friends, is not developmentally stable. Surface structures vary from adolescence to old age. Adolescents share interests and spend time in common activities. The reciprocities include intimacy that supports a sense of self-identity. Among young adults, these reciprocities are centered on work activities and family lives with children of about same age. Friendships can be said to help accomplish developmental tasks. In middle age, people invest less time and energy in friendships than in young adulthood but exchange emotional support and practical experience with friends. Social relationships have adaptive functions also in very old age as proposed by Carstensen in her socio-emotional selectivity theory; people tend to, for instance, select their social contacts to maximize emotionally meaningful experiences and avoid certain contacts in order to protect themselves from unpleasant social contacts or loss of autonomy (Lang & M. M. Baltes, 1997).

Different cultures differ in emotional closeness and openness of the relationships, as well as in values beyond them (Elbedour, Schulman, & Kedem, 1997). The role of cultural context on social relations has been described in terms of individualism–collectivism (Berry, Poortinga, Segall, & Dasen, 1992). In North American culture, which values individualism and emancipation from the family, peer groups are found more important among adolescents than in a more 'familistic' Italian culture (Claes, 1998). At an old age, correspondingly, family-related activities are preferred by Spanish people for personal free-time activity; preferences are reversed among Dutch people (Katzko, Steverink, Dittman-Kohli, & Herrera, 1998). In a culture favoring collective values, i.e., emphasizing communal feelings, social usefulness, acceptance of authority, and family values such as mutual support and commitment to the family, family values are given a higher priority than individual values. Satisfaction with friends is a weaker correlate of life satisfaction in collectivistic societies (Diener & Diener, 1995). Main changes in family occurring in the world with increased affluence are towards weakening material interdependence while emotional interdependencies may or may not remain functional (Kagitcibasi, 1996). Social security benefits replace support systems within families. For instance, sustaining elderly parents decreases in importance. It may have consequences for emotional ties.

The size of friendship network and its importance to individuals is rather stable across Western countries (Claes, 1998; Elbedour et al., 1997; Hartup & Stevens, 1997). Network size is highest in young adulthood, declines by middle age, rises at retirement, and declines again among older adults. Although the rate of social interaction decreases during old age, contacts with family members increase in emotional closeness (Hartup & Stevens, 1997). Relationships with siblings also tend to reflect age differences in social relationships, but as complementary to friendship network. Sibling relationships tend to become more distant during young adulthood when the significance of friends, spouses, and family life increases. Life events such as childbirth often tighten sibling bonds. During middle age, bonds between siblings become closer, and relationships are restored – often activated by dealing with the care of aging parents. In old age, the long-lasting nature of relationships with siblings becomes even more important, especially between sisters.

Close friends tend to remain the same over time (Cairns & Cairns, 1994). Long-term friendships that are based on shared histories are consciously maintained and preferred to the making of new friends. Individuals who have friends compared with those who do not are typically more socially competent and better adjusted, and their psychological well-being is better throughout adulthood and old age (Hartup & Stevens, 1997). In old age, friends are especially important for psychological well-being if there are no living relatives. Friendships predict job success and feelings of self-worth, and friendships can generally help individuals cope with developmental challenges in normative and non-normative developmental transitions such as entrance into family life or divorce. The developmental significance of friends is not, however, unrelated to the characteristics of friends. People have a tendency to select friends who resemble themselves although sociodemographic conditions and opportunities for socialization also affect their selection. For example, antisocial friends socialize adolescents to antisocial values and acts.

Love

A relationship that contains *intimacy*, the emotional element which involves self-disclosure and trust, *passion*, the motivational element which includes physiological arousal into sexual desire, and *commitment*, the cognitive element which is the decision to love the other, is experienced as love. These elements may occur in different strengths. Sternberg (1995) argues that people 'create' love as a story which explains the fact that couples share many kinds of love within a culture and between cultures. The similarity-attraction dynamic typical of friendships also applies to love. Lovers often resemble each other somewhat in personality traits and moderately or substantially in social attitudes and religion.

Emotions

Views on Emotions

Emotions consist of physiological, behavioral, and subjective-experiential components. There are theorists who argue that a small set of basic emotions, including anger, surprise, joy, interest, fear, sadness, and disgust, which become differentiated during the first year of life, are universal and fundamental for human motivation (Dougherty, Abe, & Izard, 1996). All theorists do not believe in the principle of basic emotions. Cross-cultural comparisons have revealed cultural effects on emotions and led to the formulation of constructionist theories of emotion which do not emphasize their biological basis. Different emotions may exist in different cultures, and factors that elicit them may differ (Mesquita & Frijda, 1992).

Individual differences in emotions can be regarded both as dispositional differences related to temperament and socio-emotional functioning, and as situationally specific reactions. *Emotionality* is related to the level of adjustment and conception of the self, and it contributes to the quality of social relationships. Achievement-related motivation and morality are also affected by emotions. Emotion is an integral part of socialization. Mechanisms involved in the regulation of one's emotions and their relation to social competence and adjustment have recently gained increasing attention among researchers. Emotion regulation can be viewed as 'the process of initiating, sustaining, modulating, or changing the occurrence, intensity, or duration of internal feeling states and emotion-related physiological processes' (Eisenberg, 1998, p. 6). (See also Chapter 12.)

Emotions in Adolescence and Adulthood

The prevalence of depressive symptoms increases in both sexes, especially in girls, at some point in early-to-middle adolescence. At the same time, there is an increase in the output of sex hormones. The adrenal cortex produces male sex hormones, called androgens, in boys and girls, but more in boys. The excretion of estrogen also increases, especially in girls. The increase in hormone output is related to negative affect. Nevertheless hormones account for negative affect less than social factors (Susman, Dorn, & Chrousos, 1991). For males, there is an association between pubertal hormones and aggressive behavior, but for females the results are less consistent. Many factors appear to modify adolescents' moods and affects.

Emotional experience is intertwined with the cognitive appraisal of situations, and there are age differences in the types of cognitive appraisals people make. The frequencies and intensities of emotional experience, especially for negative emotions, also decrease with age (Gross et al., 1997). These changes seem to be related to increased emotional control with age. Laboratory studies have confirmed some self-reported tendencies: older couples express less negativity and more affection than middle-aged couples while discussing a conflict in a laboratory situation (Carstensen, Grottman, & Levenson, 1995). Depression among older people is, however, common: more than half of the participants of the Finnish Evergreen project were classified as depressed over a five-year period among 75- and 80-year-old people. The mean score of those who died during the five-year follow-up did not differ significantly from the mean of the survivors (Heikkinen, Heikkinen, & Ruoppila, 1997).

Dimensions of Social Development

Moral Development

The quality of social interaction between people is related to the prevailing norms of society and moral reasoning in individuals. A dominant conception of moral reasoning following cognitive development, was presented by Kohlberg in the 1960s. It was comprised of three levels – preconventionality, conventional role conformity, and moral principles. The last level recognizing individual rights, contracts, laws, and ethics, is reached in adolescence, young adulthood, or never. Before his death, Kohlberg proposed an additional stage of moral development (Kohlberg & Ryncarz, 1990). It involves achieving a cosmic perspective, a sense of unity with the cosmos, nature, or God. It enables a person to think of moral issues from the standpoint of the universe as a whole and parallels the mature stage of faith as described by Fowler (1981). This stage is rare. It is reached by individuals whose commitment to humanity greatly inspires others.

Prosocial Behavior

Voluntary behavior intended to benefit others, called prosocial behavior, is motivated by empathy-related emotions (comprehension of another's emotional state) and sympathy-related emotions (feelings of concern for the distressed). Higher moral reasoning leads to altruism and moral behavior in individuals for whom moral values are central to self-understanding (Damon & Hart, 1988). Altruistic parents encourage prosociality in their children. The development of prosocial behavior has been linked to perspective-taking abilities, intelligence, the level of expressed motives for prosocial behavior, and moral reasoning (Eisenberg & Fabes, 1998). Consistency in prosocial and empathic tendencies across situations and time is already evident in adolescence.

Prosocial behavior and mature moral reasoning correlate with popularity, social competence, and self-esteem. Girls tend to be more prosocial than boys, but differences vary with the type of prosocial behavior. Prosocial values, personal norms, and one's conception of personal responsibility for assisting others motivate altruism in adulthood, but they can also be seen in adolescents who are highly committed to caring for others.

Aggression and Antisocial Behavior

Aggression is a behavior aimed at harming or injuring another person. It has adaptive and maladaptive functions; it has evolved to be part of a communication system. Studies on aggression have revealed many variables correlating with its frequency, for example, a difficult temperament, neuropsychological deficits, and psychophysiological indicators such as low resting heart rate.

Antisocial behavior is a broad construct encompassing delinquency and crime, and disruptive behavior, such as aggression, below the age of criminal responsibility (Rutter, Giller, & Hagell, 1998). It inflicts physical or mental harm or property loss or damage on others, which may or may not constitute the breaking of criminal laws (Coie & Dodge, 1998, p. 781). Antisocial behavior peaks during adolescence and declines rapidly between the ages of 18 and 25. Strengthening regulatory processes in adulthood may explain, at least in some individuals, the decrease of antisocial behavior and reorientation towards more successful development. Loeber and Stouthamer-Loeber (1998) identify three developmental types of violent individuals: (a) a life-course type, (b) a limited-duration type, and (c) a late-onset type. The life-course career criminals may continue their high rates of crime until about age 40. They begin their antisocial behavior in early life, many of them prior to age 11. The limited-duration type means that individuals outgrow aggression in late adolescence or early adulthood. The late-onset type consists of a minority of adult violent offenders who have not been aggressive or violent early in life.

Antisocial behavior is influenced by social context, by genetic factors, and by age-related determinants. It is related to unemployment and negative identity. People who can establish stable work and family lives, regardless of ethnicity, tend to end their violent criminal behavior. Life events which sever relationships with antisocial peer groups or which impose new values may be turning points that cause changes in the antisocial trajectory and advance adaptation to society.

The criminal records of violence do not include child abuse and spousal battery. There is data to suggest that about 16% of American couples are physically violent towards each other, and the rate of child abuse is about the same. Most victims of domestic violence are women, and many are killed by intimate partners. Although women at greatest risk are young, poor, and uneducated, partner abuse occurs at every level of society. Alcohol problems are often associated with such abuse, and in many cases, physical aggression toward the partner has started before marriage. Victimized women tend to have low self-confidence, little social support outside the family, and are fearful in general (Reiss & Roth, 1994).

Relatively little is known about violence against women of color. Sorenson (1996) reviews self-report surveys, which suggest that the rates of physical marital violence are 1.5 to 4 times higher for African Americans than for White Americans. For Hispanics, findings of different studies are contradictory. Sorensen remarks that data are not available for Asian American women's experiences of intimate violence. Traditional Asian values of close family ties may both discourage physical abuse at home and support hiding such problems.

15.5 Interplay of Developmental and Social Trajectories

Developmental Phases

Function-centered approaches to developmental processes may gain little understanding of how these processes, such as cognition, personality, and emotion, are interrelated, and how they are intertwined with social trajectories, such as education, family, and work. A holistic approach tries to consider human life as a system and connect age periods of development into a pattern of individual development. The most well-known holistic approach is Erikson's theory of eight lifespan stages (Erikson, 1950). Each stage involves a crisis or an age-specific challenge that should be satisfactorily resolved for optimal development. The theory states that a successful resolution of each crisis results in the refinement of a predominantly positive quality, such as trust in infancy, but it may also result in its counterpart, mistrust, to protect an individual from danger; some mistrust in the world is needed for self-protection. In this theory, the stages are more differentiated in childhood than in adulthood for which only three stages have been distinguished. The psychosocial crises to be solved in adulthood concern intimacy versus isolation (young adulthood), generativity versus stagnation (middle age), and integrity versus despair (old age). Common virtues or ego skills such as hope, will, purpose, and skill in childhood, fidelity in adolescence, and love, care, and wisdom in adulthood emerge as successful outcomes of the crises. Valsiner and Lawrence (1997) remark, however, that age stages are likely to be differentially represented in different cultures and historical times. For instance, adolescence, which is an important age period in European and North-American cultures, was identified as a cultural invention just a hundred years ago.

Another approach to adult life stages has been proposed by Levinson and his colleagues (Levinson, 1978, 1996). According to them, the passage from one developmental stage to another involves processes, which have been analyzed in terms of changes in 'life structure'. Life structure has been defined as building on things that a person finds important, for instance, work, family, and health, as well as on the values and emotions that make them important. Life structure is subjected to change during transitional periods when people reappraise and restructure important things in their lives. According to this theory, people spend about half their adult lives in transitional periods.

The theory assumes that during the early adult transition (ages 17 to 22) a person begins to define his life structure, moves out from the parents' home, and becomes independent. After a stable period in the mid-twenties a person faces a new transition period around age 30. Transitional periods occur also around ages 40, 50, and 60. Research suggests that these transitions are generally similar for men and women, but the timetable may differ and women's life structures tend to be more varied than men's.

The transition around age 50 is often called the midlife crisis. Research has, however, failed to support the inevitability of a crisis. It seems to depend on circumstances and personality rather than on age. Many women in their early fifties rate the quality of their lives as high. They are self-confident and independent. Many also experience menopause as a positive transition that opens new possibilities for the second half of life. In non-Western cultures, the mature adulthood that accompanies the responsibilities of family management, when dominance, control, and planning are at their peak, is also the period when perceived well-being peaks (Shweder, 1997).

The idea of age-related changes in adulthood has been questioned because chronological age has not been seen as very indicative of adult development. Significant life events may take place at different ages. These events structure people's lives with different timetables. The historical era and social circumstances may also have an impact on people's way of thinking and behavior as can be seen in the increase in individualism among conventionally adjusted American women between 1958 and 1989, when secular trends were strong (Roberts & Helson, 1997).

A third approach to developmental stages defines developmental tasks typical of different stages. Biological changes and social demands define social roles and typical life events in people's lives. Social demands are different at different ages, as argued by Havighurst (1948) who introduced the concept of developmental task referring to social-role demands in individuals' lives. Developmental tasks define a basic pattern of priorities for self-development across the life span, reflecting both biological changes and age-related cultural demands. Developmental tasks are different in adolescence, adulthood, and old age, and they very across cultures (Valsiner & Lawrence, 1997).

Developmental Tasks

Adolescence

Developmental tasks in adolescence include, for instance, physical maturation, heterosexual relationships, internalized morality, autonomy from parents, and career choices. Adolescence is time when the competence needed to complete developmental tasks is supported by education. Competence refers to effective adaptation to the environment indicated by close social relationships with peers, prosocial behavior, academic achievement, and a sense of self-identity (Masten & Coatsworth, 1998). The antecedents of competence include effective parenting, self-regulation, and cognitive functioning. The foundations of competence lie in early development, especially in the attachment and self-regulation of emotion. They are associated with prosocial behavior and peer popularity, as well as with academic achievement.

Emotional turmoil, conflict within the family, and alienation from and hostility toward society and adult values have been labeled adolescent rebellion. This line of thought goes back to the beginning of the twentieth century when G. Stanley Hall described adolescence as a period of 'Sturm und Drang' (storm and stress). The phenomenon is, however, much rarer than commonly thought (Offer & Schonert-Reichl, 1992). Less than 20% of teenagers fit this pattern. Parents and their adolescent children often have similar values. An authoritative parenting style, including emotional support and an age-appropriate control over the child's behavior, is associated with positive outcomes and the development of competence.

The development of manifested competence may also take place in individuals who have lived under adverse conditions typically indexed by high-risk status. This phenomenon is called *resilience*. Resilience in adolescents at risk is linked to several factors in an individual and environment, which promote competence in spite of obvious adversities or trauma. Important individual characteristics are intellectual functioning, special talents, an appealing, easy-going temperament, and faith. In the extrafamilial environment, the most important factor is a relationship with at least one caring prosocial adult. Other supporting factors are connections to prosocial organizations and attending effective schools. Within the family, a close relationship to a caring parent figure, authoritative parenting, socioeconomic advantages, and connections to extended family networks promote resilience. In the longitudinal study by Werner and Smith (1992), one-third of high risk children were resilients who grew into competent adults.

In adolescence when the rate of chronic disease is low, health problems are strongly related to lifestyle, poverty, and mental health. The use of drugs, accidents and injuries, violence, sexually transmitted diseases, suicide, and eating disorders all threaten adolescent health, as does the availability of firearms in certain societies. Long-term heavy drinking, i.e., consuming four or more drinks per day, also threatens health by resulting in disease and an increased risk of car and other accidents.

Longitudinal studies show that adolescents who begin using alcohol or drugs in their teens are likely to continue to do so into adulthood. The use of drugs is related to poorer health, delinquency, and unstable job and marital histories. Factors that predispose individuals to substance abuse include their availability, parental substance abuse, poor parenting, poor impulse control, sensation seeking, behavioral problems, school failure, peer substance abuse, and positive attitudes towards drugs (Papalia et al., 1998). Many of these factors are interrelated; for instance, poor parenting may cause poor impulse control and behavioral problems in a child which, in turn, results in school failure, choice of peers using drugs, etc.

Sexually transmitted diseases (STDs) have increased along with sexual liberation. In Western countries, adolescents have become sexually active at earlier ages, premarital sexual activity and the number of sexual partners have increased, and the double standard that once permitted more sexual freedom for males than females has been steadily eroding. Among the STDs, acquired immune deficiency syndrome (AIDS) caused by the human immunodeficiency virus (HIV) became a world-wide epidemic in the 1980s.

In wealthy societies, eating disorders have become increasingly common among adolescents. Some, especially girls, may become overly weight- and diet-conscious to the extent that they develop *anorexia nervosa*, obsessive dieting and loss of body weight, or *bulimia nervosa*, eating binges followed by attempts to avoid the high caloric intake by vomiting, exercise, or laxatives (APA, 1994). In anorexia nervosa, the body image is distorted, and the person thinks that she/he is too fat. Bulimics exhibit psychological symptoms such as shame and depression over their eating habits. The causes of eating disorders remain largely unknown. Inadequate coping skills and societal preoccupations with thinness have been offered as some factors affecting their development.

Adulthood

In adulthood, work, marriage, childbearing, and child rearing appear as developmental tasks. Two social trajectories are most central in adult lives: work and family. The balance between their demands affects people's well-being. Gender differences in the subjective importance of these trajectories are smaller than what has traditionally been believed (Papalia et al., 1998).

Work is important to people not only as livelihood but also for self-esteem and human relationships. Unemployment often affects economic situation and self-esteem, and poor economic situation and poor self-esteem mediate the relationship between unemployment and psychological distress (Kokko & Pulkkinen, 1998). Gender differences in the influence of paid work and unemployment on people's psychological well-being may even be opposite to those commonly believed in a country where women and men have equal opportunities for employment and equal rights in pay and promotion. In the Finnish Longitudinal Study of Personality and Social Development, unstable career (many changes of work place, periods of unemployment, and working positions not corresponding to one's training) had direct effects on depression, marital hostility and poor marital quality in the random sample of women (Kinnunen & Pulkkinen, 1998). In men, the effects were indirect: unstable career affected the men's lives to the extent that current economic strain increased expected financial strain, leading to greater depression and greater hostility in the marriage, and to poor marital quality. Employment itself does not, however, guarantee psychological well-being. Further analyses in the same study revealed that high time demands, low control at work, and job insecurity are linked to parenting behavior through the negative job-related affect they create. Of the indicators of negative job-related affect, job exhaustion in particular was related to child-rearing stress which, in turn, hindered child-centeredness as well as supervision in bringing up children.

Work demands may cause continuous occupational stress, which results in *burnout*. Burnout is characterized by three clusters of symptoms: (1) exhaustion (emotional, intellectual, physical) which may cause such ailments as insomnia, headaches and other somatic symptoms, and fatigue; (2) depersonalization (emotional detachment and cynicism); and (3) lowered professional accomplishment, self-efficacy, and self-esteem. Burnout can be relieved by changes in working conditions that promote more meaningful work. A balance between the demands of work and family life also supports effective functioning.

Most people marry in young adulthood. It has also become common in many countries for an unmarried couple to live together. This lifestyle is known as cohabitation. Because of an extended youth in part prolonged by education, many people do not feel prepared for marriage but want to have sexual relationships. Secular trends toward a more relaxed view of sex and away from religion in Western cultures have supported this development. There are also many people who remain single, or if they do marry, remain childless and devote their time and energy to career development and travel. In particular, married men tend to be healthier and happier than singles. The quality of the relationship affects, however, well-being: an unhappy relationship may be a burden.

Positive feelings about one's spouse, sharing goals, finding a balance between intimacy and autonomy, and a commitment to long-term marriage affect marital longevity. Divorce is, however, increasingly common in many cultures. Both marrying young and having divorced parents increase the risk of divorce. Living together before marrying does not seem to improve the quality of marriage. Many divorced people remarry, but remarriages tend to be less stable than first marriages. Remarriages have changed family structures and raised the frequency of step-parenting, which causes new role demands and conflicts; the divorce and remarriage of an adult child creates also new step-grandparenting roles.

Divorce is usually painful and demands a period of adjustment from the couple, their children, and their parents. Even grown-up children may suffer from their parents' divorce and become alienated from them. Although the majority of children whose parents have divorced come through well, there is an increased risk of adjustment problems among them which lasts until young adulthood, as longitudinal studies show.

A set of ordered stages of parenthood over the life course is known as the family cycle. The term dates back to the 1940s when Glick identified seven major events in the life cycle, such as the birth of one's children and their departure from home, and calculated age norms for their occurrence. Marital satisfaction typically declines during the years when children are born, but the relationships typically improve after the children leave home, although the 'empty nest' may at first be a source of stress, especially if the parents have failed to adequately prepare for the event. Conflicts about adult status and privacy may arise if young adults live with their parents, a frequent situation due to financial difficulties or a divorce. Relationships between children and their middle-age parents are usually positive and affectionate. Frequent contact is maintained and assistance reciprocated. A double responsibility for one's family and one's aging parents may, however, become a source of stress.

In Western culture, adult children and their parents generally live in different households if there are financial opportunities for it. Growing up in traditional extended families with two biological parents and grandparents develops familism that enhances the implementation of parental coresidence (Szinovacz, 1997). Non-Whites are more likely to express positive attitudes toward parental coresidence than Whites.

Grandchildren are sources of great pleasure for most grandparents. Although in Western countries, grandparents do not typically become very closely involved in the rearing of their grandchildren, they often play a supporting role when problems arise. The role of grandparent is not a role in the classic sense: it is not defined by social demands or voluntarily attained, and it has mostly no legal rights. Instead, contacts between grandparents and grandchildren are mediated by a middle generation (Datan, Rodheaver, & Hugher, 1987). Therefore, family disruptions threaten ties between grandparents and grandchildren, especially for paternal grandparents. The consequences of these types of disruptions on the well-being of aging grandparents and growing children have largely been neglected in research to date.

People become increasingly concerned about their health in middle age, although they are typically quite healthy. Chronic diseases increase only slightly during middle age in relation to early adulthood. High blood pressure is one health problem that does increase. It increases the risk of heart attack or stroke, and it is more common in men than in women. Another is cancer, a common cause of death in middle age. Women's risk of heart disease increases after menopause, as well as the risk of osteoporosis or loss of bone mass. When bones become thin they fracture more easily. Exercise, nutrition, and avoidance of smoking reduce the risk of osteoporosis and many other diseases. Although women have a higher life-expectancy than men, they report being ill more often than men, use health services more often, and take more medications. Health comparisons between women and men are complicated by the fact that certain health problems are gender-specific, such as those affecting the female reproductive system. Women are also more health-conscious than men.

Old Age

In old age, people have to redirect their energy towards new roles, accept their lives, and cope with the physical changes of aging. In spite of the general decline in physical functioning over time, individual differences at a given age are remarkable. Some people experience sharper and earlier declines than others; a 70-year-old may have better functional capacities than someone 20 years younger. Reasons for individual differences in functional capacities are not well known; more research would be needed, for example, for the study of the influences of racial, ethnic, and cultural factors on aging processes (Jackson, Antonucci, & Gibson, 1990).

The term *functional age* refers to a person's functional capacity compared with others the same age. The functional age may therefore be the same for people of different *chronological ages*. Since the period called old age is long and heterogeneous, three age-based substages have been differentiated by researchers: the *young old* (people aged 65 to 74), the *old old* (people aged 75 to 84), and the *oldest old* (people aged 85 or older). Age-based categorization does not, however, eliminate heterogeneity within groups because interindividual differences in functional capacities are large. Therefore, some researchers use the term young old to refer to healthy and active older adults, whereas old old refers to less capable older people, regardless of their chronological age.

In addition to functional age and chronological age, it is possible to speak of *biological age* (such as puberty), and *social age* (the various roles people assume such as teenager or grandparent). There are also different processes identified in aging. *Primary aging* is the gradual process of bodily deterioration, whereas *secondary aging* is the result of factors which are often within people's control, such as substance abuse. The secondary effects of aging can be reduced by the adoption of healthy habits. Exercise and training help maintain capacities and compensate for some age-related losses.

Biological aging theories attempt to explain why and how biological aging occurs (DiGiovanna, 1994). Genetic theories include ideas that some genes are able to control the age at which certain events occur; that the instructions in genes can be read only a limited number of times; or that there are damaged RNA and protein molecules that read the genes and spread increasing numbers of mistakes throughout the cell and the body, causing aging. There are also theories about harmful substances that accumulate in the body over a period of years and interfere with the body causing aging. Other theories state that aging is caused by hormones, particularly the hormone produced by the pituitary gland, or by the immune system which becomes weaker as it is used.

The proportion of people aged 65 or older is rapidly increasing in the world because of better nutrition, health care, and other aspects of well-being. Life expectancy at birth differs, however, in different parts of the world. For example, in 1993, it was 72 years for men and 79 for women

in the United States, 58/59 in India, and 76/82 in Japan (Aiken, 1995). Women have a higher mean longevity than men. One reason for this difference is that higher levels of certain hormones (estrogen and progesterone) help protect women from specific diseases such as heart attacks (DiGiovanna, 1994). There are also differences in male and female lifestyles.

Although longevity is generally highly valued in society, many people do not want to be old. The common stereotypes of old people in Western culture are often negative and show little understanding of elderly people's capacities. 'Old' in contemporary Western society often implies uselessness and a loss of status, whereas other societies, for example, agricultural societies, certain African tribes, or Eskimos may show great respect for the aged (Aiken, 1995). Prejudice or discrimination against the elderly is called *agism*.

Older people generally have chronic health problems, although they may have less acute health problems such as flu infections than younger people. Serious health problems limit everyday activities and cognitive functioning, and these limitations increase with age, particularly, due to disability as the consequence of multiple causes. Critical steps in functional disability can be reliably scaled as shown by a comparative study in five European countries (Ferrucci et al., 1998). Deterioration begins from activities that require dynamic balance and muscular strength and progresses to performances using hands only. Most older adults are not, however, limited in their major everyday activities by health concerns. They may even remain sexually active until their eighties if they have been sexually active during their younger years. Most older men and women can reach orgasm, although sexual activity will differ in intensity from what it was in earlier years.

Some older adults suffer from *dementia* which is the general term for cognitive and behavioral deterioration caused mostly by hypertension, stroke and other cardiovascular problems, Parkinson's disease, Alzheimer's disease, or neurological disorders. Dementia is generally irreversible, but is a disease and not merely a part of the aging process as is erroneously thought.

Different theories include contrasting conceptions of healthy aging as reviewed by M. M. Baltes and Lang (1997). The disengagement theory, proposed by Cumming and Henry in the early 1960s, maintains that there is a gradual reduction in social involvement because of the decline in physical functioning and the growing awareness of death. In contrast, the activity theory proposed by Havighurst and Albrecht in the 1950s assumes that the maintenance of activity increases the quality of aging. A more recent continuity theory by Atchley emphasizes people's need to maintain continuity or connection with the past in their life patterns. Other models of successful aging include the Eriksonian construction of integrity, Maslow's self-actualization, Rogers' meaningful life, and Ryff's integrative model based on developmental, clinical, and mental health criteria. Recent findings suggest that creative, educational, and interactive activities which facilitate a sense of control over one's life increase well-being in old age (Herzog, Franks, Markus, & Holmberg, 1998).

A holistic view adopted in the Berlin Aging Study highlights an integrative perspective on aging and sees it as a process of interrelated constancy and change involving many factors. A cross-sectional analysis of data on individuals aged 70 to 103 years showed that those endowed with more sensorimotor-cognitive and social-personality resources exhibited fewer negative aging trends, a higher level of activity, and a greater variety of activity (M. M. Baltes & Lang, 1997). The same study also shows that large interindividual differences continue into very old age. In psychological functioning (defined as intellectual functioning, personality disposition, and social relationships), the oldest old were as heterogeneous as those in their eighties. Age-associated mortality did not reduce variability in this cross-sectional study. The functional status tends, however, to decrease with increasing age, and the likelihood of broadly based dysfunctionality increases (Smith & Baltes, 1997); the functional status tends to be lower in women than in men. Physical and sensory capacities (auditory, visual, gait) account powerfully for general age-related variance in activity. In the Finnish Evergreen project (Heikkinen et al., 1997), which is part of a study called Nordic Research on Aging (NORA) including all Nordic countries, a low psychomotor speed and a low cognitive capacity were significant predictors of subsequent death during the five-year follow-up with participants aged 75 and 80 years at the baseline measurement.

Successful Development

The interplay of developmental and social trajectories forms a unique life context for each individual and produces a unique outcome of development. To understand an individual's successful career development, for example, one needs to consider other social trajectories in his/her life and immediate environment, as well as his/her psychological functioning capacities.

Successful development is not uniform but polyform.

Pathways to both successful development and the accumulation of social functioning problems have become evident in the Jyväskylä Longitudinal Study of Personality and Social Development. Based on the interviews of the participants, a mailed questionnaire, personality inventories, criminal records at ages 27 and 36, and previously collected data at ages 8 and 14 using peer nomination and parental rating techniques, several factors affecting successful career development could be identified. Initial school success coupled with high emotional regulation generally predicted both female and male career development (Pulkkinen, Ohranen, & Tolvanen, 1999). More generally, successful developmental paths had roots in high emotional and behavioral regulation in childhood, good school success, and good family environment. This pattern explained good psychosocial functioning in mid-adulthood comprising stable career, controlled drinking, good financial standing, socialization, self-esteem, satisfaction with life, and well-being. Correspondingly, low emotional regulation and home adversities in childhood was a risk factor for career development and the accumulation of other problems in social functioning (Rönkä, Kinnunen, & Pulkkinen, in press), as well as long-term unemployment (Kokko, Pulkkinen, & Puustinen, in press). Data were collected at the time of a severe economic recession when unemployment attacked one-fifth of people in Finland; those with high emotional regulation and social activity were more likely to be re-employed.

In the study of human development, the *prediction* of development or behavior is often seen as a motive for research. Future events in people's lives are, however, rarely predictable because life is complex and development is multi-factorially determined. Instead, researchers devote their energy to *explaining* and understanding the course of development and the events that are included in it (Keil, 1998). The accumulation of knowledge about developmental processes can be utilized for decision making, education, and enhancement programs that aim to improve people's lives.

Conceptualizations of successful development have been based on successful resolution of psychological crises leading finally to wisdom in old age (Erikson, 1950); accomplishment of developmental tasks (Havighurst, 1972); social and psychological adaptation (Block, 1971), and the maximization of desirable goals or outcomes and the avoidance of undesirable outcomes (Baltes et al., 1998). These conceptualizations represent different perspectives on the same lifespan process which consists of the ways in which individuals try to handle various culturally and biologically determined age-graded tasks and transitions. Successful development is exemplified within one's socio-cultural environment. Outcomes can be seen as adjustment to society. The final criterion of successful development is that an individual can see his or her life as a meaningful totality and possibly integrate it in some way into a part of the universe.

ACKNOWLEDGEMENTS

This chapter was written during my visit to the Center of Developmental Sciences, University of North Carolina, Chapel Hill, USA, and supported by its excellent working facilities. Financial support came from the Academy of Finland. I wish also to thank Sanna Oravala, M.A., for her help in the process of finalizing the paper.

RESOURCE REFERENCES

Aiken, L. R. (1995). *Aging. An introduction to gerontology*. Thousand Oaks, CA: Sage.

Baltes, P. B., Lindenberger, U., & Staudinger, U. M. (1998). Life-span theory in developmental psychology. In W. Damon (Editor-in-Chief) & R. M. Lerner (Volume Editor), *Handbook of child psychology* (Vol. 1, pp. 1029–1143). New York: Wiley.

Birren, J. E., & Schaie, K. W. (Eds.). (1990). *Handbook of the psychology of aging* (3rd ed.). San Diego, CA: Academic Press.

Elder, G. H., Jr. (1998). Life-course and human development. In W. Damon (Editor-in-Chief) & R. M. Lerner (Volume Editor), *Handbook of child psychology* (Vol. 1, pp. 939–991). New York: Wiley.

Harter, S. (1998). The development of self-representations. In W. Damon (Editor-in-Chief) & N. Eisenberg (Volume Editor), *Handbook of child psychology* (Vol. 3, pp. 553–617). New York: Wiley.

Hartup, W. W., & Stevens, N. (1997). Friendships and adaptation in the life course. *Psychological Bulletin, 121* (3), 355–370.

Kagitcibasi, C. (1996). *Family and human development across cultures: A view from the other side*. Hillsdale, NJ: Lawrence Erlbaum.

Papalia, D. E., Olds, S. W., & Feldman, R. (1998). *Human development* (7th ed.). New York: McGraw-Hill.

Pulkkinen, L. (Ed.). (1996a). *Lapsesta aikuiseksi* [From child to adult]. Jyväskylä, Finland: Atena.

Valsiner, J., & Lawrence, J. A. (1997). Human development in culture across the life span. In J. W. Berry, P. R. Dasen, & T. S. Saraswathi (Eds.), *Handbook of cross-cultural psychology* (Vol. 2, pp. 69–106). Boston, MA: Allyn & Bacon.

Journals

International Journal of Behavioral Development
Journal of Personality and Social Psychology
Psychology and Aging

ADDITIONAL LITERATURE CITED

Ackerman, P. L., & Heggestad, E. D. (1997). Intelligence, personality, and interests: Evidence for overlapping traits. *Psychological Bulletin, 121*, 219–245.

American Psychiatric Association (APA) (1994). *Diagnostic and statistical manual of mental disorders* (4th ed.) (DSM-IV). Washington, DC: APA.

Baltes, M. M., & Lang, F. R. (1997). Everyday functioning and successful aging: The impact or resources. *Psychology and Aging, 12*, 433–443.

Baltes, P. B., Staudinger, U. M., & Lindenberger, U. (1999). Lifespan psychology: Theory and application to intellectual functioning. *Annual Review of Psychology, 50*, 471–507.

Bartholomew, K., & Horowitz, L. (1991). Attachment styles among young adults: A test of a four-category model. *Journal of Personality and Social Psychology, 61*, 226–244.

Berry, J. W., Poortinga, Y. H., Segall, M. H., & Dasen, P. R. (1992). *Cross-cultural psychology: Research and applications*. New York: Cambridge University Press.

Block, J. (1971). *Lives through time*. Berkeley, CA: Bancroft Books.

Block, J. (1993). Studying personality the long way. In D. C. Funder, R. D. Parke, C. Tomlinson-Keasey, & K. Widaman (Eds.), *Studying lives through time* (pp. 9–41). Washington, DC: American Psychological Association.

Block, J. (1995). A contrarian view of the five-factor approach to personality description. *Psychological Bulletin, 117*, 187–215.

Brandtstädter, J. (1998). Action perspectives on human development. In W. Damon (Editor-in-Chief) & R. M. Lerner (Volume Editor), *Handbook of child psychology* (Vol. 1, pp. 807–863). New York: Wiley.

Bronfenbrenner, U., & Morris, P. A. (1998). The ecology of developmental processes. In W. Damon (Editor-in-Chief) & R. M. Lerner (Volume Editor), *Handbook of child psychology* (Vol. 1, pp. 993–1028). New York: Wiley.

Bühler, C. (1933). *Der menschliche Lebenslauf als psychologisches Problem*. Leipzig: Hirzel.

Cairns, R. B., & Cairns, B. D. (1994). *Lifelines and risks: Pathways of youth in our time.* New York: Harvester Wheatsheaf.

Carstensen, L. L., Gottman, J. M., & Levenson, R. W. (1995). Emotional behavior in long-term marriage. *Psychology and Aging, 10,* 140–149.

Caspi, A. (1998). Personality development across the life course. In W. Damon (Editor-in-Chief) & N. Eisenberg (Volume Editor), *Handbook of child psychology* (Vol. 3, pp. 311–388). New York: Wiley.

Claes, M. (1998). Adolescent's closeness with parents, siblings, and friends in three countries: Canada, Belgium, and Italy. *Journal of Youth and Adolescence, 27,* 165–184.

Clausen, J. A. (1993). *American lives.* New York: Free Press.

Coie, J. D., & Dodge, K. A. (1998). Aggression and antisocial behavior. In W. Damon (Editor-in-Chief) & N. Eisenberg (Volume Editor), *Handbook of child psychology* (Vol. 3, pp. 779–862). New York: Wiley.

Costa, P. T., Jr., & McCrae, R. R. (1994). Stability and change in personality from adolescence through adulthood. In C. E. Halverson, G. A. Kohnstamm, & R. P. Martin (Eds.), *The developing structure of temperament and personality from infancy to adulthood.* Hillsdale, NJ: Erlbaum.

Damon, W., & Hart, D. (1988). *Self-understanding in children and adolescence.* New York: Cambridge University Press.

Datan, N., Rodeheaver, D., & Hugher, F. (1987). Adult development and aging. *Annual Review of Psychology, 38,* 153–180.

Diehl, M., Elnick, A. B., Bourbeau, L. S., & Labouviev-Vief, G. (1998). Adult attachment styles: Their relations to family context and personality. *Journal of Personality and Social Psychology, 6,* 1656–1669.

Diener, E., & Diener, M. (1995). Cross-cultural correlates of life satisfaction and self-esteem. *Journal of Personality and Social Psychology, 68,* 653–663.

Dietz, B. E. (1996). The relationship of aging to self-esteem: The relative effects of maturation and role accumulation. *International Journal of Aging and Human Development, 43,* 249–266.

DiGiovanna, A. G. (1994). *Human aging. Biological perspectives.* New York: McGraw-Hill.

Digman, J. M. (1997). Higher-order factors of the big five. *Journal of Personality and Social Psychology, 73,* 1246–1256.

Dougherty, L. M., Abe, J., & Izard, C. E. (1996). Differential emotions theory and emotional development in adulthood and later life. In E. C. Magai & S. H. McFadden (Eds.), *Handbook of emotion: Adult development and aging* (pp. 27–41). New York: Academic Press.

Eisenberg, N. (1998). Introduction. In W. Damon (Editor-in-Chief) & N. Eisenberg (Volume Editor), *Handbook of child psychology* (Vol. 3, pp. 1–24). New York: Wiley.

Eisenberg, N., & Fabes, R. (1998). Prosocial development. In W. Damon (Editor-in-Chief) & N. Eisenberg (Volume Editor), *Handbook of child psychology* (Vol. 3, pp. 701–778). New York: Wiley.

Elbedour, S., Schulman, S., & Kedem, P. (1997). Adolescent intimacy. A cross-cultural study. *Journal of Cross-Cultural Psychology, 28,* 5–22.

Erikson, E. H. (1950). *Childhood and society.* New York: Norton.

Eysenck, H. J. (1997). Personality and experimental psychology: The unification of psychology and the possibility of a paradigm. *Journal of Personality and Social Psychology, 73,* 1224–1237.

Ferrucci, L., Guralnik, J. M., Cecchi, F., Marchionni, N., Salani, D., Kasper, J., Celli, R., Giardini, S., Heikkinen, E., Jylhä, M., & Baroni, A. (1998). Constant hierarchic patterns of physical functioning across seven populations in five countries. *Gerontology, 38,* 286–294.

Fowler, J. (1981). *Stages of faith: The psychology of human development and the quest for meaning.* New York: Harper & Row.

Gardner, H. E. (1998). Extraordinary cognitive achievements (ECA): A symbol systems approach. In W. Damon (Editor-in-Chief) & R. M. Lerner (Volume Editor), *Handbook of child psychology* (Vol. 1, pp. 415–466). New York: Wiley.

Gross, J. J., Carstensen, L. L., Pasupathi, M., Tsai, J., Götestam Skorpen, C., & Hsu, A. Y. C. (1997). Emotion and aging: Experience, expression, and control. *Psychology and Aging, 12,* 590–599.

Havighurst, R. J. (1948). *Developmental tasks and education.* New York: McKay.

Heikkinen, E., Heikkinen, R.-L., & Ruoppila, I. (Eds.). (1997). Functional capacity and health of elderly people – The Evergreen Project. *Scandinavian Journal of Social Medicine,* Supplementum 53.

Herzog, A. R., Franks, M. M., Markus, H. R., & Holmberg, D. (1998). Activities and well-being in older age: Effects of self-concept and educational attainment. *Psychology and Aging, 13,* 179–185.

Jackson, J. S., Antonucci, T. C., & Gibson, R. C. (1990). Cultural, racial, and ethnic minority influences on aging. In J. E. Birren & K. W. Schaie (Eds.), *Handbook of the psychology of aging* (3rd ed., pp. 103–123). San Diego, CA: Academic Press.

Jones, C. J., & Meredith, W. (1996). Patterns of personality change across the life span. *Psychology and Aging, 11,* 57–65.

Kagitcibasi, C. (1988). Diversity of socialization and social change. In P. R. Dasen & J. W. Berry (Eds.), *Health and cross-cultural psychology: Toward applications.* Cross-cultural research and methodology series, vol. 10 (pp. 25–47). Newbury Park, CA: Sage.

Katzko, M. W., Steverink, N., Dittmann-Kohli, F., & Herrera, R. R. (1998). The self-concept of the elderly: A cross-cultural comparison. *International*

Journal of Aging and Human Development, 46, 171–187.

Keil, F. C. (1998). Cognitive science and the origins of thought and knowledge. In W. Damon (Editor-in-Chief) & R. M. Lerner (Volume Editor), *Handbook of child psychology* (Vol. 1, pp. 341–413). New York: Wiley.

Kinnunen, U., & Pulkkinen, L. (1998). Linking economic stress to marital quality among Finnish marital couples: Mediator effects. *Journal of Family Issues, 19,* 705–724.

Kohlberg, L., & Ryncarz, R. A. (1990). Beyond justice reasoning: Moral development and consideration of a seventh stage. In C. N. Alexander & E. J. Langer (Eds.), *Higher stages of human development* (pp. 191–207). New York: Oxford University Press.

Kokko, K., & Pulkkinen, L. (1998). Unemployment and psychological distress: Mediator effects. *Journal of Adult Development, 5,* 205–217.

Kokko, K., Pulkkinen, L., & Puustinen, M. (in press). Long-term unemployment: Selection and causation. *International Journal of Behavioral Development.*

Labouvie-Vief, G. (1985). Intelligence and cognition. In J. E. Birren & K. W. Schaie (Eds.), *Handbook of the psychology of aging* (pp. 500–530). New York: Van Nostrand Reinhold.

Lang, F. R., & Baltes, M. M. (1997). Being with people and being alone in late life: Costs and benefits for everyday functioning. *International Journal of Behavioral Development, 21,* 729–746.

Levinson, D. (1978). *The seasons of a man's life.* New York: Knopf.

Levinson, D. (1996). *The seasons of a woman's life.* New York: Knopf.

Lindenberger, U., & Baltes, P. B. (1997). Intellectual functioning in old and very old age: Cross-sectional results from the Berlin Aging Study. *Psychology and Aging, 12,* 410–432.

Loeber, R., & Stouthamer-Loeber, M. (1998). Development of juvenile aggression and violence: Some common misconceptions and controversies. *American Psychologist, 53,* 242–259.

Magnusson, D., & Stattin, H. (1998). Person–context interaction theories. In W. Damon (Editor-in-Chief) & R. M. Lerner (Volume Editor), *Handbook of child psychology* (Vol. 1, pp. 685–759). New York: Wiley.

Marcia, J. E. (1980). Identity in adolescence. In J. Adelson (Ed.), *Handbook of adolescent psychology* (pp. 158–187). New York: Wiley.

Maslow, A. (1954). *Motivation and personality.* New York: Harper.

Masten, A. S., & Coatsworth, J. D. (1998). The development of competence in favorable and unfavorable environments: Lessons from research on successful children. *American Psychologist, 53,* 205–220.

Mesquita, B., & Frijda, N. H. (1992). Cultural variations in emotions: A review. *Psychological Bulletin, 112,* 179–204.

Nsamenang, A. B. (1992). *Human development in cultural context. A Third World perspective.* Newbury Park, CA: Sage.

Nurmi, J.-E. (1997). Self-definition and mental health during adolescence and young adulthood. In J. Schulenberg, J. Maggs, & K. Hurrelmann (Eds.), *Health risks and development transitions during adolescence* (pp. 395–419). Cambridge, UK: Cambridge University Press.

Offer, D., & Schonert-Reichl, K. A. (1992). Debunking the myths of adolescence: Findings from recent research. *Journal of the American Academy of Child and Adolescent Psychiatry, 31,* 1003–1014.

Pike, A., & Plomin, R. (1997). A behavioural genetic perspective on close relationships. *International Journal of Behavioral Development, 21,* 647–667.

Plomin, R., & Petrill, S. A. (1997). Genetics and intelligence: What's new? *Intelligence, 24,* 53–77.

Pulkkinen, L. (1996b). Female and male personality styles: A typological and developmental analysis. *Journal of Personality and Social Psychology, 70,* 1288–1306.

Pulkkinen, L., Ohranen, M., & Tolvanen, A. (1999). Personality antecedents of career orientation and stability among women compared to men. *Journal of Vocational Behavior, 54,* 37–58.

Reinert, G. (1979). Prolegomena to a history of life-span developmental psychology. In P. B. Baltes & O. G. Brim, Jr. (Eds.), *Life-span development and behavior* (Vol. 2, pp. 205–254). New York: Academic Press.

Reiss, A. J., Jr., & Roth, J. A. (Eds.). (1994). *Understanding and preventing violence.* Washington, DC: National Academy Press.

Roberts, B. W., & Helson, R. (1997). Changes in culture, changes in personality: The influence of individualism in a longitudinal study of women. *Journal of Personality and Social Psychology, 72,* 641–651.

Rönkä, A., Kinnunen, U., & Pulkkinen, L. (in press). The accumulation of problems of social functioning as a long-term process: Women and men compared. *International Journal of Behavioral Development.*

Rothbart, M., & Bates, J. (1998). Temperament. In W. Damon (Editor-in-Chief) & N. Eisenberg (Volume Editor), *Handbook of child psychology* (Vol. 3, pp. 105–176). New York: Wiley.

Rutter, M., Giller, H., & Hagell, A. (1998). Antisocial behavior by young people. Cambridge, UK: Cambridge University Press.

Schaie, K. W. (1994). The course of adult intellectual development. *American Psychologist, 49,* 304–313.

Shweder, R. A. (Ed.). (1997). *Welcome to middle age! (And other cultural fictions).* Chicago: Chicago University Press.

Smith, J., & Baltes, P. B. (1997). Profiles of psychological functioning in the old and oldest old. *Psychology and Aging, 12*, 458–472.

Sorenson, S. B. (1996). Violence against women. Examining ethnic differences and commonalities. *Evaluation Review, 20*, 123–145.

Sternberg, R. J. (1995). Love as a story. *Journal of Social and Personal Relationships, 12*, 541–546.

Sternberg, R. J. (1997). The concept of intelligence and its role in lifelong learning and success. *American Psychologist, 52*, 1030–1037.

Susman, E. J., Dorn, L. D., & Chrousos, G. P. (1991). Negative affect and hormone levels in young adolescents: Concurrent and predictive perspectives. *Journal of Youth and Adolescence, 20,* 167–190.

Szinovacz, M. (1997). Adult children taking parents into their homes: Effects of childhood living arrangements. *Journal of Marriage and the Family, 59*, 700–717.

Troll, L. E., & Skaff, M. M. (1997). Perceived continuity of self in very old age. *Psychology and Aging, 12*, 162–169.

Van IJzendoorn, M. H. (1997). Attachment, emergent morality, and aggression: Toward a developmental socioemotional model of antisocial behaviour. *International Journal of Behavioral Development, 21*, 703–727.

Verhaeghen, P., & Salthouse, T. A. (1997). Meta-analyses of age-cognition relations in adulthood: Estimates of linear and nonlinear age effects and structural models. *Psychological Bulletin, 122*, 231–249.

Vernon, P. A., Jang, K. L., Harries, J. A., & McCarthy, J. M. (1997). Environmental predictors of personality differences: A twin and sibling study. *Journal of Personality and Social Psychology, 72*, 177–183.

Werner, E. E., & Smith, R. S. (1992). *Overcoming the odds: High risk children from birth to adulthood.* Ithaca, NY: Cornell University Press.

York, K. L., & John, O. P. (1992). The four faces of Eve: A typological analysis of women's personality at midlife. *Journal of Personality and Social Psychology, 63*, 494–508.

Communications concerning this chapter should be addressed to: Professor Lea Pulkinnen, Department of Psychology, University of Jyväskylä, PO Box 35, FIN-40351 Jyväskylä, Finland

16

Personality and Individual Differences

ROBERT HOGAN, ALLAN R. HARKNESS, AND DAVID LUBINSKI

16.1 BASIC CONCEPTS

This chapter is about personality and individual differences, topics that are related but not identical. Personality concerns the nature of human nature; individual differences – sometimes called differential psychology (cf. Stern, 1900) – concerns analyzing the ways in which people's performance differs. In addition to social behavior, this includes individual differences in intellectual, psychomotor, perceptual, and cognitive performance. This chapter primarily focuses on personality, temperament, and intelligence, and their implications for individual differences in human performance.

Personality psychology concerns the distinctive and important characteristics of people compared with other biological species. Personality psychology is designed to answer three kinds of questions: (a) how and in what ways are people all alike, e.g., are people naturally aggressive? (b) how and in what ways are people different, e.g., what are the major dimensions of individual differences in human social behavior?; and (c) how to explain the puzzling behavior of single individuals, e.g., why did Adolf Hitler hate Jews? Most of the interesting questions we have about people are the subject of personality psychology.

How is personality defined? The word personality comes from the ancient Greek word 'persona', which referred to the mask worn by actors in Greek drama; the mask denoted an actor's part or role in a play, but left open the question of who or what was behind the mask. This suggests there are two sides to a person – that which we see in public and that which is behind the public mask. MacKinnon (1948) also noted that the word personality is defined in two very different ways – each pointing to a different but important aspects of personality. The first is personality from the outside, the manner in which a person is perceived and described by others. The second is personality from the inside, and concerns the factors inside people that explain why others perceive them as they do. This suggests that any definition of personality must take account of these two perspectives. In everyday language personality in the first sense – the observer's view – is referred to as reputation, the unique way in which each person is described by others. The terms used to describe personality in the second sense – the factors inside people that explain their characteristic behavior – differ depending on the writer, and the great debates in personality psychology concern the nature of these inner factors.

Measures of personality from the observer's and from the actor's perspective are only moderately correlated, suggesting that the two forms of personality are not identical. In addition, personality from the observer's perspective is relatively easy to study; it is studied using observer ratings, for which high levels of agreement are routinely found. In contrast, personality from the actor's perspective is hard to study because the hypothesized processes inside people cannot be directly observed; their nature must be inferred, based on sources of indirect data, whether they come from experiments or self-reports.

16.2 HISTORY

There are two separate traditions running through the history of personality psychology; they can be called the applied and the academic traditions. In the applied tradition, researchers think about personality in the context of trying to help people solve their problems. In the academic tradition, researchers study personality simply because they think it is interesting and important.

History of Applied Tradition

This tradition begins when Hippocrates, the father of Greek medicine (c. 460 B.C.E.–c. 370 B.C.E.) decided, on the basis of the physical theory of Empedocles (the world is composed of four elements: earth, air, fire, and water), that people are composed of four humors or bodily fluids: black bile, yellow bile, phlegm, and blood. Galen (130–200 C.E.) using Hippocrates' physical theory, suggested that peoples' behavior reflects the influence of these basic humors,

and problems occur when they get out of balance. Depending on which humor is predominant, this yields four types of people: those with an excess of black bile are melancholic or depressed; those with an excess of yellow bile – from the spleen – are splenetic or hostile; those with an excess of phlegm are phlegmatic or lacking in energy; and those with an excess of blood are sanguine, or cheerful and optimistic. Galen's types have been very influential; they were adopted by Immanuel Kant in his best-selling eighteenth century textbook *Anthropologie* (1798), by Wilhelm Wundt in his model of physiological psychology (1903), and by Eysenck (1970) in his taxonomy of personality types.

The ancient Greeks invented the word 'hysteria' to label medical symptoms that have no obvious physical basis. The Greeks believed that only women have hysterical symptoms; as a result, the word hysterical is related to the Greek word for uterus. The larger point is that hysterical symptoms have been recognized for at least 2,000 years and they continue to be important today, although now they are called somatization disorders. For example, the Centers for Disease Control in the US estimates that perhaps 65% of the people who seek medical attention each day are suffering from somatization disorders.

Galen and other non-Christian, non-European thinkers explained hysterical symptoms in terms of a lack of balance among the various parts of the psyche. During the Christian middle ages in Europe, however, hysterical disorders were thought to be caused by a devil who had entered a person's body, and the disorder could be treated by exorcism. Johan Joseph Gassner (1727–1779), an Austrian priest, became famous for curing poor people, many of whose symptoms were undoubtedly hysterical. A commission was formed to investigate Gassner, and it included a physician named Franz Anton Mesmer (1734–1815). Mesmer soon claimed to be able to reproduce Gassner's cures using magnets and argued that the secret to Gassner's cures was his unusual 'animal magnetism'. Mesmer developed a method for curing hysterical disorders based on magnets and his own personal magnetism. Although Mesmer was a fraud, he is credited with inventing hypnotism – originally called mesmerism.

Auguste Lieabeault (1823–1904), a French country doctor, read about hypnotism in school; he gave his patients the choice between being treated conventionally for a fee or being hypnotized for free; his practice rapidly expanded. Hippolyte Bernheim (1840–1919) studied with Lieabeault, and later proposed that hypnosis is a function of the patient's suggestibility rather than the hypnotist's personality, and that suggestibility is normally distributed in the population.

Jean-Martin Charcot (1825–1893), the best-known psychiatrist in Europe in his prime, was the director of Paris' largest psychiatric hospital, where he studied hysterics using hypnosis in the 1870s. Charcot concluded that both men and women suffer from hysterical disorders, that hysterics suffer too much to be faking, that hysteria and hypnotic susceptibility are related, and that both are caused by dissociation – an inability to integrate one's thoughts and memory due to a degeneration of the nervous system.

Charcot established hypnosis as a legitimate scientific topic; he also quarrelled with Bernheim, arguing that only neurotics could be hypnotized. Over time, Bernheim's view – that hypnotizability is a normal characteristic – prevailed. More important for this history, however, is the fact that a young doctor from Vienna named Sigmund Freud went to Paris in the winter of 1885–1886 to study with Charcot; when Freud returned to Vienna, he began using hypnosis to treat hysteria, and he began developing psychoanalysis, the first systematic theory of personality.

Freud is not well regarded by academic psychologists today, but thoughtful non-psychologists believe that he is one of the three or four most influential thinkers of the twentieth century. Freud explained psychological problems (including hysteria) in terms of powerful sexual and aggressive desires that are repressed and then reappear as physical symptoms. Three Freudian revisionists are particularly important: Alfred Adler and Karen Horney explained psychological problems in terms of disturbed social relationships (Horney especially emphasized problems that are specific to women); Carl Jung explained psychological problems in terms of frustrated religious longings.

After Freud's death, personality researchers extended Adler and Horney's views by arguing that peoples' problems are largely caused by disturbed relationships with their primary caretakers (parents) during childhood; this viewpoint, called attachment theory (Bowlby, 1983), became an important area of research at the turn of the century (Simpson & Rholes, 1998).

George Kelly's (1955) book, *The psychology of personal constructs*, stimulated the cognitive revolution in applied personality psychology. In an abrupt departure from Freud, Kelly argued that people are compelled to make conceptual sense out of their social worlds; they develop theories of what they believe others expect of them during social interaction, and then use these theories to guide their behavior. People with problems often have developed incorrect theories about what others expect, and then they have problems dealing with others. Kelly's ideas have been very influential, as seen in the writings of Walter Mischel (1990) and his students, and in the works of Julian Rotter (1966) and Albert Bandura (1982). Rotter and Bandura also developed psychometric measures of individual differences in peoples' expectations about the world – Locus of Control and Self-Efficacy – that also have been very popular and influential.

History of Academic Tradition

The applied tradition of personality research has a specific agenda – initially to explain the origins of hysterical disorders, then more generally to explain individual differences in psychological adjustment – and most of the classical theories of personality concern this problem. The academic tradition has an entirely different agenda – it is to capture the unique qualities of individuals, to describe how people differ from one another (cf. Stern, 1900). To do this, units of analysis become important – because they provide the means for comparing people. In personality psychology, two kinds of units have dominated these discussions – types and traits.

Types are coherent composites of traits; types are the discernable clusters of people found in populations, e.g., the bureaucrat, the absent-minded professor, the bohemian or hippie. Traits, on the other hand, are recurring themes in the behavior of individuals, e.g., aggressiveness, charm, conscientiousness. Types are composed of, and can always be broken down into, traits. However, it is usually difficult to examine a group of traits and decide what sort of type would be formed if they were combined. So the relationship between types and traits is intransitive – types can be decomposed into traits with some precision but the reverse is not necessarily true. Rephrasing this point, people have traits, but they fit types.

Regardless of whether we are talking about types or traits, our ability to study them scientifically depends on having available a taxonomy, a method for classifying them reliably. Consequently, the history of type theory and the history of trait theory concern the search for an agreed-upon taxonomy, a way to classify the phenomena.

Type Theory

The first theory of types that we know about was proposed by Theophrastus, a botanist and student of Aristotle; Theophrastus classified the people who were prominent in public life in Athens during the time of Alexander (356–323

B.C.E.). These types are clearly and vividly drawn, and many of them, e.g., the Flatterer, are easily recognized today. Theophrastus' types are an interesting starting point, but they are not based on systematic observations and, as a taxonomy, his types are not very comprehensive.

We mentioned earlier Hippocrates who defined four types of people based on their balance of bodily humors. Rostan (1824) developed the most influential typology after Hippocrates, based on physique or body build. He defined four types: cerebral – long and thin; muscular – square and athletic; digestive – rotund; and respiratory – a combination. Viola (1909) using more sophisticated measurement methods, reduced this typology to Rostan's first three, which Viola called microsplanchic, normosplanchic, and macrosplanchic. Following Viola, Ernst Kretschmer (1926), developed a type theory based on physique that was popular prior to World War II. He defined three types: aesthenic – an emaciated body build; athletic – a muscular build; and pyknic – a plump build. He also found relationships between the aesthenic build and schizophrenia, and between the pyknic build and manic-depression. Building on the tradition of Rostan, Viola, and Kretschmer, W. H. Sheldon (Sheldon, Dupertuis, & McDermott, 1954) also developed a typology based on body build, which he called somatotypes. He believed the somatotypes reflected underlying genetic factors, and were associated with characteristic personality styles. Long, thin people – ectomorphs – were shy and retiring and potentially disposed to schizophrenia. Square, athletically built people – mesomorphs – were aggressive and assertive and potentially disposed to paranoia. Round people – endomorphs – were jolly and fun and potentially disposed to manic-depression.

Carl Jung also developed an influential type theory in his 1923 book, *Psychological Types*. There are two features of Jung's theory that should be noted. First, it is an information-processing model; the Jungian types reflect: (a) where people deploy their attention – inward for Introverts, outward for Extraverts; (b) how they take in information – intuitively or empirically; and (c) how they evaluate information – logically or according to its personal meaning. The second thing to note about the Jungian types is that they form the basis for a very popular personality inventory – the Myers–Briggs Type Indicator, millions of copies of which are sold each year to business and educational organizations around the world.

Spranger (*Types of Men*, 1928) suggested there are six ideal types of personality, and each type is defined by a particular value orientation. The Theoretical type values truth and wants to impose rational order on the world. The Economic type values things that are useful and wants to make money. The Aesthetic type values form and harmony and wants to make life attractive. The Social type loves people and wants to help them. The Political type values power and wants to gain personal authority and influence. Finally, the Religious type values unity or oneness with the universe and wants to understand his/her relationship to the cosmos. The American personality psychologist Gordon Allport was a great enthusiast of German psychology, and he developed a personality inventory, *The Study of Values*, to measure Spranger's types. Allport's inventory enjoyed considerable popularity in the 1950s and 1960s.

Drawing on Jung, Spranger, and Allport, John Holland (1985) proposed a type theory based on peoples' interests, competencies, and values. The resemblance between Holland's types and the earlier theories are obvious: Realistic types (e.g., engineers) build, operate, and maintain things and equipment; Investigative types (e.g., scientists) use data to solve problems; Artistic types (e.g., artists) design and decorate things, and entertain people; Social types (e.g., clinical psychologists) help people; Enterprising types (e.g., politicians) persuade and manipulate people; and Conventional types (e.g., accountants) regulate and codify things. Holland's theory can classify every job in the Dictionary of Occupational Titles – it is an exhaustive taxonomy of occupations that has been extensively replicated and is generally regarded as the model theory of personality types. Holland's theory is the end point of the search for personality types that began with Theophrastus.

Trait Theory

Trait theory begins with the research of Franz Joseph Gall (1758–1828), the foremost brain anatomist of his day. Gall is best known today as the father of phrenology, a fraudulent discipline based on the notion that well-developed mental faculties can be identified by bumps or protrusions on the skull. Gall identified groups of people who were characterized by a specific trait – generosity, truthfulness, lasciviousness – and then tried to find a common denominator in the shape of their skulls. Over time he identified 27 human capacities and designed charts to show the bumps that corresponded to these capacities. The notion that bumps on the skull correspond to overdeveloped areas of the brain is, of course, nonsense. Nonetheless, Gall proposed a clear link between the brain and behavior and, while his contemporaries searched for general laws of the mind, Gall tried to identify the dimension along which people differ and to find the causes of these differences. In formulating his observations of how people differ from one another, Gall created the first taxonomy of traits.

Francis Galton (1822–1911), Charles Darwin's cousin and an enthusiastic practitioner of applied measurement, invented the foundations of modern psychometrics, including the concepts of the regression line, regression to the mean, and the correlation coefficient; and his work led directly to the development of factor analysis and modern behavior genetics. Although he studied ability and not personality, he developed methods needed to study personality traits.

The formal study of personality and individual differences as an academic discipline begins with the work of William Stern (1900, 1906). In his two founding books Stern developed a systematic framework for the study of individual differences and of psychological individuality as such. In this framework he distinguishes already between a variable-oriented and a type-oriented research approach, paralleling the later distinction between so-called R- and Q-technique of factor analysis. As to variables measuring individual differences, Stern (1900) unfolded a broad spectrum of personality indicators, including also so-called historical methods. In Part II of the book the reader is introduced to a range of statistical methods for analyzing variations and co-variations (correlations) of individual difference measures. The final part, Part III, is devoted to the study of individuality on the basis of biographical and psychological profile ('psychogram') data.

The Dutch psychologists Heymans and Wiersma published the first personality inventory in 1906; it was a checklist designed to measure individual differences in three dimensions of adjustment, and it was the prototype for personality trait measurement for the next 50 years. From 1906 until the end of World War II, personality measurement primarily focused on dimensions of psychopathology; Woodworth's (1908) Personal Data Sheet, used to screen Army recruits in World War I, was the next in this series of tests (Woodworth, 1920). Somewhat later, Thurstone developed a personality inventory (Thurstone & Thurstone, 1929) based on factor analysis – the analytical methodology invented by Spearman (1904) to study intelligence; Thurstone's inventory produced a gross score indicating the presence or absence of neurotic tendencies. Using this measure, Thurstone showed that neurotic tendencies are relatively independent of mental abilities, but are related to success in college. The most famous test in this tradition is the Minnesota Multiphasic Personality Inventory (Hathaway & McKinley,

1943), still widely used to evaluate personality, psychopathology, and the emotional stability of applicants for jobs where public safety is an issue.

William McDougall, a Scottish child prodigy and polymath, published his *Social Psychology* in 1908; despite the title, the book concerns personality. McDougall is best known today for his instinct-based theory of motivation, but he was a prolific researcher who also developed an interesting theory of personality, parts of which were adopted by later writers without attribution. Kurt Lewin's (1935) book, *A Dynamic Theory of Personality*, extends Stern's theory of 'personalism' or person theory of conscious experience, i.e., what people do depends on what is on their minds. Gordon Allport's (1937) book, *Personality: a Psychological Interpretation*, is an elaborate defense of traits. Strongly influenced by both Stern and McDougall, Allport regarded traits as conscious intentions that have a motivational force. Drawing on the German philosopher Windelband's distinction between nomothetic and idiographic analyses, Allport further distinguished between traits that describe people in general and traits that are specific to individuals, a distinction that is important when the goal of research is to characterize the distinctive features of individuals. Henry Murray's (1938) *Explorations in Personality* contains an elaborate taxonomy of needs, which are almost identical to Allport's traits, a taxonomy that is still used today.

Immediately after World War II, several researchers began studying normal personality using factor analysis. The issue here, once again, concerned the nature and number of fundamental traits underlying normal personality, i.e., the search for an adequate taxonomy of traits. This led to the development of several trait-based personality inventories, the best known of which included the 16PF (Cattell, Eber, & Tatsuoka, 1970), the Eysenck Personality Inventory (Eysenck & Eysenck, 1975), and the Guilford–Zimmerman Temperament Survey (Guilford & Zimmerman, 1949).

In the mid-1960s personality trait research went through a major crisis caused by three unrelated events. The first was the 'response set controversy' (cf. Edwards, 1959); advocates of the response set model argued that rather than measuring traits, all existing personality inventories measured individual differences in a person's desire to be well-regarded, i.e., social desirability. This argument severely challenged the methodological base of personality research. The second event was a series of behaviorist critiques of personality research, which argued that a careful review of the data provided no support for the existence of any general traits that govern, control, or explain people's behavior across situations (more about this important debate in Section 16.4 below). Third, by the mid-1960s, there were so many different personality tests in the literature, each measuring a different set of traits, that the possibility of discovering an adequate taxonomy of traits seemed hopeless.

The response set controversy was finally resolved when Block (1964), in a series of ingenious analyses, demonstrated that the basic claims of response set theory are false. Next, the reality of traits was established by research in behavior genetics showing that scales on major personality inventories had substantial heritability (cf. Loehlin, Willerman, & Horn, 1989), i.e., there is an important genetic component to personality trait measures. And finally, an obscure Air Force technical report (Tupes & Christal, 1961) provided a solution to the taxonomic issue, arguing that personality could be classified in terms of five broad traits (Adjustment, Ascendance, Agreeableness, Prudence, and Intellect/Openness). This argument, which became known as the Big Five Theory (cf. Wiggins, 1996), suggests that all existing measures of personality concern parts or combinations of the same five dimensions; this viewpoint is widely accepted by many, but not all, modern personality psychologists. Thus, many people believe that the search for a taxonomy of personality traits that began with Gall's faculties has ended with a parsimonious list of five broad dimensions.

16.3 THEORIES

Individual differences research from Stern to the present shows that people reliably differ from one another along every dimension of performance that has been studied. The major theories of personality concern why differences in social behavior occur. For purposes of exposition, these theories can be sorted into six broad categories – with apologies for the inevitable oversimplifications that this entails. These categories are: depth psychology, behaviorism, cognitive theory, trait theory, interpersonal theory, and evolutionary theory.

Depth Psychology

Depth psychology (e.g., Freudian psychoanalysis) is primarily a continental European tradition that contains many subtheories. Despite their differences, these subtheories share some important assumptions. First, they assume that the major structures of personality are primarily unconscious, that we are normally unaware of the 'true' reasons for our actions, and that a major goal in life is to become aware of these reasons. Second, in these theories, intrapsychic and interpersonal conflict is inevitable, and caused by unconscious sources. Third, these theories assume that development is important; events that happen early in life are more significant and determinative than events that happen later. Fourth, they assume that memories of these early developmental experiences persist in the unconscious and cause problems in adulthood, so that most adults have problems. Finally, these theories regard personality as very stable, over long periods of time. For traditional depth psychology, individual differences in social behavior arise from unconscious sources that are often hard to discover. Because of the emphasis on unconscious processes, depth psychology does not easily lend itself to standardized psychometric measurement and is hard to evaluate empirically.

Behaviorist Theories

Behaviorist theories are primarily a North American tradition, and behaviorism is largely defined by a point-for-point rejection of the key assumptions of depth psychology. For example, behaviorists believe that what people do depends on the circumstances they are in, and how they have learned to behave in those circumstances, rather than on underlying personality characteristics. Nor do they believe that conflict is inevitable – nothing about people is inevitable because their tendencies are learned. Behaviorist theories also conceptualize development very differently from depth psychology – early experience is no more important than later experience, what matters is how often certain forms of behavior have been successful for a person, not when they happened. Finally, because what people do depends on what they have learned, and because they are always learning, personality is not at all stable; one of the primary criticisms behaviorists make of depth psychology is that it vastly overestimates the degree to which personality is consistent over time.

People learn behaviors that are successful and repeat them until they are no longer successful. People also learn expectancies about what they, and others, will do in various circumstances; thus, individual differences in social behavior are caused by differences in learned behaviors and expectancies. Historically, a major criticism of behaviorism is the degree to which it ignores individual differences; nonetheless, among the behaviorists, Bandura and Rotter developed useful individual differences measures that have been very influential and widely used in research. The behaviorist emphasis on change is consistent with the widespread belief in American culture that people can always change and improve themselves, a set of beliefs that are not well supported by empirical data.

Cognitive Theories

Beginning with Kurt Lewin and extending through George Kelly to Walter Mischel and his students, cognitive theory tries to redefine personality psychology from the ground up. It begins with a critique of the concept of motivation, based on three points. First, motivational terms are useless when we are trying to help someone, e.g., what do you do after you have decided someone is lazy? Second, when motives are attributed to someone, the attribution will turn into a self-fulfilling prophecy, e.g., if we think a person is lazy, we will then treat the person as if he/she were lazy, thereby confirming what was initially only our hypothesis. And third, cognitive theory argues that motivational terms are unnecessary if we simply assume that people are active to begin with. This view of motivation resembles Isaac Newton's notion that gravity is a constant and physicists need not worry about it; although Newton was widely criticized at the time, his theoretical decision proved ultimately to be wise.

The essential insight of cognitive theory is that people develop theories of the world, and of other people, and then use these theories to organize their lives. Sometimes the theories are accurate, but when they are not, they cause problems. In any case, people do what is on their minds and personality research concerns discovering the laws of thought, which can be described in purely cognitive terms. Cognitive theory describes personality development very much the way behaviorists do – what is important is what is on your mind and it does not matter where it came from in a developmental sense.

Like behaviorist theory, cognitive theory believes that traditional depth psychology vastly overestimates the degree to which personality is stable. For cognitive theory, if a person changes his/her theory of the world, his/her personality will change. Cognitive theory is quite popular in the United States and the United Kingdom. It is essentially an offshoot of experimental psychology; despite the attention it ostensibly gives to individual differences, cognitive theory has had almost no influence on personality assessment, largely because the key concepts are almost impossible to operationalize with traditional psychometric methods. Because both behaviorism and cognitive theory are only peripherally interested in individual differences, this raises the possibility that they are not, in fact, theories of personality, as is widely assumed.

Trait Theory

Modern trait theory argues that social behavior is controlled in important ways by real 'neuropsychic structures' that exist inside the body. Sometimes called 'constructive realism', modern trait theory distinguishes between: (a) real traits that exist in people; (b) our theories of those traits, which are called constructs; and (c) the measures that we use to observe the traits. Trait theory argues that a person can have a high level of a trait like neuroticism, and have underlying physiological systems that make the person alert to threat and danger, and yet the person, and those who observe the person, can be unaware of this. The reports of oneself and others regarding a person's neuroticism are useful data, but they need to be supplemented with data from other sources: performance on experimental tasks, biological assays, physiological recordings, etc.

Trait theory and behavior genetics are closely linked in the study of personality. Loehlin et al. (1989), using data from many types of behavior genetic studies, estimated that slightly over 40% of the variability in the most prominent five factors of personality – personality traits – is due to genetic variation. The environmental variation that is shared within families contributed less than 10% of the variability in the five factors. Such findings support the reality of biological systems that produce consistencies in overt social behavior – and individual differences among people – and such evidence strongly challenges the behaviorist critique of traits (cf. Mischel, 1968). Some people argue that trait theories are not very 'psychological' and do not provide a link between biological traits and social behavior, but Tellegen and his colleagues propose trait theories that include motivational, perceptual, and information-processing components. Some features of modern trait theory are illustrated in the section of this chapter on temperament (Section 16.7).

Interpersonal Theory

The fundamental assumption of interpersonal theory is that personality arises out of, and is primarily expressed during, social interaction. Depth psychology, behaviorism, and cognitive theory concern intrapsychic processes; in these models other people are objects in the external world, differing from lamp posts and trees only in that they are more dangerous or more fun. In contrast, the interpersonal theorists argue that we need other people, that we live for social interaction, and the person that we become depends on feedback from others.

Social interaction is fueled by two motives: a need for approval, and a need to dominate or outperform others. Development is also important – interaction with parents and caretakers in childhood establishes core beliefs about one's competencies and feelings of self-worth. We then carry these beliefs forward into the way we deal with others in adulthood. Individual differences in personality reflect different strategies and methods for dealing with others, some of which are more productive than others. Finally, the interpersonal theorists have been very active in developing methods for measuring and classifying the differences in peoples' interpersonal behavior.

Evolutionary Theory

Models of personality based on evolutionary theory attempt to synthesize the preceding five traditions. They assume that human nature was shaped by the conditions to which our ancestors in the Pleistocene era had to adapt – people evolved as group-living animals and our culture (e.g., language and technology) and flexible intelligence gave us a substantial advantage over our animal competitors. People always live in groups, and every group has a status hierarchy; the major problem in life is to gain acceptance and approval from the other members of our social groups while at the same time gaining status and the control of resources. Acceptance and status confer reproductive benefits and are pursued during social interaction. Thus, social interaction is a major preoccupation, during which we try to build coalitions, attract support, and negotiate the status hierarchy.

Individual differences in personality reflect individual differences in temperament – which are inherited – and individual differences in strategies and behaviors designed to enhance acceptance and status – which are learned. In contrast with behaviorism, models of personality based on evolutionary theory regard personality as quite stable over long periods of time, a belief that is firmly supported by data. Personality is stable in part because it is rooted in biology; the heritability coefficients for the major dimensions of personality average about .50, suggesting that half the variance in personality scale scores is controlled by genetics. In addition, for evolutionary theory, development matters. Specifically, because people are fundamentally oriented toward social interaction, infants are born pre-wired to need attention and care. Attachment theory argues that, under normal circumstances, children become attached to their primary caretakers and develop unconscious cognitive prototypes of themselves as worthwhile and other people as trustworthy. These unconscious mental representations guide social interaction in adulthood and provide additional stability to personality.

Finally, writers in this tradition have been leading advocates of the Five-Factor Model (Wiggins, 1996), the view that the major dimensions of personality can be summarized in terms of five broad themes of Adjustment, Ascendance, Agreeableness, Prudence, and Intellectance/Openness.

16.4 TRAITS AND SITUATIONS

Starting in the late 1950s and continuing for about 15 years thereafter, personality psychology was severely criticized on many grounds, but the most vigorous line of criticism came from behaviorism. It began with a Yale University research project in the late 1920s, called the Character Education Inquiry. Thousands of school children were tested in classrooms, on playgrounds, at parties, and in experimental laboratories. The tests concerned honesty/dishonesty and each test provided children with an opportunity to cheat in some way. The major finding was that a child's performance on one task could not be predicted by its performance on another task, i.e., what children did seemed to depend on the situations they were in. If honesty is considered a trait, then this research shows that the expression of traits depends on situations. Therefore, people's behavior must be a function of situations and not personality, defined in terms of traits. Gordon Allport understood the importance of these findings and spent some time discussing the Character Education Inquiry in his 1937 book.

Personality psychologists largely ignored these findings, but Walter Mischel returned to them in his influential (1968) book; this book summarized the standard criticisms of personality psychology and set off the 'person/situation' debate which was never satisfactorily resolved – people just grew tired of it. Mischel's argument can be summarized in terms of two claims. First, if personality exists, then people's behavior should be consistent across situations; a review of the empirical literature from the Character Education Inquiry to the present reveals no such consistency. Second, if personality exists, then personality measures should be able to predict people's behavior. A review of the empirical literature shows that validity coefficients for personality measures rarely exceed a correlation of .30 and the vast majority of them are substantially smaller. Taken together, these two points strongly suggest that: (a) personality does not exist; or (b) it is essentially irrelevant as a cause of behavior. It is hard to overstate the negative impact this argument had on personality psychology in the 1970s and 1980s. Suffice it to say that, in the US, the field almost disappeared in the 1970s.

A closer examination of Mischel's argument shows that it is flawed. Consider the claim that if personality exists, then behavior should be consistent across situations. There are three problems with this proposition. First, why should behavior be consistent? Why not intentions, or values, or personal goals? Second, the question of how to define consistency in a world of continuous flux is one of the oldest problems in philosophy and seems insoluble. Third, what is a situation? The empirical literature reveals no consensus regarding how to define the term, nor is there any consensus regarding a taxonomy of situations – which means that there is no agreement even on multiple definitions. Thus, Mischel's first claim turns out to be logically odd and impossible in principle to rebut in an empirical fashion.

The second claim – that validity coefficients for personality measures rarely exceed .30 – is more interesting. In the 1960s there were thousands of personality measures available in the published literature, many of dubious technical quality, and if one lumped together the results based on all these measures, one would certainly conclude that personality measurement does not work very well. A more careful review would have led to a different conclusion, however. Specifically, the empirical literature surrounding the few technically competent inventories of normal personality available at the time contained many validity coefficients substantially in excess of .30. Today, the results are still more promising; the development of the Five-Factor Model has provided an invaluable taxonomy for organizing the empirical literature – so that measures of adjustment can be compared with one another and not, for example, with measures of extraversion. When this taxonomy is combined with the recent rise of meta-analysis as a statistical method, validity coefficients in excess of .50 summing across tests and criterion measures, have become commonplace.

Concerning Mischel's original argument, modern research reveals substantial evidence for the existence of personality and the utility of personality assessment. But for some persons outside the field of personality psychology there is some remaining confusion as reflected in the question, 'Which is the more important determinant of personality: traits or situations?'

The Fallacy of Situationism

There is a problem with the argument that people's behavior is a function of traits and situations. The problem concerns the fact that there is no agreed-upon definition or taxonomy of situations. Thus, behavior is claimed to be a function of something that has yet to be defined – even by those people who most believe in situations as explanatory concepts. As a result, the search for 'person-by-situations interactions' that so preoccupied researchers in the late 1970s seems to have been an empty exercise – because the concept of 'situation' has never been defined or given operational specification. It is very difficult systematically to link persons with situations when situations are undefined. Lewin (1935) and Murray (1938) suggested that situations should be defined in terms of how they are perceived by individuals. If so, then situations become a function of individual personality, and the person–situation debate becomes moot.

16.5 Personality Measurement and Structure

There are two primary questions in personality measurement: (a) what to measure; and (b) how to measure it? Both questions have been the subject of considerable debate. The first is a question about theoretical taste, the second is an empirical question which in principle can be answered with data.

What to Measure?

If we assume that personality assessment has a job to do, i.e., if we adopt an applied perspective, then what we measure depends on what we are trying to accomplish. For depth psychology, people are primarily motivated by unconscious wishes and desires, and this is what we should measure. Depth psychologists also believe that, when conscious controls relax, unconscious motives will appear in fantasy material: dreams, artistic creations. This belief led to the development of projective tests which are used to assess unconscious themes, desires, and aspirations.

American psychology is heavily grounded in behaviorism and American psychiatrists and clinical psychologists want to identify characteristics such as dysfunctional behaviors, conscious anxiety, and emotional distress. They generally believe people can talk about their problems and reveal them in interviews or through self-report inventories and behavioral check lists. This led to the development of standardized psychiatric inventories such as the Minnesota Multiphasic Personality Inventory, which are used as aids to diagnosis and treatment planning.

Career counselors and vocational/occupational psychologists want to measure qualities or factors that predict occupational satisfaction and success. They, therefore, measure the values, interests, and skills that characterize various well-defined occupational groups, e.g., scientists like to work alone, solve puzzles and problems, and tend not to value money, so that people who are introverted, like problem solving, and are indifferent to the profit motive are compatible with careers in science. Occupational psychologists also want to measure the characteristics that are associated with success in the various occupations, which may include such factors as intelligence, drive, creativity, and social skill. They then use this information to guide people into occupations.

Industrial psychologists overlap with the foregoing groups; they use personality assessment to solve three general categories of problems. The first is to identify people who will be undesirable employees; the goal here is to measure factors associated with absenteeism, bogus medical complaints, and tendencies toward theft, violence, and other forms of antisocial behavior. The second problem is to identify people who will perform well in specific occupations; here the goal is to develop the psychological profile of high performers in particular jobs, then use the profile to identify others who would perform well in that occupation. The third way industrial psychologists use assessment is to give individuals feedback on how to enhance and improve their overall career performance. This third case requires an extensive and in-depth assessment of all the factors that might influence career development, including cognitive ability, normal personality, abnormal personality, and values and interests.

Personality psychologists in the academic tradition want to measure traits, which they see as the building blocks of personality. Measuring traits relies heavily on factor analysis as a tool, and the goal is to identify factors that recur in different samples and languages; these factors are seen as traits. This academic orientation led to the development of the Five-Factor Model mentioned earlier, widely regarded as a substantial scientific achievement. The goal of measuring traits is very different from the goal of applied personality psychology, where the key question in measurement is validity – the

degree to which scores on a test predict measures of a desired outcome such as job success. For academic researchers, validity does not matter, the goal is to measure traits and that is sufficient unto itself. Once again, the answer to the question 'What should we measure?' depends on what we are trying to do.

How to Measure Personality?

At the beginning of this chapter we distinguished between the actor's view and the observer's view of personality, i.e., between identity and reputation.

Measuring the Observer's View of Personality

It is a relatively straightforward task to measure personality from the observer's perspective; this involves having observers rate the person in question. There are a number of well-standardized rating instruments, including the Q sorts used by clinical psychologists and the 360 degree appraisal forms used by modern industrial psychologists. Moreover, the Five-Factor Model (Wiggins, 1996) brings a useful taxonomic discipline to the rating process. Some writers suggest that the Five-Factor Model is, in fact, the natural structure of observer ratings, the innate categories in terms of which we think about and evaluate others. And this suggests that the various standardized rating instruments in use today can, at least in principle, be reconfigured in terms of five broad dimensions.

The reliability of ratings of personality depends on the number of raters and the observability of the characteristics to be rated. More raters and greater observability (e.g., talkativeness, which is observable, versus brittle ego structures, which are not) always enhance the reliability of ratings. In addition, when done correctly, these ratings tend to be stable over long time periods. And finally, ratings of personality can predict useful outcomes, i.e., they are valid as well as reliable. In fact, generally speaking, the validity of personality ratings equals or exceeds the validities of personality inventory scales.

Measuring the Actor's View of Personality

There are two models for measuring personality from the actor's perspective; these might be called the trait theory model and the empirical model. The trait theory model, which is by far the more popular, is based on two major assumptions. First, it assumes, *à la* Allport, that individual personality is configured in terms of traits – indwelling neuropsychic structures – and the goal of assessment is to measure these traits. Second, this model assumes that people can report on the degree to which various traits are salient in their lives. With these two assumptions in mind, the measurement process is relatively straightforward: one writes an initial set of items designed to reflect the trait in question; one next tests a group of people with the items; one then calculates correlations among the items and retains the items that are most highly correlated; finally, one begins again for the next trait of interest. After creating a number of trait measures in this way, one can calculate correlations among the scales and retain the scales that are most independent or uncorrelated.

This process will result in a set of homogenous or internally consistent measures of hypothesized trait dimensions that are also relatively independent – a highly desirable state of affairs for most measurement researchers. The problem with this model is that, although it maximizes scale reliabilities and independence, it tends to ignore validity – which is the bottom line in applied assessment.

The alternative and minority perspective is that the goal of assessment is not to measure traits but to predict significant outcomes: status, popularity, income, occupational performance, creativity, delinquency, leadership. Here one identifies items that discriminate between people who have high and low standing on the desired outcome, and then retains those items as scales. This model of measurement maximizes validity at the expense of scale homogeneity and scale independence. Some of the best-known tests in the history of psychological measurement have been composed in this way, including Binet's original measure of intelligence, E. K. Strong's Vocational Interest Blanks, Hathaway and McKinley's Minnesota Multiphasic Personality Inventory (Hathaway & McKinley, 1943), and Gough's California Psychological Inventory (Gough, 1987). It is, of course, possible to combine these two approaches, but it is rarely done.

The modern assessment center, which provides a comprehensive analysis of an individual personality, typically includes a variety of measurement procedures: simulations, ratings, and inventories. The modern assessment center was invented by the German Army after World War I and widely imitated in the United Kingdom and the United States. There is a rich research tradition associated with assessment centers, which when properly designed and conducted generally yield valid results, i.e., significant and useful correlations between scores for performance in the assessment center and outcome measures such as organizational status and rated creativity.

16.6 SPECIAL TOPICS

Occupational Performance

Personality psychology has been historically a part of clinical psychology and psychiatry and the history of personality measurement reflects this theme. From the beginning of the discipline in the early 1900s, personality measurement focused on assessing aspects of psychopathology. In 1943 the United States' Office of Strategic Services (today the Central Intelligence Agency) established an assessment center to screen applicants for membership in the organization. The book, *Assessment of Men* (MacKinnon, 1948) evaluated the effectiveness of the assessment center and concluded that psychopathology was not a good predictor of performance, that some highly effective individuals had experienced unusually traumatic upbringings and some undistinguished performers seemed very well-adjusted.

This lesson has been largely overlooked by researchers studying the links between personality and occupational performance, and this is partly responsible for the negative reviews in the 1960s regarding the validity of personality measures. Measures of psychopathology – anxiety, depression, and self-esteem – are largely uncorrelated with occupational performance.

For about 30 years – 1960 to 1990 – it was widely believed that personality measures were uncorrelated with significant real-life behavior. Two developments changed this perception. On the one hand, the Five-Factor Model provided the necessary taxonomy for organizing literature reviews – measures of extraversion could be compared with one another rather than with measures of conscientiousness and adjustment. On the other hand, researchers realized that certain dimensions of personality are more relevant to some occupational outcomes than to others – this is called aligning predictor variables (personality measures) with criterion variables (outcomes). Beginning in the early 1990s, researchers in the United States and Europe, using meta-analysis, organizing personality variables in terms of the Five-Factor Model, and appropriately aligning predictors with criteria, reported finding that personality reliably predicts occupational performance above and beyond the prediction afforded by cognitive variables.

Creativity

Organizations and cultures exist in environments that are constantly changing. All organizations and cultures are in competition with other organizations and cultures; in order to remain viable, they must constantly change. Groups are notoriously resistant to change; from where, then, does the stimulus for change come? It comes from the innovative people in the group or organization. In this sense, creativity is a resource for cultural and organizational survival. It then becomes a matter of some importance to be able to identify creative talent – and then to encourage it.

The Institute for Personality Assessment and Research at U.C. Berkeley was established in 1948 to study high-level effectiveness. In the 1950s and 1960s the staff of the Institute conducted a series of studies of creativity with highly significant and well-replicated results (cf. Barron, 1969). One of the best of these was a study of creativity in architects. The researchers identified, using various nomination methods, three groups of architects: the first was highly creative – as judged by a substantial number of experts; the second group had worked with the first group but was not regarded as creative; the third group was journeymen architects who had no contact with the first two groups. All of these architects went through a 2½ day assessment center. An analysis of the assessment center results revealed highly significant, cross-validated differences between the three groups with the creative people being no brighter, but substantially more troubled, ambitious, and harder working than the other groups. Moreover, these differences in early adulthood persisted through the life span – the creative group remained substantially more productive, professionally active, and well-regarded than the other two groups well into their seventies and eighties.

16.7 Temperament

Temperament involves stable individual differences that appear early in life. One of the most influential discussions of temperament was a round-table discussion in 1987 (Goldsmith et al., 1987). Goldsmith summarized the discussion in terms of four points:

1. Temperament involves individual differences.
2. Temperament consists of dispositions, that is, tendencies to engage in classes of behavior or to experience certain classes of emotion; temperament is not defined by specific behaviors.
3. Temperament is expressed most directly during infancy; later it is expressed less directly because temperament becomes subject to newly developed control processes.

4. Temperament theorists emphasize the 'biological underpinnings' and continuity of individual differences.

Goldsmith also concluded that most of the discussants regarded temperament as modifiable. But he noted that there are significant disagreements over boundaries of the temperament construct, over its boundaries with personality, and over the distinctive or defining features of temperament.

A number of the issues raised at the 1987 discussion remain quite current. On the distinction between temperament and the personality, Strelau (1987) argues that temperament is distinguishable from personality in that (1) temperament is determined by biology, whereas personality is shaped by social forces; (2) temperament is expressed in the early years and personality appears later; (3) temperament can be observed in nonhuman animals and personality cannot; (4) temperament is expressed in the style of the execution of behaviors rather than in the specific content of behaviors (although he acknowledged anxiety is an example of a temperament saturated with content); and (5) personality, but not temperament, is concerned with how behavior is directed by higher cognitive processes.

Rothbart argued that personality is built upon the foundation of temperament:

> . . . 'personality' is a far more inclusive term than 'temperament'. Personality includes important cognitive structures such as self-concept and specific expectations and attitudes that may, if they are sufficiently negative, result in frequent displays of distress even if an individual is not temperamentally predisposed toward it. Personality also includes perceptual and response strategies that mediate between the individual's biological endowment and cognitive structures and the requirements, demands, and possibilities of the environment . . . Thus, temperament and personality are seen as broadly overlapping domains of study, with temperament providing the primarily biological basis for the developing personality. (Rothbart in Goldsmith et al., 1987, p. 510)

On the other hand, Hofstee (1991) argued that if personality is defined in terms of fundamental dispositions, then the distinction between personality and temperament vanishes. The world's literature thus contains a range of opinion anchored on one end by Hofstee's contention that personality and temperament are the same, and on the other end by views that temperament is a primal organizer, a foundation for a later developing personality that is much more than temperament. Based on the view that personality and temperament are different, Angleitner and Riemann (1991) described the implications of this distinction for the measurement of temperament.

Another common assertion is that temperament should be particularly observable in infancy. That is, basic dispositions such as fearfulness should be easily observed in infancy because the child has not yet developed higher-level control processes, the elaboration of the self-concept, and so on. However, one could also argue that because infancy is the time of greatest environmental potency, when children cannot defend themselves from scratchy clothes, intrusive relatives, or aversive foods, dispositional differences are *less* likely to be observed. Certainly heritable individual differences are less detectable when potent environmental factors produce great phenotype variation. The field of behavior genetics also raises the possibility that genetic differences are powerfully enhanced by people actively selecting and modifying environments, a process that becomes prominent only later in development (Scarr & McCartney, 1983). Thus although armchair psychologists can argue one side or the other, the degree of stability and prominence of early-appearing individual differences remains an open research question, not to be resolved by definition.

Hinde, also a discussant of the 1987 round-table discussion, pointed out the problems in defining temperament by reference to its supposed biological features. A number of problems have been caused by the careless use of three terms: biological, genetic, and heritable. Unless one believes that some psychological processes are mediated by physical processes while others are mediated by metaphysical processes, it is not helpful to assert that temperament has biological underpinnings; all psychological processes have biological underpinnings or they would not exist. The general term genetics refers to molecular recipes for both individual differences and features that are shared across all members of a species, whereas heritability refers only to individual differences. Having lungs to breathe oxygen is encoded in the genome, and is thus genetically transmitted, but it is not classically heritable in humans, whereas individual differences in endurance probably has a degree of heritability. Heritability thus more specifically refers the extent to which phenotypic variation across individuals is due genetic differences between them.

Some people define temperament as individual differences that are heritable. This approach to defining temperament is not very discriminating: most well-measured behavioral traits have some degree of heritability. But the heritability of virtually all traits is well below 'perfect' heritability in which all observed differences between individuals can be accounted for by genetic differences between them. As Hinde noted, there is no natural cut-off point for deciding when a trait is heritable. Rowe (1997) reviewed research on early-appearing individual differences and concluded that, 'one-third to one-half of individual differences in temperamental traits can be attributed to genetic variation among children' (p. 378). Temperamental traits thus do not seem to have higher heritability than other human dispositions. Thus the heritability of early-appearing individual differences should be treated as a research problem to be studied, and the problems entailed in defining temperament as 'that which is heritable' should be recognized.

Others have attempted to define temperament as 'that which is stable'. However, the degree to which temperament is stable over time is another question that should be answered by research rather than by definition. Differential continuity refers to the extent to which a child retains his or her relative position in individual differences across developmental periods. This does not mean that behavior stays the same. For example, fearfulness in a one-year old may be evidenced in very different ways than fearfulness in a 13-year-old. Nevertheless, the type of continuity evaluated in this section is differential continuity, that is, maintaining one's position, high, low or medium, on a disposition across developmental periods.

Wachs (1994) summarized stability research by noting that age-to-age correlations in temperament are modest, suggesting only 4 to 9% of the variance in temperament measures is predictable over six months. Initial research on the sources of stability and change in adult positive and negative emotionality suggests that indeed, much of the stability of traits arises from genetic factors, and much of the change arises from environmental factors that are not shared by members of families (McGue, Bacon, & Lykken, 1993). Even if a dimension of individual difference shows high heritability at one developmental point, this does not imply that there will be differential continuity. Consider the stages of the butterfly's life; the transformations from larva to butterfly show that change can be the result of genetic control. The misconception that heritability implies stability seems particularly prominent in the temperament domain. But nothing known in genetics would rule out the possibility that some children might have a special temperament that is turned on for a period of time, e.g., 'a squeaky wheel gets the grease' personality, only to be shut off later. The point is that continuity of temperament must be established by research, not decided by definition.

What are the Major Dimensions of Temperament?

If one defines temperament as early-appearing psychological individual differences excluding intelligence, the problem remains of providing a list of the major dimensions that comprise temperament. At present there is no consensus. Thus we will examine the lists provided by prominent researchers and theorists who have been concerned with delineating the features of temperament. Buss and Plomin (1975) initially listed dimensions of emotionality (ranging from easily distressed to relatively phlegmatic), activity, sociability and impulsivity; impulsivity was subsequently dropped. Thomas and Chess (1977) listed nine features, most of them dimensions: rhythmicity, activity level, approach/withdrawal for novel stimuli, adaptability, sensory thresholds, predominant mood, mood intensity, distractibility, and persistence/attention. In addition to dimensions, some theorists include temperament types, such as a 'difficult' child. Thomas and Chess (1977) included three temperament types: easy, difficult, and slow to warm up.

Strelau (1983) has emphasized stylistic rather than content features of temperament; and he developed the theory and measurement instruments to apply Pavlovian concepts of the nervous system function to the study of temperament: strength of excitation, strength of inhibition, and mobility. This contrasts with a content emphasis, as found in the work of Goldsmith and Campos, who defined temperament as dispositions to experience fundamental emotions that link coherent stimulus classes with organized output classes. Goldsmith and Campos developed a list of dispositions to experience arousal of primary emotions, including: sadness, pleasure, anger, disgust, fear, interest, and activity.

Rusalov (1989) developed a measure of temperament that includes ergonicity, an ambition or achievement-like construct; social ergonicity which resembles extraversion; plasticity, resembling openness; tempo; social tempo; emotionality; and social emotionality. Gray (1991) coordinated temperament hypotheses with his three theoretical neuropsychological systems. First, there is a Behavioral Inhibition System, which generates individual differences in sensitivity to novelty and signals of punishment or nonreward. The second system is the Fight/Flight system, which responds to unconditioned aversive stimuli. Finally, the Behavioral

Approach System generates individual differences in responsiveness to signals of reward or nonpunishment.

A number of researchers have used factor analysis to examine the relationships between measures of temperament to see if some consensus might be reached regarding a set of descriptive dimensions. Ruch, Angleitner, and Strelau (1991) suggested five factors of temperament: emotional stability, rhythmicity, activity and tempo, sociability, and impulsiveness. Zuckerman, Kulhman, and Camac (1988) also suggested five factors: sociability, activity, aggression-sensation-seeking, neuroticism-anxiety, and impulsive-unsocialized-sensation seeking.

Angleitner and Ostendorf (1994) examined the relationships among a wide range of temperament measures and concluded that the Five-Factor Model of personality represented a single comprehensive framework within which measures of temperament and personality could be located. As noted earlier, the Five-Factor Model of personality is defined by the dimensions of Neuroticism, Extraversion, Agreeableness, Conscientiousness, and a fifth factor called Culture, Intellectance, or Openness.

Rothbart (1981) developed measures of smiling and laughter, fear, frustration, soothability, activity level, and duration of orienting. Ahadi and Rothbart (1994) analyzed the structure of temperament dimensions in a manner consistent with Gray's approach, and concluded that temperament dimensions can be classified as approach related (mapping onto the Five-Factor Model dimension of extroversion); anxiety-inhibition related temperament (mapping onto Neuroticism); and a third aspect, effortful control, exerting modulating effects on the other dimensions. These summary dimensions seem to correspond with Tellegen's superfactors of Positive Emotionality, Negative Emotionality, and Constraint. Rothbart, Derryberry, and Posner (1994) presented a developmental model of temperament that outlines the appearance of a generalized distress and negative affect system in the newborn period. Over the first year, more differentiated fear and frustration/anger develop from generalized distress states. The development of approach systems beginning in the second month adds the possibility of frustration when a child is unable to gain a reward. Finally, effortful control appears later because its development is tied to the maturation of attentional control systems after the tenth month.

A number of structural analyses of temperament converge on solutions that resemble four of the five factors found in the Five-Factor Model of personality (e.g., Digman & Shmelyov's, 1996, analysis of the temperament of Russian schoolchildren). These temperament findings converge with the integrative model of personality proposed by Watson, Clark, and Harkness (1994); this model is composed of Neuroticism or Negative Affectivity, Extraversion or Positive Emotionality (linked with approach systems), Conscientiousness or Constraint (linked with effortful control), and Agreeableness. Thus, one promising development is an increasing convergence between lists of the major features of temperament and lists of the major features of personality.

Recent Developments in Studying the Behavior Genetics of Temperament

Studies of the behavior genetics of early-appearing individual differences have moved beyond estimating the heritabilities of temperament traits. Recent studies show, for example, that some of the situational specificity of behavior (e.g., classroom activity level versus activity level in a laboratory) is genetic in origin (Schmitz, Saudino, Plomin, Fulker, & DeFries, 1996).

A comprehensive review of findings is beyond the scope of this chapter, however as an example of recent developments, we will describe the issue of apparent 'contrast effects' in twin studies of temperament. A large inconsistency in the literature on the behavior genetics of temperament concerns the discrepancy between twin studies and other methods. The degree of similarity in parental temperament ratings of dizygotic twins (twins resulting from two separate conceptions, as contrasted with monozygotic twins who result from a single conception that divides to become two persons) were inconsistent with similarity estimates from other methods. Comparing across multiple methods of study, the twin method produced unexpected results: dizygotic twins seemed to be *too* different. Buss and Plomin (1984) conjectured that parents amplify any existing real differences, resulting in a 'contrast effect'. Suppose one child is moderately high in fearfulness and the other is moderately low; if parents amplify the real difference by rating one child extremely high and the other extremely low in fearfulness, this would be a contrast effect. Because real differences tend to be larger between dizygotic twins than between monozygotic twins, parental ratings amplifying real differences would make dizygotic twin ratings more different than expected. Subsequent research has supported this interpretation. Saudino and Eaton (1991), using automated data collection procedures rather than ratings (automated procedures not being subject to contrast effects), showed dizygotic twin similarities to be

in line with expectations. Further, the development of measurement procedures not affected by contrast effects provides a clearer understanding of the role of environment in shaping temperament (Goldsmith, Buss, & Lemery, 1997). This maturation of research methods, in this case the ability to check the consistency of heritability estimates across methods, allowed for improvement in the measurement methods themselves.

To summarize the major developments in temperament research, structural analyses examining the list of dimensions defining temperament suggests convergence between models of temperament and the Five-Factor Model of personality. Developmental models, such as that proposed by Rothbart et al. (1994), have embedded these lists of features in a picture of dynamic change across the first years of life. The measurement of temperament has become more sophisticated through the identification and amelioration of rating contrast effects, allowing for further gains in precision.

16.8 INTELLIGENCE AND COGNITIVE ABILITY

Although this chapter begins with personality, the study of individual differences is most often associated with the study of intelligence, and this section concerns the theory, measurement, and consequences of the intelligence construct. Most people believe that the modern study of intelligence begins with Alfred Binet (1857–1911), because he developed, in 1905, the first test of general mental ability, revised the test in 1908, and refined it in 1911. Binet's instruments spawned the applied mental measurement movement, but there were some important antecedents to Binet's contribution. Earlier, for example, Esquirol distinguished between mental deficiency and mental disorders, two conditions that had often been conflated, and stressed that mental deficiencies come in degrees. In the late nineteenth century, Fechner, Weber, and Wundt tried to define the relationship between intervals of objective stimulus intensity and subjective appraisals of just noticeable differences (JNDs) in the personal experience of those stimuli. Their efforts to scale simultaneously physical and psychological phenomena (psychophysics) led to the development of psychometrics, which is based on the idea that responses to environmental cues reflect individual differences in ability, interests, and personality. The *limen* of psychophysics became the *standard error of measurement* in psychometrics (the measurement of individual differences in abilities).

Next, Frances Galton and James McKeen Cattell, among others, tried to measure intelligence by scaling individual differences in the strength of various sensory systems (Thorndike & Lohman, 1990); they used Aristotle's view that the mind is informed to the extent that one's sensory systems provide clear and reliable information. This approach did not pan out. Binet, in a creative departure, examined complex behavior, e.g., comprehension, judgment, reasoning, directly. His methods were less reliable than psychophysical assessments, but they more than made up for this in validity. Binet's insight was to use an external criterion to validate his measuring tool. Thus, Binet pioneered the empirically-keyed or external validation approach to scale construction. His external criterion was chronological age, and test items were grouped such that the typical member of each age group was able to achieve 50% correct answers on questions (items) of differential complexity. With Binet's procedure, individual differences in scale scores, or mental age (MA), were quite variable within students of similar chronological age (CA). William Stern used these components to create a ratio of mental development: MA/CA. This was later multiplied by 100 to form what we now know as the intelligence quotient (IQ), namely $IQ = MA/CA \times 100$.

Binet's approach was impressive; unlike Galton's and Cattell's psychophysical assessments of sensory systems, Binet's test predicted teacher ratings and school performance, and the progressive educational movement in America eagerly adopted it. Two of G. Stanley Hall's students, H. H. Goddard and Lewis M. Terman, promoted applied psychological testing. Although they specialized in opposite ends of the IQ spectrum (Chapman, 1988; Zenderland, 1998), they shared similar views about the need to tailor curriculum complexity and speed to individual differences in mental age. Terman later conducted one of the most famous longitudinal studies in all of psychology, devoted to the intellectually gifted (Chapman, 1988), while Goddard concentrated on the 'feeble minded' and directed the Vineland institution for training practitioners to work with this special population (Zenderland, 1998). They later joined Robert M. Yerkes to develop a cognitive ability measure for personnel selection during World War I. The Armed Forces needed to screen recruits, many of whom were illiterate; one of Terman's students, Arthur S. Otis, devised a nonverbal test of general intelligence that was used for this purpose. The group developed the Army Alpha (for literates) and Beta (for illiterates). The role mental measurements played in World War I and, subsequently, in World War II

legitimized the use of cognitive ability measures to screen people in the general public for training purposes; as a consequence, virtually every modern adult has taken some sort of cognitive ability test at some point in his or her life.

Following World War I, Terman recognized the link between the use of intellectual assessment in the military and problems in the public schools. Terman, a former teacher, understood that there is a range of ability in students who are grouped based on chronological age; he then became an advocate of homogeneous grouping based on mental age. He felt strongly that beyond two standard deviations either side of IQ's normative mean, the likelihood of encountering special students increases exponentially, and the more extreme the IQ, the more intense the need. Optimal rates of curriculum presentation, as well as its complexity, vary throughout the range of individual differences in general intelligence. With IQ centered on 100 and a standard deviation of 16, IQs extending from the bottom to the top 1% in ability cover an IQ range of approximately 63 to 137. But since IQs go beyond 200, this 74-point span only covers one-third of the possible range. Hollingworth's (1942) *Children over 180 IQ*, dramatized the unique educational needs of this special population, a need that has been empirically supported in every decade since (Benbow & Stanley, 1996).

16.9 THE NATURE OF INTELLIGENCE

American psychologists were interested primarily in the application of IQ measures to education; the early research on the nature of general intelligence came from Europe. In a groundbreaking publication, Charles Spearman (1904) showed that a dominant dimension ('g') runs through various collections of intellectual tasks (test items). Ostensibly, items used to form such groupings should be a 'hotchpotch'. Yet, all such items are positively correlated and when they are summed, the *construct-relevant* aspects of each coalesce through aggregation, whereas their *construct-irrelevant* (uncorrelated or unique) aspects vanish within the composite. Spearman and Brown formalized this property of aggregation in 1910. The Spearman–Brown Prophecy formula estimates the proportion of common or reliable variance running through a composite: $r_{tt} = kr_{xx} \div 1 + (k-1)r_{xx}$ (where: r_{tt} = common or reliable variance, r_{xx} = average item intercorrelation, and k = number of items). This formula reveals how a collection of items with uniformly light positive intercorrelations (say, averaging $r_{xx} = .15$) will form a composite dominated by common variance. Although each item on a typical intelligence test is dominated by unwanted noise, aggregation serves to amass the construct-relevant aspect (signal) from each item, while simultaneously attenuating their construct-irrelevant aspect (noise) within the composite. Aggregation *amplifies* signal, and *attenuates* noise.

At the phenotypic level, all modern intelligence tests measure essentially the same construct ('*g*') described at the turn of the century in Spearman's (1904) paper, ' "General intelligence," Objectively determined and measured' – although more efficiently and precisely. Not everyone is happy with this; some complain that this finding indicates a lack of progress, while others complain that '*g*' is simple and complex human behavior is multiply determined. Yet, given the validity data that have accrued for *g* over the years, how much additional forecasting power can be reasonably anticipated from the ability domain? Everyone agrees that, for predicting complex human behavior, many things matter, and that we must remain open to new ways to forecast performance. In the meantime, however, writers as different as Snow (1989), an educational psychologist, and Campbell (1990), an I/O psychologist, underscore the real-world significance of general intelligence:

> Given new evidence and reconsideration of old evidence, [*g*] can indeed be interpreted as 'ability to learn' as long as it is clear that these terms refer to complex processes and skills and that a somewhat different mix of these constituents may be required in different learning tasks and settings. The old view that mental tests and learning tasks measure distinctly different abilities should be discarded. (Snow, 1989, p. 22)

> General mental ability is a substantively significant determinant of individual differences in job performance for any job that includes information processing tasks. If the measure of performance reflects the information processing components of the job and any of several well-developed standardized measures used to assess general mental ability, then the relationship will be found unless the sample restricts the variances in performance or mental ability to near zero. The exact size of the relationship will be a function of the range of talent in the sample and the degree to which the job requires information processing and verbal cognitive skills. (Campbell, 1990, p. 56)

Modern research on the nature of intelligence has focused on predicting with greater precision educational outcomes, occupational training, and work performance. Other researchers have extended the network of general intelligence's external relationships to topics such as aggression, delinquency and crime, income and poverty. Some representative findings include correlations in the .70–.80 range with academic-achievement measures, .40–.70 with military training assignments, .20–.60 with work performance (higher values reflect job complexity), .30–.40 with income, and around .20 with law abidingness (see Brody, 1992; Gottfredson, 1997; Jensen, 1998, and references therein). Brand (1987, Table 2) documents a variety of *light* correlations between general intelligence and altruism, sense of humor, practical knowledge, response to psychotherapy, social skills, supermarket shopping ability (all positive correlates), and impulsivity, accident proneness, delinquency, smoking, racial prejudice, obesity (all negative correlates), among others. This diverse set of correlates reveals how individual differences in general intelligence 'pull' cascades of primary (direct) and secondary (indirect) effects. Murray's (1998) 15-year analysis of income differences between biologically related siblings (reared together) who differed on average by 12 IQ points corroborates a handful of studies using a similar control for family environment (Bouchard, 1997) – while not confounding socioeconomic status with biological relatedness.

16.10 IQ AND SOCIAL POLICY

The foregoing data are widely accepted among experts in the individual differences field (Carroll, 1993; Gottfredson, 1997; Jensen, 1998; Thorndike & Lohman, 1990). Yet research regarding general intelligence routinely stimulates contentious debate (Cronbach, 1975, *American Psychologist*), and this is likely to be with us always. Because measures of cognitive ability are used to allocate educational and vocational opportunities, they affect social policies. But psychometric data do not (and can not) dictate policies for test use. Moreover, because the test scores and criterion performance of different demographic groups differ, concern about using these tests emerged shortly after Spearman's (1904) initial article appeared (cf. Chapman, 1988; Jenkins & Paterson, 1961). Nevertheless, Robert Thorndike summarized his research findings (through the 1980s) on cognitive abilities as follows:

> [T]he great preponderance of the prediction that is possible from any set of cognitive tests is attributable to the general ability that they share. What I have called 'empirical *g*' is not merely an

interesting psychometric phenomenon, but lies at the heart of the prediction of real-life performances . . .

Remarks such as these highlight the importance of understanding general intelligence, its measurement, nature, and how best to nurture its development – because powerful scientific tools can be used wisely or unwisely, and their use is almost always accompanied by unintended (indirect) effects. So a number of wide-ranging studies have appeared over the last two decades, designed to reveal what this dimension forecasts relative to other psychological attributes. For example, John B. Carroll (1993) published his massive *Human Cognitive Abilities*, which included 467 data sets of factor-analytic work dating back to the 1920s. *Psychological Science* (1992) published a special section on 'Ability testing', as did *Current Directions in Psychological Science* (1993). The National Academy of Sciences published two book-length special reports on fairness and validity of ability testing (Hartigan & Widgor, 1989; Widgor & Garner, 1982), while the *Journal of Vocational Behavior* launched two special issues 'The *g* factor in employment' and 'Fairness in employment testing' (Gottfredson, 1986a,b; Gottfredson & Sharf, 1988, respectively). Finally, Sternberg's (1994) two-volume *Encyclopedia of Intelligence* is an excellent source for examining, systematically, the landscape of psychological concepts, findings, history, and research about intelligence. Sternberg's *Encyclopedia*, like his *Advances* series (Erlbaum), goes well beyond the psychometric assessment of cognitive abilities.

In the mid-1990s, Herrnstein and Murray (1994) published *The Bell Curve: Intelligence and class structure*, a controversial book that heightened the intensity of attention devoted to general intelligence and its assessment. Among other things, Herrnstein and Murray (1994) examined the relative predictive power of general intelligence and SES for forecasting a variety of social outcomes. Because of the controversy this volume stimulated, the American Psychological Association formed a special task force; the task force report, 'Intelligence: Knowns and unknowns' (Neisser et al., 1996), concluded that measures of general intelligence assess individual differences in 'abstract thinking or reasoning', 'the capacity to acquire knowledge', and 'problem solving ability' (Brody, 1992; Carroll, 1993; Gottfredson, 1997; Snyderman & Rothman, 1987), and that individual differences in these attributes affect facets of life outside of academic and vocational arenas, because abstract reasoning, problem solving, and rate of learning impact many aspects of life

in general, especially in a computer-driven, information-dense society.

16.11 Recent Issues in Cognitive Ability Research

Flynn Effect

Raw score increases on measures of general intelligence definitely occur over time – average scores go steadily up as time goes by. Observed scores on intelligence tests have been steadily rising cross-culturally, during most of this century, and this observation is called the 'Flynn effect', after the man who documented it. Whether these increases reflect genuine gains in general intelligence within the general population is less clear. Increases can occur due to increases on a measure's *construct-relevant* or *construct-irrelevant* variance, or both. The problem is complex; and it has generated a considerable amount of discussion (Neisser, 1998). However, the following suggests that the changes are at least in part due to construct-irrelevant aspects of measuring tools.

The magnitude of the Flynn effect is positively correlated with the amount of nonerror uniqueness of various measures of *g*. For example, population gains over time on the Raven Matrices are greater than gains on the Verbal Reasoning Composites of heterogeneous verbal tests, which, in turn, are greater than gains on broadly sampled tests of General Intelligence (aggregates of heterogeneous collections of numerical, spatial, and verbal problems). The Raven Matrices consists of approximately 50% *g* variance, whereas aggregated collections of cognitive tests approach 85%. The issue becomes more complex when we consider that test scores have also probably increased due to advances in medical care, dietary factors, and educational opportunities. Moreover, scores at the upper end of this dimension may not have increased much due to the gifted being deprived of appropriate developmental opportunities (Benbow & Stanley, 1996). Nonetheless, the Flynn effect definitely deserves intense study.

Whatever the reason for these raw score gains, the gains neither detract from nor enhance the construct validity of measures of general intelligence. Populations at different levels of ability, for example, typically show the same covariance structure with respect to the trait indicators under analysis (Lubinski, in press). It does not follow that mean changes on an individual difference dimension somehow attenuate the construct validity of measures purporting to assess it.

Vertical Inquiry

Jensen (1998) argues that basic research on general intelligence needs to identify more *fundamental* (biological) vertical paths, and develop more *ultimate* (evolutionary) explanations, for genuine advances to occur. Like other psychological constructs, general intelligence can be studied at different levels of analysis. By pooling studies of monozygotic and dizygotic twins reared together and apart, and a variety of adoption designs, the heritability of general intelligence in industrialized nations has been estimated to be between 60–80% (Bouchard, 1997). Using magnetic resonance imaging (MRI) technology, brain size controlled for body weight correlates in the high .30s with general intelligence, after removing the variance associated with body size (Jensen, 1998, pp. 146–149). Glucose metabolism is related to problem-solving behavior, and gifted people appear to engage in more efficient and less energy-expensive problem-solving behavior. Also, gifted people have enhanced right hemispheric functioning. The complexity of electroencephalograph (EEG) waves is positively correlated with g, as are the amplitude and latency of average evoked potential (AEP). Some investigators suggest that dendritic arborization (amount of branching) is correlated with g. In addition, a multidisciplinary team claims to have uncovered a DNA marker associated with g.

Proximal and Ultimate Investigations of Cognitive Ability

Bouchard and his colleagues have introduced a revision of experience producing drives (EPD) theory that concerns the development of human intelligence (Bouchard, Lykken, Tellegen, & McGue, 1996). EPD theory is a modification of the views of Hayes (1962) – a comparative psychologist who studied the language and socialization capabilities of nonhuman primates. Like all organisms, evolution designed humans to do something; inherited EPDs facilitate skill acquisition by motivating individuals toward particular kinds of experiences and developmental opportunities. Moreover, these selective sensitivities operate in a wide range of environments (because the environments children evolved in were highly variable). Bouchard et al.'s formulation is consistent with developmental theories concerning the active role individuals take in structuring their environments (see Lubinski, in press).

Other investigators propose synthesizing evolutionary psychology with chronometrical procedures for measuring inspection time (Jensen, 1998), i.e., perceptual discrimination of stimulus configurations that typically take less than one second for average adults to perform with essentially zero errors. Theoretically, elementary cognitive tasks can be used to index the time required for information processing in the nervous system. Despite the measurement issues in this area of research, it appears that the time to perform elementary cognitive tasks covaries negatively with g (faster processing is associated with higher g levels). Inspection-time measures have also been used to assess individual differences in cognitive sophistication among non-human primates.

This procedure may be a vehicle for the comparative study of the biological underpinnings of general cognitive sophistication, comparable to using sign language to study language learning in nonhuman primates. Primatologists have always recognized the range of individual differences in cognitive ability in primate groups. Premack (1983, p. 125) noted, pertaining to individual differences in language versus non-language trained groups of chimpanzees:

> Although chimpanzees vary in intelligence, we have unfortunately never had any control over this factor, having to accept all animals that are sent to us. We have, therefore, had both gifted and non-gifted animals in each group. Sarah is a bright animal by any standards, but so is Jessie, one of the non-language-trained animals. The groups are also comparable at the other end of the continuum, Peony's negative gifts being well matched by those of Luvy.

Some researchers propose that individual differences in processing stimulus equivalency (verbal/symbolic) relationships is a marker of general intelligence. If these such individual differences are linked to individual differences in CNS microstructure within and between the primate order and these, in turn, are linked to observations such as Premack's, 'all of the ingredients are in place to advance a comparative psychology of mental ability'. If individual differences in cognitive skills are linked to more fundamental biological mechanisms, we would have an especially powerful lens through which to view common phylogenetic processes involved in cognitive development. Research developments on this front will be interesting to follow, and may even assuage E. O. Wilson's (1998, p. 184) concern: '[S]ocial scientists as a whole have paid little attention to the foundations of human nature, and they have had almost no interest in its deep origins.'

RESOURCE REFERENCES

Galton, F. (1869). *Hereditary genius*. London: MacMillan.

Hogan, R., Johnson, J. A., & Briggs, S. R. (1997). *Handbook of personality psychology*. San Diego, CA: Academic Press.

Lubinski, D. (2000). Scientific and social significance of assessing individual differences in human behavior: 'Sinking shafts at a few critical points'. *Annual Review of Psychology, 51*, 405–444.

Lubinski, D., & Dawis, R. V. (1992). Aptitudes, skills, and proficiencies. In M. D. Dunnette & L. M. Hough (Eds.), *The handbook of industrial/organizational psychology* (2nd ed., pp. 1–59). Palo Alto: Consulting Psychologists Press.

Rothbart, M. K., Ahadi, S. A., & Evans, D. E. (2000). Temperament and personality: Origins and outcomes. *Journal of Personality and Social Psychology, 78*, 122–135.

ADDITIONAL LITERATURE CITED

Ahadi, S. A., & Rothbart, M. K. (1994). Temperament, development, and the Big Five. In C. F. Halverson, Jr., & G. A. Kohnstamm (Eds.), *The developing structure of temperament and personality from infancy to adulthood* (pp. 189–207). Hillsdale, NJ: Erlbaum.

Allport, G. W. (1937). *Personality: A psychological interpretation*. New York: Holt.

Angleitner, A., & Ostendorf, F. (1994). Temperament and the big five factors of personality. In C. F. Halverson, Jr., G. A. Kohnstamm, & R. P. Martin (Eds.), *The developing structure of temperament and personality from infancy to adulthood* (pp. 69–90). Hillsdale, NJ: Erlbaum.

Angleitner, A., & Riemann, R. (1991). What can we learn from the discussion of personality questionnaires for the construction of temperament inventories? In J. Strelau & A. Angleitner (Eds.), *Explorations in temperament: International perspectives on theory and measurement* (pp. 191–204). London: Plenum Press.

Bandura, A. (1982). Self-efficacy mechanism in human agency. *American Psychologist, 37*, 122–147.

Barron, F. (1969). *Creative person and creative process*. New York: Holt, Rinehart, & Winston.

Benbow, C. P., & Stanley, J. C. (1996). Inequity in equity: How 'equity' can lead to inequity for high-potential students. *Psychology, Public Policy, and Law, 2*, 249–292.

Block, J. (1964). *The challenge of response sets*. New York: Appleton-Century-Crofts.

Bouchard, T. J., Jr. (1997). IQ similarity in twins reared apart: Findings and responses to critics. In R. J. Sternberg & E. L. Grigorenko (Eds.), *Intelligence: Heredity and environment* (pp. 126–160). New York: Cambridge University Press.

Bouchard, T. J., Jr., Lykken, D. T., Tellegen, A., & McGue, M.(1996). Genes, drives, environment, and experience: EPD theory revisited. In C. P. Benbow, & D. Lubinski (Eds.), *Intellectual talent* (pp. 5–43). Baltimore: Johns Hopkins University Press.

Bowlby, J. (1983). Attachment and loss: Retrospect and prospect. *Annual Progress in Child Psychology and Child Development, 69*, 29–47.

Brand, C. (1987). The importance of general intelligence. In S. Magil & C. Magil (Eds.), *Arthur Jensen: Consensus and controversy* (pp. 251–265). New York: Falmer Press.

Brody, N. (1992). *Intelligence* (2nd ed.). San Diego, CA: Academic Press.

Buss, A. H., & Plomin, R. (1975). *A temperament theory of personality development*. New York: Wiley.

Buss, A. H., & Plomin, R. (1984). *Temperament: Early developing personality traits*. Hillsdale, NJ: Erlbaum.

Campbell, J. P. (1990). The role of theory in industrial and organizational psychology. In M. D. Dunnette & L. M. Hough (Eds.), *Handbook of industrial/organizational psychology* (2nd ed., Vol. 1, pp. 39–74). Palo Alto, CA: Consulting Psychology Press.

Carroll, J. B. (1993). *Human cognitive abilities: A survey of factor-analytic studies*. Cambridge, UK: Cambridge University Press.

Cattell, R. B., Eber, H. W., & Tatsuoka, M. M. (1970). *Handbook for the sixteen personal factor questionnaire*. Champaign, IL: Institute for Personality and Ability Testing.

Chapman, P. D. (1988). *Schools as sorters: Lewis M. Terman, applied psychology, and the intelligence testing movement, 1890–1930*. New York: New York University Press.

Chronbach, L. J. (1975). Five decades of public controversy over mental testing. *American Psychologist, 30*, 1–14.

Digman, J. M., & Shmelyov, A. G. (1996). The structure of temperament and personality in Russian Children. *Journal of Personality and Social Psychology, 71*, 341–351.

Edwards, A. (1959). *The social desirability variable in personality assessment and research*. New York: Dryden Press.

Eysenck, H. J. (1970). *The structure of human personality* (3rd ed.). London: Methuen.

Eysenck, H. J., & Eysenck, S. B. (1975). *Manual of the Eysenck Personality Questionnaire*. San Diego, CA: EITS.

Goldsmith, H. H., Buss, A. H., Plomin, R., Rothbart, M. K., Thomas, A., Chess, R., Hinde, R. A., & McCall, R. B. (1987). Roundtable: What is temperament? *Child Development, 58*, 505–529.

Goldsmith, H. H., Buss, K. A., & Lemery, K. S. (1997). Toddler and childhood temperament:

Expanded content, stronger genetic evidence, new evidence for the importance of environment. *Developmental Psychology*, *33*, 891–905.

Gottfredson, L. S. (Ed.). (1986a). The *g* factor in employment [Special issue]. *Journal of Vocational Behavior*, *29*(3), 293–450.

Gottfredson, L. S. (Ed.). (1986b). Occupational Aptitude Patterns (OAP) Map: Development and implications for a theory of job aptitude requirements (Monograph). *Journal of Vocational Behavior*, *29*, 254–291.

Gottfredson, L. S. (1997). Special issue: Intelligence and social policy. *Intelligence*, *24* (whole issue).

Gottfredson, L. S., & Sharf, J. C. (Eds.). (1988). Fairness in employment testing [Special Issue]. *Journal of Vocational Behavior*, *33*, 225–477.

Gough, H. G. (1987). *Manual for the California Psychological Inventory*. Palo Alto, CA: Consulting Psychologists Press.

Gray, J. A. (1991). The neuropsychology of temperament. In J. Strelau & A. Angleitner (Eds.), *Explorations in temperament: International perspectives on theory and measurement* (pp. 105–122). London: Plenum.

Guilford, J. P., & Zimmerman, W. S. (1949). *The Guilford–Zimmerman temperament survey*. Beverly Hills, CA: Sheridan Supply.

Hartigan, J. A., & Wigdor, A. K. (1989). *Fairness in employment testing: Validity generalization, minority issues, and the General Aptitude Test Battery*. Washington, DC: National Academy Press.

Hathaway, S. R., & McKinley, J. C. (1943). *The Minnesota Multiphasic Personality Inventory Manual*. New York: Psychological Corporation.

Hayes, K. J. (1962). Genes, drives, and intellect. *Psychological Reports*, *10*, 299–342.

Herrnstein, R. J., & Murray, C. (1994). *The bell curve*. New York: Free Press.

Hofstee, W. K. B. (1991). The concepts of personality and temperament. In J. Strelau & A. Angleitner (Eds.), *Explorations in temperament: International perspectives on theory and measurement* (pp. 177–188). London: Plenum.

Holland, J. L. (1985). *Making vocational choices*. Englewood Cliffs, NJ: Prentice-Hall.

Hollingworth, L. S. (1942). *Children above IQ 180*. New York: World Book.

Jenkins, J. J., & Paterson, D. G. (1961). *Studies in individual differences: The search for intelligence*. New York: Appleton-Century-Crofts.

Jensen, A. R. (1998). *The g factor: The science of mental ability*. Westport, CT: Praeger.

Jung, C. G. (1923). *Psychological types*. New York: Harcourt Brace.

Kelly, G. A. (1955). *The psychology of personal constructs*. New York: Norton.

Kretschmer, E. (1926). *Physique and character*. New York: Harper.

Lewin, K. (1935). *A dynamic theory of personality*. New York: Harcourt Brace.

Loehlin, J. C., Willerman, L., & Horn, J. M. (1989). Personality resemblances in adoptive families. *Journal of Personality and Social Psychology*, *53*, 961–969.

Lubinski, D. (2000). Scientific and social significance of assessing individual differences in human behavior: 'Sinking shafts at a few critical points'. *Annual Review of Psychology*, *51*, 405–444.

MacKinnon, D. W. (1948). *The assessment of men*. New York: Rhinehart & Co.

McDougall, W. (1908). *Social psychology*. London: Methuen.

McGue, M., Bacon, S., & Lykken, D. T. (1993). Personality stability and change in early adulthood: A behavior genetic analysis. *Developmental Psychology*, *29*, 96–109.

Mischel, W. (1968). *Personality and assessment*. New York: Wiley.

Mischel, W. (1990). Personality dispositions revisited. In L. A. Pervin (Ed.), *Handbook of personality* (pp. 111–134). New York: Guilford.

Murray, C. (1998). *Income, inequality, and IQ*. Washington, DC: American Enterprise Institute.

Murry, H. A. (1938). *Explorations in personality*. New York: Oxford University Press.

Neisser, U. (1998). *The rising curve: Long-term gains in IQ and related measures*. Washington, DC: APA Press.

Neisser, U., Boodoo, G., Bouchard, T. J., Jr., Boykin, A. W., Brody, N., Ceci, S. J., Halpern, D. F., Loehlin, J. C., Perloff, R., Sternberg, R. J., & Urbina, S. (1996). Intelligence: Knowns and unknowns. *American Psychologist*, *51*, 77–101.

Premack, D. (1983). The codes of man and beasts. *Behavioral and Brain Sciences*, *6*, 125–167.

Rostan, L. (1824). *Cours elementaire d'hygiene*. Paris: Bechef jeune.

Rothbart, M. K. (1981). Measurement of temperament in infancy. *Child Development*, *52*, 569–578.

Rothbart, M. K., Derryberry, D., & Posner, M. I. (1994). A psychobiological approach to the development of temperament. In J. E. Bates & T. D. Wachs (Eds.), *Temperament: Individual differences at the interface of biology and behavior* (pp. 83–116). Washington, DC: American Psychological Association.

Rotter, J. (1966). Generalized expectancies for internal versus external control of reinforcements. *Psychological Monographs*, *80* (Whole No. 609).

Rowe, D. C. (1997). Genetics, temperament, and personality. In R. Hogan, J. A. Johnson, & S. R. Briggs (Eds.), *Handbook of personality psychology*. San Diego, CA: Academic Press.

Ruch, W., Angleitner, A., & Strelaul, J. (1991). The Strelau Temperament Inventory: Validity Studies. *European Journal of Personality*, *5*, 287–308.

Rusalov, V. M. (1989). Object-related and communicative aspects of human temperament: A new questionnaire of the structure of temperament. *Personality and Individual Differences*, *10*, 817–827.

Saudino, K. J., & Eaton, W. O. (1991). Infant temperament and genetics: An objective twin study of motor activity level. *Child Development, 62,* 1167–1174.

Scarr, S., & McCartney, K. (1983). How people make their own environments: A theory of genotype-environment effects. *Child Development, 54,* 424–435.

Schmitz, S., Saudino, K. J., Plomin, R., Fulker, D. W., & DeFries, J. C. (1996). Genetic and environmental influences on temperament in middle childhood: Analyses of teacher and tester ratings. *Child Development, 67,* 409–422.

Sheldon, W. H., Dupertuis, C. W., & McDermott, E. (1954). *Atlas of men.* New York: Harper.

Simpson, J. A., & Rholes, W. S. (1998). *Attachment theory and close relationships.* New York: Guilford.

Snow, R. E. (1989). Aptitude–treatment interaction as a framework for research on individual differences in learning. In P. L. Ackerman, R. J. Sternberg, & R. G. Glasser, *Learning and individual differences* (pp. 13–59). New York: Freedman.

Snyderman, M., & Rothman, S. (1987). Survey of expert opinion on intelligence and aptitude testing. *American Psychologist, 42,* 137–144.

Spearman, C. (1904). 'General intelligence', Objectively determined and measured. *American Journal of Psychology, 15,* 201–292.

Spranger, E. (1928). *Types of men.* Halle: Niemeyer.

Stern, W. (1900). *Über die Psychologie der individuellen Differenzen.*

Stern, W. (1906). *Person und Sache: System der philosophischen Weltanschauung.*

Sternberg, R. J. (Ed.). (1994). *Encyclopedia of human intelligence* (2 vols). New York: Macmillan.

Sternberg, R. J., & Detterman, D. K. (1986). *What is intelligence? Contemporary viewpoints on its nature and definition.* Norwood, NJ: Ablex.

Strelau, J. (1983). *Temperament, personality, activity.* London: Academic Press.

Strelau, J. (1987). The concept of temperament in personality research. *European Journal of Psychology, 1,* 107–117.

Thomas, A., & Chess, S. (1977). *Temperament and development.* New York: Brunner-Mazel.

Thorndike, R. M., & Lohman, D. F. (1990). *A century of ability testing.* Chicago: Riverside.

Thurstone, L. L., & Thurstone, T. G. (1929). *Personality schedule.* Chicago: University of Chicago Press.

Tupes, E. R., & Christal, R. (1961). *Recurrent personality factors based on trait ratings* (USFD Tech. Rep. No. 67–97). Lackland, TX: Lackland Air Force Base.

Viola, G. (1909). *Le legge de correlazione morfologia del tipi individuali.* Padua: Prosperini.

Wachs, T. D. (1994). Fit, context, and the transition between temperament and personality. In C. F. Halverson, Jr., G. A. Kohnstamm, & R. P. Martin (Eds.), *The developing structure of temperament and personality from infancy to adulthood* (pp. 209–220). Hillsdale, NJ: Erlbaum.

Watson, D., Clark, L. A., & Harkness, A. R. (1994). Structures of personality and their relevance to psychopathology. *Journal of Abnormal Psychology, 103,* 18–31.

Wigdor, A. K., & Garner, W. R. (Eds.). (1982). Ability testing: Uses, consequences, and controversies, Part I. Report of the Committee, Part 2: Documentation section. Washington, DC: National Academy Press.

Wiggins, J. S. (1996). *The Five-Factor Model of personality.* New York: Guilford.

Wilson, E. O. (1998). *Consilience: The unity of knowledge.* New York: Knopf.

Woodworth, R. S. (1920). *Personal data sheet.* Chicago: Stoelting.

Wundt, W. (1903). *Grundzuege der physiologischen Psychologie* (5th ed.).

Zenderland, L. (1998). *Measuring minds: Henry Goddard and the origins of American intelligence testing.* Cambridge: Cambridge University Press.

Zukerman, M., Kuhlman, D. M., & Camac, C. (1988). What lies beyond E and N? Factor analyses of scales believed to measure basic dimensions of personality. *Journal of Personality and Social Psychology, 54,* 96–107.

Communications concerning this chapter should be addressed to: Professor Robert T. Hogan, Department of Psychology, University of Tulsa, Tulsa, OK 74104, USA

17

Social Processes and Human Behavior: Social Psychology

MICHAEL A. HOGG

17.1 STUDYING SOCIAL PSYCHOLOGY

A widely accepted and very common definition of social psychology is that it is 'the scientific investigation of how the thoughts, feelings, and behaviors of individuals are influenced, by the actual, imagined or implied presence of others'. Social psychologists study all aspects of human interaction, including verbal and nonverbal communication between people in dyads or groups; the behavior of people in groups and large-scale social categories; how people in different groups and categories treat and think about one another; how people perceive, interpret, and represent their own and others' behavior; how interaction produces shared representations of the social and physical world that shape thought and behavior; how close friendships and relation-ships develop and dissolve; how people can change one another's attitudes and behaviors; how people form a sense of who they are from their interaction with, experience of, and treatment by others; why people harm others, but can also help others.

Because the subject matter of social psychology is what goes on around us all the time, human beings are all social psychologists – we all need to have a working understanding of social psychology in order to function adequately as human beings. Some important approaches within social psychology argue that scientific social psychological theories are actually a formalization of these naive or lay theories of social psychology (e.g., Heider, 1958) and that an important way to develop theories of social psychology is simply to ask people about their explanations of the social world or to see what sorts of explanatory logic may underlie what people actually say to one another.

Another consequence of the pervasiveness of social psychology in everyday life is that there is a notable applied dimension to social psychology – many social psychologists are primarily applied (e.g., in the areas of organizations, health, family, discrimination) and almost all dabble in applications of basic research and theory. Indeed, Kurt Lewin (e.g., Lewin, 1951), the acknowledged 'father' of modern social psychology, believed that there is nothing so practical as a good theory, and advocated 'full cycle research' in which basic and applied research were closely intertwined. Lewin also believed that social psychologists should put their theories into action to help make the world a better place to live in – that people should engage in 'action research'. This latter goal is formally represented, in the United States, by the Society for the Psychological Study of Social Issues. Nevertheless the scientific heart and mainstream of social psychology is tightly conceptual and largely based on controlled laboratory experiments, which are designed to specify basic cognitive processes and social contexts and how they interact to produce specific forms of social behavior.

Research Methods

Social psychology employs the scientific method to develop and test theories, and caters research methodology to the particular research question being investigated. On the basis of hunches, personal experience, casual observation, and the study of research, a theory is developed – generally in such a way that it specifies not only what causes what, but through what process. From the theory, hypotheses are elaborated that predict that if such and such observable conditions exist (called the independent variable) then there will be such and such observable outcomes (the dependent variable). The preferred way to test predictions is by experimentation in which the independent variable is manipulated and the dependent variable measured under carefully controlled conditions, usually in a laboratory, that rule out alternative explanations for the results. Experiments are very good for establishing clean cause–effect relationships and for unpacking underlying, often cognitive, processes. Not surprisingly, the pre-eminent scholarly societies for social psychology in North America and Europe have 'experimental' in their titles: Society for Experimental Social Psychology, and European Association of Experimental Social Psychology.

Laboratory experiments strive to maximize 'experimental realism' or 'internal validity' by making the manipulation impactful and strong. However, experiments are intentionally, unrealistic in that they do not represent the richness of the real-world phenomenon being investigated – this is called 'mundane realism' or 'external validity'. Experimentation also requires tremendous care to ensure that participants' behavior is natural and automatic rather than a deliberate attempt to please the experimenter, confirm hypotheses, or project a favorable impression. To do this, social psychologists generally need to conceal hypotheses and procedures from participants – a scientifically necessary practice that attracted the emotive label of 'deception' and, using Milgram's classic obedience studies (e.g., Milgram, 1963 – see below) as the sacrificial lamb, stirred up enormous controversy in the 1960s. Although experimentation still dominates social psychology, strict ethical prescriptions have made it difficult since the early 1980s to conduct the vivid and attention-grabbing studies that characterized earlier research.

Experiments tend to use introductory psychology students as participants – this is convenient for the senior undergraduates and graduate students who actually conduct much of the research, and it is scientifically appropriate for research in which individual differences are treated as error variance and cultural forms are not the focus of study. However, even the most dedicated experimentalist feels the urge, from time to time, to see if the same processes operate in different populations. Experiments are also inappropriate for a large number of research questions – for example, it is difficult to study a riot or an established street gang in the laboratory. However, social psychologists are tenacious and inventive. One researcher tried to create a riot in the laboratory by wafting smoke under the locked door of the laboratory – some groups of participants kicked the door open and disengaged the smoke generator, and other groups calmly discussed the possibility that they were being observed!

Not surprisingly social psychologists have other research methods in their armory. These include field experiments where a variable is manipulated in a naturalistic setting outside the laboratory (e.g., the reaction of passers-by to a well-dressed or shabbily dressed experimental confederate can be measured), and a whole range of non-experimental methods. The latter include archival research (e.g., comparison of government data on TV viewing in Japan and in Britain), case studies (e.g., in-depth multi-method analysis of a specific riot), survey research (e.g., questionnaires on language use and ethnic identity), and field studies (e.g., unobtrusive observation of the behavior of traders on the floor of the stock market).

Theories in Social Psychology

Social psychological theories vary in generality, rigor, testability and general perspective or metatheory. Behaviorist theories, based on Pavlov's and Skinner's approaches to psychology, focus on situational factors that reinforce behavior and produce learning – for example, social exchange theories (see Kelley & Thibaut, 1978) analyze social behavior in terms of people's assessment of the personal costs and benefits of performing certain actions relative to other actions. Behaviorist theories are sometimes charged with incorrectly viewing people as passive targets of external influences. In response to this, cognitive theories, based on Koffka's and Köhler's Gestalt psychology of the 1930s, focus on the way that people actively interpret and change their environment through the agency of cognitive processes and cognitive representations. This perspective has a strong tradition in social psychology – it surfaces in Lewin's (1951) field theory approach to social psychology where representations of the social world motivate specific behaviors; in cognitive consistency theories of the 1950s and 1960s that view incompatible cognitions as motivating cognitive and behavioral change (see Abelson et al., 1968); in attribution theories of the 1970s that focus on people's causal explanations of behavior (see Kelley, 1967); and in contemporary social cognition that specifies in detail how cognitive processes and representations relate to social behavior (Fiske & Taylor, 1991).

As in other areas of psychology, social psychologists often try to explain social behavior in terms of enduring (now rarely innate) personality differences – for example some people conform more than others or are better leaders than others because they have conformist or leadership personalities. Most social psychologists now feel that personality is not a social psychological explanation at all – what is needed is an analysis of the interplay between situational and cognitive factors that cause apparently stable behavior patterns. Some of the strongest critics of personality or individual difference perspectives in social psychology are 'situationists' – social psychologists who focus on the way that people in groups are constituted by their immediate or more enduring social context and thus change when circumstances change. Extreme forms of this are social constructivism and discourse analysis, which virtually do away with psychology and place full explanatory load on social history or spoken language. In reality, however, most theories in social psychology are a complex mixture of perspectives, which reflect metatheory only in their theoretical emphasis.

Controversies and Debates

Social psychology sometimes appears to have an identity problem, and to be in the throes of fiery debates about what it should be doing and how it should be doing it. This makes social psychology exciting – it reflects the passionate dedication that social psychologists have for their subject. There are at least two reasons why social psychology can sometimes be heated. One is that its subject matter is people's interaction within the context of human society, and therefore social values and political ideologies impact on and frame theories. The other reason is that social psychology lies at the intersection of a number of (sub)-disciplines, including cognitive psychology, organizational psychology, sociology, political science, social anthropology, economics, developmental psychology, and sociolingusitics. To have a distinct identity social psychology needs to have a scientific niche that it alone occupies. Since many disciplines study the same phenomena as does social psychology (e.g., groups, prejudice, families, aggression, cognition), some social psychologists argue that to be distinct, social psychologists must have a distinct *way* of studying social behavior – it's how we do it, not what we do it on. The main problem is the level of explanation. Social psychology tends towards reductionism – explaining social phenomena exclusively in terms of individuals, individual cognitive processes, and in extreme cases neuropsychology. It is clear that this approach gives social psychology away to cognitive psychology or even neuropsychology. Some social psychologists, many from Europe, urge the discipline to focus on the social rather than individual dimension of social behavior (Tajfel, 1984), and to develop concepts that integrate or articulate processes that operate at the cognitive, social interactive, and societal level.

During the late 1960s and early 1970s there was a widespread crisis of confidence in social psychology which brought enduring worries into the open. Social psychologists were worried that social psychology was reductionist and immature in its theories; positivist and unsophisticated in its methods; blind to the role of language, history, and culture; inhumane and disrespectful in its treatment of research participants; and self-indulgently engaged in the explanation of trivial behaviors. The charge of positivism rested on the view that objectivity in social psychology is impossible because social psychologists are people and the subject matter of social psychology is people, ergo oneself. Therefore the scientific method is particularly inappropriate to social psychology. Out of this angst arose a diversity of 'resolutions' of the crisis – the two most successful are social cognition with its sophisticated methodologies and tight theories (e.g., Fiske & Taylor, 1991), and social perspectives that focus on culture, intergroup relations, and social identity (e.g., Tajfel, 1984). In recent years these approaches have drawn closer together. There is, however, another set of responses that radically rejects traditional social psychological methods, theories and research foci – this includes social constructionism, humanistic psychology, ethogenics, discourse analysis, and post-structuralist perspectives. These approaches are diverse but share a focus on subjectivity, language, and qualitative methods.

Historical Context

It was only in the second half of the nineteenth century that an empirical approach to the study of social behavior emerged. A group in Germany styled themselves as students of *Völkerpsychologie* (folk psychology) and focused on the collective mind (as distinct from Wundt's focus on the individual mind), defined variously as a societal way of thinking within the individual and also a form of supermentality that could enfold a whole group of people. This latter emphasis developed in the 1890s and 1900s into theories of the group mind (e.g., LeBon, McDougall), which although outmoded today still address fundamentally social psychological issues to do with the relation between the individual and the collective.

Social psychology was quickly and decisively influenced by Wundt's vision of psychology as an experimental science, and by Watson's behaviorist manifesto for psychology. Although one of the earliest programs in social psychology was at the University of Chicago, where G. H. Mead's influential symbolic interactionist perspective was developing, this 'sociological' form of social psychology became marginalized within a mainstream that viewed social psychology as a part of psychology rather than sociology, and increasingly focused on the isolated individual, observable behavior, and laboratory experimentation. This dominant form of social psychology is captured by F. H. Allport's (1924) classic text that set the agenda for modern social psychology.

In the early 1900s America ousted Germany as the powerhouse of social psychology. This shift was accelerated in the 1930s by the rise of fascism in Germany – Germany's leading social psychologists fled mainly to the United States. These emigrés included Kurt Lewin, the 'father' of experimental social psychology. This influx, coupled with research demands and questions associated with the Second World War, produced an explosion of activity, much of it applied, in social psychology that focused on small group processes (e.g., Lewin, 1951), attitudes and attitude change (e.g., the Yale attitude change program – Hovland, Janis, & Kelley, 1953), and prejudice (e.g., the authoritarian personality – Adorno, Frenkel-Brunswik, Levinson, & Sanford, 1950).

Since the late 1940s social psychology has grown at a prodigious rate, in terms of programs, publication, and significance within psychology. Although such growth embraces a diversity of research agenda, themes and perspectives, there have been dominant trends that attract attention for periods of time. During the 1950s and into the early 1960s small group research flourished (e.g., the study of cohesion, leadership, communication networks, group influence) and articulated well with a general social exchange perspective on interpersonal relations and interaction (Thibaut & Kelley, 1959). This period was also characterized by cognitive dissonance theory – building on Lewin's (1951) field theory approach to social psychology and Heider's (1958) discussion of cognitive balance, Festinger (1957) developed a cognitive dissonance perspective that traced behavior (e.g., attitude change) to motivations arising from inconsistent cognitions. This cognitive emphasis gathered strength in the mid-1960s with Jones and Davis's (1965) development of Heider's (1958) early model of people as naive or lay psychologists in the business of developing science-like causal explanations of their social world – thus was born attribution theory (e.g., Kelley, 1967) which dominated social psychology through the 1970s (see Fiske & Taylor, 1991).

Concerns about the rational model of human behavior that underpinned attribution theories, in conjunction with the crisis of confidence in social psychology of the late 1960s and early 1970s, provided fertile ground for the most recent and far-reaching cognitive revolution in social psychology – social cognition (e.g., Fiske & Taylor, 1991; Nisbett & Ross, 1980). Social cognition has tried to emulate cognitive psychology in its types of theories, and its methods of research – it focuses on the way in which people construct and are influenced by their cognitive representations of experience. The emphasis is on cognitive processes and structures within the individual – an individual who is either a cognitive miser (using the least cognitive effort to get by) or a motivated tactician (picking and choosing among cognitive processes in order to best satisfy goals), or both. The rise of social cognition in the United States since the late 1970s has been shadowed by the development in Europe of a different emphasis in social psychology, that focuses on the social dimension of human existence (e.g., Tajfel, 1984) – for example, intergroup relations, prejudice, collective representations, social identity, large-scale social categories. There is some evidence that since the early 1990s American social cognition and European intergroup approaches are finally drawing together to integrate their strengths.

Cultural and National Forms of Social Psychology

For most of the twentieth century, social psychology has been dominated by the United States. There are at least four reasons for this: (a) English is the international language of science and there are well over 250 million English speakers in the United States – Australasia, Canada, and the UK can only muster 100 million; (b) the enormous wealth of the United States has allowed a well-funded and respected research culture to thrive within an elite group of top universities; (c) early twentieth century conflicts in Europe culminated in 1930s fascism which effectively removed Europe as a significant competitor in social psychology for almost half a century; and (d) career advancement in other countries depends on American journal publication criteria and thus local forms of social psychology are inhibited.

Social psychology is done by people – people who study things which interest them and which often come from their own day-to-day experiences. The agendas and perspectives of social psychology are influenced by cultural and historical experiences. It has often been suggested that because social psychology is dominated by America, it is framed by American cultural experiences which emphasize the primacy of individuality. Other cultural milieu might produce different emphases and agendas. Indeed this has happened – most notably with the re-emergence of European social psychology. In 1945 there was effectively no European social psychology. A concerted reconstruction effort led to the birth of the European Association of Experimental Social Psychology in 1966, the launching of the *European Journal of Social Psychology* in 1971, and the *European Review of Social Psychology* in 1990. The *British Journal of Social Psychology* has also played its part, as have European social psychology textbooks (e.g., Hewstone, Stroebe, & Stephenson, 1996;

Hogg & Vaughan, 1998). Together this infrastructure has, since the mid-1980s, made Europe a major player in social psychology – a player whose contribution has been to criticize theories that explain collective phenomena purely in terms of individuality or individual cognitive processes. European social psychology has focused on intergroup relations and collective phenomena. However, there is also great, and growing, national diversity in Europe – for instance, social cognition and the study of small groups are significant themes in Germany, social representations thrives in France, and since the mid-1980s post-structuralist and discourse analytic approaches have flourished in the UK.

In Canada, social psychology is heavily influenced by the United States. However, the policy of multiculturalism, and the cultural and language context in Quebec has focused Canadian social psychologists on language, ethnicity, intergroup relations, and social identity – Canadian social psychology has some close links to European social psychology. These links with European social psychology are also to be found in Australia and New Zealand. Social psychology in Australia was initially an offshoot of British social psychology. But with Australia's post-Second World War shift of allegiance to the United States it became influenced by American social psychology. During the 1970s Australia re-focused on Asia and on its own multicultural nature, and during the 1980s there was an influx of British social psychologists fleeing Thatcher's Britain and bringing with them a European perspective. Australia is now a kaleidoscope of diverse perspectives that are strongly influenced by a focus on intergroup relations, social identity, culture, ethnicity, and language. New Zealand has been influenced by British post-structuralist and discourse analytic perspectives.

Social psychology, as a scientific debate conducted in English, has not been so well influenced by non-European or non-English speaking nations. The exception is Asia – particularly the more prosperous East Asian nations such as Hong Kong, Japan, Korea, and Taiwan. There have been recent moves to organize social psychology in Asia around a common interest in collectivist perspectives and research on culture. This has been structurally facilitated by the recent formation of the Asian Association of Social Psychology, and by the launching of the *Asian Journal of Social Psychology*. Prominent East Asian social psychologists have largely been trained in the United States, but the focus on collectivism and culture is metatheoretically closer to European social psychology and the sort of eclecticism that characterizes Australasian social psychology – indeed there are developing links between Asian and Australasian social psychology.

Nevertheless, social psychological research is overwhelmingly conducted in Western nations (North America, Europe, and Australasia). In their 1998 text, *Social psychology across cultures*, Peter Smith and Michael Bond note that only 2 to 3% of the total of research references in the top contemporary North American and European social psychology texts refer to studies conducted in non-Western cultures. The coverage of social psychology in this chapter reflects this cultural constraint.

Landmarks in Social Psychology

Although social psychology is a young science, there are some landmark studies or programs that are cited repeatedly as reference points for prolific subsequent research. A study by Triplett in 1898 is often identified as social psychology's first experiment – Triplett first discovered from analysis of published records that cyclists went faster in paced than unpaced trials, and then he went on to conduct a controlled experiment in which he had people roll in fishing line either alone or in coaction with others to see how the presence of others influenced performance. In 1936 Muzafer Sherif reported a program of experiments in which participants judged the apparent movement of a fixed point of light in a completely darkened room (the autokinetic effect) by themselves or in the presence of others. These studies showed how norms developed very rapidly to guide judgments, and how these norms persisted to have influence even when the original members of the group had all been replaced by new people. Developing this theme, Solomon Asch (1956) showed how people's judgments can be swayed by a consistent majority even when they are judging something completely unambiguous, such as which line is longest. This research showed how readily people conform to a majority. Stanley Milgram (1963) wondered whether people would conform where the consequences of conformity involved inflicting pain on others – he found that people would inflict electric shocks that they believed would be injurious to a victim simply because an experimenter had told them to do so. Milgram's focus quickly shifted from conformity to destructive obedience of commands. Similarly, Philip Zimbardo (Zimbardo, Haney, Banks, & Jaffe, 1982) found that people would readily comply with role prescriptions even if they entailed inflicting discomfort – he constructed a simulated prison in the basement of the Stanford psychology department and assigned students to prisoner or guard roles for a prolonged role-playing study that had to be curtailed after only a few days because role adherence became too extreme.

In 1939, Dollard, Doob, Miller, Mowrer, and Sears, published their frustration–aggression hypothesis. It traced prejudice and mass aggression to individual frustrations, that are expressed as aggression displaced onto targets who are weaker than the original cause of the frustration. In 1950, Adorno, Frenkel-Brunswik, Levinson and Sanford published their authoritarian personality theory. It traced prejudice and intergroup aggression to prejudiced personalities that had developed out of childhood experience of distorted family relationships involving authoritarian parenting. Later perspectives on prejudice and intergroup aggression focused on intergroup relations. In the early 1950s Muzafer Sherif (1966) conducted a series of naturalistic field experiments at boys' camps in the United States. These studies showed how mutually exclusive goal relations produced competitive behavior and intergroup conflict and stereotyping, and how superordinate goals that encouraged cooperative interaction improve intergroup relations. In 1954, Gordon Allport published a book on prejudice, which promoted meaningful and enduring equal status contact between members of social groups as a way to reduce prejudice. This recommendation was influential in the United States government's decision to desegregate the American school system.

In 1970, Henri Tajfel reported an experiment which showed that intergroup behaviors could emerge even if people were merely categorized into two non-interactive, anonymous groups on the basis of minimal and trivial criteria – categorization alone was sufficient to produce intergroup discrimination. This has become a popular paradigm in social psychology. In a typical minimal group experiment, 10 to 20 student participants who have volunteered for a one-hour study of social judgment sit at separate tables in a classroom and do not communicate or interact with one another. They complete a perception or judgment task (e.g., painting preference, dot estimation) and are ostensibly categorized into two groups on the basis of painting/painter preference or under- or over-estimation of the number of dots (in reality they are randomly categorized). They then complete a paper-and-pencil task in which they distribute points that they can think of as representing some valued resource between their own group and the other group. This is followed by a questionnaire in which they evaluate themselves, their group, and their membership in their group. Control participants are not categorized – merely aggregated by similar code number (e.g., 20s and 40s). Categorized participants show significantly greater behavioral and evaluative in-group favoritism and in-group belonging than do control participants.

Another classic study, by Stoner in 1961, challenged prevailing wisdom that conformity was all about averaging and that group decisions were cautious. Stoner found that sometimes group decisions could be more extreme and more risky than the average of the opinions held by the members of the group – groups could polarize towards extremity. In 1972 Irving Janis published an analysis of groupthink – a group decision-making phenomenon in which highly cohesive groups with overly-directive leaders can disregard optimal decision-making procedures as they blindly pursue consensus. This leads to poor decisions that can have disastrous consequences.

There are many other influential studies and publications. The brief coverage of social psychology in this chapter is necessarily framed by these influential works.

17.2 SOCIAL COGNITION AND SOCIAL EXPLANATION

Probably because social psychology allied itself very early on with general psychology, it has always placed explanatory emphasis on intra-individual cognitive processes and structures – social psychology has always been markedly cognitive. As explained in the history section above, this cognitive emphasis has taken different forms at different times – culminating in modern social cognition (Fiske & Taylor, 1991) which has dominated social psychology since the early 1980s.

Forming Impressions of People

The question of how people combine information to form impressions of other people lies at the heart of social cognition. Early research by Asch adopted a Gestalt perspective to show that some pieces of information act as *central cues* which influence the meaning of other *peripheral cues* and are disproportionately influential in impression formation. Cues can be central because people think they are more important (people have their own *personal constructs*, or implicit personality theories that identify what constellations of traits they feel are important in judging people), or because they stand out from

other information (negative information is often distinctive and thus disproportionately influential), or even because they are the first pieces of information encountered (first impressions are often hard to change – a primacy effect). There is some evidence that social norms proscribing certain impressions can inhibit the influence of central traits on impression formation – stereotypic impressions can thus sometimes be inhibited.

An initially more mechanical perspective on impression formation has been proposed by Anderson. People focus primarily on the evaluative implications (positive or negative) of pieces of information about others, and integrate this information arithmetically – the information is cognitively summed or averaged to produce an overall evaluative impression of the person. Research favors averaging, but actually goes further to suggest that the components are first subjectively weighted to reflect the context-dependent subjective importance of information in forming an impression. This weighted averaging model revisits Asch's central traits – the difference is that Asch focuses on the meaning of traits whereas Anderson focuses on their evaluative implications. Modern social cognition replaces central traits with the more general concept of schemas.

Schemas and Categories

For social psychology, a schema is a cognitive structure that represents knowledge about a concept or type of stimulus – it represents attributes and relationships among attributes. We have schemas about roles (e.g., chairperson), events (usually called 'scripts', e.g., eating at a restaurant), social groups (e.g., Norwegians), specific people (e.g., your spouse), and oneself (how we are, how we would like to be, and how we ought to be). Once invoked by contextual cues, schemas have a powerful tendency to replace data-driven or bottom-up processing (i.e., reliance on information gleaned directly from the immediate context) with theory/concept-driven or top-down processing (i.e., reliance on information provided by prior knowledge and preconceptions). In order for a schema to come into play a person, event or situation needs to be categorized as fitting a specific schema.

Social psychologists believe that categories are collections of instances that have a general appearance of similarity (called *family resemblance*), rather than a shared set of criterial attributes, and that people represent categories in terms of prototypes (an abstraction of relatively common attributes) or exemplars (a concrete instance of a category member). For example, consider the category *café* – instances are diverse but have a family resemblance, and we can represent the category as a prototype (amalgam of café attributes) or an exemplar (a specific café we have known). If an instance successfully matches a category prototype or exemplar it is categorized, and the relevant schema is activated. Categorization accentuates perceived similarities within and differences between categories. These processes, applied to the categorization of people, can produce stereotyping – people represent social categories (e.g., Canadians) as prototypes, exemplars or schemas (i.e., stereotypical images), and when an individual person is categorized as a Canadian the perceptual accentuation process in conjunction with top-down schematic processing leads to stereotypic perception of that person.

Research on schema use suggests that people relatively spontaneously employ schemas relating to social categories, roles, current mood states, easily detected features (e.g., skin color), contextually distinctive features (e.g., single male in a group of females), and schemas that are chronically accessible because they are frequently or recently used, or they relate to important aspects of self. Schemas such as these are functional and accurate enough for immediate interactive purposes in most contexts (they have *circumscribed accuracy*), and are particularly useful when quick social perceptual decisions have to be made (e.g., time pressure, distraction). However, if the perceived costs of misperception are high, people strive for greater accuracy by relying on more specific schemas or engaging in bottom-up data-driven information processing. Although people sometimes know that schemas are undesirable (e.g., derogatory stereotypes of social groups), and can actively try to avoid using them, it can be surprisingly difficult to do this. Schema use is overwhelmingly influenced by situational demands, but there are some individual differences broadly revolving around the complexity of people's representation of the social world and their predilection for quick and simple or slower and more detailed social perceptions.

People acquire schemas indirectly from other people, literature, and the media, and from encounters with category instances which make schemas more abstract, compact, richer in content, and ultimately more resistant to change. This resistance to change comes directly from the fact that schemas lend a sense of order, structure, and coherence to the social world. Rapidly changing schemas would not satisfy this need – and indeed research shows that once

fully developed, schemas are remarkably resistant to schema-disconfirming information. However, schemas are not rigidly immutable, they do change through at least three processes: (a) there can be slow change in response to new information – called *bookkeeping*, (b) a sudden cataclysmic change as the consequence of gradually accumulating information – called *conversion*, or (c) a configuration change in which new information forms the basis of a new schema nested within the original schema – called *subtyping*. Research suggests that subtyping is the most common process of schema change.

Encoding, Remembering, and Using Social Information

Social cognition is heavily influenced by salient stimuli and information because they attract attention and involve increased cognitive work. Novel, unusual, distinctive, and subjectively important stimuli/information are generally salient, and salient people are perceived more coherently, and to be more influential and more extreme. Their behavior is also considered to reflect their dispositions rather than situational constraints. Social cognition is also heavily influenced, as described above, by schemas and information that is accessible in memory. Indeed, social cognition researchers have explored the way in which people store social information in memory – this work relates closely to cognitive psychology in its reference to associative networks, long- and short-term memory, and so forth. Most directly relevant to social psychology is research which shows that we can store information about other people 'by person' or 'by group' – that is, we cluster attributes under individual people, or we cluster people under attributes of groups. One view in social psychology is that organization by group is tied largely to encounters with relative strangers and that the cognitive system strives to transform this structure into the preferred organization by person – this view reflects the traditional individualistic metatheory that places ultimate explanatory emphasis on the individual. Another view is that the two organizations coexist as distinct ways of representing social experience – this view reflects the alternative collectivist metatheory that guards against explaining groups in terms of individuals.

The cognitive decision-making processes we use to make social inferences (i.e., identify, sample, and combine information to form impressions and make judgments) have been studied in detail by social cognition researchers. A major distinction is between (a) relatively automatic top-of-the-head, schema-based, processing (also called heuristic or peripheral route processing); and (b) relatively deliberate bottom-up data-based processing (also called systematic or central route processing). Social inference research has generally specified ways in which social inference is biased and error prone because people fall short of ideal inferential processes. For instance, people are over-influenced by schemas, individual cases, and distinctive or extreme stimuli, and do not adjust inferences to accommodate more statistical information about large numbers of people (i.e., base-rate information and regression effects). One inferential bias that has been well studied is called *illusory correlation* – people tend to overestimate the co-occurrence of unusual or distinctive events (called *paired distinctiveness*) and of events which 'ought' to belong together on the basis of past experience (called *associative meaning*). Thus contextually distinctive people (a black person in a white society) and behaviors (e.g., antisocial behavior) are believed to co-occur significantly more than they actually do.

Although people are poor at making inferences they have developed cognitive decision-making shortcuts, called *heuristics* by Tversky and Kahneman (1974), that are adequate for most day-to-day interactive needs. There are three main heuristics that people use: (a) *representativeness* – people are rapidly categorized on the basis of superficial and impressionistic assessment of how well they represent the prototype or an exemplar of the category; (b) *availability* – estimates of the frequency or likelihood of an event are a function of how readily the event comes to mind; and (c) *anchoring* or *adjustment* – inferences are tied to, and disproportionately influenced by, initial standards or earlier inferences.

Causal Attribution of Behavior

Although contemporary social cognition lies at the core of social psychology, it has its critics who identify at least three limitations. First, social cognition has largely ignored the social psychological role of language and communication – people speak to one another. Second, social cognition has tended to overlook affect – people have feelings and emotions. Third, social cognition focuses on intraindividual cognitive processes and structures without properly connecting this level of analysis to human interaction, group processes, and intergroup relations – the issue of reductionism discussed earlier. Recent developments in social cognition have begun to redress these limitations. Nevertheless, the emergence of social cognition in the early

1980s itself addressed limitations in the preceding dominant paradigm, which was attribution theory (see Nisbett & Ross, 1980).

Attribution theory takes its lead from Heider (1958) who believed that in order to function adaptively, people need to have a causal understanding of the social world. People are naive or commonsense psychologists who adopt science-like methods to understand the causes and consequences of social behaviors. In doing this people are concerned to identify stable and enduring properties of people and situations that reliably produce certain behaviors. In particular they distinguish between internal/dispositional causes of behavior and external/situational causes. According to Jones and Davis's (1965) theory of *correspondent inference* people are more likely to attribute behavior internally to characteristics of the person if the behavior was freely chosen, was not socially desirable, had direct and intended impact on us, and the effects of the behavior were unlikely to be produced by other behaviors. Better known is Kelley's (1967) *covariation model* which went so far as to characterize people as naive statisticians employing analysis of variance (ANOVA) to attribute causality. People canvas three sources of information to make a decision about whether to attribute behavior internally to the person or externally to the situation: (a) *consistency* – a person must consistently behave the same way in the same situation for either the person or that situation to be a valid causal candidate; (b) *distinctiveness* – if the person's behavior is distinctive to the situation then the likely cause is the situation, but if she behaves in this way irrespective of situation then an internal attribution is warranted; and (c) *consensus* – if everyone behaves in this way in this situation then the cause is probably the situation, whereas if he is the only person behaving in this way in this situation then an internal attribution is made. Although experimental research shows that people can make attributions in this way, it does not mean that people ordinarily do make attributions in this way in everyday life.

Attribution theory has been extended in a number of ways. Stanley Schachter applied it to the experience of emotions (Schachter, 1964). He suggested that emotions involve an undifferentiated state of physiological arousal and a cognitive label that specifies the particular emotion. Thus, it should be possible to change emotions if people can be induced to attribute the physiological arousal to a different cause (i.e., label it differently) – perhaps this is why a crying (sad) child can sometimes quickly become a laughing (happy) child if a parent makes silly faces. There is some support for this idea, but subsequent research has shown that arousal is somewhat differentiated and distinctive to specific emotions, which reduces the possibility that alternative causal attributions can be made or cognitive labels accepted – the arousal associated with sadness is different to that associated with happiness. Another development of attribution theory, *self-perception theory*, suggests that people may learn about themselves by internally attributing their own behavior – I know I like seafood because I often freely eat seafood in preference to other foods, and not everyone likes seafood. One well-supported finding (the *overjustification effect*) is that if people are induced to perform a task by large rewards or harsh penalties they externally attribute their behavior and experience reduced motivation, whereas the absence of adequate external explanations for the behavior encourages increased motivation through internal attribution. Other applications of attribution theory have explored individual differences in attributional styles (people differ in the extent to which they are inclined to make internal or external attributions for their own or others behaviors) and the role of attributions in close relationships (attributional conflict and internal attribution of negative behavior seem to prevail in dysfunctional relationships).

Biases in Causal Attribution

Accumulating evidence suggests that people do not attribute causality in a rational and scientific manner – there are many biases and errors which challenge the naive-scientist model that frames the attribution approach (Nisbett & Ross, 1980). People tend to make internal attributions for others' behavior even when there are clear situational causes (the *fundamental attribution error*), and yet are quite likely to attribute their own behavior externally. People largely ignore objective consensus information in making attributions, and instead supply their own – there is a *false consensus effect* in which people assume that other people behave like they do. Finally, the entire attribution process is subject to self-serving biases aimed at protecting or enhancing self-esteem and self-image. People attribute their own or in-group members' successes internally and their failures externally, and others' or out-group members' successes externally and their failures internally. They also like to believe in a just world, and sustain this belief by tending to attribute responsibility for people's misfortunes (e.g., sickness, unemployment, poverty, rape) internally – they blame the victim.

Social Explanation

Although people *can* make causal attributions, they probably only do this when prepackaged causal knowledge does not exist, or when unusual events occur or we feel a lack of control. Generally we rely on cultural beliefs, social stereotypes, collective ideologies and social representations that automatically explain what is going on. For example, social representations are interactively elaborated, widely shared, commonsense causal understandings of complex phenomena, such as unemployment, AIDS, global warming. There are also conspiracy theories which blame various social circumstances on the intentional and organized activities of specific social groups (the so-called 'world Jewish conspiracy' is a well-documented example of a conspiracy theory). The sorts of social explanations that people give are also culturally influenced. For example, the fundamental attribution error is more prevalent in Western societies – people in Eastern societies lean more towards external attributions for people's behavior.

17.3 ATTITUDES AND PERSUASION

Attitudes are a core construct in social psychology (Eagly & Chaiken, 1993). Until the mid-1930s it was considered social psychology's most indispensable concept, and many definitions of social psychology actually defined social psychology as the study of attitudes. There are different definitions of attitude, that underpin different measurement techniques. However, most social psychologists probably agree that an attitude is a set of beliefs about an attitude object (e.g., a product, a behavior, a group) together with positive or negative feelings towards the attitude object, and perhaps some intentions to behave in certain ways towards the attitude object. Attitudes are highly functional because they integrate sets of beliefs and provide object appraisal that may help in planning action. Attitudes tend to form only around significant events or objects, and they tend to be relatively enduring structures. Attitudes tend to be more specific in terms of their referent than are values, which are much broader, more general orientations to life, (e.g., the value of freedom).

During the 1920s and 1930s attitude researchers concentrated on how to measure attitudes, and elaborated all sorts of more or less complicated methods. More recently this issue has resurfaced in a slightly different guise – how do you know whether expressed attitudes about controversial attitude objects (e.g., racial or ethnic groups, affirmative action, immigration) are people's true attitudes or merely socially desirable responses? One relatively effective method is the *bogus pipeline technique* – people complete an attitude questionnaire while they are wired up to a machine that they are (falsely) told can detect when they are lying or telling the truth. Another method capitalizes on the fact that people are quicker to decide about negative than positive descriptors in a checklist, when a stimulus they have a negative attitude towards is displayed. There are also language- and communication-based techniques which unobtrusively monitor nonverbal cues to positive and negative affect, or analyze the subtext of people's discourse about attitude objects, or measure how abstract or concrete people are in their discussion of positive or negative attributes of a group (if people dislike a group they will talk abstractly about the group's negative attributes).

Attitudes and Behavior

One might think that attitudes should predict behavior rather well – if someone says he likes running it is not unreasonable to expect frequently to encounter him running. Research, however, clearly indicates that attitudes alone are rather poor predictors of behavior. A classic case in point is a study by LaPiere, published in 1934, in which he traveled across the United States with a Chinese-American couple and was only refused service in one out of 250 establishments, yet a subsequent questionnaire returned by 128 of these establishments indicated that 92% of them would not accept Chinese customers. Research has shown that attitudes are better predictors of behavior if we focus on attitudes which are very specific to the behavior being predicted, and thus relate more to behavioral intentions.

Two related models of attitude behavior relations have been developed (see Ajzen, 1989) – Ajzen and Fishbein's *theory of reasoned action*, and Ajzen's *theory of planned behavior*. A behavior is more likely to occur if (a) the person's attitude towards the behavior is favorable, (b) the person thinks significant other individuals are also favorably inclined towards the behavior, and (c) the person believes it is relatively easy to perform the behavior (opportunity and resources exist). This model allows much better prediction of behavior from attitudes, but the correspondence is still surprisingly low. Another factor which may be important is attitude accessibility – attitudes that are strongly held, are self-relevant, and which relate to

objects with which one has had direct experience tend to be more accessible in memory and thus more influential on behavior. Finally, attitudes that define group membership may be strong predictors of behavior in contexts where people subjectively identify with the group.

Persuasion and Attitude Change

Attitudes are acquired through the socialization process; with parents, peers, social groups and, in recent decades, the mass media, playing an important role. We can acquire our attitudes through direct experience with attitude objects, classical conditioning, instrumental conditioning, observational learning (modeling), or cognitive learning. According to self-perception theory we may even learn our attitudes by internally attributing our overt behavior – 'I'm drinking tea, therefore I must have a positive attitude towards tea'. Once formed, attitudes, like schemas, are relatively enduring constructs that we use to locate ourselves in the social world and to make decisions about behavior. However, attitudes can change – otherwise advertising, propaganda, and even education would be a complete waste of time.

Almost 50 years of research on persuasive communication (since Hovland et al., 1953) has shown that people who are considered expert, trustworthy, credible, popular, or attractive are more effective in changing attitudes. The message itself may be more effective if it does not appear to be a deliberate persuasion attempt (obvious persuasion attempts, particularly when we are forewarned, can produce *reactance* or negative attitude change), if it arouses some fear, or if it is weighted towards evaluation rather than facts. If the audience is hostile or intelligent then it is worthwhile presenting both sides of the argument – otherwise one side is best. People with very low or very high self-esteem may be less susceptible to persuasion, as are people who are distracted (if the message is simple). Early findings that women were more easily persuaded than men are now conclusively attributed to other factors like familiarity with the topic of persuasion. Finally, simple messages are most effective if communicated by video, whereas complex messages are best in writing. As a rule, the persuasive communication should be catered to whether the audience is motivated or able to processes the information systematically via a central processing route, or heuristically via a peripheral processing route (e.g., Eagly & Chaiken, 1993) – for instance, where the message is complex and strong then it would help to allow the audience time and ability to process it systematically, whereas if it is simple but weak it might be better to inhibit systematic processing and encourage superficial heuristic processing.

The process of attitude change has been explored most systematically from a cognitive dissonance perspective. Cognitive dissonance theory (Festinger, 1957), which became perhaps the most studied topic in social psychology in the 1960s (see Abelson et al., 1968), states that inconsistent cognitions produce a state of dissonance – an unpleasant state of psychological tension. People strive to avoid dissonance, but when it arises they must change one or other cognition, seek additional information to bolster one or other cognition, or derogate the source of one of the cognitions. The aim is to re-establish cognitive harmony. Often one cognition is about one's attitude (e.g., towards smoking) and the other about one's behavior (e.g., I have a cigarette in my hand), in which case there is pressure on attitude change to reduce dissonance. The three best-known research paradigms for investigating attitude change through dissonance reduction are *effort justification*, *forced compliance*, and *free choice*. Together, these paradigms reveal that attitudes towards a behavior improve if people feel they have entirely freely chosen to enact the behavior, if they have exerted cognitive or physical effort to engage in the behavior, or if there was initially very little to choose between possible behaviors. In one classic experiment from the 1960s military cadets were invited to try eating grasshoppers by either a friendly and cheerful officer (no dissonance would arise – I did it to please the nice officer) or a cool and official officer (dissonance would arise) – the latter was more effective in inducing the cadets to eat more grasshoppers and to report greater liking for them. Dissonance seems to be a plausible explanation of attitude change when people behave in a markedly counter-attitudinal manner (e.g., eat grasshoppers). When the behavior is only slightly out of line with attitudes (e.g., paying just a little too much for a meal), attitude change is more likely to occur through self-perception – I have paid $50 for this meal when I really only wanted to pay $35, so I must have really enjoyed the meal.

17.4 SOCIAL INFLUENCE

Compliance and Obedience

In many ways, social psychology is the study of social influence – look at the definition of social psychology that opens this chapter. One of the most common forms of social influence involves trying to persuade someone to do something –

the idea here is not to change someone's inner attitudes, but merely to secure behavioral compliance with a simple interpersonal request (e.g., how do you persuade someone to donate money?). Generally, with small requests, people are remarkably, and 'mindlessly', compliant. However, if the request is more significant there are some tactics that can be used. One effective tactic is ingratiation – people are more likely to say 'yes' if you have succeeded in getting them to like you by, for example, praising them (i.e., flattery), drawing attention to interpersonal similarities, or linking yourself to prestigious or attractive others (i.e., basking in reflected glory, or name-dropping). Another tactic involves capitalizing on people's belief that they should reciprocate small favors (the reciprocity principle) – people are more likely to say 'yes' if you have first done something positive for them, even something trivial and uninvited. A third tactic employs two requests, in which the focal request is preceded by a priming request. Sometimes compliance can be increased when the focal request is preceded by a very small request that people are bound to comply with (the *foot-in-the-door* technique), while at other times compliance can be increased when the focal request is preceded by a very large request that people are bound *not* to comply with (the *door-in-the-face* technique). A final tactic, called *low balling*, involves first getting compliance at any price, usually by attaching all sorts of inducements to the request, and then removing the attractive inducements – having said 'yes' one is unlikely subsequently to change one's mind.

Compliance, and other forms of persuasion, are also influenced by the perceived power of the source of influence. Research has identified at least six bases of power: ability to reward compliance; ability to punish non-compliance; possession of specific pieces of information; having general expertise and knowledge; securing respect, liking and identification from others; and being a legitimate authority figure. Authority has been the focus of one of social psychology's most significant and socially meaningful pieces of research – Milgram's (1963) studies of destructive obedience of authority. Milgram discovered that quite normal people taking part in a laboratory experiment were prepared to administer electric shocks (450 V) which they believed would be injurious to another participant, simply because an authoritative experimenter told them that they must do so. By showing that apparently pathological behavior may not be due to individual pathology (the participants were 'normal'), but to particular social circumstances (the situation encouraged extreme obedience), this research places explanatory emphasis for socially unacceptable behaviors on social psychology rather than clinical or abnormal psychology. Subsequent research, exploring factors that influence obedience, suggests that social support is the single strongest moderator of the effect – obedience is strengthened if others are obedient, and massively reduced if others are disobedient. However, emblems of authority (e.g., a uniform) can secure obedience even in domains well outside their sphere of legitimate authority.

Conformity

Social influence also operates through conformity to social norms. Sherif's (1936) classic autokinetic experiments demonstrated that small groups rapidly develop norms that influence group members' judgments, and that these norms continue to influence new members even when the original members are long gone. The participants in these experiments were calling out their judgment of a highly ambiguous stimulus (the movement of a spot of light that 'appeared' to move about). People may have conformed because they were concerned about social evaluation (e.g., being liked or thought badly of) by the others in the group (called *normative social influence*), or because they were using the others' judgments to disambiguate reality (called *informational social influence*). A subsequent series of experiments by Asch (1956) controlled for informational influence – participants called out which of three comparison lines were the same length as a standard line. Although the task was unambiguous, participants were strongly inclined to conform to the unanimously erroneous judgments of five to seven preceding participants (experimental confederates).

Subsequent Asch-type experiments explored the parameters of majority influence. Conformity reaches full strength with three to five apparently independent sources of influence – larger groups are not stronger, and non-independent sources are treated as a single source. Conformity is significantly reduced if the majority is not unanimous – dissenters and deviates of almost any type can produce this effect. In one study conformity was reduced by a deviate who was virtually blind and could not actually see the stimuli. Conformity is also reduced if participants make their judgments privately. However, even when participants judged unambiguous stimuli completely privately in cubicles, they still showed some residual conformity – suggesting that the processes of informational and normative influence do not completely explain conformity. Recent research, based on

social identity theory, has suggested that conformity is the behavioral consequence of defining oneself in terms of a norm that defines membership in a self-inclusive group – in which case the 'ambiguity' of the stimulus is irrelevant, as is the absence or presence of an 'audience' for one's behavior.

Minority Influence

Conformity research mainly focuses on how a majority exerts influence. A valid question is how does a minority have influence, and thus how does social change occur? A program of research, initiated by European social psychologists Serge Moscovici (1976) and Gabriel Mugny (1982), suggests that because people dislike and avoid conflict, minorities must actively create and accentuate conflict to draw attention to themselves. In doing this they need to present a message that is consistent, but not rigidly presented, across time, modality, and members. Minorities are also more effective if they appear to be acting out of principle, and making personal sacrifices for their beliefs. These strategies disrupt majority consensus and raise uncertainty, draw attention to the minority as a group which is committed to its perspective, and convey a coherent alternative viewpoint that challenges the hegemony of majority views. It also helps if the minority can present itself as an in-group for the majority – minorities are typically vilified as outsiders. Effective minorities influence by conversion – the deviant message is superficially and publicly rejected, but is centrally and systematically processed to produce latent private attitude change that emerges behaviorally as apparent conversion to the minority.

17.5 GROUP PROCESSES

In addition to compliance, obedience and conformity, people can find that the way they perform tasks can be influenced by being in a group.

Group Performance

Social facilitation research reveals that people perform well-learned tasks better in the presence of a passive audience or group than alone, but poorly-learned tasks worse. There are competing explanations for this effect – *drive theory* suggests that people are an innate source of drive, a learned source of drive (via evaluation apprehension), or a source of attentional conflict that produces drive – drive then energizes habitual behavior patterns which may be correct (i.e., well-learned tasks) or incorrect (i.e., poorly-learned tasks). Social facilitation may also occur because of distraction and subsequent attentional narrowing that hinders performance of poorly-learned/difficult tasks, but leaves unaffected or improves performance of well-learned/easy tasks. Self-awareness and self-presentation may also play a role – social presence motivates increased effort which is able to improve performance of easy tasks, but is unable to affect difficult tasks that are hindered by anticipated poor performance.

Groups can often perform better than individuals because more hands are involved, the human resource pool is enlarged, or because people may compete, or try to compensate for a perceived lack of motivation, ability, or effort of others. However, research suggests that in many cases group performance is worse than one might expect, because members not only perform their part of the task, but have to contend with distraction and coordination problems. Another problem is *social loafing* – individual motivation can suffer in groups, particularly where the task is relatively meaningless and uninvolving, the group is large and unimportant, and individuals' contribution to the group is personally unidentifiable. Related to this is the *free-rider effect* – people selfishly take advantage of a limited public resource without contributing to its maintenance (e.g., tax evasion).

Structural Features of Groups

Groups vary in cohesion (often measured as how much people like one another), and in the nature and structure of the norms that regulate group behavior. Cohesive groups tend to retain their members and have tighter adherence to group standards – however the critical factor may be the extent to which people psychologically identify with the group and internalize its defining features as a part of their own self-concept. Group norms are relatively enduring, but change in line with changing circumstances to prescribe attitudes, feelings, and behaviors that are appropriate for group members in a particular context. Norms relating to group loyalty and central aspects of group life are usually more specific and have a narrower latitude of acceptable behavior than norms relating to more peripheral features of the group. Norms are also more forgiving of deviation among higher than lower status group members.

Almost all groups are internally structured – notably into roles that prescribe different activities that exist in relation to one another to facilitate overall group functioning. In addition to task specific roles, there are also more general roles that describe members' place in the life of the group, e.g., 'prospective member', 'newcomer', 'oldtimer', 'past member'. Rites of passage mark movement between these generic roles, which are characterized by varying degrees of mutual commitment between member and group. Roles can be very real in their consequences for role occupants. For example, Philip Zimbardo conducted a realistic role-playing study in which students were randomly assigned to be prisoners or guards in a simulated prison (Zimbardo et al., 1982) – the participants were so zealous in their adherence to role prescriptions that the study was prematurely terminated. Roles are rarely equal – some are more prestigious than others. According to *expectation states theory* role assignment in new groups is not only influenced by characteristics that relate directly to the group task (specific status characteristics, e.g., being well-organized), but also by characteristics that are more widely socially valued (diffuse status characteristics, e.g., being a doctor). Roles also define functions within a group that need to communicate with one another. Research on communication networks focuses on centralization as the critical factor. More-centralized networks have a hub person or group that regulates communication flow, whereas less-centralized networks allow free communication among all roles. Centralized networks work well for simple tasks (they liberate peripheral members to perform their role), but not for complex tasks (the hub becomes overwhelmed, delays and mis-communications occur, frustration and stress increase, peripheral members feel loss of autonomy).

Leadership

The most basic role differentiation within groups is into leaders and followers. Despite a long research tradition that attributes leadership to innate or acquired leadership personality attributes (the great person approach to leadership), there are almost no traits that are reliably associated with effective leadership in all situations. Situational perspectives that view leadership purely as a function of situational demands do better. One variant of this (*leader categorization theory*) is that we have leadership schemas for different activities and categorize people as leaders on the basis of their fit to the task-activated schema. Another variant (an application of *self-categorization theory*) is that when people identify strongly with a group they 'appoint' as leader the person who best fits their representation of a typical/ideal group member.

Interactionist perspectives view effective leaders as those whose general leadership style (the distinction is between a socio-emotional/relationship-oriented style and a task-oriented style) is best suited to situational/task demands. Fiedler's *contingency theory* states that task-oriented leaders are most effective when the situation is highly controlled and the task very well organized, and also at the other extreme of situational and task disorganization – otherwise socio-emotional leaders do best. Other approaches focus on the dynamic transactional relationship between leaders and followers. People who are disproportionately responsible for helping a group achieve its goals are rewarded by the group with the trappings of leadership in order to restore equity. Hollander suggests that part of the reward is being able to be relatively idiosyncratic and thus to be innovative – people who are highly conformist and attain leadership in a democratic manner tend to accumulate significant *idiosyncrasy credits* that they can expend once they achieve leadership. Leaders who have a high idiosyncrasy credit rating may be able to exercise what organizational psychologists call *transformational leadership* – they are able to induce significant group change because they are imbued with charisma by the group.

Group Discussion and Decision Making

A major function of groups is, through discussion, to reach a collective decision from an initial diversity of views. Research on *social decision schemes* identifies a number of implicit or explicit decision-making rules that groups can adopt to transform diversity into a group decision: (a) unanimity – discussion pressures deviants to conform; (b) majority wins – discussion confirms the majority position which becomes the group decision; (c) truth wins – discussion reveals the position that is demonstrably correct; (d) two-thirds majority – discussion establishs a two-thirds majority, that becomes the group decision; (e) first shift – the group adopts a position consistent with the direction of the first shift in opinion. On intellective tasks (there is a demonstrably correct solution, e.g., matters of fact), groups adopt truth wins. On judgmental tasks (there is no demonstrably correct solution, e.g., matters of taste), groups adopt majority wins.

The process of group discussion involves the recall of information. Because the process is subject to the process and motivation losses discussed earlier (e.g., distraction, uneven power, social loafing), group remembering is often a constructive task in which the group forges its own idiosyncratic version of the truth (a *social representation*) – a version which is internalized and carried away by group members. Some researchers suggest that there are two components to group memory – not only do members have to remember their own specialized role prescriptions (i.e., what they have to do), but they also need to know where in the group other memories are stored (i.e., where to go to access other information or expertise). This latter form of memory is called *transactive memory* – it is a shared system for encoding, storing, and retrieving information. Research suggests that because transactive memory emerges from interindividual interaction, and is essential for group functioning, groups function better if members learn together rather than individually.

One popular method to harness the potential of groups is *brainstorming* – the uninhibited generation of as many ideas as possible, regardless of quality, in an interactive group. Although it is commonly thought that brainstorming enhances individual creativity, research convincingly shows that this is not the case – people may loaf, they are distracted, and the generation of ideas is blocked by others' ideas. In fact it is more effective for people to generate ideas on their own and then pool them, rather than generate ideas interactively – electronic brainstorming may help, as may having a very heterogenous group.

Popular opinion and conformity research suggest that groups are conservative and cautious entities which exclude extremes in a ponderous process of averaging. Two phenomena that challenge this view are *groupthink* and *group polarization*. Janis (1972) has argued that highly cohesive groups that are ideologically homogenous, under stress, insulated from external influence, and lack impartial leadership and norms for proper decision-making procedures, adopt a mode of thinking (groupthink) in which the desire for unanimity overrides the motivation to adopt proper rational decision-making procedures. Such groups feel invulnerable, unanimous, and absolutely correct. They also discredit contradictory information, pressurize deviants, and stereotype outgroups. The consequence is poor decision-making procedures that produce suboptimal decisions that can have widespread disastrous consequences – particularly if the decision-making group is a government body. A related pitfall of group decision making is group polarization, which is defined as a tendency for groups to make decisions that are more extreme than the average of pre-discussion opinions in the group, in the direction initially favored by the average – group polarization extremitizes group decisions (and can sometimes shift members' enduring attitudes towards the polarized group position). Polarization does not require group interaction or discussion – it can happen on merely being exposed to a distribution of in-group positions. Polarization is particularly likely to occur when an important self-defining in-group confronts a salient out-group that holds an opposing point of view.

17.6 INTERGROUP BEHAVIOR

The study of intergroup behavior (behavior regulated by people's awareness of and identification with different social groups) is entwined with the study of prejudice and discrimination. To explain discrimination and intergroup aggression, Dollard et al. (1939) adopted a psychodynamic model to explain how individual frustrations (e.g., economic failure) produce among group members a need to aggress, which, because the cause of the frustration is usually intangible (e.g., the economy) or too powerful (e.g., a military government), is vented on a weaker and available scapegoat (e.g., immigrants). Later variants of this *frustration–aggression hypothesis* removed the psychodynamic process, and focused on frustration in the form of people's sense of *relative deprivation*. This research suggests that relative deprivation is most acute when one's expectations have been rising and there is a sudden fall in one's attainments, and that this is associated with social unrest and intergroup violence (sometimes called *revolutions of rising expectations*). People can also feel relatively deprived by comparing their attainments with those of others. Research suggests that interpersonal comparisons produce a sense of *egoistic relative deprivation* associated with individual stress and depression, whereas intergroup comparisons, between one's own reference group and relevant other groups, produce *fraternalistic relative deprivation* associated with collective behaviors and intergroup conflict.

Another psychodynamic approach to prejudice is Adorno et al.'s (1950) *authoritarian personality* theory. They argued that harsh family rearing strategies produce a love–hate conflict in children's feelings towards their parents. The conflict is resolved by idolizing parents and all power figures, despising weaker others, and striving for a rigidly unchanging and hierarchical world order. People with this authoritarian personality syndrome are predisposed to be prejudiced. Research suggests that although this syndrome does exist, its genesis in family dynamics is unconfirmed, and its relationship to prejudice is weak. By far the best predictor of

prejudice is the existence of a culture of prejudice that is legitimized by societal norms. This finding also challenges the contribution of other, non-psychodynamic, personality explanations of prejudice – for example *dogmatism*, and *closed-mindedness*.

Sherif (1966) provides an alternative perspective on intergroup behavior, based upon a series of naturalistic field experiments on conflict and cooperation at boys' camps in the United States in the early 1950s. Sherif argued that mutually exclusive goals engender competitive behavior that, at the individual level, fragments groups, and at the group level produces intergroup conflict and stereotyping. Superordinate goals requiring interdependence for their achievement produce cooperative behavior that, at the individual level, forms groups, and at the group level improves intergroup relations. The real nature of goal relations determines intergroup behavior – hence the theory is often called *realistic conflict theory*.

Other research into cooperation and competition has had people play dyadic laboratory 'games' (e.g., the prisoners dilemma, the trucking game) that are constructed to manipulate causes and consequences of cooperation or competition. This research repeatedly shows that people are so distrustful of one another that they willing adopt mutually harmful competitive strategies even when a mutually beneficial strategy is clearly available. When a number of people or groups are confronted by the dilemma of whether to cooperate or compete a *commons dilemma* can exist – if everyone cooperates a common resource (e.g., the natural environment) is preserved for all to enjoy, but if everyone competes the resource is quickly destroyed in a frenzied rush for self-gain. Research shows that self-interest almost always wins out, unless those accessing the resource derive their social identity from the entire group which has access to the resource, or there is a leader who can manage the resource. Resource destruction can also be moderated by any means that limit the number of people accessing the resource or increase the relative attractiveness of cooperation over competition. As in other areas of social psychology most cooperation/competition and dilemmas research has been conducted in Western cultures. People in non-Western societies tend to rest their decision to cooperate or compete more carefully on their relationship to their partner/opponent.

Although goal relations influence intergroup behavior, *minimal group* studies, first published by Henri Tajfel in 1970, show that competitive intergroup behavior can be an intrinsic feature of merely being categorized as a group member.

This research spawned the *social identity perspective* on group processes and intergroup relations. When category memberships are contextually salient, people categorize themselves and others in terms of contrasting in-group and out-group defining prototypes that prescribe category-appropriate perceptions, attitudes, feelings, and behaviors. This process of prototypical 'depersonalization' of self produces a sense of group identification and belonging, as well as in-group solidarity, conformity, normative behavior, ethnocentrism, in-group bias, intergroup discrimination, and perceptions of intragroup stereotypic similarity. Because groups define and evaluate who we are, intergroup relations are a continual struggle for evaluative superiority of one group over others. How the struggle is conducted, and thus the specific nature of intergroup behavior (acquiescent, competitive, conflictual, destructively aggressive), depends on people's beliefs about the stability, legitimacy, and permeability of status relations between groups.

Collective and Crowd Behavior

Social psychologists have tended to view collective behavior as irrational, aggressive, antisocial, and primitive. The general model is that people in interactive groups such as crowds are anonymous and distracted, which causes them to lose their sense of individuality and to become *deindividuated*. Deindividuation prevents people from adhering to the prosocial norms of society that usually govern our behavior, because the critical factor of identifiability which is necessary for conformity to norms is no longer present. People regress to a primitive, selfish, and uncivilized behavioral level. Research (see Zimbardo, 1970) typically manipulates anonymity (people in dark rooms, or wearing hoods and robes) to discover that deindividuation does increase aggression and antisocial behavior. The anonymity of the city has also been invoked to explain the aggression, selfishness, and rudeness that is often associated with city living.

Another perspective on the crowd is Berkowitz's *long hot summer* analysis of urban race riots in the United States during the 1960s (Berkowitz, 1972). Against a background of relative deprivation, excessive heat (an environmental stressor) amplified existing frustration and produced individual acts of aggression which were exacerbated by aggressive cues (armed police). Aggression became the dominant response which was socially facilitated by the presence of other people in the street and thus became widespread and extreme – a riot.

A rather different sort of explanation is provided by *emergent norm theory*. The essence of collective/group behavior is adherence to norms. The problem of the crowd is that it is normless, because it comprises an ad hoc collection of people who have no tradition of being together. So, where do the norms come from? One possibility is that distinctive behaviors (antisocial behavior would be distinctive due to its rarity in everyday life) attract attention and are assumed to be the appropriate norm. This raises an additional problem – for people to conform to this norm they should be identifiable, and yet most crowd research rests on the assumption that people are anonymous in the crowd. In reality, however, most crowds are not normless – they often comprise people with a shared identity and shared purpose, and thus shared norms that provide the parameters for situation-specific norms to emerge. Social identity would be particularly salient in such a crowd and so self-categorization and depersonalization may explain the generation of normative crowd behavior.

Prejudice and Conflict Reduction

Prejudice and conflict are significant social ills that produce enormous human suffering – ranging from damaged self-esteem, reduced opportunities, stigma and socio-economic disadvantage, all the way to intergroup violence, war, and genocide. Prejudices can be muted by public service propaganda and education, mainly because this conveys societal disapproval of the expression of prejudice and may allay some of the ignorance and fears that fuel prejudice. These strategies are not very effective if isolated from wider social reforms that address health, educational, occupational, and economic disadvantage.

Many people believe that prejudice can be more significantly reduced by intergroup contact – indeed the *contact hypothesis* (G. W. Allport, 1954) suggested that prolonged, cooperative, purposeful equal status contact, occurring within a framework of official institutional support for integration, should reduce prejudice and improve intergroup relations. This idea fueled the desegregation of the American education system. Almost 50 years of research on the contact hypothesis is less optimistic. Contact is very likely to consolidate or even amplify prejudices – it can confirm that the out-group is more different and less likable than anticipated (particularly if contact proponents promulgate a sanitized image of the out-group that conceals real differences), it can make people feel anxious enough to avoid further contact (*intergroup anxiety*), it can remind one that there is often a real conflict of interest between groups. A significant problem with contact is that pleasant contact with a specific out-group member rarely generalizes to the group as a whole – the contact is essentially interpersonal. However, true intergroup contact is, by definition, unlikely to be pleasant and thus change perceptions.

Another strategy to reduce prejudice is to encourage the development of a common identity based upon re-categorization, superordinate goals, or a common threat. If the in-group–out-group distinction disappears, then so does the prejudice – this is the 'melting pot' practice of assimilation or cultural monism. Although initially compelling, there are some pitfalls of this approach – superordinate goals do not reduce conflict if the groups fail to achieve the goal, and groups which furnish well-defined different identities can feel that assimilation is a threat to their distinctiveness. One way around the latter problem may be multiculturalism or cultural pluralism in which group differences are recognized and nurtured within a common superordinate identity that stresses cooperative interdependence and diversity.

One obvious way to reduce conflict between groups is for the groups or their representatives to resolve specific intergroup disagreements through discussion. Representatives can *bargain* directly with one another, but this often accentuates intergroup orientations and hinders conflict resolution – in which case a credible, respected, and impartial *mediator* can be brought in to reduce emotional heat and misperceptions and explore novel compromises and face-saving strategies. The least satisfactory resort is *arbitration*, where a powerful third party imposes a resolution. Where intergroup relations are so poor as to preclude direct interaction groups become trapped in an escalating cycle of threats and retaliation, which can only be stopped if each group advertises and makes a small concession, and then invites the other group to reciprocate. This may work because it establishes trust and engages the norm of reciprocity.

17.7 Aggression and Helping Behavior

Aggression

Theories of human aggression tend to emphasize its innate or instinctive aspects on the grounds that aggression has survival value. More popular with social psychologists are approaches that either emphasize the drive aspect of aggression, or how aggression can be learned. As we saw earlier, the *frustration–aggression hypothesis* views aggression as an automatic consequence of frustration. A more complex process is described by Zillmann's *excitation–transfer* model – arousal produced in one situation (e.g., exercise) can spill over into another context which is interpreted as requiring an aggressive response, and thus be available to drive that aggression. The most popular learning approach is Albert Bandura's *social learning theory* (Bandura, 1977) – through socialization people learn aggressive behavior directly (i.e., by being reinforced for aggressive behavior) or vicariously (i.e., by witnessing relevant others being reinforced or not censured for aggressive behavior).

Research on personality and aggression has found that people with a *Type A personality* tend, in competitive contexts, to be more aggressive than other people. Sex differences in aggression have also been a focus of study. Although there is little difference between males and females in verbal aggression, males are generally more physically aggressive than females. This is mainly attributed to sex role socialization, although there is evidence that the male hormone, testosterone, does produce more dominant behavior that can, when social norms encourage it, lead to aggressive behavior. Frustration, however caused (e.g., blocked goals, disadvantage, relative deprivation, uncomfortable climate, crowding), can also produce aggression, sometimes against targets that are entirely unrelated to the original cause of frustration. Direct provocation is another source of aggression – because it engages the reciprocity principle, even a small act of aggression can produce strong retaliation, and subsequent escalation. Disinhibition, through alcohol consumption or loss of personal identifiabilty (i.e., deindividuation), can cause people to behave in ways that are usually constrained by societal norms – for example, frustrations or aggressive attitudes that are normally kept in check may be expressed as aggression. However, much collective aggression may be better explained in terms of identification with a group that has norms that actually prescribe certain forms of aggression. Aggression can become institutionalized through official or unofficial sanctions – for example, terrorism, war, gang violence, prison culture. Generally speaking, cultural, subcultural, and group norms are powerful influences on what are considered acceptable levels or forms of expression of aggression (compare Hare Krishna with Skin Heads).

Probably the most effective moderator of aggression is the existence of cultural norms, practices, and legislation that proscribe aggressive behavior, remove societal frustrations based on social disadvantage and discrimination, and encourage non-aggressive outlets for individual frustrations.

Helping Behavior

Human aggression is balanced by a drive for people to help one another – helping is one type of prosocial behavior, which may or may not involve altruism (benefitting others at some cost to oneself). Although aggression can perhaps be reduced by facilitating helping behavior, research on helping behavior suggests that there are many factors that prevent people from helping. General theories of helping are very similar to theories of aggression – some emphasize the evolutionary advantage of helping others, while the most popular theories for social psychologists are ones that emphasize social learning through direct reinforcement, vicarious learning, and formal education.

The decision to help someone can be based on assessment of whether someone deserves help and whether the help will be effective. In order to preserve the perception of a just world, people tend to blame victims for their plight, and thus do not feel that help is deserved. This effect can be minimized by making people more aware of others' suffering, and showing how a surprisingly uncostly helpful act can effectively reduce that suffering. More effective than awareness is empathy – perceived similarity is particularly effective in making people experience others' suffering as their own, and thus provide help in order to reduce their own empathic suffering. Self-attribution processes may also play a role – internal attribution of a helpful act that one has performed helps construct a helpful personality for oneself that facilitates helping in other situations. External pressures to help others hinder this process. Helping is also increased by the existence of prosocial societal or group norms – these can be general norms of reciprocity (help those who help you) or social responsibility (help those in need), or more specific helping norms tied to the nature of a social group.

The bulk of helping research focuses on immediate situational factors that determine whether bystanders help someone who is in need of help – *bystander intervention*. This approach was given impetus by the widely reported murder of Kitty Genovese in New York in 1964 – although 38 people admitted witnessing the murder, not a single person ran to her aid. To explain bystander intervention/apathy, Darley and Latané (1968) proposed a cognitive decision-making model of helping. Bystanders (a) need to notice an event, (b) need to be able to define that event as an emergency that calls for help, (c) need to assume personal responsibility to help, and (d) need to decide what can be done. Piliavin and associates (1981) propose a *bystander calculus model* that assigns a role to arousal – emergencies make us aroused, situational factors determine how that arousal is labeled and thus what emotion is felt, and then people assess the costs and benefits of helping or not helping before deciding what to do. The presence of multiple bystanders reduces personal responsibility and is the strongest inhibitor of bystander intervention – due to diffusion of personal responsibility, fear of social blunders, and social reinforcement for inaction. In addition, the costs of not helping are reduced by the presence of other potential helpers. People tend to help more if they are alone or among friends, if situational norms or others' behavior prescribe helping, if they feel they have the skills to offer effective help, or if the personal costs of not helping are high. Other factors which increase helping include being in good mood, and assuming or recognizing that one has a leadership role in the situation. Relative to situational variables, personality and gender are poor predictors of helping

17.8 Interpersonal Processes and Close Relationships

Human beings have a strong need to affiliate with other people, through belonging to groups and developing close interpersonal relationships. The consequences of social deprivation are severely maladaptive (ranging from loneliness through psychosis), and social isolation is a potent punishment which can take many forms (e.g., solitary confinement, shunning, ostracism, the silent treatment). Research on *social comparison* processes shows that almost all knowledge we have about our ourselves, our skills, abilities, perceptions, and attitudes, comes from being able to make comparisons between ourselves and other people.

Generally, people seek out and preserve the company of people they feel they like. We tend to like others who we consider physically attractive, and who are nearby, familiar, available, and with whom we expect continued interaction. We also like people who genuinely like us (the reciprocity principle may explain this), particularly if we have relatively low self-esteem, and they grow to like us over time (the *gain–loss hypothesis*) – people who shift from less to more liking for us reduce rejection anxiety and may be perceived as being discerning. One of the most important determinants of liking is attitude or value similarity – we tend to like people who have similar attitudes and values to our own. But in contrast to this, we can also be attracted to people who satisfy our needs through having complementary qualities to our own. Research suggests that similarity is important in the early stages of a relationship, and need complementary in later stages.

A popular approach to the study of interpersonal relationships is framed by *social exchange theory* (Thibaut & Kelley, 1959). Relationships are effectively trading interactions where the partners trade goods (e.g., objects), information (e.g., advice), love (e.g., affection, warmth), money (e.g., things of value), services (e.g., activities of the body), and status (e.g., evaluative judgments). A relationship continues to the extent that both partners feel that the benefits of remaining in the relationship outweigh the costs of the relationship and the benefits of other relationships – relationships are based on complex cost-benefit analyses. Relationships are also influenced by equity considerations – people only remain in relationships if they feel that *distributive justice* exists (i.e., both partners' outcomes are proportional to their inputs – particularly that the other person is not free-riding).

Close relationships often involve love, which is difficult to study at all let alone under controlled conditions. Research distinguishes between companionate love (caring and affection arising from spending time together) and passionate/romantic love (intense absorption involving physiological arousal). The latter, romantic love, is considered to be a function of (a) the existence of a cultural concept of love, (b) physiological arousal, and (c) a culturally appropriate love object. All three conditions must exist for love to exist. Sternberg has proposed a taxonomy of love based on three dimensions: passion, commitment, and intimacy (Sternberg, 1988). Passion alone is infatuation, commitment alone is 'empty love', intimacy alone is liking, passion and commitment is fatuous love, passion and intimacy is romantic love, commitment and intimacy is companionate love, and all three together is consummate love.

The study of the development and disintegration of close relationships has tended to focus on marital satisfaction in Western-style marriages. A notable feature of distressed marriages is that partners blame each other for negative outcomes but do not dispositionally attribute positive outcomes. The warning signs of relationship dissolution are that a new life seems to be the only solution, alternative partners are available, relationship failure is expected, and there is lack of commitment to relationship continuance. Partners can respond passively by expressing relationship loyalty (waiting for things to improve) or neglect (allowing deterioration to continue), or actively by voice behavior (working at relationship improvement) or exit behavior (ending the relationship).

17.9 COMMUNICATION AND LANGUAGE

Communication and especially language are the underplayed dimensions of much conventional social psychology. Nevertheless both are obviously social psychological phenomena. The social psychology of language has tended to focus on how things are said (speech style) rather than what is said (speech content). Spoken language contains social markers that tell us something about who is speaking to whom in what context. For example, slow, precise speech suggests that we are talking to a young child, an elderly person, or a foreigner. Powerless speech (i.e., rising intonation, intensifiers, hedges, tag questions) suggests we are in the presence of a higher status person. Social markers also tell us about group memberships such as social class, ethnicity, sex, and age. Research using the *matched guise technique* (people evaluate speech extracts that are constructed to be identical in all respects except speech style, e.g., accent, dialect, language) shows that, on the basis of speech style alone we can categorize people in terms of their group membership and evaluate them accordingly. Although accommodation of speech style to communicative contexts can be largely automatic, the evaluative implications of speech style mean that we can sometimes deliberately adopt a more prestigious speech style (e.g., speaking formally in an interview).

Speech accommodation theory states that in interpersonal interactions we tend to accommodate to each other's speech styles (bilateral convergence) to improve communication and increase attraction via reciprocity and increased similarity. However, when intergroup relations are salient people with the higher prestige speech style accentuate usage of that speech style – divergence. People with the low-prestige style show upward convergence on the high-prestige variety, unless they believe that their low status position is unstable and illegitimate in which case they accentuate their own speech style – divergence. Speech accommodation in intergroup contexts reflects wider intergroup dynamics that have been extensively studied in multi-ethnic contexts containing ethnic groups for whom language is a cultural anchor point (e.g., Australia, Québec) – *ethnolinguistic identity theory*. Members of ethnolinguistic minority groups who feel that their group has low status, poor demography and little support (low *subjective ethnolinguistic vitality*), and that this is a stable and possibly legitimate state of affairs, try to pass linguistically into the dominant group by learning to be fluent speakers of the dominant group's language (the motivation to be fluent is strong, because fluency is a passport to higher status). Consequently the minority group can gradually lose its language and culture, while, because it is difficult to pass successfully, individuals are left in ethnolinguistic limbo. Where subjective ethnolinguistic vitality is high, and the legitimacy of the status quo is challenged, minority individuals promote their language and culture, and only need a working knowledge of the dominant group's language (the motivation to be fluent is weak, because fluency conflicts with pride in one's existing ethnolinguistic identity) – there is an ethnolinguistic revival.

Non-Verbal Communication

People communicate not only through what they say and how they say it, but also through postures, gestures, facial expressions, touch, and even how close they stand to one another. Verbal and non-verbal messages do not have to be consistent – sometimes they clash, and it can be difficult to know which message is 'true'. Generally, people are good at managing the verbal content of a message, but not the non-verbal channels – lies may be detected through non-verbal cues. Indeed one way to discover underlying attitudes on socially sensitive issues is to analyze non-verbal cues. Non-verbal channels tend to specialize in communicating feelings and status, and in regulating conversational turn taking. Although non-verbal communication often operates automatically without us paying conscious attention, some of us are better than others at systematically reading and strategically using non-verbal cues.

The eyes are highly informative. If someone persistently gazes at you it could mean they like you, they are trying to persuade you or ingratiate themselves, they are a higher status person trying to exert control, or they are a speaker signaling its now your turn to talk. Facial expressions are powerful communicators of universally recognizable emotions, however there are culture-specific rules that encourage or discourage the expression of emotion or specific emotions in different contexts – called *display rules*. Research indicates that although facial expression of emotion is expressive, it is also communicative – people express emotions when other people are around. The entire body can be used to illustrate spoken language (postures) or replace spoken language (gestures). For example

a relaxed, forward-leaning, face-to-face posture communicates liking, and in India a sideways tilt of the head with a simultaneous slight upswing of the head (a gesture that is distinct from the half-head shake as part of the full-head shake used for denial in most societies) means 'yes'. Touch can be used to communicate, among other things, positive affect, playfulness, or control, depending on who touches who on what part of the body, for how long, and in what context. Research indicates that higher status people touch lower status people more than vice versa, and that there are marked cross-cultural differences in the amount and pattern of touching (e.g., Italians touch more than Germans, and there is a taboo in Buddhist countries against touching the head). Finally, interpersonal distance is a potent cue to liking (people who like one another stand closer together) and to the formality of the interactive context (the greater the distance the more formal the interaction). But again, there is marked situational and cultural variation. *Intimacy equilibrium theory* suggests that if interpersonal distance is inappropriately intimate people reduce intimacy in other modalities (reduced gaze, deflected posture) – typical elevator behavior.

Conversation and Discourse

Verbal and non-verbal communication occur in face-to-face interaction. In this context, non-verbal behavior is important for regulating the flow of conversation. This can involve *attempt-suppressing* signals such as a raised hand to indicate one has not yet finished, or *back-channel communication* such as nodding to indicate that one is still listening and not intending to interrupt. Depending on context, interruptions can signify rudeness, power and influence, or involvement, interest and support. Analysis of the entire conversational event, the discourse, can reveal a subtext of meanings that tell a great deal about the context and the interactants – for example analysis of discourse can reveal bigotry that would otherwise be difficult to detect.

17.10 APPLICATIONS OF SOCIAL PSYCHOLOGY

Social psychology and social psychologists move easily between basic research, applied research, and action research. This versatility was advocated at the outset by Kurt Lewin, and has been continued by key researchers and their associates, and the discipline as a whole. It is a strength of social psychology. It is beyond the scope of this chapter to more than give a flavor of some significant areas of application. Impression formation and social inference research has been applied in the context of eyewitness testimony. Small-group decision-making research has focused on jury decision making and the legal system. Cohesion research has been applied in sports and military contexts. Aggression research has been pursued in the contexts of media violence, pornography, alcohol, soccer hooliganism, rape, and domestic violence. Attitude research has been significantly and enduringly applied in a range of areas to do with attitude measurement (survey construction), attitude change, and attitude–behavior correspondence – for example commercial and public service advertising, safe driving, safe sex, dietary and exercise behavior, tobacco smoking, and sun-related behaviors. A range of social psychological constructs, including communication and helping behavior research, have been applied to built environment design. Attribution theory has been applied in clinical settings, and other social psychological constructs have been applied to the understanding of stress and coping, and family interactions. Research on intergroup relations and prejudice has been applied in negotiation and bargaining contexts as well as race, ethnicity, and gender relations. One of the most significant applications of social psychology, particularly of group processes and intergroup relations, is to organizations – there is a relatively close link between organizational and social psychology.

RESOURCE REFERENCES

Brown, R. (1986). *Social psychology* (2nd edn). New York: Free Press.

Gilbert, D. T., Fiske, S. T., & Lindzey, G. (Eds.). (1998). *Handbook of social psychology* (4th edn.). New York: McGraw-Hill.

Hewstone, M. R. C., & Brewer, M. B. (Series Eds.). (2000). *Blackwell handbook of social psychology* (4 vols). Oxford, UK: Blackwell.

Hewstone, M. R. C., Stroebe, W., & Stephenson, G. M. (Eds.). (1996). *Introduction to social psychology* (2nd ed.). Oxford, UK: Blackwell.

Higgins, E. T., & Kruglanski, A. W. (Eds.). (1996). *Social psychology: Handbook of basic principles.* New York: Guilford.

Hogg, M. A., & Cooper, J. (Eds.). (2001). *Handbook of social psychology.* London: Sage.

Hogg, M. A., & Vaughan, G. M. (1998). *Social psychology* (2nd edn.). London: Prentice-Hall.

Kruglanski, A. W. (Series Ed.). (2000). *Key readings in social psychology* (many volumes). Philadelphia: Psychology Press.

Manstead, A. S. R., Hewstone, M. R. C., Fiske, S. T., Hogg, M. A., Reis, H. T., & Semin, G. R. (Eds.).
(1995). *The Blackwell encyclopedia of social psychology.* Oxford, UK: Blackwell.

Mugny, G., Oberlé, D., & Beauvois, J.-L. (Eds.). (1995), *La psychologie sociale.* Grenoble, France: Presses Universitaires de Grenoble.

Tesser, A. (Ed.). (1995). *Advanced social psychology.* New York: McGraw-Hill.

Key Journals

Journal of Personality and Social Psychology. Personality and Social Psychology Bulletin.

ADDITIONAL LITERATURE CITED

Abelson, R. P., Aronson, E., McGuire, W. J., Newcomb, T. M., Rosenberg, M. J., & Tannenbaum, P. H. (Eds.). (1968). *Theories of cognitive consistency: A sourcebook.* Chicago: Rand McNally.

Adorno, T. W., Frenkel-Brunswik, E., Levinson, D. J., & Sanford, R. M. (1950). *The authoritarian personality.* New York: Harper.

Ajzen, I. (1989). Attitude structure and behavior. In A. R. Pratkanis, S. J. Breckler, & A. G. Greenwald (Eds.), *Attitude structure and function* (pp. 241–274). Hillsdale, NJ: Erlbaum.

Allport, F. H. (1924). *Social psychology.* Boston, MA: Houghton-Mifflin.

Allport, G. W. (1954). *The nature of prejudice.* Reading, MA: Addison-Wesley.

Asch, S. E. (1956). Studies of independence and conformity: A minority of one against a unanimous majority. *Psychological Monographs: General and Applied, 70,* 1–70 (whole no. 416).

Bandura, A. (1977). *Social learning theory.* Englewood Cliffs, NJ: Prentice Hall.

Berkowitz, L. (1972). Frustrations, comparisons, and other sources of emotion arousal as contributors to social unrest. *Journal of Social Issues, 28,* 77–91.

Darley, J. M., & Latané, B. (1968). Bystander intervention in emergencies: Diffusion of responsibility. *Journal of Personality and Social Psychology, 8,* 377–383.

Dollard, J., Doob, L. W., Miller, N. E., Mowrer, O. H., & Sears, R. R. (1939). *Frustration and aggression.* New Haven, CT: Yale University Press.

Eagly, A. H., & Chaiken, S. (1993). *The psychology of attitudes.* San Diego, CA: Harcourt Brace Jovanovich.

Festinger, L. (1957). *A theory of cognitive dissonance.* Stanford, CA: Stanford University Press.

Fiske, S. T., & Taylor, S. E. (1991). *Social cognition* (2nd edn.). New York: McGraw-Hill.

Heider, F. (1958). *The psychology of interpersonal relations.* New York: Wiley.

Hovland, C. I., Janis, I. L., & Kelley, H. H. (1953). *Communication and persuasion.* New Haven, CT: Yale University Press.

Janis, I. L. (1972). *Victims of groupthink: A psychological study of foreign policy decisions and fiascoes.* Boston, MA: Houghton-Mifflin.

Jones, E. E., & Davis, K. E. (1965). From acts to dispositions: The attribution process in person perception. In L. Berkowitz (Ed.), *Advances in experimental social psychology* (vol. 2, pp. 219–266). New York: Academic Press.

Kelley, H. H. (1967). Attribution theory in social psychology. In D. Levine (Ed.), *Nebraska symposium on motivation* (pp. 192–238). Lincoln, NE: University of Nebraska Press.

Kelley, H. H., & Thibaut, J. (1978). *Interpersonal relations: A theory of interdependence.* New York: Wiley.

LaPiere, R. T. (1934). Attitudes vs actions. *Social Forces, 13,* 230–237.

Lewin, K. (1951). *Field theory in social science.* New York: Harper.

Milgram, S. (1963). Behavioral study of obedience. *Journal of Abnormal and Social Psychology, 67,* 371–378.

Moscovici, S. (1976). *Social influence and social change.* London: Academic Press.

Mugny, G. (1982). *The power of minorities.* London: Academic Press.

Nisbett, R. E., & Ross, L. (1980). *Human inference: Strategies and shortcomings of social judgment.* Englewood Cliffs, NJ: Prentice-Hall.

Piliavin, J. A., Dovidio, J. F., Gaertner, S. L., & Clark, R. D. III (1981). *Emergency intervention.* New York: Academic Press.

Schachter, S. (1964). The interaction of cognitive and physiological determinants of emotional state. In L. Berkowitz (Ed.), *Advances in experimental social psychology* (vol. 1, pp. 49–80). New York: Academic Press.

Sherif, M. (1936). *The psychology of social norms.* New York: Harper.

Sherif, M. (1966). *In common predicament: Social psychology of intergroup conflict and cooperation.* Boston, MA: Houghton-Mifflin.

Smith, P. B., & Bond, M. H. (1998). *Social psychology across cultures: Analysis and perspectives* (2nd edn.). London: Prentice-Hall.

Sternberg, R. J. (1988). *The triangle of love.* New York: Basic Books.

Stoner, J. A. F. (1961). A comparison of individual and group decisions including risk. Masters thesis, Massachusetts Institute of Technology.

Tajfel, H. (1970). Experiments in intergroup discrimination. *Scientific American, 223,* 96–102.

Tajfel, H. (Ed.). (1984). *The social dimension: European developments in social psychology.* Cambridge, UK: Cambridge University Press.

Thibaut, J. W., & Kelley, H. H. (1959). *The social psychology of groups.* New York: Wiley.

Triplett, N. (1898). The dynamogenic factors in pacemaking and competition. *American Journal of Psychology, 9,* 507–533.

Tversky, A., & Kahneman, D. (1974). Judgment under uncertainty: Heuristics and biases. *Science, 185,* 1124–1131.

Zillman, D. *Hostility and aggression.* Hillsdale, NJ: Erlbaum.

Zimbardo, P. G. (1970). The human choice: Individuation, reason, and order versus deindividuation, impulse, and chaos. In W. J. Arnold & D. Levine (Eds.), *Nebraska symposium on motivation 1969* (vol. 17, pp. 237–307). Lincoln, NE: University of Nebraska Press.

Zimbardo, P. G., Haney, C., Banks, W. C., & Jaffe, D. (1982). The psychology of imprisonment. In J. C. Brigham & L. Wrightsman (Eds.), *Contemporary issues in social psychology* (4th edn., pp. 230–235). Monterey, CA: Brooks/Cole.

Communications concerning this chapter should be addressed to: Professor Michael A. Hogg, School of Psychology, University of Queensland, Brisbane, QLD 4072, Australia

18

(Cross) Cultural Psychology

CIGDEM KAGITCIBASI

18.1 WHAT IS CROSS-CULTURAL PSYCHOLOGY?

Cross-cultural psychology has been variously defined. A consideration of some definitions should shed light on how the field is construed by its students. According to a definition provided in an advanced textbook of cross-cultural psychology (Berry, Poortinga, Segall, & Dasen, 1992) cross-cultural psychology 'is the study of similarities and differences in individual psychological functioning in various cultural and ethnic groups; of the relationships between psychological variables and socio-cultural, ecological, and biological variables; and of current changes in these variables' (p. 2). This is a comprehensive definition of the field, involving on the one hand a *comparative* focus on similar-

ities and differences across cultures and on the other a focus on *relating* psychological variables to environmental and even biological ones. Most researchers in the field focus on one aspect of this definition rather than others, bringing about variations in perspectives and emphases. Thus, the definition in the second edition of the *Handbook of Cross-Cultural Psychology* (Berry, 1997) states, 'Cross-cultural psychology is the systematic study of relationships between the cultural context of human development and the behaviors that become established in the repertoire of individuals growing up in a *particular culture*' (p. x) (emphases added). The comparative focus in the former definition is not explicit here.

Inherent in the above characterizations is the issue of whether a contextualistic (non-comparative) or a universalistic (comparative) perspective is preferred. This is basically a methodological problem which will be addressed later on. What is to be noted here is that this issue underlies the distinction between 'cultural' and 'cross-cultural' psychology. Though often seen as conflicting (Shweder, 1990), the two perspectives can rather be considered complementary. Cultural psychology is psychology within the cultural context, and as such all human psychology should indeed be cultural psychology, since no psychological phenomena occur in a cultural vacuum. However, as we are far from this ideal, psychological inquiry that takes cognisance of the cultural context qualifies as cultural psychology. If in such inquiry a comparative approach is used, and thus at least two cultures are implicated, even if implicitly, then we are in the realm of cross-cultural psychology (Kagitcibasi, 1996a, p. 12). Thus the use of both terms in the title '(Cross) Cultural Psychology' is intentional. With this understanding, in this chapter 'cross-cultural' will be used as a generic term unless a specific reference is made to 'cultural psychology' as such.

From the above description, it is clear that cross-cultural psychology is a general approach or outlook in psychological inquiry rather than a content area. Thus for example it is possible to talk about cross-cultural study of social or cognitive behavior or cross-cultural developmental psychology. What is distinctive in such labels is the term 'culture'.

Numerous definitions of culture have been proposed, sometimes summarized as 'the man-made part of the environment' (Herskovits, 1948). Usually the material aspects of culture, such as the built environment, as well as customs and behaviors ('explicit culture') are differentiated from culture as a symbolic meaning system. The latter refers to shared ideas and meanings, such as beliefs and values ('implicit culture') (Berry et al., 1992). An important characteristic of culture is its transmission through generations.

Culture is ubiquitous; therefore it is obvious that any human behavior is influenced by or is in response to some aspect of culture. However, the diffuse, all-inclusive nature of culture presents a problem in research. As a superordinate entity it can not serve as an independent variable or explanation (Segall, 1983), for such an explanation can turn into an empty tautology, such as 'Indians are this way because of their culture'. Therefore attempts have been made to define culture in less molar terms, that is 'unpackaging' it (Poortinga, Van de Vijver, Joe, & Van de Koppel, 1987; Whiting, 1976).

18.2 History and Present Status of Cross-Cultural Psychology

The roots of cross-cultural psychology are to be found in the nineteenth and early twentieth century European anthropology and sociology as well as psychology and evolution; philosophical antecendents go back even further. Accounts of this history can be found in a number of sources (e.g., Berry et al., 1992; Jahoda, 1990; Jahoda & Krewer, 1997; Segall, Dasen, Berry, & Poortinga, 1990). In different European countries different historical legacies are apparent. The beginnings of scientific psychology in Germany also contain the seeds of cultural psychology. For example the influential scholarly journal launched by Steinthal and Lazarus in 1860, *Zeitschrift für Völkerpsychologie und Sprachwissenschaften*, was devoted to the study of national or 'folk' psychology with an emphasis on language, customs, etc. Wundt, also, while on the one hand having founded the first experimental psychology laboratory in 1879, on the other hand was greatly interested in cultural and cross-cultural psychology, as demonstrated in his ten-volume *Völkerpsychologie* (1912–1921). Wundt tried to reveal the mental basis of cultural development, and there was a general interest at the time in understanding 'primitive culture'. Several German ethnographers studied drawings of 'savages' in South America and Africa.

In Britain, also, there was an interest in studying 'primitive peoples', as in Germany, but much more influenced by the nineteenth century 'cultural evolution' offshoots of Darwinism, espoused by Spencer. Spencer resorted to biological mechanisms to account for the origins and development of psychological and social phenomena, and in particular formed parallels between the evolutionary process of development from simple to complex life forms and the development of societies from simple/primitive to complex/civilized. The Lamarckian concept of 'the inheritance of acquired traits' was used as the basis of such evolutionary progression. Similarly, nineteenth-century British ethnologists (Tyler, Morgan, Frazer) claimed stages of cultural evolution, stressing the lower levels of 'evolutionary' development of 'savages'. These views were well accepted even though they had no scientific basis but were derived from impressionistic accounts of travellers and missionaries. They seemed to provide 'scientific' justification for British colonialism.

The first scientific study of primitives' visual perception was carried out by Rivers in the Cambridge expedition to the Torres Straits Islands (between Australia and New Guinea) in

1901. The focus on perception/sensation was mainly due to the popular assumption of the time, espoused by Spencer, that the excessive concentration of the primitive mind on sensory processes, such as better visual acuity than the Europeans, hinders the development of their higher mental processes. Yet, Rivers did not find the primitives' visual sensation/perception to be better than the Europeans' in any marked degree.

Contemporaneously with Wundt's *Völkerpsychologie*, American anthropologist Boas published *The Mind of Primitive Man* (1911). What these two important figures, from different disciplinary backgrounds, shared was a belief that despite the great difference between the cultural performances of the 'primitives' and the 'civilized' peoples, their underlying intellectual/cognitive processes are basically the same. This view, which was termed 'psychic unity' by Boas, challenged the dominant social evolutionary ideology of the time stressing the inferiority of the less-civilized peoples. The claim for the universality of thought processes, came under attack from the French scholar Levy-Bruhl in his *Les Fonctions mentales dans les Societes Inferieures* (1910). Unlike Boas, Levy-Bruhl did not carry out any fieldwork but relied on the impressionistic accounts of the day. He labelled primitive mentality 'pre-logical', reflecting an evolutionary bias and claimed a qualitative difference between the prelogical mystical thinking and the Western logical thinking. Though Levy-Bruhl later on softened some of his earlier assertions, the general thrust of his arguments remained influential.

In fact, the nineteenth century *Zeitgeist* of the inferiority of the non-literate people continued to influence the thinking of psychologists and social thinkers well into the twentieth century. In particular, the tendency to see similarities between primitives' thinking and children's (and mental patients') was rather common. It was reflected in the claim, first made by Tylor, that 'Ontogeny recapitulates phylogeny', forming an analogy between the development from childhood to adulthood and the development from 'primitive' to 'civilized' society. Known as the recapitulation theory, this view was held for example by well-known developmental psychologists in the United States, Stanley Hall and Werner in the 1940s and 1950s. Jahoda (1990) notes that 'it was not until almost the middle of the twentieth century that the doctrine of the mental inferiority of people in non-literate culture ceased to be scientifically respectable' (p. 33).

Thus the central controversy in early cross-cultural work has been whether there are fundamental differences in thinking across cultures that are critical to an understanding of human nature; or whether there are no fundamental differences in basic psychological processes, the differences being in content or performance. The former view, which emerged first but then lost popularity, has re-emerged recently in the relativistic perspective of 'cultural psychology' and 'everyday cognition' school, informed by Vygotskian thinking. In this new form, however, it does not involve an ethnocentric social evolutionist stance as before but stresses the context-specific nature of psychological processes, to be discussed later.

The study of sensation, perception, and subsequently cognition was conducted in pre-literate societies in Africa and Australia, by Western psychologists. These psychologists often worked in teams with anthropologists or utilized anthropological/ethnographic materials and data files. Quite a bit of research along these lines was conducted in the post World War II period. The research and thinking in cross-cultural psychology have therefore been closely influenced by anthropology, but not much by other social sciences such as sociology. Later work is marked by a great expansion in both topics covered, the national origins of the researchers and the locations where studies are done. Research has moved into diverse topical areas such as emotions, the self, interpersonal relations, developmental psychology, social psychology, and work and organizational psychology. In relative terms the study of basic processes, especially sensation–perception, decreased in number and importance. A continued interest in cognition is seen, however, including cognitive development, language, everyday cognition, and social cognition. As for the geographic expansion, on the one hand non-Western psychologists in growing numbers are getting involved in cultural and cross-cultural research; on the other hand, research is being conducted more in contemporary national societies, both Western and non-Western, and less in isolated pre-literate societies.

The 1970s mark the establishment of cross-cultural psychology both institutionally and as a distinct discipline. In 1971 a conference on mental testing with a cross-cultural perspective was held in Istanbul, organized by Cronbach and Drenth (1972). In 1973 the *Annual Review of Psychology* had a chapter on 'psychology and culture' for the first time. In 1972 the International Association for Cross Cultural Psychology (IACCP) was founded, with Jerome Bruner as the president, at a conference held in Hong Kong, organized by Dawson. From these beginnings this association has grown steadily with a membership of more than 700 from 71 different nations. There are also other associations involved in cross-cultural work of a general nature such as the Society for Cross-Cultural Research, International Association of Applied Psychology, or focused on subdisciplines, such as the International Society for the Study of Behavioral Development, or regional ones, such as the Inter-American Society and Asian Association of Social Psychology. Finally, the International Union of Psychological Science has a growing involvement in international psychology. These institutional structures provide supportive ground for cross-cultural research.

The great increase in publications in cross-cultural psychology, especially in the 1980s and 1990s may be even more impressive than organizational activities. Some journals are clearly cross-cultural in their mandate, such as *Journal of Cross-Cultural Psychology, Culture and Psychology, International Journal of Psychology, Cross-Cultural Research, International Journal of Behavioral Development, International Journal of Intercultural Relations, Psychology and Developing Societies, World Psychology, Applied Psychology: An International Review*. Others emphasize an international, cross-cultural outlook. They attest to the internationalization of psychology and the growing importance of cultural, cross-cultural, and ethnic perspectives in research.

A six-volume *Handbook of Cross-Cultural Psychology* was published in 1980 under the general editorship of Triandis. In 1997 a completely revised three-volume second edition (general editor: Berry) set the stage for the field. Several authored and edited textbooks are now disseminating information to an increasing number of readers. A number of reviews have appeared in the *Annual Review of Psychology* since 1973 as well as topical reviews in some mainstream journals. Cross-cultural psychology has come of age by the end of the 1990s.

18.3 THEORY AND METHOD IN CROSS-CULTURAL PSYCHOLOGY

While the historical beginnings of cross-cultural psychology might have had understanding the primitive mind and the mental basis for culture as an impetus, the more recent development of the field has had different bases and goals. Foremost among these is a reaction to the culture-bound and culture-blind nature of mainstream psychology. Psychology has traditionally followed the physical science model, aspiring toward universals in human behavior. In practice, however, this has not involved studying human behavior universally (globally) but rather within one cultural context (the Western middle class) and generalizing from it to humanity. The limitation, even the invalidity, of this approach becomes more evident as we move from basic psychological processes that are biologically based to the study of topics such as self–other relations, social cognition, etc. which are more influenced by the cultural context. Thus the above-mentioned expansion in the research topics of cross-cultural psychology was to be expected.

Since any theory that claims universality needs to be subjected to cross-cultural testing, comparative analysis is of high priority in cross-cultural methodology. Thus a significant value of cross-cultural research is its possible contribution to the generalizability of research findings and therefore theory. The theoretical basis for a comparative methodology is 'universalism', which holds that psychological processes are the same in all humans, though their manifestations in behavior may differ due to cultural factors. This view is also called the 'etic' approach in cross-cultural psychology. In contrast the 'emic' or the 'cultural relativist' approach claims that context gives meaning, thus human behavior is context specific and should be studied within culture, not comparatively.[1] These contrasting theoretical perspectives are the contemporary parallels of the nineteenth–early twentieth century central controversy discussed above.

The research methodologies associated with these different paradigms show distinctive characteristics. Cultural, emic research, such as utilized in the study of 'everyday' cognition (e.g., Childs & Greenfield, 1980; Rogoff, 1990; Scribner & Cole, 1981; for a review see Schliemann, Carraher, & Ceci, 1997) tends to be based on observations within context and descriptive, qualitative analysis. It is akin to anthropological methodology. Cross-cultural, etic research often involves hypothesis testing with comparable samples of subjects, using standardized measures (often tests or inventories and sometimes experimentation), resulting in quantitative analyses. The methodological problems encountered in the two approaches tend to be different, also. In the former, main problems are generalizability and replicability (external validity) of the findings; in the latter, sampling, equivalence (comparability), and cultural validity issues come to the fore.

Beyond the above contrasting research goals, establishing generalization of theory versus analyzing context-based dynamics, cross-cultural research can also aim specifically to uncover cross-cultural differences again for theory testing. In this approach if the cultures are known or demonstrated to vary on some theoretically meaningful variable, such as individualism–

collectivism, then this can serve as an 'experimental' manipulation whose effects on variations in some behavioral outcome can be studied.

All the methodological issues involved in psychological research with people also concern cross-cultural research, but there are also some additional ones which increase the challenge of conducting a cross-cultural study. First of all, the choice or sampling of cultures from which subjects are to be drawn should be theoretically informed, rather than being based on convenience. There is however, the additional problem of the sampling of subjects within each culture and particularly ensuring that they are comparable. For example the fact that the two samples are university students does not ensure matching in contexts as different as the United States and Sub-Saharan Africa. In the former tertiary enrollment reaches 70.4%, whereas in the latter it is as low as 2.1% (UNESCO, 1991, p. 94); thus the latter would be a much more select group. A related problem, especially in ethnic research, is the social class standing of the subjects which is often confounded by ethnicity. The differences attributed to ethnic variation may in fact be due to social class variations. For example, in a number of studies ethnic variations in parenting values are found to disappear when social class was controlled (Cashmore & Goodnow, 1986; Lambert, 1987).

Finally, equivalence of the measures and the ecological validity (Bronfenbrenner, 1979) of the testing situation present additional challenges. Equivalence has been studied extensively, and several types have been identified (see Berry et al., 1992; Poortinga, 1989; van de Vijver & Leung, 1997) where both conceptual and technical issues are involved. Basically, if some behavior is to be compared in different cultural contexts, its assessment has to have the same properties (including similar meanings and psychometric factor structures) in the two contexts. Furthermore, the testing (experimental, observational, etc.) situation should carry the same meaning in the two cultural contexts. For example, if some cognitive assessment technique is perceived by schooled subjects as an intelligence test on which they are motivated to do their best, while the same assessment technique is seen as a curious thing which does not make much sense by a group of non-schooled bushmen (and thus has no ecological validity), their behavioral outcomes are non-comparable.

What is called 'culture-fair' testing refers to this basic issue of comparability with a 'universal' standard. Several precautions such as back translations and similar administrative procedures are helpful but not sufficient for comparability. Refined conceptualization and

operationalization of equivalence in measures is required. Specifically, it is important that data sets from different cultures have similar psychometric properties, as determined for example by the similarity of factor structures underlying measurement (structural equivalence). Similarly, the measurement itself should have scalar or metric equivalence across the groups (see van de Vijver & Leung, 1997).

Going beyond these statistical and psychometric methods promoting comparability, the research question asked and how it is studied, including the research design, are also of crucial importance in cross-cultural study. Often research collaboration with local researchers helps assure that the research methodology carries the same meaning (has ecological validity) in different cultural contexts.

18.4 Basic Psychological Processes in Cultural Context

Basic psychological processes such as sensation, perception, cognition, language, motivation, and emotion have been subject to cross-cultural inquiry. Most cross-cultural research in these areas aims to develop a better understanding of the nature and extent of universals in human functioning by uncovering similarities and differences across cultures. A century of cross-cultural research in basic processes is extensive, and extensive treatments of the area are available in the Resource References. Here only some selected topics will be summarized.

Culture and Perception

Of the several areas of study in sensation and perception in which cross-cultural work has been carried out, color perception/categorization and susceptibility to visual illusions have probably stimulated most research and debate.

Color perception/categorization, an area spanning sensation, perception, and cognition, has been a battleground of nativist and empiricist theoretical perspectives, stressing the universal/biological and the experience factors, respectively. Experience in color perception has been stressed in terms of the Sapir–Whorf 'linguistic relativity hypothesis' proposing the mediation of language in color perception. From this perspective the existence of varying numbers of color names in different languages is interpreted to mean that color perception involves parallel variations, thus claiming the priority of (learned) language to perception. Berlin and Kay (1969) seriously challenged the linguistic relativity hypothesis in a study where they asked bilingual subjects from 20 different languages in the United States to generate basic color terms in their mother tongue. Then using the terms that the subjects generated themselves, they were asked to indicate on a panel with 329 differently colored chips from the Munsell system the best examples of each color. The results showed neat clusters of most typical, or focal, chips for basic colors showing similarity of foci for basic colors across languages.

Subsequent work by Rosch (1977) further questioned linguistic relativity hypothesis. She first showed that focal colors were named more rapidly and were recognized faster (i.e., had higher codability) than non-focal colors by subjects from 23 languages. Then she worked with the Dani, a tribe in New Guinea, who have only two color names, refering to white (light) and black (dark). She found that the Dani, also, recognized focal colors better than non-focal colors. Thus, even lacking a term for them in the language, focal colors are recognized clearly, implying the significance of the underlying universal physiological system in color perception.

More evidence for the role of physiological factors was provided by Bornstein (1973) who showed a correspondence between the wavelengths of the most basic focal colors obtained by Berlin and Kay (1969) and the spectral sensitivity of four types of cells found in the brains of macaque monkeys. In a further study with infants Bornstein, Kessen, and Weiskopf (1976), using habituation and dishabituation, demonstrated greater sensitivity and reaction to stimulus change which involved color category shift compared with the same amount of change in wavelength which did not involve a color category shift. Since infants have no language, any linguistic determination is not possible here.

Though there is no consensus, the weight of the evidence from early research seems to uphold the primacy of perception and neurophysiology, rather than language, in color perception. Current work on color perception is smaller in volume and involves mainly interpretations of the early research findings (Kay, Berlin, Maffi, & Merrifield, 1997) and new theoretical conceptualizations (e.g., the 'vantage theory' of MacLaury, 1992, and the evolutionary perspective of Shepard, 1992). For a current review see Russell, Deregowski, and Kinnear (1997).

Susceptibility to visual illusions (perceptions that involve a discrepancy between how an object looks and what it really is) has been another area where the empirical (experiential) and nativist (physiological) perspectives have been tested. Segall, Campbell, and Herskovits (1966) conducted a study with 14 Western and non-Western samples using several visual illusions such as the 'Müller–Lyer' and the 'vertical–horizontal' illusions. They hypothesized that visual illusions result from learned habits of inference from visual perception and thus should be subject to different environmental (ecological) influences. Specifically they reasoned that people living in modern 'carpentered' environments interpret perceived non-rectangular figures as rectangular, tend to perceive figures in perspective, as well as experiencing them as two-dimensional representation of three-dimensional objects. They indeed found greater susceptibility to visual illusions in the Western samples, supporting the 'carpentered world hypothesis'. However they also found a decrease in illusion susceptibility with age, whereas the experiential hypothesis would predict an increase in this tendency with increased environmental exposure. Other research on age trends brought up more ambiguous results.

Contrasting explanations were proposed in terms of race and physiological factors and focusing on contour detection. This ability was found to decrease with age (Pollack, 1963) and to increase with retinal pigmentation (Pollack & Silvar, 1967), the latter being related to skin color. However, Jahoda (1975) found no evidence for the retinal pigmentation hypothesis, and Stewart (1973), varying the environmental carpenteredness and keeping race constant, supported the environmental hypothesis. Though there is no consensus, the weight of evidence seems to provide support to the experiential perspective in susceptibility to visual illusions.

Other work in cross-cultural perception has involved picture perception in terms of the degree of depth perception (perspective) demonstrated in different cultural contexts, focusing especially on non-industrial groups in Africa (Hudson, 1960; Jahoda & McGurk, 1974). Cross-cultural work on perception has decreased in volume since the 1970s. However, alternative methods and more sophisticated apparatus especially for depth perception, has allowed different conceptualizations of perception in cultural contexts involving variations in environment and education. For example, picture perception is considered as a set of skills involving the use of relevant cues in a given situation (Deregowski, 1980). For a current review of cross-cultural perception and aesthetics see Russell et al. (1997).

Culture and Cognition

Cross-cultural work on cognition is extensive, being a popular research area from the very beginning and often combined with perception (see also Hatano and Inagaki, Chapter 10 in this volume).

Categorization and Sorting

Above-mentioned work on color perception/categorization (Bornstein et al., 1976; Rosch, 1977) pointed to perceptually salient color categories (focal colors) constituting natural prototypes. Such natural prototypes were also revealed in form perception/categorization in the sense that perfect squares, triangles, and circles (rather than irregular ones) (Rosch, 1977) and pure expressions of basic emotions (happiness, sadness, anger, fear, surprise, and disgust) (Ekman, 1971) were found to be better recognized, regardless of culture and language. Color, form, and basic emotions may have a physiological and evolutionary basis and thus be categorized in similar ways universally. Other categorization, as demonstrated in research on sorting, shows a stronger effect of experience and therefore more cultural variation.

The common finding in Western research of a developmental shift in sorting from color to form to shared function to taxonomic categories is not found in studies conducted in non-Western cultures especially in Africa, where sorting by color is seen most frequently even in adults, followed by sorting by form and then by function, with almost no taxonomic sorting. The most plausible explanation of this finding is in terms of differences in formal education. Color being a salient perceptual category tends to be most readily used, unless the subject has had schooling which orients him/her to search for less obvious attributes (Evans & Segall, 1969; Greenfield, Reich, & Olver, 1966). Indeed when schooling is controlled, the observed cultural differences often disappear. Similarly, when familiarity with the testing situation and materials is controlled, differences again disappear (Okonji, 1971).

Thus, the variations seem to rest more in habits, or learned orientations, than in (innate) capacities. For example a well-known anecdotal account (related by Glick) showed that the Kpelle farmers kept making functional sorting of utensils and vegetables together (because a knife is used to cut a vegetable) and saying that this is the way a wise man would do the grouping. When asked how a fool would do it, they produced a perfect taxonomic sorting. The distinction between performance and capacity, first pointed out by Tolman in the 1930s, was further stressed by the cross-cultural research of the 1960s and 1970s and is currently well accepted (e.g., Mishra, Sinha, & Berry, 1996; Wassman & Dasen, 1994). It sets the contemporary outlooks in culture and cognition apart

from the early claims of the inferiority of the 'primitives', discussed earlier.

Memory

Cross-cultural research on memory has mainly attended to serial position effects in remembering lists of names, etc. and to recall of stories. In their work with the Kpelle people of Liberia, Cole and Scribner (1974) found no serial position effects (such as primacy and recency), and no clustering into semantic categories. These are mnemonics (tools for recall) commonly used by Western subjects. The positive effects of the use of more culturally meaningful materials and instructions were noted, thus methodological factors might have played a role in the results. (See also Roediger and Meade, Chapter 7 in this volume). However, the researchers also found positive effects of schooling on serial position effects and clustering. Wagner (1981) proposed a distinction between 'hardware' and 'software' of memory. The former, as seen in short-term memory capacity may be universal, whereas the latter, such as practice and the use of mnemonics in retrieval, are control processes based on learning (culture). Wagner's research in Mexico and Morocco substantiated the hypothesis. Schooling emerges as an important factor, as it improves recall by teaching organizing principles which can serve as mnemonics in memory (Cole & Scribner, 1974). More recent work further substantiated the importance of schooling and cultural relevance in memory (for a review see Mishra, 1997).

Story recall is another topical area for the cross-cultural study of memory. Starting with Ross and Millsom's work (1970) with Ghanaian and American subjects, oral cultural tradition has been seen as improving patterned story recall. However, Mandler, Scribner, Cole, and De Forest (1980) found few differences between Liberian and American adults and children and concluded that story recall is a universal process. What accounts for the obtained cross-cultural differences appears to be whether story content is culturally relevant (Harris, Schoen, & Hensley, 1992).

Problem Solving and Reasoning

Cross-cultural research has focused mainly on conditional (syllogistic) reasoning and mathematical problem solving. Luria's work (1976) in Central Asia showed that illiterate subjects failed in deductive hypothetical reasoning tasks presented to them in the form of syllogisms. Literacy and involvement in collective farming made a difference in performance. In line with the sociohistorical school of thinking, influenced by Vygotsky, Luria claimed that schooling and more particularly literacy produced new cognitive processes, absent in their absence. Similar positive contributions of schooling to syllogistic thinking were also reported by Cole and Scribner (1974) in Liberia and by Tulviste (1978) in Estonia (see Segall et al., 1990).

However, the interpretation of this evidence as the inability of unschooled subjects to do hypothetico-deductive reasoning, as claimed by Luria, is not widely accepted. Rather, what happens is a refusal on the part of the unschooled subject to accept at face value the information presented in a hypothetical premise which goes against his/her experiential knowledge. What apparently schooling brings is a new habit of accepting and addressing hypothetical statements (logical truths, as opposed to empirical truths) as used in question–answer format in the classroom. Again, performance–ability distinction and culturally familiar tasks become relevant issues. This is the case in both verbal reasoning and also in inferential reasoning as in the use of apparatus to solve mechanical problems (Scribner & Cole, 1981). Finally some recent work on deductive reasoning has focused on linguistic factors and has shown that, notwithstanding some generally held assumptions, hypothetical reasoning is not constrained by any linguistic features of non-Western languages (Politzer, 1991).

Everyday Cognition and Mathematical Problem Solving

Mathematical problem solving has been studied in everyday life situations as a part of the larger research tradition in 'everyday cognition', informed by Vygotskian thinking. This tradition stresses contextual (emic) study of specific teaching and learning through 'guided participation' within the child's 'zone of proximal development', where in a master–apprentice relationship with an adult or someone more advanced, the child's actual level of development is extended upward within the limits of his/her potential (e.g., Childs & Greenfield, 1980; Rogoff, 1990). Observational studies have been done in such everyday apprenticeship situations as weaving, tailoring, carpentery, cooking, practical mathematics of dart players, and street vendors in many societies (for a review see Schliemann et al., 1997). Researchers in this tradition stress the importance of learning as context-dependent, goal-directed and adaptive action, and in this sense consider school learning as no different from or superior to everyday learning.

This orientation has served as a corrective to the rather ethnocentric undermining of 'indigenous' cognitive competence of people in non-Western and especially pre-literate contexts,

characteristic of the field since its beginnings. It has also helped expand our view of teaching, learning, and competence. However, if interpreted to mean that school learning is *not* important, it can feed into double standards such as formal schooling being necessary for children in Western/industrial society (because it is functional there), but not for children in preindustrial societies where parochial religious education or non-formal apprenticeships in handicrafts would do (Kagitcibasi, 1996a). School learning has greater generalizability to different situation, especially as required by more specialized work contexts in urban settings. With increasing urbanization and economic globalization, school-like cognitive habits, orientations, and skills are becoming ever more important to the development of competence. Furthermore, as research discussed above shows, schooling has a greater impact on cognitive processes such as memory, clustering, reasoning, concept formation, etc. than does any other single learning experience, including literacy (see Mishra, 1997; Scribner & Cole, 1981; Segall et al., 1990). What appears to be needed is to improve school quality. Research in India by Mishra has shown for example that cognitive performance of children from 'good' schools is better than that of children from 'ordinary' schools (see Mishra, 1997).

Cognitive Style

Cognitive style in cross-cultural psychology has focused on field dependence–independence (FI-FD) from an ecocultural framework (for a review see Berry, 1990). FI refers to greater psychological differentiation involving the tendency to be analytic and therefore less influenced by the larger field (perceptual ground), whereas FD refers to a more synthesizing orientation. In general studies have found that hunters and gatherers are more FI, compared with agriculturalists, and women are more FD than men. Western educated groups score higher on FI than non-Western and less-educated groups. Formal education, which emphasizes analytical skills, as well as child-rearing orientations involving independence, self-reliance training, and individualistic goals are implicated in the development of FI. A meta-analysis of 35 cross-cultural studies (Van Leeuwen) provided support to Berry's ecocultural framework, particularly demonstrating that the sex difference is higher in high food accumulating (agricultural) societies with greater division of labor on the basis of sex, accompanying lower status assigned to women's work and greater emphasis on compliance training for girls. Work on cognitive style has decreased in volume except for some recent research in India (see Mishra, 1997).

Culture and Emotion

Cross-cultural study of emotions has focused mainly on testing the generality of basic emotions. One type of evidence for the universality of basic emotions is based on the fact that most languages have emotion labels referring to the same commonly occurring emotions (Russell, 1991). Another type of evidence comes from cross-cultural recognition of facial expressions of emotions (Ekman, 1971). However, there is also evidence for cross-cultural variability in the recognition of some emotional expressions (Russell, 1994). While Western and non-Western literate samples were found to agree, isolated illiterate groups differed in their judgments, particularly of surprise and disgust.

An important theoretical distinction in the cross-cultural study of emotion is the potential for and the practice (expression) of emotions. In general, cross-cultural similarity (universality) is seen in the potential for different emotions, as well as in the antecedent conditions eliciting them (Mesquita, Frijda, & Scherer, 1997) though there can be culturally different meanings attributed to the same antecedent conditions which can lead to variations in emotional outcome. Emotional expression, however, should be more subject to cultural variation. Cultural norms about 'display rules' may differentially suppress, encourage, or channel the expression of emotions in specific social contexts.

Cultural differences in emotional experience and expression may be associated with emotion-related cognitive processes. For example variations in the frequency of positive or negative emotions may imply corresponding variations in the cognitive attributions regarding self-worth, etc. Thus, Americans report greater frequency of experiencing positive rather than negative affect, but no such difference is found among the Japanese (Markus & Kitayama, 1994). Moreover, the levels of both positive and negative emotion is found to be higher for Americans than for Japanese. Relevant cognitive strategies are likely to be correspondingly different. For example, Americans are found to have greater degree of self-serving bias than the Japanese who show more self-deprecating tendencies. Variations in individualism/collectivism and in norms of modesty may be relevant interpersonal dimensions mediating emotional experience and expression. Thus, 'ego-focused' emotions (such as anger, frustration, and pride) and 'other-focused' emotions (such as sympathy, shame, and feelings of interpersonal communion) are differentiated and found to be more characteristic of individualists and collectivists, respectively (Markus & Kitayama, 1991). The study of emotions in cultural contexts is not far advanced. More attention needs to be given to design and methodology issues and to studying emotions as processes rather than as stable states.

18.5 HUMAN DEVELOPMENT AND THE FAMILY

Childrearing is goal oriented; though often not explicit, this goal is becoming a competent member of a society. Cognitive and social competence are conceived as positive developmental outcomes, however, their definitions may show both similarities and differences across cultures. A great deal of cross-cultural research has focused on studying human development within the cultural context. This has constituted a methodological/theoretical perspective that is quite different from the dominant mechanistic (e.g., behavioristic) and organismic (e.g., Piagetian) paradigms in mainstream developmental psychology.

Development of Competence

In the cross-cultural study of child socialization and the development of competence, comparisons are often made between the Western/urbanized/industrial contexts and the traditional/rural contexts. Theory testing has been an important impetus in such comparative work. In particular, the cross-cultural generality of Piagetian theory has been questioned by research results which show that while the 'sensory-motor stage' of cognitive development is a strong universal, the higher stages, especially 'formal operations', may not be reached by adolescents, even adults in some preindustrial societies. Though methodological problems of comparability and equivalence and the competence–performance distinction, mentioned before, explain some of the results, this body of research has been important in pointing to the importance of cultural factors which were by and large ignored by Piagetian theory. Neo-Piagetian models combine a Piagetian qualitative-structuralist perspective (maintaining the stages of development) with functional frameworks which can take into account cultural factors (Berry et al., 1992; Dasen & Ribaupierre, 1987; Segall et al., 1990)

Quite a lot of teaching and learning of tasks in rural society is through observation and imitation, without elaborate verbal instruction or praise (LeVine, 1989; for a review see Kagitci-basi, 1996a). This is to be contrasted with the verbal, child development oriented teaching of the child in the (Western) educated/middle-class home. The developmental implications are important, particularly if almost all learning is observational. This is because such learning has limitations especially for transfer to new tasks and situations. The significance of schooling (and childrearing in general) which involves verbal instruction, abstraction, hypothetical reasoning, etc. becomes relevant here, as dis-cussed above with regard to cognitive processes in different cultural contexts.

Cultural conceptions of competence are found to vary in line with cultural values and the demands of life styles. A study by Serpell (1977) in a Zambian village showed that the children chosen by the adults as 'intelligent' were not the ones who did best on intelligence tests, even though the tests used were designed by Serpell for use in Zambia. This finding shows that the psychologist's and the villagers' concept of intelligence are very different. In traditional, closely knit society, the intelligent child is socially responsible and attuned to others' needs – this is the so-called 'African social intelli-gence'. Actually, it is not limited to Africa but is rather prevalent in most traditional collectivistic societies which value highly group well-being and interdependence rather than individual inde-pendence and self-reliance.

Harkness and Super (1992), within their framework of 'developmental niche' showed the divergent developmental results of different par-ental conceptualizations of cognitive compe-tence (ethnotheories) and their reflections in parenting in Kenya (Kokwet) and the United States. While the Kokwet children were highly skilled in household chores and taking care of infants and animals (tasks in which the urban American children would fare poorly), they did poorly on a simple cognitive test involving retelling a story, with which American children had no difficulty. Clearly children's cognitive competence in culturally valued domains gets promoted, whereas development in other domains lags behind. Thus learning and social-ization are adaptive to environmental demands. A misfit may emerge, however, when stable functional relationships or adaptive mechanisms get challenged by modifications in lifestyles accompanying social-structural and economic changes such as seen in urbanization and migra-tion. Mismatches with the school culture can be particularly problematic. Nunes (1993) found, for example, that immigrant Mexican parents in the United States believed, erroneously, that if their children are quiet and obedient, then they will succeed in school.

What seems to be needed for adjustment to schooling and modern lifestyles is an expansion of the concept of competence to include cogni-tive competence, in addition to social intelli-gence. Correspondingly, teaching and learning need to be more varied to include verbalization and reasoning (cognitive and language skills), in addition to observational learning and imitation. Applied research can help parents cultivate new orientations which can promote in children cog-nitive competence required for success in school and future specialized work in modern society (see Kagitcibasi, 1996a, Chapter 8 for an example).

Development of the Self

The antecedents of the study of self in cultural context go back to the 'Culture and Personality' school of the 1940s and 1950s. This work first involved intensive and holistic study of single cultures, and then a cross-cultural comparative approach was introduced, using the Human Relations Area Files (HRAF) (e.g., Whiting & Child, 1953). HRAF are extensive ethnographic records on a great number of preindustrial soci-eties, founded by Murdock at Yale University. The culture and personality school, which was later called 'psychological anthropology' was informed mainly by psychoanalytic theory, which turned out to be a limitation, both in terms of topics of study and methodology. Nevertheless this early work paved the way to later research, particularly in pointing to the importance of early childrearing and family pat-terns from a contextual/functional perspective.

Current work on culture and self focuses on cross-cultural variability in conceptions of the self. Since 'self' is a social product, in the sense that it emerges out of social interaction and is socially situated at any point in time, it can be expected to show cultural variation. In particular a 'relational' conceptualization of the self is a common finding in non-Western collectivistic societies, variously labeled 'the we-self', 'the group-self', 'the familial self' (in India and Japan), 'the two-person matrix' (in China), 'social selfhood' (in Africa), etc., in contrast to the individualistic selfhood of the west. Yet the west is no homogenous entity; similar distinc-tions have been made, for example, between the Northern European (Protestant) and the Medi-terranean (Latin) concepts of the person.

Different self construals refer both to self perceptions and also to the perception of others. For example, Shweder and Bourne (1984) stud-ied person concepts in India and the United States and found them to be more context-specific and relational ('socio-centric') in the former, where 'units (persons) are believed to be necessarily altered by the relations they enter into' (p. 110). Thus the American person descriptions involved more stable and abstract traits that have generality over situations, whereas the Indian descriptions reflected a more situational understanding of the changeable self. Relational concepts of self can also figure in attributions made about others' behavior.

Miller (1984), again comparing American and Indians, asked her subjects to give reasons for other's hypothetical behaviors. The results showed a preponderance of dispositional (person) attributions for Americans but situational (contextual) attributions for Indians. Apparently in more individualistic contexts persons are assumed to be the sole agents of their actions, thus the reasons for their behaviors are seen to be their own dispositions. In more collectivistic societies, however, relational concerns, such as others' expectations, etc. tend to have a greater influence on people's behavior, thus attributions regarding the causes of behavior reflect this. There are implications for moral reasoning, as well, in the sense that social responsibility in the form of beneficence is a key concept in morality for Indians but not for Americans who tend to see it as an imposition conflicting with individual freedom of choice (Miller, Bersoff, & Harwood, 1990).

The Self and the Family

A common theme underlying the above discussion is the dependence–independence dimension (Kagitcibasi, 1990; Markus & Kitayama, 1991). In cultural contexts where interdependent human/family relations are common, 'social intelligence' is valued, as discussed above, and the development of the relational self is encouraged. This contrasts with the promotion of the separated individuated self in the context of human/family pattern of independence. Why is it that some socialization contexts reinforce independence while others reinforce interdependence? A functional/contextual perspective is required to answer this question and to make an attempt to reveal some systematic patterns underlying the apparent complexity of the intricate relations between the self and the family in diverse socio-cultural settings.

Kagitcibasi (1990, 1996a) has proposed a model of family change which differentiates three ideal-typical patterns of self/family dynamics in different socio-economic contexts. In the rural-traditional context with low levels of affluence and a 'culture of relatedness' (collectivism) the family is a system of interdependent relations, particularly between generations,

through the family life cycle. Children are socialized into interdependence and loyalty to the family, since their future material support is crucial for family livelihood. Independence and autonomy in childrearing is not functional in this context. In contrast is the Western (American) middle-class family of independence where autonomy and independence training are stressed in childrearing. The model proposes that with urbanization and industrialization in collectivistic societies there is not a simple shift from the former to the latter model, as assumed by the modernization paradigm, but rather a third model emerges which synthesizes some elements of each. This is the human/family pattern of relationships characterized by independence in the material realm but interdependence in the emotional realm. Thus the resultant self is a relational-autonomous self (Kagitcibasi, 1996b). The model seems to reflect some of the complexities observed in diverse self and family patterns (e.g., LeVine, 1989; for a review see Kagitcibasi, 1996a) but needs to be substantiated by more research.

Within an individualism–collectivism framework, Markus and Kitayama (1991) proposed a similar distinction between the 'independent' and the 'interdependent' self construal and examined its consequences, particularly its implications for cognition, emotion, and motivation. This distinction has also been integrated with horizontal (egalitarian) and vertical (hierarchical) human relations and with communication styles (Singelis, Triandis, Bhawuk, & Gelfand, 1995). Beyond variations in self construals, diverse behavioral implications of individualism–collectivism have also been the topic of much research to which we now turn.

18.6 SOCIAL BEHAVIOR ACROSS CULTURES

Cross-cultural social psychological research has been most concerned about the rather culture-blind manner in which mainstream social psychology constructs theories and assumes generalities based on research with narrow samples of subjects (mostly American university students). For example, systematic programs of replication by Amir and Sharon (1987) in Israel and by Rodrigues (1982) in Brazil demonstrated the rather severe limits in the replicability of some well-known social psychological experiments. There is a need to develop a better understanding of the reasons for the cross-cultural variability that is implied by these failures of replication. Some of the theorizing in cross-cultural social psychology has endeavoured to do this.

Individualism–collectivism has served as a tool for understanding and interpreting cross-cultural variability in social behavior. It may be seen as the main paradigm for social psychological research across cultures, particularly since the early 1980s. These constructs have their antecedents in Tonnies' (1957) *Gesellschaft* and *Gemeinschaft* and were introduced into cross-cultural psychology by Hofstede's (1980) *Culture's Consequences*, to be followed by much research and theorizing, especially promoted by Triandis (for reviews see Kagitcibasi, 1997; Kim, Triandis, Kagitcibasi, Choi, & Yoon, 1994; Triandis, 1995). As a paradigm, individualism/collectivism seems to have replaced to some extent the ecocultural framework (Berry, 1990; Berry et al., 1992; Segall et al., 1990) in social psychological research. This is because, as discussed before, while earlier work on sensation, perception, cognition, and cognitive style was conducted among preindustrial groups, more directly influenced by the ecology (e.g., hunting-gathering vs. agriculture), more recent social psychological research is conducted more with similar, mainly urban, groups (e.g., students) in contemporary societies. Nevertheless, these societies often differ on cultural norms and values, particularly those arranging interpersonal relations, thus this dimension can serve as a theoretical basis for the selection of the societies in comparative research.

Conformity and Behavior in Groups

Given the variations in individualism/collectivism, as well as the related factors of socialization for independence/interdependence or loose/tight social networks in different societies, corresponding variations in social influence and conformity may be predicted. The Asch (1951) experiment (conformity to group pressure on a visual discrimination task) is the most widely replicated social psychological study in many cultures. Smith and Bond (1993) note that given the variations in subjects and procedures used in these replications, it is difficult to arrive at clear-cut results. Nevertheless, it is found in general that more conformity is obtained in collectivistic cultures and with non-student subjects (university students tend to be more individualistic than the general population in any culture). The collectivists not only engage in more compliant, conforming behavior, but they also value conformity, as demonstrated by a number of studies in non-Western countries (reviewed by Matsumoto, 1996, pp. 175–177).

However, such behavior is shown and valued not indiscriminately but mainly with 'in-groups', i.e., groups that are important for the individual, such as the family. An earlier finding by Frager (1970) of less conformity among Japanese students (compared with the original American finding) was seen as an anomaly. However, it can be explained in terms of the fact that in Frager's study the student subjects did not know each other, thus the others constituted an 'out-group', whereas in collectivistic societies conformity occurs to one's 'in-group'. In fact an important variation in self–other relations among individualistic and collectivistic people is seen in how differently they treat the in-group and the out-group – this difference is greater for the collectivists.

The significance of the group is reflected in studies of social loafing,[2] also. Studies conducted with a variety of subjects such as children, students, and managers in the US, China, Taiwan, and Japan found less social loafing in the East Asian contexts and in fact an even greater amount of effort in the group situation (reviewed by Smith & Bond, 1993, pp. 15–16). Indeed, when acceptance by the group and group goals are important for the individual, social loafing is not seen. Strong identification with and valuing the group can also have motivational outcomes. Specifically, studies show a socially-oriented, rather than an individually-oriented achievement motivation among collectivists (e.g., Phalet & Claeys, 1993; Yu & Yang, 1994). The distinctive characteristic of the socially-oriented achievement motivation is that it integrates the need for achievement with the need for extension (extending to others). Thus, when the individual achieves, both s/he and his/her group are exalted, as contrasted with the individual-oriented achievement motivation which is focused on the individual alone.

Regarding distributive justice and conflict resolution, also, meaningful differences between groups in individualistic and collectivistic societies are obtained, with equity being preferred in the former and equality in the latter (e.g., Leung & Bond, 1984). This is explained in terms of the dominant goals. The greater salience of group harmony among collectivists orients them toward equality; when the goal is defined as productivity, however, they adopt an equity orientation, also (Leung & Park, 1986). Need norm[3] is also found to be more common among collectivists (Berman, Murphy-Berman, & Singh, 1985). Greater group-orientedness in collectivistic cultures is also apparent from their greater tendency toward conflict avoidance and non-adversarial conflict resolution, believed to be most likely to reduce animosity (Leung, 1987).

A great deal of research points to higher competitive tendencies among individualists than among collectivists (e.g., Domino, 1992).

This may be related to the socially-oriented achievement motivation, mentioned before, and is for example found to be reflected in Chinese popular sayings (Ho & Chiu, 1994). Finally, the tendency to perceive consensus in group ('false consensus effect') is also found to relate to collectivism (Yamaguchi, 1994).

Social Cognition in Cultural Context

Shweder and Bourne (1984) in their study of person-perception, mentioned before, found more relational and contextualized perceptions of the person among Indians, contrasted with more abstract/trait conceptualizations among Americans. Similar results were also obtained with self-perceptions (Cousins, 1989), contrasting Japanese with Americans.

Attribution shows parallel cross-cultural variation. Miller (1984), in her study mentioned before, demonstrated that the so-called 'fundamental attribution error' (making dispositional attributions for others' behavior) is not so fundamental, after all, as she found it to be more common among Americans than among Indians. More individualistic (independent) or collectivistic (interdependent) construals of the person and interpersonal relations apparently influence social cognition.

A great deal of research finds more self-serving bias among individualists than among collectivists (reviewed by Markus & Kitayama, 1991). A factor explaining the difference is the value of modesty, prevalent in East Asian societies, where humble and even self-effacing attributions for success are seen, while self-enhancement is found to be a common tendency among Americans, also expressed in 'false uniqueness' (seeing oneself better than the average). Another factor accounting for little self-serving bias may be a low degree of 'self-focusing', as found in a study by Stipek, Weiner, and Li (1989) comparing the recollections of Chinese and American subjects. Such findings have implications for self-esteem, also; a 'collective self-esteem' might be more characteristic of collectivists than an individual self-esteem (Crocker & Luhtanen, 1990; for a comprehensive review of culture and cognition see Semin & Zwier, 1997).

Values

Values have been studied extensively in cross-cultural social psychology, both at the individual and the cultural level of analysis. The latter type of analysis has typically involved comparative study of a large number of nations. Hofstede's (1980) seminal work with IBM employees (117,000 respondents) in 50 countries and three regions has defined the agenda for this type of research. The resultant four value dimensions, 'power distance' (referring to hierarchy in interpersonal relations), 'individualism–collectivism', 'masculinity–femininity' (referring to the contrast in valuing assertiveness, achievement, etc. versus relationships and harmony), and 'uncertainty avoidance' (need for rules and certainty) are used to rank, order, and compare nations. Of these, individualism–collectivism has stimulated the most theory and research, as mentioned above. Several instruments measuring individualism–collectivism have been developed by other researchers and used extensively across cultures. Most of these also treat individualism and collectivism as values. Kagitcibasi (1997) has proposed that this is 'normative individualism/collectivism', to be differentiated from 'relational individualism/collectivism'. While the former refers to values held by a group or society, the latter refers to interpersonal relations, interpersonal distance, and the independence/interdependence of the self, as discussed previously.

In contrast to Hofstede's Western-origin value survey, Bond (Chinese Culture Connection, 1987) developed an instrument based on Chinese values. In a study conducted in 23 nations with university students, value factors corresponding to three of the four Hofstede value dimensions, power distance, individualism–collectivism, and masculinity–femininity, were obtained. A fourth factor, 'Confucian work dynamism' emerged as an East Asian emic.

A further large-scale study of values was carried out by Schwartz (1992) and many collaborators in 25 countries with nearly 60 samples. He used as a starting point the Rokeach Value Survey, from which he developed a new theory and methodology (smallest space analysis). At the individual level of analysis, single values were grouped into 10 value types according to their common goals: power, achievement, hedonism, stimulation, self-direction, universalism, benevolence, tradition, conformity, and security. Further work, with collaborators in 54 countries, has gathered data from about 44,000 respondents (teachers and university students in 121 samples). The 10 value types are found to be organized into two bipolar dimensions, 'openness to change' versus 'conservation' and 'self-transcendence' versus 'self-enhancement'. The culture level analysis of Schwartz (1994) has brought forth three further dimensions: 'conservatism versus autonomy', 'hierarchy versus egalitarianism', and 'mastery versus harmony'.

Another multi-nation value survey was conducted by Trompenaars (1985), who drew upon sociological literature and like Hofstede focused on business organizations (15,000 employees in over 50 countries). Further work by Smith, Dugan, and Trompenaars (1996) using a multi-dimensional scaling analysis derived two main dimensions, 'conservatism/egalitarian commitment' and 'loyal involvement/authoritarian involvement'.

Work on value types and dimensions is continuing using all the different approaches mentioned above and in particular searching for parallels between national values and other national characteristics (for a review see Smith & Schwartz, 1997). A word of caution is in order here; explaining national differences, as for example in the status of women, the extent of foreign aid, domestic political violence, etc., in terms of national values, as has been attempted by some researchers, may involve confusing association (correlation) with causation, as well as psychological reductionism and undermining the importance of social structural economic factors.

18.7 INDUSTRIAL ORGANIZATIONAL PSYCHOLOGY AS APPLIED CROSS-CULTURAL PSYCHOLOGY

Cross-cultural psychology is progressively more relevant for and involved in applications, in line with the current globalization of psychology. This is because, particularly as we move from theory to applications, the limits of generalization from single-culture work become more obvious. Several areas emerge as important for both research and applications. These include, among others, organizational behavior; health behavior; literacy and education; sex and gender; aggression, crime and war; intercultural communication and intergroup relations; and migration/acculturation. Space limitations preclude any extensive discussion of applied cross-cultural psychology, therefore cross-cultural industrial/organizational psychology will be briefly taken up as an example (see also Drenth and Zhong Ming, in this volume, Chapter 25, Section 12). The reader is advised to consult the third volume of the *Handbook of Cross-Cultural Psychology* (Berry, Segall, & Kagitcibasi, 1997) and other Resource References listed below for coverage of the other areas.

In the forefront of applied cross-cultural psychology is industrial/organizational (I/O) psychology. A reason for the advance of cross-cultural I/O may be the economic growth of the Pacific Rim (with collectivistic cultures) and the challenge this presents to the assumed correspondance of individualism and economic development. One approach has considered culture as external to the organization, influencing it, while another approach has looked at culture as internal to the organization, organizational culture paralleling national culture. A comparative line of research has examined cultural variation in organizational structure (Lammers & Hickson, 1979) proposing three types of organization: 'Latin', 'Anglosaxon', and 'Third World'. The first is characterized by centralization and hierarchy (classic bureaucracy); the second is more flexible with less centralization and hierarchy; and the third has paternalistic leadership and little formalization of rules (traditional).

It is possible to integrate Lammers and Hickson's typology with Hofstede's value orientations (above), where Hofstede's power reflecting distance index reflects organizational hierarchy and his uncertainty avoidance index reflects rule orientation. A fourfold typology then emerges: (1) small power distance, weak uncertainty avoidance (or weak rule orientation): Anglo (the USA, Canada, UK, Australia, Denmark, Sweden, etc.); (2) large power distance, strong uncertainty avoidance: bureaucratic (Latin) (France, Greece, Spain, Portugal, Turkey, Italy, Mexico, Columbia, Brazil, etc.); (3) weak uncertainty avoidance, large power distance: traditional (Hong Kong, Singapore, India, Philippines, Indonesia, etc.); and (4) small power distance, strong uncertainty avoidance (or high rule orientation): Germanic (Germany, Austria, Switzerland, Israel, and Finland) (Hofstede, 1983). Such typologies are substantiated by some research. However, critics question the stability of the diversity assumed by typologies and claim that similar technological requirements may override cultural factors and lead to convergence. Others (e.g., Drenth & Groenendijk, 1984) claim that technological factors influence how organizations are structured, but cultural factors affect how they function.

The study of how organizations function has focused on managerial behavior and leadership styles. Two behavioral styles have emerged in leadership research deriving from sociological and social psychological perspectives over a long period of time, which are called summarily 'concern for people' and 'concern for production'. These orientations have often been assumed to be contradictory. Research from India and Japan has provided new insights. J. B. P. Sinha (1980) proposed the concept of 'nurturant task leader' as the most effective leadership style in India where low levels of work motivation implicate a task orientation and collectivistic tendencies implicate a nurturant (concern for people) orientation for effective leadership. Similarly, in a research program

Misumi (1985) proposed that the performance (P) and maintenance (M) functions are interdependent and when both high, lead to the highest leadership effectiveness.

These perspectives show that especially in cultures with 'relational collectivism' (Kagitcibasi, 1997) group maintenance (socio-emotional) needs can not be ignored. This may turn out to be a universal, as claimed by Misumi and shown in research by Smith and Peterson (1988). What seems to vary is what specific behaviors are seen to constitute a considerate tendency (for example a supervisor talking about a subordinate's personal problems seen as caring in a collectivistic context but as breaching his privacy in an individualistic context).

Diversity in the meaning of work and work centrality has emerged in comparative research, such as the Meaning of Work Project conducted with large samples in eight countries (MOW, 1987). A rather unexpected finding was higher centrality of work in the more recently industrialized countries such as Japan and (former) Yugoslavia, with lowest scores in Britain and then Germany which were industrialized first. The rise of postmodern values in Europe, replacing capitalistic values, may be a factor here.

18.8 Summary

This chapter has endeavored the challenging task of presenting an overview of cross-cultural psychology. Though attempting to cover the main lines of influence, research, and theory, the chapter has also been necessarily selective at times, since this is a burgeoning field of inquiry, spanning an increasingly expanding scope. The examination of the historical development of the field and its main theoretical and methodological perspectives provides a better understanding of its present status. In particular, it is important to note again that cross-cultural psychology does not refer to a content area, such as social behavior, but is rather a culture-sensitive and often comparative study of human psychological phenomena. As we move from basic psychological processes, such as sensation and perception, to social behavior, the relative impact of culture increases. Thus there is a progressively increasing volume of research in such topical areas as the self, interpersonal relations, and organizational behavior across cultures. However, research in basic processes is continuing, also, focusing mainly on cognition. Whatever the topical area of inquiry, cross-cultural research promises to expand the range of variability in the behavior studied and to provide better

ground for theory testing, which in turn contribute to scientific progress in psychology.

Notes

1. The terms *etic* and *emic* were coined by Pike in analogy with phon*etics* and phon*emics* in linguistics. While phonemics is the study of sounds in a particular language, phonetics studies general aspects of sounds in languages.

2. Social loafing refers to not doing one's share of work in the anonymous group situation.

3. Need norm refers to allocation of resources on the basis of need.

Resource References

Berman, J. J. (Ed.). (1990). *Cross-cultural perspectives: Nebraska symposium on motivation, 1989.* Lincoln & London: University of Nebraska Press.

Berry, J. W. (General Ed.)
- Berry, J. W., Poortinga, Y. H., & Pandey, J. (Eds.). (1997). *Handbook of cross-cultural psychology Vol. 1: Theory and method.* Boston: Allyn & Bacon.
- Berry, J. W., Dasen, P. R., & Saraswathi, T. S. (Eds.). (1997). *Handbook of cross-cultural psychology Vol. 2: Basic processes and human development.* Boston: Allyn & Bacon.
- Berry, J. W., Segall, M. H., & Kagitcibasi, C. (Eds.). (1997). *Handbook of cross-cultural psychology Vol. 3: Social behavior and applications.* Boston: Allyn & Bacon.

Berry, J. W., Poortinga, Y. H., Segall, M. H., & Dasen, P. R. (1992). *Cross-cultural psychology: Research and applications.* New York: Cambridge University Press.

Greenfield, P. M., & Cocking, R. R. (Eds.). (1994). *Cross-cultural roots of minority child development.* Hillsdale, NJ: Lawrence Erlbaum Associates.

Kagitcibasi, C. (1996). *Family and human development across cultures: A view from the other side.* Mahwah, NJ: Lawrence Erlbaum.

Kim, U., Triandis, H. C., Kagitcibasi, C., Choi, S., & Yoon, G. (Eds.). (1994). *Individualism and collectivism: Theory, method, and applications.* Thousand Oaks, CA: Sage.

Lonner, W. J., & Malpass, R. S. (Eds.). (1994). *Psychology and culture.* Needham Heights, MA: Allyn & Bacon.

Matsumoto, D. (1996). *Culture and psychology.* Pacific Grove, CA: Brooks/Cole.

Moghaddam, F. M., Taylor, D. M., & Wright, S. C. (1993). *Social psychology in cross-cultural perspective.* New York: W. H. Freeman.

Segall, M. H., Dasen, P. R., Berry, J. W., & Poortinga, Y. H. (1990). *Human behavior in global perspective: An introduction to cross-cultural psychology.* Elmsford, NY: Pergamon.

Smith, P. B., & Bond, M. H. (1993). *Social psychology across cultures: analysis and perspectives.* Hertfordshire: Harvester Wheatsheaf.

Triandis, H. C. (General Ed.) (1980–81). *Handbook of cross-cultural psychology* (Vols. 1–6). Boston: Allyn & Bacon.

Additional Literature Cited

Amir, Y., & Sharon, I. (1987). Are social psychological laws cross-culturally valid? *Journal of Cross-Cultural Psychology, 18,* 383–470.

Asch, S. E. (1951). Effects of group pressure upon the modification and distortion of judgements. In H. Guetzkow (Ed.), *Groups, leadership and men: Research in human relations* (pp. 177–190). Pittsburgh: Carnegie Press.

Berlin, B., & Kay, P. (1969). *Basic color terms: Their universality and evolution.* Berkeley, CA: University of California Press.

Berman, J. J., Murphy-Berman, V., & Singh, P. (1985). Cross-cultural similarities and differences in perceptions of fairness. *Journal of Cross-Cultural Psychology, 16,* 55–67.

Berry, J. W. (1990). Cultural variations in cognitive style. In S. Wapner (Ed.), *Bio-psycho-social factors in cognitive style* (pp. 289–308). Hillsdale, NJ: Erlbaum.

Bornstein, M. (1973). The psychophysiological component of cultural differences in color naming and illusion susceptibility. *Behavioral Science Notes, 8,* 41–101.

Bornstein, M. H., Kessen, W. H., & Weiskopf, S. (1976). The categories of hue in infancy. *Science, 191,* 201–202.

Cashmore, J. A., & Goodnow, J. J. (1986). Influences on Australian parents' values: ethnicity versus socioeconomic status. *Journal of Cross-Cultural Psychology, 17,* 441–454.

Childs, C. P, & Greenfield, P. M. (1980). Informal modes of learning and teaching: The case of Zinacanteco weaving. In N. Warren (Ed.), *Studies in cross-cultural psychology* (vol. 2, pp. 269–316). London: Academic Press.

Chinese Culture Connection. (1987). Chinese values and the search for culture-free dimensions of culture. *Journal of Cross-Cultural Psychology, 18,* 143–164.

Cole, M., & Scribner, S. (1974). *Culture and thought: A psychological introduction.* New York: Wiley.

Cousins, S. (1989). Culture and selfhood in Japan and the US. *Journal of Personality and Social Psychology, 56,* 124–131.

Crocker, J., & Luhtanen, R. (1990). Collective self-esteem and ingroup bias. *Journal of Personality and Social Psychology, 58,* 60–67.

Cronbach, L. J., & Drenth, P. J. D. (Eds.). (1972). *Mental tests and cultural adaptation.* The Hague: Mouton.

Dasen, P. R., & de Ribaupierre, A. (1987). Neo-Piagetian theories: Cross-cultural and differential perspectives. *International Journal of Psychology, 22,* 793–832.

Deregowski, J. B. (1980). Perception. In H. C. Triandis & W. J. Lonner (Eds.), *Handbook of cross-cultural psychology* (vol. 3, 21–115). Boston: Allyn and Bacon.

Domino, G. (1992). Cooperation and competition in Chinese and American children. *Journal of Cross-Cultural Psychology, 23,* 456–467.

Drenth, P. J. D., & Groenendijk, B. (1984). Work and organizational psychology in cross-cultural perspective. In P. J. D. Drenth, H. Thierry, P. J. Willems, & C. J. De Wolff (Eds.), *Handbook of work and organizational psychology* (vol. 2, pp. 1197–1230). New York: Wiley.

Ekman, P. (1971). Universals and cultural differences in facial expressions of emotion. In J. K. Cole (Ed.), *Nebraska Symposium on Motivation* (vol. 19, pp. 207–283). Lincoln, NE: University of Nebraska Press.

Evans, J. L., & Segall, M. H. (1969). Learning to classify by color and function: A study of concept-discovery by Ganda children. *Journal of Social Psychology, 77,* 35–55.

Frager, R. (1970). Conformity and anticonformity in Japan. *Journal of Personality and Social Psychology, 15,* 203–210.

Greenfield, P. M., Reich, L. C., & Olver, R. R. (1966). On culture and equivalence II. In J. S. Bruner, R. R. Olver, & P. M. Greenfield, *Studies in cognitive growth* (pp. 270–318). New York: Wiley.

Harkness, S., & Super, C. M. (1992). The developmental niche: A theoretical framework for analyzing the household production of health. *Social Science and Medicine, 38,* 217–226.

Harris, R. J., Schoen, L. M., & Hensley, D. L. (1992). A cross-cultural study of story memory. *Journal of Cross-Cultural Psychology, 23,* 133–147.

Herskovits, M. J. (1948). *Man and his works: The science of cultural anthropology.* New York: Knopf.

Ho, D. Y.-F., & Chiu, C.-Y. (1994). Component ideas of individualism, collectivism and social organisation: An application in the study of Chinese culture. In U. Kim, H. C. Triandis, C. Kagitcibasi, S.-C. Choi, & G. Yoon (Eds.), *Individualism and collectivism: Theory, method and applications* (pp. 137–156). Thousand Oaks, CA: Sage.

Hofstede, G. (1980). *Culture's consequences.* Beverly Hills, CA: Sage.

Hofstede, G. (1983). The cultural relativity of organizational practices and theories. *Journal of International Business Studies, 14*, 75–89.

Hudson, W. (1960). Pictorial depth perception in subcultural groups in Africa. *Journal of Social Psychology, 52*, 183–208.

Jahoda, G. (1975). Retinal pigmentation and space perception: A failure to replicate. *International Journal of Psychology, 97*, 133–134.

Jahoda, G. (1990). Our forgotten ancestors. In J. J. Berman (Ed.), *Cross-cultural perspectives: Nebraska symposium on motivation, 37* (pp. 1–40). Lincoln, NE: University of Nebraska Press.

Jahoda, G., & Krewer, B. (1997). History of cross-cultural and cultural psychology. In J. W. Berry, Y. H. Poortinga, & J. Pandey (Eds.), *Handbook of cross-cultural psychology. Vol. 1: Theory and method* (pp. 1–42). Needham Heights, MA: Allyn and Bacon.

Jahoda, G., & McGurk, H. (1974). Development of pictorial depth perception: Cross-cultural replication. *Child Development, 45*, 1042–1047.

Kagitcibasi, C. (1990). Family and Socialization in Cross-cultural perspective: A model of change. In J. Berman (Ed.), *Cross-cultural perspectives: Nebraska symposium on motivation, 1989* (pp. 135–200). Lincoln, NE: Nebraska University Press.

Kagitcibasi, C. (1996a). *Family and human development across cultures: A view from the other side.* Mahwah, NJ: Lawrence Erlbaum.

Kagitcibasi, C. (1996b). The autonomous-relational self: A new synthesis. *European Psychologist, 1*(3), 180–186.

Kagitcibasi, C. (1997). Individualism and collectivism. In J. W. Berry, M. H. Segall, & C. Kagitcibasi (Eds.), *Handbook of cross-cultural psychology. Vol. 3: Social behavior and applications* (pp. 1–50). Needham Heights, MA: Allyn and Bacon.

Kay, P., Berlin, B., Maffi, L., & Merrifield, W. (1997). Color naming across languages. In C. L. Hardin & L. Maffi (Eds.), *Color categories in thought and language* (pp. 21–56). Cambridge, UK: Cambridge University Press.

Lambert, W. E. (1987). The fate of old country values in a new land: A cross-national study of child rearing. *Canadian Psychology, 28*, 9–20.

Lammers, C. J., & Hickson, D. J. (Eds.). (1979). *Organizations alike and unlike: International and interinstitutional studies in the sociology of organizations.* London: Routledge and Kegan Paul.

Leung, K. (1987). Some determinants of reactions to procedural models for conflict resolution. *Journal of Personality and Social Psychology, 53*, 898–908.

Leung, K., & Bond, M. H. (1984). The impact of cultural collectivism on reward allocation. *Journal of Personality and Social Psychology, 47*, 793–804.

Leung, K., & Park, H. J. (1986). Effects of interactional goal on choice of allocation rules: A cross-national study. *Organizational Behaviour and Human Decision Processes, 37*, 111–120.

LeVine, R. A. (1989). Cultural environments in child development. In N. Damon (Ed.), *Child development today and tomorrow.* San Francisco: Jossey-Bass.

Luria, A. R. (1976). *Cognitive development: Its cultural and social foundations.* Cambridge, MA: Harvard University Press.

MacLaury, R. E. (1992). From brightness to hue: An explanatory model of color-category evolution (article, commentaries and reply). *Current Anthropology, 33*, 137–186.

Mandler, J. M., Scribner, S., Cole, M., & De Forest, M. (1980). Cross-cultural invariance in story recall. *Child Development, 51*, 19–26.

Markus, H. R., & Kitayama, S. (1991). Culture and the self: Implications for cognition, emotion, and motivation. *Psychological Review, 98*(2), 224–253.

Markus, H. R., & Kitayama, S. (1994). The cultural construction of self and emotion: Implications for social behaviour. In S. Kitayama & M. R. Markus (Eds.), *Emotion and culture: Empirical studies of mutual influence* (pp. 89–130). Washington, DC: American Psychological Association.

Matsumoto, D. (1996). *Culture and psychology.* Pacific Grove, CA: Brooks/Cole.

Mesquita, B., Frijda, N., & Scherer, K. (1997). Culture and emotion. In J. W. Berry, P. R. Dasen, & T. S. Saraswathi (Eds.), *Handbook of cross-cultural psychology. Vol. 2: Basic processes and human development* (pp. 255–298). Needham Heights, MA: Allyn and Bacon.

Miller, J. G. (1984). Culture and the development of everyday social explanation. *Journal of Personality and Social Psychology, 46*, 961–978.

Miller, J. G., Bersoff, D. M., & Harwood, R. L. (1990). Perceptions of social responsibilities in India and the United States: Moral imperatives or personal decisions? *Journal of Personality and Social Psychology, 58*, 33–47.

Mishra, R. C. (1977). Cognition and cognitive development. In J. W. Berry, P. R. Dasen, & T. S. Saraswathi (Eds.), *Handbook of cross-cultural psychology. Vol. 2: Basic processes and human development* (pp. 255–298). Needham Heights, MA: Allyn and Bacon.

Mishra, R. C., Sinha, D., & Berry, J. W. (1996). *Ecology, acculturation and psychological adaptation: A study of Adivasi in Bihar.* New Delhi: Sage.

Misumi, J. (1985). *The behavioral science of leadership.* Ann Arbor, MI: University of Michigan Press.

MOW (Meaning of Working International Research Team). (1987). *The meaning of working.* London: Academic Press.

Nunes, T. (1993). Psychology in Latin America: The case of Brazil. *Psychology and Developing Societies, 5*, 123–134.

Okonji, O. M. (1971). The effects of familiarity on classification. *Journal of Cross-Cultural Psychology, 2,* 39–49.

Phalet, K., & Claeys, W. (1993). A comparative study of Turkish and Belgian youth. *Journal of Cross-Cultural Psychology, 24,* 319–343.

Politzer, G. (1991). Comparison of deductive abilities across language. *Journal of Cross-Cultural Psychology, 3,* 389–402.

Pollack, R. H. (1963). Contour detectability thresholds as a function of chronological age. *Perceptual and Motor Skills, 17,* 411–417.

Pollack, R. H., & Silvar, S. D. (1967). Magnitude of the Muller–Lyer illusion in children as a function of pigmentation of the fundus oculi. *Psychonomic Science, 8,* 83–84.

Poortinga, Y. H. (1989). Equivalence of cross-cultural data: An overview of basic issues. *International Journal of Psychology, 24,* 737–756.

Poortinga, Y. H., Van de Vijver, F. J. R., Joe, R. C., & Van de Koppel, J. M. H. (1987). Peeling the onion called culture: A sypnosis. In C. Kagitcibasi (Ed.), *Growth and progress in cross-cultural psychology* (pp. 22–34). Lisse: Swets & Zeitlinger.

Rodrigues, A. (1982). Replication: A neglected type of research in social psychology. *Interamerican Journal of Psychology, 16,* 91–109.

Rogoff, B. (1990). *Apprenticeship in thinking.* New York: Oxford University Press.

Rosch, E. (1977). Human categorization. In N. Warren (Ed.), *Studies in cross-cultural psychology* (vol. 1, pp. 1–49). London: Academic Press.

Ross, B. M., & Millsom, C. (1970). Repeated memory of oral prose in Ghana and New York. *International Journal of Psychology, 5,* 173–181.

Russell, J. (1991). Culture and categorisation of emotions. *Psychological Bulletin, 110,* 426–450.

Russell, J. A. (1994). Is there universal recognition from facial expression: A review of cross-cultural studies. *Psychological Bulletin, 115,* 102–141.

Russell, P., Deregowski, J., & Kinnear, P. (1997). Perception and aesthetics. In J. W. Berry, P. R. Dasen, & T. S. Saraswathi (Eds.), *Handbook of cross-cultural psychology. Vol. 2: Basic processes and human development* (pp. 107–142). Needham Heights, MA: Allyn and Bacon.

Schwartz, S. H. (1992). Universals in the structure and content of values: Theoretical advances and empirical tests in 20 countries. In M. P. Zanna (Ed.), *Advances in experimental social psychology* (vol. 25, pp. 1–65). Orlando, FL: Academic.

Schwartz, S. H. (1994). Beyond individualism/collectivism: New cultural dimensions of values. In U. Kim, H. C. Triandis, C. Kagitcibasi, S.-C. Choi, & G. Yoon (Eds.), *Individualism and collectivism: Theory, method, and applications* (pp. 85–122). Thousand Oaks, CA: Sage.

Schliemann, A., Carraher, D., & Ceci, S. J. (1997). Everyday cognition. In J. W. Berry, P. R. Dasen, & T. S. Saraswathi (Eds.), *Handbook of cross-cultural psychology. Vol. 2: Basic processes and human development* (pp. 177–216). Needham Heights, MA: Allyn and Bacon.

Scribner, S., & Cole, M. (1981). *The psychology of literacy.* Cambridge, MA: Harvard University Press.

Segall, M. H. (1983). On the search for the independent variable in cross-cultural psychology. In S. H. Irvine & J. W. Berry (Eds.), *Human assessment and cultural factors* (pp. 127–138). New York: Plenum.

Segall, M. H., Campbell, D. T., & Herskovits, M. J. (1966). *The influence of culture on visual perception.* Indianapolis: Bobbs-Mernll.

Semin, G., & Zwier, S. (1997). Social cognition. In J. W. Berry, M. H. Segall, & C. Kagitcibasi (Eds.), *Handbook of cross-cultural psychology. Vol. 3: Social behavior and applications* (pp. 51–76). Needham Heights, MA: Allyn and Bacon.

Serpell, R. (1977). Strategies for investigating intelligence in its cultural context. *Quarterly Newsletter, Institute for Comparative Human Development, 3,* 11–15.

Shepard, R. N. (1992). The perceptual organization of colors: An adaptation to regularities of the terrestial world? In J. H. Barkow, L. Cosmides, & J. Tooby (Eds.), *The adapted mind.* Oxford, UK: Oxford University Press.

Shweder, R. A. (1990). Cultural psychology – What is it? In J. W. Stigler, R. A. Shweder, & G. Herdt (Eds.), *Cultural psychology: Essays on comparative human development* (pp. 1–43). Cambridge, UK: Cambridge University Press.

Shweder, R. A., & Bourne, E. J. (1984). Does the concept of the Person vary cross culturally? In R. A. Shweder & R. A. LeVine (Eds.), *Culture theory: Essays of mind, self and emotion* (pp. 158–199). Cambridge, UK: Cambridge University Press.

Singelis, T. M., Triandis, H. C., Bhawuk, D. S., & Gelfand, M. (1995). Horizontal and vertical dimensions of individualism and collectivism: A theoretical and measurement refinement. *Cross-Cultural Research, 29,* 240–275.

Sinha, J. B. P. (1980). *The nurturant task leader.* New Delhi: Concept Publishing House.

Smith, P. B., & Bond, M. H. (1993). *Social psychology across cultures.* Hertfordshire, UK: Harvester Wheatsheaf.

Smith, P. B., Dugan, S., & Trompenaars, F. (1996). National culture and the values of organizational employees: A dimensional analysis across 43 nations. *Journal of Cross-Cultural Psychology, 27,* 231–264.

Smith, P. B., & Peterson, M. F. (1988). *Leadership, organizations and culture: An event management model.* London: Sage.

Smith, P. B., & Schwartz, S. (1997). Values. In J. W. Berry, M. H. Segall, & C. Kagitcibasi (Eds.), *Handbook of cross-cultural psychology. Vol. 3: Social behavior and applications* (pp. 77–118). Needham Heights, MA: Allyn and Bacon.

Stewart, V. M. (1973). Tests of the 'carpentered world' hypothesis by race and environment in America and Zambia. *International Journal of Psychology, 8,* 83–94.

Stipek, D., Weiner, B., & Li, K. (1989). Testing some attribution-emotion relations in the People's Republic of China. *Journal of Personality and Social Psychology, 56,* 109–116.

Tonnies, F. (1957). *Community and society* (C. P. Loomis, translator). East Lansing: Michigan State Press.

Triandis, H. C. (1995). *Individualism and collectivism.* Boulder, CO: Westview.

Trompenaars, F. (1985). *The organization of meaning and the meaning of organization: A comparative study of the conceptions of organizational structure in different cultures.* Unpublished doctoral dissertation, Wharton School of Management, University of Pennsylvannia, Philadelphia.

Tulviste, P. (1978). On the origins of theoretic syllogistic reasoning in culture and in the child. *Acta et Commentationes Universitatis Tartuensis, no. 474,* 3–22.

UNESCO (1991). *World Education Report.* Paris: UNESCO.

Van de Vijver, F. J. R., & Leung, K. (1997). Methods and data analysis of comparative research. In J. W. Berry, Y. H. Poortinga, & J. Pandey (Eds.), *Handbook of cross-cultural psychology. Vol. 1: Theory*

and method (pp. 257–300). Needham Heights, MA: Allyn and Bacon.

Wagner, D. A. (1981). Culture and memory development. In H. C. Triandis & A. Heron (Eds.), *Handbook of cross-cultural psychology: Vol. 4. Developmental psychology* (pp. 187–232). Boston: Allyn & Bacon.

Wassman, J., & Dasen, P. R. (1994). 'Hot' and 'Cold': Classification and sorting among the Yupno of Papua-New Guinea. *International Journal of Psychology, 29,* 19–38.

Whiting, B. B. (1976). The problem of the packaged variable. In K. Riegel & K. Meacham (Eds.), *The developing individual in a changing world* (vol. 1, pp. 303–309). The Hague: Mouton.

Whiting, J. W., & Child, I. (1953). *Child training and personality.* New Haven, CT: Yale University Press.

Yamaguchi, S. (1994). Collectivism among the Japanese: A perspective from the self. In U. Kim, H. C. Triandis, C. Kagitcibasi, S.-C. Choi, & G. Yoon (Eds.), *Individualism and collectivism: Theory, method, and applications* (pp. 175–178). Thousand Oaks, CA: Sage.

Yu, A.-B., & Yang, K.-S. (1994). The nature of achievement motivation in collectivistic societies. In U. Kim, H. C. Triandis, C. Kagitcibasi, S.-C. Choi, & G. Yoon (Eds.), *Individualism and collectivism: Theory, method, and applications* (pp. 239–250). Newbury Park, CA: Sage.

Communications concerning this chapter should be addressed to: Professor Cigdem Kagitcibasi, Psychology Department, Koc University, Cayir Cad. 5, 80860 Istinye, Istanbul, Turkey

19

Comparative-Evolutionary Psychology

MICHAEL C. CORBALLIS AND STEPHEN E.G. LEA

By the middle years of the twentieth century, the phrase 'comparative psychology' had come to be used to refer to any investigation of psychological processes, especially learning, in animals other than humans. Comparative psychology in its original sense, however, is concerned with comparisons of behavior and mental function across species, and this more accurate usage is now once again common. Sometimes, the aim of comparative psychology is simply to understand different species in their own right, and comparative psychologists can often provide practical information to people who keep animals or deal with them in the wild. Often, though, the aim is the more ambitious one of using comparisons between species in order to understand the evolution of psychological processes, and such use of the comparative method can properly be called 'evolutionary psychology' (Corballis & Lea, 1999). Most ambitious of all is the attempt to use comparative psychology to gain an understanding of our own, human, mental evolution, and the place of humans in relation to other species. The term evolutionary psychology is commonly restricted to this narrower sense, and in particular to the attempt to understand the contingencies that have shaped the modern human mind during the last stages of its emergence. A good deal of evolutionary psychology therefore makes little reference to other species; rather, through a process that has been dubbed 'reverse engineering', it seeks to explain the modern human mind in terms of adaptations that arose in the supposed 'hunter-gatherer' phase of hominid evolution, in the so-called 'environment of evolutionary adaptedness' of the human species.

A recurring question is whether there is a continuity of mental development between ourselves and other species, including our closest relatives, the great apes; or whether there is somehow a profound discontinuity, or dichotomy, that may even render comparative psychology largely irrelevant to understanding the human mind. The theologically inclined may see humans as closer to angels than to animals, and we are indeed often at pains to suppress the 'animal' side of our nature; moral systems often explicitly call on us to do so. But the idea of a fundamental discontinuity was given scientific and philosophical respectability by the seventeenth-century philosopher René Descartes.

19.1 A HISTORICAL PERSPECTIVE

Impressed with mechanical toys, popular at the time, Descartes asked the hypothetical question of whether it would be possible, at least in principle, to construct a mechanical replica of a human being. He concluded that it might be possible to construct a mechanical replica of an animal, even an ape, but that humans possessed a freedom of thought and action that defied explanation in mechanical terms. Religion did feature in Descartes' account, however, since he proposed that human thought must be governed, at least in part, by God-given nonmaterial forces operating through the pineal gland. He was especially impressed with the unbounded nature of language, enjoyed even by human imbeciles, but apparently unattainable by any other species. Language has continued to feature prominently in debates about continuity vs. discontinuity in human evolution, as we shall see below.

Although some of Descartes' contemporaries had supposed that humans might, after all, be just mechanical devices, it was not until Charles Darwin's theory of evolution in the mid-nineteenth century that the idea of a continuity between ourselves and other species gained prominence. Darwin himself was at first reluctant to spell out the implications for human evolution, but he evidently saw an important role for psychology, and in the first edition of *Origin of Species* he wrote:

> In the distant future I see open fields for far more important researches. Psychology will be based on a new foundation, that of the necessary acquirement of each mental power and capacity by gradation. Light will be thrown on the origin of man and his history. (Darwin, 1859, p. 488)

In later editions, he amended the second sentence of this passage to refer to 'the foundation already laid by Mr Herbert Spencer', a psychologist who had in many respects anticipated the theory of evolution.[1] It was Spencer, in fact, who coined the phrase 'survival of the fittest'. But despite this early promise, psychologists have until recently paid remarkably little attention to evolutionary theory. In his popular account of evolutionary psychology, Steven Pinker (1997) writes: 'The allergy to evolution in the social and cognitive sciences has been, I think, a barrier to understanding' (p. 23).

The first psychological laboratory was established in Leipzig in 1879 by Wilhelm Wundt, a dualist who owed more to Descartes than to Darwin, and sought to base psychology on subjects' introspective observations of their own minds – although he also carried out more objective experiments, including some on reaction time. Wundt's introspectionism was transported from Leipzig to Cornell University in the United States by an Englishman, Edward B. Titchener, and came to be known there as *Titchenerism*. These developments in mainstream psychology

did nothing to encourage a comparative approach, since by its very nature introspective psychology seems to preclude investigation of other animals.

Comparative Psychology

Perhaps not surprisingly, given Darwin's influence, comparative psychology was founded in England, and by biologists rather than psychologists. It was based on objective study rather than introspection, and much of the early interest lay in establishing a phylogenetic scale, a *scala naturae*, in which species might be ordered in terms of their intellectual prowess. In 1888, the British biologist George John Romanes published *Mental Evolution in Animals*, in which he identified some 50 levels of intellectual development, with only humans reaching the top. The next in line, apes and dogs, made it only to rung 28, followed closely by monkeys and elephants on rung 27.

In 1894, Conwy Lloyd Morgan published his *Introduction to Comparative Psychology*, which introduced his famous canon:

> In no case may we interpret an action as the outcome of a higher psychical activity, if it can be interpreted as the outcome of one which stands lower in the psychological scale. (p. 53; his italics)

Lloyd Morgan's canon has stood as a corrective to the common and perhaps wishful tendency to proclaim human-like intelligence in other animals, famously demonstrated in 1904 in the claim that a horse, known as 'Clever Hans', was capable of human-like thoughts and language ability. Its trainer, a retired schoolteacher called Wilhelm von Osten, had taught Clever Hans to answer questions by tapping out letters of the alphabet with a front hoof, with each letter represented by a different number of taps. In this manner, the animal was apparently able to answer quite sophisticated questions. The psychologist Oskar Pfungst demonstrated that van Osten, unknown even to himself, was giving subtle signals to the animal as to when to stop tapping, and so was himself generating the answers. Nevertheless, this celebrated case convinced a number of prominent scholars of the time that animals could think and even talk, if only instructed in the right way.

When Darwinian ideas began to infiltrate mainstream psychology itself, they led to the idea that thinking was governed by instincts as well as by learning, in humans as well as in nonhuman animals. The most influential of the 'instinct psychologists' was William McDougall, whose 1908 book *An Introduction to Social*

Psychology drew explicitly on Darwinian theory to develop a theory of the human mind that was based on the comparative method. McDougall systematically equated emotions and instinct, but eventually instinct psychology degenerated into the simple listing of instincts for different functions, and lacked explanatory power. The author of one text counted 1,594 instincts that had been attributed to animals and humans (Bernard, 1924).

It is not surprising, then, that instinct psychology succumbed to the relative parsimony of behaviorism, which was to dominate academic psychology, at least in North America, for most of the first half of the twentieth century (see Chapter 10). Even so, the father of behaviorism, John B. Watson, had begun his research career with the study of instinctive behaviors in the noddy and sooty terns in the Tortugas, and his first book, published in 1914, was entitled *Behavior: An Introduction to Comparative Psychology*. But the behaviorists gradually came to emphasize learning at the expense of instincts; in the *Psychological Abstracts*, entries under the term 'instinct' itself, relative to the terms 'drive', 'reinforcement', and 'motivation', dropped from 68% to 8% between 1927 and 1958 (Herrnstein, 1974). Ultimately, then, behaviorism did little to encourage comparative psychology or even evolutionary thinking. The aim was to discover common principles underlying the behavior of humans and other species, and not to dwell on differences between species that might reflect specific evolutionary adaptations.

The reluctance to pursue evolutionary theory in the early part of the twentieth century was not restricted to psychology, and it was not until the so-called 'modern synthesis' of the 1930s that evolutionary ideas returned to mainstream biology. They have been even slower to return to psychology. In the social sciences, Darwinian ideas had been tainted by the excesses of social Darwinism and the eugenics movement, promulgated by Darwin's cousin, Francis Galton, and others in the latter part of the nineteenth century. By the 1930s, this had led to sterilization laws for criminals and mental defectives in a number of countries, including Australia, Canada, Japan, Sweden, and many states in the US. Such practices, which persisted until quite recently in some countries, along with the rising threat of Nazism with its emphasis on racial purity, led to a revulsion toward social Darwinism. What Pinker (1997) calls the 'standard social science model' follows the cultural determinism of followers of Franz, such as Benedict (1935); it accounts for human behavior almost wholly in terms of culture rather than instinct, and regards culture as unpredictable in terms of geographical, economic, or ecological constraints.

Ethology

This is not to say the comparative method was totally eclipsed. Wolfgang Köhler's (1925) studies of insightful problem-solving in chimpanzees long anticipated much of the present-day work on cognitive processes in apes. Beginning in the 1930s the ethologists, who were based in zoology rather than psychology, continued to do work that largely complemented that of the behaviorists, documenting differences between species – although works such as Maier and Schneirla's (1935) classic *Principles of Animal Psychology* ensured at least some balance between learning and instinct as explanations for adaptive behaviors. In a long series of studies originating in the 1930s, Konrad Lorenz (1971) and Niko Tinbergen (1972) described a large number of instinctive behaviors, in a range of species, that seemed to owe little to conditioning or any other form of learning the comparative psychologists had studied. Activities like the following response of goslings, the egg fanning of sticklebacks, or the ways in which black-headed gulls remove egg shells, were regarded as adaptations selected because they increased reproductive success. Instinctive behaviors were often found to be dependent on innate releasing signals whose effectiveness did not depend on prior conditioning. Both authors stressed that the comparative approach was also essential to an understanding of human behavior, in marked contrast to the behaviorist notion that the mind of the human infant is a *tabula rasa*, merely awaiting the imprint of experience.

The notion that complex behavior might be purely instinctive was attacked by psychologists, such as Frank Beach (1955), who argued that it was not possible to separate instinct from learning. Nevertheless, by the 1950s, there was an increasing realization that a psychology based on a single species was unlikely to be wholly satisfactory, and it was again Beach (1965, p. 10) who asked, 'Are we building a general science of behavior or merely a science of rat learning?' Two behaviorists, Keller and Marian Breland, observed that even in experiments designed to measure pure operant conditioning, instinctive behaviors would intervene, a phenomenon they called 'instinctual drift'. They concluded their article, pertinently entitled 'The misbehavior of organisms', as follows:

> After 14 years of continuous conditioning and observing thousands of animals, it is our reluctant conclusion that the behavior of any species cannot be adequately understood, predicted, or controlled

without knowledge of its instinctive patterns, evolutionary history, and ecological niche. (Breland & Breland, 1961, p. 684)

Such observations led to modifications to the learning theory of the time, with the suggestion that evolution prepares animals to learn some things more easily than others, and that even classical conditioning is dependent on environmental contingencies, not only in the animal's experience, but in its evolutionary history as well. Nonetheless, the demonstration of such 'constraints on learning' only led to a limited impact of evolutionary theory, in part because of the confrontational nature of the interaction between the two approaches to animal behavior, in part because adaptationist arguments seemed to lead only to a fragmentation of comparative psychology – a hundred sciences of learning in a hundred species, rather than the general science of animal behavior Beach had called for.

The 'Cognitive Revolution'

The late 1950s saw another wind-change that had quite profound consequences for comparative and evolutionary psychology. Behaviorism lost its role as the dominant force in North American psychology, but not so much because of biological arguments as because of linguistic ones. In 1959, the linguist Noam Chomsky wrote a highly influential review of Skinner's (1957) book *Verbal Behavior*, an ambitious but doomed attempt to explain language in behavioristic terms. That review, along with Chomsky's other writings, was a powerful influence in persuading psychologists that language, arguably the most distinctive and sophisticated of human cognitive achievements, could not be explained in terms of associative learning. Rather, it depended on innately determined rules, better understood in terms of computation than in terms of learned connections. Chomsky's work, combined with the increasing sophistication of digital computers and the rise of artificial intelligence, brought about the so-called 'cognitive revolution' (see Chapter 10).

Chomsky argued not only that learning a language is inexplicable in terms of learning theory, but also that it is a uniquely human accomplishment, innately given. But Chomsky only took to an extreme a tendency that was widely evident in the information-processing models of cognition that emerged from the late 1950s. Such approaches had little use for evidence from species other than humans, and offered little by way of explanation for the behavior of nonhuman animals. No less than the rat-dominated learning theory that Beach deplored, they seemed to lead to a one-species

psychology, albeit with a choice of species that is more easily defended.

Actually, the cognitive revolution on animal psychology was not quite so totally at variance with conclusions from animal psychology as some of the new breed of cognitivists may have thought. Although an avowed behaviorist, Edward C. Tolman had long recognized the importance of cognitive concepts to the understanding of animal behavior. His classic work *Purposive Behavior in Animals and Men*, published in 1932, established a tradition known variously as purposive behaviorism, sign-gestalt theory, or expectancy theory. Tolman's work was influential from the 1930s into the 1950s, and he is still widely acknowledged for his view that spatial learning is governed by the establishment of cognitive maps, and not by stimulus–response learning. But it was not until after some years of elaboration of the new human cognitive psychology that some animal psychologists sought to explicitly reconcile cognitive insights with investigations of animal learning, leading to a new discipline of 'animal cognition'. This concept has been construed in two rather different ways. On the one hand, in the past three decades a huge volume of research has been devoted to fundamental processes of Pavlovian conditioning, and associative learning generally. Many leading researchers now believe that the resulting data can only be explained with the aid of cognitive concepts like representation. This approach leads to a bottom-up science of animal cognition, in which behavioral methods are rigorously applied, and cognitive conclusions drawn almost as a last resort, strictly in the spirit of Lloyd Morgan. Alternatively, the insights and concepts of cognitive psychology can be applied more directly to animal behavior, to see whether parallel analyses will prove fruitful. Whichever approach is taken, the very phrase 'animal cognition' is itself a quiet reassertion of Darwinian continuity at the mental level. But other comparative psychologists rose more directly to the challenge, and mounted an empirical assault on Chomsky's assertions about the uniqueness of language and the fundamental discontinuity it creates between humans and all other species.

19.2 Continuity versus Discontinuity in Human Evolution

As we have seen, mainstream psychology has swung sharply from one extreme to the other with respect to the question of whether humans are fundamentally different from other animals. It began with Wundt's Cartesian assumptions, swung to extreme continuity with Watson's behaviorism, then swung back to Cartesian discontinuity with the cognitive revolution. It is not surprising, then, that this issue should continue to loom large in modern comparative psychology, and especially in the study of the great apes – the species evolutionarily closest to our own.

Despite the assertions of Chomsky and his followers that there is a fundamental dichotomy between humans and all other animals, at least with respect to language, biochemical analyses have revealed an unexpectedly close genetic kinship between humans and the other great apes. By one estimate, the chimpanzee has about 99.6% of its amino acid sequences and 98.4% of its DNA nucleotide sequences in common with our own species (Goodman, 1992). Until as recently as the 1960s, it was supposed that the common ancestor of human and chimpanzee dated from some 20 million years ago, allowing plenty of time for physical and mental divergence. That estimate was revised in 1967, on the basis of biochemical evidence, to a mere five or six million years ago (Sarich & Wilson, 1967) – an estimate that has held in subsequent investigations.

These findings have led to renewed efforts to demonstrate human-like mental processes in the great apes, and have even led some to argue that the most important discontinuity lies, not between ourselves and the great apes, but between the great apes and the other primates (e.g., Byrne, 1995). Not surprisingly, much of the research effort has focused on language.

Teaching Language to Apes

At first, the battle seemed lost, as attempts to teach chimpanzees to actually talk have never been even remotely successful. For example, Catherine and Keith Hayes (Hayes, 1952) raised a chimpanzee called Viki from the age of three days until about six and a half years in their own home, treating her as one of their own children, but Viki never learned to speak more than three or four crudely articulated words. However, Viki's failure to talk might have been due to deficiencies of the vocal tract rather than to the lack of any capacity for language, and greater success was later achieved in teaching a form of manual sign language, not only to chimpanzees, but to other great apes as well. Chimpanzees have also proven fairly adept at using plastic tokens (lexigrams) to represent objects and actions, and to compose simple requests. The most impressive achievements appear to be those of a young bonobo, or pygmy chimpanzee (*Pan paniscus*), named Kanzi, who has learned to use gestures and lexigrams spontaneously while watching his mother being taught. Most of his productions, it is claimed, are not random sequences or meaningless repetitions, but are spontaneous comments, requests, or announcements. Kanzi even appears to have an understanding of spoken human language, with at least some regard to grammatical structure, at about the level of a two-year-old child (Savage-Rumbaugh & Lewin, 1994).

But even the work on gestures and tokens has not been universally accepted as demonstrating true language. Herbert Terrace (1979) analyzed the utterances of a trained chimpanzee, optimistically named Nim Chimpsky, and observed that they consist mainly of repetitions and simple sequencing of ideas. By and large, linguists and cognitive psychologists have remained unconvinced even by the exploits of Kanzi. For example, Pinker (1994) remarks that the chimpanzees, Kanzi included, 'just don't "get it" ' (p. 340). What Pinker and others argue is that all attempts to teach language to chimpanzees, or any other species, have so far produced nothing resembling *grammar*, considered the hallmark of human language.

This is not to say that chimpanzees are incapable of communication, or even symbolic representation. Derek Bickerton (1995), for example, concedes what he calls 'protolanguage' to chimpanzees, suggesting that this is a precursor to true language that is shared by two-year-old children, people with language impairment due to brain damage, and speakers of pidgins. Bickerton also argues that true language must have evolved in all-or-none fashion very recently in our evolutionary history: '. . . true language, via the emergence of syntax, was a catastrophic event, occurring within the first few generations of the species *Homo sapiens sapiens*' (p. 69).

Another to argue that language evolved late is Philip Lieberman (1991), who has claimed that the production of speech was not possible until the larynx descended in the neck, and that this adaptation, as well as concomitant changes in the brain mechanisms involved in producing speech, occurred only recently in human evolution, and perhaps only with the emergence of *H. sapiens*. According to Lieberman, even the Neanderthals of 30,000 years ago would have suffered gross speech deficits that not only kept them apart from anatomically modern humans, but led to their eventual extinction. The Neanderthals are generally considered a species distinct from *H. sapiens*, but the divergence probably took place within the past 500,000 years, suggesting that the adaptation of the vocal tract in *H. sapiens* was recent. This analysis is supported by recent evidence that the facial structure of *H. sapiens* might have been uniquely adapted to speech (D. Lieberman, 1998).

Some have argued, however, that language may have evolved, not from vocalization, but from manual gestures (e.g., Armstrong, Stokoe, & Wilcox, 1995; Corballis, 1991). As Terence Deacon (1997) points out, voluntary control over action depends on a shift from midbrain to cortical control, and in primates voluntary control over the limbs greatly exceeds that over vocalization. This could explain why apes would learn a form of sign language much more successfully than they learn anything resembling speech, even taking into account the difficulties posed by their vocal tract anatomy. The distinctive bipedal form of locomotion among even the earliest-known hominids would have freed the hands for further development of manual activity, not only for carrying things, but also for the potential development of gestural communication. There is little doubt that the sign languages of the deaf are true languages, with fully developed syntax, confirming that gesture is as much a 'natural' medium for language as is vocalization (Armstrong et al., 1995). The 'catastrophic event' that led to the dominance over *H. sapiens* over other hominid species may not have been the emergence of syntax, as Bickerton proposed, but rather the switch from a system based predominantly on manual gesture to one based on vocalization (Corballis, 1991).

Theory of Mind in Apes?

In spite of the historical prominence of language in the continuity–discontinuity debate, many primate researchers have shifted their interest from the study of language to the study of other cognitive processes. A leader in this endeavor is the one-time behaviorist, David Premack, who gave up his attempts to teach language to the chimpanzee and turned to other questions about primate cognition, such as whether or not a chimpanzee can be said to possess a 'theory of mind' (Premack & Woodruff, 1978). In some respects, questions about theory of mind resemble those about language. For example, both appear to depend on recursion. Theory of mind depends on mental propositions such as 'I know that she can see me', or 'I know that he knows that I can see her', and the phrase structure of language lends itself precisely to the expression of these kinds of embedded thoughts.

Richard W. Byrne (1995) has argued that theory of mind is in fact a necessary precursor to language. In a detailed examination of such behaviors as tactical deception and mirror self-recognition, he concludes that the great apes do indeed demonstrate evidence of theory of mind,

if not of language itself, but that other primates do not. It is for this reason that Byrne suggests that it was the emergence of the great apes, and not specifically of our hominid ancestors, that created a discontinuity in mental evolution. Unsurprisingly, Byrne's conclusions are controversial, even among comparative psychologists; for example, they have been challenged by the psychologist Celia Heyes (1998), who suggests that behaviors attributed to theory of mind can be explained in terms of learned associations.

Brain Size

In addressing the issue of continuity vs. discontinuity, some investigators have appealed to brain anatomy. It is often supposed that mental capacity might increase simply as a function of the overall size of the brain. Table 1 shows the cranial volumes of the primates, and it is clear that there is a general increase from monkeys through the lesser apes (Hylobates) to the great apes (orangutans, gorillas, and chimpanzee), and a massive increase to humans. This might seem to support the idea that any discontinuity of mental function does indeed lie between humans and the other great apes. But although humans are at the top, it may nevertheless be misleading

Table 19.1 *Cranial capacities and body weights for extant primates and for hominids*

Genus or species	Cranial capacity (cm³)	Body weight (g)
Microcebus	2	60
Phaner	7	440
Lemur	23	1,669
Samiri	24	914
Talapoin	39	1,250
Vervet	63	3,605
Cebus	76	2,437
Macaca	83	4,600
Hylobates (gibbon)	100	5,442
Pan (chimpanzee)	393	45,290
Pongo (orangutan)	418	55,000
Gorilla	465	114,450
Australopithecus afarensis	433	44,600
Australopithecus africanus	445	40,800
Australopithecus aethiopicus	410	unknown
Paranthropus boisei	487	48,600
Paranthropus robustus	530	40,200
Homo rudolfensis	781	60,000
Homo habilis	612	51,600
Homo erectus/ergaster	988	63,000
Homo neanderthalensis	1,520	71,000
Homo sapiens	1,409	65,000

Source: Beran, Gibson, and Rumbaugh (1999).

to suppose that brain size is directly proportional to intelligence. For example, the chimpanzee is generally thought to be the most intelligent of the great apes (humans excluded), but in terms of brain size comes well behind the other two great apes, the gorilla and the orangutan. Moreover, male brains tend to be larger than female ones, especially in orangutans, gorillas, and humans, yet there is no evidence for a corresponding difference in intelligence.

It has long been observed, however, that brain size depends, at least in part, on body size. In 1891, Otto Snell showed that, across different species of mammals, the logarithm of brain weight was positively and linearly related to the logarithm of body weight, with a slope of 2/3. Harry Jerison (1973) has therefore argued that, in assessing the relation between intelligence and brain size, it is necessary first to compensate for differences in body size. Following the earlier work of Eugene Dubois (1913), he proposed that the way to do this is to compute the empirical relation between brain size and body size across different species, and then express the actual brain size of a given species as a ratio of the predicted brain size. He called this the *encephalization quotient* (EQ). Based on comparative studies of the EQ, Passingham (1982) concluded that the human brain is about three times the size one would expect for a primate of our build, which he regards as 'perhaps the single most important fact about mankind' (p. 78). The EQ also restores the relatively small-bodied chimpanzee to its accustomed place next to humans, although the gap between humans and chimpanzees is considerably larger than that between chimpanzees and gorillas.

Even so, the EQ may still be a crude measure of mental capacity since it does not differentiate one part of the brain from another. In particular, the neocortex is presumably especially important in intellectual function, and Dunbar (1993) has suggested that what he calls the *neocortex ratio*, which is the ratio of the volume of neocortex to the volume of the rest of the brain, might be more indicative of mental capacity. He has shown that there is a positive relation among monkeys and primates between the neocortex ratio and the size of the social group that the animals form, suggesting that cognitive capacity establishes an upper limit to the number of individuals with which the animal can maintain personal relationships. Byrne (1995) has further shown a linear relation in primates between the neocortex ratio and the estimated prevalence of tactical deception. In humans, the ratio is 4.1:1, which is about 30% larger than that of any other primate. While this still places humans at the top of the intellectual tree, it is more suggestive

of continuity than are measures based on total brain size.

But even within the nonhuman primates, there are reasons to doubt that the neocortex ratio is an altogether adequate measure of mental capacity. For instance, it is as large in the baboon as it is in the gorilla, yet the gorilla shows much more evidence of insightful behavior. It is clear, too, that group size is not the only determinant of the neocortex ratio, since the great apes do not live in larger groups than monkeys do, and indeed the orangutan is notably solitary – although this may have been a recent adaptation. Byrne therefore suggests that while an enlarged neocortex ratio may have been selected for by social pressures, it may also reflect intelligent behavior in nonsocial contexts, such as the insightful solving of the mechanical problems posed by food-processing; this might explain why great apes are capable of insight in abstract tasks (Köhler, 1925). Indeed, one might expect actual computational power to be dependent to some extent on actual brain size, uncorrected for body size.

As Table 1 shows, the brains of the early hominids did not differ substantially from those of modern apes. For example, the absolute size of the australopithecine brain was about the same as that of the chimpanzee, although it was somewhat larger relative to body size. A significant increase in brain size did not emerge until some 2.5 million years ago, with the emergence of the hominids we place in the genus *Homo*. Again, though, interpretation of these data is complicated by differences in body size. For example, although absolute brain size increased dramatically over the successive stages from early *Homo* through to *H. sapiens*, it has been estimated that when body size is taken into account there was virtually no increase in brain size over nearly two million years of evolution in *Homo*, but then a dramatic increase from about 600,000 to 150,000 years ago. Although the Neanderthals appear to have had bigger brains than modern humans, they also had larger bodies, perhaps by as much as 24%, so that the modern human brain is slightly larger the Neanderthal brain relative to body size. There has also been a reduction in both brain and body size over the past 50,000 years.

Development of Specific Brain Regions

To understand the evolution of intelligence, Holloway (1996) argues that we should also consider specific areas of the brain relative to others. For example, the ability to 'think' independently of the immediate sensory input probably depends more on the so-called association areas of the brain than on sensory or motor areas. One such area is contained within the parietal lobe, which is concerned with spatial relations among objects. In humans, the left parietal cortex also includes part of Wernicke's area, which is critically involved in the perception and comprehension of language. The human parietal lobe is also enlarged relative to the occipital lobe, and even at the expense of it; according to Holloway (1996), the visual striate cortex in humans is only about 45% of the size one would expect in a primate with the same overall brain size. Holloway also claims that this trend had already begun in the australopithecines, but this has been challenged by Falk (1985).

Another critical association area is contained within the frontal lobe, which is greatly enlarged in the human brain relative to that in apes (Deacon, 1997). There is evidence that an endocast of the skull of *Homo rudolfensis*, the earliest-known species of *Homo*, dating from over 2 million years ago, has a human-like rather than an ape-like third frontal convolution, which is the area containing an important speech area (Broca's area) in modern humans. On this basis, Tobias (1987) argued that *H. rudolfensis* (then called *H. habilis*), had invented at least rudimentary language. This further suggests that the increase in brain size and the relative growth of association areas were driven at least in part by pressure for more effective communication, and began with the split of *Homo* from the australopithecines perhaps 2.5 million years ago. But it may have been the development of the prefrontal cortex, rather than Broca's area alone, that was critical in the evolution of the hominid mind. Deacon (1997) estimates that the human prefrontal cortex is about twice the size that would be predicted in an ape with a brain as large as a human's, and is probably the most divergently enlarged of any brain region. He argues that the development of the prefrontal cortex underlies the emergence of symbolic thinking that is unique to our species.

Cerebral Asymmetry

Another aspect of brain evolution is cerebral asymmetry; most humans are right-handed and left-cerebrally dominant for language. Since these asymmetries seem to be associated with the distinctively human attributes of toolmaking and language, respectively, it has long been supposed that they are themselves uniquely human, and further evidence of a discontinuity between humans and apes (e.g., Corballis, 1991). The idea of asymmetry as uniquely human has been somewhat eroded over the past decade. Hopkins (1996) has documented evidence of

a population bias toward right-handedness in chimpanzees (and to a lesser extent in other great apes), although McGrew and Marchant (1997) sound a note of caution. In an exhaustive meta-analysis that includes Hopkins's work, they conclude that of all the nonhuman primates studied, 'only chimpanzees show signs of a population-level bias . . . to the right, but only in captivity and only incompletely' (p. 201).

On the basis of a review of cerebral asymmetries in other primates, Bradshaw and Rogers (1993) argue for continuity between other animals and humans, although it is still possible to argue that the pattern and strength of lateral asymmetries sets humans apart. Summarizing work on anatomical asymmetries of the brain, for example, Holloway (1996) remarks that 'while asymmetries certainly exist in pongids, neither the pattern nor direction is anywhere near as strong as in Homo' (p. 94). However, it has recently been reported that the temporal planum, an important language-mediating area in humans, is larger on the left than on the right in 17 out of 18 chimpanzees examined post-mortem (Gannon, Holloway, Broadfield, & Braun, 1998).

19.3 THE IMPACT OF SOCIOBIOLOGY

As we have seen, evolutionary ideas were somewhat suppressed for much of the early part of the twentieth century, especially within the social sciences. An important influence in their revival was the publication of Edward O. Wilson's (1975) textbook and manifesto, *Sociobiology*. Taking his cue from the so-called 'modern synthesis' of the 1930s, Wilson claimed to be producing the 'new synthesis' of population genetics, behavioral ecology, and ethology. His book was widely publicized and was swiftly followed by effective popularizations, such as Richard Dawkins' (1976) *The Selfish Gene*. Suddenly, evolutionary theory was being applied to behavior in a wholly different way; sociobiology offered a new, or renewed, 'grand theory', able to generate hypotheses about a huge range of animal and, as later emerged, human behaviors.

An important precursor to Wilson's book, but somewhat neglected at the time, was George Williams' (1966) *Adaptation and Natural Selection*, which presented arguments against the idea that group selection plays a significant role in evolution. For example, behaviors that could be construed as altruistic, in which individuals act in apparently selfless ways for the good of the group, could actually be interpreted in terms of individual benefit in the longer term – virtue, in other words, could bring its own rewards. The point was elaborated by Robert Trivers (1971) with his concept of reciprocal altruism, in which a selfless act might be selected because it leads to probable reciprocation, to the ultimate benefit of both parties. Even cases of extreme altruism, in which individuals put their own lives at risk, might be interpreted in terms of the enhanced survival of the individuals' genes. In two classic papers, W. D. Hamilton (1964) argued that an altruistic trait would be adaptive if the disadvantage to the individual were outweighed by the product of the benefactor's degree of genetic relationship and the amount of benefit conferred. Hamilton's rule, as it has come to be called, is a more formal statement of a remark attributed to the British biologist J. B. S. Haldane, who is said to have declared that he would not put his life at risk for another person, but he would do so for two brothers or eight cousins, since they would equal, in total, his own genetic endowment.

But sociobiology was not universally welcomed, especially among social scientists, as it was directly antagonistic to the standard social science model, and Wilson (1975) even threatened that the biologists would take over:

> . . . sociology and the other social sciences, as well as the humanities, are the last branches of biology waiting to be included in the modern synthesis. (p. 4)

To compound the threat, Wilson argued for a reductionist approach, based on neurobiology rather than on the traditional methods of the social sciences:

> . . . having cannibalized psychology, the new neurobiology will yield an enduring set of first principles for sociology. (p. 75)

Behavioral Ecology

Not surprisingly, then, the earliest impact of sociobiology was in biology, with the emergence of a subdiscipline dubbed *behavioral ecology*, marked by the first edition of Krebs and Davies' (1987) edited volume under that title. Behavioral ecology applied the powerful and general optimizing ideas of sociobiology at a more detailed level. Unlike the earlier ethologists, however, behavioral ecologists were interested in the adaptive significance of learning as well as instincts; learning about prey densities, for example, was an essential feature of the 'optimal foraging' models that were at the core of behavioral ecology. Furthermore, the behavioral ecologists recognized the importance of what was already known, within comparative psychology, about animal learning, and this interaction was much more fruitful than the earlier study of

constraints on learning had been (Lea, 1985). For example, the so-called 'matching law', originally formulated in the context of operant conditioning, was adapted to a wide variety of species in foraging situations. Attempts to extend this to human choice, however, have been less successful; despite promising early results, in most situations human choice behavior has been found to be extensively modified, relative to animal choice, by human linguistic abilities (see Horne & Lowe, 1993).

Two further examples of the benefits of an ecological approach are especially revealing because they bear on capacities that are often considered uniquely human, but can in fact be studied within a broader comparative framework. One is birdsong, and the other is spatial memory.

Comparative Studies of Birdsong

Twenty of the 23 orders of birds inherit their calls, and develop their species-specific vocalizations even if they are raised in isolation and never hear another bird. The three exceptional orders are the perching birds (*Passeriformes*) – which include obvious songbirds such as canaries, but also mockingbirds and crows – the hummingbirds (*Trochiliformes*), and the parrots (*Psittaciformes*). In these orders, the song the bird sings depends on vocal learning, giving rise to a greater variety of song dialects. This variety is important for attracting mates and defending territory, and is in these respects necessary for reproduction and survival. The added plasticity conferred by learning gives rise to a greater diversity of specialization, and this in turn has led to a greater variety of species; the three orders of birds that learn their songs include more species than are included in the remaining 20 orders together.[2]

A phylogenetic tree of all of the species of birds shows that the three orders of birds that learn their songs are not closely related, suggesting that unlearned song is the primitive condition, and that the capacity to learn songs evolved independently in these three orders. This is known as convergent evolution. In canaries, the learning of song depends on a network of interconnected nuclei, which contain receptors for gonadal sex hormones, in the forebrain of the male bird. Similar hormone-sensitive systems have been found in many other species of songbirds, and the size of the song-control centers appears to be correlated with the variety of songs each species can acquire (DeVoogd, Krebs, Healy, & Purvis, 1993). This appears to be a product of natural selection, since the number of surviving offspring in a population of birds studied over several years was correlated with the size of the fathers' song repertoires, and so with the size of the forebrain centers (Hasselquist, Bensch, & Vonschantz, 1996).

The acquisition of song in birds has parallels with the acquisition of speech in humans; it can be sequentially complex, it depends on a critical period in development, there are variations in dialect, and in some (but not all) species of songbird it depends on asymmetric structures – the syrinx (which produces the actual sound) is innervated by the left hypoglossal nerve (Nottebohm, 1977). This need not imply, however, that there is an asymmetry in the higher centers controlling song; in at least one species, the brown thrasher, the asymmetry is at the level of muscles that gate the production of sound, implying that the lateralization of birdsong may not always be a useful model for the asymmetrical control of speech in humans (Goller & Suthers, 1995). Moreover, in birds it is only the males that sing. Even so, the independent evolution of complex communication systems, endowed with plasticity as well as a strong innate component, goes some way toward countering the idea that human language is unique.

Spatial Memory in Birds

Many animals, including mammals and birds, demonstrate considerable ability to remember specific locations, in homing and migration, foraging for specific foodstuffs, and in recovering stored food. Some of the more dramatic examples are birds that store food in caches, and later return to the caches during the winter so that they can recover enough food to enable them to survive until the spring.

In one representative study, Balda and Kamil (1989) compared cache recovery in three species of crow that are found in the forests of the southwestern United States. One species, Clark's nutcrackers, live in high-altitude forests, and store up to 33,000 pine seeds for the winter, and finding them again is critical to their survival. Another species, the pinyon jay, is found at lower altitudes where the winter climate is less severe, so that later recovery is not quite so critical. These birds store only about 20,000 seeds, but stored seeds still make up about 70 to 90% of their winter diet. A third species, the scrub jay, lives at still lower altitudes, and requires less than 60% of the cache of about 6,000 seeds that they store. Members of each species were tested in a laboratory setting in which they hid seeds in a room containing 180 holes for caching seeds. They were tested for recovery of the cached seeds after a retention interval of seven days. The nutcracker and pinyon jays were significantly more accurate at

retrieving the seeds than the scrub jays, suggesting that the different ecological niches had selected for different memory abilities. Despite being less dependent on cache recovery in their natural environment, however, the pinyon jays were rather surprisingly better than the nutcrackers, perhaps because they adopted a strategy of placing their caches close together.

Although scrub jays showed relatively poor memory, a more recent study suggests that they are able to code stored caches for the *time* at which they were stored. In a laboratory setting, the birds stored wax worms and peanuts. When retrieving the food, they preferred the wax worms if they had been recently stored and were therefore still fresh, but they preferred peanuts if the wax worms had been stored long enough to lose their freshness (Clayton & Dickinson, 1998). This result is of special interest, since the ability to encode stored information for both location and time meets two of the criteria for episodic memory, a form of memory that some have claimed to be uniquely human.

It is also of interest that there is a positive correlation between the amount of storing and the size of the hippocampus, a brain structure often identified, after Tolman, as a cognitive map (O'Keefe & Nadel, 1978). Reviewing the literature on the correlation in corvids (including jays and nutcrackers) and in parids (including chickadees and titmice), Rosenzweig, Leiman, and Breedlove (1999) conclude that 'even within closely related species, reliance on storing and recovering food appears to have been a selective pressure that has led to larger hippocampal size' (p. 141). Again this raises a question, albeit obliquely, about human uniqueness, since the hippocampus in humans has been associated with episodic memory.

Human Behavioral Ecology

In his 1975 book, Wilson devoted only a closing chapter to humans; and even when he turned to analyze human behavior specifically (Wilson, 1978), his theorizing was essentially speculative, and reminiscent of the earlier instinct psychology. For the most part it consisted of listing aspects of human behaviors, such as aggression, incest avoidance, religion, and so forth, and of arguing that they represented genetically determined predispositions that had led to increased reproductive success.

These ideas eventually led to the new discipline of human behavioral ecology, which has been defined as 'the study of the evolutionary ecology of human behavior. Its central problem is to discover the ways in which the behavior of modern humans reflects our species' natural selection' (Cronk, 1991, p. 25). Human behavioral ecology has relatively little connection with the wider discipline of behavioral ecology, discussed earlier, although some studies make direct use of the kinds of optimizing theory that were developed for the analysis of animal foraging (e.g., Winterhalder & Smith, 1981). Human behavioral ecologists are typically affiliated with anthropology rather than biology or psychology. Their general approach is to study contemporary human societies, with a focus on non-industrial societies and the few remaining hunter-gatherer societies, and to view behavior in terms of its role in maximizing reproductive success. But human behavioral ecologists also emphasize the plasticity of human behavior, and its adaptability to very different ecological and social circumstances. This adaptability is seen as dependent on the emergence of consciousness. This is not to say that the drive to increase reproductive fitness is itself conscious, but rather that it is consciousness that gives humans the unique ability to adapt to a wide variety of different contexts.

An example of this adaptability comes from Borgerhoff-Mulder's (1996) study of studies of bride-wealth payments among the Kipsigis of rural Kenya. Under conditions of plenty, when it was possible to support large families, bride-wealth payments from men reflected physical signs of fertility in the prospective brides, such as early menarche. When economic changes made large families insupportable, the preference for high fertility became unimportant, and this was reflected in reduced payments. Similarly, Crook and Crook (1988), in their study of polyandry in Tibet, have argued that polyandry is an adaptive response to low levels of subsistence and the lack of opportunity for expansion and dispersal. Such ecological arguments flow smoothly into more strictly sociobiological discussions, such as Symons' (1979) analysis of human sexuality, or Daly and Wilson's (1988) analysis of different kinds of human killing. Such modern human sociobiology differs from Wilson's original speculations by its extensive use of social statistics, but its focus on modern humans means that it lacks comparative perspective.

Evolutionary Psychology

Another development that grew out of sociobiology was evolutionary psychology, and those who identify with this movement are typically affiliated with psychology rather than anthropology. Its manifesto is the edited volume *The Adapted Mind* (Barkow, Cosmides, & Tooby, 1995), but it has reached a wider public through Steven Pinker's (1997) book *How the Mind Works*. Unlike human behavioral ecology, which stresses behavior, evolutionary psychology emphasizes the way in which the human mind has been structured by natural selection. The mind is assumed to be computational, and to comprise a number of distinct computational mechanisms, known as *adaptive specializations*, rather than as a general-purpose computational device. In these respects, evolutionary psychology owes much to the computational approach earlier adopted by David Marr (1982) in his study of vision, and by Fodor (1983) in his claim that the mind is best understood as comprised of independent, dedicated modules (Tooby & Cosmides, 1995).

The aim of the evolutionary psychology program, then, is to discover what the evolutionary specializations might be – to 'carve the mind at the joints' – and then to 'reverse engineer' these adaptations to the early environment that shaped them (Pinker, 1997). Although some aspects of the human mind, such as our capacity for visual processing, were largely formed during our pre-hominid primate ancestry, evolutionary psychologists lay particular stress on the Pleistocene – the period from about 1.6 million to about 10,000 years ago – as being especially critical to most of the distinctive aspects of the human mind. In the pre-agricultural world of the Pleistocene, our hominid forebears are thought to have existed primarily as hunter-gatherers, and for most of the Pleistocene they are thought to have lived on the African savanna (the earliest migration of *H. sapiens* out of Africa is thought to have occurred between about 60,000 and 100,000 years ago). A good deal of reverse engineering therefore has to do with how present-day dispositions might relate to conditions on the savanna. It has been proposed, for example, that we like to eat potato chips because fatty foods were scarce but nutritionally valuable during the Pleistocene; we like landscapes with trees because trees provided shade and escape from dangerous carnivores on the African savanna; our love of flowers derives from their distinctiveness as markers for edible fruit, nuts, or tubers amid the greenery of the savanna; and so on (Pinker, 1997). But there are no fossils to document the origins of these preferences, so these attempts at reverse engineering are almost entirely speculative.

A somewhat more rigorous example of reverse engineering is based on a reasoning task, known as the Wason selection task, in which people are shown cards with symbols on them. For example, they might be shown cards with *E*, *K*, *2*, and *7* showing, and asked which two cards they should turn over to check the truth of the following claim: 'If a card has a vowel on one side, then it has an even number on the other side.' In general, people perform poorly on this task; they typically turn over the cards with the *E* and the *2*, whereas the rational strategy is to turn over the cards with the *E* and the *7* (since turning over the *2* cannot disconfirm the statement, whereas turning over the *7* can). However, they are much more accurate on exactly analogous tasks that refer to social settings. For example, the cards might refer to beverages on one side and ages on the other, and the subject might be shown cards bearing the labels *beer*, *coke*, *22*, and *17*. If asked which two cards to turn over to check the truth of the statement: 'If a person is drinking beer, he or she must be over 20 years old', most people easily understand that the critical cards are those bearing the labels *beer* and *17*, as any under-age drinker will clearly understand (Cox and Griggs, 1982).

Tooby and Cosmides (1989) infer from this that reasoning of this sort does not depend on a general-purpose reasoning device, but applies specifically to situations involving social contracts. In particular, people are especially adept at strategies for detecting cheaters, such as the under-age drinker or the spouse who takes a lover. In short, there is a *cheater-detection module.* It is not quite obvious why such a module should give people an equal facility in deciding what type of stamp to put on a letter, as demonstrated in another experiment on the Wason task (Wason & Shapiro, 1971). And there remains a general problem. Experiments in evolutionary psychology are necessarily carried out with present-day human subjects, albeit sometimes in different cultural settings, and the evolutionary component has to be derived from a purely conceptual process of reverse engineering to what is known (or guessed) about social pressures operating during the Pleistocene.

A fertile ground for evolutionary psychology is that of differences between men and women in sexual strategies. It appears to be a fairly general rule across species that the sex that invests more in offspring should be the more selective in the choice of mates, and that the sex that invests less should compete more vigorously for access to mates. Buss and Schmitt (1993) find evidence across cultures that human females and males, respectively, exhibit behaviors and preferences that conform to these expectations, which can be derived from evolutionary principles. They also list other ways in which the optimal strategies for ensuring perpetuation of their genes are differently constrained in men and women.

One limitation of evolutionary psychology is its emphasis on the Pleistocene. Toward the end of the Pleistocene, from about 13,000 years ago, the human condition began to change quite radically, beginning with the domestication of wild plants and animals in the Near East. Although a few hunter-gatherer societies remain today, human societies gradually began to assume different and varied characteristics, culminating in the extraordinary cultural diversity that we see in the world today. Evolutionary psychologists have insisted that cultural differences are too recent to have a significant effect on our biological make-up, but it cannot be denied that culture nevertheless has an important impact on what we believe, how we interpret the world, and how we behave in different social settings. In stressing our common biological heritage at the expense of this cultural diversity, evolutionary psychology is often in conflict with recent traditions of postmodernism and cultural relativism in psychology and the social sciences (Pinker, 1997).

But perhaps the more important difficulty faced by evolutionary psychology is that it relies heavily on reverse engineering to a period in our prehistory about which rather little is known. If it is to progress, it will need to escape from the trap of relatively unconstrained speculation. The most obvious way of doing so is for it to rediscover its roots in a broader, comparative psychology. The key question in the evolutionary psychology of cognition is always, 'What kind of selection pressure could have produced this kind of cognitive ability?' A thoroughgoing comparative analysis allows one to ask that question, not just in a speculative way about modern humans, or in a tentative way about the very limited evidence we can find for the behavior of our hominid ancestors, but in a truly empirical, even experimental way, because we can ask it about thousands of other, extant, species. To do so of course requires us to admit that the modules of the human mind may have analogues, or even homologues, elsewhere in the animal kingdom. Such an admission should not be difficult for an evolutionary psychologist, necessarily placed on the side of Darwinian continuity, against Cartesian dualism. Oddly enough, however, it does not involve a denial of human uniqueness. To concede that some modules of the human mind may be found in other species leaves open the possibility that others (most obviously, the language module) may be unique. But even without that possibility, the most dedicated Darwinian can allow that the human mind must represent, at a minimum, a unique configuration of modules, allowing properties to emerge that cannot be paralleled in other species.

NOTES

1. In his 1855 book *The Principles of Psychology*, Spencer wrote: 'It must suffice to enunciate the belief that Life under all its forms has arisen by a progressive, unbroken evolution. . . . Save for those who still adhere to the Hebrew myth, or to the doctrines of special creation derived from it, there is no alternative but this hypothesis or no hypothesis.' (p. 578)

2. That learning should result in an increased number of species may sound Lamarckian, but probably depends on so-called 'Baldwinian evolution', first described by the American psychologist James Mark Baldwin (1895). Behavioral flexibility allows organisms to move into new ecological niches, where the selection pressures differ from those operating on their ancestors. Thus learning does not result in characteristics acquired during the organism's lifetime being passed on, as Lamarck would have it, but alters the selection pressures on future generations. Baldwinian evolution therefore does not contradict Darwinian principles of evolution by natural selection.

RESOURCE REFERENCES

Barkow, J. H., Cosmides, L., & Tooby, J. (Eds.). (1995). *The adapted mind*. New York: Oxford University Press.

Byrne, R. W. (1995). *The thinking ape: Evolutionary origins of intelligence*. Oxford: Oxford University Press.

Corballis, M. C., and Lea, S. E. G. (Eds.). (1999). *The descent of mind*. Oxford: Oxford University Press.

Deacon, T. (1997). *The symbolic species*. Harmondsworth, England: Allen Lane, Penguin Press.

Krebs, J. R., & Davies, N. B. (Eds.). (1987). *Behavioral ecology: An evolutionary approach* (4th ed.). Cambridge, MA: Blackwell Science.

Pinker, S. (1997). *How the mind works*. Harmondsworth, England: Allen Lane, Penguin Press.

Rosenzweig, M. R., Leiman, A. L., & Breedlove, M. S. (1999). *Biological psychology: An introduction to behavioral, cognitive, and clinical neuroscience* (2nd ed.). Sunderland, MA: Sinauer Associates.

Vauclair, J. (1996). *Animal cognition*. Cambridge, MA: Harvard University Press.

Wilson, E. O. (1975). *Sociobiology: The new synthesis*. Cambridge, MA: Harvard University Press.

ADDITIONAL LITERATURE CITED

Armstrong, D. F., Stokoe, W. C., & Wilcox, S. E. (1995). *Gesture and the nature of language*. Cambridge: Cambridge University Press.

Balda, R. P., & Kamil, A. C. (1989). A comparative study of cache recovery by three corvid species. *Animal Behaviour, 38*, 486–495.

Baldwin, J. M. (1895). Consciousness and evolution. *Science, 2*, 219–223.

Beach, F. A. (1955). The descent of instinct. *Psychological Review, 62*, 401–410.

Beach, F. A. (1965). The snark was a boojum. In T. E. McGill (Ed.), *Readings in animal behavior*. New York: Holt, Rinehart, and Winston.

Benedict, R. (1935). *Patterns of culture*. London: Routledge and Kegan Paul.

Beran, M. J., Gibson, K. R., & Rumbaugh, D. M. (1999). Predicting hominid intelligence from brain size. In M. C. Corballis & S. E. G. Lea (Eds.), *The descent of mind*. Oxford: Oxford University Press.

Bernard, L. L. (1924). *Instinct: A study in social psychology*. New York: Henry Holt.

Bickerton, D. (1995). *Language and human behavior*. Seattle, WA: University of Washington Press.

Borgerhoff-Mulder, M. (1996). Responses to environmental novelty: Changes in men's marriage strategies in a rural Kenyan community. In W. G. Runciman, J. Maynard Smith, & R. I. M. Dunbar (Eds.), *Evolution of social behavior patterns in primates and man*. Oxford: Oxford University Press.

Bradshaw, J. L., & Rogers, L. J. (1993). *The evolution of lateral asymmetries, language, tool use, and intellect*. Sydney, Australia: Academic Press.

Breland, K., & Breland, M. (1961). The misbehavior of organisms. *American Psychologist, 16*, 681–684.

Buss, D. M., & Schmitt, D. P. (1993). Sexual strategies theory: An evolutionary perspective on human mating. *Psychological Review, 100*, 204–232.

Chomsky, N. (1959). A review of B. F. Skinner's 'Verbal behavior.' *Language, 35*, 26–58.

Clayton, N. S., & Dickinson, A. (1998). Episodic-like memory during cache recovery by scrub jays. *Nature, 395*, 273–278.

Corballis, M. C. (1991). *The lopsided ape: Evolution of the generative mind*. New York: Oxford University Press. .

Cox, J. R., & Griggs, R. A. (1982). The effects of experience on performance in Wason's selection tasks. *Memory and Cognition, 10*, 496–502.

Cronk, L. (1991). Human behavioral ecology. *Annual Review of Anthropology, 20*, 25–53.

Crook, J. H., & Crook, S. J. (1988). Tibetan polyandry: Problems of adaptation and fitness. In L. Bezig, M. Borgerhoff Mulder, & P. Turke (Eds.), *Human reproductive behaviour*. Cambridge: Cambridge University Press.

Daly, M., & Wilson, M. (1988). *Homicide*. Hawthorne, NY: Aldine de Gruyter.

Darwin, C. (1859). *The origin of species by means of natural selection*. New York: Random House.

Dawkins, R. (1976). *The selfish gene*. Oxford: Oxford University Press.

DeVoogd, T. J., Krebs, S., Healy, S., & Purvis, A. (1993). Relations between song repertoire size and the volume of brain structures related to song: Comparative evolutionary analyses amongst oscine birds. *Proceedings of the Royal Society of London, Series B*, 254, 75–82.

Dubois, E. (1913). On the relation between the quantity of brain and the size of the body in vertebrates. *Verhandlungen des Koninklijke Academie voor Wetenschappen Amsterdam*, 16, 647.

Dunbar, R. I. M. (1993). Coevolution of neocortical size, group size and language in humans. *Behavioral and Brain Sciences*, 16, 681–736.

Falk, D. (1985). Apples, oranges, and the lunate sulcus. *American Journal of Physical Anthropology*, 67, 313–315.

Fodor, J. (1983). *The modularity of mind*. Cambridge, MA: The MIT Press.

Gannon, P. J., Holloway, R. L., Broadfield, D. C., & Braun, A. R. (1998). Asymmetry of chimpanzee planum temporale: Human-like brain pattern of Wernicke's area homolog. *Science*, 279, 220–222.

Goller, F., & Suthers, R. A. (1995). Implications for lateralization of bird song from unilateral gating of bilateral motor patterns. *Nature*, 373, 63–65.

Goodman, M. (1992). Reconstructing human evolution from proteins. In S. Jones, R. Martin, & D. Pilbeam (Eds.), *The Cambridge encyclopaedia of human evolution* (pp. 307–312). Cambridge: Cambridge University Press.

Hamilton, W. D. (1964). The genetical evolution of social behavior. *Journal of Theoretical Biology*, 7, 1–16; 17–51.

Hasselquist, D., Bensch, S., & Vonschantz, T. (1996). Correlation between male song reprtoire, extra-pair paternity, and offspring survival in the great reed warbler. *Nature*, 381, 229–232.

Hayes, C. (1952). *The ape in our house*. London: Gollancz.

Herrnstein, R. J. (1974). Nature as nurture: Behaviorism and the instinct doctrine. *Behaviorism*, 1, 23–52.

Heyes, C. M. (1998). Theory of mind in non-human primates. *Behavioral and Brain Sciences*, 21, 101–148.

Holloway, R. L. (1996). Evolution of the human brain. In A. Lock and C. R. Peters (Eds.), *Handbook of symbolic evolution* (pp. 74–125). Oxford: Oxford University Press.

Hopkins, W. D. (1996). Chimpanzee handedness revisited: 55 years since Finch (1941). *Psychonomic Bulletin and Review*, 3, 449–457.

Horne, P. J., & Lowe, C. F. (1993). Determinants of human performance on concurrent schedules. *Journal of the Experimental Analysis of Behavior*, 59, 29–60.

Jerison, H. J. (1973). *Evolution of the brain and intelligence*. New York: Academic Press.

Köhler, W. (1925). *The mentality of apes*. New York: Routledge and Kegan Paul.

Lea, S. E. G. (1985). Operant psychology and ethology: Failures and successes in interdisciplinary interaction. In C. F. Lowe, M. Richelle, D. E. Blackman, & C. M. Bradshaw (Eds.), *Behaviour analysis and contemporary psychology* (pp. 43–51). London: Erlbaum.

Lieberman, D. (1998). Sphenoid shortening and the evolution of the modern human cranial shape. *Nature*, 393, 158–162.

Lieberman, P. (1991). *Uniquely human: The evolution of speech, thought, and selfless behavior*. Cambridge, MA: Harvard University Press.

Lloyd Morgan, C. (1894). *Introduction to comparative psychology*. London: Walter Scott. (Second edition, 1903).

Lorenz, K. (1971). *Studies in animal and human behaviour, Vols. 1 and 2*. London: Methuen.

Maier, N. R. F., & Schneirla, T. C. (1935). *Principles of animal psychology*. New York: McGraw-Hill.

Marr, D. (1982). *Vision: A computational investigation into the human representation and processing of visual information*. San Francisco: Freeman.

McDougall, W. (1908). *An introduction to social psychology*. London: Methuen.

McGrew, W. C., & Marchant, L. F. (1997). On the other hand: Current issues in and a meta-analysis of the behavioral laterality of hand function in non-human primates. *Yearbook of Physical Anthropology*, 40, 201–232.

Nottebohm, F. (1977). Asymmetries for neural control of vocalization in the canary. In S. Harnad, R. W. Doty, J. Jaynes, & G. Krauthamer (Eds.), *Lateralization in the nervous system* (pp. 23–44). New York: Academic Press.

O'Keefe, J., & Nadel, L. (1978). *The hippocampus as a cognitive map*. Oxford: Clarendon Press.

Passingham, R. E. (1982). *The human primate*. San Francisco: Freeman.

Pinker, S. (1994). *The language instinct: How the mind creates language*. New York: Morrow.

Premack, D., & Woodruff, G. (1978). Does the chimpanzee have a theory of mind? *Behavioral and Brain Sciences*, 4, 515–526.

Romanes, G. J. (1888). *Mental evolution in animals*. London: Kegan Paul.

Sarich, V., & Wilson, A. C. (1967). Immunological time scale for hominid evolution. *Science*, 158, 1200–1203.

Savage-Rumbaugh, S., & Lewin, R. (1994). *Kanzi: An ape at the brink of the human mind*. New York: Wiley.

Skinner, B. F. (1957). *Verbal behavior*. New York: Appelton-Century-Crofts.

Snell, O. (1891). Das Gewicht des Gehirns und des Hirnmantels der Saugetiere in Beziehung zu deren geistigen Fahigkeiten. *Sitz. Ges. Morph. Physiol. (Munchen)*, 7, 90–94.

Spencer, H. (1855). *Principles of psychology*. London: Longman, Brown, Green, and Longman.

Symons, D. (1979). *The evolution of human sexuality.* New York: Oxford University Press.

Terrace, H. S. (1979). Is problem solving language? *Journal of the Experimental Analysis of Behavior, 31,* 161–175.

Tinbergen, N. (1972). *The animal in its world: Explorations of an ethologist 1932–1972, Vols. 1 and 2.* London: Allen and Unwin.

Tobias, P. V. (1987). The brain of *Homo habilis*: A new level of organization in human evolution. *Journal of Human Evolution, 16,* 741–761.

Tolman, E. C. (1932). *Purposive behavior in animals and men.* New York: Appleton-Century-Crofts.

Tooby, J., & Cosmides, L. (1989). Evolutionary psychology and the generation of culture, part 1. *Ethology and Sociobiology, 10,* 29–49.

Tooby, J., & Cosmides, L. (1995). Mapping the evolved functional organization of mind and brain. In M. S. Gazzaniga (Ed.), *The cognitive neuro-* sciences (pp. 1185–1210). Cambridge, MA: Bradford/MIT Press.

Trivers, R. (1971). The evolution of reciprocal altruism. *Quarterly Review of Biology, 46,* 35–57.

Wason, P., & Shapiro, D. (1971). Natural and contrived experience in a reasoning problem. *Quarterly Journal of Experimental Psychology, 23,* 63–71.

Watson, J. B. (1914). *Behavior: An introduction to comparative psychology.* New York: Holt, Rinehart, and Winston.

Williams, G. (1966). *Adaptation and natural selection: A critique of some evolutionary thought.* Princeton, NJ: Princeton University Press.

Wilson, E. O. (1978). *On human nature.* Cambridge, MA: Harvard University Press.

Winterhalder, B., & Smith, E. A. (Eds.). (1981). *Hunter-gatherer foraging strategies.* Chicago: University of Chicago Press.

Communications concerning this chapter should be addressed to: Professor Michael C. Corballis, Department of Psychology, University of Auckland, Private Bag 92019, Auckland, New Zealand

Part D
APPLIED PSYCHOLOGICAL SCIENCE

20

Psychological Assessment and Testing

KURT PAWLIK, with companion sections by
HOUCAN ZHANG, PIERRE VRIGNAUD,
VLADIMIR ROUSSALOV, AND
ROCIO FERNANDEZ-BALLESTEROS

As a technical term, 'psychological assessment' refers to methods developed to describe, record, and interpret a person's behavior, be it with respect to underlying basic dispositions (traits), to characteristics of state or change, or to such external criteria as expected success in a given training curriculum or in psychotherapeutic treatment. Methods of psychological assessment and testing constitute a major technology that grew out of psychological research, with widespread impact in educational, clinical, and industrial/organizational psychology, in counseling and, last but not least, in research itself.

In the most general sense, all assessment methods share one common feature: they are designed so as to capture the enormous variability (between persons, or within a single person) in kind and properties of behavior and to relate these observed variations to explanatory dimensions or to external criteria of psychological intervention and prediction. As a distinct field of psychology, psychological assessment comprises (1) a wide range of instruments for observing, recording, and analyzing behavioral variations; (2) formalized theories of psychological measurement underlying the design of these methods; and, finally, (3) systematic methods of psychodiagnostic inference in interpreting assessment results. In this chapter all three branches of psychological assessment will be covered and major methods of assessment will be reviewed.

Assessment methods differ in the approach taken to study behavioral variations: through direct observation, by employing self-ratings or ratings supplied from contact persons, by applying systematic behavior sampling techniques (so-called 'tests') or through studying psychophysiological correlates of behavior. In this chapter these alternative approaches are dealt with in Section 20.6 as different *data sources* for assessment. An alternative classification of assessment tools follows a typology of assessment *tasks*: developmental assessment in early or late childhood, vocational guidance testing, assessment in job selection or placement, intelligence testing, or psychological assessment in clinical contexts such as diagnostics of anxiety states. Some of these will be dealt with, albeit in an exemplary rather than exhaustive fashion, in Section 20.7.

Before reviewing different data sources and practical applications of psychological assessment, the history, heuristics, and goals of assessment will be briefly looked at (Sections 20.1 and 20.2), to be followed by the explanation of a so-called process chart of psychological assessment (Section 20.3). This will enable the reader to appreciate different functions of psychological assessment in studying and interpreting variations in human behavior. Following these three introductory sections, basic psychometric and ethical/legal standards of assessment and psychodiagnostic inference are dealt with in Section 20.4. By present understanding and professional standards, psychological assessments and tests cannot be applied responsibly without proper psychometric and ethical/legal grounding. Psychological assessment procedures in general and psychological tests in particular, must not be

mistaken for stand-alone procedures, they cannot be applied responsibly in the absence of profound psychometric qualification and sufficient familiarity with the conceptual basis of an assessment procedure, within which it has been developed and beyond which its results should not be interpreted. For example, tests of intelligence originate in specific operationalizations of what is to be understood by intelligence. Individual scores on a test of intelligence must not be interpreted beyond the limits set by the theoretical-conceptual basis of that test. Of course, from this follow also stringent rules of professional procedure as regards minimum qualifications to be requested from persons who may apply methods of assessments outside contexts of supervision (Bartram, 1998).

Not surprisingly for a field that is broad in scope and practical applications, there is a rich introductory textbook literature available (see the Resource References for a sampler). While some topics, like psychometric measurement theory or culture-fair testing of basic information-processing capacities, will hold without much variation across cultures, many assessment methods, especially in personality and clinical testing, must be viewed as ethnic-embedded and culture-related. In that case special standards have to be observed in cross-cultural testing (see also Chapter 18) and when adapting psychological tests, for example, of functions of intelligence, from one language area or culture to another (cf. Section 20.4 below). Of course, this poses also problems of presentation in this Handbook, as we look upon psychological science from an international perspective. In this chapter, the following compromise has been adopted: in the main part of the chapter (Sections 20.1–20.7) psychological assessment and testing are dealt with (1) in a generalistic manner and (2) with examples mainly from the English-language and German-language literature, simply for reasons of greater familiarity on the part of the present author. To counterbalance this unavoidable cultural bias, four further sections 20.8–20.11 provide comparative overviews of assessment methodologies in other languages, viz. Chinese (Mandarin), French, Russian, and Spanish, each one written by a distinguished author from that language region. This selection of additional language areas still cannot achieve the desirable full breadth of internationality, yet it is the authors' (and Editors'!) intention and hope that in this way at least some widening of international perspective is achieved.

Throughout this chapter the term 'behavior' is used in a generic sense, including also verbal and other expressions of internal experience, of feelings, emotions, perceptions or attitudes.

Similarly, the term 'psychological assessment' is used to cover all kinds of assessment technology, including, for example, projective techniques and objective behavior tests. 'Psychodiagnostics', as preferred in some languages, is understood as synonymous to 'assessment'. Finally, unless stated otherwise, the word 'person' is used to refer to the individual whose behavior is being assessed (thus avoiding such expressions as 'testee', 'interviewee', 'assessee', or 'subject').

20.1 History of Psychological Assessment and Testing

Individual differences in human behavior have been an object of human inquiry ever since the earliest times of human history. At the high period of ancient classics, eminent philosophers like Aristotle or Plato were intrigued by the diversity in human nature. First examples of systematic proficiency and achievement 'testing' are reported from as far back as the ancient Chinese Mandarin civil servant selection procedures (Dubois, 1966).

The historical roots of present-day psychological testing and assessment go back to 1882 and the work of Sir Francis Galton in Great Britain and to pioneer studies in individual differences, by James McKeen Cattell in 1890, in the United States. During the last decade of the nineteenth century many prototypes of what later were to become mental tests were published: for the study of individual differences in memory performance, in reasoning or speed of perception, for example. In 1897 Hermann Ebbinghaus, already famous for his monumental experimental pioneer work on human memory, devised new reasoning tests (e.g., following a sentence-completion design) to be used in school-settings. And in 1895 the French psychologist and lawyer Alfred Binet published, together with Victor Henri, the first edition of his 'échelle mentale', a scaled series of short tests designed to measure level of intellectual development in six-year-old children to guide in educational placement and counselling. At the same time we also find first attempts towards the development of assessment procedures in clinical contexts, e.g. by the German psychiatrist Emil Kraepelin.

In the following years the number of published studies on individual psychological differences expanded rapidly (cf. Pawlik, 1968), giving rise to a new branch of psychology: the study of individual differences. As early as 1900, the German psychologist William Stern published his founding text *Über Psychologie der individuellen Differenzen* ('On the psychology of individual differences'; Stern, 1900). In this book he laid a conceptual and methodological foundation also for the development of psychological assessment. The second edition of this book (Stern, 1911; see also Pawlik, 1994) still is *the* significant landmark in the early history of assessment and individual difference research.

While much early test development work was geared towards solving practical assessment problems (in the educational system, in measuring job performance and developmental potential, or in clinical contexts), another seminal publication shortly after the turn of the century by the British psychologist Charles Spearman (1904) laid the foundation for what should later become *the* first-choice assessment paradigm: psychological tests for measuring basic personal dispositions (today called traits, see Chapter 16). In his 1904 paper Spearman also developed a mathematical-statistical theory for analyzing individual differences in mental tests into two independent components: a universal component (factor) of 'general intelligence', which would be common, yet in different degree, to each and every mental test, plus a second, test-specific component (depending on test make-up, item content, mode of presentation, etc.). Spearman's paper upgraded psychological assessment from a descriptive sampling level to the level of measurement and structural analysis of individual differences. It inspired an enormous research literature on the dimensional (factorial) analysis of assessment instruments and individual difference indicators. The salient work by Sir Cyril Burt and Philip Vernon in the United Kingdom, by Leon and Thelma Q. Thurstone and Joy P. Guilford in the US, to be followed in the 1940s and 1950s by Hans J. Eysenck in the United Kingdom and Raymond B. Cattell in the US, laid the foundation for what is now confirmed empirical evidence on the multi-factor structure of human intelligence, personality/temperament, aptitudes, and motivations (Pawlik, 1968; see also Chapter 16 in this Handbook). The design of numerous methods of psychological assessment still widely in use, is rooted in this research, which has given rise to such standard assessments of intelligence as the Wechsler tests of intelligence (Wechsler, 1958), tests of psychomotor proficiency or of personality/temperament dimensions like extraversion-introversion, neuroticism, or anxiety. Early precursors in this development include, among others, the development of the first personality questionnaire (Personal Data Sheet) by Robert S. Woodworth in 1913, the first paper-and-pencil group test of intelligence (called Army Alpha Test of Intelligence) in 1914, the first multi-dimensional clinical personality questionnaire by Hathaway and McKinley (1943) in Minnesota (Minnesota Multi-Phasic Personality Inventory: MMPI), or the Differential Aptitude Test Battery by Bennett and co-workers (Bennett, Seashore, & Wesman, 1981).

One common element in these assessment developments was their primary, if not exclusive, reliance on a static cross-sectional diagnosis (so-called status assessment, studying behavior variations *between* persons). This perspective came under challenge when, in the 1950s/1960s, professional and research emphases in assessment moved away from description towards intervention, foremost in clinical contexts for evaluating new methods of counselling and psychological therapy. This called for a process-orientation in testing, that is for assessment instruments that will allow to monitor change (*within*-person variation) rather than traits (stable dispositions underlying *between*-person variations). This new test design also raised questions of psychometric measurement theory; even now these issues have not yet been brought to fully satisfactory solution.

Other lines of research progress in psychological assessment since the 1960s involve systematic construct analysis of assessment variables under study. A prime example in this respect is the assessment of anxiety, differentiating conceptually between trait (stable over time and situation) and state (varying over time and situation) anxiety, with both in turn to be contrasted from test anxiety (Spielberger, 1983). In yet another line of research, assessment techniques were developed to study behavioral variations *in situ* in a person's everyday life course or, as it has been called, 'in the field'. One motif behind this development was a growing concern for ecological validity (Barker, 1960) of assessment results, which called for sampling behavior not in an artificial laboratory situation, but in a person's natural life space. This also inspired research towards assessing individual differences in the unrestrained 'natural' stream of behavior in a person's natural environment (Pawlik, 1998).

In recent years new developments in the assessment field also became possible through the use of advanced computer technologies, mostly at the level of personal computers (PC), leading to a new assessment technology called computer-aided testing (CAT). In its simplest form, an existing paper-and-pencil test such as a personality questionnaire is loaded into a computer program that will present the test items and record the person's item responses. In its most advanced form, which employs a special adaptive psychometric test theory, a test-software (also called testware) is devised that will administer to a person only test items at a level (of item difficulty in an aptitude test or, for example, of degree of anxiousness in a personality test of anxiety) that will prove critical for measuring that trait in this specific person. Advances in testing theory and PC technology have made it possible to develop such computer-aided testing methods also for in-field applications (Pawlik, 1998).

As is true of many fields of psychology, the history of assessment and testing has also seen its share of ad hoc initiatives and even nonproductive sidelines. Two examples may suffice. In the 1920s, the Swiss psychiatrist Hermann Rorschach sought to develop an objective test of psychopathology. Following extensive clinical experience with hospitalized psychotics he settled on a series of ten plates with symmetric meaning-free graphic displays, as one would obtain by folding and subsequently unfolding a page with random ink splashes. In Rorschach's *Formdeuteversuch* (form interpretation study) patients were presented one plate after the other with the simple instruction to tell the experimenter 'what they think they could see on this plate'. In an often-quoted publication Rorschach presented evidence that a person's responses, evaluated on the basis of a detailed scoring system, would differentiate between, for example, schizophrenics and depressives. What seemed an interesting, suggestive new approach to clinical-psychological assessment later got mystified, however, when authors (mostly from depth psychological schools of thinking; cf. Chapter 16) claimed that tests of such a design would give rise to a new 'projective' personality assessment. According to their reasoning a person would perceive (interpret) a Rorschach plate according to her/his personal style of experiencing, including her/his 'unconscious' (perhaps even repressed) motives, feelings, and anxieties – as if the person would 'project' her/his own personality into her/his perception of this unstructured stimulus material. In the decades to follow, a multitude of similarly conceived 'projective tests' was developed, with most of them, as a rule, falling short in psychometric quality and not even supporting the implied projection hypothesis. Still, and despite negative psychometric quality assays, projective techniques continue to maintain a role in practical assessment work up to today, even a leading role in some regions of the world.

Another example of an assessment medium of supposedly high validity and still in use in some quarters despite its undoubtedly low to zero psychometric quality is handwriting analysis (graphology). Here again the underlying rationale seemed straightforward at first glance; obviously, the individual style of handwriting identifies a person with next-to-perfect precision – so that state authorities or banks have come to use a person's signature as proof of his/her identity. Then should not personal style of handwriting also be an indicator of a person's unique personality? Despite intuitive plausibility, this expectation has not stood empirical psychometric tests (as will be referenced briefly in Section 20.6). Still this does not seem to prevent some psychologists and, still more so, laymen and even major business firms to rely on this unreliable assessment methodology for job placement and career decisions. In addition to handwriting a wide range of other so-called expressive motions (or products thereof), such as facial expression, style of gross body motion, drawings, story completion, picture interpretation, art appreciation, etc. have been proposed, largely without great psychometric success, as alternative means for dispositional trait assessment. However recent research has shown that some of these methods, for example facial expression analysis, do contain valid variance for emotional *state* assessment, if properly recorded and scored (cf. Section 20.6).

20.2 HEURISTICS AND GOALS OF PSYCHOLOGICAL ASSESSMENT

As will be obvious from the preceding section, methods of psychological assessment may be employed for different purposes and to answer widely different types of questions. In essence, one can distinguish among the following three prototypical heuristics in psychological assessment.

(1) *Descriptive assessment:* Let us take as an example an adolescent in the final highschool year seeking vocational guidance as to which academic or professional training to take up after graduation. In a typical vocational guidance center this person will be invited to take a number of psychological tests, including a multi-dimensional interest questionnaire. In this the person will be asked to respond to a range of questions selected so as to sample salient interests and motives (for example: dealing with people vs. dealing with technical questions, working alone vs. working in groups, being interested in rural vs. urban jobs, in solving verbal-numerical vs. manual-practical problems, etc.) Often, test results will be expressed in a personal 'interest profile' which may serve, within limits of test validity, as a description of that person's interest structure. Here the purpose

and goal of the psychodiagnostic assessment is the description of a given behavioral reality. As a matter of fact, the term diagnostics (from the Greek 'diágnosis': differentiation, ability to differentiate) refers to this descriptive heuristic, as does the term 'assessment' (from 'assessing' or 'taking note of a factual state of affairs').

Obviously, mere description will only rarely suffice as a goal of assessment. In one example, the person seeking vocational guidance is not interested in her/his interest profile *per se*, but seeks to utilize this information for purposes of personal prediction (in which field of study will I be most successful and/or most satisfied?) or decision (which field of study should I choose so that it will match my personal interest profile?). Similarly, most educational, clinical and occupational/industrial assessments serve predictive or decisional purposes.

By rule of thumb, purely descriptive assessment tends to be limited to research applications, where assessment results may serve as independent or dependent variables in an experimental design or as hypothetical covariates. For example, a researcher may wish to investigate differences between high-anxiety and low-anxiety subjects in an experiment on muscular relaxation (anxiety measure as independent variable) or study the effect of a new, potentially anxiolytic drug on overt anxiety level (as dependent variable). Or a study may look into the correlation between spontaneous degree of heart beat irregularity and individual level of trait anxiety (as a covariate). In all three cases, a test of trait anxiety will be chosen under this purely descriptive heuristic.

(2) *Decision heuristic:* As explained earlier, in many practical assessment situations the psychologist seeks assessment data as information basis for optimizing decisions. The vocational guidance example speaks for itself. In a clinical setting, psychological tests may be applied to guide patient and psychologist in choosing of the most appropriate psychological therapy (for example, in the case of an anxiety syndrome) or in a treatment-related decision whether to continue or discontinue a certain psychotherapeutic intervention. Assessment-based rules of decision can be developed in different ways. In one approach one simply tabulates different assessment results (diagnostic states) against outcome categories. For example, we may relate patients' success rates in a certain method of psychotherapy against their kind or level of pre-therapy anxiety state. In more advanced decision-related assessment paradigms, decision rules will involve explanatory or predictive modeling.

(3) *Assessment for explanatory or predictive modeling:* In this case assessment results are

employed to explain how a concurrent psychological state (example: a patient's anxiety disorder) may have developed or how a person may behave at a later point in time or in a different setting. Predicting the level of professional satisfaction or success of our highschool student on the basis of her/his interest profile, presupposes a model (theory) that will relate such on-the-job criterion data to current interest test results. Provided such a model exists and has been confirmed with sufficiently strong correlations between test data and criterion data, one can extrapolate statistically (predict) that student's later job success or job satisfaction on the basis of the test results s/he obtained when still in highschool. More advanced predictive modeling will allow the psychologist (1) to predict for that student the likely job success or satisfaction across a spectrum of vocational positions, but also (2) to assign a probability estimate (level of confidence) expressing the likelihood that the predicted criterion values will in fact hold true for a student with an interest test profile as obtained.

This is the methodological paradigm followed in present-day test interpretation for purposes of criterion prediction. By contrast, solely intuitive, subjective test interpretation should be considered a practice of the past, no longer fulfilling professional standards (although, regrettably, there may still be psychologists out in the profession adhering to such a sub-standard procedure). Today validating a test against the criterion data needed in predictive modeling or prognosis is considered part of test development, which thus extends way beyond the mere selection and adaptation of test items or of questions in a questionnaire. Predictive modeling of test data for psychodiagnostic inference can amount to a very laborious undertaking, also requiring advanced theoretical sophistication on the part of the researcher as regards psychological processes of possible contribution to the criterion data in question.

A second type of modeling involves a 'postdiction' or backward modeling of earlier (antecedent) conditions to account for (or explain) assessment data at hand. For example, we may wonder about conditions earlier in the highschool student's life that contributed to her/his specific interest test profile at the time prior to graduation. In this second type of modeling, assessment test data are related backward in time to antecedent psychological or other conditions prior to the assessment. In our given example we may look into parental modeling, selective past-time learning opportunities, or the student's ability and aptitude profile (say, in the field of music or in artistic expression). In this

way, explanation can be understood as 'backward prediction' (or 'postdiction') of most likely antecedents for a given behavioral state, assessment result, or test profile.

Prediction and explanation constitute the most important and most frequently employed heuristics in interpreting psychological assessment data. This interpretation is also called psychodiagnostic inference.

We shall now turn to some further distinctions, with respect to different goals and contextual settings of psychological assessment. For the sake of simplicity they can be set out by way of three dimensional alternatives.

(1) *Assessment of status vs. assessment of process:* As explained earlier above, psychological assessments can be designed to describe a current state of behavior (status assessment; for example: intelligence profile, interest structure, or level of anxiety) or, the nature and extent of behavioral change (process assessment; for example, change in intelligence profile as a function of developmental maturation, in interest structure as a function of professional training, or in anxiety level as a function of exposure to psychotherapy). In one important variant of process assessment one studies differences in behavioral indicators across different settings or situations. For example, in a clinical treatment program one may wish to assess how a patient's anxiety profile varies across situations differing in anxiety arousal (e.g., when speaking to a friend or in front of a large auditorium).

Classical test theory (CTT; see Section 20.4 below), the measurement rationale still most commonly employed in test development, is more apt to support status assessment than process assessment, which can be accommodated more readily within the measurement format of item-response theory (IRT; see Section 20.4 below). Thus most assessment instruments still have their primary applicability in status assessment only. To a large extent, the development of process assessment techniques with satisfactory situational or developmental sensitivity is still a task for future assessment research.

(2) *Norm-referenced vs. criterion-referenced assessment:* If our highschool student answered 16 out of 20 urban-vs.-rural activity questions in the direction 'urban' – does this already indicate a disproportionally high interest in urban activities? Obviously we have to compare this result (16 out of 20) with the range of variations found in a suitable reference group (in this case: in same-aged male highschool students). In norm-referenced tests an assessment result is transformed into a standardized score expressing the

individual's result in relation to statistical distribution characteristics (cumulative percentage points; mean and standard deviation) in an appropriate reference population. These distribution characteristics are then the *statistical* norm employed for interpreting assessment data. Establishing adequate population norms constitutes an indispensable part in test development. Whenever test results vary systematically with age, gender, ethnicity, educational background, or other characteristics in the general population, special norms (for specific age groups, the two sexes, etc.) will have to be supplied.

In criterion-referenced assessment, test results are *not* expressed with reference to distribution characteristics in the population, but with reference to a behavioral criterion itself. For example, in primary-school reading instruction the educational aim (or criterion of instruction) may be mastery of words up to a certain level of reading difficulty. In a criterion-referenced reading ability test a student's test result is expressed with reference to this criterion (for example, as percentage mastery). Criterion-referenced assessment may also be the method of choice in psychotherapy outcome evaluation. An important special case of criterion-referenced assessment is program evaluation, e.g., of remedial reading ability training programs in educational research or of psychotherapeutic intervention programs in mental health research. In evaluation, assessment methods are employed to measure degrees of program goal attainment in a properly balanced field-experimental design. There is a rich reference literature available introducing the use of assessment methods in program evaluation (see Rossi & Freeman, 1993).

(3) *Sampling vs. inventory-taking in assessments:* Many assessment procedures are built on the assumption of an underlying homogeneous universe of assessment items, settings, or situations. In actual test development one follows rules of sampling from this universe. For example, in devising a vocabulary test one selects a sample of words of different difficulty levels (estimated, for example, in relative usage frequency). Provided one can set up a rational theory of item difficulty (as, for example, in some visuo-spatial test designs), this sampling can even be computerized and applied individually in adaptive CAT.

In some assessment problems the homogeneity assumption, let alone a rational item difficulty theory, cannot be meaningfully maintained. In anxiety testing, for example, we may not only like to know the level of anxiousness of a person, but also her/his individually specific profile of anxiety eliciting settings and stimuli. In other words, we do not want to rely on a representative sampling of anxiety-provoking stimuli but need to compile, as completely as possible, an inventory of all stimuli that may elicit anxiety reactions in that patient. Only in this way will we be able to devise a person-adapted psychotherapeutic intervention. Up to now, this second assessment rationale has been implemented successfully only for assessments in clinical behavior therapy. It still remains to be seen if this paradigm could not be used fruitfully also in other assessment contexts.

20.3 A PROCESS CHART OF PSYCHOLOGICAL ASSESSMENT

The practice of psychological assessment involves *considerably* and *qualitatively* more than merely administering tests, questionnaires, or behavior ratings in a uniform way. Failure to adequately conceptualize the psychodiagnostic process, from the statement of a problem to the final interpretation of results, has created considerable confusion and contributed to psychometric inadequacies of the professional practice years back.

Figure 20.1 shows a condensed summary process chart of psychological assessment according to present-day conceptualization. In this diagram five successive stages of an assessment procedure are distinguished (in rectangular frames), with connecting psychological operations shown in elliptical dishes. Straight-line top-down arrows connect typical steps in solving an assessment program, whereas bottom-up arrows indicate possible or necessary feedback loops for successive iterative optimization of the assessment.

Different from assessment in basic research, the design of an assessment in professional practice will start with a more or less coherent statement of a problem, labeled 'problem at start' in Figure 20.1. For example, parents may see a psychologist to get advice with developmental problems of their eight-year-old son. Emotional instability, phases of restlessness and lack of concentration, fits of nervousness and occasional severe tantrums are among the problem behaviors they report to the psychologist. Naturally, parents will use everyday language in describing these behavior problems and in expressing their fears and concerns. From the parents' report the psychologist will, as a first process step in assessment, deduce hypotheses about the likely nature of the boy's behavior problems, at the same time translating the problem description into scientific conceptual

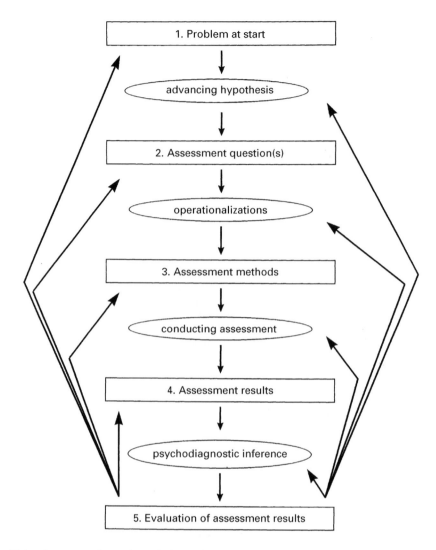

Figure 20.1   *A process chart of psychological assessment*

language with reference to behavioral science knowledge about this developmental stage. For example, the psychologist may deduce the hypothesis that the boy suffers from a symptomatology known as hyperactive attention deficit disorder. On this basis the psychologist will now translate the problem at start into specific assessment questions (in the example: testing for symptoms in sustained attention, emotional responsiveness, etc.).

The next step, 'operationalization', then calls for selecting, from among available assessment methods, a suitable set so as to access relevant behavioral indicators under the hypotheses deduced earlier. The following step, conducting the assessment, is the only routine component in this process, which may even be delegated to

assistants not holding full psychological training. This then leads to norm-referenced or criterion-referenced assessment results.

Next to deducing diagnostic hypotheses, the final step, psychodiagnostic inference, is the most demanding one in this process model. It presupposes detailed knowledge of how the results of the assessment relate to criterion data, to psychodiagnostic categories, or to explanatory concepts. At the same time the results of this inferential step open up into an over-all evaluation of assessment. For example, the hypothesis deduced initially may become confirmed or may need to be refined or even rejected. As indicated by bottom-up arrows in Figure 20.1, depending on results each subsequent step may call for iterative feedback correction of one or several earlier steps in the assessment process. For example, rejection of the hyperactivity attention deficit hypothesis may require the psychologist to restate the problem and develop alternative diagnostic hypotheses or, for example, choose a better operationalization or more advanced psychodiagnostic inference models.

Space precludes more detailed consideration of these steps and iterative feedback loops. May it suffice to say that the last step, psychodiagostic inference, has been given special research attention in recent years. For clinical psychological assessments standardized diagnostic inference systems (DSM IV, American Psychiatric Association, 1994; ICD-10, International Classification of Diseases, World Health Organization, 1990) have been developed. Specialized interpretation and prediction systems have been developed, for example, for assessment-based vocational guidance. There is reason to conclude that future development of psychological assessment methodology will depend to a growing extent on the further elaboration and creative design of systems and rules of psychodiagnostic inference. This development will widen the basis for systematic validation of the assessment process at large.

This leads us into questions of how to evaluate the quality, especially the veridicality, of psychological assessment and testing.

20.4 PSYCHOMETRIC AND ETHICAL/LEGAL STANDARDS OF ASSESSMENT AND PSYCHODIAGNOSTIC INFERENCE

Different methods of psychological assessment follow different approaches in recording and analyzing human behavior. Yet all methods touch upon a person's behavioral and personal sphere of privacy. Furthermore, personal information obtained in an assessment may become the basis for decisions of great importance for that person (cf. Section 20.2). It is for these reasons that psychological assessments must meet high standards of quality control (psychometric standards) and of ethical responsibility (legal/ethical standards). This was recognized in the 1920s/1930s. The 'Standards for Educational and Psychological Tests' developed by the American Psychological Association, currently in their 5th edition (American Psychological Association, 1985), are considered a model statement of such standards and have become a master schedule of assessment standards internationally (see also Fernandez-Ballesteros, 1997). It is current professional understanding that explicit empirical proof has to be provided for an assessment method to meet these psychometric standards to satisfactory degrees, as each and every single application of an assessment method has to follow these standards and ethical/legal provisions.

These standards and regulations are presented briefly below.

Psychometric Standards of Psychological Assessment

(1) *Objectivity of administration:* Human behavior can be open to countless influences and causes. In psychological assessment one studies human behavior to gain insight into a person's enduring dispositions (traits) or concurrent state. So special care needs to be taken to ensure that different assessment results can only be due to different trait or state make-up of the person assessed – and not due to physical or social particulars of the assessment situation, the behavior of the psychologist conducting the assessment, or any other circumstantial factor. Objectivity of administration is defined as the degree to which assessment results are independent of such extraneous factors. In developing an assessment method, special care must be taken to standardize the physical and social characteristics of the assessment situation, the way in which instructions are to be given to the person assessed, the behavior of the psychologist conducting the assessment, and the like.

Assessment methods may differ in the degree of administration objectivity. As a rule, group tests and methods employing CAT-format will show higher levels of objectivity of administration than individual performance tests (as for example, in the Wechsler intelligence test system) or methods of behavior observation and rating, respectively.

(2) *Scoring objectivity:* Scoring refers to translating observed variations of behavior into a descriptive recording system. In general, one distinguishes between qualitative and quantitative scoring. In the first, differences between scoring units are qualitative in nature (for example: technical vs. social interests). By far the majority of psychological assessment methods follow a quantitative scoring rationale, according to which scoring units differ in aspects of magnitude or intensity. In this case, assessment results are expressed in numerical form.

Depending on the scoring rationale, scoring systems differ in scaling property of assessment scores. In the most simple case (*ordinal scale*), the scoring rationale can only preserve *order* of magnitude (or intensity). For example, think of a test of twenty arithmetic problems increasing in difficulty level. Three persons solving five, ten, and fifteen of these twenty problems, respectively, most likely will differ in this order in their individual level of numerical proficiency. Yet this will not ensure that the third person surpasses the second one in trait level by the same amount as this person surpasses the first one! Obviously this would presuppose equality of distances in item difficulty level between successive items.

A scoring rationale establishes an *interval scale* if and only if equal score differences relate to equal differences in the psychological quantity to be measured. Today in many psychological tests care is taken to ascertain interval scale quality. One way to achieve this in our numerical proficiency test would be to select twenty items so that, for any item number i, the difference in item difficulty between item i and item $(i + 1)$ will be the same throughout. Constructing tests according to IRT standards can guarantee interval scale quality of test scores.

If the scoring rationale, in addition to interval scale quality, also ensures an absolute zero point of measurement, the resulting scale is called *ratio scale*. This presupposes prior knowledge about the lowest score level conceivable and ever to be found for that scoring system in human behavior. Obviously psychological measurement scales can hardly ever meet this high scale requirement. Yet, unless ratio scale quality has been established, scores must not be analyzed in a multiplicative fashion. For example, an intelligence quotient (IQ) of 140 must not be misinterpreted as indicating twice the intelligence level of an IQ of 70, as we do not know at which IQ score to locate the absolute zero level of human intelligence endowment. For the same reason, computation of score ratios such as 'following psychotherapy the anxiety level in patient X was reduced to 40% of that person's pre-therapy anxiety level' are strictly not permissible and can be highly misleading.

Scoring objectivity refers to the degree to which a scoring system provides scoring rules according to which any one observable specimen of behavior will be scored in one and only one scoring category. A frequently employed method to test for scoring objectivity is to have the same behavior record scored by several independent scorers. Then the degree of inter-scorer correspondence (correlation) can serve as a measure of scoring objectivity. In developing an assessment method the author has to demonstrate empirical proof of scoring objectivity.

(3) *Statistical norms:* With units of measurement often being arbitrary as explained above, the results of many psychodiagnostic assessment methods remain ambiguous unless norm-referenced. This involves expressing an individual score in relation to statistical distribution parameters of that score in a suitable reference or norm population. The test construction literature (see, for example, Lord & Novick, 1968) explains such different norming systems as standard raw scores (individual raw score minus population mean, divided by population standard deviation), normalized standard scores (standard score transformed so as to yield a Gaussian normal distribution in the reference population) or percentile norms (percentage of persons in the norm population yielding the same or a lower test score). Modern IQ-scores, for example, are interval scores at the level of a normalized standard score (with a mean of 100 and standard deviation of 15).

The manual of an assessment procedure has to provide detailed information on the norm population employed in standardizing the scoring system. As explained above, this may call for different sets of norms for subgroups of the population differing significantly in score distribution parameters. Before applying an assessment procedure to a new population, as a rule re-standardization should be considered obligatory. To guard against systematic differences between different age cohorts (for example, due to changes in educational systems), tests should be re-standardized at suitable intervals.

(4) *Discriminative power:* This refers to the degree to which an assessment procedure will yield different results for persons differing in the trait under study or, in the case of intra-individual assessment, yield different results for the same person in different situational states.

(5) *Internal consistency:* Of course, the different elements (components, items) of an assessment procedure should all measure the same quality or aspect of behavior. Otherwise the interpretive meaning of a test score would become ambiguous and the score itself useless. Internal consistency refers to the degree to which elements or items of an assessment procedure all measure the same aspect or quality behavior. Typically the internal consistency of a test is measured by computing the intercorrelations between test scores at item level. For a test to be consistent, each item has to correlate highly with the total score computed from all remaining test items.

(6) *Reliability:* This core psychometric criterion is defined as the degree to which assessment results are unaffected by unsystematic errors of observation, of assessment circumstances, and measurement errors. Reliability is the nucleus concept of the so-called classical test theory (CTT; see Lord & Novick, 1968). According to this theory any observed score x is the sum of two underlying components: a true

score *t* (of that person in the underlying behavior variable) plus an error component *e* (due to unintended, unsystematic causes of variation additionally affecting that person's behavior at that given assessment occasion). Then reliability is defined as the ratio of the variance of the true score component to the variance of observed scores *x*. In this sense, the reliability coefficient *R* denotes the percentage of variance in observed scores reflecting true score differences in the variable under study. Interestingly enough, this psychometric concept of error in test reliability theory is fully equivalent to the concept of error of measurement as used in ISO norms for physical and technical measurement as established by the International Standards Organisation (1981). See also Pawlik (1992). The complement $(1 - R)$ gives the percentage of error variance in raw test score variance. The positive square root of the numerator in this ratio, the standard deviation of errors *e*, is called the standard error of measurement (SEM) of an assessment method. SEM is the average amount, in raw score units, by which observed scores *x* deviate from the respective true score *t*. Knowledge of SEM can be used to compute a confidence interval within which a person's true score will lie (with chosen level of probability *p*).

A necessary condition for SEM not to exceed half of the raw score standard deviation is that the reliability *R* equals 0.75 or above. Consequently, a psychometric rule of thumb requires the reliability of a psychodiagnostic assessment method to reach or exceed 0.80. Today properly designed assessment methods, especially objective behavior tests, yield psychometric reliabilities of 0.90 and above, particularly for test measures of highly stable traits like general intelligence, visuo-spatial, or psychomotor aptitudes.

Different methods have been developed to estimate *R* in test development, most prominent among them the re-test method (yielding a stability estimate of *R*), the parallel-form method (yielding an equivalence estimate of *R*), and various internal consistency estimates of *R* (odd-even method, Kuder–Richardson coefficients). Common to all methods is their reliance on interindividual correlations as estimates of *R*. Consequently, these estimates are relative in the sense that they also depend on the degree of homogeneity/heterogeneity in the person population sampled. While originally conceptualized for trait measurement, CTT can also be expanded to provide for deriving reliability estimates for state measurement, even for within-person within-occasion measurement-reliability of an individual assessment result in a specific situation context (Buse & Pawlik, 1994).

Most psychodiagnostic assessment procedures, especially almost all psychological tests, are developed according to CTT reliability theory. While setting stringent standards for high-reliability test development, CTT carries with it also shortcomings, however. By necessity of mathematical deduction, for two CTT-designed test variables 1 and 2 the score difference $(1 - 2)$ will be less reliable than the original scores, and the drop in reliability will increase with increasing correlation between variables 1 and 2. As a consequence, CTT-designed tests yield rather unreliable difference scores in the measurement of change or process. Another disadvantage in CTT-based test development is its inability to measure person scores independent of item difficulty levels, and vice versa, at ratio scale level. These shortcomings of CTT are avoided elegantly in modern probabilistic or item-response theory (IRT) of psychological measurement, which builds on the work of Rasch, Birnbaum, Fischer, and others (see Lord & Novick, 1968; Wainer, 1990). Other than in CTT, score reliability is estimated in IRT by a maximum-likelihood error-of-estimation function. The advanced mathematical apparatus employed in IRT may be responsible for the fact that, for decades, most assessment research and applications stayed away from it. This should no longer be the case as IRT applications are now readily available in PC software programs (Wainer, 1990).

(7) *Validity:* This second most important CTT standard refers to the degree to which a psychological assessment measures that and only that psychological variable or attribute it is designed to measure. It can be shown formally that reliability is a necessary but not sufficient condition for validity (the validity of a measure cannot exceed the square root of its reliability). From a practice-oriented point of view, validity is *the* ultimate quality standard of assessment – assuring, for example, that a test of anxiety does indeed measure anxiety and, ideally, nothing but anxiety.

Again there are also several methods to estimate validity. In external or criterion validation the interindividual correlation between assessment results and the targeted criterion (for example: actual success in on-the-job training, or actual improvement in anxiety level following psychotherapy) is determined empirically. An important distinction in criterion validation refers to the temporal distance between time of assessment and time of criterion data acquisition. One speaks of concurrent (diagnostic, strictly speaking) validity when this temporal distance is negligible. (Example: validating a psychomotor aptitude test against the criterion of actual in-flight simulator performance of air pilot trainees, both types of measures taken within the same training week.) Alternatively one speaks of predictive (prognostic) validity, when time of assessment and time of criterion performance are weeks, months, or possibly years apart. In many educational, industrial, and clinical assessments this latter type of validity is of primary concern.

As expected, predictive validities will fall short of concurrent validities, with the drop in validity also being a function of temporal distance between time of assessment and time of criterion data collection. For example, predictive validities for success in professional training programs seldom exceed criterion correlations of 0.50–0.60 (and are often even lower). Provided sufficient reliability of the assessment method in question, these lower than expected predicted validities simply remind us of the necessary limits of longer-term behavioral prediction in general. Human behavior is an open system in several respects. In the course of a training program, for example, different persons may show different amounts of change in relevant basic trait scores – be it as a consequence of the training in question or for other, more individualistic reasons. Furthermore, different persons may differ in the nature and degree of change they experience (in their mental life, in psychologically relevant aspects of their social or physical environment) over the time period in question – which again will attenuate predictive criterion correlations. Given high-reliability assessment procedures, less than perfect predictive validities must not be blamed on the quality of the assessment process but simply highlight necessary, principal limits to long-range predicting of human behavior within contexts of free individuality in a free society. In this sense, predictive validation studies also tell us which diagnostic criterion can be properly predicted across which temporal or situational predictive distance. In addition, both concurrent and predictive criterion validities may be attenuated further due to imperfect criterion data reliability. When validating a test of intelligence against the criterion of intelligence ratings teachers give for their students, the reliability of criterion measures will be significantly lower than that of test measures. Within CTT it can be shown algebraically that the correlation of two variables 1 and 2 cannot exceed the square root of the product of their reliabilities R_1 and R_2. Thus insufficient criterion reliability will further attenuate external test validity.

Up to this point we have treated questions of external validity from a strict measurement point of view. In practical psychodiagnostic assessment often a less stringent mode, namely *classificatory assessment*, is fully sufficient or even more appropriate. Many clinical-psychological assessments are of such a classificatory type, for example, anxiety state in need vs. not in need of psychotherapy; patient shows vs. does not show symptoms of major depression. Also assessments in educational and industrial/organizational contexts often follow classificatory formats. As long as base rates of classificatory diagnostic classes will not differ markedly in the population of persons assessed, the percentage of correct assessment-based diagnostic classification can still justify the utility of the assessment procedure even with medium to moderate test-criterion validity correlations.

In internal validation, the validity of a new assessment method is estimated by correlating its results with other assessment methods whose validity has already been established. In construct validation the validity of an assessment method is estimated by the degree to which this method will yield empirical results in accord with hypotheses derived from the theory in which the construct is embedded. For example: If test x is indeed a valid measure of state anxiety, a psychopharmacological agent known to be anxiolytic (e.g., application of a benzodiazepine substance) should result in significant test score reduction (in a suitably balanced planned experiment). Campbell and Fiske (1959) developed a suggestive correlational model (called a multi-trait multi-method validation matrix) for construct validation which allows to separate between convergent (construct-conform) and discriminant construct validity, the latter referring to empirical proof that the measure in question is indeed unrelated to other concepts not part of the construct to be assessed.

Construct validation is the royal road to theory-guided assessment development. At the same time, systematic construct validation studies lead to substantial advances in differential psychological theory of human personality traits, of state variations, and of trait–state interactions. In this way, the last fifty years of assessment research have given rise to an even more refined understanding of central trait domains like intelligence, neurotiscism (emotional stability/lability), anxiety, or psychomotor aptitudes (see also Chapter 16).

(8) *Test fairness:* One and the same psychological test may measure different attributes in different populations. For example, performance on tests of psychomotor coordination is known to depend on different (perceptual and motor) factors in unexperienced (experimentally 'naive') subjects as compared with experienced (substantially pre-trained) subjects (Fleishman & Hempel, 1954). Differential validity diminishes test fairness, if one and the same measures

different attributes (or attributes at different levels) in different ethnic groups (Reynolds & Brown, 1984). Test fairness has also been recognized as an important limiting condition to transferring a psychodiagnostic assessment procedure (like a standard intelligence test) from one culture to an ecologically different culture. Test fairness also has implications for item translation in cross-cultural testing programs (see Chapter 18).

During the last twenty to thirty years substantial literature has accumulated on issues related to test fairness. In the most simple case, significant population differences in test validity may require different test interpretation rules or different test selection procedures to measure the same attributes in the same (fair) way in two contrasting populations. At a more complex conceptual level, problems of test fairness and ecological validity may lead one to question the usefulness and theoretical meaningfulness of comparing two different populations in tests not meeting the criterion of symmetric ecological validity. With continuing economic and social globalization, already today within the European and North American region aspects of test fairness, culture fairness, and symmetric linguistic-ecological representativeness become important issues at the psychological practitioner's level. Within the European Union assessment development has begun to concentrate on new test designs that will meet standards of cultural fairness right from the start.

(9) *Response objectivity:* Some assessment methods are more easily to fake than others. An objective intelligence test, for example, can at most be faked bad (viz. by giving incorrect or no answers to problems one would be able to master), while personality questionnaires can be faked in either direction. Response objectivity refers to the degree to which the results of a psychological assessment will be unaffected by a person's (voluntary or involuntary) response sets or faking tendencies. Since the 1950s, an enormous amount of empirical literature has accumulated on test-taking attitudes; especially in test validation special attempts have to be made to guard against response sets.

Ethical/Legal Standards

Psychodiagnostic assessment and psychological therapy are among the fields of professional psychological activity that deserve special ethical and legal consideration. Consequently, both fields of psychological practice receive attention also in national codes of professional-psychological ethics (Leach & Harbin, 1997). In some countries (for example, in Germany) also

provisions in the penal code, in the code of criminal procedure, in the civil code, or special laws pertaining to the use of electronically stored personal data are relevant.

At least the following three ethical/legal standards are considered essential universally.

(1) *Protection of personality:* As a rule, national constitutions declare an individual's right to personal integrity, with the consequence of individual rights to the protection of privacy and of personal interests. As in medicine, also in psychology diagnostic assessments must not violate these rights to personal integrity. In the past this has raised questions, for example, as to the admissibility of personality questionnaire items raising issues of sexual behavior. In case of doubt, a regional or national psychological ethics committee should weigh the necessity (or acceptability) of an assessment method vis-à-vis constitutional rights to integrity on the one hand and given psychodiagnostic assessment goals on the other hand.

(2) *Principle of informed consent:* Administering a psychodiagnostic assessment must be contingent upon the person's prior, informed, and explicit consent. (In some countries, however, the penal code or the code of criminal procedure may permit exceptions.) Analyzing or even simply observing the behavior of an identified or potentially identifiable person in a non-public situation without that person's explicit and informed consent is generally considered a violation of professional ethical standards. The relevance of this standard for hidden audio or video taping or disguised one-way mirror observation is obvious.

(3) *Principle of confidentiality:* Many national codes of professional psychological ethics highlight a person's fundamental right to have her/his data handled with absolute confidentiality. In Germany the psychologist's commitment to this confidentiality principle is even spelled out in a paragraph of the penal law, for that matter treating the psychologist like a medical doctor, a clergyman, or a barrister (Article 52, German Penal Code). Together with the foregoing two standards, the principle of confidentiality also sets rules as to how a psychologist is allowed or requested to deal with personal assessment data obtained under a third party's commission (for example, when testing a person applying for a job in an office other than that employing the psychologist conducting the assessment). Here again the principle of informed consent becomes absolutely critical. Many national professional codes of ethics also contain explicit statements on how psychological assessment data are to be filed (stored) in order to uphold principles of confidentiality and of protection of personality.

20.5 VARIABLE-DOMAINS OF PSYCHOLOGICAL ASSESSMENT

Psychodiagnostic assessment methods have been developed for a wide spectrum of trait and state variables affecting human behavior. Following a proposal by Cronbach (1949), one distinguishes between performance and personality measures, the former referring to measures of *maximum* behavior a person can maintain, the latter to measures of *typical* style of behavior. Intelligence tests are examples of performance measures, a test of extraversion–introversion or of trait anxiety examples of personality measures. While handy for descriptive purposes, this distinction must not be mistaken for a theoretical one, as trait measures of performance may in fact correlate with trait measures of personality (for example, speed of learning with level of trait anxiety). Within the limits of this distinction, the following summary list may serve to illustrate the scope of behavioral variables for which assessment procedures have been developed.

(1) *Performance variables:* These include measures of sensory processes (for example: tactile sensitivity, visual acuity, color vision proficiency, auditory intensity threshold); perceptual aptitudes (tactile texture differentiation, visual closure, visual or auditory pattern recognition, memory for faces, visuo-spatial tasks, etc.); measures of attention and concentration (tonic and phasic alertness; span of attention; distractability; double-performance tasks; vigilance performance over time); psychomotor aptitudes (including a wide variety of speed-of-reaction task designs); measures of learning and memory (short-term vs. long-term memory; memory span; intentional vs. incidental memory; visual/auditory/kinesthetic memory); assessment of cognitive performance and intelligence (next to general intelligence a wide range of primary mental abilities like verbal comprehension, word fluency, numerical ability, reasoning abilities, measures of different aspects of creativity, of social or emotional intelligence; see Chapter 16); assessment of language proficiency (developmental linguistic performance, aphasia test systems, etc.); measures of social competence.

(2) *Personality variables:* These include the assessment of primary factors of personality (especially of the so-called Big Five, cf. Chapter 16, and numerous more specific personality measurement scales); special clinical schedules and symptom checklists (to assess anxiety, symptoms of depression, schizotypic tendency, personality disorders, etc.); motivation structures and interests; styles of daily living; pastime and life goals; assessment of incisive life-events; assessment of stress tolerance and stress coping (including coping with serious illnesses and ailments); plus a wide range of still more specific assessment variables, like measures for the assessment of specific motives or specific styles of coping with illness or stressful life events.

By now even the number of psychodiagnostic assessment methods meeting high psychometric standards must already reach many tens of thousands, rendering it totally impossible to give more than an informative overview within the limitations of this chapter. Rather than enumerating hundreds of assessment procedures we shall here take a systematic look at major data sources for psychological assessment (in Section 20.6) and then briefly examine a few selected psychodiagnostic assessment problems and how they would be typically approached (in Section 20.7). For a more detailed coverage of assessment methods the reader is referred to three kinds of sources: (i) introductory texts as documented in Resource References; (ii) periodical encyclopedic resource publications such as the Mental Measurement Yearbook (Mental Measurement Yearbook 1998: Impara & Plake, 1998; now also accessible via internet at www.unl.edu/buros/catalog.html) and corresponding resource publications in languages other than English; and, most recent and most useful, (iii) electronic on-line accessible assessment method archives (as part of PsycInfo, provided by the American Psychological Association through its internet site: www.psycinfo.com or, for example, the German test data archive PSYTKOM: www.7pid.psychologie.de). To illustrate the international breadth and diversity in the field of psychological assessment, Professors Houcan Zhang, Pierre Vrignaud, Vladimir Roussalov, and Rocio Fernandez-Ballesteros accepted invitations to contribute Sections 20.8–20.11 to this chapter with overviews of Chinese-language, French-language, Russian-language, and Spanish-language assessment methods, respectively.

20.6 TEN DATA SOURCES FOR PSYCHOLOGICAL ASSESSMENT

By a rough estimate, more than 80% of all published assessment methods will be questionnaires or objective tests. As we shall see in this section, the range of possible assessment data sources extends considerably farther though. And in practical assessment work too psychologists tend to complement (cross-check or simply expand) their assessment by some or several non-questionnaire and non-test methods. For example, in clinical assessments behavior

Table 20.1   *Ten data sources in psychological assessment (adapted from Pawlik, 1998)*

Data source	Data modality			Variance accessed		
	Mental representation	Behavior	Psycho-physiology	Laboratory	Field	Response objectivity
1 Actuarial and biographical data		x			x	+
2 Behavior trace		x			x	+
3 Behavior observation		x		x	x	+/−
4 Behavior rating	x			x	x	+/−
5 Expressive behavior		x		x	x	+/−
6 Projective technique		x		x		−/+
7 Interview	x	(x)		x		−
8 Questionnaire	x	(x)		x		−
9 Objective test		x		x	x	+
10 Psychophysiological data		(x)	x	x	x	+

observation and interview data, often also psychophysiological data are considered essential additional information, as is interview and actuarial/biographical data in industrial/organizational assessments.

Table 20.1 gives a summary of ten data sources of psychological assessment which will be briefly explained below. For each data source three types of entries are given:

- data modality: whether a methods relies on mental representations (perceptions, memory, cognitive appraisal) of variations in behavior, on direct concurrent recording of behavior, or on psychophysiological measures;
- variance accessed: whether a method will study behavioral variations under (artificially) standardized and thus restricted 'laboratory' conditions (as in a typical clinical or industrial/organizational test situation) or rely on field data, i.e., variations of behavior as they occur in a person's natural life space, outside the laboratory, in the person's home, at the work place, in her/his normal daily activity; and
- response objectivity: whether data can be perfectly response-objective (+), possibly of satisfactory (+/−) or possibly not of satisfactory (−/+) response objectivity or, as a rule, deficient in response objectivity (−).

The reader is referred to Pawlik (1996, 1998) for details of this classification of data sources and to the literature referenced in Section 20.5 for details on specific assessment methods.

(1) *Actuarial and biographical data:* This category refers to descriptive data about a person's life history, educational, professional and medical record, possibly also criminal record. Age, type and years of schooling, nature of completed professional education/vocational

training, marital status, current employment and positions held in the past, leisure activities, and past illnesses and hospitalizations are examples of actuarial and biographical data. As a rule, such data is available with optimum reliability and often represents indispensable information, for example, in clinical and industrial/organizational assessments. Special biographical check list-item assessment instruments may be available in a given language and culture for special applications.

(2) *Behavior trace:* This refers to physical traces of human behavior like handwriting specimen, products of art and expression (drawings, compositions, poems or other kinds of literary products), left-overs after play in a children's playground, style (tidy or untidy, organized or 'chaotic') of self-devised living environment at home, but also attributes of a person's appearance (e.g., bitten finger nails!) and attire.

While at times perhaps intriguing, also within a wider humanistic perspective, the validity of personality assessments based on behavior traces can be rather limited. For example, graphology (handwriting analysis) has been known for a long time to fall short of acceptable validity criteria in carefully conducted validation studies (see Guilford, 1959; Rohracher, 1969). On the other hand, behavior trace variables may provide valuable information in clinical contexts and at the process stage of developing assessment hypotheses (cf. Figure 20.1).

(3) *Behavior observation:* In some sense, behavior observation will form part of each and every assessment. In the present context the word observation is used in a more restricted sense, though, referring to direct recording/monitoring, describing, and operational classification of human behavior, over and above what may be already incorporated in the scoring

rationale of a questionnaire, an interview schedule, or an objective test. Examples of behavior observation could be: studying the behavior of an autistic child in a playground setting; monitoring the behavior of a catatonic patient on a 24-hour basis; observing a trainee's performance in a newly designed work place; or self-monitoring of mood swings by a psychotherapy patient in between therapy sessions.

An enormous amount of research literature is available on the design of behavior observation schedules, on questions of time vs. event sampling in ambulatory behavior monitoring (see, for example, Fahrenberg & Myrtek, 1996; Pawlik & Buse, 1996), on alternative rationales for defining units of observation in the continuous spontaneous stream of behavior, on observer training, adequate periods of continuous other-monitored behavior observation, or on reactivity changes in behavior as a result of the observation procedure, to quote only a few.

In a way, it is regrettable that the development of self-administering questionnaires and objective tests, starting in the 1920s and 1930s, has pushed careful, systematic behavior observation to the side of the assessment process. Only in recent years, especially within clinical assessment and treatment contexts following behavior-therapeutic approaches (cf. Chapter 22), is the potential value of behavior ratings for the assessment process being re-discovered.

(4) *Behavior ratings:* In behavior rating assessments a person is asked to evaluate her/his own behavior or the behavior of another person with respect to given characteristics, judgmental scales, or checklist items. The method can be applied to concurrent behavior under direct observation (as in modern assessment center applications) or, and more typically, to the rater's explicit or anecdotal memory of the ratee's behavior at previous occasions, in (past or imagined) concrete situations, or in a general sense. Behavior rating methods may tell more about the mental representations that raters hold (developed, believe in) regarding the assessed person's behavior than about that behavior itself. A vast amount of research literature has accumulated on such research issues as raters' response sets and judgmental errors, inter-rater reliability as a function of rating format and rating scale design, on the standardized definition of rating scale units by giving sample video or audio behavior records.

Behavior ratings constitute an essential methodology in clinical and industrial/organizational psychology, in psychotherapy research and, last but not least, in basic personality research. Modern textbooks of personality research (see Chapter 16) usually give detailed accounts of how to devise behavior rating scales and how to compensate for common sources of error variance in ratings (severity vs. mildness error; central tendency error; positive or negative halo effect; semantic error; rater–attribute interaction error; and so-called logical errors, resulting from a rater's implicit theory about overlap and correlations between attributes).

(5) *Expressive behavior:* As a technical term, expressive behavior refers to variations in the way in which a person may look, move, talk, express her/his current state of emotion, feelings or motives. Making a grim-looking face, trembling, getting a red face, sweating on the forehead, walking in a hesitant way, speaking loudly or with an anxiously soft voice, would be examples of variations in expression behavior. Thereby expression refers to stylistic attributes in a person's behavior which will induce an observer to draw explicitly or implicitly inferences about that person's state of mind, emotional tension, feeling state, or the like.

Assessing another person from her/his expressive behavior has a long tradition which goes back to pre-scientific days. Chapter 16 gives examples of such early attempts to study human personality through individual differences in physique, habitual facial expression, and other bodily characteristics. Despite some intuitive plausibility (let alone culture-bound interpretative traditions!), correlations between objectively measured personality attributes and variations in physique and habitual expression do not warrant use of these variables in psychological assessment of stable personality traits (Guilford, 1959). The older German *Ausdruckspsychologie* (psychology of expression; for a summary cf. Rohracher, 1969), which hypothesized substantial physique–personality correlations, has been disproven. However, there is significant validity in expressive behavior variables for assessing *state* variations. Thus Ekman (1982), using modern time-fractioned video-analysis methods, was able to show that variations in facial expression co-vary substantially and significantly with changes in concurrent state of feeling and emotion, giving rise to objectively scorable, reliable assessments of emotional state on the basis of video-taped facial expression. More recently this approach has been extended to the study of gross bodily movement expression (Feldman & Rimé, 1991). This research is relevant also for developing teaching aids in psychological assessment and observer training.

(6) *Projective technique:* In Section 20.1 the design of the Rorschach Test (Rorschach, 1921) was introduced to illustrate a projective assessment procedure. In another procedure, the Thematic Perception Test (TAT; Murray, 1943), the person is presented pictures (some photos,

some drawings), many of them showing one or several persons in an ambiguous situation. The task of the person is to tell a story matching the picture, describing her/his perception of the situation shown, of events that would have led to this situation, and how s/he thinks the story will end.

In the 1930s and 1940s many clinical psychologists, often influenced by psychoanalysis and other forms of depth psychology, placed high expectations in such projective techniques, believing that they would induce a person to express her/his perception of the ambiguous stimulus material, thus willingly or even unwillingly 'uncovering' her/his personal individuality, including motives and emotions that the person may not even be aware of. Later, in the 1950s and 1960s, research has clearly shown that such assessment methods not only tend to lack in scoring objectivity and psychometric reliability, but – and still more important – also turned out to be of very limited validity, if any. As early as Murstein's (1963) review the underlying projection hypothesis could not be verified. Nevertheless projective tests still keep some of their appeal today, and research in the 1960s and thereafter succeeded in improving techniques like the Rorschach test at least as far as scoring objectivity and reliability are concerned (for example, Holtzman Inkblot Test: Holtzman, Thorpe, Swartz, & Herron, 1961). Furthermore thematic association techniques like the TAT maintain their status as assessment methods potentially useful for deducing assessment hypotheses. In addition, special TAT forms have been devised for assessing specific motivation variables such as achievement motivation (McClelland, 1971). In the clinical context, once their prime field of application, projective techniques are no longer considered a tenable basis for hypothesis testing and theory development, let alone therapy planning and evaluation.

(7) *Interview:* Most psychodiagnostic assessments will include an interview at least as an ancillary component – and be it only for establishing personal contact and an atmosphere of trust. Extensive research on interview structure, interviewer influences, and interviewee response biases has given rise to a spectrum of interview techniques for different purposes and assessment contexts. As a rule, clinical assessments will start out (cf. Figure 20.1) with an exploratory interview in which the psychologist will seek to focus the problem at hand and collect information for deriving assessment hypotheses. An interview is called unstructured if questions asked by the psychologist do not follow a predetermined course and, largely if not exclusively, depends on the person's responses and own interjections. Today most assessment interviews are semi-structured or fully structured. In the first case, the interviewer is guided by a schedule of questions or topics, with varying degrees of freedom as to how the psychologist may chose to follow up on the person's responses. Fully structured interviews follow an interview schedule containing all questions to be asked, often with detailed rules about which question(s) to ask next depending on a person's response to previous questions. An example of such a structured clinical interview schedule is the Structured Clinical Interview (SCID; Spitzer, Williams, & Gibbon, 1987) for clinical assessments according to the Diagnostic and Statistic Manual (DSM; cf. Section 20.1).

The less structured an interview, the richer it *may* prove in breadth of information touched upon, but the poorer its results will conform, as a rule, with standard psychometric criteria of assessment reliability. The enormous amount of literature on psychometric pitfalls in interview data and on how to improve interview schedules so as to yield more reliable assessment information is well documented (cf. Guilford, 1959). In general, structured interviews like SCID will exceed semi-structured and unstructured interviews in psychometric quality.

Interviews have also been devised as a means to introduce an assessment situation which then allows for direct behavior observation – over and above recording the person's answers. Such clinical interview and behavior observation schedules have been developed, for example, by Lorr, Klett, and McNair (1965) (see also Pawlik, 1982, pp. 302–343), by Baumann and Stieglitz (1983) or in the Present State Examination (PSE; Wing, Cooper, & Sartorius, 1974). With proper interviewer training, these combined interview–behavior observation schedules have been shown to yield high scale reliabilities (of 0.85 and above!), at the same time extracting highly valid clinical-psychological variance.

(8) *Questionnaires:* Originally, personality inventories, interest surveys, and attitude or opinion schedules were devised as structured interviews in written, following a multiple-choice response format (rather than presenting questions open-ended as in an interview proper). In a typical questionnaire each item (question or statement) will be followed by two or three response alternatives such as 'yes–do not know–no' or 'true–cannot say–untrue'. Early clinical personality questionnaires like the Minnesota Multiphasic Personality Inventory (MMPI; Hathaway & McKinley, 1943; recent revised edition by Butcher, Dahlstrom, Graham, Tellegen, & Kaemmer, 1989) drew much of their item content from confirmed clinical symptoms and syndromes. By contrast, personality questionnaires

designed to measure extraversion–introversion, neuroticism, and other personality factors in healthy normals rely on item contents from empirical (mostly factor-analytic) studies of these primary factors of personality.

As in behavior ratings, research identified a number of typical response sets also in questionnaire data, including acquiescence (readiness to chose the affirmative response alternative, regardless of content) and social desirability (preference for the socially more acceptable response alternative). One way to cope with these sources of deficient response objectivity was to introduce special validity scales (as early as the MMPI) to control for response sets in a person's protocol. Yet individual differences in response sets may – and in fact do – relate also to valid personality variance themselves. There is common agreement today that a person's responses to a questionnaire must not be interpreted as behaviorally veridical, but only within empirically established scale validities. For example, a person's response to the questionnaire item 'I frequently feel fatigued without being able to give a reason' must not be interpreted, for example, as being behaviorally indicative of the so-called fatigue syndrome. Rather subjects may differ in what they mean by 'frequently', by 'fatigued', by 'without reason', and on how broad a time and situation sample they base their response. After all, questionnaire data is assessment data about mental representations (perception, memory, evaluation) of behavior variations in a person's self-perception and self-cognition. They tell us a lot about the awareness persons develop of their own behavior which may, but need not, turn out veridical in objective behavioral terms. So the aforementioned item will carry its diagnostic value *only* as contributing to the validity of a psychometrically reliable questionnaire scale, in this case the scale 'neuroticism', with proven high clinical validity.

(9) *Objective tests:* Tests constitute the core of psychological assessment instruments; it is through them that psychological assessment has reached its level of scientific credibility and wide range of applications. A test is a sample of items, questions, problems etc. chosen so as to sample, in a representative manner, the universe of items, questions or problems indicative of the trait or state to be assessed, for example, an aptitude or personality trait or a mood state like alertness. The adjective 'objective' refers to administration, scoring, and response objectivity in test development (with the exception of possibly faking bad, see Section 20.4). Objective tests have been developed for the full spectrum of behavior variables referenced in Section 20.5; their number goes into tens of thousands.

A test is called an individual test, if it needs an examiner to administer it individually to the person assessed. Psychomotor and other performance tests are typical examples of tests still given individually. Still the most widely used intelligence test system, the Wechsler Adult Intelligent Scale (WAIS; Wechsler, 1958; and later editions) and its derivatives are administered individually throughout. The other test design, group tests, are devised so that one examiner can administer them to a number of persons (typically 20 to 30) at the same time in the same setting. Traditionally group tests were developed in so-called paper-and-pencil form, with the test items printed in a booklet and the person answering on a special answer sheet. Today the advantages of individual testing (for example, pacing and selection of items according to the person's own choice; individual timing of item responses) and of group testing (for example, higher objectivity of administration; higher assessment economy) can be combined in CAT assessment. With the exception of purely manipulative-practical tasks (as in testing psychomotor manipulative skills), almost any type of test item can be adapted to CAT, with the additional advantage of multimodel (for example, visual plus auditive) information display and efficient taylored or adaptive testing (see Section 20.4). Some important tests widely in use today will be listed in Sections 20.7–20.11 under the respective problem heading.

While the development of objective behavior tests of performance has been brought to a high level of proficiency and psychometric quality, objective behavior tests of personality still linger in a far-from-final phase of development – despite massive, continuing efforts by Eysenck, Cattell and many others (cf. Cattell & Warburton, 1965; Hundleby, Pawlik, & Cattell, 1963). There is confirmed empirical evidence to the fact that personality variables, i.e., measures of mode and style of typical behavior (rather than of optimum performance), are more difficult to assess through objective tests than through conventional questionnaire scales, behavior observations, or behavior ratings. As a consequence, recent research in objective personality test design began to concentrate on miniature-type laboratory tasks of potential validity, for example, as behavioral markers of psychopathology (Widiger & Trull, 1991).

(10) *Psychophysiological data:* All variations in behavior and conscious experience are nervous-system based, with ancillary input from the hormone and the immune system, respectively, and from peripheral organic processes (see Chapter 4 for a detailed account). This should lead us to expect that individual differences as revealed in psychological assessment

should be accessible also, and perhaps even more directly so, through monitoring psychophysiological system parameters that relate to the kind of behavior variations that an assessment is targeted at. These psychophysiological variables include measures of brain activity and brain function plasticity (electroencephalogram, EEG; functional magnetic resonance imaging, fMRI; magnetoencephalogram, MEG), of hormone and immune system parameters and response pattern, and of peripheral psychophysiological responses mediated through the autonomic nervous system (cardiovascular system response patterns: electrocardiogram, ECG; breathing parameters: pneumogram; variations in sweat gland activity: electrodermal activity, EDA; in muscle tonus: electromyogram, EMG; or in eye movements and in pupil diameter: pupillometry). Standard psychophysiology textbooks (see for example Caccioppo & Tassinary, 1990) introduce basic concepts and measurement operations. Modern computer-assisted recording and analysis of psychophysiological data facilitate on-line monitoring, often concurrent with presentation of objective tests, in an interview situation or even, by means of portable recording equipment, in a person's habitual daily life course (ambulatory psychophysiology).

In one kind of psychophysiological assessment one or several of the aforementioned psychophysiological parameters are recorded while the person is shown different stimuli. For example, one measures the orienting response in electric skin conductance (a parameter solely depending on sympathetic autonomic nervous system activity) to simple tones of medium intensity. It has been shown early, that schizophrenic patients will follow more frequently than normals a non-responder pattern, showing less clear orienting reactions than normals to these stimuli. While there are less than 10% non-responders in normals, their frequency in schizophrenics approaches 50% (Bernstein, 1987). A rich research literature has accumulated from this approach in recent years; there is reason to expect that psychophysiological assessments may one day become methods of first choice for assessing state variations, especially in clinical contexts.

Still another, more recent innovation in psychophysiological assessment refers to stable, genetically linked biological covariants of personality and aptitude development. Recent research from behavior genetics has succeeded in identifying, for the first time, circumscribed genetic markers for aspects of intellectual development or for a personality trait like extraversion–introversion (see Pawlik, 1998, for details). Surely individual differences in intellective functioning and personality formation

are determined only in part genetically (see also Chapter 16). Yet assessing the contributing genetic matrix may one day help to improve our understanding of possible or even necessary supportive behavioral intervention and should prove useful in predictive assessment.

Before closing this section, two general comments seem in order. First, the ten data sources of psychological assessment listed in Table 20.1 must not be considered mutually exchangeable. Quite to the contrary, different data sources differ substantially in their specific validity and sensitivity for some and only some assessment variables. We have seen earlier that objective tests are more suitable for assessing performance and aptitude traits, while questionnaires are more sensitive to detecting differences in personality variables. Furthermore, each data source carries with it source-specific variance, called method variance. Consequently, measures of the same trait assessed from different data sources will show lower interindividual correlations as compared with trait measures assessed through the same data source – up to the point that different traits assessed from the same source may even correlate higher than the same trait assessed through different sources! It was this problem of method variance that originally led Campbell and Fiske (1959) to devise their multitrait-multimethod matrix methodology of construct validation (cf. Section 20.4). In practical assessment work one seeks to counterbalance method-specific sources of variance by combining assessment methods from different sources, bringing together objective test and behavior observation information plus actuarial and biographical data, rather than relying solely on test data, for example.

Another comment seems in order on the column labeled 'variance accessed' in Table 20.1. Today we begin to understand that some classical validity problems in psychological assessment do not relate primarily to psychometric imperfections of assessment instruments employed, but rather to some artificiality imported into the assessment process by relying too much on laboratory-type data. It has been argued repeatedly in recent years (also by the present author; see Pawlik, 1998) that psychological assessment must open up to ambulatory or in-field data in order to directly capture sources and degrees of behavioral variation in their naturally occurring patterns of settings and co-variations. While some assessment sources (3, 4, and 5 in Table 20.1) are principally open to in-field applications, others (especially 6, 7, and 8 in Table 20.1) seem to be limited to stationary application, devoid of in-field input. Here the assessment methodology AMBU (Ambulatory Monitoring and Behavior-Test

Unit) developed by Pawlik and Buse (1996) allows one to administer, through the use of a special portable PC test technology, ultra-short chronometric performance tests together with scales for self-monitoring (of behavior and mood states, for example) and peripheral psychophysiological recording under unrestrained in-field conditions, with promising within-subject/within-occasion reliability of measurement. Fields of application range from ergonomic testing to clinical out-patient monitoring.

20.7 PRACTICAL APPLICATIONS

In this section, the reader will be introduced to some frequently used methods of psychological assessment for three frequently encountered assessment problems: testing of intellective and other aptitude functions; psychological assessment in clinical contexts; and vocational guidance testing.

(1) *Assessment of intelligence and other aptitude functions:* Clearly this is the primary domain of objective behavior tests. It was mentioned earlier (Section 20.1) that tests of cognitive and other aptitudes were among the first methods of assessment ever to be developed. Following up on the scaling proposal of mental age (age-equivalence, in months, of the number of test items solved correctly) as suggested by Binet and Henri (1896) in their prototype scale of intellectual development in early childhood, the German psychologist William Stern suggested an intelligence quotient (IQ), defined as the ratio of mental age over biological age, as a measurement concept for assessing a gross function like intelligence in a score that would be independent of the age of the person tested. When subsequent research revealed psychometric inadequacies with this formula, the US psychologist David Wechsler proposed in his test (Wechsler, 1958) an IQ computed as age-standardized normalized standard score (with mean of 100 and standard deviation of 15). Now available in re-designed and re-standardized form as Wechsler Adult Intelligence Scale (WAIS), Wechsler Intelligence Scale for Children (WISC) and Wechsler Pre-School Test of Intelligence, this test package has become *the* trend-setting intelligence test system of widest application, also internationally through numerous foreign-language adaptations. So a closer look at its assessment structure seems in order.

The WAIS, for example, contains ten individually administered tests of two kinds: verbal tests (general information, general comprehension, digit memory span, arithmetic reasoning,

finding similarities of concepts) and five performance tests (digit–symbol substitution, arranging pictures according to the sequence of a story, completing pictures, mosaic test block design, object assembly of two-dimensional puzzle pictures). A person's test performance is assessed in three IQ scores: verbal IQ, performance IQ, and total IQ. Surprisingly enough, this kind of over-all test of cognitive functioning is still maintained in practical assessment work – despite undisputable and overwhelming empirical evidence that general intelligence as a trait will only account for part, at most perhaps about 30% of individual difference variation in cognitive tests (Carroll, 1993). More recent examples of general-intelligence type tests are the Kaufman Assessment Battery (Kaufman & Kaufman, 1983, 1993) or, for example, the German-language *Begabungstestsystem* (BTS; ability test system; Horn, 1972).

An alternative, theoretically more developed approach is called differential aptitude assessment. Tests in this tradition are usually based on the results of factor-analytic multi-trait studies of intelligence, originating in the work of Thurstone, Guilford and their students. Thurstone's Primary Mental Abilities Test (PMA; Thurstone & Thurstone, 1943), the Differential Aptitude Tests Battery (DAT; Bennett et al., 1981), the Kit of Reference Tests for Cognitive Factors (French, Ekstrom, & Price, 1963) or the German *Intelligenz-Struktur-Test* 70 (IST 70; Amthauer, 1973) and, more recently, the Berliner Intelligenzstruktur-Test (BIS-Test; Jäger, Süss, & Beauducel, 1996) are typical examples of this assessment approach that provides separate standardized scales for each selected primary intelligence factor.

In addition to these tests of intellective functions, numerous more specialized aptitude tests have been developed such as the Wechsler Memory Scale (Wechsler & Stone, 1974), special performance tests for neuropsychological assessment, e.g., of brain-damaged patients (see Lezak, 1995), for assessing mentally handicapped persons and the diagnosis of dementia, as well as for special sensory and psychomotor functions (see, for example, Fleishman & Reilly, 1992).

For more information on these and other assessment procedures the reader is referred to the documentation resources listed at the beginning of Section 20.6.

(2) *Psychological assessment in clinical contexts:* In addition to some assessment questions mentioned in the preceding paragraph, in clinical psychodiagnostics one typically faces questions of testing for personality variables, for behavior disorders and/or specific symptomatologies (as in the hyperactivity attention deficit

disorder or postraumatic stress disorder syndrome, for example). The MMPI (see Section 20.6) was a classical prototype clinical personality test, which – like the Wechsler tests of intelligence – has frequently been adapted and translated into other languages. In addition, the large item stock of the MMPI (more than 550 items!) has been utilized as a base from which a great number of special questionnaire scales were developed, perhaps best known among them the Taylor Manifest Anxiety Scale (MAS; Taylor, 1953). More recent personality questionnaires used in clinical psychodiagnostics would include, for example, the 16 Personality Factors Questionnaire (16 PF; Cattell, Cattell, & Cattell, 1994; also adapted and translated into many other languages) or the German-language *Freiburger Persönlichkeitsinventar* (FPI; Fahrenberg, Hampel, & Selg, 1994).

Besides these broad-band multi-scale questionnaires numerous assessment instruments of narrower focus have been developed. Examples are the Beck Depression Inventory, assessment instruments for studying phobic or obsessive symptoms or, more recently, interview and diagnostic inference schedules implementing the DSM and ICD approaches of descriptive disease classification (cf. literature references in Section 20.6). Often introduced as *the* master-methodology of clinical psychodiagnostics, DSM IV- and ICD 10-based assessment strategies, have recently received increasing criticism because of their purely descriptive, atheoretical nature, without recourse to etiology of behavior disorders and their development. It yet remains to be seen if this criticism will give rise to novel, more etiologically oriented clinical assessment philosophies.

(3) *Assessment in vocational guidance testing and job selection/placement:* Ever since the 1920s a multitude of tests of varying conceptual bandwidth have been developed to assess specific aptitudes and interest variables related to different vocational training curricula and on-the-job work demands. In vocational guidance testing, integrated multi-dimensional systems like one inaugurated by Paul Host in the 1950s for the US State of Washington have since become a model of approach in many countries. For example, the German *Bundesanstalt für Arbeit* (Federal Office of Labor) developed its own multi-dimensional testing and prognosis system for vocational guidance counseling at senior highschool level. A similar, CAT-formatted multi-dimensional test system has been developed by the German Armed Forces Psychological Service Unit. Comparable assessment systems for guidance and placement have been devised, for example, in the UK and the US.

Compared to these broad-band assessment systems, job selection/placement testing in industrial and organizational psychology typically is narrower in scope, though more demanding in specific functions and job-related qualifications. Before implementing such an assessment system, a careful analysis of the job structure, the nature of professional demands and of contextual-situational factors is absolutely compulsory. The literature offers a developed instrumentarium for carrying out such analyses (Kleinbeck & Rutenfranz, 1987). Since the 1970s/1980s a new methodology called 'assessment center' has been introduced to provide for behavior observation, behavior rating, and interview assessment data in selected social situations deviced to mirror salient demand situations in future on-the-job performance (Lattmann, 1989). In continental Europe the assessment-center approach has even become something like *the* method of choice, in selecting, for example, persons for higher-level managerial positions. Moreover, single-stage assessment and testing is now being replaced by on-the-job personnel development programs and special trainings offered to devise a more intervention-oriented, multi-stage approach to assessment in organizational development. In CAT-formatted assessment programs for industrial/organizational selection and placement applications, also special simulation techniques (for example, in testing for interpersonal cooperation under stress conditions) are currently under development.

20.8 Chinese-Language Assessment Methods

Historical Background

About 2500 years ago, in ancient China some great thinkers and educators like Confucius (551–479 B.C.E) and Mencius (468–312 B.C.E.) pointed out the existence of individual differences and that the mind of a person can be measured. 'Scaling makes it possible to understand weight, measurement makes it possible to understand length, these are true for all things, especially true for the mind,' (Mencius) is a clear statement of the importance of the quantitative measurement of the human mind. An application of this kind of thought to the then Imperial Administrative System was the introduction of the Civil Service Examination from the early seventh century to 1905.

Psychological testing came to China along with the introduction of the Western educational system and psychology at the beginning of the twentieth century. In 1931 the Society of Psychological Testing was founded, beginning a period in which many Western tests were translated and revised for use in schools, and psychological assessment became popular in China. However, the outbreak of the Sino-Japanese war in 1937 halted the development of psychological testing, and then during the early 1950s, for ideological and political reasons, psychological testing was criticized as a pseudoscience and was totally abandoned in China. Also during the Chinese Cultural Revolution (1966–1976), Psychology was criticized as a pseudoscience and abandoned as a discipline. Only after the Cultural Revolution, was psychology rehabilitated as a science. With the advent of academic freedom, together with the demands from practical needs of society, in both educational and clinical fields, psychologists started work towards the re-establishment of psychological testing in China. Due to the shortage of well-trained personnel and tests available at that time, the Testing Commission of the Chinese Psychological Society held its first nationwide workshop in Wuhan in 1980, which can be seen as a landmark in the development of psychological testing in the People's Republic of China (see also Zhang, 1998; Zheng, 1993).

Contemporary Development

In the early 1980s, the first stage of development of psychological testing occurred in the field of education in the training of the young scholars in test construction, and to gain practical experience. Some Western tests were translated into Chinese and tried out in China; some other tests were revised and Chinese norms were developed for use in China, for example ('*' indicates the test was revised, the year indicates the time of revision or introduction into China):

*Binet–Simon Scale III (B-S Scale III), by Wu Tian-min, 1981
*Learning Ability Test for 6–8 Grades, by Lin Chuan-ding and Chen Zhong-geng, 1982
*Eysenck Personality Questionnaire (EPQ), revised by Chen Zhong-geng, 1982
*Sixteen Personality Factors Inventory (16PF), revised by Y. H. Liu and S. Y. Li, 1982
*Minnesota Multiphasic Personality Inventory (MMPI), revised by Song Wei-zen and Zhang, Miao-qing, 1984
*Wechsler Adult Intelligence Scale (WAIS), revised by Gong Yao-xian, 1984
Draw-A-Person Test, 1985
*Raven Standard Progressive Matrices (SPM), by Zhang Hou-can and Wang Xiao-ping, 1985
*Wechsler Intelligence Scale for Children (WISC), revised by Lin Chuan-ding and Zhang Hou-can, 1986

*California Personality Inventory (CPI), revised by Song Wei-zhen, 1986
Torrence Test of Creative Thinking, 1987
Raven Advanced Progressive Matrices (APM), 1988
*Wechsler Memory Scale (WMS), revised by Gong Yao-xian, 1988
*Wechsler Pre-school and Primary Scale of Intelligence (WPPSI), revised by Zhu Yue-mei, 1988
Peabody Picture Vocabulary Test (PPVT), 1989
Sensation Seeking Scale, 1990

Several years later, in order to fulfill the practical needs of society, eliminating the bias on test results from cultural differences of Western tests, besides introducing well-known foreign tests into China, some indigenous intelligence, aptitude, and personality tests were developed, for example:

*Juvenile Character Inventory, Li De-wei, 1985
*Young Children's Developmental Scale, aged 0–3 , Fan Cun-ren, 1990
*CDCC Children's Developmental Scale, aged 3–6, Zhang Hou-can and Zhou Rong, 1993
*Chinese 5-Phase Character Inventory, Xue Zhong-cheng, 1994
*Group Intelligence Test for Children, Jin Yu, 1995
*Chinese Personality Assessment Inventory, Song Wei-zhen and Zhang Miao-qing, 1995
*Mental Health Inventory (PHI), Song Wei-zhen and Zhang Miao-qing, 1995
Meta-Memory in Adulthood Questionnaire, Wu Zhenyun, 1996
*Chinese Adult Intelligence Scale (CAIS), Zhao Jie-cheng, 1997

In the field of clinical psychology, assessment and tests were used most frequently for the purpose of diagnosis. Formerly, tests were used only by psychiatrists as a kind of measurement in the diagnosis of people with mental disorders, but along with the rapid social and economic development in China, the number of people having adjustment problems to the changing environment and interpersonal relationship problems increased, and psychological counseling became a new profession where testing and assessment played important roles. Counseling centers were established and some private clinics also appeared. At present, over two-thirds of the people working in counseling clinics have their background in medicine.

Lacking knowledge in test-construction, they just adopted already existing tools for use. Thus, in addition to the tests developed in the educational field, not many new tests were developed (Zheng, 1993). Some of the rating scales for mental health used in China are shown below (* denotes tests developed by Chinese authors):

Symptom Checklist 90 (SCL-90), 1984

Self-Rating Anxiety Scale (SAS), 1984

Hamilton Anxiety Scale (HAMA), 1984

Hamilton Depression Scale (HAMD), 1984

Rorschach Inkblot Test, 1985

Self-Rating Depression Scale and Depression
Status Inventory (SDS & DSI), 1985

State-Trait Anxiety Inventory (STAI), 1986

*Life Event Scale (LES), revised by Zhang Ya-
Lin and Yang De-Sen, 1986

*Clinical Memory-Scale, revised by Xu Shu-
Lian, 1986

*Social Support Rating Scale, revised by Xiao
Shui-Yuan, 1986

*Beck Depression Inventory (BDI), revised by
Xu Jun-Mian, 1986

*Beck Anxiety Inventory (BAI), revised by
Zhang Yu-xin, 1987

*Psychological Skills Inventory for Sport
(PSIS), revised by Qiu Zhuo-ying, 1987

*Halstead–Reitan Neuropsychological Battery,
revised by Gong Yao-xian, 1987

Rutter's Children Behavior Questionnaire, 1988

Cornell Medical Index (CMI), 1988

*Test Anxiety Inventory (TAI), revised by Ye
Ren-min, 1988

Toronto Alecithymia Scale (TAS), 1990

*Family Environment Scale – Chinese revised
(FES-CV), revised by Fei Li-peng et al., 1991

*Family Adaptability and Cohesion Scale –
Chinese revised (FACESII-CV), revised by
Fei Li-peng et al., 1991

Achenbach's Child Behavior Checklist (CBCL),
1992

Interpersonal Trust Behavior Scale (ITBS), 1993

Myers–Briggs Type Indicator (MBTI), 1996

Strong–Cambell Interest Inventory (SCII), 1996

In recent years, due to the introduction of a market economy in China, the application of psychology has expanded to the field of human resource development. Theories and techniques in assessment greatly benefited the Chinese government's personnel administration, in the selection of employees, and uncovering of everyone's talent potential. As a result, psychology has gained a much better recognition from society. For the special purpose of this field, several tests and assessment systems have been developed, for example:

Leadership Behavior Scale, Xu Lian-cang, 1994

Vocational Assessment System for Managers,
Yan Gong-gu et al., 1997

Psychological Testing System for Vocational
Application, Shi Kan, 1998

Conclusion

Psychological assessment has had a long history in China. The philosophical foundation of

psychological measurement lies in the ancient Confucian ideology that mental activities can be measured. The Civil Service Examination dates back to the seventh century, and was the earliest form of educational measurement put into use in the world. Along with the introduction of modern Western psychological testing into China in the early part of the twentieth century, testing began to be a topic of research and application in the field of education. But several political events, especially the 'cultural revolution' resulted in its suspension for many years. Only after the opening up of China and the introduction of a market economy in the 1980s, did the demand for psychological measurement by society become imperative, and its application went beyond the educational field into mental health and personnel selection areas. In the meantime, regulations and a code of ethics for guiding the use of psychological testing were also established (Jing & Hu, 1998).

At the present time, research into the theory and practice of assessment, the training of qualified testing personnel, and the development of indigenous tests are being emphasized. It can be seen that the research and application of psychological assessment are expanding to a wide range of areas in China.

20.9 FRENCH-LANGUAGE ASSESSMENT METHODS

Most of the original assessment methods found in psychology are used in France with varying frequency depending on the specific professional field. In this brief synopsis of French-language methods, we do not talk in detail about the methods that have not given rise to unique developments in France, rather we insist on specific techniques, particularly in the domain of objective tests. After a general account of the history and the current situation of the tests in France, we consider the prevalent instruments existing according to the three fields of psychological evaluation: cognitive, personality, and vocational. We conclude with the presentation of a distinctive method existing in France: le bilan de compétence (the competence assessment procedure).

For each topic we give some general references allowing to explore the topic more extensively. It is always difficult in such an overview to make a choice between references in a field so rich in research and practice. We have made our choice on the basis of at least one of these three criteria: (1) offers a wide coverage of the domain (other useful references are often cited in this one); (2) presents a historical or exemplar character; (3) has been recently published. We are conscious of being unfair while discarding some very valuable publications and we hope that their authors will excuse us by understanding the difficulty of such a task.

Brief History

France has a reputation for being responsible for a major contribution to the psychological tests developed subsequent to the work of Binet and Simon (1905). In the period that followed different laboratories were established in charge of elaborating techniques and processes of selection and methods for career guidance. The work of Lahy involving the selection of tram drivers provides a good example. In the French-speaking countries, the vocational psychology field was initiated by the Belgian psychologists Christiaens and Decroly in 1908 and the educational psychology field by the Swiss psychologists Claparéde and Bovet who founded an institute in Geneva in 1912. In 1928 the psychologist, Henri Pieron created the National Institute of Career guidance (l'Institut National d'Orientation Professionnelle or INETOP) which has been responsible for a large quantity of research on tests. It is perhaps important to underline the unique application and position of the French psychologists regarding these tests which were, at the time, perceived as veritable instruments of social progress. In fact the purpose of these tests in the field of education and career guidance was to allow a more objective evaluation and thus to favor equal opportunities as regards access to training and to careers, heedless of social origin. On the other hand, opinions contrary to these were largely diffused following the events of May 1968 and led to a decline in the use of the tests which were consequently rejected by a large number of psychologists who considered them to be too heavily influenced socially. However a marked renewed interest in these tests can be observed in the 1980s due to the setting up of various structures concerned with assisting professional integration of unemployed people – in particular young people with few qualifications (see Blanchard, Francequin-Chartier, Stassinet, & Vrignaud, 1991).

The Present Situation

Several recent surveys (see for example Bruchon-Schweitzer & Ferrieux, 1991 in the professional psychology field; Castro, Meljac, & Joubert, 1996 in the clinical psychology field) have shown that the use of tests by psychologists is common in all fields of evaluation. However, it is important to point out that few of these tests are mentioned often (for example, only the Wechsler scales and the projective tests appear to be used frequently by clinicians). Nevertheless it is possible to appreciate the energy and enthusiasm of French psychometrics when reading extracts from the international conference, 'Psychological evaluation of people' organized by INETOP and a French test publisher (Editions et Applications Psychologiques; EAP) which includes more than 300 papers (Huteau, 1994). Several French journals regularly publish articles on tests and evaluations, for example: *Psychologie et Psychométrie, European Review of Applied Psychology*, and *L'Orientation Scolaire et Professionnelle*. Two test publishers are offering a wide choice of tests and questionnaires (original French tools or adaptation of famous international tools): *Les Etablissements et Applications Psychologiques* (founded in 1928) and *Les Editions du Centre de Psychologie Appliquée* (founded in 1949).

In regard to ethics, the French Society of Psychology (la Société Française de Psychologie: SFP) has recently published a code of deontology specifying the psychologist's need to use *validated* methods. The SFP is also a member of the International Commission of Tests. (Note also that the French-speaking countries are at the origin of the international movement on tests and test use, first by the creation of *Association internationale de psychotechnique* in Geneva, and more recently through the impulsion of J. Cardinet and others who founded the International Test Commission, as mentioned by J. Grégoire, 1999; see also this reference for a wide survey of test practice in French-speaking countries.)

The Cognitive Sphere

This section relies heavily for the past and present situations on Huteau and Lautrey (1999a) and for the future situation on Vrignaud (1996).

Intelligence Scale Perspectives

Returning now to the area of intelligence scales, let us recall that the second version of the scale, which was published in 1908, differed a lot from the first one: two-thirds of the items were new. A third version (1911) was published while Binet was still alive. It was only in 1949 that new norms were published for the Binet–Simon test and in 1966 that a revised version was constructed by Zazzo, Gilly, and Verba-Rad (Nouvelle Echelle Métrique de l'Intelligence). It was not until the 1960s that we saw the renewed use of Binet's test in France through the adaptation of Terman-Merril by INETOP. Currently, the most recent versions of the Wechsler scales have been subjected to an adaptation in France (Grégoire, 1992). Kaufman's K-ABC has also been adapted to suit the French-speaking country cultures. However it should be noted that for reasons of habit and more importantly motives linked to legislation (the admission in specialised education is determined by the IQ in the WISC test) the frequency of use of the Wechsler scales are largely superior of that of all the other scales.

Many of the principal tests of reasoning have been adapted for use in France: Spearman, PM38 and D48 for example. The adaptations of the General Aptitude Tests Battery (CATB) have met with little success and some have now become obsolete. On the other hand a group of tests covering the different factors of the GATB constructed by R. Bonnardel in the 1960s are widely used. The factorial series of tests have been perfected/adapted for larger surveys concerning the intellectual level of French youth (Echelle Collective de Niveau Intellectuel). In addition we can also quote here the factorial series of tests coming from the Research Department of INETOP (see Bacher & Nguyen Xuan, 1967; Richard, 1996).

Piagetian Perspectives

Jean Piaget's intelligence theory has given rise to the creation of several original tests aiming to evaluate the cognitive functions linked to the different stages of development reached by the child in the various fields defined by Piaget: thus the scale of logical thinking defined by Longeot in 1970 (*l'échelle de la pensée logique*). Two subtests in this scale come under the physical domain (conservation and pendulum); two under the logico-mathematical domain (combinatorial and probability quantification) and one under the space-representation domain (mechanical curves). The same author has also developed a version of Piagetian test using a pencil-and-paper format (on all these works, see Longeot, 1978). More recently, a scale of acquisition of numbers has been developed based on the model by Piaget: UDN II which includes elementary logic, conservation and numeration, and arithmetic tasks (Meljac & Lemmel, 1999). We mention *les inventaires Piagétiens* (Piagetian inventory) which is a set of cards describing the main Piagetian experiments and the material used (Pauli, Nathan, Droz, & Grize, 1990). Finally it is significant to mention the introduction of different movements in the analysis of verbal interaction (N. Perret-Clermont) which particularly concerns exchanges/relationships between the subject and the psychologist during the administration of a test. Learning-potential assessment has also a long tradition in French-language psychology. This current can be followed up from the 1930s with the pioneer works by A. Rey, a Swiss psychologist, and A. Ombredane, a Belgian psychologist. For example, learning-potential tests derived from the Kohs or from the Progressive Matrix have been designed (see Büchel & Paour, 1990).

Perspectives on Differential Psychology

It is important to mention the research carried out by the French school of Differential Psychology (l'École française de psychologie differentielle) which organizes an international conference every two years and also subsequently ensures the publication of the papers covered (see Huteau & Lautrey, 1999b, for example). The French school of Differential Psychology, founded by Henri Pieron and established in particular by his successor Maurice Reuchlin, has been a significant driving force behind research in the field of psychometrics. In addition to the conception of tests and experiments, differential psychology has largely contributed to the study and the circulation of psychometric methodology, in particular the analysis in common and specific factors and at present, the use of structural modeling.

The research carried out today is concerned in particular with the analysis of strategies and the resolution process of problems applied to items of cognitive tests (there are some excellent examples in a special issue of *Psychologie Française* edited by J. F. Richard (1996): *le diagnostic cognitif*). As an example of this movement it is necessary to describe the computer program, SAMUEL which can constitute a diagnosis of strategies used by subjects during a task inspired by the Kohs cubes. Using filmed recordings of the individuals selected and their verbalizations during the tests, the author, P. Rozencwajg identified three types of strategies adopted. The first was *analytical*; the original model was split up into smaller cubes, the second was *global*; the subject identified the shapes made up of several cubes; and the last strategy was *synthetic*. Using the indications recorded during a computerized test (for example, the time taken during the different tasks, the number and length of time given to consideration of the model), the program can establish a diagnostic in terms of the strategies. This is a particularly interesting approach because it not only allows a *quantitative* analysis of the cognitive aptitudes but also a *qualitative* diagnostic.

Metacognition and in particular planification has given rise to some interesting research. An exemplary procedure in this field comes from the deliveryman's test designed by E. Loarer (see Loarer, Chartier, Huteau, & Lautrey, 1995).

The participant is presented with a delivery task including receiving names of towns, and parcels (coloured cubes) to be delivered in these towns while respecting certain temporal restrictions (for example, morning only deliveries) and a model of a wooden lorry into which the parcels should be loaded. The subject must decide on the order in which he would deliver the parcels. He is then asked to load the lorry. This task is interesting because it is relatively realistic. The test has subsequently been computerized which means that a large amount of information concerning the subject's functioning can be recorded during the test. This experiment has since gained credibility by drawing on a neuropsychological study of the performance of patients with cerebral lesions that provoke dysfunction during planning activities.

Vocational Psychology

Vocational Interests

A recent and general reference on this field is the special issue edited by Bernaud, Dupont, Priou, and Vrignaud (1994): *Les questionnaires d'intérêts*. The conception and use of interest questionnaires were developed in the 1950s. At this time adaptations were established by taking the original blanks of American interests (like Strong, Kuder, or Rothwell–Miller). The Research Department of INETOP created a series of questionnaires covering the main stages of the French school system (*troisieme*: equivalent to ninth year, age 14–15 and *terminale*: equivalent to the final year of secondary school, age 17–18[1]) giving rise to several studies of school children's interests.

John Holland's model has also received wide recognition in France due to the publication of Holland's Personal Inventory (derived from John Holland's Self Directed Search) by the Swiss psychologist, J. B. Dupont in 1971. The questionnaire is unique because of its heterogeneous nature; it is divided into different categories: descriptions of self, capabilities, interests in school activities, leisure activities, types of people, etc. We also mention different computer programs designed in the field of vocational guidance that were inspired by the typology developed by Holland. For example, the program *La Station Spatiale* (Cuvillier, Tandeau de Marsac, Vrignaud, & Dellatre, 1999) is composed principally of an ergonomic questionnaire that allows the subject complete autonomy during the test (using an educational software program explaining the use of the mouse and the keyboard plus assistance throughout with access to a definition of different terms, for example). It permits the psychologist to have 15

screens of results revealing the main indicators useful for a profile interpretation based on the major concepts devised by Holland (consistency, differentiation, etc). This information, combined with the length of the study, opens up a debate concerning the importance given to the social status of certain professions and also in regard to the viewpoints developed by Gottfredson.

Holland's model has often been criticized by psychologists specializing in career guidance in France because of an inadequate lack of references to the French culture. The overlapping of the two personality characteristics, *enterprising* and *conventional* is the main difference noted regarding the theoretical model. It can be demonstrated through a study comparing the interests of young French and American people, evaluated with the help of the inventory of interests established by Strong (1985 version), that this mix-up is also present in the North American population (see Vrignaud & Bernaud, in Bernaud et al., 1994). It is not a question of a cultural difference but a lack of adequate adaptation of the theoretical model, a difference often noted during studies of the Holland model by American authors. The lack of difference between *enterprising* and *conventional* led to the creation of a unique model of interests (Larcebeau, 1983) including five different types of interests arranged in the shape of a pentagon. Holland's model has also given rise to the development of methods for the administering and the feedback of the interest questionnaires (see the Hexanime method as an example.)

Other Variables in the Vocational Field

The vocational guidance field includes many variables like motivation, maturity, and decision style. Original questionnaires, inspired by the theories, have been constructed in the French language (for an example, see particularly, Forner, 1997).

The study of decision-taking strategy Although the above movements in psychological investigation are at the border of evaluation research, we can briefly mention the evaluation of professional preferences using the models based on the subjectively expected value. The different aspects of professions that are attractive are, for the subject, the benefits to which the values are attributed. This movement has produced different instruments used to measure the area of interests. Thus the Platon program (Mullet, Barthélemy, Duponchelle, Muñoz-Sastre, & Neto, 1996) allows the user to determine the importance each subject attributes to different factors of the professions such as the salary, work, conditions, etc.

The Personality Field

Firstly, it can be said that in this field an objective questionnaire is not, according to the surveys, one of the instruments that is most often used. Methods such as the interview (structured or not), biodata, and observation techniques are more commonly applied. Projective techniques, in particular the Rorschach method and his interpretation, have given rise to important research and some more unique procedures. Surveys results reveal that unfortunately graphology is very widely used, including in the area of employment selection processes, although its lack of scientific grounding is all too well known.

With regard to the objective questionnaire, the main instruments of personality evaluation have been largely taken from Anglo-Saxon methods: Eysenck questionnaires (EPI), Guilford–Zimmerman questionnaires, and Cattell questionnaires (16PF) to name but a few. The frequent use of the Guilford–Zimmerman questionnaire is without a doubt unique to France, which can be explained by the tendency of psychologists to have great difficulty in letting go of the instruments they used during their initial training. The model of the Big Five has on the other hand given rise to the creation of some unique research instruments. For example the D5D questionnaire uses a series of five adjectives to establish a profile of the subject according to these five factors (description in five dimensions by Rolland & Mogenet, 1994). Recent methods such as the evaluation at 360° have also given rise to different adaptations.

The Competence Assessment Procedure

The competence assessment procedure represents the social change and progress of methodologies particular to France. Its uniqueness is twofold; on the one hand it concerns the integration of different methods and disciplines and on the other hand it concerns the subject's position during the evaluation process. Legislative texts published in 1991 gave everyone the right to have a free skill assessment. This assessment is aimed at everyone, whether unemployed or not, wishing to establish a professional project at whatever moment of his or her professional life. The cost of this assessment is covered by the company (in the case of an employee) or by the organization (in the case of an unemployed person). The assessment allows a triple agreement between the individual, the assessment centre, and the paying organization. The length of the assessment is 24 hours, combining different services (interviews, tests, and group work) spread out over several weeks. The person is accompanied throughout the duration of his assessment by a tutor who is there to help him understand and take stock of his performance at each stage and to define the different activities that he or she will carry out according to his or her personal needs. These activities can include interviews, taking individual or collective tests with a psychologist, an evaluation of qualifications with a teacher, and access to specific job information with active professionals. At the end of the assessment, the individual is provided with a complete written report of his achievements after discussing the conclusions with the various people involved. A description of the procedure and the methods used can be found in Lévy-Leboyer (1993). The effects of skill assessment on career planning and identity have been studied (see Lemoine, 1998).

Another procedure connected to the skill assessment is the *validation des acquis* (work experience validation). The aim of this assessment procedure is to allow a person to obtain a certification of professional knowledge which can be used to access a profession or educational and vocational training in the same way as a diploma (for a presentation and a discussion of these procedures, see Aubret & Gilbert, 1994).

Conclusion

To recap rather briefly the main ideas presented in this article, we can conclude that the psychological assessment methods in the area of tests and evaluations are caught between two trends: on the one hand is the development of some unique methods/instruments and on the other hand is the adaptation of these methods, in general Anglo-Saxon, to suit the French field of research and practice. A French specificity is without doubt the importance accorded to the person as we can see clearly demonstrated above by the procedures used in the competence assessment.

The above perspectives should be regarded by the reader as a brief overview of some of the research and methods in France as it is clear that we do not have sufficient space to do this subject full justice. We are particularly concerned with having overlooked the importance of the French-speaking world in general. Few would disagree that the techniques and methods developed have given rise to numerous fruitful exchanges between French-speaking countries, such as Belgium, Canada, France, and Switzerland, regardless of nationality. It is important to consider the common elements and the specificity of the different evaluation methods developed in each of these countries. Moreover perhaps we can conclude with a reminder that in developing countries, promoting teaching in French, there exists at present a definite current for adapting the different evaluation methods starting from French tests and questionnaires even when these are adaptations of an English-language instrument.

20.10 RUSSIAN-LANGUAGE ASSESSMENT METHODS

In Russia psychological assessment was always a problem of minor importance. Russian psychologists tried first of all to solve methodological and theoretical problems concerning the social/societal nature of the mind and thinking, the origin of intelligence, the structure of personality, etc. That is why the concepts discussed were often speculative, and it was very difficult to operationalize and assess, for example, such concepts as 'subject', 'activity', 'interiorization', 'self-control', etc. The qualitative methods (observation, talk, etc.) prevailed. The number of original tests, constructed according to psychometric procedures, is limited. The attitude to foreign tests was and still is either negative or very simplified. Often the adaptation is reduced to the translation of method. At best the adaptation includes the construction of normative distributions of the test scores. As a rule, there is no theoretical analysis of the concepts on which the test is based.

The data on the reliability and validity obtained in the country where the test was originated tend to be taken as true ones also for the Russian population. Only in the 1980s did the theoretical and practical problems of adaptation of foreign tests become an issue for discussion among Russian psychologists. Just recently specialized organizations were founded to deal with problems of psychological testing. For example, the firm Imaton (Saint-Petersburg) was founded in 1990 by the initiative of the Institute of Psychology of the Russian Academy of Sciences on the basis of the Russian Gosstandard. The main tasks of the firm are development of the original tests and the adaptation of well-known foreign tests.

All the tests (cognitive or personality) now available in the Russian language can be classified into two main categories: original and adapted. From a psychometric point of view, the tests can be divided into three levels: (A) tests containing complete (or almost complete) standardization data as well as the data on reliability and validity; (B) tests containing some psychometric information; (C) tests containing no psychometric data. It should be noted that the popularity of a test does not depend on its psychometric values. There are widely used tests for which there is no psychometric information at all, and there are tests with high psychometric standards, the application of which is very limited, however.

Below some of the tests that are well known to the majority of Russian psychologists are reviewed (see also Kirsheva & Ryubchikova, 1995; Krylov, 1990; Kulagin, 1984; Marischuk, 1984; Psychological tests, 1995; Ratanova & Shlayakhta, 1998; Shevandrin, 1998; Stolin & Shmelev, 1984). All Russian-language tests are referenced and reviewed psychometrically by Burlachuk and Morozov (1999).

Original Tests

Cognitive, Level A

'Activity Threshold Test' (T. L. Romanova, 1991) is used for diagnostics of the speed of decision making and readiness for action.

Cognitive, Level B

'Spatial Thinking Test' (I. S. Yakimanskaya, V. G. Zarkhin, H. M. Kadayas, 1991) is used for diagnostics of the level of development of spatial thinking in schoolchildren.

Cognitive, Level C

'Vygotski–Sakharov Test' (1927) is used for measuring thinking and concept formation abilities. The test is widely used in clinical and diagnostic studies.

Personality, Level A

'The Questionnaire of Terminal Values' (I. G. Senin, 1991) is used for measuring life values (prestige, social contacts, spiritual needs, etc.). 'Individual Business Style' (G. A. Grebenyuk, 1966) is used for diagnostics of the style of leadership. The test is used for selection of managers. 'Monotony Resistance Personality Test' (N. P. Fetiskin, 1991) is designed for diagnostics of personality resistance to monotony. 'Tomsk Rigidity Questionnaire' (G. V. Zalevsky, 1987) measures various aspects of rigidity. 'Formal-Dynamic Personality Inventory' (V. M. Roussalov, 1997) is used for diagnostics of formal-dynamic (temperamental) aspects of individual behavior.

Personality, Level B

'Well-being, Activity, Mood' (V. A. Doskin, N. A. Lavrentieva, V. B. Sharai, M. P. Mirroshnikova, 1973) is used for diagnostics of psycho-emotional characteristics.

'Self-Attitude Questionnaire' (V. V. Stolin, 1985) is used for diagnostics of the attitudes to oneself (self-respect, auto-sympathy, self-interest, etc.).

'Achievement Need Questionnaire' (Yu. M. Orlov, 1978) is used for measuring achievement motivation.

'Your Well-being Questionnaire' (O. S. Kopina, E. A. Suslova, E. V. Zaikina, 1995) is designed to assess psycho-emotional characteristics (attitudes to one's health, stress, satisfaction of life, etc.) in different groups of population.

'Humor Phraze Test' (A. G. Shmelev, V. S. Boldyreva, 1982) is a projective test for assessing motivational sphere (sex, money, fashion, etc.). The test is widely used for counseling.

'Personality Questionnaire of Bekhterev Institute' (1983) is designed for diagnostics of the types of attitudes to illness by the patients suffering from chronic somatic disorders.

'Mental Adaptation Disturbances Questionnaire' (A. I. Skorik, L. S. Sverdlov, 1993) is used for preliminary diagnostics of adaptation disturbances (general physical and mental comfort, depression, neurotization, etc.).

'Quality of Life' (A. G. Gladkov, V. P. Zaitsev, D. M. Aronov, M. G. Sharfnadel, 1982) is used for assessing physical, mental, and social well-being of patients suffering from heart diseases.

'The Pathocharacterological Diagnostic Questionnaire' (A. E. Lichko, 1970). The test is widely used for diagnostics of the types of psychopathology and character accentuation in adolescents.

Personality, Level C

'Time Schedule Test' (S. Ya. Rubinstein, 1979) is used to measure the structure of motivation.

Adapted Tests

Cognitive, Level A

'Heidelberger Sprachenentwicklungstest' (Grimm & Schöler, 1991) was adapted by N. B. Mikhailova (1990). The test is used for diagnostics of speech abilities in children aged from 3 to 9.

'Kognitiver Fähigkeitstest für 1. bis 3. Klassen' (Heller & Geisler, 1983) was highly modified and adapted by E. I. Shcheblanova, I. S. Averina, and E. N. Zadorina (1994). The test is designed for measuring intellectual abilities of children

aged 6–7. The Russian version received a new name: 'The test of express diagnostics of intellectual abilities'.

Cognitive, Level B

'Wechsler Adult Intelligence Scale' (Wechsler, 1958) was adapted by A. Yu. Panasyuk (1973). The test is widely used in psychological research and professional selection.

'Intelligenz-Struktur-Test' (Amthauer, 1973) was modified and adapted by K. M. Gurevich (Gurevitch & Akimova, 1987) to schoolchildren. The authors introduced a special concept of 'socio-psychological norm' (what a student of a particular social background – city, village, etc. – should know in a particular grade). The authors gave a new name to the test: 'School test of mental development'.

'Word Association Test' (popularized by Yung, 1906) was adapted by V. M. Kogan and M. S. Rogovin (1961). The test is widely used for assessing different aspects of human behavior (emotions, interests, sets, psychosexual disorders, etc.).

Cognitive, Level C

'Embedded Figure Test' (Witkin, 1954) is used (in its original form) for determining a perceptual style. The test is widely used in research of cognitive styles (P. N. Ivanov, 1985).

'Bourdon Test' (Bourdon, 1895) is widely used (in its original form) for measuring the degree of concentration and stability of attention.

'Raven Progressive Matrices' (Penrose, Raven, 1936; modified in 1982). The test is widely used (in its original form) for measuring intelligence (S. M. Morozov, 1980).

'Benton Test of Visual Retention' (1952) is widely used (in its original form) in clinics as an additional method for diagnostics of brain damage (V. M. Bleikher, I. V. Kruk, 1986).

'Sentence-Completion Techniques' (Pane, 1928; Tendler, 1930) was translated into Russian by G. G. Rumiantseva (1969). The test is widely used in clinical-diagnostic research for measuring linguistic abilities.

Personality, Level A

'Locus of Control Scale' (Rotter, 1966) was adapted by E. F. Bazhin (1984) (Bazhin, Golynkina, & Etkind, 1993). The test is widely used in personality research as well as in clinical psychodiagnostics and family counseling.

'Guilford–Zimmerman Temperament Survey' (Guilford & Zimmerman, 1949) was adapted by V. A. Ababkov, S. M. Babin, and G. L. Isurina (1993). The test is designed for measuring different aspects of temperament in the norm and patients with neurological and psychosomatic disturbances.

'Personal Orientation Inventory' (Shostrom, 1963) was adapted by A. A. Rukavishnikov (1991). The test is designed for measuring the degree of self-actualization.

'Edwards Personal Preference Schedule' (Edwards, 1959) was adapted by T. V. Kornilova, G. V. Paramei, and S. N. Enikolopov (1995) and is used for assessing various aspects of motivation (preferences).

Personality, Level B

'Purpose in Life Test' (Crambo & Macholik, 1964–1991). There are several modifications and adaptations. (K. Muzdybayev, 1891; D. A. Leontiev, 1986, 1992). The test is used for assessing different aspects of the 'meaning of life' (sense of being, future of life and responsibility, etc.).

'California Psychological Inventory' (Gough, 1956) was adapted and restandardized by N. V. Tarabrina (1989). The test measures various aspects of personality.

'Kelly Repertory Grid Technique' (Kelly, 1955). There are several modified and adapted versions (P. N. Kozlova, 1975; V. I. Pokhilko, E. O. Fedotova, 1984; V. V. Stolin, 1983). The test is used for studying personal constructs.

'Jenkins Activity Survey' (1967) was adapted by A. Goshtaus, V. Yadov, and Yu. Semenov (1972–1976). The test is used for diagnostics of the type A personality.

'Rosenzweig Picture-Frustration Study' (1945). There are several modifications and adaptations (N. V. Tarabrina, 1971; K. D. Shafranskaya, 1976). The test is widely used in research and clinical psychodiagnostics.

'State-Trait Anxiety Inventory' (Spielberger, 1983) was adapted by Yu. L. Khanin in cooperation with the author of the test (1980).

'Michigan Alcoholism Screening Test' (Selzer, 1971) was modified and standardized by A. E. Bobrov and A. N. Shurigin (1985). The test is designed for early diagnostics of pathological dependence on alcohol.

'Lüscher Farbwahl Test' (Lüscher, 1948). There were several attempts at adapting the test. The psychometric data are highly controversial (N. N. Pukhovsky, 1995).

Personality, Level C

'Sixteen Personality Factors Questionnaire' (Cattell, Cattell, & Cattell, 1994). There were several attempts of modification and adaptation of the test (Yu. M. Zabrodin and others, 1987; Vm. Roussalov, O. V. Guseva, 1990). Only half of the factors are homogeneous on the Russian

population. The test is widely used in research, professional selection and in clinical settings.

'Eysenck Personality Inventory' (1963). There are several attempts at adapting the test (I. N. Gilyasheva, 1963; A. G. Shmelev, Pokhilko, 1985; V. M. Roussalov, 1987). The adaptation process is not yet finished. The test is designed for measuring two personality scales: extraversion–introversion and emotional stability–neuroticism.

'Psychotism-Extraversion–Neuroticism' (Eysenck & Eysenck, 1968). The test was translated into Russian by an unknown author. The test is widely used, though the psychometric data are not available (Kirsheva & Ryubchikova, 1995).

'Bell Adjustment Inventory' (1938). The translation was done by A. A. Rukavishnikov and M. V. Sokolov (1991). The test measures the level of difficulties of adjustment of a person to various spheres of life.

'Life Style Index' (Plutchek, Kellerman, Conte, 1979). The translation was done by U. B. Klubova (1991). The test is designed for diagnostics of ego defense mechanisms.

'Wesenszug-Fragebogen' (Littman & Schmiescheck, 1982) is widely used for diagnostics of personality accentuations. The name of the translator is unknown. The test is widely used in clinical-psychological studies (L. F. Burlachuk, V. N. Dukhnevich, 1998).

'Crowne–Marlowe Social Desirability Scale' (1960). The test was translated and shortened by Yu. L. Khanin (1976). It is used for diagnostics of the motivation of approval.

'Leary Interpersonal Diagnosis' (1957) was modified and adapted by L. N. Sobchik (1990). The test is widely used for diagnostics of interpersonal relations and personality traits that are essential in social interactions.

'Taylor Manifest Anxiety Scale' (Taylor, 1953). The translated version by an unknown author is widely used in psychodiagnostics of sport (Khanin, 1980).

'Psychogeometric Test' (Dellinger, 1989) is used (in its original form) in psychological counseling. (A. A. Alekseeva, L. A. Gromova, 1991).

'Minnesota Multiphasic Personality Inventory' (Hathway, MacKeanly, 1943). There were several attempts at modification and adaptation of the test (F. B. Berezin, M. P. Miroshnikov, 1967; L. N. Sobchik, 1971). The test is widely used in clinical psycho-diagnostics, professional selection, and counseling.

'Rorschach Test' (Rorschach, 1921). It is widely used in clinical and psychological research. Interpretation is highly controversial (I. G. Bespalko, 1983).

'Hand Test' (Braiklin, Piotrovsky, Wagner, 1961). Adapted by the firm Imaton. The test is used for assessing human aggressive behavior.

'Thematic Apperception Test' (Murray, 1943) is widely used for differential psychodiagnostics of neuroses, psychoses and marginal states (Bespalko & Giliasheva, 1983).

20.11 SPANISH-LANGUAGE ASSESSMENT METHODS

Psychological assessment is devoted to the process of examination and scientific analysis of the behaviors and other psychological characteristics of a specific human subject or group of subjects, with the aim of describing, diagnosing, predicting, or changing relevant behaviors. In order to test assumptions about a subject's target behaviors – during this process – psychological testing and other measurement devices should be administered.

Therefore, tests and other measurement devices should be understood and undertaken in the context of the assessment process.

Psychological assessment (psychological testing included) is an ever-present subdiscipline of scientific psychology in Spain and other Spanish-speaking countries, as can be seen by considering four different types of information. First, university undergraduate programs include mandatory psychological assessment and testing courses (Blanco & Botella, 1995; Fernández-Ballesteros, 1991, 1992). Second, studies of psychologists' profiles (a survey with representative sample) show that approximately 50% of tasks conducted by Spanish psychologists concern psychological assessment and testing in applied fields such as clinical and health psychology (e.g., 'conducting interviews for clinical diagnosis'), school and educational psychology (e.g., 'individual or collective testing'); work and organizational psychology (e.g., 'administration of assessment tests'), forensic psychology (e.g., 'general diagnosis through interviews and psychological tests'); and traffic, correctional, and military psychology (e.g., 'administering psychological tests'). Third, the existence of several associations (e.g., *Sociedad Iberoamericana de Diagnóstico y Evaluación Psicológica* [Ibero-American Society of Psychological Diagnosis and Assessment]), the organization of national and international congresses and the publication of journals (e.g., *Evaluación Psicológica*[2] or *Revista Iberoamericana de Diagnóstico y Evaluación Psicológica* [Ibero-American Journal of Psychological Diagnosis and Assessment]) show the importance of psychological assessment in Spanish-speaking countries. Finally, APA test-development norms have been translated and adopted in Spain and the majority of Central and South American countries.

This section deals with several issues related to assessment methodology in the Spanish language.[3] First of all, a brief history will be presented, followed by an outline of the role of methodology in the assessment process. Also, the most important tests, techniques, and other measurement devices will be listed, and some of them described, along with a description of tests developed in English and translated into Spanish. Finally, the use of psychological tests in Spain, Portugal, and Latin America will be discussed.

Brief History of Assessment Methodology

As Carpintero (1989) pointed out, the development of psychological assessment can be traced back to the Renaissance; a Spaniard, Juan Huarte de San Juan (1575), with his book *Examen de los Ingenios para las Ciencias* (The Tryal of Wits), is a well-known precursor of psychological assessment (McReynolds, 1968). However, it is at the beginning of the twentieth century that we find the first works devoted to psychological methodology, with Madrid and Barcelona the leading centers of work in psychological assessment. From this point on, Spanish psychologists began to translate well-known tests, as well as developing some of their own. For example, at the end of the 1920s Germain and Rodrigo translated and adapted Terman's version of the Binet Intelligence Test, and during the 1940s Emilio Mira y Lopez (1949) developed the Myo-Kinetic Test for assessing personality through psycho-motor performance (see Buros, 1965). Moreover, there even took place several congresses on psychometrics. As a consequence of the Spanish Civil War (1936–39), however, a period of stagnation set in until the 1960s, from which point psychological assessment began to make great strides in its development throughout Spain.

Methodology in the Context of the Assessment Process

In the North-American tradition, psychological assessment has usually been confused with psychological testing, and therefore with assessment methodology. Nevertheless, as pointed out elsewhere, while testing and methods are primarily measurement-oriented, psychological assessment is problem- or demand-oriented and, above all, methodology refers to tests and other measurement techniques, while psychological assessment refers to a complex process of decision-making in which the psychological assessor

Table 20.2   *Tests and other assessment methodologies translated and adapted into Spanish*

Name of test	Author
Intelligence and Aptitudes	
Alexander Scale	W. P. Alexander
APT, Academic Promise Tests	M. G. Bennett, G. K. Bennett, & D. M. Clendenen et al.
Beta, Revised Beta Examination	C.-E. Kellog & N. W. Morton
Cognitive Ability Tests, Primary I & II	R. C. Throndike, E. Hagen, & I. Lorge
DAT, Differential Aptitudes Tests	M. G. Bennett, H. G. Seashore, & A. G. Wesman
D-48, Dominoes Test	P. Pichot
D-70, Dominoes Test	F. Kowrousky & P. Rennes
GCT, General Clerical Test	The Psychological Corporation Staff
G-factor Culture Fair Intelligence Tests 1/2/3	R. B. Cattell & A. K. S. Cattell
GMA, Graduate & Managerial Assessment	S. F. Blinkhorn
K-ABC, Kaufman Assessment Battery for Children	A. S. Kaufman & N. L. Kaufman
K-BIT, Kaufman Brief Intelligence Test	A. S. Kaufman & N. L. Kaufman
MacQuarrie for Mechanical Ability	T. W. MacQuarrie
Otis Self-Administering Test of Mental Ability	A. S. Otis
Progressive Matrices Tests (CPM, SPM, APM)	J. C. Raven
Primary Mental Aptitudes (PMA)	L. L. Thurstone
Seashore Measures of Musical Talents	C. E. Seashore, J. C. Saetvit, & D. Lewis
SET, Short Employment Test	G. K. Bennet & M. Gelink
TEA, SRA Test of Educational Ability	L. L. Thurstone & Th. G. Thurstone
Toni-2, Test of Non-verbal Intelligence	L. Brown, J. Sherbenou, & S. K. Johnsen
TP, Toulouse-Piéron	E. Toulouse & H. Piéron
WAIS-III, WISC-R, WPPSI, Intelligence Scales	D. Wechsler
Developmental Tests	
Batelle, Development Inventory	J. Newborg et al.
BSID, Bayley Scales of Infant Development	N. Bayley
MSCA, McCarthy Scales for Children Abilities	D. McCarthy
Personality Tests[5]	
ACS, Adolescent Coping Scales	E. Frydenberg & R. Lewis
Embedded Figure Tests (EFT, CEFT, PEFT)	H. A. Witkin & P. K. Oltman
BFQ, Big-Five Questionnaire	G. V. Caprara et al.
CAQ, Clinical Assessment Questionnaire	S. E. Krug
CAS, Child Anxiety Scale	J. S. Gillis
CDS, Child Depression Scale	M. Lang & M. Tisher
CPI, California Personality Inventory	H. G. Gough
CPQ, Child Personality Questionnaire	R. B. Porter & R. B. Cattell
EDI-2, Eating Disorders Inventory	D. M. Garner
EPI, EPQ, EPQ-R, Personality Questionnaires	H. J. Eysenck & S. B. G. Eysenck
ESPQ, Early School Personality Questionnaire	R. W. Coan & R. B. Cattell
FTT, Fairy Tales Test	C. Coulacoglou
HSPQ, High School Personality Questionnaire	R. B. Cattell, H. Beloff & R. W. Coan
IAS, Interpersonal Adjectives Scales	J. S. Wiggins
IPV, Salesmen Personality Inventory	Centre de Psychologie Appliquée
JAS, Jenkins Activity Scale	C. D. Jenkins, S. J. Zyzanski, & R. H. Rosenman
MBTI, Myers–Briggs Typological Inventory	I. Briggs-Myers & K. C. Briggs
MBI, Maslach Burnout Inventory	C. Maslach & S. E. Jackson
MCMI-II, Millon Clinical Multiaxial Inventory	Th. Millon
MMPI & MMPI-2, Multiphasic Personality Inventory	S. R. Hathaway & J. C. McKinley
PNP Questionnaire	P. Pichot
PPG-IPG, SIV, SPV, Personality and Values	L. V. Gordon
STAI, State-Trait Anxiety Inventory	C. D. Spielberger
STAIC, State-Trait Anxiety Inventory for Children	C. D. Spielberger
16-PF, 16PF-5 Personality Questionnaires	R. B. Cattell

Table 20.2   *continued*

Name of test	Author
Interest, Preferences and Attitude Tests	
Kuder-C Vocational Preferences Tests	J. F. Kuder
Manual & Motor Dexterity Tests	
Bennet Hand-Tool Dexterity Test	G. K. Bennett
Crawford Small Parts Dexterity Test	J. E. & D. M. Crawford
Stromberg Dexterity Test	E. L. Stromberg
Neuropsychological Tests	
Aphasia Test Examination	B. Ducame de Ribaucourt
Bender Gestalt Test	L. Bender
CAPE, Clifton Assessment Procedure for Elderly	A. H. Pattie & C. J. Gilleard
CMMS, Columbia Mental Maturity Scales	B. B. Burgemeister, L. H. Blum, & I. Lorge
ITPA, Illinois Test Psycholinguistic Abilities	S. A. Kirk, J. McCarthy, & W. D. Kirk
Luria–Christensen Neuropsychological Tests	A. L. Christensen
RBMT, Rivermead Behavioral Memory Test	B. Wilson, J. Cockburn, & A. Baddley
Rey Copy & Reproduction of Memory	A. Rey
Stroop Color & Word Test	C. J. Golden
TRVB, Benton Visual Retention Test	A. L. Benton
VOSP, Visual Object % Space Perception	E. K. Warrington & James
WCST, Wisconsin Card Sorting Test	D. A. Grant & E. A. Berg
Environmental Tests	
FES, WES, CIES, CES, Social Climate Scales (Family, Work, Correctional Instititions, & Classroom)	R. H. Moos

should test information about the subject, as well as testing hypotheses about target behavior with a view to satisfying a given demand, and finally testing whether a given treatment has had the expected outcome (Fernández-Ballesteros, 1997). In short, assessment methodology is the way the psychological assessor operationalizes and tests his/her hypothesis about the subject (or group of subjects). In general, this position has been assimilated into the psychological culture in Spanish-speaking psychological assessment.

Tests, Techniques, and other Measurement Devices in Spanish

We consider two types of tests, assessment techniques and other measurement devices in Spanish:

1. Tests mostly used in the United States that have been translated and adapted to the Spanish context and are available in Spain and other Spanish-speaking countries.[4] In Table 20.2, the most well-known tests already translated are listed.

2. Spaniards have also developed new tests. These tests belong to the largest domain of psychological techniques. Table 20.3 lists these tests and other methodologies in the following categories: intelligence; aptitudes (verbal, numerical, spatial and motor skills, perceptual and attentional skills); learning and memory; developmental tests; personnel selection tests; personality questionnaires; interests, preferences, attitudes and motivational tests; neuropsychological batteries; achievement tests, environmental assessment systems; observational procedures; and miscellaneous.

Unfortunately, lack of space precludes discussion or even description of these instruments. Nevertheless, the two tables can be considered as proof of the importance of psychological assessment methodology in the Spanish language.

Table 20.3 *Tests and other assessment methods developed in Spanish*

Name of test	Author
General Intelligence	
Battery of General Aptitudes	J. García Yagüe
Cards 'G'	N. García Nieto & C. Yuste
CC-78, Complex Questions	J. Crespo Vásquez
CHANGES, Test of Cognitive Flexibility	N. Seisdedos
CM-76, General Intelligence Test	J. García Yagüe
Elementary AMPE	F. Secadas
General Aptitudes, Lower Level	J. García Yagüe
IG-2, General Intelligence	TEA Publishers
TIG-1, Dominoes Test	TEA Publishers
TIG-2, Dominoes Test	TEA Publishers
TISD, Test of Data Selective Interpretation	N. Seisdedos
TEI, A & B	M. Yela
General Aptitudes Tests	
ABI, Basic Aptitudes of Computer Science	M. V. de la Cruz López
ABG-1 & 2, General Basic Aptitudes	TEA Publishers
AMD-77, Differentiated Mental Aptitudes	J. García Yagüe
AMDI, Differentiated Mental Aptitudes, Lower	J. García Yagüe
AMPE, Factorial	F. Secadas
BAC, Commercial Activity Battery	N. Seisdedos
BADYG, Battery of Differential and General Aptitudes	C. Yuste
BC, Battery for Drivers	TEA Publishers & J. L. Fernández Seara
BO, Battery of Workers	TEA Publishers
BPA, Batteries of Admission Tests (Levels 1 & 2)	N. Seisdedos
BPA, Admission Test Battery	N. Seisdedos
BS, Battery for Subordinates	TEA Publishers
Differential Battery of Intelligence	J. García Yagüe
Decatest	F. Secadas
SAE, Aptitude Test for Studying	F. Secadas
Verbal Aptitudes Tests	
COE, Comprehension of Written Orders (1 & 2)	TEA Publishers
TCV, Verbal Culture Test	TEA Publishers
Numerical Aptitudes Tests	
COINS, Numerical Aptitudes (Levels 1 & 2)	N. Seisdedos
Spatial and Mechanical Aptitudes Tests	
Development of Surfaces	M. Yela
Levers	M. Yela
Mechanics	M. Yela
Printed Puzzles	M. Yela
Solid Figure Rotation	M. Yela
Vocation Tests	F. Secadas
Perceptual and Attention Tests	
Consonants	N. Seisdedos
Faces	L. L. Thurstone & M. Yela
Identical Forms	L. L. Thurstone & M. Yela
Square of Letters	L. L. Thurstone & M. Yela
SIT-1, Situation (Spatial-Perceptual Test)	N. Seisdedos
TO-1 WORDS, Test of Observation	F. Rosel

Table 20.3 *continued*

Name of test	Author
Memory	
MAI, Immediate Auditory Memory	A. Cordero
MS-76, Immediate Memory with Meaning	J. García Yagüe & E. García Manzano
Office Orders	TEA Publishers
MY, Yuste Memory Test	C. Yuste
Manual and Motor Dexterity Tests	
Bimanual Coordination	M. Yela
Motor Speed	M. Yela
Visual Motor Coordination	M. Yela
Administrative Aptitudes Tests	
BTA, Battery of Administrative Tasks	TEA Publishers
IC, Complex Instructions	M. Yela
Personality Questionnaires	
AFA, Self-concept Scale Form A	G. Musitu, F. García, & M. Gutiérrez
AFA-5, Self-concept Scale Form 5	G. Musitu & F. García
ASPA, Coupole Assertiveness Questionnaire	M. Carrasco
CACIA, Auto-Control Questionnaire Children & Adolescents	A. Capafons & F. Silva-Moreno
CEP, Personality Questionnaire	J. L. Pinillos
CET-DE, Four-Dimensional Structural Depression Questionnaire	F. Alonso-Fernández
CPS, Situational Personality Questionnaire	J. L. Fernández-Seara, N. Seisdedos, & M. Mielgo
EAE, Stress Evaluation Scale	J. L. Fernández-Seara & M. Mielgo
EBP, Psychological Well-Being	J. Sánchez-Cánovas
EDAH, Attention-Deficit/Hyperactivity Disorder Evaluation	A. Farre & J. Narbona
ESFA, Adjective Family Satisfaction Scale	J. Barraca & L. López-Yarto
IAC, Behavior Adaptation Inventory	M. V. De La Cruz & A. Cordero
IDDA-EA, Differential Adjective Inventory for the Study of Mood	J. M. Tous & A. A. Pueyo
ISRA, Inventory of Situations & Anxiety Responses	J. J. Miguel-Tobal & A. R. Cano Vindel
MPS, Psychosocial Motivations Scale	J. Fernández-Seara
PEI, Personality Questionnaire	F. Secadas
TAMAI, Self-evaluating Multifactorial Infantile Adaptation Test	P. Hernández
TP-76 Personality Tensions	J. García Yagüe
Interests, Preferences, and Attitudes and Motivational Tests	
A-D, Questionnaire of Anti-Social/Criminal Behavior	N. Seisdedos
BAS, Battery of Socialization 1 & 2	F. Silva & M. C. Martorell
BAS, Battery of Socialization 3	F. Silva & M. C. Martorell
CETI, Study-Work Intellectual Questionnaire	C. Yuste
CHTE, Questionnaire of Study Habits & Techniques	M. Álvarez, R. Fernández, & TEA Publishers
CIPSA, Professional Interest Questionnaire	J. L. Fernández-Seara
IHE, Study Habits Inventory	F. Fernández Pozar
MPS, Psycho-social Motivational Scale	J. L. Fernández-Seara
SPS, Spanish Psycho-social Scale	N. Seisdedos
TAV, Salesman Appreciation Test	TEA Publishers
TV-76, Vocational Themes	J. Gárcia Yagüe & C. Castaño

Table 20.3   *continued*

Name of test	Author
Neuropsychological Tests	
Barcelona Test, An Integrated Neuropsychological Exam	J. Peña Casanova
EDAF, Audio-Phonological Discrimination Assessment	M. F. Brancal, F. Alcantud, A. M. Ferrer, & M. E. Quiroga
Sevilla Neuropsychological Battery	J. Leon-Carrión
TAVEC, Verbal Learning Spain-Complutense Tense	M. J. Benedet
TIDA, Daltonism Identification Test	J. Lillo-Jover
Achievement Tests	
BADIMALE, Diagnostic Battery of Reading Maturity	S. Molina-García
BAPAE 1 & 2, Battery of Tests for Scholastic Learning	M. V. De La Croz
BEHNALE, Evaluative Battery of Reading Learning	J. A. Mora
BLOC, Objective and Criterial Language Battery	M. Puyuelo, E. H. Wig, J. Renom, & A. Solanas
BP-3, Pedagogical Battery 2. Assessment of the Spanish Language in the Middle Cycle of General Basic Education	F. Fernández Pozar
CLT-CLOZE, Two Tests of Reading Comprehension	A Suárez Yañez & P. Meara
CMP, Control Test of Maturity in the Preschooler	J. Riart, I. Vendrell, & Soler I Planas
COLE, Reading Comprehension Test in the Elementary Cycle	J. Riart & M. S. Soler
EDIL-1, Exploration of Individual Reading Difficulties	M. D. González Portal
EPP, Psychomotricity Assessment in Pre-school	M. V. De La Cruz & M. C. Mazaira
EVOCA, Vocabulary Estimation	A. Suarez, N. Seisdedos, & P. Meara
LC, Comprehensive Reading	A. Lázaro Martínez
PLON, Oral Language Test of Navarra	Government of Navarra
PRESCHOOL, Diagnostic Tests	M. V. De La Cruz
PROLEC, Reading Process Battery	F. Cuetos, B. Rodríguez, & E. Ruano
READING, Tests of (Levels 1 & 2)	M. V. De La Cruz
SPELLING-2, Appreciation of Practical Knowledge	N. Seisdedos
TALE, Reading-Writing Analysis Test	J. Toro & M. Cervera
TYPING, Appreciation of Practical Knowledge	TEA Publishers
THG, Test of Graphomotor Skills	J. García Núñez & O. Leon García
TLC-M, Comprehensive Reading Test (Middle Cycle)	G. Comes & S. Sánchez
Environmental Tests	
PCA/PHS, Social Skills Evaluation Program Assessment	M. A. Verdugo
POT, Employment Orientation Assessment Program	M. A. Verdugo
SERA, Elderly Facilities Assessment System	R. Fernández-Ballesteros
Observational Systems	
EOD, Observational Developmental Scale	F. Secadas
SOC-III, Observational Family Interaction System	M. C. Cerezp & Whaler
West-Virginia/Autónoma University of Madrid Observational System	A. Martin, V. Rubio, J. M. Juan Espinosa, & M. O. Márquez
Miscellaneous	
ECP, Grading Scale	TEA Publishers
Hidden Forms	N. Seisdedos
PIP, Infantile Pre-diagnosis (Questionnaire for parents)	A. Izquierdo Martínez

The Use of Tests in Spanish-Speaking Countries

On two occasions (1978 and 1987; see Fernández-Ballesteros, 1992), surveys were carried out on Spanish psychologists in order to find out the details of their technological practices in Psychological Assessment. On both occasions the number of responses obtained was low (in 1978, out of 965 psychologists to whom questionnaires were sent, only 68 answered; in the 1987 survey, which was published in the journal *Papeles del Psicólogo*, 128 replied). Therefore, the data that follow, taken from the 1987 survey, cannot be claimed to be representative, but rather merely illustrative of some aspects of the work of Spanish psychologists using Psychological Assessment.

Regarding the tests most frequently used by those who answered the survey, 83% said that they used some of the Wechsler Scales of Intelligence, and 90% used some of the factorial tests (mainly Raven's Progressive Matrices and Thurstone's PMA); 83% also reported using Cattell's 16 PF, and only 50% Hathaway and McKinley's MMPI; 48% reported occasional use of Murray's TAT, while only 26% used the Psychodiagnostic Rorschach; finally, 50% of those surveyed indicated that they used clinical behaviorist tests (the most frequently cited being Beck's Depression Scale and Wolpe's FSS).

The above-mentioned survey also took account of the opinions of the participating psychologists regarding their expectation about the future of assessment methodology. The general opinion was that behavioral tests would be those most frequently used in the future. They also expected a certain amount of stabilization to occur in the format of intelligence and personality tests, and they believed there would be a decrease in the use of projective technology.

Recently, under the auspices of the International Test Commission (ITC) and the European Federation of Professional Psychologists Associations (EFPPA), a survey on the use of tests in several countries around the world has been carried out. The results from Spain, Portugal, and Latin America have recently been published by Prieto, Muñiz, Almeida, & Bartram (1999). Questionnaires were sent to 41 experts selected from Spain and Portugal, as well as 19 experts from Latin-American countries. Nineteen responses were received from 14 countries. Reported results showed that the use of tests is not as frequent and appropriate as it could be. Experts reported the need for the involvement of national professional psychological associations and universities to improve the use of testing. The five most frequently used tests are the

following: Wechsler Intelligence Scales (WAIS and WISC), MMPI, Rorschach Test, Raven's Progressive Matrices Test, 16 PF. This ranking is quite similar to the above-mentioned one, and is also similar to those found in English-speaking countries.

It can be concluded that there is a wide spectrum of tests and other assessment methodologies in the Spanish language that cover all psychological content; nevertheless, and despite the existence of tests constructed in Spanish, Spanish-speaking psychologists generally use tests developed in the United States.

NOTES

1. These ages are approximate, taking into account that within the French school system, pupils can be obliged to re-take a year and some can therefore be older than their classmates.

2. Transformed in 1992 into the *European Journal of Psychological Assessment*.

3. Spanish publishing companies usually have offices in all Ibero-American countries (Brazil included).

4. Some of these tests could also be standardized for other Spanish-speaking cultures, but are available all over Latin America in the Spanish adaptation.

5. For projective tests such as the Rorschach Test, TAT, Phillipson, etc. materials as well as the most well-known coding systems are available.

RESOURCE REFERENCES

Akhmedzhanov, E. P. (1996). *Psychological tests*. Moscow: List.

Almanakh of psychological tests. (1966). Moscow: KSP.

Amelang, M., & Zielinsky, W. (1997). *Psychologische Diagnostik und Intervention* (Psychological assessment and intervention). Berlin: Springer.

Anastasi, A. (1988). *Psychological testing* (6th ed.). New York: McMillan.

Berezin, F. B., Miroshnikov, M. P., & Rozhanets, R. V. (1976). *The methods of comprehensive personality assessment*. Moscow: Meditsina.

Bleikher, V. M., & Burlachuk, L. F. (1986). *Psychological diagnostic of intelligence and personality*. Kiev: Vishcha shkola.

Brickenkamp, R. (1997). *Handbuch psychologischer und pädagogischer Tests* [Handbook of tests in psychology and education]. Göttingen: Hogrefe.

Brzeziński, J. (1997). *Metodologia badań psychologicznych* [Methodology of psychological research]. Warszawa: Wydawnictwo Naukowe PWN.

Cronbach, L. J. (1949). *Essential of psychological testing* (3rd ed.). New York: Harper & Row.

Gaida, V. K., & Zakharov, V. P. (1982). *Psychological testing*. Leningrad: Leningradsky Universitet.

Hornowska, E., Kowalik, S., Matczak, A., Nowak, A., Paluchowski, W. J., Stasiakiewicz, M., & Zawadzki, B. (2000). Podstawowe metody badawcze [Basic research methods]. In J. Strelau (Ed.), *Psychologia: Podrêcznik akademicki. T. 1. Podstawy psychologii* [Psychology: Academic handbook. Vol. 1. Basis of psychology] (pp. 437–522). Gdañsk: Gdañskie Wydawnictwo Psychologiczne.

Huteau, M., & Lautrey, J. (1999a). *Evaluer l'intelligence: psychométrie cognitive*. Paris: Presses Universitaires de France.

Huteau, M., & Lautrey, J. (Eds). (1999b). *Approches différentielles en psychologie*. Rennes: Presses Universitaires de Rennes.

Impara, J. C. and Plake, B. S. (Eds.). (1998). *Thirteenth Mental Measurement Yearbook*. Nebraska: University of Nebraska Press.

Kabanov, M. M., Lichko, A. E., & Smirnov, V. M. (1983). *Methods of psychological diagnostics and correction in clinics*. Moscow: Meditsina.

Pawlik, K. (1968). *Dimensionen des Verhaltens* [Dimensions of behavior]. Bern, Switzerland: Huber.

Pawlik, K. (1992). *Psychological assessment*. In M. R. Rosenzweig (Ed.), *International psychological science* (pp. 253–287). Washington, DC: American Psychological Association.

Prieto, G., Muñiz, J., Almeida, L. S., & Bartram, D. (1999). Uso de los tests psicológicos en España, Portugal e Iberoamérica. *Revista Iberoamericana de Diagnóstico y Evaluación Psicológica, 8*, 67–82.

De Zeeuw, J. (1995). *Algemene Psychodiagnostiek* [General psychodiagnostics] (Vols. 1–3). Lisse: Swets en Zeitlinger.

ADDITIONAL LITERATURE CITED

Alekseyev, A. A., & Gromova, L. A. (1991). *Psychogeometry for managers*. Leningrad: SPb.

American Psychiatric Association. (1994). *Diagnostic and statistical manual of mental disorders* (4th ed.). Washington, DC: American Psychiatric Association.

American Psychological Association. (1985). *Standards for educational and psychological tests* (5th ed.). Washington, DC: American Psychological Association.

Amthauer, R. (1973). Intelligenz-Struktur-Test 70 (IST 70) [Intelligence structure test 70]. Göttingen: Hogrefe.

Aubret, J., & Gilbert, P. (1994). *Reconnaissance et validation des acquis*. Paris: Presses Universitaires de France.

Bacher, F., & Nguyen Xuan, A. (1967). Quelques données sur les tests d'aptitudes utilisés dans l'enquête de 1964 en classe de 3eme: IC3, V3, N3,

S3. *Bulletin de l'Institut National d'Orientation Professionelle, 23*, 219–260.

Barker, R. G. (1960). *Ecology and motivation*. Nebraska Symposium on Motivation, Lincoln, NE: University of Nebraska Press.

Bartram, D. (1998). The need for international guidelines on standards for test use: A review of European and international standards. *European Psychologist, 3*, 155–163.

Baumann, U., & Stieglitz, R. D. (1983). *Testmanual zum AMDP-System* [Test manual for the AMDP system]. Berlin: Springer.

Bazhin, E. F., Golynkina, E. A., & Etkind, A. M. (1993). *A questionnaire of the level of subjective control*. Moscow: Moskovsky Universitet.

Bennett, G. K., Seashore, H. G., & Wesman, A. G. (1981). *Differential Aptitude Tests (DAT)* (5th ed.). New York: Psychological Corporation.

Bernaud, J. L., Dupont, J. B., Priou, P., & Vrignaud, P. (1994). Les questionnaires d'intérêts professionnels. *Psychologie et Psychométrie, Numéro hors série*, 195 pages.

Bernstein, A. S. (1987). Orienting response research in schizophrenia: Where we have come and where we might go. *Schizophrenia Bulletin, 13*, 623–641.

Bespalko, I. G., & Gilyasheva, I. N. (1983). Projective methods. In M. M. Kabanov, A. E. Lichko, V. M. Smirnov (Eds.), *Methods of psychological diagnostics and correction in clinics* (pp. 116–144). Leningrad: Meditsina.

Binet, A., & Henri, V. (1896). Psychologie individuelle. *Année Psychologique, 2*, 411–465.

Binet, A., & Simon, T. (1905). Méthodes nouvelles pour le diagnostic du niveau intellectuel des anormaux. *L'Année Psychologique, 11*, 191–244.

Blanchard, S., Francequin-Chartier, G., Stassinet, G., & Vrignaud, P. (1991). *Outils et procédures de bilan pour la définition d'un projet de formation personnalisé*. Issy-les-Moulineaux: Editions et Applications Psychologiques.

Blanco, A., & Botella, J. (1995). Revisión del Plan de Estudios. *Papeles del Psicólogo, 45–46*, 120–127.

Bleikher, V. M., & Kruk, I. V. (1997). *Pathopsychological diagnostics*. Kiev: Zdorovie.

Bruchon-Schweitzer, M., & Ferrieux, D. (1991). Les méthodes d'évaluation du personnel utilisées pour le recrutement en France. *L'Orientation Scolaire et Professionnelle, 20*, 71–88.

Büchel, F., & Paour, J.-L. (Eds.). (1990). Assessment of learning and development potential: Theory and practices. *European Journal of Psychology of Education, 5*, special issue.

Burlachuk, L. F. (1997). *The introduction into projective psychology*. Kiev: Nika-Tsentr.

Burlachuk, L. F., & Morzov, S. M. (1999). *Dictionary-handbook of psychodiagnostics*. Sankt-Petersburg: Pites.

Buros, O. K. (1965). *The seventh mental measurement yearbook*. New York: Gryphone Press.

Buse, L., & Pawlik, K. (1994). Differenzierung zwischen Tages-, Setting- und Situationskonsistenz ausgewählter Verhaltensmerkmale, Maßen der Aktivierung, des Befinden und der Stimmung in Alltagssituationen [Differentiating between day, setting, and situation consistency of selected measures of behavior, of activation, of feeling, and moods in everyday-life situations]. *Diagnostica, 40,* 2–26.

Butcher, J. N., Dahlstrom, W. G., Graham, J. R., Tellegen, A., & Kaemmer, B. (1989). *Manual for administration and scoring, MMPI-2, Minnesota Multiphasic Personality Inventory-2*. Minneapolis: University of Minnesota Press.

Caccioppo, J. T., & Tassinary, L. G. (Eds.). (1990). *Principles of Psychophysiology – Physical social and interventical elements*. New York: Cambridge University Press.

Campbell, D., & Fiske, D. (1959). Convergent and discriminant validation by the multitrait-multimethod matrix. *Psychological Bulletin, 56,* 81–105.

Carpintero, H. (1989). La evolución del Psicodiagnóstico en España. *Evaluación Psicológica/Psychological Assessment, 5*(1), 3–23.

Carroll, J. B. (1993). *Human cognitive abilities*. New York: Cambridge University Press.

Castro, D., Meljac, C., & Joubert, B. (1996). Pratiques et outils des cliniciens français – les enseignements d'une enquête. *Pratiques Psychologiques, 4,* 73–80.

Cattell, R. B., Cattell, A. K., & Cattell, H. E. P. (1994). *16 PF-Test* (5th ed.). Champaign, IL: Institute for Personality and Ability Testing Inc. (IPAT).

Cattell, R. B., & Warburton, F. W. (1965). *Principles of personality measurement and a compendium of objective tests*. Champaign, IL: University of Illinois Press.

Cuvillier, B., Tandeau de Marsac, F., Vrignaud, P., & Delattre, C. (1999). *La station spatiale*. Paris: EAP.

Dubois, P. H. (1966). A test-dominated society: China, 115 BC–1905 AD. In A. Anastasi (Ed.), *Testing problems in perspective* (pp. 29–36). Washington: American Council of Education.

Dupont, J.-B. (1971). *L'Inventaire Personnel de Holland*. Issy-les-Moulineaux: Editions et Applications Psychologiques.

Ekman, P. (1982). *Emotion in the human face*. New York: Cambridge University Press.

Fahrenberg, J., Hampel, R., & Selg, H. (1994). *Freiburger Persönlichkeitsinventar. Revidierte Fassung FPI-R* [Freiburg personality inventory. Revised version FPI-R]. Göttingen: Hogrefe.

Fahrenberg, J., & Myrtek, M. (Eds.). (1996). *Ambulatory assessment*. Göttingen: Hogrefe.

Feldman, R. S., & Rimé, B. (Eds.). (1991). *Fundamentals of nonverbal behavior*. Cambridge: Cambridge University Press.

Fernández-Ballesteros, R. (1991). Enseñanza, investigación y aplicación de la evaluación psicológica. *Evaluación Psicológica/Psychological Assessment, 7,* 5–23.

Fernández-Ballesteros, R. (1992). Psychological Assessment. *Applied Psychology. An International Review, 43,* 157–174.

Fernandez-Ballesteros, R. (1997). Guidelines for the Assessment Process (GAP). *European Psychologist, 2,* 352–355.

Fleishman, E. A., & Hempel, W. E., Jr. (1954). Changes in factor structure of a complex psychomotor test as a function of practice. *Psychometrika, 19,* 239–252.

Fleishman, E. A., & Reilly, M. E. (1992). *Handbook of human abilities*. Bethesda, MD: Management Research Institute.

Forner, Y. (1997). Quelle place pour la motivation à la réussite dans l'explication des résultats au 'Bac de français'? *Revue de Psychologie de l'Education, 1,* 125–146.

French, J. W., Ekstrom, R. B. & Price, L. A. (1963). *Manual and kit of reference tests for cognitive factors*. Princeton, NJ: Educational Testing Service.

Grégoire, J. (1992). *Evaluer l'intelligence de l'enfant*. Liège: Mardaga.

Grégoire, J. (1999). Ethical and deontological codes on test use in french speaking countries. *European Journal of Psychological Assessment, 15.*

Grimm, H., & Schöler, H. (1991). *Heidelberger Sprachenentwicklungstest (HSET)*. Göttingen: Hogrefe.

Guilford, J. P. (1959). *Personality*. New York: McGraw-Hill.

Gurevich, K. M., & Akimova, M. K. (1987). *A school test of intellectual abilities (SHTUR). Methodic recommendations in the work with the test (for school psychologists)*. Moscow: Prosveshenie.

Hathaway, S. R., & McKinley, J. C. (1943). *Manual for the Minnesota multiphasic personality inventory*. New York: Psychological Corporation.

Heller, K., & Geisler, H. J. (1983). *Kognitiver Fähigkeitstest für 1. bis 3. Klassen (KFT 1–3)*. Göttingen: Hogrefe.

Holtzman, W. H., Thorpe, J. S., Swartz, J. D., & Herron, E. W. (1961). *Ink-blot perception and personality*. New York: Wiley.

Horn, W. (1972). Begabungstestsystem (BTS) (Ability test system). Göttingen: Hogrefe.

Huarte de San Juan, J. (1575). *Examen de Ingenios para las ciencias*. (The tryal of wits; Trans E. Bellamy). London: Richard Sare at Grays-Inn Gate in Holborn, 1698.

Hundleby, J. D., Pawlik, K., & Cattell, R. B. (1963). *Personality factors in objective test derives*. San Diego, CA: Knapp.

Huteau, M. (Ed.). (1994). *Actes du colloque 'L'évaluation psychologique des personnes'*. Issy-les-Moulineaux: Editions et Applications Psychologiques.

International Standards Organisation. (1981). *ISO Norm 5725: Precision of test methods*. Geneva: International Standards Organisation.

Jäger, A. O., Süss, H.-M., & Beauducel, A. (1996). Berliner Intelligenzstruktur-Test (BIS-Test) [Berlin structure of intelligence test (BIS-Test)]. Göttingen: Hogrefe.

Jing, Q. C., & Hu, P. C. (1998). The development of standards and the regulation of the practice of clinical psychology in China. In A. N. Wein (Ed.), *Comprehensive clinical psychology. Vol. 2: Professional issues* (pp. 73–83). New York: Pergamon.

Kaufman, A. S., & Kaufman, N. L. (1983). *Kaufmann assessment battery for children*. Circle Pines, MN: American Guidance Service.

Kaufman, A. S., & Kaufman, N. L. (1993). *Kaufman adolescent and adult intelligence test*. Circle Pines, MN: American Guidance Service.

Khanin, Yu. L. (1976). *A Marlowe–Crowne scale for studying the motivation of approval*. Leningrad: NII fizicheskoi kulturi.

Khanin, Yu. L. (1980). *Psychology of communication in sport*. Moscow: Fizkultura i sport.

Kirsheva, N. V., & Ryubchikova, N. V. (1995). *Psychology of personality: tests, questionnaires and methods*. Moscow: Gelikon.

Kleinbeck, O., & Rutenfranz, J. (Ed.) (1987). Arbeitspsychologie [Psychology of work]. In *Enzyklopädie der Psychologie* (vol. D/III/1). Göttingen: Hogrefe.

Kozlova, I. N. (1975). Personality as a system of constructs: some questions of J. Kelly psychological theory. In *Systems Research* (pp. 128–148). Moscow: Nauka.

Krylov, A. A. (Ed.). (1990). *Practicum in experimental and applied psychology*. Leningrad: Leningradsky Universitet.

Kulagin, B. V. (1984). *The foundations of professional psychodiagnostics*. Leningrad: Meditsina.

Larcebeau, S. (1983). Motivation et personalité [Motivation and personality]. *L'Orientation Scolaire et Professionnelle, 12*, 215–242.

Lattmann, C. (Ed.). (1989). *Das Assessment-Center-Verfahren der Eignungsbeurteilung. Sein Aufbau, seine Anwendung und sein Aussagegehalt* [The assessment-center procedure of aptitude assessment. Its design, application and validity]. Heidelberg: Physica Verlag.

Leach, M. M., & Harbin, J. J. (1997). Psychological ethics codes: A comparison of twenty-four countries. *International Journal of Psychology, 32*(3), 181–192.

Lemoine, J. (Ed). (1998). Le bilan de compétences. *European Review of Applied Psychology, 48*, Numéro spécial.

Leontiev, D. A. (1992). *A test of meaning-of-life orientations*. Moscow: Smysl.

Lévy-Leboyer, C. (1993). *Le bilan de compétences*. Paris: Editions d'Organisation.

Lezak, M. D. (1995). *Neuropsychological assessment* (3rd ed.). New York: Oxford University Press.

Lichko, A. E. (1983). Pathocharacterological diagnostic questionnaire (PDQ) for adolescents. In M. M. Kabanov, A. E. Lichko, & V. M. Smirnov (Eds.), *Methods of psychological diagnostics and correction in clinics* (pp. 81–102). Leningrad: Meditsina.

Littmann, E. M., & Schmieschek, K. (1982). *Wesenszugfragebogen (WZF)*. Göttingen: Hogrefe.

Loarer, E., Chartier, D., Huteau, M., & Lautrey, J. (1995). *Peut-on éduquer l'intelligence?* Bern: Peter Lang.

Longeot, F. (1978). *Les stades opératoires de Piaget et les facteurs de l'intelligence*. Grenoble: Presses Universitaires de Grenoble.

Lord, F. M., & Novick, M. R. (1968). *Statistical theories of mental test scores*. Reading, MA: Addison-Wesley.

Lorr, M., Klett, C. J., & McNair, D. M. (1965). *Syndromes of psychosis*. Elmsford, NY: Pergamon Press.

Marischuk, V. L., & Bludov, V. M. (1984). *Methods of psychodiagnostics in sport*. Moscow: Prosveshenie.

McClelland, D. C. (1971). *Assessing human motivation*. New York: General Learning Press.

McReynolds, P. (1968). History of psychological assessment. In P. McReynolds (Ed.), *Advances in Psychological Assessment*. Palo Alto, CA: Science and Behavior Books.

Meljac, C., & Lemmel, G. (1999). *Manuel de l'UDN II*. Paris: Editions du Centre de Psychologie Appliquée.

Methods of psychological diagnostics. (1994). Moscow: Institut Pskhologii Rossiiskoi Akademii Nauk.

Mira y Lopez (1949). *Hacia una vejez joven*. Buenos Aires: Kopeluz.

Mullet, E., Barthélemy, J.-P., Duponchelle, L., Muñoz-Sastre, M.-T., & Neto, F. (1996). Décision, choix, jugement, orientation. *L'Orientation Scolaire et Professionnelle, 25*, 169–192.

Murray, H. A. (1943). *Thematic apperception test*. Cambridge, MA: Harvard University Press.

Murstein, B. (1963). *Theory and research in projective techniques (emphasing the TAT)*. New York: Wiley.

Panasyuk, A. Yu. (1973). *Adapted version of the D. Wechsler method*. Moscow: NII Psikhiatrii MZ RSFSR.

Pauli, L., Nathan, H., Droz R., & Grize, J. B. (1990). *Inventaires piagétiens*. Paris: Editions du Centre de Psychologie Appliquée.

Pawlik, K. (1968). *Dimensionen des Verhaltens* [Dimensions of behavior]. Bern, Switzerland: Huber.

Pawlik, K. (Ed.). (1982). *Multivariate Persönlichkeitsforschung* [Multivariate personality research]. Bern, Switzerland: Huber.

Pawlik, K. (Ed.). (1994). *William Stern: Die Differentielle Psychologie in ihren methodischen Grundlagen* [William Stern: Differential psychology in its methodological foundations]. Bern, Switzerland: Huber.

Pawlik, K. (Ed.) (1996). *Grundlagen und Methoden der Differentiellen Psychologie* [Foundations and methods of differential psychology]. In *Enzyklopädie der Psychologie* (vol. C/VIII/I). Göttingen: Hogrefe.

Pawlik, K. (1998). The psychology of individual differences: The personality puzzle. In J. G. Adair, D. Bélanger, & K. L. Dion, (Eds.), *Advances in psychological science* (vol. 1, pp. 1–30). Hove, UK: Psychology Press.

Pawlik, K., & Buse, L. (1996). Verhaltensbeobachtung in Labor und Feld [Behavior observation in the laboratory and in the field]. In K. Pawlik (Ed.), *Grundlagen und Methoden der Differentiellen Psychologie. Enzyklopädie der Psychologie* (vol. C/VII/I, pp. 359–394). Göttingen: Hogrefe.

Perret-Clermont, A. N. (1979). *La construction de l'intelligence dans l'interaction sociale* [Intelligence construction through social interaction]. Bern: Peter Lang.

Pokhilko, V. I., & Fedotova, E. O. (1984). Repertory grid technique in experimental personality psychology. *Voprosi psichologii, 3*, 151–157.

Psychodiagnostic methods (in complex longitudinal studies) (1976). Leningrad: Leningradsky Universitet.

Psychological tests. (1995). Moscow: Svetoton.

Ratanova, T. A., & Shlyakhta, N. F. (1998). *Psychodiagnostic methods of personality studies.* Moscow: Flinta.

Reynolds, C. R., & Brown, R. T. (Eds.). (1984). *Perspectives on bias in mental testing.* New York: Plenum Press.

Richard, J.-F. (Ed) (1996). Le diagnostic cognitif. *Psychologie Française, 41.*

Rohracher, H. (1969). *Kleine Characterkunde* [Brief characterology] (12th ed.). Vienna: Urban & Schwarzenberg.

Rolland, J. P., & Mogenet, J. L. (1994). *D5D.* Paris: Editions du Centre de Psychologie Appliquée.

Rorschach, H. (1921). *Psychodiagnostik* [Psychodiagnostics]. Leipzig: Bucher.

Rossi, P. M., & Freeman, H. E. (1993). *Evaluation.* Beverly Hills, CA: Sage.

Rosencwajg, P., & Huteau, M. (1996). Les stratégies globale, analytique et synthétique dans les cubes de Kohs. *Psychologie Française, 41*, 57–64.

Roussalov, V. M., & Guseva, O. V. (1990). A shortened version of Cattell 16 PF (8PF). *Psichologichesky zhurnal, 1*, 34–38.

Roussalov, V. M. (1987). A new version of adaptation of EPI. *Psichologichesky zhurnal, 1*, 113–126.

Shevandrin, N. I. (1998). *Psychodiagnostics, correction and development of personality.* Moscow: Vlados.

Sobchik, L. N. (1998). *Introduction into the psychology of individuality.* Moscow: Institute of Applied Psychology.

Sobchik, L. N. (1990). *Diagnostics of interpersonal relations; modified version of interpersonal diagnostics on T. Leary.* Moscow: Meditsina.

Spearman, C. (1904). 'General intelligence', objectively determined and measured. *American Journal of Psychologie, 15*, 201–293.

Spielberger, C. D. (1983). *State-trait anxiety inventory manual.* Palo Alto, CA: Consulting Psychologists Press.

Spitzer, R. L., Williams, J. B. W., & Gibbon, M. (1987). *Instruction manual for the structural clinical interview for DSM-III-R.* New York: State Psychiatric Institute.

Stern, W. (1900). *Über Psychologie der individuellen Differenzen* [On the psychology of individual differences]. Leipzig: Barth.

Stern, W. (1911). *Die Differentielle Psychologie in ihren methodischen Grundlagen.* [Differential psychology in its methodological foundations]. (2nd ed.). Leipzig: Barth.

Stolin, V. V. (1983). *Self-consciousness of personality.* Moscow: Moskovsky Universitet.

Stolin, V. V., & Shmelev, A. G. (Eds.). (1984). *Practicum in psychodiagnostics.* Moscow: Moskovsky Universitet.

Tarabrina, N. V. (1971). An experimental study of frustration in hysteric patients. In *Clinical-psychological research of personality* (pp. 129–131). Leningrad: Leningradski Universitet.

Taylor, J. A. (1953). A personality scale of manifest anxiety. *Journal of Abnormal and Social Psychology, 48*, 285–290.

Thurstone, L. L., & Thurstone, T. G. (1943). *The Chicago tests of primary mental abilities.* Chicago: University of Chicago Press.

Vrignaud, P. (1996). Les tests au XXIéme siècle. Que peut-on attendre des évolutions méthodologiques et technologiques dans le domaine de l'évaluation psychologique des personnes? *Pratiques Psychologiques, 4*, 5–28.

Wainer, H. (1990). *Computerized adaptive testing: A primer.* Hillsdale, NJ: Lawrence Erlbaum.

Wechsler, D. (1958). *The measurement and appraisal of adult intelligence.* Baltimore, MD: Williams & Wilkens.

Wechsler, D., & Stone, C. P. (1974). *Wechsler memory scale II manual.* New York: Psychological Corporation.

Widiger, T. A., & Trull, T. J. (1991). Diagnosis and clinical assessment. *Annual Review of Psychology, 42*, 109–133.

Wing, J. K., Cooper, J. E., & Sartorius, N. (1974). *The measurement and classification of psychiatric syndrome.* New York: Cambridge University Press.

World Health Organization (1990). *International classification of diseases (ICD 10)*. Geneva: World Health Organization.

Zazzo, R., Gilly, M., & Verba-Rad, M. (1966). *Nouvelle Echelle Métrique de l'Intelligence*. Paris: Armand Colin.

Zhang, H. C. (1998). Psychological measurement in China. *International Journal of Psychology, 23,* 101–117.

Zheng, Y. (1993). *Handbook of application of clinical scales*. Changsha: Hunan Medical University Press.

Communications concerning this chapter should be addressed to: Professor Kurt Pawlik, Department of Psychology, University of Hamburg, Von-Melle-Park 11, 20146 Hamburg, Germany

21

Clinical Psychology I: Psychological Disorders: Description, Epidemiology, Etiology, and Prevention

KENNETH J. SHER AND TIM TRULL

21.1 HISTORY AND CONCEPT OF PSYCHOLOGICAL DISORDERS

Although we often think of mental disorders as a by-product of the modern industrial age, scholars have documented apparent cases of various forms of psychopathology since the beginning of recorded history. 'Observations on mental illness, the knowledge of certain clinical pictures, apparently were not wanting and were rather correct' (Zilboorg, 1941, p. 29). How-ever, explanations for these various conditions were embedded within the religious, philo-sophical, and scientific discourses of each culture and often differ dramatically from current-day conceptualizations (Vieth, 1965; Zilboorg, 1941).

Early History

Many of the major figures in the history of psychopathology are physicians who played a role in the evolution of medicine and surgery. Hippocrates (fourth century B.C.E.), the 'Father of Greek Medicine', described the symptoms of melancholia (depression), puerperal insanity (postpartum depression), and other syndromes. Perhaps most important, his division of mental diseases into two classes, mania and melancholia, was influential for the next 2,000 years. Aretaeus (first century C.E.) noted the frequent co-occurrence of mania and depression in the same individuals and presaged the recognition of what is today called bipolar disorder. He also pro-posed that certain personality traits predisposed individuals to experience specific clinical syndromes, a currently active area of research and theory. Aretaeus believed that the classification of mental disorders could be based on prognosis (course and ultimate outcome). Galen of Pergamon (second century C.E.), the famed Roman physician, described not only how physical events could affect mental states but also how mental states could affect physiological responses and chided other physicians for not knowing that 'the pulse is altered by quarrels and alarms which suddenly disturb the mind' (cited in Vieth, 1965, p. 36). Thomas Sydenham (seventeenth century), the 'English Hippocrates', argued for the importance of classifying diseases and placed the cause of certain somatic complaints (see discussion of hysteria below) in the mind. Although of interest in its own right, consideration of the history of thinking about psychopathology is especially useful if it illustrates general principles about the study of a phenomenon. With respect to the history of psychopathology, several general principles can be derived. The history of hysteria illustrates these principles quite well.

In tracing the history of 'hysteria' (a now anachronistic term that refers to conditions that would currently be classified as somatoform or dissociative disorders; see Section 21.4), Ilza Vieth (1965) carefully documented descriptions of apparent cases of hysteria from the earliest Egyptian medical papyri (dated to approximately 3,900 years ago) to the twentieth century. The term hysteria has as its root, *hystera*, the Greek word for uterus, and, for most of its history, the concept of hysteria was closely linked to aberrant positioning of the womb and female sexual functioning more generally. In following the evolution of the concept of hysteria both historically and cross-culturally, Vieth illustrates several generalizations of the history of mental illness.

First, concepts of mental illness are consistent with the larger belief systems of a culture. For example, to many ancient Greeks and Egyptians, human sexuality was viewed as a natural function and purported displacement of sexual organs from lack of sexual activity required a treatment that logically targeted this ostensibly sexual cause of hysteria. However, by the time of Augustine, Christian thought differentiated between procreation and sensuality. Consequently, it was theologically problematic to endorse sexual indulgence (an evil) as a therapeutic measure and to attribute pathologic effects to abstinence (a virtue). Although it appears that Augustine believed in both natural illness and demonic possession (i.e., did not attribute demonic possession to all forms of aberrant behavior), the role of unholy spirits in creating mental disturbances was a leading explanation for psychopathology at that time. Moreover, where natural cures were appropriate for natural illnesses, demonic possession required cures by supernatural means, like miracles.

Second, even in the face of compelling data it is often difficult to dispel widely held beliefs about psychopathology. Since antiquity, hysterical symptoms have been observed in men; a fact clearly inconsistent with a uterine cause. However, it was not until mid-way through the seventeenth century that leading physicians such as Carolus Piso and Thomas Willis began to espouse a non-uterine etiology and influenced the larger group of practitioners.

Third, it often takes many years for important ideas to become accepted. Prior to the birth of Sigmund Freud, a British physician named Robert Brudenell Carter proposed a collection of ideas on the genesis of hysteria that are remarkably similar to Freud's famed theory. Vieth suggests that Carter's ideas were 'too embarrassingly perceptive for his Victorian compatriots' (p. 200) to be given serious consideration at the time.

Fourth, individuals afflicted with various forms of psychopathology have often been discriminated against and treated cruelly. For example, both Vieth and Zilboorg document the torture unleashed upon mentally ill individuals suspected of witchcraft from the sixteenth to eighteenth century.

The Roots of Modern Nosology

Although attempts to create a classification system for mental disorders (termed a *nosology*) date back at least to Hippocrates, historians view the work of Philippe Pinel (eighteenth to nineteenth century) as seminal. In his *Treatise on Insanity* (1806), Pinel noted the considerable heterogeneity of symptoms in his patients and remarked, 'Symptoms so different, and all comprehended under the general title of insanity, required on my part, much study and discrimination.' His major work on classification, *Nosographie* (1813), classified all diseases into five groups: (1) fevers, (2) inflammations, (3) hemorrhagic diseases, (4) neuroses, and (5) organic lesions. Neuroses were divided into mania, melancholia, dementia, and idiocy and encompassed both 'moral' (i.e., psychological) and 'physical' (i.e., organic) etiologies.

Work on the classification of mental disorders accelerated after Pinel. For example, J. E. D. Esquirol (1772–1840), a student of Pinel, made important diagnostic distinctions among depressive states, distinguished between hallucinations and perceptual distortions, and introduced other important diagnostic concepts. Although many other (primarily French and German) physicians made substantial contributions to psychiatric nosology throughout the nineteenth century, the work of Emil Kraepelin (1855–1926) toward the end of that century stands out. In the second edition of his textbook in 1887, he divided mental disorders into two classes: (1) those caused by external conditions and, consequently, curable, and (2) those caused by constitutional factors and not curable. Over the next four decades Kraepelin frequently revised his textbook which grew considerably from one edition to the next, culminating in his 2,425 page ninth edition, published posthumously with Lange, in 1927. In his sixth edition (Kraepelin, 1899), he made the enduring distinction between manic-depressive illness (now termed bipolar disorder) and dementia praecox (now termed schizophrenia) largely on the basis of the course of illness. Manic-depressive illness was characterized by an episodic course with good functioning between episodes; dementia praecox was characterized by an early onset followed by a progressive, deteriorating course. Indeed, the use of prognosis to validate diagnosis is often seen as one of Kraepelin's greatest accomplishments but also one of his most problematic contributions (recall Aretaeus used such an approach 1,800 years earlier). On the one hand, 'diagnosis by prognosis' proved itself useful in making some distinctions that were ultimately validated by other means. On the other hand, the approach is circular and does little to point the way toward etiology or treatment. Nevertheless, it is clear that Kraepelin was able to synthesize many of the contributions of nineteenth-century European psychiatry and establish the foundation for contemporary approaches to the classification of mental disorders. Despite the fact that Kraepelin and his predecessors had been able to describe various forms of mental disorders, they did not do much to address the more fundamental question of 'what mental disease is?' (Zilboorg, 1941, p. 464).

21.2 DEFINING MENTAL DISORDER

Defining psychopathology is problematic for a number of reasons. First, there is no single attribute of psychopathology that is common to all of its forms. Second, there are few, if any, logically sufficient criteria for establishing the presence of psychopathology. Third, there is no clear-cut dividing line between normal and psychopathological forms of behavior.

Various approaches to defining psychopathology have been proposed and each has its strengths and weaknesses. We now consider three approaches: (1) the statistical, (2) the experience of distress, and (3) disability or dysfunction. Note that although each of these definitions are conceptually distinct, they are correlated concepts (i.e., on average, individuals classified as having a 'problem' under one approach would be classified similarly under another approach).

The *statistical approach* assumes that behaviors that are statistically infrequent or rare represent psychopathology. The simplicity of this approach is appealing. First, because determinations of 'abnormality' or 'pathology' are based on statistical infrequency, these determinations can be highly objective. This general approach is frequently employed in the interpretation of psychological test scores in the areas of intelligence and psychological distress. For example, test scores exceeding a cut-off point (often established on the basis of statistical deviance from the mean score obtained by a 'normal' sample of test-takers) are considered 'clinically significant' (i.e., abnormal or deviant). Nevertheless, this approach has several limitations. First, non-normative or statistically rare behavior can be caused by many factors and, although 'unusual', is not necessarily reflective of a pathological process. Second, when various behavioral phenomena are distributed along one or more dimensions (e.g., intelligence, psychological distress), the cut-off between normal and abnormal becomes highly arbitrary. Third, to the extent that norms vary across cultures and subcultures, it is not always clear how appropriate a given set of norms is, especially when making determinations of individuals from populations not used in the norming. Fourth, a statistical approach does not, by itself, inform us as to what dimensions of behavior are to be considered in defining abnormality. Fifth, in some situations, bidirectional deviations from a norm might be considered indicative of pathology (e.g., excessively high or excessively low blood pressure or core body temperature) while in other cases, only unidirectional deviations may indicate pathology (e.g., intelligence). A purely statistical approach, by itself, does not tell us whether we should be concerned with unidirectional or bidirectional deviations.

The *experience of distress* (e.g., sadness, anxiety, panic, anger, agitation) represents the key concept in defining psychopathology for many. Indeed, it is the experience of distress that appears to bring most individuals to seek assistance from clinical psychologists and other mental health professionals. Although, unquestionably, psychological distress is a hallmark of many important psychological disorders, it does not appear to be either a necessary or a sufficient condition for establishing the presence of psychopathology. First, many individuals who show extreme deviations in behavior and are incapable of maintaining relationships with others, holding a job, or complying with laws do not report psychological distress. In the extreme, individuals suffering from some forms of mania often report feelings of exhilaration and high levels of subjective well-being despite the fact that their erratic and reckless behavior can compromise their own and their families' standing in the community. Alternatively, extreme distress (e.g., grief over the loss of a loved one) appears to be a normal reaction to certain classes of events and therefore cannot be viewed as always representing pathology. Thus, although distress is often marked in individuals who are deemed to have certain psychological disorders and is a useful dimension of psychological adjustment, by itself it is an inadequate barometer of abnormality.

Disability or dysfunction represents a third approach to defining psychopathology. From this perspective, behavior is thought to reflect psychopathology when it results in social (i.e., interpersonal), legal, or occupational impairment. An advantage of this approach is that relatively little inference is required and that the failure to fulfill role responsibilities represents an 'ecological' assessment of an individual's functioning. However, the assessment of role functioning can be problematic. First, the threshold for determining impairment is somewhat arbitrary and determinations of dysfunction can vary across observers (although objective rating scales can be used to minimize individual rater biases). Moreover, some individuals can endure levels of distress that would incapacitate the vast majority of people. For example, some phobics who experience excessive, irrational fear in response to certain stimuli (e.g., riding on elevators, speaking in public) continue to engage in behaviors which expose them to these situations and are not obviously impaired. However, they may consistently dread their next encounter with the feared situation and are in a state of extreme discomfort during each exposure. Even those who 'suffer in silence' without any obvious behavioral impairment can still be thought to suffer from a psychological disorder.

Modern Integration

Although each of the three approaches described above has some intuitive appeal and is relevant to the definition of psychopathology, no one approach is adequate. For nosologists, scholars interested in developing a valid classification system, a sound definition of mental disorders

represents an essential first step toward this goal. However, developing such a definition is extremely difficult. Although there is no clear consensus, the working definition provided in the *Diagnostic and Statistical Manual, Fourth Edition* (DSM-IV; American Psychiatric Association, 1994) represents an amalgam of the ideas presented above and is generally consistent with the proposals of leading theorists such as Robert Spitzer and Jerome Wakefield. According to the DSM-IV:

> In DSM-IV, each of the mental disorders is conceptualized as a clinically significant behavioral or psychological syndrome or pattern that occurs in an individual and that is associated with present distress (e.g., a painful symptom) or disability (i.e., impairment in one or more important areas of functioning) or with a significantly increased risk of suffering death, pain, disability, or an important loss of freedom. In addition, this syndrome or pattern must not be merely an expectable and culturally sanctioned response to a particular event, for example, the death of a loved one. Whatever its original cause, it must currently be considered a manifestation of a behavioral, psychological, or biological dysfunction in the individual. Neither deviant behavior (e.g., political, religious, or sexual) nor conflicts that are primarily between the individual and society are mental disorders unless the deviance or conflict is a symptom of a dysfunction in the individual, as described above. (American Psychiatric Association, 1994, pp. xxi–xxii)

21.3 OVERVIEW OF MODERN NOSOLOGIES

For more than a century, psychiatric texts and other sources provided general descriptions of specific mental disorders. However, in the 1960s and early 1970s, influential studies documented that diagnoses made by clinicians are often unreliable and that there were large cross-national differences in diagnostic practices. For researchers interested in producing reproducible findings, the existing diagnostic criteria were insufficient. At Washington University in St. Louis, a group of investigators developed a set of highly explicit criteria in order to improve diagnostic reliability. These criteria, called the St. Louis criteria or the Feighner criteria, served as the basis for numerous investigations and, along with a later criteria set developed by researchers in New York and St. Louis, were the forerunners of the DSM-III. The DSM-III, published in 1980, broke tradition with earlier versions of the DSM (published in 1952 and 1968, respectively) by employing highly explicit criteria (as innovated by the Feighner criteria) and by eliminating groupings of disorders based on presumed etiology. (For example, the Freudian concept of neurosis which assumed anxiety as a primary etiological agent in certain somatoform disorders was dropped.) It also introduced the concept of multi-axial diagnosis. In 1987, the DSM-III-R was revised to address concerns raised about the DSM-III and to reflect the considerable amount of research that had taken place since its publication.

The current system of diagnosis in the United States, the DSM-IV, is currently the most widely used in psychological and psychiatric research on psychopathology and is the focus of our overview here. However, it is important to point out that the most recent edition of the *International Statistical Classification of Diseases and Related Health Problems* (ICD-10) developed by the World Health Organization is closely related to the DSM-IV due to coordination between the developers of these diagnostic systems. Although DSM-IV and ICD-10 are currently the most commonly employed diagnostic systems, researchers have long utilized specialized diagnostic criteria for research purposes (Berner et al., 1992).

Many of the distinctions and diagnostic entities described in the DSM-IV have their roots in the psychiatric literatures of the nineteenth and early twentieth century. Nevertheless, the current codification of mental disorders found in the DSM-IV reflects many recent developments in diagnostic thinking as well as the abandonment of many cherished notions (such as the Freudian concept of neurosis). Based on ever-accumulating data, each successive revision of the DSM (and the ICD) can be expected to introduce new concepts and abandon old ones. From a research perspective, it is useful to consider both the classification of disorders and their operational definitions as working hypotheses, subject to empirical testing, revision, and further testing.

21.4 DSM-IV

The current version of the DSM asks the diagnostician to provide assessments along five distinct axes, the so-called multi-axial diagnosis. *Axis I* is used for recording the clinical disorders and includes all major diagnostic categories for children and adults except for the categories of mental retardation and personality disorders. *Axis II* is used for reporting personality disorders (see discussion below) and mental retardation. *Axis III* is used for recording the presence of general medical conditions that are relevant to understanding or treating a person's mental disorder. *Axis IV* is used for recording

various life problems that are relevant to understanding or treating a person's mental disorder. Finally, *Axis V* is used for recording a patient's general level of functioning on a 100-point scale. An outline of the five axes is presented in Table 21.1. Most research in psychopathology is targeted toward the Axis I and Axis II disorders. We now provide a brief overview of several of these disorders.

Disorders Usually First Diagnosed in Infancy, Childhood, and Adolescence

The DSM-IV lists ten major categories of childhood disorder, all of which, except mental retardation, are coded on Axis I. These disorders are grouped together primarily due to their time of onset rather than by their shared symptoms. In general, they reflect problems with development and maturation

Attention-Deficit and Disruptive Behavior Disorders represent a prevalent group of disorders that are associated with problems in school and social relations. Included in this group is *Attention-Deficit/Hyperactivity Disorder*, which is characterized by prominent symptoms of inattention and/or hyperactivity-impulsivity. Also included in this group are the Disruptive Behavior Disorders which includes *Conduct Disorder*, characterized by a pattern of behavior that violates the basic rights of others or major age-appropriate societal norms or rules; and *Oppositional Defiant Disorder*, characterized by a pattern of negativistic, hostile, and defiant behavior. Disorders in this group, especially conduct disorder, show significant continuity with adult antisocial personality disorder and with substance use disorders and, thus, indicate significant risk for life-course persistent problems.

Pervasive Developmental Disorders are characterized by severe deficits and pervasive impairment in multiple areas of development including social interaction, impairment in communication, and the presence of stereotyped behavior, interests, and activities. The best known disorders in this group are *Autistic Disorder* and *Asperger's Disorder*.

Mental Retardation refers to a disorder associated with low intelligence (IQ of 70 or below) and impaired role functioning with onset before age 18. Unlike other childhood disorders, it is coded on Axis II.

Learning Disorders are characterized by academic functioning that is substantially below that expected given the person's chronological age, measured intelligence, and education.

Motor Skills Disorder is characterized by motor coordination that is substantially below

Table 21.1   *An overview of multiaxial assessment in DSM-IV*

Axis I Clinical Disorders; Other Conditions That May Be a Focus of Clinical Attention

Disorders Usually First Diagnosed in Infancy, Childhood, or Adolescence	Anxiety Disorders
	Somatoform Disorders
	Factitious Disorders
Delirium, Dementia, and Amnestic and Other Cognitive Disorders	Dissociative Disorders
	Sexual and Gender Identity Disorders
Mental Disorders Due to a General Medical Condition	Eating Disorders
	Sleep Disorders
Substance-Related Disorders	Impulse-Control Disorders Not Elsewhere Classified
Schizophrenia and Other Psychotic Disorders	Adjustment Disorders
Mood Disorders	Other Conditions That May Be a Focus of Clinical Attention

Axis II Personality Disorders (PD); Mental Retardation

Paranoid PD	Histrionic PD	PD Not Otherwise Specified
Schizoid PD	Narcissistic PD	
Schizotypal PD	Avoidant PD	Mental Retardation
Antisocial PD	Dependent PD	
Borderline PD	Obsessive-Compulsive PD	

Axis III General Medical Conditions

Axis IV Psychosocial and Environmental Problems

Problems with primary support group	Housing problems
Problems related to the social environment	Economic problems
	Problems with access to health care services
Educational problems	Problems related to interaction with the legal system/crime
Occupational problems	Other problems

Axis V Global Assessment of Functioning (1 to 100 scale)

100–91 Superior functioning in a wide range of activities . . . No symptoms

. . .

50–41 Serious symptoms OR any serious impairment in . . . functioning.

. . .

10–1 Persistent danger of severely hurting self or others OR persistent inability to maintain minimal personal hygiene OR serious suicidal act with clear expectation of death.

Adapted from American Psychiatric Association (1994). Reprinted with permission.

that expected given the person's chronological age and measured intelligence.

A number of other specific childhood disorders are delineated in the DSM-IV. *Communication Disorders* are characterized by difficulties in speech or language. *Feeding and Eating Disorders of Infancy or Early Childhood* are characterized by persistent disturbances in feeding and eating. *Tic Disorders* manifest themselves in sudden, recurrent, and stereotyped vocalizations or movements. *Elimination Disorders* include *Encopresis*, the repeated passage of feces in inappropriate places, and *Enuresis*,

the repeated voiding of urine in inappropriate places.

Other Disorders of Infancy, Childhood, or Adolescence represents a heterogeneous category that includes a number of diagnoses that do not fit well into other categories. Perhaps the most important of these, *Separation Anxiety Disorder*, is characterized by excessive anxiety surrounding separation from home or from close attachments. Another important diagnosis, *Selective Mutism*, is characterized by a consistent failure to speak in specific social situations despite speaking in other situations.

Major Axis I Disorder Categories

Schizophrenia and Other Psychotic Disorders usually onset in young adulthood and are typified by compromised perceptions of reality – psychotic symptoms such as hallucinations and delusions. Such perceptual disturbances are expressed alongside other active manifestations of disorder known as *positive* symptoms (i.e., disorganized speech and behavior, inappropriate affect). Additionally, some individuals classified with schizophrenia exhibit deficits in normal functioning – *negative* symptoms such as flat affect, decreased motivation, and poverty of speech. While positive symptoms typically respond well to medication, many theorists suggest that negative symptoms are associated with less favorable outcomes and a more recalcitrant course.

Mood Disorders are characterized by disruptive and persistent disturbances in mood. There are two major subgroups of mood, depressive disorders and bipolar disorders. Clinically, the most important type of depressive disorder is *Major Depressive Disorder* which is characterized by the presence of a depressive episode marked by depressed mood, sleep disturbance, decreased ability to experience pleasure, marked changes in weight and activity-level, inability to concentrate, and feelings of worthlessness or guilt. A less intense but more chronic form of depressive disorder is *Dysthymic Disorder* whose hallmark symptom is depressed mood 'on more days than not' over a period of at least two years.

The other major subgroup of mood disorders, bipolar disorders, are characterized by the presence or a history of *manic, hypomanic,* or *mixed episodes*. In a manic episode there is an abnormally and persistently elevated, expansive, or irritable mood. Hypomanic episodes are similar to manic episodes but are a less severe form. In mixed episodes, the symptoms of both depressive and manic episodes are met. *Bipolar I Disorder* is characterized by a history of having manic or mixed episodes. *Bipolar II Disorder* is characterized by a history of a major depressive episode, hypomanic episodes, but no history of manic or mixed episodes. In *Cyclothymic Disorder*, a less intense but chronic form of bipolar disorder, there is a persistent, fluctuating mood disturbance involving many spells of hypomanic symptoms and of depressive symptoms.

Individuals with *Anxiety Disorders* experience apprehension about future danger, adversity, or distress along with negative affect and symptoms of somatic tension. Such 'anxiety' may be diffuse or circumscribed to particular objects or situations. *Generalized Anxiety Disorder* is typified by excessive worry about a number of events or activities that occurs more days than not for a period of at least 6 months. In *Panic Disorder*, individuals experience an unexpected, discrete episode of severe apprehension or fearfulness during which many somatic symptoms occur (i.e., shortness of breath, chest pain, palpitations, feelings of 'going crazy' or smothering, etc.). Subsequently, they develop a fear of recurrent attacks or change their behavior in response to the attack. *Phobias* are characterized by significant anxiety following exposure to a particular object or situation (as in *Specific Phobia*) or a certain type of social situation (as in *Social Phobia*). *Obsesssive-Compulsive Disorder* is typified by intrusive and distressing thoughts, images, or urges (i.e., *obsessions*) and *compulsive* behaviors or thoughts designed to suppress such obsessions and relieve the tension they produce. Finally, *Post-Traumatic Stress Disorder* is marked by the re-experiencing of an extremely traumatic event with attendant symptoms of heightened arousal and avoidance of stimuli associated with the traumatic event.

Dissociative Disorders are typified by a detached sense of identity and surroundings, with disintegrated memory or consciousness. Such dissociation may manifest itself in *amnesia*, where an individual is unable to recall significant, possibly traumatic, events or personal information, or *fugue*, where an individual suddenly flees his or her home or work environment for a significant period of time during which they are unable to recall their past or their identity. In some cases, afflicted persons may assume a new identity. Finally, *Dissociative Identity Disorder* (historically, Multiple Personality Disorder) is characterized by the presence of two or more distinct personalities or identities that assume control of the individual's behavior with associated lapses in memory.

Somatoform Disorders are characterized by physical symptoms that suggest a general medical condition but cannot be fully explained by a medical condition, the effects of a substance, or another mental disorder. *Somatization Disorder* is typified by the presence of a number of persistent somatic symptoms – a combination of pain, gastrointestinal, sexual, and pseudoneurological symptoms – with onset before age 30. In *Conversion Disorder*, individuals experience physical dysfunction, such as paralysis, blindness, or muteness, without any discernable physical or organic cause. *Pain Disorder* is characterized by a clinical focus on pain, although psychological factors are deemed primarily influential on the onset, expression, maintenance, severity, and exacerbation of the pain. *Hypochondriasis* is characterized by a persistent and medically unfounded concern with present and future physical illness as well as serious misinterpretation of physical sensations and bodily functions as evidence for such concern. Finally, *Body Dysmorphic Disorder* is marked by a preoccupation with an exaggerated or imagined deficiency in physical appearance.

Substance-Use Disorders are typified by patterns of *abuse* – maladaptive use of alcohol and other psychoactive substance as well as negative consequences (social, legal, and occupational) from substance use – and *dependence* – impaired control over use, the development of tolerance to the substance, stereotyped withdrawal symptoms upon cessation of use, and preoccupation with substance use. Substances of abuse include: alcohol, amphetamines, cocaine, hallucinogens, barbiturates, marijuana, inhalants, nicotine, and opioids.

Personality Disorders

A *personality disorder* is defined as a persistent pattern of thoughts, feelings, and behavior that deviates substantially from cultural norms and that is inflexible and pervasive across situations. The conditions are stable and established by adolescence or early adulthood. Like all DSM-IV mental disorders, they must either involve significant distress or impaired role functioning. DSM-IV groups personality disorders into three major clusters or subgroups.

Cluster A includes the 'odd or eccentric' personality disorders. In *paranoid personality disorder* there is a pattern of distrust and suspiciousness of others. In *schizoid personality disorder* is there a pattern of interpersonal detachment and limited emotional expressiveness. In *schizotypal personality disorder* there is a pattern of interpersonal uneasiness, cognitive or perceptual aberrations, and behavioral eccentricities.

Cluster B includes the 'dramatic, emotional, or erratic' personality disorders, and includes the two personality disorders that have received the most attention from both clinicians and researchers. *Antisocial personality disorder* refers to a pattern of rule-breaking behavior and a disregard of others rights, needs, and feelings. Individuals with antisocial personality disorder often have severe problems in developing intimate relationships and honoring responsibilities, they often have unstable social and vocational histories, and they frequently abuse alcohol and other drugs. *Borderline personality disorder* refers to a pattern of unstable relationships, chaotic self-image, labile affectivity, and high

levels of impulsivity. Individuals with borderline personality disorders often have a history of strained interpersonal relations, suicidal gestures, depression, and substance-use disorders. *Histrionic personality disorder* refers to a pattern of excessively dramatic self-presentations and attention seeking from others. *Narcissistic personality disorder* refers to a pattern of grandiosity, need for admiration, and lack of empathy.

Cluster C includes the 'anxious or fearful' personality disorders. In *avoidant personality disorder* there is a pattern of social anxiety and fear of negative evaluation; not surprisingly, many of these individuals also have social phobias. In *dependent personality disorder* there is a pattern of submissiveness and overdependence on others. Finally, in *obsessive-compulsive personality disorder* there is a pattern of preoccupation with orderliness, perfectionism, and control.

Critique of DSM

Although the DSM represents the most widely adopted approach to diagnosis among researchers and clinicians alike, for many years there have been many respected psychologists who have been vocal critics of the DSM-III and subsequent revisions. For example, more than 20 years ago, Schacht and Nathan (1977) voiced numerous concerns about the DSM-III including its (a) epistemologic foundations strongly rooted in a medical model, (b) operationalization of specific symptoms and disorders, and (c) political and guild effects which were feared to foster psychiatric hegemony over the mental health professions (and thus marginalize the role of psychologists in the diagnosis and treatment of mental disorders). Despite psychologists bemoaning the DSM since the mid-1970s, no viable alternative has been put forward to take its place. This ostensible complacency probably reflects at least two factors. First, developing a valid diagnostic system is an extraordinarily complex endeavor, perhaps more complex than DSM critics realize. Second, the current DSM has proven to provide an extremely useful framework for epidemiologists, psychopathologists, and treatment specialists.

Still, many psychologists remain critical of the DSM and some psychologists have argued that a new diagnostic approach more firmly rooted in psychological principles is needed as an alternative approach. For example, a recent special section of an issue of the *Journal of Consulting and Clinical Psychology* (see Follette, 1996) provides a philosophical critique of the 'atheoretical' approach of the DSM and argues that a coherent theoretical framework is needed to develop a valid nosology that is testable and, therefore, more likely to advance the science of taxonomy. Obviously, given the variety of theoretical orientations that characterize the field of clinical psychology, no single 'alternative' perspective would be likely to gain wide acceptance. (Indeed, it is probable that the purported atheoretical structure of the DSM is a major factor in its acceptance.) However, the approach argued by Follette and others is that, at the very least, the widespread acceptance of DSM should be challenged and that psychologists should be active in trying to influence future revisions with findings based on alternative models of psychopathology.

21.5 EPIDEMIOLOGY OF MENTAL DISORDERS

Until recently, the extent to which individuals in the general population suffered from various mental disorders was not well known. Although data from treatment facilities (especially large psychiatric hospitals) had been used to provide estimates of the prevalence of mental disorders in the community, such statistics were problematic because (1) there is a lack of standardization of diagnostic criteria and, (2) many, if not most, individuals experiencing mental disorders never enter a formal treatment setting. Although large-scale community surveys using self-report, symptom rating scales had been used to estimate the extent of psychopathology in the community (and to examine the correlation between psychological symptoms and various risk factors), these surveys did not provide information on the prevalence of specific types of disorders. Also, because some of these studies employed cut-off points on these rating scales to provide 'caseness' estimates (i.e., the number of probable 'cases' of mental disorders in the survey), these cut-offs were highly arbitrary (see discussion of statistical approach to defining abnormality above). A few attempts to employ diagnostic interviews in large community surveys were undertaken, most notably the Stirling County (Canada) Study in 1963. However, that study rested upon the nosology of the DSM-I which, though informative, differs significantly in many ways from current nosology. Thus, until recently, the epidemiology (i.e., the study of the causes, distribution, and natural history of disorders in populations) of psychopathology was extremely limited. Population-based epidemiology of mental disorders became possible with the introduction of highly explicit diagnostic criteria sets such as DSM-III and structured diagnostic interviews designed to assess these criteria sets.

Prevalence of Major Psychological Disorders

The epidemiological concept of *prevalence* typically refers to the number of individuals in the population who have the disorder at a specific point in time, divided by an appropriate denominator (i.e., the number of people sampled) to yield a prevalence rate. In medicine, rates are frequently expressed as *point prevalence*, that is, the proportion of people who are diagnosed with a disorder on a given day of the calendar or on the day of the survey. Because many mental disorders involve episodic symptoms that do not necessarily occur on a daily basis, prevalence rates are often expressed using a temporal interval such as 6-month or 12-month prevalence (meaning that the individual met criteria for diagnosis within the past 6 or 12 months). Many research studies (especially those involving family history assessments or where family pedigrees are required for genetic analysis) employ the concept of *lifetime diagnosis* (i.e., the individual has met criteria for a given diagnosis at some point in his or her life). When prevalence rates are based on lifetime diagnosis they are called *lifetime prevalence rates*. Prevalence data are useful to researchers interested in investigating etiological hypotheses, and are helpful for determining the extent of clinically significant psychopathology. Such data are useful to public health workers assessing the need and adequacy of existing services.

In the United States, two large-scale epidemiological surveys of adults have been conducted since 1980: (1) the Epidemiologic Catchment Area survey (Robins & Regier, 1991), and (2) the National Comorbidity Survey (Kessler et al., 1994). Both of these surveys can be considered modern landmarks of mental health epidemiology and provide a wealth of data on the distribution and correlates of mental disorders in the United States. Because of the large sample sizes employed in these studies and the impact these studies have had for psychopathology research, we consider these data further.

Table 21.2 displays selected lifetime and 12-month (past year) diagnoses from the ECA and NCS. Comparison of the prevalence rates reveals some important similarities and differences. For example, in both surveys, alcohol-use disorders are the most prevalent disorder and the estimated prevalence rates for certain disorders (e.g., manic episode and antisocial personality

Table 21.2 *Selected (lifetime/past year) prevalence rates of mental disorders in the Epidemiological Catchment Area (ECA) study and the National Comorbidity Survey (NCS)*

Diagnosis	ECA study estimates using DIS/DSM-III diagnoses		NCS estimates using UM-CIDI/DSM-IIIR diagnoses	
	Lifetime	Past year	Lifetime	Past year
Major depressive episode	6.4	3.7	17.1	10.3
Manic episode	0.8	0.6	1.6	1.3
Dysthymia	3.3	–	6.4	2.5
Generalized anxiety disorder	8.5	3.8	5.1	3.1
Alcohol-use disorder	13.8	6.3	23.5	9.7
Drug-use disorder	6.2	2.5	11.9	3.6
Antisocial personality disorder	2.6	1.2	3.5	–

DIS = Diagnostic Interview Schedule. UM-CIDI = University of Michigan adaptation of the Composite International Diagnostic Interview.

ECA prevalence rates based on Table 13-7 of Robins and Regier (1991). NCS prevalence rates based on Table 2 of Kessler et al. (1994).

disorder) are roughly similar. However, there are important differences in findings as well. For example, the prevalence rates for major depressive episode are almost three times higher and the prevalence of alcohol use disorders is almost two times higher in the NCS. It is difficult to reconcile these discrepancies because of differences in the diagnostic criteria (DSM-III versus DSM-III-R) employed, differences in the assessment instruments used, differences in sampling and statistical adjustments, and possibly even secular trends in prevalence (see next section) that occurred in the interval between the two surveys. Regardless, comparison of these two studies highlights how important the specific diagnostic criteria and the means we use to assess them are on establishing the presence or absence of specific disorders in the community.

Methodological issues become even more important when we begin to compare epidemiological findings from different countries. Numerous studies investigating the epidemiology of both childhood and adult disorders have been conducted throughout the world (although primarily in North America and northern Europe). Cross-national comparisons of different rates of disorder are made difficult by differences in the sampling and ascertainment strategies utilized, the diagnostic criteria employed, and the instruments and sources of data (e.g., type of informant) used to assess diagnostic criteria. For example, a recent review of the prevalence of mental disorders in children and adolescents based on 52 studies from 20 countries yielded few consistencies in prevalence rates (Roberts, Attkisson, & Rosenblatt,

1998). Nevertheless, cross-national comparisons involving similar diagnostic methods have in some cases yielded generally consistent prevalence rates across widely varying cultures for disorders such as schizophrenia, panic disorder, and obsessive-compulsive disorder (e.g., see Weissman et al.'s, 1997, cross-national study of panic disorder). However, for other cases there are large differences in prevalence rates across cultures (e.g., Helzer & Canino's, 1992, review of cross-national studies of alcoholism). It is important to note that even accurate prevalence rates at the national level can obscure important, large regional and subcultural differences. Additionally, differences in diagnostic methods can have much larger effects than cross-national differences. For example, the difference in the prevalence rates of panic disorder provided by the ECA and the NCS was much larger than differences in the rates provided by the ECA and nine other countries using the same diagnostic method as the ECA (Weissman et al., 1997). Although the prevalence rates associated with specific diagnoses are of interest in their own right, many psychopathology researchers are more interested in the correlates of disorder as these might implicate important determinants of the onset and persistence of disorders.

Mental Disorders and Age, Sex, and Socioeconomic Variables

Both the ECA and NCS data document declines in the prevalence of mental disorders across the adult age span. For example, in both studies the youngest group of adults analyzed had approximately twice the prevalence of past-year mental disorders as the oldest group analyzed. However, interpretation of these findings is complicated because it is not clear if these age-related declines are due to (1) reduced likelihood of having a disorder as one gets older, (2) individuals born in earlier cohorts (e.g., before World War II) having had lower rates throughout their life spans, or (3) mental disorders leading to early death (and, hence, a lower proportion of older people with mental disorders).

Examination of the relation between age and lifetime prevalence rates reveals a curious finding; lifetime prevalence rates tend to be higher in younger individuals. By definition, as individuals age they cannot 'lose' a lifetime diagnosis and thus we would expect that older individuals would have higher lifetime rates of diagnosis. However, this expectation is based on several assumptions: (1) no differential mortality of those with mental disorders, (2) no cohort effect or secular trend (i.e., the likelihood of someone who is thirty-five years old and born in 1965 should be the same as someone who was born in 1940 when he was thirty-five), and (3) no recall bias whereby older individuals are less likely to recall significant symptoms of psychopathology. Unfortunately, the research literature suggests that each one of these is a possible explanation. However, the increase in the prevalence of depression and of substance-use disorders in individuals born since World War II has been replicated on several different data sets and implicates broad social forces as causal factors in psychopathology.

Epidemiological data also reveal negative gradients between measures of socioeconomic success (such as income and education) and most mental disorders studied. However, the interpretation of these associations is complex because in these relations it is not always clear if low socioeconomic success is a cause or a consequence of disorder. In some disorders where this issue has been studied extensively (e.g., schizophrenia), it appears that low socioeconomic success is largely a consequence of disorder, but not completely so. Prospective research designs and research designs that are genetically informative are best able to resolve questions regarding direction of causation.

The relation between sex and mental disorders is complex because some disorders are more prevalent in men (e.g., substance-use disorders, antisocial personality disorder) while others are more prevalent in women (e.g., mood disorders, anxiety disorders). These effects tend to be highly replicable and suggest that biological and social factors associated with sex are etiologically important in these disorders.

Comorbidity

Comorbidity refers to the phenomenon that individuals often suffer from multiple mental disorders. In the ECA study, 60% of individuals with at least one lifetime disorder had at least one additional disorder and the NCS yielded a similar statistic (56%). That is, the majority of individuals who meet diagnostic criteria are comorbid for other disorders. Because both the ECA and NCS employed a restricted subset of DSM diagnoses and, with the exception of antisocial personality, excluded the personality disorders (which tend to be highly comorbid with each other and some Axis I disorders), these comorbidity rates are probably low estimates. Additionally, treatment samples are known to have higher comorbidity than general population samples. Therefore, the typical mental health professional is likely to encounter more comorbid psychopathology than the epidemiologist.

Several reasons have been put forth to explain observed comorbidity. First, some degree of comorbidity is expected by chance alone (e.g., the joint probability of having two disorders assuming the two disorders are statistically independent). Although this type of comorbidity does not imply any meaningful etiological relation between the two disorders, it can still be important clinically. For example, the presence of one disorder can complicate the treatment of another disorder. Second, two or more disorders can co-exist simply because the diagnostic criteria for each disorder overlap (e.g., social phobia and avoidant personality disorder). Third, two or more disorders can co-exist because they are jointly caused by the same variables. For example, the personality trait of neuroticism appears to predispose individuals to a range of mental disorders. Fourth, the presence of one disorder can lead to the development of another disorder. For example, alcohol dependence appears to increase the likelihood of an anxiety disorder. Fifth, it is possible that two or more disorders reciprocally influence each other over time. That is, the presence of each disorder increases the likelihood of the other disorder occurring or persisting.

The extremely high rates of comorbidity found in the general population and in the clinic potentially pose a direct challenge to the current nosology (e.g., DSM-IV, ICD-10). That is, to comprehensively describe the extent of psychopathology in an individual, it might be necessary to assign several conceptually distinct diagnoses that appear to be interrelated at the level of symptomatology. If a purpose of a scientific taxonomy is to 'carve nature at its joints' then the current nosology might only provide a poorly resolved depiction of nature. Presumably, as our knowledge of etiology progresses, diagnosis will be based more on the causes of disorder rather than on patterns of symptoms. When this occurs, it is likely that some of the diagnostic ambiguity and overlap that characterizes current-day nosology will be minimized.

The Relation Between Childhood and Adult Psychopathology

The issue of whether childhood mental disorders are temporally limited or whether they presage continued disorder over the life course is central to understanding both the seriousness of childhood disorders and the roots of adult mental disorders. It is also possible that this type of developmental data could be useful for revising the nosology (i.e., course of disorder could prove to be a useful tool for distinguishing among related forms of disorder). However, much less is known about this topic than is desirable. Relatively few studies have prospectively followed children with mental disorders over an extended period of time. Equally problematic, the nosology of childhood disorders has been, up until recently, much less developed than the adult disorders and some important childhood diagnoses (e.g., depression) have only been recognized in recent decades.

At this point in our knowledge, several generalizations seem appropriate. First, many disorders of childhood, especially those that are related to generalized anxiety and specific fears are relatively transient. Although some highly anxious and inhibited individuals do continue to have serious problems, it is typically a small minority and the continuity is not necessarily at the level of specific symptomatology. Second, there is a strong correlation between conduct disorder in adolescence and antisocial personality disorder and substance-use disorders in adulthood. Third, although boys have a higher prevalence of disorder in most categories of childhood mental disorders, this gender pattern shifts in adulthood.

Thus, the existing literature suggests both important continuities and discontinuities in the expression of mental disorders. Our characterization of the course of mental disorders from childhood to adulthood is still crude and our understanding of the factors responsible for continuities and discontinuities is still in its infancy.

21.6 Etiological Research

Much, if not most, research in psychopathology is targeted at identifying the causes of mental disorders. Because most disorders are thought to be caused by multiple factors, it is not surprising that psychopathology research encompasses many disciplines in the social, behavioral, and biological sciences. Consequently, we discuss the study of psychopathology from each of three approaches: (1) an environmental approach, (2) a biological approach, and (3) a psychological approach. Note that these three approaches, although differing fundamentally in their emphases, are not mutually exclusive. For example, personality (a psychological construct) is strongly influenced by both environmental and biological factors. Thus, although each approach offers an important perspective and emphasizes particular classes of variables as explanatory constructs, they should not be viewed as reflecting distinct sources of influence.

Environmental Approach

Within the environmental approach we can describe three broad classes of variables: culture, stress, and parenting and socialization within the family. Although these classifications are neither mutually exclusive nor exhaustive, they provide a convenient structure for highlighting important research themes and findings.

Culture

The concept of culture is very broad and has been defined as a 'society's entire way of living'. Psychopathology researchers have focused on several key issues regarding culture. One of these refers to the question of whether or not cultural variables influence the type of mental disorders experienced by members of that culture. As John Weisz et al. (1993) have pointed out, studies of the relation between culture and psychopathology are maximally informative when cultures can be shown to differ on variables relevant to the development or expression of different forms of psychopathology. For example, Weisz and colleagues compared adolescents in Thailand (a primarily Buddhist culture where youths are taught to be self-effacing, polite, deferential to authority, and to inhibit aggression) and in the United States (where there is considerably more tolerance of aggression and other forms of undercontrolled behavior). They found that the Thai and American youths were roughly comparable in the total number of behavior problems but differed considerably in the types of problems they displayed. For example the Thai adolescents had more 'over-controlled problems' (e.g., fearfulness, lacking energy) than their American counterparts. Although Thai and American adolescents did not differ in the total number of 'under-controlled problems', American youths were more likely to show behavior problems marked by interpersonal aggression (e.g., fighting, bullying) while the Thai adolescents' undercontrolled problems tended not to have a direct interpersonal focus. These and other similar studies reveal ways in which culture can shape the expression of psychopathology.

Another aspect of the question of whether there is a relation between cultural variables and psychopathology is whether or not there are forms of psychopathology that are specific to a culture. Psychiatric texts consistently note several culture-specific syndromes. For example, *amok* (which occurs among certain peoples of the Malay Peninsula, Africa, and New Guinea) describes a condition where, after a humiliating experience, individuals go into an 'uncontrollable' rage and later have impaired memories for their behavior. (The English word *amuck* is derived from this condition.) *Koro* (which has been reported in Hong Kong, Singapore, India, and Malaysia) refers to a panic state brought on by the fear that one's genitals are retracting in the body and that this will prove fatal. Lest it be assumed that these seemingly unusual conditions appear only in non-Western, non-industrialized cultures, certain eating disorders (anorexia and bulimia nervosa) and dissociative identity disorder (formerly called multiple personality disorder) are viewed as possibly culture-specific to industrialized societies (Griffith & Gonzalez, 1994). Culture-specific syndromes are important in that they illustrate how some forms of psychopathology may be rule-governed social constructions and suggest that there are important cultural influences in the expression of psychopathology more generally.

Although much cultural research focuses on cross-national comparisons, many modern societies are culturally heterogeneous and minority group members often differ in the degree of acculturation to the larger society. Some researchers have posited that 'acculturative stress' arises from the conflicting expectations, values, norms and behaviors between minority and majority cultures. Minority groups (individuals within these groups) can vary widely in how this stress is resolved. It is believed that successful resolution of this stress involves maintenance of the minority group members' cultural identity and, ideally, positive relations with the majority culture.

Stress

The notion that stress can cause psychopathology is inherent in both popular thinking and formal theorizing. Although psychoanalytic thinking minimized the potential etiologic role of stressors in adults, the high levels of psychiatric morbidity that was documented in many soldiers and survivors of concentration camps during World War II dramatically illustrated the power of extreme traumatic stress to induce lasting behavioral disturbances.

Within the DSM, there are several types of disorders that are defined on the basis of a stress-related etiology (e.g., Acute Stress Disorder, Post-traumatic Stress Disorder, Adjustment Disorders); that is, these disorders are viewed as reflecting pathological responses to stressors. However, researchers have attempted to establish stressors as etiologic factors in virtually all major mental disorders. Indeed, for most mental disorders, the 'diathesis–stress' model is a leading etiological explanation.

Although the idea that some individuals are predisposed to develop mental disorders and the idea that stress is a causal factor in mental disorder have long been espoused, the integration of these two ideas is a relatively new concept that was first introduced into etiological theories of schizophrenia in the 1960s. This integration, the diathesis–stress theory, posits that 'stress activates a diathesis, transforming the potential of predisposition into the presence of psychopathology' (Monroe & Simons, 1991, p. 406). As Monroe and Simons note, although early theorizing in schizophrenia conceptualized the diathesis as a constitutional vulnerability, more recent research on anxiety and mood disorders has expanded the concept of diathesis to also include cognitive (e.g., see the section on *Cognitive Styles and Biases* below) and social diatheses.

Although the diathesis–stress theory remains a leading general theory of psychopathology, in recent years there has been a greater appreciation of the methodological complexities that make it difficult to evaluate the theory. First, there are individual differences in the creation of stressors. That is, not all stressors are uncontrollable, external events; many stressors are 'caused' by the individual. This phenomenon was probably first recognized by depression researchers who noted that stressors, such as job loss and arguments with spouse, often followed the onset of depressive symptoms.

However, the phenomenon is more general than depressives making their situations worse. At least one recent twin study has shown that the tendency to experience negative life events is a heritable trait; that is, genes and environment are correlated. A further complexity is raised by the fact that two individuals can experience the same event but differ in their appraisal of its stressfulness. That is, the diathesis can influence the perception of stress as well as its occurrence. These types of confounding between person and environment make it difficult to attribute causation to stressors, diatheses, or their interaction.

Intimately tied to the concept of stress are the concepts of appraisal and coping. Leading stress theorists, Richard Lazarus and Susan Folkman (1984), argue that an event or situation is only stressful when it is appraised as indicating harm or loss, threat, or challenge. Subsequent levels of stress are determined largely on the basis of ongoing reappraisals. Additionally, stressors mobilize efforts to cope. Lazarus and Folkman describe two conceptually distinct forms of coping. The first, problem-focused coping, refers to attempts to directly reduce or eliminate the problem causing the stress. The second, emotion-focused coping, refers to attempts to regulate the emotional distress resulting from a stressor. From a stress and coping perspective, situations appraised as stressors are most likely to lead to psychopathology as coping approaches fail to adequately attenuate the source of the stress, reduce one's reaction to the stress, or cause problems of their own (e.g., as in the case of substance abuse).

Parenting and Socialization within the Family

The role of parenting has been central to many theories of psychopathology. For example, in the 1940s, 1950s, and 1960s, certain parental characteristics were considered to be the primary etiological factors in schizophrenia. For example, mothers who were rejecting and hostile were thought to be 'schizophrenogenic' as were mothers who gave 'double-binding' (i.e., ambiguous and contradictory) messages to their children. Other theories posited the direct effects of pathologic spousal relationships on children as a key etiological factor.

However, contemporary research and theory on the role of the family in psychopathology tends not to attempt to correlate specific parental behaviors with specific mental disorders. Rather, the family is viewed as a context for psychological development and specific aspects of family functioning are viewed as important to the extent that they provide an adequate environment for psychological growth. As the needs of the developing child change from infancy, childhood, and adolescence, so do the functions provided by the family.

In the preschool years, child behavior problems appear to be related to the ability of parents or other caretakers to be emotionally available or responsive to their children's needs. Attachment theorists emphasize the importance of a close relationship between a child and caregivers during the first several years of life. As children get older and move toward and into adolescence, it is necessary for the family to provide for additional needs. For example, as the child develops a sense of identity independent of his or her caregivers, it is necessary for the family to be supportive of this separation while maintaining 'connectedness' (i.e., sensitivity and openness to others). Although some degree of family conflict is inevitable and provides an opportunity for modeling conflict-resolution skills, severe conflict (either spousal conflict or parent–child conflict) is associated with distress among all family members. Of particular importance to the development of externalizing problems (such as conduct disorder, substance abuse) is parental monitoring. Parental monitoring refers to a parent's knowledge of a child's activities and provides the opportunity for a parent to limit a child's involvement in activities that are risky or could cause harm. For example, the children of parents who are low monitors are more likely to be involved in delinquent activities. It has also been well documented that harsh and erratic discipline is associated with antisocial behavior. More generally, child abuse and neglect are associated with behavior problems in both boys and girls.

In relating family variables to psychopathology it is important to recognize factors that make it difficult to attribute a causal role to family variables. First, in most families, different family members share genes as well as their environment. Thus, it is possible that underlying the correlation between a parent's and a child's behavior is a shared genetic constitution that is responsible for both sets of behavior. However, even if genetic confounding can be ruled out (e.g., in studies of adoptees), establishing the direction of effect can be difficult. For example, an observed correlation between a parent's behavior and a child's (abnormal) behavior can reflect the effect of the child on the parent (and not just the effect of the parent on the child). Also, prior to the onset of manifest disorder, individuals may display subtle problems that elicit additional attention, nurturance, or criticism from a parent. Thus, what often appears to be a parent's effect on child behavior could actually be the reverse. The idea that parents and their children reciprocally influence each other over time is a central one in psychological development and cautions us against assuming the direction of effect when observing a correlation.

Biological Approach

Although the idea that various mental states arise from the brain date back to antiquity, the neurobiological view of mental disorders has probably never been stronger than it is today. Currently, powerful medications that alter brain functioning are routinely used in the treatment of many forms of psychopathology. Research using psychophysiological techniques (e.g., the electroencephalograph or EEG), structural neuroimaging techniques (e.g., CT, MRI), and functional neuroimaging techniques (e.g., PET and fMRI) has revealed associations between different brain regions and various forms of mental disorder. Finally, a large number of behavior–genetic investigations utilizing twin and adoption studies have demonstrated significant genetic contributions to most major mental disorders.

Psychopathology as Neurologic Disease

It is important to point out that many mental patients in the late nineteenth and early twentieth century had what we would today consider to be neurologic diseases (or neurological manifestations of systemic diseases). For example, paresis (a late-stage manifestation of syphilis) and pellagra (a niacin deficiency disease) often resulted in debilitating psychoses but both of these disorders are now primarily of only historical interest to psychopathologists. It is therefore understandable that some individuals believe that (at least some) mental disorders are simply yet-to-be-identified medical illnesses.

Other support for viewing mental disorders as neurologic diseases come from brain imaging studies. For example, both structural and functional brain imaging studies of schizophrenics have pointed to decreased cortical mass and decreased activity in the frontal lobes. However, brain imaging studies of mental disorders (including schizophrenia) have produced many inconsistent and unreplicated findings. Perhaps some of the problem is attributable to the heterogeneity of subjects in these studies, some to the low sample sizes that are often employed, and some to the number of statistical comparisons that are undertaken in a given experiment.

Other suggestions that certain disorders might be neurologic diseases come from studies showing an association between mental disorders and both physical trauma and medical diseases. For example, there are a number of documented cases of obsessive compulsive disorder (OCD) following head trauma. OCD has also been observed as a complication of other neurological diseases. Indeed, OCD appears to be clinically and genetically related to Tourette's syndrome, a neurologic movement disorder.

To the extent that all behaviors have neurobiological substrates, it is not surprising that various behavioral syndromes have neurological correlates. However, this is not the same as saying that any or all of these syndromes are best understood at a neurological level of explanation.

Neurotransmitter Dysfunction

Beginning with the discovery of neuroleptic drugs for the treatment of psychosis in the 1950s, there has been a steady stream of new medications developed to treat various mental disorders. Not only are many of these medications highly effective, but by understanding their mechanism of action we have developed a better understanding of the neuropharmacological underpinnings of mental disorder.

The functioning of neurotransmitters, the chemical messengers that permit communication between neurons, are implicated in many, if not most, major mental disorders. Evidence for this generalization comes from several data sources. First, drugs that have the effect of depleting levels of neurotransmitters stored in neurons can induce symptoms that mimic those of mental disorders. Similarly, there is some evidence that altered levels of neurotransmitter metabolites (i.e., the by-products of neurotransmitters after they are broken down in the body) are associated with certain pathological symptoms. For example, low levels of the main metabolite of serotonin have been associated with violence and suicide. Abnormal behavior can also be associated with excessive neurotransmitter activity. For example, the administration of some drugs functionally increases neurotransmission by mimicking the effects of specific neurotransmitters, by increasing neurotransmitter release, by inhibiting the breakdown of neurotransmitters, or by stimulating neurotransmitter receptors. Each of these manipulations can lead to pathological symptoms. There is also evidence for increased sensitivity of neurotransmitter receptors in some disorders (e.g., schizophrenia). Functionally, this could create greater neurotransmitter activity even in the absence of an excess of the neurotransmitter.

Most important clinically are the therapeutic effects of various drugs that act directly upon neurotransmitter systems. These drugs function in a number of ways including (1) increasing or decreasing the production of the neurotransmitter in the neuron, (2) decreasing the breakdown (into inactive metabolites) of the neurotransmitter in the neuron, (3) increasing or decreasing the release of the neurotransmitter into the synapse, (4) increasing or decreasing the re-uptake of the neurotransmitter back into the neuron, (5) decreasing the metabolic breakdown (catabolism) of the neurotransmitter in the synapse, and (6) increasing or decreasing the binding of a neurotransmitter with its postsynaptic receptor. In addition, therapeutic drugs can also act by potentiating longer-term changes associated with prolonged drug administration. Cooper, Bloom, and Roth (1996) provide a comprehensive overview of the method of action of a number of substances on important neurotransmitter systems.

Because of the high degree of communication among different brain regions, even drugs that directly affect highly localized neuronal systems can have indirect effects on other brain regions. It is therefore not surprising that certain medications (e.g., tricyclic antidepressants) appear to have relatively broad indications and that certain disorders (e.g., panic disorder, major depression) appear to respond to very different classes of medications. Despite these important qualifications, some generalizations can be made. (1) Drugs that tend to decrease the activity (e.g., by blocking receptors) of systems utilizing the neurotransmitter dopamine have antipsychotic effects. (2) Drugs that tend to increase the activity (e.g., by blocking reuptake or by blocking catabolism) of systems utilizing the neurotransmitters norepinephrine and serotonin often have antidepressant effects. (3) Drugs that tend to increase the activity (e.g., by their interactions with receptors) of systems utilizing the neurotransmitter GABA often have anti-anxiety effects. New medication development goes hand-in-hand with deeper understanding of the underlying neuropharmacology of mental disorders.

Genetics

Although it has been known for many years that mental disorders run in families, such family data can only demonstrate the familiality of mental disorders and not their heritability. For example, speaking Italian tends to run in families (i.e., is highly familial), but no one would suggest that there is a genetically based tendency to speak Italian as opposed to other languages. In order to establish a genetic basis, it is important to use research designs that are genetically informative; that is, where comparisons among relatives provide the data necessary for making inferences as to a genetic basis.

For many years, twin studies served as the most direct way of determining whether or not a disorder has, at least in part, a genetic basis. In the classic twin study design, the similarity of monozygotic (MZ; i.e., 'identical') twins and dizygotic (DZ; i.e., 'fraternal') twins are compared. Because MZ twins share all of their genes and DZ twins share only half their genes, greater similarity (or what is sometimes called concordance) among MZ twins than among DZ twins implies a genetic component as long as a number of other assumptions (including similarity of their environments and adequacy of sampling) are met. Another genetically informative design that has been used in psychopathology research is the adoption or cross-fostering design. In this design, the prevalence of psychopathology in adoptees is examined as a function of psychopathology in their biological parents and in their adoptive parents. If there is a significant association between psychopathology in the adoptees and their biological parents, a genetic influence is suggested; if there is a significant association between psychopathology in the adoptees and their adoptive parents, a family environment influence is suggested. Here too it is important that many assumptions are met (e.g., there is no association between the characteristics of adoptive and biological parents – that is placement is not selective; adoption occurs close to birth; and there is no interaction between adoptees and their biological parents). This design probably underestimates family environment effects because individuals with severe psychopathology are not likely to be awarded custody of adopted chidren.

For most major mental disorders (e.g., schizophrenia, the major mood disorders, anxiety disorders, alcohol-use disorders), twin and/or adoption studies have demonstrated significant genetic effects. However, these studies typically demonstrate equally, if not more, important environmental effects. For example, the concordance rates for MZ twins are far from 100% (usually less than 50%), directly establishing the importance of the environment. However, psychologists often assume that 'environment' means the family or psychosocial environment; this is not necessarily the case. Factors such as the prenatal environment and viral infections, are all part of the 'environment' in genetic terms.

However, it is equally important to recognize that effects that are ostensibly genetic do not rule out important psychological mediation of genetic effects. For example, physical attractiveness is partly genetic. If we were to find that attractive individuals suffered from depression less often than unattractive individuals, would this suggest a genetic explanation? The answer could be 'yes' and 'no'. 'Yes' in that individual differences in depression could be traced to genetic predisposition. 'No' in that the genetic effect is indirectly mediated by a psychological mechanism such as greater success in finding a good mate or greater success in various social roles. In effect, genetic influences on psychopathology are always indirect in that they must be mediated by processes causally proximal to disorder. However, the genetic mediation seems more direct when it can be traced to a missing or mutant form of a neurotransmitter receptor and less direct when environmental processes are implicated as important intervening factors.

Recent years have witnessed a revolution in molecular genetics. As a result, we are no longer primarily interested in conducting twin or adoption studies to determine whether or not a disorder has a genetic component. Today, and increasingly in the future, we are more concerned with the discovery of the specific genes that are inherited and how they act to produce mental disorders. Using several different techniques to analyze DNA (the molecular basis of genes), researchers are now in a position to correlate the presence of specific genes with specific mental disorders. The task is complicated because existing research suggests that most mental disorders are caused by multiple genes, making it very difficult to discover each individual gene that is associated with a disorder. Additionally, genetic heterogeneity (i.e., there may be alternate genetic make-ups that lead to phenotypically similar disorders) makes the search even harder. Finally, there are so many genes that the thousands of analyses undertaken in a single study can sometimes lead to false positive findings. Thus replication of positive findings is crucial. Despite these problems, it seems highly likely that in the next decade many genes associated with mental disorders will be identified. As this is done, it is likely that the nosology will be revised to distinguish among behaviorally similar syndromes that are genetically distinct.

Psychological Approaches

Psychological explanation is fundamental to an understanding of mental disorders because these are essentially disorders of mood, thought, and behavior – the core concerns of psychology. However, psychological approaches to psychopathology are preparadigmatic in that there are few basic assumptions or systems that all psychologists would accept; psychologically oriented psychopathologists often subscribe to competing schools of thought. Consequently, it is not surprising that, from a psychological perspective, there are diverse perspectives on psychopathology.

Developmental Approach

Almost 200 years ago, William Wordsworth wrote that 'The child is father of the man.' The idea that mental disorders in adulthood might have their roots in childhood was a major tenet of Freudian thought. Adult mental disorders were believed to result from unresolved conflicts arising during the stages of psychosexual development. It was believed that these conflicts could lay dormant for decades, only to erupt when activated later in life. Although this part of Freud's view of development is not widely accepted today, the idea that there are psychological stages of development and that failure to successfully negotiate a given stage will present adaptive problems at subsequent stages is currently widely held and can be traced directly back to Freud.

Evidence for the importance of developmental factors comes from several sources. For example, longitudinal studies of child behavior and personality demonstrate that various adult outcomes can be predicted, albeit typically weakly, from ratings of childhood behavior. Those childhood variables that have been the most widely investigated include temperament and attachment. Temperament refers to the fundamental response styles that form the basis of personality such as emotionality, activity level, and sociability. Attachment refers to the nature of early relationships between children and their caregivers which, at the most general level, can be categorized as reflecting secure or insecure interactional styles. Both temperament and attachment style are thought to be fairly stable across the life course and have been related to later outcomes in longitudinal studies. Although attachment is viewed as primarily an interactional process and temperament an individual difference variable, attachment styles are increasingly viewed as individual difference variables and the importance of temperament is often conceptualized with respect to its impact on social behavior.

Psychological development reveals itself over time and in the context of families, peer networks, and larger societal structures (e.g., schools, neighborhoods). From a developmental perspective, mental disorders can arise as a function of problems in any of these developmental settings as children are confronted with new roles, tasks, and responsibilities that are associated with each setting over time.

Learning

Although the belief that basic conditioning principles could explain most, if not all, mental disorders was widely held by academic clinical psychologists (especially in the United States) for much of the twentieth century, this view has increasingly fallen out of favor. Much of the decline in influence is attributable to the ascendance of cognitive psychology as well as increasing recognition of neurobiological influences in psychopathology. Nevertheless, learning perspectives continue to be a valuable explanatory system for understanding many mental disorders and symptoms.

Although classical and operant conditioning are still important explanatory concepts in understanding the etiology and maintenance of fears, addiction, and depression, these concepts are no longer viewed as sufficient explanations by most psychopathologists. First, the recognition that there are important biological constraints on learning has gained widespread acceptance. For example, it is now known that phobias do not develop simply as a function of aversive conditioning and that some classes of stimuli (e.g., animals, heights, dominant others) that have significance from an evolutionary perspective are more likely to become phobic stimuli than other potentially threatening stimuli (e.g., knives, guns). Second, there is greater acceptance of the idea that there are important types of learning beyond simple associative conditioning. For example, the fact that important learning occurs through modeling has been extensively demonstrated in different contexts. Third, in humans, symbolic instruction and logical reasoning provide additional routes to acquiring information about the world. Fourth, leading learning theorists like Robert Rescorla have pointed out that classical conditioning can be viewed from a cognitive perspective (i.e., what is conditioned are expectancies about events). These realizations have forced psychologists to place simple associative conditioning in the broader context of powerful biological constraints and cognitive functioning more generally. Perhaps the most important contribution of a learning perspective has been in the development of behavior therapies that rely extensively on conditioning principles.

Personality

Although there is considerable variability in how different theorists define personality, most formal definitions note that personality is 'internal, organized, and characteristic of an individual over time and situations . . . (and has) motivational and adaptive significance' (Watson, Clark, & Harkness, 1994, p. 18). For many years researchers have disagreed over many central questions surrounding the nature and measurement of personality, and this debate is still ongoing. At present, most psychologists subscribe to either a three-factor or five-factor model of personality. Two dimensions are common to most three- and five-factor approaches:

(a) a neuroticism or negative emotionality factor that refers to the tendency to experience negative mood states, and (b) a sociability or positive emotionality factor that refers to the tendency to experience positive emotions and manifest a high level of activity. Three-factor approaches have a third dimension that typically refers to a tendency toward impulsive and nonconforming behavior. Also similar traits appear in five-factor models; they tend to be distributed over two dimensions termed (a) conscientiousness and (b) agreeableness.

Most research on personality suggests that there is a general relation between broad personality traits like neuroticism and mental disorders; high neuroticism tends to characterize multiple disorders, but especially mood and anxiety disorders. Impulsivity is most strongly associated with diagnoses such as antisocial personality disorder and substance-use disorders that, not surprisingly, are characterized by impaired impulse control. Findings for extraversion are less consistent but it appears that low extraversion (i.e., introversion) is associated with depression and at least some anxiety disorders.

Because correlations between specific personality traits and Axis I mental disorders are typically low, researchers rarely view personality as a proximal cause of disorder. Rather, personality is increasingly being viewed as a vulnerability or protective factor that interacts with other variables to cause the onset or persistence of disorder.

The case is somewhat different with respect to Axis II personality variables where the disorders themselves are thought to reflect pathological variants of normal personality traits. However, the correspondence between DSM personality disorders and, for example, five-factor personality traits is less than desirable, leading some theorists to argue for reconceptualizing personality disorders using the five-factor model.

Information Processing Deficits

The idea that certain mental disorders represent a failure of basic information processing dates back at least to the early twentieth century when the Swiss psychiatrist, Eugen Bleuler, proposed that disturbances in the form (as opposed to content) of thought represented a core deficit in schizophrenia. Bleuler's early work led to an interest in characterizing the loose associations of schizophrenics which, in turn, led to the study of attentional deficits. For many years, the characterization of attentional dysfunction in schizophrenia was a central topic in psychopathology research.

The hypothesis that a relatively specific information-processing deficit could be responsible for a range of symptoms is an intriguing notion. It seems quite plausible that disruption of a basic cognitive resource such as attention could pose serious problems for the effective use of language, for the ability to reason abstractly, and for adequate memory functioning. Basic deficits in information processing, especially attentional processes, continue to be an active source of investigation, not only in schizophrenia research but also in other disorders where attentional problems are posited to be key symptoms of disorders (e.g., other psychoses, post-traumatic stress disorder, attention deficit disorder).

To a large extent, disrupted attentional processes are implicated (though not necessarily as a cause) in most major mental disorders. For example, a key symptom common to many forms of psychopathology is preoccupation. The content of preoccupation might differ dramatically across disorder (e.g, the depressive might be preoccupied with personal worthlessness, the phobic with possible harm, the alcoholic with having his next drink, the obsessive compulsive with contamination, the pathological gambler with 'getting even'). However, the 'tying up' of attentional resources with pathological concerns is an important phenomenon that could presumably mediate a number of consequences (e.g., impaired work performance, lack of attention to others).

Information-processing deficits have been extensively studied not only as explanatory mechanisms of symptom production but also for their localizing value for those interested in the neurological basis of mental disorders. For example, certain information processing abilities are associated with the activity of specific brain regions. Thus, the patterning of findings across a battery of cognitive tests with known neurological correlates can be used to identify possible brain areas associated with a mental disorder. Finally, self-reported problems in cognitive function, such as impaired memory, often reflect depression rather than a true deficit and many individuals with serious deficits (e.g., those with dementias such as Alzheimer's disease) commonly show little insight into the extent of their cognitive impairment. Thus it is important that psychologists not rely on self-report to assess the nature or degree of cognitive impairment.

Cognitive Styles and Biases

The idea that individuals distort information in specific ways and that these distortions are intimately related to psychopathology can be traced back to Freud's concept of defense mechanisms (i.e., unconscious strategies that distort or inhibit information that is threatening to the ego). Later psychoanalytic thinkers expanded these concepts to include more general cognitive styles that were intimately linked to personality. For example, David Shapiro (1965) described how different personality styles routinely processed information in distorted ways as a way to manage conflict.

Unlike their psychoanalytic forebears, most modern cognitive theorists, although focusing on distorted cognitions as important symptoms and putative causes of mental disorders, do not assume that information processing biases are motivated by conflict. Rather, they tend to be somewhat silent on their motivational function and instead focus on their structure and effects. Perhaps the best-known theorist in the area is Aaron Beck (1985) who proposed that depression was the result of a type of disordered thinking. Beck hypothesized that, through early learning, some individuals develop negative schemas for perceiving the world that are activated when the individual is confronted by schema-congruent negative situations. Distortions associated with such schemas include the tendency to make arbitrary inferences (e.g., making a self-disparaging attribution over a seemingly random event), selective abstractions (e.g., selectively focusing on one aspect of a complex situation to draw a negative inference about the self), overgeneralizations (e.g., making a self-damning judgment on the basis of an isolated, minor error), and magnification and minimization (e.g., overfocusing on problems and minimizing successes). Other cognitive theorists have emphasized the attributional process individuals make for personal failures and other bad events. For example, Lynn Abramson and colleagues have proposed that aversive events are likely to lead to depression if the individual tends to attribute the cause to personal (as opposed to external), stable (as opposed to transient), and global (as opposed to specific) factors. For example, a break up of a relationship is particularly likely to lead to depression if the individual blames the situation on a personal inadequacy, views the inadequacy as reflecting a chronic state of affairs, and sees it as having broad effects. Although considerable research has demonstrated that depressives frequently do tend to distort information in characteristic ways, the extent to which these cognitive styles predispose individuals to depression is less clear. That is, it appears that at least some degree of biased information processing represents the effects of depression.

Today, cognitive biases represent a leading viewpoint on the etiology of a number of different behavior problems. For example, aggressive children have been shown to exhibit biases toward inferring hostile intentions and rejection from others; individuals with panic disorder have been shown to 'catastrophize' the significance of physical sensations; phobics tend to overestimate the amount of fear they will experience in certain situations; and substance abusers tend to expect high levels of positive consequences and low levels of negative consequences from their substance use.

Although cognitions appear to be very important in determining our reactions to events and treatments that attempt to alter cognitions appear to be effective in reducing various types of mental disorders, it should not be assumed that the best way of altering cognitions is via discussion, reflection, or exhortation. For example, Albert Bandura has demonstrated that self-efficacy (i.e., a perceived ability to perform a behavior successfully) changes most in response to direct behavioral performance. Relatedly, treatment approaches that are heavily behavioral in emphasis might be effective because of cognitive changes.

21.7 Prevention of Mental Disorders

The ultimate goal of psychopathology research is the development of sufficient knowledge and appropriate technology to prevent the occurrence of mental disorders. At present this goal is a long way off, but it becomes progressively more realistic with advances in psychopathology research as well as prevention science. As is often pointed out by public health advocates, effective prevention can occur with less than complete knowledge of etiology. For example, although it would be 30 years before Robert Koch identified the bacteria responsible for causing cholera, John Snow was able to end a cholera epidemic in nineteenth-century London by removing the handle on the Broad Street pump (whose water source had been contaminated). Thus, prevention research can proceed in parallel with psychopathology research and need not wait until all etiological factors and their modes of action have been established.

Historically, the field of public health described three forms of prevention: (1) primary prevention (i.e., the reduction of new cases of disorder), (2) secondary prevention (i.e., reduction of the rate of established cases of disorder), and (3) tertiary prevention (i.e., reduction of the degree of disability associated with disorder). In other words, primary prevention meant 'prevention' in the usual sense of the word, secondary prevention meant early intervention or treatment, and tertiary prevention meant disease

management or rehabilitation. In a recent overview of research on the prevention of mental disorders, the Institute of Medicine (1994) adopted an alternative structure for conceptualizing prevention activities based on the population to be targeted. *Universal* prevention refers to prevention 'that can be advocated confidently for the general public and for all members of specific eligible groups . . . [and] in many cases . . . can be applied without professional advice or assistance. The benefits outweigh the costs for everyone' (p. 21). An example of a universal prevention measure would be adequate prenatal care for pregnant women. *Selective* prevention refers to prevention that is targeted at currently unafflicted individuals who are members of a subgroup at increased risk for developing disorder. Because of the heightened risk of the subgroup, more expensive or extensive interventions can be justified (e.g., regular assessment of drinking problems in individuals with a family history of alcoholism; preschool programs for children from poor families). *Indicated* prevention refers to prevention that is targeted at individuals who have a 'manifest' risk factor on examination that places them individually at high risk. These risk factors must not be overt signs of disorder but still represent a clinically demonstrable abnormality. For example, parent training for mothers or fathers of difficult-temperament children who do not yet demonstrate a clinical syndrome would be an example of indicated prevention.

The Institute of Medicine (1994) report lists a number of randomized controlled trials (i.e., prevention experiments) that have been carried out to date. Review of these studies, conducted over the past 20 years, reveals a considerable number of universal, selective, and indicated prevention efforts targeted towards infants, children, adolescents, and adults with various types of risk factors. The risk factors that have been targeted have been wide ranging and include economic deprivation, maternal health, nutrition, early behavior problems, early drug use, aggressive behavior, academic failure, marital distress, and bereavement, to name just a few. Many of these studies have had considerable success in reducing the level of risk factors and/or the incidence of manifest disorder.

Prevention studies are important not only because pre-empting the suffering or impairment of mental disorders is an important public health goal but also because effective prevention studies can inform our basic understanding of etiology. At their heart, prevention studies are true experiments and as such they can provide some of the strongest data on whether or not a putative cause of disorder is a 'validated' cause. For example, a correlation between parental physical abuse of a child and child psychopathology implicates but does not establish physical abuse as a possible risk factor. Nonexperimental studies that control for various confounds can be used to strengthen or weaken the case for causality. However, a true experiment that examines the effects of reducing physical abuse on later outcomes addresses many of the concerns raised earlier in this chapter (e.g., genetic correlation, reverse causation) and can often provide the most compelling data. Thus, prevention research represents not just the fruit of more basic etiological research; prevention research can be the most definitive etiological research.

RESOURCE REFERENCES

Cicchetti, D., & Cohen, D. J. (1995). *Developmental psychopathology* (vols. 1 and 2). New York: Wiley.

Clark, L. A., Watson, D., & Reynolds, S. (1995). Diagnosis and classification of psychopathology: Challenges to the current system and future directions. *Annual Review of Psychology, 47*, 371–400.

Davison, G. C., & Neale, J. M. (1998). *Abnormal psychology* (7th ed.). New York: Wiley.

Dobson, K. S., & Kendall, P. C. (1993). *Psychopathology and cognition*. San Diego, CA: Academic Press.

Freeman, C., & Tyrer, P. (1992). *Research methods in psychiatry: A beginner's guide* (2nd ed.). London: Gaskell/Royal College of Psychiatrists.

Hall, L. L. (1996). *Genetics and mental illness: Evolving issues for research and society*. New York: Plenum Press.

Sher, K. J., & Trull., T. J. (1996). Methodological issues in psychopathology research. *Annual Review of Psychology, 47*, 371–400.

Trull, T. J., & Phares, J. (in press). *Clinical psychology: Concepts, methods, and profession* (6th ed.). Pacific Grove, CA: Brooks Cole.

Wittchen, H.-U., & Unland, H. (1992). Neue Ansätze zur Symptomerfassung und Diagnosestellung nach ICD-10 und DSM-III-R: Strukturierte und standardisierte Interviews. Überblicksarbeit. [New approaches in the measurement of symptoms and diagnosis according to the ICD-10 and DSM III-R: Structured and standardized interviews. A review.] *Zeitschrift fur Klinische Psychologie: Forschung und Praxis, 20*, 321–342.

ADDITIONAL LITERATURE CITED

American Psychiatric Association (1994). *Diagnostic and statistical manual of mental disorders* (4th ed.). Washington, DC: American Psychiatric Association.

Beck, A. T. (1985). *Anxiety disorders and phobias: A cognitive perspective*. New York: Basic Books.

Berner, P., Gabriel, E., Katschnig, H., Kieffer, W., Koehler, K., Lenz, G., Nutzinger, D., Schanda, H., & Simhandl, C. (1992). *Diagnostic criteria for functional psychoses* (2nd ed.). Cambridge: Cambridge University Press (under auspices of the World Psychiatric Association).

Cooper, J. R., Bloom, F. E., & Roth, R. H. (1996). *The biochemical basis of neuropharmacology* (7th ed.). New York: Oxford.

Follette, W. C. (1996). Introduction to the special section on the development of theoretically coherent alternatives to the DSM system. *Journal of Consulting and Clinical Psychology, 64*, 117–119.

Griffith, E. E. H, & Gonzalez, C. A. (1994). Essentials of cultural psychiatry. In R. E. Hales, S. C. Yudofsky, & J. A. Talbott (Eds.), *The American Psychiatric Press textbook of psychiatry* (2nd ed., pp. 1379–1404). Washington, DC: American Psychiatric Press.

Helzer, J. E., & Canino, G. J. (1992). *Alcoholism in North America, Europe, and Asia*. New York: Oxford University Press.

Institute of Medicine (1994). *Reducing the risks for mental disorders: Frontiers for preventive intervention research*. Washington, DC: National Academy Press.

Kessler, R. C., McGonagle, K. A., Zhao, S., Nelson, C. B., Hughes, M., Eshleman, S., Wittchen, H.-U., & Kendler, K. (1994). Lifetime and 12-month prevalence of DSM-III-R psychiatric disorders in the United States: Results from the National Comorbidity Study. *Archives of General Psychiatry, 51*, 8–19.

Kraepelin, E. (1899). *Psychiatrie* (6. Aufl.). Leipzig: Barth.

Lazarus, R. S., & Folkman, S. (1984). *Stress, appraisal, and coping*. New York: Springer.

Monroe, S. M., & Simons, A. D. (1991). Diathesis-stress theories in the context of life stress research: Implications for the depressive disorders. *Psychological Bulletin, 110*, 406–425.

Roberts, R. E., Attkisson, C. C., & Rosenblatt, A. (1998). Prevalence of psychopathology among children and adolescents. *American Journal of Psychiatry, 155*, 715–725.

Robins, L., & Regier, D. A. (Eds.). (1991). *Psychiatric disorders in America: The Epidemiologic Catchment Area study*. New York: The Free Press.

Schacht, T., & Nathan, P. E. (1977). But is it good for the psychologists? Appraisal and status of DSM-III. *American Psychologist, 32*, 1017–1025.

Shapiro, D. (1965). *Neurotic styles*. New York: Basic Books.

Vieth, I. (1965). *Hysteria: History of a disease*. Chicago: University of Chicago Press.

Watson, D., Clark, L., & Harkness. (1994). Structures of personality and their relevance to psychopathology. *Journal of Abnormal Psychology, 103,* 18–31.

Weissman, M. M., Bland, R. C., Canino, G. J., Faravelli, C., Greenwald, S., Hwu, H. G., Joyce, P. R., Karam, E. G., Lee, C. K., Lellouch, J., Lepine, J. P., Newman, S. C., Oakley-Browne, M. A., Rubio-Stipec, M., Wells, J. E., Wickramaratne, P. J., Wittchen, H. U., & Yeh, E. K.

(1997). The cross-national epidemiology of panic disorder. *Archives of General Psychiatry, 54,* 305–309.

Weisz, J. R., Suwanlert, S., Chaiyasit, W., Weiss, B., et al. (1993). Behavioral and emotional problems among Thai and American adolescents: Parent reports for ages 12–26. *Journal of Abnormal Psychology, 102,* 395–403.

Zilboorg, G. (1941). *A history of medical psychology.* New York: Norton.

Communications concerning this chapter should be addressed to: Professor Kenneth J. Sher, Department of Psychology, University of Missouri, 200 S. 7th Street, Columbia, MO 65211, USA

22

Clinical Psychology II: Psychological Treatments: Research and Practice

PETER E. NATHAN, ANNE HELENE SKINSTAD, AND SARA L. DOLAN

This chapter begins with a brief historical overview of efforts over the past 50 years to identify and describe empirically supported psychological treatments. It continues with a brief consideration of the controversial development of practice guidelines, which incorporate data on empirically supported treatments in the effort to enhance both the effectiveness and the accountability of these interventions. The chapter concludes by presenting current findings on empirically supported treatments for a range of common disorders, including the childhood disorders, the alcohol-related disorders, schizophrenia, major depressive disorder, the anxiety disorders, and

the eating disorders. A table listing these disorders and their empirically supported treatments accompanies this discussion.

22.1 A Historical Overview of Efforts to Identify Empirically Supported Treatments

British psychologist Hans Eysenck's initial critical evaluation of the effects of psychotherapy
(Eysenck, 1952), followed by subsequent reviews
in 1960 and 1969, served as a benchmark of the
sorry state of outcome research at the time. The
1960 review is remembered best for two remarkable conclusions. First, Eysenck determined the
neuroses' spontaneous remission rate – the rate
at which they disappear without treatment –
which he used as a benchmark against which to
compare the effects of psychotherapy. His controversial conclusion: '. . . roughly two-thirds of
a group of neurotic patients will recover or
improve to a marked extent within about two
years of the onset of their illness' in the absence
of treatment (1952, p. 322).

Eysenck's re-analysis of treatment data also
led him to calculate that '. . . patients treated by
means of psychoanalysis improved to the extent
of 44%; patients treated eclectically – by a
combination of methods – improved to the
extent of 64%; patients treated only custodially
or by general practitioners improved to the extent
of 72%.' Accordingly, 'there thus appears to
be an inverse correlation between recovery and
psychotherapy' (1952, p. 322). Eysenck's controversial 1952 conclusion, essentially repeated
in 1960 and 1969: the psychotherapies in widest
use at mid-century are largely ineffective.

Eysenck's 1952 review was engaged by
numerous critics, who focused on the inadequate
methodology of the outcome studies on which
he based his conclusions. Few of these studies
were controlled. The nature and severity of the
conditions treated were inadequately described
(due partly to the low reliability of diagnosis at
the time). The treatments that were provided were
insufficiently detailed. And treatment follow-ups
were generally inadequate. Nonetheless, Eysenck
insisted that, despite the shortcomings of their
research bases, his calculations pointed in only
one direction: 'They fail to prove that psychotherapy, Freudian or otherwise, facilitates the
recovery of neurotic patients' (1952, p. 323).

The 1973 meeting of the American Psychopathological Association featured a presentation
by Luborsky, Singer, and Luborsky (1976) pro-
vocatively titled 'Comparative studies of psychotherapies: Is it true that "everyone has won
and all must have prizes." ' It reiterated several

familiar themes of 1970s psychotherapy research:
all psychotherapies work to some extent, differences among psychotherapies in effectiveness
are often not found, and more adequate research
methodologies must be developed before a true
picture of psychotherapy effectiveness can be
achieved.

Luborsky and his colleagues confined their
review to 'studies in which some attention was
paid to the main requirements of controlled
comparative research.' These requirements included many of the design elements of contemporary outcome studies today, including random
assignment of subjects to treatments, controls,
and blind outcome assessment. Unlike the best
designed of today's studies, the studies Luborsky
and his colleagues reviewed generally lacked
methods for ensuring that the treatment was
delivered as intended. As well, the period of
post-treatment follow-up was rarely extended,
and follow-up assessments generally focused on
non-specific rather than the targeted behaviors
we prefer to assess nowadays.

Meta-analysis, introduced a year later by
Smith and Glass (1977), was designed to minimize the methodological shortcomings of many
of the psychotherapy outcome studies of the
time. Smith and Glass's 1977 article integrated
findings from almost 400 independent outcome
studies to produce an overall 'effect size' for
each of a large number of psychotherapy outcome measures. (Effect size is, in essence, a
statistically derived estimate of the robustness of
an intervention.) It reported that the average
outcome study '. . . showed a .68 standard
deviation superiority of the treated group over
the control group' (1977, p. 756). This finding
convinced Smith and Glass that psychotherapy
works – especially since they also reported that
the average patient achieved a better outcome
than 75% of untreated controls.

Smith and Glass's initial study of meta-
analysis was well received by many for several
reasons. Its findings were based on a very substantial sample size. It introduced an innovative
statistical method, meta-analysis, designed to
minimize the impact of the methodological
shortcomings of the therapy outcome studies of
the time and transform qualitative judgments
into quantitative ones. And it attempted, for the
first time, to quantify the impact of treatments
by means of the effect size estimation. Nonetheless, the 1977 study was also strongly criticized.
Among the most telling of the criticisms was
Rachman and Wilson's (1980), who took strong
exception to Smith and Glass' uncritical acceptance of the flawed methodology of many of the
studies they analyzed. Rachman and Wilson also
lamented Smith and Glass's decision to endorse
Luborsky, Singer, and Luborsky's views on the

positive effects of psychotherapy, despite seemingly insufficient evidence. They also questioned Smith and Glass's unexplained failure to include some of the best-designed behavior therapy outcome studies of the early 1970s in their analysis.

Rachman and Wilson offered an underwhelming assessment of the effectiveness of psychotherapy at the conclusion of their 1980 review of outcomes of psychoanalytic treatment, Rogerian psychotherapy, psychotherapy with psychotic patients, behavior therapy, and cognitive behavior therapy.

> Since the First Edition was published (in 1971), some slight progress has been made in the attempt to produce evidence to support the claims made on behalf of psychotherapy in general . . . Nevertheless, it is our view that modest evidence now supports the claim that psychotherapy is capable of producing some beneficial changes – but the negative results still outnumber the positive findings, and both of these are exceeded by reports that are beyond interpretation. (Rachman & Wilson, 1980, p. 259)

The first edition of this book (Rachman, 1971) had lent strong support to Eysenck's earlier claims of psychotherapy's ineffectiveness. Hence, it is noteworthy that improvements in the methodology of outcome research, coupled with the development of more effective behavioral treatments, led Rachman and Wilson to express even this degree of cautious optimism in 1980. Rachman and Wilson were particularly impressed by the emerging data on behavior therapy outcomes:

> There are well-established methods for reducing anxieties and fears of various sorts, good progress has been made in establishing an equally powerful method for dealing with obsessions and compulsions, and significant advances have been made in dealing with some sexual dysfunctions. (p. 261)

Howard, Kopta, Krause, and Orlinsky reported the results of the first dose–effect study of psychotherapy in 1986. In the report's preface, the authors note 'a growing consensus in the psychotherapy research literature that psychotherapeutic treatment is generally beneficial to patients.' However, '. . . to date, there has been no systematic attempt to specify the mathematical form of this dose–effect relationship or to determine its accuracy.' Confirming the dose–effect relationship would clearly constitute strong additional evidence for the efficacy of psychotherapy. To do so, Howard and his colleagues analyzed 15 therapy outcome studies, concluding that:

> . . . 10% to 18% of patients could be expected to have shown some improvement after the first session

> of psychotherapy . . . by eight sessions, 48% to 58% of patients would be expected to have measurably improved . . . (and) about 75% of patients should have shown measurable improvements by the end of six months of once-weekly psychotherapy. (Howard et al., 1986, p. 162)

A confound of time with number of sessions and an exclusive reliance on global ratings of improvement by therapists and patients detract from these findings. Nonetheless, this first quantitative determination of a dose–effect relationship for psychotherapy (like that demonstrated repeatedly for pharmacological treatment) constituted another empirical voice of support for the efficacy of psychotherapy.

In the same issue of *American Psychologist*, Stiles, Shapiro and Elliott (1986) again asked a familiar question: 'Are all psychotherapies equivalent?' Their answer was the same as that of Luborsky, Singer, and Luborsky. The outcome data to date still '. . . appear to support the conclusion that outcomes of diverse therapies are generally similar' (p. 165). In other words, little more than a decade ago, the views of clinical scientists continued to reflect the continuing failure of efforts to differentiate effective from ineffective treatments for specific disorders, as they had since Eysenck's 1952 review. Stiles' conclusion was especially surprising in view of strong evidence that Rachman and Wilson (1980) and other proponents of behavior therapy had marshaled years earlier pointing to the superior efficacy of behavior therapy for several common behavioral disorders.

The 180,000 subscribers of *Consumer Reports*, an American magazine that evaluates the quality of a broad range of consumer goods and services, were sent a questionnaire in 1994 asking them to respond to a series of questions about their experiences with mental health professionals, physicians, medications, and self-help groups. This effort constituted the largest survey of mental health treatment outcomes to date. Its most notable findings, published in the November, 1995, issue of the magazine, included the following:

- Almost half of the respondents whose self-described emotional state was 'very poor' or 'fairly poor' reported significant improvement following therapy.
- The longer psychotherapy lasted, the more it helped.
- Psychotherapy alone worked as well as combined psychotherapy and pharmacotherapy.

These findings suggest very strongly that psychotherapy is effective. Regrettably, however, the study had significant methodological problems that detract from this positive conclusion. A mail survey touching on matters this sensitive and complex, a substantially-undefined and essentially-undiagnosed group of respondents, the absence of an untreated control group, and outcome questions that focused on generalized 'improvement' rather than specific outcomes targeted to symptoms all raise serious concerns. Most troubling, however, was the very low rate of response to the mailed questionnaire: Only 4,100 (slightly more than 2%) of the 180,000 subscribers to the magazine reported seeking professional help or joining groups, while only 2,900 (about 1.5%) reported actually consulting a mental health professional. These numbers are so low that it seems clear that only a portion of the *Consumer Reports* subscribers with therapy experience responded to the survey. Perhaps more of those who felt especially positive about their psychotherapy experiences responded, thereby skewing the findings in a positive direction. In the absence of data on the universe of *Consumer Reports* subscribers who sought professional help for their emotional problems, the results of the survey must be viewed with considerable caution.

By contrast, Martin Seligman, a consultant to the project, believes it 'complements the (more traditional) efficacy method, (so that) the best features of these two methods can be combined into a more ideal method that will best provide empirical validation of psychotherapy' (Seligman, 1995, p. 965). Here Seligman draws attention to differences between efficacy studies, the traditional highly controlled 'gold standard' for judging psychotherapy outcomes, and effectiveness studies, which reflect feasibility and clinical utility in the real world. The *Consumer Reports* survey comprised an effectiveness study, although it was not particularly well designed. Nonetheless, the distinction between efficacy and effectiveness studies is important, Seligman writes, because efficacy studies show us one part of the psychotherapy elephant while effectiveness studies show us another. Nathan, Stuart, and Dolan (in press) have completed a comprehensive historical review of efforts to distinguish between efficacy and effectiveness studies; they emphasize the difficulty at times of separating the two, concluding that perceived differences between them in some instances may be more semantic than real.

22.2 Empirically Supported Treatments and Practice Guidelines: The Continuing Controversy

As this brief review of the history of efforts to identify empirically supported psychological treatments suggests, marked advances have been made in both the quality of the methods employed to assess psychotherapy outcomes and the number and efficacy of the behavior change methods themselves. Not surprisingly, as more effective treatments have been developed, pressures on providers of psychological and psychiatric services to use them have increased. Giving impetus to these pressures is the dramatic recent growth in American society of expectations of increased professional accountability. For the first time, mental health professionals are now expected to demonstrate proof of the efficacy of their diagnostic and treatment methods in return for reimbursement for these services. As a consequence, within the past decade, a number of mental health practice guidelines incorporating empirically supported treatments have appeared in the United States. At least one, developed by the Swedish Psychiatric Association, has also appeared in Europe. This section briefly describes three of the most influential of the American guidelines and assesses their current strengths and weaknesses, as well as their potential for greater ultimate usefulness.

The AHCPR *Depression in Primary Care* Guidelines (1993)

The Agency for Health Care Policy and Research (AHCPR) *Depression in Primary Care* Guidelines (Depression Guideline Panel, 1993) were created to inform primary care physicians and the general public about the diagnosis and treatment of depression. Although clinical depression is diagnosed and treated much more often by primary care physicians and nurses than by mental health professionals in the United States, primary care health professionals are often unaware of the best treatment practices for these conditions (Clinton, McCormick, & Besteman, 1994). Accordingly, the AHCPR guidelines were designed to convey the empirical data on best practices for depression in primary care settings.

Both the popular press and several physician groups responded favorably to the AHCPR guidelines. Psychologists also recognized the AHCPR guidelines shortly after they appeared, describing them in detail (Clinton, McCormick, & Besteman, 1994) and offering comprehensive analyses for (Schulberg & Rush, 1994) and against (Munoz, Hollon, McGrath, Rehm, & VandenBos, 1994).

Munoz and his colleagues expressed serious concerns about the pamphlets designed for primary care physicians and patients. They observed that, 'in these shorter publications, the balanced presentation of the longer documents is lost and a consistent biomedical bias appears evident that is likely to lead patients and their physicians to opt for pharmacological interventions to the exclusion of other alternative treatments' (Munoz et al., 1994, p. 43). Kingsbury (1995) responded with support for the AHCPR guidelines' emphasis on medication, in recognition of the substantial numbers of depressed patients who do not comply with referrals for outpatient psychotherapy. Others (e.g., Antonuccio, 1995; Karon & Teixeira, 1995), however, agreed that the guidelines ignored the equal or superior effectiveness of psychotherapy for depression in favor of medication.

The American Psychiatric Association Practice Guidelines (1993, 1994, 1995, 1996, 1997)

The American Psychiatric Association has published practice guidelines for the treatment of major depressive disorder in adults (1993); bipolar disorder (1994b); alcohol, cocaine, and opioid abuse and dependence (1995); nicotine dependence (1996); and schizophrenia (1997). Each guideline provides a brief introductory section on disease definition, epidemiology, and natural history; a lengthier section detailing treatment principles and options; and a concluding section summarizing research directions.

All five psychiatric practice guidelines stress adherence whenever possible to the empirical data on treatment outcomes, although all envision occasions when clinical judgment factors would outweigh research findings. This implicit continuum – at one end of which are decisions determined entirely by empirical findings and, at the other, decisions influenced entirely by clinical considerations – relates in some ways to the continuing controversy over the worth of efficacy studies as against effectiveness studies.

These guidelines also rate the methodological adequacy of the outcome literature cited. The major depressive disorder guideline, like the others, describes three 'categories of endorsement' based on research design and methodology.

> The three categories represent varying levels of clinical confidence regarding the efficacy of the treatment for the disorder and conditions described. [I] indicates recommended with substantial clinical confidence; [II] indicates recommended with moderate clinical confidence; [III] indicates options that may be recommended on the basis of individual circumstances. (APA, 1993, p. 19)

The reaction of psychiatrists to the psychiatric guidelines has generally been positive. Reasons include the familiarity of physicians with practice guidelines, which are common in physical medicine, and the long history of efforts, overseen by the Food and Drug Administration, to establish the efficacy of drug treatments by means of established evaluation protocols. However, psychologist Jacqueline Persons and her colleagues (1996) take a distinctly more negative view. On evaluating both the AHCPR and the psychiatric guidelines for major depression, they concluded that the psychiatric guideline undervalues the proven efficacy of cognitive, behavioral, brief psychodynamic, and group therapies in the treatment of depression. Moreover, 'both guidelines understate the value of psychotherapy alone in the treatment of more severely depressed outpatients' while the psychiatric guideline 'overvalues the role of combined psychotherapy-pharmacotherapy regimens . . . and makes recommendations about choosing among psychotherapies that are not well supported by empirical evidence' (Persons, Thase, & Crits-Christoph, 1996, p. 283). Rush (1996), among others, offers rebuttal, observing both that clinical judgments of the complexity required to treat depression ought not be made from empirical findings alone and that the psychiatric guideline is not a prescriptive standard of care.

The Division of Clinical Psychology Task Force Reports (1995, 1996, 1998)

Training in and Dissemination of Empirically Validated Psychological Treatments: Report and Recommendations was published in 1995. Produced by a Task Force of Division 12, the Division of Clinical Psychology of the American Psychological Association, it proposed a preliminary list of empirically supported psychosocial treatments. Treatments were allocated to one of two evaluative categories ('well-established' or 'probably efficacious') based on very specific 'criteria for empirically-validated treatments' designed to reflect the adequacy of the research underlying claims of treatment efficacy. The 1995 *Task Force Report* identified 22 well-established treatments for 21 different syndromes, and seven probably efficacious treatments for the same number of disorders. With the exception of family education programs for schizophrenia (designed primarily to provide practical guidance on how to enhance the compliance of family members with schizophrenia with their medication regimens) and interpersonal therapy for bulimia and for depression (interpersonal therapy is described later in this chapter), all the remaining well-established psychosocial treatments are behavioral or cognitive behavioral. Similarly, all but the brief psychodynamic therapies listed as probably efficacious are behavioral or cognitive behavioral.

Prominent American psychotherapy researcher Sol Garfield (1996) subsequently published a detailed analysis of the 1995 Division 12 Report. It criticized the language of the Task Force report as overly strong and its recommendations as premature. Garfield questioned the Task Force's decision to emphasize validated therapies for specific conditions, which he felt implies more knowledge of the factors that produce or facilitate positive change than is warranted by the state of our knowledge. He reminded his readers of 'the questionable reliability and validity of the fourth edition of the *Diagnostic and Statistical Manual of Mental Disorders*' (DSM-IV; APA, 1994a), because it might have led to diagnostically heterogeneous treatment groups in key outcome studies. Garfield lamented the inclusion of treatment manuals in studies of well-established treatments, believing that they idealize and, thus, distort psychotherapy. Finally, Garfield took issue with the Task Force's focus on techniques, which he felt failed to acknowledge the more important role common or nonspecific factors like those specific to therapist or patient play in determining therapy outcomes. Many other critics of empirically supported treatments take the same position: non-specific factors have garnered substantial support through the years as influential determinants of therapy outcomes (Frank, 1971, 1973; Greenberg, 1994; Orlinsky & Howard, 1975).

A 1996 update to the Division 12 list added eight 'well-established' treatments and 19 'probably efficacious' treatments; all but five are behavioral or cognitive behavioral. The 1996 update also qualified the 1995 and 1996 lists by referring to them as 'far from complete', especially regarding children's problems. The Task Force also urged that the lists 'not be employed as the basis for decisions concerning reimbursable treatments', since they cannot 'substitute for educators' and practitioners' own decisions about what is the most appropriate treatment for a given client'. This qualification, like the similar one in the psychiatric guidelines, was clearly intended to convey the conviction that efficacy studies alone, on which most of these decisions were made, are not always sufficient for making clinical decisions.

A second update of the Division 12 list was published in 1998. While it endorsed a number of additional behavioral and cognitive behavioral treatments, it included non-behavioral couples treatments – which involve spouses or partners in treatment together – for three disorders, psychological interventions for severely mentally ill patients, and health psychology interventions, thereby broadening the scope of approved treatments. The 1998 update also addressed more directly the efficacy/effectiveness controversy on which it had indirectly touched in 1996, acknowledging that while its decisions were based largely on the results of efficacy studies, it recognized the importance ultimately of integrating the results of effectiveness studies in its decision-making.

22.3 EMPIRICALLY SUPPORTED TREATMENTS AND PRACTICE GUIDELINES: CURRENT STATUS, FUTURE PROSPECTS

Almost 50 years separate Eysenck's initial landmark review of psychotherapy outcomes from this chapter. Over those years, widespread pessimism over the effects of psychotherapy and the informational value of research on psychotherapy outcomes has become much more positive in the face of markedly more rigorous outcome research methods and a growing array of empirically supported psychosocial treatments. During the last decade in the United States, these substantial advances have had a significant, albeit unintended, consequence: the controversial development of practice guidelines.

We have highlighted above the concerns of psychologists and others about the scientific adequacy of the research bases underlying empirically supported treatments. Psychologists have raised other, distinctly more professional, concerns about these lists as well. For example, Nathan (1998) pointed out their clear potential to impose constraints on the decision-making of clinicians, even though they establish a desirable empirical standard by which the adequacy of a proposed program of treatment can be judged. It also seems likely, Nathan (1998) observed, that practice guidelines and empirically supported treatments may disenfranchise some practitioners, specifically, those whose therapeutic approaches have not been empirically supported. Finally, as we note in this chapter as well as in Nathan (1998), the apparent lack of consensus on the manner in which lists of empirically supported treatments are to be utilized in clinical settings represents another substantial problem. In essence, it has to do with how empirical findings and clinical judgments are weighed and integrated when clinical decisions have to be made in the real world. While the drafters of all of the practice guidelines reviewed above alert their readers to this problem, they offer no suggestions for its solution.

Few psychologists question whether empirically supported treatments and practice guidelines have the potential to enhance the effectiveness and accountability of our interventions. However, achievement of this potential clearly depends on the continued maturation of the research base that underlies practice guidelines, so that this research can provide solutions to the formidable problems that currently prevent the full acceptance of guidelines. Nonetheless, as many knowledgeable psychologists have observed, the availability of empirical data on treatment outcomes, despite their shortcomings, must be exploited as we plan our treatments. The fruits of those efforts comprise the remainder of this chapter: summaries of the status of findings on empirically supported psychological treatments for a broad range of DSM-IV disorders.

22.4 Current Data on Empirically Supported Treatments

Research on Empirically Supported Treatments: No Longer Exclusively North American

In a review of recent developments in psychology around the world, Rosenzweig (1999) identifies an increasing demand for accountability now imposed on the sciences. Society now expects the sciences, including psychology, to prove their relevance to social and economic well being in order to merit financial and social support. Rosenzweig (1999) is convinced that the recent emphasis American clinical psychologists (and psychiatrists) have placed on empirical demonstrations of the effectiveness of their treatments epitomizes this development.

Rosenzweig (1999) cites Beutler and Machado (1992) in the course of this discussion. On completing an earlier review of international psychotherapy research, Beutler and Machado (1992) concluded that few researchers outside North America had investigated treatment outcomes with the methodological sophistication of North American researchers that requires randomized clinical trials, manualized treatments, and diagnostically homogeneous treatment groups. As a consequence, few non-North American studies were considered well enough designed to permit their inclusion in reviews of research on empirically supported treatments.

As what follows in this chapter will suggest, however, that situation appears to be changing. In fact, quite a number of references to state-of-the-art European psychotherapy outcome studies

are included in the following survey of current data on empirically supported treatments.

Criteria for Judging the Methodological Adequacy of Outcome Studies

The summaries of findings on empirically supported treatments that follow reflect more extended presentations of these data in *A Guide to Treatments that Work* (Nathan & Gorman, 1998). Early in that volume, the editors detail the criteria by which chapter authors were asked to assess the methodological adequacy of the treatment outcome research they reviewed. A condensed version of those criteria is reproduced here:

> *Type 1 Studies*: These studies involve a randomized, prospective clinical trial (RCT), comparison groups with random assignment, blinded assessments, clear presentation of exclusion and inclusion criteria, state-of-the-art diagnostic methods, adequate sample size to offer statistical power, and clearly described statistical methods. *Type 2 Studies*: These studies involve clinical trials in which an intervention is made, but some aspect of the Type 1 study requirement is missing. *Type 3 Studies*: Methodologically limited, these are open treatment studies aimed at obtaining pilot data. Because they are highly subject to observer bias, they can usually do little more than indicate whether a treatment is worth pursuing in a more rigorous design. *Type 4 Studies*: These are reviews with secondary data analysis, useful especially if the data analysis techniques are sophisticated. *Type 5 Studies*: These are reviews without secondary data analysis. *Type 6 Studies*: These constitute a wide variety of reports of marginal value, including case studies, essays and opinion papers. (Nathan & Gorman, 1998, pp. 19–20)

Knowledgeable readers will doubtless observe that single-subject research designs do not appear in this listing. While these designs have shown their utility in the development of a number of efficacious behavioral treatment procedures (e.g., Rachman, 1971; Rachman & Wilson, 1980), they have been less useful in the quest for valid comparisons between or among treatments in efficacy.

The syndromes whose empirically supported treatments are described below and listed in Table 22.1 were chosen for inclusion because (1) their high prevalence make them common problems for large numbers of persons, and (2) treatments for them have been identified for which substantial empirical support exists. The order in which the syndromes and their treatments are presented reflects the order in which they appear in DSM-IV.

Table 22.1   *Empirically supported treatments*

Syndromes	Psychosocial treatments	Pharmacologic treatments
Alcohol-Use Disorders	*Cognitive-behavioral treatments* help patients shape and adapt to their life circumstances. Two recent multisite evaluations also suggest that *12-step treatment* may be as effective as cognitive-behavioral and motivational enhancement treatment.	*Naltrexone,* a recently FDA-approved therapy for alcohol abuse and dependence, diminishes craving early in the abstinence process, but works best when combined with psychosocial and/or 12-step approaches.
Bipolar Disorder	While pharmacological interventions are treatments of choice for this disorder, psychosocial treatments, including psychoeducation and cognitive-behavior therapy for medication adherence, are helpful ancillary treatments.	*Lithium* is effective in reducing the symptoms of acute mania in bipolar disorder. *Valproate* has also been shown to be effective in reducing symptoms of mania. *Lithium* is also effective with a substantial percentage of bipolar patients (e.g., 35–50% within a year) in preventing or reducing the frequency of recurrent affective episodes, although side effects have been a problem with drug compliance. *Lithium and several antidepressants* have shown moderate effectiveness in chronic bipolar depression.
Bulimia Nervosa (BN)	*Manual-based cognitive-behavioral therapy (CBT)* is most effective in eliminating the core features of BN: roughly half the patients receiving CBT ease binge eating and purging; long-term maintenance of improvement is reasonably good.	*Several different classes of antidepressant drugs* produce significant but short-term reduction in binge eating and purging.
Childhood Attention-Deficit Hyperactivity Disorder (ADHD)	*Contingency management* produces impressive behavioral and academic gains in specialized classrooms so long as contingencies are enforced; it may also enable a reduction in the stimulant dosage needed for optimal classroom behavior.	*Psychostimulants* (*e.g., methyphenidate, dexedrine, and magnesium pemoline*) show short-term efficacy in reducing overactivity, increasing concentration and prosocial behavior, and eliminating disruptive classroom behavior. They also improve longer-term behavioral and academic outcomes.
Conduct Disorder in Children	*Cognitive Problem-Solving Skills Training* (CPSST) with impulsive, aggressive, and conduct disorder (CT) children and adolescents, *parent management training* (*PMT*), with the parents of a variety of troubled children and adolescents, *functional family therapy (FFT)*, with difficult-to-treat CD populations, and *multisystemic therapy* (*MST*), with troubled families and their troubled adolescents have all been used with success with this population.	
Generalized Anxiety Disorder (GAD)	*Cognitive-behavior therapy* (combining relaxation exercises and cognitive therapy), which aims to bring the worry process under control, is most efficacious.	The *benzodiazepines* reduce the anxiety and worry symptoms of GAD; *buspirone* appears to be comparable to the benzodiazepines in alleviating GAD symptoms. Both, however, have a substantial abuse potential. The *tricyclic antidepressants* also show promise in the treatment of the symptoms of GAD.
Major Depressive Disorder (MDD)	Interventions utilizing behavior therapy, cognitive-behavior therapy, and interpersonal therapy have all yielded substantial reductions in scores on the two major depression rating scales, as well as in the percent of patients meeting MDD criteria post-treatment; all three also produce significant maintenance of effect after discontinuation of treatment.	Because of their narrow safety margin and significant drug-induced adverse side effects, both the tricyclic antidepressants (TCAs) and the monoamine oxidase inhibitors (MAOIs), formerly treatments of choice for MDD, have been largely replaced by selective serotonin reuptake inhibitors (SSRIs). These drugs work as well as the TCAs, but have substantially fewer adverse side effects.

Table 22.1 *continued*

Syndromes	Psychosocial treatments	Pharmacologic treatments
Obsessive Compulsive Disorder (OCD)	*Cognitive-behavioral therapy* involving exposure and ritual prevention methods reduce or eliminate the obsessions and behavioral and mental rituals of OCD.	Approximately 40–60% of OCD patients respond to *SSRIs*, with mean improvement in obsessions and compulsions of approximately 20–40%. Combined psychosocial-pharmacologic treatments appear to work especially well together.
Panic Disorder with and without Agoraphobia	*Situational in vivo exposure* substantially reduces symptoms of panic disorder with or without agoraphobia. *Cognitive-behavioral treatments* which focus on education about the nature of anxiety and panic and provide some form of exposure and coping skills acquisition are of proven effectiveness.	*Tricyclic antidepressants and monoamine oxidase inhibitors* reduce the number of panic attacks and anticipatory anxiety and phobic avoidance, although side effects cause patients to drop from clinical trials. *High potency benzodiazepines (e.g., alprazolam)* have been found to eliminate panic attacks in 55–75% of patients. *Selective Serotonin Reuptake Inhibitors (SSRIs)* have more recently shown positive effects on panic frequency, generalized anxiety disability, and phobic avoidance.
Post-Traumatic Stress Disorder (PTSD)	*Exposure therapies (systematic desensitization, flooding, prolonged exposure, and implosive therapy)* and, to a lesser extent, *anxiety management techniques (both cognitive and behavioral strategies)* reduce PTSD symptoms, including anxiety and depression, and increase social functioning.	*Antidepressants (SSRIs, TCAs, and MAOIs)* reduce both PTSD symptoms and those of comorbid conditions; they also make it easier for patients to benefit from psychotherapy.
Schizophrenia	*Behavior therapy and social learning/token economy programs* help structure, support, and reinforce prosocial behaviors in treating refractory persons with schizophrenia. *Structured educational family interventions* help maintain gains achieved with medication and customary case management. *Social skills training* enables persons with schizophrenia to acquire instrumental and affiliative skills to improve functioning in their communities.	*Conventional phenothiazine antipsychotic medications* markedly reduce the positive symptoms of schizophrenia and significantly decrease the risk of symptomatic relapse and rehospitalization; however, serious neurological side effects make these drugs difficult for many patients to tolerate. More recently, a group of *atypical antipsychotics drugs (e.g., clozapine, risperidone, and olanzapine)* have demonstrated comparable efficacy with significantly lower risk of adverse neurological events, especially in treating the negative symptoms of schizophrenia.
Social Phobia	*Exposure-based procedures* reduce or eliminate symptoms of social phobia. Other common treatment approaches include *social skills training, relaxation techniques,* and *multicomponent cognitive-behavioral treatments.*	*Medications* from three different drug families (an MAOI, a benzodiazepine, and two SSRIs) have shown effectiveness in treating the symptoms of social phobia.
Specific Phobias	*Exposure-based procedures, particularly in vivo exposure,* reduce or eliminate phobic behavior	
Substance-Use Disorders		*Nicotine gum and the nicotine patch* assist with smoking cessation efforts. *Methadone treatment* is an effective maintenance option following detoxification from heroin, especially when combined with psychosocial treatment designed to facilitate retention and compliance and address the psychological and social problems that accompany addiction.

22.5 CHILDHOOD DISORDERS

Childhood Attention Deficit Hyperactivity Disorder (ADHD)

Most of the empirical research on psychological treatments for childhood attention deficit hyperactivity disorder (ADHD) has focused on direct contingency management in specialized classroom settings (e.g., Hinshaw, Klein, & Abikoff, 1998). So long as contingencies are enforced, impressive behavioral and academic gains for ADHD children have been reported. Children concentrate and attend better and leave their seats and disrupt other children less often, so they are able to do better schoolwork. However, when the contingencies are withdrawn, the behavioral and academic gains are generally not maintained.

Extensive research exploring the academic and behavioral consequences of combined stimulant medication (generally, methylphenidate, whose U.S. brand name is Ritalin) and *direct contingency management*, which involves the systematic application of reward and punishment to modify behavior, has also been reported (e.g., Pelham, Carlson, Sams, Dixon, & Hoza, 1993). When combined treatment is provided, behavioral and academic gains of substantially greater magnitude than those achieved by contingency management alone are typically the result. Additionally, contingency management procedures may permit a reduction in the dosage level of methylphenidate, another desirable feature of combined treatment.

Two other psychological treatments for ADHD in children have also been explored, although neither has yet been shown to be effective by a substantial number of well-designed outcome studies. *Clinical behavior therapy* teaches parents contingency management and behavior shaping (which involves modifying behavior in small steps by systematic reinforcement) and helps teachers develop skills in classroom management techniques. *Multimodal treatments* for ADHD may include social skills training (in which a range of assertive and interpersonal skills to facilitate social interaction are taught), remedial tutoring, organizational skills training, and individual psychotherapy for the child. Parents receive parent management training, which is designed to teach them how to use reward and punishment systematically to change their child's behavior; home-based reinforcement programs for targeted school behaviors are also common. The relatively few outcome studies which have been done of these two treatment have been of only fair methodological quality,

so they do not provide an adequate basis for overall claims of efficacy for these procedures.

Overall, stimulant medication has shown itself to be effective for treating both the behavioral and academic deficits associated with ADHD in a large number of Type 1 studies (e.g., Vyborova, Nahunek, Drtilkova, Balastikova, & Misurec, 1984). Direct contingency management in the classroom, evaluated for the most part by Type 2 and Type 3 studies, appears to be a useful adjunct to stimulant medication and may even permit a reduction in medication dosage.

Conduct Disorder

Four psychological treatments for conduct disorder (CD) in children have been employed in recent years (Kazdin, 1998). Conduct disorder describes a recurrent behavior pattern in childhood or adolescence of violation of the basic rights of others as well as important social norms or rules; the syndrome often leads to juvenile delinquency (Lundman, 1984; Rutter & Giller, 1983).

Cognitive problem-solving skills training (PSST) presumes that aggressive children and adolescents diagnosed with CD experience distortions and deficiencies in various cognitive processes. Accordingly, this treatment aims to help the CD child or adolescent develop interpersonal cognitive problem-solving skills. Several randomized clinical trials (RCTs) of PSST have shown that it significantly reduces aggressive and antisocial behavior at home, at school, and in the community; these gains have persisted for up to a year (Kazdin, 1993).

Parent management training (PMT) aims to train parents to modify their child's behavior in the home. The therapist trains parents in specific methods designed to alter their interactions with the child in order to increase appropriate social behavior and decrease pathological behavior, on the assumption that CD behavior is developed and maintained in the home by maladaptive interactions between parents and their children. A large number of Type 1 RCTs of PMT over the past 25 years (e.g., Patterson, Dishion, & Chamberlain, 1993) have shown marked improvements on a variety of measures in the behavior of children whose parents received PMT.

Functional family therapy (FFT) conceptualizes clinical problems from the perspective of the functions they serve in the family system. The child's problem behaviors are conceptualized by FFT as the means by which important interpersonal functions within the family are carried out. Maladaptive family processes prevent a more direct and successful way of fulfilling important functions. Accordingly, the goals of FFT are to modify family communication and interaction patterns so that the family functions more effectively. FFT, based on learning theory, identifies specific stimuli and responses that can be used to bring about these changes. Relatively few outcome studies to date have evaluated FFT (e.g., Alexander, Holtzworth-Munroe, & Jameson, 1994). However, those that have been completed have generally been of good methodological quality, and clear effects with difficult groups, including delinquent adolescents and multiple-offender delinquents, have been observed.

Multisystematic therapy (MST) assumes, like FFT, that conduct disorder reflects a breakdown in the functioning of the family system. Accordingly, this family-based treatment uses several family therapy techniques to identify family problems, increase communication among family members, build cohesion among family members, and modify family members' interactions. Several controlled studies of MST (e.g., Borduin et al., 1995) show that the treatment leads to positive, sustained changes in seriously problematic adolescent behavior.

Type 1 RCTs have shown that each of these four treatments is capable of changing conduct-disordered behavior in positive directions, although PMT has been studied to a substantially greater extent than the other three techniques. However, the research has not always shown that the positive changes are of sufficient magnitude to have clinical significance. Moreover, follow-up periods have generally not extended to more than a year, so the long-term effects of these treatments are uncertain.

22.6 ALCOHOL-RELATED DISORDERS

Cognitive Behavioral Treatments for Alcohol-Use Disorders

Fifteen psychological treatments for alcohol abuse and dependence have been examined in three or more Type 1 and Type 2 studies (Finney & Moos, 1998). Most effective are three cognitive behavioral treatments that help patients adapt to their life circumstances. *Social skills training* (Smith & McCrady, 1991) helps patients develop better assertive and communication skills, on the assumption that deficits in social skills contribute to the depression and lowered self-esteem that can be precursors to abusive drinking. *Community reinforcement* (Azrin, Sisson, Meyers, & Godley, 1982), which has taken a variety of forms, provides patients access to interpersonal, vocational, and economic

reinforcers in their environments contingent on their continued sobriety, willingness to take Antabuse, or both. (Antabuse is a drug which interferes with the metabolism of alcohol; ingesting Antabuse every day makes it impossible to drink alcohol without suffering very unpleasant physiological consequences.) *Behavioral marital therapy* (O'Farrell, Choquette, Cutter, Brown, & McCourt, 1993) simultaneously addresses the alcoholic spouse's alcohol abuse and the disordered marital relationship it contributes to by means of behavioral contracts designed to provide the alcoholic spouse access to a range of reinforcers in return for agreed-upon changes in behavior.

Two Large-Scale Randomized Clinical Trials

Only recently have large-scale randomized clinical trials of alcoholism treatments, the 'gold standard' for treatment outcomes, been undertaken. Recently, results from two such studies, the National Institute on Alcohol Abuse and Alcoholism's Project MATCH (Project MATCH Research Group, 1993, 1997a, 1997b, 1998) and the Veterans Administration's Cooperative Study (Ouimette, Finney, & Moos, 1997), were reported.

Project MATCH

Project MATCH was a large national multi-site clinical trial designed to evaluate a set of patient-treatment matching hypotheses. *A priori* hypotheses linking 11 client attributes to three treatments proposed that certain attributes would be associated with better outcomes when patients received one of the treatments rather than either of the other two. Project MATCH's secondary purpose was to compare outcomes of three different, manual-guided, individually delivered 12-week treatments. *Cognitive Behavioral Coping Skills Treatment* (CBT) was based on social learning theory and viewed drinking behavior as functionally related to major problems in an individual's life; it emphasized overcoming skills deficits and increasing the ability to cope with situations that commonly precipitate relapse. *Motivational Enhancement Therapy* (MET) was based on principles of motivational psychology and focused on producing internally-motivated change. *Twelve-Step Facilitation* (TSF) was grounded in the concept of alcoholism as a spiritual and medical disease with stated objectives of fostering acceptance of the disease of alcoholism, developing a commitment to participate in AA and beginning to work through the 12 steps. Detailed treatment manuals were provided for each therapist participating in the study (Kadden et al., 1992; Miller, Zweben, Di Clemente, & Rychtarik, 1992; Nowinski, Baker, & Carroll, 1992) to ensure to the best extent possible that different therapists at different sites would deliver the same treatment in the same way.

Two independent, parallel matching studies were conducted, one with 952 patients (72% male) recruited from outpatient settings, the other with 774 patients (80% male) in aftercare treatment after a period of inpatient treatment. Patients were contacted for follow-up every three months for a year after the 12-week treatment period; as noted above, primary outcome measures were percent days abstinent and drinks per drinking day. At the 12-month mark, 92% and 93%, respectively, of patients originally treated were successfully contacted. Overall results were described as follows:

> Significant and sustained improvements in drinking outcomes were achieved from baseline to one-year post-treatment by the clients assigned to each of (the) well-defined and individually delivered psychosocial treatments. There was little difference in outcomes by type of treatment. (Project MATCH Research Group, 1997a, p. 7)

Drinking days for the aftercare group dropped from about four out of five days before treatment to about one out of 20 following treatment; drinking days for the outpatient group declined from about three out of four days pre-treatment to about one out of four post-treatment days. Drinks per drinking day for the aftercare group dropped from 15–20 during the pre-treatment period to 2–3 drinks per drinking day post-treatment; the comparable figures for the outpatient group were 11–13 and 3–4 drinks. About 35% of the aftercare subjects and 19% of the outpatient subjects reported complete abstinence throughout the 12 follow-up months.

At a 39-month follow-up of the outpatient group (Project MATCH Research Group, 1998), 806 subjects of the original 952 in that group were contacted successfully. Almost 30% reported complete abstinence during the three months preceding the follow-up (an increase in the percent of these subjects who were abstinent at the 12-month mark), meaning that slightly more than 70% of the sample had consumed alcohol during that period. Drinks on drinking days for this group averaged 4.21, a marked reduction from pre-treatment levels but an increase over the comparable figures at the 12-month mark.

Overall, it is clear that a substantial majority of Project MATCH clients were consuming alcohol throughout the 12-month and 39-month follow-up periods. Despite the positive changes in drinking behavior that followed treatment,

these findings are worrisome. Most studies of recovering alcoholics have concluded that those who continue to drink after treatment, however minimally, are at substantial risk at some point to resume an abusive drinking pattern (Nathan & Skinstad, 1987; Vaillant, 1995).

Veterans Administration Cooperative Study

Ouimette et al. (1997) compared the effectiveness of 12-step, cognitive behavioral (C-B), and combined 12-step C-B models of substance abuse treatment in a non-random clinical trial of 3,018 detoxified inpatients already enrolled in substance-abuse treatment programs at 15 Department of Veterans Affairs Medical Centers (VAMC). The 15 sites were selected because they offered 12-step, cognitive behavioral, and combined cognitive behavioral inpatient treatment programs that met the investigators' criteria for quality and theoretical integrity. Desired length of stay in the programs ranged from 21 to 28 days; all provided both individual and group therapy and all were multidisciplinary in staffing. Follow-up of treatment extended for a year.

Although 12-step patients were somewhat more likely to be abstinent and to be employed at the one-year follow-up mark, the three treatments yielded equivalent reductions in substance use and improvements in most other areas of functioning by both the end of inpatient treatment and the one-year follow-up. Patients with substance-abuse diagnoses alone, those with comorbid psychiatric diagnoses, and those who had not entered treatment on their own volition all showed similar improvement at one-year follow-up, regardless of type of treatment received.

However, by the end of the one-year follow-up, only 25–30% of the patients were judged to be without a substance-abuse problem, only 23–29% were in remission from their substance-use disorder, and only 18–25% had been able to maintain abstinence. While these figures represent marked improvements over pre-treatment rates, they are nonetheless troubling. As we already noted, a great deal of research suggests that many or most recovering alcoholics who continue to drink following treatment in even a controlled fashion will ultimately return to abusive drinking.

22.7 SCHIZOPHRENIA

Treatment of schizophrenia with anti-psychotic drugs, studied by countless Type 1 RCTs, has been the disorder's treatment of choice for 40 years (Bjorndal et al., 1980; Sheitman, Kinon, Ridgway, & Lieberman, 1998). New 'atypical' anti-psychotic drugs that work at least as well as the older antipsychotics but offer substantially less risk of serious neurological side effects have recently been introduced (e.g., Ceskova & Svestka, 1993). Numerous, well-designed studies have also pointed to a significant role for behavioral treatments for schizophrenia (Kopelowicz & Liberman, 1998; Wunderlich, Wiedemann, & Buchkremer, 1996).

Several Type 1 RCTs and literally hundreds of less well-controlled case studies have established the value of *behavior modification programs*, even for severely ill, hospitalized persons with schizophrenia (Brenner, Hodel, & Roder, 1990). Typically, these programs are designed to reduce the frequency of disruptive and/or psychotic behaviors and increase the frequency of adaptive, prosocial behaviors by systematically reinforcing desired behaviors and ignoring or punishing unwanted behaviors. One of the most familiar are *token economies*, in which material and social reinforcers are made available to individual patients or groups of patients when they emit specific prosocial behaviors (Menditto, Valdes, & Beck, 1994; Paul & Lentz, 1977). While these treatments do not cure the disorder, they make it possible for severely ill patients to maintain a substantially higher quality of life in institutional settings so long as the behavioral contingencies controlling patients' behavior remain in place.

A number of behavioral methods have also been developed to engage families in the rehabilitation and treatment of their family member with schizophrenia. These *structured family programs* typically have several goals. Those goals include educating family members about schizophrenia and how to cope with it. They also include helping family members utilize available community resources more effectively, use stress management techniques to deal with the stress associated with schizophrenia in the family; and develop more effective communication patterns among themselves and with their family member with schizophrenia. Several Type 1 RCTs have shown that better outcomes are achieved when structured, educational family interventions are added to anti-psychotic medication and traditional case management (Randolph et al., 1994).

Social skills training enables persons with schizophrenia in partial remission from their symptoms to function better in community and family settings by helping them acquire more effective communication and assertion skills (Mueser, Wallace, & Liberman, 1995). Many Type 1 and Type 2 RCTs (e.g., Eckman et al., 1992) have shown that persons with chronic schizophrenia living in the community can acquire these skills and that doing so reduces

relapse rates and increases a range of quality of life indicators.

22.8 MAJOR DEPRESSIVE DISORDER

Two major meta-analyses and at least two Type 1 or Type 2 RCTs each have shown behavior therapy (BT), cognitive behavior therapy (CBT), and interpersonal therapy (IPT) to be efficacious for the treatment of major depression (Craighead, Craighead, & Ilardi, 1998).

Scores of Type 1 RCTs have established the effectiveness of anti-depressant medication with patients with major depressive disorder (Nemeroff & Schatzberg, 1998). However, tricyclic anti-depressants (TCAs), the first consistently effective medications for this serious disorder, have now largely been replaced as treatments of choice by selective serotonin reuptake inhibitors (SSRIs). The SSRIs are as effective as TCAs but do not cause many of the serious side effects of the TCAs (Rush et al., 1994).

Behavior Therapy

Behavior therapy for depression aims to improve social and communication skills, increase appropriate assertive behavior and response-contingent positive reinforcement for adaptive behaviors, and decrease negative life experiences. Lewinsohn and Gotlib (1995) and Rehm (1977) have developed behavior therapy treatments for depression. While these treatments have been supported by a few well-designed outcome studies, they have been largely overshadowed more recently by substantially more and stronger studies of cognitive behavior therapy (CBT) and interpersonal therapy (IPT).

Cognitive Behavior Therapy

Beck's *cognitive behavior therapy* (Beck, Rush, Shaw, & Emery, 1979) is the most thoroughly explored psychological treatment for depression. A short-term treatment that typically extends over 16–20 sessions during 12–16 weeks, its primary goal is to change the depressed individual's negative view of his or her current and future world. Patients are taught self-monitoring early in treatment, so they can recognize logical errors in their thinking and identify the principal schemas underlying their positive and negative thoughts. (A schema is an underlying belief system about oneself or the world that filters and organizes one's experiences.) The focus then shifts to trying to change the negative schemas thought to be responsible for the patient's major depressive disorder. Toward the end of therapy, the focus again shifts to identification and practice of cognitive strategies designed to prevent relapse (Teasdale, Fennell, Hibbert, & Amies, 1984).

A substantial number of RCTs have compared the efficacy of CBT to treatment with TCAs (e.g., Hollon et al., 1992). The essential finding in almost all these studies is that CBT works as well as the TCAs in alleviating major depressive disorder in outpatients. Typically, 50–70% of patients completing CBT no longer meet the diagnostic criteria for major depressive disorder; this success rate approximates that of TCA therapy. Moreover, CBT appears to confer some protection against a recurrence of depression, in that only 20–30% of CBT patients relapse during the year following treatment.

However, one of the largest, most widely-cited tests of treatments for major depressive disorder, the NIMH Treatment of Depression Collaborative Research Program (TDCRP; Shea et al., 1992) yielded results at variance with the findings cited above. Two hundred and fifty outpatients were randomly assigned to one of four 16-week treatment conditions: CBT, IPT, a TCA plus clinical management (IMP-CM), or pill-placebo plus clinical management (PLA-CM). The three active treatments were comparable in alleviating depression following treatment, although only IPT and IMP-CM produced greater reductions in depression than the placebo condition and then only for some measures. At an 18-month follow-up, none of the active treatments was superior to the placebo condition. The follow-up outcomes show all treatments in the NIMH study to be substantially weaker than those examined in other long-term studies of depression treatment. Most observers now point to a site-by-treatment-by-severity interaction in the NIMH study to explain these anomalous findings (Elkin, Gibbons, Shea, & Shaw, 1996). Despite these anomalous findings, however, most clinicians believe that CBT is a treatment of choice for patients with major depressive disorder, although many believe it ought to be combined with anti-depressant medication when treating severely depressed patients.

Interpersonal Therapy

Interpersonal therapy for depression (Klerman, Weissman, Rounsaville, & Chevron, 1984), which emphasizes the reciprocal relations between biological and psychosocial factors in depression, posits that patients' interpersonal relationships play important roles in major depressive disorder. As a consequence, IPT aims

to resolve difficulties in interpersonal functioning, including unresolved grief, disputes, role transitions, and social isolation.

Two RCTs of IPT for the acute treatment of major depressive disorder have been reported. The first (Weissman et al., 1979) compared IPT, a TCA, combined TCA-IPT, and a control condition over a 16-week treatment period. All three active treatments yielded better outcomes than the control condition, with the combined drug–psychotherapy treatment doing a bit better than either drugs or psychotherapy alone. The second – and most often cited – test of IPT was the NIMH study (Shea et al., 1992). It showed that, on completion of treatment, IPT and TCA tended to yield slightly greater reductions in depressive symptoms than either CBT or the placebo although, after 18 months, those differences had disappeared and the active treatments were not associated with better outcomes than the placebo. However, as noted above, the likelihood of a confounding interaction among site, treatment type, and severity of disorder makes the NIMH data extremely difficult to interpret.

IPT has also been evaluated as a maintenance therapy following recovery from major depressive disorder. Frank and her colleagues (1990) found that the likelihood of relapse following monthly IPT maintenance treatment of patients with major depressive disorder over a 36-month period decreased significantly.

22.9 Bipolar Disorder

Pharmacological interventions, which include lithium carbonate and similar drugs designed to stabilize mood and prevent recurrences of mania and depression, are generally agreed to represent the treatment of choice for bipolar disorder (Keck & McElroy, 1998; Priebe, Wildgrube, & Mueller-Oerlinghausen, 1989). For patients who do not respond to mood-stabilizing agents, benzodiazepines, typical anti-psychotics, and atypical anti-psychotics have all been reported to help in selected cases.

The principal role of psychological treatments for bipolar disorder is to provide patients and their families with *psychoeducation*: information about the disorder, its pharmacological treatments, and the treatments' side effects (Craighead, Miklowitz, Vajk, & Frank, 1998). This information is important since many patients on long-term lithium maintenance do not adhere to their treatment regimen because of the formidable side effects of lithium (Goodwin & Jamison, 1990); most of these individuals ultimately relapse. A large number of case reports and other Type 2 and Type 3 studies have shown that psychoeducation has a positive effect on medication adherence among patients with bipolar disorder.

Five controlled clinical trials are now under way to evaluate the effectiveness of individual and family therapy; these studies have reported encouraging preliminary data suggesting that these psychosocial interventions may be of value in the treatment of bipolar disorder (Craighead et al., 1998).

22.10 Anxiety Disorders

There are voluminous data on outcomes of behavioral and cognitive behavioral treatments for the diverse group of anxiety disorders, which include panic disorder, agoraphobia with panic attacks, specific and social phobic disorder, generalized anxiety disorder, obsessive compulsive disorder, and post-traumatic stress disorder (PTSD). For the most part they are derived from Type 1 and Type 2 studies and are extremely encouraging (Barlow, Esler, & Vitali, 1998).

Specific pharmacological treatments have been developed for these disorders as well (Roy-Byrne & Cowley, 1998). The TCAs, the benzodiazepines, especially alprazolam, and the SSRIs are the current pharmacological treatments of choice for panic disorder. The benzodiazepines have been studied intensively as treatments for generalized anxiety disorder. No pharmacological intervention appears to be effective for specific phobia. The MAO inhibitor phenelzine has shown efficacy in three RCTs for social phobia (e.g., Fahlen, Nilsson, Borg, Humber, & Pauli, 1995).

Panic Disorder

A large number of well-designed Type 1 RCTs have established the efficacy of situational in vivo exposure for persons with panic disorder with or without agoraphobia (Barlow & Craske, 1994). (Agoraphobia is defined as extreme fear of places or situations in which help might not be available should an incapacitating or embarrassing event occur.) A similarly substantial number of excellent studies have demonstrated the efficacy of cognitive behavior therapy for persons with panic disorder (Barlow & Craske, 1994; Clark et al., 1994). (Panic disorder involves the sudden feeling of intense fear accompanied by physiological symptoms and thoughts of losing control or dying.) Although research has also been conducted on combined psychosocial-pharmacological treatments for these disorders (e.g., Clark et al., 1994), the incremental value

of combined treatments over psychological treatments has not been proven.

Situational in vivo exposure for agoraphobia and panic disorder with agoraphobia initially requires construction of a hierarchy of the feared activities or situations the patient has chosen to avoid. Patients are then taught *behavioral coping strategies* (which might involve efforts to modify or eliminate fearful cognitions that lack justification) to deal with the fear-inducing situations and activities. Armed with effective coping mechanisms, the patient is then encouraged to confront the feared situations while utilizing the coping procedures he or she has acquired. Although most patients can undertake this in vivo desensitization by themselves or with a family member or friend, in severe cases the therapist may have to accompany the patient. While few patients achieve complete remission of symptoms at the end of exposure treatment, most achieve substantial clinical gains that tend to last for lengthy periods (e.g., Fava, Zielezny, Savron, & Grandi, 1995).

During the last decade, researchers have also explored a range of strategies to improve the effectiveness of exposure-based procedures for agoraphobia (Barlow et al., 1998). Relaxation training, cognitive therapy components, and breathing retraining have all been added to the exposure-based strategies, generally without enhancing outcomes. Other researchers have modified the pace of situational in vivo exposure treatment by contrasting massed, intensive exposure sessions with spaced, graduated ones; again, the empirical literature has not pointed to a consistent advantage of one or the other. Finally, researchers have explored briefer, more self-directed exposure-based treatments, again, with inconsistent results.

The cognitive behavioral treatments for panic disorder have tended to focus on education about anxiety and panic, cognitive therapy, and some exposure and coping skills training. Barlow and Craske (1994) developed what they called *panic control treatment* (PCT). PCT exposes patients to interoceptive (internal, physiological) sensations like those experienced in panic attacks, includes cognitive restructuring that addresses misconceptions about panic and anxiety, and breathing retraining that reduces the likelihood of hyperventilation (rapid breathing) and has a calming effect. Several controlled studies of PCT (e.g., Craske, Brown, & Barlow, 1991) have shown PCT to generate significantly more and longer panic-free periods in patients with panic disorder than other treatments, including pharmacological treatments. Several Type 1 RCTs have also established the efficacy of more traditional cognitive therapy for panic disorder. In particular, Clark and his colleagues have developed a treatment designed to modify patients' appraisals of bodily sensations during panic states in ways similar to PCT, although greater emphasis is put on the cognitive therapy component of treatment. Results of controlled studies of this approach (e.g., Clark et al., 1994) have been very positive as judged by the percent of patients who are panic-free following treatment and after lengthy follow-up periods.

Specific Phobias

Quite a few well-designed studies have also established the efficacy of exposure-based procedures, particularly in vivo exposure, in the treatment of the specific phobias (Antony & Barlow, 1996). Over the past decade, in vivo exposure has proven successful in eliminating animal, height, flying, dental, choking, and blood-injury-injection phobias (Barlow et al., 1998).

Social Phobia

Social phobia is the most common of all the anxiety disorders and the third most common mental disorder (Kessler et al., 1994), so its successful treatment would clearly have a major impact on the quality of human life. A variety of cognitive behavioral treatments have been employed, including social skills training (SST), relaxation training, exposure-based procedures, and multi-component cognitive behavioral packages. Of these treatments, Heimberg and Juster (1995) conclude that only the exposure-based procedures appear to yield positive changes in social phobias of greater magnitude than those induced by control or comparison treatments. Barlow and Lehman (1996) add that combined treatments may be more effective than single treatments, including combined exposure-based treatments and anti-anxiety drugs.

Generalized Anxiety Disorder

Given the widespread prevalence of generalized anxiety disorder (GAD), surprisingly few studies of its treatment have been undertaken, probably because its diagnostic criteria have changed markedly over the past 15 years (Brown, O'Leary, & Barlow, 1993). In a set of studies of highest quality comparing potentially efficacious treatments (Barlow, Rapee, & Brown, 1992), significant differences among these treatments were usually not shown. Treatments included relaxation training, cognitive behavior therapy, and pharmacological treatment. One of the most important continuing questions is the role of the

benzodiazepines in the treatment of this condition. While these drugs do provide relief from anxiety, they are also highly dependency inducing. While there have been reports that combining pharmacological and psychological treatments yields better outcomes over the long term than either alone (Roy-Byrne & Cowley, 1998), these reports have not been definitive, so more research is needed.

Obsessive Compulsive Disorder

Three meta-analyses, a number of comprehensive literature reviews, and a large number of Type 1 and Type 2 RCTs point to the efficacy of *exposure and ritual/response prevention* (EX/RP) in the treatment of obsessive compulsive disorder (OCD) (Franklin & Foa, 1998). First reported by Meyer (1966), EX/RP involves prolonged exposure to obsessional cues, combined with strict prevention of compulsive rituals following the exposure. Thus, EX/RP appears to confront two different aspects of the obsessive compulsive syndrome (Foa, Steketee, Grayson, Turner, & Latimer, 1984). However, data on the value of adding imaginal exposure to in vivo exposure to maintain treatment gains are in conflict. While Foa and Goldstein (1978) reported that imaginal exposure did help maintain gains, de Araujo, Ito, Marks, and Deale (1995) failed to find a positive effect. Researchers have also studied the impact of adding cognitive techniques to EX/RP in treating OCD, generally concluding that CBT does not add much if anything to the efficacy of EX/PR.

Since many Type 1 RCTs have also demonstrated the efficacy of the SSRIs in the treatment of OCD (Rauch & Jenike, 1998), the efficacy of EX/PR and pharmacological treatments alone or in combination has also been studied. Unfortunately, most of the studies designed to weigh the relative efficacy of EX/RP and drug treatment for OCD in the same population group have been burdened by design and methodology problems that prevent unequivocal interpretation of their results. As well, no study comparing these two treatment modalities has yet demonstrated long-term superiority for combined pharmacological and exposure-based treatments, even though many authorities recommend combined treatments.

Post-Traumatic Stress Disorder (PTSD)

Several Type 1 and Type 2 RCTs suggest that exposure-based treatments are also the most effective psychosocial treatments for post-traumatic stress disorder (PTSD). A few studies have also indicated that cognitive and behavioral techniques for anxiety management may also prove efficacious (Keane, 1998). Eye-movement desensitization and reprocessing (EMDR) is a controversial new approach to PTSD (Shapiro, 1995). While the results of some studies of EMDR to date have been promising, the research has consisted largely of open clinical trials rather than RCTs, so the role of EMDR in the treatment of PTSD remains uncertain. Research on psychopharmacologic agents for the management of PTSD is in its early stages; no single agent has emerged as the clear pharmacological treatment of choice for PTSD (Yehuda, Marshall, & Giller, 1998).

The lengthy history of successful treatment of many of the anxiety disorders with exposure-based treatments, including systematic desensitization, flooding, in vivo exposure, implosive therapy, and related methods (Barlow, 1988) makes it unsurprising that similar procedures should be employed successfully with patients with PTSD. Initial research involved single-case trials of systematic exposure to memories of traumatic events reported by veterans who had experienced combat (e.g., Black & Keane, 1982). These studies were followed by three Type 1 RCTs. The first compared exposure therapy, anxiety management therapy, and a wait-list control in the treatment of combat-related PTSD (Keane, Fairbank, Caddell, & Zimering, 1989). The second compared exposure therapy, hypnotherapy, and psychodynamic treatment as treatments for patients who had experienced a traumatic event (Brom, Kleber, & Defares, 1989). And the third compared exposure, anxiety management/stress inoculation, supportive counseling, and a wait-list condition to treat rape-induced PTSD (Foa, Rothbaum, Riggs, & Murdock, 1991). Exposure-based therapy yielded the best outcomes in all three trials.

22.11 EATING DISORDERS

The quantity and quality of treatment outcome research on the two major eating disorders, anorexia nervosa (AN) and bulimia nervosa (BN), differ markedly (Wilson & Fairburn, 1998). The outcome literature on treatments for AN, which aim to restore adequate eating habits and normal weight and to resolve the individual or social problems which may be contributing to the disorder, is made up largely of modestly designed, uncontrolled studies. As a result, no efficacious treatments for AN have been identified. By contrast, research on treatments for BN, which are designed to instill healthy eating habits and resolve associated interpersonal problems, is replete with Type 1 and Type 2 RCTs.

These trials have shown CBT to be the treatment of choice for BN. It eliminates bingeing (the uncontrolled consumption of unusually large amounts of food) and purging (self-induced vomiting or laxative misuse designed to control weight) in half or more of BN patients and also improves associated behavioral problems like depression. Other well-designed trials have indicated that anti-depressant drugs reduce bingeing and purging in the short term, although their long-term effectiveness remains uncertain. Little or no data have indicated to date that combining CBT and anti-depressant medication enhances outcomes for BN.

A few RCTs of outpatient treatment for AN, including individual psychotherapy, family therapy, BT, and CBT, have also been reported. Unfortunately, the studies' methodological shortcomings have led experts (e.g., Wilson & Fairburn, 1998) to conclude that effective outpatient treatments for AN have yet to be demonstrated.

The best documented psychosocial treatment for BN is CBT. Virtually all current CBT for BN is derived from the pioneering work of British psychiatrist Christopher Fairburn (Fairburn, 1981), which identified the crucial role of both cognitive and behavioral factors in BN. Central to this treatment approach is recognition of the extreme personal value BN patients attach to idealized body shape and low body weight. As a consequence, the treatment addresses more than bingeing and purging. Instead, it involves an integrated sequence of cognitive and behavioral interventions that aim to restore normal weight and a healthy capacity for accurate appraisal of body shape and weight. In a review of 10 studies of CBT for BN, Craighead and Agras (1991) found CBT to produce an average reduction in purging of 79% and a 57% remission rate. A review of nine other studies published subsequently (Wilson & Fairburn, 1998) indicated a mean reduction in purging of 83.5% and a 47.5% remission rate; corresponding estimates for bingeing were 79% and 62%, respectively.

Wilson and Fairburn (1998) also reviewed results from six controlled studies in which CBT was directly compared with anti-depressant drug treatments for BN. Their conclusion is that CBT is more acceptable to patients, leads to lower dropout rates, and is superior to treatment with a single anti-depressant. They also concluded that combining CBT with anti-depressants is significantly more effective than medication alone, that CBT and medication are not superior to CBT plus pill placebo, and that maintenance of change over the long term is better with CBT than anti-depressants.

The most thoroughly studied pharmacological treatments for BN are the anti-depressants, including the TCAs, the MAO inhibitors, the SSRIs, and the atypical anti-depressants. Although the original rationale for using these drugs for this condition – that patients with BN are depressed – has now been largely rejected, these drugs have nonetheless been found to reduce binge eating and purging to a significantly greater extent than pill placebo. Devlin and Walsh (1995) reviewed 14 outcome studies, finding the anti-depressants to reduce binge eating by a mean of 61.4%, with an average remission rate of 22%. Purging was reduced an average of 58.9%, with an average remission rate of 34%. Different classes of anti-depressants appeared to be equally effective. Unfortunately, neither the long-term effects nor the mechanisms by which the anti-depressants exert their positive impact on BN has yet been identified.

22.12 SUMMARY AND CONCLUSIONS

Psychologists' efforts to identify empirically supported psychological treatments over the past 50 years have gradually revealed more robust outcome research methods and been accompanied by the concurrent development of more effective treatments. Practice guidelines reflecting empirical findings on both pharmacological and psychological treatments are an important contemporary consequence of these efforts. While practice guidelines foster therapeutic accountability and encourage adoption of best current therapeutic practices, their empirical bases, diverse standards of proof, and potential to constrain clinical decision-making have been questioned. After critically reviewing three influential current sets of U.S. practice guidelines, the chapter reviewed research on empirically supported treatments for the childhood disorders, the alcohol-related disorders, schizophrenia, major depressive disorder, the anxiety disorders, and the eating disorders. All are common syndromes for which effective psychological treatments have been identified.

RESOURCE REFERENCES

Barlow, D. H., & Craske, M. G. (1994). *Mastery of your anxiety and panic*. Albany, NY: Graywind Publications.

Bergin, A. E., & Garfield, S. L. (Eds.). (1994). *Handbook of psychotherapy and behavior change* (4th ed.). New York: Wiley.

Eysenck, H. J. (1952). The effects of psychotherapy: An evaluation. *Journal of Consulting Psychology, 16*, 319–324.

Eysenck, H. J. (1969). *The effects of psychotherapy*. New York: Science House.

Garfield, S. L. (1996). Some problems associated with 'validated' forms of psychotherapy. *Clinical Psychology: Science and Practice, 3*, 218–229.

Nathan, P. E., & Gorman, J. M. (Eds.). (1998). *A guide to treatments that work*. Oxford: Oxford University Press.

Nathan, P. E., Gorman, J. M., & Salkind, N. J. (1999). *Treating mental disorders: A guide to what works*. Oxford: Oxford University Press.

Rachman, S., & Wilson, G. T. (1980). *The effects of the psychological therapies* (2nd ed.). Oxford: Pergamon Press.

Wilson, G. T. (1995). Empirically supported treatments as a basis for clinical practice: Problems and prospects. In S. C. Hayes, V. M. Follette, R. M. Dawes, & K. E. Grady (Eds.), *Scientific standards of psychological practice: Issues and recommendations* (pp. 163–196). Reno, NV: Context Press.

ADDITIONAL LITERATURE CITED

Alexander, J. F., Holtzworth-Munroe, A., & Jameson, P. B. (1994). The process and outcome of marital and family therapy research: Review and evaluation. In A. E. Bergin & S. L. Garfield (Eds.), *Handbook of psychotherapy and behavior change* (4th ed., pp. 595–630). New York: Wiley.

American Psychiatric Association. (1993). Practice guidelines for the treatment of major depressive disorder in adults. *American Journal of Psychiatry, 150* (No. 4, Supplement), 1–26.

American Psychiatric Association. (1994a). *Diagnostic and statistical manual of mental disorders* (4th ed.). Washington, DC: American Psychiatric Association.

American Psychiatric Association. (1994b). Practice guideline for the treatment of patients with bipolar disorder. *American Journal of Psychiatry, 151* (No. 12, Supplement), 1–36.

American Psychiatric Association. (1995). Practice guideline for the treatment of patients with substance use disorders: Alcohol, cocaine, opioids. *American Journal of Psychiatry, 152* (No. 11, Supplement), 1–59.

American Psychiatric Association. (1996). Practice guideline for the treatment of patients with nicotine dependence. *American Journal of Psychiatry, 153* (No. 10, Supplement), 1–31.

American Psychiatric Association. (1997). Practice guideline for the treatment of patients with schizophrenia. *American Journal of Psychiatry, 154* (No. 4, Supplement), 1–63.

Antonuccio, D. (1995). Psychotherapy for depression: No stronger medicine. *American Psychologist, 50,* 450–452.

Antony, M. M., & Barlow, D. H. (1996). Specific phobia. In V. E. Caballo & R. M. Turner (Eds.), *International handbook of cognitive/behavioral treatment of psychiatric disorders.* Madrid, Spain: Siglio XXI.

Azrin, N. H., Sisson, R. W., Meyers, R., & Godley, M. (1982). Alcoholism treatment by disulfiram and community reinforcement therapy. *Journal of Behavior Therapy and Experimental Psychiatry, 13,* 105–112.

Barlow, D. H. (1988). *Anxiety and its disorders: The nature and treatment of anxiety and panic.* New York: Guilford Press.

Barlow, D. H., Esler, J. L., & Vitali, A. E. (1998). Psychosocial treatments for panic disorders, phobias, and generalized anxiety disorder. In P. E. Nathan & J. M. Gorman (Eds.), *A guide to treatments that work* (pp. 288–318). Oxford: Oxford University Press.

Barlow, D. H., & Lehman, C. (1996). Advances in the psychosocial treatment of anxiety disorders: Implications for national health care. *Archives of General Psychiatry, 53,* 727–735.

Barlow, D. H., Rapee, R. M., & Brown, T. A. (1992). Behavioral treatment of generalized anxiety disorder. *Behavior Therapy, 23,* 551–570.

Beck, A. T., Rush, A. J., Shaw, B. F., & Emery, G. (1979). *Cognitive therapy of depression: A treatment manual.* New York: Guilford Press.

Beutler, L. E., & Machado, P. P. P. (1992). Research on psychotherapy. In M. R. Rosenzweig (Ed.), *International psychological research: Progress, problems, and prospects* (pp. 227–252). Washington, DC: American Psychological Association.

Black, J. L., & Keane, T. M. (1982). Implosive therapy in the treatment of combat related fears in a World War II veteran. *Journal of Behavior Therapy and Experimental Psychiatry, 13,* 163–165.

Borduin, C. M., Mann, B. J., Cone, L. T., Henggeler, S. W., Fucci, B. R., Blaske, D. M., & Williams, R. A. (1995). Multisystematic treatment of serious juvenile offenders: Long-term prevention of criminality and violence. *Journal of Consulting and Clinical Psychology, 63,* 569–578.

Brenner, H., Hodel, B., & Roder, V. (1990). Integrated cognitive and behavioral interventions in treatment of schizophrenia. *Psychosocial Rehabilitation Journal, 13,* 41–43.

Brom, D., Kleber, R. J., & Defares, P. B. (1989). Brief psychotherapy for posttraumatic stress disorders. *Journal of Consulting and Clinical Psychology, 57,* 607–612.

Brown, T. A., O'Leary, T. A., & Barlow, D. H. (1993). Cognitive behavioral treatment of generalized anxiety disorder. In D. H. Barlow (Ed.), *Clinical handbook of psychological disorders* (2nd ed.). New York: Guilford Publications.

Ceskova, E., & Svestka, J. (1993). Double-blind comparison of risperidone and haloperidol in schizophrenic and schizoaffective psychoses. *Pharmacopsychiatry, 26,* 121–124.

Clark, D. M., Salkovskis, P. M., Hackmann, A., Middleton, H., Anastasiades, P., & Gelder, M. (1994). A comparison of cognitive therapy, applied relaxation, and imipramine in the treatment of panic disorder. *British Journal of Psychiatry, 164,* 759–769.

Clinton, J. J., McCormick, K., & Besteman, J. (1994). Enhancing clinical practice: The role of practice guidelines. *American Psychologist, 49,* 30–33.

Consumer Reports Editors. (1995). Mental health: Does therapy help? *Consumer Reports, 60,* 734–737.

Craighead, L. W., & Agras, W. S. (1991). Mechanisms of action in cognitive behavioral and pharmacological interventions for obesity and bulimia nervosa. *Journal of Consulting and Clinical Psychology, 59,* 115–125.

Craighead, W. E., Craighead, L. W., & Ilardi, S. S. (1998). Psychosocial treatments for major depressive disorder. In P. E. Nathan & J. M. Gorman (Eds.), *A guide to treatments that work* (pp. 226–239). Oxford: Oxford University Press.

Craighead, W. E., Miklowitz, D. J., Vajk, F. C., & Frank, E. (1998). Psychosocial treatments for bipolar disorder. In P. E. Nathan & J. M. Gorman (Eds.), *A guide to treatments that work* (pp. 240–248). Oxford: Oxford University Press.

Craske, M. G., Brown, T. A., & Barlow, D. H. (1991). Behavioral treatment of panic disorder: A two-year follow-up. *Behavior Therapy, 22,* 289–304.

De Araujo, L. A., Ito, L. M., Marks, I. M., & Deale, A. (1995). Does imagined exposure to the consequences of not ritualising enhance live exposure for OCD? *British Journal of Psychiatry, 167,* 65–70.

Depression Guideline Panel. (1993). *Depression in Primary Care: Treatment of Major Depression.* Rockville, MD: US DHHS, Agency for Health Care Policy and Research.

Devlin, M. J., & Walsh, B. T. (1995). Medication treatment for eating disorders. *Journal of Mental Health, 4,* 459–469.

Division 12 Task Force. (1995). Training in and dissemination of empirically-validated psychological treatments: Report and recommendations. *The Clinical Psychologist, 48,* 3–23.

Division 12 Task Force. (1996). An update on empirically validated therapies. *The Clinical Psychologist, 49,* 5–18.

Division 12 Task Force. (1998). Update on empirically validated therapies, II. *The Clinical Psychologist, 51,* 3–16.

Eckman, T. A., Wirshing, W. C., Marder, S. R., Liberman, R. P., et al. (1992). Techniques for training schizophrenic patients in illness self-management: A controlled trial. *American Journal of Psychiatry, 149,* 1549–1555.

Elkin, I., Gibbons, R. D., Shea, M. T., & Shaw, B. F. (1996). Science is not a trial (but it can be sometimes a tribulation). *Journal of Consulting and Clinical Psychology, 64*, 92–103.

Eysenck, H. J. (1960). *Behavior therapy and the neuroses*. Oxford: Pergamon Press.

Fahlen, T., Nilsson, H. L., Borg, K., Humber, M., & Pauli, U. (1995). Social phobia: The clinical efficacy and tolerability of the monoamine oxidase-A and serotonin uptake inhibitor brofaromine. *Acta Scandinavica, 92*, 351–358.

Fairburn, C. G. (1981). A cognitive behavioural approach to the management of bulimia. *Psychological Medicine, 11*, 707–711.

Fava, G. A., Zielezny, M., Savron, G., & Grandi, S. (1995). Long-term effects of behavioural treatment for panic disorder with agoraphobia. *British Journal of Psychiatry, 166*, 87–92.

Finney, J. W., & Moos, R. H. (1998). Psychosocial treatments for alcohol use disorders. In P. E. Nathan & J. M. Gorman (Eds.), *A guide to treatments that work* (pp. 156–166). Oxford: Oxford University Press.

Foa, E. B., & Goldstein, A. (1978). Continuous exposure and complete response prevention in the treatment of obsessive-compulsive neurosis. *Behavior Therapy, 9*, 821–829.

Foa, E. B., Rothbaum, B. O., Riggs, D. S., & Murdock, T. B. (1991). Treatment of posttraumatic stress disorder in rape victims: A comparison between cognitive-behavioral procedures and counseling. *Journal of Consulting and Clinical Psychology, 59*, 715–723.

Foa, E. B., Steketee, G., Grayson, J. B., Turner, R. M., & Latimer, P. (1984). Deliberate exposure and blocking of obsessive-compulsive rituals: Immediate and long-term effects. *Behavior Therapy, 15*, 450–472.

Frank, E., Kupfer, D. J., Perel, T. M., Cornes, C. L., Jarrett, D. J., Mallinger, A., Thase, M. E., McEachran, A. B., & Grochocinski, V. J. (1990). Three-year outcomes for maintenance therapies in recurrent depression. *Archives of General Psychiatry, 47*, 1093–1099.

Frank, J. D. (1971). Therapeutic factors in psychotherapy. *American Journal of Psychotherapy, 25*, 350–361.

Frank, J. D. (1973). *Persuasion and healing: A comparative study of psychotherapy* (rev. ed.). Baltimore, MD: Johns Hopkins University Press.

Franklin, M. E., & Foa, E. B. (1998). Cognitive behavioral treatments for obsessive compulsive disorder. In P. E. Nathan & J. M. Gorman (Eds.), *A guide to treatments that work* (pp. 339–357). Oxford: Oxford University Press.

Goodwin, F. K., & Jamison, K. R. (1990). *Manic-depressive illness*. Oxford: Oxford University Press.

Greenberg, J. (1994). Psychotherapy research: A clinician's view. In P. F. Talley, H. H. Strupp, & S. F. Butler (Eds.), *Psychotherapy research and practice: Bridging the gap* (pp. 1–18). New York: Basic Books.

Heimberg, R. G., & Juster, H. P. (1995). Cognitive behavioral treatments: Literature review. In R. G. Heimberg, M. R. Liebowitz, D. A. Hope, & F. R. Schneier (Eds.), *Social phobia: Diagnosis, assessment and treatment*. New York: Guilford Press.

Hinshaw, S. P., Klein, R. G., & Abikoff, H. (1998). Childhood attention deficit hyperactivity disorder: Nonpharmacological and combination treatments. In P. E. Nathan & J. M. Gorman (Eds.), *A guide to treatments that work* (pp. 26–41). Oxford: Oxford University Press.

Hollon, S. D., DeRubeis, R. J., Evans, M. D., Wiemer, M. J., et al. (1992). Cognitive therapy and pharmacotherapy for depression: Singly and in combination. *Archives of General Psychiatry, 49*, 774–781.

Howard, K. I., Kopta, S. M., Krause, M. S., & Orlinsky, D. E. (1986). The dose-effect relationship in psychotherapy. *American Psychologist, 41*, 159–164.

Kadden, R., Carroll, K. M., Donovan, D., Cooney, N., Monti, P., Abrams, D., Litt, M., & Hester, R. (1992). *Cognitive behavioral coping skills therapy manual: A clinical research guide for therapists treating individuals with alcohol abuse and dependence*. NIAAA Project MATCH Monograph, Vol. 3, DHHS Publication No. (ADM) 92-1895. Washington, DC: U.S. Government Printing Office.

Karon, B. P., & Teixeira, M. A. (1995). 'Guidelines for the treatment of depression in primary care' and the APA response. *American Psychologist, 50*, 453–455.

Kazdin, A. E. (1993). Treatment of conduct disorder: Progress and directions in psychotherapy research. *Development and psychopathology, 5*, 277–310.

Kazdin, A. E. (1998). Psychosocial treatments for conduct disorder in children. In P. E. Nathan & J. M. Gorman (Eds.), *A guide to treatments that work* (pp. 65–89). Oxford: Oxford University Press.

Keane, T. M. (1998). Psychological and behavioral treatments of post-traumatic stress disorder. In P. E. Nathan & J. M. Gorman (Eds.), *A guide to treatments that work* (pp. 398–407). Oxford: Oxford University Press.

Keane, T. M., Fairbank, J. A., Caddell, J. M., & Zimering, R. T. (1989). Implosive (flooding) therapy reduces symptoms of PTSD in Vietnam combat veterans. *Behavior Therapy, 20*, 245–260.

Keck, P. E., & McElroy, S. L. (1998). Pharmacological treatment of bipolar disorders. In P. E. Nathan & J. M. Gorman (Eds.), *A guide to treatments that work* (pp. 249–269). Oxford: Oxford University Press.

Kessler, R. C., McGonagle, K. A., Zhao, S., Nelson, C. B., et al. (1994). Lifetime and 12-month prevalence of DSM-III-R psychiatric disorders in the United States: Results from the national comorbidity survey. *Archives of General Psychiatry, 51*, 8–19.

Kingsbury, S. J. (1995). Bias in the guidelines or bias in the response? *American Psychologist, 50,* 455–456.

Klerman, G. L., Weissman, M. M., Rounsaville, B. J., & Chevron, E. S. (1984). *Interpersonal psychotherapy of depression.* New York: Basic Books.

Kopelowicz, A., & Liberman, R. P. (1998). Psychosocial treatments for schizophrenia. In P. E. Nathan & J. M. Gorman (Eds.), *A guide to treatments that work* (pp. 190–211). Oxford: Oxford University Press.

Lewinsohn, P. M., & Gotlib, I. H. (1995). Behavioral theory and treatment of depression. In E. E. Becker & W. R. Leber (Eds.), *Handbook of depression* (pp. 352–375). New York: Guilford Press.

Luborsky, L., Singer, B., & Luborsky, L. (1976). Comparative studies of psychotherapies: Is it true that 'everybody has won and all must have prizes'? In R. L. Spitzer & D. F. Klein (Eds.), *Evaluation of psychological therapies* (pp. 3–22). Baltimore: Johns Hopkins University Press.

Lundman, R. J. (1984). *Prevention and control of juvenile delinquency.* London: Oxford University Press.

Menditto, A. A., Valdes, L. A., & Beck, N. C. (1994). Implementing a comprehensive social-learning program within the forensic psychiatric service of Fulton State Hospital. In P. W. Corrigan & R. P. Liberman (Eds.), *Behavior therapy in psychiatric hospitals* (pp. 61–78). New York: Springer.

Meyer, V. (1966). Modification of expectations in cases with obsessional rituals. *Behaviour Research and Therapy, 4,* 273–280.

Miller, W. R., Zweben, A., DiClemente, C. C., & Rychtarik, R. G. (1992). *Motivational enhancement therapy manual: A clinical research guide for therapists treating individuals with alcohol abuse and dependence.* NIAAA Project MATCH Monograph, Vol. 2, DHHS Publication No. (ADM) 92-1894. Washington, DC: U.S. Government Printing Office.

Mueser, K. T., Wallace, C. J., & Liberman, R. P. (1995). New developments in social skills training. *Behaviour Change, 12,* 31–40.

Munoz, R. F., Hollon, S. D., McGrath, E., Rehm, L. P., & VandenBos, G. R. (1994). On the AHCPR *Depression in primary care* guidelines: Further considerations for practitioners. *American Psychologist, 49,* 42–61.

Nathan, P. E. (1998). Practice guidelines: Not yet ideal. *American Psychologist, 53,* 290–299.

Nathan, P. E., & Gorman, J. M. (Eds.). (1998). *A guide to treatments that work.* Oxford: Oxford University Press.

Nathan, P. E., & Skinstad, A. H. (1987). Outcomes of treatment for alcohol problems: Current methods, problems, and results. *Journal of Consulting and Clinical Psychology, 55,* 332–340.

Nathan, P. E., Stuart, S. P., & Dolan, S. L. (in press). Research on psychotherapy efficacy and effectiveness: Between Scylla and Charybdis? *Psychological Bulletin.*

Nemeroff, C. B., & Schatzberg, A. F. (1998). Pharmacological treatment of unipolar depression. In P. E. Nathan & J. M. Gorman (Eds.), *A guide to treatments that work* (pp. 212–225). Oxford: Oxford University Press.

Nowinski, J., Baker, S., & Carroll, K. (1992). *Twelve-step facilitation therapy manual: A clinical research guide for therapists treating individuals with alcohol abuse and dependence.* NIAAA Project MATCH Monograph, Vol. 1, DHHS Publication No. (ADM) 92-1893. Washington, DC: U.S. Government Printing Office.

O'Farrell, T. J., Choquette, K. A., Cutter, H. S. G., Brown, E. D., & McCourt, W. F. (1993). Behavioral Marital Therapy with and without additional couples relapse prevention sessions for alcoholics and their wives. *Journal of Studies on Alcohol, 54,* 652–666.

Orlinsky, D. E., & Howard, K. I. (1975). *Varieties of psychotherapeutic experience.* New York: Teachers College Press.

Ouimette, P. C., Finney, J. W., & Moos, R. H. (1997). Twelve-step and cognitive-behavioral treatment for substance abuse: A comparison of treatment effectiveness. *Journal of Consulting and Clinical Psychology, 65,* 230–240.

Patterson, G. R., Dishion, T. J., & Chamberlain, P. (1993). Outcomes and methodological issues relating to treatment of antisocial children. In T. R. Giles (Ed.), *Handbook of effective psychotherapy* (pp. 43–87). New York: Plenum.

Paul, G. L., & Lentz, R. J. (1977). *Psychosocial treatment of chronic mental patients: Milieu versus social-learning programs.* Cambridge, MA: Harvard University Press.

Pelham, W. E., Carlson, C., Sams, S. E., Dixon, M. J., & Hoza, B. (1993). Separate and combined effects of methylphenidate and behavior modification on boys with attention-deficit hyperactivity disorder in the classroom. *Journal of Consulting and Clinical Psychology, 61,* 506–515.

Persons, J. B., Thase, M. E., & Crits-Christoph, P. (1996). The role of psychotherapy in the treatment of depression. *Archives of General Psychiatry, 53,* 283–290.

Priebe, S., Wildgrube, C., & Mueller-Oerlinghausen, B. (1989). Lithium prophylaxis and expressed emotion. *British Journal of Psychiatry, 154,* 396–399.

Project MATCH Research Group. (1993). Project MATCH: Rationale and methods for a multisite clinical trial matching patients to alcoholism treatment. *Alcoholism: Clinical and Experimental Research, 17,* 1130–1145.

Project MATCH Research Group. (1997a). Matching alcoholism treatment to client/heterogeneity: Project

MATCH posttreatment drinking outcomes. *Journal of Studies on Alcohol, 58,* 7–29.

Project MATCH Research Group. (1997b). Project MATCH secondary *a priori* hypotheses. *Addiction, 92,* 1671–1698.

Project MATCH Research Group. (1998). Matching alcoholism treatments to client heterogeneity: Project MATCH three-year drinking outcomes. *Alcoholism: Clinical and Experimental Research, 22,* 1300–1311.

Rachman, S. (1971). *The effects of the psychological therapies.* Oxford: Pergamon Press.

Randolph, E., Eth, S., Glynn, S., Paz, G., Van Vort, W., Shaner, A., et al. (1994). Efficacy of behavioral family management in reducing relapse in veteran schizophrenics. *British Journal of Psychiatry, 164,* 501–506.

Rauch, S. L., & Jenike, M. A. (1998). Pharmacological treatment of obsessive compulsive disorder. In P. E. Nathan & J. M. Gorman (Eds.), *A guide to treatments that work* (pp. 358–376). Oxford: Oxford University Press.

Rehm, L. P. (1977). A self-control model of depression. *Behavior Therapy, 8,* 787–804.

Rosenzweig, M. R. (1999). Continuity and change in the development of psychology around the world. *American Psychologist, 54,* 252–259.

Roy-Byrne, P. P., & Cowley, D. S. (1998). Pharmacological treatment of panic, generalized anxiety, and phobic disorders. In P. E. Nathan & J. M. Gorman (Eds.), *A guide to treatments that work* (pp. 319–338). Oxford: Oxford University Press.

Rush, J. A. (1996). Commentary. *Archives of General Psychiatry, 53,* 298–300.

Rush, J. A., & the Depression Guideline Panel of the Agency for Health Care Policy and Research. (1994). Synopsis of the clinical practice guidelines for diagnosis and treatment of depression in primary care. *Archives of Family Medicine, 3,* 85–92.

Rutter, M., & Giller, H. (1983). *Juvenile delinquency: Trends and perspectives.* New York: Penguin Books.

Schulberg, H. C., & Rush, A. J. (1994). Clinical practice guidelines for managing major depression in primary care practice. *American Psychologist, 49,* 34–41.

Seligman, M. E. P. (1995). The effectiveness of psychotherapy: the *Consumer Reports* survey. *American Psychologist, 50,* 965–974.

Shapiro, F. (1995). *Eye movement desensitization and reprocessing: Basic principles, protocols, and procedures.* New York: Guilford Press.

Shea, M. T., Elkin, I., Imber, S. D., Sotsky, S. M., et al. (1992). Course of depressive symptoms over follow-up: Findings from the National Institute of Mental Health Treatment of Depression Collaborative Research Program. *Archives of General Psychiatry, 49,* 782–787.

Sheitman, B. B., Kinon, B. J., Ridgway, B. A., & Lieberman, J. A. (1998). Pharmacological treatments of schizophrenia. In P. E. Nathan & J. M. Gorman (Eds.), *A guide to treatments that work* (pp. 167–189). Oxford: Oxford University Press.

Smith, D. E., & McCrady, B. S. (1991). Cognitive impairment among alcoholics: Impact on drink refusal skill acquisition and treatment outcome. *Addictive Behaviors, 16,* 265–274.

Smith, M. L., & Glass, G. V. (1977). Meta-analysis of psychotherapy outcome studies. *American Psychologist, 32,* 752–760.

Stiles, W. B., Shapiro, D. A., & Elliott, R. (1986). 'Are all psychotherapies equivalent?' *American Psychologist, 41,* 165–180.

Teasdale, J. D., Fennell, M. J., Hibbert, G. A., & Amies, P. L. (1984). Cognitive therapy for major depressive disorder in primary care. *British Journal of Psychiatry, 144,* 400–406.

Vaillant, G. E. (1995). *The natural history of alcoholism revisited.* Cambridge, MA: Harvard University Press.

Vyborova, L., Nahunek, K., Drtilkova, I., Balastikova, B., & Misurec, J. (1984). Intraindividual comparison of 21-day application of amphetamine and methylphenidate in hyperkinetic children. *Activas Nervosa Superior, 26,* 268–269.

Weissman, M. M., Prusoff, B. A., DiMascio, A., Neu, C., Goklaney, M., & Klerman, G. L. (1979). The efficacy of drugs and psychotherapy in the treatment of acute depressive episodes. *American Journal of Psychiatry, 136,* 555–558.

Wilson, G. T., & Fairburn, C. G. (1998). Treatments for eating disorders. In P. E. Nathan & J. M. Gorman (Eds.), *Treatments for eating disorders* (pp. 501–530). Oxford: Oxford University Press.

Wunderlich, U., Wiedemann, G., & Buchkremer, G. (1996). Are psychosocial methods of intervention effective in schizophrenic patients? A meta-analysis. *Verhaltenstherapie, 6,* 4–13.

Yehuda, R., Marshall, R., & Giller, E. L., Jr. (1998). Psychopharmacological treatment of post traumatic stress disorder. In P. E. Nathan & J. M. Gorman (Eds.), *A guide to treatments that work* (pp. 375–397). Oxford: Oxford University Press.

ABBREVIATIONS

ADHD:	Attention deficit hyperactivity disorder
AHCPR:	U.S. Agency for Health Care Policy and Research
AN:	Anorexia nervosa
BN:	Bulimia nervosa
BT:	Behavior therapy
CBT:	Cognitive Behavioral Coping Skills Treatment, a Project MATCH treatment
CD:	Conduct disorder

DSM:	*Diagnostic and Statistical Manual of Mental Disorders* (American Psychiatric Association)	NIMH:	U.S. National Institute of Mental Health
		OCD:	Obsessive compulsive disorder
		PCT:	Panic control treatment
EMDR:	Eye-movement desensitization and reprocessing treatment	PLA-CM:	A TDCRP treatment group that received pill-placebo plus clinical management
EX/RP:	Exposure and ritual/response prevention treatment	PMT:	Parent management training
		PSST:	Cognitive problem-solving skills training
FFT:	Functional family therapy	PTSD:	Post-traumatic stress disorder
GAD:	Generalized anxiety disorder	RCT:	Randomized clinical trial
IMP-CM:	A TDCRP treatment group that received a TCA plus clinical management	SSRI:	Selective serotonin reuptake inhibitor
		SST:	Social skills training
IPT:	Interpersonal Therapy	TCA:	Tricyclic anti-depressant
MAO inhibitor:	Monoamine oxidase inhibitor	TDCRP:	Treatment of Depression Collaborative Research Program
MET:	Motivational Enhancement Therapy, a Project MATCH treatment	TSF:	Twelve-Step Facilitation, a Project MATCH treatment
MST:	Multisystematic therapy	VAMC:	U.S. Veterans Affairs Medical Centers

Communications concerning this chapter should be addressed to: Professor Peter E. Nathan, Department of Psychology, University of Iowa, E119 Seashore Hall, Iowa City, Iowa 52242, USA

23

Health Psychology

RALF SCHWARZER AND BENICIO GUTIÉRREZ-DOÑA

23.1 HEALTH PSYCHOLOGY AS A SCIENTIFIC DISCIPLINE

The Emergence of the Field of Health Psychology

Health Psychology emerged in the 1970s as a response to a number of factors, one of them the *changing pattern of illness and death* in industrialized nations. In former times, infectious diseases such as influenza, pneumonia, tuberculosis, and gastroenteritis were the leading causes of death. Later, in the second half of the twentieth century, conditions such as heart disease, cancer, stroke, chronic obstructive pulmonary disease, as well as accidents became the leading causes of death. These are chronic diseases, illnesses, or injuries related to lifestyle. Lifestyle choices such as smoking, drinking, overeating, and underexercising cause millions of preventable deaths per year. Health psychologists have the opportunity of helping to prevent many of these deaths. Human behavior has moved into the focus of prevention and rehabilitation attempts. Behavior change is the subject of psychological, not medical, research, and therefore the new field of Health Psychology has received a great deal of attention within and outside the scientific community.

A second factor that facilitated the rise of the discipline was the escalating *costs of medical care*. It became clear that society could not, in the long run, afford public health care based on expensive advanced medical technology. At the same time, psychology succeeded in designing behavioral interventions that proved to be more cost-effective. Changing people's lifestyles to prevent the onset of illness is the preferred method.

A third factor was the emergence of a new understanding of health and illness. Health is no longer seen as the mere absence of illness, but rather as the presence of well-being, although the medical profession still largely adheres to a biomedical model. This model reduces the focus to pathology instead of the causes of well-being and regards mind and body as separate entities. A paradigm shift has taken place within the social sciences, from the biomedical model to the *biopsychosocial model* that regards health and illness as resulting from an interplay of biological, psychological, and social determinants, which implies that mind and body cannot be separated when it comes to an understanding of health-related processes. Health can now rather be seen as an active achievement, and Health Psychology follows this new model and applies advanced research methodology to unveil the complex relationships inherent in this approach.

These three factors, among others, are believed to have contributed to the development of Health Psychology as a field within psychology. Established formally in 1978 as Division 38 within the American Psychological Association (APA), it has grown rapidly since then, as can be seen by the program and the attendance of the annual meetings. In 1986, the International Association for Applied Psychology (IAAP) also established a Division of Health Psychology with a global focus. In the same year, the European Health Psychology Society (EHPS) was founded. EHPS holds annual meetings attended by a large number of European health psychologists and guests from abroad. Meetings have taken place in The Netherlands, Germany, the United Kingdom, Switzerland, Belgium, Spain, Norway, Ireland, France, Austria, and Italy. Activities can be monitored at the website: www.ehps.net. Most European countries have, in addition, their own professional or academic health psychology societies that also hold frequent meetings. Austria was the first country where the professional title 'Health Psychologist' was officially introduced in 1991. On a global scale, there are other health psychology societies linked to the mainstream, for example in Japan, Canada, Australia, and New Zealand. Most others, however, are less visible. In 1994, the International Society of Health Psychology Research (ISHPR) was founded, strongly influenced by Japanese leaders in this field, with the aim of integrating groups in developing parts of the world.

More evidence for the emergence of the field of Health Psychology is given by the number of new journals. The APA Division 38 flagship journal, founded in 1982, is called *Health Psychology*, and it has more than 10,000 subscribers. Its European counterpart, *Psychology and Health: An International Review*, which is linked to the EHPS, was launched in 1987. More recently, various English-language periodicals have been launched, such as *International Journal of Behavioral Medicine, Journal of Health Psychology, British Journal of Health Psychology, Journal of Occupational Health Psychology, Journal of Health Communication, Anxiety, Stress, and Coping, Japanese Health Psychology,* and *Psychology, Health and Medicine.* In addition, non-English-language periodicals are published such as *Gedrag* (in the Netherlands), *Zeitschrift für Gesundheitspsychologie* (in Germany) and *Psicologia della Salute* (in Italy).

Also, many textbooks have been produced, some of them with multiple editions within a short time (e.g., Taylor, 1998, four editions). In addition to these publications, several internet online services reflect the high demand for information about this field (e.g., www.apa.org, www.ehps.net).

In Latin America, Health Psychology has grown out of both the public health policies derived from the Pan American Health Organization (PHO) and the regional policies of local governments, universities, and so-called nongovernmental organizations (NGO). Research development is a function of the priorities that these organizations consider or define.

There are also specific conditions (e.g., economic, geographic, environmental, and political) that determine the development of research programs. Therefore, not only behavioral prevention or intervention programs oriented toward reducing epidemic diseases (e.g., the spread of tropical diseases) are urgent, but also fighting against the serious impact of frequent natural disasters (e.g., earthquakes or hurricanes) or the unpredictable dynamics of an unstable political and economical system.

The theoretical and methodological development of Health Psychology in Latin America has received a strong influence from Behavioral Medicine, Psychosomatics, and transactional models of stress and coping (Lazarus, 1991). Activities and research advances can be monitored on several websites (e.g., http://www.psy.utexas.edu/psy/RLP/RLPSpanish.html).

Definition of Health Psychology and Its Relationships to Other Disciplines

Health Psychology is a field within psychology that is devoted to understanding psychological influences on health-related processes, such as why people become ill, how they respond to illness, how they recover from a disease or adjust to chronic illness, or how they stay healthy in the first place. Health Psychology deals with the etiology and correlates of health, illness, and disability, with the prevention and treatment of diseases, with readjustment during and after illness, and with health promotion.

Three basic questions are asked in Health Psychology research: (a) who becomes sick and who stays well? (b) among the sick, who recovers and why? and (c) how can illness be prevented or recovery be promoted? (Adler & Matthews, 1994). Health psychologists conduct research on the origins and correlates of diseases. They identify personality or behavioral antecedents that influence the pathogenesis of certain illnesses. Health psychologists analyze the adoption and maintenance of health behaviors (e.g., physical exercise, good nutrition, condom use, or dental hygiene) and explore the reasons why people adhere to misbehaviors or risk behaviors (e.g., why they continue to smoke or fail to abstain from alcohol). Health promotion and the prevention of illness are, therefore, agendas for research and practice, as is the improvement of the health care system in general. A popular definition of Health Psychology is:

> Health Psychology is the aggregate of the specific educational, scientific and professional contributions of the discipline of psychology to the promotion and maintenance of health, the prevention and treatment of illness, the identification of etiologic and diagnostic correlates of health, illness, and related dysfunction and the improvement of the health care system and health policy formation. (Matarazzo, 1980, p. 815)

Before there was a formal discipline of Health Psychology, other research areas attended to some of its subject matters. For example, *Medical Psychology* used to be the main branch in charge of applying psychological knowledge to the medical profession and of providing the means for psychological assessment of patients and an evaluation of treatment outcomes. Many researchers studied psychosomatics, a paradigm strongly influenced by psychoanalysis that attempted to identify psychological precursors of illness. Today, Medical Psychology seems to become more and more integrated into Health Psychology as a subfield devoted to the study of psychological factors in the illness experience. *Behavioral Medicine*, historically based on learning theory, studied the conditions that modified and maintained health and illness behaviors. Nowadays, this has become a broad interdisciplinary collaborative effort to study all kinds of health- and illness-related phenomena. Health Psychology is one of several disciplines that contribute to this effort, along with medicine, pharmacology, epidemiology, social work, health education, sociology, and public health (Schwarzer, 1997). The major difference between Behavioral Medicine and Health Psychology is that the former is interdisciplinary, whereas the latter is a field within psychology.

23.2 Precursors of Illness and Resources for Health

An overview of factors that influence health and illness follows. Personal and social resources are described that can buffer the experience of stress. The negative impact of stress on health is

well-documented today, as are the ways of coping with stress and illness. Moreover, it has been argued that some persons are more disposed than others to fall prey to certain conditions. This is discussed under the heading of disease-prone personality.

The Disease-Prone Personality

The onset of diseases such as cancer or coronary heart disease is caused by a number of factors, including a genetic predisposition. In the absence of the major predictors, such as a family history of that particular disease, personality characteristics assume greater importance. There is evidence that a disposition for maladaptive coping with stress, the chronic expression of negative emotions, and poor social relations play a role in the development of illness and in the impairment of recovery from illness (Friedman, 1990). Depression, hostility, anger expression, and cynical distrust have been related to morbidity. It is important to note, however, that negative emotions need not necessarily be only the precursors of illness, but they can also be the consequence of illness. An association between depression and cancer, for example, does not come as a surprise since almost everyone becomes depressed to some extent after learning that he or she has cancer. Prospective studies, nevertheless, have found that stressed, depressed, or helpless people are somewhat more at risk than joyful or enthusiastic persons, which is due to the fact that the former tend to develop a compromised immune system that cannot cope well with infectious agents and tumor cells (Cohen & Herbert, 1996).

Cancer

Research on the association between personality and cancer has pointed to the possibility that antiemotional, repressed, defensive, and conflict-avoiding individuals may be especially prone to developing cancer. Eysenck (1994) hypothesized that a risk behavior such as smoking might interact with personality, which would imply that smokers are not directly at risk for lung cancer unless their personality predisposes them for this disease. While this is a controversial issue, other research has confirmed some association between a personality profile, labeled Type C, and cancer (Temoshok & Dreher, 1992). It is argued that a strong need for harmonious social relationships and a tendency not to express emotions might, over a period of decades, facilitate the onset of tumors. A recent study in Spain, although cross-sectional, illustrates this relationship (Fernandez-Ballesteros, Ruiz, & Garde, 1998). The authors compared healthy

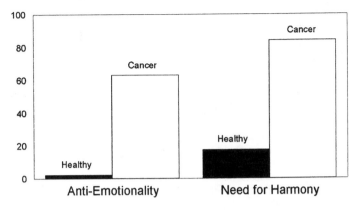

Figure 23.1   *Personality characteristics of breast cancer patients (Fernandez-Ballesteros et al., 1998)*

women with breast cancer patients. Figure 23.1 shows that healthy women tend to have lower scores on anti-emotionality and need for harmony than women diagnosed with breast cancer.

This study cannot uncover the cause–effect relationship because cancer develops slowly over many years. It might be possible that personality dispositions follow the pathogenesis instead of preceding it. It is of note, however, that some of the breast cancer patients were questioned before they knew about their diagnosis, which means that their high anti-emotionality scores cannot constitute a mere response to the threatening diagnosis.

Cardiac Disease

Another pathogenic pathway to morbidity and mortality lies in coronary-prone attitudes and behaviors. It was found as early as in the 1970s that ambitious, hard-driving, competitive, hostile, impatient, and aggressive persons, labeled Type A individuals, were more likely to suffer from a myocardial infarct than their counterparts, labeled Type B individuals. In two long-term prospective studies with thousands of participants, the Western Collaborative Group Study in California and the Framingham Study on the East Coast of the United States, empirical evidence emerged that Type A individuals were about twice as likely to die from a heart attack than their counterparts, after controlling for age, blood pressure, cholesterol levels, and smoking. This convinced the National Heart, Lung, and Blood Institute in 1981 to confirm publicly that Type A is associated with heart disease, which was the first time that the medical profession acknowledged the existence of a psychosocial

risk factor for physical illness. This event created much enthusiasm in the young discipline of Health Psychology and stimulated further research. However, soon afterwards, several other independent studies were unable to replicate the previous findings, among them the Multiple Risk Factor Intervention Trial, the Multicenter Post-Infarction Program, and the Aspirin Myocardial Infarct Study (see Matthews & Haynes, 1986, for details).

Nevertheless, further research has convinced investigators that coronary diseases are influenced by psychosocial risk factors such as personality dispositions and coping behaviors (Siegrist, 1996). Hostility, anger expression, and cynical distrust appear to be the prime candidates, instead of the Type A construct. Taking this for granted, the next step was to identify the physiological mediators that convert personality and behavioral risk factors into physical illness. Hostile individuals, for example, have been found to have more elevated cholesterol levels than others, which might be one reason for their increased morbidity risk. The mediating mechanisms are subject to further research.

In general, behaviors can be seen as responses to life stress. If someone is ambitious, hard-driving, competitive, hostile, impatient, and aggressive, this is based on one's appraisal of the situation and one's perceived resources to cope with the situational demands. Hostile behaviors and cynicism are particular coping behaviors of individuals who are vulnerable to stress in a unique way. A thorough study of stress and coping, therefore, is a prerequisite for our understanding of health-compromising behaviors as well as of personality precursors of illness.

Stress, Coping, and Health

Cognitive-Transactional Stress Theory

Stress has been defined as a particular relationship between a person and the environment that this person appraises as taxing or exceeding his or her resources and endangering his or her well-being (Lazarus, 1991; Lazarus & Folkman, 1984). Appraisals are determined by perceiving environmental demands and personal resources simultaneously. They can change over time due to coping effectiveness, altered requirements, or improvements in personal abilities. This cognitive-relational theory emphasizes the continuous, reciprocal nature of the interaction between the person and the environment.

Cognitive appraisals include two component processes, called by Lazarus (1991) primary and secondary appraisals. *Primary appraisal* refers to the stakes a person has in a certain encounter. In primary appraisals, a situation is perceived as being either irrelevant, benign-positive, or stressful. Those events classified as stressful can be further subdivided into the categories of benefit, challenge, threat, and harm/loss. A stress-relevant situation is appraised as challenging when it mobilizes physical and psychological activity and involvement. In the appraisal of *challenge*, a person may see an opportunity to prove herself or himself, anticipating gain, mastery, or personal growth from the venture. The situation is experienced as pleasant, exciting, and interesting, and the person is hopeful, eager, and confident to meet the demands. *Threat* is experienced when future harm or loss is anticipated. In the experience of *harm/loss*, some damage to the person has already occurred. Damages can be injury, illness, or loss of valued persons, important objects, self-worth, or social standing.

Primary appraisals are mirrored simultaneously by *secondary appraisals* that refer to one's available coping options for dealing with stress, that is, one's perceived resources to cope with the demands at hand. The individual evaluates the competence, social support, and material or other resources required to adapt to the circumstances and to establish an equilibrium between person and environment. A patient who has suffered a myocardial infarct, for example, might perceive his spouse as the best resource to readjust from the event. Instead of primary and secondary appraisal, the terms 'demand appraisal' and 'resource appraisal' might be more meaningful (Schwarzer, 1992). Hobfoll (1989) has expanded the stress and coping theory with respect to the conservation of resources as the main human motive in the struggle with stressful encounters.

Coping With Stress

Different ways of coping have been found to be more or less adaptive. In a meta-analysis, Suls and Fletcher (1985) have compiled studies that examined the effects of various coping modes on several measures of adjustment to illness. The authors conclude that *avoidance* coping strategies seem to be more adaptive in the short run, whereas *attentive-confrontative* coping is more adaptive in the long run. It remains unclear, however, how the specific coping responses of a patient struggling with a disease can be classified into broader categories. There are many attempts to reduce the total of possible coping responses to a parsimonious set of coping dimensions. Some researchers have come up with two basic dimensions, such as *instrumental, attentive, vigilant,* or *confrontative coping* on the one hand, in contrast to *avoidance, palliative,* and *emotional coping* on the other (for an overview, see Schwarzer & Schwarzer, 1996). A well-known approach has been put forward by Lazarus and Folkman (1984), who discriminate between *problem-focused* and *emotion-focused* coping. Another conceptual distinction has been suggested between *assimilative* and *accommodative* coping, the former aiming at an alteration of the environment to oneself, and the latter aiming at an alteration of oneself to the environment. This pair has also been coined 'mastery versus meaning' or 'primary control versus secondary control'. These coping preferences may occur in a certain time order, for example when individuals first try to alter the demands that are at stake, and, after failing, turn inward to reinterpret their plight and find subjective meaning in it.

Coping also has a temporal aspect. One can cope before a stressful event takes place, while it is happening (e.g., during the progress of a disease), or afterwards. Beehr and McGrath (1996) distinguish five situations that create a particular temporal context: (a) *preventive coping*: long before the stressful event occurs or might occur; for example, a smoker might quit well in time to avoid the risk of lung cancer; (b) *anticipatory coping*: when the event is anticipated soon; for example, someone might take a tranquilizer while waiting for surgery; (c) *dynamic coping*: while the event is ongoing; for example, diverting attention to reduce chronic pain; (d) *reactive coping*: after the event has happened; for example, changing one's life after losing a limb; and (e) *residual coping*: long afterwards, by contending with long-run effects; for example, controlling one's intrusive thoughts years after a traumatic accident has happened.

There are many other attempts to conceptualize coping dimensions, and those mentioned above may serve as examples. Which of the above dimensions is suitable for a valid description of an actual coping process depends on a number of factors, among them the particular stress situation, one's history of coping with similar situations, and one's personal and social coping resources, or the opposite, one's specific vulnerability.

Personality Resources and Health

Some people become sick and others stay healthy because they differ in resources associated with specific personality characteristics. It has been found that some individuals can cope better with life and resist illness due to a pattern of personality characteristics such as hardiness (a profile of challenge, commitment, and control), sense of coherence, and optimism. In the following, three kinds of optimism are described in more detail. It is hypothesized that such beliefs may buffer pathogenesis and prevent or alleviate diseases through complex mechanisms, either by altering physiological parameters (such as immune parameters) or by altering health behaviors. Some individuals have been found to be 'self-healing personalities' (Friedman, 1990).

Optimistic Explanatory Style

People develop depression if they acquire a depressive attributional response style (Seligman, 1991). This style is composed of three dimensions: locus of control (internal versus external), stability (stable versus variable), and globality (global versus specific). Habitual responses to negative events in terms of internal, stable, and global attributions ('I am a loser and always will be') are coded as indicators for depressive affect. Nondepressives tend to attribute negative events rather to external, variable and specific factors ('The circumstances have recently been unfortunate'). This is called an *optimistic explanatory style* that counts as a protective factor against stress and illness. Optimists attribute good events rather to internal, stable, and global causes, that is, optimists make self-serving causal attributions.

In many studies, optimistic explanatory style has been related positively to health and negatively to illness. But the causal link between optimism and health is not well established. One assumption is that people with an optimistic explanatory style take control of their lives and adopt healthy practices that, in turn, lead to positive health outcomes in the long run. Another assumption is that optimists show different physiological reactions than pessimists. Kamen-Siegel, Rodin, Seligman, and Dwyer (1991) have studied the relationship between explanatory style and immune response in older adults. They found that pessimistic explanatory style was related to poorer immune function. Health behaviors, however, were almost uncorrelated with explanatory style. This result points to the possibility that the missing link between optimism and health might be rather of a physiological than a behavioral nature. This finding is in line with earlier studies that found a compromised immune status among humans and animals who had been made helpless or who were hopeless and depressed. In spite of impressive research that underscores the close association between explanatory style and health, it is not clear how this construct would fit as an integral part of a health behavior theory. Explanatory style seems to be a moderate predictor of health, except when it comes to preventive behaviors. It offers little guidance on how to change health behaviors.

Dispositional Optimism

The common-sense notion of optimism can be expressed in statements such as 'I'm always optimistic about my future,' a sample item taken from a psychometric scale developed by Scheier and Carver (1985). In contrast to explanatory style, this view of optimism explicitly pertains to expectancies and reflects a positive outlook on the future. The scientific concept is derived from a comprehensive theory of behavioral self-regulation that uses outcome expectancies as major ingredients. According to this theory, people strive for goals as long as they see them as attainable and as long as they believe that their actions will produce the desired outcome. Expectancies can be generalized across a variety of situations and can remain stable over time. Therefore, the label 'dispositional optimism' was chosen, defined as a stable tendency to believe that one will generally experience good outcomes in life. People who have a favorable outlook on life are considered to cope better with stress and illness, to invest more effort to prevent harm, and to enjoy better health than those with negative generalized outcome expectancies.

Indeed, there is ample evidence that dispositional optimism is associated with improved coping. Scheier et al. (1989) followed up a group of male heart patients who underwent bypass surgery. At four points in time, optimists were compared with pessimists, having been identified before surgery. In the first week after surgery, the optimists recovered faster and were quicker to get up and ambulate. After six months, the life of the optimists had almost normalized in terms of work and exercise, whereas this process took longer for the pessimists. After five years, optimists reported superior quality of life, better sleep, less pain, and more frequent health behaviors. The authors explain these benign effects of optimism with a more adaptive coping style. Even before the operation, the optimistic patients made plans and set goals for the time to come, whereas the pessimists paid more heed to their current emotions.

Another study among breast cancer patients yielded similar results (Carver et al., 1993). Dispositional optimism turned out to be a good predictor for recovery and adaptation. Most studies report positive associations between optimism and psychological as well as physical well-being, and preliminary data also point to a relationship with health habits.

Perceived Self-Efficacy

Numerous research studies have found that a strong sense of personal efficacy is related to better health, higher achievement, and more social integration. Perceived self-efficacy represents the key construct in social cognitive theory (Bandura, 1997). It has been applied to such diverse areas as school achievement, emotional disorders, mental and physical health, career choice, and sociopolitical change.

Behavioral change is facilitated by a personal sense of control. If people believe that they can take action to solve a problem instrumentally, they become more inclined to do so and feel more committed to this decision. While outcome expectancies refer to the perception of the possible consequences of one's action, perceived self-efficacy pertains to personal action control or agency. A person who believes in being able to make an event happen can conduct a healthier and self-determined life course. This 'can do'-cognition mirrors a sense of control over one's environment. It reflects the belief of being able to master challenging demands by means of adaptive action. It can also be regarded as an optimistic view of one's capability to deal with stress.

The relationship between self-efficacy and specific health outcomes, such as recovery from surgery or adaptation to chronic disease, has been studied. Patients with high efficacy beliefs are better able to control pain than those with low self-efficacy. Self-efficacy has been shown to affect blood pressure, heart rate, and serum catecholamine levels in coping with challenging or threatening situations. Cognitive-behavioral treatment of patients with rheumatoid arthritis enhanced their efficacy beliefs, reduced pain and joint inflammation, and improved psychosocial functioning. Optimistic self-beliefs have turned

out to be influential in the rehabilitation of chronic obstructive pulmonary disease patients. Recovery of cardiovascular function in post-coronary patients is similarly enhanced by beliefs in one's physical and cardiac efficacy. Obviously, perceived self-efficacy predicts the degree of therapeutic change in a variety of settings (Bandura, 1997).

These three kinds of optimistic beliefs were described here in some detail because they reflect the current thinking about personal resources and the mind–body relationship. Firm beliefs in oneself and the world guide emotions and behaviors and may have long-lasting effects on health and illness.

Social Resources and Health

Social support can assist coping and exert beneficial effects on various health outcomes. Social support has been defined in various ways, for example as resources provided by others, as coping assistance, or as an exchange of resources intended to enhance the well-being of the recipient. Several types of social support have been investigated, such as instrumental support (e.g., assist with a problem), tangible support (e.g., donate goods), informational support (e.g., give advice), emotional support (e.g., give reassurance), among others.

Social support has been found to be advantageous for patients during recovery from heart surgery. Kulik and Mahler (1989) studied men who underwent coronary artery bypass surgery. On the average, those who were often visited by their spouses were released somewhat earlier from the hospital than those who received only a few visits. In a longitudinal study, the same authors also found positive effects of emotional support after surgery. Schröder, Schwarzer, and Endler (1997) studied cardiac patients and their spouses over a half-year period before and after heart surgery, and they found that resourceful spouses seemed to transfer their resilient personality to the patients as part of a dyadic coping process.

The extent to which individuals are integrated in their communities and to which their social relationships are strong and supportive is associated with health. Maintaining close personal relationships to others can be a social resource factor that can, to a certain degree, protect against illness and premature death. There is a large body of empirical evidence that indicates such a beneficial influence of *social integration* on health. Starting with the well-known Alameda County Study (Berkman & Breslow, 1983), eight community-based prospective epidemiological investigations have documented a link between lack of social integration on the one hand and morbidity and all-cause mortality on the other. Those who are the most isolated socially are at the highest risk for a variety of diseases and fatal outcomes.

There is also growing evidence about the causal pathways that involve social factors in the development of disease, although further research is needed to understand the mechanisms that render social ties beneficial for the organism. Social embeddedness, or the lack of it, can influence the onset, progression, or recovery from illness. For example, several major studies have found a link between social integration and survival rates of patients who had experienced a myocardial infarct (MI). Ruberman, Weinblatt, Goldberg, and Chaudhary (1984) studied male survivors of an acute MI and found that cardiac patients who were socially isolated were more than twice as likely to die over a three-year period than those who were socially integrated. In a Swedish study of cardiac patients, it was found that those who were socially isolated had a three times higher ten-year mortality rate than those who were socially integrated (Orth-Gomer, Unden, & Edwards, 1988). Diagnosis of coronary artery disease and subsequent death was linked to marital status (Williams et al., 1992). Those who were single or lacked a confidant were more than three times as likely to die within five years compared with those who had a close confidant or who were married. Marital status and recurrent cardiac events were also linked in a study by Case et al. (1992), who identified a higher risk of cardiac deaths and nonfatal infarctions among those who lived alone. In another prospective study among MI patients, it was found that mortality rates within a six-month period were related to the social support reported by these patients (Berkman, Leo-Summers, & Horwitz, 1992). They identified the number of persons representing major sources of emotional support. In analyzing the data, the researchers distinguished men and women with one, two, and more than two such sources. There was a consistent pattern of death rates, the highest of which was associated with social isolation and the lowest of which pertained to two or more sources of emotional support, independent of age, gender, comorbidity, and severity of MI.

These five studies have focused on the *survival time* after a critical event. Obviously, the recovery process can be modified by the presence of a supportive social network. A sense of belonging and intimacy is able to facilitate the coping process one way or the other. Physiological or behavioral mechanisms have been mentioned as potential pathways for this facilitation. Among the multiple physiological pathways, an immunological and a neuroendocrine link have been investigated. It is known that losses and bereavement are followed by *immune depression*, which compromises in particular natural killer cell activity and cellular immunity. This, in turn, reduces overall host resistance, so that the individual becomes more susceptible to a variety of diseases, including infections and cancer. The quality of social relationships, for example marital quality, has been found a predictor of immune functioning. Social stress, in general, tends to suppress immune functioning (Cohen & Herbert, 1996).

The neuroendocrine system is closely related to high *cardiovascular reactivity* and physiological arousal, which are seen as antecedents of cardiac events. In a study by Seeman et al. (1994), emotional support was associated with neuroendocrine parameters, such as urinary levels of epinephrine, norepinephrine, and cortisol in a sample of elderly people. The link with emotional support was stronger than the link with instrumental support or mere social integration.

The behavioral pathway has been suggested by studies where social networks were stimulating health behaviors that prevented the onset of illness, slowed its progression, or influenced the recovery process. For example, abstinence after *smoking cessation* was facilitated by social support (Mermelstein, Cohen, Lichtenstein, Baer, & Kamarck, 1986). *Alcohol consumption* was lower in socially embedded persons (Berkman & Breslow, 1983), although other studies have found that social reference groups can trigger more risky behaviors, including alcohol consumption (Schwarzer, Jerusalem, & Kleine, 1990). Participation in *cancer screenings* can also be promoted by social ties (Suarez et al., 1994).

Physical exercise is among the health behaviors that have a close link to social integration and social support. Perceived support by family and friends can help in developing the intention to exercise as well as initiating the behavior (Sallis, Hovell, & Hofstetter, 1992). Long-term participation in exercise programs or the maintenance of self-directed exercise is probably more strongly determined by actual instrumental support than by perceived and informational support (Fuchs, 1997). Duncan and McAuley (1993) have found that social support influences exercise behaviors indirectly by improving one's self-efficacy, which might be an important mediator in this process. The reason could be that not only a sense of belonging and intimacy is perceived as supportive, but also being verbally persuaded that one is competent or the social modeling of competent behaviors.

23.3 Health Behaviors

Risky Lifestyles and Addictive Behaviors

Many health conditions are caused by behaviors, for example problem drinking, substance use, smoking, reckless driving, overeating, or unprotected sexual intercourse. Health Psychology research has identified a number of risk factors for such behaviors. A risk factor is a personal, social, or environmental characteristic that is related to a higher rate of the critical behavior. *Substance use or abuse*, in studies in the US, was associated with the following 15 factors (Wills, 1998): (1) male gender, (2) white ethnicity, (3) lower socioeconomic status, (4) family history of substance abuse, (5) temperament (high activity level, negative emotionality), (6) poor parental relationship and supervision, (7) early onset of substance use, (8) poor self-control, (9) novelty seeking and risk taking, (10) anger, hostility, and aggression, (11) avoidance and helpless coping, (12) tolerance for deviance, (13) conduct disorder and antisocial personality disorder, (14) negative life events, and (15) affiliation with peer users. Obviously, there is no single cause, which makes it difficult to predict the onset and course of risk behaviors.

Each of the health-compromising behaviors can be a target for interventions. However, a single behavior cannot be easily removed from one's life without replacing it by something else. Specific health-enhancing behaviors need to be adopted, such as physical exercise, weight control, preventive nutrition, dental hygiene, condom use, or accident-preventive measures. Moreover, a particular behavior constitutes an integral part of one's lifestyle. Thus, risky and healthy lifestyles should be the units of analyses. *Coronary-prone behavior*, for example, describes a pattern that consists of a sedentary lifestyle, a high-fat, high-cholesterol diet, overeating, smoking, and a maladaptive way of coping with stress (the latter is also a characteristic of the Type A personality). The *adolescent lifestyle*, for example, is characterized by risk-taking, such as careless driving, unprotected sex, and the exploration of drugs. There are *gay lifestyles*, *senior citizen lifestyles*, and so on, which reflect clusters of behaviors that are more frequent in these subgroups than in others. Behavioral epidemiology describes the frequencies and modalities of all health-compromising and health-enhancing behaviors, and their hazards and benefits are well-documented in the research literature. The major challenge for Health Psychology is the systematic modification of such behaviors.

Self-Regulated Health Behavior Change

The adoption of health behaviors (e.g., physical exercise, condom use, not smoking, dieting, etc.) is often viewed too simplistically as an individual's response to a health threat. Individuals become aware that their lifestyle puts them at risk for a life-threatening disease. Consequently, they are believed to make a deliberate decision to refrain from risk behaviors in favor of recommended precautions. This common-sense view of behavioral change is based on the questionable belief that humans are rational beings who perceive a risk and then respond to it in the most reasonable manner. In fact, studies show that risk perception is a poor predictor of behavioral change (Hahn & Renner, 1998). This state of affairs has encouraged psychologists to design more complex prediction models that include a number of determinants of action (for reviews, see Schwarzer, 1992; Wallston, 1994; Weinstein, 1993). Changing one's health behavior is considered to be a difficult self-regulation process. In Health Psychology research, attempts are being made to model such processes with the aim to understand the mechanisms of how people are motivated to change their risk behaviors, and how they become encouraged to cope with barriers and setbacks. Health behavior models are designed to predict and explain the adoption of novel or difficult health behaviors and the adherence to medical regimens. In the past, the focus has been on identifying an optimal set of predictors that included constructs such as attitude, social norm, disease severity, personal vulnerability, behavioral intention, etc. The most prominent approaches were the Health Belief Model, the Theory of Reasoned Action, the Theory of Planned Behavior, and Protection Motivation Theory (for an overview of these models, see Conner & Norman, 1996). It is a common understanding that there are several necessary ingredients for all health behavior models, among them (a) behavioral intentions, (b) perceived self-efficacy, and (c) outcome expectancies.

However, the focus on static prediction cannot account for changes during the course of time. Thus, many theorists have made an attempt to consider process characteristics that might add substantially to the predictive power of such constructs. The *Transtheoretical Model of Behavior Change* (DiClemente & Prochaska, 1982) has become the most popular stage model. Its main feature is the implication that different types of cognitions may be important at different stages of the health behavior change process. It includes five discrete stages of health behavior change that are defined in terms of one's past behavior and future plans (precontemplation, contemplation, preparation, action, maintenance). For example, at the *precontemplation stage*, a drinker does not intend to stop consuming alcohol in the future. At the *contemplation stage*, a drinker thinks about quitting sometime within the next six months, but does not make any specific plans for behavior change. At the *preparation stage*, the drinker resolves to quit within the next six months. The *action stage* includes individuals who have taken successful action for any period of time. If this abstinence has lasted for more than six months, the person is categorized as being in the *maintenance stage*. The model, which also includes self-efficacy and other relevant features, has been applied successfully to a broad range of health behaviors, with particular success for smoking cessation. However, it has been argued that the notion of stages within this theory might be flawed or circular, in that the stages are not genuinely qualitative, but are rather arbitrary distinctions within a continuous process (Weinstein, Rothman, & Sutton, 1998). Instead, these 'stages' might be better understood as 'process heuristics' to underscore the nature of the entire model. That is, the model can serve as a useful heuristic that describes a health behavior change process, which has not been the major focus of health behavior theories so far. In redirecting the attention to a self-regulatory process, the transtheoretical model has served an important purpose for applied settings. The postintentional, preactional phase ('preparation') may be the

most challenging stage for researchers and professionals because it is exactly in this phase where an intention is or is not translated into an action – depending on the circumstances. Planning and initiative, but also volatility, hesitation, and procrastination characterize this phase.

Intervention research in The Netherlands has dwelt on the stage approach in conjunction with social-cognitive theory. One recent finding on *smoking cessation* will be cited here as a good example (Dijkstra, De Vries, Roijackers, & Breukelen, 1998). In an experimental study, several groups of smokers who were identified as 'immotives', 'precontemplators', 'contemplators', or 'preparers' were given health messages ('immotives' are those who are absolutely determined to remain smokers). One group received *information on outcomes* of quitting, and another group received *self-efficacy-enhancing information*. Within each group, there were smokers in all four stages. Ten weeks later, their abstinence was assessed by the questionnaire item 'Have you smoked in the last seven days (even one puff)?' Participants were told that there would be biochemical verification of their responses. It turned out that quite a few had quit smoking. This was true for the two intervention groups and for all four stages within these conditions. Figure 23.2 decomposes the percentages of ex-smokers. As expected, the number of quitters increased with stages. Moreover, at the preparation stage, self-efficacy information provided the best means to motivate smokers to quit, whereas at the previous stages there was no significant difference between the two treatment conditions. The idea was to identify the optimal intervention strategy by matching individuals at different stages to different conditions designed to stimulate either outcome beliefs or optimistic

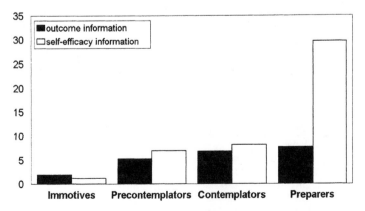

Percent of ex-smokers 10 weeks post-treatment

Figure 23.2 *Effects of different health messages at different levels of readiness for change on smoking cessation (Dijkstra et al., 1998)*

self-beliefs. The results are promising in this direction.

Other modern health behavior theories pay more attention to postintentional processes, which is in line with action theories (e.g., Kuhl, 1992). The *Health Action Process Approach* (HAPA; Schwarzer, 1992, 1999; Schwarzer & Fuchs, 1996), for example, represents a generic framework, also based on social cognitive theory and an explicit self-regulation process view. Health behavior change is subdivided into two processes: (a) the motivation phase, where intentions are developed, and (b) the volition phase, where these intentions are translated into action. The development of an intention or goal is a motivational process quite different from the subsequent preparation, performance, and evaluation of the desired action. In fact, the translation of intention into action appears to be the most challenging research issue. In the *motivation phase*, the question is how to move people to enter into the necessary contemplation process. Risk communication is still the technique practiced most often in health education. Making people believe that they are at risk for a certain disease is expected to bring about change. However, risk perception can backfire if individuals feel overwhelmed by the threat. Instead, they may choose to respond with defense or reactance. Some degree of risk perception can set the stage for subsequent contemplation and motivation to change, but it must be accompanied by other cognitions, in particular by outcome expectancies and perceived self-efficacy (Bandura, 1997). In the motivation phase, people choose which actions to take, whereas in the action or *volition phase* they plan the details, act, persist, possibly fail, and then recover. When a preference for a particular health behavior has been shaped, the intention needs to be transformed into detailed instructions on how to perform the desired action. Mental process simulation can bring people on track and ease them into the desired but difficult activity. Self-efficacy beliefs influence the cognitive construction of specific action plans, for example by visualizing scenarios that may guide goal attainment (Bandura, 1997). These postdecisional, preactional cognitions are necessary because otherwise the person would act impulsively in a trial-and-error fashion and would not know where to allocate the available resources.

When an action is being performed, self-efficacy determines the amount of effort invested and the level of perseverance. People who harbor self-doubts are more inclined to anticipate failure scenarios, worry about possible performance deficiencies, and abort their attempts prematurely. People with an optimistic sense of self-efficacy, on the other hand, visualize success scenarios that guide the action and let them persevere, even in the face of obstacles. They recover quickly when running into unforeseen difficulties.

This health behavior change model is regarded as a heuristic to better understand the complex mechanisms that operate when people become motivated to change and when they attempt to resist temptations. It applies to all health-compromising and health-enhancing behaviors.

Health Promotion and Health Education

'An ounce of prevention is worth a pound of cure.' It is a truism that an investment in prevention pays off. Yet many people rely on expensive cures by health care providers because they do not feel responsible for their own health. They believe that there will be effective treatments for all ailments and do not realize that the cure, if possible at all, will be costly in terms of discomfort, time, money, and other resources. Since most chronic diseases, including the major killers heart disease and cancer, are at least partially caused by lifestyles, preventive health behaviors can make a difference. This is true even more so if the preventive focus is on quality of life, not just length of life. Therefore, people must be convinced to make informed and responsible choices that lead to improved health.

Health promotion is an umbrella term that includes all educational and political measures to assist people in modifying their lifestyle toward a state of optimal health. For example, public health efforts can aim at the creation of supportive environments or at limitations to the access of health-compromising foods or drugs. In comparison, *health education* represents a more narrow concept. It comprises all teaching and learning arrangements that facilitate voluntary health behavior change. By this, individuals and groups are offered opportunities, knowledge, skills, and resources to help them refrain from risk behaviors and adopt health behaviors in order to pursue a continuous improvement of their health and wellness. Health education can take place in a variety of settings, including schools and workplaces, and it can be best performed by Health Psychologists or by educators with training in Health Psychology.

Four modalities of health promotion are distinguished: (a) one-to-one approach, (b) small group intervention, (c) community-wide campaign, and (d) public policy measures. The wider the approach, the broader and more cost-effective the impact can be. However, each of the four modalities can be the most appropriate one, depending on the particular problem and the target population. For an addicted smoker who suffers from a physical condition, a clinical, individual setting might be most efficient, but when it comes to reducing the average cholesterol intake of the entire population, for example, community-wide or other broad-range public health approaches (such as media campaigns) are preferred. It is also important to find cost-effective ways of targeting mainly those people who are most responsive to interventions at the right point in time ('teachable moments'). Moreover, risk populations, where interventions would be most effective, need to be identified. For example, gays constitute a risk population for HIV infection, teenagers are at risk for developing smoking and drug use habits, and the elderly are a risk population for a sedentary lifestyle. On the other hand, research resources need to be allocated to uncover the reasons for nonresponsiveness of some target groups.

Seen from a global perspective, it is not affordable to choose one-to-one interventions to change risk behaviors in millions of people in countries where health services are undeveloped. The primary role of Health Psychologists in Third World countries is at the level of designing and evaluating theory-based interventions by using the mass media or other educational means that reach larger groups. There is a particular challenge to reach also those who are refractory to any behavior changes. There is, for example, remarkable progress in the habitual condom use of risk populations in some parts of Asia (e.g., Thailand), after major educational efforts had been undertaken.

23.4 SUMMARY AND OUTLOOK

During its short history, Health Psychology has made substantial progress in establishing itself as a discipline. In particular, coping with chronic illness, behavioral etiology of certain diseases, and adoption and maintenance of health behaviors have been targets for research and practice. However, there is no magic bullet available that could serve as an immediate remedy to alter risk behaviors because human cognitions, emotions, and behaviors are highly complex and cannot be changed by a quick-fix approach.

The emergence of dynamic health behavior theories that describe the processes of behavior change is promising. These theories aim to identify the most powerful components within programs intended to bring about change and to tailor the intervention to a particular phase where the individual is optimally predisposed

for health messages and social influence. Modern change programs consider the cognitive and emotional prerequisites and barriers, and they help people set ambitious health goals, make realistic action plans, support strategies for maintenance, and facilitate recovery from setbacks. Health habits or risk behaviors should not be seen as isolated phenomena, but should be regarded as part of one's lifestyle that may have a functional value in coping with life. Simply applying a technology to remove a bad habit does not account for the fact that the habit is embedded in one's lifestyle and may fulfill an important role. Further, intervention models should be long-lasting, comprehensive, and cost-effective.

Life is in general more or less stressful, and continuous stress may eventually result in acute or chronic illness or in physical dysfunction. Stress compromises the immune system, among others, and renders people more vulnerable toward infections and neoplastic diseases. Exposure to environmental or social stressors (e.g., job stress) is one aspect, individual differences in coping with stress is another ('It's not the load that breaks you down, it's the way you carry it'). Health Psychology deals with the various pathways that translate the experience of stress into physiological malfunctioning and physical illness. It also investigates the resources that may buffer stress, for instance competence, beliefs, and social support. Improving social networks along with the individual's skills to mobilize them and use them becomes an important agenda for Health Psychology.

Coping with chronic illness is also a resource-driven process. It has been found that resourceful patients recover more quickly after surgery and readjust better to long-term disability or terminal disease (Schröder et al., 1997). Health Psychology can provide the knowledge of critical mechanisms, help people prepare for stressful medical interventions, and guide them through a difficult life course. If recovery is not possible, the focus needs to be on quality of life. If life is unbearable, there must be ways to allow patients, doctors, and relatives to collaborate on the ethically controversial issue of dignified dying by one's own will.

It is important to nurture and develop further communication and collaboration between the various disciplines involved, such as Health Psychology, medicine, and public health, as well as health services. The particular contribution that Health Psychology is able to make has not yet been fully recognized and acknowledged. Health Psychology is deeply rooted in promising and powerful psychological theories, and it adheres to high methodological standards that make it especially suitable for the advancement of health sciences and health practice.

RESOURCE REFERENCES

Adler, N., & Matthews, K. (1994). Health psychology: Why do some people get sick and some stay well? *Annual Review of Psychology, 45*, 229–259.

Bishop, G. (1994). *Health psychology. Integrating mind and body.* Boston, MA: Allyn & Bacon.

Cohen, S., & Herbert, T. B. (1996). Psychological factors and physical disease from the perspective of human psychoneuroimmunology. *Annual Review of Psychology, 47*, 113–142.

Conner, M., & Norman, P. (Eds.). (1996). *Predicting health behavior.* Buckingham, UK: Open University Press.

Friedman, H. S. (Ed.). (1998). *Encyclopedia of mental health.* San Diego, CA: Academic Press.

Ogden, J. (1996). *Health psychology. A textbook.* Buckingham, UK: Open University Press.

Petrie, K. J., & Weinman, J. A. (Eds.). (1997). *Perceptions of health and illness.* Amsterdam, The Netherlands: Harwood Academic Publishers.

Schwarzer, R. (Ed.). (1997). *Gesundheitspsychologie. Ein Lehrbuch* (2nd ed.) [Health psychology. A textbook]. Göttingen, Germany: Hogrefe.

Taylor, S. E. (1998). *Health psychology* (4th ed.). New York: McGraw-Hill.

ADDITIONAL LITERATURE CITED

Bandura, A. (1997). *Self-efficacy: The exercise of control.* New York: Freeman.

Beehr, T. A., & McGrath, J. E. (1996). The methodology of research on coping: Conceptual, strategic, and operational-level issues. In M. Zeidner & N. S. Endler (Eds.), *Handbook of coping – Theory, research, applications* (pp. 65–82). New York: Wiley.

Berkman, L. F., & Breslow, L. (1983). *Health and ways of living: The Alameda County Study.* London: Oxford University Press.

Berkman, L. F., Leo-Summers, L., & Horwitz, R. I. (1992). Emotional support and survival following myocardial infarction: A prospective population-based study of the elderly. *Annual Review of International Medicine, 117*, 1003–1009.

Carver, C. S., Pozo, C., Harris, S. D., Noriega, V., Scheier, M. F., Robinson, D. S., Ketcham, A. S., Moffat, F. L., & Clark, K. C. (1993). How coping mediates the effect of optimism on distress: A study of women with early stage breast cancer. *Journal of Personality and Social Psychology, 65*, 375–390.

Case, R. B., Moss, A. J., Case, N., et al. (1992). Living alone after myocardial infarction. *Journal of the American Medical Association, 267*, 515–519.

DiClemente, C. C., & Prochaska, J. O. (1982). Self-change and therapy change of smoking behaviour: A comparison of processes of change in cessation and maintenance. *Addictive Behaviours, 7*, 133–142.

Dijkstra, A., De Vries, H., Roijackers, J., & Breukelen, G. van (1998). Tailored interventions to communicate stage-matched information to smokers in different motivational stages. *Journal of Consulting and Clinical Psychology, 66*(3), 42–58.

Duncan, T. E., & McAuley, E. (1993). Social support and efficacy cognitions in exercise adherence: A latent growth curve analysis. *Journal of Behavioral Medicine, 16*, 199–218.

Eysenck, H. J. (1994). Cancer, personality and stress: Prediction and prevention. *Advances in Behaviour Research and Therapy, 16*, 167–215.

Fernandez-Ballesteros, R., Ruiz, M. A., & Garde, S. (1998). Emotional expression in healthy women and those with breast cancer. *British Journal of Health Psychology, 3*, 41–50.

Friedman, H. (Ed.). (1990). *Personality and disease.* New York: Wiley.

Fuchs, R. (1997). *Psychologie und körperliche Bewegung* [Psychology and physical exercise]. Göttingen, Germany: Hogrefe.

Hahn, A., & Renner, B. (1998). Perception of health risks: How smoker status affects defensive optimism. *Anxiety, Stress, and Coping, 11*, 93–112.

Hobfoll, S. E. (1989). Conservation of resources: A new attempt at conceptualizing stress. *American Psychologist, 44*(3), 513–524.

Kamen-Siegel, L., Rodin, J., Seligman, M. E. P., & Dwyer, J. (1991). Explanatory style and cell-mediated immunity in elderly men and women. *Health Psychology, 10*, 229–235.

Kuhl, J. (1992). A theory of self-regulation: Action versus state orientation, self-discrimination, and some applications. *Applied Psychology: An International Review, 41*, 95–173.

Kulik, J. A., & Mahler, H. I. M. (1989). Social support and recovery from surgery. *Health Psychology, 8*, 221–238.

Lazarus, R. S. (1991). *Emotion and adaptation.* London: Oxford University Press.

Lazarus, R. S., & Folkman, S. (1984). *Stress, appraisal, and coping.* New York: Springer.

Matarazzo, J. D. (1980). Behavioral health and behavior medicine: Frontiers for a new health psychology. *American Psychologist, 35*, 807–817.

Matthews, K. A., & Haynes, S. G. (1986). Type A behavior pattern and coronary disease risk. *American Journal of Epidemiology, 123*, 923–960.

Mermelstein, R. J., Cohen, S., Lichtenstein, E., Baer, J. S., & Kamarck, T. (1986). Social support and smoking cessation and maintenance. *Journal of Consulting and Clinical Psychology, 54*(4), 447–453.

Orth-Gomer, K., Unden, A. L., & Edwards, M. E. (1988). Social isolation and mortality in ischemic heart disease. *Acta Medicine of Scandinavia, 224,* 205–215.

Ruberman, W., Weinblatt, E., Goldberg, J. D., & Chaudhary, B. S. (1984). Psychological influences on mortality after myocardial infarction. *New England Journal of Medicine, 311,* 552–559.

Sallis, J. F., Hovell, M. F., & Hofstetter, C. R. (1992). Predictors of adoption and maintenance of vigorous physical activity in men and women. *Preventive Medicine, 21,* 237–251.

Scheier, M. F., & Carver, C. S. (1985). Optimism, coping, and health: Assessment and implications of generalized outcome expectancies. *Health Psychology, 4,* 219–247.

Scheier, M. F., Matthews, K. A., Owens, J., Magovern, G. J. Sr., Lefebre, R. C., Abbott, R. A., & Carver, C. S. (1989). Dispositional optimism and recovery from coronary artery bypass surgery: The beneficial effects on physical and psychological well-being. *Journal of Personality and Social Psychology, 57,* 1024–1040.

Schröder, K., Schwarzer, R., & Endler, N. S. (1997). Predicting cardiac patients' quality of life from the characteristics of their spouses. *Journal of Health Psychology, 2*(2), 231–244.

Schwarzer, R. (Ed.). (1992). *Self-efficacy: Thought control of action.* Washington, DC: Hemisphere.

Schwarzer, R. (1999). Self-regulatory processes in the adoption and maintenance of health behaviors: The role of optimism, goals, and threats. *Journal of Health Psychology, 4*(2), 115–127.

Schwarzer, R., & Fuchs, R. (1996). Self-efficacy and health behaviours. In M. Conner & P. Norman (Eds.), *Predicting health behaviour* (pp. 163–196). Buckingham, UK: Open University Press.

Schwarzer, R., Jerusalem, M., & Kleine, D. (1990). Predicting adolescent health complaints by personality and behaviors. *Psychology and Health: An International Journal, 4,* 233–244.

Schwarzer, R., & Schwarzer, C. (1996). A critical survey of coping instruments. In M. Zeidner & N. S. Endler (Eds.), *Handbook of coping – Theory,* research, applications (pp. 107–132). New York: Wiley.

Seeman, T. E., Berkman, L. F., Blazer, D., et al. (1994). Social ties and support and neuroendocrine function: The MacArthur studies of successful aging. *Annual of Behavioral Medicine, 16,* 95–106.

Seligman, M. E. P. (1991). *Learned optimism.* New York: Knopf.

Siegrist, J. (1996). *Soziale Krisen und Gesundheit* [Social crises and health]. Göttingen, Germany: Hogrefe.

Suarez, L., Lloyd, L., Weiss, N., et al. (1994). Effect of social networks on cancer-screening behavior of older Mexican-American women. *Journal of the National Cancer Institute, 86,* 775–779.

Suls, J., & Fletcher, B. (1985). The relative efficacy of avoidant and nonavoidant coping strategies: A meta-analysis. *Health Psychology, 4,* 249–288.

Temoshok, L., & Dreher, H. (1992). *The type C connection.* New York: Random House.

Wallston, K. A. (1994). Theoretically based strategies for health behavior change. In M. P. O'Donnell & J. S. Harris (Eds.), *Health promotion in the workplace* (2nd ed., pp. 185–203). Albany, NY: Delmar.

Weinstein, N. D. (1993). Testing four competing theories of health-protective behaviour. *Health Psychology, 12,* 324–333.

Weinstein, N. D., Rothman, A. J., & Sutton, S. R. (1998). Stage theories of health behavior: Conceptual and methodological issues. *Health Psychology, 17*(3), 290–299.

Williams, R. B., Barefoot, J. C., Califf, R. M., et al. (1992). Prognostic importance of social and economic resources among medically treated patients with angiographically documented coronary artery disease. *Journal of the American Medical Association, 267,* 520–524.

Wills, T. A. (1998). Substance abuse. In H. S. Friedman (Ed.), *Encyclopedia of mental health* (pp. 607–619). San Diego, CA: Academic Press.

Communications concerning this chapter should be addressed to: Professor Ralf Schwarzer, Freie Universität Berlin, Institut für Arbeits-, Organisations- und Gesundheitspsychologie – WE 10, Habelschwerdter Allee 45, 14195 Berlin, Germany

24

Psychology in Education and Instruction

ROBERT L. BURDEN

One area of human endeavor to which psychologists have devoted a considerable amount of time and both academic and professional investment is that of education. From its earliest beginnings in Europe and the USA psychology has been represented by pioneers dedicated to solving some of the most complex mysteries of human development. How do people learn? Do babies, children, and adults learn in the same way? Is the process of human learning basically the same as that of animals? Why do some children seem to learn very quickly whilst others struggle to master even the simplest mental tasks? How much, if anything, can we learn without being taught? What makes a good teacher? Are some forms of learning more difficult or more worthwhile than others? How much of what we learn is shaped by our cultural environment?

These and thousands of similar questions have been investigated in one way or another by psychologists at various times throughout the past century. Because such investigations can legitimately be considered to be related to the process of becoming educated, they have tended to be seen as representing that branch of psychology normally referred to as *educational psychology*, although the dividing lines between educational, developmental, social, and even clinical psychology are not always easy to distinguish.

Educational psychology is a far more complex area than its title might seem to imply. At first sight, the marriage of psychological theories, principles, and methods to various aspects of educational practice appears to be relatively straightforward and uncontentious. Indeed, such a long-held assumption would seem to underpin a recent and widely accepted definition of educational psychology, produced by the American Psychological Association (APA), which refers to 'the application of psychology to education by focusing on the development, evaluation and application of theories and principles of learning and instruction that can enhance lifelong learning' (Kaplan, 1990).

However, a few moments' reflection should reveal that such a definition begs a number of important questions. Firstly, it suggests that a narrow focus on learning and instruction represents those areas of education alone to which psychology can and should be applied. Secondly, in fostering a simple additive model, it denies the possibility that educational psychology might exist as a unique discipline with its own developed theories and methods. This definition might also be interpreted as suggesting that there is general agreement amongst psychologists in their understanding of what is involved in successful learning and instruction, when little could be further from the truth. In fact, as will be demonstrated in the next section, the history of educational psychology can be largely represented in terms of contrasting theories about what is meant by learning and how humans learn.

The first purpose of this chapter, therefore, will be to trace some important historical developments in educational psychology from the work of the early pioneers who attempted to construct general theories of learning which could be applied right across the phylogenetic scale. In parallel with this has been an associated interest in theories of teaching or, as it has been commonly referred to in the United States, instruction. Subsequent developments in Europe, and even more recently in non-Western societies, have led firstly to an emphasis upon the individual within the learning process and then to a focus upon the importance of context and culture, as will be revealed in a later section. Further issues which will be explored relate to the practical applicability of psychological theories within education and the evolution of *school psychology* as a profession of applied educational psychologists, the nature and appropriateness of different forms of research within educational psychology, and, finally, a reconceptualization of the discipline which is grounded more within recent developmental, social, and educational theory than within a traditional psychological approach based upon the physical sciences.

24.1 Historical Overview

In many ways the history of educational psychology, in its early years at least, mirrors the evolution of theories of learning. Phye (1993) suggests, for example, that conceptions of learning have evolved from an essentially transactional perspective, as epitomized in the early writings of William James and John Dewey, through the environment-focused emphasis of Skinnerian behaviorism, leading to an inner-centered reaction of cognitive approaches, only to return once more to transactional perspectives as provided by the socio-cultural theories of Vygotsky and his followers.

To begin at the beginning, it could be argued that much of early American psychology was synonymous with educational psychology. Certainly, the definition by William James of psychology as 'the science of mental life' in his seminal text *The Principles of Psychology* (1890) lent itself naturally to the investigation of such questions as 'How do people learn?' James is considered by many to be the father of modern psychology, at least in the USA, who conceived of mind as a function rather than an entity and emphasized the dynamic nature of the interplay between accumulated habits and conscious thoughts. By doing so he sought to synthesize empiricist/reductionist and holistic views of thinking and learning. In one famous metaphor, he likened thoughts to ripples or waves on a lake formed by the oscillatory dynamics of the brain and nervous system. He later attempted to relate his *functionalist* ideas to education in a series of highly influential talks to teachers, thereby placing educational psychology at the very center of the newly developing discipline of psychology.

Many of James' ideas were taken up and built upon by John Dewey who developed the notion of action and of learners as active participants functioning in a cyclical, transactional manner with their environments. Thinking was thereby interpreted as a form of action to be encouraged within the educational context. For Dewey, engagement in problem-solving activity genuinely arising within specific contexts was one of the primary functions of education. Here the role of the teacher is to act as a facilitator in enabling students to solve the problems that they meet, rather than as an instructor aiming to achieve specific, pre-determined goals.

At this point we can see a division emerging between the fundamental beliefs of the early pioneers in educational psychology as to how learning should be conceived and studied and the importance of the role played by the teacher or instructor in this process. It could be argued that much of educational psychology since that time has been devoted to one or another aspect of that debate.

Another important distinction that began to emerge at this time was the differing emphasis that succeeding theorists placed upon the importance of *thinking* in the learning process. Dewey in particular emphasized the involvement of thinking as essential in developing learning in a broader context than the mere accumulation of isolated skills. He saw thinking as itself being stimulated by engagement with genuine problem-solving activities, with its enhancement therefore becoming a primary function of education.

Educational psychology, however, began to be pulled in another direction, reflecting an increasing determination by mainstream psychology to be recognized as a science on a par with the natural sciences. One of the earliest and most influential exponents of taking a scientific approach to educational psychology was Edward Thorndike, considered by many to be the founder of educational psychology as a separate discipline. Through his 40 years of research into such areas as attention, memory, and learning habits and his experimental approach to teacher training, Thorndike promulgated an empiricist approach to developing knowledge in the new discipline, an approach which was firmly rooted in theories of learning derived from a reductionist perspective. In this way he developed such influential psychological constructs as learning curves, feedback and reinforcement, and massed vs. spaced learning (Walberg & Haertel, 1992).

For Thorndike, educational psychology was seen as providing 'knowledge of the original nature of man and of the laws of modifiability or learning, in the case of intellect, character, and skill' (Thorndike, 1913, p. 1), thereby setting the scene for much of what was to follow. One consequence was a longstanding emphasis upon the importance of empirical and scientific study for educational psychology with the aim of discovering and organizing new knowledge related to pedagogy. This also led in Thorndike's case and in those of many subsequent educational psychologists to the production of textbooks on the application of psychological principles to a variety of school subject areas such as mathematics and literacy.

It should be noted at this point that educational psychology was developing elsewhere than in the United States. The work of Alfred Binet in France in constructing what is generally recognized as the world's first intelligence test was taken up by Terman in the United States and later by Burt in the UK as a means of highly significant social intervention. In the USA this led to the Army Alpha Examination and Terman's lifelong work on the origins and consequences of giftedness, whilst in the UK several generations of professional educational psychologists based the bulk of their contributions to schools on their understanding (often misguided) of the predictive validity of the IQ. Moreover, the whole of the British secondary educational system was restructured after World War II on the basis of ability testing at the age of 11 as the best possible predictor of later academic success.

Within the United States, however, an even more powerful force was emerging with the rise of *behaviorism*. The roots of this approach can be traced back to early Associationist ideas and the learning theories of Hull, Spence, Guthrie, and others (see Hilgard & Bower, 1966, for a thorough review of such theories) and to Soviet work, particularly that of Ivan Pavlov, on classical conditioning. The strongest early advocate of behaviorism was J. B. Watson who rejected all mentalistic concepts of thought and claimed instead that learning and behavior could best be accounted for in terms of stimulus–response contingencies.

These early ideas were taken up by B. F. Skinner who is generally considered to be the central figure in the rise of behaviorism as the predominant force in educational psychology in the United States (and to a somewhat lesser extent in the UK and the rest of the world) during the 1950s, 1960s, and early 1970s. Moreover, it is still the case that many ideas arising from Skinnerian behaviorism, such as the importance of reinforcement in learning and instruction, the relative effectiveness of rewards and punishments, criterion-referenced testing, and objectives-based curricular activities, dominate much of current educational debate.

The unique contribution that Skinner made to behaviorism was to introduce the notion of *operants*, i.e., the range of behaviors that organisms perform or are capable of performing. By shifting the emphasis from the stimulus in the S–R (stimulus–response) chain to a focus upon the ways in which behavior is shaped by the consequences of previous behavior, i.e., by emphasizing the importance of the environment, Skinner was able to represent learning in terms of a change in response rate following reinforcement. Learning was therefore seen as only that behavior which was observable, with short shrift being given to considerations of hidden purposes or meanings behind any actions. It was not that Skinner rejected such mentalistic notions, but that he saw them as unhelpful and attempted instead to account for all human activities in environmental terms.

In directing his ideas towards the improvement of instruction in schools (for behaviorism is essentially concerned with ways in which the instructor as reinforcing agent can manipulate and control environmental contingencies), Skinner suggested four simple procedures which he incorporated into his ideas on *programmed learning*. These were that

- teachers should make explicit what is to be taught;
- tasks should be broken down into small, sequential steps;
- students should be encouraged to work at their own pace by means of individualized learning programs;
- learning should be 'programmed' by incorporating the above procedures and providing immediate positive reinforcement based as nearly as possible on 100% success.

Programmed learning achieved a brief spell of success, but proved to be of limited attraction to most teachers interacting with their students in more meaningful ways. It did have a continuing powerful influence within the field of foreign language learning, however, where the popular approach known as *audiolingualism* was based upon the development of good language habits involving pattern drills, memorization of dialogues, or choral repetition of structural patterns, all of which were accompanied by abundant 'reinforcing' praise. Nevertheless, as in other educational areas, the passive role afforded to the learner and the lack of attention to the application of meaningful cognitive strategies in learning a new language meant that here too the influence of behaviorism was inevitably limited.

Partly as a reaction to behaviorism led by the distinguished linguist Noam Chomsky, but also quite independently in Europe, a cognitive revolution was taking place in the 1960s as an alternative approach to understanding how learning occurs. Although *cognitive* theory is commonly presented as the main significant rival to behaviorism, it would nevertheless be far too simplistic to present this as one coherent approach or even several related approaches. What cognitive theories of learning have in common is a concern with how the human mind thinks and learns. (Even to make this point is to suggest a mind/body dualism with which not all cognitive psychologists would agree.) How they approach that particular issue, however, is vastly different. At the same time, it should be noted that some forms of cognitive theory are constantly evolving and building upon what has gone before.

In the USA cognitive psychology came to be largely synonymous with *information-processing* models of the mind. Returning to Dewey's earlier preoccupation with problem-solving, Herbert Simon, one of the creators of the concept of artificial intelligence, began in the 1960s to simulate on the computer possible ways in which the mind might deal with such problems. From this a whole range of possible applications to human learning were developed, particularly with reference to such areas as attention, memory, knowledge acquisition, and reading. Subsequent work became directed towards the differences between novice and expert learners and to ways in which cognitive and metacognitive strategies might be usefully employed for overcoming various forms of learning difficulties (Walberg & Haertel, 1992).

Despite the refreshing emphasis upon the active role of the learner within the learning process that information-processing approaches were able to bring to bear, in their extreme form they nevertheless placed little or no emphasis upon the ways in which individuals developed the power to think and learn nor upon the

personal sense that individuals made of learning opportunities. By contrast, the *radical constructivist* approach of the Swiss developmental psychologist, Jean Piaget, emphasized the ways in which right from birth human infants began to explore their environments through various senses and thereby construct their own personal knowledge of the world. Piaget's *genetic epistemology* is far too complex to describe in a few brief paragraphs and the interested reader is referred to Elkind (1976) and Furth (1970) for excellent summaries of various key aspects of his work and its contribution to education. The important point to emphasize here is the main underlying assumption of constructivism that individuals are actively involved throughout their lives in constructing personal meaning from their experiences.

In many respects Piaget was much more concerned with understanding how knowledge is constructed than with the practical applications of his theories. Nevertheless, he has had a profound effect upon pedagogical practice in Europe, particularly during the 1960s. Some of the resultant assumptions were entirely sensible, such as the importance of taking account of learners' unique ways of constructing meaning, the relationship between thinking and learning, the nature of developmental stages and the need to match the requirements of any task to the cognitive level of which a learner is capable. Piagetian concepts such as *schema, assimilation,* and *accommodation* have also made a useful contribution to our understanding of educational processes. However, there have also been misinterpretations of Piagetian theory, the most dangerous of which has been the assumption in some quarters that there is no place for direct instruction in teaching since children must be left to learn at their own rate. It is also possible that Piaget, particularly in his early work, underestimated the importance of language and the social context in the development of thought.

An important figure in introducing the work of Piaget to American audiences has been Jerome Bruner, who became a persuasive advocate for the discovery approach to learning. A true educationalist, like Dewey before him, Bruner considered the process of education to be at least as important as its product. Recognizing that learning in schools should be seen to have a purpose, Bruner posed the challenge for educators to find the optimum conditions for learning. He offered advice on the structure of the curriculum as well as on ways in which learners could be motivated and helped to remember what they had learned. An original thinker in his own right, Bruner also extended aspects of Piagetian theory by suggesting that educators needed to take into account different modes of thinking – *enactive, iconic,* and *symbolic* modes of thought.

Bruner can also be considered a significant 'bridging' figure in the history of educational psychology because of his discovery on a trip to the Soviet Union in the 1960s of the work of the great Russian educational psychology Lev Vygotsky and his part in arranging for the translation of Vygotsky's key work *Thought and Language* into English. For Vygotsky the socio-cultural background within which learning took place was of vital importance, as also was the application of language in the development of thought. In contrast to Piaget, Vygotsky empha-sized the social context into which children are born and the way in which their thinking was shaped by that context. In particular, Vygotsky was interested in the ways in which more com-petent adults or peers guided the novice child into and through what he termed the *zone of proximal development*, that level of skill or knowledge which is just beyond that with which the learner is currently capable of coping.

With Vygotsky we can see the pedagogical seesaw swing back once more to the importance of the teacher in the learning process. The term used by Vygotsky was *mediation*, which he considered took place by means of various tools, the most important of which was language, as well as by other semiotic means. This concept of mediation has been independently developed by the Israeli psychologist and educator, Reuven Feuerstein in his theory of *structural cognitive modifiability*. Feuerstein combined elements of Piagetian and Vygotskian theory with aspects of behavioral analysis and reinforcement to pro-duce a cognitive development program known as *Instrumental Enrichment* together with a form of dynamic assessment which is implemented by means of his *Learning Potential Assessment Device* (LPAD). Essentially, Feuerstein argues that any person of any age, however handi-capped, can become a fully effective learner, the key to which lies in the efficiency of the *mediation* process by which that person is taught. Much of Feuerstein's later work was devoted to the identification of key aspects of mediated learning experiences which underpin his intervention program.

A final few words in this historical overview should be afforded to a group of psychologists working in parallel with their behaviorist and cognitive counterparts but emphasizing far more the holistic, affective aspects of human develop-ment and education. Referred to in general as *humanistic* psychologists, this group includes such significant figures as Abraham Maslow and Carl Rogers. Rogers in particular emphasized that independence, creativity, and self-reliance are most likely to flourish in learning situations where external criticism is kept to a minimum and where self-evaluation is encouraged. At the same time, he considered that the most socially useful kind of learning to prepare young people to cope with the demands of the modern world is learning about the process of learning itself. This, he felt, could best be accomplished in an atmosphere of 'unconditional positive regard'. Thus a vitally important element of all good teaching is to convey warmth and empathy towards the learner in order to establish con-fidence and a relationship of trust.

This overview of some historically central figures and ideas influencing the development and direction of educational psychology over its first hundred or so years has revealed both its cyclical and often contradictory nature. The predominance of one set of ideas over another appears to have been as much due to the exigencies of time, place, and fashion as to any coherent sense of knowledge progression or the emergence of an overarching meta-theory.

24.2 EDUCATIONAL THEORY VERSUS PSYCHOLOGICAL PRACTICE

One of the dilemmas faced by educational psy-chology is reflected in the title of a highly influential textbook, *Educational Psychology: A realistic approach* (Good & Brophy, 1977). What was recognized by these authors was the gap that many educational practitioners noted between theories of learning and the practice of teaching. They begin with the basic assumption that the key to successful teaching is the *inte-gration* of concepts into *teaching strategies* that are responsive to the learning needs of particular groups of students. Thus, they stress the need to interpret psychological concepts so that they apply to specific learning settings and emphasize pragmatic decision-making by teachers faced by realistic problems, constraints and limitations in students, in classes, and in themselves.

Good and Brophy take an eclectic approach in seeking to draw together various theories, concepts, and research findings in educational psychology in so far as these enable them to offer concrete advice to teachers. Their overall approach is nevertheless objectives-based in that each chapter of their text begins with a brief list of specific behavioral objectives that will have been attained once the reader has mastered the material provided in that chapter. Moreover, the successful teacher in their terms is one who makes her or his goals explicit, uses class work as a means of attaining these goals, and uses feedback to determine how well the goals are being achieved. Task-analysis is seen as a helpful means of sequencing activities, but emphasis is placed also on the importance of what the student brings to the learning situation and the constraints of the learning context.

Good and Brophy's classic text is a first-class example of this particular genre in that it represents much that has been found to be of value in the application of psychological theory to education. However, it also illustrates some of the inherent weaknesses in that chapters are grouped in various sections side by side without any explicit coherent thread drawing them together. This, after all, is one of the features of eclecticism. Thus, there is a section on various aspects of child development, followed by a section contrasting behavioral and cognitive approaches to learning, and sections on motivation, classroom management, instruction, individual differences, and measurement and evaluation. The advice to teachers under each of these headings is often excellent, but the depth of psychological theory upon which it is based is not always readily apparent, particularly if one seeks a coherent thread which binds the various sections together.

One severe and influential critic of his own field of educational psychology has been David Ausubel, who described it as 'a superficial, ill digested and typically disjointed and watered-down miscellany of general psychology, learning theory, developmental psychology, social psychology, psychological measurement . . . and child centered education' (Ausubel, 1968, p. 1). This withering attack was one which received substantial support from many in the 1960s and 1970s as highlighting the fact that educational psychology had lost its way. In trying to apply 'psychological science' to every educational issue under the sun, educational psychology, it was claimed, had become a ragbag of studies and dogma unconnected by any form of coherent theoretical structure.

The approach taken by Ausubel was to focus more narrowly but in far greater depth than many of his contemporaries on what actually took place in classrooms, most specifically in a cognitive approach to school learning. His work was even more specifically concerned with *meaningful symbolic* learning which occurred both by means of direct instruction and by discovery. From this, it should be noted, he deliberately excluded the learning of values and attitudes.

This tension between practical relevance and theoretical coherence is one which has bedevilled educational psychology from its earliest beginnings. In seeking to classify itself as a science on a par with the natural sciences, mainstream psychology has tended to take the

empirical route in its acceptance of what constitutes evidence and to favor by patterns-testing, experimental designs in its pursuit of that evidence. In seeking respectability it has therefore allied itself philosophically with logical positivism and has constructed its theories accordingly. This assumption of rational objectivity is not one, however, which necessarily fits easily with everyone's conceptions of education. Here, for example, values have a central role to play, as do beliefs and the search for meaning.

Moreover, the goals of education can be viewed as somewhat at variance with the view of psychology as an objective science. If, for example, two primary educational goals are seen as the intergenerational transmission of culture and the preparation of people to meet the learning demands of a rapidly changing world, then a more integrated, theory-driven conceptualization of educational psychology may be called for. In place of the 'middleman' conception of James and Dewey, linking a science to an art by some form of bridging process, or of the view of educational psychology as a 'masterscience', acting as some kind of 'umbrella' for psychologists and other scientists who just happen to be interested in the problems of education, there is a strong case to be made for educational psychology as a discipline in its own right.

A valiant attempt to get to grips with this dilemma has been made by a working party commissioned by the British Psychological Society to provide evidence to the United Kingdom Council for the Accreditation of Teacher Education (Tomlinson, Edwards, Finn, Smith, & Wilkinson, 1992). Whilst acknowledging that pedagogy must be seen as pluralist and inter-disciplinary in its resources, the document produced by this group argues for the centrality of psychology in that a psychological perspective is by definition concerned with the nature of action and experience within and between individuals. The document begins broadly by suggesting that teachers need to have practically applicable understanding of

- the nature of the intended learning outcomes they are attempting to achieve;
- the learning experiences and activities that can lead to these acquisitions;
- the internal and external influences on action which may affect these activities; and
- the ways learners vary as individuals and groups.

Given such understanding, teachers should be in a position to identify helpful strategies for managing effective learning activity which is appropriately matched to particular pupils, teaching aims and contexts, and effectively assessed for progress and achievement.

From a psychological perspective, intended learning outcomes can be viewed as cognitive, behavioral, and affective (knowledge, skills, and attitudes). The learning experiences and activities will entail the acquisition of concepts, knowledge, and understanding, the development of skills and learning strategies, and the shaping up of attitudes. Internal and external influences on action reflect the nature of motivational processes, social communication and group processes, and the effect of school organization and climate. The importance of the nature of individual and developmental variation among learners is revealed in a consideration of special educational needs as these relate to aims and processes of learning and teaching, equal opportunities, provision and issues relating to race, gender, and class.

Teachers need to be able to deploy a range of teaching tactics, strategies, and styles in order to achieve particular purposes. These will include explanation, questioning, the management of group discussion, and various forms of teacher–pupil interaction including the appropriate use of rewards and sanctions. Appropriate matching of tasks to pupils requires not only an awareness of individual pupil differences and an ability to analyze tasks, but also a critical awareness of the potential effects of different forms of pupil grouping for learning. Finally, it is essential that teachers understand the differences between formative and summative assessment and can carry these out by means of norm-referenced and criterion-referenced techniques on their pupils' and their own work and encourage their pupils to do the same.

A particularly helpful aspect of this kind of approach is that it provides a comprehensive framework within which the complex nature of the teaching–learning process can be encompassed. As such it represents one form of the *social interactionist* model represented in Figure 24.1.

This model suggests that there are four key elements involved in the educational process: *teachers*, *learners*, *tasks (or activities)*, and *contexts*, all of which constantly interact in a dynamic manner. Teachers bring to this process their beliefs and attitudes about education, about schools, about learner potential, and about their own capabilities. They also bring their own particular interests, values, and abilities. Each individual learner brings her or his own characteristics and orientations towards learning and towards schools as institutions. Schools and other educational institutions, families, and communities are the main contexts within which learning takes place and, as such, exert a powerful influence upon the nature of what is learnt and upon the teaching–learning process. Within such con-

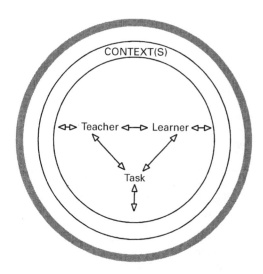

Figure 24.1 *A social interactionist model of learning*

texts both the formal and informal (or 'hidden') curriculum determine the nature of the learning tasks and activities, the implementation of which is itself influenced by the teacher's beliefs and other characteristics and the learner's ability and willingness to learn. The purpose of educational psychology can be seen, therefore, as providing information about each of these elements together with a deeper level of understanding about how such knowledge can be employed to enhance the educational process.

The question nevertheless remains as to how helpful information and ideas acruing from psychological theory and research can best be made available to those more centrally involved in the process of education – teachers, parents, and the learners themselves. Attempts to face up to this issue have led to the separation of educational psychology into two distinct, but not always complementary strands (Burden, 1994). These are most commonly referred to as *educational* and *school* psychology, although the latter descriptor tends to vary from one part of the world to another; those who are termed school psychologists in the USA are called psycho-pedagogists in Italy, psychological counsellors in Portugal, and guidance officers in parts of Australia. In the UK, somewhat confusingly, both groups are referred to as educational psychologists, despite the fact that their terms of reference, their professional orientation, and even their main focus of interest are likely to differ markedly.

Although it is not the function of this chapter to describe the evolution and subsequent contribution of school psychology to education (see Saigh & Oakland, 1989, and Burden, 1994, for a review of international perspectives in this area), a brief overview of the main differences between the two groups should throw further light on some of the dilemmas alluded to earlier. As has been demonstrated in a previous section, the academic study of psychology in education has given rise to considerable research and theory building on ways of enhancing teaching and learning in particular, which tends to be disseminated in academic books and journals from university departments of psychology and education. In practical terms the information generated by such writings is most likely to be passed on to teachers in pre-service training courses or through research for higher degrees. Students demonstrating an interest in the practical manifestation of psychological knowledge to educational settings whilst undertaking first degree courses in psychology, on the other hand, are offered the opportunity of further study and training to become school psychologists. In the United States this normally entails study to at least Master's, but preferably Doctoral level. In the UK a similar pattern has emerged, with the additional requirement of at least three years' teaching experience. There is, however, considerable variation across the rest of the world in pre-service requirements for working as a school psychologist.

School psychologists are traditionally employed by local school boards or government education ministries and are based in schools, specialist clinics, or psychology service centers. From these bases they seek to provide advice and support of a psychological nature to schools, families, and communities in promoting the cognitive, social, and emotional development of children. In practice, particularly where statutory requirements for extra funding depends upon a psychological assessment and recommendation, the role of the school psychologist has tended to become rather more limited than would ideally be the case. In large measure, this situation appears not to have changed since a seminal paper by Bardon (1983) described school psychology as 'a specialty in search of an identity'.

The main differentiating issue here is most likely to be one of focus. How this focus is determined is inevitably a result of historical, economic, and socio-cultural factors. School psychologists tend to view themselves as applied educational psychologists. However, if we consider the development of applied educational psychology in the UK from its beginnings in the 1920s, it becomes clear that the overriding interest of the first appointed UK educational psychologist, Cyril Burt, in the development and employment of psychometric tests had a profound and long-standing influence on the future direction of professional practice. Similarly, the

introduction of psychodynamic ideas into educational psychology training a few years later led to the establishment of the Child Guidance movement which held sway until the mid-1970s. Thus, issues of assessment and therapeutic intervention became two major components of the work of the applied educational (school) psychologist in the UK for more than half a century.

It will not be possible to gain a proper understanding of the complexity of the issues surrounding the one-hundred-year history of educational psychology without an awareness of this major and, to many, incomprehensible division. It has led on the one hand to a view of educational psychology as a somewhat esoteric, academic subject divorced from the practical problems faced by teachers and learners in school settings and, on the other, to a view of school psychology as an essentially atheoretical profession seeking in an often futile manner to act as a 'fire-brigade' service to the ills of the educational system or as a much-maligned gatekeeper to sparse educational resources.

Neither of these extreme views is entirely appropriate, but each contains a germ of truth which has been more or less prevalent at various times within the history of both branches of educational psychology. A major task for both professions continues to be that of finding ways to draw them more closely together to develop a coherent theoretical foundation for applied practice within educational contexts such that illogical and unhelpful boundaries are removed. This issue will be returned to in the final section, but first we must turn to a consideration of differing approaches to psychological research and their applicability to educational issues.

24.3 RESEARCH

Educational psychology has been both helped and hindered in its close association with and dependence upon the notions of science and attendant research methodology prevalent within mainstream psychology. In particular, the legitimization of experimental and quasi-experimental research designs within the traditional logical-positivist paradigm has placed great emphasis upon the collection of empirical data and the recording of observable behavior at the expense of more introspective methods. This, in turn, has led to the proliferation of what has come to be termed *process–product* research (Shulman, 1986), seeking to identify the nature of relationships between teaching performance and student achievement. Examples of research within this tradition include examinations of the ways in which measurable student learning outcomes are affected by specific teacher actions, by the amount of 'academically involved' time and by aspects of classroom ecology. In his summary of research in this field, Creemers (1991) concludes that variation in teaching behaviors relates systematically to variation in learning outcomes both in cognitive and affective domains. However, there is still no common agreement within the literature as to what makes an excellent, good, or effective teacher.

A significant weakness of many process–product studies is that they seek to establish causality, often by means of correlation techniques, which at best can only indicate that an association is likely to exist between selected variables. Efforts to improve the sophistication of such studies led naturally to the application of *meta-analyses*, whereby data from a large number of studies are gathered and submitted to statistical analysis in a search for underlying stable relationships which go beyond the limitations of studies on particular teachers working in particular contexts. Other high-powered statistical techniques such as multiple regression analysis and structural equation modeling also make it possible to move beyond simple measures of association.

Two examples of meta-analytic studies which are pertinent to the concerns of the present chapter were carried out by the Australian educational psychologist John Hattie and his colleagues. In the first study (Hansford & Hattie, 1982) a meta-analysis was carried out on 128 studies into the relationship between measures of self-concept and measures of performance and achievement. This is an area of particular relevance to educational psychology because it is commonly assumed that such a relationship exists, even though the causal direction of that relationship is open to considerable dispute. It also illustrates very clearly many of the aspects of process–product research – the transformation of concepts like achievement and self-esteem into numbers by means of standardized tests or structured questionnaires, the application of those tests to matched samples of experimental and control groups, and the manipulation of the resultant data by means of appropriate statistical techniques.

By means of meta-analysis, Hansford and Hattie were able to draw upon a combined sample of over 2,000 subjects and produce a database of over 1,000 correlations between self-ratings and performance measures. By this means they came to draw the authoritative conclusion that a small but significant positive relationship exists between self-concept and achievement. More recent research has tended to suggest that initially the former will tend to be a reflection of

the latter but that over time a two-way reciprocal relationship develops.

Another meta-analytical study (Hattie & Marsh, 1996) examined 58 investigations into the relationship between research and teaching in universities, and synthesized their results. Here it was found that only 20% of the 498 correlations examined were significant, which led to the conclusion that, at best, research and teaching are very loosely coupled. Even single cases of 'the quintessential academician Nobel Prize winner who can enthrall an undergraduate class' were few and far between. The highest correlations were found between research and the presentation aspects of teaching, where good researchers were seen as a little more likely to be better prepared as teachers and to have better presentation skills than non-researchers.

As a result of a meta-analysis of some 8,000 comparative process–product studies, Fraser (1991) was able to identify nine factors as the chief influences on cognitive, affective, and behavioral learning. These factors were conveniently grouped under three headings:

- *student aptitude*, which included ability (or prior achievement as measured by psychometric tests), development (as indexed by chronological age or stage of maturation), and motivation;
- *instruction*, which included the amount of time in which students were engaged in learning, and the quality of instructional experience (including psychological and curricular aspects);
- *psychological environments*, which included the curriculum of the home, the morale of the classroom social group, the influence of the peer group, and optimum leisure-time television viewing.

There is clearly a close correspondence between most of these factors and those identified earlier within the social interactionist model.

The main alternative to process–product research studies has been offered by what are generally termed *interpretative-meaning centered* approaches (Shulman, 1986). Such research is sometimes referred to as 'post-positivist' or even, by its detractors, unscientific, in that it begins from a very different set of assumptions about the nature of knowledge and the ways in which this is constructed.

In contrast to the essentially pragmatic and often atheoretical nature of many process–product research studies, interpretative researchers view learning as a qualitative transformation of understandings rather than a quantitative accretion of information. Thus teaching ceases to be seen as a means of providing instruction and becomes instead a way of facilitating new understandings. Within this paradigm both teachers and students are viewed as learners in the sense that they actively construct their own meanings within every educational situation (Gergen, 1985). There are obvious parallels between these alternative approaches to research and the differences between behaviorist and constructivist theories of learning described in Section 24.2.

Interpretative research within educational psychology has tended to emphasize the ways in which learners seek to make sense of and bring meaning to their educational experiences. Research and theory in the area of motivation, for example, has been transformed by a change in emphasis from studies focusing on drive-reduction or reinforcement contingencies to one in which the cognitive involvement and decision-making processes of individuals are seen to play a central part (Ames & Ames, 1989). The search for effective ways of promoting self-directed learning has similarly benefited from a constructivist approach (Candy, 1991), as has the teaching of school curriculum subjects such as maths and science, particularly where emphasis is placed on what has come to be termed 'situated cognition' (Lave & Wenger, 1991). At the same time, a growth in interest in teacher belief systems and, in particular, the notion of teachers as 'reflective practitioners' (Schön, 1983) arose directly from this alternative interpretative approach to research.

Process–product and interpretative-meaning centered approaches to research are generally considered to be antithetical in that they represent different paradigmatic views of the world. However, a strong case has been made for combining the two approaches and selecting methods from each which will best suit the needs of any particular investigation (Denzin & Lincoln, 1994). Here the researcher is seen as 'bricoleur', perfectly entitled to collect large-scale empirical data and submit this to quantitative analysis in order to seek answers to one set of questions, and then justified in carrying out in-depth qualitative analyses of the meanings that the participants are constructing of the process under investigation. According to this perspective, the value of the research findings is likely to be enhanced by such a marriage of approaches.

A good example of this kind of combined research is provided by Mevarech and Kramarski (1997) in their description of their innovative instructional method for teaching mathematics in heterogeneous classrooms and their investigation into its effects on students' mathematics achievement. Based on social cognition and metacognition theories, the method consisted of three interdependent components: metacognitive activities, peer interpretation, and systematic provision of feedback-corrective enrichment. Two studies were carried out with seventh-grade students. The first focused on in-depth analyses of students' information processing under different learning conditions, the second investigated the development of students' mathematical reasoning over a full academic year. Both studies demonstrated significant improvements by the experimental groups in comparison with their control group peers. The authors conclude that all students can be taught higher cognitive processes (in maths) in heterogeneous classes without implementing tracking (setting) by ability. However, they emphasize also the necessity for individual teacher, departmental, and whole school commitment to the underlying principles of the particular program – in this case the principles of social cognition and metacognition.

It should be apparent that a central issue here has been one of whether educational psychology research should begin with questions about human activity in educational settings which it seeks to answer with all the means at its disposal, or whether it should be theory driven and seek to investigate the applicability of various psychological and developmental theories to issues and problems within education. As with the development of often conflicting theories of learning, much early research in educational psychology tended to fall between one or the other of these two extremes. This was a situation which existed in Europe as well as in the United States, as a review of forty years of research in educational psychology in Finland testifies (Olkinuora & Lehtinen, 1997).

24.4 A Wider International Perspective

The vast majority of textbooks written about educational psychology together with most of the research-related journals represent a tradition that is essentially positivist in its orientation and steeped in the culture of the United States and, to a lesser extent, Western Europe. As such they encourage an approach to theory and research which mirrors that of the natural sciences whilst taking as given certain virtues associated with a particular kind of formal education. Typical of such virtues are liberalism, rational morality, and the attainment of individual autonomy.

An alternative perspective which is more illustrative of traditional Eastern cultures is that of collectivism, reflected in the Confucian philosophy prevalent in such countries as China and Japan. In contrast to the Western emphasis upon the rights of the individual, emotional independence, personal initiative, and the search for self-fulfillment, collectivist societies stress collective identity, group decision-making, emotional dependence upon significant others, and the importance of roles, duties, and obligations.

Such cultural distinctions play a highly significant, if largely unrecognized part in the conceptualization and application of psychology to education in different parts of the world. Thus, in the construction and development of the self-concept, for example, a traditional Western view holds to the belief that every individual is a separate entity from every other and defined in terms of that individual's own internal thoughts, feelings, and actions. A mentally healthy individual tends to be seen as one who strives for autonomy and achieves independence from close early family ties. By contrast, an Eastern (Confucian) view of self emphasizes collectivistic values and interdependence, where duty to one's in-group is considered a primary virtue and continuous, close relationships with one's family and friends are paramount.

The cultural transmission of such norms is clearly reflected in child-rearing practices and parent–child relationships. This in turn influences the nature of interpersonal interactions and the educative process. Individuals in Confucian societies are encouraged to harness self-interests and personal goals for the promotion of social harmony and collective good. Social harmony is seen as vitally important and great emphasis is placed within the family upon responsibility for one's children's actions in this respect.

Different forms of educational achievement can be seen to be related to these differing underlying cultural philosophies. On the one hand, individual achievement is viewed within Confucian philosophy as a form of moral virtue which is mainly achieved through one's own efforts and the support of one's family and friends. On the other hand, the notion of effort is widened to include a sense of responsibility to the group to which one belongs, i.e., one works on behalf of others as well as oneself. This sense of social-oriented achievement motivation has been cited as an important underlying factor in the remarkably high general attainment level of students in many Eastern countries in mathematics in particular.

It has been argued also that the ability of individuals from certain cultural and ethnic backgrounds to function far more effectively outside of formal school settings may be accounted for by reference to such cultural considerations. In their longitudinal study of the educational progress of native Hawaiian students within the formal U.S. school system, Tharp, Gallimore and their colleagues clearly show how early

learning and development within a context of 'shared functioning', where the emphasis is upon collaboration and cooperation, is at variance with the individualistic, competitive environment pertaining in many schools. (See Gallimore, Tharp, & Rueda, 1989, for a summary of this work.) The authors draw helpfully upon Vygotskian socio-cultural theory to suggest ways in which children who may be seen as disadvantaged in this respect can be helped to function more effectively in mainstream schools.

The importance of the cultural context of learning becomes more and more apparent the further that we move in an educational sense from Western systems and assumptions. Research into the mathematical abilities of 'street' children in Brazil, for example, has shown them to be far more capable in their natural environments than would ever have been predicted by their performance in school. The potential implications of this for taking a truly international perspective on educational psychology has been clearly spelt out by Serpel (1993, p. xii) when he states 'An indigenous theoretical conceptualisation of human development and socialisation is an essential adjunct to the adaptation of exogenous institutions for endogenous progress in the field of education.'

In his efforts to apply educational psychology in a rural area of Zambia, East Africa, Serpel came to recognize the importance of gaining a context-related understanding of such notions as educational success, intelligent behavior, and the implicit psychology of the caregivers. Eurocentric views about the nature of learning, the applicability of standard assessment techniques, and the goals of education were found to be not only inappropriate but even seriously misleading. The point to be made here is that universal assumptions about the application of psychology to education are simply not warranted.

24.5 TOWARDS A MORE COHERENT FRAMEWORK

If we return at this point to the academic–practitioner divide referred to earlier, we can see that a central theme running through the history of educational psychology's search for an identity has been the lack of coherence between theory, research, and practice. Towards the end of the twentieth century it became clear that this was an issue which needed to be settled if educational psychology was to continue to develop as a discipline in its own right. A social interactionist approach would appear to offer a helpful framework for tackling this dilemma.

Firstly, in drawing upon the socio-cultural theories of Vygotsky and Feuerstein, each of the elements of teacher, learner, task, and context are considered to play a significant part in the educational process. A consideration of the purposes of education becomes an essential starting point for the development of theory and the identification of appropriate research and action. It thus becomes clear that educational systems reflect the cultural and historical contexts within which they exist and by which they are shaped. Educational psychology therefore stands in relation to sociology, history, and anthropology as much as it does to 'pure' psychology. In the terms of a great psychological pioneer, Wilhelm Wundt, it should be seen as a representative of *Geistewissenschaften* (the cultural sciences) rather than of *Naturwissenschaften* (the natural sciences).

A consideration of the aims of education from a socio-cultural perspective fits well with the first point made by the British Psychological Society report of Tomlinson et al. described earlier, namely that teachers need to be clear about the nature of learning outcomes that they wish their students to attain. Different learning goals will require different learning activities and experiences and will be achieved by different means. Acceptance of this point removes educational psychology once again from the realms of 'objective science' and places it within the real world where people act on the basis of values, feelings, and ideology as much as out of habit or as a result of contingent reinforcements.

This is an issue that has been faced more squarely by school psychologists than by the majority of educational psychologists. The International School Psychology Association (ISPA), for example, has a concern for the rights of the child as one of its central tenets. Thus, the United Nations Convention on the Rights of the Child provides a fundamental set of principles by which school psychologists across the world define their role.

The notion of *teacher-as-mediator* proposed by both Vygotsky and Feuerstein makes possible the incorporation of a strong constructivist perspective within which beliefs, feelings, and attitudes can be seen as central. It is in keeping, moreover, with such radical ideas as the *critical pedagogy* of Paulo Freire (1970). Freire's social pedagogy defined education as one place where the individual and society are constructed – a social action which can empower people to bring about social change, and to advance democracy as they advance their literacy and their knowledge. The purpose of education for Freire is to develop *critical consciousness*. Therefore, pedagogy must be participatory, critical,

context-bound, democratic, dialogic, multicultural, research-oriented, activist, and affective (Freire & Faundex, 1989). At a practical level, therefore, one of the primary tasks of the teacher-as-mediator is to teach students how to think effectively for themselves and to teach them to learn how to learn.

A strong lead in this respect has been taken by Feuerstein, who claims to have identified a number of essential aspects of *mediated learning experiences* (MLE), which are seen as essential in making learning truly educational. In presenting any learning task, the teacher should have a clear intention of what is to be learnt which is understood and reciprocated by the learners. The teacher needs to make learners aware of the significance of the task so that they can see the value of it to them personally, and in a broader cultural context. In addition, learners must be aware of the way in which the learning experience will have wider relevance to them beyond the immediate time and place. These essential aspects of MLE will be enhanced by the development of several other features in learners, including a sense of competence, the ability to take control of their own behavior, seeking, setting and achieving personal goals, the search for new challenges, a recognition of their own uniqueness, and the development of sharing behavior.

This chapter has presented just a few illustrative examples of some noteworthy historical events, significant theorists, and alternative perspectives on educational psychology. It is not meant to be, nor can any such brief overview ever be, truly representative of a consensual viewpoint. Readers should, therefore, have little difficulty in funding any one of a number of texts in fundamental disagreement with this author's reluctant conclusion that educational psychology cannot honestly be said to have yet achieved its early promise.

It may well be that William James was making a significant point which has far too long been overlooked when he wrote in one of his talks to teachers on psychology

> You make a great, a very great mistake, if you think that psychology, being the science of the mind's laws, is something from which you can deduce definite programs and schemes and methods of instruction for immediate schoolroom use. Psychology is a science, and teaching is an art; and sciences never generate arts directly out of themselves. (James, 1899, pp. 23–24)

With this proviso in mind, an alternative starting point for the development of educational psychology in the twenty-first century might take the following form. Educational psychology is the study of how and why people think and feel and act in the ways that they do within, and as a result of, educational transactions. It is not a 'hard' science but a hermeneutical form of enquiry which seeks to provide meaningful interpretations of the teaching and learning processes. It is always grounded within a culture, and is not and cannot be culture free.

Applied educational psychology seeks to draw upon the insights revealed by such enquiry to promote helpful exchanges with those involved in the educational process, and value-driven changes to the education system.

LITERATURE CITED

Ames, C., & Ames, R. (Eds.). (1989). *Research on motivation in education, Volume 3. Goals and cognitions*. London: Academic Press.

Ausubel, D. P. (1968). *Educational psychology: A cognitive view*. New York: Holt.

Bardon, J. I. (1983). Psychology applied to education: A specialty in search of an identity. *American Psychologist, 38*, 185–196.

Burden, R. L. (1994). Trends and developments in educational psychology: An international perspective. *School Psychology International, 15*, 293–347.

Candy, P. C. (1991). *Self-direction for life-long learning*. San Francisco: Jossey-Bass.

Creemers, B. P. M. (1991). *Effectieve Instructie*. Den Haag: Stichting voor Onderzock van het Ondernigs.

Denzin, N. K., & Lincoln, Y. S. (1994). *Handbook of qualitative research*. London: Sage.

Elkind, D. (1976). *Child development and education*. New York: Oxford University Press.

Fraser, B. J. (1991). Two decades of classroom research. In B. J. Fraser & H. J. Walberg (Eds.), *Educational environments: Evaluation, antecedents, consequences*. Oxford: Pergamon Press.

Freire, P. (1970). *Pedagogy of the oppressed*. New York: Continuum Press.

Freire, P., & Faundex, A. (1989). *Learning to question*. New York: Continuum Press.

Furth, H. (1970). *Piaget for teachers*. Englewood Cliffs, NJ: Prentice Hall.

Gallimore, R., Tharp, R., & Rueda, R. (1989). The social context of cognitive functioning in the lives of mildly handicapped persons. In D. Sugden (Ed.), *Cognitive approaches in special education*. Lewes: Falmer Press.

Gergen, K. J. (1985). The social constructionist movement in modern psychology. *American Psychologist, 40*(3), 266–75

Good, T. L., & Brophy, J. E. (1977). *Educational psychology: A realistic approach*. New York: Holt, Rinehart and Winston.

Hansford, B. C., & Hattie, J. A. (1982). The relationship between self and achievement/performance measures. *Review of Educational Research, 52*(1), 123–142.

Hattie, J. A., & Marsh, H. W. (1996). The relationship between research and teaching: A meta-analysis. *Review of Educational Research, 66*(4), 507–542.

Hilgard, E. R., & Bower, G. H. (1966). *Theories of learning* (3rd ed.). New York: Appleton Century Crofts.

James, W. (1890/1950). *The principles of psychology*. New York: Dover Publications.

James, W. (1899/1958). *Talks to teachers on psychology*. New York: Norson.

Kaplan, P. S. (1990). *Educational psychology for tomorrow's teacher*. St Paul, MN: West Publications.

Lave, J., & Wenger, E. (1991). *Situated learning: Legitimate peripheral participation*. Cambridge: Cambridge University Press

Mevarech, Z. R., & Kramarski, B. (1997). IMPROVE: A multidimensional method for teaching mathematics in heterogeneous classrooms. *American Educational Research Journal, 34*(2), 365–394.

Olkinuora, E., & Lehtinen, E. (1997). Forty years of research in educational psychology in Finland: A selected overview. *Scandinavian Journal of Educational Research, 41*(3–4), 273–293.

Phye, G. D. (1993). *Handbook of academic learning*. San Diego, CA: Academic Press.

Saigh, P., & Oakland, T. (Eds.). (1989). *International perspectives on psychology in the schools*. Hillsdale, NJ: Erlbaum.

Schön, D. A. (1983) *The reflective practitioner: How professionals think in action*. London: Temple Smith.

Serpel, R. (1993). *The significance of schooling: Life journeys in an African society*. Cambridge: Cambridge University Press.

Shulman, L. S. (1986). Paradigms and research programs in the study of teaching. In M. C. Whitrock (Ed.), *Handbook of research on teaching* (3rd ed.). New York: Wiley.

Thorndike, E. L. (1913). *Educational psychology*. New York: Teachers College, Columbia University.

Tomlinson, P., Edwards, A., Finn, G., Smith, L., & Wilkinson, E. (1992). *Psychological aspects of beginning teacher competence*. Submission by the Bristol Psychological Society to the UK Council for the Accreditation of Teacher Education. Leicester: British Psychological Society.

Walberg, H. J., & Haertel, G. D. (1992). Educational psychology's first century. *Journal of Educational Psychology, 84*(1), 6–19.

Communications concerning this chapter should be addressed to: Professor Robert L. Burden, School of Education, University of Exeter, Heavitree Road, Exeter EX1 2LU, UK

25

Work and Organizational Psychology

PIETER J.D. DRENTH AND WANG ZHONG MING

25.1 INTRODUCTION

The organizational psychology of work is a twentieth-century product. With the rapid development of industrialized society, the growing number of larger enterprises and the increasing complexity of production processes so typical of this century, company directors have learned, sometimes by bitter experience, that economic and technical models alone are not enough to understand and control these developments within their organizations. Directors and managers have turned to social science and to psychologists in particular to help them gain insight into workers' individual needs and motives, into the complexity of social interplay, and into the conditions likely to facilitate the development of satisfied workers and harmonious as well as productive workgroups. They have asked psychologists to develop methods for optimizing man–machine interactions, valid and reliable procedures for assessing and selecting personnel, and effective methods for the training and development of employees. They have also asked them to examine organizational culture and working conditions and to suggest ways of measuring and improving them, to advise on the best type of leadership behavior, and to find out how best to market their products or recruit new employees. In other words, an appreciation grew that concern for the human side of an enterprise was as essential for the survival of industrial organizations as their concern for technical or financial issues.

Psychologists working on these issues gradually united and organized themselves into a special subdiscipline of psychology, which was first called 'industrial psychology' (or its equivalent in a number of other languages: *Betriebspsychologie* in German, *bedrijfspsychologie* in Dutch). Later the broader term 'Industrial and Organizational (I/O) psychology' became more current in the USA, whereas in Europe the term 'Work and Organizational (W&O) psychology' was used more widely.

Since the beginning of this century, when the first modest attempts were made to answer such questions and to render such services, W&O psychology has grown continuously. W&O psychologists currently constitute the second largest category of psychologists in the world after clinical psychologists, and in many Western European universities W&O psychology is one of the two most preferred specializations within psychology. Of course, this is partly determined by the better prospects for graduates on the labor market, but this also clearly reflects the importance of the contribution made by W&O psychology as perceived by industry and by public and governmental administrations.

25.2 DEFINITION AND DOMAIN

W&O psychology refers to the specialization within psychology that is specifically concerned with human behavior at work in or in connection with a work organization. It is sometimes asked why a special subdiscipline had to be created (or had to emerge) to deal with this behavior. Why such a special interest and why so much special attention?

The arguments are twofold. A first motive stems from the significant position that 'work' has in most lives. This can be taken literally; in a great many cases, some 40 years of work experience, preceded by an ever-increasing number of preparatory years of schooling, and in many instances even followed by an extended (often voluntary) contribution to the economy or to society in general, indicate the core position of work in a person's lifetime. Moreover, a great many workers spend the major part of their daily waking hours either in or in relation to their working role: preparing for work, commuting to or from work, or at work. This is not to say that the present situation will not change. Working times will become more flexible, the total number of hours spent at the workplace or in the office may decrease, the distinction between working and learning will become less apparent, retirement age may become more variable or less distinct, etc. but none of these developments alters the fact that, in terms of time spent and energy invested, the work role will remain a central one in a person's life.

A second argument may be found in the salient position which work occupies in the psychological sense. In all the countries taking part in the international comparative study 'Meaning of Working' (MOW, 1987) the work role is described as highly central in one's life, taking only a second position after 'family'. Similar findings were reported in the longitudinal, cross-national comparative 'European Value Study' (Ester, Halman, & de Moor, 1993). This finding does not come as a surprise to anyone who takes cognizance of the often intense emotional reactions to the loss of the work role, either through unemployment or because of physical disability.

Even retirement, whether voluntary or compulsory, is a far from gratifying experience for many employees.

At the same time it should be realized that we are dealing with a very large and diverse scientific field, only part of which has yet been clearly delineated. The large extent of this scientific field stems from the enormous diversity of its subject: people working in organizations. The large variety in kinds of work, types of organizations, working conditions, and social interactions, as well as individual differences, create a complex and intricate field of study.

The large differences in kinds of work, for instance, are reflected in the enormous variety of occupations and professions that exist. The *Dictionary of Occupational Titles* (1965) lists tens of thousands of descriptions of occupations, divided into 22 work areas and 114 trait groups. And of course, this list does not include the many new functions created by the developments in new information technologies, automation, and computing that have taken place since 1965.

Organizations differ widely in nature (private or public, privately owned or officially listed, etc.), structure (size, type of hierarchy, location, etc.), culture (democratic, output-oriented, bureaucratic, etc.), and product or service (industrial products, raw materials, services, banking). The variation in working conditions is equally large, varying from conveyer belts to operating rooms, from motor cars to space vehicles, and from offices to marketplaces. Looking at modern developments, even more radical changes are in the offing; people in one organization no longer work at the same location, or they may operate in networks that connect different organizations. More and more traditional organizational tasks are being 'outsourced' and carried out by consultants, interim employees, and project workers. It is sometimes even difficult to define the exact boundaries of an organization; a reason why the term 'boundaryless organizations' has become *en vogue*.

As far as individuals are concerned, one sees about as much variety in work organizations as in society in general, with the exception of the disabled, the very young, and the very old. Workers differ in their capacities, education and training, experience, needs and expectations, personality, attitudes, and values. They have different regional, cultural, and ethnic backgrounds. They may be male or female, young or old, high or lower class, healthy, sick or handicapped, and they all have their individual parts to play in what is supposed to be the harmonious symphony of the working organization as a whole.

This short description of the great variety in individuals and situations which can be found in work organizations should make it clear that work and organizational psychology is concerned with a highly complex field of study. Many of the subjects in this specialization have been studied at one time or another, and although some sub-areas of this field have been extensively explored, little is yet known about others.

As was mentioned in the introduction, in Europe the subdiscipline under discussion is now generally referred to as 'work and organizational psychology' rather than the previously used term 'industrial psychology'. This shift in terminology is not without significance; it indicates a conspicuous change in thinking and orientation. First, of course, it illustrates the widening of interest in the subject. In the early 1960s Leavitt (Leavitt, 1961) was already arguing in favor of a merger of classical 'industrial psychology' with 'organizational psychology'. Similar pleas could be heard in the chapter by Leavitt and Bass in their 1964 *Annual Review* article. A little later, Porter also expressed the hope that a marriage between 'personnel-differential' and 'social-organizational' orientations and interests would be contracted (Porter, 1966). In fact, that is exactly what happened in the following years, and this is correctly reflected in the alteration of the name.

A second shift occurred in the orientation of 'industrial' psychologists when they no longer paid exclusive or primary attention to profit-making production and sales organizations. Today, service organizations (banks, consultancy firms, insurance companies), hospitals, schools, governmental agencies, sports organizations, members' associations, and others constitute just as much the field of interest of W&O psychologists as do commercial firms.

Third, the value orientation and guiding principles of W&O psychologists have undergone an important change. They no longer work exclusively on behalf of company management, but have turned their attention rather to the proper functioning of interaction processes in the organization as a whole. In the classical dilemma of 'client' versus 'organization' (e.g., in personnel selection, performance appraisal, industrial relations, conflict management), today's W&O psychologists are less inclined to think in terms of 'either–or' (and consequently allow the organizational or management point of view to prevail), but rather prefer a 'both–and' viewpoint. They try to think of the client system as encompassing both its individuals (with their needs, expectations, and interests) and its organization (with its requirements, expectations, and interests). W&O psychologists of the 1980s and 1990s put themselves in a position to serve both

parties, rather than just one (see also Drenth, 1987, p. 267).

25.3 RESEARCH METHODOLOGY

W&O psychology is often referred to as an applied science, like any other field-oriented specialization within psychology such as clinical psychology, educational psychology, forensic psychology, and the like.

And to quite some extent this is true. If one accepts the distinction between applied and pure scientific research as being determined by the origin of the research question – being either a practical difficulty, problem, or dilemma (applied science), or scientific curiosity, an unsolved theoretical problem, or a need for more theoretical insight (pure science) – then much of W&O psychology is indeed applied research. Most W&O research in the areas of testing and selection, training, performance evaluation, worker motivation and satisfaction, ergonomics, leadership, accidents and safety, organizational processes and decision making, consumer behaviour, and the like is initiated by practical problems or requests, and is also intended to lead to practical decisions, useful advice, or instruments; they are both field-induced and solution-oriented. Nevertheless, it is also true that the basic disciplines in psychology, representing the more purely scientific side of psychology (including psychonomics, developmental psychology, social psychology, and personality theory), often play an invaluable role in clarifying and deepening the insights and findings of W&O psychology.

Two remarks should be made here. First, it has to be pointed out that in scientific terms there is nothing wrong with, or second-rate about, applied research. Indeed, formally speaking there is no difference between pure and applied research. They apply the same standards and norms, and both types of research lead to generalizable insights and laws. The only difference is whether they start with a practical or a theoretical problem, and whether or not they intend to provide a helping hand in solving a practical problem.

Second, it cannot be denied that W&O psychology has also made a substantial contribution to theoretical and scientific developments in psychology in general. Plenty of examples of practical experience and insights stimulating theoretical, experimental, or psychometric developments can be given. In fact, psychometric and test-theoretical developments would never have taken place without the stimulation of the need for the large-scale assessment and selection of personnel. Social psychological theory has benefited greatly from research into inter-group behavior and interactive processes in organizations. Experimental psychology has been extensively stimulated by studies of task requirements, optimal man–machine systems, and information processes in organizational decision making. This is simply to say that not only is applied research a valid type of research in its own right, but also that there is much interaction and mutual stimulation between applied and pure research.

Of course, a sharp distinction should be made between applied research and the application and use of this research as this takes place in practice; in the latter, the criteria involved are the usefulness or efficacy of the application of the findings, and no longer simply their veracity, as in the former. In this capacity, organizational developers, personnel selection psychologists, management trainers, and stress counselors are not scientists, but social practitioners, whose decisions and actions are also founded on personal, social, and economic norms and values. We have elaborated on this distinction extensively elsewhere; the interested reader is referred to these publications (Drenth, 1996, 1997).

25.4 Sub-Specializations

Over the course of time, differentiation within the field of W&O psychology has led to more or less independent sub-specializations. Today, W&O psychologists may identify themselves as 'ergonomists', 'personnel selection specialists', or 'organization developers'. These titles refer to large areas within the field of W&O psychology which have developed into more or less autonomous specializations. Other subfields have not developed into such autonomous entities (as yet), but nevertheless indicate further differentiations within the field. The following section will provide an overview of these sub-specializations and the topics to be covered herein.

Four aspects can be distinguished in the description of the domain as given in the second section (see also Drenth, Thierry, & de Wolff, 1998): (1) the individual and individual differences in behavior, (2) work, task and function, (3) group and organizational processes, and (4) the organization and its environment. In fact, this distinction in focus also gives an indication of the historical development of W&O psychology. In the early years of W&O psychology the main emphasis was on the individual, enforced by the development of the instruments (tests, scales, appraisal systems) to be used for assessment, evaluation, and selection purposes.

Stimulated by insights from experimental psychology, interest widened to include the study of ergonomic problems and human factors in the work setting. The view of the worker as a social individual who is part of a larger social and organizational system, functioning in interaction with other individuals and subsystems, led to the further development of the social and organizational psychological approach in the study of organizations. Finally, it was acknowledged that organizations do not exist in a societal vacuum. They interact with other organizations, governments, markets, customers, unions, educational institutions – in short, with a wider environment. This wider environment has also become of interest to W&O psychologists in more recent times.

The following sections give a more detailed overview of these four sub-specializations.

Personnel Psychology

In this section the emphasis is on the individual and on individual differences. One may think here of dispositional characteristics (intellectual abilities and personality traits), habitual characteristics, i.e., stable characteristics, but learned in interaction with the environment (aptitudes, knowledge, attitudes, habits), and motivational characteristics: shorter or longer during physical or mental conditions which cause a certain level of activity or specific behavior (hunger, aspiration level, anxiety) (see Roe, 1984).

As we have said, personnel psychology has a long history which goes back to the early days of applied psychology. Not surprisingly, in older textbooks on 'industrial psychology' (Meijers, 1920; Tiffin, 1942; Viteles, 1932), much attention is devoted to issues in personnel psychology. The European Network of Professors in W&O psychology (ENOP) has developed a teaching model for their discipline, in which personnel psychology was described as follows: personnel psychology concerns the relationship between persons and the organization, in particular the establishment of the relationship, its development, and its termination. The focus is on 'employees', i.e., those with whom the organization has a temporal relationship (Roe, Coetsier, Levy-Leboyer, Peiro, & Wilpert, 1994).

Although the total field of W&O psychology has widened to incorporate other social and organizational issues, this classical domain of personnel psychology has always continued to attract the attention of many practitioners and researchers. This has resulted in an ever-increasing body of knowledge. Handbooks, specialized monographs and journals such as

Personnel Psychology, the *Journal of Applied Psychology* and the *Journal of Occupational Psychology* attest to this substantial and much-researched field of specialization.

The following topics can generally be found in this area.

Personnel Selection

This term refers to those organizational activities which aim towards choosing people to fill certain posts, often by making use of psychological instruments such as psychological tests, interviews, questionnaires, personality measures, assessment centres, and the like, and often employing different kinds of psychometric prediction functions and utility models. Psychological selection has developed from a rather isolated 'measurement and prediction' paradigm to a much more integrated part of human resource management in which the critical analysis of the criterion, the incorporation of dynamic criteria and the need for situational selection, and the relationship with other personnel policy issues (fairness, openness, diversity, employability) or practices (training, career development) are emphasized (Herriot, 1989).

Appraisal and Assessment

Obtaining insight into how employees perform, into their qualities and shortcomings, and into their potential for further development and growth, is of prime importance for an organization. Psychology has contributed significantly to the quality of personnel evaluation and assessment by developing tools and instruments, by suggesting methods and procedures, but above all by providing the necessary sagacity with regard to the psychological mechanisms of the assessment and appraisal process. This has often led to a better insight into employees and their performance, and therefore to an improved foundation of the decisions to be made on this basis (see, for instance, a collection of articles on the subject in Berk, 1986).

Socialization, Training and Development

Very seldom does a school-leaver or graduate have the exact competencies, knowledge, and skills needed for the function or office to be held. Specific further training is almost invariably needed. Moreover, every company or organization has its 'culture', its written and unwritten rules and traditions, to which a newcomer has to adapt and socialize. Moreover, the dynamic nature of job requirements, the frequent introduction of new technologies and the rapid change of applied information systems actually require continuous learning on the part of the employee. In the course of his or her career an employee will also be often faced with new functions and new requirements, for which training or retraining will be needed. In other words, socialization, training, and retraining constitute a permanent and serious concern for any organization that wants its members to perform as well as possible. Psychologists have been able to assist in this respect by applying their knowledge about learning and the development of skills and competencies, about attitudinal change, and about social adaptation processes, hence contributing to the fit between individual and organization.

Work Attitudes and Motivation

These concepts refer to another classic topic in W&O psychology: the measurement of work attitudes and work motivation. The original emphasis was put on the measurement of satisfaction; more specifically, satisfaction with work content, payment, co-workers, supervisor, promotion opportunities, and work conditions. This was firstly defended for its own sake; workers were entitled to be satisfied with what the organization offered to satisfy their needs. But it was also defended for 'external' reasons; it was thought that satisfaction would also be a determinant of hard work and good performance. It was only later, and convincingly defended in Vroom's (1964) book *Work and Motivation*, that a clear distinction was made between satisfaction and motivation; a happy worker is not necessarily a hard worker, and dissatisfaction does not necessarily lead to lower performance. Determinants of performance, i.e., the sum of forces that produce and maintain the efforts expended in particular behaviors or performances, are subsumed under the concept of 'motivation'. Many useful theories of work motivation have been derived from the more general theories of motivation developed in the experimental laboratory. Thierry (1998) classifies these along two dimensions: in the first place content (e.g., need theories) versus process (e.g., goal setting), and in the second place reinforcement (e.g., Skinner's behavior modification) versus cognitive theories (e.g., equity or expectancy theories). In the meantime it has become clear that if one wants to understand what makes people work and work hard, and which incentives are functional and why, then motivation is a more useful concept than satisfaction.

Human Resources Management

The concern for personnel, often described today as 'human resources management', has an individual as well as an organizational dimension. In an approach which emphasizes the individual dimension, the career of individual employees is the object of investigation. Topics like career choice, career management, promotion strategies, management development, and life-span psychology (developmental phases during adulthood) fall within this chapter. Of course, there are points of contact with other related fields such as selection, training, and appraisal.

In the organizational orientation, issues having respect to personnel in organizations are approached from a more institutional perspective, and include proper personnel planning, the optimal composition of the work force now and in the foreseeable future, optimal age and educational distribution, a balance between male and female, and social policy with respect to minority groups or handicapped workers. Some of the subjects in this area that are especially pertinent nowadays are:

- women and work, as a specification of the more general issue of gender differences and work;
- the older worker in the organization, including the question of how the older worker can be trained or retrained and kept motivated to keep working satisfactorily at higher ages;
- equal opportunities for and fair treatment of members of minority groups;
- work and employment, with specific attention to the problem of unemployment and its social and psychological consequences.

Work Psychology

Like personnel psychology, work psychology dates back to the early days of applied psychology. Whereas personnel psychology was rooted in an interest in individual differences and its instrumental base of 'tests and measurement', work psychology originated from a more experimental tradition which emerged in time and motion studies, fatigue research and safety research. Numerous studies have since been published and a substantial body of knowledge has been established in this particular area.

In the American literature both the personnel and the work psychology orientations have developed strongly, although with some prevalence for the personnel tradition. In a number of European countries the work psychology tradition has often prevailed. In the German journal *Zeitschrift für angewandte Psychologie* and the French journal *Le Travail Humain*, both leading journals in the field of W&O psychology, emphasis is much more on ergonomics and human factors than on training, selection, and other human resources topics.

In middle and eastern Europe this preference for experimental work studies was even stronger, at least before the fall of communism and the disintegration of the Soviet Union. In those countries, research into personnel psychological and organizational psychological questions was subject to a strong political taboo. All matters related to personnel and organizational policy were under central control and did not allow for research that might undermine political doctrine. Relatively value-free experimental work psychology was clearly less dangerous and therefore less vulnerable. In Eastern Germany and other Eastern European countries, a strong tradition and an advanced body of knowledge in experimental work psychology therefore emerged (Hacker, 1986).

The following sections within work psychology can be identified.

Task and Job Analysis

The difference between task analysis and job analysis is that of a lower order versus a higher order analysis (see e.g., Jewell & Siegall, 1990). A task is a piece of work assigned to an individual which has to be completed within a certain time and which has to meet some standard of quality. The tasks performed by any employee define a position. Positions that are more or less alike form a job. Groups of jobs are job families. The general term 'job analysis' refers to the attempt to seek and to provide information about the tasks and their requirements with respect to the various jobs and job families in organizations. For W&O psychology purposes, these analyses are made in terms of psychological abilities and competencies as well as psychological needs and motives.

The results of these analyses are of fundamental importance to many applications in W&O psychology: they form the starting point for the development or choice of selection instruments, for the definition of the content of training courses, for remuneration systems, for the evaluation of individual performances, and so on. For many of these applications, job analysis provides the necessary elements for further measures or practices.

Ergonomics and Job Design

Ergonomics, or as it is often referred to in the US 'human factors psychology', deals with the individual as an information-processing or moving system which interacts with operating systems, machines or information technology. Its aim is to fit the job to the worker, rather than fitting the worker to the job by means of selection, training, and adaptation.

This field has developed rapidly since its origin in the beginning of the twentieth century. It grew out of the classic time and motion studies which were aimed at finding the best way to perform a job, i.e., with maximum rapidity and minimal waste. The focus was on the study of physical and mental workload, human errors, and the effect of different work conditions. The worker operated a machine or apparatus and the latter did the work. In the course of time, the combination of man and machine were seen more as a 'system' with varying distributions of tasks. Sometimes the roles were reversed: the man did the work and the machine did the guidance and the controlling. Moreover, with the rapid development of new technologies and information systems, greater cognitive and decision-making demands were placed on the operators, while the total system became much more complex, demanding, and interrelated with other subsystems within the total production or operating process.

The design of work based upon ergonomic principles has accordingly changed throughout this period. It originally aimed at adapting the tasks and machines to the primarily physical and perceptual capabilities of the worker. Later these requirements were enlarged so as to include the psychological and social needs of the worker: the quality of work movement. Later again, the worker and the machine were seen as a single integrated operating system: the systems approach. At present the entire organization is seen as a large and complex system in which human, technical, and organizational components, each with their own demands and limitations, have to be integrated and optimized. This is the modern form of the socio-technical approach as originally developed at the Tavistock Institute of Human Relations, London, UK.

Accidents and Safety

This sub-specialization has developed from general ergonomics into a separate field of study, partly because it is a phenomenon often associated with grave personal and economic consequences. Originally, much attention was directed towards accidents themselves: their causes and, consequently, their prevention. From the W&O psychological perspective, it was particularly the 'human error' which was studied.

However, it has gradually become clear that 'accidents' were not the proper starting point for the study of industrial safety. The number of accidents is often too small to make proper statistical analyses, chance factors play too important a role, and there are a great many 'near accidents' which are not registered but which are just as relevant as actual accidents.

This focus on accidents meant that an excessive amount of attention was given to the immediate determinants (human errors), to their amendment, and to the workers that 'caused' the accidents. The present-day approach to industrial safety regards it, rather, as resulting from a deliberate management philosophy and practice in which safe operation and good operation are basically identical and in which safety management is the combined responsibility of all company employees.

Work and Health Psychology

This combination of health psychology and work psychology is a fairly new independent sub-discipline, although some thirty years ago Abt and Riess (1971) had already pointed out the usefulness of combining clinical psychological and organizational psychological knowledge in their book *Clinical Psychology in Industrial Organizations*. One of today's key words in this respect is 'work stress', or rather – since a certain degree of tension is normal or even desirable – 'work distress', which manifests itself in physical, psychological or social disfunction. The first possible determinant in this respect discussed in the literature is 'workload', and its psychological consequences. Other sources of unhealthy disfunction, such as the consequences of conflicts, work conditions, post-traumatic syndromes, burnout, unemployment or threats of unemployment, strong dissatisfaction with work, supervisor or co-workers, have also become the subjects of increasing attention. A significant broadening of the horizon of the work and health psychologist is stimulated by the consideration that health should be seen not merely as the absence of disease, but, in accordance with the definition of the 1987 constitution of the WHO, as 'a complete state of physical, mental and social wellbeing'.

Automation

Another 'offspring' of ergonomics that has developed into a more or less independent field of interest is the study of automation and its effects on work and the worker. The term 'automation' refers to the application of sophisticated technical resources in entirely or largely self-regulating processes, eliminating or reducing human intervention in the direct production process (Koopman & Algera, 1998). In the automation of production processes as well as in office automation, both the collection, storage and retrieval of information and the related decision making, previously handled by human beings, are taken over by the automated system or the computer.

The effects of automation on the work itself, on modes of steering and control, on the employee who has to work in such systems, on the capacities and skills needed to operate them, on the requirements for the new man–machine interface systems, on the need to develop user-friendly software as well as early warning systems in case of malfunctions, have been analyzed in an increasing number of publications over the last 15 years. Questions like the wider impact of automation on the organization as a whole and on employment opportunities, and how to smoothly introduce and implement plans for automation in existing organizations, have also become the subject of extensive research.

Organizational Psychology

Systematic analyses of organizations, their formal structure, and the roles of their members, have long been carried out in other disciplines; economics, organizational theory, and business administration studies have produced a fairly good insight into how organizations are built and how they operate. Again, the term 'organization' should not be restricted to industrial companies, although most of the organization theories stem from studies of the latter, but should be understood to include social clubs, hospitals, armies, schools, churches, and the like, all of which are organizations, albeit with specific structures and objectives.

It was only after World War II that industrial psychology more systematically turned its attention to organizational factors and tried to incorporate these into the study of work behavior. After all, the central constituents of organizations are people, not machines, buildings, telephone lines, or other infrastructural hardware. Not only do people create organizations, they are also in turn influenced by these creations; the way they work, the way they interact with co-workers, subordinates and supervisors, and the way they define and play their roles is to a large extent determined by the nature, goal and culture of the organization they belong to. This attention has been strongly reinforced by a growing interest in social psychology in general and by the Human Relations Movement in the US and the early work in Sociotechnics at the Tavistock Institute in London in particular.

This field is sometimes referred to as 'organizational behavior' (see for instance, Bobbitt, Breinholt, Doktor, & McNaul, 1978). However, this term is somewhat confusing, since it includes the behavior of individuals or groups in organizations (with the individual or group as unit of analysis) as well as the 'behavior' of organizations themselves (with the organization as unit of analysis). Organizational psychology focuses on the interaction between individuals or groups of individuals and the organization, but always from the perspective of the former. Organization theories as such do not fall within the remit of organizational psychology, although, of course, knowledge of organization theories is an important condition for understanding the behavior of individuals in organizations.

This organizational psychological orientation has created an active and productive subdivision of W&O psychology. A large number of books have been written and new journals have been started in this field (*Organization Studies, Organizational Behavior and Human Performance, Administrative Science Quarterly, Human Relations* and many others). If one compares the classical books and readers in 'industrial psychology' with the more recent published ones, one sees a significant increase in organizational topics. In the earliest publications these topics were actually completely absent, whereas for instance in the first edition of Dunnette's *Handbook*, published in 1976, as in Dubin's *Handbook* published in the same year, more than half of the space devoted to the content of W&O psychology deals with social-organizational issues.

The following clusters of topics can be distinguished within this particular domain.

Organization Theories and Models

As was stated above, organization theories as such do not belong to the field of organizational psychology, but a knowledge and understanding of organizational principles and processes form a precondition for understanding the organizational behavior of an organization's members. Much attention is therefore paid to the analysis of organizational characteristics and their influence on human behavior and performance.

In most definitions of organizations the following elements are recognized as essential. Individuals collaborate towards a common goal, the work and tasks are differentiated and divided over the individuals, there is a 'binding structure' which integrates the specific tasks, and there is some continuity over time (see for instance Veen & Korver, 1998). Organizations may vary in terms of their formal or structural characteristics, in size, in goals, in type of product or service, in composition, in age and many other characteristics; all these differences have been studied with respect to the consequences and requirements for their members.

However, a more basic framework for understanding the interactions between individuals and organizations is provided by the conceptual approach to organizations. An example of such an approach is 'scientific management', a system in which human capacities are utilized maximally by structuring tasks, controlling performances, and remunerating individuals according to the work done. Organizations can also be seen as systems which have to be ruled by hierarchical structures and preset rules, as in the bureaucratic approach. Other approaches emphasize the needs of working members and focus on ways in which these can be reconciled with organizational goals, as in the human relations movement. Other views again stress the importance of achieving performance targets and meeting objectives while leaving considerable freedom for people's own creativity and initiative. Organizations can also be seen as systems in permanent interaction (reaction and anticipation) with the environment, as in the contingency theory, or as unstable, opportunistic 'adhocracies', or as systems for 'sense-making' by their members, or even as garbage cans. Naturally, each of these different perspectives on organizations will cast a distinctive light on the human factor in organizations.

Leadership and Decision Making

The study of leadership has a long tradition in W&O psychology; the subject was being studied by I/O psychologists even before organizational psychology had been defined as a separate subfield of W&O psychology. Researchers have focused on a description of the activities and functions of leaders. They have analysed the traits which distinguish leaders from non-leaders, or, more interesting for promotion and training purposes, effective from ineffective leaders. They have also studied a number of styles, such as task-orientation, people-orientation, the charismatic inspirational style, or the various participative styles of leadership.

The latter is strongly related to issues of decision making, since participation almost always refers to the decision-making process in which the subordinate takes some part. Views on decision making have developed from the classical rational model, describing the procedures and parameters leading to maximum output, via the organizational model, which stresses a number of restrictions of this rational model mainly due to the insufficiency of the information-processing capacity of decision-makers, to the arena model, in which it is acknowledged that various players in the decision-making process may have divergent or sometimes even conflicting objectives; they form coalitions and follow strategies that turn decision making into a set of political processes in which negotiations (and conflicts) play a central role.

It is now generally accepted that the effectiveness of leadership is contingent upon a number of situational and organizational characteristics. In fact, leadership itself is part of an organizational process. Leader behavior is strongly determined (and restricted) by the structure, technology, roles, control mechanisms, and other characteristics of the environment.

Organizational Development and Organizational Design

Organizations should be seen as open systems which have to adapt to changes in the environment if they are to survive. These changes may be of a cultural, political/legal, economic, technological, or physical (climate, resources) nature (Katz & Kahn, 1978).

Organizational psychologists have developed a number of methods and instruments to facilitate this adaptation process, which is then called 'planned change'. These methods can be either processual or structural. The former are directed towards changes in the attitudes and behavior of employees, as well as towards organizational processes such as communication, decision making, and conflict management. They often result in a more open, communicative and participative climate. The latter are more directed towards changing the formal structural aspects of the organization, such as tasks, role definitions, role relations, job content, and operational procedures. They deal less with the development process or strategy, and more with an analysis of how problems could be solved, how new tasks could be performed and how to overcome organizational shortcomings.

Another, somewhat related, distinction is that between development in which the goals are less concrete and more abstract and general (e.g., to improve the organization's decision-making capacity, creativity, and problem-solving ability), generally referred to as 'organizational development', on the one hand; and the construction, introduction and implementation of a totally new organization, resulting in a new, stable situation, on the other. The latter is called 'organizational design'.

It has become clear that with the growing number and magnitude of change processes in organizations, the need for methods and instruments with which to assess progress and the eventual success of the change has also increased. Such methods focus on the measurement of the change process itself, on obstacles and resistance to the acceptance and implementation of change, and on the shorter- and longer-term effects of the organizational development interventions.

Organizational Culture

A fairly new, but fast growing chapter within organizational psychology is concerned with organizational culture. The concept is borrowed from anthropology and refers to the basic and relatively stable patterns of values and beliefs within an organization.

Two perspectives in the treatment of organizational culture can be distinguished. The first sees culture as a variable, as a characteristic of the organization. Various specific aspects within this variable can be distinguished, such as, for instance, those offered by the matrix based on Quinn's (1988) two polar dimensions 'external versus internal' and 'flexibility versus control', leading to the four 'cultures': support, innovation, goal orientation, and rule orientation. Another approach is the more social psychological analysis of the processes of problem-solving, learning, and adaptation within organizations by Schein (1992).

In the second perspective, organizational culture is treated as a root metaphor; the organization *is* a culture. Authors sometimes refer to organizations as systems of knowledge or cognitive enterprises whose individual members store their experiences in 'organizational memory maps'. Others speak of organizations as patterns of symbolic discourse, and ways of understanding work-related experiences by individual members. Anyway, the objective in this perspective is to understand the constructed realities, and not to analyze the instrumental meaning of culture as related to (for instance) organizational effectiveness or the satisfaction of its members.

Industrial Relations

This subject deals with those interrelationships between the various layers within industrial organizations which affect the process of reaching and implementing decisions. These decisions may refer to all kinds of issues (day-to-day work aspects, tactical medium-term problems, or long-term strategic issues) and all layers within the organization (direct supervisor–superior relations, higher and middle management interactions, and the negotiation of management with representatives of the employees, either through a works council or through a system of shop stewards, welfare committees, a central or local union, or any other form of representation). The subject of industrial relations is therefore strongly associated with concepts such as 'worker participation' and 'industrial democracy'.

The literature on industrial democracy has focused on various processual aspects, including: (1) its objectives and motives (are they principal and political (structural democracy) or do they aim at the improvement of effective decision making or workers' well-being (functional democracy)?), (2) the level of participation (the right to be informed, the right to advise, the right to vote, the right to exercise a veto), and (3) the effectiveness of different systems of industrial democracy.

Particularly the last of these questions has been extensively researched in Europe. Quite a variety of formal systems of industrial democracy exist in Europe, and the question of the extent to which these systems have led to power equalization and/or employees' involvement in decision making has been analyzed cross-nationally and longitudinally by the international research group, Industrial Democracy in Europe (IDE, 1981, 1993).

The Organization and Its Environment

A last and relatively new chapter in organizational psychology devotes attention to the relationship between the organization and its complex and multifaceted environment. Early W&O psychology was confined to what happened within the organization, and rarely was any attention paid to its relationship to the external environment. This has since been seen as an unjustified restriction of the domain. The boundaries of the system in which the interactions between individuals or groups take place do not coincide with the factory gates or the offices's revolving doors. The organization as such is also in constant interaction with its environment. Some go even further, and state that the organization creates its own environment. 'Environment' in this sense may refer to the economic market and customers, to the labour market and potential employees, to other collaborating or competing organizations, and to the outside socio-political world, including supra-national, national, or local governments, pressure groups, and political movements.

This fourth area of attention has not yet developed clear sub-specializations, as have the previous three. It encompasses rather a combination of (rather recently developed) lines of research and interest, and a systematic treatment will have to confine itself to mentioning a number of themes rather than clearly defined sections. The following themes can be listed.

Contingency Theories

This theory is based on the presumption that there is no one best way to organize, but that the best form of organization depends on the fit with the environment. In some earlier writings this 'fit' was based on normative views, the propagation of freedom, autonomy and decentralization as stimulants for entrepreneurship and flexible adaptation to the environment. Later approaches, called structural contingency theories, focused more on the study of empirically demonstrated optimal fit models between the organization and the environment (Pennings, 1998).

Organizational Field and Networks

Almost any organization is part of a supra-organizational field or network. Interest can be focused on the organizational field as such, consisting of the strategically interdependent organizations. But attention can also be directed towards the cooperative interactions between the organizations making up an organizational network. Players in this network field can have different forms of interrelationship. They can be mutually or unilaterally dependent; this dependence can be horizontal (both need each other on an equal footing, such as in the free market structure) or vertical (e.g., different stages in a production chain). They also have different forms of interaction, ranging from cooperation to negotiating and bargaining and to power struggles, disruptive strategies and authoritative control.

Communication and Image Building

Many W&O psychologists make use of modern techniques of communication and marketing in building the image of the organization. The image can concern the work climate and work conditions (aiming at creating a positive image of the organization for potential employees), the incorporation of ethical and social objectives in their mission (so as to please national or local governments), or specific measures to avoid possible harm to the environment, to further the health of employees, or to promote the prudent use of animals or raw materials in production processes (so as to face confrontation with action groups successfully). Many of today's large or multinational companies have included such 'rules of ethical conduct' in their corporate mission.

Economic Psychology

Related to the previous theme is the sub-specialization of economic psychology, sometimes referred to as 'consumer behavior' or as 'marketing psychology'. In fact this branch of W&O psychology also deals with 'communications', but its primary aim is to study (and in practice to influence) individual customers or clients and their economic decisions (buying, saving, spending, allocating) under conditions of scarcity. The difference between economic psychology and economics is that the latter deals with economic behavior at a high level of abstraction (of systems, companies, or nations), and the former focuses on individual decisions at the micro-level. Economic psychologists have successfully found their way into the worlds of marketing, advertising, company–customer relations, and so on.

A fairly recent theme that fits within this last section is *cross-cultural W&O psychology*, i.e., the study of the extent to which cultural differences determine organizational characteristics or the behavior of the members of the organization, and to what extent we find differences or similarities under different cultural conditions. Since it is our presumption that this subject is of particular interest to an international audience we will devote a separate and more extensive section to this subject.

25.5 CROSS-CULTURAL WORK AND ORGANIZATIONAL PSYCHOLOGY

In recent years, research and applications in work and organizational psychology have developed rapidly in the area of economic development and cross-cultural management. Considerable efforts are being made in terms of conceptual development and methodological refinement with respect to cross-cultural studies. Work and organizational psychology has placed new emphasis on the cultural embeddedness of values and work attitudes, team effectiveness and leadership, organizational decision making, personnel assessment, and Human Resource Management in general.

Cross-cultural organizational psychology is concerned with two basic questions: first, do organizations located in different countries differ with respect to organizational characteristics, to the behavior of its members, or to the interrelationship between the two; and second, can these differences be explained in terms of culture (see Drenth & den Hartog, 1998)?

In order to answer both questions, it is not enough to investigate whether organizations differ cross-nationally. The problem is that not all national differences can be considered as cultural differences, in spite of the fact that these two words often are used synonymously. Nations may differ in language, legislation, education, religions, geographic and climatic variables, and economically, technologically, and in many other ways. These variables may be related to culture, but they cannot be equated with it. One has to define culture on the basis of a reasoned choice. A widely accepted definition is Kroeber and Parson's 'patterns of roles and norms embedded in certain paramount values' (Kroeber & Parson, 1958).

The following section will present a more specific treatment of some of the prevalent issues in cross-cultural W&O psychology.

Cultural Dimensions and Organizations

Several cultural dimensions have shown their usefulness and relevance in understanding national and cultural differences in behavior and attitudes within organizations. The following selection of fairly independent cultural dimensions, which are relevant for understanding cross-cultural differences in organizations, can be put forward on the basis of an analysis of the relevant literature (Hofstede, 1980, 1991; House et al., 1998; Inglehart, 1997; Schwartz & Sagiv, 1995; Triandis, 1994; Trompenaars, 1993):

1. collectivism versus individualism (is the primary concern in life oneself and one's immediate family, or the wider groups to which one belongs?);
2. egalitarianism versus power distance (should power be distributed equally or unequally in society and organizations?);
3. uncertainty avoidance (do people feel threatened by ambiguous situations and are they trying to avoid uncertainty through formal rules?);
4. masculine control versus harmony (rational and power control of people and environment versus harmonious and affective relations with other people and nature);
5. universalism versus particularism (can what is good and true be defined and applied everywhere, or do unique conditions and relationships always have to be taken into consideration in order to determine what is good and true?);
6. discipline versus individual autonomy (soberness and adherence to moral values versus emphasis on intellectual and moral independence);
7. neutral versus affective relationships (the extent to which culture allows people to express their emotions or forces them to keep their emotions and affections under strict control);
8. achievement versus ascription (are people evaluated by their functional performance or by their roles, status, or formal characteristics?);
9. materialism versus postmaterialism (emphasis on economic goals and financial rewards versus an emphasis on a much

more broadly-defined well-being objective and non-material values);
10. future orientation (the extent to which the (more distant) future is an important orientation in the choice of behavior and decision making).

Cultural Values and Work Attitudes

Work attitudes have been widely studied in cross-cultural W&O psychology. However, most cross-cultural studies of cultural values and attitudes use scales adopted or modified from Western-based cultural values. Many of these studies therefore actually start from the premise that Western values can be generalized and studied globally. In fact, this was the case in a well-known early study by Hofstede (1980), which was based on measures for satisfaction and well-being in a Western company (IBM). It was only later that he and Bond included typical Asian measures in studying Asian cultures' consequences (Hofstede, 1991).

In another study, Bond (1988) analyzed survey data from a large Asian sample and found two common factors: (a) social integration versus culture inwardness; (b) reputation versus morality. Triandis (1996) and his colleagues also studied the dimension collectivism–individualism and identified three strong etic factors: separation from in-groups, independence, and personal competence.

Huang (1995) supported the view that Asian cultures have specific characteristics which influence their organizational behavior. He concluded that:

*   Asian-based cultural values are characterized as inside- and family-oriented, whereas Western-based cultural values are more outside- and social-oriented;
*   Asian-based cultural values are more relationship-oriented while Western-based cultural values are more task-oriented.

However, he also observed a shift in Asian-based cultural values form harmony-orientedness to competition-orientedness and from a collectivistic to an individualistic orientation. It seems that in this respect Asian-based cultural values are becoming more similar to Western-based cultural values.

Cross-Cultural Leadership and Decision Making

As was stated earlier, organizational decision making and participation have been widely researched from a cross-cultural perspective. The motivation for comparing management in different cultures arises because indigenous local organizations need to design management systems that are able to handle newly emerging ownership arrangements (Smith & Wang, 1996).

In the early days, models of managerial leadership implicitly treated the manager as an individual agent and tended to ignore the broader social context which made such influences possible.

House (1995) notes that almost all prevailing theories of leadership and most empirical evidence is rather North American in character, that is, 'individualistic rather than collectivistic; emphasizing assumptions of rationality rather than ascetics, religion, or superstition; stated in terms of individual rather than group incentives; stressing follower responsibilities rather than rights; assuming hedonistic rather than altruistic motivation and assuming centrality of work and democratic value orientation'. Many cultures do not share these assumptions. 'As a result there is a growing awareness of a need for a better understanding of the way in which leadership is enacted in various cultures and a need for an empirically grounded theory to explain differential leader behavior and effectiveness across cultures' (see for instance Misumi, 1985).

Nevertheless, a leader–subordinate or leader–group relationship is a thoroughly interpersonal and social phenomenon, and therefore deeply embedded in the social and cultural environment. It would be difficult to see how attempts to influence and stimulate workers or groups of workers could be abstracted from this cultural context. A good example is given by Leung, Smith, Wang, and Sun (1996), who argue that in Asian joint ventures a new construct for distributive justice is needed in treating personnel. They propose the concept of comparative distributive justice, as opposed to the traditional concept of performance-based distributive justice, in order to capture the social comparison processes that are salient in Asian joint ventures.

Of course, similarity also exists. In a comparative study on power distribution and the effects of participative decision making in China and the UK it was shown that in both countries participative decision making had similar positive effects upon management effectiveness and that there were comparable distributions of decision-making power along different decision-making stages, across organizational levels and concerning various decision tasks (Wang & Heller, 1993).

Personnel Assessment

A recent significant trend in cross-cultural W&O psychology has been a shift of psychological assessment from general testing using translated and adapted Western tests to more specific work-oriented personnel assessment based upon indigenous work behavior analysis. For example, in a personnel assessment project sponsored by the Personnel Testing Center under the Ministry of Personnel in China, a comprehensive test inventory of specific Chinese management abilities and skills has been developed. Four core management skills (planning, organizing, leading, and controlling) together with three specific skills needed in Chinese work situations (relationship skills, teamwork skills, and time management skills) were identified (Wang, 1996a). Another important dimension in Chinese personnel assessment is the stronger utilization of a situational design. Wang and his associates (1998) used such a situational scenario design in the Chinese Microsoft Assessment Process. This design was reflected in testing strategic thinking ability, team-negotiation skills, and group value-orientation. A managerial model of managerial competence was then developed with 'cultural sensitivity' as the main dimension of joint venture management competencies.

Another area in personnel assessment in which a culture-specific approach may be needed is the theory and measurement of personality. While most recent studies in this field relate to the 'big five' categorization, it is not at all clear whether these five factor dimensions fit to non-Western (for instance, Chinese) traditions and culture. It may very well be that a re-examination of Western personality theories in non-Western contexts will reveal the need for much more specific conceptualizations and measures (Wang, 1996b).

Culture and Human Resource Management

The last subject to be discussed in this context is the definition and use of Human Resource Management (HRM) practices. Management tools such as HRM were long regarded as universals which could be applied anywhere across the globe. The continuing development of the international market, however, has contributed to the belief that successful tools for managing personnel in one country do not necessarily have the same impact in another. Models of HRM have often taken on an individualistic flavor by concentrating on job analysis, staffing, performance appraisal, and compensation, thereby de-emphasizing activities at group and company level such as communication, teambuilding, and cultural values.

Erez (1994) illustrates the contextual boundaries for applying managerial tools by defining context in terms of task and cultural characteristics. HRM practices will only lead to preferred behavior of employees when applied in the right context. In a different context HRM practices will have a different meaning and different effects. The definition of the elements comprising high-commitment strategies is dependent on contextual knowledge such as insight into local organizational structures, cultural values, and labor regulations.

This observation was supported by a comparative study of HRM practices in Chinese and Dutch industrial companies (see Verburg et al., 1999). The results show considerable differences between China and the Netherlands in the HRM practices of industrial enterprises. The organizational culture of the companies studied also varies between the two countries and the differences found are clearly in line with differences at the national cultural level.

25.6 FUTURE DEVELOPMENTS

As this chapter has shown, W&O psychology has grown into a mature and widely recognized specialization within psychology. We have seen a number of trends in this development that testify to its maturity (see also Bass & Drenth, 1987), and these trends will most certainly continue in the future. These trends include:

- Increasing theoretical and scientific sophistication. Before the 1960s many W&O psychology handbooks were practical manuals, with a strong emphasis on 'tips and tricks' and 'getting it done' rather than on providing a solid theoretical basis for understanding people's behavior in organizations. This has changed. Granted, as we have seen in Section 25.3, that a natural tension between research and application does exist, it is still fair to say that the fundamental requirements for the scientific acquisition of knowledge and the embeddedness in general psychological theories have now become widely accepted in W&O psychology.

- Differentiation, both in terms of research methods and analysis procedures and in terms of conceptualizations and theoretical models. Methodological differentiation will become clear to anyone who takes notice of the elaborate data collection and analysis techniques which are available and in use, stimulated in particular by the exponential growth of available computer support. The best illustrative example of theoretical differentiation is probably the widely accepted contingency approach. It is increasingly widely recognized that general laws and rules have to be specified or 'contextualized' in the light of specific organizational or environmental contingencies.

- Integration, as the counterpart of the differentiation just mentioned. W&O psychology has also gradually learned to incorporate loose pieces of knowledge and experience into a more integrated theoretical framework. To give a few examples: We have already seen the integration of personnel and organizational psychology. Many previously separated elements of W&O psychology, such as selection, training, and development are now being considered from an integrative career perspective. Individual training and organizational development are viewed from an interactive prospect. The present-day approach of organizational design integrates the production, information, and control dimensions.

- Internationalization. It has to be acknowledged that many present-day insights and instruments in W&O psychology have an American signature, although at the same time a European origin of the line or school of thought often cannot be denied (see also Wilpert, 1990). The US will undoubtedly continue to play a dominant role in the advancement of W&O psychology, but at the same time there is a growing awareness that the phenomena under study in this field are embedded in culture. It is being increasingly widely recognized that one must adapt the methods and procedures used to influence people and change systems to the cultural context in which they operate. This even applies to the methods and procedures used to research the individual and organizational processes.

- Future orientation. W&O psychologists have almost always been concerned with innovations and new developments; in fact, their expertise was and is often called in to assist organizations in dealing with these developments. Innovation, resistance to change, new technologies and work, flexibility, new types of contracts, attitudes and values of the worker in the future, adaptation to new markets, products and services, new types of work and work contracts (telework, virtual offices, distance work, telemeetings, electronic communication), etc. have been and will continue to be central topics on the agenda of the practitioner as well as the researcher in W&O psychology.

In actual fact it would be quite fair to say that W&O psychologists have often been the originators of change. W&O psychologists were among the first to warn against the negative consequences of Taylor's 'scientific management'. They took a lead in pointing out the importance of the quality of working life, the possibility of improving work performance and decision making by promoting the involvement and participation of personnel, in showing that safety policy and accident prevention cannot be confined to the training and conditioning of individual workers but has to be seen as a matter of integral concern for the entire social and organizational system, in warning about the limits of human information capacity and mental load, in indicating the various ways people can learn to cope with stress, in stressing the need to adapt learning and work tasks to older workers and the possibilities for doing so. This list could be extended almost endlessly with examples of new developments in human resource management.

What we are trying to say is that W&O psychologists have often been the forerunner in creating new insights and new ways of dealing with people in organizations. It is our conviction that in the future they will continue to play this role, so inherent to their responsibility: to develop insight into, and to promote the conditions for, an optimal functioning of the individual in organizations.

Let us end this chapter with a brief discussion of the future identity of W&O psychology, a subject which has been dealt with more extensively elsewhere (Drenth, 1997), but which also deserves some attention in this review article. The issue here is that there is a growing interest in W&O psychology outside mainstream psychology, both in training and in the work context. W&O psychologists are increasingly identifying themselves less as psychologists and more as organizational specialists, analysts, or consultants. They more often attend management and business conferences than psychology meetings. Organizational psychology is taught more outside conventional disciplinary psychology programmes (e.g., in MBA and management courses) than within them.

Such developments have driven organizational psychology beyond its original domain and have weakened its identity as a psychological discipline. Interdisciplinarity has become a fashionable motto. Often it is implied that pure psychology is not meaningful, problem-oriented, or relevant enough. Interdisciplinary training is then seen as being more concerned with real-life issues. 'Real-life problems aren't bothered about disciplinary boundaries', as is often said.

The question is: is this a desirable development and should it be encouraged? In answer, it should first be recognized that broadening the orientation of the organizational psychologist so as to include insight into business, management, economic, political, and social problems should be appreciated as a desirable or even a necessary advancement. Moreover, it cannot be denied that organizational psychology would benefit from developing a more problem-oriented attitude and the political skills needed to operate in a business environment and to implement findings in practice, and from a greater capacity to translate everyday problems into analyzable questions. In addition, spreading the organizational 'gospel' in other faculties and schools should also be welcomed. Insights developed and decisions taken in adjacent scientific fields are certainly improved if knowledge of the 'human factor' is incorporated into them.

However, it is our opinion that this should not lead to the abandonment of the monodisciplinary identity of W&O psychology. In our opinion, the contribution of the organizational psychologist can best be safeguarded if training is based on a solid, disciplinary education in psychology. This education should focus on three dimensions, the unique combination of which gives the contribution of the W&O psychologist an added value.

The first dimension refers to the distinction between intra- and interindividual behavior. Organizational processes are influenced by both types of factors: individual motives, needs, and expectancies as well as interindividual interactions: collaboration, competition, and conflicts. The second dimension refers to the difference between the analytical knowledge of static psychological structures and functions on the one hand, and attention to processes of development and change on the other. Change can be brought about by natural growth and development as well as by deliberate intervention (laboratory or field experiments). The third dimension relates to the body of knowledge and insight resulting from a long tradition of reflection and experimentation in psychology on the one hand, and to the methodological and statistical tradition with an emphasis on instrument development, research design, and data analysis on the other.

These three dimensions form a cube which encompasses the eight basic competencies in W&O psychology as a scientific discipline, as illustrated in Figure 25.1. As can be seen, another dimension is added, indicated by dotted lines. This dimension comprises the four practical skills for diagnosing and understanding as well as influencing or changing human behavior in organizations. The lines are dotted since this dimension does not relate to the generation of generalizable knowledge, but to practical diagnostic or intervention competencies, which allow

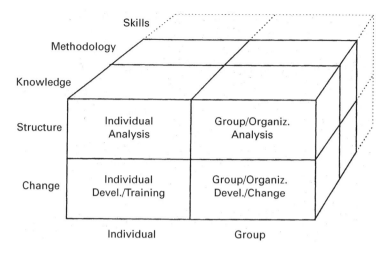

Figure 25.1 *Cube illustrating psychological and professional competences (from Drenth, 1997, p. 305, with permission of the publisher Psychology Press)*

for the professional contribution of the W&O psychologist.

It should be stressed again that the added value of the contribution of the W&O psychologist as a researcher or as a professional practitioner results from the unique combination of qualities which are represented in the different boxes within the competence cube. It is our opinion, therefore, that in the definition of W&O psychology as a scientific discipline, as well as in academic and professional training in W&O psychology, a proper balance between all these competencies and qualities has to be pursued. W&O psychology will then be able to retain its psychological identity. It will also be able, through the better understanding of human behavior in organizations, to contribute both to the proper functioning of organizations and to the well-being of their members.

Literature Cited

An * refers to a more general introduction or handbook in (a sub-specialization of) W&O psychology, published in the last 15 years.

Abt, L. E., & Riess, B. F. (1971). *Clinical psychology in industrial organizations.* New York: Grune & Stretton.

Bass, B. M., & Drenth, P. J. D. (1987). *Advances in organizational psychology.* Newbury Park, CA: Sage.

* Berk, R. A. (1986). *Performance assessment: Methods and applications.* Baltimore: Johns Hopkins University Press.

* Bobbitt, H. R., Breinholt, R. H., Doktor, R. H., & McNaul, J. P. (1978). *Organizational behavior* (2nd ed.). Englewood Cliffs, NJ: Prentice-Hall.

Bond, M. H. (1988). *The psychology of the Chinese people.* Hong Kong: Oxford University Press.

Dictionary of occupational titles. (1965). Washington, DC: Department of Labor.

Drenth, P. J. D. (1987). Conclusions and perspectives. In B. M. Bass & P. J. D. Drenth, *Advances in organizational psychology.* Newbury Park, CA: Sage.

Drenth, P. J. D. (1996). Psychology as a science: truthful or useful? *European Psychologist, 1,* 3–13. Also in: J. Georgas, M. Mauthhouli, E. Beseregis, & A. Kokkeri (Eds.), *Contemporary psychology in Europe* (pp. 23–40). Seattle: Hogrefe & Huber.

Drenth, P. J. D. (1997). Psychology of work and organizations; scientific inquiry and professional care. In J. G. Adair, K. Dion, & D. Bélanger (Eds.), *Advances in psychological science: Social, personal and cultural aspects* (pp. 295–306). Hove: Psychological Press.

Drenth, P. J. D., & den Hartog, D. N. (1998). *Culture and organizational differences.* In W. J. Lonner, D. N. Dinnel, D. K. Forkays & S. A. Hayes (Eds.), *Merging past, present and future* (pp. 489–502). Lisse: Swets & Zeitlinger.

* Drenth, P. J. D., Thierry, H., & de Wolff, C. J. (1998). *Handbook of work and organizational psychology* (2nd ed.). Vol. I, Introduction, 104 pp., Vol. II, Work psychology, 310 pp., Vol. III, Personnel psychology, 422 pp., Vol. IV, Organizational psychology, 496 pp. Hove: Psychology Press.

Dubin, R. (1976). *Handbook of work, organization and society.* Chicago: Rand McNally.

Dunnette, M. (1976). *Handbook of industrial and organizational psychology* (1st ed.). Chicago: Rand McNally.

Erez, M. (1994). Toward a model of cross-cultural industrial and organizational psychology. In H. C. Triandis, M. D. Dunnette, & L. M. Hough (Eds.), *Handbook of industrial and organizational psychology* (2nd ed., vol. 4, pp. 559–607). Palo Alto, CA: Consulting Psychologists Press.

Ester, P., Halman, L., & de Moor, R. (Eds.). (1993). *The individualizing society*. Tilburg: Tilburg University Press.

Hacker, W. (1986). *Arbeitspsychologie: Psychische Regulation von Arbeitstätigkeiten* [Work psychology: Psychological regulation of work activities]. Berlin/DDR: Deutscher Verlag der Wissenschaften.

* Herriot, P. (1989). *Assessment and selection in organizations*. Chichester: Wiley.

* Hofstede, G. (1980). *Culture's consequences: International differences in work-related values*. Beverly Hills, CA: Sage.

Hofstede, G. (1991). *Cultures and organizations: Software of the mind*. London: McGraw-Hill.

House, R. J. (1995). Leadership in the 21st century: A speculative enquiry. In A. Howard (Ed.), *The changing nature of work*. San Francisco: Jossey-Bass.

House, R. J., Hanges, P. J., Ruiz-Quintanilla, S. A., Dorfman, P. W., Javidan, M., Dickson, M., and 170 co-authors. (1998). Cultural influences on leadership and organizations: Project GLOBE. In W. Mobley (Ed.), *Advances in global leadership* (vol. 1). London: JAI Press.

Huang, K. L. (1995). A comparison of work values between Taiwan and mainland employees. In Kuo-shu Yang (Ed.), *Organizational psychology and behavior, indigenous psychological research in Chinese societies* (vol. 4). Taiwan: Guiguan Press.

IDE-International Research Group (1981). *Industrial democracy in Europe*, Vol. I. *Industrial relations in Europe*, Vol. II. Oxford: Oxford University Press.

IDE-International Research Group (1993). *Industrial democracy in Europe, revisited*. Oxford: Oxford University Press.

Inglehart, R. (1997). *Modernization and post-modernization*. Princeton: Princeton University Press.

* Jewell, L. N., & Siegall, M. (1990). *Contemporary industrial/organizational psychology* (2nd ed.). St. Paul: West Publishing Company.

* Katz, D., & Kahn, R. L. (1978). *The social psychology of organizations* (2nd ed.). New York: Wiley.

Koopman, P. L., & Algera, J. A. (1998). Automation: Socio-organizational aspects. In P. J. D. Drenth, H. Thierry, & C. J. de Wolff, *Handbook of work and organizational psychology* (2nd ed., vol. IV, pp. 429–460). Hove: Psychology Press.

Kroeber, A. L., & Parson, T. (1958). The concept of culture and of a social system. *American Sociological Review*, *23*, 582–583.

Leavitt, H. J. (1961). *Toward organisational psychology*. Pittsburg: Carnegy Institute of Technology.

Leavitt, H. J., & Bass, B. M. (1964). Organizational psychology. In P. H. Mussen & M. R. Rosenzweig (Eds.), *Annual review of psychology*, *15*. Palo Alto, CA: Annual Reviews.

Leung, K., Smith, P. B., Wang, Z. M., & Sun, H. (1996). Job satisfaction in joint venture hotels in China: An organizational justice analysis. *Journal of International Business Studies*, *27*, 947–962.

Meijers, C. S. (1920). *Mind and work*. London: University of London Press.

Misumi, J. (1985). With M. F. Peterson (Ed.), *The behavioral science of leadership*. Ann Arbor, MI: University of Michigan Press.

MOW International Research Team (1987). *Meaning of working. A cross national study*. London: Academic Press.

Pennings, J. M. (1998). Structural contingency theory. In P. J. D. Drenth, H. Thierry, & C. J. de Wolff, *Handbook of work and organizational psychology* (vol. IV, pp. 39–60). Hove: Psychology Press.

Porter, L. W. (1966). Personnel management. In P. R. Farnsworth, O. McNemar, & Q. McNemar (Eds.), *Annual Review of Psychology* (vol. 17). Palo Alto, CA: Ann. Reviews.

Quinn, R. E. (1988). *Beyond rational management*. San Francisco: Jossey-Bass.

Roe, R. A. (1984). Individual characteristics. In P. J. D. Drenth, H. Thierry, & C. J. de Wolff, *Handbook of work and organizational psychology* (pp. 103–130). Chichester: Wiley.

Roe, R. A., Coetsier, P., Levy-Leboyer, C. Peiro, J. M., & Wilpert, B. (1994). The teaching of work and organizational psychology in Europe. *The European Work and Organizational Psychologist*, *4*, 355–365.

Schein, E. (1992). *Organizational culture and leadership*. San Francisco: Jossey-Bass.

Schwartz,, S. H., & Sagiv, L. (1995). Identifying culture-specifics in the content and structure of values. *Journal of Cross-Cultural Psychology*, *26*, 92–116.

Smith, P. B., & Wang, Z. M. (1996). Chinese leadership and organizational structures. In M. Bond (Ed.), *Handbook of Chinese psychology* (pp. 322–338). Hong Kong: Oxford University Press.

Thierry, H. (1998). Motivation and satisfaction. In P. J. D. Drenth, H. Thierry, & C. J. de Wolff, *Handbook of work and organizational psychology* (2nd ed., vol. IV, pp. 253–289). Hove: Psychology Press.

Tiffin, J. (1942). *Industrial psychology*. Englewood Cliffs, NJ: Prentice-Hall.

* Triandis, H. (1994). *Culture and social behavior*. New York: McGraw-Hill.

Triandis, H. C. (1996). Cross-cultural industrial and organizational psychology. In M. D. Dunnette & L. M. Hough (Eds.), *Handbook of industrial and organizational psychology* (2nd ed., vol. 4). Palo Alto, CA: Consulting Psychologists Press.

Trompenaars, F. (1993). *Riding the waves of culture.* London: Economist Books.

Veen, P., & Korver, T. (1998). Theories of organizations. In P. J. D. Drenth, H. Thierry, & C. J. de Wolff, *Handbook of work and organizational psychology* (2nd ed., vol. IV, pp. 5–38). Hove: Psychology Press.

Verburg, R. M., Drenth, P. J. D., Koopman, P. L., van Muijen, J. J., & Wang, Z. M. (1999). Managing human resources across cultures: A comparative analysis of practices in industrial enterprises in China and the Netherlands. *The International Journal of Human Resource Management, 10,* 391–410.

Viteles, M. S. (1932). *Industrial psychology.* New York: Norton.

Vroom, V. (1964). *Work and motivation.* New York: Wiley.

Wang, Z. M. (1996a). Assessment of managerial skills for Chinese state-owned enterprises. Hangzhou University, unpublished report to the Testing Center of the Ministry of Personnel, China.

Wang, Z. M. (1996b). Culture, economic reform and the role of industrial and organizational psychology in China. In M. D. Dunnette & L. M. Hough (Eds.), *Handbook of industrial and organizational psychology* (2nd ed., vol. 4). Palo Alto, CA: Consulting Psychologists Press.

Wang, Z. M. (1998). Situational design for the microsoft (China) assessment process. Hangzhou University, unpublished report to Microsoft Greater China.

Wang, Z. M., & Heller, F. A. (1993). Patterns of power distribution in managerial decision making in Chinese and British industrial organizations. *The International Journal of Human Resource Management, 4,* 113–128.

Wilpert, B. (1990). How European is work and organizational psychology? In P. J. D. Drenth, J. A. Sergeant, & R. J. Takens, *European perspectives in psychology* (vol. 3, pp. 3–20). Chichester: Wiley.

In addition to the general introductory publications indicated with an * above we present hereafter some more recent titles for further reading.

Anderson, N., & Herriot, P. (1997). *International handbook of selection and assessment.* Chichester: Wiley.

Arnold, J., Cooper, C. L., & Robertson, I. T. (1995). *Work psychology: Understanding human behavior in the workplace* (2nd ed.). London: Pitman Publishing.

Berry, L. M., & Houston, J. P. (1993). *Psychology at work.* Madison: Brown & Benckmark.

Dunnette, M. D., & Hough, L. M. (Eds.). (1990). *Handbook of industrial and organizational psychology* (2nd ed., vols. I–IV). Chicago: Rand McNally.

Greif, G., Holling, H., & Nicholson, N. (1989). *Arbeits- und Organisationspsychologie* [Work and organizational psychology]. München: Psychologie Verlags Union.

Guion, R. M. (1998). *Assessment, measurement, and prediction for personnel decisions.* Mahevah, London: Lawrence Erlbaum.

Miner, J. M. (1992). *Industrial-organizational psychology.* New York: McGraw-Hill.

Nicholson, N. (Ed.). (1995). *Encyclopedic dictionary of organisational behaviour.* Cambridge, MA: Blackwell.

Porteus, M. (1997). *Occupational psychology.* Hemel Hempstead: Prentice-Hall Europe.

Pugh, D. S., & Hickson, D. J. (Eds.). (1993). *Great writers on organizations.* Brookfield/Adershof: Dartmouth.

Semin, G., & Friedler, K. (Eds.). (1996). *Applied social psychology.* London: Sage.

Smither, R. M. (1990). *The psychology of work and human performance.* New York: Harper Collins.

Spector, P. E. (1996). *Industrial and organizational psychology: Research and practice.* New York: Wiley.

Weick, K. E. (1995). *Sensemaking in organizations.* Thousand Oaks, CA: Sage.

Wilpert, B. (1995). Organizational behavior. *Annual Review of Psychology, 46,* 59–90.

Communications concerning this chapter should be addressed to: Professor Pieter J. D. Drenth, Faculty of Psychology and Pedagogics, Department of Work and Organizational Psychology – Vrije Universiteit, De Boelelaan 1081c, NL-1081 HV Amsterdam, The Netherlands

26

Applied Social Psychology

JOSÉ M. PRIETO, MICHEL SABOURIN,
LENORE E. A. WALKER, JUAN I. ARAGONÉS,
AND MARIA AMERIGO

26.1 INTRODUCTION: TWO OF A KIND

Two Pioneers

There are two pioneering figures in the domain of applied psychology: Hugo Munsterberg and Edouard Claparède. Hugo Munsterberg (1863–1916) is considered the senior pioneer because he began his experimental research in applied psychology in 1885 in the laboratory at the University of Freiburg in Germany. He was later invited by William James to conduct applied psychology research at Harvard University. Munsterberg became a consultant in a variety of areas including fatigue and accident analysis, business and consumer behavior, forensic issues and dilemmas, aviation psychology as well as psychological therapy.

The second pioneering figure was Edouard Claparède (1873–1940) who created the journal *Archives de Psychologie* in 1901 and in 1908 became a professor of psychology at the University of Geneva. His main disciple and successor was Jean Piaget. Claparède's field of study and expertise was educational and school psychology, stressing a functional perspective to understand learning and intelligent behavior. He became a well-known educational consultant in many countries under the aegis of several international organizations. Claparède suggested how psychological knowledge could be used to intervene actively in the treatment of individuals and groups with real life troubles and to solve problems in business, education, and government. In 1920 Claparède founded the International Association of Psychotechnics (that is, psychological technologies) which afterwards became the International Association of Applied Psychology (http://www.iaapsy.org).[1]

Two Frameworks

Social psychology got its name in 1908 from the title of two books published separately in London (authored by William McDougall, a psychologist) and in New York (authored by E. A. Ross, a sociologist). This name for an area of applied psychology gained rapid acceptance:

for instance, in 1921 the *Journal of Abnormal Psychology* became the *Journal of Abnormal and Social Psychology*. It emerged as a new label subsuming other customary terms.

Initially, social psychologists studied social instincts as the way to gain a comprehensive understanding of the collective efforts of individuals as well as groups. In the 1920s, for instance, the concept of a *group mind* became the focus of analysis, implying the existence of a group consciousness that exceeded the individual consciousness of group members. A methodological and conceptual distance developed between those social psychologists studying group behavior and those psychologists studying individual and group differences. Both disciplines started to drift apart. Social psychologists claimed that the behavior of a group cannot be understood just by knowing the set of complementary or incompatible characteristics of its individual members. Differential psychologists opposed the concept of *syntality* which is the group equivalent to the personality of the individual. By learning the characteristics of the group, it will improve the ability to predict what that group will do in some very specific circumstances under scrutiny. Social psychologists learned to analyze the collective behavior of a stable group in terms of process variables and social structure. In contrast, differential psychologists analyzed ability and personality traits of its members that supported the attractiveness and cohesiveness of the group, evident through performance and interactions. Social psychologists highlighted, for instance, that a given group itself could have its own degree of concern for something (group mind). Differential psychologists highlighted, by contrast, that only individuals in the group can indicate such concern and as a whole, the group will demonstrate its concern in a way that may be forecast (syntality). In other words, is a group considered to lead its members into being 'corrupted and deceitful' a leading group or do corrupted and deceitful leaders belong to such a particular leading group?

This distinction is just the second example of two distinct ways of developing applied social psychology. Conventionally, 'social psychologists' viewed themselves as psycho-social agents involved in intervention research programs. By contrast, for decades, 'differential psychologists' have been known as 'applied psychologists'. If their methods are combined, then the title 'Applied Social Psychology' can be used to describe intervention research and practice that deals directly with the facts themselves.

Two Pacesetters

Kurt Lewin (1890–1947) is considered one of the pacesetters in the domain of applied social psychology because he emphasized the usefulness of an experimental and experiential perspective in the analysis of social behavior through action research (Lewin, 1951). Lewin advocated that the method to be used by an applied social psychologist is not just to be an observer but to join in the group and become just another participant. He believed that the actual process of actions generated by a specific group is itself the subject of psychological research. As a consequence, the set of activities undertaken by groups appointed or organized to solve specific problems or to attain distinct goals become the focus of the applied social psychologist's interventions. Lewin stated that the best way for the applied social psychologist to intervene was to both participate in and observe the group's reflection of their experience as well as the way they memorize their actions and its results. The result of both kinds of intervention is that applied social psychologists become experts in action-group processes and in action-learning groups and so can contribute what they have learned to increase the quality of life in an affluent society.

A second international pacesetter in applied social psychology has been Edwin Fleishman (1927–) known for his application of the experimental and multivariate perspective in the analysis of the individual and the group performance. Fleishman has advocated that applied social psychologists employ standard scientific and technological methods, using tasks and measures that make it possible to study individuals and situations reliably in real life settings. Applied social psychologists are external observers or at most, very indirect participants in the workgroup being studied. Factors affecting individual or group performance are the main subject of analysis; once identified and validated, such factors are viewed as psychological dimensions or constructs leading to improved generalizations and predictions in program interventions and in decision-making processes where new but related tasks and situations are taken into account. The focus of analysis is human performance in a wide variety of settings (Fleishman & Quaintance, 1984). The objective is to develop taxonomies that, when merged with appropriate sets of quantitative data and a strategic outlook, might be useful for forecasting purposes. Under this framework, the world of human actions and social behavior is not chaotic, improbable, and inaccessible. The result of this methodological approach is that applied social psychologists can become experts who successfully predict and generalize about human performance, the touchstone that can increase the quality of life in affluent societies.

Lewin and Fleishman present two quite different and seemingly incompatible research and intervention traditions in social applied psychology, but both perspectives have been present throughout the twentieth century when psychologists have dealt with a large variety of issues. For instance:

1. Changes in food habits may be enhanced by fostering focus groups discussing the advantages of the new product compared with other products. In this context, the consumer psychologist plays a visible role during the discussions. But also changes in food habits may be enhanced by supplying the new product and other competing products at no cost and then analyzing consumption patterns during a given period through a follow up of purchases and returns. In this context, the consumer psychologist may remain invisible for the sample of people testing the new product.

2. Stress symptoms may be addressed by sport psychologists fostering group discussions among teammates and by analyzing rational and irrational fears before and during an important match against a competing team. Successful learning is the consequence of a reorganization of the perception of stressors and of the generation of a new insight. The psychologist plays the role of facilitator in group discussions. An optional strategy used by other sport psychologists has been to assess individual stress symptoms in each member of the team and then train the team member in coping strategies taking into consideration differentially the predisposition to succeed or fail by setting aside rational and irrational fears before and during an important match. Successful learning is the consequence of adequate training instructions to facilitate coping strategies; the stressors are considered mere stimuli. The psychologist plays the role of assessor.

3. Organizational and health psychologists may study the degree of satisfaction among patients in a hospital by getting patients together in small group sessions, and inviting them to comment on direct or indirect examples of satisfactory or regrettable health services received during the treatment period. An optional approach is to interview the patients in the room by asking them to enunciate examples of agreeable manners and sensitivity they have felt during their stay in the hospital. Another possibility is to administer an exit survey to every patient and analyze the answers by specialties, by buildings, by shifts, by seasons. The outcome will differ according to the strategy launched. When

patients are granted the possibility of commenting using specific examples, strong distinctions and subtle nuances flow in the group dynamics; somehow the organizational and health psychologist chairing the meeting becomes another participant and may be viewed as such by the other members in the group. By contrast, patients usually would not view the interviewing psychologist as a participant in the examples set down as a reaction to questions such as 'were you pleasantly surprised by your doctor when he or she did . . .?' But in fact that very question only looks for an answer about positive feelings and may encourage one particular answer over another. Although administering a survey might create an impression of neutrality by the absence of the psychologist, each time generic questions such as 'are you satisfied with . . .?' are posed, two out of three people tend to respond showing a general sentiment of contentment. Answering a survey with a positive mood is a friendly way to project a good image before the pollster.

These are three instances showing that the same real life issue may be examined by social applied psychologists following in the footsteps of two quite distant schools in the academic milieu but quite close frameworks in psychological practice.

Bringing out Psychological Products

A critical issue is the understanding of how psychological products are generated to fill a gap in applied and social settings. Figure 26.1 provides the hidden cues that are rarely highlighted (Low, 1992): an idea in a form with a demand.

The first ingredient is *ideas*. While teaching or doing research, psychologists get used to pondering notions, conceptions, models, theoretical frameworks, ways of describing or explaining human cognition, emotion and action. The outcome of such mental activity is a set of ideas

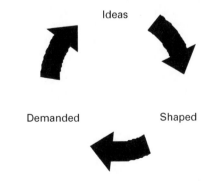

Figure 26.1 *Applied social psychology: generating psychological products*

revealing the inner relationships between events, actions, or phenomena. Society subsidizes the learning process of university graduates expecting they will become advanced experts who are full of ideas and know how to elaborate and refine the flow of ideas when they stimulate creative thinking. In one way or another, the business of university students and graduates is the world of ideas. However, this is not enough; it is essential to know how to shape and structure these ideas.

The second ingredient is *shaping*. Ideas alone survive in the books and journals, dreaming until they wake up on a bookshelf. Psychological ideas must be transformed, shaped, organized, and structured to become an actual psychological product. Through the form, an idea becomes something and gets an identity. Intelligence or projective tests, graphic rating scales, interview schemes, individual or group exercises, protocols, the syllabus and goals of a seminar, the report to the client, the scientific paper, all are tangible and psychological products. Each has a distinct form, a structure, a layout, a procedure, a cost. The output is an applied and social technology. This is the origin of expressions such as 'psychotechnics' and 'psychotechnology'. The artificer works out together several ideas in a long chain of decisions, some related to psychology and some to the commercial side of the final product (Prieto & Martinez-Arias, 1997). A wrong decision in the process of shaping up the set of interrelated ideas underlying any psychological product may ruin its availability or acceptance. An idea without a given form is only a ghost. Quite often the process of developing and shaping ideas remains under the control of professors, not of students, on the campus. The psychotechnological approach is an unresolved matter that young graduates learn to handle through a period of supervised practice or through trial and error. Currently the syllabus, in the campus, deals with psychology, not with psychotechnology!

The third ingredient is the existence of an actual *demand*. Successful applications of psychological knowledge are backed by the societal demand; such a good or service must improve the quality of life of individuals, groups, or organizations. Applied social psychology fails when there is the social perception that the product supplied might be nice, interesting, innovative but irrelevant for the well-being of the targeted audience. If the goods or service launched obtains the support of grateful or responsive customers it rises to the occasion and the program is welcome. The immediate consequence is jobs, in the public or the private sector. It is the touch of the master.

Figure 26.1 illustrates, in a loop, how an applied psychological product exists if one or several ideas are interrelated and shaped together, generating a unique form that is backed gradually by the demand. It is sought and needed. It has a name and is identified by a logo or by a trademark; it may be bought, exchanged, donated, or stolen. If there is no demand, the product ends packed in the chest of souvenirs. If there is no demand and no form, the idea is a succession of images, of thoughts, of cognitive emotions, not yet a professional plan, a program, a course of action, a psychological tool. The three threads weave the fabric of psychological products.

26.2 APPLIED SOCIAL PSYCHOLOGY: THE JANUS CLOTH

To understand the section it is helpful to remember the typical ambiguous figures produced and disseminated by Gestalt psychology: some people see the old lady, for instance, and others see the young woman. The concept underlines the perceptual dichotomy of the original figure; each vision is meaningful but only when viewed separately. However, the concept also stresses the perceptual polarity in the image: each vision is ephemerally true but requires the evanescent presence of the complementary image. Both have an actual but chimerical appearance. Understanding becomes, just, a matter of discernment and perspicacity; perception is in the eye of the beholder. The four-dimensional reality cannot be captured gratuitously!

Goods and services created by the applied social psychologist nourish the coexistence of Janus-faced profiles. This is not a matter of dichotomy (two mutually exclusive pairs), but of polarity (a Janus cloth, that is, a worsted fabric each side of which has a different color). Applied social psychology also pursues the logic of paradoxes.

Psychological Science as well as Psychological Technology

Applied social psychology utilizes the null hypothesis to verify the adequacy of propositions and models in a given subject. The focus is the aseptic analysis of contrasted facts through valid measures or reliable databases. Researchers, consultants, or practitioners, when explaining or predicting what happens at the individual, group, or organizational level, claim a value-free profile. But the same researchers, consultants, or practitioners currently handle advanced knowledge expertly to deal with and solve individual, group, or societal problems by changing situation A (not desirable) into situation B (highly desirable). Under such circumstances, the psychological product is intended to contribute to an increase in the quality of life of the society or the customer. The focus is the analysis of facts highlighted by values, which quite often are under the influence of political, deontological, and benevolent as well as self-interested motives. As a consequence applied social psychology does adopt a value orientation technological profile in the process of explaining or predicting what happens at the individual, group, or organizational level.

A typical example is the study of how alcohol influences driving behavior. Traffic psychologists may gradually increase drivers' intake of alcohol and analyze their behavioral patterns in a car-simulator. The covariance between errors and alcohol consumption is studied and critical levels of alcohol are determined empirically. This is within the framework of psychology as a scientific field of inquiry. In a similar vein, traffic psychologists may study the outcomes of alcohol tests administered at the roadside by police. Within the framework of psychology as a technological field of inquiry, they use statistical methods to find the critical level of alcohol consumption that impairs tests of balance, and they may submit suggestions to politicians or authorities in their role as assistants to policy makers. Science fixes the standard from the analysis of facts, mainly in the laboratory. Technology fixes the standard by combining facts, judgments, and values within the framework of a strategy of road safety. The scientific perspective studies and may explain the subject, whereas the technological perspective fixes and may solve the problem.

Human Behavior and Human Performance

For decades, many researchers, consultants, and practitioners emphasized that human behavior was the basic unit of analysis. The focus of empirical study or inquiry has been observable activities as well as responses to internal or external stimuli. The result is a profile of applied social psychology as the science of human behavior. At the same time, human performance has also been the basic unit of analysis for many other researchers, consultants, and practitioners. They use it as the dependent variable when they have had to persuade present or potential customers about the 'ad hoc' suitability of their expertise. Human performance becomes the basic unit of analysis for applied social psychologists paying attention to those activities leading

to a result (Campbell, McCloy, Oppler, & Sager, 1993). As soon as there is a task or a challenge, a person's performance emerges and can be studied. Human performance may be the outcome of a thoughtful strategy, of a sincere engagement, of ad-libbing, but also of a theatrical play. Children and adults concern themselves with the minutiae of playing as well as of reaching goals daily. Human performance can be seen when applied social psychologists design and evaluate intervention programs to influence the degree of change in individuals or groups. Thus, an understanding of applied social psychology would not be complete without a profile of applied social psychology as providing a technology of human performance. Human performance is always observable and measurable, because it points to specific actions contributing or failing to attain the expected result. By contrast, human behavior is not always observable but inferred, as is the case sometimes in cognitive and emotional behavior.

A typical example occurs when health psychologists analyze the nexus between stress and smoking patterns among health professionals and they find the occurrence of stable relationships. But, also they may be requested to predict the occurrence of symptoms of stress that negatively affect the otherwise stable and friendly interaction between medical and nursing staff in a hospital if smoking in public becomes formally forbidden within the premises. The first example deals with behavioral and the second with performance issues in the workplace.

Psychological Knowledge as well as Psychological Achievements

The main purpose pursued in rigorous research and practice is often said to be the expansion of the body of scientific knowledge in applied social psychology. Journals and conventions sponsored by national and international associations push towards this advancement. Excellence is strengthened after the existence and the convergence of contrasted knowledge in the discipline. In fact, this is the realm of hypotheses and predictions emanating from theories or models and validated after thorough examination and investigation into the matter. However, unlike in basic science, the excellence of a discipline is recognized by society only if there is a series of continuous accomplishments and successes led by well-known professionals involved in problem-solving programs (Dorken, 1986; Prieto, 1992). Their achievements are compared with those of other competing professionals in similar domains of expertise. Success is not measured as a matter of public opinion or mass media but rather, it is a matter of presence or absence in problem-solving and decision-making committees. It is a matter of inclusion or exclusion in strategic actions and plans launched by policy makers in the region. It is a matter of high visibility or clandestine working when sound knowledge is taken into consideration when dealing with societal issues and dilemmas. Achievements exist if psychologists achieve the intended goals they have been pursuing through applied and social actions or when they complete a creditable action. Achievements tend to be attributed directly to the expert or the leading researcher involved. Achievements are understood as a contribution to progress or fulfillment, as masterpieces.

A good example is how testing procedures succeed in being selected for vocational guidance or personnel selection. Sometimes instructors, supervisors, superintendents, personnel managers, military officers, and others, years if not decades before scientific knowledge about assessment, evaluation, and psychometrics has been standardized, sponsor an approach. A comprehensive body of knowledge has been developed as a consequence of the systematic analysis of accomplishments and failures. A comparison of textbooks on psychometrics published in the 1920s and in the 1990s shows real progress in the development of new sets of formulas and indices but the mathematical background still remains the same. Computers add sophistication in testing and evaluation methodologies, for instance, but the general framework remains the same. In fact, the large majority of findings published in contemporary psychometric journals are rarely used in applied social psychology. These findings create good basic science but do not significantly improve the decision-making processes, accomplishments or achievements. The authors do not reach the audience of policy makers, and this is a critical issue concerning the survival of any scientific or technological discipline. An achievement is the support that consultant psychologists obtain when they renew a contract, when a psychological approach becomes a local, regional, or national standard in the field, when a psychological expression for identifying workplace events ('sexual harassment', 'creativity', IQ or EQ for instance) is welcomed and accepted in many languages, discourses, daily talk, or legislation. A way of verifying the achievements of applied social psychologists is to search and find out how psychological terminologies and frameworks appear in the minutes and norms enacted within organizations, within society, by the parliament, the ministry, the chief executive officer. When done, this follow-up often raises the researcher's spirit. However, it is convenient to stress that achievements are both of a professional and a political nature.

These three dyads, taken together, value applied social psychology both as (a) a behavioral science whose main focus is the production of sound knowledge in the context of scientific discoveries and advancements; and (b) a behavioral technology focused on the attainment of persuasive achievements in the context of improving the quality of life in the society.

It is not mere duality or the coexistence of two ways of being an applied social psychologist. Rather, it is two equal and valid ways of understanding the role and goals of applied social psychology within the scientific community and within an affluent society. One way cannot triumph over the other nor merge with the other. In each field, applied social psychologists serve those goals and needs fitting their techniques and frameworks and avoid extending their approaches beyond their established expertise (Dorken, 1986). In this way they design and promote specific psychological programs to deal with real life problems, with issues in the laboratory or with interventions in open field studies and actions. A smile is the fire escape for all ambiguities.

26.3 APPLIED SOCIAL PSYCHOLOGY: MAKING A LONG STORY SHORT

The list of subspecialties that may be placed within the umbrella of applied social psychology is quite long and continues to grow. The terminology used has changed at different phases of the history of each subspecialty and, furthermore, from English to non-English language (see, for instance, the search engine located at: http://www.cop.es/database/ or the homepage of the International Union of Psychological Science, at: http://www.iupsys.org). Some areas are described in other chapters of this Handbook. There are some areas that warrant attention, especially since they have had a sufficient number of practitioners to become a division within the International Association of Applied Psychology (IAAP). Audience and membership is a non-intrusive measure of consolidation and soundness. The IAAP is the oldest worldwide association of scholars and practitioners, identifying themselves as applied social psychologists, from 94 countries. Further details may be found at: http://www.iaapsy.org/.

These are the 14 divisions of the IAAP and chapters where their fields are mentioned in this Handbook:

1. Organizational psychology (Chapter 25).
2. Psychological assessment and evaluation (Chapter 20).
3. Psychology and national development (briefly in this chapter).
4. Environmental psychology (extensively in this chapter).
5. Educational, instructional, and school psychology (Chapter 24).
6. Clinical and community psychology (clinical psychology, Chapters 21 and 22; community psychology briefly in this chapter).
7. Applied gerontology (Chapter 15).
8. Health psychology (Chapter 23).
9. Economic psychology (briefly in this chapter).
10. Psychology and law (extensively in this chapter).
11. Political psychology (briefly in this chapter).
12. Sport psychology (briefly in this chapter).
13. Traffic and transportation psychology (briefly in this chapter).
14. Applied cognitive psychology (briefly in this chapter).

Describing precise details of each subspecialty area would require a handbook, already in progress, for each field. Several possibilities were considered. Finally, the first author of this chapter decided (a) to introduce in this section some basic tenets of those areas not approached in other chapters of this Handbook and (b) to devote the remaining two sections to a more detailed study of forensic and law psychology (written by Michel Sabourin and Lenore E. A. Walker) and to environmental psychology (written by Juan I. Aragonés and María Amérigo).

Each sub-discipline of expertise in applied social psychology has been approached in this section paying some attention to historic circumstances and focusing the attention on the standard contributions expected from scholars and practitioners acting as experts in the specific field. It is a concisely presented sketch of the expertise that seems to be already consolidated through the professional profile (COP, 1998; electronic version, http://www.cop.es/perfiles/).

Psychology and National Development

There appears to be a direct overlap between the strengthening of affluent societies and the strengthening of applied social psychology as a scientific and technological field of research and expertise. In fact, the large majority of professional projects and programs in applied social psychology may be categorized within the service sector of the economy. A majority of long-term research and action projects that have attained high visibility and an aura of respectability were subsidized by public funding in developed countries.

It is not only a question of a lack of resources and job opportunities in developing countries. During the twentieth century, dictatorships and theocratic governments imprisoned or forced into exile a large number of scholars and practitioners in psychology, notably in Spain, several Latin American, some Asian and Arab countries. There were also many cases of graduates in psychology for whom it was more convenient to stay abroad than come back home because they were considered 'persona non grata' by their field of expertise. Perhaps this is because many of the psychological findings appear to be laden with the politics of democratically, culturally, or economically advanced settings.

It is not clear that applied social psychology only reflects a way of life in advanced and open societies. The 24 International Congresses of Applied Psychology, held during the twentieth century, have provided an important forum to exchange working hypotheses, predictions, and analyses among scholars and practitioners testing the same or quite similar models in countries with different kinds of economic or governmental structures (Adair & Kagitcibasi, 1995). The result has created an area of expertise in studying sensitive issues in developing countries such as (a) factors facilitating progress; (b) individual and community development programs; (c) the psychosocial role of institutions; (d) psychosocial challenges in periods of transitions; (e) transformation processes in post-communist countries; (f) ethnocentrism and psychology; (g) the role of women in democratization processes; (h) the transfer of research information from developed to developing countries; (i) psychotherapy and ethnic minorities; (j) diversity values, mentalities, and ideologies; (k) psychological crises in refugees and war victims; (l) human rights and democracy; and (m) acculturation and adaptation.

Cross-cultural psychology (Chapter 18 in this Handbook) and psychology and national development share many methodological techniques around the observation, study or comparison of specific psychological issues (Triandis, 1993). However there are important differences in the focus. Cross-cultural psychology is focused on the analysis of positive facts, on the comparison of patterns between persons or groups of different cultures or settings, and it tries to avoid alignments around political issues while acknowledging differences. Psychology and national development is focused on the analysis of complex phenomena, on screening the latent causes of behavioral, cognitive, emotional, or social patterns, and it welcomes the challenge of analyzing political conflicts and their impact on individuals and society.

A typical example of these differences may be detected by a content analysis of congresses sponsored by the Interamerican Psychological Society (IPS) before and after 1980. In the 1960s and 1970s the program dealt mostly with cross-cultural and language comparisons between North and South American countries. The influence of what has been called 'liberation theology' and the bankruptcies of military regimes changed the perspective. The focus of attention moved towards using psychology to understand problems in daily living; unfairness and injustice affecting second-class citizens, aboriginal people, and impoverished masses; dilemmas, threats, and vested interests obstructing or favoring societal progress, and personal growth or family well-being. Another example can be observed by analyzing the focus at the European Congresses of Psychology sponsored during the 1990s by the European Federation of Professional Psychologists Associations (EFPPA, http://www.efppa.org/). Before the fall of the Berlin Wall, there was a prevalence of papers analyzing cross-cultural differences between Eastern and Western European countries; papers prevailed analyzing the consequences of political and economic transition from real socialism to capitalism or liberalism.

There is a trap set to scholars trained in developed countries when they return home. Many of them try to transfer what they have learned. Only a minority develop indigenous models and methods adequate to deal with current challenges and problems requiring a sound psychological approach adjusted to the near by surroundings (Kim & Berry, 1993). Their contributions actually facilitate and impend progress in developing countries. Their ideas are shaped to meet the societal demands. A good example is the contribution of Jyuji Misumi to Japanese management techniques. His research on group dynamics and small group processes was welcomed by many businesses and industries to increase production and quality.

Further information concerning new trends in the analysis and follow-up of psychological contributions to national development may be found at the Society for the Psychological Study of Social Issues (http://www.spssi.org), the APA Division 52 of International Psychology (http://www.tamu-commerce.edu/orgs/div52.html) and the Society for the Study of Peace, Conflict and Violence, APA Division 48, Peace Psychology (http://moon.pepperdine.edu/ ~ mstimac/Peace-Psychology.html); see also Chapter 27 in this Handbook.

Community Psychology

Health and social problems quite often come together and then it becomes somehow artificial to approach and treat each facet separately or to focus the attention only on the individual. Community psychology addresses both well-being as well as health issues, combining social and institutional perspectives and highlighting the importance of social systems and environmental influences for enhancing wellness. The initiative may be transferred to the hands of direct or indirect relatives, to the solidarity of people suffering a similar problem, to certain degrees of empowerment in delicate circumstances, to psychosocial feelings of identity, pride, and dignity present in the community. Community research and action sometimes is the point of departure for a reactive and curative outlook or for a proactive and preventive reorganization in normal or abnormal courses of events. It is also a matter of switching to a scientific or a technological way of understanding and outreaching health and social well-being issues and dilemmas.

Since the mid-1960s, community psychologists have developed a large and diversified set of procedures and techniques to analyze, evaluate, and intervene in complex and dynamic processes favoring or obstructing the quality of life and the well-being of groups and individuals in a given community (COP, 1998). There are several purposes to this subspecialty: (a) increasing the awareness of the people involved; (b) training them in those skills, strategies, and competencies that are helpful when they analyze delicate social realities or when they try to find adequate solutions; (c) predicting and reducing the probability of high-risk situations for some members of the community; (d) providing additional institutional and welfare support where needed. Community psychologists attempt to prevent problems from occurring in the first place or where they have appeared, lower the risk of their negative impact on individuals, families, and community groups.

Community psychologists intervene with community members, caregivers, individuals, and families of groups of people in distress such as: (a) minors requiring an analysis of sensitive circumstances and a support to overcome severe weaknesses or conflicts in the family, launching programs of adoption, family and foster care; (b) aging men and women and their caregivers needing to make the decision whether to live alone or with partial or complete assistance in geriatric units; (c) people evidencing challenges from disabilities or deficiencies needing psychological training to deal with daily life as well as occupational issues and designing programs to promote the acceptance and the integration of these persons in the school, the workplace, the community; (d) women requiring special aid programs to guarantee the fulfilment of their human, civil, or social rights; (e) young men and women in transition from the educational to the occupational setting, needing orientation and guidance to deal with sensitive issues such as crime-prevention, school-failure, drug-addiction, sexual life, suicide, healthy attitudes, and behavioural patterns; (f) ethnic minorities, immigrants, and refugees requiring programs to deal with the psychological consequences of their exclusion from a given community and their integration in that or in another community; (g) drug-addicts, granting them ambulatory care as well as hospitalization, assessing their progress in the process of recovery, supplying support and training to their relatives.

Community psychologists use methods such as need analysis, group counseling, group problem-solving, family counseling and therapy, program evaluation, transaction and mediation as well as arbitration, surveys and inventories, discussion groups, the Delphi technique, behavior mapping, cognitive rehearsal, successive approximations, and the like. The kind of functions they perform in the organizations where they are employed may identify them as consultants, advocates, agents of change, supervisors of programs, facilitators of community enhancement processes, program managers and evaluators, designers of training and development projects, or even epidemiologists. There are major differences among countries and governments concerning the acceptance, support and feasibility of community psychology plans, actions, and involvement.

Democratic societies, where policy makers highlight mainly civil rights, devote less attention and financial support to these programs than those where policy makers endorse formally both civil and social rights. Theocratic societies sanction such programs under the heading of charity and beneficence or by allocating them to charitable institutions. An updated overview of this discipline by subjects as well as by countries has been edited by López-Cabanas and Chacón (1997). Communist societies have considered these kinds of programs rather irrelevant, usually making a passing reference within broader and generic schemes of policy-making in the country.

Further information concerning new trends in community psychology may be found online at: http://www.apa.org/divisions/div27/ (Society for Community and Research Action), http://www.geocities.com/CollegePark/Library/3543/contact.html (community psychology web ring), http://www.cmmtypsych.net/ (community psychology net), and http://www.wiley.com/journals/casp/ Home.html (community and applied psychology journal).

Economic Psychology

The expression 'Economic Psychology' can be traced back to 1901, because it was the title of the course taught by G. Tarde at the University of Paris and published the following year. The expression 'The Psychology of Advertising' was the title of an article published in 1900, by H. Gale, from the University of Minnesota. W. D. Scott was the first psychologist, specializing in advertising psychology, employed by a publishing firm also in 1901. In the 1920s, John B. Watson (1878–1958), the founder of Behaviorism, was hired by a cosmetic firm to work in the area of advertising and marketing research, once he was forced to abandon the direction of his laboratory at the Johns Hopkins University because of the aftermath of a love affair. It is clear that this has been one of the pioneering fields in moving applied social psychology to a scientific or a technological frame of reference. In 1981, the *Journal of Economic Psychology* was launched, becoming the main forum.

At present 'economic psychology', 'consumer psychology', 'business psychology', 'marketing psychology' are viewed as different titles identifying a sphere of research and intervention within the realm of the acquisition, management, and distribution of wealth. The focus of analysis is economic behavior, studying its antecedents, and forecasting its consequences (Van Raaj, 1999). Another perspective heightens 'economic psychology' as the broad trade name for applied social psychology because it establishes the comprehensive framework. 'Homo economicus' is the subject who borrows, buys, earns, donates, exchanges, gambles, invests, lends, saves, spends, transacts, and works. Under this premise, economic psychology would be considered the trunk and each discipline a branch focused on a specific range of inputs and outputs in real life issues and dilemmas affecting human cognition, emotion, and behavior.

In this chapter, however, economic psychology is just used as the label for a specific discipline. It studies how people are influenced by the economy and what psychological processes are involved in the economic behavior of people when they make decisions looking for a better quality of life and increased well-being. The psychologists practicing in this field analyze and follow up (a) beliefs, values, preferences, attitudes, choices, plans, purposes, and factors underlying the economic behavior of citizens, producers, and consumers; (b) the consequence of foresight, decisions, pressures, oscillations, and legislation influencing or shaping the economic behavior of citizens, producers, and consumers; (c) the inducement and satisfaction of economic needs and goals among producers, citizens, and consumers.

The main areas of psychological research and action in this discipline can be organized in three categories:

1. The analysis of individual as well as family members' behavior in the role of consumers. The main subjects are the study of psychological factors and processes underlying the choice of goods and services, the loyalty to brand names and trademarks, the usefulness of the information and its understandability, complaints and reputation damage, suitable and satisfactory purchases, savings and investments, borrowing and over-indebtedness via credit cards, risks, and mortgages, insurance policies, testaments, and beneficiaries.

2. The analysis of entrepreneurial initiatives, strategies and action to introduce, maintain, or increase the presence of goods and services produced in the national or the international market. Some of the main subjects approached are sales strategies, advertising campaigns, investment plans, returns and refunds, price control, start-up competency profiles, and decision making inside and outside the firm.

3. The analysis of the economic behavior and attitudes of citizens concerning payment and evasion of taxes, periods of inflation or depression, reaction to economic measures or norms, unemployment subsidies, use of social funds, corruption and public funds squandering, and compulsive gambling.

There is a bias towards psychological studies focused on the micro-economic level, which permits keeping a certain distance from studies at the macro-economic level, preferred by sociologists and economists.

Economic psychologists use experimental designs such as single and double blind to test specific attributes or perceptual aspects of a product as well as trademark loyalty. Experimental designs are also used to ascertain price discrimination among similar goods of different sizes, to fix the typography and colors used or to maintain a balance between fashion and ergonomics in the design. The impact of an advertising campaign may be contrasted through pre-test and post-test designs. Sales force allocation schemes also have been validated experimentally. Survey researchers use cross-sectional studies to compare, for instance, potential customers contacted by phone, by mail, or face to face in the street, or to compare different modalities of

items or of wording. In a similar vein, survey researchers also use longitudinal studies of a panel of consumers' or retailers' meetings. Observational methods are also used to record consumer behaviors, for example, in a shopping center, by using video cameras, creating artificially hot and cold points of sale, or measuring the after effects of a promotion in several shops. Pseudo-sales are used to test the effectiveness of training programs among vendors, to identify regular customers, or test the adequacy of customer service department. There is a technique known as 'dustbin check' that contrasts items marked by customers in a survey and what is found in the garbage can.

Economic psychologists use various techniques such as questionnaires, surveys, behavior ratings, semantic differentials, the contents of shopping carts, and word-building tests to gather and analyze quantitative data. But they also use interviews, group discussions, behavior records, projective techniques, shopping lists, word association tests, protocols, and agendas to gather and analyze qualitative data. Sophisticated electronic tools, such as cookies and bootstrap tracers, have been developed to continue gathering data on consumer behavior online via the Internet.

Economic psychologists are often employed to fulfill several functions such as managers and consultants in the area of consumer analysis and marketing, in the role of program designers, researchers, program evaluators, developers of products and strategies, and advisors assessing needs and addiction patterns. Antonides, van Raaij and Maital (1997) summarize the state of the art of the discipline and describe new advances and challenges in a large number of sectors. Further information concerning new trends in economic psychology may be found online at: http://cwis.kub.nl/ ~ fsw_1/eco/links.htm (economic psychology links), and http://www. eiasm.be/iarep.html (International Association for Research in Economic Psychology, IAREP).

Political Psychology

Political Psychology and Social Defense was the title of the book published in 1910, in France, by G. Le Bon who supported the idea that the core issue of study in political psychology is the knowledge of how to govern people. Le Bon believed that the masterpiece and essential textbook for the discipline was Nicolo B. Machiavelli's *The Prince* published in 1532. In a similar vein, G. Wallas published in the UK in 1914 a book entitled *The Great Society: A Psychological Analysis*. In the US, H. D. Lasswell is considered the father of political psychology after the publication of his book on

Psychopathology and Politics which had a strong influence from psychoanalysis.

There have been a large number of recurrent subjects described by researchers and practitioners, which concern the political functioning of individuals as well as groups. Cognitive theory, psychoanalysis, and learning provide the background for four out of five researches published in the main journal of the field, *Political Psychology*, launched in 1980 (Boehnke & Bar-Tal, 1998).

Shifts in public opinion, belief, and value systems in a country or its evolution during periods of political transition have become classic. The analysis of political discourse, propaganda, and affiliation has also had a huge impact since latent ideologies and manipulation strategies have been used. There has been continuity in analyzing the influence of mass media in short-term opinions and attitudes, in long-term cognitive effects, and in beliefs and representation schema. The study of leadership and participation issues concerning motivation, power and influence, identification, self-esteem, and decision making has been frequently examined. Within the context of industrial democracy, for instance, some of the leadership and participation studies in work settings contributed to the dialogue between Eastern and Western European countries (Wilpert, Kudat, & Özkan, 1978) and some of them continue doing research on the psychological aspects present in the transition from 'real socialism'.

Studying the normal and abnormal personalities of political figures has been another target, paying some attention to the emotional catharsis generated in the general public by details of their private lives, for instance a wedding, a scandalous love affair, or a sudden death. The socialization process of making political choices, electoral preferences, and voting behavior has also been a favorite topic to study.

The issue of corruption in the government has been studied by psychologists as a situational phenomenon, usually looking at the behavior as a set of factors and circumstances favoring dishonesty and outlaws in sensitive affairs decided by top policy makers in both public or private institutions, but also in sensationalizing daily life affairs. The focus is on behaviors, situations, beliefs and values, and social perception of morally correct and corrupted conduct. The situation may prove to be both a criminal event in the biography of a leading figure or party but also a psychosocial failure for the society itself, causing them to give up hope.

Issues such as ethnocentrism, racism, nationalism, separatism, terrorism, and the interplay between majorities and minorities have been also approached, contributing to an in-depth understanding facilitating the planning of actions for peacemaking and peace building. Comparative studies on Puritanism, tolerance, and privacy in Anglo and non-Anglo cultures, in democratic or theocratic societies, in rural and urban milieus have been examined. The role and public image of governmental versus non-governmental agencies in dealing with aid programs dealing with refugees, war victims, and survivors of natural catastrophes is an increasingly popular subject area here. Delinquency and right-wing extremism in advanced societies have attracted attention under a preventive perspective.

Methodologically, political psychologists make use of a large number of techniques such as surveys, experiments in the laboratory, outdoor quasi-experiments and field studies, simulations, games, interviews by phone, attitude scales, content analysis, case studies, and psychoanalytical re-interpretation of leading figures. They switch both to a scientific and a technological way of studying the political life, trends, and events.

A controversial subject is the issue of using psychobiographies of leaders, a genre launched by Sigmund Freud in 1910 with his study of Leonardo da Vinci. This was followed by a psychological analysis of Moses, and then Eric Erikson published his analysis of Martin Luther as a young man in 1958. Since then, there have been many other retrospective and historical psychological studies of well-known public figures such as Hitler, Gandhi, and Robespierre, just to name a few. Some of these psychoanalytical biographies of historical figures or psychopathological assessment of contemporary political leaders have become best-sellers, drawing public attention to the field, but this genre of psychobiographies has also brought some strong discredit to the discipline within the scientific community (Jiménez-Burillo, 1996).

The 'case study' technique has been used to recount notorious failures in politics, such as the Group-thinking syndrome in the Bay of Pigs crisis, and the irrelevance of highly reliable sources in the decline of the Shah Reza Pahlavi or in President Nixon's impeachment process. These were post hoc studies with the purpose of learning through the analysis of mistakes. This genre has been welcomed and even gained reputation within the scientific community.

Further information concerning new trends in political psychology may be found online at: http://ispp.org/ISPP/ (International Society of Political Psychology), http://www.pr.erau.edu/ ~ security/ (International Bulletin of Political Psychology), and http://www.polisci.umn.edu/ polipsyc/index.html (Center for the Study of Political Psychology).

Sport Psychology

The first World Congress on sport psychology was held in Rome, in 1965, and this event was a milestone. Also, the International Society of Sport Psychology took off. However, pioneering psychological research may be traced back to 1895 when tests of reaction time were used by G. W. Fitz to predict sporting abilities and trainability. Studies on the influence of competitors' presence in the performance of cyclists or the influence of athletic activities in the character of children in reform school were performed between 1898 and 1900 in the US. Similar approaches were launched in Europe, where P. Jusserand published a book on the psychology of football in 1901 and in 1913 Baron Pierre de Coubertin, father of the contemporary Olympic Games, published his first collection of essays on sport psychology.

The subjects in the variety of psychological studies carried out are not only about the sportsmen and women (both professional and amateurs), but also coaches, referees, managers of clubs and sport federations, and audiences. Sport psychologists examine the past and present performance of individuals but also the past and present interactions that occur among stakeholders in sporting events and settings.

The following areas of study have helped shape the field of sport psychology (COP, 1998): (a) the role of psychological factors involved in the personal growth and peak performance of sportsmen and women as well as sportsmanship; (b) the role of motivational factors and learning experiences in the interactions held between coaches and sportsmen and women as well as coaching effectiveness; (c) the role of cognitive and sensorimotor factors influencing the interpretations and decisions made by referees; (d) the role of organizational and management factors favoring or obstructing sport activities and interest; (e) the role of the spectators and fans as facilitators or as troublemakers in stadiums, stressing the analysis of mobs and violence; (f) the positive or negative psychological consequences of success, failures, or injuries among men and women performing physical exercises or participating in sport activities as a hobby, as maintenance, or as fitness during their life-span; (g) the usefulness of sports and physical exercises as a therapeutic resource for people with certain disabilities or handicaps and in the clinical practice.

The analysis of individual differences to identify the personal characteristics and cognitive styles of successful sportsmen and women took the lead in the discipline until the 1960s:

the output was a list of traits and tests considered useful to assess and sponsor potential top performance athletes. In the 1970s the study of psychobiological factors prospered by paying attention to bio-electric potentials and biofeedback, chemical changes induced by psychological states, bio-engineering procedures that may enhance sporting performance, as well as to the action of psychotropic drugs in drugged athletes. In the 1980s the cognitive theory of learning stressed the importance of knowing and awareness to maximize sport performance and training. The output was a list of new constructs and original ways of perceiving, conceiving, judging, and imagining sporting situations and events: cognitive maps, cognitive controls, cognitive mediations, cognitive needs, cognitive rehearsal, cognitive restructuring, cognitive schema, and so on. In the early 1990s social learning theory, social-inquiry model, social-exchange theory, and social-comparison theory started to sway and dominate, emphasizing the role of social influences and interactions, the role of reciprocity and expectations of reward, and the comparative worth of sporting achievements. By the year 2000, great strides have been made developing new psychological instruments specific to the sport and exercise environment, setting aside generic assessment instruments, not sensitive enough to the demands of sport. The use of virtual reality in implementing visualization and modeling training is another advanced technological innovation.

The fall of the Berlin Wall brought an unexpected finding. For years it was considered that the high performance of athletes nurtured and trained inside communist countries could be attributed to advance programs of psychological support developed ad hoc and in secrecy. This account was based on well-known early findings of A. Puni and P. Rudik during the 1920s and the creation in 1930 of a Research Institute of Physical Education in Moscow. There were very specific findings concerning individuals or teams that were rarely generalizable to other groups of athletes. The salient presence of sport psychologists in a large expedition of technical personnel appears to have been overestimated because if they did exist, they were conspicuous by their absence in other national expeditions of experts.

Sport psychologists use experimental designs in the laboratory to isolate psychobiological factors, cognitive processes, and specific characteristics of peak performers. They also use field studies, surveys, games trainers' play, panel groups, and so on to observe and describe deeds and accomplishments in the gymnasium and the stadium. They perform psychological assessment using questionnaires, tests, interviews, self-observation and self-report inventories, psycho-physiological protocols, and reconstruction methods, combining scientific and technological backgrounds in procedures and tools.

Sport psychologists are employed by clubs, federations, or institutes to perform several functions and responsibilities. They know how to optimize competence and performance among sportsmen and women. They assess them, design treatment compatible with training protocols, do research, give expertise to coaches and other staff, and assist the athletes when dealing with the mass media and when adjusting time-tables and agendas during long-term training periods. Psychological expertise may also facilitate the transition of athletes from the challenges and pressures of peak performance to those of a normal life, which is a quite delicate period if they have been involved in the front line of gold medals and awards. Models and methods used in industrial and organizational psychology are also used to understand sporting organizations and the managerial role of coaches.

Sport psychologists also know how to assist children and teenagers in the process of becoming involved in sports as play. They take advantage of psychological knowledge in the area of human learning, motivation, and satisfaction. They assess relatives, coaches, physiotherapists and other technical staff, and policy makers, paying special attention to transitory disabilities or permanent handicaps. In a similar vein they may advise people to participate in sport activities in their leisure time to help overcome drug-addiction, alcoholism, depression, anxiety or stress, sleep disorders, obesity, and a sedentary lifestyle to adopt maintenance, fitness, or rehabilitation. The contribution of sport psychologists has also been welcome in the design of campaigns promoting sport activities in the community and in redesigning indoor and outdoor space used by sports enthusiasts, taking into consideration age differences, handicaps, and disabilities. A conventional activity is the organization and development of training programs and seminars addressed to the stakeholders of the sport activities

The Achilles' heel of sport psychology may be its visibility in the mass media. Journalists tend to oversimplify when trying to understand what happens in the arena when an athlete succeeds or fails. Quite often interviewees have psychological references on the tip of their tongues and the result is that the expertise of the sport psychologist may be heightened or obscured categorically, without nuances. An updated source for further reading is the book edited by Cruz-Feliu (1997).

Further information concerning new trends in sport psychology may be found online at: http: //www.aaasponline.org/index2.html (Association for the Advancement of Applied Sport Psychology), and http://www.psyc.unt.edu/apadiv47/ (Exercise and Sport Psychology, APA Division 47).

Traffic and Transport Psychology

L. M. Patrizi, an Italian occupational physician, who stressed the importance of testing the persistence of attention, launched the interest in the psychological assessment of tramway and automobile drivers for the first time in 1900. The first regulation of automobile traffic, enacted in Germany in 1910 included several sensorimotor and character traits that were to be examined in order to obtain a driver's license. By 1915 the American Association for Labor Legislation invited Hugo Munsterberg to design a procedure to assess the 'mental disposition and psychic tone' of tramway drivers. The conclusions and findings gained at the end of the 2nd International Congress on Psychotechnics held in Barcelona in 1921 were included in the traffic rules enacted by the Mayor of Barcelona a few months afterwards. This resulted in every tramway and taxi driver having to pass several psychological tests. Probably this was the first time that psychological findings were adopted immediately into a rule promulgated by local authorities.

There are two ways of seeking information in this discipline: the prevention of accidents or the effectiveness of driving performance. These must be understood as complementary expressions of the contributions expected from psychologists involved in this area. Both are two sides of the same coin. The more conventional approach has been the compulsory psychological testing of professional drivers who are recidivists in traffic accidents. Spain seems to be the only country where psychological testing is obligatory to obtain or renew the drivers' license. More advanced approaches in preventing traffic accidents have included their analysis using the study of biases induced by reporting procedures, ways of optimizing the reconstruction of events and the understanding of how witnesses or victims account and recall what happened, and the improvement of emergency care assistance and rehabilitation programs geared to the victims and survivors.

In a similar vein, the influence of drowsiness, fatigue, emotional states, and other reactions including alcohol or tobacco consumption, drug-addiction, and prescribed drugs on traffic safety have been also studied. New technologies introduced on the road and streets, the design and redesign of infrastructures, the ergonomic design of vehicles, the adequacy of sign-posting and lighting have been also studied, taking into consideration vision and human perception, motor reactions, and decision making while driving.

Psychological models have been examined and used to improve programs of educational safety among children and teenagers that deal with their behavior as passengers, pedestrians, or bikers. Advertising campaigns concerning safety in the road and the street have been analyzed and improved through the use of psychological hints and contributions.

Traffic psychologists are employed by driver assessment centers, clinics devoted to the recovery of accident victims, driving schools, training centers for professional drivers, insurance companies, railway and bus companies, governmental agencies, and traffic research centers. Some psychologists have designed workshops to deal with fear of flying which have obtained the financial support of airlines. High-speed trains have also used the contribution of psychologists to assess cognitive and behavioral patterns detected among engineer drivers when facing an absence of stimulation in highly automated trains. An overview of how this field has been developing during the last decade is summarized in the book edited by Montoro-Gonzalez, Carbonell-Vaya, Sanmartin Arce, and Tortosa-Gil (1995). This is a field where the technological and short-term perspective prevails over a long-term and scientific strategy.

Further information concerning new trends in traffic psychology may be found online at: http://www.surrey.ac.uk/Psychology/Traffic_Psychology/ (IAAP, Division 13, Traffic Psychology), and http://www.soc.hawaii.edu/leonj/leonj/leonpsy/traffic/tpintro.html (traffic psychology at the University of Hawaii).

Applied Cognitive Psychology

Many psychology departments, centers, and institutes of applied social psychology around the world regard themselves as focused on the study of processes such as attention, perception, learning and memory, and the identification of structures and representations that facilitate or impede the satisfactory functioning of the human mind in action. Today, this field has numerous connections with information processing, cybernetics, and information technologies, linking scientific and technological approaches in the study of human behavior and performance.

In 1903 a new term 'psychotechnics' started to be used by psychologists when they referred to applications of sound psychological principles in the cognitive and emotional capability

or trainability of people. These psychologists used their expertise to develop advanced ways of handling, controlling, or improving human performance in the workplace, educational settings, and in the prevention of accidents. They devised and employed innovative techniques that were a forerunner of personnel assessment, guidance, training, and safety at work. If the focus of analysis and intervention was on the moldable plasticity of the individual, the approach was better known as *subjective psychotechnics*, which is the attempt to figure out how to adjust the individual to the job. If the focus was on the multifaceted 'shapeability' of any situation to actual or potential incumbents or clients, *objective psychotechnics* was the stage name, stressing how to reshape and redesign the job matching up to the individual.

Both lines of research and action have continued, bringing forth a new specialty under different names such as 'ergonomics', 'cognitive ergonomics', and 'psychological telematics' in Europe and 'engineering psychology', 'human factors engineering', and 'cognitive engineering' in the US. Each name identifies a period, a perspective, and a way of investigating the problems and dilemmas people face when they have to handle new complex equipment. The purpose has been that of understanding and optimizing person–machine interactions, control of human errors, study of human efficiency in working environments, effect of fatigue and boredom in daily tasks, interface between users and computers, compatibility between controls and displays, and elaboration of design guidelines as a cost-effective alternative to long or complex training programs. Human cognition and emotion are involved in the transmission of messages, retrieving online information, determining the presence and location of people or objects, organizing databases, capturing and archiving documents, authoring hypertext documents and multimedia, making calculations, analyzing or broadcasting daily life or workplace events, and problem analysis and decision making.

Although the analysis of information processing in real life settings began many centuries ago, starting with Sumerian cuneiform writing and Egyptian hieroglyphs, at the end of the twentieth century, it continues when people devour the PC screen with their eyes scrutinizing the dynamic and multimedia documents available online. There is an agreement about the label of this new field of research and action, 'knowledge management' as well as 'knowledge engineering'. It is the study of how knowledge is authored, published, catalogued, and recovered online on demand and the study of how net-users reach, manage, and make the most of online knowledge when deciding what must be done, how, and when. Even in the analysis and follow-up of high-tech crimes, psychological profiling is based upon the cognitive, emotional, and behavioral clues left by offenders.

A second pioneering approach dates back to the second half of the nineteenth century when Gustav T. Fechner (1801–1887) and disciples began to generate standard techniques and measures to study sensations evoked by physical stimuli (Chapter 5). From the very beginning the field was named *psychophysics* and the purpose was to investigate the relationship between a given sensation and the intensity of the eliciting stimulus. The main laws and principles, the large majority of the related measures, the experimental work in the laboratory and the practical knowledge accumulated in real life settings have been in force during the twentieth century as a consequence of its weight and usefulness, for instance, in the food, beverage, and textile sectors. Fechner's notion of 'the just noticeable difference' as the basic unit to measure and discriminate between sensations remains the criterion in the process of creating illusions and persuading potential consumers of the adequacy of certain artificial flavors, colors, or textures produced to look or taste just like similar but different natural flavors, colors, and textures.

Psychophysical methods have been used by some firms in the computer sector to study patterns in visual and auditory information processing to improve monitors, images, sounds, animations, and so on broadcast via the Internet. For instance, advances in virtual reality would be considered not possible from a conventional perspective in the psychological study of human perception: human subjects are used to performing visual rotations of objects up to 180 grades but very rarely up to 360 grades up and down or backward and forward. However this is a common standard accomplished in virtual reality by the touch of a click in the mouse. Many rotations, which are classified as impossible in classical manuals on perception, are a common feature in TV ads, attracting the attention of the audience who are rarely aware that they are viewing special effects. The paradox is that psychophysics nowadays is a very active research area in some corporate research and development departments and consulting firms but not in university psychology departments. They cling to other and more conventional areas of study. Stable and consolidated findings do not attract the attention of those basic researchers who are more concerned with moving beyond the present knowledge and state of the art!

A third pioneering approach was started by Paul Broca (1824–1880) stressing the brain–behavior relationship, a new field, labeled by the middle of the twentieth century neuropsychology (Chapter 4). The conventional approach has been the careful study of given lesions in specific regions of the brain to find out associated changes in human cognition, emotion, or behavior. Advanced approaches combine, for instance, electrical signals recorded at the forehead to facilitate the monitoring of cursor movements by brain-injured patients. A mental interface device has been developed to allow these severely impaired patients to move around virtually in Internet, whereas they stay in the same physical room. The same basic approach, sometimes combined with video-based eyetracking, is used nowadays to enable individuals with severe speech and mobility deficiencies to communicate and to cooperate with others, an achievement which was absolutely impossible only a couple of years ago. This is only an example of how networked computers are already used as prostheses for people with brain injuries or with functional or organic disabilities. New labels are coming out such as 'Applied Neuropsychology', 'Neuro-ergonomics', and 'Applied Cognitive Bioengineering'.

Networked computers may be used to facilitate psychological and medical assistance to people in isolation in an airplane, to grant the continuous training programs addressed to experts residing in low-income countries, to facilitate interactions and follow-up among teleworkers (Prieto & Simon, 1997). The new generation of online computers may introduce even illiterate people to the new realm of new information technologies at a fairly low cost. It is not only a matter of developing user-friendly techniques, but determination of human limits and potentials driven by the goal of creating interfaces that better suit excellence in human performance. This area uses both on- and off-line computer-based resources and support facilities for designing advanced methods and sophisticated systems to support multiple users interacting and performing complex and collaborative tasks in a world some still consider too artificial and virtual, while others see the genuine and real in a different way.

This is an area where the terminology is still confusing. In the US the expression 'cyber-psychology' has received support among those viewing this label as a blend of cybernetics and psychology and those accepting it as a blend of the cyberspace culture and psychology. In the European Union another expression, 'psychology and telematics' (that is, distant and automatic transmission of digital data) has been coined without too much success. By now, applied cognitive psychology seems to be a compromise expression clearing up the subject.

Further information concerning new trends in applied cognitive psychology may be found online at: http://rcswww.urz.tu-dresden.de/ ~ cogsci/ iaap-acp/iaap-acp.html (IAAP, Division 14, Applied Cognitive Psychology), http://info.lut. ac.uk/departments/hu/links/erglinks.html (ergonomics, resource links), and http://www.neuro psychologycentral.com/index.html (neuropsychology central).

26.4 FORENSIC AND LEGAL PSYCHOLOGY: BEYOND DOUBT

The field of forensic and legal psychology has grown dramatically as an applied field of psychology since the early 1900s when social psychologists began studying the behavior of individuals or groups who deviate from societal norms. The field of criminology, which first encompassed this research on deviancy, gave rise to the broader applied psychology field that deals directly with the entire interface between psychology and the law, commonly called forensic or legal psychology. The fields of social, experimental, and clinical psychology interact together with the law in forensic psychology. Since the early 1970s, the field of forensic psychology has developed into a major area of research and practice for psychologists in various parts of the world, switching to the scientific or to the technological perspective. Sustained research efforts in some areas, such as perception and eyewitness testimony or the perceptions of credibility, increased significantly. In many countries, the recognition of the usefulness of clinical and social psychological expertise in the courtrooms and the admissibility of expert testimony from psychologists to assist in applying legal standards has made major gains over the preceding decades. Techniques such as psychological assessment, measurement of competency and insanity, and prediction of dangerousness, utilizing the many studies on deviancy and criminology have been modified for forensic use. A set of guidelines for the forensic psychologist has been promulgated by the American Psychological Association's Division 41, the Society for Psychology and the Law (APA, 1991), and the Division of Forensic Psychology at the Spanish Psychological Association (COP, 1998) (http://www.apa.org/div41 and http://www.cop.es/perfiles/).

More and more, psychologists and attorneys have found some psychological issues to have a common relevance. An illustration of this rapprochement between both disciplines is the fact that in recent years, many of the better known universities (in the USA and certain Canadian provinces, for instance) are now offering students either the possibility of entering a joint program in psychology (Ph.D.) and in law (J.D.). Another modality is a subspecialty area in clinical and professional psychology training programs, for instance at the Spanish Psychological Association (SPA). Considered a specialty encompassing both science and practice, the forensic psychologist can obtain diplomate credentials and contribute to the research in the area of psychological jurisprudence.

Brief Historical Perspective

Ever since Hugo Munsterberg published in 1908 his provocative best-seller *On the Witness Stand*, forensic psychology has become a subject of interest in affluent societies. The field developed slowly at first, partly because of the differences in methodology and partly because of the difficulties that the legal profession initially had toward this perceived intrusion into their territory (Bartol & Bartol, 1987). In the 1920s a psychologist, Donald Slesinger and a lawyer, Robert Hutchins, published numerous papers on legal psychology together and thus began changing the initial hostile relationship between psychology and law.

In Europe, during the 1900s experimental psychologists such as Alfred Binet in France, William Stern in Germany, and Francisco Santamaría in Spain became interested in the psychology of testimony. They replicated separately the first known forensic experiment that had originally been conducted in the United States by James McKeen Cattell in 1895 dealing with the specific conditions explaining how testimony can be inaccurate. Stern later proceeded to establish the very first journal dealing with forensic issues, and more particularly with the psychology of testimony. This journal broadened its scope and in 1908 became the first journal of applied psychology in German. Santamaría lectured and researched on psychology at the School of Criminology of the University of Madrid. During the same period, psychologists in several European countries also were being asked to become expert witnesses and to testify in criminal cases both on matters of fact and on matters of opinion.

Psychologists differ from other 'fact' witnesses in that they are usually able to offer their 'opinions' that are based on the facts. Obviously, the psychologist's interpretation of the facts that become opinion is designed to influence the jury's findings, an observation that has to be considered when the court decides whether or not to admit such expert testimony in a particular case.

Clinical psychologist Grace Fernald and psychiatrist William Healy established the first clinic in the US for youthful offenders in 1909. At the request of the criminal justice system and the courts, other psychologists were developing mental tests to administer to criminals and delinquents. Mental testing also became one of the main screening devices used in the selection of police officers.

Mental measurement was not the only area of interaction between psychology and the legal system, especially in Europe. For instance, during the early 1910s Professors Karl Marbe, at the University of Wurzburg, and Luis Simarro, at the University of Madrid became the first experimental psychologists to testify in a civil suit.

Only after World War II have psychologists become recognized as expert witnesses on the US legal scene, although there were some unsuccessful attempts to get psychologists admitted to give testimony as early as the 1920s. In 1954, there were two important cases that opened the door even further. In the first, Hidden vs. Mutual Life Insurance Co., psychological expertise was welcomed in a civil case and the psychologist permitted to give his opinion on the mental status of the plaintiff. In the second, a crucial case in the legal struggle against school segregation, Brown vs. Board of Education, psychologists and other social scientists were allowed to testify after a bitter debate. The best-known contribution to this trial was Kenneth and Mamie Clark's presentation of the results of their famous doll experiment on the effects of segregation. This case made it clear that the scientific and technological research provided by psychologists was an important addition to the clinical findings of psychiatrists.

The Areas of Psycholegal Research

Kagehiro and Laufer (1992) made an informal content analysis of the major journals publishing psycholegal work and noted that almost one third of all the articles published dealt with either expert witnessing, jury decision making, and eyewitness testimony. Empirical research published could be subsumed under two categories: mental health and court-related processes.

Jury Selection and Jury Dynamics

Starting with the pioneering efforts of Marston in 1917, the jury decision-making process and its offshoot, the jury selection procedures, has been one of the most frequently studied areas in legal psychology, despite the observation that in the real world, trial by jury is a rare event from a statistical perspective.

There has been an extensive body of research on the efficacy of different types of juries around the world, often using experimental analogue studies to help understand the psychology of juries and how they weigh evidence. The fact that the dynamics of jury deliberations can usually be understood by social psychological concepts and theories related to the functioning of small groups and persuasive communication strategies, probably explains why this area is of particular interest to psychologists.

Modern American research on the jury system actually begun in the 1950s with what came to be known as the Chicago Jury Project. Since, traditionally, jury deliberations are held 'in camera' (behind closed doors), researchers on this project actually obtained permission from the judge and attorneys to secretly record the deliberations in several civil cases. However, when this became known, public opinion indicated outrage and the issue was eventually debated before the influential U.S. Senate Judiciary Committee. Many states enacted laws forbidding the recording of jury deliberations even for research purposes. So, in view of the limited access to jurors and to ensure the proper study of jury dynamics, new techniques, such as archival methods and jury simulation with mock cases, were developed and frequently used in the decades that followed.

A substantial amount of research around the world has been conducted to specify the impact of the individual differences of jurors on their verdicts and to look at ways of improving the jury-selection process. Most of the practitioners who consult in this area believe that they are more successful in eliminating those prospective jurors who would not render a good verdict for their client rather than in choosing those who would be sympathetic and vote to support their client's position. Many think that there are very few modest or inconsistent effects (related to demographic or personal factors) that can actually be used for prediction purposes, thereby limiting the potential impact of psychologically related selection strategies on the outcome of a trial. Others argue that good strategies can be developed from juror characteristics and successfully used to enable the prediction of verdicts.

In a number of studies, a positive attitude towards the death penalty has been shown to be associated with a greater likelihood of convicting the defendant. Also, it has been shown that a specific attitude towards one element of a case, for example about sexual abuse when listening to a rape case, can have a strong predictive value. In the Netherlands, for example, there has been research to show that police officers and mental health professionals have very different attitudes towards crime prevention. The police believe that punishment has more of a deterrent effect while mental health professionals stress the efficacy of rehabilitation. In a Canadian study that concentrated on the impact of introducing no evidence, general social science evidence, and psychological evidence of the individual person on juror's decisions, it was found that those who had both clinical and research evidence were most likely to find battered women who killed their partners not guilty by reason of self-defense (see Kagehiro & Laufer, 1992). The follow-up on the National Jury Project suggests that in civil cases, the views, either of personal or social responsibility, expressed by the jurors to explain their attribution to individuals or to environmental/social factors for adversity, seem to be related to the verdicts.

The direct involvement in the early 1970s of sociologists and psychologists in the Harrisburg Seven Trial, the first 'political' trial during the Vietnam War years, opened the way to 'scientific or systematic jury selection'. Methods, such as public opinion surveys, juror profiles, rating of non-verbal behavior, were developed to help attorneys select jurors. These techniques, which have since been technologically refined and elaborated, have been successfully used in many trials, but still remain quite controversial. Whereas lawyers and their clients are generally satisfied by the advantages they believe are associated with using these methods, many psychologists believe that the claims of their effectiveness have generally been exaggerated, notwithstanding the fact that under certain circumstances psychologists can be useful in trial preparation and jury selection.

Some of the very exciting research work that has been conducted in recent years has dealt with the development of jury decision-making models. Many of these theoretical models (such as the information integration theory, the Bayesian approach, the story model, the algebraic model) have generated important research efforts and the results obtained help us better to understand juror decision processes. With the refinement of statistical analysis procedures, virtual reality developments, and the sophistication used in data gathering, there is no doubt that effectiveness will improve and that research should continue to monitor this important area of application.

Eyewitness Testimony

It is well known that eyewitness testimony is one of the most powerful types of evidence that can be introduced in the courtroom and that it is the single most important factor responsible for convicting an accused person, rightly or wrongly. In recent years, some excellent reviews have been published (Cutler & Penrod, 1995;

Pope & Brown, 1998; Ross, Read, & Toglia, 1994) that we strongly recommend to the interested reader.

When evaluating the accuracy of the eyewitness, it is common to examine the conclusions drawn to the three different stages of the memory process, pointing along the way to the factors that impact the level of accuracy.

1. *Acquisition*: During the acquisition stage, many variables can affect the encoding of eyewitness memories including both characteristics of the event itself and those related to the witness. A better opportunity to observe the event and a longer exposure time yields a stronger relation to memory accuracy. But this relationship tends to be moderated by the increased complexity of the scene observed, or by the presence of an important element, such as a weapon or blood, that draws the attention away from a critical item, such as the face of the perpetrator. Strong and reliable differences have been found in studies conducted on the effects of cross-race identification. The main conclusion is that own-race recognitions are more accurate than other-race identifications.

2. *Storage*: The storage phase of the eyewitness memory trace, i.e., the interval between the end of the encoding and its subsequent access, has also had extensive research conducted on the impact of misleading verbal information on witness recollection that is often called 'the misinformation effect'. This research suggests that new information given at the storage stage can certainly influence the accuracy of the report of the witness.

3. *Retrieval*: Finally, during retrieval, the witness is asked to recollect the initial event with as much precision as possible. Research here has concentrated on finding ways to enhance this retrieval process. Many potentially helpful techniques or enhancement procedures have been examined, like for instance, hypnosis, guided memory, and recent refinements of this latter procedure such as the 'cognitive interview'. Studies show that while hypnosis does not appear to facilitate recognition performance, it sometimes helps promote eyewitness recall. On the other hand, the cognitive interview approach does appear to provide better recall for details, in some studies 40 to 45% better recall, but does not seem to influence face recognition.

The main findings of studies carried out in the laboratory have yielded the identification of potential biases, related to (a) lineup instructions, (b) quality and number of foils, (c) effect of clothing, (d) the type of presentation (simultaneous or sequential), and (e) the investigator. Biased lineup instructions, for instance, can have a profound effect on false identification rates, and sequential presentation of suspects yields much better results in terms of correct identifications than the traditional simultaneous presentation.

The application of these laboratory findings to legal situations have been less helpful when attempting to measure the credibility of witness memories when violence or abuse is experienced. This is especially true for children's memories of sexual abuse. Often clinicians around the world have found that victims of violence (particularly those who have been repeatedly abused by family members or those in a position of authority and trust) sometimes do and other times do not remember what happened during any particular incident. Researchers state that repressed memories of trauma do not fit the memory acquisition model described above and demonstrate by analogy studies of traumatic but non-abusive experiments that it cannot happen. Therapists, on the other hand, state that variability in memory for some traumatic events does occur and is even observable during treatment and therefore, insist that it does happen and in fact, is a sign of the credibility and authenticity of the reports. New research on the physiological effects of trauma including the impact of the biochemical secretions at the time of the abuse indicates that the cognitive model of memory storage and retrieval is not appropriate under these conditions, especially if the events are perceived as life-threatening rather than just unpleasant or traumatic without the threat of survival to the person.

Factors Affecting Juror Belief

The believability of jurors regarding eyewitness testimony can be affected by witness confidence, memory for peripheral details, cross-examination, and witness age. The most potent influence undoubtedly comes from witness confidence. The fact that a particular witness indicates during his or her testimony that he or she is absolutely certain that the suspect is the guilty person has an enormous influence on the jurors. For most people, eyewitness confidence is the single most important predictor of identification accuracy, even if research has shown that confidence in one's ability to make a correct identification is usually a poor predictor of the accuracy of the identification; meta-analytic studies show correlations that range from .00 to .25.

Usually, the more an eyewitness provides specific details, even peripheral and unimportant ones, the more people are convinced about credibility. But some researchers have found that people believe that eyewitnesses who pay attention to trivial details were less likely to have paid proper attention to the face of the suspect!

What happens if an efficient attorney discredits an eyewitness during cross-examination? The classical study conducted by Loftus in 1974 found that cross-examination completely discrediting an eyewitness (e.g., indicating that he had very poor vision and was not wearing his eyeglasses at the time of the event) did not do very much to alter the conviction rate (68%) by comparison with the unchallenged presence of an eyewitness (72%). Both these conditions differed significantly from the mere presentation of circumstantial evidence. Replication studies conducted more recently did show that a good cross-examination can significantly reduce the conviction rate.

A substantial number of studies have examined the effect of the age of the witness, with an emphasis on looking at how well children remember and what effects their testimony has on jurors. It was found that correct identification improved with age, while false identification declined. However, many studies have shown that children's skills at observation and memory are not as defective as was thought. Moreover, their suggestibility seems related to particular situations and styles of questioning. When studies on people's perception of children's testimony are reviewed, little about the credibility of children's testimony can be concluded. It seems that the individual differences related to the perceived competence of children, as well as their quality of verbal expression is most important.

Applications to Practice: Expert Witnesses

Memon (1998) suggests that the increase in the use of experts is directly related to the research in forensic psychology that shows that both the inquisitorial and adversarial methods of presenting evidence, which permits vigorous cross-examination, prevents the expert from being more believable than other witnesses. The adversarial method is more common in those countries that follow the British Common Law and the inquisitorial mode prevails in those countries that follow the Napoleonic code. In the adversarial mode, it is critical for the psychologist to remain objective during the assessment phase to avoid even the appearance of bias during the testimony phase of trials (Walker, 1994).

Qualifying an expert witness before testimony is given has been a requirement of the courts where the judge may not have appointed the psychologist, although where juries are the decision-makers, it is common for experts to try to impress them by reciting their qualifications prior to their testimony. In the US, the Frye test has been used to qualify experts, named after the case that created its standards (Frye v. US). The judge is expected to rely on the scientific credibility of the expert's testimony based on a consensus of the relevant scientists, usually using publication of psychological research or opinions in peer-reviewed journals or testimony of other psychologists upon which to base their decision. Some jurisdictions also required the expert to have certain credentials such as certification, for example chartered status in the British Psychological Society or in the Spanish Psychological Society, an academic appointment in Greece, or state licensure in the US. On the other hand, there are others who believe that psychological testimony is not scientifically sound and should not be permitted in the courts at all. In the early 1990s there was a debate on the admissibility of psychological assessment data in the courts, published in the *American Psychologist* as well as in *Science*, which presented both sides of the argument. Thus, although admissibility of experts has been based on published US case decisions, in fact the forensic world often looks to them for guidance and trends as a behavioral technology.

Other Forensic Psychology Areas

There are a large number of areas where psychologists can practice forensic psychology in addition to being 'expert witnesses' in trials and that list continues to grow. The following sections briefly describe the main roles and functions.

Behavioral Trial Consultants

This broader area is where the psychologist, using psychological knowledge of human behavior, helps attorneys prepare their trial strategies in addition to selecting jurors. This includes consultation about the persuasiveness of the evidence – both the fact pattern as well as the way it is presented. Community attitudes towards certain types of behavior may be researched by systematically gathering information using focus groups, telephone surveys, or even door-to-door and community observations. Everything from the global attitudes about the specific legal issues raised by the case to how a particular type of dress including the color of the clothes worn by witnesses and attorneys may be covered in these strategy sessions. Orders of presentation of witnesses, organization of material to be presented, creation of demonstrative evidence including charts and pictures, and types of food to serve the jury, all are possible consultation topics.

Consultation with Judges in Cases Involving Access to Children

Another area of consultation for psychologists is in helping judges arrive at the difficult decisions they must make by providing both empirical and clinical psychological data relevant to the law the judges must follow. Assessment of children has historically been an area in which psychologists have practiced. Psychologists have applied this knowledge base to assist the court in making decisions about who gets access to the children who come before them. One popular example is in child custody and visitation decisions and access to children who are involved in the juvenile justice system. Here psychologists are more likely to use clinical judgment that might be based originally on research data, primarily because there is little longitudinal data about the impact of access to one or both parents on the development of children.

Interestingly, there are some data concerning exposure to abusive parents on subsequent delinquency and use of violence, which is consistently ignored by the courts even when psychologists attempt to present it, such as is the case with battered women whose children are exposed to violent fathers. Rather, confirmation of one's particular beliefs about what really is 'in the best interests of the child', which is supposed to be the legal standard, often gets confused with the 'interests of the father' or the 'interests of the mother' while not taking the issue of domestic violence seriously. In some cases, abusive fathers have been given unsupervised access to their children, because the state had a more compelling interest in their ability to provide financial support than in the child's other psychological needs. Educating professionals about the dangers of violence in the family is a fertile ground for psychologists with expertise in this area around the world (Walker, 1999).

Rehabilitation Programs for Victims and Perpetrators of Crimes of Abuse

Psychologists have become critical partners in areas of the law where rehabilitation is a more appropriate goal. In domestic violence and rape cases, for example, the policy around the world has been to provide groups for women victims to help them heal from any trauma that occurred as a result of the assault. Psychologists consult with or actually conduct many of these groups, with clients referred by the legal system. In many countries, perpetrators of these crimes are given the opportunity to attend group therapy to help them stop their violent behavior, whether in prison, such as the sexual offender's treatment programs, or while on probation, such as batterer's treatment programs. Again, psychologists provide actual treatment or consultation in the development of these programs with the referrals coming from the criminal justice system (Walker, 1994).

Amicus Curiae Briefs and Other Forms of Written Testimony

Sometimes it is not appropriate to give expert witness testimony in the court but rather, provide the judge with important information that may assist in resolving the legal issues in a case either at the trial or appellate levels. This procedure is known as 'Amicus Curiae'. In some countries, the only form of expert testimony is the report submitted by the psychologist. Here cross-examination is not possible. In appellate cases cross-examination of the expert is of less importance than at the trial level itself. Psychologists may be asked to write amicus briefs in support of an appellate issue on which psychological research can provide important information to assist the court in making decisions.

In some cases, the interest has to do with professional matters while in other cases it is more likely to use psychological knowledge to help promote the public interest. For example, psychological research demonstrates that discrimination against people because of the color of their skin, their culture, their sexual orientation, or their gender can have long-lasting psychological impact. Other areas in which psychologists have written briefs include forced psychotropic medication, permitting consenting adults to practice sex with each other without government interference, unfairness of the implementation of death penalty laws, proper assessment techniques by practitioners in cases such as use of anatomically-explicit dolls and closed-circuit television on children's testimony, cognitive capacities of children to give reliable and valid testimony, and consent to medical procedures such as abortion, desegregation of public schools, impact of sexual harassment in the workplace on women, psychological legitimacy of the battered woman syndrome, and issues concerning insanity and diagnosis of mental disorders. A more complete list of cases is available from the APA, Legal Affairs Office (http://www.apa.org/).

Training for Judges, Attorneys and Others in the Legal Profession Including Police Psychology

Judges in most countries are required to spend some time in training seminars designed to help them to deal with the many different types of cases brought before them. Psychologists may be hired to present information that is useful and helpful to the judges whether it is personal or professional. The same is true for other members of the legal profession including lawyers of the various bar associations. Although the topic area might change from time to time, psychologists are often quite comfortable in providing consultation on cases or in other areas of their expertise. Often this leads to requests to develop more formal training workshops. New training programs in psychology departments are teaching students to develop specialty areas and the APA, the Canadian Psychological Association (CPA) and SPA, for instance, are encouraging practitioners to develop a specialty niche where they can develop a reputation for their expertise rather than the old general model (http://www.apa.div42.org/).

A new and fertile area for psychologists to practice is with law enforcement officers in the criminal justice field. Police psychology is a specialized branch of psychology that applies psychological principles to working with police who are clearly in a dangerous and high stress position. Psychologists have researched the impact of a stressful occupation such as police work. There are many different ways to help police deal with issues internal to their department as well as internal to themselves, including teaching stress-reduction techniques. It is also helpful to assist the police department in selecting officers who will be as highly effective as possible and will remain on duty, considering the high level of training necessary before they become good officers.

Attorneys and others may also call upon the psychologist to consult with them so that they are better educated in a particular area of expertise for the psychologist or perhaps, in general. Often the attorneys as well as the client are both clients of the forensic psychologist. This makes it important to separate forensic and clinical work so that there is no appearance of or danger of bias towards one or the other.

Assessment of Psychological Injury for Damages

Another important area for clinical forensic psychologists is to assess the psychological or neuropsychological injuries that someone might have from an accident or other form of trauma.

Shapiro (1999) has provided a good basic introduction to using standardized psychological tests to conduct forensic psychological evaluations. Others have concentrated in the criminal arena although their suggestions can be applied to civil matters.

Battered women syndrome, rape trauma syndrome, and personal injury torts require a specialized evaluation and a written report or perhaps live testimony from an expert. While it is common in North America for psychologists to give expert witness testimony in deposition or at trial, in other countries, an expert can submit a written report to the court to demonstrate that a person has suffered and the injuries are outlined to assist the court in attempting to obtain financial restitution for the person concerned.

Competency and duress are two other issues important in the civil courts for psychologists. When someone enters into a contract, such as a financial agreement prior to marriage (prenuptial agreement) it is important for it to occur without any coercion or duress. However, sometimes people are coerced into signing such contracts and then attempt to break the agreement. This most often occurs during business disputes or a divorce action. A psychological evaluation that includes a clinical interview and some other psychological assessment may assist in determining whether or not someone was so frightened that she or he signed documents without understanding their meaning. Or, in some cases, it is possible to determine the competency of someone who has knowingly signed documents, for example after a head injury or during a particular point in the debilitating process of dementia.

Assessment of Criminal Responsibility

Psychologists have provided psychological data to help solve criminal cases. Most countries provide for mental illness exceptions (incompetence and insanity) to their criminal laws and hold the person less responsible for their criminal acts if psychological reasons can be demonstrated. Important issues arise for the forensic practitioners that are less important for the psychotherapist, particularly in assessing for the reliability and validity of the information gained in the evaluation.

Therefore, the psychological issues raised by the detection of malingering and deception become important here (Shapiro, 1999). It is often difficult for psychologists to meet the requirement to assess for legally defined conditions such as 'competency' and 'insanity' rather than just assess for mental illness. Competency is defined by statute or case law and, therefore, it takes more than just a clinical

finding of mental illness to meet the requirements and forensic psychologists must follow the law. Insanity is even more problematic as it is a legal construct without any firm definition (Melton, Petrila, Poythress, & Slobogin, 1997). Insanity is a rarely used defense, but when it is used, psychologists, just like psychiatrists, often play an important role in the assessment and expert witness testimony via written report or live testimony.

Further information concerning new trends in forensic psychology may be found online at: http://www-personal.umich.edu/ ~ degues/project4.html (guide to forensic psychology), http://flash.lakeheadu.ca/ ~ pals/forensics/links. htm (forensic psychology resources), http://www. ozemail.com.au/ ~ dwillsh/ (forensic psychology resources links), and http://www-psicologia. psibo.unibo.it/jure.htm (forensic and law psychology), and the Domestic Violence Institute, with world-wide affiliate centers for training, research, and policy in this area: http://www. dviworld.org.

26.5 Environmental Psychology: As Large as Life

The environment includes everything that surrounds people, and environmental psychology considers it in specifically socio-physical terms. Thus, the subject involves analyzing behavior wherever it occurs: in rooms, buildings, offices, hospitals, classrooms, streets, elevators, means of transport, parks, natural spaces, or any other places which people occupy. Environmental psychology studies something, which, in most cases, people are unable to define, despite the fact that they know where they are, are able to describe it, and move about within the place. It may be said that the environment affects, and is at the same time affected by, behavior, but that its influence is not recognized. In brief, environmental psychology can be defined as the field that studies the reciprocal relationships between people's behavior and the socio-physical environment, whether it is natural or built.

One aspect that distinguishes environmental psychology can be found in Darley and Gilbert (1985) where it is regarded not as a subdiscipline of psychology, as is the case with social psychology, but as a grouping of various areas of research with a high degree of cohesion. Nevertheless, the relationship between social and environmental psychology is a very close one, since the latter emphasizes psycho-social processes, particularly in communication, and frequently refers to intervening variables such as attitude to explain relationships between environment and behavior.

Some of the significant general characteristics, which distinguish environmental psychology, are as follows (Darley & Gilbert, 1985; Stokols, 1995):

1. It studies the relationships between behavior and environment where the latter is considered from a holistic perspective; that is to say, as people experience it in their daily lives, and thus more attention is paid to the relationship between the elements as units of analysis than to their components.
2. It takes into account the numerous possible relationships between environment and behavior; that is to say, how environment influences behavior and how behavior produces changes in an environment.
3. Having begun with what was clearly an applied orientation, its evolution has generated concepts and relationships between them have led environmental psychology to develop, somehow, as a basic discipline. However, within the subject, a dialectic tension can be detected between the scientific and the technological perspective, although this is always driven more by practice than theory.
4. There are many disciplines that are interested in the relationships between the individual and the environment, which means that environmental psychology is part of a multi-disciplinary and multi-faceted field. Consequently, numerous concepts and laws are adopted from other disciplines such as geography, biology, architecture, town planning, etc.
5. The underlying objectives of most developments and studies relate to improving quality of life and the environment.

An adequate starting point would be to take the two terms, environment and behavior, to describe the field. We may refer to three classic domains in what concerns the environment: (a) the natural environment, which is untouched by people, or where there is hardly any human impact; (b) the built environment, which mainly covers fields relating to architecture, interior design, and town planning; and (c) the social environment, which refers to physical space in order to define situations of interaction. Three different fields can be distinguished around human behavior: (a) individual processes (perception, cognition and emotion); (b) social processes relating to inter-personal relationships (personal space, territorialism, overcrowding, etc.); and (c) societal processes such as urban life, residential matters, resource management, etc.

Evolution and Thematic Development of Environmental Psychology

By consensus, 1960 is the year in which this new field was shaped. Three periods will be considered to provide a temporal framework facilitating the understanding of the process whereby environmental psychology developed.

Pre-History of Environmental Psychology (before 1960)

Experimental psychology was still in a premature phase at the end of the nineteenth century, but leading authors such as Fechner and Wundt underlined the importance of physical stimuli in studies of perception. Similarly in sociology, during the same period, there were references to the lamentable conditions in which the poor were living in London. Subsequently, studies on urban life in Chicago by the School of Human Ecology showed the importance of socio-physical variables in explaining aspects relating to residential quality. The influences of physical factors such as climate, temperature, height, or landscape on several aspects of behavior are classic references, which were approached in the pioneering work of W. Hellpach in Germany during the 1910s.

The development of the Gestalt School constituted a qualitative leap by taking into consideration a holistic concept to explain behavior. Two of its indirect followers, Egon Brunswik and Kurt Lewin, played a decisive role in the development of this field. Brunswik coined the term environmental psychology in 1943 and, with his 'Brunswik lens' model, emphasized the active role of individuals in structuring perception of the environment. Lewin stressed the role of the internal representation that people have of the environment in order to move around the 'vital space'. Moreover, his influence on Barker makes him worthy to be considered a primary figure when seeking to establish the origins of environmental psychology.

One classic study, which is famous within the world of psychology, was that carried out in the 1930s at the Hawthorne Works of Western Electric in Chicago. This study looked into the effects of light and other aspects of environmental design on human behavior. Although the results are primarily of interest to work and organizational psychologists, subsequent studies have again shown the interest of social sciences in matters relating to environmental design. For example, in the United Kingdom, studies were carried out, during the post World War II reconstruction period where, by means of questionnaires, they succeeded in influencing the legal norms on how dwellings should be constructed in order to exploit natural light better.

The late 1940s and the 1950s saw the emergence of a number of researchers who established the framework from which environmental psychology developed. In 1947, Barker and Wright founded the Midwest Psychological Field Station, which was to yield ecological psychology, another nickname for environmental psychology. During the same period, Tolman's work on cognitive maps gave rise to further developments, present in the work of the town planner, Kevin Lynch. H. Osmond studied how the layout of furniture can facilitate or impede interaction between subjects sharing a dwelling. Around the same time, E. T. Hall published his book *The Salient Language*, describing how space is used in different cultures and R. Sommer conceived his studies on 'personal space'. In Europe, Terence Lee presented his doctoral dissertation on the Study of the Urban Neighborhood at Cambridge University. These studies are at the crossroads of what is or is not environmental psychology, since they are the precedents leading to the strengthening of the field in the following decade.

The Period of Institutionalization (1960–1980)

During this period, environmental psychology was consolidated and regarded as an advanced discipline in its own right within the realm of psychology. A series of events in society occurred, particularly in the US, and in social sciences as a whole, which favored the development of environmental psychology. Thus, the awareness amongst numerous social groups of prevailing social problems led to the promotion of country life as opposed to urban life. On the other hand, the 'crisis of relevance' in social psychology encouraged research outside the laboratory and led to the development of field study researches, where naturalistic and interdisciplinary methods came to the fore.

Amongst the main milestones reached in the US during the 1960s it is convenient to highlight the following: (a) the first Utah conference in 1961 on 'Architectural Psychology and Psychiatry. A National Exploratory Research Conference'; (b) the publication of a monographic issue of the *Journal of Social Issues* edited by Kates and Wohlwill; (c) the first meeting of the Environmental Design Research Association (EDRA) which was held in 1968 in North Carolina; (d) the first scientific journal on the subject which appeared in 1969, under the title *Environment and Behavior*; (e) the first book edited in 1970 by Proshansky, Ittelson and Rivlin on

Environmental Psychology: Man and his Physical Setting. In the UK in 1963, the British Psychological Society sponsored various symposia on the subject. At this stage, it was more a matter of a psychology of the building environment or of architecture – as it was called at that time – than of an environmental psychology as it is called now.

A landmark study of this period was that which followed the failure of the Pruitt-Igoe development in St. Louis, Missouri (USA). Rainwater published the main findings in 1966 as did Yancey in a controversial article presented to the American Psychological Association (APA) in 1971. Pruitt-Igoe, a large public housing project consisting of 43 buildings, each 11 stories high, was constructed between 1955 and 1956. The development was designed to house around 2,500 families who were living in very poor conditions in three-story blocks downtown. The architecture of the development was awarded a prize for public housing design, but, paradoxically, soon afterwards, the development was declared uninhabitable and it had to be demolished. The problem was not related to defects in its construction, but to the behavior that the inhabitants began to display. The degree of vandalism committed by the residents themselves was the reason for its demolition. Studies designed to investigate the reasons for this failure showed that the cause of such vandalism stemmed from the lack of social control over the space promoted by the very design of the building. The required level of social control had, however, been present in their previous dwellings. By the way, behavioral and motivational aspects behind vandalic actions have been studied in depth (Levy-Leboyer, 1984).

Based on this work, many studies showed that a great deal of the fear of crime experienced by public housing residents can be directly attributed to architectural design. In contrast, the old ghettos and slum districts, which seem to grow in a haphazard way, without any sanitary standards or minimal degree of comfort, seem, by virtue of their spatial layout, to offer an area where a tightly woven social network develops, providing a degree of security to the inhabitants. The social cohesion that characterizes such urban and architectural developments leads to a greater sense of social control. Many studies have shown that feelings of fear and danger experienced by public housing residents are inversely proportional to the existence of a wide social network in the neighborhood.

According to Sommer (1997), it was in 1973 that the term environmental psychology was consolidated and embraced other terms such as architectural psychology, man–environment relationships, and ecological psychology. In the mid-1970s, Division 34 of the APA was created under the title of 'Population and Environmental Psychology'. In the United Kingdom, postgraduate courses on the subject were launched at the University of Surrey in 1973.

The Period of Advancement and Development (from 1980 to 2000)

The 1980s and 1990s have seen great progress in environmental psychology. Periodic reviews appear approximately every four years in the *Annual Review of Psychology*, chronicling the most important findings within the field.

In the 1980s there were three key moments. The *Journal of Environmental Psychology* was published in the UK, in 1981, which, together with *Environment and Behavior*, were to become the two most important means of dissemination for research. Other significant landmarks were the publication of the series *Human Behavior and Environment: Advances in Theory and Research* and, later, in 1987, of another series entitled *Advances in Environment, Behavior, and Design Psychology*. The third important event was the appearance of the *Handbook of Environmental Psychology* edited by Stokols and Altman (1987).

From that point on, environmental psychology may be regarded as a consolidated field, an academic and research subject in many of the world's universities, and one which has means of expression which are more or less agreed on by those who practice it.

At the end of the twentieth century, 'green' issues and ecology have been the topics receiving most attention (Pol, 1993). The middle classes in Western society now share the concerns of those social movements that were present when environmental psychology emerged and this has quite possibly influenced the new direction taken in this field. Psycho-environmental research concentrates on investigating values and attitudes towards the environment and its relationship with pro-environmental behavior. The so-called 'new environmental paradigm' reflects an alternative set of beliefs and values associated with conservation and the environment. One of the most frequently obtained results concerns the fact that the high scores obtained amongst the population for environmental concern do not correspond to recycling or energy-saving behavior. Some explanation for this discrepancy would seem to lie in the existence of different dimensions in understanding environmental values: on the one hand, are egotistical or anthropocentric tendencies, and, on the other, are ecocentric orientations. Both place great value on the environment, but for different motives: whilst the former value the environment because of its contribution to human well-being and the satisfaction of human needs, the latter value it for its transcendental dimension rather than its utilitarian worth.

Further information concerning new trends in environmental psychology may be found online at: http://www.psy.gu.se/iaap/envpsych.htm (IAAP, Division 2, Environmental Psychology), http://luna.cas.usf.edu/ ~ miles/envpsych.htm (environmental psychology links), and http://www.sosig.ac.uk/roads/subject-listing/UK/enpsych.html (environmental psychology links).

Theoretical Approaches

It may be said that, given the characteristics of environmental psychology, there are multiple theoretical and methodological approaches to the subject, which impede integrated discourse on the large quantity of results obtained. Altman and Rogoff (1987) outlined the different perspectives. They highlight four different perspectives which they term 'World Views in Psychology' to explain each of the different ways of understanding the relationship between the environment and the individual.

The first perspective is called the 'Trait World View'. The focus is on studies bringing out psychological processes, cognitive characteristics, and personality qualities, where situational aspects have little significance. Predictions are made on the basis of psychological processes, and thus this would include all those studies focused on the person as the basic unit of analysis.

The second perspective is called the 'Interactional World View', and this is the approach most commonly used by the end of the twentieth century. It takes into account the relationships amongst three different interrelated fields: psychological processes, environmental frameworks, and contextual factors. This is the perspective most frequently adopted in psycho-environmental research. These range from studies of cognition or emotion relating to the environment (cognitive maps, attitudes, stress, etc.), via theories such as reactance, learned helplessness, or mere mechanisms for regulating personal space, to learning theories themselves.

The third perspective is the 'Organismic World View'. In this case, the focus of psychological studies are on the dynamic and holistic systems in which personal and environmental components exhibit complex, reciprocal relationships as well as influences. This view may be regarded as attempting to stay closer to the objectives of environmental psychology, in its holistic approach and in its analysis of the reciprocal relationships between the two elements of the headline, but taking into account the fact that this 'view' is of a systemic nature, where the individual and the environment are composed of related elements. The work of Moos on institutional environments was noticed as a prototype in this perspective.

Finally, there is the 'Transactional World View'. This approach emphasizes studies focused on the changing relations among psychological and environmental aspects of holistic unities. The unit of psychological analysis is holistic entities. That is, it deals with persons, psychological processes, and environments involved. The transactional whole is not fragmented in separate elements; it appears in the confluence of mutually embedded factors that depend on one another. There is a correspondence by definition and meaning. This approach would be the most appropriate for studying the behavior–environment relationship from a holistic perspective, but few studies follow these marks. Although many psychologists consider it as having high potential, the majority of them make generalized theoretical comments but with little empirical research. Examples of research which does exemplify this approach are the anthropological studies carried out by Rapoport (1977) and the ecological psychology developed by Barker.

While it may be the case that the range of perspectives described above offers the possibility of situating most studies in environmental psychology, it is also true that there have been other efforts along the same lines, such as the work of Saegert and Winkel (1990). These authors differentiate three different ways of studying behavior–environment relationships: (a) the adaptation paradigm, which covers stressors, perception, cognition, and environmental emotion; all of this based on the fact that 'the goal of biological and psychological survival motivates behavior' (p. 446); (b) the environment as opportunity structure for goal-directed action. In this case it is a question of studying 'the relationship between the behavioral requirements of the active and goal-directed person and the qualities of the environment' (p. 452); (c) 'sociocultural paradigms', which include all those studies that emphasize 'the person as a social agent rather than an autonomous individual having needs for survival or desires to carry out personal projects' (p. 457). The important thing is to study environmental problems by considering the individual as a member of a social structure.

More recently, Sundstrom, Bell, Busby, and Asmus (1996), have made another attempt to classify the different theories or approaches, which have been used in studies to date. In addition to recording how new approaches are being incorporated into environmental psychology, these authors also recognize that environmental psychologists are a long way from reaching a theoretical consensus, and that there are a variety of approaches. In their judgement there are six notably influential approaches: arousal, environmental load, stress and adaptation, privacy-regulation, ecological psychology and behavior setting theory, and transactional approach.

These various ways of approaching the subjects investigated by environmental psychologists demonstrate, at least at the present time, the difficulty of finding a single approach, which can be adopted by the majority. The selection of one approach or another, and thus of one methodology or another, will depend on the underlying concept of person, the environment being studied, and how the relationship between the two is understood.

Research Methods and Techniques

Environmental psychology shares the methodological framework of psychology as a science and as a technology. However, there are certain factors that characterize psycho-environmental research and differentiate it from other areas:

1. Environmental psychology studies environment–behavior relationships as global unities, and thus the fragmented study, in isolation, of 'stimulus–response', so frequently used in other areas of psychology, here proves very inappropriate.

2. Environmental psychology research mainly takes place in the natural context, in the environment where the behavior is displayed.

3. It has a more applied and technological focus than other areas of psychology, considering that the object of study in environmental psychology is not exclusive to the field, but that other subjects have played an active part in its development. This has favored a pluri-methodological panorama, which serves to increase the complexity when seeking methodological unity.

The three methods most frequently used in environmental psychology are laboratory, field, and correlational studies. The first method includes studies relating to personal space (crowding, personal distance) and the impact of physical environment on behavior (e.g., effects of noise or temperature on performance, aggression, etc.). In field studies, the laboratory is replaced by the natural environment, particularly in the area of responsible ecological behavior, where studies often assess the efficacy of programs designed to increase such ecological behavior (use of public transport, energy-saving, recycling, etc.) in public places (streets, cafeterias, communities) or in the home. Finally, correlational studies usually relate environmental variables (physical resources, geographical factors, designs of environments, etc.) with socio-demographic variables or individual differences (fear of crime, perception or evaluation of environments, evaluation of energy consumption, etc.). Similarly, this method is also used in trans-cultural psycho-environmental studies and in those concerning environmental risk perception.

With regard to research techniques, recent handbooks classify those used in environmental psychology into two broad groups: auto-reporting (questionnaires, interviews, scales) and observational techniques. Observational techniques fall into three types, depending on whether the research is focused on the physical environment (scene of behavior), the behavior of the subject (prototypical behavior), or both (behavior map).

The evaluation of occupied environments, or Post-Occupancy Evaluation (POE) is a sound example of the methodological application of psycho-environmental research. The objective of evaluations of this type is to ascertain the extent to which the design of a building effectively fulfills the purposes for which it was first designed. The process by which a POE is carried out involves the following steps: (a) analysis and interpretation of the affective and cognitive judgements and the behaviors of the people who interact with the building to be evaluated; (b) comparison of this data with the objectives for which the building was constructed, thereby establishing the criteria for the appropriateness of the building to the needs of its users; (c) establishment of the characteristics of the building and its main problems, thereby allowing future results to be predicted in similar buildings and neighborhoods; and (d) introduction of the necessary correctives.

The *walkthrough* is the technique most frequently employed in this kind of evaluation. It is an unstructured interview that uses the physical environment as an incitement to help the subjects articulate their reactions to the milieu. A tour of the building to be evaluated is arranged, in which a number of people interested in or affected by the building take part: architects, designers, the building managers, users, etc. In addition, the group is asked to gather all available information concerning the building. Subsequently, the participants attend an initial meeting to explain the reasons for the walkthrough; thereafter, they proceed to walk through the building. During this walkthrough, a series of open questions are posed to the participants; their responses are recorded on previously coded papers. Finally, there is a review session, in which the various stakeholders make certain recommendations, until agreement is reached on what specific actions are required with regard to the building.

This method helps to show the importance of the users' opinions, as well as facilitating a degree of accord between the various parties, but it has the disadvantage that it is very difficult to make comparisons between different places and times. In this sense, the POE is a type of ad hoc evaluation, carried out in a particular space and at a particular time, and it seeks to obtain very specific results about the setting evaluated. This is one of the main criticisms made of POE, although the accumulation of results obtained from multiple POEs may serve as a guide for future developments. Thus, the POE becomes a type of evaluation, which can be used not only for diagnostic, but also for prognostic purposes. Thus, a situation is reached where the POE does not merely provide an evaluation of a particular occupied environment, but constitutes genuine research, which can be applied to help maximize the available resources in designing a building.

Acknowledgements

The main author acknowledges the feedback and comments from Gloria Balague (President IAAP Division on Sport Psychology), Klaus Boehnke (Secretary IAAP Division of Political Psychology), Fernando Chacón (President, COP, Madrid, Community Psychology), Uichol Kim (President IAAP Division on Psychology and National Development), Boris Velichkovsky (President IAAP Division on Applied Cognitive Psychology), Fernando Rambla and Socorro D. González (my assistants in this project).

A modified and expanded version of the two sections devoted to the historical perspective and the areas of research in forensic and law psychology are available in Sabourin and Walker (1999).

Note

1. We have included several references to WWW homepages that, in some cases, may require an automatic translation engine such as that available at http://www.alis.com/.

RESOURCE REFERENCES

Aragonés, J. I., & Amérigo, M. (Eds.). *Psicología ambiental* [Environmental psychology]. Madrid: Pirámide.

Bryant, F. B., Edwards, J., Scott Tindale, R., Posavac, E. J., Heath, L., Henderson, E., & Balcazar-Suarez, Y. (Eds.). (1992). *Methodological issues in applied social psychology*. New York: Plenum Press.

Cairns, R. B., Bergman L. R., & Kagan J. (1998). *Methods and models for studying the individual*. Thousand Oaks, CA: Sage.

Guastello, S. J. (1995). *Chaos, catastrophe and human affairs: applications of nonlinear dynamics to work, organizations and social evolution*. Mahwah, NJ: Lawrence Erlbaum.

Hobfoll, S. E. (1998). *Stress, culture and community: Psychology and philosophy of stress*. New York: Plenum Press.

Huck, S. W., & Sandler, H. M. (1979). *Rival hypotheses: Alternative interpretations of data based conclusions*. New York: HarperCollins.

Kirchler, E. (1999). *Wirtschaftspsychologie. Grundlagen der ökonomischen Psychologie* [Economic psychology: Essentials of economic psychology]. Göttingen: Hogrefe.

Miller, D. C. (1991). *Handbook of research design and social measurement* (5th ed.). Newbury Park, CA: Sage.

Morales, J. F., Blanco, A., Huici Casal, C., & Fernández Dols, J. (1985). *Psicología social aplicada* [Applied social psychology]. Bilbao: Desclée de Brouwer.

Oskamp, S., & Schultz, P. W. (1998). *Applied social psychology*. New York: Prentice-Hall.

Reuchlin, M. (1999). *Traité de psychologie appliquée* [Handbook of applied psychology] (vols 1–10). Paris: Presse Universitaires de France.

Smith, P. B., & Bond, M. H. (1998). *Social psychology across cultures* (2nd ed.). London: Prentice-Hall.

West, M. (1996). *Handbook of work group psychology*. Chichester, UK: Wiley.

ADDITIONAL LITERATURE CITED

Adair, J., & Kagitcibasi, C. (1995). National development of psychology: factors facilitating and impeding progress in developing countries. *International Journal of Psychology*, *30*(6) (Special issue).

Altman, I., & Rogoff, B. (1987). World views in psychology: Trait, interactional, organismic and transactional perspectives. In D. Stokols & I. Altman (Eds.), *Handbook of environmental psychology* (pp. 7–40). New York: Wiley.

Antonides, G., Van Raaij, W. J., & Maital, S. (1997). *Advances in economic psychology*. New York: Wiley.

APA, Committee on Ethical Guidelines for Forensic Psychology (1991). Specialty guidelines for forensic psychologists. *Law and Human Behavior*, *15*, 655–665.

Bartol, C. R., & Bartol, A. M. (1987). History of forensic psychology. In I. B. Weiner & A. K. Hess (Eds.), *Handbook of forensic psychology* (pp. 3–21). New York: Wiley.

Boehnke, K., & Bar-Tal, D. (Eds.). (1998). Political psychology. *Applied Psychology: An International Review*, *47*(1) (Special Issue).

Campbell, J. P., McCloy, R. A., Oppler, S. H., & Sager, C. E. (1993). A theory of performance. In N. Schmitt & W. C. Borman (Eds.), *Personnel selection in organizations* (pp. 34–70). San Francisco, CA: Jossey-Bass.

COP. (1998). *Perfiles profesionales del psicólogo*. Madrid: Colegio Oficial de Psicólogos.

Cruz-Feliu, J. (Ed.). (1997). *Psicología del deporte* [Sport psychology]. Madrid: Síntesis.

Cutler, B. L., & Penrod, S. D. (1995). *Mistaken identification: The eyewitness, psychology, and the law*. Cambridge, MA : Cambridge University Press.

Darley, J. M., & Gilbert, D. T. (1985). Social psychological aspects of environmental psychology. In G. Lindzey & E. Aronson (Eds.), *Handbook of Social Psychology* (3rd ed., pp. 949–991). New York: Random House.

Dorken, H. (Ed.). (1986). *Professional psychology in transition*. San Francisco, CA: Jossey-Bass.

Fleishman, E. A., & Quaintance, M. K. (1984). *Taxonomies of human performance*. Orlando, FL: Academic.

Hellpach, W. (1911). *Die Geopsychischen erscheinungen*. Leipzig: Engelmann.

Jiménez-Burillo, F. (1996). Psicología política [Political psychology]. In J. L. Alvaro, A. Garrido, & J. R. Torregrosa (Eds.), *Psicología social aplicada* [Applied social psychology] (pp. 219–252). Madrid: McGraw-Hill.

Kagehiro, D. K., & Laufer, W. S. (Eds.). (1992). *Handbook of psychology and law*. New York: Springer-Verlag.

Kim, U., & Berry, J. W. (1993). *Indigenous psychologies: Experience and research in cultural context*. Newbury Park, CA: Sage.

Levy-Leboyer, C. (Ed.). (1984). *Vandalism: Behavior and motivations*. Amsterdam: Elsevier.

Lewin, K. (1951). *Field theory in social science*. New York: Harper and Row.

Loftus, E. F. (1974). Reconstructing memory: The incredible eyewitness. *Psychology Today*, December, 117–119.

López-Cabanas, M., & Chacón, F. (1997). *Intervención psicosocial y servicios sociales: un enfoque participativo* [Psychosocial intervention and social services: a participation]. Madrid: Síntesis.

Low, A. (1992). *Zen and creative management.* Tokyo: Charles E. Tuttle.

Melton, G. B., Petrila, J., Poythress, N. G., & Slobogin, C. (1997). *Psychological evaluations for the courts: A handbook for mental health professionals and lawyers* (2nd ed.). New York: Guilford Press.

Memon, A. (1998). Expert testimony. In A. Memon, A. Vrij, & R. Bull (Eds.), *Psychology and law: Truthfulness, accuracy and credibility* (pp. 210–225). London: McGraw-Hill.

Montoro-González, L., Carbonell-Vaya, E., Sanmartín Arce, J., & Tortosa-Gil F. M. (Eds). (1995). *Seguridad vial: del factor humano a las nuevas tecnologías* [Traffic safety: from human factors to new technologies]. Madrid: Síntesis.

Pol, E. (1993). *Environmental psychology in Europe: From architectural psychology to green psychology.* London: Avebury.

Pope, K., & Brown, L. (1998). *The accuracy of recovered memory in child sexual abuse cases.* Washington, DC: American Psychological Association.

Prieto, J. M. (1992). A market-based competition in applied psychology. In B. Wilpert, H. Motoaki, & J. Misumi, *General psychology and environmental psychology* (pp. 55–69). Hove, UK: Erlbaum,

Prieto, J. M., & Martínez-Arias, R. (1997) Those things yonder are not giants, but decision makers in international teams. In P. C. Earley & M. Erez, *New perspectives on international industrial/ organizational psychology* (pp. 410–445). San Francisco, CA: New Lexington Press.

Prieto, J. M., & Simón, C. (1997) Network and its implications for assessment. In N. Anderson & P. Herriot, *International handbook of selection and assessment* (pp. 97–124). Chichester, UK: Wiley.

Proshansky, H. M., Ittelson, W. H., & Rivlin, L. G. (Eds.). (1970). *Environmental psychology: People and their physical settings.* New York: Holt, Rinehart & Winston.

Rainwater, L. (1966). Fear and the house-as-haven in the lower class. *Journal of the American Institute of Planners, 32,* 23–31.

Rapoport, A. (1977). *Human aspects of urban form: Towards a man–environment approach to human form and design.* New York: Pergamon.

Ross, D. F., Read, J. D., & Toglia, M. P. (Eds.). (1994). *Adult eyewitness testimony: Current trends and developments.* Cambridge, MA: Cambridge University Press.

Sabourin, M., & Walker, L. E. A. (1999). Recherches contemporaines en psychologie légale [Contemporary research in legal psychology]. In L. Brunet (Ed.), *L'expertise psycholégale: Balises méthodologiques et déontologiques* [Psycholegal expertise: Deontological and methodological frameworks]. Montreal, Canada: Presses de l'Université du Québec.

Saegert, S., & Winkel, G. H. (1990). Environmental psychology. *Annual Review of Psychology, 41,* 441–477.

Shapiro, D. (1999). *Criminal responsibility evaluations: A manual for practice.* Sarasota, FL: Professional Resources Exchange.

Sommer, R. (1997). Benchmarks in environmental psychology. *Journal of Environmental Psychology, 17,* 1–10.

Stokols, D. (1995). The paradox of environmental psychology. *American Psychologist, 50,* 821–837.

Stokols, D., & Altman, I. (Eds.). (1987). *Handbook of environmental psychology.* New York: Wiley.

Sundstrom, E., Bell, P. A., Busby, P. L., & Asmus, C. (1996). Environmental psychology 1989–1994. *Annual Review of Psychology, 47,* 485–512.

Triandis, H. C. (1993). *Culture and social behavior.* New York: McGraw-Hill.

Van Raaj, W. F. (1999) Economic psychology. *Applied Psychology: An International Review, 48*(3) (Special Issue).

Walker, L. E. A. (1994). *Abused women and survivor therapy: A practical guide for the psychotherapist.* Washington, DC: American Psychological Association.

Walker, L. E. A. (1999). Psychology and domestic violence around the world. *American Psychologist, 54,* 21–29.

Wilpert, B., Kudat, A., & Özkan, Y. (1978). *Workers' participation in an internationalized economy.* Kent, OH: Kent State University Press.

Yancey, W. L. (1971). Architecture, interaction and social control: the case of a large-scale public housing project. *Environment and Behavior, 3,* 3–21.

Communications concerning this chapter should be addressed to: Professor José M. Prieto, Department of Psychology, Complutense University of Madrid, Despacho 2218, Campus Somosaguas, E-28223 Madrid, Spain

27

Contributions of Psychology to Peace and Nonviolent Conflict Resolution

MICHAEL G. WESSELLS

Today millions of people live in what are best described as systems of violence in which violence pervades multiple levels, including the family, community, and societal levels. One of the great challenges facing humanity is to convert systems of violence into cultures of peace, not only ending physical, psychological, and structural violence but also creating conditions and processes that enable human well-being, protection of human rights, and sustainable development.

Psychological science has much to contribute to the construction of peace and the resolution and prevention of destructive conflict. In recent decades, psychological research has advanced analyses of causes of war and inter-group conflict, dynamics of oppression and injustice, impacts of violence, processes of conflict escalation and de-escalation, and methods for building cooperation and resolving conflicts without resort to violence, among many other areas.

Issues of peace and conflict, however, are multidisciplinary and require analyses that emphasize the interpenetration between micro-level processes and macro-level institutions and processes in a dynamic social system. This chapter develops a systems analytic framework that situates the contributions of psychological research in multidisciplinary perspective, analyzes causes of violence at levels such as the family, community, and society, and identifies processes that contribute to peace at multiple levels.

27.1 WAR

War has multiple causes, including political, historical, economic, social, and psychological processes. Most analyses of war, particularly wars fought between states, have emphasized power struggles, political conflicts over realistic divergences of interest, and competition over scarce resources such as land and water (Levy, 1989; Lynn-Jones & Miller, 1995). Resource scarcity is increasing and is likely to amplify poverty and the North–South gap in wealth (Homer-Dixon, 1994), and growing environmental degradation creates problems such as environmental refugees that increase social pressures and conflict (El-Hinnawi, 1985). Further, anthropological evidence indicates that although as many as 20% of preindustrial societies have no history of organized war (Ross, 1993), increasing pressures for land competition have led previously non-warring groups such as the Fore people of New Guinea to take up arms (Sorenson, 1978).

As important as realistic conflicts are, protracted conflict damages the relationship between adversaries, and the damaged relationships bring a host of negative psychological dynamics into play that become integral, self-perpetuating parts of the conflict process (Kelman, 1997a; Staub, 1989). In this respect, war and destructive conflict reflect a mixture of objective and subjective elements. Analysis of subjective elements is a natural focus for psychological research, which has adapted its methodologies to fit real-world problems that do not permit careful isolation of variables and that have a rich historical, political, and cultural context.

The interplay between objective and subjective elements has become particularly conspicuous in the brutal ethnopolitical wars that surfaced in the latter three decades of the twentieth century. Objective oppression of ethnic groups and denial of access of minority groups to resources is a major determinant of ethnopolitical wars (Gurr, 1993; Horowitz, 1985). Land shortages, overcrowding, difficult economic circumstances, and privileging along lines of social class and ethnicity have helped to fuel conflicts such as the 1994 Rwandan genocide (Prunier, 1995; Smith, 1998). Ethnic struggles, however, are intensely psychological and often center around issues of identity, social memory, and group victimization. Each ethnic group, really an 'imagined community' (B. Anderson, 1991), honors its own culture, origin myths, and traditions, which provide a culturally constructed space in which people find their social identity, meaning, and security. Social psychological research indicates that even in the absence of material bases of conflict, people naturally divide themselves into in-groups and out-groups (Tajfel, 1982). Although ethnic identity and divisions do not themselves cause fighting, human needs theory has emphasized that armed conflict occurs when basic needs for security or positive social identity go unmet (Burton, 1990). This occurs in contexts of actual or perceived victimization, where remembered wrongs at the hands of the Other become a psychological warrant for revenge, fighting to protect one's group, or human rights abuses such as ethnic cleansing and mass rapes. As people participate in violence, they become increasingly capable of committing heinous acts (Staub, 1989).

In the wars of the 1990s in the former Yugoslavia, for example, both Serbs and Croats celebrated memories or 'chosen traumas' (Volkan, 1997) of their historic victimization by the Other. Each group integrated a sense of victimization into its social identity, increasing its fears about its collective survival. Political leaders on both sides exploited these fears to their own advantage. The survival fears, coupled with

the increasing polarization of communities by ethnicity, unleashed powerful nationalist sentiments that had been held in check largely by superpower domination during the Cold War. In the post-Cold War era, ethnonationalism erupted in many regions out of desire for 'patria' that would be sovereign, protected from adversaries, and enabling of the fullest expression of the cultural values of one's ethnic group (Kelman, 1997b). Thus psychological processes have contributed to the splintering of states that has characterized the post-Cold War era.

These processes of mass victimization, collective memory, and socialization for war are particularly powerful at present due to changes in the nature of armed conflict (Wessells, 1998a). In current intra-state conflicts, now the dominant form of war (Wallensteen & Sollenburg, 1998), nearly 90% of war casualties are civilians (Garfield and Neugut, 1997; Sivard, 1991), and mass victimization of civilians by attack, displacement, loss, and landmines plants the seeds of future conflicts. Further, the fighting occurs mostly with light weapons such as AK-47 assault rifles, and the combatants are increasingly children reared in environments that normalize violence, banditry, and war (Cairns, 1996; Klare, 1999; Wessells, 1998b).

With regard to international relations, subjective influences are visible at multiple levels. Both national leaders and political elites within the government bureaucracies that make decisions about war in industrialized societies are subject to a variety of biases that contribute to departures from strictly rational decision-making. Consistent with prospect theory (Kahneman & Tversky, 1979), leaders frequently take excessive risk to avoid losses (Levy, 1992). Research conducted by political scientists and psychologists has indicated that amidst realistic conflicts of interest, leaders of competing nations experience powerful fears, which motivate misperceptions regarding their adversaries' motives, strength, and willingness to fight (Jervis, 1976; Jervis, Lebow, & Stein, 1985). These misperceptions can be particularly dangerous in crises, leading some analysts to criticize policies such as nuclear deterrence (White, 1984). In addition, increased international tensions can lead to cognitive constriction as exhibited, for example, in the reduction of complexity of views toward the adversary in political speeches (Tetlock, 1985). Attributional biases are also pervasive. During the Cold War, both U.S. and Soviet leaders imputed the worst motives to their adversaries' behavior even in cases in which there may have been peaceful intent (White, 1984). Small group processes may also bias decision-making by leaders. Some evidence indicates that leadership groups having a strong espirit de corps and a charismatic leader may, in a crisis situation, engage in groupthink, a biased decisional process characterized by premature consensus, a sense of invulnerability, failure to weigh moral concerns, internal suppression of dissent, inadequate attention to problems, and poor contingency planning (Janis, 1982).

In many societies, particularly those having democratic governments, leaders alone do not make war. Publics also have to be mobilized for war, and numerous psychological processes are influential in this regard. Both political elites and political cultures encourage patriotism, which entails positive sentiments towards one's nation and a sense of obligation to protect it (Bar-Tal & Staub, 1997). In times of crisis, public symbols and political rhetoric stir patriotic sentiments and prepare the people to make sacrifices in war. Both individuals and groups construct social meaning and find social identity and cohesion through patriotism (Reykowski, 1997). But extreme forms of patriotism can lead to silencing of dissent, anti-intellectualism, and discrimination against out-groups defined as a threat to national security (Gozman, 1997).

A particularly powerful tool for public mobilization for war is enemy imaging, the construction of dehumanized images or beliefs that portray the Other as thoroughly diabolical, untrustworthy, evil and as manageable only through violence (Silverstein, 1989; White, 1984). Enemy images have sociocultural roots, become part of the reigning ideology, and find expression in mass media (Szalay & Mir-Djalali, 1991). By dehumanizing the Other, enemy images reduce moral restraints against killing and ill treatment. Both superpowers cultivated enemy images throughout the Cold War (White, 1984), and more recently, U.S. leaders used negative images of Saddam Hussein to win public support for the Gulf War (Manheim, 1993). Enemy imaging also played a prominent role in the 1994 Rwandan genocide, as the Hutu-dominated regime spread demonic images of Tutsis by radio and other means, preparing the way psychologically for the attempted extermination of the Tutsis (Prunier, 1995).

27.2 VIOLENCE

Aside from war, psychological processes influence violence at many levels. In criminology, psychological research has complemented multi-disciplinary investigations by analyzing the interaction of personal and situational determinants of violence. Physical violence occurs at much higher frequency in men than women (Archer,

1994), and longitudinal studies indicate remarkable stability in aggressiveness and violence in males from two to eighteen years (Loeber & Hay, 1997; Olweus, 1979). Childhood violence correlates with various forms of violence in adulthood, including partner assault and conviction for violent crimes by age 32 years (Farrington, 1994). This remarkable consistency of aggression and violence has encouraged the search for criminal personalities and attempts at criminal profiling, which have had modest success in regard to crimes such as serial rape and serial sexual homicide (Pinizzotto & Finkel, 1990). Still, most psychological research has emphasized the importance of situational influences and of family, community, and peer determinants of violent behavior. Many violent crimes are impulsive and incited by situations that produce intense anger, frustration, or fear (Berkowitz, 1993). Similarly, heightened levels of aggression and violence often occur in disadvantaged neighborhoods where people experience multiple psychosocial and economic stressors, where relative deprivation is pervasive, and where violence becomes an instrument for attaining not only material goods but also personal power and recognition (Campbell, 1986; Gilligan, 1996).

Psychological research has also advanced analysis of problems such as gang violence, which is rooted in historic patterns of discrimination and economic injustice (Huff, 1990). Psychological analyses have contributed by illuminating the manner in which young people are socialized into gangs, the interplay between personality and gang participation, dynamics of conformity, compliance, and obedience that lead individuals to participate in gang violence, and the needs for belonging, power, and social identity that may be met partially through gang membership (Goldstein, 1991). They have also helped to illuminate the psychological functions and meanings associated with the issues of territory and honor over which gangs frequently fight (Goldstein & Soriano, 1994).

More broadly, societal violence has been examined through the lens of systems theory (Miller, 1978; Rapoport, 1989), which interconnects psychological research with research on institutions. This research has yielded more comprehensive understanding of structural violence (Galtung, 1969) – psychological violence, social oppression, and physical damage owing to institutionalized inequalities and denial of access to basic service such as health care. Structural violence is particularly conspicuous in the '-isms' of racism, classism, sexism, and militarism. In each of these, psychological processes contribute to structural violence, and structural violence enables direct, physical violence.

Sociological studies of the institutional, legal, and economic bases of sexism, for example, have emphasized patriarchy and macro-social power differentials between men and women (M. Anderson, 1993). These studies have been complemented by psychological investigations of gendered identities, socialization practices, and dynamics around gender issues (Unger & Crawford, 1992). In addition, sexist institutions set the stage for direct violence at various levels, as evidenced in domestic violence against women, a global phenomenon (Walker, 1999). Men often use spouse battering as a strategy (objectionably) for maintaining power and control in the family. This strategy is grounded in patriarchy, socially constructed beliefs about men's rightful position of dominance, socialization into gendered identities and roles, and institutionalized patterns of injustice towards women (Koss et al., 1994).

In regard to militarism, research has documented processes of violence glorification, the heroization of military deeds, the integration of violence into men's roles, and the socialization of soldiers for obedience and watching out for fellow troops (Archer, 1994; Kellett, 1990; Kelman & Hamilton, 1989; Lorentzen & Turpin, 1998; Reardon, 1985). Further, psychological processes are evident in militaristic regimes' use of state-sponsored violence to control populations through policies of terror and political repression (Ardila, 1996; Lira, 1988). The state may define social reality through state lies (Martín-Baró, 1994), and dissenters are treated as criminals or terrorists. At the individual level, torture is often used to destroy the identity and meaning patterns of dissenters (Sveaass, 1994) and to insure that others learn to adhere to the state line.

States have no monopoly on militarism, which is cultivated by many non-state groups and paramilitary organizations. Also, in democratic countries, psychological processes contribute to an insidious form of militarism in the streets. For example, many U.S. cities are saturated with guns, gangs, and violent crime, which serve both to normalize violence and to set the context for socialization in the streets into lives of violence (Berkowitz, 1993; Campbell, 1986).

27.3 CONFLICT MITIGATION AND RESOLUTION

Law is one of the primary means for handling conflicts without resort to violence. Extensive research on psychology and law has grown up around issues such as mental competency to stand trial, psychological assessment, jury selection, family law, and psychology of corrections (Kapardis, 1997). In some cases, psychological research has cast new light on ancient practices. For example, cognitive research on eyewitness testimony has revealed a variety of biases in memory, including possible distorting effects of information introduced by post-event questions and discussions (Loftus, 1979). Psychological research has also encouraged alternate means of dispute resolution through the use of professional mediators (third parties) rather than adversarial legal proceedings, which may strain already troubled relationships. Some evidence indicates that divorcing couples are happier with mediated settlements, which they regard as more fair, less damaging of relationship, and more likely to be complied with (Emery & Wyer, 1987; Kelly & Gigy, 1989).

At the societal and international levels, law is a useful but limited means of handling conflicts in a constructive manner. Societal law is a principal venue for achieving justice, which is closely connected with conflict resolution (Bunker & Rubin, 1995; Deutsch, 1985). Citizens' willingness to obey law and use the legal system to handle conflicts depends on perceptions of fairness and procedural justice (Tyler, 1990). As illustrated by racist societies, however, law can itself become a tool of injustice that sparks armed rebellion or encourages nonviolent social movements such as the U.S. civil rights movement, which was animated partly by psychological processes and enabled changes in law (Rubin, Pruitt, & Kim, 1994). In intra-societal wars, the opposition groups challenge the legitimacy of governmental laws, and legal means are poorly suited to addressing the psychological issues of identity and fear that fuel conflicts in communities following the signing of treaties (Kelman, 1997a). In many international conflicts, willingness to adjudicate conflict via international law is often limited by lack of political will, perceptions that the adversary will not obey law, or attachment of higher value to national law.

Beyond legal means, a variety of sophisticated tools exist for nonviolent conflict mitigation, resolution, and prevention. Among these are diplomacy (Barston, 1988), negotiation (Carnevale & Pruitt, 1992), mediation (Zartman & Rasmussen, 1997), interactive problem-solving (Fisher, 1997), contact across lines of conflict (Pettigrew, 1998), cooperation on superordinate goals (Johnson & Johnson, 1989; Sherif, 1966), and unilateral initiatives (Osgood, 1962). Which tools are most appropriate depends on the situation, the kind of issues involved in the conflict, and whether the parties have an orientation that is cooperative, individualistic, or competitive (Deutsch, 1994). Analysis of how conflicts may be contained and resolved requires consideration of the social context, including its political, historical, cultural, economic, and religious elements.

Culture also plays a key role in determining which approaches to conflict resolution are most appropriate and effective in a particular context (Cohen, 1997). For example, collectivistic, high-context cultures favor the use of collaborative strategies and maintenance of harmony. In high-context cultures, communication often occurs implicitly through context rather than through what is said directly, and emphasis is on non-verbal reactions, how the perceiver is responding, and avoidance of confrontation and competition. In contrast, individualist, low-context cultures favor more direct, clear communications and emphasis is on what is said rather than on how it is said or other aspects of context (Ting-Toomey, 1988). In high-context cultures, confrontational, argumentative styles of handling conflict are avoided, whereas these styles may be preferred in low-context cultures. Just as culture shapes modes of conflict, it also shapes approaches to conflict mitigation and resolution (Fry & Björkqvist, 1997; Jandt & Pederson, 1996; Sponsel & Gregor, 1994), which are passed on through processes such as social learning.

Psychological research has helped to elucidate why various methods succeed, the conditions under which particular methods work, and the psychological processes that mediate changes in conflictual relationships. For example, negotiation is often not possible or limited in scope in very intense conflicts since the parties mistrust each other and avoid making concessions to prevent image loss. In this context, mediation is often the more appropriate method since an effective mediator may be perceived by the parties as willing to oppose intransigence and cheating and as being in a position to broker an outcome that is more acceptable than the hurting stalemate that the parties would otherwise confront (Rubin et al., 1994). Face-saving plays an important role in mediation, as the mediator may suggest concessions, thereby avoiding any appearance of weakness among the parties. Effective mediators use social influence processes such as 'carrots and sticks', a mixture of promised rewards for conflict-reducing actions and promised punishments for intransigence, to move toward an agreement.

Formal agreements by themselves, however, do not make for peace, which is frequently undermined by polarized communities, powerful fears, and damaged inter-group relationships. Settlement of a particular dispute, particularly if achieved through power bargaining, may manage the conflict but do little to achieve conflict

resolution, which requires changing a hostile relationship (Fisher, 1994). Official diplomacy has limited ability to resolve conflicts since external political pressures constrain negotiation. Moreover, what is said in public dialogues can evoke backlashes that undermine a peace process, and treaties signed between leaders may make little change in the polarization, fear, and hostile patterns of interaction that characterize divided societies and communities (Kelman, 1997a). For these reasons, psychologists have helped to develop methods of unofficial diplomacy that contribute to conflict resolution and enable official diplomacy before, during, and following formal negotiations and mediations.

A particularly useful tool of unofficial diplomacy is the interactive problem-solving workshop (Fisher, 1997) pioneered by psychologists such as Herbert Kelman (1996). In regard to the Israeli–Palestinian conflict, a typical workshop brings together three to six Israelis with an equal number of Palestinians for two-and-a-half days of private dialogue facilitated by social scientists. The participants are well-respected political influentials who hold no official positions, are free to explore various options, and are likely to assume official political leadership positions. Through careful analytic, problem-solving discussion, the participants examine the main issues at stake in the conflict, explore their concerns and fears, and identify possible solutions and steps that might help to overcome the psychological and political barriers on both sides. Empathy, problem-solving, and collaborative exploration of 'what-if' questions are encouraged. Following the workshops, participants have taken their new learning about the other side back into their communities, beginning the arduous process of community transformation that is essential for handling and preventing intercommunal conflict. The workshops have been instrumental in establishing positive communication and empathy, altering dehumanizing stereotypes of the other, and stimulating constructive dialogue across conflict lines in highly segregated societies. They have also helped set the stage for official negotiations and for official back-channel, secret meetings such as those which led to the Oslo Accords.

Psychology also has much to contribute to tasks of conflict prevention such as preventive diplomacy (Lund, 1996), early warning and intervention of bystanders, and development of prosocial behaviors and caring societies (Staub, 1996), education for peace (Wagner & Christie, 1994), and systemic integration of processes of nonviolent conflict resolution (Deutsch, 1994). In the next millennium, one of the main challenges of social science research is to improve strategies for prevention of violence and destructive conflict.

RESOURCE REFERENCES

Christie, D., Wagner, R. V., & Winter, D. (Eds.). (in press). *Peace, conflict, and violence: Peace psychology for the 21st century*. Englewood Cliffs, NJ: Prentice-Hall.

Galtung, J. (1996). *Peace by peaceful means: Peace and conflict, development and civilization*. London: Sage.

Garbarino, J. (1999). *Lost boys: Why our sons turn violent and how we can save them*. New York: Free Press.

Kelman, H. C., & Hamilton, V. L. (1989). *Crimes of obedience: Toward a social psychology of authority and responsibility*. New Haven: Yale University Press.

Leavitt, L. A., & Fox, N. A. (Eds.). (1993). *The psychological effects of war and violence on children*. Hillsdale, NJ: Erlbaum.

Lorentzen, L. A., & Turpin, J. (Eds.). (1998). *The women and war reader*. New York: New York University Press.

Marsella, A. J., Bornemann, T., Ekblad, S., & Orley, J. (Eds.). (1994). *Amidst peril and pain: The mental health of the world's refugees*. Washington, DC: American Psychological Association.

Martin-Baró, I. (1983). *Acción e Ideología: Psicología Social desde Centroamérica*. San Salvador: UCA Editores.

Montville, J. V. (Ed.). (1991). *Conflict and peacemaking in multiethnic societies*. Lexington, MA: Lexington Books.

Pruitt, D. G., & Carnevale, P. J. (1993). *Negotiation in social conflict*. Buckingham, England: Open University Press.

Raviv, A., Oppenheimer, L., & Bar-Tal, D. (Eds.). (1999). *How children understand war and peace: A call for international peace education*. San Francisco: Jossey-Bass.

Smith, M. B. (1991). *Values, self, and society: Toward a humanist social psychology*. London: Transaction.

ADDITIONAL LITERATURE CITED

Anderson, B. (1991). *Imagined communities*. London: Verso.

Anderson, M. (1993). *Thinking about women: Sociological perspectives on sex and gender* (3rd ed.). New York: Macmillan.

Archer, J. (Ed.). (1994). *Male violence*. London: Routledge.

Ardila, R. (1996). Political psychology: The Latin American perspective. *Political Psychology, 17*(2), 339–351.

Barston, R. P. (1988). *Modern diplomacy*. London: Longman.

Bar-Tal, D., & Staub, E. (Eds.). (1997). *Patriotism in the lives of individuals and nations*. Chicago: Nelson-Hall.

Berkowitz, L. (1993). *Aggression: Its causes, consequences, and control*. New York: McGraw-Hill.

Bunker, B. B., & Rubin, J. Z. (Eds.). (1995). *Conflict, cooperation, and justice*. San Francisco: Jossey-Bass.

Burton, J. W. (Ed.). (1990). *Conflict: Human needs theory*. New York: St. Martin's.

Cairns, E. (1996). *Children and political violence*. Oxford: Blackwell.

Campbell, A. (1986). The streets and violence. In A. Campbell & J. J. Gibbs (Eds.), *Violent transactions: The limits of personality* (pp. 115–132). New York: Basil Blackwell.

Carnevale, P. J., & Pruitt, D. G. (1992). Negotiation and mediation. *Annual Review of Psychology, 43*, 531–582.

Cohen, R. (1997). *Negotiating across cultures* (rev. ed.). Washington, DC: U.S. Institute of Peace Press.

Deutsch, M. (1985). *Distributive justice: A social psychological perspective*. New Haven, CT: Yale University Press.

Deutsch, M. (1994). Constructive conflict resolution: Principles, training, and research. *Journal of Social Issues, 50*, 13–32.

El-Hinnawi, E. (1985). *Environmental refugees*. New York: United Nations Development Program.

Emery, R. E., & Wyer, M. M. (1987). Child custody mediation and litigation: An experimental evaluation of the experience of parents. *Journal of Consulting and Clinical Psychology, 2*, 179–186.

Farrington, D. P. (1994). Childhood, adolescent, and adult features of violent males. In L. R. Huesmann (Ed.), *Aggressive behavior: Current perspectives* (pp. 215–240). New York: Plenum.

Fisher, R. J. (1994). Generic principles for resolving intergroup conflict. *Journal of Social Issues, 50*(1), 47–66.

Fisher, R. J. (1997). *Interactive conflict resolution*. Syracuse, NY: Syracuse University Press.

Fry, D. P., & Björkqvist, K. (Eds.). (1997). *Cultural variation in conflict resolution*. Mahwah, NJ: Lawrence Erlbaum.

Galtung, J. (1969). Violence, peace, and peace research. *Journal of Peace Research, 3*, 167–191.

Garfield, R. M., & Neugut, A. I. (1997). The human consequences of war. In B. S. Levy & V. W. Sidel (Eds.), *War and public health* (pp. 27–38). New York: Oxford University Press.

Gilligan, J. (1996). *Violence*. New York: Grosset/Putnam.

Goldstein, A. P. (1991). *Gangs: A psychological perspective*. Champaign, IL: Research Press.

Goldstein, A. P., & Soriano, F. I. (1994). Juvenile gangs. In L. D. Eron, J. H. Gentry, & P. Schlegel (Eds.), *Reason to hope* (pp. 315–333). Washington, DC: American Psychological Association.

Gozman, L. (1997). Russian patriotism: Forward to the past. In D. Bar-Tal & E. Staub (Eds.), *Patriotism in the lives of individuals and nations* (pp. 293–308). Chicago: Nelson-Hall.

Gurr, T. R. (1993). *Minorities at risk: A global view of ethnopolitical conflicts*. Washington, DC: United States Institute of Peace Press.

Homer-Dixon, T. (1994). Environmental scarcity and intergroup conflict. In M. T. Klare & D. C. Thomas (Eds.), *World security* (2nd ed., pp. 290–313). New York: St. Martin's.

Horowitz, D. (1985). *Ethnic groups in conflict*. Berkeley, CA: University of California Press.

Huff, C. R. (Ed.). (1990). *Gangs in America*. London: Sage.

Jandt, F. E., & Pedersen, P. B. (Eds.). (1996). *Constructive conflict management: Asia-Pacific cases*. Thousand Oaks, CA: Sage.

Janis, I. L. (1982). *Groupthink* (2nd ed.). Boston: Houghton Mifflin.

Jervis, R. (1976). *Perception and misperception in international politics*. Princeton, NJ: Princeton University Press.

Jervis, R., Lebow, R. N., & Stein, J. G. (1985). *Psychology & deterrence*. Baltimore: Johns Hopkins University Press.

Johnson, D. W., & Johnson, R. T. (1989). *Cooperation and competition: Theory and research*. Edina, MN: Interaction Book Company.

Kahneman, D., & Tversky, A. (1979). Prospect theory: An analysis of decision under risk. *Econometrica*, *47*, 263–291.

Kapardis, A. (1997). *Psychology and law: A critical introduction*. Cambridge: Cambridge University Press.

Kellett, A. (1990). The soldier in battle: Motivational and behavioral aspects of the combat experience. In B. Glad (Ed.), *Psychological dimensions of war* (pp. 215–235). Newbury Park, CA: Sage.

Kelly, J. B., & Gigy, L. L. (1989). Divorce mediation: Characteristics of clients and outcomes. In K. Kressel & D. G. Pruitt (Eds.), *Mediation research* (pp. 263–283). San Francisco: Jossey-Bass.

Kelman, H. C. (1996). The interactive problem-solving approach. In C. A. Crocker, F. O. Hampson, & P. Aall (Eds.), *Managing global chaos* (pp. 501–519). Washington, DC: U.S. Institute of Peace Press.

Kelman, H. C. (1997a). Social-psychological dimensions of international conflict. In I. W. Zartman & J. L. Rasmussen (Eds.), *Peacemaking in international conflict* (pp. 191–237). Washington, DC: U.S. Institute of Peace Press.

Kelman, H. C. (1997b). Nationalism, patriotism, and national identity: Social-psychological dimensions. In D. Bar-Tal & E. Staub (Eds.), *Patriotism in the lives of individuals and nations* (pp. 165–189). Chicago: Nelson-Hall.

Kelman, H. C., & Hamilton, V. L. (1989). *Crimes of obedience*. New Haven, CT: Yale University Press.

Klare, M. (1999). The Kalashnikov age. *The Bulletin of the Atomic Scientists*, *55*(1), 18–22.

Koss, M. P., Goodman, L. A., Browne, A., Fitzgerald, L. F., Keita, G. P., & Russo, N. F. (1994). *No safe haven: Male violence against women at home, at work, and in the community*. Washington, DC: American Psychological Association.

Levy, J. S. (1989). The causes of war: A review of theories and evidence. In P. E. Tetlock, J. L. Husbands, R. Jervis, P. C. Stern, & C. Tilly (Eds.), *Behavior, society and nuclear war* (vol. 1, pp. 209–333). New York: Oxford University Press.

Levy, J. S. (1992). An introduction to prospect theory. *Political Psychology*, *13*(2), 171–186.

Lira, E. (1988). Consecuencias psicosociales de la represión política en Chile [Psychosocial consequences of political repression in Chile]. *Revista de Psicología de El Salvador*, *28*, 143–159.

Loeber, R., & Hay, D. (1977). Key issues in the development of aggression and violence from childhood to early adulthood. *Annual Review of Psychology*, *48*, 371–410.

Loftus, E. R. (1979). *Eyewitness testimony*. Cambridge, MA: Harvard University Press.

Lorentzen, L. A., & Turpin, J. (Eds.). (1998). *The women and war reader*. New York: New York University Press.

Lund, M. S. (1996). *Preventing violent conflicts: A strategy for preventive diplomacy*. Washington, DC: U.S. Institute of Peace Press.

Lynn-Jones, S. M., & Miller, S. E. (Eds.). (1995). *Global dangers*. Cambridge, MA: MIT Press.

Manheim, J. B. (1993). The war of images: Strategic communication in the Gulf conflict. In S. A. Renshon (Ed.), *The political psychology of the Gulf War* (pp. 155–171). Pittsburgh, PA: University of Pittsburgh Press.

Martín-Baró, I. (1994). Public opinion research as a de-ideologizing instrument. In A. Aron & S. Corne (Eds.), *Writings for a liberation psychology: Ignacio Martín-Baró* (pp. 186–197). Cambridge, MA: Harvard University Press.

Miller, J. G. (1978). *Living systems*. New York: McGraw-Hill.

Olweus, D. (1979). Stability of aggressive reaction patterns in males: A review. *Psychological Bulletin*, *86*, 852–875.

Osgood, C. E. (1962). *Alternative to war or surrender*. Urbana, IL: University of Illinois Press.

Pettigrew, T. F. (1998). Intergroup contact theory. *Annual Review of Psychology*, *49*, 65–85.

Pinizzotto, A. J., & Finkel, N. J. (1990). Criminal personality profiling: An outcome and process study. *Law and Human Behavior, 14,* 215–234.

Prunier, G. (1995). *The Rwanda crisis.* New York: Columbia University Press.

Rapoport, A. (1989). *The origins of violence.* New York: Paragon House.

Reardon, B. A. (1985). *Sexism and the war system.* New York: Teachers College Press.

Reykowski, J. (1997). Patriotism and the collective system of meanings. In D. Bar-Tal & E. Staub (Eds.), *Patriotism in the lives of individuals and nations* (pp. 293–308). Chicago: Nelson-Hall.

Ross, M. H. (1993). *The culture of conflict.* New Haven, CT: Yale University Press.

Rubin, J. Z., Pruitt, D. G., & Kim, S. H. (1994). *Social conflict: Escalation, stalemate, and settlement* (2nd ed.). New York: McGraw-Hill.

Sherif, M. (1966). *In common predicament: Social psychology of intergroup conflict and cooperation.* Boston: Houghton Mifflin.

Silverstein, B. (1989). Enemy images: The psychology of U. S. attitudes and cognitions reagarding the Soviet Union. *American Psychologist, 44*(6), 903–913.

Sivard, R. L. (1991). *World military and social expenditures 1991.* Washington, DC: World Priorities.

Smith, D. N. (1998). The psychocultural roots of genocide: Legitimacy and crisis in Rwanda. *American Psychologist, 53*(7), 743–753.

Sorenson, E. (1978). Cooperation and freedom among the Fore of New Guinea. In A. Montagu (Ed.), *Learning non-aggression: The experience of non-literate societies* (pp. 12–30). New York: Oxford University Press.

Sponsel, L. E., & Gregor, T. (Eds.). (1994). *The anthropology of peace and nonviolence.* Boulder, CO: Lynne Rienner.

Staub, E. (1989). *The roots of evil: The origins of genocide and other group violence.* Cambridge: Cambridge University Press.

Staub, E. (1996). The psychological and cultural roots of group violence and the creation of caring societies and peaceful group relations. In T. Sponsel (Ed.), *A natural history of peace* (pp. 129–155). Nashville, TN: Vanderbilt University Press.

Sveaass, N. (1994). The organized destruction of meaning. In N. J. Lavik, M. Nygard, N. Sveaass, & E. Fannemel (Eds.), *Pain and survival: Human rights violations and mental health* (pp. 43–64). Oslo: Scandinavian University Press.

Szalay, L. B., & Mir-Djalali, E. (1991). Image of the enemy: Critical parameters, cultural variations. In R. W. Rieber (Ed.), *The psychology of war and peace* (pp. 213–250). New York: Plenum.

Tajfel, H. (1982). *Social identity and intergroup relations.* New York: Cambridge University Press.

Tetlock, P. E. (1985). Integrative complexity of American and Soviet foreign policy rhetorics: A time-series analysis. *Journal of Personality and Social Psychology, 49,* 1565–1585.

Ting-Toomey, S. (1988). Intercultural conflict styles: A face-negotiation theory. In Y. Kim & W. Gudykunst (Eds.), *Theories in intercultural communication* (pp. 213–235). Newbury Park, CA: Sage.

Tyler, T. R. (1990). *Why people obey the law.* New Haven, CT: Yale University Press.

Unger, R., & Crawford, M. (1992). *Women and gender: A feminist psychology.* New York: McGraw-Hill.

Volkan, V. (1997). *Bloodlines: From ethnic pride to ethnic terrorism.* New York: Farrar, Straus and Giroux.

Wagner, R. V., & Christie, D. J. (1994). Psychology and peace. In M. T. Klare (Ed.), *Peace & world security studies: A curriculum guide* (6th ed., pp. 230–242). London: Lynne Rienner.

Walker, L. E. (1999). Psychology and domestic violence around the world. *American Psychologist, 54*(1), 21–29.

Wallensteen, P., & Sollenberg, M. (1998). Armed conflicts and regional conflict complexes, 1989–97. *Journal of Peace Research, 35*(5), 621–634.

Wessels, M. G. (1998a). The changing nature of armed conflict and its implications for children: The Graça Machel/UN Study. *Peace and Conflict: Journal of Peace Psychology, 4*(4), 321–334.

Wessells, M. G. (1998b). Children, armed conflict, and peace. *Journal of Peace Research, 35,* 635–646.

White, R. K. (1984). *Fearful warriors: A psychological profile of U.S.–Soviet relations.* New York: Free Press.

Zartman, I. W., & Rasmussen, J. L. (Eds.). (1997). *Peacemaking in international conflict: Methods & techniques.* Washington, DC: U.S. Institute of Peace Press.

Communications concerning this chapter should be addressed to: Professor Michael G. Wessells, Randolph-Macon College, Department of Psychology, Ashland, VA 23005, USA

28

Psychology as a Profession

INGRID LUNT

28.1 The Emergence of Psychology as a Profession

Over the past fifty years there has been an extremely rapid and substantial development and expansion of psychology as a profession. Emerging from a predominantly academic discipline in the early part of the twentieth century, psychology has rapidly become an applied profession, to the point where at the end of the century a significant majority of psychologists work as practitioners in professional contexts. Indeed, for the first half of the century, until about 1950, most psychologists held posts teaching and doing research in universities or colleges; however, today, in the United States, for example, only about 33% of the 100,000 psychologists with doctoral degrees work in academic settings, while the remaining 67% are deployed in a wide variety of practitioner work settings and contexts. The proportion of psychologists now working in academic settings may be even lower in many countries of the Western world, while in developing countries there may be an even stronger emphasis on practitioner and professional psychology (Rosenzweig, 1992; Wilpert & Lunt, 1998), where social needs and economic circumstances demand a concentration on practical problems.

Professional psychologists work in settings which include private clinical or consulting practice, the state or local government service in the health, social welfare and education services, universities, industry, private organizations and companies, and a growing range of contexts in which psychology has been applied by practitioners. This growing number of different contexts has led to a growth in specialization of psychologists (see below). In turn, the growth in specialization has led to an increase in the number of specialist qualifications, and in the demand for specialist post-graduate education and training.

In most countries, psychology became rapidly 'professionalized' following World War II, a period when psychologists increasingly became involved in various social service domains, in attempts to solve individual and social problems (Louw, 1997a). Thus, from the 1950s on, we see a growth in the health-service-provider areas and a relative decline in the traditional academic/research areas (Rosenzweig, 1992). Clinical, educational and organizational psychologists constituted the earliest groups of professional psychologists. More recently, professional psychology has become increasingly diversified and specialized with professional groups of counseling, environmental, forensic, health, sports and traffic psychologists, and a growing trend of specialization with a growth in specialist education and training and professionalization within specialties.

For the present purposes we define professionalization as the development of the use of skills based on a unique body of theoretical knowledge, education and training in those skills, competence ensured by examination, a code of professional conduct, orientation toward the public good, a professional organization (Millerson, 1964). We see that over the recent decades and across the world, psychologists increasingly aspire to full professional status. There are a number of trends which demonstrate this growing professionalization. These include: pressures in most countries for legal recognition and regulation of psychologists, an increase in level of qualification and length of education and training required for professional practice, a growing concern with ethical issues, pressures to develop systems to facilitate psychologists' mobility between different countries and therefore for mutual recognition of the equivalence of qualifications, and a growing specialization and differentiation within professional psychology.

Most countries have aspired to increased professionalization through legal regulation and ethical codes, higher qualifications, and the institutionalization of psychology in universities and professional associations. Many countries now have laws which regulate psychologists, most countries have developed codes of ethics through their national psychologist association, and in most countries, the education and qualifications for psychologists have progressively increased in scope and status to a high level; indeed, many countries and psychological specialties require doctoral level qualification for professional practice. For example, doctoral level education is required for practice as a clinical psychologist in the USA and the UK, increasingly in Canada, and will be required in South Africa within the next four years; this trend appears likely to spread to other countries. In Australia, six years' university education plus two years' supervised experience is usually the

requirement for membership of any specialist professional college of the Australian Psychological Society (APS), while from January 2000 six years' university education is required for basic membership of APS. In European countries, there is considerable variation in the pattern of education and training for professional psychologists (e.g., Lunt, 1997; Newstead & Makkinen, 1997), though there are moves for more common standards, while many of the former colonial countries have until recently followed the pattern of education of the colonizing countries (Leung & Zhang, 1995).

It is well known that psychology first emerged as a discipline in Europe which dominated its development until the middle of the twentieth century; following World War II the USA succeeded Europe as the leader and has dominated the field up to the present. Traditional psychology as a discipline and a profession is permeated with Euro-American cultural values that champion rational, liberal, and individualistic ideals (Kim, 1995) and thus was basically non-existent in its traditional form in non-Western countries before World War II. However, it is only relatively recently that the implications of fundamental differences between individualistic and collectivistic cultures for psychology have been emphasized, and the potential links between folk and scientific epistemology allowed expression, and the importance of indigenous psychologies brought to the fore. Thus, in many non-Western countries, psychology as a profession has emerged only recently, and it is only now becoming apparent that Western modes of professionalization may not be the most appropriate or culturally relevant for all countries.

Definition and Scope of Professional Psychology

Robert M. Yerkes frequently referred to the work of academic psychologists as the 'profession of psychologists' (Yerkes, 1918), and the term is frequently used to cover both scientist and practitioner psychologists. This chapter will mainly refer to 'professional psychologists' as the group of psychologists who apply the findings of the science of psychology, and who work directly or indirectly with clients in a predominantly practitioner, though including teaching, role. As stated above, this has been the direction of the major expansion of psychology, and its professionalization has led to a strong focus in all countries on this practitioner or professional role. However it has been stated that the scope of professional psychology has become restricted over the years to the 'practice' of psychology (Evans, Staudt Sexton, & Cadwallader, 1992), and in some countries restricted to or dominated by clinical psychology.

This definition fits in with definitions of 'professional' provided by the wider literature which suggests the distinguishing features of a 'profession' to be a unique body of knowledge and set of skills (for gate-keeping and standard-setting), a code of conduct, self-regulation and disciplinary procedures for its members (Freidson, 1994; Millerson, 1964). The first occupations to be considered professions were theology, medicine, and law, which early on gained the status of 'learned professions'; these were followed in the nineteenth century by architecture and engineering, and in this century by a proliferation of other occupations claiming or aspiring to professional status. Psychologists have become increasingly professionalized in all countries; this professionalization has manifested itself through an increase in the length of the education and training period (for example, see Cumming, Siddler, & Hyslop, 1997; EFPPA, 1990; Martin, 1989), pressures for regulation of the practice and the profession (EFPPA, 1997b; Lindsay, 1995; Pulverich, 1998), the development of codes of ethics (e.g., Lindsay, 1996; Sinclair, 1993), and an increase in political activity in relation to other professionals.

The Relationship between Scientists and Practitioners

Although there are those who would suggest that there is a fundamental separation between basic research and applied practice (e.g., Schönpflug, 1993), the majority of professional psychologists consider that science forms an integral foundation and base for the practice of psychology. This model, which originated in part with Witmer's clinic in the USA in the 1890s and was articulated much later at a conference in Boulder, Colorado, in 1949, led to a widespread commitment to a 'scientist-practitioner' model of professional psychology. This model dominates major countries in the world and their practice of psychology (e.g., Cumming et al., 1997; Lunt, 1998a). The Boulder conference of 1949 clearly marked a further stage in the professionalization of American clinical psychology, and led to an exclusive definition of 'clinical psychologist' in the USA; this was claimed to be in order to 'safeguard the public as well as the profession against the still greater evils that are bound to arise if the profession cannot define what the title "clinical psychologist" stands for' (Raimy, 1950, p. 38). Protection of the title of

'psychologist' is an aspiration of a growing number of psychology associations which seek legal regulation for their members.

The 'scientist-professional' or 'scientist-practitioner' model dominated clinical psychology in the USA, United Kingdom, and Australia, and later many other countries in Europe and across the world. Thus, for example, there was a presumed relationship between the development of new psychological knowledge such as attachment theory, locus of control, anxiety, learning theories, and the application of this knowledge, together with theories of change such as behaviorism and psychoanalysis, which supported the early development of clinical psychology; the scientific basis of mental testing led to the early development of educational psychology; while understanding of the science of selection and the science of human factors and later of organizations led to the field of work and organizational psychology. Not only was scientific knowledge assumed to be the source of new applications, but it was also claimed to be necessary to the practice of professional psychology, hence in part the lengthy education and training requirements for professional psychologists. The model has been subjected to criticism (e.g., Dawes, 1994; Pilgrim & Treacher, 1992) and, as Schönpflug (1993) has pointed out, the relationship between science and application is not straightforward. This relationship is embodied in the nature of national psychology associations (see below), some of which combine scientific and practitioner interests in one body, while others have separate associations for science and practice aspects of the discipline.

Professional Identity of Professional Psychologists

Within the health sector, clinical psychologists developed their role alongside medical professionals, in particular psychiatrists. In many countries there has been a struggle for psychologists to develop and maintain their autonomy as a separate profession. This has taken different forms according to the different social, economic, and employment contexts. Historically, psychologists have in some countries had to defer to their medical colleagues, either in their role as administrators of test and assessment procedures, or in their struggle to gain reimbursement privileges for psychological treatment through health insurance. However, in the majority of countries, professional psychologists assert their professional identity as a science-based profession, and have gained status through their lengthy education and training and through their professional organizations.

28.2 DIFFERENT GROUPS OF PROFESSIONAL PSYCHOLOGISTS

Although clinical psychology dominates the practitioner domain in all countries (Wilpert & Lunt, 1998), in many countries professional psychologists have become increasingly differentiated and specialized, with specialist patterns of education and training for the different branches. This section provides very brief information on the major specializations within professional psychology, within a context of rapid growth in specialist subfields. Again, it is necessary to be clear as to the definition of 'professional psychologist' as one who provides a psychological service directly or indirectly to a client. In the UK, for example, these professional groups are defined by the British Psychological Society (BPS) through its professional Divisions which differ in structure from its scientific 'Sections'; the professional Divisions are defined through the possession of a separate route of education and training leading to a specialist qualification and title; there are currently Divisions for clinical, counseling, educational, forensic, health, occupational, teaching psychology, with sports psychology developing its own route (BPS, 1995). This provides one definition of 'professional psychology' which is used by Shimmin and Wallis in their account of the development of professional status for occupational psychology (Shimmin & Wallis, 1994).

Clinical Psychologists

Clinical psychologists (for many the 'prototype' professional psychologists) constitute the earliest group of professional psychologists seeking to apply the findings of the science of psychology in a practitioner or client context. The founder of clinical psychology (and school psychology) is widely held to be Lightmer Witmer, a professor at the University of Pennsylvania, who founded a psychological clinic in 1896, and proposed to a meeting of the American Psychological Association (APA) that year that 'the principles of psychology should be used to help people individually' (Routh, 1994). In the UK, Hans Eysenck is generally considered to have founded clinical psychology at the Maudsley Hospital in London in the late 1940s and early 1950s, where a strong tradition of behavior therapy dominated the profession for several

decades, although the earlier psychoanalytic tradition was maintained at the Tavistock Clinic also in London. As noted above, clinical psychologists emerged as a major group in the 1950s, in the United Kingdom as part of the post-war development of the Welfare State, and in other countries also as a response to some of the problems resulting from the war. This was a period when professional associations of psychologists were founded in many countries (see below).

Clinical psychology has evolved in many countries over its fifty years into a professionalized and specialized activity, with growing sub-specialisms in clinical neuropsychology, drug and addiction rehabilitation, gerontological psychology, and community psychology (see below). As mentioned, in most countries, it is a science-based profession, relying on thoroughly verified research findings, careful evaluation of models and procedures, and the use of hypothesis testing in assessment and intervention. This is not necessarily the model in all countries, and there are a number of countries where a more hermeneutic tradition prevails, and a long tradition of clinical psychologists using often highly sophisticated psychoanalytic models continues. There is furthermore debate within the profession itself as to the appropriateness of the 'pure' scientific approach to the alleviation of human problems and distress (see for example Pilgrim & Treacher, 1992).

Although a substantial part of clinical psychologists' work in most countries is as psychotherapists for children, adults, couples, and families, they also play an important role in work with people with learning difficulties, work with offenders, work in organizational change and training, work with older clients in the field of gerontology, and in the field of disaster and crisis. Clinical psychologists have themselves specialized and developed specialisms in further subfields such as clinical neuropsychology, forensic psychology, learning disability, child mental health, adult mental health, and gerontology, with the development of post-qualification training and specialist titles.

Clinical psychologists have become professionalized through the growth of specialist organizations, usually within a wider psychologist association. Clinical psychology was established by 1945 as Division 12 of the American Psychological Association (APA), and as an early Division of the International Association of Applied Psychology (IAAP); in the UK, the British Psychological Society's Division of Clinical Psychology was formed in 1970, though clinical psychologists had long belonged to the Medical

Section of BPS and later the Division of Educational and Child Psychology. 1998 saw the formation of the International Society for Clinical Psychology.

Work and Organizational Psychologists

The group of psychologists concerned with human behavior and experience in organized work settings started with the name 'industrial psychologists', or its equivalent in other languages. The name later became 'industrial and organizational psychologists' in the USA, and 'work and organizational psychologists' in Europe, while in the UK the name 'occupational psychologists', is still held today by many professionals and by the relevant Division of the British Psychological Society. However, the more widely used name 'work and organizational psychologists' is perhaps a more accurate reflection of their field of activity, and is in more common use internationally (and see Drenth and Wang, Chapter 25). This is the second largest category of psychologists after clinical psychologists and is a fast-growing sector in psychology across the world.

Work and organizational psychologists are concerned with human behavior at work, and may specialize in human factors and the interaction of humans with machines, in understanding and working with groups and organizations, in appraisal, assessment and selection, personnel issues, and in training and development, and human resources management. This field of professional work developed early this century, both in the USA and in Europe. The first President of the British Psychological Society was the occupational psychologist C. S. Myers in 1920, the founder and first director of the National Institute of Industrial Psychology (NIIP) in 1921 in London, UK. The expansion of this field in the UK was based in the 1920s mainly on two institutions in London, the NIIP, and the industrial Health Research Board of the Medical Research Council, both founded at about the same time. These developments were paralleled in other countries.

The APA's Division 14, Industrial and Organizational Psychology, was an early Division of the Association (and the Society of Industrial and Organizational Psychology (SIOP) is a major organization in the field). In the UK the BPS has both a Division of Occupational Psychology and an Occupational Psychology Section, while in Europe the European Association of Work and Organizational Psychology (EAWOP) provides further manifestation of the institutionalization of the subfield, and internationally, Division 1 of the IAAP is the Division of Work and Organizational Psychology.

Educational (School) Psychologists

Educational psychology has also been claimed to originate with Lightmer Witmer's clinic in the 1890s, though substantively it may be said to originate with the work of early pioneers in the field of psychometrics such as Sully in the US, Binet in France, and Burt who was appointed as the first school psychologist in the UK in 1913. Early school psychology was influenced by 'particular paradigmatic approaches to learning, most notably a cognitive perspective relating success or failure on school learning tasks to the individual's level of intelligence as measured by standardized tests' (Burden, 1994, p. 303). This paradigm dominated the profession of school psychology for many decades; the survey undertaken by the United Nations Educational Scientific and Cultural Organization (UNESCO) and the International Bureau of Education (IBE) in 1948 indicated that the main function of school psychologists across the world at that time was the assessment and diagnosis of exceptional children for the purpose of classifying and treating various educationally related difficulties, often through placement in special provision (UNESCO/IBE, 1948). The survey was followed by a specially convened UNESCO conference in Hamburg (Wall, 1956) which attempted to establish concrete goals for guiding the provision of school psychological services.

A major survey carried out in the early 1990s (Oakland & Cunningham, 1992) of 54 developed and developing countries suggested that school psychologists 'appear to value the traditional roles accorded them, particularly those relating to assessment and intervention' (p. 122), and that psychometric tests provided a major tool in their work. They estimated that the 87,000 school psychologists working throughout the world represented a 100% increase in a period of just over ten years (Catterall, 1977–79), and that this increase was predicted to continue. The school psychologist respondents in this survey generally emphasized their commitment to a scientist-practitioner model in which scientific knowledge forms the basis for practice (Oakland, 1992), a commitment reiterated in the major handbook in the field: 'school psychology must first and foremost be built on the foundations of scientific psychology' (Reynolds & Gutkin, 1999).

Although assessment continues to be a central function of school psychologists, over the past twenty years there has been some dissatisfaction with traditional psychometric approaches to assessment, with the development of curriculum-related approaches (e.g., Shapiro & Elliott, 1999) and more recently dynamic assessment (Campione & Brown, 1987) in order to emphasize the context of learning and the interactive nature of pupils' learning. Simultaneously, many school psychologists have developed consultation as an approach to their work with schools (e.g., Gutkin and Curtis, 1999) and have developed approaches to working with schools as organizations based on systems theories (e.g., Apter, 1982; Burden, 1981).

As early Divisions of the APA, both Educational Psychology as Division 15 and School Psychology as Division 16 existed by 1945, while the International School Psychology Association (ISPA) is a flourishing international organization with its own journal and conferences; the Division of Educational and Child Psychology of the British Psychological Society (DECP of BPS) was formed in the 1940s, and an early Division of IAAP, the oldest international organization of psychologists is the Division of Educational, School and Instructional Psychology.

Counseling Psychologists

Counseling psychology has been a rapidly growing field of psychology in many countries over the past ten years. In Australia, the membership of the Australian Board of Counseling Psychology has grown rapidly, while in both the USA and the UK, numbers belonging to this professional subgroup have doubled during the 1990s (Pickard & Carroll, 1994; Tyler, 1972). Counseling psychology may probably be said to have originated with the work of Carl Rogers and his holistic approach to the person, which led to the development of client-centered work (e.g., Rogers, 1980). This is one of the fast-growing fields of professional psychology across all countries.

Again, APA Division 17 of Counseling Psychology existed as early as 1945, though the UK Division of Counseling Psychology was not formed until 1982.

Health Psychologists

With the growing emphasis on health and on prevention rather than therapy, the sub-specialism of health psychology has grown rapidly in the past decade. It emerged in the 1970s as a response to the changes in patterns of health and illness and awareness of the psychological aspects of major diseases and causes of death. Health psychologists are defined variously in different countries, with some countries defining health psychology as a subfield of clinical psychology, others as a separate group, and still other countries effectively replacing the term 'clinical psychology' by 'health psychology'. In all countries this is a rapidly growing field. Health psychology is the study of psychological and behavioral processes in health, illness, and health care. With the increasing awareness of the contribution of psychological factors to health, and the power of health promotion and attention to life style in mental and physical well-being, health psychologists contribute with research and intervention strategies in a range of areas. These include the following: health risk behaviors, health protective enhancing behaviors, health-related cognitions, processes influencing health care delivery, psychological aspects of illness, and stress factors (Johnston, 1994).

There are Divisions of Health Psychology in both APA and in BPS, the IAAP has a Division of Health Psychology, and the European Health Psychology Society (EHPS) and the International Health Psychology Society (IHPS) bring together health psychologists at the European and international level.

Teaching and Research Psychologists

The majority of psychologists for the first half of the twentieth century were engaged in teaching and research, and this remains a significant source of employment for psychologists who normally require a PhD to enter university teaching. In most countries teaching psychology is restricted to university level, though in both the USA and the UK there are some programs at high school level. Psychologists are engaged in research in universities, in research units funded by government, private industry or funding councils or bodies, in hospitals and clinics, and in a range of settings. A significant amount of applied psychology research has direct practical application and may be used to improve drug safety, transport safety, accident prevention, and so on. In most countries the number of universities and therefore university and college programs in psychology have increased significantly over the past twenty years, and psychology continues to be one of the most popular subjects for university study.

Other Fields

As mentioned above, professional psychology is being differentiated into further subfields, such as traffic psychology which exists as a field in a number of European countries where traffic psychologists are involved in driver diagnostics and selection, driver improvement and rehabilitation, traffic safety work, and research work on safety and evaluation of human–machine interfaces (EFPPA, 1997a; Risser, 1998). In a number of European countries, there are attempts to develop this area as a full professional field with its own post-graduate education, and its own definition of the field and those entitled to practice in this field. Indeed the Traffic Psychology Section of one European country states its explicit objectives as: safeguarding the existing areas of activity of traffic psychologists, opening up of new areas of activity, and asserting and securing the legal recognition of the profession. Other fields such as environmental psychology, sports psychology, consumer psychology, and disaster psychology are developing in the same way, becoming increasingly professionalized with a claim to a specific area of work and specific qualifications. It is not simply a matter of applying psychology in different contexts and settings, but rather the professionalization of the subfield, with the development of specialist training and specialist titles which aim to protect the field of activity.

28.3 REGULATIONS AND LAWS FOR PSYCHOLOGISTS

Certification and Licensing

With increased professionalization of psychologists' work there have been increasing pressures in all countries to develop laws and regulations which at minimum restrict the title of psychologist to those with certain qualifications, which may restrict the field of work to those holding the title, and which aim to protect the public from unqualified practitioners. Professional regulation sets out the terms and conditions by which members of the profession are recognized and may practice, and has two purposes: to identify those with the levels of education and training deemed necessary to practice, and to enforce minimum standards of behavior through a code of conduct and a disciplinary procedure. Thus in most countries there have been attempts to define a certain level of education and qualification, to use this as the basis for a license, and to make the possession of such qualification and license mandatory for practice as a professional psychologist.

The first psychology law was introduced in 1945 in the state of Connecticut in the USA. Credentialling and licensing procedures are now well developed across the USA, where licensing is arranged at the state level by the State Registration Boards; these form an alliance of state, territorial, and provincial agencies responsible for the licensure and certification of psychologists throughout the US and Canada, the Association of State and Provincial Psychology Boards (ASPPB), formerly the American Association of State Psychology. Although its original purpose was to produce the Examination for Professional Practice in Psychology (EPPP), which is used by most boards in assessing candidates for licensure and certification, it is now a world leader in the regulation of psychologists, and serves to obtain, interpret, and disseminate information on legal and regulatory matters.

In the USA, the National Register of Health Service Providers in Psychology which is a private credentialling organization, offers a national credential which determines whether psychologists have met certain educational, training, and state/provincial licensing standards and have no evidence of having violated ethical or professional conduct codes. Following a 'grandparenting' period between 1974–1978, the current criteria for listing are:

- be currently, actively licensed, certified, or registered by a state/provincial board of examiners of psychology at the independent practice level of psychology; and
- have completed a doctoral degree in psychology from a regionally accredited educational institution that meets the Guidelines for Defining a Doctoral degree in Psychology; and
- have completed two years (3,000 hours) of supervised experience in health services in psychology, of which one year (1,500 hours) is in an organized health service training program or internship and one year (1,500 hours) is at the postdoctoral level.

A similar organization exists in Canada, the Canadian Register of Health Service Providers in Psychology, with similar requirements. Between the 1960s and the 1990s, legislation was enacted to regulate the practice of psychology in each of Canada's ten provinces and in the Northwest territories.

In many countries of Africa, psychological practice has adopted the model provided by the UK (in Anglophone countries) or France (Francophone countries) with university education following a similar pattern. Most African countries do not yet have regulation for psychologists. However, the profession of psychology has been regulated for over twenty years in both Zimbabwe and South Africa. In Zimbabwe psychology has been controlled since 1971 by the Psychological Practices Act, which is administered by full-time staff of the Health Professions Council, and all psychologists are required to have an Honours degree in psychology plus post-graduate training which includes supervised practice to be registered. In South Africa, statutory recognition was granted to psychology as a profession in 1975, with two forms of registration, a voluntary Register through the South African Psychological Association (SAPA), a body formed in 1948, the other a statutory register kept by the South African Medical and Dental Council (SAMDC), now the Health Professions Council (Louw, 1990, 1997a, 1997b; Richter et al., 1998). The Council's Professional Board for Psychology is charged by statute to register those wishing to use the title 'psychologist' and to restrict specified diagnostic and therapeutic activities to registered psychologists, and therefore exercises statutory control over the profession of psychology. The qualification for registration is a Master's degree plus twelve months internship at an accredited institution, thus requiring a minimum of six years, though this is likely to change to doctoral level requirement in the future. Recent developments in that country and the formation of a new society, the Psychological Society of South Africa (PsySSA) have led to renewed negotiations concerning regulation of the profession of psychology, which could provide a model for other African countries in their aspirations to develop the profession.

The situation is different in Europe where each country works with a different system and where there is a range of regulatory and licensing practice (see for example, McPherson, 1998; Pulverich, 1995, 1998). A survey of regulations for psychologists in European countries (EFPPA, 1997b) demonstrated the wide range of legal recognition and regulation in the sample of European psychological associations, while highlighting the common direction of state regulation of this professional group. The first European state to regulate psychology was the German Democratic Republic in 1967; individual countries enacted individual regulation over the following decades, and have reached different stages in the development of statutory regulation. At the present time, there is some form of regulation of psychology either in place or proposed in every European state where there is a well-developed profession of psychology, usually clinical psychology (McPherson, 1998). However, there is no European system of regulation, nor is there likely to be so, since the orientation of the European Union is counter to pan-European regulation and in favor of the principle of subsidiarity (devolving to member

states the responsibility for regulation), and procedures to promote cross-border recognition (see below).

In the United Kingdom, the British Psychological Society is the professional body for all psychologists; in 1987 it amended its Charter to permit it to provide a Register for all those recognized as Chartered Psychologists. In the absence of a law protecting the title of 'psychologist', Chartered Psychologist status fulfils a similar role, and forms the basis of the legal status which is currently being sought in the UK. This means that the public is protected through the existence of a Register of Chartered Psychologists, albeit voluntary, which guarantees the qualifications and the disciplinary procedures under which psychologists practice in the United Kingdom. The concept of a 'chartered' profession is widely used in the United Kingdom, and refers to the role of professional bodies in defining the education and qualifications required to practice in a particular field, and the regulation of this practice through an ethical code and disciplinary procedures with which members undertake to comply. Professional self-regulation of this kind is widespread in the United Kingdom, though the late 1990s have seen pressures for greater accountability and external control in the wake of a number of well-publicized cases of malpractice.

This is not the place to discuss the relative merits of regulation by government ministry, and self-regulation through a national professional association, though there is a substantial and growing literature on this topic, and there are growing pressures within governments to question the principle of self-governing professions and the balance between economic self-interest and protection of the public.

28.4　QUALIFICATIONS AND MOBILITY

Although the qualifications of psychologists in all countries have increased over the past fifty years, with doctoral qualifications required for practice as a clinical psychologist in both the USA and the UK, and about to be required in South Africa, requirements vary across the world. An increasing proportion of new Doctorates in psychology in the USA come from Professional Schools which are set up outside universities specifically for professional training of psychologists (Peterson, 1991). At the present time, although countries such as Australia, Norway, and the UK, for example, have developed professional doctorates for clinical psychology training, these continue to be organized through universities. The USA and the UK have well-developed systems of accreditation which aim to ensure the quality and standards of postgraduate programs across the country. The variation in patterns of qualification across the world makes mobility and evaluation of equivalence of qualifications difficult (see Hall, Lunt, & Ritchie, 1999). Nevertheless increased globalization and regional directives to promote free movement of goods and services provide the impetus for the development of systems for the recognition of qualifications, and the political direction is towards greater mobility across international boundaries.

Systems for facilitating mobility across borders are well worked out in the USA and Canada. As mentioned above, the private credentialling organization in the USA, the National Register of Health Service Providers in Psychology, and similarly the Canadian Register of Health Service Providers in Canada offers a national credential that determines whether psychologists have met certain minimum standards, and therefore promotes mobility for individual psychologists across the USA, or across Canada, at least in the health field, and at least for doctoral programs. The standards have been adopted by the APA and the Association of State and Provincial Psychology Boards (ASPPB). More recently, the North American Free Trade Agreement (NAFTA) seeks to promote mobility between the USA, Canada, and Mexico, thus covering a large area of the world's psychologists. Similarly, in Canada, the Agreement on Internal Trade (AIT) aims to remove barriers to free movement among the provinces and territories of Canada; the Psychology Sectoral Work Group on AIT is attempting to implement the Agreement by achieving bilateral or multilateral agreements among already similar jurisdictions, and by producing a framework aimed to cover all jurisdictions.

In Europe, the Treaty of Rome which established the European Community in 1957 aspired to a situation of freedom to work anywhere in the European Community; this has been realized through Directive 89/48/EEC which requires European member states to provide mechanisms for the recognition of qualifications, and aims to remove barriers to movement between states. Although there was initially a hope that professional qualifications could be harmonized across Europe, experience demonstrated otherwise, and the Directive now operates on the basis of 'mutual recognition'. Thus each member state of the European Union (15) and increasingly other countries in Europe, for example those in the European Free Trade Agreement (EFTA) are required to provide systems for recognition of qualifications; in practice language provides a major barrier to mobility of psychologists across European borders. There are some moves currently to develop a common framework of qualification for psychologists across Europe, which could in the future lead to a common qualification and certification as a psychologist, though these are at a very early stage (Lunt, 1998b, 1999).

At the present time, regional groupings are developing their own systems for recognizing equivalence of qualifications; the assumption is that as large regional groupings develop their own procedures for mobility and recognition, this will lead to increased internationalization, and enhanced professional standards for all countries.

28.5 ETHICS, ETHICAL CODES, AND DISCIPLINARY PROCEDURES

With growing professionalization of psychology, national psychology associations have increasingly developed codes of ethics to govern the conduct of their members (e.g., Francis, 1999; Leach & Harbin, 1997). This is a feature of professionalization adopted by all aspiring professional groups, claiming that this places the welfare of the public before the interests of the profession itself. The development of psychology from an academic discipline to a more professional activity has led to the growth of a number of different professional subgroups as already mentioned, with an increasing range and complexity of potential ethical concerns. Sinclair (1993) reviewed articles listed in *Psychological Abstracts* from 1927 to draw a picture of the evolution of interest in ethical issues and codes of ethics. She states that 'very few articles on ethical responsibilities or ethics codes (appeared) prior to the end of World War II' (p. 175), a period when, as we have seen, professional psychology began to develop rapidly. Since that time there has been a growing concern with ethics, and a growing literature on the subject.

It is widely recognized that there are two different purposes for ethical codes: first, the regulation of inappropriate behavior through defining minimal expectations and rules of conduct; second, the promotion of high standards or optimal behavior. The first has a regulatory and discipline function, the second is aspirational.

The earliest Code of Ethics in psychology was that developed by the APA, following the creation of a new Committee on Ethical Standards for Psychology in 1948. This Committee set out criteria that the Code should meet which included the following:

- that it should be an expression of the best ethical practice in the field of psychology as judged by a large representative sample of members of the APA;
- that it should be empirically developed;
- that it should involve wide participation by APA members in its formulation.

The empirical approach taken by the APA in 1948 was unusual and different from other professions which had tended to begin with a committee of experts and the development of a set of rules. 7,500 members of the APA were asked 'to describe a situation that they know of first-hand in which a psychologist made a decision having ethical implications, and to indicate what the correspondent perceived as being the ethical issue involved' (Crawford, 1992). This exercise led to the adoption of the Ethical Standards of Psychology published in 1953 (APA, 1953); since then, a number of revisions have led to the present code (APA, 1992) which consists of the following six General Principles: (i) Competence, (ii) Integrity, (iii) Professional and Scientific Responsibility, (iv) Respect for People's Rights and Dignity, (v) Concern for others' Welfare, (vi) Social Responsibility, and eight categorical Standards: (i) General Standards, (ii) Evaluation, Assessment or Intervention, (iii) Advertising and other Public Statements, (iv) Therapy, (v) Privacy and Confidentiality, (vi) Teaching, Training, Research and Publishing, (vii) Forensic Activities, (viii) Resolving Ethical Issues.

Through the 1970s and 1980s national psychological associations developed their own codes; comparisons have indicated that they have much in common (Leach & Harbin, 1997; Lindsay, 1996; Sinclair, 1993). However, in their comparison of the psychology ethics codes of 24 countries, Leach and Harbin (1997) found that, although there were major similarities between the codes of different psychology associations, the Canadian code was most similar to that of the USA, while the Code of the Chinese Psychological Society was the most dissimilar. For example, all of the US principles were found in Australia, Canada, Israel, and South Africa, while none were found in China. These authors assumed a universalist position, 'positing that some ethical principles and standards will overlap with one another regardless of country and culture, whereas other ethical principles and standards will be unique to a particular culture' (p. 182).

Within Europe, the European Federation of Professional Psychologists' Associations (EFPPA), a federation of thirty national psychology associations (see below) decided to attempt the development of a common ethical code for the member associations of the Federation. This work culminated in the European MetaCode of Ethics (EFPPA, 1995) which was accepted by EFPPA Member Associations in 1995, and which all member associations agreed to adopt, modifying their own codes where necessary. The European MetaCode articulates the common ethical principles of respect for a person's rights and dignity, competence, responsibility, integrity, and specifies the content of national ethical codes (Lindsay, 1996), thus providing a consistent foundation of ethical guidelines at least in this region.

Although the Code of the Canadian Psychological Association (CPA) is similar to that of the USA, the CPA having used the Code of the APA for many years until their own Code was adopted in 1986 (revised in 1991), it has excited interest in the international community for nine features which appear to be unique (Sinclair, 1998). These are:

- setting objectives based on a critical analysis of the international and interdisciplinary literature on codes of ethics;
- inclusion of an overriding ethic of a social contract;
- use of an empirical methodology in developing the Code;
- organization of the Code round four ethical principles;
- differential weighting of the four ethical principles;
- inclusion of a model for ethical decision-making;
- inclusion of a role for personal conscience;
- inclusion of both minimum and idealized standards;
- presentation of the Code as an umbrella document.

However, the mere existence of codes of ethics does not necessarily guarantee good conduct; as mentioned Codes may provide 'bottom-line' rules or proscriptions for behavior or aspirational guidelines. The increasing complexities of professional practice, the growing criticism of professionals by clients and consumers, and the political distrust of professionals has led to the publication of manuals such as that by Keith-Spiegel and Koocher (1985) who suggest that ethics codes tend to be fairly blunt instruments and may create conceptual confusion in their attempt to be all things to all people (p. 2). Manuals such as this provide case examples and examples of ethical dilemmas in order to sensitize psychologists to the complexity of the issues involved in professional practice.

Countries vary in their implementation of disciplinary procedures; for some countries these are administered by a government department, others have a Professional Board, while still others administer the investigatory and disciplinary procedures within the psychological association. In South Africa, for example, registration of psychologists has been through the Medical and Dental Council (now the Health Professions Council) which has its own Professional Board, separate from the Psychological Association. On the other hand, in the UK the BPS is seeking legal registration of psychologists and aspires to retain the disciplinary function within its own society, as do some other professions in this country, and to maintain the functions which are carried out by the BPS for the voluntary Register.

28.6 INSTITUTIONALIZATION OF PSYCHOLOGY

From early beginnings of groups of psychologists (mainly academic) forming associations or societies which provided a forum to meet and to give papers and discuss scientific research, the profession of psychology has become gradually more institutionalized through this century. This institutionalization was demonstrated early on by the foundation of Chairs and departments of psychology in universities, and by the formation of societies and associations to bring together psychologists and more recently to represent their interest and their professional identity. This section will focus mainly on the growth of professional associations which emerged particularly in the 1940s and 1950s in response to the enormous increase in the numbers of professional psychologists.

National Professional Associations in Psychology

As with other professional groups, the role of national professional associations of psychologists is becoming increasingly important in the professionalization of the field. The psychology associations of most countries started with scientific or 'learned' societies formed as early as the APA (1892) (Benjafield, 1996; Evans et al., 1992) when 'a small gathering of academicians met on July 8, 1892, in the study of G. Stanley Hall and formed the American Psychological Association' at a time 'when the new, experimental psychology was still in its infancy in America' (Evans et al., 1992). The APA had a membership of 31 when it was founded in 1892; in its first fifty years 3,000 members joined, whereas in its second fifty years over 130,000 members have joined. A similar increase in the second half of this century is demonstrated in

the BPS. This was founded in the UK in 1901, and its membership has increased exponentially in recent years. Other European countries formed scientific societies of psychology early in the twentieth century, for example in Germany the Deutsche Gesellschaft für Psychologie, in Italy the Societa de Psicologia Italiana, and in France the Societè Francaise de Psychologie. Learned societies exist primarily to 'advance scientific psychological research and to further the co-operation of investigators in the different branches of psychology' (BPS objects as stated in Knight, 1954) or 'the advancement of psychology as a science' (APA objects) and do not act to set professional standards for practitioners.

In many countries the emergence of psychology as a profession led to a split or the emergence of a separate association which was intended to meet the needs of professional psychologists. Thus in the USA 'the perception was that "private practitioners" had come to dominate the APA by 1975 (and t)he Council and the APA found themselves engaged in major conflicts in the period 1970 to 1975 as the 'practitioner' segment moved their agenda regarding professional autonomy to the fore' (Evans et al., 1992, p. 241). The APS formed in 1988 in reaction to the perceived focus of the APA on the needs and interests of professional psychologists, especially clinical psychologists (Evans et al., 1992). In Australia, the Australian Psychological Society formed out of the Australian Branch of the BPS in the 1970s, and now has a comprehensive structure and service provision, uniting scientists and practitioners, with separate science and profession Directorates. In South Africa, although the first sub-department of psychology was established in the University of Stellenbosch in 1917, the first society of psychologists, the South African Psychological Association, was formed in 1948, and this country has had a number of different psychology associations in part reflecting its own political situation until the formation of the Psychological Society of South Africa in 1994, a body which aimed to bring together a number of earlier associations. In other African countries, there have been loose associations formed during the 1970s and 1980s, many using the British model, for example the Zimbabwe Psychological Association which was formed in 1971.

Different and separate organizations, more like guilds or unions, formed in many European countries in the 1940s and 1950s; these organizations developed an explicit concern to enforce professional standards by restricting membership to those with appropriate training. Thus in the 1940s and 1950s associations formed in Germany, in Norway (in 1938),

Sweden, Denmark, and Finland reflecting the growing professionalization of psychology. In countries of southern Europe, there has been a tendency to form professional 'colleges' (e.g., the 'colegio' in Spain), or 'orders' (the 'ordine' in Italy) which also demonstrate the professionalization of the field. In the UK, the BPS has remained an organization providing for both scientists and practitioner or professional psychologists, with a Scientific Board and a Professional Board to meet the specific and separate interests of these groups within one organization.

In the past fifty years, most national associations of psychologists have played an active role in seeking legislation and regulation for psychologists, frequently engaging in political and lobby activity, contributing to the drafting of legislation, and in some cases determining the level of qualifications. Many national associations now have relatively large offices, and carry out a wide range of professional and sometimes political activity.

Regional and International Associations

The recent decades have seen a growing interest in regional and international activity in psychology. The organization of this occurs both at the scientific level, and more recently at the professional level. It is worth mentioning that there are a number of different international and regional organizations representing different interests and aspects of psychology and psychologists.

There are two major 'federal' organizations, providing federations of national psychology societies/associations: IUPsyS (the International Union of Psychological Science) and EFPPA (the European Federation of Professional Psychologists Associations). The oldest international association of psychology is the International Association of Applied Psychology (IAAP) which was founded in 1920 and which is an individual membership association with 14 Divisions of different specialist interest in applied psychology; there is a growing number of international 'specialist topic' organizations, such as the International Society for the Study of Behavioral Development (ISSPD) and regional specialist topic organizations, particularly in Europe, such as the European Association of Work and Organizational Psychology (EAWOP) or the European Health Psychology Society (EHPS). There are also other regional associations such as the InterAmerican Society of Psychology (SIP) which bring together individual psychologists from the region. The majority of these organizations hold congresses and publish newsletters or journals thus contributing to the dissemination of the discipline, and providing a forum to bring together psychologists in professional gatherings.

IUPsyS

The International Union of Psychological Science is a federation of national scientific societies, which aims to represent psychology in its full breadth as a science and as a profession. It grew out of the International Congress Committee which had been responsible for organizing the International Congress of Psychology starting in Paris in 1889. After World War II, at the ICP in Edinburgh in 1948, participants decided to organize an International Union of Psychological Science, similar to other scientific unions. The IUPsyS was founded by 11 Charter members at the International Congress of Psychology in Stockholm in 1951, and now has members from 64 countries (1999) and carries out a wide range of activities to promote and develop the discipline at an international level.

The aims of the IUPsyS are:

- to develop the exchange of ideas and scientific information between psychologists of different countries, and in particular, to organize International Congresses, and other meetings, on subjects of general or special interest in psychology;
- to contribute to psychological documentation in different countries by fostering exchange of publications of all kinds, including reviews, films, and biographies;
- to aid scholars of different countries to go abroad to universities, laboratories, libraries and other institutions;
- to foster the exchange of students and of young research workers;
- to collaborate with other international and national organizations in matters of mutual interest;
- to engage in such other activities as will further the development of the science of psychology.

The Union demonstrates the increasing institutionalization and thus professionalization of psychology as a discipline through its scientific activity.

The other federal organization is EFPPA which has considerable overlap in membership with the IUPsyS within Europe, in part because of the integrated focus of several national psychology associations (see above).

EFPPA

The European Federation of Professional Psychologists' Associations (EFPPA) is a major regional federation involved in professional psychology. This is a federation of psychology associations, founded in 1981, and which now covers all the countries of Western Europe, increasing numbers of countries from former East Europe, and of course plays a growing role within the European Union. There are 30 member associations of EFPPA (1999) representing over 100,000 psychologists across Europe. The member associations of EFPPA are various in nature and focus; as mentioned above, in some countries there are separate organizations for the science and the practice or 'profession' of psychology, while in others these different groups belong to the same organization.

The aims of EFPPA are:

- to promote communication and cooperation between member associations in Europe, and to contribute to their development;
- to further the establishment of ethical codes of practice for psychologists, and to promote the application of psychology as a means of improving the well-being of those to whom psychologists offer services;
- to promote the furtherance of psychology and its application, with particular reference to professional training and the professional status of psychologists;
- to support the interests of psychology and its application in relation to any European or international organizations concerned with specifying requirements for the professional practice of psychology;
- to support member associations in promoting the interests of psychology within their own countries;
- to facilitate contacts with international bodies of psychology;
- to promote the development of professional psychology in all its different areas and subject matters and, as appropriate, to assist in the coordination of this activity.

The development of EFPPA and its evolving activities and focus reflect the growing professionalisation of psychology in Europe, particularly though not only on the professional practitioner aspect, and EFPPA itself represents both the profession and the science of psychology (EFPPA Statutes article 3), (see EFPPA, 1999).

SIP

Another major regional grouping is the Inter-American Society of Psychology/Sociedad Interamericana de Psicologia (SIP), founded almost fifty years ago, which brings together psychologists in North, Central, and South America, and which holds conferences every two years. However, unlike EFPPA, SIP does not have a political professional focus, since it provides a forum for individual psychologists to meet rather than for national psychology associations to cooperate. The implementation of the NAFTA agreement mentioned above may give this regional organization a sharper focus and a greater involvement in professional activities of this kind.

With greater professionalization and globalization there are other regional groups of psychologists, for example in the Asia-Pacific region. These institutional trends highlight the need for a balance between national, regional, and international concerns and activities.

28.7 CONCLUSIONS

The past fifty years have seen the establishment of psychology as a profession, and its development to full professional status, and an enormous growth in the numbers of psychologists working in professional contexts across the world. This period has also seen the growth of professional organizations both at a national level, and more recently at a regional and international level. In the majority of countries there are provisions or proposals for the regulation of professional psychologists usually through governmental ministries, particularly in the health field. Protection and regulation of the title is more common than regulation of the field of activities, a trend in line with current political and consumer pressures to promote competition and to increase the rights of consumers to choose providers. Regulation of the profession has been accompanied by the development of codes of ethics, and guidelines and manuals which promote the development of ethical practice and are used in the discipline and education of psychologists in this field. While the status of psychologists has been enhanced through an increase in the length of their education and training, and the demands required prior to recognition as competent to practice, a growing specialization within the field leads to demands for further specialist training, and in some cases further specialist titles, usually given at the present time by national professional associations such as those in Germany (BDP), the Netherlands (NIP), Norway (NPF), and the UK (BPS), all of whom grant specialist titles following recognized post-graduate education.

These trends seem likely to continue. What is also likely to increase in the next century is the internationalization of professional psychology with growing opportunities for movement between countries, and cooperation across national borders. It is also likely that psychologists will expand their activity into further fields of practice, partly as a result of new scientific knowledge, partly as a result of the political professional process of job expansion.

LITERATURE CITED

American Psychological Association. (1953). *Ethical Standards for Psychologists.* Washington, DC: American Psychological Association.

American Psychological Association. (1992). Ethical principles for psychologists and code of conduct. *American Psychologist, 47,* 1597–1611.

Apter, S. J. (1982). *Troubled children, troubled systems.* Oxford: Pergamon Press.

Benjafield, J. G. (1996). *A history of psychology.* Needham Heights, MA: Allyn & Bacon.

British Psychological Society. (1995). *Professional psychology handbook.* Leicester: British Psychological Society.

Burden, R. L. (1981). Systems theory and its relevance to schools. In B. Gillham (Ed.), *Problem behavior in the secondary school: A systems approach.* London: Croom Helm.

Burden, R. L. (1994). Educational psychology trends. *School Psychology International, 15*(4), 293–347.

Campione, J. C., & Brown, A. L. (1987). Linking dynamic assessment with school achievement. In C. Lidz (Ed.), *Dynamic assessment. An interactional approach to evaluating learning potential.* New York: Guilford Press.

Catterall, C. S. (Ed.). (1977–79). *Psychology in the schools in international perspective.* Columbus, OH: International School Psychology Steering Committee.

Crawford, M. (1992). Rapid growth and change at the American Psychological Association: 1945 to 1970. In R. Evans, V. Staudt Sexton, & T. Cadwallader (Eds.), 100 Years. *The American Psychological Association: A historical perspective.* Washington, DC: American Psychological Association.

Cumming, G., Siddle, D., & Hyslop, W. (1997). Psychological science in Australia. *International Journal of Psychology, 32*(6), 409–424.

Dawes, R. M. (1994). *House of cards. Psychology and psychotherapy built on myth.* New York: Free Press.

EFPPA. (1990). *Optimal standards for the professional training in psychology.* Brussels: EFPPA.

EFPPA. (1995). *European metacode of ethics.* Brussels: EFPPA.

EFPPA. (1997a). *Final report of the task force on traffic psychology.* Brussels: EFPPA.

EFPPA. (1997b). *Inventory of regulations in the field of psychology in European countries.* Bonn: Deutscher Psychologen Verlag GmbH.

EFPPA. (1999). *About EFPPA. Booklet 1.* Brussels: EFPPA.

Evans, R., Staudt Sexton, V., & Cadwallader, T. (1992). *100 Years. The American Psychological Association: A historical perspective.* Washington, DC: American Psychological Association.

Francis, R. (1999). *Ethics for psychologists: A handbook.* Leicester: British Psychological Society.

Freidson, E. (1994). *Professionalism reborn: Theory, prophecy and policy.* London: Polity Press.

Gutkin, T. B., & Curtis, M. J. (1999). School-based consultation theory and practice: the art and science of indirect service delivery. In C. R. Reynolds & T. B. Gutkin, *The handbook of school psychology* (3rd ed.). New York: Wiley.

Hall, J., Lunt, I., & Ritchie, P. (1999). Cross-border mobility and credentialling of psychologists. Paper presented to VI European Congress of Psychology, Rome, July 1999.

Johnston, M. (1994). Current trends in health psychology. *The Psychologist, 7,* 114–118.

Keith-Spiegel, P., & Koocher, G. (1985). *Ethics in Psychology. Professional standards and cases.* Hillsdale, NJ: Lawrence Erlbaum Associates.

Kim, U. (1995). Psychology science and culture: Cross-cultural analysis of national psychologies. *International Journal of Psychology, 30*(6), 663–679.

Knight, R. (1954). The British Psychological Society: Problems and prospects. *Bulletin of the BPS, 24,* 1–8.

Leach, M., & Harbin, J. (1997). Psychological ethics codes: A comparison of twenty-four countries. *International Journal of Psychology, 32*(3), 181–192.

Leung, K., & Zhang, J. (1995). Systemic considerations: Factors facilitating and impeding the development of psychology in developing countries. *International Journal of Psychology, 30*(6), 693–706.

Lindsay, G. (1995). Statutory registration of psychologists: A Parliamentary Bill. *The Psychologist, 8*(8), 353–355.

Lindsay, G. (1996). Psychology as an ethical discipline and profession. *European Psychologist, 1*(2), 79–88.

Louw, J. (1990). *Professionalizing psychology.* Pretoria: Human Sciences Research Council.

Louw, J. (1997a). Regulating professional conduct Part I: Codes of ethics of national psychology associations in South Africa South African Journal of Psychology 27,3,183–188.

Louw, J. (1997b). Regulating professional conduct Part II: The Professional Board for Psychology in South Africa. *South African Journal of Psychology, 27*(3), 189–195.

Lunt, I. (1997). Education and training for psychologists in Europe: Optimal or minimal standards. *News from EFPPA, 11*(3), 6–10.

Lunt, I. (1998a). History and emerging trends in education and training for clinical psychology in the European Union. In A. S. Bullock & M. Hersen

(Eds.), *Comprehensive clinical psychology*. Oxford: Persimmon Press.

Lunt, I. (1998b). Education and qualifications for psychologists in Europe and implications for mobility across member states. Paper presented at the International Congress of Applied Psychology, San Francisco, July 1998.

Lunt, I. (1999). Mobility in Europe: A challenge and an opportunity. Paper presented at VIth European Congress of Psychology, Rome, July 1999.

Martin, P. R. (1989). 'Specialist' clinical psychologists: Upgrading training in clinical psychology. *The Australian Psychologist*, 24(1), 3–11.

McPherson, F. (1998). Thirty years of regulating clinical psychology in Europe. *Clinical Psychology Forum*, 113, 13–15.

Millerson, G. (1964). *The qualifying associations: A study in professionalization*. London: Routledge and Kegan Paul.

Newstead, S., & Makkinen, S. (1997). Psychology teaching in Europe. *European Psychologist*, 2(1), 3–10.

Oakland, T. D. (1992). Priorities for international school psychology. *School Psychology International*, 13(2), 171–177.

Oakland, T. D., & Cunningham, J. L. (1992). A survey of school psychology in developed and developing countries. *School Psychology International*, 13(2), 99–130.

Peterson, D. R. (1991). Connection and disconnection of research and practice in the education of professional psychologists. *American Psychologist*, 46(4), 422–429.

Pickard, E., & Carroll, M. (1994). Counseling psychology. In P. Spurgeon, R. Davies, & T. Chapman (Eds.), *Elements of applied psychology*. Chur, Switzerland: Harwood Academic Publishers.

Pilgrim, D., & Treacher, A. (1992). *Clinical psychology observed*. London: Routledge.

Pulverich, G. (1995). The Council Directive on a general system of professional education and training of at least three years' duration (89/48/EEC): Meanings and effects for psychologists in Europe. Symposium on regulation and education for psychologists at the 23rd International Congress of Applied Psychology, Madrid, July 1994. *News from EFPPA*, 9(1).

Pulverich, G. (1998). Basic legal conditions for psychologists in European countries. *European Psychologist*, 3(2), 164–166.

Raimy, V. C. (Ed.). (1950). *Training in clinical psychology*. New York: Prentice-Hall.

Reynolds, C. R., & Gutkin, T. B. (1999). *The handbook of school psychology* (3rd edn.). New York: Wiley.

Richter, L., Griesel, R., Durrheim, K., Wilson, M., Surendorff, N., & Asafo-Agyei, L. (1998). Employment opportunities for psychology graduates in South Africa: A contemporary analysis. *South African Journal of Psychology*, 28(1), 1–7.

Risser, R. (1998). EFPPA Task Force on Traffic Psychology in Europe. *European Psychologist*, 3(2), 170–174.

Rogers, C. (1980). *A way of being*. Boston: Houghton Mifflin.

Rosenzweig, M. (Ed.). (1992). *International psychological science. Progress, problems, and prospects*. Washington, DC: American Psychological Association.

Routh, D. K. (1994). *Clinical psychology since 1917. Science, practice, and organization*. New York: Plenum Press.

Schönpflug, W. (1993). Applied psychology: Newcomer with a long tradition. *Applied Psychology: An International Review*, 42(1), 5–30.

Shapiro, E. S., & Elliott, S. N. (1999). Curriculum-based assessment and other performance-based assessment strategies. In C. R. Reynolds & T. B. Gutkin, *The handbook of school psychology* (3rd ed.). New York: Wiley.

Shimmin, S., & Wallis, D. (1994). *Fifty years of occupational psychology in Britain*. Leicester: British Psychological Society Books.

Sinclair, C. (1993). Codes of ethics and standards of practice. In K. Dobson & D. Dobson (Eds.), *Professional psychology in Canada*. Göttingen: Hogrefe and Huber.

Sinclair, C. (1998). Nine unique features of the Canadian code of ethics for psychologists. *Canadian Psychology*, 39(3), 167–176.

Tyler, K. (1972). Reflections on counseling psychology. *The Counseling Psychologist*, 3(4), 6–11.

UNESCO/IBE. (1948). *School psychologists*. Publication no. 105. Paris: UNESCO/IBE.

Wall, W. D. (1956). *Psychological services for schools*. New York: University Press for UNESCO.

Wand, B. (1993). The nature of regulation and entrance criteria. In K. Dobson & D. Dobson (Eds.), *Professional psychology in Canada*. Göttingen: Hogrefe and Huber.

Wilpert, B., & Lunt, I. (1998). World study of applied psychology. Unpublished report to International Association of Applied Psychology.

Yerkes, R. M. (1918). Psychology in relation to war. *Psychological Review*, 25, 85–115.

Communications concerning this chapter should be addressed to: Dr Ingrid Lunt, Institute of Education, 25 Woburn Square, London WC1H 0AA, UK

Part E
PSYCHOLOGY IN TRANS-DISCIPLINARY CONTEXTS

29

Theoretical Psychology

HENDERIKUS J. STAM

29.1 THEORY AND FOUNDATIONS OF MODERN PSYCHOLOGY

The place of theory in modern psychology is both obvious and problematic. It is obvious because scientific psychology seems clearly premised upon if not preoccupied with formulating and testing theory. As Pawlik and Rosenzweig note in the first chapter, theories are constructed to give an explanation of phenomena and hence are to be preferred to mere hunches, hypotheses, or other approximations to explanations. In addition, the natural sciences proceed on a model of explicit theory development, even if such theories are often in the form of mathematical and formalized statements. Contemporary psychology features a wide variety of uses

of the term 'theory,' not all of which are equally aligned with conceptions of scientific explanation. This chapter will attempt to clarify both the necessity of theory and its multiple uses. Just as Sigmund Koch noted in the 1970s that psychology is not so much a single discipline as a set of 'psychological studies' (Koch, 1976), so is theory in psychology no longer a single enterprise. In order to understand this state of affairs it is necessary to examine some key definitions and assumptions that play a crucial role in theory development as well as the recent history of the development of theory in the philosophy of science. In addition, theory development in psychology is intimately related to the manner in which methods have been developed, accepted, and propagated in the discipline. At several points then the discussion will consider the impact of method on theory.

The Problematic Nature of Theory

Three influential views of theory that have been prevalent in the twentieth century hold theories to be (a) reducible to observables, (b) used as instruments to do things in the world, or (c) statements about things that really exist. Reductionism, instrumentalism, and realism, as the most prominent theories about theories in science had considerable influence on philosophers' attempts to explain how it is that scientists generate theories that are true or useful or predictive of the world. Modeling themselves on the ideal scientist, these accounts still generate some discussion among philosophers of science, not so much because they are still upheld as true instances of how science works but for the lessons they teach about how not to do philosophy of science (Stam, 1996).

The 'received view' of the philosophy of science held that observation generates empirical facts that are explained at a higher level by empirical generalizations that are in turn explained by theories which contain unobservables (Salmon, 1989). This approach created problems for the logical empiricists. The philosophers Carnap and Hempel made various stabs at arguing for the necessity of theory through the notion of 'inductive systematization', and by arguing that scientific language contains both observational and theoretical vocabularies (Salmon, 1989).

The received view has been largely abandoned as a result of the arguments that scientific theories are underdetermined by the data, as exemplified by the physicist Duhem and the philosopher Quine (the Duhem–Quine thesis; see Quine, 1953), or alternatively, as a result of the work of philosophers such as Kuhn, Hanson, and others who have argued that observations are theory-laden and historically constituted. The first issue consists of the problem that theories can be maintained in the face of (almost) any evidence so long as adjustments are made elsewhere in the system. This follows from the argument that any given theory is embedded in a web of collateral assumptions and hence conclusive refutation is not possible. The thesis that observations are theory-laden has two parts, one that observations, in order to count as observations, require auxillary assumptions such as measurement theories and suppositions about the nature of observation (Suppe, 1974). This amounts to saying again that theories are underdetermined by data (Knorr-Cetina & Mulkay, 1983). However, theory-ladenness

also refers to the claim that what 'counts as relevant and proper evidence is partly determined by the "theory or family of theories" which the evidence is supposed to test' (p. 4). One implication drawn from this is that 'observations cannot serve as independent arbiters in questions of theory choice if their relevance, their descriptive identification and their proper measurement depend on the theories involved' (1983, p. 4; for a further discussion see Stam, 1996).

The Inheritance from the Received View in Psychology

Theory is far too frequently understood in psychology by reference to a version of positivism (loosely modeled on the philosophical version of logical positivism) that came to dominate the field in mid-century. According to the philosophical version of logical positivism, a theory is really no more than an axiomatized collection of sentences that has a specified relationship to a set of observables. This view was never explicitly accepted in psychology insofar as there was not a determined or formal attempt to introduce this model as the way of doing science. Instead, the nineteenth-century positivism of Ernst Mach was gradually modified and introduced into psychological research through behaviorism with an explicit emphasis on observation as the key element of scientific research (Danziger, 1990; Mills, 1998; O'Neil, 1995). Observations gradually became strictly separated from theory, especially in the work of behaviorists such as Hull who adopted a 'deductive-nomonological' framework. Theories in this context came to mean statements that had a specific relationship to the events to be explained, a deductive-nomonological relationship. In the ideal case the theory was a universal law that could act as a 'covering law' that explains the events under consideration. Theory and observation were then to be related in strictly logical terms (see Bem & Looren de Jong, 1997, for an introduction).

Although this model was often taken to be the ideal, in fact very little psychological research after Hull matched its prescriptions. Instead, the development of inferential statistics and the demise of behaviorism as an all-encompassing theory for psychology led to a much more liberal approach in understanding theoretical claims. Although the emphases on observation and quantification persisted and were strengthened by post-World War II generations of psychologists, inferential statistics encouraged the wider use of theoretical models or 'hypotheses' in psychology and discouraged formal theorization. The advent of cognitivism in the 1960s and 1970s re-introduced theory and soon formalized functional analyses, analyses that came to rely on and required the kind of statistical averaging used in tests of statistical inference.

Statistical Inference and Theory

In order to understand the development of statistical inference and its impact on psychological theory we need to understand the gradual importance of the use of aggregate scores as descriptors of psychological properties. As Danziger (1990) has argued this did not come without a price. One deleterious consequence of the widespread adoption of statistical inference techniques in psychology was their restriction of theoretical developments in the discipline (Gigerenzer, 1993; Stam & Pasay, 1998). In response to the demand for applied knowledge, research groups were constituted whose purpose was to serve as vehicles for comparing groups with each other. For example, research in intelligence demanded some conception of normative levels for the development of intelligence tests. Individual scores came to be reported in the aggregate and deviations were construed as 'error'. Aggregate scores however make it difficult to develop concepts about intra-individual processes and these were the most important to the development of the discipline. Danziger (1990) gives an account of how the introduction of inferential statistics solved this problem for psychologists, namely, it allowed the identification of psychological properties with the hypothetical distributions of statistical analysis. In other words, individual scores no longer mattered but rather the distribution of scores came to represent the theoretical processes at hand. For example, such processes as memory could be captured not by studying individual acts of remembering but by comparing how different groups ('experimental conditions') of individuals performed on some restricted task such as learning a list of nonsense syllables. The resulting functional and abstract theoretical notion was one that no longer referred to any single participant in the experiment but instead to some abstract property of 'memory'.

One major consequence of the implicit adoption of a positivist notion of theory as an explanatory device, requiring confirmation through observation combined with the use of statistical inference, was that theory remained a largely simplified affair. However sophisticated one's psychological notions, the indiscriminate use of tests of statistical inference led to a mechanical

and routine use of the technique that by its very nature forecloses rather than advances theory (Gigerenzer, 1993). Psychological theory remains constrained because the techniques of adjudication between theories require simple or simplified models and hypotheses.

New Developments in Psychological Theory

Although I will describe these two movements in more detail below, it is important to note here the two broad developments in psychological theorizing that characterize modern psychology. The major development in psychological theory that changed the center of the discipline was the advent of cognitive psychology. With the adoption of cognitive and representational problems in psychology, the possibility of functional analyses made available a wider variety of tools within which theory could develop. In particular, the notion that internal functions were not unlike cybernetic feedback systems allowed the development of complicated internal representations a place in theory and research. In addition it, along with computer modeling, allowed for the wider development of theoretical models that were often partial simulations of theoretical concepts. These in themselves were not tied to entire theoretical research programs as had been the case within behaviorism (although even here this was not always clear; see Mills, 1998). The subsequent liberalization of theory was partly influenced by nascent disciplines such as linguistics, where Chomsky's theory of transformational-generative grammar had a major impact, and philosophy generally where renewed interest in the problems of mind and cognition proved a major component of cognitive science.

The second major development in psychological theorizing (to be discussed below) came from the distinct dissatisfaction in human psychology with the legacy of behaviorism. Historically such dissatisfactions were already present in the discipline but under the influence of humanistic psychologies, critical theory, and post-positivistic approaches in the social sciences, theory came to be seen as a vehicle for re-describing the very subject matter of psychology, subjectivity. In this development theory was not a kind of scientific tool which required a rigorous testing protocol but rather theory was itself a form of doing psychology. Empirical programs loosely associated with this form of psychology have developed under the rubric of qualitative approaches but in the first instance this movement means to do nothing more than refashion psychology in the name of a meaning focused, socially relevant, and descriptive enterprise.

29.2 PHILOSOPHY OF SCIENCE IN PSYCHOLOGY

A number of crucial concepts play a role in the current understanding of the philosophy of science as applied to psychological theory. Although they are not self-consciously applied in psychological research they are often invoked as a way of accounting for current views of psychological science. In addition they have recast the manner in which theory is understood in the philosophy of psychology. The most important of these issues can best be captured by discussing reductionism and determinism. These two categories automatically raise a number of other issues for psychologists such as the nature of the mental, the intentional and so on, issues I do not have the space to discuss further here (see recommended readings below).

Reductionism is the activity of taking statements of one sort, that is, statements characterizing a phenomenon or practice in a certain language, and transposing or translating these to statements of another sort where the latter are taken to be characteristic of a simpler, clearer or perhaps more accurate or more widely recognized or recognizable language. Thus, when we reduce statements of the sort 'there is a relationship between the unbalanced force applied to an object and resultant acceleration of that object' to:

$$F = M \times A,$$

then we have a precise mathematical relation that we recognize as Newton's second law of motion, force equals mass times acceleration. The latter expression is much to be preferred to the former in the practice of physics for obvious reasons of clarity and predictability.

Yet there are difficulties with this simple definition of reductionism and these have to do with what precisely the reduction means. In effect, is the translation a redescription, that is, an analytical reduction or is it a physical reduction, a model of actual processes? (See Robinson, 1985, for a discussion.) For example, let us take Rotter's (1954) Social Learning Theory formulation of

$$BPx, S1, Ra = f(Ex, Ra, S1 \& RVa, S1).$$

In words this formulation indicates that the potential for behavior x to occur in situation 1 in relation to reinforcement a is a function of the expectancy of the occurrence of reinforcement a following behavior x in situation 1 and the value of reinforcement a in situation 1. Although this formula might serve as a shorthand way of capturing Rotter's theory it also misleads since none of the components of this formula are exact mathematical expressions with precise empirical referents. On the other hand, this formulation is theoretic. It expresses something of interest to the psychologist but only within the context of social learning theory. In this sense it serves a heuristic function and cannot be seen as constituting a physical reduction. It does not model some process in nature in a mathematical way nor does it even serve the same analytic reduction that psychophysical equations might serve. In this sense, we can take Fechner's psychophysical law to be different again for it does serve an analytic purpose. Fechner's law (in its logarithmic form) is given as

$$R = k \log S$$

By showing that the magnitude of a sensation is a linear function of the intensity of a stimulus the researcher is able to pursue precise relationships, as has in fact been done for over 100 years. Certain predictions from the psychophysical law allow the researcher to pursue further questions, refine the relationships for different sensory domains, determine their limits, and so on (Robinson, 1985). Despite this the psychophysical law has no direct physical relationship to the sensory organs.

Psychology and Reductionism

A useful statement on reductionism within psychology is Margolis's (1984). I take his principle claim to be that 'all systematic efforts to describe, identify, and explain the phenomena of sentience and intelligence and the nature of the organisms and systems that exhibit sentience and intelligence are focused on two issues: (1) whether such phenomena and such entities are purely physical in nature; (2) whether in the context of scientific explanation, it is possible to account for such phenomena in terms adequate for explanation in the fundamental physical sciences' (p. 8). The utility of this definition is that it differentiates between ontological reductionism, or the affirmative response to (1) above and methodological reductionism, or the affirmative response to (2) above. It is in principle possible to be ontologically reductionist without being methodologically so, as in the case where one might argue that the obstacles to (2) are too great to be overcome. On the other hand it is also possible to argue that psychology ought to strive to achieve methodological reductionism while leaving the ontological question unresolved (or seeing it as unresolvable). The classic materialist-reductivist position is one that answers in the affirmative to both (1) and (2). As should be clear, however, it is not the case that the classic materialist-reductivist position is the only position that psychologists can take on this question.

The question of reductionism has always been a difficult one in psychology because it is intimately connected with the question of dualism. Cartesian dualism is typically taken to be the position that there are two distinct substances required to account for psychological phenomena, those of a bodily or physical nature and those of a non-material nature. All major versions of psychology have had some strategy to avoid this position since it is distinctly disadvantageous to parsimonious and scientific theorizing. The problem has frequently been that in order to avoid Cartesian dualism, psychologists have seen a form of radical reductionism as their only solution. Even the parallelism of early psychologists such as Titchener was taken as wholly unsatisfactory. In taking on board a material-reductivist position, psychologists have often found themselves being unable to give a reasonable account of what the lay-person takes for granted, namely the givenness of experience.

Post-positivist philosophers of psychology as well as cognitive scientists have gradually come to reject the either/or proposition inherent in the dualism versus reductionism debate. Instead, what some have proposed is that psychology ought to proceed under the assumptions of a nonreductive materialism, that is, a materialism that concedes that certain properties that are 'not reducible to physical properties – for instance, informational properties, functional properties, linguistic properties, cultural properties, as well as narrowly mental properties' are nonetheless real properties (Margolis, 1984, p. 10). In addition, argues Margolis, this allows us to distinguish between ontic dualism and attribute dualism where the former is Cartesian dualism or a dualism of substances and hence a position to be avoided and the latter is a 'dualism (or pluralism) of properties or attributes signifying only that entities of some internal complexity, though perhaps composed entirely of matter, are capable of exhibiting qualities, properties, and relations that cannot in principle, be characterized in purely physical, or material, terms' (1984, p. 10). In this manner one can be a materialist without requiring that all properties and phenomena of interest be reducible to or explained only in strictly material terms even though, in principle, all such phenomena are composed of matter. (This too is an entirely open question of course since whatever the

sciences say matter is must itself be open to continual revision.)

The claim of attribute dualism is driven by pragmatic interests since, for most of the social sciences, we seek explanations at a level far beyond that of the strictly material. Historically, worries about dualism have driven psychologists to sometimes absurd positions. The more radical versions of behaviorism as well as more recent claims for eliminativist materialism have, in their attempt to remove all speculation of mental content, foreclosed discussion of the most interesting of psychological questions and topics. Hence the escape to functionalism in most psychological research. I will take up this topic below but before I do there is a second major issue in the philosophy of science that has traditionally had a bearing on psychological research.

Psychology and Determinism

Psychological explanations come in many varieties and the concept of cause plays a loose role in these explanations. For example, let us take what, on the surface appears to be a simple action, Mary abruptly ends her conversation with John. An account of this action based on Hullian habit formation will be based on terms, principles, and assumptions radically different from an account based on cognitive information-processing terms or a parallel distributed processing model. Each of these will again be radically different from an account that finds its inspiration in the five-factor model of personality or one of its variants currently in vogue (e.g., McCrae, 1992). We might also say that the incident just precedes an epileptic seizure which would bring us into another explanatory realm entirely, just as different from the preceding if we were to say that Mary has just broken a long relationship with John. We could also invoke theories of cognition, motivation, or other, related explanatory constructs (see Robinson, 1985; Stam, 1990). To understand the conflicting nature of these accounts requires a brief foray into the problems of causation and determinism.

One of the problems for the social scientist is not just that the 'theories' above are different but that the very basis of these accounts presume different kinds of mechanisms that determine the nature of the explanation. In most standard accounts of the philosophy of science, the following definition of scientific determinism typically holds, namely that it 'requires (1) a complete description of the present state of the system, and (2) knowledge of the laws governing it, which together enable prediction of a future state of the system to be made' (Valentine, 1992, p. 16). Such a definition makes clear that determinism aims to describe fully some aspect of the universe under consideration such that reasonably certain predictions of its future can be made. Nevertheless, this does not yet settle the notion of what constitutes a 'causal explanation', a problem frequently paired with determinism. Suffice it to say at this juncture that the notion of a cause remains contested (e.g., Salmon, 1989) although more about its relevance below.

The problem for psychology is to ascertain whether strict determinism holds for properties, dispositions, and capacities that may not be capable of description solely in physical terms, are not strictly or always observable, are linked with central states, and yet still play a role in the explanation of human action (cf., Margolis, 1984, p. 42). The distinction between hard and soft determinism has been rescued from incoherence recently by Dan Robinson (1985) although in practice the distinction has long been in play. This is because the so-called hard determinist position requires that conditions exist such that, at the level of human behavior, nothing else could happen. Such a position requires the rejection of any kind of voluntarism or the possibility that human agency is useful for understanding individual actions, or as Robinson has it, hard determinism 'denies the authenticity of human action sequences' (1985, p. 43). He defends in turn a version of the incorrigibility thesis which states simply that in explaining any action such as Mary's conclusion of her conversation with John, above, the actors' first-person reports of their sensations are incorrigible, that is, they cannot be shown to be wrong on independent grounds. The authenticity of the first-person reports then is established by grounding it in the actor's own statements, feelings, desires, intentions, and so on. This does not postpone the inevitable questions of a determinist psychology so much as it makes it impossible to deny that questions of intending agents cannot be wished away by reference to physical or biological laws if one is to understand human persons. Primarily this is because all such references to law-like features of human activity miss the point that understanding is impossible (and cannot be replaced by explanation) precisely because persons assign moral characteristics to their own actions, that is, their own actions are always cast as an intended set of events. Even if persons are (sometimes) shown to be wrong about their own activities, it remains the case that actions which

rely on the causal laws of nature are not reducible to these laws.

29.3 'SYSTEMS' IN THE HISTORY OF TWENTIETH-CENTURY PSYCHOLOGY

Until recently theories of psychology in the twentieth century were readily captured by the concept of 'systems', a reference to groups of theories that vied with each other for dominance in psychology (e.g., behaviorism, functionalism, etc.). The psychological systems, however, started their long decline after World War II and by the 1980s had disappeared from practical usage except for their citation in various 'history and systems' textbooks. This was certainly not because the major questions raised by those systems had been solved or that the systems could in some way be reconciled. Instead, it appeared as if it was precisely because those systems could not be reconciled and its problems remained unresolved that they were eventually abandoned for simpler, reduced models and theories governing not all of human psychology but theories that proscribed limited domains of the discipline. By then the grand systems of the pre-war era were indeed fodder for historical texts. Thus, while Heidbreder (1933) could write confidently over sixty years ago about 'seven psychologies', those distinctions began to break down rapidly with the continuing dominance of behaviorism. Hence so-called 'systems' such as Gestalt psychology, functionalism, and structuralism gradually disappeared as separate entities and their most compelling insights or their most useful discoveries were integrated into a methodologically homogenous discipline that was at least nominally behavioral.

This transformation of twentieth-century psychology to what I have called a methodologically homogenous discipline was marked by a number of important developments. Perhaps the most important of these was the end of the hegemony of what Koch always referred to (in a phrase he coined) as the Age of Theory which lasted from 1930 to 1945. In his own words, the Age of Theory was (Koch, 1985, p. 931) a time in which psychology

. . . had achieved a remarkable constriction of substantive interests. The vast majority of theoretico-experimental psychologists concentrated research attention on elementary 'laws' of learning and, to some extent, motivation, in the belief that all significant phenomena associated with other traditionally distinguished problems and processes could ultimately be treated as 'secondary derivations' from S-R learning principles.

This constriction of interests meant that the age of theory was primarily the age of theories of learning, and not theories of many of the other substantive processes and problems that could have constituted a basis for psychology and that would gradually come to the fore in the last forty years of the twentieth century. This is not to say that there were no activities in such areas as cognition, personality and social psychology, physiology, and sensation-perception but rather that developments here were typically secondary to that of the learning theorists.

The End of Behaviorism and the Beginning of Pluralism

A consequence of the hegemony of neo-behaviorism was the end of schools and systems of psychology within academic, experimental North American psychology. When this version of psychology became an export-product, especially in post World War II Europe, it was sold as a single enterprise with a unified theory and a scientific methodology. It should be noted however that theoretical versions of behaviorism never found a strong audience in European countries, even those countries in northern Europe where psychology as a whole did take root. And despite the fact that it was being promoted as a unitary scientific enterprise to the rest of the world, North American social and intellectual developments of the 1950s ensured that the single-science ideology of psychology was gradually modified. These were the outcome of the sudden development and popularity of clinical psychology after the war and the increased demand for more relevance elsewhere. Cognitive science ensured a solid footing for cognitive psychology and the neurosciences ensured the relevance of what are now studies of brain–behavior relationships. Currently there are almost a million psychologists in the world and the majority of these function in applied settings (see Pawlik & Rosenzweig, Chapter 1). What has remained is a theoretically de-centered discipline that nevertheless is still methodologically uniform, despite the rising pressure from what is broadly (but somewhat misleadingly) labeled as qualitative psychology.

In order to explore further the major theoretical developments of twentieth-century psychology, the following sections will more closely examine behaviorism and cognitivism. These two general approaches (rather than theories in and of themselves) have influenced a number of

trends in psychology and continue to determine the nature of the discipline in surprising ways.

29.4 Varieties of Behaviorism: The Search for Foundations

With characteristic confidence, J. R. Kantor proclaimed in 1968 that 'by behaviorism we understand the study of the behavior of some confrontable thing or process; thus the term "behaviorism" is equivalent to the term "science" ' (Kantor, 1968, p. 152). Although a pitch for Kantor's version of behaviorism it was also a sign of the continuing and still unresolved issue of the labels that characterized behaviorism both during its dominance in psychology and in the remainder of the twentieth century. Neobehaviorism, radical behaviorism, logical behaviorism, and methodological behaviorism were terms that were frequently applied to different programs. These terms emphasized either methodological constraints placed on psychology, the irrelevance of mental terms, the reducability of mental terms, and so on. I will purposely restrict myself to discussing some of the fundamental tenets of the theories of Watson, Hull, and Skinner. In this manner I will have occasion to cover the major (but certainly not all) theoretical solutions to the question of the nature of psychological properties that behaviorism offered psychology. For a more detailed historical description of all of the various positions in behaviorism see the series of books edited by Wozniak (1993a, 1993b, 1994). For a more detailed contextual analysis of behaviorism see Mills (1998).

Historical Considerations

The history of behaviorism is only now beginning to find interested authors and to date most of these have consisted of former participants turned chroniclers. And as any political historian will confirm, the witness is not necessarily the best analyst. A thorough historical analysis is, in part, still unavailable because, as Mills (1998) has argued, elements of behaviorism are still very much with the discipline of psychology. Methodologically, the historical development of research methods coincided with the hegemony of behaviorism and learning theory. Their research strategies proved instructive for other areas of psychology that would develop research based on the use of experimental designs that grouped individuals and collected aggregate measures. Furthermore, despite its self-proclaimed overthrow of behaviorism in the 1970s, cognitive psychology turned to functional analyses that often reflected a characterization of psychological phenomena that were different only in name from behaviorist descriptions. Hence elements of behaviorism are still very much part of what makes up the mainstream of psychology. This is sometimes characterized as 'methodological behaviorism' or the notion orginally proposed by Skinner that whatever mental ('private') events there may be, they can be accounted for solely by reference to public, observable behaviors.

The historical considerations must be tempered here by geographical ones. European psychology was more eclectic and indeed, until the 1950s there were alternative traditions, including phenomenological ones, that continued to exist in various psychology departments. Hence the historical portrait that follows is largely focused on North America.

The questions of a comparative psychology – of the differences and similarities between humans and other animals – are also invoked in any history of behaviorism. But comparative work rapidly became a form of research that isolated and restricted the animal so that it could be used to answer behavior-theoretic questions. Thorndike inaugurated a new set of relationships between the psychologist and the animal in the creation of the field of experimental animal psychology in his dissertation in 1898. His work was not just a precursor of behaviorism but was the beginning of a convention that treats animals as abstract devices for introducing concepts that were to become common in human psychology. Animals were to become organisms of convenience upon which psychologists could script a variety of processes that were made 'visible' in ways that were not possible with human beings. Thorndike (1898) argued against anecdotalism, anthropomorphism, and introspectionism but in the creation of a new technology and in the concern with measurement and experimentation, his methods and explanations replaced anthropomorphism with mechanomorphism and theriomorphism (mechanicotheriomorphism). Mechanomorphism is the exclusive attribution of mechanistic properties to psychological phenomena whereas theriomorphism is the attribution of the qualities of nonhuman animals to human beings (English & English, 1958). Mechanicotheriomorphism is the ascription of mechanical properties to phenomena that are psychological in nature in nonhuman animals that are, in turn, used to explain human psychological phenomena (e.g., instinct and habit; see Stam & Kalmanovitch, 1998).

What Did Behavioral Explanations Accomplish?

The emphasis on animals as the primary source of data in early North American behaviorist research made it possible to limit the kinds of questions that were asked of the research. I am deliberately restricting my scope here to what needs to be seen as the fundamental issue about the nature of mind by behaviorists and the answer to which laid the foundations for the entire edifice of behaviorism. (I am also leaving aside the technical and social context of behaviorism and psychology's continuing insecurity about its status as a 'science' that it temporarily cured.) The theoretical questions thus are first, whether explanations of behavior can indeed be provided by the language of behaviorism and whether any references to central states (including physiological ones) are required. Second, is it possible to eliminate all references to mental or cognitive events in the name of science?

John Watson's fundamental thesis was, in his most theoretical writings (e.g., Watson, 1913) , a strictly reductive one for a psychology of organisms. By this Watson appeared to mean the outright dismissal of mental concepts and all references to other internal, psychological functions of the 'organism'. Instead Watson claimed that psychology could get along just fine by references to fundamental principles whose origins lay in physiology (such as the notion of reflex or that of the fundamental emotions which he discussed later, in the 1920s, after he was forced out of the academy, e.g., Watson, 1925). Watson's target was of course the functionalism and structuralism of his day but as more contemporary commentators have made clear, behaviorism was already established in all but name by the time Watson came to write his proclamation in 1913. It was predated by various uses of the term 'behaviorism' and a general readiness to accept restrictions in methodology to undercut the problems associated with 'introspectionism'. Nevertheless, Watson's expulsion of consciousness was never clear, a problem that would continue to haunt behaviorism. He vacillated between an outright rejection of consciousness as a scientific problem in its own right to treating it as epiphenomenal (non-causal) to psychological properties of interest. In his positive program he introduced North American psychology to a version of Pavlov's conditioned reflex which provided the mechanism Watson needed to make his research program cohere. But Watson's formulations were unprogrammatic and would lead Tolman to characterize Watson's behaviorism as 'molecular behaviorism' as opposed to a more molar behaviorism that focused on behavior as the unit of analysis. Watson's more difficult claims such as his notion that thought could be explained as a form of subvocal speech made him an easy target for those who saw it as only a 'muscle-twitch psychology'.

The Hull–Spence formulation of behaviorism that dominated so much of psychology during the Age of Theories was a formalization of a deductive theory of learning. The formal deductive system, especially as expressed in the *Principles of Behavior* (Hull, 1943) consisted of a set of principles (such as habit and drive reduction) that were capable of giving an equivalent translation of psychological terms expressed in ordinary language. This, combined with the search for what were believed to be universal elementary laws of learning and the immediate success of the psychologists' version of operationism furnished the framework for mainstream psychological theorizing in mid-century. The demise of this particular frame was long in coming, its downfall predicted and detailed in works by Koch and others (e.g., Koch, 1959). Tolman and Guthrie were also important contenders in the Age of Theory and although lack of space precludes a discussion here, their work too was eclipsed by the coming 'cognitive revolution'.

Skinner's position remained, to the last, one which was clearly defined around the two problems noted above, namely, the place of central states and the elimination of the mental in an explanation of behavior. Although having argued that theories were unnecessary (Skinner, 1950), Skinner built his work around a set of simple but enduring theoretical principles. These included his rejection of the hypothetico-deductive method in favor of the study of individual organisms who responded in a free-response situation, the rejection of all references to cognitive or central states, all combined with an emphasis on schedules of reinforcement (Ferster & Skinner, 1957).

Skinner's work has been subjected to extended criticism for the past forty years, criticism that he himself astutely but unfortunately refused to answer during his lifetime. In summary, Skinner's elimination of central states has long been rejected by both behaviorists and cognitivists. The arguments here focus on the logical indispensability of central states (Nelson, 1969) and the impossibility of giving a causal explanation without dispositional concepts (see Margolis, 1984). The objections to the elimination of the cognitive have focused on the notion that admitting the mental does not entail dualism and that the intentional dimensions of human activity have to be smuggled in to behavioral accounts, after having been eliminated up front,

in order to make these accounts understood. Hence animal and human properties and dispositions 'must be linked with internal, central states of organisms distinct from their determinate behavior' and 'must play a causal role in the empirical explanation of actual behavior' (Margolis, 1984, p. 42).

Having thus dispensed with the arguments against addressing internal states, and having found a respectable metaphorical device (a computing machine that serves as a cybernetic device) as well as allies in linguistics and the philosophy of mind, psychologists once again addressed themselves to the problems of mind and cognition.

29.5 COGNITIVISM AND FUNCTIONALISM IN PSYCHOLOGY: MIND THE GAP

Cognitive psychology and its putative role in the broad field that is now ambiguously labelled as cognitive science are theoretical projects whose outcome is far from known. A substantial shift has already occurred in cognitive theory away from representational theory and towards connectionist theories or towards the cognitive neurosciences. Despite this shift, the theoretical work continues to be substantial. Cognitive psychology is without a doubt the major preoccupation in mainstream, experimental psychology. I will first outline a prominent feature of cognitive (and many other) explanations in psychology, namely their functional character.

Functionalism and the Computational Theory of Mind

One of the greatest difficulties in understanding functionalism is that the term is used in twentieth-century psychology for a dizzying array of positions. These include (a) relating to or being a member of the so-called functionalism 'school' which was initiated at the turn of the century by, among others, James Angell; (b) having to do with or related to evolutionary properties, as in, the evolutionary 'function' of a trait; (c) applied, as in being 'functional' for something; (d) referring to the criterion of 'functional equivalence' between machine processes and cognitive processes requiring not just equivalent outputs but equivalent processes between the two; (e) referring to explanations, as in Skinner's use of 'functional explanations' that are different from functional properties; (f) a teleological functionalism that is explicitly biological in orientation in opposition to machine functionalism; (g) an explicit realist form of functionalism such as Putnam's earlier work which ascribed functional states realistically; and so on. Here I can note only the overlap with cognitive accounts in psychology and the importance functionalism played in establishing a modern cognitive psychology. Needless to say I will not nearly exhaust the discussion of functionalism. Clear discussions of the many ways in which functionalism is used and confused in psychology are, unfortunately, not available.

Cognition became firmly associated with functionalism through the work of Jerry Fodor (e.g., Fodor, 1975) in philosophy who together with Zenon Pylyshyn (e.g., Pylyshyn, 1984) in psychology and others provided the foundation for a computational theory. One of the cornerstones of this theory was that cognitive states are instantiated on some physical system but need not be related in a one-to-one fashion to a particular physical system. Hence we might model particular mental processes on a computer in the hope that the same functions can be ascribed to brain states. Nevertheless functional states (cognitions) are real in the same way that software is real and hence the independence of cognitions from particular instantiations does not make them any less real than the phenomena of the neurosciences. Cognitions are equally deserving of scientific status while at the same time they ensure the autonomy of cognitive psychology. Fodor (1975) added to this his notion of the 'language of thought' which is the claim that one consequence of our representational and computational minds is that there must be a primal language of thought that consists of computations for every cognition. This primitive language is entirely symbolic and entails a version of Platonism with all of its attendant problems.

In the classical computational architecture therefore we typically find three levels: first, a semantic (knowledge) level which is a level of meaning and goals; second, a symbol level where the semantic is encoded into symbolic expressions; and third, the 'platform' or the physical level. The model is premised on the notion that the second or symbolic level preserves semantic content. This means that the symbolic expressions can be translated into semantic content under appropriate conditions. Hence the necessity of a language of thought in Fodor's sense.

The problem then is to explain how a physical system behaves in ways that correspond to knowledge-level principles while it is simultaneously governed by physical laws and hence not a mysterious or dualistic entity. Symbolic approaches to cognition argue that knowledge is physically realized. According to Fodor, symbols must be structured like a language. Thus we have a physical symbol system. It is at once symbolic and realized on a physical architecture. In addition, the symbolic level must be cognitively impenetrable, that is architecture must not be altered by cognitive operations itself. These run like a program on the physical system.

It is clear that functionalism took on an important position with the rise of cognitivism, although it was never clear that psychologists took much notice (see for example a paper on cognition by Gleitman, 1992, which makes no mention of functionalism). Research in cognitive psychology proceeded quite apart from the discussions held by cognitive scientists and philosophers and their theoretical formulations were relatively independent functional formulations in the sense that they were descriptive, heuristic properties of mind that had an implied reductive relation to a physiological base. The work of psychologists such as Newell went no further than specifying that humans have symbol systems; that different architectures (i.e., physical structures) may support different symbol systems, and that within these architectures programs exist that correspond to psychologically meaningful actions and thoughts (Newell, 1980).

The reason for this discrepancy between the philosophical, theoretical justification and the psychological laboratory is not entirely mysterious. Psychologists have not adopted a rigorous or formal explanatory framework in part because their empirical commitments were grounded in a neobehavioral framework. The continuing use of operationism and aggregate, inferential statistics derived from highly controlled and hence abstract experimental conditions meant that cognitive theory on the computational model frequently meant, in practice, the use of reaction times, simple memory or perceptual tasks, attentional tasks and so on that were not dissimilar from those used by earlier neobehaviorists. More recent changes in cognitive science however have begun to change both theory and research practice.

Cognition, Now and Then

Theories of cognition have splintered and regrouped in recent years with significant consequences for psychology. The inadequacies of the symbolic or computational model are clearly not universally agreed upon, yet the presence of entirely different forms of analysis and research has led to the gradual decline of the traditional computational model. What is contentious in the latter model is the emphasis on propositions and the putative independence of cognitions. Indeed, with advances in the neurosciences some advocates have argued that no theory of cognition is worth considering that does not take fundamental neurological processes and limits into account. The sudden influx of biologists and philosophers who have ressurected consciousness as a legitimate topic (e.g., Edelman, 1992; Llinás & Churchland, 1996; Shapiro, 1997) has brought psychological questions to the forefront of an interdisciplinary forum that includes researchers identified with neuroscience, cognitive science, philosophy, and psychology.

Connectionism or the theory of (hypothetical) neural networks is based on a loose conception of how the nervous system purportedly works. In effect, connectionist models hypothesize a network of activations that is primarily composed of nodes and connections between these nodes. According to David Rumelhart (1989) connectionist models use an abstract neuron as their starting point. Their model is 'neurally inspired'. But of course neurons are much slower than computers since the former operate in the range of milliseconds whereas computer components operate in the scale of nanoseconds, that is, 10^6 times faster than neurons. Given the complexity of brains and the speed with which they work, the processes to be modeled or the algorithms must involve parallel processes, that is, many things occurring simultaneously.

The constraints on knowledge are in the connections between units themselves rather than in the state of the system as is the case in conventional computers. Thus long-term storage exists in connections. According to Rumelhart (1989) there are seven components to connectionist systems: (1) a set of processing units, (2) a state of activation defined over these units, (3) an output function for each unit, (4) a pattern of connectivity among units, (5) an activation rule that combines inputs with the current state of the unit to produce a new level of activation, (6) a learning rule that tells the patterns of connectivity how they are to be modified, and (7) an environment in which the system must operate.

The way these micro-features come together in a connectionist model does not depend on a central level of symbol processing. Instead symbolic-level information is 'spread' over units whose connections determine the appropriate use of such information. In addition, the inputs are similar to traditional cognitive models and the outputs send signals out of the system. There is a third kind of processing unit, a hidden unit, that is not 'visible' outside the system but that is postulated to exist between inputs and outputs and that is crucial to whatever is being modeled. That is because the hidden units determine the pattern of connectivity (Rumelhart,

1989). In its emphasis on developing new connections and modifying existing connections, these models simply seek the best or most robust network to model the phenomenon at hand. Network models are better at modeling perceptual-motor skills than symbolic models which, in turn, are better at modeling complex cognitive tasks.

Current work on connectionist models has advanced rapidly but it is still not clear if these models will entirely surpass the traditional computational, symbolic theories as a model of cognition (e.g., Fodor & Pylyshyn, 1988; Quartz & Sejnowski, 1997). Indeed, there are arguments that the two approaches to cognition can coexist in a single theory of cognition. There are also arguments that any reference to representation is unnecessary in a final scientific version of cognition (see Bem & Looren de Jong, 1997, for an account of these controversies). It is far too soon to know what the eventual outcome of these debates will be and the future of cognitive psychology remains to be determined. What has become increasingly clear however is that this will include interdisciplinary collaboration with the neurosciences and philosophy especially now that the problem of consciousness has re-entered the debate. One guiding assumption of this work is that any theory of cognition will require that connections be made between cognitive and neural levels of description and that through the constraints these levels impose on each other a satisfactory theory will emerge (Churchland & Sejnowski, 1988; Quartz & Sejnowski, 1997).

Alternatively, a continuing objection to theorizing the cognitive realm comes from theoretical traditions that view the attempt to provide an infrapsychological account of the cognitive capacities of human agents as essentially incomplete (e.g., Gergen & Gigerenzer, 1991; Smythe, 1992). Most succinctly put, the objections to cognitivism as a sole enterprise for the elucidation of the mental life of human beings is that cognitive phenomena are themselves made possible only insofar as those who have them participate in social practices and these practices in some fundamental way depend on this participation. In addition, such practices are not amenable to reductive analysis at the level of individuals and the investigator (as well as the investigation) participates in those same practices (e.g., Edwards & Potter, 1992). Regardless of the strengths of the cognitive research enterprise and all it has accomplished, the reflexive nature of human psychology then requires us to turn to the uniquely human and social world for theories in this domain.

29.6 Theories in Personality and Social Psychology: Traditions and Counter-Themes

Among the most contested theories in psychology are those that belong to Social Psychology and Personality Psychology. Although the mainstream (particularly in North America) in each sub-discipline has more or less created an artificial consensus by focusing strictly on experimentation and quantitative research, it is clear that there are still a host of unresolved ontological and epistemological problems that remain to be acknowledged. By virtue of their suppression these problems continually reappear in various forms of critique, alternative theories and the production of counter-positions, many of which are short-lived. In the next section I will discuss some of these alternative positions, here I want to note the major themes that have dominated social and personality psychology. In this space I can only look for meta-theoretical themes and will not discuss the wide array of theoretical positions within these sub-disciplines.

Social Psychology

The predominant theoretical approaches in social psychology are focused on individuals and their cognitions. Indeed most textbooks of social psychology still cite the definition first proferred by Gordon Allport in his history chapter in earlier editions of the *Handbook of Social Psychology* (see Lubek, 1993). This definition, which takes social psychology to be the study of the way in which people's thoughts, feelings, and behaviors are influenced by 'the real or imagined presence of others', is entirely individualist. It extends Floyd Allport's (1924) definition that social psychology is 'a part of the psychology of the individual' (p. 4). Social psychologists frequently imply that their research is the mirror image to sociologists' research when the latter study societies and cultures, although most such defences are left for undergraduate textbooks (e.g., Aronson, Wilson, & Akert, 1997). Unfortunately, individualistic definitions severely limit social psychology's capacity to research or otherwise understand truly social phenomena such as the creation of institutions, cultures, and other social phenomena and their relationship to the individuals that create them and are, in turn, constituted by them (e.g., Stam, 1987).

Historically then, social psychology has limited itself to theories focusing on internal and individual, cognitive or cognitive-like processes.

This theoretical orientation however was also tied up in a complex way with experimentation which became the preferred method of proceeding in social psychology after the end of World War II (Lubek & Stam, 1995; Stam & Lubek, 1992). Following the death of Lewin, social psychological research studies within psychology became increasingly manipulative, deceptive, and consisted more frequently of controlled group research. This was coupled with a sense of insecurity about experimental rigor, particularly in the use of artificially manipulated variables, and is reflected in aggressive proselytizing by social psychologists. The use of high profile, ludic experiments of great ingenuity gradually distinguishes social psychology from other areas of psychology and from other forms of social psychology such as those in sociology (Lubek & Stam, 1995; Stam, Lubek, & Radtke, 1998).

The new rigorous social psychology made it possible for highly complex individual cognitive and cognitive-like structures to be posited as theoretical entities. Prior to World War II, Kurt Lewin's field theory had come to have considerable impact in the United States. Using the 'constructive method', a method focused on relationships between people or people and objects, Lewin argued that one must analyze situations as wholes, not isolated elements. The approach was 'dynamic', that is, examining underlying forces and tensions. Finally, the entire approach was mathematical, or at least capable of being modeled in terms of topological and vector concepts (see Lewin, 1997).

Field theory was complex and mathematically difficult. It also contained some concepts at odds with the dominant conceptions of persons then reigning in behaviorism, that is, persons as complex automata. After the death of Lewin, cognitive consistency theories rapidly replaced field theory and along with them came individualist models far less concerned with social interaction. The prevalent conception within cognitive consistency theories consisted of the notion that inconsistent cognitions aroused an unpleasant psychological state that, in turn, produces behaviors designed to achieve consistency. The state of inconsistency formulated within this set of theories included cognitive imbalance (Heider), asymmetry (Newcomb), incongruence (Osgood), and most influential, cognitive dissonance (Festinger; see Shaw & Costanzo, 1982, for a description of the classic positions).

Attribution theories are equally important in social psychology by virtue of their focus on internal attributions for behavior. Heider's (1958) original work as well as that of others such as Jones and Davis (1965; Theory of Correspondent Inference) and Kelley (1972; Theory of External Attribution) was based on the conceptual analysis that interpersonal relations are primarily determined by people's interpretations of the behavior of others. People seek invariance in the action of those around them and do so by primarily attributing their actions to stable internal characteristics. 'The fundamental attribution error' (Ross, 1978) was an important development in attribution research in that the finding that perceivers overattribute behavior to the personal dispositions of actors led to a large number of studies of 'bias' in the attribution process. A host of other theories compete to account for social processes, such as Social Comparison Theory (originally formulated by Festinger but still influential in research today), various models and theories of attitude change and of social persuasion. In addition, a host of theories and models address more limited domains of 'social behavior' such as interpersonal attraction and group processes.

What is remarkable about the tremendous quantity of literature published in social psychology in the past fifty years is its failure to adequately characterize or capture precisely what makes an act, a thought, a feeling, or an utterance social in the first place. Even in group research the very definition of a 'group' is no more than two or more people present in the same space. With such an impoverished understanding of how anything comes to be and is maintained as 'social' it is not surprising therefore that an enduring critique of social psychology has continued and continues to this day (Gergen, 1973; Parker & Shotter, 1990). Unfortunately most social psychologists have responded to the 'crisis' in their midst by ignoring it, simply exacerbating the very real ontological and epistemological problems faced by this subdiscipline. By its very incapacity to address the relationship between social, cultural, and institutional phenomena and our constitution as individuals, social psychology (in psychology) remains abstract, individualist, and incapable of addressing real social concerns and issues in all except the most general and abstract fashion. I will discuss various alternative conceptions that have arisen in response to this below.

Personality Psychology

Even more so than Social Psychology, the field of Personality has such a long and rich tradition that the reader is primarily referred to other sources (e.g., Hogan, Johnson, & Briggs, 1997). I will note only major trends here and offer some tentative comments about its directions.

Although the idea of a separate sub-discipline of 'personality' owes a great deal to Gordon

Allport, it was also politically indebted to behaviorism which as a mechanistic and positivistic enterprise precluded the discussion of persons altogether. The practicing psychologist could not wait for the behaviorist to produce the final laws of behavior; what was needed were practical studies of motivation and dynamics as well as individual differences. In addition, German psychology prior to World War II included the study of 'character', so important for selecting civil servants, officers, and the like. Personality theories were also entwined in traditions of 'abnormal' personality through the work of Morton Prince and Henry Murray and the testing movement had already demonstrated the potential of measuring elements of personality. And finally, an ambiguous relationship existed between North American psychology and psychoanalysis, the popularity of which ensured that psychologists were put upon to give their own account of personal dynamics if these were not to be of the psychoanalytic variety. This was crucial particularly during the time when psychiatry had all but appropriated psychoanalytic techniques and training as its own.

Gordon Allport and Henry Murray reflect two very different approaches that demarcate the origins of the field of personality theory. Whereas Allport was concerned with the unity and wholeness of the person and self ('the proprium'), Murray saw personality organized around the concepts of 'need', 'press', and 'thema'. Allport's theoretical work attempted to give the notion of the self a life outside of psychodynamic theory and within North American academic psychology. Hence it was rational and orderly, focused primarily on the issue of the self and the problem of traits. What survived of Allport's theory however was the notion of a trait, which Allport conceived of as a real organizing structure. The trait concept merged with testing methods and along with the influential work of psychologists such as Hans Eysenk and Raymond Cattell, among others, a focus on constructs and construct measurement and definition came to dominate personality psychology. The wide availability of factor analysis and other high-speed computer programs that allow for the rapid manipulation of personality scale data have greatly aided the development of trait research, including the current preoccupation with the 'five-factor' model, the theory that there are only five fundamental factors to human personality (e.g., McCrae, 1992).

Despite the dominance of personality by trait conceptions, the field as a whole spent approximately twenty years in retreat in the face of a series of powerful critiques (see McAdams, 1997). Most important of these was Mischel's (1968) book which argued that personality traits and dispositions, although stable on average between people, can vary tremendously across situations. Hence it is situational variance in individual behavior that best predicts the behavior of individuals. Mischel modified his position substantially over the years (e.g., Mischel, 1973), but the ensuing debate (often referred to as the situationism debate) was resolved more or less by a kind of tacit agreement among personality researchers that behavior is a function of both persons and situations and their interaction (hence the term 'interactionism'). What this allowed researchers to do was focus on the empirical issues involved, namely to assess the extent that traits are predictive of behavior, to assess cross-situational consistency, use moderator variables, and so on (McAdams, 1997). What interactionism specifically prevented was an examination of the real conceptual confusion that underlay the debate in the first place. Both the notion of trait (as personal disposition) and the conceptual limits of what we know when we measure 'situations' are vague and fuzzy at best.

In addition to these developments, it is in these areas of human psychology that the dominance of North American concepts, theories, research, and practices is most often seen as a restriction on indigenous psychologies elsewhere in the world. The drive for a universal and natural conception of human being is often seen as a normative aspect of the psychologists' work rather than as concepts that require defence, elaboration, and theoretical explication. Even such major handbooks as the *International Handbook of Personality and Intelligence* (Saklofske & Zeidner, 1995) are premised on standard conceptions drawn from the English-speaking, academic world. What is most urgently required is a reconsideration of more fundamental theoretical questions, such as the notion of persons and the cultural and historical heritage as well as constraints that such concepts have given us (see, for example, Smythe, 1998).

29.7 POST-FOUNDATIONALISM: HERMENEUTICS, FEMINISM AND SOCIAL CONSTRUCTIONISM

A range of positions that maintain that the human subject is essentially a social or meaning-making (and hence a historical) subject have vied for a footing in the discipline for most of the twentieth century. Indeed the roots of these traditions are present in the work of Wundt (particularly his *Völkerpsychologie*) and James, and have manifested themselves in early phenomenological

psychology prior to mid-century and in the humanist traditions after World War II. It continues in various Marxist and critical psychological strands from the 1950s on and in feminist, post-positivist and more generally, postmodernist conceptions of psychology. In the current preoccupations with culture and the cross-fertilization between the Social Sciences and Cultural Studies are new discussions of subjectivity, embodiment, and meaning that have been fashioned and now have a maturity and interdisciplinary character that would have been inconceivable even a decade ago (e.g., Bayer & Shotter, 1998; Stam, 1998).

Despite this proliferation and maturation, these traditions have not had a great influence on the psychology produced in the English-speaking world. Instead, separate traditions have emerged around the mainstream of the discipline that, although marginal to it, continue to thrive both in and out of Anglophone psychology. In this section I will describe briefly three major developments but this is in no way meant to be a comprehensive list or program.

Hermeneutics

As a position in philosophy, hermeneutics has a long history. But it is not a psychology and requires considerable theoretical explication before it can serve as a satisfactory psychological enterprise. For this reason there are a variety of traditions that have emerged out of an ontological (as opposed to merely epistemological) hermeneutic framework through the work of Martin Heidegger and Hans-Georg Gadamer. Paul Ricoeur was influential in showing how hermeneutics could be brought to bear on questions in the social sciences. He argued that the objects of the social sciences are constituted by meaningful action and that this form of action shares a number of constitutive features of texts. Once considered as text the methodology proper to the social sciences are akin to the interpretation of texts or, more immediately, discourse. In addition, our knowledge of the social world is colored by the fact that this knowledge is produced by those who are part of the social world. By being part of that social world we are in a relation of belonging which, according to Ricoeur, gives the social sciences their hermeneutic character and means we can never fully stand outside of our objects of investigation (Ricoeur, 1981).

Hermeneutics brings a number of crucial issues to psychology, but not in a direct way. Several commentators have noted that hermeneutic-like inquiries are involved in social constructionism, phenomenological studies (which often are not phenomenological in the theoretical sense but more properly hermeneutic), qualitative research, and areas of psychology that are primarily focused on the meaning-making activities of human beings such as research on psychotherapy. In addition, hermeneutic inquiries can clarify why theoretical blind spots and dead ends exist in other areas of the discipline (e.g., Smythe, 1992). Despite the commonalities however it is difficult to point to a coherent enterprise that goes by the name 'hermeneutic psychology'. More important is the grounding that hermeneutic studies can give to the problems of and relations between, understanding, lived experience, the 'human sciences', and life itself (see, e.g., Mos, 1996; Stancombe & White, 1998). In addition, what characterizes hermeneutic work, and that which makes it incommensurate with the experimental traditions of psychology, is its unfolding within the 'hermeneutic circle'. A single 'fact' never stands alone but always in relation to a larger context, frame, or theory. We understand the 'fact' by moving from theory to fact and back again, enlarging our understanding of the theory by reference to the 'fact'. Likewise we never understand a text without foreknowledge that alerts us to the features we find important, yet at the same time the text moves beyond this background knowledge to new horizons of intelligibility. On this view psychological research methodology is second to the interpretative act (see Messer, Sass, & Woolfolk, 1988, for a discussion).

Feminism in Psychology

Of all the political movements that have had an impact on the academy in the past decades, feminism appears to be the most important and has led to the most far-reaching changes, certainly in a North American context and perhaps more broadly as well. In addition, it has been a model for other social movements and as its analyses have become more diverse and embedded in scholarly communities it serves as a continual reminder of the contextual, political, and socially embedded nature of knowledge. Feminism has also altered psychological theory and theorizing, not just through its insistence that hidden but powerful masculine ideals be unmasked but also for feminists' outright questioning of the phallocentric bases of epistemology and science (see, e.g., Harding, 1991). Psychology has been profoundly affected by feminist research and theory, both at the level of research practices and topics and at the level of theory. Nevertheless, as Morawski (1994) points out, feminist research and theory are not always welcome in the mainstream and are frequently caught up in a critique that places them in an artificial binary of politics–science.

Within the discipline at large, feminism has largely been visible at the level of empirical research. This attempts to restore to psychological research those who have been underrepresented and to eliminate biases by examining sex and gender differences and examine women's experiences as an end in itself (e.g., Belenky, Clinchy, Goldberger, & Tarule, 1986; Gilligan, 1982). Morawski (1994) rightly notes however that this work is frequently appropriated into the mainstream or is ignored, in neither case making the changes and adjustments to the discipline desired by feminist psychologists. More recent feminist analyses in psychology are exploring the more fundamental and foundational epistemological and ontological questions at the base of the discipline, just as this is happening elsewhere in the social sciences (see, for example, Flax, 1990; Morawski & Steele, 1991; Radtke & Stam, 1994; Wilkinson & Kitzinger, 1995). In addition, the relationship between such foundational questions and psychological practices and research form an essential part of this analysis.

Social Constructionism

The last 'new movement' I want to consider is also one that has generated a fair degree of debate, perhaps because it is frequently targeted as the one alternative associated with postmodernism and all that this term entails. It is also the most visible alternative movement in English-speaking psychology. There is no one theory associated with social constructionism however but as a set of theories it has in common a general structure or set of problems with which it is associated. In the remaining space I will consider some of these as well as describing several specific positions.

The social constructionist is most immediately concerned with the problem of language and the conclusion, drawn from modern philosophy, that what one utters as a speaker is drawn from and relies on the cultural experience of a particular historical society. No one member of that society can internalize this shifting experience. The problem is, in part, Wittgensteinian and based on his arguments about private language. Language is not only inseparable from considerations of actual societal life but the practices of a linguistic group make it possible to have a meaningful language. Meanings are located in the practices of a society and mental events, however we characterize them, are embedded in the discursive practices of a human community (Gergen, 1985; Shotter, 1993). Those practices cannot be accounted for solely in terms of the infrapsychological powers of the members of such a community, although such an interpretation of the mental does not rule out the possibility of a less ambitious account of cognitive capacities. Language then appears to be unique and a requirement for the emergence of human aptitudes and capabilities as well as being always open to improvisation, revision, and interpretation due to its embeddedness in history and culture (cf., Harré, 1984; Margolis, 1984; Ricoeur, 1981).

It was Berger and Luckmann (1966) who gave the label to constructionist positions. By extending Mannheim's analysis of the interested nature of knowledge to everyday life, they viewed individuals as self-producing while simultaneously the product of social structures. Their sociological analysis was as concerned with the micro-world of the ordinary as with the structures of society and it enabled a range of questions to be addressed under the banner of the 'social construction of reality'. Psychologists such as Gergen extended this analysis to psychological categories by claiming that 'social constructionism . . . begins with radical doubt in the taken-for-granted world – whether in the sciences or in daily life – and in a specialized way acts as a form of social criticism. Constructionism asks one to suspend belief that commonly accepted categories or understandings receive their warrant through observation' (Gergen, 1985, p. 267). Instead, argues Gergen, an account of the world or self is sustained on the inconstancies of social processes. And social processes are forms of cultural life; they always remain indeterminate. Our descriptions of them have a function within the relationships, rituals, and activities of social life.

There are several competing accounts of social constructionism however which try to specify more precisely the origin of our social life. For example, Rom Harré has argued that the 'fundamental human reality is a conversation, effectively without beginning or end, to which, from time to time, individuals may make contributions' (Harré, 1984, p. 20). The personal, mental, and emotional are appropriated from the conversational flow of our daily lives and on Harré's account, the features and properties of mind are explicitly derived from the features of public conversation. Furthermore that conversation is as real as any other object of scientific inquiry. Argues Harré, 'the production of psychological phenomena, such as emotions, decisions, attitudes, personality displays, and so on, in discourse depends upon the skill of the

actors, their relative moral standing in the community, and the story lines that unfold' (Harré & Gillett, 1994, p. 27). Social constructionists have also turned to Vygotsky and Bakhtin for a developmental-dialogical account of social life. In this vein Shotter (1993, 1995) argues that thought is constituted in language as a form of inner speech and is part of the contingent flow of continuous human interaction. Inner lives exist in-between a world and our bodies; our dialogue with others is a form of 'joint action'.

Much recent constructionist work has explicitly taken a focus on discourse and discourse analysis. This has become constituted as 'discursive psychology', a form of doing psychology that sees talk not as expressions of the underlying cognitive states of a speaker, but takes expressions to be occasioned and situated constructions 'whose precise nature makes sense to participants and analysts alike in terms of the social action these descriptions accomplish' (Edwards & Potter, 1992, p. 2). Discursive psychologists are engaged in understanding the function and construction of talk in context and in recasting such traditional topics as memory and attributions through the micro-analysis of psychological talk.

29.8 Conclusions

The tremendous range and depth of problems addressed in theoretical psychology today make it unwise, if not impossible, to attempt a comprehensive overview (see also Slife & Williams, 1997). I have chosen what I think are some representative and key problems, the development of which have implications for the entire discipline or perhaps better said, the entire range of 'psychological studies'. I have omitted many topics perhaps equally deserving but requiring commentary of such length that it would be impossible to include. For example, the theoretical problems of applied and clinical psychology are not only extensive but take place in the context of a continual interplay of theory–practice–research. Theory here is often a case of puzzle solving and must be generated and modified in the field. At the same time, the political and social realities of practice make it very difficult to ask certain questions about the nature of practice and the role it plays in social structures and institutions. It is precisely for these reasons that forms of critical psychology still demand our attention (e.g., Fox & Prilleltensky, 1997). Their voices of dissent remind us that neither psychological theories nor research or practice are conducted in the abstract.

Psychology not only affects those who would be its clients but also our self-understandings. A discipline whose work is not only popularized but taught to such large numbers of undergraduates around the world, must, in ways not yet clear, filter through to our experiences of subjectivity. Theorizing is the first step in articulating not just what our subjective worlds are but what they can be. For embedded in our theoretical understanding is an ever-present teleological question: once a theory specifies the nature of psychological being does it not, ipso facto, also specify the nature of psychological becoming? On those grounds alone theoretical psychology is and will continue to be an important endeavor in an increasingly 'global' psychology.

Resource References

Bem, S., & Looren de Jong, H. (1997). *Theoretical issues in psychology: An introduction*. London: Sage.

Robinson, D. N. (1985). *Philosophy of psychology*. New York: Columbia.

Slife, B. D., & Williams, R. N. (1995). *What's behind the research: Discovering hidden assumptions in the behavioral sciences*. Thousand Oaks, CA: Sage

Valentine, E. R. (1992). *Conceptual issues in psychology* (2nd ed.). London: Routledge.

Recent volumes of the *Proceedings of the International Society for Theoretical Psychology*

Lubek, I., van Hezewijk, R., Pheterson, G., & Tolman, C. W. (Eds.). (1995). *Trends and issues in theoretical psychology*. New York: Springer Publishing.

Stam, H. J., Mos, L. J., Thorngate, W., & Kaplan, B. (Eds.). (1993). *Recent trends in theoretical psychology* (vol. III). New York: Springer-Verlag.

Tolman, C. W., Cherry, F., van Hezewijk, R., & Lubek, I. (Eds.). (1996). *Problems of theoretical psychology*. Toronto: Captus University Publications.

Journals that cover a range of theoretical problems

Behavioral and Brain Sciences
Journal for the Theory of Social Behavior
Philosophical Psychology
Psychological Review
Theory & Psychology

Additional Literature Cited

Allport, F. H. (1924). *Social psychology*. Boston: Houghton Mifflin.

Aronson, E., Wilson, T. D., & Akert, R. M. (1997). *Social psychology* (2nd ed.). New York: Longman.

Bayer, B. M., & Shotter, J. (Eds.). (1998). *Reconstructing the psychological subject: Bodies, practices and technologies*. London: Sage.

Belenky, M. F., Clinchy, B. M., Goldberger, N. R., & Tarule, J. M. (1986). *Women's ways of knowing: The development of self, voice, and mind*. New York: Basic Books.

Berger, P. L., & Luckmann, T. (1966). *The social construction of reality*. New York: Doubleday.

Churchland, P. S., & Sejnowski, T. J. (1988). Perspectives on cognitive neuroscience. *Science, 242*, 741–745.

Danziger, K. (1990). *Constructing the subject: Historical origins of psychological research*. New York: Cambridge University Press.

Edelman, G. (1992). *Bright air, brilliant fire*. New York: Harper Collins.

Edwards, D., & Potter, J. (1992). *Discursive psychology*. London: Sage.

English, H. B., & English, A. V. (1958). *A comprehensive dictionary of psychological and psychoanalytical terms*. London: Longmans, Green.

Ferster, C. B., & Skinner, B. F. (1957). *Schedules of reinforcement*. New York: Appleton-Century-Crofts.

Flax, J. (1990). *Thinking fragments: Psychoanalysis, feminism, and postmodernism in the contemporary west*. Berkeley, CA: University of California Press.

Fodor, J. (1975). *The language of thought*. New York: Crowell.

Fodor, J., & Pylyshyn, Z. (1988). Connectionism and cognitive architecture: A critical analysis. *Cognition, 28*, 3–71.

Fox, D., & Prilleltensky, I. (1997). *Critical psychology: An introduction*. London: Sage.

Gergen, K. J. (1973). Social psychology as history. *Journal of Personality and Social Psychology, 26*, 309–320.

Gergen, K. J. (1985). The social constructionist movement in modern psychology. *American Psychologist, 40*, 266–275.

Gergen, K. J., & Gigerenzer, G. (Eds.). (1991). Cognitivism and its discontents. Special Issue. *Theory & Psychology, 1*, 403–569.

Gigerenzer, G. (1993). The superego, the ego, and the id in statistical reasoning. In G. Keren & C. Lewis (Eds.), *A handbook for data analysis in the behavioral sciences: Methodological issues*. Hillsdale, NJ: Erlbaum.

Gilligan, C. (1982). *In a different voice: Psychological theory and women's development*. Cambridge: Harvard University Press.

Gleitman, H. (1992). Some trends in the study of cognition. In S. Koch & D. E. Leary (Eds.), *A century of psychology as science* (pp. 420–436).

Washington, DC: American Psychological Association.

Harding, S. (1991). *Whose science? Whose knowledge? Thinking from women's lives*. Ithaca, NY: Cornell University Press.

Harré, R. (1984). *Personal being: A theory for individual psychology*. Cambridge, MA: Harvard University Press.

Harré, R., & Gillett, G. (1994). *The discursive mind*. Thousand Oaks, CA: Sage.

Heidbreder, E. (1933). *Seven psychologies*. New York: Appleton.

Heider, F. (1958). *The psychology of interpersonal relations*. New York: Wiley.

Hogan, R., Johnson, J., & Briggs, S. (Eds.). (1997). *Handbook of personality psychology*. San Diego, CA: Academic Press.

Hull, C. L. (1943). *Principles of behavior*. New York: Appleton-Century-Crofts.

Jones, E. E., & Davis, K. E. (1965). From acts to dispositions. In L. Berkowitz (Ed.), *Advances in social psychology* (vol. 2). New York: Academic Press.

Kantor, J. R. (1968). Behaviorism in the history of psychology. *The Psychological Record*, *18*, 151–166.

Kelley, H. H. (1972). *Causal schemata and the attribution process*. Morristown, NJ: General Learning Press.

Knorr-Cetina, K. D., & Mulkay, M. (1983). Introduction: Emerging principles in social studies of science. In K. D. Knorr-Cetina & M. Mulkay (Eds.), *Science observed* (pp. 1–17). London: Sage.

Koch, S. (Ed.) (1959). *Psychology: A study of science* (6 vols.). New York: McGraw-Hill.

Koch, S. (1976). Language communities, search cells, and the psychological studies. In W. J. Arnold (Ed.), *Nebraska symposium on motivation* (Vol. 23). Lincoln, NE: University of Nebraska Press.

Koch, S. (1985). Afterword. In S. Koch & D. E. Leary (Eds.), *A century of psychology as science* (pp. 928–950). Washington, DC: American Psychological Association.

Lewin, K. (1997). *Resolving social conflicts & field theory in social science*. Washington, DC: American Psychological Association. (Originally published 1948 and 1951.)

Llinás, R., & Churchland, P. S. (Eds.). (1996). *The mind-brain continuum*. Cambridge, MA: MIT Press.

Lubek, I. (1993). Social psychology textbooks: An historical and social psychological analysis of conceptual filtering, consensus formation, career gatekeeping and conservatism in science. In H. J. Stam, L. P. Mos, W. Thorngate, & B. Kaplan (Eds.), *Recent trends in theoretical psychology* (vol. III, pp. 359–378). New York: Springer-Verlag.

Lubek, I., & Stam, H. J. (1995). Ludicro-experimentation in social psychology: Sober scientific versus playful prescriptions. In I. Lubek, R. van Hezewijk, G. Pheterson, & C. Tolman (Eds.),

Trends and issues in theoretical psychology (pp. 171–180). New York: Springer.

Margolis, J. (1984). *Philosophy of psychology*. Englewood Cliffs, NJ: Prentice-Hall.

McAdams, D. P. (1997). A conceptual history of personality psychology. In R. Hogan, J. Johnson, & S. Briggs (Eds.), *Handbook of personality psychology* (pp. 3–39). San Diego, CA: Academic Press.

McCrae, R. R. (Ed.). (1992). *The five-factor model: A special issue of the Journal of Personality*. Durham, NC: Duke University Press.

Messer, S. B., Sass, L. A., & Woolfolk, R. L. (Eds.). (1988). *Hermeneutics and psychological theory*. New Brunswick, NJ: Rutgers University Press.

Mills, J. A. (1998). *Control: A history of behavioral psychology*. New York: New York University Press.

Mischel, W. (1968). *Personality and assessment*. New York: Wiley.

Mischel, W. (1973). Toward a cognitive social learning reconceptualization of personality. *Psychological Review*, *80*, 252–282.

Morawski, J. G. (1994). *Practicing feminisms, reconstructing psychology: Notes on a liminal science*. Ann Arbor, MI: University of Michigan Press.

Morawski, J. G., & Steele, R. S. (1991). The one or the other? Textual analysis of masculine power and femine empowerment. *Theory & Psychology*, *1*, 132–144.

Mos, L. P. (1996). Immanent critique of experience: Dilthey's hermeneutics. In C. W. Tolman, F. Cherry, R. van Hezewijk, & I. Lubek (Eds.), *Problems of theoretical psychology* (pp. 368–378). North York, ON: Captus University Publications.

Nelson, R. J. (1969). Behaviorism is false. *Journal of Philosophy*, *66*.

Newell, A. (1980). Physical symbol systems. *Cognitive Science*, *4*, 135–183.

O'Neil, W. M. (1995). American behaviorism: A historical and critical analysis. *Theory & Psychology*, *5*, 285–306.

Parker, I., & Shotter, J. (1990). *Deconstructing social psychology*. London: Routledge.

Pylyshyn, Z. (1984). *Computation and cognition: Toward a foundation for cognitive science*. Cambridge, MA: MIT Press.

Quartz, S. R., & Sejnowski, T. J. (1997). The neural basis of cognitive development: A constructivist manifesto. *Behavioral and Brain Sciences*, *20*, 537–596.

Quine, W. V. O. (1953). Two dogmas of empiricism. In W. V. O. Quine, *From a logical point of view* (pp. 20–46). Cambridge, MA: Harvard University Press.

Radtke, H. L., & Stam, H. J. (Eds.), (1994). *Power/gender: Social relations in theory and practice*. London: Sage Publications.

Ricoeur, P. (1981). *Hermenuetics & the human sciences* (ed. and trans. by J. B. Thompson). Cambridge: Cambridge University Press.

Ross, L. (1978). The intuitive psychologist and his shortcomings. In L. Berkowitz (Ed.), *Cognitive* theories in social psychology. New York: Academic Press.

Rotter, J. B. (1954). *Social learning and clinical psychology.* Englewood Cliffs, NY: Prentice-Hall.

Rumelhart, D. E. (1989). The architecture of mind: A connectionist approach. In M. I. Posner (Ed.), *Foundations of cognitive science* (p. 133–159). Cambridge, MA: MIT Press.

Saklofske, D. H., & Zeidner, M. (Eds.). (1995). *International handbook of personality and intelligence.* New York: Plenum Press.

Salmon, W. C. (1989). Four decades of scientific explanation. In P. Kitcher & W. C. Salmon (Eds.), *Scientific explanation: Minnesota studies in the philosophy of science* (vol. 13, pp. 3–219). Minneapolis, MN: University of Minnesota Press.

Shapiro, Y. (1997). The consciousness hype: What do we want explained? *Theory & Psychology, 7,* 837–856.

Shaw, M. E., & Costanzo, P. R. (1982). *Theories of social psychology* (2nd ed.). Singapore: McGraw-Hill.

Shotter, J. (1993). *Cultural politics of everyday life: Social constructionism, rhetoric and knowing of the third kind.* Toronto: University of Toronto Press.

Shotter, J. (1995). In conversation: Joint action, shared intentionality and ethics. *Theory & Psychology, 5,* 49–73.

Skinner, B. F. (1950). Are theories of learning necessary? *Psychological Review, 57,* 193–216.

Slife, B. D., & Williams, R. N. (1997). Toward a theoretical psychology: Should a subdiscipline be formally recognized? *American Psychologist, 52,* 117–129.

Smythe, W. E. (1992). Conceptions of interpretation in cognitive theories of representation. *Theory & Psychology, 2,* 339–362.

Smythe, W. E. (Ed.). (1998). *Toward a psychology of persons.* Mahwah, NJ: Lawrence Erlbaum Associates.

Stam, H. J. (1987). The psychology of control: A textual critique. In H. J. Stam, T. B. Rogers, & K. J. Gergen (Eds.), *The analysis of psychological theory: Metapsychological perspectives* (pp. 131–156). Washington, DC: Hemisphere.

Stam, H. J. (1990). What distinguishes lay persons' psychological explanations from those of psychologists? In W. J. Baker, M. E. Hyland, R. van Hezewijk, & S. Terwee (Eds.), *Recent trends in theoretical psychology* (vol. 2, pp. 97–106). New York: Springer-Verlag.

Stam, H. J. (1996). Theory and practice. In C. W. Tolman, F. Cherry, R. van Hezewijk, & I. Lubek (Eds.), *Problems of theoretical psychology* (pp. 24–32). North York, ON: Captus University Publications.

Stam, H. J. (Ed.). (1998). *The body and psychology.* London: Sage.

Stam, H. J., & Kalmanovitch, T. (1998). E. L. Thorndike and the origins of animal psychology: On the nature of the animal in psychology. *American Psychologist, 53,* 1135–1144.

Stam, H. J., & Lubek, I. (1992). A textual analysis of the development of experimentation in social psychology. Paper presented at the annual meeting of the Cheiron Society, Windsor, June 1992.

Stam, H. J., Lubek, I., & Radtke, H. L. (1998). Repopulating social psychology texts: Disembodied 'subjects' and embodied subjectivity. In B. M. Bayer & J. Shotter (Eds.), *Reconstructing the psychological subject: Bodies, practices and technologies* (pp. 153–186). London: Sage.

Stam, H. J., & Pasay, G. A. (1998). The historical case against null-hypothesis significance testing. *Behavioral and Brain Sciences, 21,* 219–220.

Stancombe, J., & White, S. (1998). Psychotherapy without foundations? Hermeneutics, discourse and the end of certainty. *Theory & Psychology, 5,* 579–599.

Suppe, W. (1974). *The structure of scientific theories.* Urbana, IL: University of Illinois Press.

Thorndike, E. L. (1898). Animal intelligence: An experimental study of the associative processes in animals. *Psychological Monographs, 2* (4, Whole No. 8).

Watson, J. B. (1913). Psychology as the behaviorist views it. *Psychological Review, 20,* 158–177.

Watson, J. B. (1925). *Behaviorism.* New York: Norton.

Wilkinson, S., & Kitzinger, C. (Eds.). (1995). *Feminism and discourse: Psychological perspectives.* London: Sage.

Wozniak, R. H. (Ed.). (1993a). *Theoretical roots of early behaviourism: Functionalism, the critique of introspectionism, and the nature and evolution of consciousness.* London: Routledge/Thoemmes Press.

Wozniak, R. H. (Ed.). (1993b). *Experimental and comparative roots of early behaviourism: Studies of animal and infant behaviour.* London: Routledge/Thoemmes Press.

Wozniak, R. H. (Ed.). (1994). *Reflex, habit and implicit response: The early elaboration of theoretical and methodological behaviourism, 1915–1928.* London: Routledge/Thoemmes Press.

Communications concerning this chapter should be addressed to: Professor Hank J. Stam, Department of Psychology, University of Calgary, 2500 University Drive, Calgary, Alberta, Canada T2N 1N4

30

International Psychology

QICHENG JING

Psychology is international in many respects, including its history, its active presence in many countries – both developing and industrial – and its aspirations. The International Union of Psychological Science (IUPsyS) now includes organizations that represent 66 national communities of psychologists. The IUPsyS traces its history back to the first International Congress of Psychology, held in Paris in 1889, just ten years after Wilhelm Wundt established the first formal laboratory of psychology (Rosenzweig, Holtzman, Sabourin, & Bélanger, 2000). But the history of psychology in a more general sense goes back to antiquity, as we will review briefly.

Although psychology is present around the world, it differs in its development and its emphases among the regions of the world. These characteristics of psychology have been determined in part by the cultural backgrounds of different regions and in part by their political and economic histories. In the recent past psychology was even banned under some political circumstances, and has had to struggle to make a comeback. The current levels of development of psychology in different countries correlate with national economic status and human development, as we will see in this chapter.

International psychological organizations promote the development of psychology through their meetings and publications, and foster cross-national understanding and goodwill by organizing international cooperation and exchange of scholars.

30.1 ANCIENT ROOTS OF PSYCHOLOGY

The earliest attempts to explain natural events date back to a time when our ancestors struggled for survival amidst powerful natural forces. Our early primitive predecessors who lived on earth hundreds of thousands of years ago were subordinated by natural forces and dependent on the mercy of nature for their subsistence. Abundance or disaster depended upon environmental conditions such as storm, blizzard, drought, flood, and other natural incidents. Some explanations had to be given as to how nature acted to cause its effects upon human beings. This forced primitive people to project human attributes onto nature, thinking that all natural phenomena are alive and possess some kind of animated forces. Looking at all of nature as though it were alive is called animism, and the projection of human traits onto nature is called anthropomorphism. There were also other early attempts to explain natural phenomena, however, most of the explanations were supernatural beliefs not much different from animism and anthropomorphism, such as work of magic, superstitious worship, and mystical assumptions. Animism and anthropomorphism existed all through history and still exist among some primitive societies in some secluded parts of the world. With the attempts to explain nature there were also attempts to explain one's own mind and behavior. Some primitive people believe that there is a spirit or soul dwelling inside the body that animates the body and leaves it at death. Because one stops breathing at death, some people believed that the soul is a form of vapor which escapes the body after death. At death one no longer casts shadow on the ground, so some believed that one's shadow is the soul, and avoided casting a shadow in a river while walking on its bank, fearing that crocodiles may swallow up the shadow. These may be seen as the earliest forms of psychological thinking.

However, the systematic study of nature and the human behavior occurred only two to three thousand years ago by ancient philosophers both in the West and in the East. Coincidentally, great thinkers in Greece, China, and India advanced theories about the human mind and behavior almost at the same time, around 300 B.C.E. to 500 B.C.E. during a time some have called the 'axial age' (Fairbank, 1992). The Greek philosophers Plato (437–347 B.C.E.) and Aristotle (384–321 B.C.E.), their contemporaries in China, Confucius (551–479 B.C.E.) and Mencius (372–289 B.C.E.), and the great Indian teacher the Buddha (*c.* 500 B.C.E.) were the most prestigious among these philosophers.

Greek Philosophers

The Greek philosophers were considered as the first scholars who offered natural instead of supernatural explanations for natural phenomena, and with them explanations of the mind. Most of the early Greek philosophers were materialists, primitive or sophisticated; they searched for the primary elements from which everything was made. Thales (624–546 B.C.E.) assumed the element was water, Democritus (460–370 B.C.E.) thought it was the atom, and Hippocrates (460–375 B.C.E.) and Empedocles (554–495 B.C.E.) advanced four primary elements: water, earth, fire, and air. Plato (437–347

B.C.E.) particularly elaborated on the essence of the human mind and thought that our experience was manifestation of pure ideas that existed in the abstract. Plato believed the soul is immortal and had a rational component. To Plato, all knowledge is innate and can be attained only through introspection, that is, through reminiscence of the experience the soul had before entering the body. Plato upheld a dualism that divided the human being into a body that was material, and a mind (soul) that contained pure knowledge.

Aristotle (384–322 B.C.E.), a student of Plato, was the first philosopher to treat extensively many topics that were later to become part of psychology. His book *De Anima* is considered to be the first book of psychology. Aristotle maintained that the soul was the source of life, all living things possess a soul. There were three kinds of souls: (1) the vegetative or nutritive soul, possessed by plants; (2) the sensitive soul, possessed by animals. Animals acquire information about the environment through the five senses: sight, hearing, taste, touch, and smell. Animals also respond to the environment; (3) the rational soul, possessed only by humans, which provides all of the functions of the other two souls, but in addition it has the capability of thinking. Through active reasoning the rational soul could accomplish the abstraction of principles from experience. For Aristotle, everything in nature has a purpose, that is they are teleologically determined. The cause of the purpose was a primary mover which set nature in motion.

The views of Plato and Aristotle concerning the sources of knowledge set the stage for epistemological inquiry that has lasted until the present time. The Platonian philosophy can be seen as the forerunner of British empiricism. The Aristotelian theory of the immortality of the soul was succeeded by the scholastic philosophers. However, the Greek notion of psyche or soul is strikingly different from the modern notion of the mind. For the Greeks, all living things, including plants and the lower animals have a soul. The Greeks were concerned with the distinction between what is alive and what is not alive, while the primary concern of contemporary psychologists is the distinction between what possesses mind and what does not, such that material objects and plants do not have a mind, hence there is no psychology of inanimate objects.

Chinese Confucian Ideology

Psychological thought in ancient China appeared in diverse philosophical, educational, political, and other writings. A distinctive feature of ancient Chinese philosophy relating to psychology was the discussion of human nature and of how human beings are being shaped by education. The great Chinese thinker Confucius and his successor Mencius had profound influence on the development of China's cultural history. Confucius himself did not leave us with very many writings. After he died, his disciples collected his teachings and sayings and compiled them in a book known as *The Analects*. Confucian ideology is not a religion but ethical principles to guide the proper behavior of individuals in society. Even to this day the behaviors of Chinese in Asian societies conform, to a greater or lesser degree, to this ideology.

Confucius said 'human nature is similar, habits are far apart'. He stressed the basic equality of human beings at birth, and considered individual differences to be the result of training and environmental influence, and not due to inborn, inherent qualities. Confucius believed that all people were subject to molding and self-improvement, and education plays an important role in molding one's behavior. All people were, in principle, capable of achieving the same level through learning and self-cultivation. In his view, human social interaction is guided by a value system called *Li* (convention or propriety). Sages and rulers who have mastered *Li* are the models of behavior from which people learn. Confucian ethics stressed the hierarchical authority of the ruler who holds absolute power over his subjects, just as the father is the authority in the family. In the moral system, when people have acquired *Ren* (benevolence), the highest level of moral development is reached. With *Dao* (the way), the harmony between the natural and social aspects of human nature is achieved. Confucius taught people to achieve the ideal states of ethical and moral standards to live in a harmonious society.

Mencius claimed that humans were born with a good nature, they become good if developed in a proper way, but by following bad examples they may become bad. Mencius' mother moved house several times simply to have a good neighbor for her son to follow. Xun Zi (298–238 B.C.E.) proposed that human nature is malevolent and should not be allowed to run its own course, rather human behavior needs to be corrected to the right course. Human nature, specifically the relation between nature and nurture, has always been a topic for discussion in Chinese philosophy. These discussions on human nature centered on the role of education in molding personality. Confucian rationalism, as well as later Neo-Confucianism, was the official Chinese

philosophy for more than 2,000 years. The thinking of these Chinese philosophers exemplifies the historical roots of modern Chinese educational methods, particularly having laid the ground for Chinese educational psychology.

Indian Buddhism

The Indian ideas of the mind have been elaborated in a conceptual context derived from purely religious concerns. As far back as 1500 B.C.E. there was psychological thinking in ancient Indian philosophy and religious writings. In the *Bhagavad Gita* (*c.* 1500 B.C.E.), a treatise on the nature of human reason, the world of matter and individual consciousness are embodied in the same spiritual reality. In the religio-philosophical treatise *Upanishads* (*c.* 800 B.C.E.) the nature of self-consciousness was discussed. Particularly, the religious teachings of Buddhism (*c.* 500 B.C.E.) exerted great influence on Eastern ethical and moral values. It should be noted that the Buddhist religious practices are the roots of some modern medicinal and therapeutic ideas.

Buddhism, originated in India and later spreading to China and Japan, presented systematic elaboration on the nature of the soul and its relation to the material world. The word Buddha is a general term meaning one who is enlightened or awakened. It applied to the founder of Buddhism known as Sakyamuni, a prince of a small kingdom spanning northern India and Nepal. Sakyamuni's personal name was Siddhartha (*c.* 560–*c.* 480 B.C.E.). Siddhartha outlined his doctrine of the Four Noble Truths. The first Noble Truth is suffering (duhkha), that human existence is painful, that all beings, humans and animals, are caught up in *Samsara*, a cycle of rebirth, that each living thing lives through a series of lives, which can occur in various forms both in this world and the future world. The second Noble Truth is that suffering itself has a cause. *Karma*, meaning action or moral retribution, is the moral quality of actions performed in past lives that determines the happiness or suffering experienced thereafter. The third Noble Truth is that this chain of suffering can cease. The Buddhists called this end of suffering *Nirvana* and conceived of it as a cessation of rebirth, an escape from *Samsara*. The fourth Noble Truth is that this cessation of rebirth can be brought about by ethical and disciplinary practices. There are eight kinds of forbidden behaviors from which one must abstain to escape rebirth, namely, killing, stealing, adultery and lust, exaggeration in speech, drinking, retiring on luxurious bedding, fancy dressing and enjoying song and dance, and eating inappropriate food. These disciplinary practices, combined with training in concentration and meditation, lead to an ultimate state called *Moksa*, meaning spiritual release or liberation, a state which is transformed into enlightened wisdom (Kitagawa & Strong, 1984).

The later Yoga practice (*c.* 300 C.E.), as was emphasized by certain Buddhist systems, refers to a method self-cultivation of gaining release from the bondage of *Karma* and rebirth. Yoga teaches practices of breath and posture control designed to allow one to concentrate without having the mind distracted by extraneous things. By progressively concentrating on more abstract ideas, the yogi achieves higher and higher meditative states, culminating in a trance state that constitutes liberation. At more advanced stages of this practice, the Yogis are said to be endowed with extrasensory powers. Zen Buddhism is a sectarian movement of the Buddhist religion originated in China, which flourished during the seventh century and spread to India and Japan; it stresses the practice of meditation as the means to enlightenment. *Emphasizeda* is the practice of contemplative sitting for meditation. Monks of this sect sit quietly in a cross-legged position for days and months and suspend all actions and thoughts to achieve enlightenment. It is Zen Buddhism which had great impact on modern psychotherapy practices. Many Eastern psychotherapy practices have their roots in Zen Buddhism and Yoga practices; the Chinese Qi Gong and the Japanese Morita therapy are such examples. In more recent times, one also sees the spread of Zen practices to the West.

30.2 THE FOUNDING OF MODERN PSYCHOLOGY

Wundt at Leipzig and the Spread of Psychology Around the World

In 1879, Wilhelm Wundt in Germany founded the first psychological laboratory in the world. Wundt established the Psychologisches Institut in Leipzig with a few rooms and some equipment for psychological demonstrations. Even earlier, in 1875, William James also had a room set up for psychological experimentation at Harvard University. Nevertheless, it is generally acknowledged that Wundt was the founder of modern experimental psychology, and Leipzig was called the 'Mecca of the new science'

(Jaroschewski, 1975). This was justified on the ground that not only did Wundt start psychological experimentation himself, but he also trained the men who were to become important names in the subsequent history of psychology around the world. These included Emil Kraepelin, Oswald Külpe, Ernst Meumann, and Hugo Münsterberg, who were members of the first generation of German psychologists. The Americans included Stanley Hall, James McKeen Cattell, George Ladd, Frank Angell, and the Englishman E. B. Titchener, who became leaders of the first generation of American psychology. Others who studied with Wundt in Leipzig were the Russians Georgy I. Chelpanov and Nikolay N. Lange, who became the founders of Russian psychology; Dimitry N. Uznadze from Georgia; Friedrich Kiesow from Italy; Ernst Durr from Switzerland; Matataro Matsumoto from Japan (Lück, Miller, & Rechtien, 1984); Alfred Lehman from Denmark, who established the first psychological laboratories in 1886 in Copenhagen (Koppe, 1987); and the famous scholar Cai Yuanpei from China. Psychological laboratories, patterned upon Leipzig, and founded by men trained at Leipzig, were beginning to be established in Germany, America, Japan, China, India, and many other countries around the world in the late nineteenth century and the early twentieth century.

Vladimir M. Bekhterev set up the first Russian psychological laboratory in Kazan in 1885. In 1912, the first Russian Psychological Institute was opened in Moscow. Georgy I. Chelpanov, professor of Imperial Moscow University, was its first director. This Institute later became the Psychological Institute of the Russian Academy of Education. Prominent Russian psychologists Lev S. Vygotsky, Alexander R. Luria, and Alexey N. Leontiev all worked in this Institute (Brushlinskii, 1995).

Prominent men from Asian countries, who either studied directly under Wundt or under the influence of the Wundtian tradition, founded experimental psychology in their home countries. Amane Nishi (1829–1897), after returning from Europe, coined the Japanese term 'shinri-gaku' for psychology that is now well established in Japan. Yujiro Motora (1859–1912), the first fully accredited psychologist in Japan, assumed the lectureship in psychology at University of Tokyo. He established the first psychology laboratory in Japan in 1900. Motora, who first studied in Germany, earned his Ph.D. degree at Johns Hopkins in 1885 under Stanley Hall. Matataro Matsumoto (1865–1943), a student of Wundt, became the first chair of the Department of Psychology of University of

Tokyo in 1918 (Azuma & Imada, 1994; Kaneko, 1987). Notably, the Chinese student in Leipzig, Cai Yuanpai, later became the President of Peking University, and with his support Chen Daqi established China's first psychological laboratory in 1917 (X. H. Yang, 1998). Another Chinese psychologist, Zhang Yaoxiang who founded the Chinese Psychological Society in 1921, was a student at Columbia in 1916 just before the retirement of James McKeen Cattell. In India, the first psychological laboratory was established in Calcutta University in 1915 by N. N. Sengupta, a student under Münsterberg at Harvard University (Sinha, 1987).

British and French Psychology

From the 1880s to the early twentieth century, as Germany and the United States led the way in the new psychology, Britain and France followed, but more slowly in a rather different path. At the turn of the century, British philosophical psychology still resisted the experimental approach. Instead, the evolutionary theories proposed by Charles Darwin and others just before Wundt established his experimental psychology had a direct and lasting influence on British psychology. Under the influence of evolutionary theory, Darwin's cousin Francis Galton's statistical study on individual differences, further developed by Karl Pearson, led to the technique of coefficient of correlation, which has become one of the most important statistical tools in all fields of science. Only in 1897, 18 years after the founding of Wundt's laboratory, did James Sully in University College in London and W. H. Rivers in Cambridge establish the first psychological laboratories in the United Kingdom. In 1906, Charles Spearman pursued the measurement of intelligence in the London laboratory where he later developed factor analysis. Oxford had no psychological laboratory until 1936. Instead of following the Wundtian tradition, Great Britain's early experimental psychology developed along the line of psychometrics (Boring, 1957).

In France, early psychology ran the course of clinical psychology. The French physician Jean Charcot, famous for the study of hypnotism and hysteria, and later Theodule Ribot and Pierre Janet advocated a psychology centered on treatment of mental diseases. The first chair of experimental and comparative psychology was created for Ribot in 1887 at College de France. In 1889 the French government set up the first psychological laboratory under Henri Beaunis who was succeeded by Alfred Binet. In 1901, Janet organized the French Psychological Society (Trognon, 1987).

Psychological Associations

From the above simple overview of the early days of psychology as a modern science, it can be seen that the nations whose scholars were under direct influence of German and American psychology were early to establish psychological laboratories or offer courses in psychology in universities. This is also true for the establishment of national psychological organizations. It is no wonder that the earliest psychological associations were established on the European continent and North America. National organizations were formed in some of the leading industrialized nations before World War I. The

Table 30.1 *Years when certain national psychological associations were founded*

Year	Countries
1892	United States
1901	France, United Kingdom
1904	Germany
1908	Argentina
1910	Italy
1921	China
1925	India
1926	Japan
1928	Hungary
1934	Norway
1939	Canada
1943	Switzerland
1945	Australia, Brazil
1946	Netherlands, Korea
1947	Belgium, Denmark
1948	Poland, Egypt
1949	South Africa
1950	Yugoslavia
1951	Mexico
1952	Finland, Spain
1953	Austria, Uruguay
1954	Iceland, Peru
1955	Sweden, Colombia
1956	Turkey
1957	Soviet Union, Venezuela
1958	Czechoslovakia, Israel
1960	Indonesia
1962	Philippines
1963	Greece
1968	Hong Kong (China), Iran, Pakistan
1969	Bulgaria
1971	Zimbabwe
1975	Dominican Republic, Paraguay
1979	Ireland, Singapore
1981	Nicaragua

American Psychological Association, founded in 1892, was the first psychological association in the world. Other countries which had psychologists who studied in Europe or America were also early to establish psychological associations. Notably, China, Japan, and India had psychologists who studied in Germany or America, and on returning to their home countries established their psychological societies quite early in the twentieth century. By the end of the 1950s, most industrialized countries had a national psychological association, whereas in Latin America, Africa, and most third world countries, psychology mainly developed after World War II (Pawlik, 1985; Sinha 1987). Table 30.1 shows that in the 102 years between 1879 when Wundt founded the first psychological laboratory and 1981, only 13 national associations were established before the end of World War II, while most of the national associations were established later (Rosenzweig, 1992b, p. 50).

30.3 DETERMINANTS IN THE DEVELOPMENT OF PSYCHOLOGY

Psychology and National Development

The development of science is dependent upon the economic development of a country. This is especially true in the fields of natural science where enormous financial support is needed for basic and applied research. Generally, the support for psychology is only secondary on the national agenda compared with the pure sciences and engineering, thus making psychology all the more dependent upon the society's economic growth, for only after the basic survival needs of the people have been met can there be investment for the advances in the field of psychology. When a country's economy is underdeveloped, the attention is usually directed toward more important problems of developing industry, commerce, and agriculture in order to improve basic living conditions. The development of psychology in some third world countries, such as China and India, although started early, remained stagnant when compared with other industrialized countries. Fu and Jing (1994) have noted that the ratio of psychologists to the general population is significantly higher in developed countries than in developing countries. This demonstrates that with the improvement of a country's economy, as it becomes capable to invest more in basic research in psychology, the society at the same time develops a clear need for application of psychology.

The Gross National Product/capita (GNP/capita) reflects a country's economic development, and we can assume that the number of psychologists in a country reflects the development of psychology of that country. A strong correlation should exist between the GNP/capita of a country and the number of psychologists in that country. Another strong indicator of national development is the human development level of a country. The United Nations Development Programme (UNDP) rates countries annually on a Human Development Index (HDI), which takes into account the factors of (a) life expectancy at birth, (b) adult literacy and rate of school enrolment, and (c) adjusted gross domestic product per capita. Of 174 countries rated in the Human Development Report of UNDP, 43 countries rated high on the HDI, and 36 (84%) of those have membership in the IUPsyS, 37 countries rated low on the HDI and only one (3%) has membership in IUPsyS. Thus, high human development level guarantees a sufficient psychological community to justify membership in IUPsyS. As of 1999 the International Union of Psychological Science (IUPsyS) had 66 national members. The membership in a national society may not reflect the total number of psychologists in a country; in some countries the discrepancy is quite great, for example in Argentina where the membership in the national psychological society is only 100, but the actual number of psychologists is about 37,000. Similarly, in France there are only 1,100 members in the French Psychological Society, whereas the total number of psychologists is about 30,000. Usually the total number of psychologists in a country is much greater than the psychologists enrolled in its national association. From data available, Table 30.2 shows the GNP/capita, HDI, total number of psychologists, membership in its national society, population, and the number of psychologists per million population of 32 countries. Statistics showed that the correlation between GNP/capita and number of psychologists/million population was .44, whereas the correlation between HDI and number of psychologists/million population was .51. Thus, it seems that both GNP/capita and HDI are comprehensive indicators of national development and good predictors of the relative number of psychologists (psychologists/million population) and the level of development of psychology in a country. Furthermore, both correlations would undoubtedly have been higher if more developing countries had provided information to the survey, thus increasing the range of the data.

Table 30.3 shows the 10 countries with the highest number of psychologists per million population; all have high GNP/capita and high

Table 30.2　*Relationship between national development and psychology in 32 countries*

Country	GNP/capita US$ (1994)[1]	HDI (1998)[2]	Total number psychologists (1998)[3]	Membership in national society (1998)[4]	Population (million) (1995)[5]	Psychologists/ million population
Argentina	8100	0.888	37000	100	34.6	1069.4
Australia	18000	0.932	12000	12500	18.1	663.0
Austria	24630	0.933	4000	1500	8.0	500.0
Belgium	22870	0.933	3987	500	10.1	394.8
Bulgaria	1250	0.789	4500	500	8.8	511.4
Canada	19510	0.960	16000	4300	29.5	542.4
China	530	0.650	3500	3500	1221.5	2.9
Colombia	1670	0.850	12000	900	35.1	341.9
Croatia	2560	0.759	1200	–	4.5	266.7
Czechoslovakia	3200	0.884	1060	1000	10.3	102.9
Estonia	2820	0.758	600	58	1.5	400.0
Finland	18850	0.942	4300	1500	5.1	843.1
France	23420	0.946	30000	1100	58.0	517.2
Georgia	580	0.633	780	–	5.5	141.8
Germany	25580	0.925	45000	22000	81.6	551.5
Greece	7700	0.924	1600	260	10.5	152.4
Israel	13530	0.930	1039	850	3.6	288.6
Italy	19300	0.922	30000	2600	57.2	524.5
Japan	34630	0.940	12000	5800	125.1	95.9
Korea	8260	0.894	1100	1200	45.0	24.4
Mexico	4180	0.855	11500	1025	93.7	122.7
Netherlands	22010	0.941	20000	8000	15.5	1290.3
New Zealand	13350	0.939	1700	700	3.6	472.2
Norway	26390	0.943	3200	3526	4.3	744.2
Portugal	9320	0.892	8000	252	9.8	816.3
Romania	1270	0.767	2000	500	22.8	87.7
Singapore	22500	0.896	1700	120	2.8	607.1
Slovenia	7040	0.887	1300	420	1.9	684.2
Spain	13440	0.935	30000	500	39.6	757.6
Uganda	190	0.340	100	100	21.3	4.7
USA	25880	0.943	174900	114000	263.3	664.3
Venezuela	2760	0.860	6145	3938	21.8	281.9

[1] UNICEF Report, 1997.
[2] Human Development Report, 1998.
[3] IUPsyS Survey, 1998.
[4] IUPsyS Report, 1998.
[5] China Statistical Yearbook, 1996.

HDI. Switzerland and Japan, the two countries having the highest GNP/capita, $37,930 and $34,630, have only 55.6 and 46.4 national society members per million population respectively, which suggests they have too few psychologists compared with their economic power. India and Pakistan have the fewest psychologists per million population; their GNP/capita are less than $500. When considering the number of psychologists in a country, it should be noted that the amount of training of a psychologist differs greatly among countries. In the US most psychologists have a Ph.D. degree, while in

other countries a psychologist may only have a M.S. or M.A. degree.

Rosenzweig (1982) showed that from 1970 to 1980 the 36 IUPsyS member countries' membership increased from 53,219 to 101,521; the increase is almost all in industrial countries. In our analysis of 32 countries, 26 are developed countries, only six are developing countries in Asia and Latin America. The average number of psychologists per million population is 512.7 for developed countries, compared with 129.8 psychologists per million population for developing countries.

Table 30.3 *Countries with highest number of psychologists per million population*

Country	Psychologists/ million population	GNP/capita (US$)	HDI
Netherlands	1290.3	22010	0.941
Argentina	1069.4	8110	0.888
Finland	843.1	18850	0.942
Portugal	816.3	9320	0.892
Spain	757.6	13440	0.935
Norway	744.2	13350	0.939
Slovenia	684.2	7040	0.887
USA	664.3	25880	0.943
Australia	663.0	18000	0.932
Singapore	607.1	22500	0.896

Political–Cultural Influences

Another approach to the determinants of the development of psychology follows along the line of thought of the sociologist Max Weber (1930) in which cultural legitimization of individualism is seen as playing a major role in the development of modern society. In a study by Frank, Meyer, and Miyahara (1995) it is argued that the prominent feature of modern social thought and cultural ideology is the promotion of individualism, encouraging individuals to be autonomous and uncontrolled, and the legitimization of society in which the individual is seen as a central constitutive element. Because of the association between political–cultural modernization and the professionalized concern with the individual, variations in the institutionalization of individualism affect variations in the prominence of psychology. A proof of this is that the greatest expansion of psychology occurred only after the development of the modern individualist nation-state.

Several causal mechanisms may relate political–cultural individualism to the prevalence of psychology. (1) Leaders at the state level in individualist societies responsible for promoting economic growth and political development are likely to support scientific analyses of the individual; psychological analyses are called for in evaluating individual qualities or incentives to improve national competitiveness. (2) Managers in business and industry in individualist societies are more likely to contemplate psychologically-based improvements in motivation, skill training or worker development. In medicine, elites become concerned with psychological factors affecting health choices. (3) Individuals in such societies tend to view their own mental structures or psychological problems with the help of behavioral analyses for explanation. A multiple-indicator

model was constructed to test cross-nationally among 89 countries the relationship between levels of national political–cultural individualism and the prevalence of psychology. The effect of individualism on the prevalence of psychology turns out to be very large, that political–cultural systems emphasizing the individual tend to sustain professionalized and scientific psychology. However, many Far Eastern countries are dominated by collectivist Confucian culture; it is doubtful if the individualist polity approach applies to the development of psychology in these countries. Perhaps the level of national development is a better predictor for the development of psychology in a country.

Psychology in the Former Soviet Union

A better example of the strong political–cultural influence on psychology is the psychology in the former Soviet Union. As psychology was developing in Europe, America, and other countries around the world in patterns of the Wundtian tradition or under the influence of European philosophical thinking, the Russian Revolution in 1917 shaped another course of development of psychology which not only dominated all the republics in the Soviet Union, but after World War II took over all eastern European countries, as well as Cuba, Vietnam, and mainland China. These socialist countries tried to build a Marxist psychology. Karl Marx (1818–1883) in his monumental book *Das Kapital* (Marx, 1953) maintained that material production is the driving force for social development, and production relations among people are important in the process of social development. Production relations implied that all people are involved in the process of class struggle which brings about revolution to promote social progress. Marxism stressed 'social existence determines social consciousness', that is, the mind of a human being is determined by the position one occupies in his social environment. Besides Marxist theory, the ideology of the founder of the Russian Communist party Vladimir I. Lenin (1870–1924) was also taken as a guiding principle for Soviet psychology. Lenin's theory of knowledge promulgated in the book *Materialism and Empirio-Criticism* (Lenin, 1951) stated that consciousness is the function of the brain, it is a reflection of the objective world. This was called the theory of reflection in Soviet psychology.

After the Russian revolution, Vladimir M. Bekhterev was the first to give support to the new Soviet government and tried to establish a materialistic psychology. In 1918 he established the Institute of Brain Research in St. Petersburg and brought forth the concepts 'objective psychology' and 'reflexology'. Konstantin N. Kornilov in 1921 and Petrovich Blonsky in 1923 first introduced dialectical materialism into psychology. Later, Sergei L. Rubenstein, Alexey N. Leontiev, Boris Teplov, Boris Lomov, and others also tried to establish a Marxist psychology. The Marxist foundations of psychology involved the principles of determinism, reflective nature of the mind, integration of consciousness and activity, unity of the subjective and objective, and social historical development of the mind (Lomov, 1972). During this period some important contributions were made in the fields of educational psychology and psychoneurology, such as the cultural-historical theory of Lev Vygotsky and the neurological studies of Alexander Luria.

During the course of the development of Soviet psychology, there were campaigns organized by the Soviet authority to criticize the so-called bourgeois idealistic ideologies. As noted above, the political purges and liquidation launched in the 1920s and 1930s during Stalin's rule affected science in general, and the biological and behavioral sciences in particular. Lenin criticized the Taylor system practiced in industry, and psychotechnology was banned. A resolution, 'On pedological distortions in the system of the People's Commissariat for Education' was passed in 1936 in which pedology, a combination of pedagogy and child psychology, was denounced. One of the pretexts was the use of tests to assess children's intelligence, for psychological tests are said to be tools for discrimination against children of the working class. Social psychology was abandoned by calling it a pseudoscience to replace historical materialism. As the persecution continued, many were arrested, imprisoned, and exiled. Stalinist dogmatism inhibited the development of psychology and led to fruitless discussions centered around the interpretation of quotations from the classics of Marx and Lenin. Only as late as 1942 did Rubenstein organize a department of psychology in Moscow University. In 1945, he set up the first psychological laboratory in the Institute of Philosophy in the Soviet Academy of Sciences, the forerunner of the current Institute of Psychology of the Russian Academy of Sciences founded in 1971. In 1981, Rubenstein, although claiming to be a Marxist psychologist, was attacked for departing from official ideology and released from office (Brushlinskii, 1995; Lomov, 1987).

Another major event was the joint conference of the Soviet Academy of Sciences and Soviet Academy of Medical Sciences held in 1950. A resolution was passed to reform psychology on the basis of the theory of Ivan P. Pavlov. Meanwhile, in China immediately after the founding of the People's Republic in 1949, psychology was also to be reformed under the guidance of dialectical materialism and on the basis of the theory of Pavlov. In the Soviet Union this set the direction of recognizing psychological functions as the product of higher nervous activity. Pavlov's theory of the two signal systems laid the ground for the study of language. The first signal system is the conditioned response to sensory stimuli, the second signal system involves an abstraction process resulting in symbolic language activity. When the cognitive revolution first occurred in the United States in the 1950s Soviet philosophers and psychologists were not slow in reacting against it by labeling computer simulation of cognitive processes as vulgar materialism, and commented on the impossibility of artificial intelligence (Simon, 1991). On the contrary, Simon and Jing (1988) tried to show that dialectical materialism could be compatible with cognitive psychology.

Marxist psychology denotes special mention because after World War II it was the state policy for almost all communist countries. Some countries, such as the Soviet Union, Cuba, Czechoslovak, and China, more strictly held to this doctrine, while other countries, such as Poland and Yugoslavia, were more liberal. After Stalin's death in 1953, the liberalization and reform movements that followed made behavioral sciences more free to accept new ideas, and psychology took a new turn in rehabilitating some previously abandoned disciplines and introduced new branches of psychology (Brozek & Rahmani, 1976). In 1991, after the dissolution of the Soviet Union, Marxist–Leninist psychology no longer holds an authoritative position in the eastern European countries, although it is still held in China and some other countries around the world in various forms.

30.4 Cross-Cultural Psychology

Cross-cultural psychology is the study of culture's effects on human behavior. More specifically, it is the empirical study of members of various culture groups with identifiable experiences which lead to predictable and significant similarities and differences in behavior (Brislin, 1987). Defined more broadly, it comprises many ways of studying culture as an important context for human psychological development and behavior (Segall, Lonner, & Berry, 1998). Cross-cultural psychology consists mostly of diverse forms of comparative research in order to discern the influence of various cultural factors on human development and behavior. As we have noted before, modern scientific psychology was first developed in the West and became the main force of psychology, hence called mainstream psychology. It is argued that this psychology was mainly a Euro-American product of a specific social milieu that characterizes advanced industrial societies. In other parts of the world the Western influence was overwhelming, teaching was based on Western textbooks, new researches were largely imitative, and replications of Western studies and research results were accepted for granted. What goes in the name of psychology today mainly reflects the theories and ideas of the United States. However, the study of human behavior must include observations made all around the world, not just in a few highly industrialized nations. Many scholars have questioned the external validity and generalizability of the principles of mainstream psychology transplanted to a different sociocultural soil. It was found that many descriptions of mental functioning emerging out of American laboratory research do not hold very well for subjects in other cultures. One good example is the use of so-called standardized tests developed in Western industrialized countries, which are usually normed on middle-class children in the United States. Considering the social context in which test scores are to be used, these tests cannot be fair when applied to children from quite different cultures. It would be difficult to make inferences about children's underlying competencies and their native ability as compared with some other cultural groups. Furthermore, apart from being monocultural and ethnocentric, mainstream psychology almost completely disregards research done in other countries and particularly in foreign languages.

Cross-cultural psychology studies the culture-specific factors in understanding and explaining human behavior and in accordance with the concepts derived from those cultures. Special attention has been focused on perspectives that are non-Western and not rooted in the Judeo-Christian tradition that provide the basis for modern psychology (Sinha, 1981; Sinha & Kao, 1997). Following the linguist Pike (1967), many cross-cultural psychologists used the terms *etic* and *emic* to describe the relation between culture-specific and culture-universal approaches in psychology. Emics and etics refer to the two goals of cross-cultural research. The emic approach is to describe behavior in terms that are meaningful to members of a particular culture, with attention to what the people themselves value as important as well as what is familiar to them. Insight into a culture cannot be gained by using foreign tools; the tools must be indigenous. The

etic approach is to compare behavior in that culture with behavior in another or all cultures, to document valid principles for all cultures and to establish theoretical frameworks useful in comparing human behavior in various cultures (Berry, 1984). Westerners studying another culture yet not knowing much of that culture are instances of what has been termed an 'imposed etic' or 'Euro-American emics' (Berry, 1978). The best approach to cross-cultural research is a collaboration of both the members of the home country who can obtain the data and decode them from an 'insiders' view, and the 'outsiders' who can observe and interpret data from the position of an outsider 'looking in' (Adler, 1982). For cross-cultural research to be meaningful, the first essential step is to carry out many emic studies from within the culture, and then supplement this with a comparative framework.

In the last quarter of the twentieth century some psychologists in Asia began trying to establish indigenous psychology. Because of the questionable applicability of Euro-American psychological theories to the third world countries, a revolt is underway to build an indigenous psychology in the study of a society's own problems by native psychologists who are familiar with the cultural environment and using methods suitable to the solution of these problems. In Taiwan China, Yang Kuo Shu (1993) led the way in this movement. He proposed a Sinolized psychology or indigenous psychology of the Chinese people that included psychologists from mainland, Taiwan, and Hong Kong China to study the specific behaviors of Chinese people in these societies. Chinese are different from Westerners in that they have different cultural historical backgrounds. Chinese living in different parts of China have the same cultural roots, although under different influences. In Taiwan China the American influence is predominant, Hong Kong was a British colony, and the mainland preserves the Chinese tradition under a socialist political system. Psychology is to study the ethno-national behavioral patterns of the Chinese people, such as moral judgment, the value of the 'face', social behavior, ways of interaction, etc. The movement attracted supporters in Hong Kong (C. F. Yang, 1993). Alternatively, in mainland China, Pan Shu (1987) proposed the construction of psychology with Chinese characteristics, that psychology should be guided by Marxism and dialectical materialism to solve problems relevant to Chinese society, and should not be merely the following of Western models. There are also calls for indigenization of psychology from other countries (Azuma & Imada, 1994; Diaz-Guerrero, 1977, 1994). As Sinha puts it 'the process of indigenization can be viewed as a "battle for consciousness", a challenge to Western intellectual domination, and a search to restore the true identity of people' (Sinha, 1994).

30.5 INTERNATIONAL DIMENSIONS OF PSYCHOLOGY

International Organization of Psychology: IUPsyS

Almost from the beginning of psychology as a modern science, international meetings of psychologists were organized to facilitate the exchange of ideas. Only ten years after the founding of the first psychological laboratory in Leipzig in 1879, the first International Congress of Psychology was held in Paris in 1889. This was even earlier than the establishment of the American Psychological Association in 1902. The second international congress was held in London in 1892, and the third in Munich in 1896. Then it was held every three to four years in Europe or North America until the 11th Congress in Paris in 1937, when the series of congresses was interrupted by World War II. After World War II, at the 13th International Congress of Psychology which took place in Stockholm in 1951, the International Union of Psychological Science (IUPsyS) was formed with 11 national organizations as charter members. The Union took over the responsibility of sponsoring International Congresses of Psychology at regular intervals (now every four years). The 27th Congress in Stockholm in 2000 will be followed by the 28th Congress in Beijing, one of the few international congresses held outside of economically highly developed countries.

The IUPsyS joined the major international scientific body, the International Council of Science (ICSU) in 1981, and is a founding member of the International Social Science Council (ISSC). It has working relations with United Nations Educational, Scientific and Cultural Organization (UNESCO) and the World Health Organization (WHO). As an ICSU member, the IUPsyS and its activities have to observe the principle of the universality of science. The principle of free circulation of scientists stipulates that scientists from all over the world have the right to join and take part in international academic activities without discrimination based on citizenship, religion, creed, political stance, race, ethnic origin, color, language, age, or sex.

As of 1999, the IUPsyS has 66 national members, which may be national associations, federations, or societies of scientific psychology (IUPsyS, 1998; Rosenzweig et al., 2000). Each country can have only one such organization admitted to IUPsyS. A number of organizations are also affiliated with the IUPsyS. The IUPsyS cooperates with affiliated organizations in various ways, such as the planning of congresses and conferences and collaborating in special projects. An affiliated organization must be regional or global in its coverage, have individuals rather than national organizations as members. The organizations affiliated with IUPsyS are:

1. International Association of Applied Psychology (IAAP)
2. Interamerican Society of Psychology (SIP)
3. Association de Psychologie Scientifique de Langue Francaise (APSLF)
4. International Council of Psychologists (ICP)
5. International Association for Cross-Cultural Psychology (IACCP)
6. European Association of Experimental Social Psychology
7. International Society of Comparative Psychology
8. International Society for the Study of Behavioral Development (ISSBD)
9. European Association of Personality Psychology
10. European Association of Psychological Assessment
11. International Neuropsychological Society.

These affiliates of IUPsyS cover many of the major international and regional organizations of psychological science in the world. They convene meetings every two to four years. Due to the rapid expansion and branching out of psychology in recent years, many other disciplinary, inter-disciplinary, and regional organizations in psychology are playing important roles in organizing scientific meetings and promoting exchanges. The European Federation of Professional Psychologists' Associations (EFPPA) was founded in 1981; it presently includes associations from 25 European countries. A major objective of EFPPA is to reduce differences between European countries in the standards of training and professional practice of psychologists. EFPPA in cooperation with IUPsyS organizes the biennial European Congress of Psychology. Other regional groups include the Afro-Asian Psychological Association, the Asia-Oceania Psychological Association and the Asian Association of Social Psychology. A Pan-Arab Psychology Association is in preparation.

Common Characteristics in the Development of Psychology

Although modern psychology of different countries and regions developed under different circumstances and originated at different times, there are shared characteristics in the development of psychology. First, each country's psychology is historically linked, sometimes deeply rooted, to indigenous philosophical, ethical, and cultural background (Pawlik & d'Ydewalle, 1996). This can be seen in Western psychology which has its roots in European or American philosophy, and some branches of natural science. The early pioneers of psychology were either philosopher or scientist (physicist and physiologist) turned psychologists, such as William James, Wilhelm Wundt, or Gustav Fechner. In Eastern countries modern psychology, although first introduced from the West, added in its development some aspects of the ideology of Buddhism or Confucianism, giving rise to indigenous psychology. In the foreseeable future, along with the globalization process and increase in international exchanges there will be more convergence in the structure and content of the study of behavior and consciousness, and more commonalities than differences may exist in international psychology. Second, psychology as a science of human behavior and consciousness transcends both natural science and social science. This two-sidedness of psychological science is a major, constituent characteristic of psychology as a science and as a profession. Thus, psychology has to share its object of study, 'behavior', within a wide family of sister disciplines, including sociology, ethology, ethnology or anthropology, linguistics, physiology, and brain sciences. Studying behavior and consciousness as a joint function of organismic and social factors defines psychology as a unique discipline of science attracting a wide range of interests from scientists of various disciplines. And there may be an increase in the study of the social aspects of human behavior as more pressing societal problems are becoming evident in modern society. There is good reason to believe that, in the time to come, the task force of psychologists in the world may be one of the greatest in number among all disciplines of science. Third, psychology first developed as a basic scientific approach, answering questions about consciousness and behavior mainly to satisfy the quest for knowledge and then gradually extended to applied fields. Now, psychology finds its potential of development both as a basic science and as an applied profession grown out of the demands of society. Psychology is both a science and a profession. Which

part of this developmental trend is stronger depends upon national investment in science and the effectiveness of psychology in solving health, industrial, and societal problems. Generally speaking, in the economically more developed countries there is a better investment for basic research in psychology.

A fact from history that should be noted is that the 'two-sided' nature of psychology as a science spanning across social and natural sciences makes it especially sensitive to social and political crises, making it more vulnerable to attack at times of political turmoil. When political turmoil and infringement of academic freedom occur in a country, it is the social sciences, and psychology in particular, that are affected first, such as the attack on sociology and psychology during the Stalin period in the 1930s, and in Germany in the 1930s when many eminent psychologists emigrated to America. During the Chinese Cultural Revolution in the 1960s, psychology was completely eradicated for almost a decade. As a discipline for explaining the cause of human behavior, which may run contrary to designated authoritative principles, the development of psychology is especially dependent on intellectual freedom in a country. For historians of psychology, research should be launched to find out under what circumstances these crises in psychology occurred, and what are their consequences for the development of psychology.

Promotion of Cross-National Understanding and Goodwill

Another core function of international psychology is promoting cross-national understanding and goodwill among people. International cooperation and exchange of persons and knowledge in psychology serve the interest of developing cross-national understanding and goodwill among people of different nationality, ethnic, or other backgrounds. Psychology has been opening up to and has become a partner in many such initiatives. The International Union of Psychological Science (IUPsyS) is the main body that promotes cooperation and exchange among psychologists across nations. The International Association of Applied Psychology (IAAP), the International Association of Cross-Cultural Psychology (IACCP), and the International Council of Psychologists (ICP) have been founded to serve this function of international psychology as well. IUPsyS, besides organizing international congresses of psychology in different parts of the world, in collaboration with other international or national psychological organizations also organizes Advanced

Research and Training Seminars (ARTS). This program promotes attendance at the international congresses and training of scholars from low-income countries. ARTS programs take place every two years in conjunction with the International Congress of Psychology and the International Congress of Applied Psychology. ARTS meetings are organized in the form of workshops with different themes at its meetings. These international congresses, regional conferences, and workshops of international nature greatly facilitate the cooperation and exchange of experience among different nations, especially giving more opportunity to young psychologists in the developing world to be able to participate in international exchanges.

30.6 THE FUTURE OF PSYCHOLOGICAL SCIENCE

Since Wilhelm Wundt established the first psychological laboratory in 1879, psychology has just celebrated its 120th birthday. From the early days of its inception psychology has developed a variety of schools. In the early part of the twentieth century psychologists witnessed the heydays of Gestalt psychology, Behaviorism, Psychoanalysis, and humanistic psychology. Behaviorism gained the upper hand for a while in the United States by claiming the goal of psychology to be the prediction and control of behavior. Soon Behaviorism encountered a crisis in the limited plausibility of explaining complex human behavior on the basis of simple elementary stimulus–response units obtained from laboratory animal experiments. Gestalt psychology and Psychoanalysis still have followers but only in certain areas of research and application.

Psychology has grown into a discipline so rich and varied in its approaches that it is difficult to describe the field in simple language. Researchers are more prone to be eclectic in their approaches to existing problems than strongly adhering to any one theory or system. With the onset of the cognitive revolution, big strides were made in disclosing the information-processing functions of the mind. With the advancement of computer science and information technology, new tools such as functional magnetic resonance imaging (fMRI) and positron emission tomography (PET) became available for brain research, giving new hope to discover the relation between brain functions and behavior, which may shed light on the underlying mechanisms of behavior and consciousness. A new age in psychology in the third millennium may grow out of the collaboration

between cognitive psychology and neuroscience. And in the applied arena psychology is gaining an ever larger field to contribute to the welfare of society.

Modern psychology may be seen as divided into two camps; one camp sees man as a functioning organism; the other camp sees man as an active social person. These camps are not in opposition, rather they seek to complement each other. To the first camp belong the biological psychologists or neuropsychologists; its adherents are integrated in the study of biological functions, make use of animals as well as humans as ways to explore human psychology, and take control experimentation as the generally accepted method. They have reached a consensus as to their methodology and a standard to assess research results. If this part of psychology is to be separated from the all-embracing extended psychology, and to declare independence, then, to use Thomas S. Kuhn's term (Kuhn, 1962), it may be said that the biological psychologists are developing their part of psychology into a paradigmatic science. (See Chapter 4.)

But psychology is by nature a far more complex science. There is hardly any social behavior independent of particular socio-cultural systems. Hence a second camp of psychologists should exist to complement the first; it consists of humane psychologists, including social, clinical, counseling psychologists, and a host of others that concern with the social nature of man. It looks more at the purposive behavior of the person and tries to develop its potentialities. It adopts survey, observation, social experiment, and whatever other tools are available as methodology. This is a loosely organized group, diverse in views, and adopts a wide range of theories. This group of psychologists contributes more to the practical needs of society than the biological psychologists. (See Chapter 3.)

Now, at the start of the twenty-first century, adherents of cross-cultural psychology and indigenous psychology challenge the validity of mainstream psychology. Psychology faces not only disciplinary diversification, but also geographical and cultural diversification. Indeed, a true science of psychology must take into account observations made in various parts of the world. One must admit that cross-cultural studies are central to the development of psychology. The question is: are the behavioral differences of different cultural groups really so big as to entail a completely new science of psychology? In the process of globalization and rapid information exchanges in the new century, people are linked closer in space and time, and no part can be independent from other parts of the world. Along with the economic development of third world countries, more psychological contributions will be added to world psychology and be freed from Euro-American limitations. Psychologists from various parts of the world can develop their own theories and make significant contributions. Cross-cultural studies may, eventually, join forces with mainstream psychology and both offer more powerful universal theories. 'Cross-cultural psychology will be shown to have succeeded when it disappears. For, when the whole field of psychology becomes truly international and genuinely intercultural – in other words, when it becomes truly a science of human behavior – cross-cultural psychology will have achieved its aims and become redundant' (Segall et al., 1998). Among all the complexities in the development of the science of psychology, the diversification of the discipline reflects a rich and varied psychology that is helping to understand many aspects of human behavior and consciousness.

RESOURCE REFERENCES

Gao, J. F. (Ed.). (1985). *History of Chinese psychology*. Beijing: People's Educational Publishers. (In Chinese).

Gilgen, A. R., & Gilgen, C. K. (Eds.). (1987). *International handbook of psychology*. New York: Greenwood Press.

Kao, H. S. R., & Sinha, D. (Eds.). (1997). *Asian perspectives on psychology*. New Delhi: Sage Publications.

Rosenzweig, M. R. (Ed.). (1992a). *International psychological science: Progress, problems, and prospects*. Washington, DC: American Psychological Association.

Sexton, V. S., & Misiak, H. (Eds.). (1976). *Psychology around the world*. Monterey, CA: Brooks/Cole.

ADDITIONAL LITERATURE CITED

Adler, L. L. (Ed.). (1982). *Cross-cultural research at issue*. New York: Academic Press.

Azuma, H., & Imada, H. (1994). Origins and development of psychology in Japan: The interaction between Western science and the Japanese cultural heritage. *International Journal of Psychology, 29,* 707–715.

Berry, J. W. (1978). Social psychology: Comparative, societal and universal. *Canadian Psychological Review, 19*(2), 93–104.

Berry, J. W. (1984). Toward a universal psychology of cognitive competence. *International Journal of Psychology, 6,* 193–197.

Boring, E. G. (1957). *A history of experimental psychology* (2nd ed.). New York: Appleton-Century Crofts.

Brislin, R. W. (1987). Cross-cultural psychology. In R. J. Corsini (Ed.), *Concise encyclopedia of psychology* (pp. 274–278). New York: Wiley.

Brozek, J., & Rahmani, L. (1976). Soviet Russia. In V. S. Sexton & H. Misiak (Eds.), *Psychology around the world* (pp. 370–388). Monterey, CA: Brooks/Cole.

Brushlinsky, A. (1995). Man as an object of investigation. *Herald of the Russian Academy of Sciences, 65,* 424–431.

Diaz-Guerrero, R. (1977). A Mexican psychology. *American Psychologist, 32,* 934–944.

Diaz-Guerrero, R. (1994). Origins and development of psychology in Latin America. *International Journal of Psychology, 29,* 717–727.

Fairbank, J. K. (1992). *China: A new history*. Cambridge, MA: Belknap Press.

Frank, D. J., Meyer, J. W., & Miyahara, D. (1995). The individualist polity and the prevalence of professionalized psychology: A cross-national study. *American Sociological Review, 60,* 360–377.

Fu, X. L., & Jing, Q. C. (1994). The relation between psychology and the development of economy, science and technology. *Acta Psychologica Sinica, 26*(2), 208–218. (In Chinese).

IUPsyS. (1998). International Union of Psychological Science: National Members and Affiliates.

Jaroschewski, M. G. (1975). *Psychologie im 20. Jahrhundert* [Psychology in the 20th century]. Berlin: Volk und Wissen.

Kaneko, T. (1987). Japan. In A. R. Gilgen & C. K. Gilgen (Eds.), *International handbook of psychology* (pp. 274–296). New York: Greenwood Press.

Kitagawa, J. M., & Strong, J. S. (1984). Buddhism. In *Academic American encyclopedia* (vol. 3, pp. 539–543). Danbury, CT: Grolier Inc.

Koppe, S. (1987). Denmark. In A. R. Gilgen & C. K. Gilgen (Eds.), *International handbook of psychology* (pp. 161–171). New York: Greenwood Press.

Kuhn, T. S. (1962). *The structure of scientific revolutions*. Chicago: University of Chicago Press.

Lenin, V. I. (1951). *Materialism and empiriocriticism*. Moscow: Government Press. (In Russian).

Lomov, B. F. (1972). Present status and future development of psychology in the USSR in the light of the decisions of the 24th Congress of the CPSU. *Soviet Psychology, 10,* 329–358.

Lomov, B. F. (1987). Soviet Union. In A. R. Gilgen & C. K. Gilgen (Eds.), *International handbook of psychology* (pp. 418–439). New York: Greenwood Press.

Lück, H. E., Miller, R., & Rechtien, W. (1984). *Geschichte der Psychologie* [History of Psychology]. München: Ruban & Schwarzenberg.

Marx, K. (1953). *Das Kapital*. Band 1, 2, 3. Berlin: Dietz Verlag.

Pan, S. (1987). *Selected psychological papers of Pan Shu*. Jiangsu: Jiangsu Educational Publishers. (In Chinese).

Pawlik, K. (1985). *International directory of psychologists*. Amsterdam: North-Holland.

Pawlik, K., & d'Ydewalle, G. (1996). Psychology and the global commons: Perspectives of international psychology. *American Psychologist, 51*, 488–495.

Pike, K. L. (1967). *Language in relation to a unified theory of the structure of human behavior*. The Hague, the Netherlands: Mouton.

Rosenzweig, M. R. (1982). Trends in development and status of psychology: An international perspective. *International Journal of Psychology, 17*, 117–140.

Rosenzweig, M. R. (1992b). Resources for psychological science around the world. In M. R. Rosenzweig (Ed.), *International psychological science: Progress, problems, and prospects*. Washington, DC: American Psychological Association.

Rosenzweig, M. R., Holtzman, W. H., Sabourin, M., & Bélanger, D. (2000). *History of the International Union of Psychological Science (IUPsyS)*. Hove, England: Psychology Press.

Segall, M. H., Lonner, W. J., & Berry, J. W. (1998). Cross-cultural psychology as a scholarly discipline: On the flowering of culture in behavioral research. *American Psychologist, 53*, 1101–1110.

Simon, H. A. (1991). *Models of my life*. USA: Basic Books.

Simon, H. A., & Jing, Q. C. (1988). Recognizing, thinking, and learning as information processes. *Psikhologiskii Ruannal, 9*, 33–46. (In Russian).

Sinha, D. (1981). Non-Western perspectives in psychology: Why, what and whither? *Journal of Indian Psychology, 3*, 1–9.

Sinha, D. (1987). India. In A. R. Gilgen & C. K. Gilgen (Eds.), *International handbook of psychology* (pp. 239–257). New York: Greenwood Press.

Sinha, D. (1994). Origins and development of psychology in India: Outgrowing the alien framework. *International Journal of Psychology, 29*, 695–705.

Sinha, D., & Kao, H. S. R. (1997). The journey to the East – An introduction. In H. S. R. Kao & D. Sinha (Eds.), *Asian perspectives on psychology* (pp. 9–22). New Delhi: Sage Publications.

Trognon, A. (1987). France. In A. R. Gilgen & C. K. Gilgen (Eds.), *International handbook of psychology* (pp. 184–207). New York: Greenwood Press.

Weber, M. (1930). *The protestant ethic and the spirit of capitalism*. New York: Scribner.

Yang, C. F. (1993). On how to deepen the study in indigenous psychology. In K. S. Yang (Ed.), *Indigenous psychological research in Chinese societies* (pp. 122–183). Taibei: Gui Guan Book Co. (In Chinese).

Yang, K. S. (1993).Why are we constructing indigenous psychology of the Chinese people. In K. S. Yang (Ed.), *Indigenous psychological research in Chinese societies* (pp. 6–88). Taibei: Gui Guan Book Co. (In Chinese).

Yang, X. H. (1998). On the contribution of Cai Yuanpei as a pioneer in the history of contemporary Chinese psychology. *Psychological Science, 21*, 293–296. (In Chinese).

Communications concerning this chapter should be addressed to: Professor Qicheng Jing, Institue of Psychology, Chinese Academy of Sciences, Beijing, 100012, China

31

Psychological Science in Cross-Disciplinary Contexts

MICHEL DENIS

31.1 INTRODUCTION: THREE LEVELS OF CROSS-DISCIPLINARY INTERACTIONS

Psychology belongs to a rich family of disciplines that includes biology and the life sciences, as well as the human and social sciences, and it has recently been extended to the engineering sciences. Psychology has always been in contact with other disciplines, first with those from which it developed historically, such as philosophy, and then with those whose links are immediately apparent, such as psychiatry, as a practice and a science devoted to psychological dysfunctioning. Other links have always been active in the domains of learning and education.

As both a basic science and an applications-oriented science, psychology is naturally in touch with the scientists and practitioners devoted to remediation and increasing human potential. Even in the basic research contexts of psychophysiology and more recently neuroscience, the background idea remains that elaborating fundamental knowledge is likely to serve intervention and remediation.

As a scientific discipline, psychology has forged its identity during the rather short century of its existence. This chapter explores the idea that psychology, like any other discipline, derives its existence and identity not only from the features that are specific to it (that is, a set of domains and a set of methods), but also from the topics that it shares with other disciplines. Thus, psychology depends for part of its existence on its relations with its neighbor disciplines. This interaction with other disciplines has resulted in some concepts related to cross-disciplinary exchange becoming more prominent in the last decades than they were before. This is also true for the whole field of science. It is useful to clarify the terminology here, and to distinguish among several possible levels of interactions that may occur between a discipline (here, psychology) and one or several others.

The reference to *pluridisciplinary* research is frequently found in these contexts. In general, the term merely refers to situations or contexts involving more than one discipline. The use of this term implies nothing about the form of the joint involvement, or the degree of its reciprocity, or whether the joint venture serves truly common objectives. It simply delineates a domain of research and the several disciplines that provide their respective points of view on the domain. A plurality of methods is implemented to attack the issue under investigation, at different levels of analysis.

In some cases, one may wish to refer to the fact that not only are several disciplines involved in a project, but that they are engaged in a more integrated cooperation to solve a common problem. Here, the underlying (or, preferably, explicit) idea is that of a common enterprise, in which not only several disciplines share their resources, but that the final outcome essentially depends on this cooperation. The trend, then, is to use the concept of *interdisciplinary* research to express such stronger integration and convergence on the part of the disciplines involved. However, each discipline maintains its identity in the partnership.

In interdisciplinary projects, a new question may at some point be considered. The issue is whether this converging process is intended to maintain each discipline as a separate entity, or whether the joint efforts reflect a new broader approach, which integrates the capacities of the individual sciences involved in the project. The concept of a *transdisciplinary* approach may emerge in such contexts. It is a more ambitious concept, maybe also more difficult to circumscribe. The idea is that the work developed in an interdisciplinary project may force the partners to 'cross the divide' between disciplines and delineate a new domain that encompasses several disciplines (or parts of them). A common language, which is not the original language of each individual partner, is to be forged, going 'beyond' individual disciplines, perhaps to found a new science.

Whatever the degree of integration of projects involving the cooperation of psychology with other disciplines, it is important to clarify whether pluridisciplinarity (or one of its more integrated versions) is an intrinsic goal. While some scientists favor cooperation among disciplines in principle, an alternate view is that there is no a priori virtue in pluridisciplinarity. Its virtue depends on the relevance of making disciplines converge to resolve a specific issue that a single discipline cannot. Pluridisciplinarity is thus to be seen as a sort of 'metamethod', that is to be used simply to answer research questions that require this approach. Actually, some of the questions that psychologists face are intrinsic to their own endeavor and do not need any special contribution from other disciplines. This, for instance, is the case when psychology assigns to itself the task of finding an adequate method for measuring intelligence, or for describing a child's behavior. In some other cases, a psychologist may wish to develop a model of a cognitive function, while taking care that the model is realistic, that is, compatible with what is currently known of brain functioning. This requires cooperation with neuroscience, and this cooperation must be specified in such a way that the partners approach the same level of a scientific reality, or close enough levels. Similarly, when engineers have to design software that is to be used by ordinary people, the role of psychology is to make sure that the level of cognitive processing required by the software is compatible with human cognitive capacities. This latter example has the additional advantage of revealing that pluridisciplinary or interdisciplinary projects may respond to a plurality of scientific motivations. While the engineer may simply feel committed to designing artificial functional systems, without being interested in human cognition itself, the aim of the psychologist is to provide accounts of the cognitive functions, as a domain of natural sciences, some of these functions being likely to be involved when a person interacts with artificial systems. Psychological science may thus contribute to a joint effort that goes beyond the establishment of scientific knowledge per se. It takes part in a broader concert that aims to improve the conditions in which human beings interact with their surrounding world.

31.2 PSYCHOLOGY AND NEUROSCIENCE

Most of the disciplines gathered under the generic label of neuroscience take account of the research and concepts of psychology, and the reciprocal is true as well. Cognitive functions can well be analyzed at a rather abstract level, independently of the physical reality of the brain that supports their functioning. This approach, isolated from any reference to the brain, is useful for understanding the algorithms that underlie the functioning of any 'cognitive agent', whether its support is biological or artefactual. However, there has been a strong tendency in recent years to claim that researchers must at some point take into account the constraints imposed by the biological systems underlying cognitive functions. Neuroscience is assigned the task of identifying the biological infrastructures of these functions (cf. Kosslyn & Andersen, 1992).

The progress of research in neuroscience has been rapid and considerable over the last two decades. Part of this progress can be attributed to the enormous effort devoted to the comprehension of neurological disease and the invention of efficient treatments. This concern was also connected to the investigation of the effects of aging on neurological and psychological functions. A major goal for a growing number of neuroscientists is to understand the neurological basis of cognitive functions (perception, attention, memory, action), which includes how they are implemented in the architecture of the brain (cf. Kosslyn & Koenig, 1992).

The rapid progress made in this domain is undoubtedly due to the increased emphasis on model building, and the development of highly sophisticated techniques, in particular those based on functional neuroimaging. For instance, the positron emission tomography (PET) first offered rich information on the cerebral regions involved in psychiatric syndromes (such as depression or anxiety). But the greatest value of neuroimaging techniques is their use to examine normal people. It is then possible to identify the cerebral structures activated during the execution of behavioral or cognitive tasks, such as in visual attention, mental imagery, language comprehension, motor activity, or decision processes. New techniques, such as functional magnetic resonance imaging (fMRI) and magnetoencephalography (MEG), are also used with normal people, and make it possible to overcome the current limitations of PET in temporal accuracy (cf. Toga & Mazziotta, 1996).

Visual attention, visual perception, and motor control, are all examples of domains where cerebral mechanisms are also quite usefully studied by recording neuron activity in awake animals. Crucial to the understanding of psychological functions, some studies have shown that the cell responses in some highly integrated cortical regions may reflect great selectivity, that is, specific classes of complex stimuli (for instance, faces) can activate specific neurons. Our understanding of cognitive functions has also benefited from new developments in anatomical techniques and knowledge of the biochemical mechanisms involved in synaptic plasticity and long-term potentiation.

The growing effort of neuroscience to understand cerebral functioning in terms of coordinated information-processing systems is essential to the development of psychological theory. Computational neuroscience is orienting itself towards analyzing the coding of sensory and motor information in the brain. The information gained from this approach has important implications for researchers attempting to design information-processing systems directly inspired by the concepts established by neuroscience. This is the case of the connectionist (or neuromimetic) systems, to which more and more psychologists are contributing. The concept of a 'neuronal computer' has become common in this community. This is probably a domain in which interdisciplinary integration is especially advanced, and is on its way to producing some form of transdisciplinarity, attempting to establish connectionism as a field and discipline on its own, 'beyond' the individual contributions of the disciplines involved in the process (cf. Churchland & Sejnowski, 1992).

One of the most remarkable trends in neuroscience is that it is more and more involved in attempts to understand cognitive behavior that implies a high degree of integration. This is important for psychology, and may explain the success of initiatives to establish long-term sustained cooperation between psychologists and neuroscientists. Hence, a growing number of psychologists tend to describe themselves as cognitive neuroscientists. It is worth stressing that the majority of the members of the Society of Cognitive Neuroscience, which was founded a few years ago in the United States, are psychologists and neuropsychologists. The domains covered by this community are the effects of brain lesions in humans and animals, electrophysiological recordings in animals, and neuroimaging in normal humans. The picture that emerges is that of a genuine cooperation among scientists of different backgrounds to link brain, mind, and behavior. This trio, after all, sounds like a good description of the objectives of psychology in general. The same set of psychological functions form the program of psychology and neuroscience, thus justifying the launching of integrated actions. This kind of integration probably reflects genuine interdisciplinarity, in that the same concepts are investigated at two distinct levels of their implementation, that is, cognitive and neuronal. Each discipline keeps control and use of its methods in this joint approach, but the models of cognition and the experimental designs are elaborated jointly. Each discipline attacks the phenomena at the level for which it is specialized and methodologically equipped, but without ignoring that other levels of description are relevant from the alternate perspective. This balance is very valuable, and it is important to encourage it, inasmuch as it contributes to defining the field of investigation in both biological and psychological terms.

There are also more recent trends. For instance, it is well established that the internal chemical environment of a person shapes his/her nervous states and behavior. The external chemical environment (such as olfactory signals) also influences individual and group behavior. Promising collaborations have started with biochemistry, that is, the study of the chemistry specific to biological systems, and biological chemistry, with the creation of synthetic molecules that control biological activities. Psychology has obviously much to contribute to this kind of cooperative research. Lastly, there are links between psychology and neuropharmacology. The perspective here is to produce molecules likely to repair altered cognitive functions (in particular, in the domain of memory).

31.3 Psychology, Computer Science, and Artificial Intelligence

Human cognition expresses itself in natural contexts (such as when people solve problems in natural environments or social contexts), but it also has many opportunities to reveal its capacities when interacting with human-made devices or artefacts. Artificial systems that are capable of generating 'intelligent' outputs are becoming more and more available to everyone. Psychology must obviously interact with the 'sciences of the artificial', first of all computer science and artificial intelligence (AI). This is because it has become important for engineers to create artificial systems which behave like cognitive agents endowed with rational capacities. These systems must also contain representations and processing modes that are functionally compatible with those of human beings (cf. Osherson, Stob, & Weinstein, 1986; Russell & Norvig, 1995; Winston, 1984).

The human mind is frequently confronted with incomplete, uncertain, or partly contradictory information. Nevertheless, it is capable of conducting a variety of modes of reasoning in order to solve problems. The mechanisms by which the human mind achieves such processing and adapts to an uncertain world are typically opaque to people. Psychological science attempts to discover the algorithms underlying reasoning processes, whether they are productive of optimal solutions or not. The objective of AI is to formalize reasoning in a rigorous, efficient manner, so that computers can reason and produce outputs that satisfy explicit rational criteria. Complementarily, by relying on formal models of reasoning, psychologists try to understand how people reason, including an analysis of their 'errors' and 'contradictions' in scientific accounts. This is considered to be a crucial component in the process of developing human–machine communication systems, as well as computer-based instructional devices. Although computer science may not have been originally prepared to value the analysis of the errors produced by an intelligent system, it has now developed a more explicit interest in the mechanisms which cause errors in human reasoning.

Not only has AI come to value the data collected and models proposed by psychologists, but the results obtained by AI for formalizing reasoning are of great interest for psychologists themselves. This is a good context for the development of theoretical frameworks encompassing the variety of modes of reasoning, but also for providing a more solid epistemological basis for the analysis of natural reasoning and argumentation.

An important domain in this cross-disciplinary context is the automatic processing of natural language. Originally, this domain was considered to be just part of computer science. Nowadays, it is agreed by both psychologists and computer scientists that understanding how humans process natural language is a prerequisite for building systems capable of producing similar behavior. In particular, language-processing systems can only be efficient if they produce appropriate inferences based on the inputs provided to them. Similarly, the 'behavior' of the systems must offer outputs that make it possible for their users to perform the same type of inferences as those they make when processing natural language. Psychologists, and more specifically psycholinguists, play an important role in this endeavor. They contribute to the view that, beyond superficial comprehension, it is crucial for any intelligent system to access the meaning and deep implications of the message, including the goals, intentions, and strategies of its author.

The most fruitful relationships between psychology and AI are those which take place in the framework of 'cognitive science' (CS), that is the project interrelating the family of disciplines concerned by the ways in which intelligent systems or organisms acquire, store, and make use of knowledge for adaptive purposes (cf. Posner, 1989; Stillings et al., 1987). Artificial systems are intended to produce intelligent behavior, not necessarily by mimicking the processes believed to occur in a human mind. However, when AI researchers become engaged in interdisciplinary projects, then psychology is more than likely to be a key participant. One reason is that the human mind is the first (and probably most sophisticated) cognitive system that has ever been approached as a scientific object. Psychology is not only greatly concerned in most current programs in CS, but it is quite central to them, especially in the projects that develop computational models in the areas of perception, language comprehension, memory, and problem solving. Such programs may also combine psychology and computer science with physical and life sciences in the area of neural networks (cf. Bechtel & Graham, 1998; Sun & Bookman, 1994).

The importance of maintaining close contacts between psychology and AI in the domain of CS is justified by the capacity of psychology to address issues at both the theoretical and the empirical level. There are good epistemological reasons for the involvement of psychology. Psychology investigates human cognitive functions and provides data for modeling processes that are relevant to AI. In addition, human cognition is by far the most well-developed example of cognitive function, which makes it possible to provide models that inform computer science. Another set of reasons is the methodological expertise of psychologists in collecting and analyzing empirical data. Psychological researchers are recognized by AI researchers as rigorous and well-trained research methodologists. Thus, because it provides both the core theoretical and empirical basis for advancing the field, psychology is a prerequisite for any program in which AI will attempt to build intelligent artificial systems, especially if these systems are intended to mimic some of the human cognitive capacities (cf. Denis, 1998).

Psychology is biased to human forms of cognition and intelligence by its very nature, and requires little computational expertise. However, the computational approach is gaining popularity and consideration in contemporary cognitive psychology (which may be a result of a growing interaction with AI). Psychology may contribute its basic experimental nature and strong research methodology to joint projects with computer science, but its great strength is its ability to model mental processes at different levels of abstraction. In this respect, any common project may benefit from the unique integrative capacity of psychology and its care in maintaining the place of the human being at the center of CS. Despite the development of computers and information technology, or perhaps because this development, it is clear that the human being

remains central in CS, thanks to the involvement of psychology.

31.4 PSYCHOLOGY, ERGONOMICS, AND HUMAN–MACHINE COMMUNICATION

Improving communication between humans and artificial devices is an important task. The researchers whose aim is to endow machines with faculties similar to (or compatible with) human faculties have to deal with a number of problems, such as the automatic processing of speech, written language, visual information, or gesture. The current trend in human–machine communication (HMC) research is to consider these different modes of communication in an integrated fashion (rather than independently). This tendency is favored by the fact that quite similar methods for shape recognition can be applied to these different domains. Furthermore, a growing number of interactive systems actually call upon multiple modes of communication (such as vision + language, or speech + pointing, etc.) (cf. Maybury, 1993).

HMC should not be seen as a discipline, but rather as a set of problems. It is an extremely interdisciplinary field, which has to take into account three terms of a situation: a user, a machine, and the object of the user's activity. The aim of HMC researchers is to specify the constraints on the interactions between a user and a machine, given the assigned task or activity. The growing need for new software and interfaces in HMC offers a number of opportunities for psychology to identify the cognitive difficulties likely to be engendered by such systems, and to propose ways of circumventing these difficulties. Knowledge based on ergonomics is of unique value here, as it has to solve problems at the very junction of cognition and communication. There is an important social aspect of this issue, given the key position of computers in new professional environments. This situation creates an opportunity for using knowledge acquired in cognitive psychology to design devices that enhance the quality of working conditions and increase the reliability of human–machine systems. Psychology helps HMC to identify a key issue, that is, the compatibility between the languages used in the interactions between the user and the machine, and the representational and processing capacities of the users' cognitive system (cf. Card, Moran, & Newell, 1983; Carroll, 1991).

Early research in ergonomics extensively investigated the motor components of working situations. When ergonomics turned towards more cognitive issues, the researchers mainly focused on training in professional contexts and on the development of software suited to the users' cognitive capacities. This evolution paralleled a shift in perspective, moving from an approach mainly concerned with the repairing of ill-adjusted situations to a perspective where ergonomics plays a role in the very conception and design of systems. Cognitive psychology and ergonomics also have an important role in assessing the relevance of the results collected in ergonomic research to real work situations. Another important part of cognitive ergonomics is interested in knowledge contents, such as scientific knowledge in education or pragmatic knowledge in professional contexts. There, it is highly important to verify the compatibility between the designers' and the users' knowledge. A related field is that of instructional devices for professional activities, where it is important to account not only for public or explicit expert knowledge, but also for private or implicit procedural knowledge (cf. Rasmussen, 1986; Wickens, 1984).

Psychology is becoming more and more involved in applications that require consideration of the expectations or queries of the industry. Hence, human factors and ergonomics are essential issues in research and development. Psychologists are involved in conducting user-oriented surveys and evaluating systems. Cognitive psychologists may also prove to be especially valuable in refining the human–system interaction aspect of system design. The difference between cognitive psychologists and engineers in refining the human–system features of a design is that the latter usually rely on user feedback and trial and error. In contrast, cognitive psychologists are armed with psychological principles to guide the design and reduce the risk of errors by avoiding potential pitfalls they have learned through experimental studies.

This is, in fact, a feature that is of growing importance, as a contrast to the classical methods used in the design of human–machine systems. The former methods tended to emphasize the technical aspects (such as the electronics of the system), giving secondary importance to the perceptual, motor, and cognitive characteristics of the user. It rapidly became apparent that an approach focusing primarily on the technological aspects is limited. Many iterations are needed to produce really functional systems, due to the neglect of including both the user and the task from the outset of the designing process. The new trend is to explicitly include the constraints of the user and the task early in the design, that is, to adapt the systems to their future users. But this does not imply that the psychologist should ignore the economical, technical, and temporal constraints that the designers must take into account (cf. Helander, 1988; Norman & Draper, 1986).

In conjunction with the system designer, the psychologist works to elaborate a 'model of the user', which offers an abstract description of the actual functioning of the cognitive system in the considered task. A 'model of the task' is also constructed, based on detailed analysis of the objective of the user. These preliminary formulations force the designer and the psychologist to make explicit the steps to be followed by the users when they process information and respond to the system. The combination of the two models provides a basis for designing the optimal configuration of the information to be displayed by the system (which pieces of information to deliver, which media to use, which modes to call upon jointly, in which temporal sequence). The articulation of the two models also makes it possible to formulate predictions of any incident likely to occur during processing, whether the incident concerns the user or the task.

To summarize, in the many cases where psychology is invited to contribute to technology-oriented research, its first role is to provide theories and tools for modeling a user's knowledge and ways of handling a task. Then, psychology contributes to design and development by helping engineers design more user-centered systems. It may also study the organizational impact of new systems (for instance, the impact of a new system on the users and on the organization as a whole).

31.5 PSYCHOLOGY AND SCIENCES OF LANGUAGE

Language is a major domain in which psychology interacts with other disciplines, the first of which is linguistics. One good reason for placing language at the core of interdisciplinary research involving psychology is its status of a specific human activity. As a consequence, many disciplines are likely to converge on this very particular object. For instance, lexical processing is more and more approached by interdisciplinary programs that combine behavioral analysis, electrophysiological methods, and connectionist modeling. At a higher level of complexity, language comprehension and production are approached as complementary aspects of a common underlying system, on the elucidation of which linguistics (including computational linguistics) and several branches of psychology may share interests. Some specialization normally takes place in such converging processes.

While linguists describe the product, psycho-linguists attempt to specify how language is generated and understood by the brain and why it has evolved in the way it has. Computer scientists, for their part, build systems that are intended to process natural language by using mechanisms that mimic the human mind, in addition to mechanisms of their own (cf. Gleitman & Liberman, 1995).

Two broad perspectives are usually contrasted in the sciences of language. On the one hand, language is mainly considered to be a symbolic activity that occurs in contexts where it is important to take into account the speaker's perceptual–cognitive system and the social interactions in which the speaker is involved. This perspective is characteristic of the theories dedicated to the elaboration of 'cognitive grammars' (cf. Langacker, 1987–1991). On the other hand, emphasis is placed on identifying the formal properties of natural languages. One possible extension of this approach is to implement these properties in computers in order to simulate comprehension processes (cf. Kintsch, 1998). These two perspectives correspond to two aspects of an interdisciplinary approach to language, namely, the analysis of cognitive and socio-cognitive representations involved in the relationships among language, perception, and action, and the modeling of processes underlying language production and comprehension. The two perspectives are closely knit in a number of applied domains (such as expert systems, databases, hypertexts, speech synthesis, etc.).

Psychology is making special contributions to a number of fields in the domain of language. One area is the ontogenetic development of language, and the way it is related to cognitive development in general (cf. Fletcher & Mac-Whinney, 1995). Cross-linguistic studies are also developing well in psychology, with the aim of revealing the basic cognitive processes that underlie the discourse structures of different languages and the semantic representations that are associated with them. Another domain is the study of the disorders of language, in which neuropsychology and neurology are closely interacting with psychology. Still another important domain is that of the comparative approach and the investigation of language capacities in animals.

The contribution of psychology in interdisciplinary linguistic research is to consider language as a reflection of human intelligence and cognition. In the analysis and modeling of perception, memory, and learning, it is crucial to consider that quite large parts of cognition depend on language, and that language is also a privileged mode for expressing thought in social

contexts. The cognitive status of language is thus a primary fact that provides guidelines for its approach by scientists taking part in cognitive science projects. A cognitive approach to language cannot be based solely on models restricted to grammar and syntactic regulations and that ignore the relationships of the speakers with meaning. At the same time, by placing emphasis on the semantic components of language, this does not mean that the syntactic constraints are only of secondary importance in the construction of meaningful statements. Lastly, it is important to acknowledge that the intricate relationships between syntax and semantics take place in pragmatic contexts, that is, they are dependent on concrete situations and on the speakers' intention to adjust their messages to these situations (cf. Garnham, 1985; Levelt, 1989).

Accounting for the cognitive status of language implies two correlated sets of operations on the part of psychologists and linguists. The first set consists of modeling the processes by which language creates and communicates knowledge. The second set of operations consists of identifying the processes by which language helps a person to build and organize his/her own knowledge (which includes knowledge shared with other members of a community as well as idiosyncratic knowledge). These processes are essential for the interactions of speakers with their environment. The major point is the intricate relationship between the two facets of language, as a system of communication and as a system of symbolic representation of objects, events, and actions. Language is probably the most sophisticated system used to serve these two purposes, which justifies the special consideration it requires from the cognitive sciences.

An important objective in which linguistics and psychology cooperate is the definition and classification of the functions of language, and the sequence in which these functions appear during language acquisition. These functions include instrumental ones, in which language is used to obtain some form of satisfaction (for instance, obtain a desired object). Other functions are linked to communicating, that is, establishing and maintaining interactions with other people in a social environment. Still other functions of language are the acquisition and manipulation of knowledge, through exploring the physical environment or creating imaginary worlds. More sophisticated cognitive operations are those by which speakers not only declare representational contents, but also express their position relative to these contents (such as in argumentation).

Another special contribution of psychology is to develop models of the cognitive architecture that include non-linguistic modes of symbolic representation, endowed with distinct functional properties. This is the case of the models including analogue representational systems in addition to the linguistic system. Psychology, then, has to include in the models adequate translation procedures that make it possible for speakers and listeners to perform complex tasks, such as generating linguistic outputs that describe multi-dimensional configurations, or construct visuo-spatial images from verbal descriptions. Such articulations between differently structured internal representations are also an important issue in AI, when a computer is required to perform translations between linguistic and perceptual inputs.

31.6 Psychology, Philosophy, and Logic

Psychology and philosophy obviously share a number of notions and concepts, although the corresponding objects are approached by the two disciplines with rather different methods. When scientific psychology became autonomous with respect to philosophy, by developing its own methodological tools and proof-based argumentation, philosophy pursued its investigation of crucial issues, such as the nature of the human mind and the functioning of thinking. This created a context favorable to the maintenance of interdisciplinary relationships between the two disciplines. During the first century of its existence as a scientific discipline, psychology has built a body of knowledge based on systematic observation of behavior in natural and experimental settings. However, philosophers have only fairly recently become aware of the scientific knowledge established by psychologists and reformulated some of their issues by taking into account psychological data obtained by empirical methods, and not solely by intuitive or introspective approaches.

To take an example, an issue of interest for both psychology and philosophy is the nature of mental activity. Philosophy tends to take two main properties into account when dealing with this issue, consciousness and intentionality. A mental state is described as being specific to a *conscious* subject; it is also an *intentional* state in that it bears upon things and evokes them in the form of representations (cf. Baars, 1988; Dretske, 1988). Psychology and psychophysiology have considerable information on consciousness and the measurement of its varying states. They also have methods for dealing with

the study of mental representations, not by 'capturing' them as observable entities, but as constructs inferred from the covariations between situations and responses. Cognitive psychology postulates that such internal representations have a functional role in behavior, although there seems to be no intrinsic need for them to be conscious in order to have behavioral consequences. For instance, priming effects obtained when stimuli are presented below the perceptual threshold generate new questions for philosophy and, more broadly, the disciplines which aim at elucidating what is a mental state and how mental representations determine behavior.

One of the most important tenets of the so-called 'philosophy of the mind', which has considerable relevance for cognitive psychology, is that mental phenomena should be considered from a 'functional' perspective, that is, they should be accounted for essentially by the functions they serve in a mental system. According to this approach, mental states are causal in shaping behavioral outcomes, although they cannot be viewed solely as 'precursors' of behavior. They must also be analyzed for their own properties and functional characteristics, in line with the view that more important than behavior itself are the mechanisms by which internal states articulate to one another to trigger behavioral responses. This concept creates an epistemological context that favors an attempt to analyze causal relations among mental states. A consequence of that approach is that the relevance of a psychological level of explanation is recognized, distinct from a neurobiological level, without denying that the two levels certainly involve causal relationships. The functional perspective thus promotes the idea that psychological phenomena do have neurobiological counterparts, but cannot be reduced to them in principle (cf. Rey, 1996). This approach departs from the former 'physicalist' philosophical perspective, according to which mental states should simply be identified with cerebral states. Obviously, through these discussions, philosophical concepts have had a direct impact on issues that were in the scope of scientific psychology.

The early steps in the development of cognitive science were marked by the postulate that there is a 'language of thought' (cf. Fodor, 1975). This concept was used by both psychologists and philosophers to account for the way humans create and use internal representations of the world. The dominant conception favored a view of the language of thought as being encoded in the human brain just like a formal language is encoded in a computer. This approach involved efforts to specify the syntactic structure of that language, by defining predicates, quantifiers, logical connectors, etc., that should be combined to form higher-order, more complex entities, equivalent to sentences, but expressed in propositional terms. The propositional format of the language of thought is generally claimed to have a greater expressive power than other representational formats, in particular mental images. On the other hand, the analog structure of images gives them a power that propositions do not have, in particular when continuous dimensions of the world are represented by the mind.

Whereas philosophy covers a wide spectrum of mental phenomena, from sensory to higher cognitive processes, logic essentially focuses on reasoning (cf. Overton, 1990). Logicians are interested in systems based on three main components: a language (typically, propositional), a deductive device applying inference rules to formulas of that language, and a set of procedures computing the truth value of these formulas. Logic and psychology were bound to develop mutual relationships because of the common objectives of the operations undertaken by logic systems and human reasoners, that is, to produce valid conclusions from combining informational inputs in an appropriate manner. Cognitivism has employed the concept of the brain as a deductive system governed by logical principles from its very outset.

As a science of formal reasoning, logic traditionally excludes from its scope any reference to psychological processes. However, the development of scientific psychology has created a new context, in which the mind is assessed for its deductive capacities, and thus compared with a computer. Experimental psychology also pointed to behavioral features suggesting that the human mind performs sub-optimally according to the rules of logic. In short, ordinary people are not intuitive logicians. Systematic errors and biases in deductive and probabilistic reasoning forced researchers to acknowledge that only a limited part of human reasoning is governed by the principles of logic. The theory of the 'mental logic' was thus faced with the somewhat provocative view that some forms of reasoning at least can be performed without any recourse to formal logic. The concept of a 'mental model' was proposed to account for the actual deductive capacities of ordinary people when they do not apply the formal rules of inference (cf. Johnson-Laird & Byrne, 1991). Advances in psychological accounts of natural reasoning were thus very dependent on the capacity of psychologists to exchange concepts with logicians.

31.7 PSYCHOLOGY, SOCIOLOGY, POLITICAL SCIENCE, AND ECONOMICS

There are many opportunities for human beings to become part of social groups. In fact, they are generally obliged to do so. It has long been acknowledged that the study of human cognition and behavior must take into account the social dimension of the contexts where they take place. Contemporary social psychology illustrates the need to consider the contextual and social factors in any approach to behavior and its underlying cognitive mechanisms.

An individual's personal identity is regulated by social factors. Autobiographical memory is closely connected to the personal experience of individuals as members of groups. Also important is the social regulation of inter-group perceptions and relationships. The organization, values, and modes of functioning of socioeconomic, national, or ethnic groups are studied by social sciences, mainly sociology. The fact that people usually belong to groups has psychological consequences that are the main object of investigation by social psychology. For instance, people tend to classify other people as members of social categories. The consequence is that when a person interacts with another one (even remotely, such as when a judgment is expressed on that person), the alleged characteristics of that person's group or social category are as much considered as his/her personal characteristics. Furthermore, a person's perception or judgment of other people is to some extent shaped by that person's belonging to a social category. These factors have an important impact on the mutual representations of social groups. Psychosocial research assesses the representational dimension of groups, which is likely to enrich the models developed in sociology.

One interesting example of a domain shared by sociology and psychology is ethnocentrism, which implies that a person attributes different features to the group he/she belongs to and to other groups. The social status of a group relative to others is also thought to affect the rate of ethnocentrism of that group, as well as its perception of the homogeneity of other groups. The relations among groups are governed by asymmetries in their status and powership in natural social contexts. The feeling of belonging to one's group is more marked in groups of low social status, whereas members of high-status groups tend to perceive more distinct features among themselves. Sociological research has much to do in delineating the macro-features that affect the perception of groups by individual members of these groups (such as socioeconomic variables), and consequently the like-lihood that institutions that rule a society formally recognize the existence of these groups. Psychology provides its unique expert-ise in making evident the perceptual biases or stereotypes that may affect the judgments of members of one group on members of other groups. Such powerful psychosocial mechan-isms may have crucial consequences in the social transmission of inter-group perceptions and judgments (cf. Devine, Ostrom, & Hamil-ton, 1994; Mackie & Hamilton, 1993; Tajfel, 1982).

The cooperation of psychology with other social sciences is of special significance in sev-eral applied domains. One example is work organization and its effects on productivity. Pro-ductive work is a work in which people cooper-ate. It is important for psychology and sociology to better understand the way to improve mutual perception of co-workers and to promote inter- and intra-group comprehension, and to reduce resistance to change. This joint approach may shed light on the relationships among productiv-ity, work satisfaction, and work organization. In industrial societies, not only are automated production systems developing rapidly, but dramatic changes also take place in patterns of work organization. Work is a domain where communication patterns and authority relation-ships are changing; workers' motivation and satisfaction are also changing. Behavioral and social science research can help identify what motivates productivity for individuals and for work groups, and more generally provide infor-mation on the relationships among productivity, work satisfaction, and work organization.

Another domain where psychologists and social scientists may profitably address common issues is the domain of political science. There is a growing interest for assessing the situations in which groups with divergent interests or values are required to interact or reach com-promises. Psychology may help political scien-tists by attracting their attention on factors that hinder communication and make mutual percep-tion more difficult, especially in tense contexts. This occurs when leaders or other agents respon-sible for making decisions must simultaneously process a cognitive task (e.g., compare a variety of options, evaluate risks) and an emotional dimension (which, in fact, is part of the percep-tion of most social situations). The classic stud-ies on predictive reasoning are an example of empirical facts that should demonstrate to polit-ical scientists the susceptibility of decision mak-ing to undesirable reasoning biases (cf. Kahne-man, Slovic, & Tversky, 1982). Such factors are particularly relevant in situations of negotiation and conflict resolution.

The domain of economics is also open to interdisciplinary exchange with cognitive psy-chology and, more generally, cognitive science. Both economists and ordinary people must make economic decisions, most frequently in com-plex, uncertain environments. The issue is whether ordinary people perform rationally when making decisions, by systematically seek-ing to maximize rewards and minimize losses. This strategy is expected of rational economic agents. Psychological research shows that people, in fact, exhibit limited rationality in this domain and frequently fail when confronted with quite simple decision-making tasks. Irra-tional decision making occurs because people's reasoning is biased by whether descriptions of the choices to be made draw their attention to positive or negative outcomes. Highly salient, but irrelevant information also affects decision making, since the limited processing capacities of the human mind prevent people considering less salient, but relevant information. The value of understanding the cognitive processes in-volved in decision making is that it allows researchers to introduce the human factor into their accounts of economic mechanisms. Appli-cations can then be considered by developing interactive systems to help decision making that simulate human behavior in various types of economic situations (cf. Hoffman, McCabe, & Smith, 1995; Simon, 1983).

31.8 PSYCHOLOGY, ANTHROPOLOGY, AND GEOGRAPHY

Psychology and anthropology are both con-cerned with the human mind. While psychology primarily investigates human mental capacities through their individual manifestations, anthro-pology devotes its efforts to cultures, as mani-festations of these capacities in communities of people. The data collected by ethnography have long been valued for their capacity to reveal the variety of human experience, but anthropology is engaged in a distinct program, to account for the variation of such experience from a theoret-ical point of view.

Although the projects of psychology and anthropology are distinct from each other, they converge on a number of points. Anthropology aims to construct a science of the specificities of humans, both their universality and their varia-tions. Psychology is similarly concerned by the universal (to establish general laws of psycho-logical function) and the individual (to account for the variations in human capacities and behavior). After a long period during which anthropology remained isolated from psychology, the dominant branch of the discipline, 'cultural anthropology', is increasingly taking into account those issues related to human cognition and the variety of its expressions. Based on the premises that cognition is always culturally situated, investigations of new populations are intended to understand their perception of the world and also their perception of *their* world.

Nowadays, the objects studied by cognitive anthropology (such as perception, thinking, and the construction of knowledge) are quite similar to those of cognitive psychology. These domains are mainly approached by anthropologists in natural settings, but the fact that their description may require observations that meet the standards of empirical methodology is fully accepted, the objective being to evaluate the degree to which culture influences the expression of human cognition. For instance, people in populations that rely heavily on an oral tradition are better at remembering verbal information than those in other cultures. This is restricted, however, to their memory of narratives (and not other verbal materials). This suggests that differences among populations with different traditions reflect cultural rather than psychological differences.

One of the most extensively investigated domains of cognition is categorization. To take a famous example, the classification of colors varies considerably among languages and cultures. The fact that each language segments the color continuum in a specific way has long been taken as supporting the relativistic view that no universal constraints weigh on color perception. However, anthropologists have also considered the hypothesis that perception is based on a small number of universal, fundamental concepts. The experiments carried out by psychologists in collaboration with anthropologists have confirmed that there is a universal set of focal colors underlying every lexicon of colors, beyond their diversity (cf. Berlin & Kay, 1969; Rosch & Lloyd, 1978).

The cognitive structures shaped by culture include 'mental schemas' or 'models of the world'. These models are knowledge structures that are taken for granted and shared by the members of a society. They have a great adaptive value, in that they help generate inferences in situations that contain only partial information. Such models play a major role in people's understanding of the world and generating behavior. The relevant point for both psychologists and anthropologists is that schemas may vary greatly among cultures, but observations converge on the universal availability of such schemas in all cultures (cf. Holland & Quinn, 1987).

Cultural models are closely related to the domain of beliefs. A belief that is considered to be rational in a given culture (and is thus a candidate for the status of 'knowledge') may seem irrational in another. Anthropological research has forced us to consider that the criteria of rationality applied to beliefs vary widely among cultures. In some cultures, it suffices for a belief to have internal coherence and to be coherent with the other beliefs of the person to be considered 'rational'. Cognitive psychology provides conceptual guidelines for differentiating between the concepts of 'belief' and 'knowledge', and to account for the situations in which they interact. Anthropology documents the difficulties arising when people are confronted with the beliefs held by people from another culture.

The concept of variability is also important in other social sciences, in particular geography. Beyond the description of geographic objects, geographers are paying more and more attention to people's interactions with their environments. The development of 'cognitive geography' is correlated with an increase in interest in human activities in these environments, and in the way people create representations and communicate with each other about these environments. These issues are most relevant for psychologists, whose aim is to account for the mechanisms by which people generate and use internal representations (or 'cognitive maps') of the external world. Geography is a special field of application for the study of mental representations of space.

Psychologists interested in spatial cognition have considered the various contexts in which learning of spatial environments takes place. Navigation is the primary and most common source of spatial knowledge for most species. Humans also rely on symbolic substitutes for spatial environments, such as maps. They also acquire spatial knowledge from verbal descriptions. Psychology develops empirical methods to assess the specific merits of each type of learning, but also to reveal their common features. In particular, research in this domain considers the capacity of representational subsystems endowed with different functional characteristics to cooperate within a single cognitive system (cf. Bloom, Peterson, Nadel, & Garrett, 1996; Portugali, 1996).

Psychologists and geographers also cooperate in the design of artefacts used to represent space and assist people's navigation in unfamiliar environments. For instance, cartographers may profit from empirical investigations into the formats of map representations that are the easiest to process and memorize. With additional input from computer scientists, these investigations have direct applications in the design of geographic information systems and on-board navigational aid systems (cf. Barfield & Dingus, 1998; Freksa & Mark, 1999). Geography offers a wide range of other subjects for collaboration with psychology and other social sciences, such as the physical and psychological effects of natural hazards, the organization of industrial space, the perception of the safety of living environments, and the human factors involved in urban development and urban life.

31.9 Conclusion

This chapter has reviewed a number of scientific domains in which psychology is cooperating with other sciences. There are probably research domains that have not been mentioned and deserve consideration for the development of joint efforts between psychology and other disciplines. For the time being, the wide spectrum of domains in which psychology interacts in order to solve problems shared with other disciplines is impressive. This is probably due to one important feature of psychology, its diversity and the number of branches that have developed within it. This situation enables psychology to attack problems at different levels of analysis, from microlevels to highly integrated levels. It also provides a unique opportunity for psychology to develop a wide range of interactions with other disciplines.

Most of the examples of interactions cited above may be labeled as pluridisciplinary or interdisciplinary. Psychology clearly has a great capacity to become involved in true scientific interactions with other disciplines. This contrasts with the long-term projects aiming at establishing genuinely transdisciplinary collaborations. The most frequent forms of interactions in current research illustrate the benefits resulting from sharing the exploration of well-specified fields, and in some cases sharing the concepts related to these fields with other disciplines. To be productive in both the short and long terms, this converging process must respect the other disciplines, their specific aims, concepts, and methods.

Resource References

D'Andrade, R. (1995). *Cognitive anthropology*. Cambridge, England: Cambridge University Press.

Delacour, J. (1998). *Une introduction aux neurosciences cognitives* [An introduction to cognitive neuroscience]. Brussels: De Boeck.

Edelman, G. (1989). *The remembered present: A biological theory of consciousness*. New York: Basic Books.

Engel, P. (1994). *Introduction à la philosophie de l'esprit* [Introduction to philosophy of the mind]. Paris: La Découverte.

Gazzaniga, M. S. (Ed.). (1996). *The cognitive neurosciences*. Cambridge, MA: MIT Press.

Le Ny, J.-F. (1989). *Science cognitive et compréhension du langage* [Cognitive science and language comprehension]. Paris: Presses Universitaires de France.

Osherson, D. N. (Ed.). (1995–1997). *An invitation to cognitive science* (4 vols.). Cambridge, MA: MIT Press.

Sabah, G. (1988–1989). *L'intelligence artificielle et le langage* (2 vols.) [Artificial intelligence and language]. Paris: Hermès.

Sowa, J. (1991). *Principles of semantic networks*. San Mateo, CA: Morgan Kaufman.

Sperber, D. (1982). *Le savoir des anthropologues* [Anthropologists' knowledge]. Paris: Hermann.

Tomasello, M. (1998). *The new psychology of language: Cognitive and functional approaches to language structure*. Mahwah, NJ: Erlbaum.

Additional Literature Cited

Baars, B. (1988). *A cognitive theory of consciousness*. Cambridge, England: Cambridge University Press.

Barfield, W., & Dingus, T. A. (Eds.). (1998). *Human factors in intelligent transportation systems*. Mahwah, NJ : Erlbaum.

Bechtel, W., & Graham, G. (Eds.). (1998). *A companion to cognitive science*. Oxford: Blackwell.

Berlin, B., & Kay, P. (1969). *Basic color terms: Their universality and evolution*. Berkeley, CA: University of California Press.

Bloom, P., Peterson, M. A., Nadel, L., & Garrett, M. F. (Eds.). (1996). *Language and space*. Cambridge, MA: MIT Press.

Card, S. K., Moran, T. P., & Newell, A. L. (1983). *The psychology of human–computer interaction*. Hillsdale, NJ: Erlbaum.

Carroll, J. M. (Ed.). (1991). *Designing interaction: Psychology at the human–computer interface*. Cambridge, England: Cambridge University Press.

Churchland, P. S., & Sejnowski, T. J. (1992). *The computational brain*. Cambridge, MA: MIT Press.

Denis, M. (1998). The place and role of psychology in cognitive science: An international survey. *International Journal of Psychology, 33*, 377–395.

Devine, P., Ostrom, T., & Hamilton, D. (Eds.). (1994). *Social cognition: Impact on social psychology*. San Diego, CA: Academic Press.

Dretske, F. (1988). *Explaining behavior: Reasons in a world of causes*. Cambridge, MA: MIT Press.

Fletcher, P., & MacWhinney, B. (Eds.). (1995). *The handbook of child language*. Oxford: Blackwell.

Fodor, J. (1975). *The language of thought*. New York: Crowell.

Freksa, C., & Mark, D. M. (Eds.). (1999). *Spatial information theory: Cognitive and computational foundations of geographic information science*. Berlin: Springer.

Garnham, A. (1985). *Psycholinguistics: Central topics*. London: Methuen.

Gleitman, L. R., & Liberman, M. (Eds.). (1995). *An invitation to cognitive science. Vol. 1: Language*. Cambridge, MA: MIT Press.

Helander, M. (Ed.). (1988). *Handbook of human–computer interaction*. Amsterdam: North-Holland.

Hoffman, E., McCabe, K., & Smith, V. (1995). *Behavioral foundations of reciprocity: Experimental economics and evolutionary psychology*. Cambridge, MA: MIT Press.

Holland, D., & Quinn, N. (Eds.). (1987). *Cultural models in language and thought*. Cambridge, England: Cambridge University Press.

Johnson-Laird, P. N., & Byrne, R. M. J. (1991). *Deduction*. Hillsdale, NJ: Erlbaum.

Kahneman, D., Slovic, P., & Tversky, A. (Eds.). (1982). *Judgment under uncertainty: Heuristics and biases*. Cambridge, England: Cambridge University Press.

Kintsch, W. (1998). *Comprehension: A paradigm for cognition*. Cambridge, England: Cambridge University Press.

Kosslyn, S. M., & Andersen, R. A. (Eds.). (1992). *Frontiers in cognitive neuroscience*. Cambridge, MA: MIT Press.

Kosslyn, S. M., & Koenig, O. (1992). *Wet mind: The new cognitive neuroscience*. New York: Free Press.

Langacker, R. (1987–1991). *Foundations of cognitive grammar* (2 vols.). Stanford, CA: Stanford University Press.

Levelt, W. J. M. (1989). *Speaking: From intention to articulation*. Cambridge, MA: MIT Press.

Mackie, D. M., & Hamilton, D. L. (Eds.). (1993). *Affect, cognition, and stereotyping: Interactive processes in group perception*. San Diego, CA: Academic Press.

Maybury, M. T. (Ed.). (1993). *Intelligent multimedia interfaces*. Cambridge, MA: MIT Press.

Norman, D. A., & Draper, S. (Eds.). (1986). *User-centered system design: New perspectives in human–computer interaction*. Hillsdale, NJ: Erlbaum.

Osherson, D., Stob, M., & Weinstein, S. (1986). *Systems that learn*. Cambridge, MA: MIT Press.

Overton, W. F. (Ed.). (1990). *Reasoning, necessity, and logic*. Hillsdale, NJ: Erlbaum.

Portugali, J. (Ed.). (1996). *The construction of cognitive maps*. Dordrecht, The Netherlands: Kluwer.

Posner, M. I. (Ed.). (1989). *Foundations of cognitive science*. Cambridge, MA: MIT Press.

Rasmussen, J. (1986). *Information processing and human–machine interaction: An approach to cognitive engineering*. Amsterdam: North-Holland.

Rey, G. (1996). *Contemporary philosophy of mind: A contentiously classical approach*. Oxford: Blackwell.

Rosch, E., & Lloyd, B. B. (Eds.). (1978). *Cognition and categorization*. Hillsdale, NJ: Erlbaum.

Russell, S., & Norvig, P. (1995). *Artificial intelligence: A modern approach*. Englewood Cliffs, NJ: Prentice-Hall.

Simon, H. A. (1983). *Reason in human affairs*. Stanford, CA: Stanford University Press.

Stillings, N. A., Feinstein, M. H., Garfield, J. L., Rissland, E. L., Rosenbaum, D. A., Weisler, S. E., & Baker-Ward, J. (1987). *Cognitive science: An introduction*. Cambridge, MA: MIT Press.

Sun, R., & Bookman, L. (Eds.). (1994). *Computational architectures integrating neural and symbolic processes*. Boston: Kluwer.

Tajfel, H. (1982). *Social identity and intergroup relations*. Cambridge, England: Cambridge University Press.

Toga, A. W., & Mazziotta, J. C. (1996). *Brain mapping: The methods*. San Diego, CA: Academic Press.

Wickens, C. D. (1984). *Engineering psychology and human performance*. Columbus, OH: Charles Merill.

Winston, P. H. (1984). *Artificial intelligence*. Reading, MA: Addison-Wesley.

Communications concerning this chapter should be addressed to: Professor Michel Denis, Groupe Cognition Humaine, LIMSI-CNRS, Université de Paris-Sud, BP 133, F-91403 Orsay Cedex, France

Author Index

Subject Index